Immigration and Nationality Law

Immigration and Nationality Law

Cases and Materials

FIFTH EDITION

Richard A. Boswell
PROFESSOR OF LAW
UNIVERSITY OF CALIFORNIA
HASTINGS COLLEGE OF THE LAW

CAROLINA ACADEMIC PRESS
Durham, North Carolina

ISBN 978-1-5310-1132-1
eISBN 978-1-53101-133-8
LCCN 2018939843

Carolina Academic Press, LLC
700 Kent Street
Durham, North Carolina 27701
Telephone (919) 489-7486
Fax (919) 493-5668
www.cap-press.com

Printed in the United States of America

To my parents Dorothy E. Boswell and William P. Boswell who have taught me so much about love and the value of all human beings.

and

To Karen, with love and appreciation for her ever constant support.

R.A.B.

Contents

Acknowledgments

It would not be an exaggeration to say that at no time in the last century has immigration been on the front page more than it is today. At the same time that immigration has played such a dominant force in our political discourse, it is both complex and barely understood. More than 40 years ago the late Judge Irving R. Kaufman of the Second Circuit noted "the striking resemblance between some of the laws we are called upon to interpret and King Minos's labyrinth in ancient Crete." *Lok v. INS*, 548 F.3d 37 (2d Cir. 1977). The judge went on to compare the immigration laws with the Internal Revenue Code. Since Judge Kaufman made that observation, the laws have only become more complex and confusing.

All of this is occurring in a time when communication and human interaction is accelerating on a global scale. When a war or natural disaster breaks out immigration laws are implicated. When a US or foreign corporation reorganizes and needs to bring key employees to manage it operations, immigration laws need to be consulted. When a President asserts that the admission of certain foreign nationals implicates our national security, immigration laws are invoked. When a US citizen or resident marries and wishes to live in this country with their foreign spouse, a complicated set of legal and procedural hurdles will need to be overcome. These are but a few examples of how immigration laws impact on our daily lives—this text represents an attempt to aid in making this body of law more accessible.

Since beginning my work in this field I have been constantly moved and inspired by the immigrants and their life stories of perseverance and tenacity. Each person has a story which will resonate with anyone who is open to being inspired. I hope that reading these stories of human migration might lead to a deeper examination and understanding of this complex body of law. Such an examination might yield to more humane immigration laws.

As is the case with any book there are more people to thank than there is space to acknowledge. I will try by first thanking the souls who constitute the flesh and blood behind each case (and hypothetical) which appear on these pages. For each petitioner, respondent, appellant or plaintiff, there are countless other loved ones and family members whose futures were forever changed by the decisions which are represented here. I am indebted to the luminaries of this field who have inspired me and left their indelible marks—the late Charles Gordon, Jack Wasserman, David Carliner and Maurice Roberts. Appreciation and respect are also extended to my friend Ira Kurzban who as a contemporary has been a source of wisdom, encouragement and admiration. I also wish to thank the countless students who I have had the privilege to engage with in an effort to try to better understand our immigration laws. I want to acknowledge and thank the research support that I have received from the Hastings Law Library staff and many research assistants who over the years have helped to locate sometimes obscure but important information. My deepest appreciation and love go to my life partner, Karen Musalo who has been with me from the very first edition—her inspiration and support has sustained me and without which this work could not have been completed.

Notwithstanding all of these wonderful and dedicated supporters on this project I assume full responsibility for any errors, omissions or misstatements that might be found within these pages.

Richard A. Boswell

Immigration and Nationality Law

Chapter 1

Introduction

These materials are designed to present a survey of the cases, statutes, and procedures in immigration and nationality law. It is fair to say that anyone who studies this subject matter will not become an immigration law expert in one semester. Seasoned practitioners in the field acknowledge that it takes many years to master the intricacies of immigration law.

This subject matter is considered by many to rival the complexity of tax and social security law. Indeed, immigration and tax law have developed in a similar manner in that each section is built upon the other, each having a myriad of exceptions. For example, each of the numerous deportability and inadmissibility provisions overlap and contain complicated waiver provisions depending on the applicant's family ties in the United States. The result of this type of scheme is that the Immigration and Nationality Act has developed into a quilt-like patchwork of confusing rules.

Some find it helpful to have a copy of the relevant statute and regulations to accompany the casebook. Where it is helpful, the actual language from the statutory section, regulation or agency interpretation are reprinted in this volume.[1]

Immigration Reform

For well over two decades, Congress has debated the enactment of substantial reform of the Immigration and Nationality Act.[2] As of this writing, the comprehensive

1. The policy instructions for USCIS are referred to as the Adjudicator's Field Manual (AFM), while those for the Wage and Hour Division of the Department of Labor, which enforces labor standards provisions applicable to persons under nonimmigrant work visas, are referred to as the Field Operations Handbook (FOH). Policy instructions for the Department of State, which are used by consular officers, are called the Foreign Affairs Manual (FAM). A separate companion volume called the "Selected Statutory and Regulatory Materials on Immigration and Nationality Law" is available.

2. The Immigration and Nationality Act, as amended, will hereafter be referred to as the "Act." The basic statute is commonly referred to as the McCarran-Walter Act of 1952, Pub. L. No. 82-414, 66 Stat. 163 (1952). The most important amendments to the basic statute since its enactment in 1952 include the Acts of Sept. 11, 1957, 7 Stat. 639; Oct. 3, 1965, 79 Stat. 911; Oct. 20, 1976, Pub. L. No. 94-571, 90 Stat. 2703; Oct. 5, 1978, Pub. L. No. 95-412, 92 Stat. 907; Refugee Act of 1980, enacted March 17,1980, Pub. L. No. 96-212, 94 Stat. 102; Immigration and Nationality Amendments of 1981, enacted December 29, 1981, Pub. L. No. 97-116, 95 Stat. 1611. Immigration Reform and Control Act of 1986, enacted Nov. 6, 1986, Pub. L. No. 99-603, 100 Stat. 3359; Immigration Marriage Fraud Amendments of 1986, enacted Nov. 10, 1986, Pub. L. No. 99-639, 100 Stat. 3537; Immigration and Nationality Act Amendments of 1986, enacted Nov. 14, 1986, Pub. L. No. 99-653, 100 Stat. 3655;

reform efforts have been unsuccessful. References to the changes enacted in 1986 will be referred to under a variety of headings: Simpson-Mazzoli, Simpson-Rodino, the Immigration Reform and Control Act of 1986 or simply "Reform Legislation." The legislation enacted in 1990 will be referred to as either the "1990 Act" or the "Immigration Act of 1990." Beginning in 1996, Congress began enacting sweeping changes to restrict immigrants' rights in the United States with the Anti-Terrorism and Effective Death Penalty Act of 1996, sometimes referred to as "AEDPA", and the Illegal Immigration Reform and Immigrant Responsibility Act of 1996, or "IIRAIRA." AEDPA established a summary procedure to prevent the admission of certain persons without a hearing as well as wide-ranging restrictions for foreigners with criminal records. IIRAIRA enhanced the U.S. Citizenship and Immigration Services's enforcement power, limited judicial review, created new grounds of inadmissibility and deportability and limited relief from removal and waivers of removal.

In 2000, the 106th Congress made numerous amendments to the immigration laws, creating additional categories of nonimmigrant visas including additional visas for high-tech workers in the H-1B visa category, providing relief for certain immigrants adversely affected by the immigration legislation of 1996, modifying rules of acquisition of citizenship by foreign-born children, allowing certain nonimmigrants seeking

---

the United States Canada Free-Trade Agreement Implementation Act of 1988, enacted Sept. 28, 1988, Pub. L. No. 100-449, 102 Stat. 1851, and ratified by the Canadian government, effective Jan. 1, 1989; the Immigration Technical Corrections Act of 1988, enacted Oct. 24, 1988, Pub. L. No. 100-525, 102 Stat. 2609; the Anti-Drug Abuse Act of 1988, enacted Nov. 18, 1988, enacted Nov. 15, 1988, Pub. L. No, 100-658, 102 Stat. 3908; the Immigration Act of 1990, Pub. L. No. 101-649, 104 Stat. 4978; the Anti-Terrorism and Effective Death Penalty Act of 1996, Pub. L. No. 104-132, 110 Stat. 279; the Illegal Immigration Reform and Immigrant Responsibility Act of 1996, Pub. L. No. 104-208, 110 Stat. 3009; Religious Workers Act of 1997, Pub. L. No. 105-54, 111 Stat. 1175 (1997); Nicaraguan Adjustment and Central American Relief Act, Pub. L. No. 105-100, 111 Stat. 2160, as amended by Pub. L. No. 105-139, 111 Stat. 2644 (1997); Haitian Refugee Immigration Fairness Act of 1998, Pub. L. No. 105-277, 112 Stat. 2681 (1998); Torture Victims Relief Act of 1998, Pub. L. 105-320, 112 Stat. 3016 (1998); International Religious Freedom Act of 1998, Pub. L. No. 105-292, 112 Stat. 27871 (1998); American Competitiveness in the 21st Century Act, Pub. L. No. 106-313, 114 Stat. 1251 (2000); Victims of Trafficking and Violence Protection Act of 2000, Pub. L. No. 106-386, 114 Stat. 1464 (2000); Child Citizenship Act of 2000, Pub. L. No. 106-395, 114 Stat. 1631 (2000); Legal Immigration Family Equity Act ("LIFE"), Pub. L. 106-553, 114 Stat. 2762 (2000), as amended by Pub. L. 106-554, 114 Stat. 2763 (2000); Uniting and Strengthening America by Providing Appropriate Tools Required to Intercept and Obstruct Terrorism (USA PATRIOT Act) of 2001, Pub. L. No. 107-56, 115 Stat. 272 (2001); Enhanced Border Security and Visa Entry Reform Act of 2002 (Pub. L. No. 107-173, 116 Stat. 543 (2002); Child Status Protection Act, Pub. L. 107-208, 116 Stat. 927 (2002); Homeland Security Act of 2002, Pub. L. No. 207-296, 116 Stat. 2135 (2002); Homeland Security Act of 2002 Amendments Act, Pub. L. 108-7, 117 Stat. 11 (2003); National Defense Authorization Act for Fiscal Year 2004 (Naturalization and Other Immigration Benefits for Military Personnel and Families), Pub. L. 108-136, 117 Stat. 1392 (2003); REAL ID Act of 2005, Pub. L. No. 109-13, 119 Stat. 231 (2005); Violence Against Women and DOJ Reauthorization Act of 2005, Pub. L. No. 109-162, 119 Stat. 2960 (2006); COMPETE Act of 2006, Pub. L. No. 109-463, 120 Stat. 3477 (2006); The United States Global Leadership Against HIV/AIDS, Tuberculosis and Malaria Reauthorization Act of 2008, Pub. L. No. 110-293, 122 Stat. 2918, 2963, § 305 (2008); William Wilberforce Trafficking Victims Protection Reauthorization Act of 2008, Pub. L. No. 110-457, 122 Stat. 5044 (2008); Violence Against Women Reauthorization Act of 2013, Pub. L. No. 113-4, 127 Stat. 54 (2013).

medical treatment (at no expense to the government) to remain in the United States and providing additional protection for victims of torture and slavery and battered spouses and children.[3] Following the attacks of September 11, 2001, Congress enacted the USA Patriot Act, which expanded the definition of terrorist activity and focused on restricting and more closely monitoring the activity of foreigners in the country.[4] In 2005, with the stated purpose of enhancing border security, Congress enacted far-reaching legislation attempting to restrict access to identification documents by undocumented persons and to limit asylum relief in legislation known as the REAL ID Act.[5] Most recently in 2013, a broad reform proposal was passed with bi-partisan support in the U.S. Senate but failed due to inaction in the House of Representatives.[6] Largely due to the legislative impasses, the Obama Administration instituted a number of regulatory and Executive actions to alleviate some of the pressures on the legal migration system. With the election of a new President in 2016, it is not clear what type if any reform might be enacted.

Restructuring of "INS" into the Department of Homeland Security

In 2002, Congress passed and the President signed legislation creating a new Department of Homeland Security (DHS).[7] As a result of the legislation, many of the functions previously found within the Immigration and Naturalization Service (INS) were moved into the DHS and divided between U.S. Citizenship and Immigration Services (USCIS), U.S. Customs and Border Protection (CBP) and U.S. Immigration and Customs Enforcement (ICE).[8] Within the purview of USCIS are the adjudicatory functions under the immigration laws, such as change of status, permanent residency

3. The major amendments which were enacted by the 106th Congress include the following: Civil Asset Forfeiture Reform Act of 2000, Pub. L. No. 106-185, § 18(a), 114 Stat. 222 (2000); Immigration Services and Infrastructure Improvements Act of 2000, Pub. L. No. 106-313, § 106(c)(1), 114 Stat. 1251 (2000); Victims of Trafficking and Violence Protection Act of 2000, Pub. L. No. 106-386, Title V, §§ 1501–13, 114 Stat. 1464, 1518–1536 (2000); Child Citizenship Act of 2000, Pub. L. No. 106-395, 104 Stat. 1631 (2000); International Patient Act of 2000, Pub. L. No. 106-406, 114 Stat. 1755 (2000); Immigration and Nationality Act—Amendment, Pub. L. No. 106-448, 114 Stat. 1939 (2000); Special Immigrant Status for Certain United States International Broadcasting Employees, Pub. L. No. 106-536, 114 Stat. 2560 (2000); Legal Immigration Family Equity Act, Pub. L. No. 106-553, § 1101–04, 114 Stat. 2762A-141 (2000); Pub. L. No. 106-554, § 1(a)(1), 114 Stat. 2763 (2000).

4. See USA Patriot Act, Pub. L. No. 107-56, 115 Stat. 272 (2001); Enhanced Border Security and Visa Entry Reform Act of 2002, Pub. L. No. 107-173, 116 Stat. 543, 116 Stat. 543 (2002).

5. See Real ID Act of 2005, Pub. L. No. 109-13 (2005). The legislation was part of the Emergency Supplemental Military Appropriations bill to support the military involvement in Iraq.

6. See Border Security, Economic Opportunity, and Immigration Modernization Act of 2013, S.744, 113th Cong. (2013). The legislation would have granted temporary status to the large population of undocumented immigrants in the U.S. and added substantially to the number of border agents.

7. See Homeland Security Act of 2002, Pub. L. No. 107-296, 116 Stat. 2135 (2002).

8. See 68 Fed. Reg. 9824 (2003).

and naturalization.[9] CBP deals with the inspection of persons arriving at the country's borders,[10] while ICE functions to enforce the immigration laws by conducting worksite inspections, investigating immigration law violations and implementing removal orders.[11]

The concern for reorganizing the bureaucracy responsible for immigration had been a persistent issue for decades. Under the Clinton Administration, the INS had started to develop plans for restructuring its bureaucracy at both the headquarters in Washington, D.C. and in its field offices by separating the enforcement and service functions. It was not until after the events of September 11, 2001 when it became imperative to create a super domestic security agency that INS was reorganized into separate divisions within DHS.[12] These divisions were Customs and Border Patrol (CBP), Immigrations and Customs Enforcement (ICE) and Customs and Immigration Services (USCIS).

What remained untouched in the reorganization were the functions of Consular officers, Public Health Officers, Department of Labor (DOL) officials, Immigration Judges and the Board of Immigration Appeals, which remain in the agencies where they existed prior to the legislation. Consular functions remain within the Department of State (DOS), public health remains at the Public Health Service (PHS), labor certification remains at DOL and immigration judges and the Board of Immigration Appeals remain at the Department of Justice (DOJ). It remains to be seen what, if any, additional changes will be made to the agencies responsible for enforcing the immigration laws and whether the constant problems which plagued legacy INS will persist in USCIS, CBP and ICE.

Division of Responsibilities between the Departments of State and Homeland Security

As will be seen, there are a number of government agencies responsible for interpreting the immigration laws. This amalgam of government agencies with different roles in the immigration process create overlapping jurisdiction and sometimes confusion in understanding what the correct or best interpretation might be. Following the restructuring of INS into DHS, the President provided notice to Congress that a Memorandum of Understanding between the DOS and DHS[13] had been entered into, which provides for a clearer delimitation of the authority between consular and DHS

9. For more information on USCIS's jurisdiction, visit www.uscis.gov.

10. For a more in-depth discussion of CBP's functions, visit www.cbp.gov.

11. For a more detailed description of ICE's mandate, visit www.ice.gov.

12. For a more detailed article which describes the political and security concerns leading to the reorganization and raises some of the future challenges to the new agency, see David A. Martin, *Immigration Policy and the Homeland Security Act Reorganization: An Early Agenda for Practical Improvements*, 80 Interpreter Releases 601–18 (2003).

13. *See* 68 Fed. Reg. 56519 (2003).

Chart 1 U.S. Department of Homeland Security

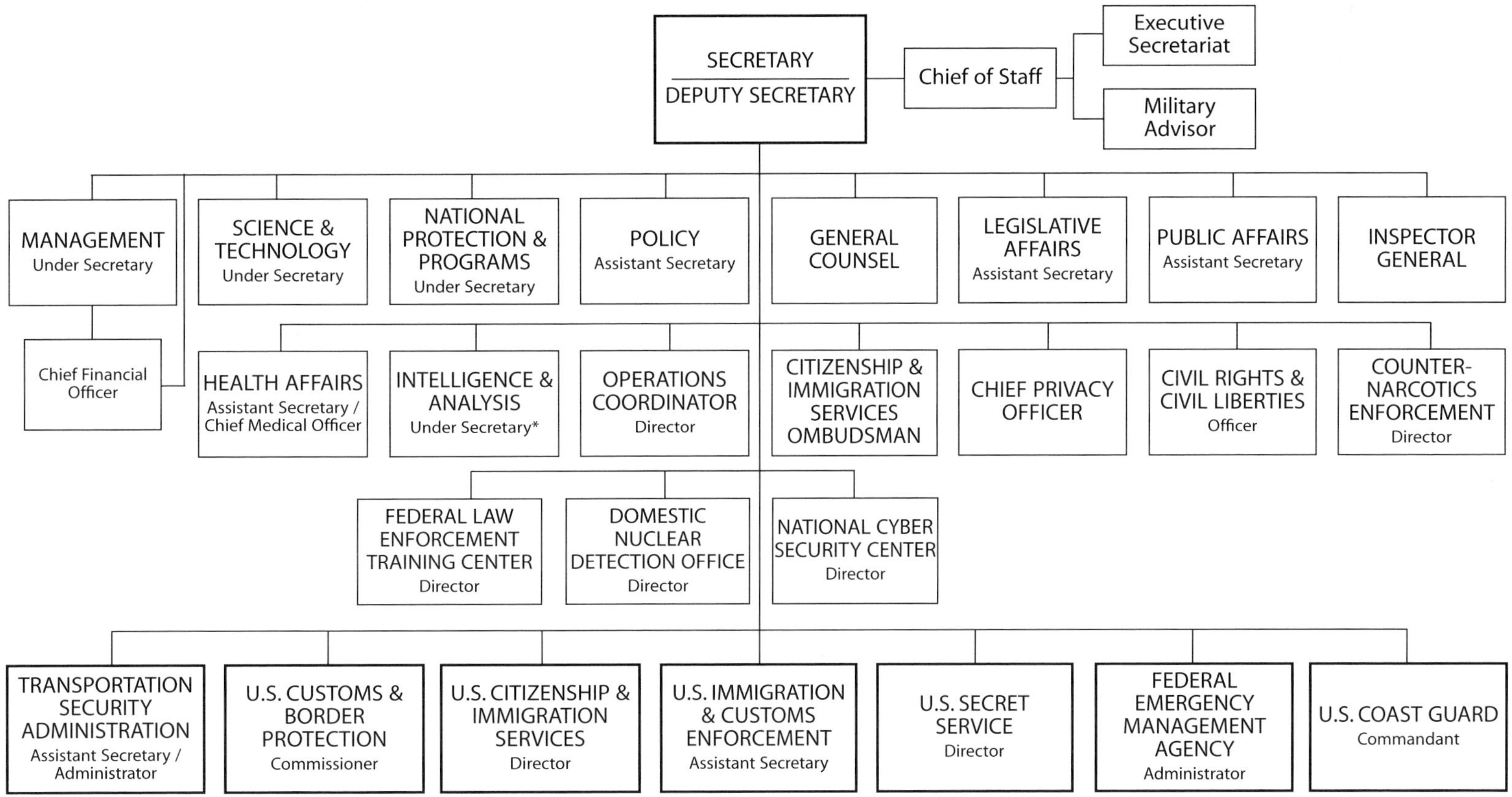

*Under Secretary for Intelligence & Analysis title created by the Implementing Recommendations of the 9/11 Commission Act of 2007. Pub. L. NO. 110-53, 121 Stat. 266 (2007).

officers in the issuance of visas and admission of non-citizens to the United States. Specifically, the Memorandum provides that DHS will have final responsibility on visa guidance to consular officials concerning eligibility for nonimmigrant and immigrant visas. The two agencies will share guidance over cultural and training programs under 8 U.S.C. §§ 1101(a)(15)(Q)(ii), (S)(ii), with the Secretary of State having full responsibility regarding diplomatic, transit, NATO, exchange visitor and investor and trade visas. Further, DHS will have final responsibility over guidance of what constitutes material support under the terrorism provisions.

A Multitude of Government Agencies

The study of immigration law is more complicated than other areas of law, because most immigration questions involve procedures of at least five agencies of the executive branch. These agencies are the Department of Homeland Security, Department of Justice, Department of Labor, Department of State and Public Health Service.[14]

Department of Homeland Security

DHS is responsible for both the enforcement of the immigration laws and conferral of immigration benefits. The Secretary of Homeland Security, the cabinet level officer who oversees DHS, determines the policy and overall management of the agency. As indicated previously, DHS is divided into three components: USCIS, CBP and ICE. Within the USCIS is the Administrative Appeals Office (AAO), which is responsible for administrative review of certain types of decisions under the agency's jurisdiction.[15]

Department of Justice's Executive Office for Immigration Review

Separate from DHS is the Executive Office for Immigration Review (EOIR), which has an adjudicatory function. The EOIR was created by the Attorney General in January 1983[16] and consists of immigration judges (IJs) who perform hearing functions and the Board of Immigration Appeals (BIA) which acts as an administrative review

---

14. The Public Health Service is within the Department of Health and Human Services. In labor certification cases, which are discussed in Chapter 8, the employer seeking certification for temporary or permanent workers must apply first through a state employment training service office. Administrative review may involve the Executive Office for Immigration Review, a separate branch of the Department of Justice, or the Board of Labor Certification Appeals, a separate branch of the Department of Labor. *See* Chapter 12.

15. The administrative review process will be explored in greater detail in Chapter 12.

16. The separation of the immigration judges and Board of Immigration Appeals from legacy INS became effective January 9, 1983. 60 INTERPRETER RELEASES 155 (1983). This separation was due to criticism by the private bar as well as immigration judges, who complained of pressures being imposed on them by legacy INS. *See, e.g.*, *Asylum Adjudication: Hearings before the Subcommittee on Immigration and Refugee Policy of the Senate Committee on the Judiciary,* 97th Cong., 1st Sess. 259–69 (1981) (statement of Ralph Farb, former member, Board of Immigration Appeals).

body. The immigration judges decide questions of admissibility and deportability as well as certain cases involving bonds for individuals seeking admission.[17] The BIA reviews decisions of immigration judges and is the final administrative appellate body for certain cases under the immigration laws.[18] Also housed within DOJ is the Office of Special Counsel, which is responsible for adjudicating immigrants' employment discrimination claims, and the Office of the Chief Administrative Hearing Office, which is responsible for adjudicating cases involving employers hiring illegal immigrants.[19] The Office of Special Counsel operates separately from the EOIR even though it is part of DOJ.

Department of Labor

The Act provides that persons who are coming to the United States to perform work must be certified as not displacing or adversely affecting the wages and working conditions of U.S. workers.[20] It also provides that temporary workers entering the country must be similarly certified.[21] The responsibility for issuing the certification that the statutory provisions have been fulfilled rests with the Secretary of Labor.[22] The procedures and requirements involved in the temporary and permanent labor certifications will be discussed in Chapters 6 and 8.

The labor certification process involves a recruitment survey, which is initially carried out by the local or state employment training agency where the job is located. The section within DOL responsible for providing the necessary information to the Secretary is the Employment Training Administration (ETA). Accordingly, the individual and the employer or his attorney are required to deal with state as well as federal bureaucracy. The country is divided into regions, and each of the regions is headed by a regional certifying officer who bears the responsibility of assuring that the requirements of 8 U.S.C. § 1182(a)(5) are met. In the event that the labor certification application is denied by the regional certifying officer, the sponsoring employer may request a hearing before an administrative law judge.[23]

---

17. The jurisdiction of immigration judges will be discussed in more detail in Chapters 3–5 and 13. These sections relate to determining grounds of inadmissibility (Chapter 3) and deportability (Chapter 4) and whether a person will be granted asylum (Chapter 5).

18. The complexities of the administrative review scheme are discussed at greater length in Chapter 12.

19. *See* 8 U.S.C. § 1324b, Sec. 274B.

20. 8 U.S.C. § 1182(a)(5), Sec. 212(a)(5) of the Act. It should also be noted that there is a statutory presumption that all persons coming to the United States are immigrants and therefore must be certified by the Department of Labor as not taking away jobs from U.S. workers. The exceptions from the labor certification requirement are discussed in Chapter 8.

21. 8 U.S.C. § 1184(c), Sec. 214(c) of the Act. *See also* 8 C.F.R. § 214.2(h)(3).

22. The historical role of the Department of Labor has been that of protecting the interests of workers, and a major voice for these workers is organized labor. For this reason, the obvious agency to be charged with administering this certification process is DOL.

23. The administrative appeals process within DOL will be discussed in the chapter on employment-based immigrants (Chapter 8).

Department of State

The INA created the Bureau of Consular Affairs within DOS to administer U.S. immigration laws overseas.[24] U.S. consular officers serving at embassies and consulates abroad, in addition to having other duties, are also responsible for the issuance of immigrant and nonimmigrant visas to persons seeking permission to come to the United States.

Adverse visa decisions made by U.S. consuls are not appealable to the federal courts. The only recourse for an interested party is to seek an advisory opinion from the DOS Visa Office. As will be discussed later, these opinions are only advisory and do not bind the consular officers.[25]

Public Health Service

The immigration laws prevent persons who are or have been afflicted with certain psychological and medical problems from entering the United States.[26] It is the sole responsibility of PHS under the Department of Health and Human Services to make determinations regarding the medical and psychological conditions of persons seeking admission. These determinations are only reviewable by a panel of doctors under PHS.

A Historical Perspective

The immigration laws have been called discriminatory on racial and national origin grounds.[27] As seen from the following discussion by the U.S. Civil Rights Commission, political, economic and social factors bear heavily on the question of immigration reform. Anti-immigrant sentiment has ebbed and flowed, and various racial or ethnic groups have been targeted or disfavored throughout the history of the United States.

---

24. 8 U.S.C. § 1104, Sec. 104.

25. The role of consular officers in the immigrant and nonimmigrant visa issuing process are discussed in Chapters 6 and 7.

26. 8 U.S.C. § 1224, Sec. 234 of the Act, deals with the authority of the Public Health Service in the "inspection" of persons entering the United States. 8 U.S.C. § 1182(a)(1), Sec. 212 (a)(1) is the statutory section which prohibits the admission of certain persons with psychological and medical problems. These issues will be discussed further in Chapter 3.

27. Charles Gordon, *The Need to Modernize our Immigration Laws,* 13 San Diego L. Rev. 1 (1975); Bill Ong Hing, *Racial Disparity: The Unaddressed Issue of the Simpson-Mazzoli Bill,* 1 La Raza L.J. 21 (1983).

The Tarnished Golden Door: Civil Rights Issues in Immigration

U.S. Commission on Civil Rights, 7–12 (1980)

The Early Years

During the formative years of this country's growth, immigration was encouraged with little restraint. Any restrictions on immigration in the 1700s were the result of selection standards established by each colonial settlement. The only Federal regulation of immigration in this period lasted only *2* years and came from the Alien Act of 1798, which gave the President the authority to expel aliens who posed a threat to national security.[2]

Immigrants from northern and western Europe began to trickle into the country as a result of the faltering economic conditions within their own countries. In Germany, unfavorable economic prospects in industry and trade, combined with political unrest drove many of its nationals to seek opportunities to ply their trades here. In Ireland, the problems of the economy, compounded by several successive potato crop failures in the 1840s, sent thousands of Irish to seaports where ships bound for the United States were docked. For other European nationals, the emigration from their native countries received impetus not only from adverse economic conditions at home but also from favorable stories of free land and good wages in America.

The Nativist Movements

As a result of the large numbers of Catholics who emigrated from Europe, a nativist movement began in the 1830s. It advocated immigration restriction to prevent further arrivals of Catholics into this country. Anti-Catholicism was a very popular theme, and many Catholics and Catholic institutions suffered violent attacks from nativist sympathizers. The movement, however, did not gain great political strength and its goal of curbing immigration did not materialize.

Immigrants in the mid-19th century did not come only from northern and western Europe. In China, political unrest and the decline in agricultural productivity spawned the immigration of Chinese to American shores. The numbers of Chinese immigrants steadily increased after the so-called Opium War, due not only to the Chinese economy, but also to the widespread stories of available employment, good wages, and the discovery of gold at Sutter's Mill, which filtered in through arrivals from the Western nations.

The nativist movement of the 1830s resurfaced in the late 1840s and developed into a political party, the Know-Nothing Party. Its western adherents added an anti-Chinese theme to the eastern anti-Catholic sentiment. But once again, the nativist movement, while acquiring local political strength, failed in its attempts to enact legislation curbing immigration. On the local level, however, the cry of "America

2. Ch. 58, 1 Stat. 570 (1798).

for Americans" often led to discriminatory State statutes that penalized certain racially identifiable groups.[3] As an example, California adopted licensing statutes for foreign miners and fishermen, which were almost exclusively enforced against Chinese.

In the mid-1850s, the Know-Nothing Party lost steam as a result of a division over the question of slavery, the most important issue of that time. The nativist movement and anti-foreign sentiment receded because of the slavery issue and the Civil War. It maintained this secondary role until the Panic of 1873 struck.

Chinese Exclusion

The depression economy of the 1870s was blamed on aliens who were accused of driving wages to a substandard level as well as taking away jobs that "belonged" to white Americans. While the economic charges were not totally without basis, reality shows that most aliens did not compete with white labor for "desirable" white jobs. Instead, aliens usually were relegated to the most menial employment.[4]

The primary target was the Chinese, whose high racial visibility, coupled with cultural dissimilarity and lack of political power, made them more than an adequate scapegoat for the economic problems of the 1870s.[5] Newspapers adopted the exhortations of labor leaders, blaming the Chinese for the economic plight of the working class. Workers released their frustrations and anger on the Chinese, particularly in the West. Finally, politicians succumbed to the growing cry for exclusion of Chinese.

Congress responded by passing the Chinese Exclusion Act of 1882.[6] That act suspended immigration of Chinese laborers for 10 years, except for those who were in the country on November 17, 1880. Those who were not lawfully entitled to reside in the United States were subject to deportation. Chinese immigrants were also prohibited from obtaining United States citizenship after the effective date of the act.

The 1882 act was amended in 1884 to cover all subjects of China and Chinese who resided in any other foreign country.[7] Then in 1888, another act was enacted that extended the suspension of immigration for all Chinese except Chinese officials, merchants, students, teachers, and travelers for pleasure.[8] Supplemental legislation to

---

3. Mary Roberts Coolidge, *Chinese Immigration* (1909), pp. 69–82. Some municipalities also adopted ordinances that discriminated against Chinese.As an example, a San Francisco municipal ordinance, subsequently held unconstitutional in *Yick Wo v. Hopkins*, 118 U.S. 356 (1886), was enacted to regulate the operation of public laundries but in practice was enforced almost exclusively against Chinese.

4. As one author noted, "[b]efore the late 1870's the Chinese engaged only in such work as white laborers refused to perform. Thus, the Chinese not only were noninjurious competitors but in effect were benefactors to the white laborer." S.W. Kung, *Chinese in American Life: Some Aspects of Their History, Status, Problems and Contributions* (1962), p. 68.

5. Carey McWilliams, *Brothers Under the Skin* (rev. 1951), pp. 101–03.

6. Ch. 126, 22 Stat. 58 (1882).

7. Ch. 220, 23 Stat. 115 (1884).

8. Ch. 1015, 25 Stat. 476 (1888).

that act also prohibited Chinese laborers from reentering the country, as provided for in the 1882 act, unless they reentered prior to the effective date of the legislation.[9]

Senator Matthew C. Butler of South Carolina summed up the congressional efforts to exclude Chinese by stating:

> [I]t seems to me that this whole Chinese business has been a matter of political advantage, and we have not been governed by that deliberation which it would seem to me the gravity of the question requires. In other words, there is a very important Presidential election pending. One House of Congress passes an act driving these poor devils into the Pacific Ocean, and the other House comes up and says, "Yes, we will drive them further into the Pacific Ocean, notwithstanding the treaties between the two governments."[10]

Nevertheless, the Chinese exclusion law was extended in 1892 and 1902, and in 1904 it was extended indefinitely.[11]

Although challenged by American residents of Chinese ancestry, the provisions of these exclusion acts were usually upheld by judicial decisions. For example, the 1892 act mandated that Chinese laborers obtain certificates of residency within 1 year after the passage of the act or face deportation.[12] In order to obtain the certificate, the testimony of one credible white witness was required to establish that the Chinese laborer was an American resident prior to the passage of the act. That requirement was upheld by the United States Supreme Court in *Fong Yue Ting v. United States*, 149 U.S. 698 (1893).

Literacy Tests and the Asiatic Barred Zone

The racial nature of immigration laws clearly manifested itself in further restrictions on prospective immigrants who were either from Asian countries or of Asian descent. In addition to extending the statutory life of the Chinese exclusion law, the 1902 act also applied that law to American territorial possessions, thereby prohibiting not only the immigration of noncitizen Chinese laborers from "such island territory to the mainland territory," but also "from one portion of the island territory of the United States to another portion of said island territory." Soon after, Japanese were restricted from free immigration to the United States by the "Gentleman's Agreement" negotiated between the respective governments in 1907. Additional evidence would be provided by the prohibition of immigration from countries in the Asia-Pacific Triangle as established by the Immigration Act of 1917.[13]

During this period, congressional attempts were also made to prevent blacks from immigrating to this country. In 1915 an amendment to exclude "all members of the African or black race" from admission to the United States was introduced in the Senate during its deliberations on a proposed immigration bill. The Senate approved

9. Ch. 1064, 25 Stat. 504 (1888).
10. 19 Cong. Rec. 8218 (1888).
11. *See* 27 Stat. 25 (1892), 32 Stat. 176 (1902), and 33 Stat. 428 (1904) respectively.
12. Ch. 60, 27 Stat. 25 (1892).
13. Ch. 29, 39 Stat. 874 (1917).

the amendment on a 29 to 25 vote, but it was later defeated in the House by a 253 to 74 vote, after intensive lobbying by the NAACP.

In 1917 Congress codified existing immigration laws in the Immigration Act of that year.[14] That act retained all the prior grounds for inadmissibility and added illiterates to the list of those ineligible to immigrate, as a response to the influx of immigrants from southern and eastern Europe. Because of a fear that American standards would be lowered by these new immigrants who were believed to be racially "inassimilable" and illiterate, any alien who was over 16 and could not read was excluded. The other important feature of this statute was the creation of the Asia Pacific Triangle, an Asiatic barred zone, designed to exclude Asians completely from immigration to the United States. The only exemptions from this zone were from an area that included Persia and parts of Afghanistan and Russia.

The 1917 immigration law reflected the movement of American immigration policy toward the curbing of free immigration. Free immigration, particularly from nations that were culturally dissimilar to the northern and western European background of most Americans, was popularly believed to be the root of both the economic problems and the social problems confronting this country.

The National Origins Quota System

Four years later, Congress created a temporary quota law that limited the number of aliens of any nationality who could immigrate to 3 percent of the United States residents of that nationality living in the country in 1910.[15] The total annual immigration allowable in any one year was set at 350,000. Western Hemisphere aliens were exempt from the quota if their country of origin was an independent nation and the alien had resided there at least 1 year.

The clear intent of the 1921 quota law was to confine immigration as much as possible to western and northern European stock. As the minority report noted:

> The obvious purpose of this discrimination is the adoption of an unfounded anthropological theory that the nations which are favored are the progeny of fictitious and hitherto unsuspected Nordic ancestors, while those discriminated against are not classified as belonging to that mythical ancestral stock. No scientific evidence worthy of consideration was introduced to substantiate this pseudoscientific proposition. It is pure fiction and the creation of a journalistic imagination....
>
> The majority report insinuates that some of those who have come from foreign countries are non-assimilable or slow of assimilation. No facts are offered in support of such a statement. The preponderance of testimony adduced before the committee is to the contrary.[16]

14. Ch. 29, 39 Stat. 374 (1917).
15. Ch. 8, 42 Stat. 5 (1921).
16. As reprinted in the legislative history of the INA at 1952 U.S.C.C.A.N. 1653, 1668.

Notwithstanding these objections, Congress made the temporary quota a permanent one with the enactment of the 1924 National Origins Act.[17] A ceiling of 150,000 immigrants per year was imposed. Quotas for each nationality group were 2 percent of the total members of that nationality residing in the United States according to the 1889 census. Again, Western Hemisphere aliens were exempt from the quotas (thus, classified as "nonquota" immigrants). Any prospective immigrant was required to obtain a sponsor in this country and to obtain a visa from an American consulate office abroad. Entering the country without a visa and in violation of the law subjected the entrant to deportation without regard to the time of entry (no statute of limitation). Another provision, prohibiting the immigration of aliens ineligible for citizenship, completely closed the door on Japanese immigration, since the Supreme Court had ruled that Japanese were ineligible to become naturalized citizens. Prior to the 1924 act, Japanese immigration had been subjected to "voluntary" restraint by the Gentleman's Agreement negotiated between the Japanese Government and President Theodore Roosevelt.

In addition to its expressed discriminatory provisions, the 1924 law was also criticized as discriminatory against blacks in general and against black West Indians in particular.

The Mexican "Repatriation" Campaign

Although Mexican Americans have a long history of residence within present United States territory,[18] Mexican immigration to this country is of relatively recent vintage. Mexican citizens began immigrating to this country in significant numbers after 1909 because of economic conditions as well as the violence and political upheaval of the Mexican Revolution. These refugees were welcomed by Americans, for they helped to alleviate the labor shortage caused by the First World War. The spirit of acceptance lasted only a short time, however. Spurred by the economic distress of the Great Depression, Federal immigration officials expelled hundreds of thousands of persons of Mexican descent from this country through increased Border Patrol raids and other immigration law enforcement techniques. To mollify public objection to the mass expulsions, this program was called the "repatriation" campaign. Approximately 500,000 persons were "repatriated" to Mexico, with more than half of them being United States citizens.

Erosion of Certain Discriminatory Patterns

Prior to the next recodification of the immigration laws, there were several congressional enactments that cut away at the discriminatory barriers established by the

---

17. Ch. 190, 43 Stat. 153 (1924).

18. Under the Treaty of Guadalupe Hidalgo, many Mexican citizens became U.S. citizens after the annexation of territory by the United States following the Mexican War. Leo Grebler, Joan W. Moore & Ralph C. Guzman, *The Mexican American People*, pp. 40–41 (1970). The Treaty of Guadalupe Hidalgo is reprinted in Wayne Moquin, *A Documentary History of the Mexican Americans*, p. 183 (1971).

national origins system. In 1943 the Chinese Exclusion Act was repealed, allowing a quota of 105 Chinese to immigrate annually to this country and declaring Chinese eligible for naturalization.[19] The War Brides Act of 1945 permitted the immigration of 118,000 spouses and children of military servicemen. In 1946 Congress enacted legislation granting eligibility for naturalization to Filipinos and to races indigenous to India.[20] A Presidential proclamation in that same year increased the Filipino quota from 50 to 100. In 1948 the Displaced Persons Act provided for the entry of approximately 400,000 refugees from Germany, Italy, and Austria (an additional 214,000 refugees were later admitted to the United States).[21]

The McCarran-Walter Act of 1952

The McCarran-Walter Act of 1952, the basic law in effect today, codified the immigration laws under a single statute.[22] It established three principles for immigration policy: (1) the reunification of families, (2) the protection of the domestic labor force, and (3) the immigration of persons with needed skills. However, it retained the concept of the national origins system, as well as unrestricted immigration from the Western Hemisphere. An important provision of the statute removed the bar to immigration and citizenship for races that had been denied those privileges prior to that time. Asian countries, nevertheless, were still discriminated against, for prospective immigrants whose ancestry was one-half of any Far Eastern race were chargeable to minimal quotas for that nation, regardless of the birthplace of the immigrant.

"Operation Wetback"[23]

Soon after the repatriation campaigns of the 1930s, the United States entered the Second World War. Mobilization for the war effort produced a labor shortage that resulted in a shift in American attitudes toward immigration from Mexico. Once again Mexican nationals were welcomed with open arms. However, this "open arms" policy was just as short lived as before.

In the 1950s many Americans were alarmed by the number of immigrants from Mexico. As a result, then United States Attorney General Herbert Brownell, Jr., launched "Operation Wetback," to expel Mexicans from this country. Among those caught up in the expulsion campaign were American citizens of Mexican descent who were forced to leave the country of their birth. To ensure the effectiveness of the expulsion process, many of those apprehended were denied a hearing to assert their constitutional rights and to present evidence that would have prevented their deportation. More than 1 million persons of Mexican descent were expelled from this country in 1954 at the height of "Operation Wetback."

---

19. Ch. 344, 57 Stat. 600 (1943).

20. *See* 59 Stat. 659 (1945), 60 Stat. 1353, and 60 Stat. 416 (1946) respectively.

21. Ch 647, 62 Stat. 1009 (1948).

22. 66 Stat. 163 (1952).

23. [Authors Note:] The term "wetback" was used by the U.S. Attorney General at the time and is an extremely derogatory term.

The 1965 Amendments

The national origins immigration quota system generated opposition from the time of its inception, condemned for its attempts to maintain the existing racial composition of the United States. Finally, in 1965, amendments to the McCarran-Walter Act abolished the national origins systems as well as the Asiatic barred zone.[24] Nevertheless, numerical restrictions were still imposed to limit annual immigration. The Eastern Hemisphere was subject to an overall limitation of 170,000 and a limit of 20,000 per country. Further, colonial territories were limited to 1 percent of the total available to the mother country (later raised 3 percent or 600 immigrants in the 1976 amendments). The Western Hemisphere, for the first time, was subject to an overall limitation of 120,000 annually, although no individual per-country limits were imposed. In place of the national origins system, Congress created a seven category preference system giving immigration priority to relatives of United States residents and immigrants with needed talents or skills. The 20,000 limitation per country and the colonial limitations, as well as the preference for relatives of Americans preferred under the former selections process, have been referred to by critics as "the last vestiges of the national origins system" because they perpetuate the racial discrimination produced by the national origins system.

Restricting Mexican Immigration

After 1965 the economic conditions in the United States changed. With the economic crunch felt by many Americans, the cry for more restrictive immigration laws resurfaced. The difference from the 19th century situation is that the brunt of the attacks is now focused on Mexicans, not Chinese. High "guesstimates" of the number of undocumented Mexican aliens entering the United States, many of which originated from Immigration and Naturalization Service sources, have been the subject of press coverage.

As a partial response to the demand for "stemming the tide" of Mexican immigration, Congress amended the Immigration and Nationality Act in 1976, imposing the seven category preference system and the 20,000 numerical limitation per country on Western Hemisphere nations.[25] Legal immigration from Mexico, which had been more than 40,000 people per year, with a waiting list 2 years long, was thus cut by over 50 percent.

Recent Revisions of the Immigrant Quota System

Although the annual per-country limitations have remained intact, Congress did amend the Immigration and Nationality Act of 1978 to eliminate the hemispheric quotas of 170,000 for Eastern Hemisphere countries and 120,000 for Western Hemisphere countries. Those hemispheric ceilings were replaced with an overall annual worldwide ceiling of 290,000.

In 1980 the immigrant quota system was further revised by the enactment of the Refugee Act. In addition to broadening the definition of refugee, that statute eliminated the seventh preference visa category by establishing a separate worldwide ceiling for

24. Pub. L. No. 89-236, 79 Stat. 911 (1965).
25. Pub. L. No. 94-571, 90 Stat. 2703 (1976).

refugee admissions to this country. It also reduced the annual worldwide ceiling for the remaining six preference categories to 270,000 visas, and it increased the number of visas allocated to the second preference to 26 percent.[26]

The preceding article by the Civil Rights Commission concludes with a reference to the Refugee Act of 1980. Three major statutory changes, which will be presented in these materials, were later enacted. These amendments were the Immigration Reform and Control Act of 1986, the Immigration Act of 1990, and the 1996 Amendments. The 1986 Act was designed to enhance the enforcement powers of the INS, and the 1990 enactments were intended to modestly increase the immigration quotas.[28]

Questions

1. The immigration laws only provide for the unification of families where the alien is the spouse, offspring or sibling of a U.S. citizen or the spouse or unmarried child of a lawful permanent resident. These provisions have been criticized as attempting to prevent the influx of "too many" racial minorities. Is this criticism valid? Would this criticism be valid if it was established that during periods of previous immigration (when Europeans were immigrating in large numbers) the family relationship restrictions did not exist?

2. Since 1975, there has been extensive discussion about changing our laws to prevent illegal immigration. Currently, the trend seems to be moving toward making both legal and illegal immigration more difficult. Is it possible to place realistic controls on illegal immigration in a country with more than 6,000 miles of land borders in the north and south?

Toward a Global View of the "Immigration Problem"

In the preceding section we considered the history of U.S. immigration policy. In addition to having a historical perspective it may be helpful to taking a global view of migration. It should be understood immigration is purely and simply the movement of people from one country to another. Migration has occurred since the beginning of civilization and will undoubtedly continue into the foreseeable future. There are many motivations behind the decision of an individual or a family to move from one place to another. An individual's reasons for migrating may include fear of persecution or prosecution, civil war in one's homeland, desire to join family in another country

---

26. Refugee Act of 1980, Pub. L. No. 96-212.

28. Some have described the 1986 amendments as controlling illegal immigration and the 1990 Act as providing for increased legal immigration.

or simply a wish to better one's economic status. At the same time, the policies underlying the immigration laws of virtually every nation are designed to frustrate this natural movement by placing specific controls on migration.

The charts which appear on the following pages provide basic information on refugee flows, labor migration, and the phenomena that propels migration around the world as well as information on refugee and other migration to the United States. The graphs do not include data on world migration motivated by family reunification. Even a cursory review of these charts should lead the reader to the conclusion that the migration flows to the United States are relatively small when considered in the global context. This does not mean, however, that illegal immigration is not a problem for the United States. One should view the immigration problems from a global perspective and remember that those who migrate to this country have in all likelihood traveled through and/or stayed in other countries. The consequence of this extensive human movement is that all countries in the migrants' path will experience some effect. In this regard, it might be helpful to consider the impact of immigration on the sending and receiving countries as well as on the countries of transit.

Graph 1. In this first chart, we see data comparing the migration rates between a number of industrialized or developed countries. One of the arguments raised by demographers is that it is more useful to compare migration rates to not just the size of the country but also to the size of its economy.

Graph 1 Net Migration Rate per 1,000
(CIA World Factbook 2017)

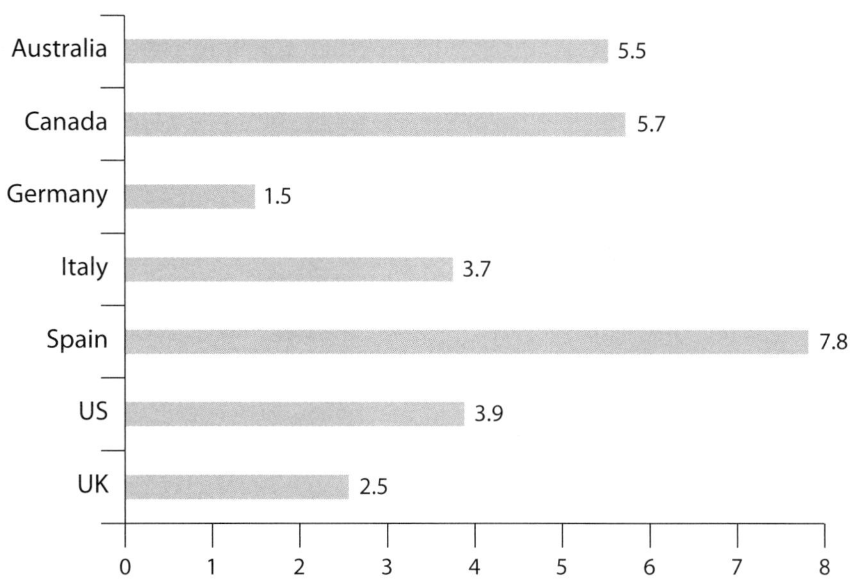

Graph 2. The flip side of the preceding chart is to understand the outflow of migrants to see some of the sending nations. While some countries receive larger numbers of

migrants, others have a large outflow of people. The graph does not attempt to explain the cause for this movement, but some of the forces include the search for work, political unrest, and limited opportunities in the home country. Consider the positive effects of outward migration for the sending country. These could include money which returns to the country from those who find increased opportunity overseas.

Graph 2 Net Emigration Rate per 1,000 (CIA World Factbook 2017)

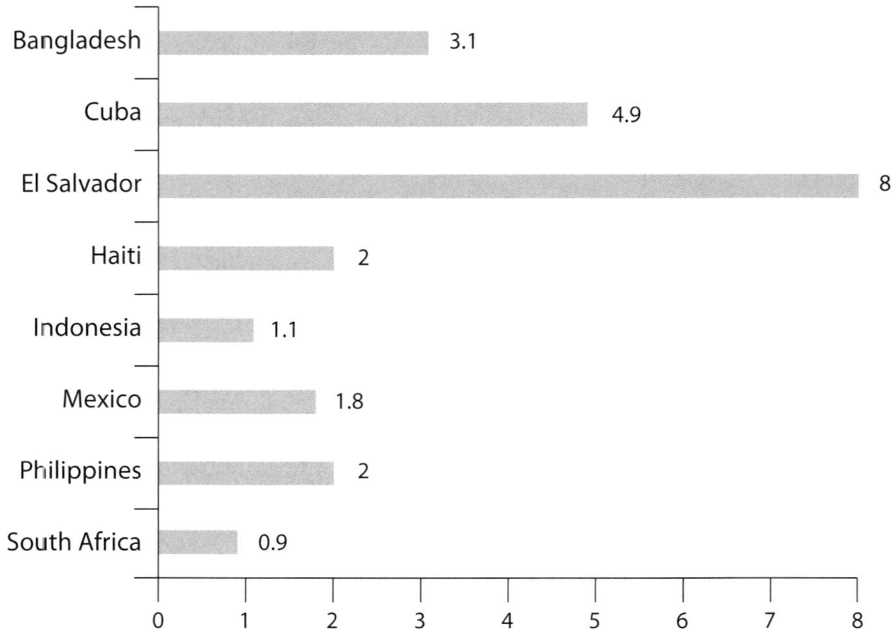

Graph 3. This graph which was extracted from a United Nations report shows the changes in migration patterns and how the source countries have shifted.

Most of the world's migrants live in a relatively small number of countries. In 2017, more than 50 per cent of all international migrants in the world were living in just ten countries or areas, while only twenty countries or areas hosted 67 per cent of the global number of international migrants. The largest number of international migrants resided in the United States of America: 50 million, equal to 19 per cent of the world's total. Saudi Arabia, Germany and the Russian Federation hosted the second, third and fourth largest numbers of migrants worldwide (around 12 million each), followed by the United Kingdom of Great Britain and Northern Ireland (nearly 9 million), and the United Arab Emirates (8 million). Of the twenty largest countries of destination of international migrants worldwide, nine a relocated in Asia, seven in Europe, two in Northern America, and one each in Africa and Oceania.

United Nations, Department of Economic and Social Affairs, Population Division, International Migration Report 12–13 (2017).

Graph 3 Twenty largest countries or areas of origin of international migrants, 2000 and 2017, number of migrants (millions)

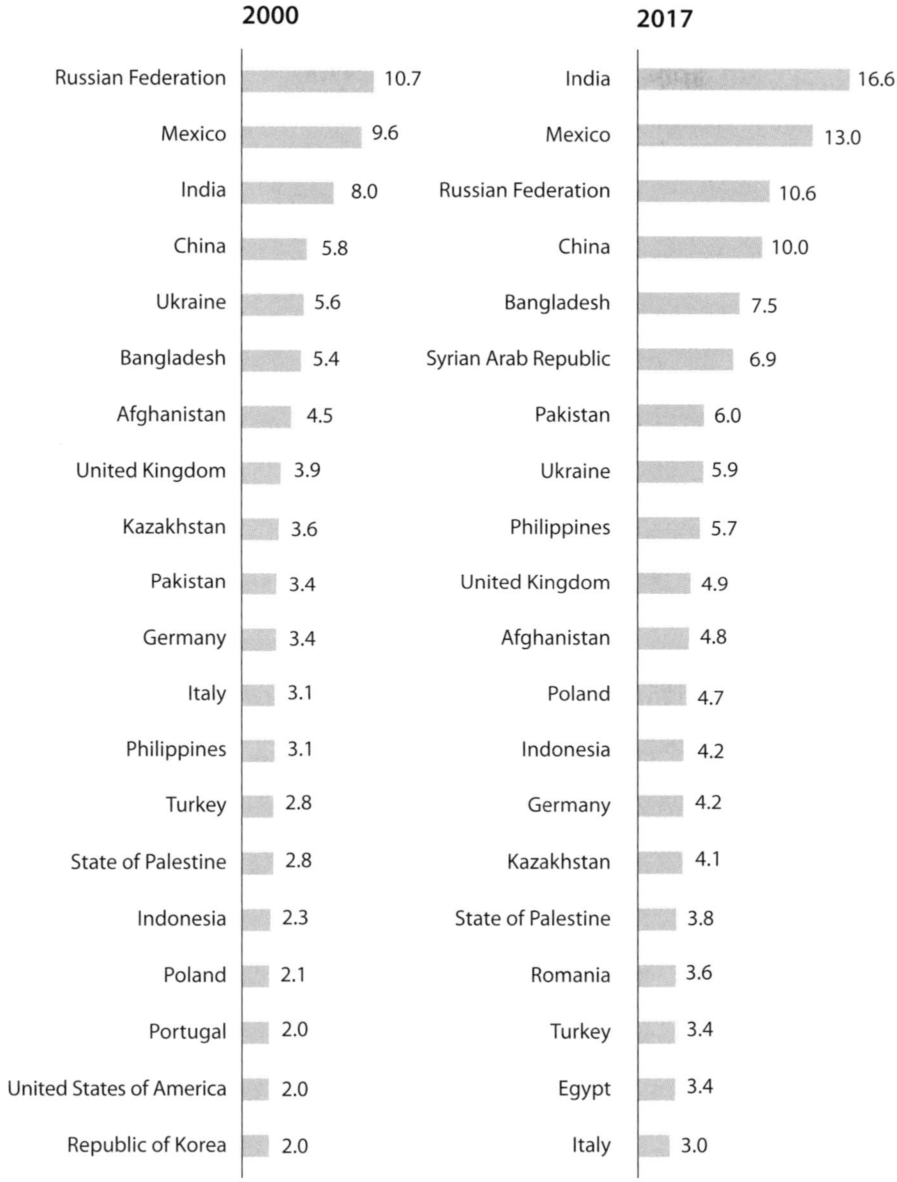

Source: United Nations (2017a).

Graph 4. A significant portion of migration is a consequence of armed conflicts, whether in the form of cross border or internal fighting. This graph excerpts the data of the number of refugees per 1,000 of the host country's population. Here we see what refugee workers know all too well—most refugees remain close to the conflicted areas. Another reality is that developing countries are the least burdened by refugee flight, for a comparatively small number of people are able to find their way to Europe, the United States or Canada.

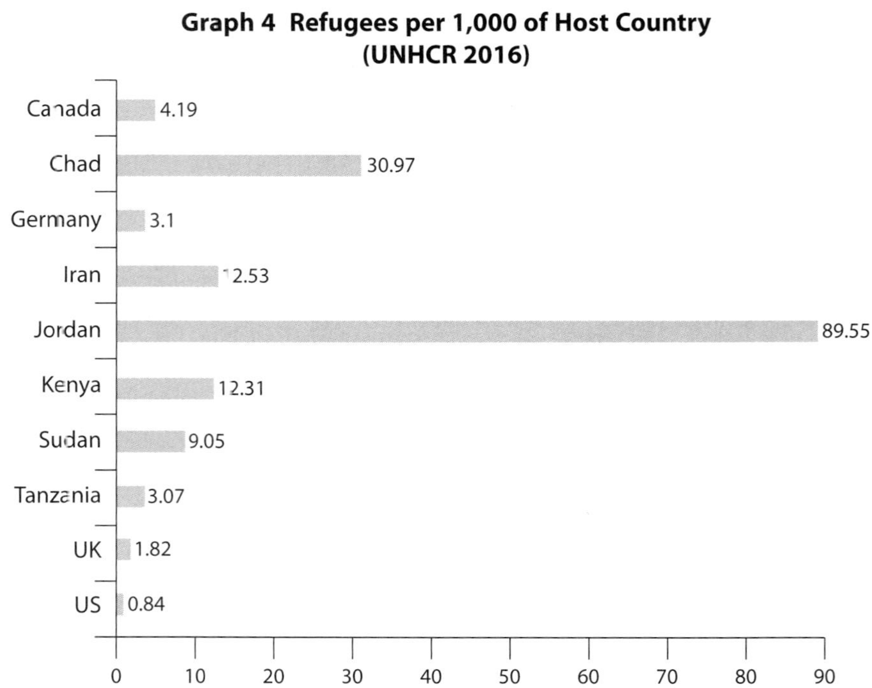

Graph 5. This final graph provides information on a growing phenomena which is the importance of the funds that migrants receive and send back to their home countries. This graph presents the foreign remittances as a percentage of each of these country's gross domestic product. Some of the poorest of nations literally survive on the money that their citizens send back into their economies.

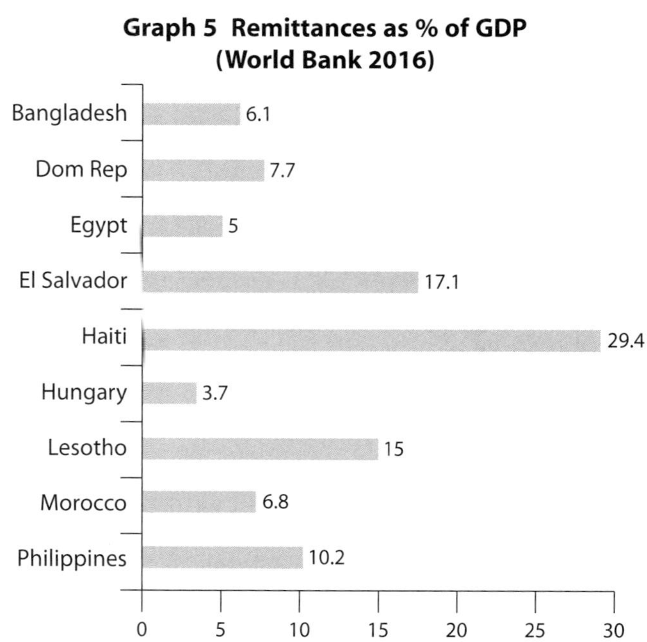

Sharon Stanton Russell, International Migration: Global Trends and National Responses

20 Fletcher F. World Aff. 1 (1996)
 Footnotes have been omitted.

As recently as the late 1980s, scholars and politicians alike tended to view migration, especially international migration, as a subject of peripheral interest. In the academic world, the fact that migration involves aspects of demography, economics, political science, sociology, and anthropology placed it firmly at the margins of—or in the interstices between—mainstream social science disciplines. Moreover, because migration defied monocausal explanations and attracted little funding for academic research, the subject captured the attention of relatively few scholars. Among politicians, migration was considered "low politics," part of the province of social affairs ministries, labor attaches, human rights nongovernmental organizations, church groups, ethnic politicians, international humanitarian organizations, and the like.

Only a few years later, migration issues have come to be found increasingly on the desks of presidents, prime ministers, kings, finance ministers, parliamentarians, and other participants in "high politics." Migration has also become a "hot topic" among a growing number of researchers and academics. Why has international migration achieved this new level of prominence, not only in academic and policy circles, but among general populations in developed and developing countries alike? After all, only a small minority of the world's people, roughly 2 percent, ever move across national boundaries as migrants. Even in extreme or catastrophic cases, such as those of Afghanistan, El Salvador, and Cuba, the proportion of citizens who leave their country seldom exceeds 10 to 25 percent.

One reason for migration's heightened salience is that international population movements are posing some fundamental challenges to:

the search for a "new world order" out of the change and uncertainty that has accompanied the end of the Cold War;

the post-World War II system of sovereign nation-states;

the international refugee regime; and

the political survival of governments and parties in migrant-receiving countries.

A second reason for migration's higher profile is the growing potential for international migration, driven by three major forces:

Deepening economic divides between countries. The gap between rich and poor countries, as measured by real per capita income, has widened steadily over the past 40 years.

Widening demographic differentials. These are perhaps best reflected in the gap between rapid labor force growth in developing countries and slow growth in industrialized countries.

Sharpening political differentials. These are evident in the differences between countries governed by the rule of law, with active participation by the civil society, and those characterized by weak legal systems, human rights abuses, and violent domestic conflicts.

However, population pressures and economic and political differentials are not the whole story. Other factors are also amplifying, precipitating, and perpetuating international migration flows. These include global networks of communication, transportation, and people-moving intermediaries; growing international trade links; and the collapse of empires, the failure of states, and the resurgence of nationalisms. Although control measures shape and modulate international population movements, the combined effect of these driving forces and amplifying factors has led to a third reason why international migration has become a hot topic: the number of migrants has increased, at an accelerating rate of growth.

Global Trends

In 1965, there were approximately 75 million international migrants, including the foreign-born, foreign nationals, and official refugees. By 1990, their numbers had swelled to nearly 120 million, equivalent in size to the population of Bangladesh, the ninth most populous country in the world. Between 1985 and 1990 alone, the total stock of migrants increased by about 15 million people or 2.6 percent per year, a rate of increase higher than the 2.2 percent annual rate of natural increase in the populations of less-developed countries. A recent International Labour Office (ILO) analysis of labor migration between 1970 and 1990 provides evidence that the geographical scope of economically motivated migration is spreading as well. This study found a striking 53 percent increase in the number of countries participating in international migration, as senders, receivers, or both. More than half (84 out of 155) of the countries in the analysis were actively involved in migration streams as of 1990. It is expected that the data for 1990–1995 will show a large increase in both the number of migrants and the number of countries involved in migration, partly as a result of reclassification following the breakup of the Soviet Union and the former Yugoslavia.

The world's international migrants are distributed across all regions of the globe: 37 percent in Asia and North Africa; 21 percent in Eastern and Western Europe; 20 percent in the United States and Canada; 11 percent in sub-Saharan Africa; 6 percent in Latin America and the Caribbean; and 4 percent in Oceania. More than half of all international migrants are in developing countries. Contrary to the common perception of international migrants as young adult males, between 40 and 60 percent of all international migrants worldwide—and over half of all refugees—are women and girls.

From the mid-1980s through the early 1990s, Asia produced nearly half the world's refugees, but their numbers have fallen from almost 10 million in 1993 to under 8 million in 1995, largely as the result of repatriation of Afghans from Pakistan and

Iran. Labor migrants continue to return to the Arab Gulf. Despite the massive departure of the Palestinian population from Kuwait during the 1990–1991 Gulf crisis, by January 1995 there were nearly 1.2 million expatriates in Kuwait and Kuwaitis were once again a minority in their own land (a mere 37 percent of the total population). East Asia continues to be an especially dynamic region of population mobility. For example, despite Japan's recent economic woes, the stock of foreign workers there doubled from 300,000 in 1990 to 600,000 in 1993. Taiwan had virtually no guest workers in 1990, but had 316,000 by 1995. The last of the Vietnamese "boat people" in Southeast Asia and Hong Kong are being repatriated or resettled, and Vietnam's leaders have indicated that the country now intends to become a major labor exporter. The number of Koreans emigrating to the United States has dropped dramatically from a high of 36,000 annually in the mid-1980s to only 11,000 in 1994. Since 1991, between 5,000 and 6,500 per year have become "return migrants," leaving the United States for Korea.

The Korean case illustrates the broader point that, over long periods of time, as countries develop, they appear to pass through what is called the "migration transition"—going from being sending countries, to both sending and receiving, and finally receiving countries. In China, however, where there are already approximately 100 million internal migrants, 20 million of whom are located in booming coastal cities, the prospects for such a transition are a long way off. This new internal mobility has ramifications for international migration: during the early 1990s, well-organized human smuggling operations involving 30 countries are estimated to have delivered approximately half a million illegal Chinese migrants to Europe, the former Soviet Union, and North America. Another 100,000 have reportedly entered Thailand, with smaller numbers to other destinations in Asia.

Africa as a whole, and sub-Saharan Africa in particular, continues to be distinctive for its production of refugees—more than 80 percent of the world's total at the beginning of 1995—and for the volatile and sometimes appalling nature of these population movements. During 1994, some 2 million refugees fled Rwanda in the fastest exodus of its size ever recorded; in April, for example, nearly a quarter of a million poured into Tanzania in one 24-hour period. There were also significant numbers of new refugees from Burundi, Liberia, Sudan, Somalia, Mali, and Sierra Leone, all but a fraction of whom have remained in neighboring countries. At the same time, there have been some promising developments in the region: nearly three-quarters of a million refugees repatriated to Mozambique during 1994, while smaller numbers repatriated to Burundi, Somalia, Ethiopia, Eritrea, and Togo.

Despite the visibility of refugee situations in Africa, not all African migrants are refugees; there are long-standing as well as recent population movements between African countries that are largely economically motivated. Well-established migration streams include those from Burkina Faso, Mali, and Guinea to Cote d'Ivoire and those from Botswana, Lesotho, and Swaziland to South Africa. More recent developments include the movement into South Africa of as many as 2 million illegal migrants from all parts of the continent.

Migration from North Africa has been predominantly labor migration and mostly toward European destinations. Indeed, migration across the Mediterranean basin is a major focus of concern in Europe, prompting great interest in whether and how trade, financial aid, and development assistance might be deployed to help stem these migratory flows. Within North Africa, Libya has been a regional pole of attraction from time to time, notably for Tunisians. Recently, however, Libya has expelled Palestinian, Egyptian, and Sudanese workers for both economic and political reasons.

With regard to Latin America and the Caribbean, Mexico is the principal sending country, and the United States is the country of overwhelming attraction. Nevertheless, there is also a considerable, and growing, amount of economic migration among Latin American countries, notably to Argentina and Venezuela, some of it facilitated by regional trade agreements such as the Andean Pact (between Bolivia, Ecuador, Peru, and Venezuela) and the Mercado Comun del Cono Sur (MERCOSUR) among the countries of the Southern Cone. The number of officially designated refugees in the region continues to decline and stood at just over 100,000 at the end of 1994. At the same time, there are several notable cases of significant international movements in 1994 as a result of deteriorating political and economic conditions. Haiti and Cuba are perhaps the two most prominent examples.

The United States, Canada, and Australia are the so-called traditional countries of permanent immigration. As of the 1990 U.S. census, the foreign-born population stood at about 20 million, approximately 8 percent of the total population. Since then, and especially following passage of the 1990 Immigration Act, there has been a substantial rise in the number of persons who entered the United States for lawful permanent residence—from 674,000 in 1990 to 877,000 in 1993, compared to about 600,000 per year in the latter half of the 1980s, and 360,000 per year in the late 1960s. These figures do not include asylum seekers (another 144,000 in 1993), people admitted on non-immigrant visas, or those unlawfully resident in the United States who legalized under provisions of the Immigration Control and Reform Act of 1986 (which has added another 3 million persons in the past decade). The figures also do not include continuing net flows of illegal migrants, whose stock was estimated to be about 3.4 million in 1992 and growing at a rate of 300,000 per year.

With regard to legal, permanent immigration to the United States, Mexico headed the list of major source countries between 1956 and 1993. In 1991, Mexico briefly dropped to second place, after the Philippines. Mexico, Asia, and Central America together now account for over half of the foreign-born population in the United States—a dramatic shift from 1970, when 60 percent of foreign-born residents were from Europe. These numbers and their composition form the backdrop for current heated policy debates on U.S. immigration reform.

Canada held more or less to its targeted intake of about 250,000 persons per year in 1992 and 1993, but annual immigration to Australia has dropped. Australian intake was only 63,000 in fiscal year 1993–1994, an historically low level generally explained by economic recession and high unemployment, both of which have made Australia a less attractive destination for migrants in recent years. Like the United States, both Canada and Australia have experienced a notable shift to Asian source countries over the past decade. Although annual intake in both Canada and Australia is much lower than in the United States, the proportions of foreign-born in the total populations are considerably higher—over 16 percent in Canada and 22 percent in Australia.

Migration to Western Europe has undergone several dynamic shifts in recent years. Europe initiated relatively large-scale labor recruitment in the years after World War II in response to labor shortages and the needs of post-war reconstruction. In the late 1960s and early 1970s, West European countries were admitting upwards of 1 million people annually—ostensibly on a temporary basis under "guest-worker" programs. Large numbers of these were from Turkey, Yugoslavia, and the southern European countries—Greece, Italy, Spain, and Portugal.

Such recruitment was halted or slowed during the early 1970s because of rising public concern and the economic recession that followed the oil price rises of the period. The inflow continued, however, primarily because of provisions allowing for family reunification. Between 800,000 and 900,000 people per year were admitted throughout the late 1970s and early 1980s. By the late 1980s, average annual inflows had risen dramatically to more than 1 million per year and in 1992 exceeded 1.7 million. Family reunification continued to be the major component of admissions in most countries, followed by workers and refugees, but the numbers were also swelled by new east-west flows and asylum seekers. The number of people arriving in Europe and lodging claims for political asylum began to rise dramatically in the mid-1980s, reaching nearly 700,000 in 1992. Although so-called "recognition rates" are low, with only a small proportion of asylum seekers granted refugee status, until recently most rejected asylum seekers (and others awaiting adjudication of their cases) remained in the host countries. Since 1987, migration has accounted for more than 60 percent of Western Europe's total population growth. Yet to this day, puzzling as it might seem, European countries insist (unlike the United States, Canada, and Australia, and despite evidence to the contrary) that they are not "countries of immigration."

Since 1993, however, the inflow of foreign-born populations to Europe has begun to level off in most countries, especially in Germany and France, the largest receivers. By 1994, the number of asylum seekers also had dropped to less than half its 1992 level. West European states are concerned, nevertheless, that illegal immigration may be on the rise. One estimate puts the stock of illegal immigrants in the region between 2.5 and 3 million; other estimates run as high as 5.5 million.

Several other important features of recent migration to Western Europe should be noted. First, the share of foreigners from non-European Union member countries has increased substantially. As their numbers have increased, certain nationalities have gained importance relative to groups that migrated earlier—for example, Iranians and Sri Lankans in Norway and Sweden; Moroccans, Senegalese, and Vietnamese in France; Africans from the former Portuguese colonies of Angola and Cape Verde in Portugal. New and growing east-west flows are especially important for Germany, Austria, and Sweden. Second, as in North America and Australia, migration of highly skilled workers is becoming more common. And third, recourse to temporary worker programs is also becoming more popular—notwithstanding the fact that such programs in the 1960s and early 1970s were not entirely successful, in the sense that "the guests came to stay."

Changes have also occurred in Central and Eastern Europe, which has been emerging as a regional pole of attraction since 1993. The Czech Republic, Hungary, Poland, Bulgaria, and Russia have all begun to receive labor migrants from elsewhere in the region and from developing countries, skilled workers from developed countries, and the return migration of former emigrants. Net immigration to the Russian Federation alone was 916,000 in 1994 and 963,000 in 1995, with Kazakhstan, Ukraine, and the Central Asian republics being the main countries of origin.

With respect to Europe as a whole, upwards of 800,000 refugees from Bosnia-Herzegovina were being hosted in the region at the end of 1994, in addition to the 1.3 million Bosnians internally displaced. They are a sobering reminder that all the control mechanisms in the world cannot rule out such volatile flows.

In conclusion, international migration today is characterized by several trends:

- Globalization. International migration is a worldwide phenomenon, affecting developing as well as industrialized countries.
- Diversification. The directions of migration are not simply toward industrialized countries; as of the mid-1980s, just over half of all migrants were in developing countries. A growing number of countries are participating in migration streams.
- Acceleration. The number of international migrants of all types appears to be growing. The official refugee population rose dramatically from just over 8 million in 1980 to more than 14 million at the beginning of 1995 (down from a high of 18 million in 1993) and the number of internally displaced is growing.

National Responses

Trying to make broad and simple generalizations about international migration, a complex and shifting subject, is a challenge under any circumstances, particularly when looking at national responses. A given country's declared policies toward migration and the control mechanisms it employs to manage migration are usually the products of intense and heated political debate within that country.

One measure of national responses on a global basis may be found by consulting the section on International Migration Policies in the World Population Monitoring Report, which presents findings based on regular, periodic surveys of governments, conducted by the U.N. Population Division. According to the 1993 Monitoring Report, the percentage of countries that view levels of immigration as too high grew significantly in the late 1970s and early 1980s, and has continued to rise, reaching nearly 23 percent in 1993. Some countries that view immigration levels as satisfactory nonetheless have policies to lower immigration; consequently, the percentage of governments with such policies is even higher—35 percent in 1993. This has contributed to the general perception that countries around the globe are becoming more "restrictionist," especially in the face of economic uncertainty and adverse public reactions to immigration. However, this should not obscure the fact that most countries view their current levels of immigration as satisfactory and have policies to maintain those levels. Also, a small percentage of countries view the level of immigration as too low and have policies to raise it. The latter include Equatorial Guinea, Namibia, Israel, Argentina, Uruguay, Guyana, Canada, and New Zealand. Nor is restrictionism concentrated in industrialized countries. Of the 39 countries that officially view immigration as too high and consciously intervene to lower it, only 13 are developed countries. The percentage of foreigners in a population is not necessarily a good predictor of national response (although obviously at the individual country level it can play a role in immigration debates). Perhaps paradoxically, the median percentage of foreign-born persons in countries with policies to raise immigration is 11, while it is only 4 percent in countries with policies to reduce immigration.

Countries also have views and policies about the emigration of their own citizens. In 1993, the majority viewed the prevailing levels of emigration as satisfactory and had policies to maintain them; approximately 20 percent viewed emigration as too high and intervened to lower it, while just over 3 percent acknowledged official efforts to encourage emigration. The latter include Korea, Indonesia, Pakistan, and Turkey.

In trying to generalize about responses to international migration at the country level, one can make a broad distinction between countries of origin and countries of destination, although a growing number of countries are in both categories. Regardless of their officially stated views and policies, a number of countries—from Barbados to the Philippines—have encouraged labor emigration as an outlet for their rapidly expanding labor forces and as a source of hard currency remittance inflows. In 1990, total global remittance credits through official channels were over $71 billion, second in value only to trade in crude oil; net flows to developing countries were nearly $37 billion, over two-thirds the value of official development assistance that year. In other words, remittances are important and growing mechanisms for the transfer of resources from developed to developing countries.

Some governments also tacitly welcome the voluntary departure of certain ethnic or political groups, as in the cases of Azeris from Turkey and Palestinians from Jordan. At the extremes, governments have been known to forcibly expel residents and even citizens, often to achieve cultural homogeneity or ethnic dominance. Ethnic cleansing in Bosnia is but one recent example—the practice has a long history, including expulsion of the Jews from Spain in the fifteenth century and expulsion of the Protestant Huguenots from Catholic France in the seventeenth century.

Although emigration has some clear benefits for countries of origin, they are also naturally ambivalent about the phenomenon. They often decry the loss of human capital and in recent years have been confronted with the financial downside of dependence on remittances. This downside centers on their increasing vulnerability to sudden changes in countries of destination, as seen most dramatically with the repatriation and/or expulsion of migrants during the 1990–1991 Gulf crisis.

Reactions in countries of destination vary widely, can change with time, and may differ depending on the sources and circumstances of the migrants. In both developed and developing countries, those with booming economies and labor shortages have initially welcomed labor migrants, only to become less welcoming or even hostile to immigrants when economic conditions (and with them, domestic political conditions) deteriorate.

Reactions to refugees and other forced migrants can also change over time. For years, Thailand hosted hundreds of thousands of Indochinese refugees coming across its eastern border. However, by the late 1980s, resettlement in third countries had slowed and in 1988, Thailand (along with Malaysia) began to repel boatloads of Indochinese attempting to reach its shores. National responses may also be different toward different groups. For example, the United States has admitted very few Haitians or Guatemalans as refugees but for three decades admitted Cubans, granting them virtually automatic adjustment to permanent resident alien status.

Beyond these generalizations about national responses, it is necessary to look at some of the dynamics within countries that help shape those responses. This may be termed the political economy of responses to migration. Five broad groups of potential actors can be distinguished: governmental actors, including elected officials at the federal, provincial, and local levels and politicians of both the ruling and opposition parties; employers and business interests; organized labor; migrant and other allied interest groups; and the general public.

The interplay among and within these groups of actors is often complex and unpredictable, and the groups are by no means monolithic in their stances on particular issues. Governments, especially at the federal or national level, tend to view the determination of who may enter and under what conditions they may remain as a fundamental sovereign right of states. But beyond agreement on this general principle, there is much debate and dissention. The current furor surrounding immigration reform in the United States is an immediate example. Tensions have developed between those who formulate national immigration policy in Washington and local government officials, supported by public opinion, in states such as California, Texas, and Florida. These localities feel unfairly and excessively burdened by the inflows of immigrants that have resulted from national immigration policies and they want to see the levels reduced. Yet elected officials in New York, a state with one of the largest concentrations of migrants, have come out strongly in favor of continued high levels of immigration, which they view as contributing to their state's economy. There are similarly divergent views (both in the United States and in other industrialized countries) about whether or not illegal as well as legal migrants should be eligible for social benefits such as health, education, and welfare services.

Employers and business communities around the globe tend to be among the staunchest supporters of migratory movements because of their ongoing interest in cheap and readily available labor. Their influence on national policy can be considerable. In countries as diverse as the United States, Malaysia, and those of Western Europe, agribusiness interests have lobbied hard against the introduction of restrictions on entry and against employer sanctions for hiring illegal workers. The views of organized labor are less predictable. Many labor unions in the United States argue that migrants take jobs away from native-born workers; they opposed the North American Free Trade Agreement on this basis. Yet others are recognizing migrant workers, both legal and illegal, as a new source of energy to revitalize dwindling union membership roles. Similarly, labor unions in Kuwait (whose power has been limited in any event) have tended to take a positive view of migrants. Already-established migrant communities also exert pressures on the formulation of national responses. In Fiji, the long-resident Indian population and native Fijians have united in opposition to the prime minister's recent proposal to encourage immigration of Chinese from Hong Kong.

Indeed, immigration policy debates often create strange bedfellows. A recent New York Times article observed that, "As Congress ... considers anti-immigration measures, it is facing resistance from a surprising alliance of high-technology manufacturers, religious leaders, conservative think tanks, civil liberties organizations and tiny, grass-roots immigrant groups." Added to such cauldrons of domestic debate are the foreign policy dimensions that often accompany international migration and that, in turn, feed back into domestic responses. When the Cuban government began allowing large numbers of people to flee the country by boat in 1994, President Clinton reversed the long-standing U.S. policy of admitting Cubans with virtually automatic rights to permanent residence. In doing so, he faces the potential wrath of the Cuban-American community at the ballot box in 1996. Within the past year, Philippine president Fidel Ramos has similarly faced crises in both the foreign policy and domestic arenas over the arrests, convictions, and in one case execution of Filipina domestic workers in Singapore and the United Arab Emirates.

Members of the general public, at least in pluralistic societies, have the opportunity to register their views through electoral processes. In California, they did so in 1994 through Proposition 187, which sought to eliminate the provision of social, educational, and health services to illegal aliens; in Switzerland and France, they have done so through the rising numbers of votes cast for the anti-immigrant Auto and National Front parties, respectively. At the end of the day, national responses are fundamentally influenced by "policymakers' and citizens' concerns for the preservation of a particular national identity (or identities) and widely shared values and for maintaining control over political institutions." Even countries that take a positive view toward the entry of non-nationals want to be seen as being in control of the process.

Control Measures

All countries have a range of control measures from which to select. Different observers offer different classifications of such mechanisms. In his new book, The Global Migration Crisis, Myron Weiner divides these broadly into rules of entry and rules of exit. Along a spectrum from lax to tight, rules of entry may be unrestricted (the United States in the nineteenth century), promotional (Israel with respect to Jews), restrictive but permissive (such as allowing for family reunification), unwanted (as in the case of massive refugee inflows), or prohibitive (as in Turkey's response to Iraqi Kurds in the spring of 1991). Ranging from tight to lax, rules of exit may be prohibitive (common practice among totalitarian states), selective (restricting the emigration of the highly skilled or permitting the emigration of certain groups), permissive (typical of Western democracies), promotional (as in the case of some labor-exporting countries), or expulsive (Indians and other Asians from East Africa).

Another approach, put forward by Aristide Zolberg, distinguishes between "direct controls" and "remote controls," depending upon where they are exercised. Direct controls include those exercised by virtually every country at land border crossings, ports, and airports. Another direct control measure is the round-up and deportation of illegal migrants and rejected asylum seekers. This mechanism has a long history in many developing countries but has also recently found favor in the industrialized democracies.

Remote controls are of three general types. First, passports and visas were widely introduced in the United States and other Western countries during the nineteenth century. Second, "carrier sanctions" require that airlines, ships, and other carriers assume responsibility for validating that each passenger has the travel documents needed to enter the country of destination. Failure to do so results in monetary fines and obligates the carrier to return the traveller at its own expense. Finally, intelligence has been used in countries such as Kuwait where "security checks" of prospective migrants are common and involve the issuance of "Good Conduct Certificates" and "Endorsements" from Kuwaiti embassies in migrants' countries of origin. Historically, intelligence measures have not been widely used in industrial democracies, but that is changing with the advent of computerized technologies that permit the "tracking" of migrants (such as the EURODOC system) and increased international cooperation among law enforcement officials (through Interpol, for example). To Zolberg's classification, we might add those "remote" and much longer-term controls that consist of efforts to stem migration through fostering economic development in countries of migrant origin, and a fourth category of interior controls, such as residence permits, work permits, identity cards, and practices such as permitting employers to retain and hold a worker's passport (common in the Gulf states).

In the wake of the asylum crisis of the late 1980s and early 1990s, European and North American countries have introduced a number of other control mechanisms. These include the following: expedited asylum procedures to screen prospective asylum seekers at points of entry and to exclude those whose claims are patently "frivolous" or "manifestly unfounded"; off-shore screening (in countries of origin, in third countries, or on the high seas), as was used by the United States in the Haitian and Cuban crises of 1994; and lists of "safe countries" determined to pose little or no risk of persecution. Asylum claimants from designated safe countries are provided with "fasttrack" adjudication of their claims (for example, Romanians seeking asylum in Germany), while those who pass through a safe country (such as Bosnians attempting to enter Germany through Austria) are returned to that safe country for processing of their claims. The safe country approach is now embodied in the Dublin

Convention, as well as in numerous bilateral agreements between West European countries and their eastern neighbors.

The subject of control mechanisms, like immigration itself, is hotly debated. There are at least two sets of issues: how vigorously they should be implemented and how effectively they work. In the industrial democracies, views on some of these control mechanisms have changed markedly in recent years as the number of migrants has grown and public reactions to migration have become more negative. Only several years ago, the idea of chartering a plane to remove rejected asylum seekers was unthinkable, but France and Germany have done just that recently. Views on the use of certain mechanisms also differ sharply in countries with different political cultures. Countries such as France and Sweden have long had systems of national identity documents (cards identifying the bearer) for citizens and resident aliens alike and these are widely accepted as normal. In the United States, by contrast, any hint of such measures is widely resisted. Even the proposal to verify a worker's social security number prior to employment—which the bipartisan U.S. Commission on Immigration Reform (established by the Immigration Act of 1990) has recommended be pilot-tested—has drawn fire from civil libertarians and conservatives alike as an infringement on personal liberty.

Despite such differences, on balance there appears to be a growing convergence among countries in the policy instruments used for controlling migration, especially illegal migration and refugee flows. This is not accidental or even simply the result of a diffusion effect. Within Europe, the convergence of control mechanisms came at the same time the European Union was being forged, when the need arose to harmonize national policies with an eye toward the emergence of common community policies. Among industrial countries more broadly, there has been a great deal of transnational dialogue on control mechanisms among policymakers in both longstanding forums such as the Organization for Security and Cooperation in Europe and new, ad hoc groups such as the Inter-governmental Consultations on Asylum, Refugee, and Migration Policies in Europe, North America, and Australia. Growing international cooperation to stem terrorism and international trafficking in migrants, along with the awareness that the policies of one country or region may have an impact on those of another, provide further impetus for convergence. In this respect, although the system of sovereign states is still very much alive, it may be incomplete to talk about national responses. The outlines of supranational responses are visible.

Regarding whether or not control mechanisms work, there are two camps. On one side, Wayne Cornelius, Philip Martin, and James Hollifield argue in their new book, Controlling Immigration, that such measures do not work and that there is a growing gap between the stated goals of immigration policies and their actual outcomes. The other side, which includes Aristide Zolberg, Myron Weiner, and Michael Teitelbaum, believes that control mechanisms can and do work. On balance, it may be argued, the burden of evidence lies with the latter group—witness, for example, the decline in immigration and asylum statistics in Western Europe over the last two years. Were it not for the presence of controls on entry, the volume of international migration would likely be even greater than it is. Ultimately, the gap is less between stated policies and outcomes than between stated policies and implemented policies. The real issue may be to what extent internal political debates within liberal democracies permit policymakers to implement control measures, even when general public opinion favors them.

International migration is likely to continue to be a matter of high politics. The demographic, economic, and political differentials that drive the potential for international population movements show no signs of abating any time soon. The continued emergence of a global economy, the liberalization of world trade and transition economies, and the process of development itself add further impetus to such movements. The responsibilities of states to their citizens abroad and the presence of growing foreign populations within their territories raise both foreign and domestic national policy issues that promise to pose challenges for a long time to come.

R. George Wright, Federal Immigration Law and the Case for Open Entry

27 Loy. L.A. L. Rev. 1265 (1994)

Footnotes have been omitted.

I. Introduction

The most basic features of United States immigration law generate continuing controversy. Public debate over federal statutory limits on entry into the United States is ongoing and frequently passionate. The practical importance of the subject seems undeniable. The lives or welfare of many people are directly implicated. Many legal and political philosophers, as well as immigration specialists, however, shy away from some of the most fundamental issues of moral limits on immigration.

A possible explanation for this inattention may be that many students of basic immigration policy half-consciously perceive that broad legal restrictions on entry into the United States cannot be morally justified. These persons also assume that opening legal entry into the United States would require current United States residents to endure a painful sacrifice of important interests and privileges. Admittedly, academic calls for collective self-sacrifice are not unknown. In the immigration context, however, the direct beneficiaries of an open entry policy do not currently vote or maintain an organized presence in the United States. Calls for an open entry policy are therefore understandably not particularly common.

This Article seeks to broaden the debate not only by arguing for an open entry policy, but also, perhaps surprisingly, by arguing that a carefully crafted version of an open entry policy need not involve costs to current citizens so substantial as to practically disqualify such a policy.

It is widely assumed that an open entry policy would simply result in "swamping the lifeboat"; that is, in the abrogation of national sovereignty, in enormous costs in unemployment, in reduced wage rates and other economic and welfare costs, in jeopardizing our national cultural identity, and in slowing or reversing progressive political and social change. Each of these obvious concerns requires a different response, and each is addressed separately below.

The defense of an open entry policy is thus multifaceted. But it may be of general interest to think about the possibility of "decoupling" an open entry policy from various more or less related areas of government policy, including minimum wage rates, benefits eligibility, and voting rights. Once this decoupling process is undertaken, it becomes clear that various costs of open entry can be minimized or redistributed in ways that enhance the appeal of an open entry policy.

This Article concludes by examining the moral arbitrariness of restrictions on immigration and by constructing a broad-based affirmative moral case for open entry. It is hoped that over time, the public debate over limitations on immigration can be broadened, deepened, and otherwise enhanced.

II. The Feared Consequences of Open Entry

A. Preliminary Observations

Recent debate over United States immigration law has raised important issues of public policy. There should, however, be no illusions as to the remarkably narrow scope of the debate. Current United States immigration policy may seem generous, relative to that of many other nations. But this should not obscure the fact that the mainstream, contemporary immigration debate focuses only upon various substantially restrictive immigration policies. What might reasonably be referred to—with sensible qualifications—as an open entry policy of any sort is not typically considered a viable option.

Given the limitations on judicial decision making, it is not surprising that the courts do not take an open immigration policy seriously. The apparent indifference of most major legal and moral philosophers is, however, less justifiable. To the extent that such writers ignore immigration questions, or merely assume the implausibility of any open entry policy, this indifference should be called into question. This Article therefore seeks to expand interest in the most basic assumptions underlying the law of immigration, and in the viability of some forms of an open entry policy.

Substantial legal restriction of immigration is not a clear reflection of historical tradition in the United States. Currently, of course, entry into the United States is subject to legal restriction. Alien immigration was, however, essentially unrestricted at least at the federal level until 1875, with the first general immigration statute following only in 1882. Legal restrictions on the total annual amount of immigration into the United States were not imposed until 1921.

Plainly, matters such as United States population density, international wage differentials, government benefit programs, and the demand for unskilled labor do not now stand as they did during our first century. Each of these considerations bears legitimately upon United States immigration law and policy. It would therefore be absurd to argue that since an open entry policy was once viable, it must remain viable today.

Still, the historical fact of roughly a century of open entry into the United States has some force against certain kinds of cultural, as opposed to economic, arguments against an open entry policy. Both cultural and economic concerns are examined below. For the moment, it suffices to observe that in light of our first century of open entry, any argument that the United States ethos or the United States community requires rigorous cultural restrictiveness in immigration is implausible. Whether the United States ethos in fact requires, or at least suggests, abolishing such restrictiveness is taken up below.

For some time now, admittedly, federal immigration law has imposed substantial restrictions on immigration. Since 1990 specified annual ceilings or maxima are imposed on most important categories of immigrants. Although statutory provision is made for the granting of asylum to a class of refugees, granting such asylum remains within the discretion of the Attorney General. More broadly, persons deemed illegally present, border arrivals temporarily paroled into the United States, and would-be entrants interdicted on the high seas are subject to deportation or exclusion on the basis of correspondingly minimal hearing rights.

In general, the substantive legal rights of even the most desperate individuals seeking initial entry into the United States have been thought to be modest. The Supreme Court has thus observed, in apparently anachronistic language, that "an alien seeking initial admission to the United States requests a privilege and has no constitutional rights regarding his application, for the power to admit or exclude aliens is a sovereign prerogative." Indeed, this judicial position is frequently encountered. It has even been suggested that "Congress can bar aliens from entering the United States for discriminatory and arbitrary reasons, even those that might be condemned as a denial of equal protection or due process if used for purposes other than immigration policy."

Taken literally, this doctrine would validate, for example, an entry scheme based on the willingness of potential entrants to undergo severe and prolonged physical torture. It is, therefore, not surprising that some writers have expressed sympathy for the idea of constitutional restrictions on immigration criteria and procedures. Regardless, this Article will show the sheer feasibility and moral attractiveness of some forms of open entry policy, without launching prematurely into a debate as to the constitutional status of such a policy.

B. Open Entry and National Sovereignty

What sort of open entry policy, then, could be thought feasible and morally attractive? Assuming the continued existence of nation-states, legitimate military defense must be distinguished from unjust foreign invasion. As one writer has observed, "It would be something of a joke to refer to ... defensive military action as 'immigration restriction.'" It is possible, of course, to refer to any substantial influx of entrants as an "invasion," but such concerns seem to raise the sorts of cultural or communitarian concerns that are addressed below, rather than military security in a narrow sense.

Admittedly, there may be intermediate cases in which, for example, a country seeks to export its prison or mental hospitalization costs by forcing, persuading, or merely allowing massive numbers of these undesired residents to emigrate to a particular recipient state. The best guide in such cases will be our sense of whether, as in the classic immigrant case, the decision to enter was made exclusively by each would-be entrant, even if under the press of circumstance, or whether the entry is ultimately traceable to a donor-government policy of seeking to externalize perceived costs by encouraging emigration. Whether a foreign government is seeking on a major scale to manipulate a generous United States entry policy should not, in practice, be unusually difficult to determine. A genuine open entry policy, then, need not invite foreign exploitation.

This argument can be expanded, though, by considering whether an open entry policy is in all contexts consistent with the idea of national sovereignty. Courts have frequently held that the power to limit immigration, or to deny entry, is a necessary, inherent aspect of national sovereignty. With this doctrine I take no issue. It is important, however, to recognize how little this doctrine, by itself, actually says. It should be clear that the mere possession of a power, in this case of limiting entry, does not require the actual exercise of that power in practice.

Thus, we might equally grant that the fully sovereign government of a territory necessarily must possess the authority to inflict legal punishments, including the death penalty. It would hardly follow, however, that a state is no longer sovereign if, perhaps by statute or by constitutional amendment, it consistently declines to impose, or constitutionally disables itself from imposing, the death penalty.

Similarly, a government could remain sovereign if it freely and conscientiously chose a policy of open entry, even if such a border policy was written into its constitution. Such a policy could represent an authoritative, deliberate act of self-definition and self-determination by the public in its sovereign capacity. Such a choice seems at the very least as compatible with genuine national sovereignty as the current United States policy of nominally asserting complete legal border control while in practice exerting only minimal control over the entry and departure of undocumented persons.

Thus, the idea of sovereignty itself does not require any particular degree of actual openness or closure of borders, any more than sovereignty itself requires, for example, any particular approach to population policy. A community may, in its sovereign capacity, choose to extend its scope to encompass a broadly defined or even partially self-selected class of current outsiders. A broad, or in some respects open-ended, community self-definition need not amount to an abrogation of community sovereignty. It should thus be clear that the relevant fear is not that open entry jeopardizes national sovereignty, but that open entry may threaten community self-preservation as a defined, distinctive culture.

C. Open Entry and National Cultural Character

I have suggested above that open entry need not countenance manipulation or invasion by foreign powers, and that open entry is compatible with self-determination and self-definition at the national level. Instead, the real worry seems to be that open entry may lead to a failure to preserve the nation's basic character. Open entry might, it is thought, transform a society culturally beyond recognition in allegedly undesirable ways.

First, it is believed that open entry, or merely excessive, rapid immigration, might lead to adverse changes in the receiving country's political culture. Assume for the purposes of this discussion that the receiving country's political culture is, to some sufficient degree, genuinely or objectively good. Without this assumption, mere political self-preservation would carry little moral weight. Even on this assumption it is difficult to see why current residents have some sort of absolute right against adverse political-cultural changes not stemming from foreign invasion or manipulation. Convincing arguments must be made why protecting against adverse political-cultural changes is genuinely incompatible with all forms of open entry policy, and why the harms of such cultural changes outweigh or outrank all possible rights and interests of all would-be immigrants who are to be barred. It is not immediately obvious why person A should be protected from a less attractive political culture at the cost of starvation, poverty, or repression of person B.

These matters are pursued in general terms below. For the moment, I merely assert that through what I call decoupling, the United States might combine an open entry policy with a variety of legal measures designed to minimize the risk that immigration will slow or reverse any momentum toward progressive political change within the United States.

A broader challenge to an open entry policy raises the prospect of adverse cultural, and not merely political-cultural, changes flowing from allegedly excessive immigration. The desire to limit immigration may reflect "a concern that cultural change should not proceed so rapidly as to destabilize United States society." This broader culturally based challenge is an important one, and cannot be evaded by questioning whether genuine cultural stability is currently possible for the United States at any level of immigration, by questioning whether we can clearly distinguish between cultural stability and instability, or even by demanding to know why our being spared cultural instability should trump the rights and interests of would-be immigrants.

In some measure, of course, concerns for cultural stability may simply mask "paranoia, xenophobia, and racism," along with unwarranted national chauvinism. In other cases, concern for cultural stability may depend upon a romantic, unrealistic view of the extent to which the contemporary United States constitutes a culturally uniform genuine community. It may be unreasonable to accuse an open entry policy of undermining a national community if the United States would not remotely approach a genuine community at any level of immigration.

It is, however, certainly possible to argue that an open entry policy would greatly increase the current level of ethnic conflict within the United States, resulting in greatly enhanced ethnic violence, hostile separatism, and cultural polarization. Examples of nation-states torn by such sectarian division are, unfortunately, not difficult to cite. The problem of cultural conflict sufficient to justify restrictions on entry is addressed in stages below.

Two preliminary points can be made regarding the issue of whether cultural conflict justifies restrictions on entry. First, it is apparently difficult to find an era in United

States history in which it could not be soberly judged that social or cultural conflict was threatening our sense of community. Yet, in retrospect, what may have struck us at the time as the loss of valued solidarity may later seem a neutral or even valuable cultural development. Second, and relatedly, given that dubious collective track record in recognizing unredeemed loss of community, and in view of the interests of the would-be entrants at stake, application of something like a demanding "clear and present danger" test may be appropriate if entry is to be restricted based on fear of sufficiently severe cultural conflicts that would presumably not otherwise occur.

Cultural change is always threatening to a society, and has of course been a constant feature of life in the United States. The consensus, however, is that the cultural changes wrought by immigration have been generally beneficial least in retrospect. It is important to ask directly, though, whether the United States ethos is genuinely compatible with an open entry policy.

It is of course impossible to fairly summarize the United States ethos in general. Certain strands, qualities, and themes, however, can be identified. Certain currents seem dominant over time. It does not take long, for example, for Michael Walzer's analogy of the United States to an elite university, "besieged by applicants," to begin to break down. It may be that for an elite university to avoid compromising its distinct mission, it must reject an open admissions policy in favor of selectivity. And it is certainly possible to speak of national aspirations or perfectionism, or of overridingly important national cultural goals.

But the United States ethos simply does not require analogous attempts, futile or successful, at selectivity among entrants. One way of explaining this would be to say that the United States ethos is by its nature not concretely perfectionist; another would be that there is no set of cultural priorities or substantive goals, held in common, to which immigration policy might be accommodated. We could just as well say, however, that substantive or perfectionist dimensions of the United States ethos—our highest and best public selves—are compatible with, and may actually require, an open entry policy.

There is certainly no point in denying historic and contemporary United States cultural strands opposed to substantial, broad-based immigration. The benefit of hindsight, however, invariably leaves most of us with a collective sense of embarrassment over such impulses. Other deeper, cultural themes that we tend to be prouder of in moments of reflection, have long run in the direction of diversity, pluralism, heterogeneity, and inclusion. Professor Frederick Whelan has observed that "diversity in the sense of ethnic and cultural pluralism has always been an important aspect of the American tradition." Immigration has obviously been a crucial source of that renewing diversity. Professor Whelan has further recognized that "an ongoing tradition of diverse immigration is arguably part of the very identity of the democratic community of the United States."

Plainly, the United States has been an immigrant society, a multiracial and multicultural society, and will surely remain so regardless of future immigration policy. Diversity and pluralism are not merely facts, but basic societal values. Although we can hardly predict the precise demographic effects of a shift to open entry, it seems reasonable to suppose that open entry would implicitly enhance cultural diversity in crucial respects. Nor would we necessarily be optimizing diversity by significantly restricting entry, even if the formulae for priorities among entrants were maximally sensitive to any recognized underrepresentation of various groups within United States society. It is not entirely clear that even if group A is uncontroversially assumed to be underrepresented relative to group B, diversity is really better served by admitting twenty As and no Bs, as opposed to fifty of each. Threshold levels may matter as much as percentages.

Admittedly, it is possible that just the increase in immigration attributable to an open entry policy may lead to additional cultural conflict. Such additional cultural conflict may be thought to somehow morally outweigh the rights and interests of the additional potential immigrants. Increases in immigration, whether enhancing diversity or not, may well lead to social friction, as in the case of contemporary Germany.

There is, however, some reason not to be unduly fearful of such a prospect. Recall first that the United States political system involves not merely federalism, but the far more radical—and initially counterintuitive—notion that increasing the number and the diversity of Madisonian "factions" actually tends to discourage the worst, most disruptive political and cultural outcomes. The rough idea is that the greater the number and variety of groups, the more difficult it will be for any single group or coalition to communicate, coordinate, and combine in such a way as to subvert the broader public interest. Enhancing diversity by multiplying factions through an open entry policy could thus lead to long-term social and political stability.

Certainly it would be unrealistic to simply view all immigrants as themselves constituting a large, organized, unified faction, regardless of their political rights or lack thereof. As one writer has suggested, "The class of resident aliens, to begin with, includes enormously variegated groups in terms of country of origin, reason for emigrating, age, race, income and so on; they are likely to have more in common with particular groups of citizens than they are with each other." Nor is it clear that financially well-off, well-educated, English-speaking, established immigrants will have a strict identity of interest with other immigrants lacking these advantages, even if they are of the same national or ethnic group. Thus, although an open entry policy might in a limited sense increase the low-level frictions of factional activity, it might also dampen the adverse effects of faction overall. In sum, the "absorptive capacity" of a state for additional, more diverse immigration is partly a function of whether the political system is designed to operate best in an environment of many and diverse factions, as ours presumably was.

Other processes may also tend to mitigate social conflict related to immigration. Whether future immigrants incline toward assimilation or not, they will likely tend—at least for a time—to engage in geographical and cultural "enclaving," in which new immigrants voluntarily seek first the community of others with similar backgrounds. The voluntary concentration of immigrants of a particular background in a particular area or areas is presumably, in many respects, in their social and economic interest. Thus, the inevitable strains of immigration are not felt on a geographically uniform basis. At least initially, such strains and their costs would fall on or even be naturally reduced or avoided in immigrant communities themselves, rather than on areas of the country with small or nonexistent recent immigrant communities. Whatever its deficiencies, this voluntary enclaving phenomenon would seem to mitigate any broader, society-wide cultural strains of immigration.

Additionally, the degree to which the sheer number of new immigrants would promote cultural conflicts should not be overestimated. An open entry policy is not a compelled entry policy, or even a subsidized entry policy. The number of persons who would voluntarily leave their native land to live permanently in the United States under an open entry policy, independent of any incentives or disincentives available to any government, including our own, should not be casually assumed to be enormous.

Without denying the disparities in opportunity available in the United States and the poorest nations, it remains true that persons "who are immersed in a particular way of life will find it difficult to reject it, or to sever their emotional ties with it." Professor Alan Dowty elaborates the point in the following common-sense terms:

Most people have no inclination to leave their native soil, no matter how onerous conditions become. Would-be emigrants must fight off the ties of family, the comfort of familiar surroundings, the rootedness in one's culture, the security of being among "one's own," and the power of plain inertia. Conversely, being uprooted carries daunting prospects: adjusting to alien ways, learning a new language, the absence of kith and kin, the sheer uncertainty of it all. One implication, of course, is that a merely open but unsubsidized entry policy may disproportionately benefit persons other than the most chronically poor. To the extent that poverty is associated with traditionalism or limited exposure to modern technological culture, these persons may tend to be among those least willing and able to emigrate.

It is plausible to assume that as communication technologies expand, more people will be made aware of the opportunities afforded by life in the United States. On the other hand, better communications may also reinforce any perceptions of the United States as a strange, culturally or spiritually alien, and perhaps occasionally dangerous, place. In any event, the desire not to enter or remain permanently in the United States depends not solely upon ignorance, but upon basic values.

Finally, it is worth briefly mentioning in this context an argument that is further developed below. The actual level and composition of immigration under an open entry policy will likely depend, over time, on a wide range of practically alterable United States government policies regarding matters such as minimum wage rates, industry subsidies, health and welfare benefits, and various political, civic, and voting rights. Thus, it is extremely important to decouple the potential effects of an open entry policy from any particular set of such background policies. The consequences of an open entry policy may vary widely, depending upon which background assumptions are chosen. For various reasons, then, assuming an inevitable "tidal wave" of permanent new immigrants under any open entry policy is unrealistic.

D. Open Entry, Employment, and Economics

Whatever the importance of broad cultural conflicts, there is clearly a sense in which narrow economic and employment-related issues are fundamental to evaluating immigration policies. These concerns are multidimensional. Among the most prominent concerns are fears of job displacement of native workers by immigrants, fears that increased job competition with immigrants will significantly reduce United States wage rates, and a variety of fears to the effect that an open entry policy would involve enormous net economic costs, at least to current citizens.

As to the first of these concerns, the available evidence of displacement of native workers by new entrants is, perhaps surprisingly, quite weak. Professor George Borjas has concluded that "modern econometrics cannot detect a single shred of evidence that immigrants have a sizable adverse impact on the earnings and employment opportunities of native citizens in the United States." Viewing matters of employment as simply a zero-sum competition between immigrants and native U.S. citizens, or African-American workers in particular, is thus a gross oversimplification at best.

Job competition may, for example, be muted by any willingness of immigrants to take jobs that would otherwise go unfilled or abolished. More positively, immigrants generate economic demand for the employment of nonimmigrants, start new businesses that employ other persons, and in general enhance long-term capital formation. To the extent that these benefits occur only in the long run, politicians facing reelection campaigns in the short term may tend to unduly discount such benefits when legislating on immigration policy, to the prejudice of the public interest. More generally, the nonvoting status of persons wishing to enter the United States tends to bias immigration policy into morally undervaluing the interests of would-be entrants.

Relatedly, there is understandable concern that increased immigration would significantly drive down wages and working conditions. But for reasons analogous to those referred to above in connection with issues of job displacement, such effects at best are difficult to document. Immigration can in fact have positive effects on general wage levels. Although the matter is not free from doubt, it has been argued that "a 10-percent increase in the number of immigrants increases the average African-American wage by about .2 percent." On the other hand, the same increase in immigration may also have a small adverse effect on the wages of African-American wage earners who are young, and there certainly can be no guarantee that these wage effects must remain constant at any level and composition of immigration. It seems clear, though, that any such adverse effects on wage levels of young African-Americans could be completely negated or compensated for by other federal tax, training, job development, or transfer programs, without reducing immigration. Funding for such compensatory programs could draw upon the fact that reductions in wage rates may generate increased profits, or may benefit consumers in the form of lower prices of goods manufactured with such labor.

Finally, whether an open entry policy would have other extremely harmful economic consequences, on net, is doubtful in the extreme. Such have hardly been the consequences of immigration historically. And while it is possible to argue that current or prospective immigrants will make fewer significant contributions, or will otherwise acquit themselves less gloriously than past waves of immigrants, this argument itself has greeted virtually every generation of United States immigrants. Any argument that recent immigrants have adapted poorly or that they will not, in the aggregate, continue the past pattern of immigrant success seems premature at best. There is no obvious reason why future entrants would, for example, be less interested in long-term educational investments in their own human capital, and in that of their children, than native-born citizens currently seem to be.

In the meantime, new immigrants add to the local, state, and federal tax bases, and reduce every citizen's share of the cost of public goods, such as defense, that are to some degree insensitive to population size. Given our enormous current national debt, new entrants are in effect agreeing to help bear the cost of past U.S. consumption, the enjoyment of which they presumably did not directly share. If the United States is to "grow" its way out of such indebtedness by effectively competing in an increasingly international, multilingual, and multicultural economy, future immigrants ultimately have an even more significant role in the process.

As is true of any policy, open entry involves some costs that would not be incurred under a more restrictive immigration policy. I have shown above how, at least in certain cases, job competition may produce winners and losers. In such cases, and more generally, sound public policy may require that the direct and indirect beneficiaries of an open entry policy fully or partially compensate those who suffer loss from such a policy. The basic point is simply that the choice need not be between foregoing an open entry policy or allowing all costs of such a policy to remain on those who initially bear them. All of these costs can be shifted by governmental action, through subsidies, taxes, redistributive programs, or other mechanisms. Fairly judging an open entry policy thus requires the critic of open entry to consider the morally attractive, feasible mechanisms by which costs of open entry may be shifted.

Even more broadly, an assessment of an open entry policy requires breaking any arbitrary or contingent linkage between immigration policy and any other government policy. The right to enter the country must be conceptually decoupled from other areas of law and policy. By way of analogy, consider arguments in favor of capital punishment that emphasize, for example, the relatively short sentences served by some murderers, the possibility of the subsequent murder of prison guards, or the failure of prison inmates to contribute to their own maintenance, or to make even symbolic restitution to the families of their victims.

But to reasonably evaluate capital punishment, a critic must, among other things, consider feasible alternative correctional worlds without capital punishment, but in which murderers serve genuine life terms, are physically isolated from prison guards, and to the extent possible, make such restitution from their own labor.

Similarly, it is important to evaluate open entry policies in the context of alternative feasible sets of any related background policies that may dramatically affect the attractiveness of an open entry policy. Fundamental principles of economics suggest, for example, that the number of entrants may be alterable by modifications in the broad system of benefits awaiting new entrants.

If the general public, for example, is unwilling to tolerate the level of immigration attributable to the attraction of particular levels of welfare or other benefits for new entrants, the public may respond either by limiting immigration, or to some limited degree, by reducing welfare or other benefit levels available to future entrants. If it wishes to, the public could minimize other perceived costs of open entry by, for example, enforcing higher or lower minimum wage rates—generally or in particular industries.

There is, admittedly, no guarantee that the public will be willing to accept open entry on the basis of a package of rights and benefits for future entrants that is even minimally consistent with the demands of justice or the equal protection rights of future entrants. The public should at least be able to grasp the utter foolishness of denying benefits, such as vaccinations and other forms of health care, and education, when providing such benefits would have important positive externalities. At least emergency provision of basic life necessities may be politically feasible.

Whether the public could insist, to any degree, on reducing benefits available to future entrants while still acting justly toward those entrants—and not unconstitutionally conditioning their entry—is of course controversial. Such a course hardly seems morally attractive. Under the United States Constitution, it is generally impermissible to favor established state residents over new entrants to a state. Still, it seems irresponsible to ignore the possibility that insisting on equal benefit rights for future new entrants may mean, as a matter of practical politics, that no open entry policy can be enacted. Realistically, the only viable choice may be between open entry with a minimally reduced benefits package for future new entrants only, and a more restrictive immigration policy.

Faced with this choice, the case for open entry is surprisingly strong. For example, consider the choices based on fair and equal consideration of "the interests of all those affected, either directly or indirectly, whether as an immediate result of the policy, or in the long run." The enhanced or preserved benefit levels available to those lucky enough to gain entry in the future must somehow be considered in the context of the assumed public refusal to grant entry to some number of future would-be entrants. It is hardly implausible that denying entry works a more substantial hardship than allowing entry, but only at reduced government benefit levels.

Insisting upon full benefits for future new entrants, even if this inevitably means denying entry to many others, actually has a lottery-like quality. Such a policy promotes extreme disparities in well-being. Independent of anyone's efforts or deserts, there arises a favored or "jackpot" class of persons who both enter and find relatively great benefit programs available, and a large "loser" class of persons who are denied entry and, of course, those high benefit levels. Such a system seems not so much liberal or generous as morally arbitrary. When we then add in any obligations we may have to ensure that the United States remains a place of great economic opportunity for future generations of natives and immigrants alike, the case for paying large benefits to future new immigrants—if at the inevitable expense of restricting immigration and the jeopardy of future generations—seems even more dubious. There seems no clear reason, in particular, to favor new immigrants at the expense of persons who will consider the possibility of immigrating over the next several generations.

This, however, is not the end of any moral complications. It may be either practically necessary or morally desirable to take the further step of decoupling open entry even from voting rights for future first generation immigrants, at least for a time, at any level of government. Doubtless it is at least initially appealing to require that "every new immigrant ... be offered the opportunities of citizenship." But the general populace may become convinced that new entrants may, through voting, undermine general liberal democratic goals, or liberal democracy itself. More pointedly, subordinated or oppressed groups within the United States may fear that enfranchisement of many new immigrants from illiberal cultures may retard or reverse contemporary progressive political trends. The point of such franchise restrictions, of course, is not to facilitate oppression of new entrants, but to protect fragile and developing recognition of the rights of current minority citizens.

At a minimum, potential entrants are entitled, prior to entry, to a reasonably clear and reliable description of the relevant limitations, if any, to be imposed on their franchise and other civic rights. Such disclosure would at least allow potential entrants to make an informed choice as to entry, without clearly denying their constitutional rights upon entry. Presumably, any necessary franchise restrictions may deter at least a few potential entrants, while being understandably viewed by others as a small price to pay.

III. Open Entry and Obligations to Neighbors and Strangers

To show that an open entry policy is feasible is not, admittedly, to show that it is morally or constitutionally sound. It has been argued that "it is in its immigration laws that a state most starkly asserts the primacy of state interest over universal principles of justice." Few states, however, would concede the injustice of their failure to adopt an open entry policy. One obvious line of defense would be for states to argue that just as persons owe stronger moral obligations to their own family members than to strangers, so states bear stronger moral obligations to their own citizens or current residents than to foreigners.

With the general idea of specially stringent obligations to one's dependents or to those to whom one has special commitments, there need be no quarrel. Certainly, a principled unwillingness to, for example, rescue one's own innocent relatives first would commonly be thought peculiar. We generally know the needs, resources, and limitations of our compatriots better than those of distant strangers, so we may be able to aid those near to us more effectively and at lower cost. It is also possible that seeking to extend the bonds of moral loyalty too far would result in indifference to nearby suffering. Finally, we should be wary of pressing too hard against even an arbitrary or apparently irrational but widespread bias in favor of those close to us.

These considerations, however, do not substantially undermine the moral case for open borders. The logic of open borders does not depend upon some unappealing or unsustainable version of universalism or absolute impartiality among persons. We need not maintain that relationships, voluntary or involuntary, are of no special moral import, or that cosmopolitan concerns must invariably trump narrower, more parochial interests.

The more appropriate argument is instead, roughly, that the interests of would-be voluntary entrants into the United States cannot be dismissed or flatly subordinated to all legitimate interests of current United States citizens or residents. Thus the issue need not be thought of as whether foreigners are in all respects and for all purposes the precise moral equals of citizens, but again rather roughly, whether foreigners or would-be entrants are morally entitled to at least some relevant level of concern and respect with regard to their vital interests.

An open entry policy thus need not be incompatible with national loyalties, patriotism, or even with national chauvinism. Nor need open entry undermine our ability to form what the philosopher Michael Sandel has described as identity-constitutive attachments. Most clearly, we need not view the assets of our fellow citizens merely as resources that ought to be placed at the unfettered disposal of any would-be entrant.

Part of the resistance to open entry may stem from a misleading dichotomy between special moral obligations owed to particular persons bearing particular statuses and general moral obligations owed universally. An open entry policy implicitly refers only to a class of persons voluntarily desirous of and otherwise capable of entering the United States. Obligations could be owed to such persons distinct from those owed to all humans, all rational agents, or all moral persons. Thus we may owe what can in a sense be called relativized or dependent obligations to all would-be entrants. We might call our obligations to such persons particularized or special obligations, as we might call our obligations to our own family.

No plausible moral or legal rule absolutely subordinates our obligations to broad groups of people to those we bear only to a few, or absolutely subordinates the distant to the near. We have admittedly become used to the idea that in immigration cases, conservation of the public fisc may suffice to justify refusal of entry. In these cases, more localized rights or interests are thought to trump broader concerns. But cases such as *Shapiro v. Thompson* and *Plyler v. Doe* can sensibly be read as endorsing a contrary result. At the national level, *Shapiro* concludes that "a State may no more try to fence out those indigents who seek higher welfare benefits than it may try to fence out indigents generally." And while *Plyler* concludes that a state's denial of public education to undocumented children actually undermines the broader public interest, the case can be read as finding no state interest sufficiently substantial to outweigh the harm visited upon the undocumented children, even if denying such children a public school education would tend to preserve the public fisc.

Thus, strength of moral obligation is not invariably a function of proximity, spatial or cultural. Martyrs, for example, may fail to provide for the welfare of their immediate relatives. If we could, with the push of a button, permanently end torture of a large group of distant strangers, somehow at the unavoidable cost of breaking a promise to some friends and at some minimal cost to those friends, we might well seem justified in doing so. More generally, it is hardly clear that promoting the narrow national interest should invariably be the aim of public policies bearing upon human rights and upon important interests of persons beyond our national borders. Pointing to the real or alleged sovereignty of the nation-state simply begs the question. Even if we recognize the fact of national legal sovereignty, it remains "a mystery why we should regard the national point of view as having the kind of significance for morality that attaches naturally to the personal point of view."

It may well be that positive international law remains more comfortable with the idea of states, as opposed to individual persons, as the bearers and enforcers of rights. There is, however, a strong countervailing tendency to recognize persons as rights bearers. There is as well a tendency to recognize that some of these rights are held simply by virtue of one's status as a person, or at least upon grounds independent of the arbitrary contingency of one's place of birth or native citizenship. Finally, there is a tendency to recognize a moral right, or otherwise attach substantial moral weight, to every person's right to broad freedom of movement.

Familiar legal policy recognizes in some contexts the general moral arbitrariness of distinguishing among persons on grounds of national origin. The ultimate moral arbitrariness of deliberately conferring or withholding the most substantial benefits on the basis of national origin or place of birth in the context of immigration is less clearly established. Allegations of discrimination on the arbitrary basis of national origin arise in the context of relative shares of a more or less fixed total ceiling of immigrants annually. It is less common, however, to go beyond disputes among groups as to their fair relative shares of an assumedly fixed total sum of immigrants to the broader issue of the moral arbitrariness of any restrictive entry policy.

In general, neither United States immigration law, nor the academic criticism of the law, has come to grips with the apparent moral arbitrariness of allowing many persons to undeservedly suffer absolute or relative poverty, rather than permit them merely to enter the United States if they are otherwise able, where others with the equally undeserved good fortune to have been born in the United States resist even a largely passive or negative accommodation of the undeservedly less fortunate.

Of course, the issue of whether or when persons may be left, or made, to suffer even grievous harm by virtue of circumstances for which they cannot reasonably be held responsible is a broad one, extending well beyond the scope of this Article. Few writers in any context go so far as to seek to completely eliminate all effects of all undeserved circumstances. Clearly, an open entry policy need not seek, for example, to compensate all entrants into the United States so as to neutralize all blameless suffering ever incurred by those entrants above some equitable baseline level. In many cases voluntary entry into the United States on any reasonable terms might well be thought by itself to outweigh one's net accumulated undeserved misfortunes. At a minimum allowing entry into the United States may often constitute at least a significant contribution toward redressing any such net imbalance of blameless misfortune.

An open entry policy is thus itself a broad attack on the problem of morally arbitrary suffering and inequality. Such a policy—however justified in terms of charity, utility, liberty, equality, autonomy, and self-realization, or rights to freedom of movement—begins with Kant's recognition that "the birth is no deed of him who is born." Kant speaks of "the right all men have, of demanding of others to be admitted into their society; a right founded upon that of the common possession of the surface of the earth ... because originally one has not a greater right to a country than another." As a potential qualification though, Kant suggests elsewhere that a government may encourage immigration over popular opposition as long as "the private ownership of the land of the natives is not diminished." Certainly, an open entry policy need not involve anything like forced sales or condemning land for the benefit of new entrants.

Ultimately, an open entry policy emphasizes not the arbitrary contingencies of geopolitical natality, but the unconditional dignity of each person. Respecting such dignity, for Kant, may require some degree of societal sacrifice or cost. An open entry policy not only promotes human dignity in an exceptionally broad fashion, but also broadly promotes what Kant takes to be the purpose of law itself—"to guarantee each individual a maximum sphere of external freedom."

The contemporary philosopher John Rawls follows Kant in seeking to control the influence of morally arbitrary contingencies on one's life chances. Rawls writes that "the arbitrariness of the world must be corrected for by adjusting the circumstances of the initial contractual situation" under which the basic principles of justice are to be derived. Notoriously, though, Rawls does not attempt to consider the implications of his basic assumptions for most questions of international or global justice or immigration.

Ultimately, Rawls's analysis must come to terms with the argument that if, for example, one's genetic limitations or inherited wealth are morally arbitrary, severe deprivations imposed solely on the basis of place of birth are equally arbitrary. If the logic, as opposed to the letter, of Rawls's argument were to be extended internationally, freedom of movement not merely within but between nations might be considered among the Rawlsian basic liberties.

Setting aside the problem of whether Rawls's deepest insights are compatible with sovereign nation-states, Rawls's own theory would thus seem to suggest that "nationality is just one further deep contingency (like genetic endowment, race, gender, and social class)." Whether Rawls's most basic assumptions really imply an open entry policy would then depend upon whether such a policy advances the basic interests of an assumed continuum of relatively disadvantaged persons and would not overtax our abilities to comply with such a policy choice. Ultimately, the most basic Rawlsian principles might well suggest an open entry policy, if not more radical innovations.

Thus consistent forms of Kantianism, libertarianism, egalitarianism, certain natural rights or natural law theories, and even Rawlsianism may lead in the direction of open borders. Whether standard forms of utilitarianism tend in the same direction is unclear. The answer may depend most fundamentally upon whether we are to aim at maximizing the welfare of all persons everywhere affected by our border policy, or only of all persons currently within the boundaries of our decision-making community.

Of course, a utilitarian who proposes to ignore the welfare of foreigners in the utilitarian calculus must face a powerful objection of arbitrariness. To the extent that the utilitarian wishes to maximize, over any time frame, something like average or total utility, even discounting for uncertainties, it is difficult to say why a unit of local pain counts for more than a unit of foreign pain. An open entry policy, when suitably qualified as by our discussion above, seems fully compatible with otherwise viable and attractive forms of utilitarianism.

IV. Conclusion

The basic lines of the argument for a radical revision of United States immigration law and policy seem clear, primarily because the reasoning supporting the current restrictive policies seems to have no historical or moral justification. An open entry policy may actually bring greater benefits to United States society as a whole, and any costs imposed on particular segments to society can certainly be addressed through legislative cost-shifting measures. It cannot be pretended, however, that no loose ends remain. Certainly, not all possible arguments against an open entry policy have been ventilated. Nor have I sorted out all the differences between open entry policies and policies that moderately restrict entry while aiming at diversity among immigrants, or the relationships between immigration policy and international wealth redistribution, foreign aid, or terms of trade. Finally, I have not considered the extent to which the arguments raised above may or may not apply to other societies, such as Germany, Australia, Canada, or Japan.

However, an open entry policy need not have the adverse effects many critics predict. Indeed, as shown above, legislative responses can ameliorate any disproportionate burdens on particular segments caused by such a policy. The current morally arbitrary restrictions on immigration are not a reasoned response to the immigration issue. An open entry policy strips away such arbitrariness and leads to deeper and more enlightened debate on immigration.

No doubt there is an important difference between appreciating the feasibility and moral logic of a legal rule of free entry, and being psychologically "ready" to collectively implement such a rule in practice. In this area as in others, though, the defense of legal privilege may over time come to be recognized as ultimately unconvincing. At such a point, a law of immigration based upon a policy of open entry would be recognized as the embodiment of moral common sense.

Glossary of Common Terms in Immigration Law

There are many words which will appear foreign to a new reader of immigration law. The following list is a short glossary which attempts to "loosely" define some of the more troublesome terms used in immigration. The terms of art will be clarified after reviewing the cases and materials.

Adjustment of Status. An immigration benefit accorded as a matter of discretion to certain persons in the United States, which allows them to have their status changed from that of a parolee or nonimmigrant to that of a lawful permanent resident without having to leave the country. Adjustment of status is a term of art. Certain lawful permanent residents may have their status "adjusted" to that of a nonimmigrant. This benefit should be distinguished from "change of status," which generally applies to nonimmigrants moving from one nonimmigrant status to another.[29] The procedure for obtaining permanent residency through adjustment of status while a person is in removal proceedings is called "cancellation of removal."

Arrival-Departure Record (I-94). A form issued to foreign nationals upon arrival at the time of inspection. Information on the form indicates the person's admission status and the period of authorized stay. Formerly a handwritten document, since April, 2013, for those arriving by sea or air it is not issued in paper form but in an electronic format and is available to the traveler on the U.S. Customs and Border Protection (CBP) website (*www.cbp.gov/I94*). *See* Chapter 3.

Asylum. A discretionary benefit accorded to certain persons in the United States who demonstrate that they are unable or unwilling to return to their country on account of persecution or a well-founded fear of persecution based on race, religion, nationality, membership in a particular social group, or political opinion.[30] One year after the receipt of asylum status, asylees may apply for lawful permanent residence. *See* Chapter 5.

The REAL ID Act[31] altered the standards and evidentiary burdens governing asylum, withholding of removal, and other discretionary forms of relief from removal. It requires asylum applicants to demonstrate that one of the enumerated grounds was or will be "at least one central reason" for their persecution, and allows immigration judges to require credible asylum and withholding applicants to obtain corroborating evidence "unless the applicant does not have the evidence and cannot reasonably obtain the evidence."[32]

Border Crossing Card (BCC). An identity card issued to a foreign national who is lawfully admitted for permanent residence, or to a foreign national who is a res-

29. *See* 8 U.S.C. § 1255, Sec. 245.

30. 8 U.S.C. § 1158, INA § 208. *See also* 8 U.S.C. § 1101(a)(42), INA § 101(a)(42) (defining the term "refugee").

31. Pub. L. No. 109-13, 119 Stat. 231 (May 11, 2005).

32. 8 U.S.C. § 1158(b)(1)(B), INA § 208(b)(1)(B).

ident in Mexico or Canada, by a consular officer or an immigration officer for the purpose of crossing the border from Canada or Mexico. The biometric BCC is a laminated, credit-card-style document with many security features and has a validity period of 10 years. Called a "laser visa," the card is both a BCC and a B-1/B-2 visitor visa. Mexican visitors to the United States, whether traveling to the border region or beyond, receive a laser visa.

U.S. Customs and Border Protection (CBP). The administrative agency under the U.S. Department of Homeland Security (DHS) which has as its primary function, the inspection of persons and things brought into the United States. *See* Chapter 2.

U.S. Citizenship and Immigration Services (USCIS). The administrative agency which is part of the U.S. Department of Homeland Security responsible for overseeing immigration benefits under the INA. *See* Chapter 2.

Deferred Action. Extraordinary relief in the form of prosecutorial discretion where the government takes no action to remove a person although the person may be technically inadmissible or deportable. The relief may be granted in cases with compelling humanitarian factors. A person under deferred action is considered to be lawfully present in the United States for purposes of applying for certain public benefits.[33]

Deferred Action for Childhood Arrivals (DACA). A special form of deferred action created by the Obama Administration in 2012 to allow certain persons who had come to the United States as children to apply for and receive deferred action consideration.

Deferred Action for Parents of Americans and Lawful Permanent Residents (DAPA). A special form of deferred action established by the Obama Administration in 2014 that would allow certain parents of U.S. citizens and lawful permanent residents to remain in the United States. The program is expected to protect up to 4.4 million persons from removal. DAPA relief was enjoined by a federal judge in 2015, and that decision was revised by a federal appellate court and the stay remained in place. The appellate court decision remains in effect as a result of a deadlocked Supreme Court in 2016.[34]

Deferred Enforced Departure. A non-statutory form of relief from removal granted to persons of certain nationalities present in the United States for compelling humanitarian reasons usually involving natural disaster or civil unrest. *See* Chapter 10. (*See also* Extended Voluntary Departure).

U.S. Department of Homeland Security (DHS). The agency into which legacy Immigration and Naturalization Service (legacy INS) was folded effective March 1, 2003. The benefits functions of legacy INS transferred to the U.S. Citizenship

---

33. 8 CFR § 102.12(a)(4)(v).

34. *See Texas v. U.S.*, 86 F. Supp. 3d 591 (S.D. Tex. 2015), 809 F.3d 134 (5th Cir. 2015), *U.S. v. Texas*, 136 S. Ct 2271 (2016), *reh'g denied* 137 S. Ct. 285 (2016).

and Immigration Services (USCIS), while the enforcement functions transferred to CBP and U.S. Immigration and Customs Enforcement (ICE). *See* Chapter 2.

Derivative Citizenship. Citizenship conveyed to children through the naturalization of parents or, under certain circumstances, to foreign-born children adopted by U.S. citizen parents, provided certain conditions are met.[35] *See* Chapter 11.

Deportation. The removal, ejectment or transfer of a person from a country because her presence is deemed inconsistent with the public welfare. Prior to the 1996 Amendments, the term "deportation" was used to describe the ejectment of a person who had managed to gain entry to the United States either legally or illegally. The 1996 Act replaced the term "deportation" with "removal." Deportation is not considered to be a form of punishment. Grounds of deportability are set out at 8 U.S.C. § 1227, Sec. 237 and are discussed in Chapter 4.

Diversity Lottery. The generic name given to the immigrant visa lottery program established by the Immigration Act of 1990[36] that makes available up to 55,000 immigrant visas per federal fiscal year to persons from low-admission states and low-admission regions.[37] The Diversity Immigrant Visa Lottery (DV) program is administered by the U.S. Department of State (DOS), which establishes the rules for the lottery and tracks the available visa numbers.

Exclusion. The procedure existing prior to the 1996 Immigration Act for the ejectment of persons seeking admission to the United States. The term "exclusion" under current immigration law refers to the various bases for finding persons inadmissible to the United States. Grounds for inadmissibility are set out at 8 U.S.C. § 1182, Sec. 212 and are discussed in Chapter 3.

Extended Voluntary Departure. A non-statutory form of relief where individuals from a designated country were granted work authorization and temporary relief from removal due to civil unrest, natural disaster or other compelling humanitarian factors. Compare with Temporary Protected Status (TPS), which is provided for under the Immigration and Nationality Act (INA). This relief has also been termed "Deferred Enforced Departure."[38] *See* Chapter 10.

Immediate Relatives. A category of immigrants not subject to the annual quotas and made up of spouses and minor unmarried children of U.S. citizens. Also included as immediate relatives are parents of U.S. citizens where the petitioning son or daughter is at least 21 years of age.[39] *See* Chapter 7.

Immigrant. A person coming to the United States to reside. Within the meaning of the Immigration and Nationality Act, as amended, "immigrant" means any person who is not a U.S. citizen, except one who is within one of the classes of nonimmigrants. This characterization of immigrants shifts the burden to the person

35. 8 U.S.C. § 1431, INA § 320; 8 CFR § 320.

36. Pub. L. No. 101-649, 104 Stat. 4978 (Nov. 29, 1990).

37. 8 U.S.C. § 1153(c), INA § 203(c).

38. *See e.g.*, 75 Fed. Reg. 15715 (2010).

39. INA § 201(b)(2)(A)(i).

seeking admission to establish her clear eligibility.[40] Nonimmigrants are those with a residence abroad who can prove that they will be coming for a temporary (short and definable) period of time and fit into narrowly defined categories enumerated in the statute. Generally, an immigrant is one who cannot establish her eligibility for nonimmigrant status. The inability to establish such eligibility will require the person to meet the requirements of either having specific family ties with a U.S. citizen or lawful permanent resident (preference eligibility) or a sponsoring employer in the United States and a job which will not displace or adversely affect U.S. workers. *See also* Labor Certification, Nonimmigrant and Preference Petition.

Immigrant Visa. Permission obtained from a U.S. consul (abroad) to seek admission to the United States. A visa is issued subsequent to establishing eligibility for admission on a permanent basis under the Immigration and Nationality Act, as amended. *See also* Preference Categories, Labor Certification and Visa.

U.S. Immigration and Customs Enforcement (ICE). The administrative agency under DHS primarily responsible for the enforcement of the immigration laws within the United States. This is to be contrasted with the determination of whether a noncitizen is eligible for immigration benefits. *See* Chapter 2.

Immigration Judge. Sometimes referred to in the statute and Code of Federal Regulations as "Special Inquiry Officer," the person responsible for deciding questions involving bond, exclusion and removal. While in the past, immigration judges were employed by INS, they are now employed by EOIR.

Labor Certification. The process by which some immigrants are approved for entry to the United States. In order for these immigrants to come to the country (other than those who qualify as immigrants based on their family ties with U.S. citizens or lawful permanent residents), they must establish the following: (1) an employer is willing to hire them in a job for which they are qualified; (2) there are no equally qualified U.S. workers for the job which is being offered; and (3) the job will not adversely affect the wage rate or working conditions of U.S. workers (the employer must therefore be offering the job at the "prevailing wage" in the particular market). An employer's obtaining a labor certification does not entitle the person to admission if there is an annual quota on the numbers of foreign workers who may be admitted to the country. In 2004, new regulations were implemented by DOL to obtain labor certifications.[41] *See also* Preference Categories.

Laser Visa. *See* Border Crossing Card.

Lawful Permanent Resident. A person accorded the benefit of being able to reside in the United States on a permanent basis. Such a person may engage in employment but may not vote in U.S. elections. Lawful permanent resident status is the status gained by a person who is admitted or paroled to the country with an immigrant

---

40. *See* 8 U.S.C. § 1101(a)(15), Sec. 101(a)(15).
41. 69 Fed. Reg. 77325 (2004).

visa, a refugee or asylee or a person who has resided in the United States for over ten years and is able to prove a requisite level of hardship. Lawful permanent resident status may be taken away following the commission of certain acts or through "abandonment."

Nonimmigrant. A person who can establish that she has a residence abroad which she has no intention of abandoning, is coming to the United States for a temporary period and fits into specifically defined categories under the Immigration and Nationality Act, as amended.[42] Some of the nonimmigrant categories are students, tourists, treaty investors and foreign government officials. *Also see* Immigrant.

Parole. Permission granted by the Attorney General which allows a person to physically enter the United States yet still be considered to have not legally entered the country. Parole is a legal fiction. In the legal sense, a person paroled into the country is treated as if she were still at the border's edge seeking permission to enter.[43] *See* Chapter 3.

PERM. *See* Program Electronic Review Management

Preference Categories. Immigrant visas are allocated on the basis of an annual quota. In order to qualify for admission, the intending immigrant must show that (1) she is married to a lawful permanent resident or is the unmarried son or daughter of a lawful permanent resident; (2) she is the son, daughter or sibling of a U.S. citizen (irrespective of marital status); or (3) her employer has obtained a labor certification for her eventual employment in the United States. Whether the person meets the quota restriction will depend on her relationship with a U.S. citizen or lawful permanent resident or the skilled or unskilled nature of the employment. *See* Labor Certification; *also see* Chapters 7 and 8.

Preference Petition. In order to determine the preference category to which a person is entitled, an application or petition must first be submitted to USCIS. The preference petition may be referred to as a family or employment-based preference petition. *See* Preference Categories.

Primary Inspection. The first or initial examination at a port of entry where a person arriving is subjected to questions to determine whether they may be admitted. *See* Chapter 3.

Program Electronic Review Management (PERM). A system established, effective March 28, 2005, for filing applications for labor certification. PERM uses an automated computer system to scan attestation forms filed by employers regarding their compliance with all regulatory requirements.[44] *See* Chapter 8.

Provisional Waiver. Sometimes referred to as a "provisional unlawful presence waiver," was a procedure established in March 2013, allowing spouses, children, and parents of U.S. citizens who were immigrant visa applicants and who were oth-

---

42. *See* 8 U.S.C. § 1101(a)(15), Sec. 101(a)(15).
43. *See* 8 U.S.C. § 1182(d)(5), Sec. 212(d)(5).
44. 20 CFR Parts 655 and 656.

erwise subject to the unlawful presence ground of inadmissibility at INA §212(a)(9)(B)(i) to obtain a waiver prior to being interviewed for their immigrant visa.[45]

Quotas. There are annual numerical restrictions on many forms of immigration status. Certain nonimmigrant categories are restricted to a set number of persons who may be admitted in any given fiscal year. Similarly, the number of persons who may be granted permanent residence is also restricted and allocated between the family and employment categories. Strict attention is paid to the immigrant category, as well as to making sure that persons are issued visas in the order in which they applied and that no more than 25,620 (7 percent of the total) are issued to nationals of any one country in a given fiscal year. *See* Preference Categories. *See* Chapters 7 and 8.

Refugee. A person outside of the United States who is unable or unwilling to return to her country because of persecution or a well-founded fear of persecution on account of race, religion, nationality, membership in a particular social group or political opinion.[46] Refugee admission to the country is based upon annual allocations as established between the executive and legislative branches. A refugee, once admitted, may apply for permanent resident status after one year. *See* Chapter 5.

Removal. The procedure used to eject persons who are seeking admission as well as those who have been admitted to the United States. Prior to enactment of the 1996 Act, the terms "deportation" and "exclusion" were used. *See* Chapters 3 and 4.

Restriction on Removal. A remedy available to persons able to establish that their life or freedom would be threatened on account of race, religion, nationality, membership in a particular social group or political opinion if returned to their home country.[47] Restriction on removal does not confer the person a right to stay in the United States, but she may be removed to any other country willing to accept her. Formerly called "withholding of deportation." *See* Chapter 5.

Secondary Inspection. The procedure beyond the initial screening to determine whether a person will be admitted. At "secondary inspection," applicants for admission are subjected to additional questioning to determine their eligibility for admission. *See* Chapter 3.

Unlawful Presence. Presence in the United States after the expiration of the authorized period of stay, or presence in the United States without having been admitted or paroled. The period of authorized stay, usually noted on Form I-94 or I-94W, must end on a date certain. Thus, Canadians admitted without being issued an I-94, and F, J, and M students and exchange visitors admitted for "duration of status" (D/S) who overstay, do not accrue unlawful presence until and

---

45. 8 CFR §212.7.
46. 8 U.S.C. §1101(a)(42), Sec. 101(a)(42).
47. 8 U.S.C. §1253(h), Sec. 243(h).

unless an immigration judge or a DHS official determines and formally finds such person to be "out of status" or in violation of their status (*e.g.*, the F-1 student who works without authorization). Depending on the period of unlawful presence, a person may be barred from re-admission for a period of three or ten years.[48]

Visa. A document which evidences permission obtained from a U.S. consul (abroad) to seek admission to the United States at a designated port of entry. A visa may be either a nonimmigrant or immigrant visa and merely allows one to attempt to seek admission at a port of entry. The visa is an official endorsement upon a document or passport certifying that the bearer has been examined and is permitted to proceed for purposes of seeking admission.

Visas Viper. The "Visas Viper Terrorist Reporting Program" was a mechanism created in response to the deficiencies discovered in the aftermath of the 1993 World Trade Center bombing. The program was designed to provide a way "for routinely and consistently bringing suspected terrorists" to the consular section's attention for the purpose of entering names into the DOS "Consular Lookout and Support System" (CLASS) and into the CBP "Interagency Border Inspection System" (IBIS).[49]

Withholding of Removal. A remedy available to persons who establish that their lives or freedom would be threatened if deported to their home country on account of race, religion, nationality, membership in a particular social group, or political opinion.[50] The use of the term "withholding" was a reference to the relief under the statute prior to the enactment of IIRAIRA in 1996 which was "withholding of deportation." The relief does not confer a right to remain in the United States; a person granted withholding of removal may be removed to any country, other than their home country, that is willing to accept them. *See also* Restriction on Removal." *See* Chapter 10.

Work Permit. There is no single document in U.S. immigration law that is a "work permit." Citizens, nationals, and lawful permanent residents are automatically authorized to engage in employment in the United States. Certain nonimmigrant visa categories include, as an incident of status, employment authorization either with or without limitation to a particular employer or after application and approval by USCIS. Virtually all employment authorization for nonimmigrants or undocumented foreign nationals (where authorized) is limited as to time, and most is limited as to the nature of employer and employment. Other foreign nationals physically present in the United States may have the right to apply for an Employment Authorization Document.

---

48. 8 U.S.C. § 1182(a)(9)(B), INA § 212(a)(9)(B).
49. 9 FAM 40.37 N1.1.
50. 8 U.S.C. § 1231(b)(3), INA § 241(b)(3).

Throughout this text and often in the excerpted cases you will see references to the "Immigration and Nationality Act" or the "INA." This reference is to the Congressional Bill creating the immigration laws. These provisions are cross referenced below to the codifications found in the U.S. Code. Most often the US Code provision will be given with a brief cross-reference to the INA section. You should be aware that these are mere cross references and not a reference to a separate statutory provision. Below is a conversion table between the US Code and the Immigration and Nationality Act.

Immigration and Nationality Act Conversion Table

INA Sec.	*Title 8, U.S. Code*	*Description*
101	1101	Definitions
103	1103	Powers and Duties of Attorney General and Commissioner
104	1104	Powers and Duties Sect'y of State
Title II, Chap. 1—Selection System		
201	1151	Worldwide level of immigration
202	1152	Numerical limitation to any single foreign state
203	1153	Allocation of immigrant visas
204	1154	Procedure for granting immigrant status
205	1155	Revocation of approval of petitions
207	1157	Refugees Admissions
208	1158	Asylum Procedures
209	1159	Adjustment of Status for Refugees
Chap. 2—Qualifications for Admission of Aliens; Travel Control of Citizens and Aliens		
212	1182	Classes Ineligible for Visas and admission; Waivers
213A	1183a	Requirements for Affidavit of support
214	1184	Admission of Nonimmigrants
216	1186	Conditional Permanent Residence for Certain spouses and sons and daughters
216A	1186a	Conditional Permanent Residence for certain alien entrepreneurs, spouses, and children
217	1187	Visa waiver pilot program for certain visitors
218	1188	Admission of temporary H-2a workers
219	1189	Designation of foreign terrorist organization
Chap. 3—Issuance of Entry Documents		
221	1201	Issuance of Visas
222	1202	Applications for visas
223	1203	Reentry Permits
Chap. 4—Inspection; Apprehension; Examination; Exclusion; and Removal		
231	1221	List of and citizen passengers arriving and departing
232	1222	Detention of aliens for physical and mental examination
233	1223	Entry through or from foreign territory and adjacent islands
234	1224	Designation of ports of entry for aliens arriving by aircraft
235	1225	Inspection by immigration officers; expedited removal of inadmissible arriving aliens; referral for hearing
235A	1225a	Preinspection at Foreign Airports
236	1226	Apprehension and detention of aliens
237	1227	General classes of deportable aliens
238	1228	Expedited removal of aliens convicted of aggravated felonies

239	1229	Initiation of removal proceedings
240	1229a	Removal proceedings
240A	1229b	Cancellation of removal; adjustment of status
240B	1229c	Voluntary departure
241	1231	Detention and removal of aliens ordered removed
242	1252	Judicial review of orders of removal
243	1253	Penalties related to removal
244	1254	Temporary protected status

Chap. 5—Adjustment and change of status

245	1255	Adjustment of status of nonimmigrant to that of person admitted for permanent residence
245A	1255a	Adjustment of status of certain entrants before January 1, 1982, to that of person admitted for lawful residence
246	1256	Rescission of adjustment of status
248	1258	Change of nonimmigrant classification
249	1259	Record of admission for permanent residence in the case of certain aliens who entered the united states prior to July 1, 1924 or January 1, 1972

Chap. 7—Registration of Aliens

261	1301	Aliens seeking entry into the United States
262	1302	Registration of aliens in the United States
263	1303	Provisions governing registration of special groups
264	1304	Forms and procedure
265	1305	Notices of change of address
266	1306	Penalties

Chap. 8—General Penalty Provisions

272	1322	Bringing in aliens subject to denial of admission on a health related ground
273	1323	Unlawful bringing of aliens into United States
274	1324	Bringing in and harboring certain aliens
274A	1324a	Unlawful employment of aliens
274B	1324b	Unfair immigration-related employment practices
274C	1324c	Penalties for document fraud
274D	1324d	Civil penalties for failure to depart
275	1325	Entry of alien at improper time or place; misrepresentation and concealment of facts
276	1326	Reentry of removed alien
277	1327	Aiding or assisting certain aliens to enter the United States
278	1328	Importation of alien for immoral purpose
279	1329	Jurisdiction of district courts
287	1357	Powers of immigration officers and employees
291	1361	Burden of proof
292	1362	Right to counsel

Title III, Chap. 1—Nationality at Birth and by Collective Naturalization

301	1401	National and Citizens of the United States at Birth
302	1402	Persons born in Puerto Rico on or after April 11, 1899
303	1403	Persons born in the canal zone or Republic of Panama on or after February 26, 1904
304	1404	Persons Born in Alaska on or after March 30, 1867
305	1405	Persons Born in Hawaii
306	1406	Persons living in and born in the Virgin Islands

307	1407	Persons living in and born in Guam
308	1408	Nationals but not citizens of the united states at birth
309	1409	Children Born out of Wedlock

Chap. 2—Nationality Through Naturalization

310	1421	Naturalization Authority
311	1422	Eligibility for Naturalization
312	1423	Requirement as to Understanding the English Language, History, Principles, and Form of Government of the United States
313	1424	Prohibition Upon the Naturalization of Persons Opposed to Government or Law, or Who Favor Totalitarian Forms of Government
314	1425	Ineligibility to Naturalization of Deserters from the Armed Forces of the United States
315	1426	Alien Relieved from Training and Service in the Armed Forces of the United States because of Alienage Barred from Citizenship
316	1427	Requirements as to Residence, Good Moral Character, Attachment to the Principles of the Constitution, and Favorable Disposition to the United States
317	1428	Temporary Absence of Persons Performing Religious Duties
318	1429	Prerequisites to Naturalization; Burden of Proof
319	1430	Married Persons and Employees of Certain Nonprofit Organizations
320	1431	Children Born Outside of the United States and Residing Permanently in the United States; Conditions Under which Citizenship Automatically Acquired
322	1433	Children Born and Residing Outside the United States; Conditions for Acquiring Certificate of Citizenship
324	1435	Former Citizens of United States Regaining United States Citizenship
325	1436	Nationals but not Citizens of the United States; Residence within Outlying Possessions
326	1437	Resident Philippine Citizens Excepted from Certain Requirements
327	1438	Former United States Citizens Losing Citizenship by Entering the Armed Forces of Foreign Countries During World War II
328	1439	Naturalization through Service in the Armed Forces of the United States
329	1440	Naturalization through Active-Duty Service in the Armed Forces during World War I, World War II, the Korean Hostilities, the Vietnam Hostilities, or in other periods of Military Hostilities
329A	1440	Posthumous Citizenship through Death While on Active-duty Service in the Armed Forces during World War I, Word War II, the Korean Hostilities, the Vietnam Hostilities, or in other periods of Military Hostilities
330	1441	Constructive Residence through Service on Certain United States Vessels
331	1442	Alien Enemies; Naturalization under Specified Conditions Conditions and Procedure
332	1443	Procedural and Administrative Provisions; Executive Functions
333	1444	Photographs
334	1445	Application for Naturalization; Declaration of Intention
335	1446	Investigation of Applicants; Examinations of Applicants
336	1447	Hearings on Denials of Applications for Naturalization
337	1448	Oath of Renunciation and Allegiance
338	1449	Certificate of Naturalization; Contents
339	1450	Functions and Duties of Clerks and Records of Declaration of Intention and Applications for Naturalization
340	1451	Revocation of Naturalization

341	1452	Certificates of Citizenship or U.S. Non-citizen National Status; Procedure
342	1453	Cancellation of Certificates Issued by the Attorney General, the Commissioner or a Deputy Commissioner; Action not to affect Citizenship Status
343	1454	Documents and Copies Issued by the Attorney General
344	1455	Fiscal Provisions
345	[repealed]	
346		
347		
348	[repealed]	

Chap. 3—Loss of Nationality

349	1481	Loss of Nationality by Native-born or Naturalized Citizen
350	[repealed]	
351	1483	Restrictions on Loss of Nationality
356	1488	Nationality Lost Solely from Performance of Acts or Fulfilment of Conditions
357	1489	Application of Treaties; Exceptions

Chap. 4—Miscellaneous

358	1501	Certificate of Diplomatic or Consular Officer of the United States as to Loss of American Nationality Under Chapter IV Nationality Act of 1940, or Under Chapter 3 of this Title
359	1502	Certificate of Nationality for a Person not a Naturalized Citizen for use in Proceedings of a Foreign State
360	1503	Judicial Proceedings for Declaration of United States Nationality in Event of Denial of Rights and Privileges as National
361	1504	Cancellation of United States Passports and Consular Reports of Birth

Chap. V—Alien Terrorist Removal Procedure

501	1531	Definitions
502	1532	Establishment of removal court
503	1533	Removal court procedure
504	1534	Removal hearing.
505	1535	Appeals
506	1536	Custody and release pending removal hearing
507	1537	Custody and release after removal hearing

Chapter 2

Immigrants' Rights in the Social Context

Introduction

This chapter examines immigrants' rights apart from the formal immigration proceedings to which a large part of this book has been devoted. We will examine the rights of persons who are not citizens of the United States as they pertain to employment, education and public benefits. Implicated in this analysis are attempts by state governments and others to place restrictions on persons who are not citizens of the United States or who may not be in a lawful immigration status.[1]

A. Employment Discrimination and Non-Citizens

Although federal statutes may be invoked to remedy employment discrimination suffered by non-citizens, among the most important developments regarding employment discrimination against immigrants was the enactment of the anti-discrimination provisions contained in the Immigration Reform and Control Act of 1986 (IRCA).[2] This section focuses primarily on IRCA's anti-discrimination provisions and how they relate to other federal statutes prohibiting employment discrimination, such as Title VII of the Civil Rights Act of 1964,[3] the Civil Rights Act of 1991[4] and the Civil Rights Act of 1866 ("Section 1981").[5]

This section is intended only as an overview. The law of employment discrimination is complex, and the relevant federal statutes overlap and interact in ways that are

1. As will be seen in our later discussion, noncitizens include lawful permanent residents. Within this group of persons are those who have been admitted legally or whose permission to remain has expired, and others who may have entered illegally. Within this group of undocumented persons, those in the country illegally may be eligible to have their status made legal through an administrative process.

2. Pub. L. 99-603, 100 Stat. 3359 (1986).

3. Pub. L. No. 88-352, 78 Stat. 252 (Title VI, Section 601) Title VI, Section 601 provides that "No person in the United States shall, on grounds of race, color, or national origin be excluded from participation in, be denied the benefits of, or be subjected to discrimination under any program or activity receiving Federal financial assistance."

4. Pub. L. No. 102-166, 1038 Stat. 1071 (1991) (codified at 42 U.S.C. § 2000e *et seq*).

5. 14 Stat. 27, ch. 31 (1866) (codified at 42 U.S.C. § 1981).

often very complicated, with each of these statutes protecting different classes of individuals and covering different types of employment-related discriminatory activity. Complicating matters further is the fact that employment discrimination law, as a whole, is subject to quite rapid change, either by amendment to applicable statutes or through the decisions of courts. Notwithstanding the more than two decade history of IRCA, there is not a wide body of case law interpreting its anti-discrimination provisions. Part of this may be due in large part to the evidentiary challenges in making out a successful discrimination claim. Nevertheless, we will explore the statutes and cases to provide a general overview of employment discrimination law as it relates to immigrants and non-citizens.

1. Title VII of the Civil Rights Act of 1964

Title VII of the Civil Rights Act of 1964, which was amended in 1991,[6] is the most comprehensive federal anti-discrimination statute. It prohibits employers of fifteen or more employees from discriminating on the basis of race, color, religion, sex or national origin.

As will be seen, the law distinguishes between national origin and alienage discrimination. National origin discrimination is the differential treatment of an individual on the basis of "the physical, cultural or linguistic characteristics of a national origin group."[7] Alienage discrimination, on the other hand, entails differential treatment, regardless of national origin or ancestry, because of a person's citizenship status.

Although IRCA applies only to recruiting, hiring, referral for a fee or discharge, Title VII applies to these and almost all other aspects of employment, including wages or salary, benefits, promotion and working conditions. Title VII is enforced by an administrative agency, the Equal Employment Opportunity Commission (EEOC).

Title VII, however, does not cover citizenship status or alienage discrimination.[8] Thus, persons who suffer such discrimination must proceed under IRCA, which is the only federal statute that expressly prohibits citizenship status discrimination. Although the regulations implementing IRCA provide for relief from employer retaliation, the statute itself contains no provision expressly corresponding to Title VII's proscription of retaliation against employees who assert their equal employment rights.[9]

In *Hoffman Plastic Compounds v. NLRB*, 535 U.S. 137 (2002) which addressed the application of the National Labor Relations Act (NLRA),[10] the Court explored questions regarding the legal remedies to which an undocumented person may avail himself even if they are able to prove discrimination. In Hoffman, the Court recog-

6. Among other things, the 1991 Act's stated purpose was "to strengthen and improve Federal civil rights laws, to provide for damages in cases of intentional employment discrimination, to clarify provisions regarding disparate impact actions." Pub. L. No. 102-166, 1038 Stat. 1071 (1991)

7. 29 C.F.R. § 1601.1.

8. *Espinoza v. Farah Manufacturing Co.*, 414 U.S. 86 (1973).

9. *See* 28 C.F.R. § 44.201.

10. 29 U.S.C. § 151 et. seq.

nized that while undocumented workers were employees under the NLRA, they were not entitled to back-pay awards. This means that while employers are prohibited from unfair labor practices, the NLRA did not permit the award of back-pay for violations where the employees were not legally authorized to work in the United States.[11] The courts have not been clear following *Hoffman* as to whether Title VII applies to undocumented workers.[12]

2. Section 1981 and Employment Discrimination

Persons who suffer employment-related discrimination on the basis of race, national origin and possibly of alienage may also be protected by 42 U.S.C. § 1981. Because of its expansive language in guaranteeing all "persons" the same right "to make and enforce contracts ... as is enjoyed by white citizens," Section 1981 has been recognized as prohibiting discrimination in the employment context.

Although the Supreme Court has revisited the question of whether Section 1981 reaches private action, it is now clear that Section 1981 may be used as a remedy for employment discrimination in the private sector. In *Patterson v. McLean Credit Union,*[13] the Supreme Court reaffirmed the validity of Section 1981's application to and prohibition of private racial discrimination but only as to hiring and discharge. The Court interpreted the statute to exclude from its coverage discrimination related to conditions of employment. Thus, although it is still a very important tool in remedying employment discrimination in the private sector, Section 1981 has been substantially limited in its scope and no longer applies to all aspects of the employment relationship.

Furthermore, for non-citizens who suffer some type of employment discrimination, Section 1981's applicability to alienage discrimination (i.e., in addition to discrimination on the basis of race and color) is still an open question. The Supreme Court, prior to enactment of the 1991 Act, denied *certiorari* when the issue was presented in *Bhandari v. First National Bank of Commerce.*[14] The Court declined review of a decision of the Fifth Circuit, which held that Section 1981 was not intended to reach private discrimination on the basis of alienage. Later the Fourth Circuit in *Duane v. Gov't Employees Ins. Co.*[15] disagreed with *Bhandari*, holding that

11. 535 U.S. at 151.

12. *See Rivera v. Nibco, Inc.*, 364 F.3d 1057, (9th Cir. 2004), *cert denied*, 544 U.S. 905 (2005) (prohibited defendant lawyers from questioning plaintiff about her immigration status in discovery); *but see Egbuna v. Time-Life Libraries, Inc.*, 153 F.3d 184 (4th Cir. 1998), *cert. denied* 525 U.S. 1142 (1999). A number of lower court decisions have upheld the right of undocumented workers to pursue Title VII claims. *See Iweala v. Operational Technologies Services, Inc.*, 634 F. Supp. 2d 73 (D.D.C. 2009); *Escobar v. Spartan Security Service*; 281 F. Supp. 2d 895 (S.D. Tex. 2003); *Olvera-Morales v. Sterling Onions, Inc.*, 322 F. Supp. 2d 211 (N.D.N.Y. 2004)

13. 491 U.S. 164 (1989).

14. 887 F.2d 609 (5th Cir. 1989) (*en banc*) (on remand), *cert. denied,* 494 U.S. 1061 (1990) (White and O'Connor dissenting to the denial *of certiorari*).

15. 37 F.3d 1036 (4th Cir. 1994).

private discrimination was prohibited. In *Anderson v. Conboy*,[16] the Second Circuit found that Section 1981 did apply to private actions. While another Circuit could interpret the Act and its 1991 amendments as not encompassing private alienage discrimination, such discrimination involving state action has been interpreted to include foreigners within its coverage, at least with respect to those lawfully in this country.[17]

3. Unfair Immigration-Related Employment Practices

As was noted earlier, the 1986 Amendments made it unlawful for employers to hire undocumented or "unauthorized" persons.[18] The law imposes a series of escalating fines, potentially leading to criminal sanctions, on employers who violate its mandate. Congress believed that the threat of sanctions created a risk that employers might refuse to hire or would discriminate against persons who appear foreign, have foreign-sounding names or speak with a foreign accent or in a foreign language. Consequently, Congress included the anti-discrimination provisions in IRCA as a counterbalance to employer sanctions.[19]

These "unfair immigration-related employment practices" provisions create a new cause of action prohibiting discrimination on the basis of citizenship status and, in certain more limited instances, on the basis of national origin.[20] A special administrative process for prosecuting claims under the Act was established. The statute provides that it is an unfair immigration-related employment practice to discriminate with respect to hiring, recruitment, referral for a fee or discharge because of a person's national origin or citizenship status. Protection against discrimination based on citizenship status extends to all citizens and "intending citizens" (as defined in the statute) as long as the "persons or entities" employ more than three persons.

In addition to creating a new cause of action for citizenship status discrimination, the Act, as mentioned above, also expands the available protection against national

---

16. 156 F.3d 167 (2d Cir. 1998), *cert. granted sub. nom. United Bhd. of Carpenters & Joiners of America v. Anderson*, 526 U.S. 1086 (1998), *cert. dismissed* 527 U.S. 1030 (1999).

17. *Takahashi v. Fish and Game Commission*, 334 U.S. 410, 419 (1948); *cf.* 42 U.S.C. § 1983.

18. *See* 8 U.S.C. § 1324a, Sec. 274A.

19. The legislative history of the Act reveals that the anti-discrimination provision was one of the most controversial aspects of the bill and nearly led to its defeat. Opponents of the provision argued that existing federal statutes provided immigrants with sufficient protection against discrimination and that this type of "civil rights legislation" should not be included within an immigration reform law. Proponents, however, argued that the existing federal statutes, none of which unambiguously prohibited private discrimination on the basis of alienage, were clearly insufficient because of their limited coverage and complex enforcement procedures. Gilbert Paul Carrasco, *The Golden Moment of Legalization*, X In Defense of the Alien 32, 35 (1988); Donald R. Stacy, *The Standard for Proving an Unfair Immigration-Related Employment Practice Under IRCA: Disparate Impact or Intent*, 4 Lab. Law. 271 (1988).

20. *See* 8 U.S.C. § 1324b, Sec. 274B.

origin discrimination by providing that employers with more than three employees who are not covered under Title VII of the Civil Rights Act[21] will now be subject to IRCA's prohibition against national origin discrimination. However, because Title VII already prohibits employers with fifteen or more employees from discriminating on the basis of national origin, this expanded protection applies only to claims against employers of between four and fourteen employees.

One source of controversy with regard to claims of employment discrimination brought under the anti-discrimination provisions of IRCA is the proper standard of proof applicable to such cases. The Act itself does not explicitly state what type of showing is required to establish that an employer engaged in unlawful discrimination. However, under long-settled Title VII standards, an individual can prove unlawful discrimination by showing either "disparate treatment" or "disparate impact." Thus, under Title VII, a claimant can either prove that an employer intentionally discriminated based upon some unlawful criterion such as national origin or, using disparate impact analysis, that the effect of the employer's activity, even though neutral on its face, was discriminatory.

Although disparate impact analysis is well accepted under Title VII[22] (after which IRCA was modeled), both President Reagan and his Justice Department took the position that IRCA claimants may not use the disparate impact standard to establish unlawful discrimination. When President Reagan signed the bill into law on November 6, 1986, he attempted to create something in the nature of legislative history by including in his signing statement his understanding of what Congress intended by certain of the more important sections of the Act. The President stated that he understood section 274B (the Act's anti-discrimination provisions) to require a "'discriminatory intent' standard of proof" and that "it would be improper to use the 'disparate impact' theory of recovery."[23] Thus, the President concluded, "a facially neutral employee selection practice that is employed without discriminatory intent will be permissible under the provisions of section 274B."[24]

While this view has been criticized, the statute requires that the discrimination be intentional.[25] The immigration related anti-discrimination statute removed the pos-

21. 42 U.S.C. § 2000e *et seq.*

22. *Griggs v. Duke Power Co.*, 401 U.S. 424, 431 (1971); *but see Wards Cove Packing Company, Inc. v. Atonio*, 490 U.S. 642, 646 (1989).

23. *President's Statement on Signing S. 1200 into Law*, 22 Weekly Comp. Pres. Doc. 1534 (Nov. 10, 1986).

24. This conclusion, however, is not based on legislative history. Moreover, as a commentary on interpretation of the statute that was not considered by Congress, the presidential signing statement is not a part of the legislative history and, accordingly, should be given little, if any, weight by the courts when interpreting this statute. 2A C. Sands, Sutherland's Statutes and Statutory Construction § 48.05 (N. Singer 4th ed. 1984). Furthermore, the sponsor of section 274B has emphatically rejected the President's construction. *See* Barney Frank, *The Anti-Discrimination Amendment*, X In Defense of the Alien 67 (1988).

25. 28 C.F.R. § 44.200(a).

sibility of using disparate impact in cases where the employer has required the protected employee to produce more documents than required by law.[26] And, although the issue is likely to inspire further litigation, at least one district court has already held that both disparate treatment and disparate impact analysis may be used in IRCA cases.[27] In resolving the question, courts will likely focus on the fact that IRCA's "pattern or practice" language, which tracks the language found in Title VII, has not generally been held to require a showing of intentional discrimination in the Title VII context. Thus, such a showing should not be required in the context of 274B anti-discrimination cases.

The following administrative law judge's decision is fairly representative of the issues likely to be litigated further in the implementation of the statute's anti-discrimination provisions. Because the following case is an administrative rather than a judicial opinion, undue weight should not be placed on the conclusions reached. In addition, after the case was decided, Congress removed the requirement that the complainant file a notice of intention to become a citizen in order to seek relief for discrimination.[28] However, the case does explore the more important issues in alienage discrimination.

In re Charge of Zeki Yeni Komsu v. Mesa Airlines

No.88-2000001, No. 88-2000002, 1 OCAHO 74 (1989)

MORSE, J.

Background

... [8 U.S.C. 1324b] was enacted to create new causes of action arising out of any "unfair immigration-related employment practice," 8 U.S.C. § 1324b(a)(1), and to broaden "... the Title VII protections against national origin discrimination ... because of the concern of some Members that people of 'foreign' appearance might be made more vulnerable" to employment discrimination "by the imposition of [employer] sanctions." "Joint Explanatory Statement of the Committee of Conference," Conference Report, Immigration Reform and Control Act of 1986, H.R.Rep. No. 99-1000, 99th Cong., 2d Sess., at 87 (1986).

Practices newly prohibited are those which discriminate against an individual on the basis of that individual's national origin or, in the case of a citizen or national of the United States or an "intending citizen...., because of such individual's citizenship status." 8 U.S.C. § 1324b(a)(1). Section 1324b(a) provides that it is a violation of law, subject to specified exceptions, to discriminate against any individual with respect to hiring, recruitment, referral for a fee, or discharge from employment because of that individual's national origin or citizenship status. The individuals protected against

26. 8 U.S.C. § 1324b(a)(6), Sec. 274B(a)(6).

27. *LULAC v. Pasadena Independent School District,* 662 F. Supp. 443, 449 n. 6, *motion deferred,* 672 F. Supp. 280 (S.D. Tex. 1987).

28. While the law does not require that the person have filed papers for naturalization, she may not receive protection under the statute if she fails to file within six months of eligibility to apply for citizenship. *See* 8 U.S.C. § 1324b(a)(3)(B)(i), Sec. 274B(a)(3)(B)(i).

discrimination are U.S. citizens or nationals and those aliens who (1) have been admitted for permanent residence, (2) have been granted the status of aliens lawfully admitted for temporary residence, as applicants for amnesty, (3) have been admitted as refugees, or (4) have been granted asylum provided that each such individual has evidenced "an intention to become a citizen of the United States through completing a declaration of intention to become a citizen ..." *Id.* at § 1324b(a)(3).

IRCA directed the President to appoint within the Department of Justice a Special Counsel for Immigration-Related Unfair Employment Practices (Special Counsel, or OSC), responsible for investigating charges, issuing complaints and prosecuting cases before administrative law judges, and authorized to seek judicial enforcement of orders issued by such judges. *Id.* at §§ 1324b(c) and (j)(1).

Remedies provided for breach of the duty not to discriminate, which the administrative law judge may impose upon determining that the respondent has engaged in an unfair immigration-related employment practice include not only relief on behalf of covered individuals but also liability to the United States upon a finding of a "pattern or practice of discriminatory activity." *Id.* at § 1324b(d)(2). The present case raises questions of first impression under 8 U.S.C. § 1324b with respect both to relief on behalf of the individual complainant, Mr. Zeki Yeni Komsu (charging party, or Komsu), and to liability to the government.

Procedural Summary

The United States, by OSC, to vindicate the public interest and on behalf of Komsu filed two complaints with the Office of the Chief Administrative Hearing Officer (OCAHO) on January 12, 1988, against Mesa Airlines (respondent, or Mesa). The Special Counsel, in effect, asserts in Docket 88200001 that Mesa engaged in a pattern and practice of discrimination in its hiring of airline pilots by promulgating and adhering to a policy of failure to consider for employment those applicants, including Komsu, who are not citizens of the United States, at any time that qualified applicants were available who were citizens of the United States. In Docket 88200002, the Special Counsel contends that Komsu was not hired as a pilot because Mesa, applying its U.S. citizen-only policy, rejected his employment application.

* * *

Jurisdiction Established

There is no claim here arising out of national origin status. Rather, Mesa is charged with breach of its duty not to discriminate against Komsu by rejecting his application for the reason that he was not a U.S. citizen. It is undisputed that he was at all times relevant to this case a citizen of a nation other than the United States, during all of which time Mesa employed more than fourteen individuals.

A preliminary question, not previously addressed judicially, challenges availability of § 1324b relief in cases like the present one where enforcement of employer sanctions is not directly implicated. At least one commentator has suggested that under the view that the antidiscrimination provisions were adopted "solely to counterbalance IRCA's employer sanctions provisions," only discrimination arising in the context of employer sanctions would be actionable. Pivec, "Handling Immigration-Related Employment Discrimination Claims," Immigration Briefings (April 1988), at 2.

That suggestion is said to have support in the legislative history of IRCA. For example, the Conference Report, H.R.Rep. No. 99-1000, *supra*, at 87, explains that the antidiscrimination provisions of IRCA "... are a complement to the sanctions provisions, and must be considered in this context," and notes that if, as provided by IRCA, "the sanctions are repealed by joint resolution, the antidiscrimination provisions will also expire, the justification for them having been removed." As reflected by the Conference Report, *id.* at 87–88, it is a commonplace that § 1324b had its genesis in apprehension that enactment of employer sanctions, 8 U.S.C. § 1324a, might be perceived to generate discrimination. See also House Committee on the Judiciary, Immigration Control and Legalization Amendments Act of 1986, H.R.Rep. No. 99-682, 99th Cong., 2d Sess., Pt. 1, at 68 (1986).

Legislative sunsetting of IRCA's employer sanctions program would terminate the antidiscrimination provisions as well. But the conferees pointed out that "[t]he antidiscrimination provisions would also be repealed in the event of a joint resolution approving a GAO finding that the sanctions had resulted in no significant discrimination, or that the administration of the antidiscrimination provisions had resulted in an unreasonable burden on employers." Conference Report, H.R.Rep. No. 99-1000, *supra*, at 87. In either of such situations, sanctions could continue despite repeal of the causes of action enacted at 8 U.S.C. § 1324b.

* * *

Nothing contained in the unusually structured statutory mechanism for legislative inquiry into the continued viability of either employer sanctions or antidiscrimination provisions, 8 U.S.C. §§ 1324a(m) and (n), spells out or necessarily implies a requirement that causes of action arising under section 1324b must proximately result from enactment (or, implementation) of section 1324a. Nothing contained in IRCA limits causes of action under section 1324b to claims arising out of employer responses to the employer sanctions program mandated by section 1324a. Nothing constrains me to look behind a remedial statute for a limitation that would be inconsistent with the plain words of the statute, 8 U.S.C. § 1324b(a)(1), or included within the catalogue of exceptions to its sweep, 8 U.S.C. §§ 1324b(a)(2) and (4). For all the foregoing reasons, I conclude that 8 U.S.C. § 1324b confers jurisdiction upon administrative law judges to adjudicate complaints whether or not the alleged discriminatory practices implicate either the text or the administration of 8 U.S.C. § 1324a.

This conclusion is consistent also with the expressed views of the Department of Justice in the preamble to the rule establishing the "... standards and procedures for the enforcement of section 102...." That rulemaking issued in 28 C.F.R. Part 44, at 52 Fed.Reg. 37402 et seq. (October 6, 1987), made clear the Department's understanding that Congress banned "... all intentional discrimination in light of the likely difficulty for a charging party or the Special Counsel to prove that such discrimination stemmed directly from an employer's desire to avoid sanctions." *Id.* at 37,405.

Standing of the Charging Party as an Intending Citizen

Very few of the material facts developed on the record are undisputed. It is unquestioned, however, that Mr. Komsu, who was born on March 19, 1960, in Turkey, and attended high school and aeronautical college in Denmark, lawfully entered the United States in November 1985, on a tourist visa. In July 1986, Komsu married and was issued a temporary resident permit; he has been a permanent resident alien of the United States since at least November 1986.

As a lawfully admitted permanent resident alien he was eligible to qualify as an intending citizen as that term is understood under IRCA. The parties disagree as to whether he evidenced his intent to qualify as an intending citizen in time to obtain standing to maintain this citizenship discrimination charge under IRCA.

Mr. Komsu concededly did not formally evidence his intent to become a citizen prior to October 28, 1987, the date he executed an INS Form N-300, "Application to File Declaration of Intention." Previously, in December 1986 he applied to Mesa for employment as a pilot. Late in March 1987 he filed an updated resume.

... Section 1324b(a)(3) excludes from the definition of intending citizen an alien who fails to apply for naturalization within six months of the date the alien first becomes eligible to apply for naturalization or within six months after November 6, 1986, whichever is later. Similarly excluded is an alien who applied on a timely basis but who does not obtain naturalization within 2 years after the date of the application subject to exception provided that the alien can establish that he/she is actively pursuing naturalization.

* * *

The Department of Justice, in an interim final rule adopted as final, with changes, has subsequently amended its position on the timing of the filing of an I-772. See 53 Fed.Reg. 48248, November 30, 1988. The revised rule to be codified at 28 C.F.R. §44.101(c)(2)(ii) establishes that the declaration of intention filing requirement is satisfied as long as the declaration is completed and filed not later than the filing of the charge with OSC. Contrary to its prior position, the Department no longer requires that a declaration be completed and filed before the occurrence of the alleged discrimination....

If the Special Counsel fails to file a complaint before an administrative law judge, "... the person making the charge may.... file a complaint directly before ..." the judge. *Id.* at §1324b(d)(2). In the instant action, Komsu filed his charge of discrimination with OSC on November 18, 1987. Exh. 37. OSC's filing of the two complaints with the OCAHO on January 12, 1988, was clearly within the statutorily prescribed 120-day period from receipt of the charge during which the Special Counsel is to investigate and determine whether or not to file a complaint with respect to the charge.

As Komsu has been found to be an intending citizen with standing to bring a citizenship discrimination claim under IRCA, OSC has standing to file a complaint on Komsu's behalf, Case No. 88200002. In addition, by virtue of its power to "... conduct investigations respecting unfair immigration-related employment practices and, based on such an investigation.... file a complaint ..." before an administrative law judge, 8 U.S.C. § 1324b(d)(1), Special Counsel has standing to investigate a charge or proceed on its own initiative and, presumptively, to file a complaint alleging a pattern or practice of discrimination by Mesa.

* * *

IRCA provides no definition of the pattern or practice formulation enacted at section 102, 8 U.S.C. § 1324b. However, the House Judiciary Committee did discuss its understanding of the term as provided in section 101 with respect both to criminal and civil injunctive liability under 8 U.S.C. § 1324a(f) arising out of violations of prohibitions against employment of unauthorized aliens:

> The term "pattern or practice" has received substantial judicial construction, since the term appears in the Voting Right [sic] Act (42 U.S.C. 1971 et seq.), the Civil Rights Act of 1964 (42 U.S.C. 2000 et seq.), and the Fair Housing Act of 1968 (42 U.S.C. 3601 et seq.). The Committee emphasizes that it intends to follow the judicial construction of that term as set forth in *U.S. v. Mayton*, 335 F.2d 153 (1964), *International Brotherhood of Teamsters v. U.S.*, 431 U.S. 324, and *U.S. v. International Association of Ironworkers Local No. 1*, 438 F.2d 679 (1971). These cases all indicate that the term "pattern or practice" has its generic meaning and shall apply to regular, repeated and intentional activities, but does not include isolated, sporadic or accidental acts. The same interpretation of "pattern or practice" shall apply when that term is used in this bill with regard to the injunctive remedy that may be sought by the Attorney General for recruitment, referral or employment violations, as well as for certain unfair immigration-related employment practices.

H.R.Rep. No. 99-682, *supra*, at 59.

... [A] threshold inquiry must be resolved, i.e., whether Special Counsel may properly maintain a pattern or practice cause of action. This inquiry derives from the peculiar positioning in the statute of the sole provision dealing with pattern or practice in discrimination cases:

> Private actions—
>
> If the Special Counsel, after receiving such a charge respecting an unfair immigration-related employment practice which alleges knowing and intentional discriminatory activity or a pattern or practice of discriminatory activity, has not filed a complaint before an administrative law judge with respect to such charge within such 120-day period, the person making the charge may (subject to paragraph (3)) file a complaint directly before such a judge.

8 U.S.C. § 1324b(d)(2).

It may be argued that by such placement under the subsection entitled "Private actions," Congress contemplated that a complaint alleging "a pattern or practice of discriminatory activity" might be filed only by "the person making the charge" and not by the Special Counsel. I think otherwise.

Absent some such indication in the legislative history, it would be inconsistent with the thrust of the protections sought by IRCA to conclude that Special Counsel was to be limited to prosecuting only individualized actions before administrative law judges. Nor should it be assumed that Congress intended to clothe individuals to the exclusion of the newly created statutory officer with authority to initiate actions which reflect "regular, repeated and intentional activities" (as defined by the House Judiciary Committee, H.R.Rep. 99-682, *supra*, at 59). Patently, pattern or practice jurisdiction implicates causes of action initiated by or prosecuted to vindicate the public interest in eliminating ongoing discriminatory practices. See, e.g., *EEOC v. United Parcel Service*, 860 F.2d 372 (10th Cir.1988).

Considering that filing of any charge with the OSC is a condition precedent to filing with a judge, I am unable to conclude that Congress intended that the charging party but not the Special Counsel might maintain an action for "a pattern or practice of discriminatory activity." Moreover, in the preceding subsection, 8 U.S.C. § 1324b(c)(2), assigning duties to the Special Counsel, IRCA charges OSC with "... investigation of charges and issuance of complaints under this section and in respect of the prosecution of all such complaints before administrative law judges...." There are no words of limitation to suggest that "such complaints" exclude the pattern or practice cases contemplated at subsection (d)(2). I do not overlook that (d)(2) is introduced by the catch-line "Private actions," but I am unable to conclude that those words inform the substantive text.

The Charging Party was Unlawfully Denied Employment on Citizenship Grounds

In an undated prehearing statement, Eric Trigg, promoted to director of operations prior to that statement, candidly expressed Mesa's hiring practices as applied to Zeki Yeni Komsu.

> Mr. Komsu was not hired for two reasons. The first reason is that he was not a citizen of the United States and Mesa had more then [sic] enough qualified U.S. citizens applying for those positions that were available. It is the policy of Mesa to hire only U.S. citizens if a sufficient number of qualified citizens is available to fill the positions needed. The second reason Mr. Komsu was not hired is because of his constant and irritating phone calls to me. These numerous phone calls left me with an unfavorable impression of Mr. Komsu.

Exh. 17.

Within a week of Komsu's filing with EEOC, Larry Risley, in his capacity as Mesa's president, on August 27, 1987, in a letter to EEOC, acknowledged that:

> It is the policy of Mesa Airlines, Inc., to hire U.S. citizens only unless the available employee pool is not adequate at the time. During the past 12 months we have not experienced any shortage of U.S. citizen applicants from which to hire.
>
> It is our understanding that there are no acts, laws or statutus (sic) that prohibit this policy. We therefore request this charge be dismissed as Mr.

> Yenikomsu was not hired due to his non-citizen status and not because of his national origin—Turkish.

Thus, months after Mesa became aware of Komsu's charge of discrimination, Gary Risley, asserting that "[t]he Justice Department is attempting to write the U.S. citizen preference out of the statute ..." *id.*, unambiguously described Mesa's practices in a way which I can only understand as reflecting the view that wholesale exclusion of non-U.S. candidates complied with the law so long as any qualified citizen candidates had also applied. Larry L. Risley, president of Mesa since its founding in 1982, conceded as much.

On the witness stand, Gary Risley asserted he had been mistaken as to Mesa's practices, impeaching as erroneous his broadside, omnibus letter as well as documentary and oral evidence of other Mesa officials. I am unpersuaded by his after-the-fact recantations. Mesa both enunciated and practiced invidious discrimination against non-U.S. citizens. Even after Komsu filed his charges, Mesa officials continued to contend that their employment practices were lawful because the U.S. citizens they hired were as qualified as the non-U.S. citizen candidates. Exhibits 10–12, acknowledging Mesa's hiring preference, reflect a discriminatory hiring policy on their face.

... Accordingly, I reject as lacking in trustworthiness the testimony of Gary Risley and others that the prior iterations by himself and others of Mesa's employment policy and practices were erroneous. In so deciding, I need not disbelieve Gary Risley's repudiation of his earlier statement that Mesa maintained two physically separate applicant pools. It is sufficient that Mesa implemented its stated policy of preferring U.S. citizen candidates by failing to compare qualifications of non-U.S. citizen candidates with those of citizen candidates.

It follows without question that Mesa's pilot hiring practices fall outside and fail to qualify for the exception provided at 8 U.S.C. § 1324b(a)(4):

> ... it is not an unfair immigration-related employment practice for a person or other entity to prefer to hire, recruit, or refer an individual who is a citizen or national of the United States over another individual who is an alien if the two individuals are equally qualified.

* * *

Mesa's commitment to hiring U.S. pilots to the exclusion of non-U.S. citizens so long as the supply of qualified citizens meets the demand in no way satisfies the exception. The plain words of the exception are inescapable: the employer avoids liability for discrimination if, but only if, there has been a comparison of qualifications as the result of which the selected citizen is found to have qualifications not less than equal to the non-selected alleged discriminate. Here there was no such comparison.

* * *

On the record before me it is a certainty that Komsu was not rejected on the basis of pilot qualifications in head-to-head competition with any one or more of the U.S. citizen candidates who were selected during the pendency of his application from

December 1986 to August 1987, or during any interval in between. I conclude from the testimony of Mesa's witnesses that their evaluation of Komsu's qualifications was after the fact, after he was rejected on citizenship grounds, and not before.

* * *

The results reached in the cases first heard under new legislation such as this will by definition establish precedent. To the extent that any one case turns on unique facts, of course, its precedential significance is reduced. This may be one such case because with the passage of time after enactment of IRCA on November 6, 1986, it may be supposed that employers will be less candid than was Mesa in trumpeting to non-U.S. citizen candidates and to public authorities their unwillingness to hire non-U.S. citizens.

* * *

Accordingly, I find and conclude that Mr. Komsu was knowingly and intentionally denied employment for the sole reason that he was not a citizen of the United States.

* * *

Where as here the discrimination has been proven, it is the teaching of cases involving Title VII that the burden is on the putative employer to persuade that even absent the discrimination it would not have hired the charging party. See, e.g., *McDonnell-Douglas Corp. v. Green*, 411 U.S. 792 (1973); *Int'l Bhd. of Teamsters v. United States*, 431 U.S. 324, (1977); *Texas Dep't of Community Affairs v. Burdine*, 450 U.S. 248 (1981); *Lowe v. City of Monrovia*, 775 F.2d 998 (9th Cir. 1986); *Rich v. Martin Marietta Corp.*, 522 F.2d 333 (10th Cir. 1975).

McDonnell-Douglas, supra, is the seminal case that articulated a four part formula to establish a prima facie showing of discriminatory disparate treatment in Title VII causes of action. An individual or class plaintiff must demonstrate: (1) that he/she belongs to a protected class; (2) that he/she applied for and was qualified for a position for which the putative employer was seeking applicants; (3) that despite being qualified, he/she was rejected; and (4) that after such rejection, the position remained available and the employer continued to seek applicants from individuals having the plaintiff's qualifications. 411 U.S. at 802. The burden of proof is divided into three stages. At the first stage, the charging party must make a prima facie showing of discrimination by satisfying the four criteria enumerated above. After that showing is made, the second stage shifts the burden to the employer "to articulate some legitimate, nondiscriminatory reason for the employee's rejection." *Id.* The third stage returns the burden to the plaintiff to disprove the putative employer's explanation as pretextual, i.e., the pretext or gloss designed to conceal an underlying discriminatory motivation.

The Supreme Court recently reversed the D.C. Circuit as having held erroneously that an employer found to have allowed a discriminatory motive to play a part in an employment decision must prove by clear and convincing evidence that it would have made the same decision absent the discrimination. By a plurality decision, six justices recently instructed that an employer in a mixed motive case who proves by a preponderance of the evidence that it would have made the same employment decision if it had not taken the prohibited discriminatory consideration into account may avoid a finding of liability. *Price Waterhouse v. Hopkins, supra.*

The plurality noted that *McDonald v. Santa Fe Trail Transportation Co.*, 427 U.S. 273 (1976) "... dealt with the question whether the employer's stated reason for its decision was the reason for its action; unlike the case before us today, therefore, *McDonald* did not involve mixed motives. This difference is decisive in distinguishing this case from those involving 'pretext.'" *Hopkins, supra*, 109 S.Ct. at 1785 n. 6. While "but for" analysis may be critical to a pretext case, e.g., *McDonald, supra*, "[w]here a decision was the product of a mixture of legitimate and illegitimate motives, however, it simply makes no sense to ask whether the legitimate reason was 'the "true reason"'... for the decision—which is the question asked by Burdine." *Hopkins, supra*, at 1788–89.

* * *

Justices White and O'Connor each separately concurred in the judgment of the Court. Justice White agreed that the plurality opinion of Justice Brennan "is not a departure from and does not require a modification of the Court's holdings.... [in *McDonnell Douglas* and *Burdine*]...," even though they were pretext cases, involving the search for the one "true" motive behind the employment decision. *Id.*, concurring op. at 1795. He disagreed, however, that the employer must carry its burden through objective evidence, suggesting that "where the legitimate motive found would have been ample grounds for the action taken, and the employer credibly testifies that the action would have been taken for the legitimate reasons alone, this should be ample proof." *Id.* at 1796.

Justice O'Connor disagreed with the plurality as to the analysis to be utilized by a court to determine when a claimant's proof warrants shifting the burden of persuasion to the employer. Title VII prohibits employment decisions made "because of" prohibited considerations, i.e., race, color, religion, sex or national origin. Writing that "[b]ased on its misreading of the words 'because of' in the statute.... the plurality appears to conclude that if a decisional process is 'tainted' by awareness of sex or race in any way, the employer has violated the statute, and Title VII thus commands that the burden shift to the employer...," she concluded instead that the burden shifts only when a disparate treatment claimant shows "by direct evidence that an illegitimate criterion was a substantial factor in the decision." *Id.*, concurring op. at 1804. "Only then would the burden of proof shift to the defendant to prove that the decision would have been justified by other, wholly legitimate considerations." *Id.* at 1805

* * *

Even assuming that the law were as Justices White and O'Connor understand it to be, I am satisfied that the record before me proves that Mesa's motive not to hire non-U.S. pilots "was a substantial factor in the adverse employment action." *Hopkins, supra*, White, J., concurring op. at 1795.

That the improper motive, the discriminatory animus, was a substantial factor, if not the only one, in Mesa's hiring decisions is established here....

Pattern or Practice Applied

The question to be decided is whether I am authorized to find a pattern or practice of unlawful discrimination on the basis that individuals presumptively eligible for protection of remedial legislation, but not proven to have qualified, may, nevertheless, comprise the universe of individuals on whose behalf it may be found that an employer practiced such a pattern or practice.

An analogy which suggests inclusion in the class to be counted for pattern or practice purposes of individuals ineligible to maintain an action is found in policy guidance recently issued by the EEOC. Discussing IRCA's impact on remedies available to undocumented aliens under Title VII, the Commission has applied the analysis in *Sure-Tan v. NLRB*, 467 U.S. 883 (1984), which held that undocumented workers were employees for the purposes of, and, therefore, had standing to maintain claims under, the National Labor Relations Act.

EEOC explains that Title VII remedies are intended to discourage employment discrimination both (1) by providing disincentives to potential future discrimination and (2) by restoring an individual charging party as nearly as possible to the position that individual would have been in but for the discrimination. As to both, EEOC explains that Title VII protection is applicable to undocumented workers because if it were not:

> ... a discriminatory atmosphere might be created in the work place which would violate not only the rights of undocumented workers but also the rights of authorized workers. Therefore, it is essential to the goals of both Title VII and IRCA that undocumented aliens continue to be covered by Title VII.

EEOC Policy Guidance: Effect of the Immigration Reform and Control Act of 1986 (IRCA) on the Remedies Available to Undocumented Aliens Under Title VII, at 5, April 26, 1989, see Interpreter Releases, Vol. 66, No. 23, June 19, 1989, at 655–56.

* * *

OSC relies on a recent opinion of the Tenth Circuit which sustained authority of the EEOC to maintain a pattern or practice action even where it lacked any ascertainable member of the class to be protected. Without concluding here that precedents implicating EEOC standing necessarily inform IRCA jurisdiction, it cannot be doubted that the court's analysis is instructive, especially in this circuit. In *EEOC v. United Parcel Service, supra*, the court reversed the district court for having granted summary judgment dismissing EEOC's suit for racial discrimination where the only identified individual injured by defendant's conduct had settled his claim....

* * *

In my judgment, IRCA prohibits unfair immigration-related employment practices against aliens (other than unauthorized aliens) without regard to whether they qualify as intending citizens. Interpreting and applying this remedial statute, it appears that protection is provided in the sense of traditional remedies to obtain "make whole" relief only for intending citizens; pattern or practice liability is provided in context of any alien (other than an unauthorized alien) perceived to be the victim of unfair immigration-related employment practices.

* * *

It follows that a pattern or practice of discrimination may arise without proof that more than one alien, as to whom the practice in question impacted, qualifies as an intending citizen within the meaning of section 102. Accordingly, the pattern or practice claim, clearly established, is found to have been proven as a matter of law.

Notes

1. While the 1990 Act removed the requirement that the complainant file a notice of intention to become a U.S. citizen, can it truly be said that the "intending citizen" requirement was removed? Read through the statute [8 U.S.C. § 1324b(a)(3)(B)] and see if you can define who are the beneficiaries of the statute. Does it include U.S. citizens or ethnic minorities? Is it intended to proscribe national origin discrimination? What would happen if a company discriminated against certain employees because it preferred to hire permanent residents; would this be in violation of the anti-discrimination provisions? According to one view, the hiring of a natural born citizen over someone who was naturalized is actionable. *Nickman v. Mesa Air Group,* 9 OCAHO 351 (2004). However, the employer's unwillingness to go through the non-immigrant or immigrant labor certification requirement is not considered actionable by the Special Counsel. Letter Deputy Special Counsel Baldwin, 15 BENDER'S IMMIGR. BULL 1057, 1114 (2010).

2. It is an unfair immigration-related employment practice, referred to as "document abuse," for an employer seeking to avoid sanctions to require more proof of work authorization than is deemed sufficient under the statute under 8 U.S.C. § 1324b(a)(6).[29] *In Re Charge of Valdivia-Sanchez v. LASA Marketing Firms,* No. 88-200061 (Exec. Off. for Imm. Rev. November 27, 1989) reached that conclusion. In that case, the charging party responded to an employment referral agency's advertisement and presented a driver's license, social security card and letters indicating her intent to apply for legalization. She was turned away because she did not have further documentation. She subsequently applied for legalization and then returned to the agency. The agency again requested more proof of work authorization even though she had an I-688A (temporary work permit). Although the administrative law judge did not find that LASA had knowingly discriminated against Ms. Valdivia, he nevertheless concluded that Section 274B had been violated based on LASA's uninformed understanding of what kinds of immigration-related employment documents were required to evince employment authorization in accordance with IRCA, "thus resulting in Ms. Valdivia being rejected with respect to employment for an *illegitimate,* statutorily prohibited reason, i.e., disparate treatment on account of citizenship status" (emphasis in original). Similarly, an employer was found to be in

---

29. Section 274B(a)(6); 28 C.F.R. § 44.200(a)(3).

violation where it fired a person who had been granted asylum and whose employment authorization had expired, though he had proof of a request for extension of the employment authorization document.[30] The court reasoned that employment authorization extensions in such cases were routine.

3. As previously mentioned, at the time that the *Komsu* case was brought, there had been relatively few Section 274B discrimination cases filed and processed by the Office of the Special Counsel (OSC) and even fewer that had reached the federal courts. *Komsu* was the first ever dealing with the Act's anti-discrimination provision and was actually filed before the administrative structure provided for in the Act was fully established. This lag in implementation of the OSC explains why the district court exercised its jurisdiction and heard the case even though the plaintiffs had not exhausted all of their administrative remedies as was required under the Act, which provides that exhaustion is a statutory prerequisite to judicial review.

4. **Private actions.** Amendments enacted under the 1990 Act require the Special Counsel to notify the complainant within 120 days after receiving the charge of its intent not to file a complaint before the Administrative Law Judge (ALJ). The complainant then has 90 days after receiving such notification to file her complaint directly before the ALJ. During this 90 day period, the Special Counsel may continue to investigate the charge and file a complaint before the ALJ.

5. *Komsu v. Mesa* also addressed the issue of equitable tolling and held that the 180-day time limit for filing a charge with the OSC is not a jurisdictional requirement but more in the nature of a statute of limitations that is subject to waiver, estoppel and equitable tolling. Accordingly, the ALJ held that the filing of a charge with the EEOC tolled the running of the 180-day limitation period for filing a charge with the OSC. The OSC and EEOC have since filed a Memorandum of Understanding that allows individuals to file charges with the EEOC, which are then referred to the OSC if later determined to have been filed with the wrong agency. The 180-day statute of limitations is tolled while the EEOC has the charge. Similarly, the limitations period is tolled if the charge is erroneously filed with the OSC instead of the EEOC.[31]

6. Mesa Airlines appealed the ALJ decision, but their appeal was dismissed by the Court as untimely filed. 8 U.S.C. § 1324(b)(I)(1) provides that a petition for review must be filed from an ALJ's decision "[n]ot later than 60 days after the entry of such final order." The Judge had signed his decision on July 24, 1989 and had served the decision on the parties the following day. On September 25, 1989, Mesa filed a petition for review with the Clerk of the Tenth Circuit Court of Appeals. The Tenth Circuit held that the 60-day requirement was jurisdictional and that the period would begin with the ALJ's signing of the order and not on the day that the decision was received.[32]

30. *Getahun v. OCAHO*, 124 F.3d 591 (3d Cir. 1997).

31. *See* 54 Fed. Reg. 32,499 (1989).

32. *Mesa Airlines v. U.S.*, 951 F.2d 1186 (10th Cir. 1991).

7. In *Romo v. Todd Corp.,*[33] the ALJ acknowledged that the availability of the disparate impact standard in anti-discrimination cases is still in dispute. The ALJ nevertheless stated that the dispute could not be resolved in the case before him in view of the result reached on the record that the complainant failed to qualify as a protected individual under section 102.

8. **Defenses and Appeals.** State and Native American tribes enjoy sovereign immunity from the statute's coverage. States do so under the 11th Amendment. *Hensel v. OCAHO*, 38 F.3d 505, 508 (10th Cir. 1994). The statute does not explicitly divest tribes of their sovereign immunity. *Quais Ibrahim Alhameed v. Grand Traverse Resort & Casino*, 10 OCAHO 1126 (2008). Other defenses include the statute of limitations. Adverse decisions must be appealed within 60 days after entry of the ALJ order with the federal appeals court where the violation occurred or where the employer resides or conducts business.[34]

9. **Protection of Undocumented Workers Under Other Federal Labor Legislation.** How the undocumented in the work force will fare under other federal labor legislation will depend on the particular statute invoked. In an earlier case pre-dating IRCA, the Supreme Court held that the National Labor Relations Act (NLRA) protected undocumented workers.[35] However while the employees may receive back pay, their reinstatement is conditioned on their eligibility to work.[36] In *Patel v. Quality Inn South,*[37] a federal circuit court reversed a district court decision that had held that undocumented workers are not protected under the Fair Labor Standards Act (FLSA). The district court had reasoned that to give the protection of the FLSA to undocumented persons would encourage illegal immigration and thus undermine the policies behind the INA as amended by IRCA. In reversing, the circuit court concluded that extending FLSA's protection to the undocumented is perfectly consistent with the goals of IRCA, as it removes any incentive employers might have in hiring persons unlawfully in this country. The court held that if the undocumented are paid substandard wages, they can sue their employers in an action under the FLSA. The court thus concluded that undocumented persons should be entitled to the full range of available remedies under the statute without regard to their immigration status. It found that such a result would be consistent with the policies of IRCA and *Sure-Tan, supra.*[38]

---

33. 1 OCAHO 25 (1988), *aff'd sub nom., United States v. Todd Corporation,* 900 F.2d 164 (9th Cir. 1990).

34. 28 C.F.R. §68.57; *Curuta v. OCAHO,* 398 F.3d 329 (5th Cir. 2005).

35. *See Sure-Tan Inc. v. NLRB,* 467 U.S. 883 (1984).

36. *NLRB v. APRA Fuel Oil Buyers Group, Inc.* 134 F.3d 50 (1997); *but see Del Rey Tortilleria v. NLRB*, 976 F.2d 1115 (7th Cir. 1992).

37. 846 F.2d 700 (11th Cir. 1988), *cert. denied,* 489 U.S. 1011 (1989).

38. For additional discussion of *Sure-Tan* in a post-IRCA era, *see* Alan A. Stevens, *Give Me Your Tired, Your Poor, Your Destitute Laborers Ready to be Exploited: The Failure of International Human Rights Law to Protect the Rights of Illegal Aliens in American Jurisprudence,* 14 Emory Int'l L. Rev. 405 (2000); Richard E. Blum, *Labor Standards Enforcement and the Results of Labor Migration,* 63 N.Y.U. L. Rev. 1342 (1988); L. Tracy Harris, *Conflict or Double Deterrence? FLSA Protection of Illegal Aliens and the Immigration Reform and Control Act,* 72 Minn. L. Rev. 900 (1988); Charnesky, *Protection for Undocumented Workers Under the FLSA: An Evaluation in Light of IRCA,* 25 San Diego L. Rev.

10. ***Attorney Fees.*** The prevailing party in an unfair immigration-related employment practice case filed with the Office of the Chief Administrative Hearing Officer (OCAHO) may be awarded attorney's fees if the losing party's argument was without reasonable foundation in law or fact. The standard requires a showing that the aggrieved position was frivolous, unreasonable or without foundation.[39]

B. Education

The "American people have always regarded education and [the] acquisition of knowledge as matters of supreme importance."[40] Public schools have served as vehicles by which social, political and cultural ideals have been disseminated and preserved. In *Brown v. Board of Education*,[41] the Court unanimously recognized that "[c]ompulsory school attendance laws and the great expenditures for education both demonstrate our recognition of the importance of education to our democratic society...." However, the Supreme Court has never held that public education is a fundamental right. In *San Antonio Independent School Dist. v. Rodriguez*,[42] the Court held that education is not a fundamental right and, furthermore, that poverty, standing alone, does not constitute a suspect classification. These are the two strands upon which violations of the equal protection clause of the fourteenth amendment are predicated.

The Court in *San Antonio* implied that had there been an absolute deprivation of education imposed on a particular group, this might be determined to be an impairment of a fundamental right. The plaintiffs in *San Antonio* had claimed that Texas' system of financing public education violated equal protection, because it relied on local property taxes. Districts with high property tax bases, therefore, could spend and did spend more on education than those districts with low property tax bases. Nevertheless, the Court held that there was no denial of a fundamental right, stating that "we have no indication that the [low taxation] system fails to provide each child with an opportunity to acquire the basic minimal skills."[43] Justice Powell, speaking for the Court in *San Antonio,* went on to define a "suspect class" as a "discrete and insular" minority that has historically suffered from "unequal treatment" or is in a position of "political powerlessness" requiring judicial protection from the majority's political processes. Thus, adult citizens have some political power but undocumented aliens do not because they are not entitled to vote.

The children of undocumented persons seem to fit within Powell's definition of "suspect class." Similar to illegitimate children, they not only have suffered from un-

---

379 (1988). *See also NLRB v. Ashkenazy Property Management Corporation,* 817 F.2d 74 (9th Cir. 1987).

39. *See U.S. v. General Dynamics Corp.*, 3 OCAHO 517 (1993); *Jones v. Dewitt Nursing Home*, 1 OCAHO 189 (1990).

40. *Meyer v. Nebraska*, 262 U.S. 390, 400 (1923).

41. 347 U.S. 483, 493 (1954).

42. 411 U.S. 1, 35 (1973).

43. 411 U.S. at 36–37.

equal treatment but are relegated to a state of helplessness, political and otherwise. However, as the following case demonstrates, the Court has gone to great lengths to avoid reaching the conclusion that the undocumented constitute a suspect class.

James Plyer, Superintendent of the Tyler Independent School District and Its Board of Trustees et al. v. J. and R. Doe, et al.

457 U.S. 202 (1982)

[The United States District Court for the Eastern District of Texas, Judge William Wayne Justice, held for plaintiffs, Mexican undocumented children excluded from Texas public schools. On appeal, the Fifth Circuit affirmed.]

Justice BRENNAN delivered the opinion of the Court.

The question presented by these cases is whether, consistent with the Equal Protection Clause of the Fourteenth Amendment, Texas may deny to undocumented school-age children the free public education that it provides to children who are citizens of the United States or legally admitted inadmissibles.

* * *

In May 1975, the Texas Legislature revised its education laws to withhold from local school districts any state funds for the education of children who were not "legally admitted" into the United States. The 1975 revision also authorized local school districts to deny enrollment in their public schools to children not "legally admitted" to the country. Tex. Educ. Code Ann. § 21.031 (Vernon Supp. 1981).

* * *

The Fourteenth Amendment provides that "[n]o State shall.... deprive any person of life, liberty, or property, without due process of law; nor deny to any person within its jurisdiction the equal protection of the laws." Appellants argue.... that undocumented aliens because of their immigration status, are not "persons within the jurisdiction" of the State of Texas, and that they therefore have no right to the equal protection of Texas law. We reject this argument. Whatever his status under the immigration laws, an alien is surely a "person" in any ordinary sense of that term. Aliens, even aliens whose presence in this country is unlawful, have long been recognized as "persons" guaranteed due process of law by the Fifth and Fourteenth Amendments. *Shaughnessy v. Mezei*, 345 U.S. 206, 212 (1953)....

Appellants seek to distinguish our prior cases, emphasizing that the Equal Protection Clause directs a State to afford its protection to persons within its jurisdiction while the Due Process Clauses of the Fifth and Fourteenth Amendments contain no such assertedly limiting phrase.

* * *

... We have never suggested that the class of persons who might avail themselves of the equal protection guarantee is less than coextensive with that entitled to due process. To the contrary, we have recognized that both provisions.... protect an identical class of persons, and reach every exercise of state authority.

* * *

There is simply no support for appellants' suggestion that "due process" is somehow of greater stature than "equal protection" and therefore available to a larger class of persons. To the contrary, each aspect of the Fourteenth Amendment reflects an elementary limitation on state power. To permit a State to employ the phrase "within its jurisdiction" in order to identify subclasses of persons whom it would define as beyond its jurisdiction.... would undermine the principal purpose for which the Equal Protection Clause was incorporated in the Fourteenth Amendment. The Equal Protection Clause was intended to work nothing less than the abolition of all caste-based and invidious class-based legislation. That objective is fundamentally at odds with the power the State asserts here....

* * *

... In applying the Equal Protection Clause to most forms of state action, we thus seek only the assurance that the classification at issue bears some fair relationship to legitimate public purpose.

But we would not be faithful to our obligations under the Fourteenth Amendment if we applied so deferential a standard to every classification. The Equal Protection Clause was intended as a restriction on state legislative action inconsistent with elemental constitutional premises. Thus we have treated as presumptively invidious those classifications that disadvantage a "suspect class,"[1] or that impinge upon the exercise of a "fundamental right." With respect to such classifications, it is appropriate to enforce the mandate of equal protection by requiring the State to demonstrate that its classification has been precisely tailored to serve a compelling governmental interest. In addition, we have recognized that certain forms of legislative classification, while not facially invidious, nonetheless give rise to recurring constitutional difficulties; in these limited circumstances we have sought the assurance that the classification reflects a reasoned judgment consistent with the ideal of equal protection by inquiring whether it may fairly be viewed as furthering a substantial interest of the State. We turn to a consideration of the standard appropriate for the evaluation of § 21.031.

* * *

... [I]ncapability or lax enforcement of the laws barring entry ... [and] ... failure to establish an effective bar to the employment of undocumented aliens, has resulted in the creation of a substantial "shadow population" ... numbering in the millions.... The existence of such an underclass presents most difficult problems for a Nation that prides itself on adherence to principles of equality under law.[2]

---

1. Several formulations might explain our treatment of certain classifications as "suspect."

2. We reject the claim that "illegal aliens" are a "suspect class." ... Unlike most of the classifications that we have recognized as suspect, entry into this class, by virtue of entry into this country, is the product of voluntary action. Indeed, entry into the class is itself a crime....

The children who are plaintiffs in these cases are special members of this underclass. Persuasive arguments support the view that a State may withhold its beneficence from those whose very presence within the United States is the product of their own unlawful conduct. These arguments do not apply with the same force to classifications imposing disabilities on.... minor children.... [T]he children who are plaintiffs in these cases "can affect neither their parents' conduct nor their own status." *Trimble v. Gordon*, 430 U.S. 762, 770 (1977).

* * *

Section 21.031 is directed against children, and imposes its discriminatory burden on the basis of a legal characteristic over which children can have little control. It is thus difficult to conceive of a rational justification for penalizing these children for their presence within the United States. Yet that appears to be precisely the effect of § 21.031.

Public education is not a "right" granted.... by the Constitution. *San Antonio Independent School Dist. v. Rodriguez*, 411 U.S. 1, 35 (1973). But neither is it merely some governmental "benefit" indistinguishable from other forms of social welfare legislation. Both the importance of education in maintaining our basic institutions, and the lasting impact of its deprivation on the life of the child, mark the distinction.... [E]ducation provides the basic tools by which individuals might lead economically productive lives to the benefit of us all.... We cannot ignore the significant social costs borne by our Nation when select groups are denied the means to absorb the values and skills upon which our social order rests.

... [B]y depriving the children of any disfavored group of an education, we foreclose the means by which that group might raise the level of esteem in which it is held by the majority.

* * *

Illiteracy is an enduring disability. The inability to read and write will handicap the individual deprived of a basic education each and every day of his life....

* * *

... Undocumented aliens cannot be treated as a suspect class because their presence in this country in violation of federal law is not a "constitutional irrelevancy." Nor is education a fundamental right; a State need not justify by compelling necessity every variation in the manner in which education is provided to its population.... [M]ore is involved in these cases than the abstract question whether § 21.031 discriminates against a suspect class, or whether education is a fundamental right....

In determining the rationality of § 21.031, we may appropriately take into account its costs to the Nation and to the innocent children who are its victims. In light of these countervailing costs, the discrimination contained in § 21.031 can hardly be considered rational unless it furthers some substantial goal of the State.

... Indeed, in the State's view, Congress' apparent disapproval of the presence of these children within the United States, and the evasion of the federal regulatory program that is the mark of undocumented status, provides authority for its decisions to impose upon them special disabilities. Faced with an equal protection challenge respecting the treatment of aliens, we agree that the courts must be attentive to congressional policy; the exercise of congressional power might well affect the State's prerogatives to afford differential treatment to a particular class of aliens. But we are unable to find in the congressional immigration scheme any statement of policy that might weigh significantly in arriving at an equal protection balance concerning the State's authority to deprive these children of an education.

* * *

... In light of the discretionary federal power to grant relief from deportation, a State cannot realistically determine that any particular undocumented child will in fact be deported until after deportation proceedings have been completed. It would of course be most difficult for the State to justify a denial of education to a child enjoying an inchoate federal permission to remain.

We are reluctant to impute to Congress the intention to withhold from these children, for so long as they are present in this country through no fault of their own, access to a basic education....

Appellants argue that the classification at issue furthers an interest in "preservation of the State's limited resources for the education of its lawful residents." Of course, a concern for the preservation of resources standing alone can hardly justify the classification used in allocating those resources....

... While a State might have an interest in mitigating the potential harsh economic effects of sudden shifts in population, § 21.031 hardly offers an effective method of dealing with an urgent demographic or economic problem. There is no evidence in the record suggesting that illegal entrants impose any significant burden on the State's economy.... [E]ven ... assum[ing] that the net impact of illegal aliens on the economy of the State is negative, we think it clear that "[c]harging tuition to undocumented children constitutes a ludicrously ineffectual attempt to stem the tide of illegal immigration."

... Of course, even if improvement in the quality of education were a likely result of barring some number of children from the schools of the State, the State must support its selection of this group as the appropriate target for exclusion. In terms of educational cost and need, however, undocumented children are "basically indistinguishable" from legally resident alien children.

Finally, appellants suggest that undocumented children are appropriately singled out because their unlawful presence [makes] them less likely than other children to remain within the boundaries of the State, and to put their education to productive social or political use within the State.... [T]he record is clear that many of the undocumented children disabled by this classification will remain in this country indefinitely, and that some will become lawful residents or citizens of the United States. It is difficult to understand precisely what the State hopes to achieve by promoting the creation and perpetuation of a subclass of illiterates within our boundaries, surely adding to the problems and costs of unemployment, welfare, and crime....

... Accordingly, the judgment of the Court of Appeals in each of these cases is Affirmed.

Justice MARSHALL, concurring.

While I join the Court's opinion, I do so without in any way retreating from my opinion in *San Antonio Independent School District v. Rodriguez*, 411 U.S. 1, 70–133 (1973) (dissenting opinion)....

Justice BLACKMUN, concurring.

I join the opinion and judgment of the Court.

* * *

I joined Justice Powell's opinion for the Court in *Rodriguez*, and I continue to believe that it provides the appropriate model for resolving most equal protection disputes. Classifications infringing substantive constitutional rights necessarily will be invalid, if not by force of the Equal Protection Clause, then through operation of other provisions of the Constitution. Conversely, classifications bearing on nonconstitutional interests—even those involving "the most basic economic needs of impoverished human beings," *Dandridge v. Williams*, 397 U.S. 471, 485 (1970)—generally are not subject to special treatment under the Equal Protection Clause, because they are not distinguishable in any relevant way from other regulation in "the area of economics and social welfare." *Ibid.* With all this said, however, I believe the Court's experience has demonstrated that the Rodriguez formulation does not settle every issue of "fundamental rights" arising under the Equal Protection Clause.

* * *

[D]enial of an education is the analogue of denial of the right to vote: the former relegates the individual to second-class social status; the latter places him at a permanent political disadvantage.

* * *

Justice POWELL, concurring.

I join the opinion of the Court, and write separately to emphasize the unique character of the cases before us.

The classification in question severely disadvantages children who are the victims of a combination of circumstances.... Perhaps because of the intractability of the problem Congress—vested by the Constitution with the responsibility of protecting our borders and legislating with respect to aliens—has not provided effective leadership in dealing with this problem. Although the analogy is not perfect, our holding today does find support in decisions of this Court with respect to the status of illegitimates....

... The classification at issue deprives a group of children of the opportunity for education afforded all other children.... A legislative classification that threatens the creation of an underclass of future citizens and residents cannot be reconciled with one of the fundamental purposes of the Fourteenth Amendment.

* * *

Chief Justice Burger, with whom Justice White, Justice Rehnquist, and Justice O'Connor join, dissenting.

Were it our business to set the Nation's social policy, I would agree without hesitation that it is senseless for an enlightened society to deprive any children—including illegal aliens—of an elementary education. I fully agree that it would be folly—and wrong—to tolerate creation of a segment of society made up of illiterate persons, many having a limited or no command of our language. However, the Constitution does not constitute us as "Platonic Guardians" nor does it vest in this Court the authority to strike down laws because they do not meet our standards of desirable social policy, "wisdom," or "common sense." See *TVA v. Hill*, 437 U.S. 153, 194–195 (1978). We trespass on the assigned function of the political branches under our structure of limited and separated powers when we assume a policymaking role as the Court does today.

* * *

... I have no quarrel with the conclusion that the Equal Protection Clause of the Fourteenth Amendment applies to aliens who, after their illegal entry into this country, are indeed physically "within the jurisdiction" of a state. However, as the Court concedes, this "only begins the inquiry...."

The dispositive issue in these cases, simply put, is whether, for purposes of allocating its finite resources, a state has a legitimate reason to differentiate between persons who are lawfully within the state and those who are unlawfully there.

* * *

The Court first suggests that these illegal alien children, although not a suspect class, are entitled to special solicitude under the Equal Protection Clause because they lack "control" over or "responsibility" for their unlawful entry into this country. Similarly, the Court appears to take the position that § 21.031 is presumptively "irrational" because it has the effect of imposing "penalties" on "innocent" children.

... Illegality of presence in the United States does not—and need not—depend on some amorphous concept of "guilt" or "innocence" concerning an alien's entry. Similarly, a state's use of federal immigration status as a basis for legislative classification is not necessarily rendered suspect for its failure to take such factors into account.

... This Court has recognized that in allocating governmental benefits to a given class of aliens, one "may take into account the character of the relationship between the alien and this country." *Mathews v. Diaz*, 426 U.S. 67 (1976). When that "relationship" is a federally prohibited one, there can, of course, be no presumption that a state has a constitutional duty to include illegal aliens among the recipients of its governmental benefits.

The second strand of the Court's analysis rests on the premise that, although public education is not a constitutionally guaranteed right, "neither is it merely some governmental 'benefit' indistinguishable from other forms of social welfare legislation."

The importance of education is beyond dispute. Yet we have held repeatedly that the importance of a governmental service does not elevate it to the status of a "fundamental right" for purposes of equal protection analysis.... Moreover, the Court points to no meaningful way to distinguish between education and other governmental benefits in this context. Is the Court suggesting that education is more "fundamental" than food, shelter, or medical care?

The Equal Protection Clause guarantees similar treatment of similarly situated persons, but it does not mandate a constitutional hierarchy of governmental services. The central question in these cases, as in every equal protection case not involving truly fundamental rights "explicitly or implicitly guaranteed by the Constitution," *San Antonio Independent School Dist.*, *supra*, 411 U.S., at 33–34, is whether there is some legitimate basis for legislative distinction between different classes of persons....

The State contends primarily that § 21.031 serves to prevent undue depletion of its limited revenues available for education, and to preserve the fiscal integrity of the State's school-financing system against an ever-increasing flood of illegal aliens—over whose entry or continued presence it has no control. Of course such fiscal concerns alone could not justify discrimination against a suspect class or an arbitrary and irrational denial of benefits to a particular group of persons. Yet I assume no Member of this Court would argue that prudent conservation of finite state revenues is per se an illegitimate goal.... The significant question here is whether the requirement of tuition from illegal aliens who attend the public schools—as well as from residents of other states, for example—is a rational and reasonable means of furthering the State's legitimate fiscal ends.

* * *

... The Court has failed to offer even a plausible explanation why illegality of residence in this country is not a factor that may legitimately bear upon the bona fides of state residence and entitlement to the benefits of lawful residence....

It is significant that the Federal Government has seen fit to exclude illegal aliens from numerous social welfare programs, such as the food stamp program, ... the old-age assistance, aid to families with dependent children, aid to the blind, aid to the permanently and totally disabled, and supplemental security income programs, the Medicare hospital insurance benefits program, and the Medicaid hospital insurance benefits for the aged and disabled program....

The Court maintains—as if this were the issue—that "barring undocumented children from local schools would not necessarily improve the quality of education provided in those schools." ... However, the legitimacy of barring illegal aliens from programs such as Medicare or Medicaid does not depend on a showing that the barrier would "improve the quality" of medical care given to persons lawfully entitled to participate in such programs.

* * *

The Constitution does not provide a cure for every social ill, nor does it vest judges with a mandate to try to remedy every social problem.... Today's cases.... present yet another example of unwarranted judicial action which in the long run tends to contribute to the weakening of our political processes....

While the "specter of a permanent caste" of illegal Mexican residents of the United States is indeed a disturbing one, it is but one segment of a larger problem, which is for the political branches to solve.... Yet instead of allowing the political processes to run their course—albeit with some delay—the Court seeks to do Congress' job for it, compensating for congressional inaction. It is not unreasonable to think that this encourages the political branches to pass their problems to the Judiciary.

Notes

1. The Court determined that undocumented persons were not a "suspect class" for purposes of equal protection analysis. In contrast to the involuntary nature of membership in other suspect classes, the undocumented person committed a voluntary, albeit illegal, act of entry. The Court asserted that their illegal status was not a constitutional irrelevancy because Congress has the power to deny admission to persons into the United States. In refusing to recognize undocumented persons as a suspect class, the Court avoided the strict scrutiny analysis.

2. It appears that the Court has combined the two factors in *Plyler*, namely, a disadvantaged group (the undocumented) and an important interest (education), to justify its use of intermediate scrutiny. It seems from the majority decision that the Court applied nearly strict scrutiny based on these factors despite particular facts that involved a non-suspect classification and a non-fundamental right. In both Blackmun and Powell's concurrences, the Justices urged that the majority opinion be read narrowly in that the case possessed these unique characteristics. Did the Court in *Plyler v. Doe* muddy the waters of equal protection analysis?

3. In *Plyler*, the Court held that undocumented children in Texas could not be statutorily denied an education. Also noteworthy is the unreported 1985 decision in *Leticia A. v. Board of Regents of the University of California*,[44] where the California Constitution was held to prohibit a state institution of higher learning from refusing to provide an education to undocumented persons. In a later case, undocumented students were precluded from receiving in-state residency for tuition purposes in the California State University system. In 2001, the California legislature enacted § 68130.5 of the Education Code, which provides that certain undocumented students may be eligible to attend community colleges and the California State University and pay the resident student fees. The legislation requires that the person attended a high school in California for at least three years, graduated from such a school, is not in the United States as a nonimmigrant student and is able to show that she is in the process of obtaining legal status. The statute was challenged in an action filed in a California court and was found to be in violation of the equal protection clause of the State's constitution.[45]

---

44. Action No. 588-982-4 (Alameda County).

45. *See Martinez v. Regents of Univ. of Calif.*, 83 Cal. Rptr. 3d 518 (Cal. Ct. App. 2008); *see also American Ass'n. of Women (AAW) v. Board of Trustees of the Cal. St. Univ.*, 38 Cal. Rptr. 2d 15 (1995).

4. The equal protection clause speaks in terms of "persons." The Fifth Amendment's due process clause also refers to "persons" and was the basis of the decision in *Bolling v. Sharpe*,[46] in which the Court held that African-American students in the District of Columbia could not be denied equal educational opportunity. How, then, can "persons" be denied other "rights" such as the right to entitlements or other benefits?[47]

5. In *Shapiro v. Thompson*,[48] the Court stated that "Congress may not authorize the States to violate the Equal Protection Clause." There, the Court invalidated the laws of two states and the District of Columbia that denied welfare benefits to residents who had not resided in the jurisdiction for at least a year, because the laws *impinged* on the fundamental right of travel. There, the Court applied the strict scrutiny tier of review and found that the interests asserted by the states did not constitute a compelling governmental interest sufficient to support the one-year waiting period that the statutes required. Contrary to *Shapiro v. Thompson*, did the Court in *Plyler* indicate that Congress may, in certain circumstances, authorize states to violate the equal protection clause by sanctioning statutes such as the subject statute in *Plyler?* Or can one reconcile the two decisions?

6. What might have been the result if the federal government had prohibited the use of federal funds for education of undocumented children?

7. The Court in *Plyler* places some reliance on the assertion that the undocumented should not be treated as a "suspect class," because "entry into the class is itself a crime."[49] Is such reliance justified if the misdemeanor of "entry without inspection"[50] is not a continuing offense?[51]

C. Access to Public Benefits

As will be discussed in subsequent chapters, most persons who are not citizens coming to the United States must establish that they are able to support themselves without relying on public assistance.[52] Those who manage to gain admission may be

---

For an excellent discussion of the cases on this issue, *see* Michael A. Olivas, *Storytelling Out of School: Undocumented College Residency, Race and Reaction*, 22 Hastings Const. L.Q. 1019 (1995).

46. 347 U.S. 497 (1954).

47. *See e.g., Mathews v. Diaz,* 426 U.S. 67 (1976).

48. 394 U.S. 614, 618 (1969).

49. 457 U.S. 202, 219.

50. 8 U.S.C. § 1325.

51. *See U.S. v. Rincon-Jimenez,* 595 F.2d 1192 (9th Cir. 1979) (holding that violation of 8 U.S.C. § 1325 is completed at the time of entry, and subsequent to such time, the appropriate sanction is removal which is a civil proceeding).

52. 8 U.S.C. § 1182(a)(4)(A), Sec. 212(a)(4)(A), provides that certain persons are inadmissible unless they are able to establish that they are "not likely at any time to become public charges." 8 U.S.C. § 1227(a)(5), Sec. 237(a)(5), further provides a grounds for removal for a person who within five years after admission "has become a public charge from causes not affirmatively shown to have arisen since entry."

"removed" from the country if "within five years after entry [they] become a public charge from causes not affirmatively shown to have arisen after entry."[53]

Beyond the implications regarding immigration status, however, the law of public benefits as applied to aliens is fraught with nuances. The threshold question of eligibility for benefits is often dependent on the immigration status of the applicant. Although such eligibility requirements are usually determined by immigration status as defined by the Immigration and Nationality Act, in some cases, courts have carved out their own eligibility classifications.[54]

The extent to which public entitlements may be limited on the basis of immigration status is largely a question of whether the benefit at issue was enacted by the federal or state government. In 1996, Congress enacted sweeping changes to public entitlement programs for citizens as well as permanent residents. Some of the more far-reaching changes which would have precluded permanent residents from accessing certain programs were revoked in 1997. Perhaps what is most important about the rights of immigrants to access public benefits is to understand how these issues should be analyzed.

As demonstrated in the case of *Graham v. Richardson*, if a state bases eligibility requirements for public entitlements on citizenship status, such legislation is subject to challenge as a denial of equal protection under the Fourteenth Amendment. Congress, on the other hand, may draw distinctions based on alienage when establishing eligibility requirements for federal benefit programs. As the Supreme Court's decision in *Mathews v. Diaz* illustrates, equal protection takes on quite a different meaning within the terms of the Fifth Amendment's due process clause when the federal sovereign acts.

John O. Graham, Commissioner, Department of Public Welfare, State of Arizona v. Carmen Richardson

403 U.S. 365 (1971)

Mr. Justice Blackmun delivered the opinion of the Court.

* * *

... The issue here is whether the Equal Protection Clause of the Fourteenth Amendment prevents a State from conditioning welfare benefits either (a) upon the beneficiary's possession of United States citizenship, or (b) if the beneficiary is an alien, upon his having resided in this country for a specified number of years....

No. 609. This case, from Arizona, concerns the State's participation in federal categorical assistance programs. These programs originate with the Social Security Act

53. 8 U.S.C. § 1227(a)(5), Sec. 237(a)(5).

54. For example, prior to the 1996 immigration amendments, a determination of whether an applicant was deemed to be in the country "permanently residing under color of law" (PRUCOL) was the governing criterion in many statutory entitlements programs. *See Holley v. Lavine*, 553 F.2d 845 (2d Cir. 1977), *cert. denied*, 435 U.S. 947 (1978). Janet Calvo, *Alien Status Restrictions on Eligibility for Federally Funded Assistance Programs*, 16 N.Y.U. Rev. L. & Soc. Change 395 (1988).

of 1935, 49 Stat. 620, as amended, 42 U.S.C., c. 7. They are supported in part by federal grants-in-aid and are administered by the States under federal guidelines. Arizona Rev. Stat. Ann., Tit. 46, Art. 2, as amended, provides for assistance to persons permanently and totally disabled (APTD). See 42 U.S.C. §§ 1351–1355. Arizona Rev. Stat. Ann. § 46-233 (Supp. 1970–1971), as amended in 1962, reads:

> A. No person shall be entitled to general assistance who does not meet and maintain the following requirements:
>
> 1. Is a citizen of the United States, or has resided in the United States a total of fifteen years....

A like eligibility provision conditioned upon citizenship or durational residence appears in § 46-252(2), providing old-age assistance, and in § 46-272(4), providing assistance to the needy blind. See 42 U.S.C. §§ 1201–1206, 1381–1385.

* * *

The three-judge court upheld Mrs. Richardson's motion for summary judgment on equal protection grounds. *Richardson v. Graham*, 313 F.Supp. 34 (Ariz. 1970). It did so in reliance on this Court's opinions in *Takahashi v. Fish & Game Comm'n*, 334 U.S. 410 (1948), and *Shapiro v. Thompson*, 394 U.S. 618 (1969)....

No. 727. This case, from Pennsylvania, concerns that portion of a general assistance program that is not federally supported. The relevant statute is § 432(2) of the Pennsylvania Public Welfare Code, Pa. Stat. Ann., Tit. 62, § 432(2) (1968) originally enacted in 1939. It provides that those eligible for assistance shall be (1) needy persons who qualify under the federally supported categorical assistance programs and (2) those other needy persons who are citizens of the United States. Assistance to the latter group is funded wholly by the Commonwealth.

* * *

... The Fourteenth Amendment provides, "[N]or shall any State deprive any person of life, liberty, or property, without due process of law; nor deny to any person within its jurisdiction the equal protection of the laws." It has long been settled, and it is not disputed here, that the term "person" in this context encompasses lawfully admitted resident aliens as well as citizens of the United States and entitles both citizens and aliens to the equal protection of the laws of the State in which they reside. *Yick Wo v. Hopkins*, 118 U.S. 356, 369 (1886). Nor is it disputed that the Arizona and Pennsylvania statutes in question create two classes of needy persons, indistinguishable except with respect to whether they are or are not citizens of this country. Otherwise qualified United States citizens living in Arizona are entitled to federally funded categorical assistance benefits without regard to length of national residency, but aliens must have lived in this country for 15 years in order to qualify for aid. United States citizens living in Pennsylvania, unable to meet the requirements for federally funded benefits, may be eligible for state-supported general assistance, but resident aliens as a class are precluded from that assistance. Under traditional equal protection principles, a State retains broad discretion to classify as long as its classification has a reasonable basis.... This is so in "the area of economics and social welfare." *Dandridge v. Williams*, 397 U.S. 471, 485 (1970). But the Court's decisions have established that classifications based on alienage, like those based on nationality or race, are inherently suspect and subject to close judicial scrutiny. Aliens as a class are a prime example of a "discrete and insular" minority (see *United States v. Carolene Products Co.*, 304 U.S. 144, 152–153, n.4 (1938)) for whom such heightened judicial solicitude is appropriate. Accordingly, it was said in *Takahashi*, 334 U.S., at 420, that "the power of a state to apply its laws exclusively to its alien inhabitants as a class is confined within narrow limits."

Arizona and Pennsylvania seek to justify their restrictions on the eligibility of aliens for public assistance solely on the basis of a State's "special public interest" in favoring its own citizens over aliens in the distribution of limited resources such as welfare benefits. It Is true that this Court on occasion has upheld state statutes that treat citizens and noncitizens differently, the ground for distinction having been that such laws were necessary to protect special interests of the State or its citizens. Thus, in *Truax v. Raich*, 239 U.S. 33 (1915), the Court, in striking down an Arizona statute restricting the employment of aliens, emphasized that "[t]he discrimination defined by the act does not pertain to the regulation or distribution of the public domain, or of the common property or resources of the people of the state, the enjoyment of which may be limited to its citizens as against both aliens and the citizens of other states." 239 U.S., at 39–40....

Takahashi v. Fish & Game Comm'n, 334 U.S. 410 (1948), however, cast doubt on the continuing validity of the special public-interest doctrine in all contexts. There the Court held that California's purported ownership of fish in the ocean off its shores was not such a special public interest as would justify prohibiting aliens from making a living by fishing in those waters while permitting all others to do so. It was said:

> "The Fourteenth Amendment and the laws adopted under its authority thus embody a general policy that all persons lawfully in this country shall abide 'in any state' on an equality of legal privileges with all citizens under nondiscriminatory laws." 334 U.S., at 420.

Whatever may be the contemporary vitality of the special public-interest doctrine in other contexts after *Takahashi*, we conclude that a State's desire to preserve limited welfare benefits for its own citizens is inadequate to justify Pennsylvania's making noncitizens ineligible for public assistance, and Arizona's restricting benefits to citizens and longtime resident aliens....

[A]s the Court recognized in *Shapiro*:

> "[A] State has a valid interest in preserving the fiscal integrity of its programs. It may legitimately attempt to limit its expenditures, whether for public assistance, public education, or any other program. But a State may not accomplish such a purpose by invidious distinctions between classes of its citizens.... The saving of welfare costs cannot justify an otherwise invidious classification." 394 U.S., at 633.

Since an alien as well as a citizen is a "person" for equal protection purposes, a concern for fiscal integrity is no more compelling a justification for the questioned classification in these cases than it was in *Shapiro*.

... It is enough to say that the classification involved in *Shapiro* was subjected to strict scrutiny under the compelling state interest test, not because it was based on any suspect criterion such as race, nationality, or alienage, but because it impinged upon the fundamental right of interstate movement.... The classifications involved in the instant cases, on the other hand, are inherently suspect and are therefore subject to strict judicial scrutiny whether or not a fundamental right is impaired....

We agree with the three-judge court in the Pennsylvania case that the "justification of limiting expenses is particularly inappropriate and unreasonable when the discriminated class consists of aliens. Aliens like citizens pay taxes and may be called into the armed forces. Unlike the short-term residents in *Shapiro,* aliens may live within a state for many years, work in the state and contribute to the economic growth of the state." 321 F.Supp. at 253. See also *Purdy & Fitzpatrick v. California*, 71 Cal. 2d 566, 581–582, 79 Cal. Rptr. 77, 456 P.2d 645, 656 (1969). There can be no "special public interest" in tax revenues to which aliens have contributed on an equal basis with the residents of the State.

Accordingly, we hold that a state statute that denies welfare benefits to resident aliens and one that denies them to aliens who have not resided in the United States for a specified number of years violate the Equal Protection Clause.

An additional reason why the state statutes at issue in these cases do not withstand constitutional scrutiny emerges from the area of federal-state relations. The National Government has "broad constitutional powers in determining what aliens shall be admitted to the United States, the period they may remain, regulation of their conduct before naturalization, and the terms and conditions of their naturalization." *Takahashi v. Fish & Game Comm'n*, 334 U.S., at 419; *Hines v. Davidowitz*, 312 U.S. 52, 66 (1941). Pursuant to that power, Congress has provided, as part of a comprehensive plan for the regulation of immigration and naturalization, that "[a]liens who are paupers, professional beggars, or vagrants" or aliens who "are likely at any time to become public charges" shall be excluded from admission into the United States, 8 U.S.C. §§ 1182(a)(8) and 1182(a)(15), and that any alien lawfully admitted shall be deported who "has within five years after entry become a public charge from causes not affirmatively shown to have arisen after entry...." 8 U.S.C. § 1251(a)(8). Admission of aliens likely to become public charges may be conditioned upon the posting of a bond or cash deposit. 8 U.S.C. § 1183. But Congress has not seen fit to impose any burden or restriction on aliens who become indigent after their entry into the United States. Rather, it has broadly declared: "All persons within the jurisdiction of the United States shall have the same right in every State and Territory.... to the full and equal benefit of all laws and proceedings for the security of persons and property as is enjoyed by white citizens...." 42 U.S.C. § 1981. The protection of this statute has been held to extend to aliens as well as to citizens. *Takahashi*, 334 U.S., at 419 n.7....

State laws that restrict the eligibility of aliens for welfare benefits merely because of their alienage conflict with these overriding national policies in an area constitutionally entrusted to the Federal Government. In *Hines v. Davidowitz*, 312 U.S., at 66–67, where this Court struck down a Pennsylvania alien registration statute (enacted in 1939, as was the statute under challenge in No. 727) on grounds of federal preemption, it was observed that "where the federal government, in the exercise of its superior authority in this field, has enacted a complete scheme of regulation ... states cannot, inconsistently with the purpose of Congress, conflict or interfere with, curtail or complement, the federal law, or enforce additional or auxiliary regulations." And in *Takahashi* it was said that the States

> "can neither add to nor take from the conditions lawfully imposed by Congress upon admission, naturalization and residence of aliens in the United States or the several states. State laws which impose discriminatory burdens upon the entrance or residence of aliens lawfully within the United States conflict with this constitutionally derived federal power to regulate immigration, and have accordingly been held invalid." 334 U.S., at 419.

Congress has broadly declared as federal policy that lawfully admitted resident aliens who become public charges for causes arising after their entry are not subject to deportation, and that as long as they are here they are entitled to the full and equal benefit of all state laws for the security of persons and property. The state statutes at issue in the instant cases impose auxiliary burdens upon the entrance or residence of aliens who suffer the distress, after entry, of economic dependency on public assistance....

In *Truax* the Court considered the "reasonableness" of a state restriction on the employment of aliens in terms of its effect on the right of a lawfully admitted alien to live where he chooses:

> ... The assertion of an authority to deny to aliens the opportunity of earning a livelihood when lawfully admitted to the state would be tantamount to the assertion of the right to deny them entrance and abode, for in ordinary cases they cannot live where they cannot work....

239 U.S., at 42. The same is true here, for in the ordinary case an alien, becoming indigent and unable to work, will be unable to live where, because of discriminatory denial of public assistance, he cannot "secure the necessities of life, including food, clothing and shelter." State alien residency requirements that either deny welfare benefits to noncitizens or condition them on longtime residency, equate with the assertion of a right, inconsistent with federal policy, to deny entrance and abode. Since such laws encroach upon exclusive federal power, they are constitutionally impermissible.

Arizona suggests, finally, that its 15-year durational residency requirement for aliens is actually authorized by federal law. Reliance is placed on § 1402(b) of the Social Security Act of 1935, added by the Act of Aug. 28, 1950, § 351, 64 Stat. 556, as amended, 42 U.S.C. § 1352(b). That section provides:

> The Secretary shall approve any plan which fulfills the conditions specified in subsection (a) of this section, except that he shall not approve any plan

which imposes, as a condition of eligibility for aid to the permanently and totally disabled under the plan—

(2) Any citizenship requirement which excludes any citizen of the United States.[1]

* * *

It is apparent from this that Congress' principal concern in 1935 was to prevent the States from distinguishing between native-born American citizens and naturalized citizens in the distribution of welfare benefits. It may be assumed that Congress was motivated by a similar concern in 1950 when it enacted § 1402(b). As for the indication in the 1935 Committee Reports that the States, in their discretion, could withhold benefits from noncitizens, certain members of Congress simply may have been expressing their understanding of the law only insofar as it had then developed, that is, before Takahashi was decided. But if § 1402(b), as well as the identical provisions for old-age assistance and aid to the blind, were to be read so as to authorize discriminatory treatment of aliens at the option of the States, Takahashi demonstrates that serious constitutional questions are presented. Although the Federal Government admittedly has broad constitutional power to determine what aliens shall be admitted to the United States, the period they may remain, and the terms and conditions of their naturalization, Congress does not have the power to authorize the individual States to violate the Equal Protection Clause. Shapiro v. Thompson, 394 U.S., at 641. Under Art. I, § 8, cl. 4, of the Constitution, Congress' power is to "establish an uniform Rule of Naturalization." A congressional enactment construed so as to permit state legislatures to adopt divergent laws on the subject of citizenship requirements for federally supported welfare programs would appear to contravene this explicit constitutional requirement of uniformity....

The judgments appealed from are affirmed.

Mr. Justice HARLAN joins in Parts III and IV of the Court's opinion, and in the judgment of the Court.

---

1. Pursuant to his rulemaking power under the Social Security Act, 42 U.S.C. § 1302, the Secretary of Health, Education, and Welfare adopted the following regulations, upon which Arizona also relies:

> *3720. Requirements for State Plans*
>
> A State plan under titles I, X, XIV, and XVI may not impose, as a condition of eligibility, any citizenship requirement which excludes any citizen of the United States."
>
> 3730. *Interpretation of Requirement*
>
> State plans need not contain a citizenship requirement. The purpose of IV-3720 is to ensure that where such a requirement is imposed, an otherwise eligible citizen of the United States, regardless of how (by birth or naturalization) or when citizenship was obtained, shall not be disqualified from receiving aid or assistance under titles I, X, XIV and XVI. Where there is an eligibility requirement applicable to noncitizens, State plans may, as an alternative to excluding all noncitizens, provide for qualifying noncitizens, otherwise eligible, who have resided in the United States for a specific number of years.

HEW Handbook of Public Assistance Administration, pt. IV.

F. David Mathews, Secretary of the Department of Health, Education, and Welfare v. Santiago Diaz et al.

426 U.S. 67 (1976)

Mr. Justice Stevens delivered the opinion of the Court.

The question presented by the Secretary's appeal is whether Congress may condition an alien's eligibility for participation in a federal medical insurance program on continuous residence in the United States for a five-year period and admission for permanent residence. The District Court held that the first condition was unconstitutional and that it could not be severed from the second. Since we conclude that both conditions are constitutional, we reverse.

Each of the appellees is a resident alien who was lawfully admitted to the United States less than five years ago. Appellees Diaz and Clara are Cuban refugees who remain in this country at the discretion of the Attorney General; appellee Espinosa has been admitted for permanent residence. All three are over 65 years old and have been denied enrollment in the Medicare Part B supplemental medical insurance program established by § 1831 *et seq.* of the Social Security Act of 1935, 49 Stat. 620, as added, 79 Stat. 301, and as amended, 42 U.S.C. 1395j *et seq.* (1970 ed. and Supp. IV).[1] They brought this action to challenge the statutory basis for that denial. Specifically, they attack 42 U.S.C. § 1395o (2) (1970 ed., Supp. IV), which grants eligibility to resident citizens who are 65 or older but denies eligibility to comparable aliens unless they have been admitted for permanent residence and also have resided in the United States for at least five years.[2] Appellees Diaz and Clara meet neither requirement; appellee Espinosa meets only the first.

* * *

The District Court held that the five-year residence requirement violated the Due Process Clause of the Fifth Amendment[3] and that since it could not be severed from the requirement of admission for permanent residence, the alien-eligibility provisions

---

1. The Medicare Part B medical insurance program for the aged covers a part of the cost of certain physicians' services, home health care, outpatient physical therapy, and other medical and health care. 42 U.S.C. § 1395k (1970 ed. and Supp. IV). The program supplements the Medicare Part A hospital insurance plan, § 1811 *et seq.* of the Social Security Act of 1935, 49 Stat. 620, as added, 79 Stat. 291, and as amended, 42 U.S.C. § 1395c *et seq.*(1970 ed. and Supp. IV), and it is financed in equal parts by the United States and by monthly premiums paid by individuals aged 65 or older who choose to enroll. 42 U.S.C. § 1395r(b) (1970 ed., Supp. IV).

2. Title 42 U.S.C. § 1395o (1970 ed. and Supp. IV) provides:

> "Every individual who—(1) is entitled to hospital insurance benefits under Part A, or (2) has attained age 65 and is a resident of the United States, and is either (A) a citizen or (B) an alien lawfully admitted for permanent residence who has resided in the United States continuously during the 5 years immediately preceding the month in which he applies for enrollment under this part, is eligible to enroll in the insurance program established by this part.:

This case does not raise any issues involving subsection (1).

3. "[N]or shall any person ... be deprived of life, liberty, or property, without due process of the law...." U.S. Const., Amendment. 5.

of § 1395o (2)(B) were entirely unenforceable. *Diaz v. Weinberger*, 361 F.Supp. 1 (1973). The District Court reasoned that "even though fourteenth amendment notions of equal protection are not entirely congruent with fifth amendment concepts of due process," *id.*, at 9, the danger of unjustifiable discrimination against aliens in the enactment of welfare programs is so great, in view of their complete lack of representation in the political process, that this federal statute should be tested under the same pledge of equal protection as a state statute. So tested, the court concluded that the statute was invalid because it was not both rationally based and free from invidious discrimination. It rejected the desire to preserve the fiscal integrity of the program, or to treat some aliens as less deserving than others, as adequate justification for the statute. Accordingly, the court enjoined the Secretary from refusing to enroll members of the class and subclass represented by appellees.

* * *

There are literally millions of aliens within the jurisdiction of the United States. The Fifth Amendment, as well as the Fourteenth Amendment, protects every one of these persons from deprivation of life, liberty, or property without due process of law. Even one whose presence in this country is unlawful, involuntary, or transitory is entitled to that constitutional protection.

The fact that all persons, aliens and citizens alike, are protected by the Due Process Clause does not lead to the further conclusion that all aliens are entitled to enjoy all the advantages of citizenship or, indeed, to the conclusion that all aliens must be placed in a single homogeneous legal classification. For a host of constitutional and statutory provisions rest on the premise that a legitimate distinction between citizens and aliens may justify attributes and benefits for one class not accorded to the other;[4] and the class of aliens is itself a heterogeneous multitude of persons with a wide-ranging variety of ties to this country.

In the exercise of its broad power over naturalization and immigration, Congress regularly makes rules that would be unacceptable if applied to citizens. The exclusion of aliens and the reservation of the power to deport have no permissible counterpart in the Federal Government's power to regulate the conduct of its own citizenry. The fact that an Act of Congress treats aliens differently from citizens does not in itself imply that such disparate treatment is "invidious."

In particular, the fact that Congress has provided some welfare benefits for citizens does not require it to provide like benefits for *all aliens*. Neither the overnight visitor, the unfriendly agent of a hostile foreign power, the resident diplomat, nor the illegal entrant, can advance even a colorable constitutional claim to a share in the bounty that a conscientious sovereign makes available to its own citizens and *some* of its guests. The decision to share that bounty with our guests may take into account the

---

4. The Constitution protects the privileges and immunities only of citizens, Amdt. 14, § 1; *see* Art. IV, § 2, cl. 1, and the right to vote only of citizens. Amdts. 15, 19, 24, 26. It requires that Representatives have been citizens for seven years, Art. I, § 2, cl. 2, and Senators citizens for nine, Art. I, § 3, cl. 3, and that the President be a "natural born Citizen." Art. II, § 1, cl. 5.

character of the relationship between the alien and this country: Congress may decide that as the alien's tie grows stronger, so does the strength of his claim to an equal share of that munificence.

The real question presented by this case is not whether discrimination between citizens and aliens is permissible; rather, it is whether the statutory discrimination within the class of aliens—allowing benefits to some aliens but not to others—is permissible. We turn to that question.

For reasons long recognized as valid, the responsibility for regulating the relationship between the United States and our alien visitors has been committed to the political branches of the Federal Government.[5] Since decisions in these matters may implicate our relations with foreign powers, and since a wide variety of classifications must be defined in the light of changing political and economic circumstances, such decisions are frequently of a character more appropriate to either the Legislature or the Executive than to the Judiciary. This very case illustrates the need for flexibility in policy choices rather than the rigidity often characteristic of constitutional adjudication. Appellees Diaz and Clara are but two of over 440,000 Cuban refugees who arrived in the United States between 1961 and 1972. And the Cuban parolees are but one of several categories of aliens who have been admitted in order to make a humane response to a natural catastrophe or an international political situation. Any rule of constitutional law that would inhibit the flexibility of the political branches of government to respond to changing world conditions should be adopted only with the greatest caution. The reasons that preclude judicial review of political questions also dictate a narrow standard of review of decisions made by the Congress or the President in the area of immigration and naturalization....

We may assume that the five-year line drawn by Congress is longer than necessary to protect the fiscal integrity of the program. We may also assume that unnecessary hardship is incurred by persons just short of qualifying. But it remains true that some line is essential, that any line must produce some harsh and apparently arbitrary consequences, and, of greatest importance, that those who qualify under the test Congress has chosen may reasonably be presumed to have a greater affinity with the United States than those who do not. In short, citizens and those who are most like citizens qualify. Those who are less like citizens do not.

The task of classifying persons for medical benefits, like the task of drawing lines for federal tax purposes, inevitably requires that some persons who have an almost equally strong claim to favored treatment be placed on different sides of the line; the differences between the eligible and the ineligible are differences in degree rather than

5. "[A]ny policy toward aliens is vitally and intricately interwoven with contemporaneous policies in regard to the conduct of foreign relations, the war power, and the maintenance of a republican form of government. Such matters are so exclusively entrusted to the political branches of government as to be largely immune from judicial inquiry or interference." *Harisiades v. Shaughnessy, supra*, 342 U.S., at 588–589.

differences in the character of their respective claims. When this kind of policy choice must be made, we are especially reluctant to question the exercise of congressional judgment. In this case, since appellees have not identified a principled basis for prescribing a different standard than the one selected by Congress, they have, in effect, merely invited us to substitute our judgment for that of Congress in deciding which aliens shall be eligible to participate in the supplementary insurance program on the same conditions as citizens. We decline the invitation.

The cases on which appellees rely are consistent with our conclusion that this statutory classification does not deprive them of liberty or property without due process of law.

Graham v. Richardson, 403 U.S. 365, provides the strongest support for appellees' position. That case holds that state statutes that deny welfare benefits to resident aliens, or to aliens not meeting a requirement of durational residence within the United States, violate the Equal Protection Clause of the Fourteenth Amendment and encroach upon the exclusive federal power over the entrance and residence of aliens. Of course, the latter ground of decision actually supports our holding today that it is the business of the political branches of the Federal Government, rather than that of either the States or the Federal judiciary, to regulate the conditions of entry and residence of aliens. The equal protection analysis also involves significantly different considerations because it concerns the relationship between aliens and the States rather than between aliens and the Federal Government.

Insofar as state welfare policy is concerned,[6] there is little, if any, basis for treating persons who are citizens of another State differently from persons who are citizens of another country. Both groups are noncitizens as far as the State's interests in administering its welfare programs are concerned. Thus, a division by a State of the category of persons who are not citizens of that State into subcategories of United States citizens and aliens has no apparent justification, whereas, a comparable classification by the Federal Government is a routine and normally legitimate part of its business. Furthermore, whereas the Constitution inhibits every State's power to restrict travel across its own borders, Congress is explicitly empowered to exercise that type of control over travel across the borders of the United States.

The distinction between the constitutional limits on state power and the constitutional grant of power to the Federal Government also explains why appellees' reliance on *Memorial Hospital v. Maricopa County*, 415 U.S. 250, is misplaced. That case involved Arizona's requirement of durational residence within a county in order to receive nonemergency medical care at the county's expense. No question of alienage was involved. Since the sole basis for the classification between residents impinged

6. We have left open the question whether a State may prohibit aliens from holding elective or important nonelective positions or whether a State may, in some circumstances, consider the alien status of an applicant or employee in making an individualized employment decision.

on the constitutionally guaranteed right to travel within the United States, the holding in *Shapiro v. Thompson*, 394 U.S. 618, required that it be justified by a compelling state interest.[7] Finding no such justification, we held that the requirement violated the Equal Protection Clause. This case, however, involves no state impairment of the right to travel nor indeed any impairment whatever of the right to travel within the United States; the predicate for the equal protection analysis in those cases is simply not present. Contrary to appellees' characterization, it is not "political hypocrisy" to recognize that the Fourteenth Amendment's limits on state powers are substantially different from the constitutional provisions applicable to the federal power over immigration and naturalization.

Finally, we reject the suggestion that *U.S. Dept. of Agriculture v. Moreno*, 413 U.S. 528, lends relevant support to appellees' claim. No question involving alienage was presented in that case. Rather, we found that the denial of food stamps to households containing unrelated members was not only unsupported by any rational basis but actually was intended to discriminate against certain politically unpopular groups. This case involves no impairment of the freedom of association of either citizens or aliens.

We hold that § 1395o (2)(B) has not deprived appellees of liberty or property without due process of law.

The judgment of the District Court is Reversed.

Notes

1. In light of *Mathews*, is there any doubt whether Congress has power to disqualify lawful temporary and permanent residents from public benefits as specified in subsection A?

2. As to subsection B, can a Fifth Amendment challenge be made regarding the provision itself? Does this section of the law actually require any action?

3. Is legislation enacted by a state on the authority of subsection B constitutional? Or is Congress here attempting "to authorize the individual States to violate the Equal Protection Clause"?[55]

---

7. In *Shapiro v. Thompson*, we held that state-imposed requirements of durational residence within the State for receipt of welfare benefits denied equal protection because such requirements unconstitutionally burdened the right to travel interstate. Since the requirements applied to aliens and citizens alike, we did not decide whether the right to travel interstate was conferred only upon citizens. However, our holding was predicated expressly on the requirement "that all citizens be free to travel throughout the length and breadth of our land uninhibited by statutes, rules, or regulations which unreasonably burden or restrict this movement." 394 U.S., at 629.

55. *Graham v. Richardson*, 403 U.S. 365, 382 (1971); *Shapiro v. Thompson*, 394 U.S. 618, 641 (1969).

4. Does Congress have the authority to constrict the extent of Fourteenth Amendment equal protection under its Section 5 "power to enforce, by appropriate legislation"?[56] This has been referred to as the "one-way ratchet theory."[57]

5. Is it necessary that a state's disqualification of foreigners from eligibility for public benefits be consistent with federal law or policy? Does it matter whether or not the federal law is preemptive?[58]

6. The Court has carved out a substantial exception to the general rule of *Graham* that alienage is a suspect classification. This "public" or "political" function exception has been applied for the most part to state restrictions based on alienage regarding public employment.[59]

7. As the Court notes in *Mathews,* many provisions of the Constitution refer to "citizens."[60] Yet, the Fifth Amendment refers to "persons." Can the result in *Mathews* be reconciled with the plain language of the due process clause of the Fifth Amendment, which has been interpreted to include an equal protection component?[61]

8. Does it make any sense to consider non-U.S. citizens "persons" for purposes of Fourteenth Amendment analysis but to change the interpretation of the same term for purposes of Fifth Amendment equal protection analysis when the challenged action in both instances is identical but for the "perpetrator" (state in one, federal in the other)?

1. Federal Restrictions on Non-Citizens Access to Public Benefits

In July 1996, Congress enacted the Personal Responsibility and Work Opportunity Reconciliation Act[62] (PRA) followed by IIRAIRA, the two of which together made

---

56. *See Mississippi University for Women v. Hogan,* 458 U.S. 718, 732–33 (1982) (Section "5 grants Congress no power to restrict, abrogate, or dilute these guarantees," *quoting Katzenbach v. Morgan,* 384 U.S. 641, 651 n.10 (1966)).

57. Lawrence Tribe, American Constitutional Law 344–45 (2d ed. 1988). The ratchet theory refers to the principle articulated in Katzenbach v. Morgan, 384 U.S. 641, 651, n. 10 (1966) that Congress may expand on rights recognized by the Supreme Court as required under the Constitution but may not "ratchet" them down. *See also* Roger C. Hartley, *Congressional Devolution of Immigration Policymaking: a Separation of Powers Critique,* 2 Duke J. Const'l L. & Pub. Poly' 93, 110 (2007).

58. *See De Canas v. Bica,* 424 U.S. 351 (1976) (state's restriction on employment of those not lawful residents of the United States not preempted by federal law or policy).

59. *See,* e.g., *Foley v. Connelie,* 435 U.S. 291 (1978) (state troopers); *Ambach v. Norwick,* 441 U.S. 68 (1979) (public school teachers); *Cabell v. Chavez-Salido,* 454 U.S. 432 (1982) (deputy probation officers); *but see Bernal v. Fainter,* 467 U.S. 216 (1984) (notaries public).

60. 426 U.S. at 78 n.12.

61. *Bolling v. Sharpe,* 347 U.S. 497 (1954).

62. Pub. L. No. 104-193, 110 Stat. 2105 (1996).

significant changes to the federal welfare statutes as well as the consequences to non-citizens for accessing welfare programs. The welfare law changes were significant both to lawful permanent residents and U.S. citizens. In the two years following the enactment of the PRA, some of its harshest restrictions were ameliorated by Congress.[63] The eligibility requirements are very complicated and vary from program to program, but the general limits and requirements for receiving benefits are the following:

> All persons, irrespective of their citizenship or alienage, are subject to a five-year lifetime cap of benefits.
>
> Generally, non-citizens are not eligible to receive benefits under any "means-tested" assistance programs unless they fall within a specific group of "qualified aliens." Some of these "qualified aliens" may be eligible for a limited set of benefits if they were already receiving benefits when the statutes were enacted (August 22, 1996). Some persons who were lawfully residing in the United States on August 22, 1996, may be eligible for disability benefits if they later become disabled.
>
> The basic statutory requirement for a person to be a "qualified alien" for receiving benefits (other than emergency medical assistance) is that the person come within one of the following categories:[64] (1) lawful permanent residence; (2) refugee; (3) asylum; (4) withholding of removal; (5) present in the United States for at least one year; (6) Cuban/Haitian entrants; or (7) certain battered spouses or children.
>
> Persons who meet the "qualified alien" definition but entered the United States after the statute was enacted are barred from receiving any means-tested benefits or Supplemental Security Income (SSI) benefits until they have been in the United States for five years. After the five-year period, the income of the person's sponsor as indicated on the affidavit of support is to be treated as income of the person applying for the assistance benefit to determine her eligibility.[65]
>
> States are authorized to deny "qualified aliens" from state-funded public benefit programs.[66]

---

63. Non-citizen Benefit Clarification and Other Technical Amendments Act of 1998, Pub. L. No. 105-306 (1998); Balanced Budget Act of 1997, Pub. L. No. 105-33 (1977).

64. These various immigration statuses were defined under the definitional headings in Chapter 1 and are further discussed in these materials.

65. This "deeming" of income will render most applicants ineligible for the public benefit because the statute requires that signers of the affidavit of support be able to show that they have the ability to ,maintain the immigrant at a level not less than 125% of the poverty level. *See* 8 U.S.C. § 1183a(a)(1), Sec. 213A(a)(1). The affidavit of support is enforceable until the person becomes a citizen of the United States.

66. *See* Sec. 412(a) of the Personal Responsibility and Work Opportunity Reconciliation Act, Pub. L. No. 104-193, 110 Stat. 2105 (1996).

D. The Interplay between State and Federal Government in Enacting Laws Affecting Non-Citizens

Over the years, there have been repeated efforts by states to impose restrictions on immigration. This has been fueled, in part, by economic downturns and shifts in the racial mix of the overall population. One example of these tensions occurred in 1995 in the State of California when voters enacted a ballot initiative known as "Proposition 187." Proposition 187 had as its primary purpose the restriction of access by undocumented persons to health, education and other public benefits, including the reporting of undocumented persons to federal immigration officials. Immediately upon passage, the initiative was challenged in federal court and much of its provisions were enjoined in *League of United Latin American Citizens (LULAC) v. Wilson*.[67] The segments which were not enjoined were those requiring public post-secondary educational institutions to verify the immigration status and to limit access to unauthorized non-citizens in the U.S.[68]

Following the District Court's decision in *LULAC*, Congress enacted the Personal Responsibility and Work Opportunity Reconciliation Act of 1996 (PRA),[69] and the defendants in *LULAC* sought reconsideration. Judge Pfaelzer, in rejecting their claims, held that PRA preempted portions of Proposition 187 which called for the denial of social services and post-secondary education. The court held further that the portion of the initiative which denied public elementary and secondary education to certain undocumented persons was invalid, as were those portions denying public and health benefits to "aliens in the United States in violation of federal law." The only part of the initiative which withstood challenge by the plaintiffs was the section which penalized persons for using false documents to conceal their true citizenship or resident alien status.

One of the focal points of the immigration debate of the last several years has been the enactment of state and local laws against foreigners who are present in the United States without legal permission. According to one scholar, in 2006, more than seventy-eight bills were approved in thirty-three different states.[70] The number of introduced legislation during this same period was more than 570.

---

67. 908 F. Supp. 755, 763 (C.D. Cal. 1995) (partial grant of summary judgment in favor of plaintiffs), motion for reconsideration granted in 997 F. Supp. 1244 (C.D. Cal. 1997). For a copy of the full text of the ballot initiative see 908 F. Supp at 786.

68. 908 F. Supp. at 774. For an interesting article exploring the issue raised in *LULAC*, see Elizabeth Hull, *The Unkindest Cuts: the 1996 Welfare Reform Acts Impact on Resident Aliens*, 33 Gonz. L. Rev. 471, 500 (1998).

69. Pub. L. No. 104-193, § 1601, 110 Stat. 2105 (1996) At times, this statute may be referred to as "PRA".

70. *See* Raquel Aldana, *On Rights, Federal Ctizenship and the "Alien,"* 46 Wash. L.J. 263, 284 (2007).

While these efforts have been stymied in the federal courts, opponents have been forced to seek injunctive relief in multiple federal courts each time legislation has been introduced.[71]

Some state and local legislation come in the form of tenancy restrictions which prohibit landlords from renting to undocumented immigrants. Others have attempted to place restrictions on employers who hire undocumented workers through the revocation or suspension of the employer's business license. Consider the following case and the notes which follow to better understand the approach to analyzing these questions.

Arizona, et al. v. United States

567 U.S. 387 (2012)

KENNEDY, J., delivered the opinion of the Court, in which ROBERTS, C.J., and GINSBURG, BREYER and SOTOMAYOR joined. SCALIA, J., THOMAS, J., and ALITO, J., filed opinions concurring in part and dissenting in part. KAGAN, J. took no part in the consideration or decision of the case.

To address pressing issues related to the large number of aliens within its borders who do not have a lawful right to be in this country, the State of Arizona in 2010 enacted a statute called the Support Our Law Enforcement and Safe Neighborhoods Act. The law is often referred to as S.B. 1070, the version introduced in the state senate. See also H. 2162 (2010) (amending S. 1070). Its stated purpose is to "discourage and deter the unlawful entry and presence of aliens and economic activity by persons unlawfully present in the United States." Note following Ariz. Rev. Stat. Ann. § 11-1051 (West 2012). The law's provisions establish an official state policy of "attrition through enforcement." *Ibid.* The question before the Court is whether federal law preempts and renders invalid four separate provisions of the state law.

The United States filed this suit against Arizona, seeking to enjoin S.B. 1070 as preempted. Four provisions of the law are at issue here. Two create new state offenses. Section 3 makes failure to comply with federal alien-registration requirements a state misdemeanor. Ariz. Rev. Stat. Ann. § 13-1509 (West Supp.2011). Section 5, in relevant part, makes it a misdemeanor for an unauthorized alien to seek or engage in work in the State; this provision is referred to as § 5(C). See § 13-2928(C). Two other provisions give specific arrest authority and investigative duties with respect to certain

---

71. *Lozano v. City of Hazleton*, 724 F.3d 297 (3d Cir. 2013) (enjoining housing and employment restrictions in Pennsylvania city); *U.S. v. South Carolina*, 720 F.3d 518 (4th Cir. 2013) (enjoining state immigration enactments as preempted); *U.S. v. Alabama*, 691 F.3d 1269, 1282–97 (11th Cir. 2012) (enjoining multiple provisions of Alabama statute). For an excellent article exploring these issues, see Joshua Herndon, *Broken Border: De Canas v. Bica and the Standards that Govern the Validity of State, Measures Designed to Deter Undocumented Immigration*, 12 TEX. HISPANIC J. L. & POL'Y 31 (2006).

aliens to state and local law enforcement officers. Section 6 authorizes officers to arrest without a warrant a person "the officer has probable cause to believe ... has committed any public offense that makes the person removable from the United States." § 13-3883(A)(5). Section 2(B) provides that officers who conduct a stop, detention, or arrest must in some circumstances make efforts to verify the person's immigration status with the Federal Government. See § 11-1051(B) (West 2012).

The United States District Court for the District of Arizona issued a preliminary injunction preventing the four provisions at issue from taking effect. 703 F.Supp.2d 980, 1008 (2010). The Court of Appeals for the Ninth Circuit affirmed. 641 F.3d 339, 366 (2011). It agreed that the United States had established a likelihood of success on its preemption claims. The Court of Appeals was unanimous in its conclusion that §§ 3 and 5(C) were likely preempted. Judge Bea dissented from the decision to uphold the preliminary injunction against §§ 2(B) and 6. This Court granted certiorari to resolve important questions concerning the interaction of state and federal power with respect to the law of immigration and alien status. 565 U.S. ___, 132 S.Ct. 845 (2011).

The Government of the United States has broad, undoubted power over the subject of immigration and the status of aliens. See *Toll v. Moreno,* 458 U.S. 1, 10 (1982); see generally S. Legomsky & C. Rodríguez, Immigration and Refugee Law and Policy 115–132 (5th ed. 2009). This authority rests, in part, on the National Government's constitutional power to "establish an uniform Rule of Naturalization," U.S. Const., Art. I, § 8, cl. 4, and its inherent power as sovereign to control and conduct relations with foreign nations, see *Toll, supra,* at 10 (citing *United States v. Curtiss-Wright Export Corp.,* 299 U.S. 304, 318 (1936)).

The federal power to determine immigration policy is well settled. Immigration policy can affect trade, investment, tourism, and diplomatic relations for the entire Nation, as well as the perceptions and expectations of aliens in this country who seek the full protection of its laws. See, *e.g.,* Brief for Argentina et al. as *Amici Curiae;* see also *Harisiades v. Shaughnessy,* 342 U.S. 580, 588–589 (1952). Perceived mistreatment of aliens in the United States may lead to harmful reciprocal treatment of American citizens abroad. See Brief for Madeleine K. Albright et al. as *Amici Curiae* 24–30.

It is fundamental that foreign countries concerned about the status, safety, and security of their nationals in the United States must be able to confer and communicate on this subject with one national sovereign, not the 50 separate States. See *Chy Lung v. Freeman,* 92 U.S. 275, 279–280 (1876); see also The Federalist No. 3, p. 39 (C. Rossiter ed. 2003) (J. Jay) (observing that federal power would be necessary in part because "bordering States ... under the impulse of sudden irritation, and a quick sense of apparent interest or injury" might take action that would undermine foreign relations). This Court has reaffirmed that "[o]ne of the most important and delicate of all international relationships ... has to do with the protection of the just rights of a country's own nationals when those nationals are in another country." *Hines v. Davidowitz,* 312 U.S. 52, 64 (1941).

Federal governance of immigration and alien status is extensive and complex. Congress has specified categories of aliens who may not be admitted to the United States. See 8 U.S.C. § 1182. Unlawful entry and unlawful reentry into the country are federal offenses. §§ 1325, 1326. Once here, aliens are required to register with the Federal Government and to carry proof of status on their person. See §§ 1301–1306. Failure to do so is a federal misdemeanor. §§ 1304(e), 1306(a). Federal law also authorizes States to deny noncitizens a range of public benefits, § 1622; and it imposes sanctions on employers who hire unauthorized workers, § 1324a.

Congress has specified which aliens may be removed from the United States and the procedures for doing so. Aliens may be removed if they were inadmissible at the time of entry, have been convicted of certain crimes, or meet other criteria set by federal law. See § 1227. Removal is a civil, not criminal, matter. A principal feature of the removal system is the broad discretion exercised by immigration officials. See Brief for Former Commissioners of the United States Immigration and Naturalization Service as *Amici Curiae* 8–13 (hereinafter Brief for Former INS Commissioners). Federal officials, as an initial matter, must decide whether it makes sense to pursue removal at all. If removal proceedings commence, aliens may seek asylum and other discretionary relief allowing them to remain in the country or at least to leave without formal removal. See § 1229a(c)(4); see also, *e.g.*, §§ 1158 (asylum), 1229b (cancellation of removal), 1229c (voluntary departure).

Discretion in the enforcement of immigration law embraces immediate human concerns. Unauthorized workers trying to support their families, for example, likely pose less danger than alien smugglers or aliens who commit a serious crime. The equities of an individual case may turn on many factors, including whether the alien has children born in the United States, long ties to the community, or a record of distinguished military service. Some discretionary decisions involve policy choices that bear on this Nation's international relations. Returning an alien to his own country may be deemed inappropriate even where he has committed a removable offense or fails to meet the criteria for admission. The foreign state may be mired in civil war, complicit in political persecution, or enduring conditions that create a real risk that the alien or his family will be harmed upon return. The dynamic nature of relations with other countries requires the Executive Branch to ensure that enforcement policies are consistent with this Nation's foreign policy with respect to these and other realities.

Agencies in the Department of Homeland Security play a major role in enforcing the country's immigration laws. United States Customs and Border Protection (CBP) is responsible for determining the admissibility of aliens and securing the country's borders. See Dept. of Homeland Security, Office of Immigration Statistics, Immigration Enforcement Actions: 2010, p. 1 (2011). In 2010, CBP's Border Patrol apprehended almost half a million people. *Id.*, at 3. Immigration and Customs Enforcement (ICE), a second agency, "conducts criminal investigations involving the enforcement of immigration-related statutes." *Id.*, at 2. ICE also operates the Law Enforcement Support Center. LESC, as the Center is known, provides immigration status information to federal, state, and local officials around the clock. See App. 91. ICE officers are responsible "for the identification, apprehension, and removal of illegal aliens from the United States." Immigration Enforcement Actions, *supra,* at 2. Hundreds of thousands of aliens are removed by the Federal Government every year. See *id.,* at 4 (reporting there were 387,242 removals, and 476,405 returns without a removal order, in 2010).

The pervasiveness of federal regulation does not diminish the importance of immigration policy to the States. Arizona bears many of the consequences of unlawful immigration. Hundreds of thousands of deportable aliens are apprehended in Arizona each year. Dept. of Homeland Security, Office of Immigration Statistics, 2010 Yearbook of Immigration Statistics 93 (2011) (Table 35). Unauthorized aliens who remain in the State comprise, by one estimate, almost six percent of the population. See Passel & Cohn, Pew Hispanic Center, U.S. Unauthorized Immigration Flows Are Down Sharply Since Mid-Decade 3 (2010). And in the State's most populous county, these aliens are reported to be responsible for a disproportionate share of serious crime. See, *e.g.,* Camarota & Vaughan, Center for Immigration Studies, Immigration and Crime: Assessing a Conflicted Situation 16 (2009) (Table 3) (estimating that unauthorized aliens comprise 8.9% of the population and are responsible for 21.8% of the felonies in Maricopa County, which includes Phoenix).

* * *

Federalism, central to the constitutional design, adopts the principle that both the National and State Governments have elements of sovereignty the other is bound to respect. See *Gregory v. Ashcroft,* 501 U.S. 452, 457 (1991); *U.S. Term Limits, Inc. v. Thornton,* 514 U.S. 779, 838 (1995) (Kennedy, J., concurring). From the existence of two sovereigns follows the possibility that laws can be in conflict or at cross-purposes. The Supremacy Clause provides a clear rule that federal law "shall be the supreme Law of the Land; and the Judges in every State shall be bound thereby, any Thing in the Constitution or Laws of any State to the Contrary notwithstanding." Art. VI, cl. 2. Under this principle, Congress has the power to preempt state law. See *Crosby v. National Foreign Trade Council,* 530 U.S. 363, 372 (2000); *Gibbons v. Ogden,* 9 Wheat. 1, 210–211 (1824). There is no doubt that Congress may withdraw specified powers from the States by enacting a statute containing an express preemption provision. See, *e.g., Chamber of Commerce of United States of America v. Whiting,* 563 U.S. ___, ___, 131 S.Ct. 1968, 1974–1975 (2011).

State law must also give way to federal law in at least two other circumstances. First, the States are precluded from regulating conduct in a field that Congress, acting within its proper authority, has determined must be regulated by its exclusive governance. See *Gade v. National Solid Wastes Management Assn.,* 505 U.S. 88, 115 (1992). The intent to displace state law altogether can be inferred from a framework of regulation "so pervasive ... that Congress left no room for the States to supplement it" or where there is a "federal interest ... so dominant that the federal system will be assumed to preclude enforcement of state laws on the same subject." *Rice v. Santa Fe Elevator Corp.,* 331 U.S. 218, 230 (1947); see *English v. General Elec. Co.,* 496 U.S. 72, 79 (1990).

Second, state laws are preempted when they conflict with federal law. *Crosby, supra,* at 372. This includes cases where "compliance with both federal and state regulations is a physical impossibility," *Florida Lime & Avocado Growers, Inc. v. Paul,* 373 U.S. 132, 142–143 (1963), and those instances where the challenged state law "stands as an obstacle to the accomplishment and execution of the full purposes and objectives of Congress," *Hines,* 312 U.S., at 67; see also *Crosby, supra,* at 373 ("What is a sufficient obstacle is a matter of judgment, to be informed by examining the federal statute as a whole and identifying its purpose and intended effects"). In preemption analysis, courts should assume that "the historic police powers of the States" are not superseded "unless that was the clear and manifest purpose of Congress." *Rice, supra,* at 230; see *Wyeth v. Levine,* 555 U.S. 555, 565 (2009).

The four challenged provisions of the state law each must be examined under these preemption principles.

Section 3 of S.B. 1070 creates a new state misdemeanor. It forbids the "willful failure to complete or carry an alien registration document ... in violation of 8 United States Code section 1304(e) or 1306(a)." Ariz. Rev. Stat. Ann. § 11-1509(A) (West Supp.2011). In effect, § 3 adds a state-law penalty for conduct proscribed by federal law. The United States contends that this state enforcement mechanism intrudes on the field of alien registration, a field in which Congress has left no room for States to regulate. See Brief for United States 27, 31.

The Court discussed federal alien-registration requirements in *Hines v. Davidowitz,* 312 U.S. 52. In 1940, as international conflict spread, Congress added to federal immigration law a "complete system for alien registration." *Id.,* at 70. The new federal law struck a careful balance. It punished an alien's willful failure to register but did not require aliens to carry identification cards. There were also limits on the sharing of registration records and fingerprints. The Court found that Congress intended the federal plan for registration to be a "single integrated and all-embracing system." *Id.,* at 74. Because this "complete scheme ... for the registration of aliens" touched on foreign relations, it did not allow the States to "curtail or complement" federal law or to "enforce additional or auxiliary regulations." *Id.,* at 66–67. As a consequence, the Court ruled that Pennsylvania could not enforce its own alien-registration program. See *id.,* at 59, 74.

The present regime of federal regulation is not identical to the statutory framework considered in *Hines,* but it remains comprehensive. Federal law now includes a requirement that aliens carry proof of registration. 8 U.S.C. § 1304(e). Other aspects, however, have stayed the same. Aliens who remain in the country for more than 30 days must apply for registration and be fingerprinted. Compare § 1302(a) with *id.,* § 452(a) (1940 ed.). Detailed information is required, and any change of address has to be reported to the Federal Government. Compare §§ 1304(a), 1305(a) (2006 ed.), with *id.,* §§ 455(a), 456 (1940 ed.). The statute continues to provide penalties for the willful failure to register. Compare § 1306(a) (2006 ed.), with *id.,* § 457 (1940 ed.).

* * *

Federal law makes a single sovereign responsible for maintaining a comprehensive and unified system to keep track of aliens within the Nation's borders. If § 3 of the Arizona statute were valid, every State could give itself independent authority to prosecute federal registration violations, "diminish[ing] the [Federal Government]'s control over enforcement" and "detract[ing] from the 'integrated scheme of regulation' created by Congress." *Wisconsin Dept. of Industry v. Gould Inc.,* 475 U.S. 282, 288–289 (1986). Even if a State may make violation of federal law a crime in some instances, it cannot do so in a field (like the field of alien registration) that has been occupied by federal law. See *California v. Zook,* 336 U.S. 725, 730–731, 733 (1949); see also *In re Loney,* 134 U.S. 372, 375–376 (1890) (States may not impose their own punishment for perjury in federal courts).

* * *

There is a further intrusion upon the federal scheme. Even where federal authorities believe prosecution is appropriate, there is an inconsistency between § 3 and federal law with respect to penalties. Under federal law, the failure to carry registration papers is a misdemeanor that may be punished by a fine, imprisonment, or a term of probation. See 8 U.S.C. § 1304(e) (2006 ed.); 18 U.S.C. § 3561. State law, by contrast, rules out probation as a possible sentence (and also eliminates the possibility of a pardon). See Ariz. Rev. Stat. Ann. § 13-1509(D) (West Supp.2011). This state framework of sanctions creates a conflict with the plan Congress put in place. See *Wisconsin Dept., supra,* at 286 ("[C]onflict is imminent whenever two separate remedies are brought to bear on the same activity" (internal quotation marks omitted)).

These specific conflicts between state and federal law simply underscore the reason for field preemption. As it did in *Hines,* the Court now concludes that, with respect to the subject of alien registration, Congress intended to preclude States from "complement[ing] the federal law, or enforc[ing] additional or auxiliary regulations." 312 U.S., at 66–67, 61 S.Ct. 399. Section 3 is preempted by federal law.

Unlike § 3, which replicates federal statutory requirements, § 5(C) enacts a state criminal prohibition where no federal counterpart exists. The provision makes it a state misdemeanor for "an unauthorized alien to knowingly apply for work, solicit work in a public place or perform work as an employee or independent contractor" in Arizona. Ariz. Rev. Stat. Ann. § 13-2928(C) (West Supp. 2011). Violations can be punished by a $2,500 fine and incarceration for up to six months. See § 13-2928(F); see also §§ 13-707(A)(1) (West 2010); 13-802(A); 13-902(A)(5). The United States contends that the provision upsets the balance struck by the Immigration Reform and Control Act of 1986 (IRCA) and must be preempted as an obstacle to the federal plan of regulation and control.

When there was no comprehensive federal program regulating the employment of unauthorized aliens, this Court found that a State had authority to pass its own laws on the subject. In 1971, for example, California passed a law imposing civil penalties on the employment of aliens who were "not entitled to lawful residence in the United States if such employment would have an adverse effect on lawful resident workers." 1971 Cal. Stats. ch. 1442, § 1(a). The law was upheld against a preemption challenge in *De Canas v. Bica,* 424 U.S. 351 (1976). *De Canas* recognized that "States possess broad authority under their police powers to regulate the employment relationship to protect workers within the State." *Id.,* at 356. At that point, however, the Federal Government had expressed no more than "a peripheral concern with [the] employment of illegal entrants." *Id.,* at 360; see *Whiting,* 563 U.S., at ___, 131 S.Ct., at 1974.

* * *

The legislative background of IRCA underscores the fact that Congress made a deliberate choice not to impose criminal penalties on aliens who seek, or engage in, unauthorized employment. A commission established by Congress to study immigration policy and to make recommendations concluded these penalties would be "unnecessary and unworkable." U.S. Immigration Policy and the National Interest: The Final Report and Recommendations of the Select Commission on Immigration and Refugee Policy with Supplemental Views by Commissioners 65–66 (1981); see Pub.L. 95-412, § 4, 92 Stat. 907. Proposals to make unauthorized work a criminal offense were debated and discussed during the long process of drafting IRCA. See Brief for Service Employees International Union et al. as *Amici Curiae* 9–12. But Congress rejected them. See, *e.g.,* 119 Cong. Rec. 14184 (1973) (statement of Rep. Dennis). In the end, IRCA's framework reflects a considered judgment that making criminals out of aliens engaged in unauthorized work—aliens who already face the possibility of employer exploitation because of their removable status—would be inconsistent with federal policy and objectives....

* * *

The ordinary principles of preemption include the well-settled proposition that a state law is preempted where it "stands as an obstacle to the accomplishment and execution of the full purposes and objectives of Congress." *Hines,* 312 U.S., at 67. Under § 5(C) of S.B. 1070, Arizona law would interfere with the careful balance struck by Congress with respect to unauthorized employment of aliens. Although § 5(C) attempts to achieve one of the same goals as federal law—the deterrence of unlawful employment—it involves a conflict in the method of enforcement.... The correct instruction to draw from the text, structure, and history of IRCA is that Congress decided it would be inappropriate to impose criminal penalties on aliens who seek or engage in unauthorized employment. It follows that a state law to the contrary is an obstacle to the regulatory system Congress chose. See *Puerto Rico Dept. of Consumer Affairs v. Isla Petroleum Corp.,* 485 U.S. 495, 503 (1988) ("Where a comprehensive federal scheme intentionally leaves a portion of the regulated field without controls, *then* the pre-emptive inference can be drawn—not from federal inaction alone, but from inaction joined with action"). Section 5(C) is preempted by federal law.

Section 6 of S.B. 1070 provides that a state officer, "without a warrant, may arrest a person if the officer has probable cause to believe ... [the person] has committed any public offense that makes [him] removable from the United States." Ariz. Rev. Stat.

Ann. § 13-3883(A)(5) (West Supp. 2011). The United States argues that arrests authorized by this statute would be an obstacle to the removal system Congress created.

As a general rule, it is not a crime for a removable alien to remain present in the United States. See *INS v. Lopez-Mendoza,* 468 U.S. 1032, 1038 (1984). If the police stop someone based on nothing more than possible removability, the usual predicate for an arrest is absent. When an alien is suspected of being removable, a federal official issues an administrative document called a Notice to Appear. See 8 U.S.C. § 1229(a); 8 CFR § 239.1(a) (2012). The form does not authorize an arrest. Instead, it gives the alien information about the proceedings, including the time and date of the removal hearing. See 8 U.S.C. § 1229(a)(1). If an alien fails to appear, an *in absentia* order may direct removal. § 1229a(5)(A).

The federal statutory structure instructs when it is appropriate to arrest an alien during the removal process. For example, the Attorney General can exercise discretion to issue a warrant for an alien's arrest and detention "pending a decision on whether the alien is to be removed from the United States." 8 U.S.C. § 1226(a); see Memorandum from John Morton, Director, ICE, to All Field Office Directors et al., Exercising Prosecutorial Discretion Consistent with the Civil Immigration Enforcement Priorities of the Agency for the Apprehension, Detention, and Removal of Aliens (June 17, 2011) (hereinafter 2011 ICE Memorandum) (describing factors informing this and related decisions). And if an alien is ordered removed after a hearing, the Attorney General will issue a warrant. See 8 CFR § 241.2(a)(1). In both instances, the warrants are executed by federal officers who have received training in the enforcement of immigration law. See §§ 241.2(b), 287.5(e)(3). If no federal warrant has been issued, those officers have more limited authority. See 8 U.S.C. § 1357(a). They may arrest an alien for being "in the United States in violation of any [immigration] law or regulation," for example, but only where the alien "is likely to escape before a warrant can be obtained." § 1357(a)(2).

Section 6 attempts to provide state officers even greater authority to arrest aliens on the basis of possible removability than Congress has given to trained federal immigration officers. Under state law, officers who believe an alien is removable by reason of some "public offense" would have the power to conduct an arrest on that basis regardless of whether a federal warrant has issued or the alien is likely to escape. This state authority could be exercised without any input from the Federal Government about whether an arrest is warranted in a particular case. This would allow the State to achieve its own immigration policy. The result could be unnecessary harassment of some aliens (for instance, a veteran, college student, or someone assisting with a criminal investigation) whom federal officials determine should not be removed.

* * *

By authorizing state officers to decide whether an alien should be detained for being removable, § 6 violates the principle that the removal process is entrusted to the discretion of the Federal Government. See, *e.g., Reno v. American-Arab Anti-Discrimination Comm.,* 525 U.S. 471, 483–484 (1999); see also Brief for Former INS

Commissioners 8–13. A decision on removability requires a determination whether it is appropriate to allow a foreign national to continue living in the United States. Decisions of this nature touch on foreign relations and must be made with one voice. See *Jama v. Immigration and Customs Enforcement,* 543 U.S. 335, 348 (2005) ("Removal decisions, including the selection of a removed alien's destination, may implicate [the Nation's] relations with foreign powers and require consideration of changing political and economic circumstances" (internal quotation marks omitted)); see also *Galvan v. Press,* 347 U.S. 522, 531 (1954) ("Policies pertaining to the entry of aliens and their right to remain here are ... entrusted exclusively to Congress ..."); *Truax v. Raich,* 239 U.S. 33, 42 (1915) ("The authority to control immigration—to admit or exclude aliens—is vested solely in the Federal Government").

In defense of §6, Arizona notes a federal statute permitting state officers to "cooperate with the Attorney General in the identification, apprehension, detention, or removal of aliens not lawfully present in the United States." 8 U.S.C. §1357(g)(10)(B). There may be some ambiguity as to what constitutes cooperation under the federal law; but no coherent understanding of the term would incorporate the unilateral decision of state officers to arrest an alien for being removable absent any request, approval, or other instruction from the Federal Government....

* * *

Section 2(B) of S.B. 1070 requires state officers to make a "reasonable attempt ... to determine the immigration status" of any person they stop, detain, or arrest on some other legitimate basis if "reasonable suspicion exists that the person is an alien and is unlawfully present in the United States." Ariz. Rev. Stat. Ann. §11-1051(B) (West 2012). The law also provides that "[a]ny person who is arrested shall have the person's immigration status determined before the person is released." *Ibid.* The accepted way to perform these status checks is to contact ICE, which maintains a database of immigration records.

Three limits are built into the state provision. First, a detainee is presumed not to be an alien unlawfully present in the United States if he or she provides a valid Arizona driver's license or similar identification. Second, officers "may not consider race, color or national origin ... except to the extent permitted by the United States [and] Arizona Constitution[s]." *Ibid.* Third, the provisions must be "implemented in a manner consistent with federal law regulating immigration, protecting the civil rights of all persons and respecting the privileges and immunities of United States citizens." §11-1051(L) (West 2012).

The United States and its *amici* contend that, even with these limits, the State's verification requirements pose an obstacle to the framework Congress put in place. The first concern is the mandatory nature of the status checks. The second is the possibility of prolonged detention while the checks are being performed.

Consultation between federal and state officials is an important feature of the immigration system. Congress has made clear that no formal agreement or special training needs to be in place for state officers to "communicate with the [Federal

Government] regarding the immigration status of any individual, including reporting knowledge that a particular alien is not lawfully present in the United States." 8 U.S.C. § 1357(g)(10)(A). And Congress has obligated ICE to respond to any request made by state officials for verification of a person's citizenship or immigration status. See § 1373(c); see also § 1226(d)(1)(A) (requiring a system for determining whether individuals arrested for aggravated felonies are aliens). ICE's Law Enforcement Support Center operates "24 hours a day, seven days a week, 365 days a year" and provides, among other things, "immigration status, identity information and real-time assistance to local, state and federal law enforcement agencies." ICE, Fact Sheet: Law Enforcement Support Center (May 29, 2012), online at http://www.ice.gov/news/ library/factsheets/lesc.htm. LESC responded to more than one million requests for information in 2009 alone. App. 93.

The United States argues that making status verification mandatory interferes with the federal immigration scheme. It is true that § 2(B) does not allow state officers to consider federal enforcement priorities in deciding whether to contact ICE about someone they have detained. See Brief for United States 47–50. In other words, the officers must make an inquiry even in cases where it seems unlikely that the Attorney General would have the alien removed....

Congress has done nothing to suggest it is inappropriate to communicate with ICE in these situations, however. Indeed, it has encouraged the sharing of information about possible immigration violations. See 8 U.S.C. § 1357(g)(10)(A). A federal statute regulating the public benefits provided to qualified aliens in fact instructs that "no State or local government entity may be prohibited, or in any way restricted, from sending to or receiving from [ICE] information regarding the immigration status, lawful or unlawful, of an alien in the United States." § 1644. The federal scheme thus leaves room for a policy requiring state officials to contact ICE as a routine matter. Cf. *Whiting,* 563 U.S., at ___, 131 S.Ct., at 1985–1986 (rejecting argument that federal law preempted Arizona's requirement that employers determine whether employees were eligible to work through the federal E-Verify system where the Federal Government had encouraged its use).

* * *

The nature and timing of this case counsel caution in evaluating the validity of § 2(B). The Federal Government has brought suit against a sovereign State to challenge the provision even before the law has gone into effect. There is a basic uncertainty about what the law means and how it will be enforced. At this stage, without the benefit of a definitive interpretation from the state courts, it would be inappropriate to assume § 2(B) will be construed in a way that creates a conflict with federal law. Cf. *Fox v. Washington,* 236 U.S. 273, 277 (1915) ("So far as statutes fairly may be construed in such a way as to avoid doubtful constitutional questions they should be so construed; and it is to be presumed that state laws will be construed in that way by the state courts" (citation omitted)). As a result, the United States cannot prevail in its current challenge. See *Huron Portland Cement Co. v. Detroit,* 362 U.S. 440, 446 (1960) ("To hold otherwise would be to ignore the teaching of this Court's decisions which enjoin seeking out conflicts between state and federal regulation where none clearly exists"). This opinion does not foreclose other preemption and constitutional challenges to the law as interpreted and applied after it goes into effect.

* * *

The United States has established that §§ 3, 5(C), and 6 of S.B. 1070 are preempted. It was improper, however, to enjoin § 2(B) before the state courts had an opportunity to construe it and without some showing that enforcement of the provision in fact conflicts with federal immigration law and its objectives.

The judgment of the Court of Appeals for the Ninth Circuit is affirmed in part and reversed in part. The case is remanded for further proceedings consistent with this opinion.

It is so ordered.

Notes

1. In *Arizona*, the Court cites to *De Canas v. Bica*.[72] In *De Canas*, the Court set out a test to be applied in determining whether the state law may stand. Does the state law regulate immigration? Did Congress in enacting the federal statute intend to "oust" the state from the field? Does the state law conflict with federal law or is it an obstacle to Congress' objective? If any of these exist, the state law must be rejected. *De Canas v. Bica*, 424 U.S. 351, 355–359 (1976).

2. In *U.S. Chamber of Commerce v. Whiting*, 563 U.S. 582 (2011), which was cited by the Court in *Arizona*, the Court applied the *De Canas* test and approved Arizona's state business licensing rules. The rules allowed for the revocation of a company's business license for the knowing and intentional hiring of an "unauthorized alien." The Court held that the state law was not preempted by federal immigration law and was within the state's authority to license businesses. The state law further mandated businesses to use the E-verify program which the Court concluded was encouraged under federal law. *Id.* at 608–611.

3. **Driver's Licenses.** Following the attacks on the World Trade Center on September 11, 2001, it was revealed that a number of the hijackers had obtained driver's licenses and used them as identification documents to board their flights. For a number of years, the undocumented access to a driver's license or other form of "ID" has become most controversial. On one hand, having some form of identification is increasingly essential for anyone moving about, whether it is to go to work or go about their daily activities. On the other hand, for would-be terrorists, having a secure form of identification allows them to go about their activities with less concern. Unlike many countries, the U.S. has no national identification document, and the primary document used to identify a person is a state-issued driver's license or identification card. In response to

---

72. 424 U.S. 351 (1976).

these challenges, in 2005, Congress passed the Real ID Act of 2005.[73] The legislation was controversial for a variety of reasons, including the fact that it went beyond the purpose described in its title.[74] The statute established federal standards for state issued driver's licenses requiring "facial image capture" and security features using common machine-readable technology. It also required that the licenses could only be issued to persons who could prove their U.S. citizenship, lawful permanent residency, temporary residency, pending or approved asylum status, refugee status, lawful non-immigrant status, pending or approved application for permanent residency or temporary protected status. Temporary licenses may be issued for not more than one year. Persons who are applicants for asylum, temporary protected status or temporary or conditional residence may not be issued a driver's license valid for more than one year.

Besides criticism leveled at the Real ID Act by immigration advocates and civil libertarians, some security consultants noted that identity theft could increase as a result of the uniformity of driver's licenses mandated by the legislation. According to these opponents, the requirement of a "common machine-readable technology" which will be accessible to businesses with whom one does transactions will allow this information to become part of the commercial database stream, making it easier to engage in identity theft.[75]

E. Secured Communities and Sanctuary Cities

With growing populations of undocumented persons, many local law enforcement officials have been struggling with how to balance crime prevention and victim protection. On one hand, witnesses are needed to prosecute crimes, but if the witness is undocumented they may be less willing to come forward. While immigration law provides some protection for these witnesses, many local law enforcement officials do not want to be perceived as immigration enforcement agents out of concern for losing trust within communities. In 1996, as part of IIRAIRA, Congress gave authority to the Attorney General to enter into cooperative agreements with state and local law enforcement to carry out some of the functions normally carried out by ICE.[76] Beginning in 2003, in a program called Secure Communities, ICE began entering into Memoranda Agreements with local law enforcement, primarily focused on non-citizens with crim-

73. Pub. L. No. 109-13 (2005).

74. As will be discussed in other sections of this text, the Real ID Act also amended other parts of the INA, limiting relief for asylum seekers, curtailing judicial review in immigration matters and expanding the definition of terrorism for purposes of denying, removing or preventing noncitizens from obtaining legal status.

75. *See* Lisa Vaas, Analysts: Real ID Could Help ID Thieves, Eweek.com, May 6, 2005, available online at https://perma.cc/2SZZ-CUUN; Nat'l Conference of State Legislatures, 2006 State Legislation Related to Immigration: Enacted and Vetoed, available online at https://perma.cc/K8BK-TQSN.

76. *See* 8 U.S.C. § 1357(g), Sec. 287(g). Under the statute, state and local officers could be authorized to identify, arrest and detain certain non-citizens.

inal records, to refer them for the institution of removal proceedings.[77] Secure Communities was discontinued in 2014 following a great deal of controversy, and a new program called the Priority Enforcement Program (PEP) was instituted. PEP relied on the same agreements and procedures previously entered into but with different enforcement priorities.[78] In January 2017, the new President issued Executive Orders ending the PEP program, reinstituting Secured Communities, and changing the enforcement priorities of the agency to detain as many non-citizens as possible.[79] In the wake of these various enforcement efforts, some local governments chose instead to refuse to cooperate with federal immigration enforcement efforts either by abandoning their prior agreements or refusing overtures to enter into new ones. Cities opting for this approach have become known as "Sanctuary Cities." The term as used here is meant to cover municipalities or other subdivisions that have expressly enacted ordinances or policies that prohibit the use of their own funds or resources from being used to enforce the immigration laws. Given the heightened enforcement priorities and the resistance in different parts of the country to the manner in which federal law is being implemented, the following case reflects at least one response taken by the federal government and the counter-response taken by local officials.

County of Santa Clara et al. v. Donald J. Trump, et al.

250 F. Supp. 3d 497 (N.D. Cal. 2017)

William H. Orrick, United States District Judge

Introduction

This case involves Executive Order 13768, "Enhancing Public Safety in the Interior of the United States," which, in addition to outlining a number of immigration enforcement policies, purports to "[e]nsure that jurisdictions that fail to comply with applicable Federal law do not receive Federal funds, except as mandated by law" and to establish a procedure whereby "sanctuary jurisdictions" shall be ineligible to receive federal grants. Executive Order 13768, 82 Fed. Reg. 8799 (Jan. 25, 2017) (the "Executive Order"). In two related actions, the County of Santa Clara and the City and County of San Francisco have challenged Section 9 of the Executive Order as facially unconstitutional and have brought motions for preliminary injunction seeking to enjoin its enforcement. See *County of Santa Clara v. Trump*, No. 17-cv-0574-WHO; *City and County of San Francisco v. Trump*, 17-cv-0485-WHO.

---

77. *See* https://www.ice.gov/secure-communities (last visited Dec. 31, 2017). Under Secure Communities, the FBI would forward the fingerprint information it received from local law enforcement to DHS which in turn would determine which cases on which to initiate enforcement actions.

78. *See* Shadi Masri, *ICE's Initiation of Secure Communities Program Draws More Criticism than Praise*, 25 Geo. Imm. L.J. 533 (2011).

79. *See* Memorandum from DHS Sect'y John Kelly, Implementing the President's Border Security and Immigration Enforcement Improvements Policies (Feb. 20, 2017), at https://www.dhs.gov/sites/default/files/publications/17_0220_S1_Implementing-the-Presidents-Border-Security-Immigration-Enforcement-Improvement-Policies.pdf (last visited Dec. 31, 2017).

The Counties challenge the enforcement provision of the Order, Section 9(a), on several grounds: first, it violates the separation of powers doctrine enshrined in the Constitution because it improperly seeks to wield congressional spending powers; second, it is so overbroad and coercive that even if the President had spending powers, the Order would clearly exceed them and violate the Tenth Amendment's prohibition against commandeering local jurisdictions; third, it is so vague and standardless that it violates the Fifth Amendment's Due Process Clause and is void for vagueness; and, finally, because it seeks to deprive local jurisdictions of congressionally allocated funds without any notice or opportunity to be heard, it violates the procedural due process requirements of the Fifth Amendment.

The Government does not respond to the Counties' constitutional challenges but argues that the Counties lack standing because the Executive Order did not change existing law and because the Counties have not been named "sanctuary jurisdictions" pursuant to the Order. It explained for the first time at oral argument that the Order is merely an exercise of the President's "bully pulpit" to highlight a changed approach to immigration enforcement. Under this interpretation, Section 9(a) applies only to three federal grants in the Departments of Justice and Homeland Security that already have conditions requiring compliance with 8 U.S.C. 1373. This interpretation renders the Order toothless; the Government can already enforce these three grants by the terms of those grants and can enforce 8 U.S.C. 1373 to the extent legally possible under the terms of existing law. Counsel disavowed any right through the Order for the Government to affect any other part of the billions of dollars in federal funds the Counties receive every year.

* * *

The Executive Order

On January 25, 2017, President Donald J. Trump issued Executive Order 13768, "Enhancing Public Safety in the Interior of the United States." See Harris Decl. ¶ 2; Ex. A ("EO") (SC Dkt. No. 36-1). In outlining the Executive Order's purpose, Section 1 reads, in part, "Sanctuary jurisdictions across the United States willfully violate Federal law in an attempt to shield aliens from removal from the United States." EO § 1. Section 2 states that the policy of the executive branch is to "[e]nsure that jurisdictions that fail to comply with applicable Federal law do not receive Federal funds, except as mandated by law." EO § 2(c).

Section 9, titled "Sanctuary Jurisdictions" lays out this policy in more detail. It reads:

> Sec. 9. Sanctuary Jurisdictions. It is the policy of the executive branch to ensure, to the fullest extent of the law, that a State, or a political subdivision of a State, shall comply with 8 U.S.C. 1373.
>
> (a) In furtherance of this policy, the Attorney General and the Secretary, in their discretion and to the extent consistent with law, shall ensure that jurisdictions that willfully refuse to comply with 8 U.S.C. 1373 (sanctuary jurisdictions) are not eligible to receive Federal grants, except as deemed necessary for law enforcement purposes by the Attorney General or the Sec-

> retary. The Secretary has the authority to designate, in his discretion and to the extent consistent with law, a jurisdiction as a sanctuary jurisdiction. The Attorney General shall take appropriate enforcement action against any entity that violates 8 U.S.C. 1373, or which has in effect a statute, policy, or practice that prevents or hinders the enforcement of Federal law.
>
> (b) To better inform the public regarding the public safety threats associated with sanctuary jurisdictions, the Secretary shall utilize the Declined Detainer Outcome Report or its equivalent and, on a weekly basis, make public a comprehensive list of criminal actions committed by aliens and any jurisdiction that ignored or otherwise failed to honor any detainers with respect to such aliens.
>
> (c) The Director of the Office of Management and Budget is directed to obtain and provide relevant and responsive information on all Federal grant money that currently is received by any sanctuary jurisdiction.

EO § 9.

Section 3 of the Order, titled "Definitions," incorporates the definitions listed in 8 U.S.C. § 1101. EO § 3. Section 1101 does not define "sanctuary jurisdiction." The term is not defined anywhere in the Executive Order. Similarly, neither section 1101 nor the Order defines what it means for a jurisdiction to "willfully refuse to comply" with Section 1373 or for a policy to "prevent[ ] or hinder[ ] the enforcement of Federal law." EO § 9(a).

Section 1373

Section 1373, to which Section 9 refers, prohibits local governments from restricting government officials or entities from communicating immigration status information to ICE. It states in relevant part:

> (a) In General. Notwithstanding any other provision of Federal, State, or local law, a Federal, State, or local government entity or official may not prohibit, or in any way restrict, any government entity or official from sending to, or receiving from, the Immigration and Naturalization Service information regarding the citizenship or immigration status, lawful or unlawful, of any individual.
>
> (b) Additional Authority of Government Entities. Notwithstanding any other provision of Federal, State, or local law, no person or agency may prohibit, or in any way restrict, a Federal, State, or local government entity from doing any of the following with respect to information regarding the immigration status, lawful or unlawful, of any individual:
>
> (1) Sending such information to, or requesting or receiving such information from, the Immigration and Naturalization Service.
>
> (2) Maintaining such information.
>
> (3) Exchanging such information with any other Federal, State, or local government entity.

8 U.S.C. 1373.

In July, 2016, the U.S. Department of Justice issued guidance linking two federal grant programs, the State Criminal Alien Assistance Program ("SCAAP") and Edward Byrne Memorial Justice Assistance Grant ("JAG") to compliance with Section 1373.2 This guidance states that all applicants for these two grant programs are required to "assure and certify compliance with all applicable federal statutes, including Section 1373, as well as all applicable federal regulations, policies, guidelines, and requirements." *Id.* The Department has indicated that the Community Oriented Policing Services Grant (COPS) is also conditioned on compliance with Section 1373.

Civil Detainer Requests

An ICE civil detainer request asks a local law enforcement agency to continue to hold an inmate who is in local jail because of actual or suspected violations of state criminal laws for up to 48 hours after his or her scheduled release so that ICE can determine if it wants to take that individual into custody. See 8 C.F.R. § 287.7; Neusel Decl. ¶ 9; Marquez Decl., Ex. C at 3 (SC Dkt. No. 29-3). ICE civil detainer requests are voluntary and local governments are not required to honor them. See 8 C.F.R. § 287.7(a); *Galarza v. Szalczyk*, 745 F.3d 634, 643 (3d Cir. 2014) ("[S]ettled constitutional law clearly establishes that [immigration detainers] must be deemed requests" because any other interpretation would render them unconstitutional under the Tenth Amendment). Several courts have held that it is a violation of the Fourth Amendment for local jurisdictions to hold suspected or actual removable aliens subject to civil detainer requests because civil detainer requests are often not supported by an individualized determination of probable cause that a crime has been committed. See *Morales v. Chadbourne*, 793 F.3d 208, 215–217 (1st Cir. 2015); *Miranda-Olivares v. Clackamas Cnty.*, No. 3:12-cv-02317-ST, 2014 WL 1414305, at *9–11 (D. Or. Apr. 11, 2014). ICE does not reimburse local jurisdictions for the cost of detaining individuals in response to a civil detainer request and does not indemnify local jurisdictions for potential liability they could face for related Fourth Amendment violations. See 8 C.F.R. § 287.7(e); Marquez Decl. ¶¶ 21–15 & Exs. B–D.

The Counties' Policies

A. Santa Clara's Policies

Santa Clara asserts that its local policies and practices with regard to federal immigration enforcement are at odds with the Executive Order's provisions regarding Section 1373. SC Mot. at 5. (SC Dkt. No. 26). In 2010, the Santa Clara County Board of Supervisors adopted a Resolution prohibiting Santa Clara employees from using County resources to transmit any information to ICE that was collected in the course of providing critical services or benefits. Marquez Decl. ¶ 27 (SC Dkt. No. 29) & Ex. G (SC Dkt. No. 29-7); Neusel Decl. ¶ 7 (SC Dkt. No. 31); L. Smith Decl. ¶ 6 (SC Dkt. No. 35). The Resolution also prohibits employees from initiating an inquiry or enforcement action based solely on the individual's actual or suspected immigration status, national origin, race or ethnicity, or English-speaking ability, or from using County resources to pursue an individual solely because of an actual or suspected violation of immigration law. *Id.* In October, 2016, after receiving DOJ guidance that JAG and SCAAP funds would be conditioned on compliance with Section 1373, Santa Clara decided not to participate in those programs. Marquez Decl. ¶ 29 & Ex. H (SC Dkt. No. 29-8).

Santa Clara also asserts that its policies with regard to ICE civil detainer requests are inconsistent with the Executive Order and the President's stated immigration enforcement agenda. Prior to late 2011, Santa Clara responded to and honored ICE civil detainer requests, housing an average of 135 additional inmates each day at a daily cost of approximately $159 per inmate. Neusel Decl. ¶ 4. When the County raised concerns about the costs associated with complying with detainer requests and potential civil liability, ICE confirmed that it would not reimburse the County or indemnify it for the associated costs and liabilities. Marquez Decl. ¶¶ 21–15 & Exs. B–D.

Santa Clara subsequently convened a task force and adopted a new policy where the County agreed to honor requests for individuals with serious or violent felony convictions, but only if ICE would reimburse the County for the cost of holding those individuals. Neusel Decl. ¶ 6; Marquez Decl. ¶ 26 & Ex. E. ICE has never agreed to reimburse the County for any costs, so since November 2011 the County has declined to honor all ICE detainer requests. *Id.*

B. San Francisco's Policies

San Francisco's sanctuary city policies are contained in Chapters 12H and 12I of its Administrative Code. Eisenberg Decl. Exs. A–B (SF Dkt. No. 28). The stated purpose of these laws is "to foster respect and trust between law enforcement and residents, to protect limited local resources, to encourage cooperation between residents and City officials, including especially law enforcement and public health officers and employees, and to ensure community security, and due process for all." S.F. Admin Code § 12I.1.

As relevant to Section 1373, Chapter 12H prohibits San Francisco departments, agencies, commissions, officers, and employees from using San Francisco funds or resources to assist in enforcing federal immigration law or gathering or disseminating information regarding an individual's release status, or other confidential identifying information (which as defined does not include immigration status), unless such assistance is required by federal or state law. S.F. Admin Code § 12H.2. Although Chapter 12H previously prohibited city employees from sharing information regarding individuals' immigration status, the San Francisco Board of Supervisors removed this restriction in July, 2016, due to concerns that the provision violated Section 1373.

With regard to civil detainer requests, Chapter 12I prohibits San Francisco law enforcement from detaining an individual, otherwise eligible for release from custody, solely on the basis of a civil immigration detainer request. S.F. Admin Code § 12I.3. It also prohibits local law enforcement from providing ICE with advanced notice that an individual will be released from custody, unless the individual meets certain criteria. S.F. Admin Code § 12I.3. Chapter 12I.3(e) provides that a "[l]aw enforcement official shall not arrest or detain an individual, or provide any individual's personal information to a federal immigration officer, on the basis of an administrative warrant, prior deportation order, or other civil immigration document based solely on alleged violations of the civil provisions of immigration laws." S.F. Admin Code § 12I.3.(e). San Francisco explains that it adopted these policies due to concerns that holding people in response to civil detainers would violate the Fourth Amendment and require it to dedicate scarce law enforcement personnel and resources to holding these individuals. Hennessy Decl. ¶ 11 (SF Dkt. No. 24).

The Counties' Federal Funding

A. Santa Clara's Federal Funding

In the 2015–2016 fiscal year, Santa Clara received approximately $1.7 billion in federal and federally dependent funds, making up roughly 35% of the County's total revenues. J. Smith Decl. ¶ 6; Marquez Decl. ¶ 8. This figure includes federal funds provided through entitlement programs.

Most of the County's federal funds are used to provide essential services to its residents. Marquez Decl. ¶¶ 5–8. In support of its motion, the County includes a number of declarations outlining how a loss of any substantial amount of federal funding would force it to make substantial cut backs to safety-net programs and essential services and would require it to lay off thousands of employees. It highlights that the County's Valley Medical Center, the only public safety-net healthcare provider in the County, relies on $1 billion in federal funds each year, which covers up to 70% of its total annual costs. Lorenz Decl. ¶¶ 3, 7 (SC Dkt. No. 28). A loss of all federal funds would shut down Valley Medical Center and cut off the only healthcare option for thousands of poor, elderly, and vulnerable people in the County. *Id.* ¶ 8. It further highlights that Santa Clara's Social Services Agency, which provides various services to vulnerable residents, including child welfare and protection, aid to needy families, and support for disabled children, adults and the elderly, receives roughly 40% of its budget, $300 million, from federal funds. Menicocci Decl. ¶ 5 (SC Dkt. No. 30). The County's Public Health Department receives 40% of its budget and $38 million in federal funds. And the County's Office of Emergency Services, whose job is to prepare for and respond to disasters such as earthquakes and terrorism, receives more than two-thirds of its budget from federal funds. Reed Decl. ¶¶ 3–20 (SC Dkt. No. 32).

In the 2014–2015 fiscal year, the County received over $565 million in non-entitlement federal grants. See Marquez Decl. Ex. A at 11–12 (SC Dkt. No. 29-1) (showing $338 million in federal grants subject to OMB auditing requirements and an additional $227 million in federal grants through the Department of Housing and Urban Development). This $565 million represents approximately 11% of the County's budget.

B. San Francisco's Federal Funding

San Francisco's yearly budget is approximately $9.6 billion; it receives approximately $1.2 billion of this from the federal government. Rosenfield Decl. ¶ 9 (SF Dkt. No. 22). San Francisco uses these federal funds to provide vital services such as medical care, social services, and meals to vulnerable residents, to maintain and upgrade roads and public transportation, and to make needed seismic upgrades. Whitehouse Decl. ¶ 16 (SF Dkt. No. 23). Losing all, or a substantial amount, of federal funds would have significant effects on core San Francisco programs: federal funds make up 100% of Medicare for San Francisco residents, Rosenfield Decl. ¶ 29; 30% of the budget for San Francisco's Department of Emergency Management, id. ¶¶ 25–27; 33% of the budget for San Francisco's Human Services Agency, id. ¶¶ 13–18; and 40% of the budget for San Francisco's Department of Public Health, *id.* ¶¶ 19–24.

Approximately 20% of these federal funds, or $240 million, are from federal grants. Id. ¶ 29. San Francisco also receives $800 million each year in federal multi-year grants, primarily for public infrastructure projects. *Id.* ¶ 11.

* * *

Legal Standard

"A plaintiff seeking a preliminary injunction must establish that he is likely to succeed on the merits, that he is likely to suffer irreparable harm in the absence of preliminary relief, that the balance of equities tips in his favor, and that an injunction is in the public interest." *Winter v. Nat'l Res. Def. Council, Inc.*, 555 U.S. 7, 20 (2008). This has been interpreted as a four-part conjunctive test, not a four-factor balancing test. However, the Ninth Circuit has held that a plaintiff may also obtain an injunction if he has demonstrated "serious questions going to the merits" that the balance of hardships "tips sharply" in his favor, that he is likely to suffer irreparable harm, and that an injunction is in the public interest. See *Alliance for the Wild Rockies v. Cottrell*, 632 F.3d 1127, 1131–35 (9th Cir. 2011).

* * *

The Government's primary defense is that the Order does not change the law, but merely directs the Attorney General and Secretary to enforce existing law. In its briefing, the Government emphasized Section 9(a)'s provision that it will be implemented "to the extent consistent with law." It argued that to the extent the Order directs the Attorney General and Secretary to newly condition federal funds on compliance with Section 1373, it could not lawfully do so and so it does not. It asserted, "If the grant language does not require compliance with Section 1373, the Executive Order does not purport to give the Secretary or Attorney General the unilateral authority to alter those terms." By this interpretation, Section 9 simply directs the Attorney General and Secretary to ensure that grants that are already conditioned on compliance with Section 1373 are not remitted to jurisdictions that fail to meet that requirement. At the hearing, the Government went further and explicitly disclaimed the ability under the Executive Order to add conditions to grants authorized by Congress or to enforce the Order against any but three grant programs, SCAAP, JAG and COPS. Government counsel urged me to adopt this narrow reading of the Order, arguing that well-established rules of construction require courts to adopt narrow readings when broader ones would read in constitutional problems.

Where a construction of a statute "would raise serious constitutional problems, the Court will construe the statute to avoid such problems unless such construction is plainly contrary to the intent of Congress." *Edward J. DeBartolo Corp. v. Florida Gulf Coast Bldg. & Const. Trades Council*, 485 U.S. 568, 575 (1988). "[A]s between two possible interpretations of a statute, by one of which it would be unconstitutional and by the other valid, our plain duty is to adopt that which will save the Act." *Blodgett v. Holden*, 275 U.S. 142, 148 (1927). The primary purpose of the doctrine is to "minimize disagreement between the branches by preserving congressional enactments that might otherwise founder on constitutional objections." *Almendarez-Torres v. U.S.*, 523 U.S. 224, 238 (1998).

This canon is followed out of respect for Congress, which we assume legislates in the light of constitutional limitations." *Rust v. Sullivan*, 500 U.S. 173, 191 (1991). This canon of construction is limited; to adopt an alternate construction the statute must be "readily susceptible" to that construction. *United States ex rel. Attorney General v. Delaware & Hudson Co.*, 213 U.S. 366, 409 (1909). It is not the job of the courts "to insert missing terms into the statute or adopt an interpretation precluded by [its] plain language." *Foti v. City of Menlo Park*, 146 F.3d 629, 639 (9th Cir. 1998).

As a preliminary matter, a narrow construction does not limit a plaintiffs' standing to challenge a law that is subject to multiple interpretations. See *Virginia v. American Booksellers Ass'n, Inc.*, 484 U.S. 383, 392 (1988) (noting that a plaintiff's standing may be based on its interpretation of the statute even when a narrower interpretation is offered). Therefore, the Government's proposed narrow construction does not destroy justiciability.

* * *

While the Government urges that the Order "does not purport to give the Secretary or Attorney General the unilateral authority" to impose new conditions on federal grants, that is exactly what the Order purports to do. It directs the Attorney General and the Secretary to ensure that "sanctuary jurisdictions" are "not eligible to receive" federal grants. EO § 9(a). Whether a jurisdiction is eligible to receive federal grants is determined by the conditions on those grants and the characteristics, acts, and choices of the jurisdiction. See Black's Law Dictionary 634 (10th ed. 2014) (defining "eligible" as "Fit and proper to be selected or to receive a benefit."). Section 9(a)'s language directing the Attorney General and Secretary to ensure that jurisdictions that "willfully refuse to comply" with Section 1373 are "not eligible" for federal grants therefore purports to delegate to the Attorney General and the Secretary the authority to place a new condition on federal grants, compliance with Section 1373. And as Government counsel agreed at the hearing, the power to place conditions on funds belongs exclusively to Congress.

The Government attempts to read out all of Section 9(a)'s unconstitutional directives to render it an ominous, misleading, and ultimately toothless threat. It urges that Section 9(a) can be saved by reading the defunding provision narrowly and "consistent with law," so that all it does is direct the Attorney General and Secretary to enforce existing grant conditions. But this interpretation is in conflict with the Order's express language and is plainly not what the Order says. The defunding provision is entirely inconsistent with law in its stated purpose and directives because it instructs the Attorney General and the Secretary to do something that only Congress has the authority to do—place new conditions on federal funds. If Section 9(a) does not direct the Attorney General and Secretary to place new conditions on federal funds then it only authorizes them to do something they already have the power to do, enforce existing grant requirements. Effectively, the Government argues that Section 9(a) is "valid" and does not raise constitutional issues as long as it does nothing at all. But a construction so narrow that it renders a legal action legally meaningless cannot possibly be reasonable and is clearly inconsistent with the Order's broad intent.

At the hearing, Government counsel argued that the Order applies only to grants issued by the Department of Justice and the Department of Homeland Security because it is directed only at the Attorney General and Secretary of Homeland Security. This reading is similarly implausible. Nothing in Section 9(a) limits the "Federal grants" affected to those only given though the Departments of Justice and Homeland Security. The Department of Justice is responsible for federal law enforcement throughout the country, not just within its own Department. So when the Attorney General is directed to "ensure that jurisdictions that willfully refuse to comply with 8 U.S.C. 1373 (sanctuary jurisdictions) are not eligible to receive Federal grants, except as deemed necessary for law enforcement purposes by the Attorney General or the Secretary" and to "take appropriate enforcement action against any entity that violates 8 U.S.C. 1373, or which has in effect a statute, policy, or practice that prevents or hinders the enforcement of Federal law," it is not reasonable to interpret the directive as applying solely to law enforcement grants that the Attorney General and Secretary are specifically given authority to exempt from the Order.

Nor is counsel's narrow interpretation supported by the rest of the Order. Two examples suffice. Section 9(c) instructs the Director of the Office of Management and Budget "to obtain and provide relevant and responsive information on all Federal grant money that currently is received by any sanctuary jurisdiction." This directive is not limited to grants issued by the Departments of Justice and Homeland Security. And Section 2(c) announces a policy to "ensure that jurisdictions that fail to comply with applicable Federal law do not receive Federal funds, except as mandated by law." The Order's structure and language make clear that a "sanctuary jurisdiction," which the Secretary will eventually define, should change its policies or risk loss of all federal grants, and Section 9(a) provides the means to do so.

... At the hearing, Government counsel explained that the Order is an example of the President's use of the bully pulpit and, even if read narrowly to have no legal effect, serves the purpose of highlighting the President's focus on immigration enforcement. While the President is entitled to highlight his policy priorities, an Executive Order carries the force of law. Adopting the Government's proposed reading would transform an Order that purports to create real legal obligations into a mere policy statement and would work to mislead individuals who are not able to conclude, by reading Section 9(a) itself, that it is fully self-cancelling and carries no legal weight.

* * *

The Government's construction is not reasonable. It requires a complete rewriting of the Order's language and does not "save" any part of Section 9(a)' s legal effect. There is no doubt that Section 9(a), as written, changes the law.

* * *

The Counties' claims implicate a constitutional interest, the rights of states and local governments to determine their own local policies and enforcement priorities pursuant to the Tenth Amendment. See *Alfred L. Snapp & Son, Inc. v. Puerto Rico, ex rel., Barez*, 458 U.S. 592, 601 (1982) (highlighting that states have a sovereign interest in "the exercise of sovereign power over individuals and entities within the relevant jurisdiction—this involves the power to create and enforce a legal code, both civil and criminal"); see also *New York v. United States*, 505 U.S. 144, 157–158 (1992) ("[T]he Tenth Amendment confirms that the power of the Federal Government is subject to limits that may, in a given instance, reserve power to the States.").

* * *

The Counties have demonstrated that their sanctuary policies reflect their local judgment of what policies and practices are most effective for maintaining public safety and community health. Because they argue that the Executive Order seeks to undermine this judgment by attempting to compel them to change their policies and enforce the Federal government's immigration laws in violation of the Tenth Amendment, their claims implicate a constitutional interest. See *Virginia ex rel. Cuccinelli v. Sebelius*, 656 F.3d 253, 269 (4th Cir. 2011) ("when a federal law interferes with a state's exercise of its sovereign 'power to create and enforce a legal code' [] it inflict[s] on the state the requisite injury-in-fact."); *Ohio ex rel. Celebrezze v. U.S. Dep't of Transp.*, 766 F.2d 228, 233 (6th Cir. 1985) (Ohio had standing to litigate the constitutionality of its own law where "effective enforcement of the Ohio statute" was rendered "uncertain by the formal position of the [U.S. Department of Transportation] that the Ohio statute is preempted" as "threatened injury to a State's enforcement of its safety laws" constitutes an injury-in-fact).

Likelihood of Success on the Merits

Conclusion

The Counties have demonstrated that they are likely to succeed on the merits of their challenge to Section 9(a) of the Executive Order, that they will suffer irreparable harm absent an injunction, and that the balance of harms and public interest weigh in their favor. The Counties' motions for a nationwide preliminary injunction, enjoining enforcement of Section 9(a), are Granted. The defendants (other than the President) are enjoined from enforcing Section 9(a) of the Executive Order against jurisdictions they deem as sanctuary jurisdictions. This injunction does not impact the Government's ability to use lawful means to enforce existing conditions of federal grants or 8 U.S.C. 1373, nor does it restrict the Secretary from developing regulations or preparing guidance on designating a jurisdiction as a "sanctuary jurisdiction."

Notes

1. The reasoning in *County of Santa Clara* has at least been partially followed by other federal district courts addressing the requirements imposed by the Department of Justice by municipalities seeking federal grants. See *City of Philadelphia v. Sessions*, 2017 WL 5489476 (E.D. Pa. 2017); *City of Seattle v. Sessions*, 2017 WL 4700144 (W.D. Wash. 2017); *City of Chicago v. Sessions*, 264 F. Supp. 3d 933 (N.D. Ill. 2017). While *Santa Clara* involved an interpretation of the impact of the President's Executive Order, *City of Chicago* enjoined requirements of notice and access to correctional facilities. The *City of Chicago* court did not grant an injunction on the Attorney General's requirement that the city certify its compliance with a federal mandate that the city would share information regarding the citizenship status of individuals encountered by city officials. 264 F. Supp. 3d at 949.

2. For interesting articles on the subject, see Ming H. Chen, *Trust in Immigration Enforcement: State Noncooperation and Sanctuary Cities After Secure Communities*, 91 Chi. Kent L. Rev. 13 (2016); Bill Ong Hing, *Immigration Sanctuary Policies: Constitutional and Representative of Good Policing and Good Public Policy*, 2 U.C. Irvine L. Rev. 247 (2012); Rose Cuison Villazor, *"Sanctuary Cities" and Local Citizenship*, 37 Fordham Urb. L.J. 573 (2010).

Chapter 3

Admissibility and Removal

On the Statue of Liberty is inscribed a verse which entreats the world to give the United States its "tired ... poor ... [and] huddled masses...."[1] As was seen in the previous discussion by the U.S. Civil Rights Commission in *The Tarnished Golden Door* in Chapter 1, this verse may have been more appropriate to a much earlier period in our history. The grounds for admissibility and deportability are the core of U.S. immigration law, for these provide the basis for determining who is allowed to enter and who may remain.[2] Laws and policies which govern who may enter and remain in a nation reflect, in part, a nation's future and hence are the subjects of great controversy.[3] Participation in this debate requires a clear understanding of the admissibility provisions. Even upon careful review, the reader will find it difficult to see a cohesive pattern in the statute. Our discussion will therefore begin with an attempt to describe

---

1. Not like the brazen giant of Greek fame,
With conquering limbs astride from land to land;
Here at our sea-washed, sunset gates shall stand
A mighty woman with a torch, whose flame
Is the imprisoned lightning, and her name
Mother of Exiles. From her beacon-hand
Glows world-wide welcome; her mild eyes command
The air-bridged harbor that twin cities frame.
"Keep, ancient lands, your storied pomp!" cries she
With silent lips. "Give me your tired, your poor,
Your huddled masses yearning to breathe free,
The wretched refuse of your teeming shore.
Send these, the homeless, tempest-tost to me,
I lift my lamp beside the golden door!"

Emma Lazarus, The New Colossus (1883).

2. One of the major changes made by the 1996 Amendments was the replacement of the word "inadmissible" for the word "excludable." The 1996 Amendments also use the term "removal hearings" to describe the procedure which had been formerly described as "exclusion" or "deportation" hearings. As a result, the pre-1996 cases and discussion will use the older terminology.

3. One scholar has argued that the reason that the United States has had great difficulty in developing a coherent immigration policy is because the choices tug at the moral fabric of the nation, thereby making the issue particularly difficult to harmonize. *See* Fuchs, *Immigration Policy and the Rule of Law,* 44 U. Pitt. L. Rev. 433, 433 (1983); Christopher J. Coyne & Peter J. Boettke, *Institutions, Immigration, and Identity,* 2 N.Y.U. J.L. & Liberty 131, 135 (2006). Perhaps the 2016 Presidential election cycle brought out these tensions. Lindsay Pérez Huber, *"Make America Great Again!": Donald Trump, Racist Nativism and the Virulent Adherence to White Supremacy Amid U.S. Demographic Change,* 10 Charleston L. Rev. 215 (2016).

the statutory scheme which provides the foundation for understanding the provisions relating to inadmissibility.[4]

A. Substantive Grounds of Inadmissibility

The inadmissibility grounds should be viewed as an expression by this country of those it does not like, abhors or otherwise feels should not be allowed to become a part of this society. It is, by omission, an expression of the categories of individuals who might make up a perfect society. When studying these substantive grounds, it must be understood that from a legal standpoint, every nation has been recognized to have broad powers to permit only those people whom it wishes to allow to enter the country.[5] One should also remember that none of the grounds of inadmissibility apply to U.S. citizens.[6] Thus, when a person seeks admission, she has the burden of establishing that she is either a citizen or not inadmissible under the grounds of inadmissibility.[7]

A review of 8 U.S.C. § 1182(a), Sec. 212(a) will certainly lead the reader to conclude that the grounds for inadmissibility encompass virtually every type of person. In an effort to make sense of the myriad grounds, our discussion will focus on the six general categories synthesized below, which are based upon a strong concern that certain people should not be allowed to come to this country.

Economic

Political, Foreign Policy and Security

Health

Criminal

---

4. The substantive grounds for inadmissibility are found at 8 U.S.C. § 1182(a), Sec. 212(a). The procedures for removal are found at 8 U.S.C. §§ 1229 and 1229a, Sections 239–40.

5. Many scholars have criticized the cases which have upheld this absolutist rule. *See* H.L. Hart, *The Power of Congress to Limit the Jurisdiction of Federal Courts: An Exercise in Dialectic*, 66 Harv. L. Rev. 1362, 1392–96 (1953); James Nafziger, *The General Admission of Aliens Under International Law*, 77 Am. J. Int'l L. 804, 823–29 (1983); David Martin, *Due Process and Membership in the National Community: Political Asylum and Beyond*, 44 U. Pitt. L. Rev. 165, 173–80 (1983); Richard A. Boswell, *Rethinking Exclusion: The Rights of Cuban Refugees Facing Indefinite Detention in the United States*, 17 Vand. J. Transnt'l L. 925, 942–49 (1984); Michael Scaperlanda, *Polishing the Tarnished Golden Door*, 1993 Wis. L. Rev. 165 (1993); Charles D. Weisselberg, *The Exclusion and Detention from the Lives of Ellen Knauff and Ignatz Mezei*, 143 U. Pa. L. Rev. 933 (1995). However, there is also ongoing debate about the current strength of the plenary power doctrine. *See* Gabriel J. Chin, *Segregation's Last Stronghold: Racial Discrimination and the Constitutional Law of Immigration*, 46 UCLA L. Rev. 1 (1998); Gabriel J. Chin, *Is There a Plenary Power Doctrine? A Tentative Apology and Prediction for Our Strange but Unexceptional Constitutional Immigration Law*, 14 Geo. Immigr. L.J. 257 (2000); Peter J. Spiro, *Explaining the End of Plenary Power*, 16 Geo. Immigr. L.J. 339 (2002); Kif Augustine-Adams, *The Plenary Power Doctrine After September 11*, 38 U.C. Davis L. Rev. 701 (2005).

6. *Gegiow v. Uhl*, 239 U.S. 3 (1915). A returning U.S. citizen unable to prove her citizenship could have problems.

7. 8 U.S.C. § 1361, Sec. 291.

Quasi-Criminal or Moral

Miscellaneous

Keep in mind that even though the inadmissibility grounds are very broad, there are some ameliorative provisions that will allow some people to immigrate to the United States if, notwithstanding their inadmissibility, they are fleeing persecution, have family ties with a U.S. citizen or permanent resident or can meet certain hardship requirements. Some of these legal mechanisms for avoiding the application of the inadmissibility grounds are called "waivers." These waivers will be touched on briefly at the end of each grounds of inadmissibility section below and will be explored in greater detail in Chapter 10. At the outset, it is worth noting that most of the inadmissibility grounds can be waived in the case of nonimmigrants.[8] In addition, there are broad waivers available to persons who have been long-term lawful permanent residents,[9] were granted status as refugees or asylees,[10] are certain long-term residents able to establish the requisite levels of hardship,[11] are battered spouses and children of U.S. citizens and permanent residents, are victims of trafficking,[12] are assisting law enforcement in the prosecution of criminal organizations or terrorism[13] or are the victims of criminal activity and helpful or likely to be helpful in the prosecution of the crime.[14]

1. Economic

One of the broadest categories for inadmissibility is the provision which prohibits the admission of persons who are "likely to become a public charge."[15] To assure that

8. See 8 U.S.C. §§ 1182(d)(1) and (3), Sections 212(d)(1) and (3).

9. 8 U.S.C. § 1229b(a), Sec. 240A(a).

10. 8 U.S.C. § 1159(c), Sec. 209(c). This provision allows for waivers for humanitarian purposes to assure family unity of most grounds of inadmissibility with the exception of the security grounds, which include terrorism, foreign policy, Nazi persecution, participants in genocide or extra-judicial killing, torture and trafficking in controlled substances.

11. 8 U.S.C. § 1229b(b), Sec. 240A(b).

12. The beneficiary is granted a "T" nonimmigrant visa and the Secretary may grant a waiver if she considers it to be in the national interest. The waiver is for all grounds of inadmissibility with the exception of Nazis, persons who have committed genocide, acts of torture or extrajudicial killings, persons falling under the security-related grounds of inadmissibility, participants in child abduction and former U.S. citizens who renounced their citizenship to avoid taxation. The ground of inadmissibility must be related to or caused by the incidents of victimization. 8 U.S.C. § 1182(d)(13), Sec. 212(d)(13). This visa is described further in Chapter 6.

13. 8 U.S.C. § 1182(d)(1), Sec. 212(d)(1). The waiver covers all grounds of inadmissibility with the exception of the provisions for those involved in Nazi persecution, genocide or the commission of acts of torture or extrajudicial killings. These waivers are granted "in the national interest" and available to persons who are beneficiaries of the "S" nonimmigrant visas, which is for persons who assist in the prosecution of an individual criminal organization or enterprise or terrorism. This visa is described further in Chapter 6.

14. The person receives a "U" visa. The "U" visa recipient may have all grounds of inadmissibility waived except for Nazi activity or participation in genocide or acts of extra-judicial killing. 8 U.S.C. § 1182(d)(14). The "U" visa is described more fully in Chapter 6.

15. *See* 8 U.S.C. § 1182(a)(4), Sec. 212(a)(4).

such persons are not admitted, consular and immigration officers are empowered to require these applicants to obtain "affidavits of support" from their sponsors, assuring that in the event the applicant does fall into distress, the sponsor will be responsible for the costs incurred by the government.[16] While there have not been any cases challenging the enforceability of the affidavit of support, the law clearly makes it enforceable.[17] Another group of persons rendered inadmissible are those who are not being admitted under the family preference categories (discussed in Chapter 7), are coming to enter the labor force and are unable to obtain a labor certification, which is described in greater detail in Chapter 8. The certification is issued upon proof that there are no ready, willing and able U.S. workers for the position being offered to the person coming to the United States.[18]

Waivers of the economic grounds. Other than the broad nonimmigrant waivers, the only way that a person may avoid the public charge provisions is by posting a bond set by the Secretary of the Department of Homeland Security (DHS).[19] Otherwise the applicant for admission is required to establish that she will not likely become a public charge.

2. Political, Foreign Policy and Security

Among the more controversial grounds of inadmissibility have been political and foreign policy or "ideological" grounds.[20] This broad category prohibits the admission of those who present a potential threat to the government or merely hold ideas that Congress and the President have deemed to be abhorrent. Included within this category are persons whose admission and proposed activity the Secretary of State has reasonable grounds to believe would pose "potentially serious adverse foreign policy consequences for the United States."[21] Others who fall into this category are applicants who are or were affiliated with the "Communist or other totalitarian party" as well as persons who are deemed to be "terrorists."[22] Prior law prohibited the admission

16. The affidavit of support is executed by the sponsor, who is required to prove that she has sufficient resources to support the applicant at 125% of the poverty income guidelines. *See generally* 8 U.S.C. § 1183a, Sec. 213A. The poverty income guidelines are issued annually by the federal government and are available at http://aspe.hhs.gov/poverty.

17. See 8 U.S.C. §§ 1183a(a) and (e), Sections 213A(a) and (e). The affidavit is binding on the "affiant" until the person becomes a citizen or after the person has credited payments into social security for the equivalent of ten years, whichever is earlier. *Id.*

18. *See* 8 U.S.C. § 1182(a)(5), Sec. 212(a)(5).

19. 8 U.S.C. § 1183, Sec. 213.

20. Kevin R. Johnson, *The Antiterrorism Act, The Immigration Reform Act, and Ideological Regulation in the Immigration Laws: Important Lessons for Citizens and Noncitizens*, 28 St. Mary's L. J. 822, 870–78 (1997).

21. 8 U.S.C. § 1182(a)(3)(C), Sec. 212(a)(3)(C).

22. *See* 8 U.S.C. §§ 1182(a)(3)(D)(I) and 1182(a)(3)(B), Sections 212(a)(3)(D)(I) and 212(a)(3)(B). Communist membership requires that the membership was voluntary, a meaningful association and relatively recent to the application for immigrant admission. Acts of terrorism include being a member of a terrorist organization, encouraging others to engage in terrorist activities, preparing for the commission of terrorist activities and committing acts that provide material support to future acts of ter-

of Communists even as nonimmigrants.[23] Also falling within this category for inadmissibility are Nazis, former Nazis or persons who have committed genocide.[24] Further, a provision of the Cuban Liberty and Democratic Solidarity Act of 1996 prohibits the admission of persons and family members whom the Secretary of State determines have confiscated or been involved in the confiscation of property to which there is a claim of ownership by a U.S. national or Cuban government.[25]

Following the events of September 11, 2001, Congress passed the USA Patriot Act and then the REAL ID Act of 2005.[26] The USA Patriot Act broadened the inadmissibility grounds for terrorism, prohibiting the admission of representatives of groups who had used their positions to endorse terrorism.[27] Under the REAL ID Act, the definitions of what constitutes terrorist organizations and terrorist activities were broadened further to include the endorsement or encouragement of others to engage in terrorism.[28]

Specifically, the REAL ID Act of 2005 expanded the definition of what it means to "engage in terrorist activity" and made it easier for the government to find inadmissible any alien who solicited for or provided material support to any member of a terrorist organization.[29] Prior to its enactment, aliens who provided support to a member of an organization and not the organization directly may be considered as not engaging in terrorist activity if they could show that they did not know or could not reasonably have known that the support was going to further terrorist activities. Representatives of terrorist organizations were found inadmissible only if they publicly endorsed terrorist acts that the Secretary of State determined undermined efforts by the United States to reduce or eliminate terrorist activities. Under the amended statute, persons who endorse or persuade others to support terrorist activities are inadmissible regardless of whether they are in a position of prominence within the country or their endorsement undermines U.S. efforts to reduce terrorist activities as required by the prior statute. Furthermore, persons who received military-type training from or on behalf of an organization that could be designated a terrorist organization at the time of the

---

rorism. *Id.* Officers, officials, representatives and spokespersons of the Palestine Liberation Organization (PLO) are considered persons engaged in terrorist activities. 8 U.S.C. § 1182(a)(3)(B)(i)(IX), Sec. 212(a)(3)(B)(i)(IX).

A more controversial statute enacted by Congress was the Cuban Liberty and Democratic Solidarity (Libertad) Act of 1996, Pub. L. No. 104-114, 110 Stat. 785 (1996), which makes inadmissible anyone whom the Secretary of State determines (after March 12, 1996) has confiscated property, traffics in confiscated property or is the corporate officer, principal or shareholder with a controlling interest in an entity involved in the confiscation of property in Cuba. *See also* 61 Fed. Reg. 30,655–56 (1996).

23. *See Abourezk v. Reagan*, 785 F.2d 1043 (D.C. Cir. 1986), *aff'd*, 479 U.S. 1016 (1987); *Kleindienst v. Mandel*, 408 U.S. 753 (1972).

24. *See* 8 U.S.C. § 1182(a)(3)(E), Sec. 212(a)(3)(E).

25. Pub. L. No. 104-114, § 401, 110 Stat. 785, 822–24 (1996).

26. REAL ID Act of 2005, Pub. L. No. 109-13, § 103, 119 Stat. 231, 306–309 (2005).

27. 8 U.S.C. § 1182(a)(3)(B)(i)(IV)(bb), Sec. 212(a)(3)(B)(i)(IV)(bb).

28. REAL ID Act of 2005, Pub. L. No. 109-13, § 103, 119 Stat. 231, 306–309 (2005). Changes to 8 U.S.C. § 1182(a)(3)(B) were effective on the enactment date of the statute (May 11, 2005) and applied to removal proceedings instituted before or after such date and to acts constituting grounds for inadmissibility occurring before or after such date.

29. 8 U.S.C. § 1182(a)(3)(B)(iv), Sec. 212(a)(3)(B)(iv)

training would also be found inadmissible. In order to rebut one's engagement in terrorist activities, the non-citizen must be able to show by clear and convincing evidence, a higher standard than that required by the prior law, that she did not and could not have reasonably known that her support would further terrorist activities. The Act also broadened the definition of "terrorist organization" under 8 U.S.C. § 1182(a)(3)(B)(vi) to significantly increase the types of groups that could constitute a terrorist organization, notwithstanding the designation by the Secretary of State. Under prior law, a terrorist organization included groups that committed, incited, prepared, planned or gathered information for a terrorist activity; however, the Real ID Act would also deem groups that solicited funds or membership or provided material support for terrorist activities or organizations as terrorist organizations.

Waivers of political, foreign policy and security grounds. The broad nonimmigrant waiver previously described can waive all but the inadmissibility provision related to those coming to engage in espionage or to overthrow the U.S. government.[30] A discretionary waiver is available to immigrant members of a totalitarian party where the person is the parent, spouse, son, daughter, brother or sister of a U.S. citizen spouse or child of an alien lawfully admitted for permanent residence for humanitarian, family unity or public interest purposes.[31] The inadmissibility grounds relating to the Cuban Liberty and Democratic Solidarity Act may be waived for medical reasons or for purposes of litigating property claims.[32]

3. Health

Persons having a communicable disease of public health significance are inadmissible, as such persons would pose a risk to the community.[33] Due to advances in modern science and public health education, the risk of mass infection is limited. Consequently, fewer persons will actually be found inadmissible under this provision. Historically, decisions of inadmissibility under the health grounds have been delegated to doctors within the Public Health Service. In the last two decades, however, these provisions have been the subject of a great deal of political influences. In the recent past, the health grounds have been used to exclude homosexuals[34] and persons infected with HIV.[35]

30. 8 U.S.C. § 1182(d)(3)(A), Sec. 212(d)(3)(A).

31. 8 U.S.C. § 1182(a)(3)(D)(iv), Sec. 212(a)(3)(D)(iv).

32. Pub. L. No. 104-114, § 401(c), 110 Stat. 785, 824 (1996).

33. 8 U.S.C. § 1182(a)(1), Sec. 212(a)(1).

34. The exclusion of homosexuals was originally accomplished by defining homosexuality as a psychological disorder. When the medical community changed its position on this application of the "psychological" grounds for inadmissibility, political pressure was applied to reverse the new medical interpretation. *See* Samuel M. Silvers, *The Exclusion and Expulsion of Homosexual Aliens*, 15 Colum Hum. Rts. L. Rev. 295 (1984). Presently, homosexuality is not a ground for inadmissibility. Robert Foss, *The Demise of Homosexual Exclusion: New Possibilities for Gay and Lesbian Immigration*, 29 Harv. C.R.-C.L. L. Rev. 439 (1994).

35. *See* 8 U.S.C. § 1182(a)(1)(i), Sec. 212(a)(1)(i). The United States Global Leadership Against HIV/AIDS, Tuberculosis and Malaria Reauthorization Act of 2008, Pub. L. No. 110-293, § 305, 122

Also encompassed within this ground of inadmissibility are applicants for admission who are unable to show that they have been vaccinated,[36] who suffer from physical or mental disorders[37] or who are drug abusers.[38]

In reviewing these health grounds for inadmissibility, it is important to bear in mind the possible overlap with some of the other provisions. For example, applicants who suffer from a psychological or physical condition may, as a result, fall into the economic grounds due to the severity or advanced nature of their conditions.[39] Similarly, persons with medical conditions such as alcoholism or drug addiction may be inadmissible for their prior drug-related criminal behavior.

Waivers of health grounds. A number of waivers are available for the health grounds in addition to those broadly available to long-term residents. Persons seeking admission who are the spouse or unmarried child of a U.S. citizen or lawful permanent resident or a person issued an immigrant visa are eligible for this waiver.[40] The vaccination provision can be waived where the Secretary of Health and Human Services (HHS) certifies that it would not be medically appropriate or where it is contrary to the person's religious or moral convictions.[41] Finally, for persons found inadmissible due to a physical or mental disorder, a discretionary waiver may be obtained from the Secretary of DHS in consultation with the Secretary of HHS, which may also include the posting of a bond.[42] There is no waiver for persons who are drug abusers; however, someone who no longer engages in abuse may be admissible.[43]

4. Criminal

While crimes have been a basis for inadmissibility since the earliest immigration laws, the subject has received even greater attention in recent years. The statute is quite broad, as it precludes the admission of persons who have been convicted of or admit to acts which would constitute a crime involving moral turpitude or would

---

Stat. 2918, 2963 (2008), amended the statutory requirement that persons infected with HIV be inadmissible to the United States. However, HHS continues to list HIV as a "communicable disease of public health significance," though it is currently working to amend this. In the meantime, DHS finalized a regulation in October 2008, which provides a waiver for otherwise eligible aliens who are HIV-positive to enter the United States on short-term visas. *See* 73 Fed. Reg. 58023 (Oct. 6, 2008).

36. 8 U.S.C. § 1182(a)(1)(A)(ii), Sec. 212(a)(1)(A)(ii).

37. 8 U.S.C. § 1182(a)(1)(A)(iii), Sec. 212(a)(1)(A)(iii).

38. 8 U.S.C. § 1182(a)(1)(A)(iv), Sec. 212(a)(1)(A)(iv). A drug abuser is someone who engages in the non-medical use of a controlled substance under Section 202 of the Controlled Substance Act. *See* 42 C.F.R. § 34.2(g). However, it does not include experimentation but may include alcohol abuse.

39. *See* Rebecca Kidder, *Administrative Discretion Gone Awry: The Reintroduction of the Public Charge Exclusion for HIV-Positive Refugees and Asylees*, 106 YALE L.J. 389, 390 (1996).

40. 8 U.S.C. § 1182(g)(1), Sec. 212(g)(1). The Secretary is authorized to also require the posting of a bond in appropriate cases. *Id.*

41. 8 U.S.C. § 1182(g)(2)(C), Sec. 212(g)(2)(C).

42. 8 U.S.C. § 1182(g)(3), Sec. 212(g)(3).

43. The Department of State takes the position that a person must not have used a substance in the last three years. *See* 9 F.A.M. § 40.11 note 9.1(c).

violate any law "relating to a controlled substance."[44] A crime involving moral turpitude is one which is *malum in se*, where the act is intrinsically wrong, as opposed to *malum prohibitum*, where the act is made wrong by statute.[45] A conviction must be final, meaning that the case is not on appeal and the period for appeal has passed. Moreover, a person would still be inadmissible if he was convicted of more than one crime where the aggregate sentence of confinement was more than five years, irrespective of whether the crimes involved moral turpitude.[46]

Drug-related inadmissibility grounds include situations where the person is someone whom the consular officer "knows or has reason to believe is or has been an illicit trafficker in any such controlled substance or is or has been a knowing assister, abettor, conspirator, or colluder."[47] Therefore, even if a person was not convicted of drug trafficking, she may still be found to be inadmissible.[48] Also included within this category are persons whom a consular officer or the Attorney General knows or has reason to believe has aided, assisted or colluded in the "severe forms of trafficking in persons" as defined in 22 U.S.C. § 7102.[49]

Crimes Involving Moral Turpitude. The statute, while not defining "crime[s] involving moral turpitude," provides that a non-citizen convicted for such a crime is inadmissible.[50] The approach to determining whether a crime involves moral turpitude is imprecise and difficult to apply with uniformity due to inharmonious court and administrative decisions. In the first instance the analysis of what constitutes such a crime requires a review of the statute under which the person was convicted without regard to supplementary facts such as the circumstances of the persons case, transcripts and other extraneous information. This type of examination is called a "categorical approach" and to find moral turpitude the crime must include "reprehensible conduct and some degree of scienter." When the analysis includes the review of supplementary facts is referred to as a "modified categorical approach." The description of how these cases should be ex-

44. 8 U.S.C. § 1182(a)(2)(A)(i), Sec. 212(a)(2)(A)(i). Exempted from this definition are situations where the single crime occurred before the person's eighteenth birthday and the person was released from confinement five years prior to the request for admission; also exempted are situations where the person committed a single crime, the maximum possible penalty was one year imprisonment and the person served not more than six months. 8 U.S.C. § 1182(a)(2)(A)(ii), Sec. 212(a)(2)(A)(ii). This second exemption is known as the petty offense exception and is described later in Chapter 10.

45. *Matter of Franklin*, 20 I. & N. Dec. 867 (BIA 1994), *aff'd* 72 F.3d 571 (8th Cir. 1995). Whether a crime is one involving moral turpitude is a question of law and is reviewable *de novo* by a reviewing court. *Hamdan v. INS*, 98 F.3d 183, 185 (5th Cir. 1996); *Goldeshtein v. INS*, 8 F.3d 645 (9th Cir. 1993).

46. 8 U.S.C. § 1182(a)(2)(B), Sec. 212(a)(2)(B). The person would be inadmissible if he were sentenced to five years but only served two years imprisonment.

47. *See* 8 U.S.C. § 1182(a)(2)(C), Sec. 212(a)(2)(C).

48. *See Nuñez-Payan v. INS*, 815 F.2d 384 (5th Cir. 1987) (deferred adjudication statute did not preclude its use in determining inadmissibility); *Castano v. INS*, 956 F.2d 236 (11th Cir. 1992).

49. *See* 8 U.S.C. § 1182(a)(2)(H), Sec. 212(a)(2)(H). The statute also prohibits the admission of the spouse or child of a trafficker who benefitted financially or otherwise from trafficking in the previous five years and knew or should have known that the benefit was derived from such activity. This prohibition does not apply to children who were minors at the time.

50. 8 U.S.C. § 1182(a)(2), Sec. 212(a)(2).

amined was set forth by the BIA in *Matter of Silva-Treviño*,[51] where it held that the categorical approach would be used in the Third and Fifth Circuits and the modified categorical under some circumstances in other Circuits. The Board stated the rule as follows:

> In evaluating the criminal statute under the categorical approach, unless circuit court law dictates otherwise, we apply the realistic probability test. This requires us to focus on the minimum conduct that has a realistic probability of being prosecuted under the statute of conviction, rather than on the facts underlying the respondent's particular violation of that statute. [*citing Moncrieffe v. Holder*, 569 U.S. 184 (2013)]... In cases where the statute of conviction includes some crimes that involve moral turpitude and some that do not, adjudicators must determine if the statute is divisible and thus susceptible to a modified categorical analysis. Under such an analysis, resort to the record of conviction is permitted to identify the statutory provision that the respondent was convicted of violating. [*citing Descamps v. U.S.*, 570 U.S. 254 (2013)]

Waivers for criminal grounds. Waivers for the criminal grounds of inadmissibility are much narrower. The most common waiver for the criminal grounds is cancellation of removal for long-term permanent residents, which requires that the person has been a lawful permanent resident for at least five years and a continuous resident of the United States for at least seven years.[52] Refugees and asylees may also obtain a waiver of most of the criminal grounds of inadmissibility with the exception of the provisions for drug traffickers.[53] Another basis for obtaining a waiver is where the person who is otherwise eligible for an immigrant visa is the spouse, parent or child of a U.S. citizen or lawful permanent resident and is able to establish that the family member would experience extreme hardship if the applicant's admission is denied. This waiver is effective for crimes involving moral turpitude, except for murder, torture, multiple criminal convictions or for a single offense involving simple possession of 30 grams or less of marihuana.[54]

5. Quasi-Criminal or Moral

The quasi-criminal or moral grounds are designed to prevent the admission of persons who have committed acts or engaged in behavior are contrary to the norms of society as established by Congress when it passed the Act. Included within this group are persons

51. 26 I. & N. Dec. 826, 831-33 (BIA 2016).

52. 8 U.S.C. § 1229b(a), Sec. 240A(a). The seven years of continuous residency stops at the time when the person is served with the notice to appear or upon the commission of the crime. This waiver is also available for certain grounds of deportability but is not available for aggravated felons.

53. 8 U.S.C. § 1159(c).

54. 8 U.S.C. § 1182(h)(1)(B), Sec. 212(h)(1)(B). This waiver is not available to a person who was previously admitted to the United States as a permanent resident and who subsequently committed an aggravated felony or who has not lawfully resided in the country for a period of at least seven years immediately preceding the date that proceedings were initiated for her removal. The provision has withstood constitutional challenge asserting a violation of the Equal Protection clause. *See Latu v. Ashcroft*, 375 F.3d 1012 (10th Cir. 2004); *Taniguchi v. Schultz*, 303 F.3d 950, 958 (9th Cir. 2002).

who come to the United States to practice polygamy[55] or who have engaged in or sought to engage in prostitution within ten years of their application for admission.[56] The Immigration Act of 1990 removed the inadmissibility ground for persons who were entering the United States to perform "immoral sex acts."[57] Applicants (including their spouse and children) who, while serving as a foreign government official, were responsible for or carried out particularly severe violations of religious freedom as defined in the International Religious Freedom Act of 1998 within the preceding two-year period are also inadmissible. Further included within this category are persons who have or tried to obtain a visa or other documentation through fraud or misrepresentation.[58]

Waivers for quasi-criminal grounds. The prostitution grounds for inadmissibility may be waived either upon a showing of extreme hardship to the spouse, parent or child of a U.S. citizen or lawful permanent resident or if the prostitution acts which the person committed preceded the application for admission by more than fifteen years. Persons who are coming to practice polygamy may not obtain a waiver.

6. Miscellaneous[59]

The grounds of inadmissibility under the miscellaneous category is an ever expanding group of acts which can be divided into immigration law violators and other persons who Congress has determined should not be admitted. The immigration violator category includes persons who (1) do not have valid documentation to enter the United States;[60] (2) were previously removed;[61] (3) are accompanying an inadmissible person;[62] (4) are stowaways;[63] (5) are found in the country but were not ad-

---

55. 8 U.S.C. § 1182(a)(10)(A), Sec. 212(a)(10)(A). Prior to 1990, the law also precluded the admission of persons who were "polygamists" or who "advocated" polygamy.

56. 8 U.S.C. § 1182(a)(2)(D), Sec. 212(a)(2)(D). The bar also extends to persons who are otherwise involved in or received proceeds from prostitution. 8 U.S.C. § 1182(a)(2)(D)(ii), Sec. 212(a)(2)(D)(ii). A person who is coming to engage in any other unlawful commercialized vice, whether or not related to prostitution, is also inadmissible. 8 U.S.C. § 1182(a)(2)(D)(iii), Sec. 212(a)(2)(D)(iii).

57. This was formerly codified at 8 U.S.C. § 1182(a)(13), Sec. 212(a)(13).

58. 8 U.S.C. § 1182(a)(6)(C), Sec. 212(a)(6)(C).

59. The immigration statute itself uses the term "miscellaneous" to describe some of the grounds of inadmissibility described here. The organization here represents not the statute's organization but the author's view of a more coherent way to view the grounds of inadmissibility.

60. 8 U.S.C. § 1182(a)(7), Sec. 212(a)(7).

61. 8 U.S.C. § 1182(a)(9)(A), Sec. 212(a)(9)(A). The statute describes a number of different forms of removal. The first is "expedited" removal under 8 U.S.C. § 1225; this procedure contemplates that a person who has been removed would be inadmissible for five years after removal. If the person was removed a second time, then she would be inadmissible for twenty years. If she was removed as an aggravated felon, she would not be able to return at any time. *See* 8 U.S.C. § 1182(a)(9)(A)(i). The second form of removal is a regular removal proceeding, where a person ordered removed may not return to the United States for ten years, and a second removal order would bar her return for twenty years. A person removed as an aggravated felon would be unable to return permanently.

62. 8 U.S.C. § 1182(a)(10)(B), Sec. 212(a)(10)(B).

63. 8 U.S.C. § 1182(a)(6)(D), Sec. 212(a)(6)(D). A stowaway is someone who travels without consent. 8 U.S.C. § 1101(a)(49).

mitted or paroled;[64] (6) knowingly encouraged, induced or assisted someone's entry to the United States in violation of the law;[65] (7) have been in the country in an unlawful status for more than 180 days or more than one year and later seeks readmission;[66] (8) failed to attend their removal hearing without reasonable cause;[67] and (9) are student visa abusers.[68] Within the second group are graduates of non-approved foreign medical schools seeking to practice their profession,[69] uncertified foreign health care workers,[70] persons previously admitted as exchange visitors and subject to the two-year foreign residency requirement,[71] draft evaders,[72] former citizens who renounced their citizenship to avoid taxes[73] and persons who have falsely claimed U.S. citizenship "for any purpose or benefit under [the] Act."[74]

64. 8 U.S.C. § 1182(a)(6)(A), Sec. 212(a)(6)(A).

65. 8 U.S.C. § 1182(a)(6)(E), Sec. 212(a)(6)(E). In addition to being an immigration violation, smuggling can also be a crime. *See* 8 U.S.C. §§ 1324(a)(1)(A)(ii)–(iii), Sections 212(a)(1)(A)(ii)–(iii). The illegal acts include illegally bringing in a person or transporting, harboring or encouraging someone to enter or reside in the United States. Penalties for these violations can range from five to twenty years imprisonment. If death occurs in the smuggling, the possibility of the death sentence exists.

66. 8 U.S.C. § 1182(a)(9)(B), Sec. 212(a)(9)(B). Unlawful presence for more than 180 days and less than one year triggers a three-year bar to readmission. 8 U.S.C. § 1182(a)(9)(B)(i)(I), Sec. 212(a)(9)(B)(i)(I). A person who has been in unlawful status for one year or more is subject to a ten-year bar. 8 U.S.C. § 1182(a)(9)(B)(i)(II), Sec. 212(a)(9)(B)(i)(II).

67. 8 U.S.C. § 1182(a)(6)(B). This ground of inadmissibility renders the person ineligible for readmission and inadmissible for five years following the person's departure or removal.

68. 8 U.S.C. § 1182(a)(6)(G), Sec. 212(a)(6)(G). A student visa abuser is not someone who violates the terms of their student visa but is someone who was admitted under a student visa to attend a private elementary or secondary institution but then transfers to a public institution without permission from DHS. A person may only attend a public elementary or secondary institution if she pays the institution the full cost of the educational program. 8 U.S.C. § 1184(m)(2). A student visa abuser is inadmissible for five years, and this only applies to student visas issued under IIRAIRA.

69. 8 U.S.C. § 1182(a)(5)(B),Sec. 212(a)(5)(B). The provision requires that the person pass parts I, II and III of the U.S. Medical Licensing Exam (USMLE) exam. This inadmissibility ground only applies to persons who are coming to perform services as a member of the profession. Therefore, someone immigrating under the family preference would not be subject to the bar.

70. 8 U.S.C. § 1182(a)(5)(C), Sec. 212(a)(5)(C). Non-physicians working in the healthcare profession are required to have been certified as having equivalent training. In addition, they are required to pass a predictor licensing exam accepted by many states or to have an actual state license in the state where they will work. 8 C.F.R. § 1212.5.

71. 8 U.S.C. § 1182(e), Sec. 212(e). The restrictions apply to certain persons admitted under the "J" Exchange Visitor nonimmigrant visa. Those subject to the foreign residency requirement are ineligible for immigrant visas or permanent residency and may not be issued nonimmigrant visas as temporary workers (H) or intracompany transfers (L) until they have fulfilled the required two-year foreign residency or obtained a waiver. Those subject to the two-year residency requirement are those whose education was financed in whole or in part by the United States or the government of their nationality or last residence; it may also include persons who at the time of admission was studying in a field on a list of professions from their country on the Department of State's Skills List. The residency requirement also applies to persons coming to the United States to receive graduate medical training after January 10, 1977. The "J" visa is described in greater detail in Chapter 6.

72. 8 U.S.C. § 1182(a)(8)(B), Sec. 212(a)(8)(B).

73. 8 U.S.C. § 1182(a)(10)(E), Sec. 212(a)(10)E).

74. 8 U.S.C. § 1182(a)(6)(C)(ii), Sec. 212(a)(6)(C)(ii). The statute provides an exception where the natural or adoptive parents were citizens, and the person mistakenly believed that she was a U.S. citizen and relied thereupon.

Waivers of miscellaneous grounds for inadmissibility. As with the other grounds of inadmissibility, most of the miscellaneous grounds are amenable to some type of waiver. Within the first group of immigration law violators is the group of persons who have arrived without proper documentation, a provision which is not amenable to a waiver. As will be seen later, such a person may only seek relief from removal in the form of asylum or some other protection.[75] If the person has been previously removed, under the statute, she may only return during the restricted period if she first obtains permission from the Secretary.[76] Persons who are battered spouses or children or beneficiaries of "U," "S" or "T" visas may have this bar to admission waived. Persons who are inadmissible due to a prior unlawful presence may seek a waiver of the bar if they are the spouse or child of a U. S. citizen or lawful permanent resident and can establish that the refusal of admission would result in extreme hardship to the citizen or lawful resident spouse or child of such alien.[77] As with other removal bars, this provision does not apply to asylees, battered children or spouses or beneficiaries of "S," "T" and "U" visas.

The two-year foreign residency requirement applicable to certain persons admitted under the exchange visitor program may be waived upon a favorable recommendation from the Department of State. The waiver is discretionary and may be obtained upon a showing of one or more of the following: (1) the person would be subject to persecution in her home country; (2) exceptional hardship would result to the person's U.S. citizen or permanent resident spouse or child; (3) the country to which the person "owes" the two-year residency issues a "no objection statement; (4) a U.S. government agency requests the waiver; or (5) the person is an international medical graduate and a state or federal agency needs her services in a medically-underserved area.[78] A person who engages in smuggling may have the inadmissibility grounds waived for humanitarian purposes to assure family unity or for the public interest if the person smuggled was their spouse, parent or child.[79]

B. The Process of Determining Admissibility

A clear understanding of the legal principles established in the cases which follow will form a building block for mastering immigration law. Some examples of recent

---

75. These benefits will be discussed in Chapter 5.

76. 8 U.S.C. § 1182(a)(9)(iii), Sec. 212(a)(9)(iii). This is known as consent to reapply for admission. The statute is not written as a waiver and is termed an "exception," yet it provides that consent must be given for the person to reapply for admission, which is equivalent to a waiver of the bar to admission.

77. 8 U.S.C. § 1182(a)(9)(B)(v), Sec. 212(a)(9)(B)(v).

78. The waiver is explored in greater detail in Chapter 10.

79. 8 U.S.C. § 1182(d)(11), Sec. 212(d)(11). The requisite family relationship described in the statute must have existed at the time the smuggling occurred. *Moran v. Ashcroft*, 395 F.3d 1089 (9th Cir. 2005). The statute uses the terms "son or daughter."

issues which implicate admissibility are the questions of testing persons seeking admission for HIV, detaining people for long periods indefinitely, banning the admission of controversial foreign political figures, controlling international terrorism and deporting naturalized U.S. citizens found to have participated in Nazi activities during World War II.

In order to understand the term "inadmissibility," one must first understand how a person can gain entry into the United States. There are only two ways to come to this country. The first is by applying for a visa before a U.S. consul abroad.[80] There the applicant is questioned to ensure that she does not fall within one of the grounds of inadmissibility, and if all goes well, is issued a visa to come to this country to attempt to gain admission. Generally, it is at the consular interview that a determination is made that a waiver might be necessary.[81] Following receipt of the visa, she would travel to a port of entry by air, sea or land and would be questioned a second time by the CBP to determine her admissibility.[82]

The second way to come into the United States is to not apply for a visa but attempt to gain entry without one. A person who comes without a visa is faced with a very serious dilemma. When she arrives at the border (if she attempts to enter at a designated port), she would be found inadmissible for not having a visa.[83] Even if the applicant manages to gain entry into the country, she remains subject to the grounds of inadmissibility, since she was not legally admitted.[84]

CBP's questioning of a person at the border is called "inspection."[85] In most cases, this inspection process is done without the person having the benefit of counsel. It has been clearly established that throughout this inspection process, the applicant has no constitutional protection as she is merely "knocking at the door";

---

80. The *only* way for a person to obtain a visa is by application before a U.S. consul abroad. USCIS does not have any visa-issuing authority.

81. As will be seen later, procedural amendments instituted in 2013 provide for some persons to seek a waiver prior to their interview before the consular officer overseas. Dree K. Collopy, *I-601A Provisional Unlawful Presence Waivers: A Practitioner's Guide for Preserving Family Unity*, 3-06 Immigr. Briefings 1 (June 2013). This topic will be covered in greater detail in the discussion on waivers of grounds of inadmissibility in Chapter 10.

82. One change made in the 1990 Act was that all applicants denied a visa by a consul or denied admission by an immigration officer must be presented with a written notice stating the determination and specific provision under which the applicant is inadmissible for entry or ineligible for adjustment of status. *See* 8 U.S.C. § 1182(b), Sec. 212(b).

83. As will be discussed in Chapter 4, a person who manages to physically enter without a visa will be subject to "removal" as a person present without admission and remains subject to grounds of inadmissibility. 8 U.S.C. § 1182(a)(6)(A)(i), Sec. 212(a)(6)(A)(i); 8 C.F.R. § 235.1(f)(2).

84. 8 U.S.C. § 1182(a)(6)(A)(i), Sec. 212(a)(6)(A)(i); 8 C.F.R. § 235.1(f)(2).

85. Inspection is not defined in the statute but is implicit within the statutory sections dealing with the procedure used by a CBP officer in determining a person's admissibility. It may include interrogation, perusal of documents and other means of assuring that the applicant is clearly entitled to land. *See* 1 Charles Gordon, Stanley Mailman, Stephen Yale-Loehr & Ronald Wada, Immigration Law and Procedure, § 1.03 (Matthew Bender rev. ed. 2017); 8 U.S.C. § 1225, Sec. 235.

she does not even have the rights afforded a non-U.S. citizen already in the United States.[86]

Understandably, this process before both the U.S. consul and the immigration inspector at the border is very quick. The process is so fast that numerous persons otherwise inadmissible manage to gain entry. The person arriving at the border has the burden of showing that she is "clearly and beyond a doubt entitled to be admitted and is not inadmissible."[87] If she is not entitled to land, or cannot establish to the satisfaction of the immigration inspector that she is admissible, she may be given the opportunity to withdraw her application for entry, summarily removed, bound over to an immigration judge for a removal hearing or paroled into the country until completion of the inspection process at a local CBP office. The term "parole" is a legal fiction, as it is a method of allowing a person to physically enter the United States, while at the same time not providing her the legal advantages of being "within" the country.[88] Parole is convenient in allowing inadmissible persons to physically enter the country rather than being detained while their admission is being considered.

The admissibility grounds remain relevant in certain circumstances, even if a person was legally admitted to the United States. Persons seeking to adjust their status to lawful permanent resident status following admission are required to overcome the inadmissibility provisions.[89]

1. The "Removal" Hearing

The hearing to determine whether a person is admissible is conducted by an immigration judge (sometimes referred to as a special inquiry officer). The judge's jurisdiction is defined at 8 U.S.C. § 1229a(a)(1), Sec. 240(a). As stated earlier, the applicant has the burden of proving clearly and beyond a doubt that she is admissible to the United States. She is permitted to have an attorney present and is given the opportunity to present evidence and cross-examine witnesses.[90] In removal hearings,

86. The term "knocking at the door" is used to illustrate that the right of a person who is not a citizen of the United States but who wishes to enter is analogous to the right of a stranger seeking permission to enter one's home.

87. 8 U.S.C. § 1229a(c)(2)(A), Sec. 240(c)(2)(A).

88. The legal advantages are discussed in Chapter 4. Briefly stated, they are primarily procedural. A person who has "made an entry" will be accorded constitutional protection, entitled to judicial review of the deportation order and may be entitled to cancellation of removal *(see* Chapter 10) or adjustment of status to that of a lawful permanent resident (*see* Chapter 9). A person under parole may be allowed to stay in the United States despite the fact that she has no other legal basis to remain. In addition, she may be able to apply for lawful permanent residence at a later date.

89. 8 U.S.C. § 1255, Sec. 245.

90. Although the applicant has a right to counsel in removal proceedings under the statute, the government will not provide an attorney. *See* 8 U.S.C. §§ 1252(b)(2) and 1362, Sec. 242 and 292. While one may not have a constitutional right to counsel in removal proceedings to determine admissibility, that right arguably exists for persons who are within the United States. *See Castaneda-Delgado v. INS,* 525 F.2d 1295 (7th Cir. 1975); *Cheung v. INS,* 418 F.2d 460 (D.C. Cir. 1969); *but see Matter of Santos,* 19 I. & N. Dec. 105 (BIA 1984).

strict rules of evidence are not followed, and it is the responsibility of the immigration judge to determine admissibility based upon the weight of evidence provided at the hearing. At the conclusion of the proceeding, the judge may immediately make an oral or written decision, whereupon the person will have thirty days to file an appeal with the BIA.[91] A removal order entered in absentia is not subject to appeal. We will explore the removal hearing in more detail in Chapter 4.

C. The Plenary Power Doctrine: The Power to Determine Who Is Admissible?

At the center of any discussion about who Congress considers admissible and the procedural protections that should be afforded to those who might wish to come to this country is a legal doctrine commonly referred to as the "Plenary Power Doctrine." The two cases which follow vividly present the power and to which branches it is accorded. The first of these cases, *Chae Chan Ping v. U.S.*,[92] was decided in 1889 and involved non-citizens who were the equivalent of present day lawful permanent residents who were denied readmission to the U.S. as a result of changes in the law enacted following their departure. The second case, *Shaughnessy v. Mezei*,[93] also involved a lawful resident permanently denied readmission and detention on security grounds.

The Chinese Exclusion Case: Chae Chan Ping v. United States

130 U.S. 581 (1889)

Mr. Justice Field delivered the opinion of the Court.

This case comes before us on appeal from an order of the circuit court of the United States for the Northern district of California, refusing to release the appellant, on a writ of habeas corpus, from his alleged unlawful detention by Capt. Walker, master of the steam-ship Belgic, lying within the harbor of San Francisco. The appellant is a subject of the emperor of China, and a laborer by occupation. He resided at San Francisco, Cal., following his occupation, from some time in 1875 until June 2, 1887, when he left for China on the steam-ship Gaelic, having in his possession a certificate in terms entitling him to return to the United States, bearing date on that day, duly issued to him by the collector of customs of the port of San Francisco, pursuant to the provisions of section 4 of the restriction act of May 6, 1882, as amended by the act of July 5, 1884, (22 St. p. 59, c. 126; 23 St. p. 115, c. 220.) On the 7th of September, 1888, the appellant, on his return to California, sailed from Hong Kong in the steam-ship Belgic, which arrived within the port of San Francisco on the 8th of October following. On his arrival he presented to the proper custom-house officers

91. 8 C.F.R. § 1240.15.
92. 130 U.S. 581 (1889).
93. 345 U.S. 206 (1953).

his certificate, and demanded permission to land. The collector of the port refused the permit, solely on the ground that under the act of congress approved October 1, 1888, supplementary to the restriction acts of 1882 and 1884, the certificate had been annulled, and his right to land abrogated, and he had been thereby forbidden again to enter the United States. 25 St. p. 504, c. 1064. The captain of the steam-ship, therefore, detained the appellant on board the steamer. Thereupon a petition on his behalf was presented to the circuit court of the United States for the Northern district of California, alleging that he was unlawfully restrained of his liberty, and praying that a writ of habeas corpus might be issued directed to the master of the steam-ship, commanding him to have the body of the appellant, with the cause of his detention, before the court at a time and place designated, to do and receive what might there be considered in the premises. A writ was accordingly issued, and in obedience to it the body of the appellant was produced before the court. Upon the hearing which followed, the court, after finding the facts substantially as stated, held as conclusions of law that the appellant was not entitled to enter the United States, and was not unlawfully restrained of his liberty, and ordered that he be remanded to the custody of the master of the steam-ship from which he had been taken under the writ. From this order an appeal was taken to this court.

The appeal involves a consideration of the validity of the act of congress of October 1, 1888, prohibiting Chinese laborers from entering the United States who had departed before its passage, having a certificate issued under the act of 1882 as amended by the act of 1884, granting them permission to return. The validity of the act is assailed as being in effect an expulsion from the country of Chinese laborers, in violation of existing treaties between the United States and the government of China, and of rights vested in them under the laws of congress.

It will serve to present with greater clearness the nature and force of the objections to the act if a brief statement be made of the general character of the treaties between the two countries, and of the legislation of congress to carry them into execution. The first treaty between the United States and the empire of China was concluded on the 3d of July, 1844, and ratified in December of the following year. 8 St. 592. Previous to that time there had been an extensive commerce between the two nations, that to China being confined to a single port. It was not, however, attended by any serious disturbances between our people there and the Chinese. In August, 1842, as the result of a war between England and China, a treaty was concluded stipulating for peace and friendship between them, and, among other things, that British subjects, with their families and establishments, should be allowed to reside for the purpose of carrying on mercantile pursuits at the five principal ports of the empire. 6 Hert. Treaties, 221. Actuated by a desire to establish by treaty friendly relations between the United States and the Chinese empire, and to secure to our people the same commercial privileges which had been thus conceded to British subjects, congress placed at the disposal of the president the means to enable him to establish future commercial relations between the two countries, "on terms of national equal reciprocity." Act March, 1843, c. 90, (5 St. 624.) A mission was accordingly sent by him to China, at the head of which was placed Mr. Caleb Cushing, a gentleman of large experience in public affairs. He found the Chinese government ready to concede by treaty to the United States all that had been reluctantly yielded to England through compulsion. As the result of his negotiations, the treaty of 1844 was concluded. It stipulated, among other things, that there should be a "perfect, permanent, and universal peace, and a sincere and cordial amity," between the two nations; that the five principal ports of the empire should be opened to the citizens of the United States, who should be permitted to reside with their families and trade there, and to proceed with their vessels and merchandise to and from any foreign port and either of said five ports; and while peaceably attending to their affairs should receive the protection of the Chinese authorities. Senate Document No. 138, 28th Cong. 2d Sess. The treaty between England and China did not have the effect of securing permanent peace and friendship between those countries. British subjects in China were often subjected, not only to the violence of mobs, but to insults and outrages from local authorities of the country, which led to retaliatory measures for the punishment of the aggressors. To such an extent were these measures carried, and such resistance offered to them, that in 1856 the two countries were in open war. England then determined with the co-operation of France, between which countries there seemed to be perfect accord, to secure from the government of China, among other things, a recognition of the right of other powers to be represented there by accredited ministers, an extension of commercial intercourse with that country, and stipulations for religious freedom to all foreigners there, and for the suppression of piracy. England requested of the president the concurrence and active co-operation of the United States similar to that which France had accorded, and to authorize our naval and political authorities to act in concert with the allied forces. As this proposition involved a participation in existing hostilities, the request could not be acceded to, and the secretary of state in his communication to the English government explained that the war-making power of the United States was not vested in the president, but in congress, and that he had no authority, therefore, to order aggressive hostilities to be undertaken. But as the rights of citizens of the United States might be seriously affected by the results of existing hostilities, and commercial intercourse between the United States and China be disturbed, it was deemed advisable to send to China a minister plenipotentiary to represent our government, and watch our interests there. Accordingly, Mr. William B. Reed, of Philadelphia, was appointed such minister, and instructed, while abstaining from any direct interference, to aid by peaceful cooperation the objects the allied forces were seeking to accomplish. Senate Document No. 47, 35th Cong. 1st Sess. Through him a new treaty was negotiated with the Chinese government. It was concluded in June, 1858, and ratified in August of the following year. 12 St. 1023. It reiterated the pledges of peace and friendship between the two nations, renewed the promise of protection to all citizens of the United States in China peaceably attending to their affairs, and stipulated for security to Christians in the profession of their religion.

Neither the treaty of 1844 nor that of 1858 touched upon the migration and emigration of the citizens and subjects of the two nations, respectively, from one country to the other. But in 1868 a great change in the relations of the two nations was made in that respect. In that year a mission from China, composed of distinguished functionaries of that empire, came to the United States with the professed object of establishing closer relations between the two countries and their peoples. At its head was placed Mr. Anson Burlingame, an eminent citizen of the United States, who had at one time represented this country as commissioner to China. He resigned his office under our government to accept the position tendered to him by the Chinese government. The mission was hailed in the United States as the harbinger of a new era in the history of China,—as the opening up to free intercourse with other nations and peoples a country that for ages had been isolated and closed against foreigners, who were allowed to have intercourse and to trade with the Chinese only at a few designated places; and the belief was general, and confidently expressed, that great benefits would follow to the world generally, and especially to the United States. On its arrival in Washington, additional articles to the treaty of 1858 were agreed upon, which gave expression to the general desire that the two nations and their peoples should be drawn closer together. The new articles, eight in number, were agreed to on the 28th of July, 1868, and ratifications of them were exchanged at Peking in November of the following year. 16 St. 739. Of these articles, the fifth, sixth, and seventh are as follows: "Art. 5. The United States of America and the emperor of China cordially recognize the inherent and inalienable right of man to change his home and allegiance, and also the mutual advantage of the free migration and emigration of their citizens and subjects respectively from the one country to the other for purposes of curiosity, of trade, or as permanent residents. The high contracting parties, therefore, join in reprobating any other than an entirely voluntary emigration for these purposes. They consequently agree to pass laws making it a penal offense for a citizen of the United States or Chinese subjects to take Chinese subjects either to the United States or to any other foreign country, or for a Chinese subject or citizen of the United States to take citizens of the United States to China or to any other foreign country, without their free and voluntary consent, respectively. Art. 6. Citizens of the United States visiting or residing in China shall enjoy the same privileges, immunities, or exemptions in respect to travel or residence as may there be enjoyed by the citizens or subjects of the most favored nation; and, reciprocally, Chinese subjects visiting or residing in the United shall enjoy the same privileges, immunities, and exemptions in respect to travel or residence as may there be enjoyed by the citizens or subjects of the most favored nation. But nothing herein contained shall be held to confer naturalization upon citizens of the United States in China, nor upon the subjects of China in the United States. Art. 7 Citizens of the United States shall enjoy all the privileges of the public educational institutions under the control of the government of China, and, reciprocally, Chinese subjects shall enjoy all the privileges of the public educational institutions under the control of the government of the United States, which are enjoyed in the respective countries by the citizens or subjects of the most favored nation. The citizens of the United States may freely establish and maintain schools within the empire of China at those places where foreigners are by treaty permitted to reside; and, reciprocally, Chinese subjects may enjoy the same privileges and immunities in the United States."

But notwithstanding these strong expressions of friendship and good will, and the desire they evince for free intercourse, events were transpiring on the Pacific coast which soon dissipated the anticipations indulged as to the benefits to follow the immigration of Chinese to this country. The previous treaties of 1844 and 1858 were confined principally to mutual declarations of peace and friendship, and to stipulations for commercial intercourse at certain ports in China, and for protection to our citizens while peaceably attending to their affairs. It was not until the additional articles of 1868 were adopted that any public declaration was made by the two nations that there were advantages in the free migration and emigration of their citizens and subjects, respectively, from one country to the other, and stipulations given that each should enjoy in the country of the other, with respect to travel or residence, the "privileges, immunities, and exemptions" enjoyed by citizens or subjects of the most favored nation. Whatever modifications have since been made to these general provisions have been caused by a well-founded apprehension—from the experience of years—that a limitation to the immigration of certain classes from China was essential to the peace of the community on the Pacific coast, and possibly to the preservation of our civilization there....

The discovery of gold in California in 1848, as is well known, was followed by a large immigration thither from all parts of the world, attracted not only by the hope of gain from the mines, but from the great prices paid for all kinds of labor. The news of the discovery penetrated China, and laborers came from there in great numbers, a few with their own means, but by far the greater number under contract with employers, for whose benefit they worked. These laborers readily secured employment, and, as domestic servants, and in various kinds of outdoor work, proved to be exceedingly useful. For some years little opposition was made to them, except when they sought to work in the mines, but, as their numbers increased, they began to engage in various mechanical pursuits and trades, and thus came in competition with our artisans and mechanics, as well as our laborers in the field. The competition steadily increased as the laborers came in crowds on each steamer that arrived from China, or Hong Kong, an adjacent English port. They were generally industrious and frugal. Not being accompanied by families, except in rare instances, their expenses were small; and they were content with the simplest fare, such as would not suffice for our laborers and artisans. The competition between them and our people was for this reason altogether in their favor, and the consequent irritation, proportionately deep and bitter, was followed, in many cases, by open conflicts, to the great disturbance of the public peace. The differences of race added greatly to the difficulties of the situation. Notwithstanding the favorable provisions of the new articles of the treaty of 1868, by which all the privileges, immunities, and exemptions were extended to subjects of China in the United States which were accorded to citizens or subjects of the most favored nation, they remained strangers in the land, residing apart by themselves, and adhering to the customs and usages of their own country. It seemed impossible for them to assimilate with our people, or to make any change in their habits or modes of living. As they grew in numbers each year the people of the coast saw, or believed they saw, in the facility of immigration, and in the crowded millions of China, where population presses upon the means of subsistence, great danger that at no distant day that portion of our country would be overrun by them, unless prompt action was taken to restrict their immigration. The people there accordingly petitioned earnestly for protective legislation.

In December, 1878, the convention which framed the present constitution of California, being in session, took this subject up, and memorialized congress upon it, setting forth, in substance, that the presence of Chinese laborers had a baneful effect upon the material interests of the state, and upon public morals; that their immigration was in numbers approaching the character of an Oriental invasion, and was a menace to our civilization; that the discontent from this cause was not confined to any political party, or to any class or nationality, but was well nigh universal; that they retained the habits and customs of their own country, and in fact constituted a Chinese settlement within the state, without any interest in our country or its institutions; and praying congress to take measures to prevent their further immigration. This memorial was presented to congress in February, 1879. So urgent and constant were the prayers for relief against existing and anticipated evils, both from the public authorities of the Pacific coast and from private individuals, that congress was impelled to act on the subject. Many persons, however, both in and out of congress, were of opinion that, so long as the treaty remained unmodified, legislation restricting immigration would be a breach of faith with China. A statute was accordingly passed appropriating money to send commissioners to China to act with our minister there in negotiating and concluding by treaty a settlement of such matters of interest between the two governments as might be confided to them. 21 St. p. 133, c. 88. Such commissioners were appointed, and as the result of their negotiations the supplementary treaty of November 17, 1880, was concluded and ratified in May of the following year. 22 St. 826. It declares in its first article that "Whenever, in the opinion of the government of the United States, the coming of Chinese laborers to the United States, or their residence therein, affects or threatens to affect the interests of that country, or to endanger the good order of the said country or of any locality within the territory thereof, the government of China agrees that the government of the United States may regulate, limit, or suspend such coming or residence, but may not absolutely prohibit it. The limitation or suspension shall be reasonable, and shall apply only to Chinese who may go to the United States as laborers, other classes not being included in the limitations. Legislation taken in regard to Chinese laborers will be of such a character only as is necessary to enforce the regulation, limitation, or suspension of immigration, and immigrants shall not be subject to personal maltreatment or abuse." In its second article it declares that "Chinese subjects, whether proceeding to the United States as teachers, students, merchants, or from curiosity, together with their body and household servants, and Chinese laborers who are now in the United States, shall be allowed to go and come of their own free will and accord, and shall be accorded all the rights, privileges, immunities, and exemptions which are accorded to the citizens and subjects of the most favored nation."

The government of China thus agreed that, notwithstanding the stipulations of former treaties, the United States might regulate, limit, or suspend the coming of

Chinese laborers, or their residence therein, without absolutely forbidding it, whenever in their opinion the interests of the country, or of any part of it, might require such action. Legislation for such regulation, limitation, or suspension was intrusted to the discretion of our government, with the condition that it should only be such as might be necessary for that purpose, and that the immigrants should not be maltreated or abused. On the 6th of May, 1882, an act of congress was approved, to carry this supplementary treaty into effect. 22 St. 58, c. 126. It is entitled "An act to execute certain treaty stipulations relating to Chinese." Its first section declares that after 90 days from the passage of the act, and for the period of 10 years from its date, the coming of Chinese laborers to the United States is suspended, and that it shall be unlawful for any such laborer to come, or, having come, to remain within the United States. The second makes it a misdemeanor, punishable by fine, to which imprisonment may be added, for the master of any vessel knowingly to bring within the United States from a foreign country, and land, any such Chinese laborer. The third provides that those two sections shall not apply to Chinese laborers who were in the United States November 17, 1880, or who shall come within 90 days after the passage of the act. The fourth declares that, for the purpose of identifying the laborers who were here on the 17th of November, 1880, or who should come within the 90 days mentioned, and to furnish them with "the proper evidence" of their right to go from and come to the United States, the "collector of customs of the district from which any such Chinese laborer shall depart from the United States shall, in person or by deputy, go on board each vessel having on board any such Chinese laborer and cleared or about to sail from his district for a foreign port, and on such vessel make a list of all such Chinese laborers, which shall be entered in registry books to be kept for that purpose, in which shall be stated the name, age, occupation, last place of residence, physical marks or peculiarities, and all facts necessary for the identification of each of such Chinese laborers, which books shall be safely kept in the custom-house;" and each laborer thus departing shall be entitled to receive, from the collector or his deputy, a certificate containing such particulars, corresponding with the registry, as may serve to identify him. "The certificate herein provided for," says the section, "shall entitle the Chinese laborer to whom the same is issued to return to and reenter the United States upon producing and delivering the same to the collector of customs of the district at which such Chinese laborer shall seek to re-enter."

* * *

The validity of this act, as already mentioned, is assailed, as being in effect an expulsion from the country of Chinese laborers, in violation of existing treaties between the United States and the government of China, and of rights vested in them under the laws of congress. The objection that the act is in conflict with the treaties was earnestly pressed in the court below, and the answer to it constitutes the principal part of its opinion. 36 Fed. Rep. 431. Here the objection made is that the act of 1888 impairs a right vested under the treaty of 1880, as a law of the United States, and the statutes of 1882 and of 1884 passed in execution of it. It must be conceded that the act of 1888 is in contravention of express stipulations of the treaty of 1868, and of the supplemental treaty of 1880, but it is not on that account invalid, or to be restricted in its enforcement. The treaties were of no greater legal obligation than the act of congress. By the constitution, laws made in pursuance thereof, and treaties made under the authority of the United States, are both declared to be the supreme law of the land, and no paramount authority is given to one over the other. A treaty, it is true, is in its nature a contract between nations, and is often merely promissory in its character, requiring legislation to carry its stipulations into effect. Such legislation will be open to future repeal or amendment. If the treaty operates by its own force, and relates to a subject within the power of congress, it can be deemed in that particular only the equivalent of a legislative act, to be repealed or modified at the pleasure of congress. In either case the last expression of the sovereign will must control.

The effect of legislation upon conflicting treaty stipulations was elaborately considered in the *Head-Money Cases*, and it was there adjudged "that, so far as a treaty made by the United States with any foreign nation can become the subject of judicial cognizance in the courts of this country, it is subject to such acts as congress may pass for its enforcement, modification, or repeal." 112 U. S. 580, 599, 5 Sup. Ct. Rep. 247. This doctrine was affirmed and followed in *Whitney v. Robertson*, 124 U. S. 190, 195, 8 Sup. Ct. Rep. 456. It will not be presumed that the legislative department of the government will lightly pass laws which are in conflict with the treaties of the country; but that circumstances may arise which would not only justify the government in disregarding their stipulations, but demand in the interests of the country that it should do so, there can be no question....

* * *

... This court is not a censor of the morals of other departments of the government; it is not invested with any authority to pass judgment upon the motives of their conduct. When once it is established that congress possesses the power to pass an act, our province ends with its construction and its application to cases as they are presented for determination. Congress has the power under the constitution to declare war, and in two instances where the power has been exercised—in the war of 1812 against Great Britain, and in 1846 against Mexico—the propriety and wisdom and justice of its action were vehemently assailed by some of the ablest and best men in the country, but no one doubted the legality of the proceeding, and any imputation by this or any other court of the United States upon the motives of the members of congress who in either case voted for the declaration, would have been justly the cause of animadversion. We do not mean to intimate that the moral aspects of legislative acts may not be proper subjects of consideration. Undoubtedly they may be, at proper times and places, before the public, in the halls of congress, and in all the modes by which the public mind can be influenced. Public opinion thus enlightened, brought to bear upon legislation, will do more than all other causes to prevent abuses; but the province of the courts is to pass upon the validity of laws, not to make them, and, when their validity is established, to declare their meaning and apply their provisions. All else lies beyond their domain.

* * *

While under our constitution and form of government the great mass of local matters is controlled by local authorities, the United States, in their relation to foreign countries and their subjects or citizens, are one nation, invested with powers which belong to independent nations, the exercise of which can be invoked for the maintenance of its absolute independence and security throughout its entire territory. The powers to declare war, make treaties, suppress insurrection, repel invasion, regulate foreign commerce, secure republican governments to the states, and admit subjects of other nations to citizenship, are all sovereign powers, restricted in their exercise only by the constitution itself and considerations of public policy and justice which control, more or less, the conduct of all civilized nations.... The people have declared that in the exercise of all powers given for these objects it is supreme. It can, then, in effecting these objects, legitimately control all individuals or governments within the American territory. The constitution and laws of a state, so far as they are repugnant to the constitution and laws of the United States, are absolutely void. These states are constituent parts of the United States. They are members of one great empire,—for some purposes sovereign, for some purposes subordinate." The same view is expressed in a different form by Mr. Justice Bradley, in *Knox v. Lee*, 12 Wall. 457, 555, where he observes that "the United States is not only a government, but it is a national government, and the only government in this country that has the character of nationality. It is invested with power over all the foreign relations of the country, war, peace, and negotiations and intercourse with other nations; all of which are forbidden to the state governments. It has jurisdiction over all those general subjects of legislation and sovereignty which affect the interests of the whole people equally and alike, and which require uniformity of regulations and laws, such as the coinage, weights, and measures, bankruptcies, the postal system, patent and copyright laws, the public lands, and interstate commerce; all which subjects are expressly or impliedly prohibited to the state governments. It has power to suppress insurrections, as well as to repel invasions, and to organize, arm, discipline, and call into service the militia of the whole country. The president is charged with the duty and invested with the power to take care that the laws be faithfully executed. The judiciary has jurisdiction to decide controversies between the states, and between their respective citizens, as well as questions of national concern; and the government is clothed with power to guaranty to every state a republican government, and to protect each of them against invasion and domestic violence."

The control of local matters being left to local authorities, and national matters being intrusted to the government of the Union, the problem of free institutions existing over a widely extended country, having different climates and varied interests, has been happily solved. For local interests the several states of the Union exist, but for national purposes, embracing our relations with foreign nations, we are but one people, one nation, one power. To preserve its independence, and give security against foreign aggression and encroachment, is the highest duty of every nation, and to attain these ends nearly all other considerations are to be subordinated. It matters not in what form such aggression and encroachment come, whether from the foreign nation acting in its national character, or from vast hordes of its people crowding in upon us. The government, possessing the powers which are to be exercised for protection and security, is clothed with authority to determine the occasion on which the powers shall be called forth; and its determinations, so far as the subjects affected are concerned, are necessarily conclusive upon all its departments and officers. If, therefore, the government of the United States, through its legislative department, considers the presence of foreigners of a different race in this country, who will not assimilate with us, to be dangerous to its peace and security, their exclusion is not to be stayed because at the time there are no actual hostilities with the nation of which the foreigners are subjects. The existence of war would render the necessity of the proceeding only more obvious and pressing....

The power of the government to exclude foreigners from the country whenever, in its judgment, the public interests require such exclusion, has been asserted in repeated instances, and never denied by the executive or legislative departments. In a communication made in December, 1852, to Mr. A. Dudley Mann, at one time a special agent of the department of state in Europe, Mr. Everett, then secretary of state under President Fillmore, writes: "This government could never give up the right of excluding foreigners whose presence it might deem a source of danger to the United States." "Nor will this government consider such exclusion of American citizens from Russia necessarily a matter of diplomatic complaint to that country." In a dispatch to Mr. Fay, our minister to Switzerland, in March, 1856, Mr. Marcy, secretary of state under President Pierce, writes: "Every society possesses the undoubted right to determine who shall compose its members, and it is exercised by all nations, both in peace and war." "It may always be questionable whether a resort to this power is warranted by the circumstances, or what department of the government is empowered to exert it; but there can be no doubt that it is possessed by all nations, and that each may decide for itself when the occasion arises demanding its exercise." In a communication in September, 1869, to Mr. Washburne, our minister to France, Mr. Fish, secretary of state under President Grant, uses this language: "The control of the people within its limits, and the right to expel from its territory persons who are dangerous to the peace of the state, are too clearly within the essential attributes of sovereignty to be seriously contested. Strangers visiting or sojourning in a foreign country voluntarily submit themselves to its laws and customs, and the municipal laws of France, authorizing the expulsion of strangers, are not of such recent date, nor has the exercise of the power by the government of France been so infrequent, that sojourners within her territory can claim surprise when the power is put in force." In a communication to Mr. Foster, our minister to Mexico, in July, 1879, Mr. Evarts, secretary of state under President Hayes, referring to the power vested in the constitution of Mexico to expel objectionable foreigners, says: "The admission that, as that constitution now stands and is interpreted, foreigners who render themselves harmful or objectionable to the general government must expect to be liable to the exercise of the power adverted to, even in time of peace, remains, and no good reason is seen for departing from that conclusion now. But, while there may be no expedient basis on which to found objection, on principle and in advance of a special case thereunder, to the constitutional right thus asserted by Mexico, yet the manner of carrying out such asserted right may be highly objectionable. You would be fully justified in making earnest remonstrances should a citizen of the United States be expelled from Mexican territory without just steps to assure the grounds of such expulsion, and in bringing the fact to the immediate knowledge of the department." ... As to criminals, the power of exclusion has always been exercised, even in the absence of any statute on the subject. In a dispatch to Mr. Cramer, our minister to Switzerland, in December, 1881, Mr. Blaine, secretary of state under President Arthur, writes: "While, under the constitution and the laws, this country is open to the honest and the industrious immigrant, it has no room outside of its prisons or almshouses for depraved and incorrigible criminals or hopelessly dependent paupers who may have become a pest or burden, or both, to their own country." Whart. International Dig., *supra.*

The power of exclusion of foreigners being an incident of sovereignty belonging to the government of the United States as a part of those sovereign powers delegated by the constitution, the right to its exercise at any time when, in the judgment of the government, the interests of the country require it, cannot be granted away or restrained on behalf of any one. The powers of government are delegated in trust to the United States, and are incapable of transfer to any other parties. They cannot be abandoned or surrendered. Nor can their exercise be hampered, when needed for the public good, by any considerations of private interest. The exercise of these public trusts is not the subject of barter or contract. Whatever license, therefore, Chinese laborers may have obtained, previous to the act of October 1, 1888, to return to the United States after their departure, is held at the will of the government, revocable at any time, at its pleasure. Whether a proper consideration by our government of its previous laws, or a proper respect for the nation whose subjects are affected by its action, ought to have qualified its inhibition, and made it applicable only to persons departing from the country after the passage of the act, are not questions for judicial determination. If there be any just ground of complaint on the part of China, it must be made to the political department of our government, which is alone competent to act upon the subject. The rights and interests created by a treaty, which have become so vested that its expiration or abrogation will not destroy or impair them, are such as are connected with and lie in property capable of sale and transfer, or other disposition, not such as are personal and untransferable in their character. Thus, in the *Head-Money Cases*, the court speaks of certain rights being in some instances conferred upon the citizens or subjects of one nation residing in the territorial limits of the other, which are "capable of enforcement as between private parties in the courts of the country." "An illustration of this character," it adds, "is found in treaties which regulate the mutual rights of citizens and subjects of the contracting nations in regard to rights of property by descent or inheritance, when the individuals concerned are aliens." 112 U. S. 580, 598, 5 Sup. Ct. Rep. 247. The passage cited by counsel from the language of Mr. Justice Washington in *Society v. New Haven*, 8 Wheat. 464, 493, also illustrates this doctrine. There the learned justice observes that, "if real estate be purchased or secured under a treaty, it would be most mischievous to admit that the extinguishment of the treaty extinguished the right to such estate. In truth, it no more affects such rights than the repeal of a municipal law affects rights acquired under it." Of this doctrine there can be no question in this court; but far different is this case, where a continued suspension of the exercise of a governmental power is insisted upon as a right, because, by the favor and consent of the government, it has not heretofore been exerted with respect to the appellant or to the class to which he belongs. Between property rights not affected by the termination or abrogation of a treaty, and expectations of benefits from the continuance of existing legislation, there is as wide a difference as between realization and hopes.

During the argument reference was made by counsel to the alien law of June 25, 1798, and to opinions expressed at the time by men of great ability and learning against its constitutionality. 1 St. 570, c. 58. We do not attach importance to those opinions in their bearing upon this case. The act vested in the president power to order all such aliens as he should judge dangerous to the peace and safety of the United States, or should have reasonable grounds to suspect were concerned in any treasonable or secret machination against the government, to depart out of the territory of the United States within such time as should be expressed in his order. There were other provisions also distinguishing it from the act under consideration. The act was passed during a period of great political excitement, and it was attacked and defended with great zeal and ability. It is enough, however, to say that it is entirely different from the act before us, and the validity of its provisions was never brought to the test of judicial decision in the courts of the United States. Order affirmed.

Notes

1. One issue which arose in *The Chinese Exclusion Case* was the extent to which the Chinese Exclusion Act affected an earlier treaty which existed between the United States and China at the time. The Court noted a now well-established principle when it stated:

> It must be conceded that the act of 1888 is in contravention of express stipulations of the treaty of 1868, and of the supplemental treaty of 1880, but it is not on that account invalid, or to be restricted in its enforcement. The treaties were of no greater legal obligation than the act of congress. By the constitution, laws made in pursuance thereof, and treaties made under the authority of the United States, are both declared to be the supreme law of the land, and no paramount authority is given to one over the other. A treaty, it is true, is in its nature a contract between nations, and is often merely promissory in its character, requiring legislation to carry its stipulations into effect. Such legislation will be open to future repeal or amendment. If the treaty operates by its own force, and relates to a subject within the power of congress, it can be deemed in that particular only the equivalent of a legislative act, to be repealed or modified at the pleasure of congress. In either case the last expression of the sovereign will control.

For additional clarification on this point, *see* Restatement (Third) of the Foreign Relations Law of the United States § 115 (2009); *Head-Money Cases*, 112 U.S. 580, 599 (1884); *Whitney v. Robertson*, 124 U.S. 190 (1888).

2. It cannot be presumed that Congress will lightly pass laws which are in conflict with treaties; thus, the courts will strain interpretation of a statute to avoid overturning a treaty unless there is a clear legislative directive otherwise.[94]

3. The power to determine who may be admitted is broad and extensive but it is a power which rests in the Congress and is viewed as inherent in the very notion of national sovereignty. *Nishimura Ekiu v. U.S.*, 142 U.S 651, 658 (1892). The Constitution has been interpreted as separately conferring power to regulate immigration through the Commerce and War Powers Clauses—Art. I, § 8, clause 3 (Commerce Clause),[95] Art. I, § 9, clause 1 (War Powers).[96] Courts have also recognized the power as being an incident of the foreign policy powers inherent in all nations.[97]

Shaughnessy, Dist. Dir. of Immigration and Naturalization v. United States ex rel. Mezei

345 U.S. 206 (1953)

Mr. Justice Clark delivered the opinion of the Court.

This case concerns an alien immigrant permanently excluded from the United States on security grounds but stranded in his temporary haven on Ellis Island because other countries will not take him back. The issue is whether the Attorney General's continued exclusion of respondent without a hearing amounts to an unlawful detention, so that courts may admit him temporarily to the United States on bond until arrangements are made for his departure abroad. After a hearing on respondent's petition for a writ of habeas corpus, the District Court so held and authorized his temporary admission on $5,000 bond. The Court of Appeals affirmed that action, but directed reconsideration of the terms of the parole. Accordingly, the District Court entered a modified order reducing bond to $3,000 and permitting respondent to travel and reside in Buffalo, New York. Bond was posted and respondent released. Because of resultant serious problems in the enforcement of the immigration laws, we granted certiorari. 344 U.S. 809.

Respondent's present dilemma springs from these circumstances: Though, as the District Court observed, "[t]here is a certain vagueness about [his] history", respondent

---

94. *See Chae Chan Ping v. United States*, 130 U.S. 581, 600 (1889) ("It will not be presumed that the legislative department of the government will lightly pass laws which are in conflict with the treaties of the country."); *Murray v. Schooner Charming Betsy*, 6 U.S. 64, 118 (1804) ("[A]n act of Congress ought never to be construed to violate the law of nations if any other possible construction remains.").

95. *See Passenger Cases*, 48 U.S. 283 (1849); *Head Money Cases*, 112 U.S. 580 (1884).

96. While the War Power is conferred on Congress which in turn through statute authorizes the removal and arrest of "enemy aliens" at 50 U.S.C. § 21, the Court has held that it does not confer the power to strip a citizen of their citizenship. *Trop v. Dulles*, 356 U.S. 86, 91–92 (1958).

97. *Arizona v. U.S.*, 567 U.S. 387, 397, 423 (2012).

seemingly was born in Gibraltar of Hungarian or Rumanian parents and lived in the United States from 1923 to 1948. In May of that year he sailed for Europe, apparently to visit his dying mother in Rumania. Denied entry there, he remained in Hungary for some 19 months, due to "difficulty in securing an exit permit." Finally, armed with a quota immigration visa issued by the American Consul in Budapest, he proceeded to France and boarded the Ile de France in Le Havre bound for New York. Upon arrival on February 9, 1950, he was temporarily excluded from the United States by an immigration inspector acting pursuant to the Passport Act as amended and regulations thereunder. Pending disposition of his case he was received at Ellis Island. After reviewing the evidence, the Attorney General on May 10, 1950, ordered the temporary exclusion to be made permanent without a hearing before a board of special inquiry, on the "basis of information of a confidential nature, the disclosure of which would be prejudicial to the public interest." That determination rested on a finding that respondent's entry would be prejudicial to the public interest for security reasons. But thus far all attempts to effect respondent's departure have failed: Twice he shipped out to return whence he came; France and Great Britain refused him permission to land. The State Department has unsuccessfully negotiated with Hungary for his readmission. Respondent personally applied for entry to about a dozen Latin American countries but all turned him down. So in June 1951 respondent advised the Immigration and Naturalization Service that he would exert no further efforts to depart. In short, respondent sat on Ellis Island because this country shut him out and others were unwilling to take him in.

Asserting unlawful confinement on Ellis Island, he sought relief through a series of habeas corpus proceedings. After four unsuccessful efforts on respondent's part, the United States District Court for the Southern District of New York on November 9, 1951, sustained the writ. The District Judge, vexed by the problem of "an alien who has no place to go", did not question the validity of the exclusion order but deemed further "detention" after 21 months excessive and justifiable only by affirmative proof of respondent's danger to the public safety. When the Government declined to divulge such evidence, even in camera, the District Court directed respondent's conditional parole on bond. By a divided vote, the Court of Appeals affirmed. Postulating that the power to hold could never be broader than the power to remove or shut out and that to "continue an alien's confinement beyond that moment when deportation becomes patently impossible is to deprive him of his liberty", the court found respondent's "confinement" no longer justifiable as a means of removal elsewhere, thus not authorized by statute, and in violation of due process. Judge Learned Hand, dissenting, took a different view: The Attorney General's order was one of "exclusion" and not "deportation"; respondent's transfer from ship to shore on Ellis Island conferred no additional rights; in fact, no alien so situated "can force us to admit him at all."

Courts have long recognized the power to expel or exclude aliens as a fundamental sovereign attribute exercised by the Government's political departments largely immune from judicial control. The *Chinese Exclusion Case* (*Chae Chan Ping v. United States*), 1889, 130 U.S. 581; *Fong Yue Ting v. United States*, 1893, 149 U.S. 698; 905;

United States ex rel. Knauff v. Shaughnessy, 1950, 338 U.S. 537; *Harisiades v. Shaughnessy*, 1952, 342 U.S. 580. In the exercise of these powers, Congress expressly authorized the President to impose additional restrictions on aliens entering or leaving the United States during periods of international tension and strife. That authorization, originally enacted in the Passport Act of 1918, continues in effect during the present emergency. Under it, the Attorney General, acting for the President, may shut out aliens whose "entry would be prejudicial to the interest of the United States". And he may exclude without a hearing when the exclusion is based on confidential information the disclosure of which may be prejudicial to the public interest. The Attorney General in this case proceeded in accord with these provisions; he made the necessary determinations and barred the alien from entering the United States.

It is true that aliens who have once passed through our gates, even illegally, may be expelled only after proceedings conforming to traditional standards of fairness encompassed in due process of law. The *Japanese Immigrant Case* (*Kaoru Yamataya v. Fisher*), 1903, 189 U.S. 86, 100–101; *Wong Yang Sung v. McGrath*, 1950, 339 U.S. 33, 49–50; *Kwong Hai Chew v. Colding*, 1953, 344 U.S. 590, 598. But an alien on the threshold of initial entry stands on a different footing: "Whatever the procedure authorized by Congress is, it is due process as far as an alien denied entry is concerned". *United States ex rel. Knauff v. Shaughnessy, supra*, 338 U.S. at page 544; *Nishimura Ekiu v. United States*, 1892, 142 U.S. 651, 660. And because the action of the executive officer under such authority is final and conclusive, the Attorney General cannot be compelled to disclose the evidence underlying his determinations in an exclusion case; "it is not within the province of any court, unless expressly authorized by law, to review the determination of the political branch of the Government". *United States ex rel. Knauff v. Shaughnessy, supra*, 338 U.S. at page 543; *Nishimura Ekiu v. United States, supra*, 142 U.S. at page 660. In a case such as this, courts cannot retry the determination of the Attorney General. *United States ex rel. Knauff v. Shaughnessy, supra*, 338 U.S. at page 546; *Ludecke v. Watkins*, 1948, 335 U.S. 160, 171–172.

Neither respondent's harborage on Ellis Island nor his prior residence here transforms this into something other than an exclusion proceeding. Concededly, his movements are restrained by authority of the United States, and he may by habeas corpus test the validity of his exclusion. But that is true whether he enjoys temporary refuge on land, *Nishimura Ekiu v. United States, supra*, or remains continuously aboard ship. *United States v. Jung Ah Lung*, 1888, 124 U.S. 621, 626; *Chin Yow v. United States*, 1908, 208 U.S. 8, 12. In sum, harborage at Ellis Island is not an entry into the *United States. Kaplan v. Tod*, 1925, 267 U.S. 228, 230; *United States v. Ju Toy*, 1905, 198 U.S. 253, 263; *Nishimura Ekiu v. United States, supra*, 142 U.S. at page 661. For purposes of the immigration laws, moreover, the legal incidents of an alien's entry remain unaltered whether he has been here once before or not. He is an entering alien just the same, and may be excluded if unqualified for admission under existing immigration laws. E.g., *Lem Moon Sing v. United States*, 1895, 158 U.S. 538, 547–548; *United States ex rel. Polymeris v. Trudell*, 1932, 284 U.S. 279.

To be sure, a lawful resident alien may not captiously be deprived of his constitutional rights to procedural due process. *Kwong Hai Chew v. Colding*, 1953, 344 U.S. 590, 601; Cf. *Delgadillo v. Carmichael*, 1947, 332 U.S. 388. Only the other day we held that under some circumstances temporary absence from our shores cannot constitutionally deprive a returning lawfully resident alien of his right to be heard. *Kwong Hai Chew v. Colding, supra*. Chew, an alien seaman admitted by an Act of Congress to permanent residence in the United States, signed articles of maritime employment as chief steward on a vessel of American registry with home port in New York City. Though cleared by the Coast Guard for his voyage, on his return from four months at sea he was "excluded" without a hearing on security grounds. On the facts of that case, including reference to § 307(d)(2) of the Nationality Act of 1940, 8 U.S.C.A. § 707(d)(2), we felt justified in "assimilating" his status for constitutional purposes to that of continuously present alien residents entitled to hearings at least before an executive or administrative tribunal. *Id.*, 344 U.S. at pages 596, 599–601. Accordingly, to escape constitutional conflict we held the administrative regulations authorizing exclusion without hearing in certain security cases inapplicable to aliens so protected by the Fifth Amendment. *Id.*, 344 U.S. at page 600.

But respondent's history here drastically differs from that disclosed in Chew's case. Unlike Chew who with full security clearance and documentation pursued his vocation for four months aboard an American ship, respondent, apparently without authorization or reentry papers, simply left the United States and remained behind the Iron Curtain for 19 months. Moreover, while § 307 of the 1940 Nationality Act regards maritime service such as Chew's to be continuous residence for naturalization purposes, that section deems protracted absence such as respondent's a clear break in an alien's continuous residence here. In such circumstances, we have no difficulty in holding respondent an entrant alien or "assimilated to (that) status" for constitutional purposes. *Id.*, 344 U.S. at page 599. That being so, the Attorney General may lawfully exclude respondent without a hearing as authorized by the emergency regulations promulgated pursuant to the Passport Act. Nor need he disclose the evidence upon which that determination rests.

* * *

... While the Government might keep entrants by sea aboard the vessel pending determination of their admissibility, resulting hardships to the alien and inconvenience to the carrier persuaded Congress to adopt a more generous course. By statute it authorized, in cases such as this, aliens' temporary removal from ship to shore. But such temporary harborage, an act of legislative grace, bestows no additional rights. Congress meticulously specified that such shelter ashore "shall not be considered a landing" nor relieve the vessel of the duty to transport back the alien if ultimately excluded. And this Court has long considered such temporary arrangements as not affecting an alien's status; he is treated as if stopped at the border.

Thus we do not think that respondent's continued exclusion deprives him of any statutory or constitutional right. It is true that resident aliens temporarily detained pending expeditious consummation of deportation proceedings may be released on bond by the Attorney General whose discretion is subject to judicial review. *Carlson v. Landon*, 1952, 342 U.S. 524. By that procedure aliens uprooted from our midst may rejoin the community until the Government effects their leave. An exclusion proceeding grounded on danger to the national security, however, presents different considerations; neither the rationale nor the statutory authority for such release exists. Ordinarily to admit an alien barred from entry on security grounds nullifies the very purpose of the exclusion proceeding; Congress in 1950 declined to include such authority in the statute. That exclusion by the United States plus other nations inhospitality results in present hardship cannot be ignored. But, the times being what they are, Congress may well have felt that other countries ought not shift the onus to us; that an alien in respondent's position is no more ours than theirs. Whatever our individual estimate of that policy and the fears on which it rests, respondent's right to enter the United States depends on the congressional will, and courts cannot substitute their judgment for the legislative mandate.

Notes

1. The provision under which Shaughnessy was excluded has since been modified and falls under the heading of "security grounds."[98] The law as presently written provides that:

> (A) Any alien who a consular officer or the Attorney General knows, or has reasonable ground to believe, seeks to enter the United States to engage solely, principally, or incidentally in—
>
> (i) any activity (I) to violate any law of the United States relating to espionage or sabotage or (II) to violate or evade any law prohibiting the export from the United States of goods, technology, or sensitive information,
>
> (ii) any other unlawful activity, or
>
> (iii) any activity a purpose of which is the opposition to, or the control or overthrow of, the Government of the United States by force, violence, or other unlawful means, is inadmissible.

2. The procedures for determining whether a person poses a risk to the national security are described in the statute at 8 U.S.C. § 1225(c), Sec. 235(c). This section provides for review of the determination by the Attorney General and, if necessary, the further determination of some issues by an immigration judge.[99] Compare the procedures used in cases involving national security with those for expedited removal, which are described at 8 U.S.C. § 1225(b), Sec. 235(b).

3. 8 U.S.C. § 1182(f) confers broad powers on the President to suspend "the entry of any aliens or of any class of aliens into the United States [whose admission] would

---

98. See 8 U.S.C. § 1182(a)(3), Sec. 212(a)(3).
99. See 8 U.S.C. §§ 1225(c)(2)(B) and (C), Sections 235(c)(2)(B) and (C).

be detrimental to the interests of the United States...." Historically, this power has only been used to suspend the admission of more narrowly proscribed groups.[100] Until its invocation in 2017, its broadest application was used to interdict boats on the high seas bringing Haitian asylum seekers in 1992.[101] In January, March and September of 2017, the President signed a series of Executive Orders which have become known as the "Travel Bans."[102] These Executive Orders were part of an effort to ban the admission of refugees and nationals from a number of predominantly Muslim countries in the region of the Middle East. Each version of the ban resulted in a lower federal court's imposition of a restraining order to all or significant parts of the ban, with a federal appellate court's modification of the order and then the government's appeal to the Supreme Court.[103] At this writing, the third version of the ban is on appeal, and the government is seeking certiorari before the Supreme Court.[104]

1. Parole of Persons into the United States

In *Shaughnessy v. Mezei*, the Court referred to a procedure called "parole" whereby the person was allowed to be removed from the vessel pending the ultimate outcome of his case. Although parole was not statutorily authorized until 1952, it has been used by the executive branch since perhaps 1875 upon the implementation of the first inadmissibility statutes.

---

100. *See, e.g.*, Exec. Order No. 13,664, Blocking Property of Certain Persons With Respect to South Sudan, 79 Fed. Reg. 19,283 (Apr. 7, 2014); Exec. Order No. 13,660, Blocking Property of Certain Persons Contributing to the Situation in Ukraine, 79 Fed. Reg. 13,493 (Mar. 10, 2014) (suspending the admission of certain persons undermining the democratic process in the Ukraine); Exec. Order No. 13,628, Authorizing the Implementation of Certain Sanctions Set Forth in the Iran Threat Reduction and Syria Human Rights Act of 2012 and Additional Sanctions With Respect to Iran, 77 Fed. Reg. 62,139 (Oct. 12, 2012) (suspending entry to certain human rights abusers or those engaging in free speech censorship in Iran); Proclamation No. 5377, Suspension of Entry as Nonimmigrants by Officers or Employees of the Government of Cuba or the Communist Party of Cuba, 50 Fed. Reg. 41,329 (Oct. 10, 1985).

101. Exec. Order No. 12,807, Interdiction of Illegal Aliens, 57 Fed. Reg. 23,133 (May 24, 1992). The challenge to the policy is discussed more broadly in *Sale v. Haitian Ctrs. Council*, 509 U.S. 155 (1993), in Chapter 5.

102. Exec. Order No. 13,769, Protecting the Nation from Foreign Terrorist Entry into the United States, 82 Fed. Reg. 8977 (Jan. 27, 2017); Executive Order No.13,780, Protecting the Nation from Foreign Terrorist Entry into the United States, 82 Fed. Reg. 13,209 (Mar. 6, 2017); Proclamation No. 9645, Enhancing Vetting Capabilities and Processes for Detecting Attempted Entry Into the United States by Terrorists or Other Public-Safety Threats, 82 Fed. Reg. 45161 (Sept. 24, 2017).

103. See *State of Hawaii v. Trump*, 245 F. Supp. 3d 1227 (D. Hawaii 2017), *aff'd in part, vacated in part, remanded*, 859 F.3d 741 (9th Cir. 2017); *Int'l Refugee Assistance v. Trump*, 857 F.3d 554 (4th Cir. 2017), stayed and briefing schedule set sub nom. *Trump v. Int'l Refugee Assistance Project*, 137 S. Ct. 2080 (2017).

104. David S. Rubenstein & Pratheepan Gulasekaram, *Immigration Exceptionalism*, 111 Nw. U. L. Rev. 583 (2017).

As was seen in *Mezei*, whether a person is considered within or without the United States is of paramount significance. Although the parole power has not undergone serious scrutiny by the courts, its use by the executive has raised many issues as to the treatment of an applicant who is seeking admission at the border. The effective parole statute is provided below and should be helpful prior to reviewing the following case.

1. The statutory authority for parole is contained in 8 U.S.C. § 1182(d)(5), Sec. 212(d)(5) and provides that:

> (A) The Attorney General may, except as provided in subparagraph (B) or in [8 U.S.C. § 1184(f)], in his discretion parole into the United States temporarily under such conditions as he may prescribe for emergent reasons or for reasons deemed strictly in the public interest any alien applying for admission to the United States, but such parole of such alien shall not be regarded as an admission of the alien and when the purposes of such parole shall, in the opinion of the Attorney General, have been served the alien shall forthwith return or be returned to the custody from which he was paroled and thereafter his case shall continue to be dealt with in the same manner as that of any other applicant for admission to the United States.
>
> (B) The Attorney General may not parole into the United States an alien who is a refugee unless the Attorney General determines that compelling reasons in the public interest with respect to that particular alien require that the alien be paroled into the United States rather than be admitted as a refugee under section 1157 of this title.

2. Whether and under what conditions parole may be granted is the subject of some debate. In *Paktorovics v. Murff*,[105] an appellate court held that due to the special circumstances under which Hungarian refugees were admitted as parolees, the court would continue limits on the method used by the government in its revocation of the benefit. Notwithstanding this decision, *Paktorovics* has been viewed narrowly.[106] While a formal hearing is not required for the revocation of parole, the regulations require that written notice be given.[107] Of what value is this revocation notice if the parolee does not have a right to be heard by USCIS?

3. A brief digression into some successful (or partially successful) challenges in parole cases may be helpful both in understanding parole and the importance of procedure in immigration cases. The agency's failure to follow its own regulations in the revocation of parole may amount to a violation of the rights conferred under the statute.[108] Similarly, an allegation that the agency's action amounted to rulemaking

---

105. 260 F.2d 610 (2d Cir. 1958).

106. *Ahrens v. Rojas*, 292 F.2d 406 (5th Cir. 1961); *Matter of Castellon*, 17 I. & N. Dec. 616 (BIA 1981).

107. *See* 8 C.F.R. § 212.5(d)(4).

108. *Moret v. Karn*, 746 F.2d 989 (3d Cir. 1984).

in violation of the Administrative Procedure Act may be reviewed.[109] Similarly, courts have reviewed parole decisions where there is an allegation of a violation of a person's rights under both the statute and the Constitution.[110]

4. As was noted earlier, one of the arguments that was successful in *Paktorovics* was that the Hungarian parolees had been invited to the United States. In the case of the members of the Mariel boatlift, a similar argument was made, and evidence was presented that President Carter had, in effect, invited the refugees to the United States. This argument was rejected by an appellate court in *Garcia-Mir v. Meese.*[111]

> The long-range implications of such a holding would be both profound and dangerous. It is a hallmark of our system of government that certain rights and liberties are enshrined in the social compact. These guarantees may be expanded or contracted through any of several constitutionally provided-for processes. But to give countenance to the notion that one of the political branches can simply wave a magic wand and "create" (and by implication extinguish) constitutional rights would be to undo completely the notion of limited government through separated, checked and balanced powers. This is a step we decline to take.
>
> * * *
>
> ... While in any event we decline to be bound by that holding, that case is inapposite because there is a critical distinction between the situation in Paktorovics and the instant case. While in both cases the President made public pronouncements to the effect that a certain ethnic group was welcome to come to America, in Paktorovics Congress [later] enacted legislation endorsing the extraordinary action of the President with respect to these Hungarian refugees.

In light of the cases noted above, is *Paktorovics* good law today?

D. Determining Admissibility for Detention or Removal

In 2001, the Supreme Court held in *Zadvydas v. Davis*[112] that the removal statute did not contemplate indefinite detention for persons who had been admitted or were found in the United States. [*Zadvydas* is discussed in Chapter 4]. After *Zadvydas*, the question remained as to whether indefinite detention would be permissible for persons

109. *Louis v. Nelson*, 544 F. Supp. 973 (S.D. Fla. 1982), *rev'd in part aff'd in part sub nom. Jean v. Nelson*, 711 F.2d 1455 (11th Cir. 1983), *aff'd Jean v. Nelson*, 472 U.S. 846 (1985).

110. *Nguyen Da Yen v. Kissinger*, 528 F.2d 1194 (9th Cir. 1975); *also see Gutierrez v. Ilchert*, 702 F. Supp. 787 (N.D. Cal. 1988).

111. 788 F.2d 1446 (11th Cir. 1986).

112. 533 U.S. 678 (2001).

who had not yet been admitted to the country. In 2005, the Court answered that question in *Clark v. Martinez*, which is excerpted below.

Neil Clark, Field Dir., Immigration and Custom Enforcement, et al. v. Sergio Suarez Martinez

543 U.S. 371 (2005)*

Justice O'Connor concurred and filed opinion.

Justice Thomas dissented and filed opinion, in which Chief Justice Rehnquist joined in part.

Justice SCALIA delivered the opinion of the Court.

An alien arriving in the United States must be inspected by an immigration official, 66 Stat. 198, as amended, 8 U.S.C. § 1225(a)(3), and, unless he is found "clearly and beyond a doubt entitled to be admitted," must generally undergo removal proceedings to determine admissibility, § 1225(b)(2)(A). Meanwhile the alien may be detained, subject to the Secretary's discretionary authority to parole him into the country. *See* 8 U.S.C. § 1182(d)(5); 8 CFR § 212.5 (2004). If, at the conclusion of removal proceedings, the alien is determined to be inadmissible and ordered removed, the law provides that the Secretary of Homeland Security "shall remove the alien from the United States within a period of 90 days," 8 U.S.C. § 1231(a)(1)(A). These cases concern the Secretary's authority to continue to detain an inadmissible alien subject to a removal order after the 90-day removal period has elapsed.

I.

Sergio Suarez Martinez (respondent in No. 03-878) and Daniel Benitez (petitioner in No. 03-7434) arrived in the United States from Cuba in June 1980 as part of the Mariel boatlift, see *Palma v. Verdeyen*, 676 F.2d 100, 101 (C.A.4 1982) (describing circumstances of Mariel boatlift), and were paroled into the country pursuant to the Attorney General's authority under 8 U.S.C. § 1182(d)(5).[1] *See* Pet. for Cert. in No. 03-878, p. 7; *Benitez v. Wallis*, 337 F.3d 1289, 1290 (C.A.11 2003). Until 1996, federal law permitted Cubans who were paroled into the United States to adjust their status to that of lawful permanent resident after one year. See Cuban Refugee Adjustment Act, 80 Stat. 1161, as amended, notes following 8 U.S.C. § 1255. Neither Martinez nor Benitez qualified for this adjustment, however, because, by the time they applied, both men had become inadmissible because of prior criminal convictions in the

---

* Some footnotes have been omitted.

1. The authorities described herein as having been exercised by the Attorney General and the Immigration and Naturalization Service (INS) now reside in the Secretary of Homeland Security (hereinafter Secretary) and divisions of his Department (Bureau of Immigration and Customs Enforcement and Bureau of Citizenship and Immigration Services). *See* Homeland Security Act of 2002, §§ 441(2), 442(a)(3), 451(b), 116 Stat. 2192, 6 U.S.C. §§ 251(2), 252(a)(3), 271(b) (2000 ed., Supp. II).

United States. When Martinez sought adjustment in 1991, he had been convicted of assault with a deadly weapon in Rhode Island and burglary in California, Pet. for Cert. in No. 03-878, at 7; when Benitez sought adjustment in 1985, he had been convicted of grand theft in Florida, 337 F.3d, at 1290. Both men were convicted of additional felonies after their adjustment applications were denied: Martinez of petty theft with a prior conviction (1996), assault with a deadly weapon (1998), and attempted oral copulation by force (1999), see Pet. for Cert. in No. 03-878, at 7–8; Benitez of two counts of armed robbery, armed burglary of a conveyance, armed burglary of a structure, aggravated battery, carrying a concealed firearm, unlawful possession of a firearm while engaged in a criminal offense, and unlawful possession, sale, or delivery of a firearm with an altered serial number (1993), see 337 F.3d, at 1290–1291.

The Attorney General revoked Martinez's parole in December 2000. Martinez was taken into custody by the INS, and removal proceedings were commenced against him. Pet. for Cert. in No. 03-878, at 8. An Immigration Judge found him inadmissible by reason of his prior convictions, § 1182(a)(2)(B), and lack of sufficient documentation, § 1182(a)(7)(A)(i)(I), and ordered him removed to Cuba. Martinez did not appeal. Pet. for Cert. in No. 03-878, at 8. The INS continued to detain him after expiration of the 90-day removal period, and he remained in custody until he was released pursuant to the District Court order that was affirmed by the Court of Appeals' decision on review here. *Id.*, at 9.

Benitez's parole was revoked in 1993 (shortly after he was imprisoned for his convictions of that year), and the INS immediately initiated removal proceedings against him. In December 1994, an Immigration Judge determined Benitez to be excludable and ordered him deported under §§ 1182(a)(2)(B) and 1182(a)(7)(A)(i)(I) (1994 ed. and Supp. V). 337 F.3d, at 1291. Benitez did not seek further review. At the completion of his state prison term, the INS took him into custody for removal, and he continued in custody after expiration of the 90-day removal period. Ibid. In September 2003, Benitez received notification that he was eligible for parole, contingent on his completion of a drug-abuse treatment program. Letter from Paul D. Clement, Acting Solicitor General, to William K. Suter, Clerk of Court, 1 (Nov. 3, 2004). Benitez completed the program while his case was pending before this Court, and shortly after completion was paroled for a period of one year. Ibid. On October 15, 2004, two days after argument in this Court, Benitez was released from custody to sponsoring family members.[3] *Id.*, at 2.

3. Despite Benitez's release on a 1-year parole, this case continues to present a live case or controversy. If Benitez is correct, as his suit contends, that the Government lacks the authority to continue to detain him, he would have to be released, and could not be taken back into custody unless he violated the conditions of release (in which case detention would be authorized by 8 U.S.C. § 1253), or his detention became necessary to effectuate his removal (in which case detention would once again be authorized by § 1231(a)(6)). His current release, however, is not only limited to one year, but subject to the Secretary's discretionary authority to terminate. See 8 CFR § 212.12(h) (2004) (preserving discretion to revoke parole). Thus, Benitez "continue[s] to have a personal stake in the

Both aliens filed a petition for a writ of habeas corpus under 28 U.S.C. § 2241 to challenge their detention beyond the 90-day removal period. In Martinez's case, the District Court for the District of Oregon accepted that removal was not reasonably foreseeable, and ordered the INS to release Martinez under conditions that the INS believed appropriate. *Martinez v. Smith*, No. CV 02-972-PA (Oct. 30, 2002), App. to Pet. for Cert. in No. 03-878, p. 2a. The Court of Appeals for the Ninth Circuit summarily affirmed, citing its decision in *Xi v. INS*, 298 F.3d 832 (2002). *Martinez v. Ashcroft*, No. 03-35053, 2003 WL 23892563 (Aug. 18, 2003), App. to Pet. for Cert. in No. 03-878, at 1A. In Benitez's case, the District Court for the Northern District of Florida also concluded that removal would not occur in the "foreseeable future," but nonetheless denied the petition. *Benitez v. Wallis*, Case No. 5:02cv19 MMP (July 11, 2002), pp. 2, 4, App. in No. 03-7434, pp. 45, 48. The Court of Appeals for the Eleventh Circuit affirmed, agreeing with the dissent in *Xi*. *Benitez v. Wallis*, 337 F.3d 1289 (2003). We granted certiorari in both cases. *Benitez v. Wallis*, 540 U.S. 1147 (2004); *Crawford v. Martinez*, 540 U.S. 1217 (2004).

II.

Title 8 U.S.C. § 1231(a)(6) provides, in relevant part, as follows:

> An alien ordered removed who is inadmissible under section 1182 of this title, removable under section 1227(a)(1)(C), 1227(a)(2), or 1227(a)(4) of this title or who has been determined by the [Secretary] to be a risk to the community or unlikely to comply with the order of removal, may be detained beyond the removal period and, if released, shall be subject to the terms of supervision in paragraph (3).

By its terms, this provision applies to three categories of aliens: (1) those ordered removed who are inadmissible under § 1182, (2) those ordered removed who are removable under § 1227(a)(1)(C), 1227(a)(2), or 1227(a)(4), and (3) those ordered removed whom the Secretary determines to be either a risk to the community or a flight risk. In *Zadvydas v. Davis*, 533 U.S. 678 (2001), the Court interpreted this provision to authorize the Attorney General (now the Secretary) to detain aliens in the second category only as long as "reasonably necessary" to remove them from the country. *Id.*, at 689, 699. The statute's use of "may," the Court said, "suggests discretion," but "not necessarily ... unlimited discretion. In that respect, the word 'may' is ambiguous." *Id.*, at 697. In light of that perceived ambiguity and the "serious constitutional threat" the Court believed to be posed by indefinite detention of aliens who had been admitted to the country, *id.*, at 699, the Court interpreted the statute to permit only detention that is related to the statute's "basic purpose [of] effectuating an alien's removal," *id.*, at 696–699. "[O]nce removal is no longer reasonably foreseeable, continued detention is no longer authorized." *Id.*, at 699. The Court further held that the presumptive period during which the detention of an alien is reasonably necessary to effectuate his removal is six months; after that, the alien is eligible for

---

outcome" of his petition. *Lewis v. Continental Bank Corp.*, 494 U.S. 472, 477–478 (1990) (internal quotation marks omitted).

conditional release if he can demonstrate that there is "no significant likelihood of removal in the reasonably foreseeable future." *Id.*, at 701.

The question presented by these cases, and the question that evoked contradictory answers from the Ninth and Eleventh Circuits, is whether this construction of § 1231(a)(6) that we applied to the second category of aliens covered by the statute applies as well to the first—that is, to the category of aliens "ordered removed who are inadmissible under [§] 1182." We think the answer must be yes. The operative language of § 1231(a)(6), "may be detained beyond the removal period," applies without differentiation to all three categories of aliens that are its subject. To give these same words a different meaning for each category would be to invent a statute rather than interpret one. As the Court in *Zadvydas* recognized, the statute can be construed "literally" to authorize indefinite detention, *id.*, at 689, or (as the Court ultimately held) it can be read to "suggest [less than] unlimited discretion" to detain, *id.*, at 697. It cannot, however, be interpreted to do both at the same time.

The dissent's belief that *Zadvydas* compels this result rests primarily on that case's statement that "[a]liens who have not yet gained initial admission to this country would present a very different question," 533 U.S., at 682. See *post*, at 729–730, 731 (opinion of Thomas, J.). This mistakes the reservation of a question with its answer. Neither the opinion of the Court nor the dissent in *Zadvydas* so much as hints that the Court adopted the novel interpretation of § 1231(a)(6) proposed by today's dissent. The opinion in that case considered whether § 1231(a)(6) permitted the Government to detain removable aliens indefinitely; relying on ambiguities in the statutory text and the canon that statutes should be interpreted to avoid constitutional doubts, the opinion held that it did not. Despite the dissent's repeated claims that § 1231(a)(6) could not be given a different reading for inadmissible aliens, see *Zadvydas, supra*, at 710, 716–717, the Court refused to decide that question—the question we answer today. It is indeed different from the question decided in *Zadvydas*, but because the statutory text provides for no distinction between admitted and nonadmitted aliens, we find that it results in the same answer.[4]

The dissent's contention that our reading of *Zadvydas* is "implausible," *post*, at 730, is hard to reconcile with the fact that it is the identical reading espoused by the *Zadvydas* dissenters, who included the author of today's dissent. Worse still, what the *Zadvydas* dissent did find "not ... plausible" was precisely the reading adopted by today's dissent:

> [T]he majority's logic might be that inadmissible and removable aliens can be treated differently. Yet it is not a plausible construction of § 1231(a)(6) to imply a time limit as to one class but not to another. The text does not admit of this

4. The dissent is quite wrong in saying, *post*, at 730, that the *Zadvydas* Court's belief that § 1231(a)(6) did not apply to all aliens is evidenced by its statement that it did not "consider terrorism or other special circumstances where special arrangements might be made for forms of preventive detention," 533 U.S., at 695. The Court's interpretation of § 1231(a)(6) did not affect the detention of alien terrorists for the simple reason that sustained detention of alien terrorists is a "special arrangement" authorized by a different statutory provision, 8 U.S.C. § 1537(b)(2)(C). See *Zadvydas*, 533 U.S., at 697.

> possibility. As a result, it is difficult to see why '[a]liens who have not yet gained initial admission to this country would present a very different question.'

Zadvydas, 533 U.S., at 710–711 (Kennedy, J., dissenting).

The *Zadvydas* dissent later concluded that the release of "Mariel Cubans and other illegal, inadmissible aliens ... would seem *a necessary consequence of the majority's construction of the statute*." *Id.*, at 717 (emphasis added). Tellingly, the *Zadvydas* majority did not negate either charge.

The Government, joined by the dissent, argues that the statutory purpose and the constitutional concerns that influenced our statutory construction in *Zadvydas* are not present for aliens, such as Martinez and Benitez, who have not been admitted to the United States. Be that as it may, it cannot justify giving the same detention provision a different meaning when such aliens are involved. It is not at all unusual to give a statute's ambiguous language a limiting construction called for by one of the statute's applications, even though other of the statute's applications, standing alone, would not support the same limitation. The lowest common denominator, as it were, must govern. See, e.g., *Leocal v. Ashcroft*, 543 U.S. ___, ___, 125 S.Ct. 377, 384, n. 8 (2004) (explaining that, if a statute has criminal applications, "the rule of lenity applies" to the Court's interpretation of the statute even in immigration cases "[b]ecause we must interpret the statute consistently, whether we encounter its application in a criminal or noncriminal context"); *United States v. Thompson/Center Arms Co.*, 504 U.S. 505, 517–518, and n. 10 (1992) (plurality opinion) (employing the rule of lenity to interpret "a tax statute ... in a civil setting" because the statute "has criminal applications"); id., at 519, (Scalia, J., concurring in judgment) (also invoking the rule of lenity). In other words, when deciding which of two plausible statutory constructions to adopt, a court must consider the necessary consequences of its choice. If one of them would raise a multitude of constitutional problems, the other should prevail—whether or not those constitutional problems pertain to the particular litigant before the Court.

The dissent takes issue with this maxim of statutory construction on the ground that it allows litigants to "attack statutes as constitutionally invalid based on constitutional doubts concerning other litigants or factual circumstances" and thereby to effect an "end run around black-letter constitutional doctrine governing facial and as-applied constitutional challenges." *Post*, at 733. This accusation misconceives—and fundamentally so—the role played by the canon of constitutional avoidance in statutory interpretation. The canon is not a method of adjudicating constitutional questions by other means. See, e.g., *NLRB v. Catholic Bishop of Chicago*, 440 U.S. 490, 502 (1979) (refusing to engage in extended analysis in the process of applying the avoidance canon "as we would were we considering the constitutional issue"); see also Vermeule, *Saving Constructions*, 85 Geo. L.J.1945, 1960–1961 (1997) (providing examples of cases where the Court construed a statute narrowly to avoid a constitutional question ultimately resolved in favor of the broader reading). Indeed, one of the canon's chief justifications is that it allows courts to avoid the decision of constitutional questions. It is a tool for choosing between competing plausible interpretations of a statutory text, resting on the reasonable presumption that Congress did not intend the alternative which raises serious constitutional doubts. See *Rust v. Sullivan*, 500 U.S. 173 (1991); *Edward J. DeBartolo Corp. v. Florida Gulf Coast Building & Constr. Trades Council*, 485 U.S. 568, 575 (1988). The canon is thus a means of giving effect to congressional intent, not of subverting it. And when a litigant invokes the canon of avoidance, he is not attempting to vindicate the constitutional rights of others, as the dissent believes; he seeks to vindicate his own statutory rights. We find little to recommend the novel interpretive approach advocated by the dissent, which would render every statute a chameleon, its meaning subject to change depending on the presence or absence of constitutional concerns in each individual case. Cf. *Harris v. United States*, 536 U.S. 545, 556 (2002) (rejecting "a dynamic view of statutory interpretation, under which the text might mean one thing when enacted yet another if the prevailing view of the Constitution later changed").

In support of its contention that we can give § 1231(a)(6) a different meaning when it is applied to nonadmitted aliens, the Government relies most prominently upon our decision in *Crowell v. Benson*, 285 U.S. 22 (1932). Brief for Petitioners in No. 03-878, p. 29; Brief for Respondent in No. 03-7434, p. 29. That case involved a statutory provision that gave the Deputy Commissioner of the United States Employees' Compensation Commission " 'full power and authority to hear and determine all questions in respect of' " claims under the Longshoremen's and Harbor Workers' Compensation Act. 285 U.S., at 62. The question presented was whether this provision precluded review of the Deputy Commissioner's determination that the claimant was an employee, and hence covered by the Act. The Court held that, although the statute could be read to bar judicial review altogether, it was also susceptible of a narrower reading that permitted judicial review of the fact of employment, which was an "essential condition precedent to the right to make the claim." *Ibid.* The Court adopted the latter construction in order to avoid serious constitutional questions that it believed would be raised by total preclusion of judicial review. *Ibid.* This holding does not produce a statute that bears two different meanings, depending on the presence or absence of a constitutional question. Always, and as applied to all claimants, it permits judicial review of the employment finding. What corresponds to *Crowell v. Benson*'s holding that the fact of employment is judicially reviewable is *Zadvydas*'s holding that detention cannot be continued once removal is no longer reasonably foreseeable—and like the one, the other applies in all cases.

The dissent, on the other hand, relies on our recent cases interpreting 28 U.S.C. § 1367(d). *Raygor v. Regents of Univ. of Minn.*, 534 U.S. 533 (2002), held that this provision does not include, in its tolling of limitations periods, claims against States that have not waived their immunity from suit in federal court, because the statutory language fails to make " 'unmistakably clear,' " as it must in provisions subjecting States to suit, that such States were covered. Id., at 543–546. A subsequent decision, *Jinks v. Richland County*, 538 U.S. 456 (2003), held that the tolling provision does apply to claims against political subdivisions of States, since the requirement of the unmistakably clear statement did not apply to those entities. *Id.*, at 466. This progression of decisions does not remotely establish that § 1367(d) has two different meanings, equivalent to the unlimited detention/limited detention meanings of

§ 1231(a)(6) urged upon us here. They hold that the single and unchanging disposition of § 1367(d) (the tolling of limitations periods) does not apply to claims against States that have not consented to be sued in federal court.

We also reject the Government's argument that, under *Zadvydas*, § 1231(a)(6) "authorizes detention until it approaches constitutional limits." Brief for Petitioners in No. 03-878, at 27–28; Brief for Respondent in No. 03-7434, at 27–28. The Government provides no citation to support that description of the case—and none exists. *Zadvydas* did not hold that the statute authorizes detention until it approaches constitutional limits; it held that, since interpreting the statute to authorize indefinite detention (one plausible reading) would approach constitutional limits, the statute should be read (in line with the other plausible reading) to authorize detention only for a period consistent with the purpose of effectuating removal. 533 U.S., at 697–699. If we were, as the Government seems to believe, free to "interpret" statutes as becoming inoperative when they "approach constitutional limits," we would be able to spare ourselves the necessity of ever finding a statute unconstitutional as applied. And the doctrine that statutes should be construed to contain substantive dispositions that do not raise constitutional difficulty would be a thing of the past; no need for such caution, since—whatever the substantive dispositions are—they become inoperative when constitutional limits are "approached." That is not the legal world we live in. The canon of constitutional avoidance comes into play only when, after the application of ordinary textual analysis, the statute is found to be susceptible of more than one construction; and the canon functions as a means of choosing between them. See, e.g., *Almendarez-Torres v. United States*, 523 U.S. 224, 237–238 (1998); *United States ex rel. Attorney General v. Delaware & Hudson Co.*, 213 U.S. 366, 408 (1909). In *Zadvydas*, it was the statute's text read in light of its purpose, not some implicit statutory command to avoid approaching constitutional limits, which produced the rule that the Secretary may detain aliens only for the period reasonably necessary to bring about their removal. See 533 U.S., at 697–699.

In passing in its briefs, but more intensively at oral argument, the Government sought to justify its continued detention of these aliens on the authority of § 1182(d)(5)(A).[7] Even assuming that an alien who is subject to a final order of removal is an "alien applying for admission" and therefore eligible for parole under this provision, we find nothing in this text that affirmatively authorizes detention,

---

7. Section 1182(d)(5)(A) reads as follows:

> The [Secretary] may ... in his discretion parole into the United States temporarily under such conditions as he may prescribe only on a case-by-case basis for urgent humanitarian reasons or significant public benefit any alien applying for admission to the United States, but such parole of such alien shall not be regarded as an admission of the alien and when the purposes of such parole shall, in the opinion of the [Secretary], have been served the alien shall forthwith return or be returned to the custody from which he was paroled and thereafter his case shall continue to be dealt with in the same manner as that of any other applicant for admission to the United States.

much less indefinite detention. To the contrary, it provides that, when parole is revoked, "the alien shall ... be returned to the custody from which he was paroled and thereafter his case shall continue to be dealt with in the same manner as that of any other applicant for admission." § 1182(d)(5)(A) (emphasis added). The manner in which the case of any other applicant would be "dealt with" beyond the 90-day removal period is prescribed by § 1231(a)(6), which we interpreted in *Zadvydas* and have interpreted above.

The Government fears that the security of our borders will be compromised if it must release into the country inadmissible aliens who cannot be removed. If that is so, Congress can attend to it. But for this Court to sanction indefinite detention in the face of *Zadvydas* would establish within our jurisprudence, beyond the power of Congress to remedy, the dangerous principle that judges can give the same statutory text different meanings in different cases.

Since the Government has suggested no reason why the period of time reasonably necessary to effect removal is longer for an inadmissible alien, the 6-month presumptive detention period we prescribed in *Zadvydas* applies. See 533 U.S., at 699–701, 121 S.Ct. 2491. Both Martinez and Benitez were detained well beyond six months after their removal orders became final. The Government having brought forward nothing to indicate that a substantial likelihood of removal subsists despite the passage of six months (indeed, it concedes that it is no longer even involved in repatriation negotiations with Cuba); and the District Court in each case having determined that removal to Cuba is not reasonably foreseeable; the petitions for habeas corpus should have been granted. Accordingly, we affirm the judgment of the Ninth Circuit, reverse the judgment of the Eleventh Circuit, and remand both cases for proceedings consistent with this opinion.

Justice O'CONNOR, concurring.

I join the Court's opinion. I write separately to emphasize that, even under the current statutory scheme, it is possible for the Government to detain inadmissible aliens for more than six months after they have been ordered removed. For one thing, the 6-month presumption we described in *Zadvydas v. Davis*, 533 U.S. 678 (2001), is just that—a presumption.

The Court notes that the Government has not suggested here any reason why it takes longer to effect removal of inadmissible aliens than it does to effect removal of other aliens. It is conceivable, however, that a longer period is "reasonably necessary," *id.*, at 689, to effect removal of inadmissible aliens as a class. If the Government shows that to be true, then detention beyond six months will be lawful within the meaning we ascribed to 8 U.S.C. § 1231(a)(6) in *Zadvydas*.

Moreover, the Government has other statutory means for detaining aliens whose removal is not foreseeable and whose presence poses security risks. Upon certifying that he has "reasonable grounds to believe" an alien has engaged in certain terrorist or other dangerous activity specified by statute, 8 U.S.C. § 1226a(a)(3) (2000 ed., Supp. II), the Secretary of Homeland Security may detain that alien for successive six-month periods "if the release of the alien will threaten the national security of the United States or the safety of the community or any person," § 1226a(a)(6).

Finally, any alien released as a result of today's holding remains subject to the conditions of supervised release. See 8 U.S.C. § 1231(a)(3); 8 CFR § 241.5 (2004). And, if he fails to comply with the conditions of release, he will be subject to criminal penalties—including further detention. See 8 U.S.C. § 1253(b); *Zadvydas, supra*, at 695 ("We nowhere deny the right of Congress ... to subject [aliens] to supervision within conditions when released from detention, or to incarcerate them where appropriate for violations of those conditions").

E. Expedited Removal— Removal without Hearing

In 1996 in the IIRAIRA, Congress enacted the expedited removal statute, which permits the summary return of certain persons seeking admission to the United States.[113] Expedited removal applies to all "arriving aliens"[114] who are inadmissible for fraud or misrepresentation in seeking to procure a visa, other documentation or admission to the United States.[115] Expedited removal also applies to stowaways who express a fear of persecution or an intent to apply for asylum.[116] As originally enacted, the procedures did not apply to Cubans who arrived in the United States by air[117] or to pre-April 1, 1997 parolees.[118] Under most circumstances, unaccompanied minors are also exempt from expedited removal.[119]

---

113. This law has been codified at 8 U.S.C. § 1225.

114. An "arriving alien" is defined as one "who seeks admission to or transit through the United States ... at a port of entry." 8 C.F.R. § 1.1(q). "Arriving aliens" include persons interdicted in international or U.S. waters. Sec. 235(a)(1).

115. 8 U.S.C. § 1225(b)(1)(A)(I), Sec. 235(b)(1)(A)(I). The statute refers to persons who are inadmissible under 8 U.S.C. §§ 1182(a)(6)(C), Sec. 212(a)(6)(C) (fraud or misrepresentation) or 1182(a)(7), Sec. 212(a)(7) (lack of valid or suitable documentation).

116. 8 U.S.C. § 1225(a)(2), Sec. 235(a)(2).

117. By its terms the expedited removal procedures were not applicable to such persons who were citizens of a country "with whose government the United States does not have full diplomatic relations." *See* 8 U.S.C. § 1225(b)(1)(F), Sec. 235(b)(1)(F) 8 C.F.R. § 235.3(b)(1)(i). On July 20, 2015 the United States and Cuba renewed full diplomatic relations, leaving in place pre-enacted economic sanctions. *See* Press Briefing by Press Secretary Josh Earnest, July 20, 2015, http://www.presidency.ucsb.edu/ws/index.php?pid=110477. On January 17, 2017, the Department of Homeland Security issued a final rule eliminating the exception for expedited removal for Cubans arriving by air. *See* Eliminating Exception to Expedited Removal Authority for Cuban Nationals Arriving by Air, 82 Fed. Reg. 4,769 (Jan. 17, 2017).

118. Office of Field Operations, INS Memorandum: Policy Concerning Pre-1997 Parolees (June 30, 1997), reprinted in 74 Interpreter Releases 1528 (Aug. 18, 1997). *See also* 8 C.F.R. § 1.1(q).

119. *See* Office of Programs, INS Memorandum: Unaccompanied Minors Subject to Expedited Removal (Aug. 21, 1997) reprinted in Karen Musalo & Deborah Anker, The Expedited Removal

The INA permits the Attorney General to apply expedited removal to persons who entered without inspection and cannot establish that they have been physically present in the United States continuously for the two-year period immediately prior to the date of the determination of inadmissibility.[120] Pursuant to this authority, legacy "INS" issued regulations in 2002 applying expedited removal to certain persons arriving by sea who had not been admitted, paroled or present in the country for at least two years prior to an inadmissibility determination.[121] The ostensive justification for the issuance of the notice was to deter illegal migration by sea of non-Cuban immigrants who reached the U.S. shore,[122] as this notice was published in the federal register following an incident in the fall of 2002 when Haitian asylum seekers were discovered on shore in South Florida. This expansion in applying expedited removal was the first time this provision had been invoked.[123]

In August 2004, expedited removal was further expanded to apply to additional persons present in the United States who had not been admitted or paroled following inspection by an immigration officer at a designated port of entry, are encountered by an immigration officer within one hundred air miles of a U.S. international land border and have not established to the satisfaction of an immigration officer that they have been physically present in the United States continuously for the fourteen-day period immediately prior to the date of encounter.[124] These regulations were issued under the broad umbrella of enhancing national security and public safety. While these statutory provisions and regulations contemplate that a person who has illegally entered the country should be treated as continuing to seek admission and, therefore, remain subject to expedited removal, the constitutionality of these provisions have yet to be determined.[125]

Study: Report on the First Year of Implementation of Expedited Removal (Attachment 1) (1998).

120. 8 U.S.C. § 1225(b)(1)(A)(iii), Sec. 235(b)(1)(A)(iii).

121. *See* Notice Designating Certain Aliens Subject to Expedited Removal under Section 235(b)(1)(A)(iii), 67 Fed. Reg. 68,924 (2002)

122. While Cubans arriving by air are not subject to expedited removal, the notice by the Attorney General specifically exempts Cubans arriving by sea because of the "longstanding U.S. policy to treat Cubans differently from other aliens."

123. *See* Notice Designating Certain Aliens Subject to Expedited Removal under Section 235(b)(1)(A)(iii), 67 Fed. Reg. 68,924 (2002).

124. *See* 69 Fed. Reg. 48,877 (2004).

125. Prior to the enactment of the 1996 Amendments, it was well settled that all persons who had managed to gain entry were entitled to constitutional protections. *Plyer v. Doe,* 457 U.S. 202, 210 (1982). While the INA as amended in 1996 authorizes DHS under limited circumstances to apply expedited removal, persons who have physically entered the country without formal admission may still be entitled to certain constitutional protections, a position which was recently recognized by the Court. *See Zadvydas v. Davis*, 533 U.S. 678, 693–94 (2001) ("[A]liens who have once passed through our gates, even illegally, may be expelled only after proceedings conforming to traditional standards of fairness encompassed in due process of law") (citing *Shaughnessy v. Mezei*, 345 U.S. 206, 212 (1953)). There is some question as to whether those who are physically present in the United States outside of parole may be deprived of the rights under the Constitution.

In January of 2017, the White House issued two Executive Orders providing the framework for a significant expansion of the immigration enforcement powers.[126] Together these orders call on federal agencies to change how immigration law is enforced. Some of the provisions have been explored previously in our exploration of the Executive Branch's efforts to limit what are called "Sanctuary Cities," but this discussion will focus on the most far reaching of the enforcement tools to be invoked by the Trump Administration, which involve the expansion of expedited removal. As was explained previously, expedited removal is by its very terms the absence of any due process. An immigration officer makes a determination which is not reviewable by anyone other than her supervisor, and that decision results in the person being removed from the country. The only situation where a person's case is subject to more careful scrutiny is when they are afforded a "credible fear" interview to determine whether they may be able to have a removal hearing to determine their eligibility for asylum. Outside of the asylum context, there is no administrative or judicial review.

The power being invoked was a provision of the original expedited removal statute which authorized its expansion upon notice in the Federal Register.[127] This expansion of expedited removal has yet to be tested in the courts. The invocation of this authority will place the due process stripping provisions squarely before a federal court for review. Heretofore, even persons unlawfully in the U.S. were considered "persons" entitled to constitutional due process to determine whether they were deportable and subject to removal. How a court might deal with a specific set of facts is not clear, but the statute first places the burden on the non-citizen to "affirmatively show" to the "satisfaction of an immigration officer" that they have been physically present in the U.S. for at least two years. It is not clear what that showing might be, but the statute does not contemplate any review of the officer's determination by anyone, including by an administrative review tribunal.

1. The Application of Expedited Removal

CBP officers conduct initial examinations of all arriving individuals at primary inspection and route persons whose inadmissibility is in question to secondary inspection for further questioning. During secondary inspection, applicants determined by an immigration officer to be subject to expedited removal may be ordered removed without further process. Under INA § 212(a)(9)(A)(I), the removal order becomes final upon a supervisor's approval and bars reentry to the United States for five years. 8 U.S.C. § 1225(a)(3), Sec. 235(a)(3) permits the withdrawal of an application for admission at the discretion of the Attorney General, in which case the applicant may depart without being subject to the five-year bar on reentry.

126. *See* Border Security and Immigration Enforcement Improvements, Exec. Order No. 13,767, 82 Fed. Reg. 8,793 (Jan. 25, 2017); Enhancing Public Safety in the Interior of the United States, Exec. Order No. 13,768, 82 Fed. Reg. 8,799 (Jan. 25, 2017).

127. 8 U.S.C. §§ 1225(b)(1)(A)(iii)(I) and (II), Sec. 235(b)(1)(A)(iii)(I) and (II).

Pursuant to the law, there are two groups of persons subject to expedited removal who are provided with additional procedural protections and not immediately returned: (1) those who express a fear of persecution or an intention to apply for asylum and (2) those who claim a right to reside in the United States based on citizenship, permanent resident, asylum or refugee status.[128] Applicants claiming lawful status must have their claims verified by an immigration officer,[129] and if the immigration officer is unable to verify a person's status, the person is referred to an immigration judge.[130] Those who express a fear of return or a desire to apply for asylum are referred to a "credible fear" interview to determine if they will be allowed to present their claims through the regular process provided by law to apply for asylum,[131] restriction on removal[132] or protection under the Torture Convention.[133] A "credible fear of persecution" is established if "there is a significant possibility, taking into account the credibility of the statements made by the alien in support of the alien's claim and such other facts as are known to the officer, that the alien could establish eligibility for asylum under Section 208."[134] If it is determined that a person does not have a credible fear of persecution, he may request *de novo* review by an immigration judge. The statute precludes any further administrative or judicial review.[135] Once a determination is made, there is no appeal except where the person claims a fear of persecution or claims to be a lawful permanent resident or U.S. citizen. These regulations as applied to U.S. citizens in the context of expedited removal raise due process issues that have not yet been resolved in the courts.[136]

Those who are found to have a credible fear of persecution will have their applications for asylum and related protections heard by an immigration judge in removal proceedings under 8 U.S.C. § 1229a, Sec. 240. Those who fail to establish a credible fear during the credible fear process or whose claims to lawful status are not verified

---

128. 8 U.S.C. §§ 1225(b)(1)(A)(ii) and (b)(1)(C), Sec. 235(b)(1)(A)(ii) and (b)(1)(C); 8 C.F.R. § 235.3(b)(5).

129. 8 C.F.R. §§ 235.3(b)(5), 1235.3(b)(5).

130. *Id.*

131. *See* 8 U.S.C. § 1158, Sec. 208.

132. *See* 8 U.S.C. § 1231(b)(3), Sec. 241(b)(3).

133. *See* Pub. L. No. 105-277, § 242(a) (Oct. 19, 1998); 8 C.F.R. § 208 (interim regulations); Convention Against Torture and Other Cruel, Inhuman or Degrading Treatment or Punishment, Feb. 4, 1985, 1465 U.N.T.S. 85, 23 I.L.M. 1027, *modified* 24 I.L.M. 535, G.A. Res. 39/46, U.N. GAOR, 39th Sess., Supp. No. 51 at 197, U.N. Doc. A/39/51 (1985).

134. 8 U.S.C. § 1225(b)(1)(B)(v), Sec. 235(b)(1)(B)(v).

135. 8 U.S.C. § 1225(b)(1)(C), Sec. 235(b)(1)(C).

136. *See, e.g., Agosto v. INS*, 436 U.S. 748 (1978); *Rusk v. Cort*, 369 U.S. 367 (1962). Some due process concerns are highlighted in a case which preceded the 1996 Act. In *Hernandez v. Cremer*, 913 F.2d 230 (5th Cir. 1990) *reh'g denied*, 925 F.2d 1461 (5th Cir. 1991), a federal court affirmed an injunction against the INS in San Antonio, which established a set of special procedures to be applied to persons at the border who claimed U.S. citizenship. The special procedures contemplated the institution of new verification procedures, a hearing before an immigration judge as well as federal court review.

by an inspector or immigration judge will be summarily removed from the United States.

The statute provides for mandatory detention, until removal, of all persons subject to expedited removal proceedings.[137] A limited form of parole (release from detention) is available for individuals subject to expedited removal in accordance with 8 U.S.C. § 1182(d)(5), Sec. 212(d)(5) if "the Attorney General determines, in the exercise of discretion, that parole is required to meet a medical emergency or is necessary for a legitimate law enforcement objective."[138] A person who establishes a credible fear of persecution is no longer subject to expedited removal proceedings but to regular removal proceedings under 8 U.S.C. § 1229a, Sec. 240. Therefore, a person who establishes a credible fear of persecution may be eligible for parole "under normal parole criteria."

The following case involved a challenge to the expedited removal statute. The case was brought by immigrant assistance organizations and individuals. Under special provisions of IIRAIRA a challenge to expedited removal had to be brought in U.S. District Court for the District of Columbia and was limited to the its constitutionality and conformance with legislative intent.[139]

Note

As was noted previously, the statute limits judicial review of expedited removal to one single action brought in the federal circuit within 60 days of the federal notice expanding expedited removal. The statute further precludes individual and class action review.[140] What remains available to an aggrieved party is *habeas* review. Notwithstanding the potential constitutional challenges that might be made to an expansion of expedited removal, a litigant to whom it was being applied could be expected to show that they were deprived of a real immigration benefit as a result of the violation of their due process rights. Would it be enough to show that one's procedural rights had been violated even though the person was unable to make out a case for remaining in the U.S.?[141]

---

137. 8 U.S.C. § 1225(b)(1)(B)(iii)(IV), Sec. 235(b)(1)(B)(iii)(IV); 8 C.F.R. § 235.3(b)(2)(iii). Prior to the credible fear interview, if there is insufficient detention space to detain an individual who arrived at a land port of entry, the individual may be required to wait in Canada or Mexico pending a final determination of her claim. However, those persons who make false claims or unverified claims to U.S. citizenship lawful permanent residency, asylee or refugee status and persons whose fear of persecution is "related to" Canada or Mexico will be detained in the United States. Office of the Deputy Commissioner, INS Memorandum: Implementation of Expedited Removal (Mar. 31, 1997) (Attachment 3 to First Year Report, *supra* note 3); INS, Inspector's Field Manual 17–33 (Oct. 1998).

138. 8 C.F.R. §§ 235.3(b)(2)(iii), (b)(4)(ii).

139. *See* 8 U.S.C. § 1252(e)(3), Sec. 242(e)(3).

140. 8 U.S.C. § 1252(e), Sec. 242(e).

141. Ebba Gebisa, *Constitutional Concerns with the Enforcement and Expansion of Expedited Removal*, 2007 U. Chi. Legal F. 565, 576–80 (2007); Jennifer Lee Koh, *Removal in the Shadows of Immigration Court*, 90 S. Cal. L. Rev 181 (2017).

F. The Significance of Admission into the United States

The Meaning of "Entry"

Prior to the enactment of IIRAIRA, the Immigration and Nationality Act defined the term "entry" at section 101(a)(13), 8 U.S.C. § 1101(a)(13) as:

> ... any coming of an alien into the United States, from a foreign port or place or from an outlying possession, whether voluntarily or otherwise, except that an alien having a lawful permanent residence in the United States shall not be regarded as making an entry into the United States for the purposes of the immigration laws if the alien proves to the satisfaction of the Attorney General that his departure to a foreign port or place or to an outlying possession was not intended or reasonably to be expected by him or his presence in a foreign port or place or in an outlying possession was not voluntary: Provided, That no person whose departure from the United States was occasioned by deportation proceedings, extradition, or other legal process shall be held to be entitled to such exception.

The 1996 legislation replaced the term "entry" with "admission":

> (A) The terms "admission" and "admitted" mean, with respect to an alien, the lawful entry of the alien into the United States after inspection and authorization by an immigration officer.
>
> (B) An alien who is paroled under section 212(d)(5) or permitted to land temporarily as an alien crewman shall not be considered to have been admitted.
>
> (C) An alien lawfully admitted for permanent residence in the United States shall not be regarded as seeking an admission into the United States for purposes of the immigration laws unless the alien—
>
>> (i) has abandoned or relinquished that status,
>>
>> (ii) has been absent from the United States for a continuous period in excess of 180 days,
>>
>> (iii) has engaged in illegal activity after having departed the United States,
>>
>> (iv) has departed from the United States while under legal process seeking removal of the alien from the United States, including removal proceedings under this Act and extradition proceedings,
>>
>> (v) has committed an offense identified in section 212(a)(2), unless since such offense the alien has been granted relief under section 212(h) or 240A(a), or
>>
>> (vi) is attempting to enter at a time or place other than as designated by immigration officers or has not been admitted to the United States after inspection and authorization by an immigration officer.

G. The Reentry Doctrine

Prior to the enactment of IIRAIRA, lawful permanent residents returning to the United States were not regarded as seeking a new admission if their trip abroad was "innocent, casual, and brief," as established in *Rosenberg v. Fleuti.*[142] In *Fleuti*, the returning lawful permanent resident was a homosexual, which was a ground of inadmissibility but not of deportability. Because the Court ruled that his trip to Mexico was innocent, casual and brief, Fleuti was not regarded as requesting a new admission upon his return but was treated as if he never left the country.

Following the 1996 amendments, a lawful permanent resident returning to the United States will not be regarded as requesting a new admission unless she (1) has abandoned or relinquished her permanent residency, (2) has been absent from the United States for over 180 days, (3) has engaged in illegal activity following her departure from the country, (4) has departed following institution of removal or extradition proceedings, (5) has committed a crime listed under the criminal grounds of inadmissibility and has not been granted a waiver or cancellation of removal, or (6) is attempting to enter or has entered the United States without inspection and authorization by an immigration officer.[143]

When applying the inadmissibility provisions, a lawful permanent resident is afforded more constitutional rights than other returning noncitizens, as established in the following case.

Michael Landon, Dist. Director, INS v. Maria Antonieta Plasencia

459 U.S. 21 (1982)

O'Connor, J., delivered the opinion of the Court, in which Burger, C. J., and Brennan, White, Blackmun, Powell, Rehnquist, and Stevens, JJ., joined. Marshall, J., filed an opinion concurring in part and dissenting in part,

Respondent Maria Antonieta Plasencia, a citizen of El Salvador, entered the United States as a permanent resident alien in March, 1970. She established a home in Los Angeles with her husband, a United States citizen, and their minor children. On June 27, 1975, she and her husband travelled to Tijuana, Mexico. During their brief stay in Mexico, they met with several Mexican and Salvadoran nationals and made arrangements to assist their illegal entry into the United States. She agreed to transport the aliens to Los Angeles and furnished some of the aliens with alien registration receipt cards that belonged to her children. When she and her husband attempted to cross the international border at 9:27 on the evening of June 29, 1975, an INS officer at the port of entry found six nonresident aliens in the Plasencias' car. The INS detained the respondent for further inquiry pursuant to § 235(b) of the Immigration and Nationality Act of 1952, 66 Stat. 182, as amended, 8 U.S.C. § 1101 et seq. ("Act"). In a

---

142. 374 U.S. 449 (1963).

143. 8 U.S.C. § 1101(a)(13)(C), Sec. 101(a)(13)(C).

notice dated June 30, 1975, the INS charged her under § 212(a)(31) of the Act, 8 U.S.C. § 1182(a)(31), which provides for the exclusion of any alien seeking admission "who at any time shall have, knowingly and for gain, encouraged, induced, assisted, abetted, or aided any other alien to enter or to try to enter the United States in violation of law," and gave notice that it would hold an exclusion hearing at 11:00 a.m. on June 30, 1975.

An immigration law judge conducted the scheduled exclusion hearing. After hearing testimony from the respondent, her husband, and three of the aliens found in the Plasencias' car, the judge found "clear, convincing and unequivocal" evidence that the respondent did "knowingly and for gain encourage, induce, assist, abet, or aid nonresident aliens" to enter or try to enter the United States in violation of law. He also found that the respondent's trip to Mexico was a "meaningful departure" from the United States and that her return to this country was therefore an "entry" within the meaning of § 101(a)(13), 8 U.S.C. § 1101(a)(13). On the basis of these findings, he ordered her "excluded and deported."

* * *

The respondent contends that she was entitled to have the question of her admissibility litigated in a deportation hearing, where she would be the beneficiary of the procedural protections and the substantive rights outlined above. Our analysis of whether she is entitled to a deportation rather than an exclusion hearing begins with the language of the Act. Section 235 of the Act, 8 U.S.C. § 1225, permits the INS to examine "(*a*)*ll* aliens" who seek "admission or *readmission* to" the United States and empowers immigration officers to take evidence concerning the privilege of any person suspected of being an alien "to enter, *reenter*, pass through, or reside" in the United States. *Ibid.* (emphasis added). Moreover, "every alien" who does not appear "to be clearly and beyond a doubt entitled to land shall be detained" for further inquiry. *Ibid.* If an alien is so detained, the Act directs the special inquiry officer to determine whether the arriving alien "shall be allowed to enter or shall be excluded and deported." Section 236(a), 8 U.S.C. § 1226(a). The proceeding before that officer, the exclusion hearing, is by statute "the sole and exclusive procedure for determining admissibility of a person to the United States...." *Ibid.*

* * *

The language and history of the Act ... clearly reflect a congressional intent that, whether or not the alien is a permanent resident, admissibility shall be determined in an exclusion hearing. Nothing in the statutory language or the legislative history suggests that the respondent's status as a permanent resident entitles her to a suspension of the exclusion hearing or requires the INS to proceed only through a deportation hearing. Under the terms of the Act, the INS properly proceeded in an exclusion hearing to determine whether respondent was attempting to "enter" the United States and whether she was excludable.

To avoid the impact of the statute, the respondent contends, and the Court of Appeals agreed, that unless she was "entering," she was not subject to exclusion proceedings, and that prior decisions of this Court indicate that she is entitled to have the question of "entry" decided in deportation proceedings. The parties agree that only "entering" aliens are subject to exclusion. See Brief for Petitioner at 19. That view accords with the language of the statute, which describes the exclusion hearing as one to determine whether the applicant "shall be allowed to *enter* or shall be excluded and deported." Section 236(a), 8 U.S.C. § 1226(a) (emphasis added). But the respondent's contention that the question of entry can be determined only in deportation proceedings reflects a misconception of our decisions.

In *Rosenberg v. Fleuti*, 374 U.S. 449 (1963), we faced the question whether a resident alien's return from an afternoon trip across the border was an "entry" for immigration law purposes. The definition of that term was the same then as it is now: it means "any coming of an alien into the United States ... except that an alien having a lawful permanent residence in the United States shall not be regarded as making an entry into the United States for the purposes of the immigration laws if the alien proves to the satisfaction of the Attorney General that his departure to a foreign port or place or to an outlying possession was not intended or reasonably to be expected by him...." Section 101(a)(13), 8 U.S.C. § 1101(a) (13). We held in *Fleuti* that the "intent exception" refers to an intent to depart in a "manner which can be regarded as meaningfully interruptive of the alien's permanent residence." 374 U.S. at 462. Thus, an "innocent, casual, and brief excursion" by a resident alien outside this country's borders would not subject him to the consequences of an "entry" on his return. Ibid. If, however, "the purpose of leaving the country is to accomplish some object which is itself contrary to some policy reflected in our immigration laws, it would appear that the interruption of residence thereby occurring would properly be regarded as meaningful." *Ibid.* That distinction both protects resident aliens from "unsuspected risks and unintended consequences of ... a wholly innocent action," *ibid.*, and gives effect to the language of § 101(a)(13).

The government has argued in this case that Plasencia violated the immigration laws by attempting to smuggle aliens for gain. Therefore, her departure was "meaningfully interruptive" of her residence, she was attempting an "entry," and she was subject to exclusion proceedings. And, the government urges, under § 212(a)(31), 8 U.S.C. § 1182(a)(31), she was excludable because she had attempted to smuggle aliens for gain. Plasencia, on the other hand, argues that it would "violat(e) both the scope and spirit," Brief for the Respondent at 15, of *Fleuti* to permit the INS to litigate questions of "entry" in exclusion proceedings.

The Court of Appeals viewed *Fleuti* as a deportation case rather than an exclusion case, 637 F.2d, at 1288, and therefore not relevant in deciding whether the question of "entry" could be determined in exclusion proceedings. For guidance on that decision, the Court of Appeals turned to *Kwong Hai Chew v. Colding*, 344 U.S. 590 (1953), which it read to hold that a resident alien returning from a brief trip "could not be excluded without the procedural due process to which he would have been entitled had he never left the country"—i.e., in this case, a deportation proceeding. 637 F.2d, at 1288. The court concluded that Plasencia was entitled to litigate her admissibility in deportation proceedings. It would be "circular" and "unfair," thought the court, to allow the INS to litigate the question of "entry" in exclusion proceedings when that question also went to the merits of the respondent's admissibility. *Id.*, at 1288–1289.

We disagree. The reasoning of *Chew* was only that a resident alien returning from a brief trip has a right to due process just as would a continuously present resident alien. It does not create a right to identical treatment for these two differently situated groups of aliens. As the Ninth Circuit seemed to recognize, if the respondent here was making an "entry," she would be subject to exclusion proceedings. It is no more "circular" to allow the immigration judge in the exclusion proceeding to determine whether the alien is making an entry than it is for any court to decide that it has jurisdiction when the facts relevant to the determination of jurisdiction are also relevant to the merits. Thus, in *United States v. Sing Tuck*, 194 U.S. 161 (1904), this Court held that an immigration inspector could make a determination whether an applicant for admission was an alien or a citizen, although only aliens were subject to exclusion. Cf. *Land v. Dollar*, 330 U.S. 731, 739 (1947) (district court has jurisdiction to determine its jurisdiction by proceeding to a decision on the merits). Nor is it in any way "unfair" to decide the question of entry in exclusion proceedings as long as those proceedings themselves are fair. Finally, the use of exclusion proceedings violates neither the "scope" nor the "spirit" of *Fleuti*. As the Court of Appeals held, that case only defined "entry" and did not designate the forum for deciding questions of entry. The statutory scheme is clear: Congress intended that the determinations of both "entry" and the existence of grounds for exclusion could be made at an exclusion hearing.

Our determination that the respondent is not entitled to a deportation proceeding does not, however, resolve this case. In challenging her exclusion in the District Court, Plasencia argued not only that she was entitled to a deportation proceeding but also that she was denied due process in her exclusion hearing. See Joint Appendix 5, at P 9; Record at 19, 20, 23. We agree with Plasencia that under the circumstances of this case, she can invoke the Due Process Clause on returning to this country, although we do not decide the contours of the process that is due or whether the process accorded Plasencia was insufficient.

This Court has long held that an alien seeking initial admission to the United States requests a privilege and has no constitutional rights regarding his application, for the power to admit or exclude aliens is a sovereign prerogative. See, e.g., *United States ex rel. Knauff v. Shaughnessy*, 338 U.S. 537, 542 (1950). Our recent decisions confirm that view. See, e.g., *Fiallo v. Bell*, 430 U.S. 787, 792 (1977); *Kleindienst v. Mandel*, 408 U.S. 753 (1972). As we explained in *Johnson v. Eisentrager*, 339 U.S. 763, 770 (1950), however, once an alien gains admission to our country and begins to develop the ties that go with permanent residence his constitutional status changes accordingly. Our cases have frequently suggested that a continuously present resident alien is entitled to a fair hearing when threatened with deportation, see, e.g., *United States ex rel. Tisi v. Tod*, 264 U.S. 131, 133, 134 (1924); *Low Wah Suey v. Backus*, 225 U.S. 460,

468 (1912) (hearing may be conclusive "when fairly conducted"); see also *Kwong Hai Chew*, 344 U.S., at 598 n. 8, and, although we have only rarely held that the procedures provided by the executive were inadequate, we developed the rule that a continuously present permanent resident alien has a right to due process in such a situation. See, e.g., *United States ex rel. Vajtauer v. Commissioner of Immigration*, 273 U.S. 103, 106 (1927); *The Japanese Immigrant Case*, 189 U.S. 86, 100–101 (1903); see also *Wong Yang Sung v. McGrath*, 339 U.S. 33, 49–50 (1950); *Bridges v. Wixon*, 326 U.S. 135, 153–154 (1945).

The question of the procedures due a returning resident alien arose in *Kwong Hai Chew v. Colding, supra*. There, the regulations permitted the exclusion of an arriving alien without a hearing. We interpreted those regulations not to apply to Chew, a permanent resident alien who was returning from a five-month voyage abroad as a crewman on an American merchant ship. We reasoned that, "For purposes of his constitutional right to due process, we assimilate petitioner's status to that of an alien continuously residing and physically present in the United States." 344 U.S., at 596. Then, to avoid constitutional problems, we construed the regulation as inapplicable. Although the holding was one of regulatory interpretation, the rationale was one of constitutional law. Any doubts that *Chew* recognized constitutional rights in the resident alien returning from a brief trip abroad were dispelled by *Rosenberg v. Fleuti, supra*, where we described *Chew* as holding "that the returning resident alien is entitled as a matter of due process to a hearing on the charges underlying any attempt to exclude him." 374 U.S., at 460.

If the permanent resident alien's absence is extended, of course, he may lose his entitlement to "assimilat[ion of his] status," *Kwong Hai Chew v. Colding, supra*, 344 U.S., at 596, to that of an alien continuously residing and physically present in the United States. In *Shaughnessy v. United States ex rel. Mezei*, 345 U.S. 206 (1953), this Court rejected the argument of an alien who had left the country for some twenty months that he was entitled to due process in assessing his right to admission on his return. We did not suggest that no returning resident alien has a right to due process, for we explicitly reaffirmed *Chew*. We need not now decide the scope of *Mezei*; it does not govern this case, for Plasencia was absent from the country only a few days, and the United States has conceded that she has a right to due process, see Transcript of Oral Argument at 6, 9, 14; Brief for the Petitioner at 9–10, 20–21.

The constitutional sufficiency of procedures provided in any situation, of course, varies with the circumstances. See, e.g., *Lassiter v. Department of Social Services*, 452 U.S. 18, 24–25 (1981); *Greenholtz v. Nebraska Penal Inmates*, 442 U.S. 1, 12 (1979). In evaluating the procedures in any case, the courts must consider the interest at stake for the individual, the risk of an erroneous deprivation of the interest through the procedures used as well as the probable value of additional or different procedural safeguards, and the interest of the government in using the current procedures rather than additional or different procedures. *Mathews v. Eldridge*, 424 U.S. 319, 334–335 (1976). Plasencia's interest here is, without question, a weighty one. She stands to lose the right "to stay and live and work in this land of freedom," *Bridges v. Wixon*, *supra*, 326 U.S., at 154. Further, she may lose the right to rejoin her immediate family, a right that ranks high among the interests of the individual....

Plasencia questions three aspects of the procedures that the government employed in depriving her of these interests. First, she contends that the immigration law judge placed the burden of proof upon her. In a later proceeding in *Chew*, the Court of Appeals for the District of Columbia Circuit held, without mention of the Due Process Clause, that, under the law of the case, *Chew* was entitled to a hearing at which the INS was the moving party and bore the burden of proof. *Kwong Hai Chew v. Rogers*, 257 F.2d 606 (CADC 1958). The BIA has accepted that decision, and although the Act provides that the burden of proof is on the alien in an exclusion proceeding, § 291, 8 U.S.C. § 1361, the BIA has followed the practice of placing the burden on the government when the alien is a permanent resident alien. See, e.g., *In re Salazar, supra*, at 169; *In re Kane*, 15 I & N Dec. 258, 264 (BIA 1975); *In re Becerra-Miranda*, 12 I & N Dec. 358, 363–364, 366 (BIA 1967). There is no explicit statement of the placement of the burden of proof in the Attorney General's regulations or in the immigration law judge's opinion in this case and no finding on the issue below.

Second, Plasencia contends that the notice provided her was inadequate. She apparently had less than eleven hours' notice of the charges and the hearing. The regulations do not require any advance notice of the charges against the alien in an exclusion hearing, and the BIA has held that it is sufficient that the alien have notice of the charges at the hearing, In re Salazar, supra, at 169. The United States has argued to us that Plasencia could have sought a continuance. It concedes, however, that there is no explicit statutory or regulatory authorization for a continuance.

* * *

If the exclusion hearing is to ensure fairness, it must provide Plasencia an opportunity to present her case effectively, though at the same time it cannot impose an undue burden on the government. It would not, however, be appropriate for us to decide now whether the new regulation on the right to notice of free legal services is of constitutional magnitude or whether the remaining procedures provided comport with the Due Process Clause. Before this Court, the parties have devoted their attention to the entitlement to a deportation hearing rather than to the sufficiency of the procedures in the exclusion hearing. Whether the several hours' notice gave Plasencia a realistic opportunity to prepare her case for effective presentation in the circumstances of an exclusion hearing is a question we are not now in a position to answer. Nor has the government explained the burdens that it might face in providing more elaborate procedures. Thus, although we recognize the gravity of Plasencia's interest, the other factors relevant to due process analysis—the risk of erroneous deprivation, the efficacy of additional procedural safeguards, and the government's interest in providing no further procedures—have not been adequately presented to permit us to assess the sufficiency of the hearing. We remand to the Court of Appeals to allow the parties to explore whether Plasencia was accorded due process under all of the circumstances.

Justice Marshall, concurring in part and dissenting in part.

I agree that the Immigration and Nationality Act permitted the INS to proceed against respondent in an exclusion proceeding. The question then remains whether the exclusion proceeding held in this case satisfied the minimum requirements of the Due Process Clause. While I agree that the Court need not decide the precise contours of the process that would be constitutionally sufficient, I would not hesitate to decide that the process accorded Plasencia was insufficient.

The Court has already set out the standards to be applied in resolving the question. Therefore, rather than just remand, I would first hold that respondent was denied due process because she was not given adequate and timely notice of the charges against her and of her right to retain counsel and to present a defense.

While the type of hearing required by due process depends upon a balancing of the competing interests at stake, due process requires "at a minimum ... that deprivation of life, liberty or property by adjudication be preceded by notice and opportunity for hearing." *Mullane v. Central Hanover Bank & Trust Co.*, 339 U.S. 306, 313 (1950). See, e.g., *Bell v. Burson*, 402 U.S. 535, 542 (1971). Permanent resident aliens who are detained upon reentry into this country clearly are entitled to adequate notice in advance of an exclusion proceeding. To satisfy due process, notice must "clarify what the charges are" in a manner adequate to apprise the individual of the basis for the government's proposed action. *Wolff v. McDonnell*, 418 U.S. 539, 564 (1974). Notice must be provided sufficiently in advance of the hearing to "give the charged party a chance to marshal the facts in his defense." *Id.*, at 563, 564 (prisoners charged with disciplinary violations must be given "advance written notice of the claimed violation"). See, e.g., *Goldberg v. Kelly*, 397 U.S. 254, 267–268 (1970) (welfare recipients must be given "timely and adequate notice detailing the reasons for a proposed termination"); *In re Gault*, 387 U.S. 1, 33 (1967) (juvenile must be given notice of "the specific charge or factual allegations" to be considered at delinquency hearing "at the earliest practicable time, and in any event sufficiently in advance of the hearing to permit preparation").

* * *

These procedures deprived Plasencia of a fair opportunity to show that she was not excludable under the standards set forth in the Immigration and Nationality Act. Because Plasencia was not given adequate notice of the standards for exclusion or of her right to retain counsel and present a defense, she had neither time nor opportunity to prepare a response to the government's case. The procedures employed here virtually assured that the Government attorney would present his case without factual or legal opposition.

When a permanent resident alien's substantial interest in remaining in this country is at stake, the Due Process Clause forbids the Government to stack the deck in this fashion. Only a compelling need for truly summary action could justify this one-sided proceeding. In fact, the Government's haste in proceeding against Plasencia could be explained only by its desire to avoid the minimal administrative and financial burden of providing her adequate notice and an opportunity to prepare for the hearing. Although the various other government interests identified by the Court may be served by the exclusion of those who fail to meet the eligibility requirements set out in the Immigration and Nationality Act, they are not served by procedures that deny a permanent resident alien a fair opportunity to demonstrate that she meets those eligibility requirements.

Notes

1. Congress incorporated the standards set out in *Plasencia* when it enacted 8 U.S.C. § 1101(a)(13) into the immigration statute in 1996. While the Court in *Plasencia* refers to the *Fleuti* case throughout its decision for the principle that a lawful permanent resident who is returning to the United States from a brief and casual trip abroad is not subject to the grounds of inadmissibility. *Fleuti*, however, is no longer good law, since it has been supplanted by the statute.[144] In *Matter of Collado*,[145] the Board of Immigration Appeals declared the *Fleuti* doctrine was no longer relevant. *Collado* involved a lawful permanent resident who had been convicted of a crime described under 8 U.S.C. § 1182(a)(2), Sec. 212(a)(2), nearly twenty years before his most recent trip abroad. IIRAIRA's inadmissibility provisions were retroactive in that the statute encompassed crimes committed at any time irrespective of whether at the time committed the crimes would have rendered the person inadmissible. In *Richardson v. Reno*,[146] a District Court held that a lawful permanent resident who had a criminal conviction and had been detained without bond as a person seeking admission was entitled to due process protection. The Fifth Circuit reversed the District Court in *Richardson v. Reno*,[147] and the Supreme Court granted certiorari, vacated the Fifth Circuit's decision and remanded the case.[148] Given that the Court's remand of the *Richardson* case was to consider a habeas corpus jurisdictional question, it is not clear that a definitive ruling on 8 U.S.C. § 1101(a)(13) will be forthcoming.

2. **The burden of proof in cases involving LPRs.** As was noted earlier, the statute places the burden of proof on the applicant for admission.[149] However, in cases involving returning lawful permanent residents, it is not so clear. For example, the burden is on the government to show that a lawful permanent resident has abandoned her LPR status. In cases preceding the enactment of IIRAIRA, the burden was on the government to show inadmissibility.[150] In a case where a returning LPR who was charged with encouraging, assisting or aiding his brother's admission into the United

---

144. *De Vega v. Gonzales*, 503 F.3d 45, 46 (1st Cir. 2007); *Othi v. Holder*, 734 F.3d 259, 261 (4th Cir. 2013); *Heredia v. Sessions*, 865 F.3d 60 (2d Cir. 2017).

145. 21 I. & N. Dec. 1061 (BIA 1997).

146. 994 F.Supp. 1466 (S.D. Fla. 1998).

147. 162 F.3d 1338 (5th Cir. 1998).

148. *See Richardson v. Reno*, 526 U.S. 1142 (1999).

149. 8 U.S.C. § 1229a(c)(2)(A), Sec. 240(c)(2)(A).

150. *Molina v. Sewell*, 983 F.3d 676, 678 (5th Cir. 1993).

States in violation of 8 U.S.C. § 1182(a)(6)(E)(i), Sec. 212(a)(6)(E)(i), a circuit panel side-stepped the questioning by determining that the government did establish their case by clear, convincing and unequivocal evidence."[151]

Some Procedural Questions

1. Consider the following: A arrives at LAX (Los Angeles International Airport) and is refused admission as a person traveling without a visa. The airline was directed to detain A, as she was from the People's Republic of China and traveling to Guatemala via Tokyo and Los Angeles. A escapes from the airline's custody. B arrives at LAX and is paroled for further inspection. B never appears for her interview with the immigration officer. C arrives at LAX, is first paroled and placed in a detention center; she escapes from the detention center and is paroled to a "half-way house." Three years pass, and C disappears. Five years later, she is discovered by the USCIS. How should A, B and C be treated? Are any of these persons entitled to removal proceedings? If so, when proceedings are instituted, what will be the government's burden of proof? What will be the burden on the applicant?[152]

2. A applies abroad for a visa to enter the United States. She is granted a (B-2) tourist visa. Upon arrival she is questioned by a CBP inspector. The official does not advise A about any legal rights which she might have. Instead, she verbally berates A. She then forces open A's luggage, searches through it and finds a letter which states a job offer from a business in the United States. The inspector decides to exclude A. Was the CBPs officer's actions proper? Does A have any cognizable legal defenses to the search or the institution of removal proceedings?

3. B is paroled into the United States for humanitarian reasons. Four months later, B receives a letter from a local district director stating that she must leave the country, because her parole has been revoked. No explanation is given for the parole revocation. What rights, if any, does B have? Upon revocation of her parole, what must B show in order to be allowed to remain in the United States?

Some Final Substantive Questions

1. The "political" grounds for inadmissibility prohibit Communists, persons prejudicial to the national interest or national security or those presenting a danger to the United States from being allowed to enter the country. Also included in this category are anarchists or those who would likely overthrow by force or violence the government of the United States. What could be the reason for including the multitude of provisions found at 8 U.S.C. § 1182(a)(3)? Are these provisions overlapping and redundant? What would you submit as alternatives?

2. At one time the "health" grounds for inadmissibility prohibited the admission of persons using the terms "mentally retarded," "psychopathic personality," "insane" or "persons who have had one or more attacks of insanity." The statute was amended in

151. *See Sandoval-Loffredo v. Gonzales*, 414 F.3d 892 (8th Cir. 2005).

152. *See In re Tanahan*, 18 I. & N. Dec. 339 (BIA 1981).

1990 to reflect changes in psychology and medical science which had occurred decades earlier, and the terms "physical or mental disorder and behavior" are now used. Similarly, there was a great deal of controversy relating to the denial of admission of homosexuals on grounds of their being "afflicted" with psychopathic personality disorder. Historically, the ability of Congress to exclude such persons has had constitutional support.[153] Current rulings by the U.S. Public Health Service, which was charged with defining what is and is not a "psychopathic personality disorder," revised its medical interpretations so as not to include homosexuals within the disorder. Is this type of statutory delegation for purposes of defining a psychological personality disorder proper? If it is proper, could the Public Health Service later revise its determination to permit the denial of admission of homosexuals? Would such a revision be proper?[154]

3. The criminal grounds for inadmissibility prohibit the admission of those persons who have been convicted of a crime involving moral turpitude (other than political offenses).[155] A crime involving moral turpitude is interpreted as a crime which is *malum in se* as opposed to a crime which is *malum prohibitum. Malum in se* is defined as an act or case involving illegality by the very nature of the transaction upon principles of natural, moral and public law.[155]

The criminal grounds for inadmissibility are divided into five subcategories.[157] Persons in the following categories are inadmissible:

> *Crimes generally*—Any person who has been convicted or admits the commission of the essential elements of a crime involving moral turpitude or a violation or conspiracy to violate any law relating to a controlled substance. Excepted from this definition are where one crime was committed while the person was under the age of 18, where the crime was committed more than five years prior to the application for admission *or* where the maximum possible penalty for the crime did not exceed one year and the applicant was not sentenced to more than six months.
>
> *Multiple convictions*—Any person convicted of two or more offenses, whether the conviction was in a single trial or whether the offenses arose from a single scheme of misconduct, irrespective of whether the offenses involved moral turpitude for which the aggregate sentence of confinement actually imposed was five years or more.

---

153. *Boutilier v. INS*, 387 U.S. 118 (1967).

154. For differences in treatment of this very controversial issue, *see Lesbian/Gay Freedom Day Comm. v. INS*, 541 F.Supp. 569 (N.D. Cal. 1982) *aff'd*, 714 F.2d 1470 (9th Cir. 1983); *Matter of Longstaff*, 716 F.2d 1439 (5th Cir. 1983). *See also* Robert Foss, *The Demise of Homosexual Exclusion: New Possibility for Gay and Lesbian Immigration*, 29 Harv. C.R.-C.L. L. Rev. 439 (1994).

155. See 8 U.S.C. § 1182(a)(9), Sec. 212.

156. *See* Black's Law Dictionary 112 (5th ed. 1968).

157. The criminal grounds for inadmissibility can be found generally at 8 U.S.C. § 1182(a)(2), Sec. 212(a)(2).

Traffickers in controlled substances—Any person who the consular or immigration officer knows or has reason to believe is or has been an illicit trafficker in a controlled substance.

Prostitutes or persons involved in commercialized vice—Any person who is coming to the United States principally or incidentally to engage in prostitution or has engaged in prostitution within ten years from her application for admission (or adjustment of status). This provision also provides for the denial of admission to persons involved in "pimping" and those who engage in "any other unlawful commercialized vice whether or not related to prostitution."

Persons involved in serious criminal activity and who have asserted immunity from prosecution—Any person who has committed serious criminal offenses as defined in Section 101(h), who asserted immunity from criminal jurisdiction. Presumably, this provision applies to foreign diplomats asserting immunity from criminal prosecution.

4. The power to exclude rests solely with Congress, and the courts cannot inquire into the constitutionality of the inadmissibility grounds. Would it be proper for Congress to establish a new ground for inadmissibility based upon the color of a person's eyes or skin?[158]

H. Procedures to Determine Admissibility—Flow Charts

Chart 1 presents the process of admission, which begins with the arrival of the person at the border or "port of entry." The applicant is first "inspected" by a CBP officer. At that point, a determination is made as to whether the person will be admitted. If the person is not admitted, she will either be placed in detention or allowed to remain free in parole status pending final determination of her admission. If the person is entitled to have a hearing to determine her admissibility, the hearing will be before an immigration judge. If the person is subject to expedited removal (see Charts 3 and 4), she will be removed according to those procedures.

Chart 1 General Procedure to Determine Admissibility

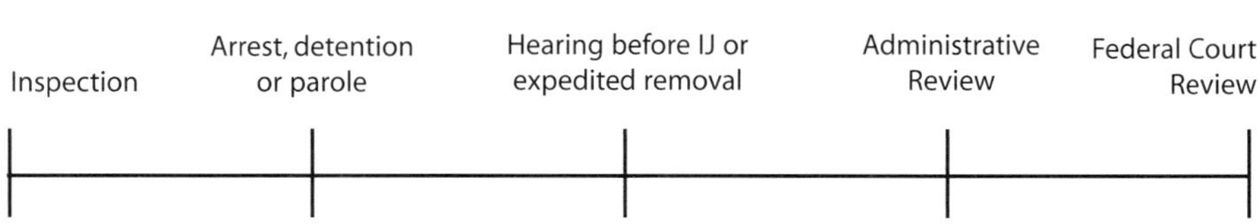

158. *See Fiallo v. Bell,* 430 U.S. 787 (1977); 1 C. Gordon & S. Mailman, Immigration Law & Procedure 1–10 (rev. ed. 1990); *see also* Jack Wasserman, Immigration Law and Procedure 211 (1979).

Chart 2 presents what occurs in the removal proceeding as a follow-up from the previous chart. In the process of inspection, the CBP officer first determines whether the person is an "alien" under the immigration laws. This chart only presents the removal proceeding as it relates to someone who is seeking admission. (Removal proceedings as they relate to someone who has been admitted are presented in Chapter 4.) A person who is not an "alien" is not subject to the immigration laws and therefore cannot be placed in these proceedings. A person's presentation of a valid U.S. passport establishes prima facie evidence of U.S. citizenship. A lawful permanent resident is an alien and remains subject to the procedures described here. The next question is whether or not the person meets the definition of admission as defined in 8 U.S.C. § 1101(a)(13), Sec. 101(a)(13). The statute requires that the non-citizen show that she is "clearly and beyond a doubt entitled to be admitted."[159] If a person arrives and is in possession of a valid visa and passport, they have met their initial burden. *Matter of Walsh & Pollard.*[160] If the person has a visa, the government must come forward with some basis for questioning the person's admissibility, whereupon the burden then shifts to the applicant to show that she is admissible.

Chart 2 Removal Proceedings
(Admission)

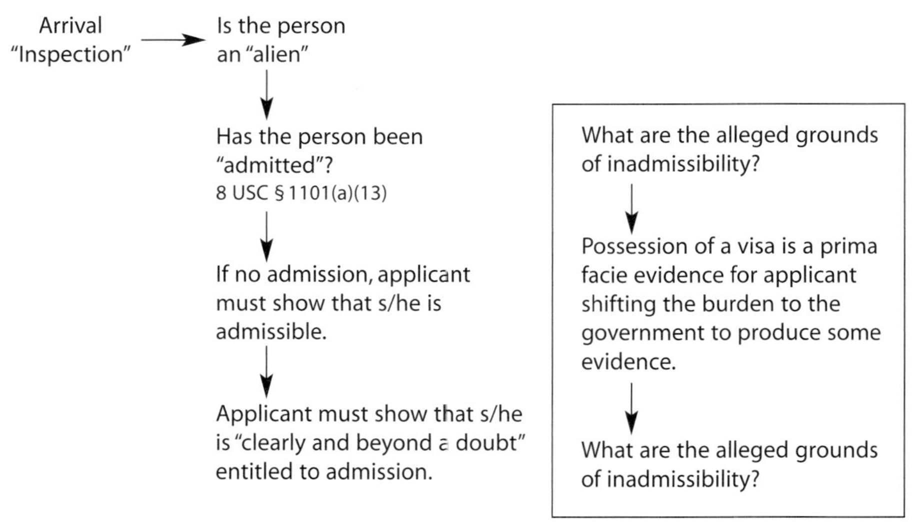

Chart 3. This chart presents what happens when a person arrives at inspection and is determined to have obtained her visa through fraud or misrepresentation or to have no travel documents. The determination of whether the person should be removed without the benefit of having a hearing before an immigration judge is made at "secondary" inspection.

159. 8 U.S.C. § 1229a(c)(2), Sec. 240(a)(c)(2).
160. 20 I. & N. Dec. 60, 62–63 (BIA 1988).

Chart 3 Expedited Removal
(no claim of persecution or claimed status as a citizen or lawful permanent resident)

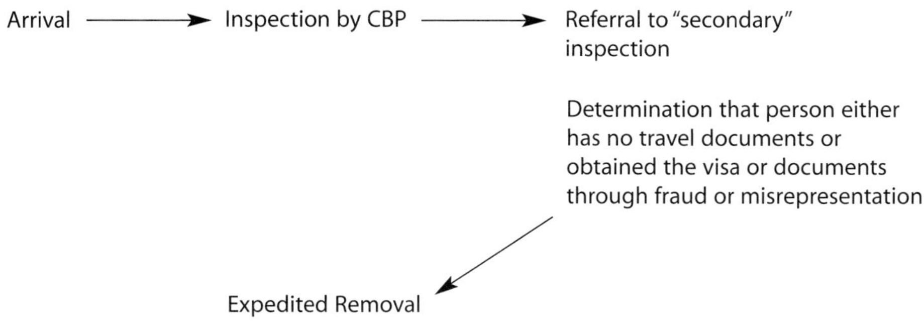

Chart 4. Expedited removal, or removal without a hearing, occurs when either the person arrives without documents or the immigration inspector believes that she has obtained her visa based on fraud or misrepresentation. This chart presents the procedures for expedited removal where the person has made a claim of possible persecution in her home country. The person arrives at the port of entry and presents herself for inspection. If she expresses a fear of persecution, she is sent over to be interviewed by an asylum officer. The asylum officer interviews the applicant to determine whether she has a "credible fear" of persecution.[161] If the person is unable to make a case for "credible fear," then the immigration judge re-evaluates the case to determine whether the standard has been met. If the judge is satisfied that the applicant has a credible fear, then the applicant is allowed to proceed in a regular removal hearing to present her asylum claim. However, if the person fails to meet the standard, she is ordered removed under expedited removal.

Chart 4 Expedited Removal
(for person claiming fear of persecution)

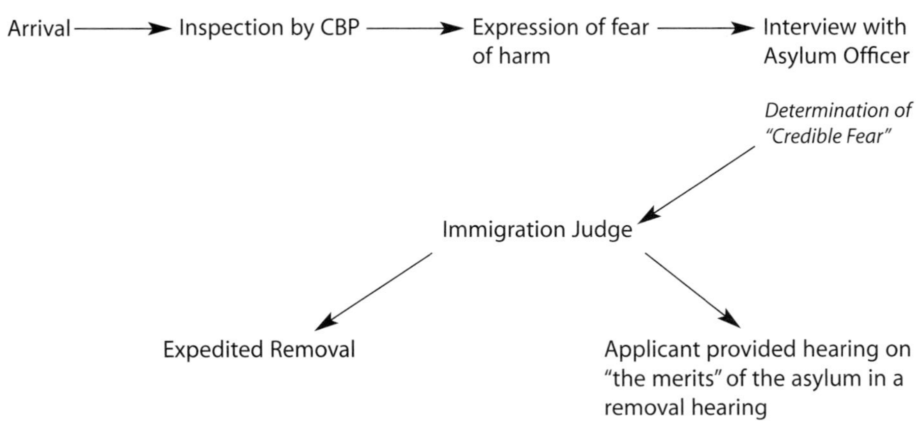

161. 8 U.S.C. § 1225(b)(1)(B)(v), Sec. 235(b)(1)(B)(v).

Chart 5. A person who is otherwise subject to expedited removal and presents a claim of U.S. citizenship, permanent residency asylum or refugee status is not subject to expedited removal. The person's claim is heard by an immigration judge, where she is either found admissible or subject to removal.

Chart 5 Expedited Removal

(Claimed Status Review: claim of U.S. citizenship, LPR status, asylee or refugee)

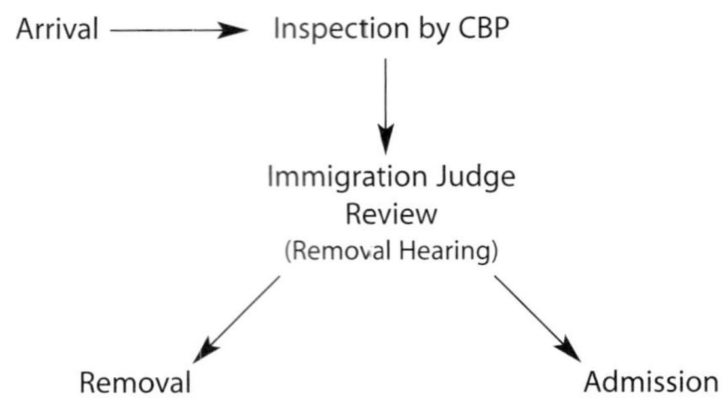

I. Problem Exercises

Exercise 1

The Case of Carlos Uribe

Carlos Uribe is a native and citizen of Guatemala and was born on January 1, (yr. -25). His mother Doris came to the United States in the (yr. -23) after she and Carlos' father had separated. After being here for a short while, she was able to get her permanent residency as a live-in household domestic and child tutor for a wealthy family in Mountain View, California. Doris became a permanent resident on January 1, (yr. -21). Carlos' father would not let him have anything to do with his mother while he was growing up, and for her own safety, she stayed away from her son and the child's father. Life was very difficult for Carlos growing up under his father, and he eventually ran away from home living on the streets of Guatemala City through much of his teen years.

During this time, he was severely abused and, as is common for many street children, he first fell into sniffing gasoline, then glue and other chemicals and eventually was forced into prostitution. Through the help of a local human rights organization, Doris was able to find her son and submitted what is called a "second preference" family-based petition to bring him to the United States as an immigrant. (The second preference application is for the unmarried children of lawful permanent residents.) The preference petition was approved, and Carlos is awaiting his immigrant visa interview in Guatemala City which has been scheduled for December 1 of (yr. -0).

Doris learns that you are a compassionate person and well versed in at least certain sections of the Immigration and Nationality Act and comes to you for help. You tell her that you are only a law student, and she says that you should not worry—"just think of this as if it were a typical law school hypothetical question." She explains that she really needs your help.

She explains that Carlos' situation is very desperate and that she really needs to bring him to the U.S. and to remove him from certain bad characters in Guatemala. She tells you that she does not believe that he was ever convicted of any crimes other than prostitution in Guatemala but that he was forced to do these things. She explains further that while he used to be addicted to some of the chemicals that he was sniffing, he is now clean. As a result of the substances that he was using, he now has some medical problems and experiences occasional seizures. She believes that she would like to get him into some type of medical treatment here in the U.S.

After you inquire about her income, you learn that she is presently working and earns approximately $1,600 per month and receives free room and board with the family for whom she is working in Mountain View, California. You ask her a few more questions, and she tells you that she has two DUI (driving while under the influence) convictions and one shoplifting conviction and that all of these occurred after respectively in January of (yr. -16), (yr. -18) and (yr. -19). Her plan is to travel to Guatemala to be with Carlos when he has his formal interview at the US Embassy in Guatemala City for his immigrant visa.

Give Doris advice on any difficulties that either she or her son Carlos might face as they relate to the grounds of inadmissibility how you would try to help them address them.

Vehicle Code

§ 23152. Driving under influence; blood alcohol percentage; presumptions

(a) It is unlawful for a person who is under the influence of any alcoholic beverage to drive a vehicle.

(b) It is unlawful for a person who has 0.08 percent or more, by weight, of alcohol in his or her blood to drive a vehicle.

For purposes of this article and Section 34501.16, percent, by weight, of alcohol in a person's blood is based upon grams of alcohol per 100 milliliters of blood or grams of alcohol per 210 liters of breath.

In any prosecution under this subdivision, it is a rebuttable presumption that the person had 0.08 percent or more, by weight, of alcohol in his or her blood at the time of driving the vehicle if the person had 0.08 percent or more, by weight, of alcohol in his or her blood at the time of the performance of a chemical test within three hours after the driving.

(c) It is unlawful for a person who is addicted to the use of any drug to drive a vehicle. This subdivision shall not apply to a person who is participating in a narcotic treatment program approved pursuant to Article 3 (commencing with Section 11875) of Chapter 1 of Part 3 of Division 10.5 of the Health and Safety Code.

(d) It is unlawful for a person who has 0.04 percent or more, by weight, of alcohol in his or her blood to drive a commercial motor vehicle, as defined in Section 15210. In a prosecution under this subdivision, it is a rebuttable presumption that the person had 0.04 percent or more, by weight, of alcohol in his or her blood at the time of driving the vehicle if the person had 0.04 percent or more, by weight, of alcohol in his or her blood at the time of the performance of a chemical test within three hours after the driving.

* * *

§ 459.5. Shoplifting

(a) Notwithstanding Section 459, shoplifting is defined as entering a commercial establishment with intent to commit larceny while that establishment is open during regular business hours, where the value of the property that is taken or intended to be taken does not exceed nine hundred fifty dollars ($950). Any other entry into a commercial establishment with intent to commit larceny is burglary. Shoplifting shall be punished as a misdemeanor, except that a person with one or more prior convictions for an offense specified in clause (iv) of subparagraph (C) of paragraph (2) of subdivision (e) of Section 667 or for an offense requiring registration pursuant to subdivision (c) of Section 290 may be punished pursuant to subdivision (h) of Section 1170.

(b) Any act of shoplifting as defined in subdivision (a) shall be charged as shoplifting. No person who is charged with shoplifting may also be charged with burglary or theft of the same property.

Exercise 2

Aaron is a native and citizen of Country A and was born on January 1, (yr. -30). He has traveled to the United States on numerous occasions as a tourist to visit with family and friends in various parts of the country. In July (yr. -10), he applied for and received a student visa to study at the University of California, at Berkeley. The purpose of his study program was to pursue a graduate degree in mechanical engineering. In obtaining his visa, Aaron presented a number of papers to the U.S. Vice-Consul in Country A, such as bank records and documentation of his parents' ability to support him as a student in the United States. He also provided a statement to the effect that following his studies he would be rehired by his employer, the Union Carbide Company of Country A. As part of the settlement following his dismissal, Union Carbide Company provided him with an undisclosed monetary payment and a letter promising to rehire him even though, in fact, there was no position for him. Aaron, as an employee, had uncovered information implicating the company in a bribery scheme of Country A officials for which the company officers could have been held criminally responsible under the federal Foreign Corrupt Practices Act of the United States. Under the settlement agreement, which was not uncommon under laws of Country A, Aaron was prohibited from discussing its terms with anyone under penalty of having to return a sum of money and to pay a fine for the disclosure.

Aaron was admitted to the United States in August (yr. -10) as a nonimmigrant student and began his studies later than month. While studying at U.C. Berkeley, Aaron met Bridget in one of his classes. Bridget was born in Oakland, California, and is a U.S. citizen. Aaron and Bridget hit it off very well, and after several years and following a meeting of their respective families, decided to get married.

Aaron and Bridget decide that it might be a good idea to consult with a lawyer regarding their situation. After spending some time talking with Aaron and Bridget, you learn the above-mentioned information and the following: (1) at the age of 18, Aaron was arrested and convicted for the crime of selling foreign currency, which was a violation of Section 1.2.1 of Country A's Penal Code (a copy of which is provided below), for which he was sentenced to 18 months in prison—he was released from prison after having served 12 months of his sentence on account of "good behavior"; (2) Aaron's arrest and conviction for the violation of the currency laws was related to an investigation of gangs by Country A authorities; (3) Aaron was a member of the Principe gang and the proceeds of the currency exchange was part of a larger scheme of raising money for other gang activity; (4) Aaron has had no contact with the Principe gang or any of its members since his arrest and conviction; and (5) Aaron is unaware of the gang's activities other than the foreign currency exchange activity. After conducting research on these matters, you learn that the Principe gang was named as a terrorist organization by the U.S. Secretary of State on January 1, (yr. -10), pursuant to procedures set forth in 8 U.S.C. § 1189(a). See 8 U.S.C. § 1189, Sec. 219, for more information on the designation of terrorist organizations.

Section 1.2.1 of the Penal Code of Country A provides

> Any person who engages in the intentional sale, transfer, or exchange of foreign currency for gain without having first been licensed to engage in such activity by the Ministry of the Treasury shall be guilty of the crime of currency fraud. Such persons shall be sentenced to a term of imprisonment of not less than 18 months. However, the sentencing judge shall have the authority to reduce the term of imprisonment at his or her own discretion.

Provide Aaron and Bridget advice only relevant to the grounds of inadmissibility. (Do not discuss alternatives to removal or the grounds of deportability.)

Exercise 3

A, a U.S. citizen, marries B, a citizen of Germany. They file a petition requesting that B be able to "adjust her status" and obtain lawful permanent resident (LPR) status without having to first return to the U.S. consulate in Germany for an immigrant visa interview. While the petition is pending, A and B decide to visit B's elderly parents in Germany. They call USCIS to inquire if they may leave the country while B's petition is pending and are told that they may.

A and B travel to Germany. In Germany, B receives a tourist visa to return to the United States. Upon her return in March, B is questioned by CBP officers at the airport. She is paroled into the country and asked to return for "inspection" on April

15th. When she returns, B is taken into custody by immigration officials, imprisoned for a week and chained to an airplane seat as she is returned to Germany.

How would you explain to B why she was returned to Germany and the procedure that was used to remove her?

Chapter 4

Removal after Admission

Introduction

In the previous chapter, we explored the substantive grounds of inadmissibility, the available waivers and the important procedural rights of persons facing removal. In this section, we will look at the provisions under the immigration statute which provide for the removal of persons following their admission to the country. Our discussion, while not fully exploring the available waivers, will briefly describe them and elaborate on the removal procedure as it relates to this section. In this section we will for the first time explore the law of search, seizure, arrest and detention as well the hearing to determine removability. Where the substantive grounds for removal applicable to the pre-admission process were called grounds of "inadmissibility," those relevant in the post-admission stage are termed grounds of "deportability."

According to the INA, the grounds of deportability become relevant after a person's lawful "admission" to the United States.[1] While it was noted in the previous chapter that certain persons not yet admitted could be removed without regard to due process (without a hearing), once a person has been admitted or is physically within the U.S., she is entitled to some type of removal proceeding.[2] This difference in treatment as between those seeking admission and those who have been admitted is reinforced by the language of the statute.[3] Moreover, as was noted in the previous chapter, once a person has physically entered the United States outside of parole, she may be entitled to constitutional protections as she is treated as a "person" within the United States.[4]

---

1. The INA provides that the grounds of deportability apply to persons "in and admitted" to the United States. *See* 8 U.S.C. §§ 1227(a), Sec. 237(a). 8 U.S.C. § 1101(a)(13)(A), Sec. 101(a)(13)(A) defines admission as "the lawful entry of the alien into the United States after inspection and authorization."

2. See 8 U.S.C. § 1225(b)(1)(A)(iii), Sec. 235(b)(1)(A)(iii). Obviously, if someone does not wish to stay in the United States, she is free to depart voluntarily. Furthermore, the statute provides for voluntary departure either before or after a finding of deportability has been entered. *See* 8 U.S.C. § 1254(e), Sec. 244; 8 C.F.R. § 244.

3. The statute does not apply expedited removal to persons who have been admitted. As will be seen later, nonresident aggravated felons are subject to a summary removal proceeding. *See* 8 U.S.C. § 1228(b), Sec. 238(b). As was discussed in the previous chapter, the INA authorizes the expansion of expedited removal to certain non-citizens who have not been lawfully admitted. 8 U.S.C. § 1225(b)(1)(A)(iii), Sec. 235(b)(1)(A)(iii).

4. *See Yick Wo v. Hopkins*, 118 U.S. 356 (1886); *Zadvydas v. Davis*, 533 U.S. 678, 693–94 (2001). The terms used in the Constitution are "people" and "persons." *See* U.S. Constitution, Amendment IV ("The right of the people to be secure in the persons ..."); U.S. Constitution, Amendment V ("No person shall be held to answer for capital, or otherwise infamous crime unless ...").

A. Substantive Grounds of Deportability and Waivers[5]

The substantive grounds for deportability are much narrower than those for admissibility.[6] Although the grounds are narrower, it has been said that there are more than 700 separate grounds of deportation.[7] The breadth of the grounds of deportability are more expansive than they might appear at first glance, both because the deportability grounds absorb the inadmissibility grounds and because there are many subsections within each section.[8] The following points provide an additional framework within which the statute and cases should be read:

1. Even after a person manages to gain admission to the United States, each time she leaves the country, she is subject to the inadmissibility provisions when she returns.

3. Unlike the inadmissibility grounds where the applicant is required to establish her admissibility, in order to sustain its burden, the government must establish by clear, unequivocal and convincing evidence that one of the grounds of deportability have been met.[9]

4. A person who is granted status as a lawful permanent resident may still be subject to both the inadmissibility and the deportability provisions depending on whether or not she is considered to be seeking a new admission.[10] The only way a person can remove herself from being subject to the immigration laws is to lawfully obtain U.S. citizenship.

5. Even if a person is properly admitted to the United States under a visa, she will become subject to removal if she violates the terms of the visa under which she was admitted[11] or fails to "maintain" her status.[12]

---

5. All of the grounds of deportability will not be explored here. For a comprehensive listing of the deportability grounds, consult 8 U.S.C. § 1227(a), Sec. 237(a).

6. The grounds of deportability are found at 8 U.S.C. § 1227(a), Sec. 237(a).

7. *See* Jack Wasserman, *The Undemocratic, Illogical and Arbitrary Laws of the United States,* 3 INT'L LAW. 254 (1969). *See also* Charles Gordon, *The Need to Modernize Our Immigration Laws,* 13 SAN DIEGO L. REV. 1, 2 (1975).

8. *See e.g.* 8 U.S.C. § 1227(a)(1)(A), Sec. 237(a)(1)(A). This provision provides that a person who was inadmissible at the time of admission becomes deportable.

9. *Woodby v. INS,* 385 U.S. 276 (1966); *Jaggernauth v. Atty. Gen'l,* 432 F.3d 1346 (11th Cir. 2005).

10. If a person is considered to be seeking admission, her removal will be governed by one or more of the grounds of inadmissibility. If she has already been admitted, then at least one of the grounds of deportability must be met. Exceptions are made for lawful permanent residents who travel abroad on a brief trip of less than 180 days and who are not inadmissible under one of the criminal grounds as described in 8 U.S.C. § 1101(a)(13). Prior to the enactment of IIRAIRA, this was known as the *Fleuti* doctrine. *See Rosenberg v. Fleuti,* 374 U.S. 449 (1963). The Fleuti doctrine did not survive the enactment of IIRAIRA according to the BIA, and BIA's interpretation of the Act is entitled to *Chevron* deference. *See Camins v. Gonzalez,* 500 F.3d 872, 884 (9th Cir. 2007); *Malagon de Fuentes v. Gonzalez,* 462 F.3d 498, 501 (5th Cir. 2006); *Olatunji v. Ashcroft,* 387 F.3d 383, 395–96 (4th Cir. 2004); *Tineo v. Ashcroft,* 350 F.3d 382, 397 (3rd Cir. 2003); *Matter of Collado-Muñoz,* 21 I. & N. Dec. 1061 (BIA 1997). In addition, lawful permanent residents and others may avail themselves of waivers of the grounds of deportability or inadmissibility. These waivers are discussed later in greater detail in this chapter.

11. 8 U.S.C. § 1227(a)(1)(B), Sec. 237(a)(1)(B).

12. 8 U.S.C. § 1227(a)(1)(C), Sec. 237(a)(1)(C). The requirements for acquiring and maintaining nonimmigrant status are discussed in more detail in Chapter 6.

6. There is no statute of limitation for the grounds of inadmissibility or deportability. If it is later learned that a person was inadmissible or deportable, she may still be subject to removal notwithstanding the fact that she was inspected and admitted to the United States as someone who was "inadmissible at the time of entry."[13]

The discussion which follows sets forth the substantive grounds for deportability. The presentation will be organized around many of the same categories which were used to describe the inadmissibility grounds. In reviewing the deportability provisions, you will find that while many of the categories mirror those found in the inadmissibility section, there are some deportability provisions which are unique.

The first principle which needs to be understood before analyzing the individual deportability categories is that when a court interprets the deportability grounds, it will apply ambiguities in the statutory language in favor of the person charged with removal.[14] A second principle is that many of the grounds of deportability are amenable to some kind of a waiver, particularly for long-term permanent residents and certain victims of domestic violence.[15] The relief available for long-term permanents residents is called cancellation of removal and sometimes characterized as "relief from removal", and it is available to persons who have resided in the United States for at least seven years, where at least five of those years have been as a lawful permanent resident.[16] Cancellation has additional requirements but generally is not available for those facing removal as aggravated felons or for security reasons.[17] These various mechanisms to avoid removal and to waive the grounds of deportability are briefly touched upon here and will be explored in greater depth in Chapter 10.

Economic Grounds. While a person may be refused admission because an immigration inspector or consular officer believes that she is likely to become a public

---

13. 8 U.S.C. § 1227(a)(1)(A), Sec. 237(a)(1)(A).

14. This is otherwise known as the "Rule of Lenity." The Rule of Lenity is a canon of statutory construction which directs that ambiguities in criminal statutes be interpreted in favor of the defendant. A similar rule of "lenity" has been recognized in immigration cases resulting in the same interpretation of deportation statutes. *See* Brian Slocum, *The Immigration Rule of Lenity and Chevron Deference*, 17 Geo. Imm. L. J. 519–20 (2003).

15. The specific requirements are explored more extensively in Chapter 10. The special rule for battered spouses or those subjected to extreme cruelty by a spouse or parent who is a U.S. citizen or permanent resident allows the person to avoid most grounds of deportability with the exception of those involving crimes, aggravated felonies or national security. See 8 U.S.C. § 1229b(b)(2).

16. A second form of relief from removal is available to long-term, non-permanent residents of at least ten years who can establish that their removal would cause exceptional and extremely unusual hardship to their U.S. citizen or permanent resident, spouse, child or parent. This remedy will also be explored in greater detail in Chapter 10. 8 U.S.C. § 1229b(b), Sec. 240A(b).

17. Additional bars include those who were admitted as exchange visitors but did not fulfill the residency requirement, those who entered under the J nonimmigrant visa for medical training but were inadmissible under 8 U.S.C. § 1182(a)(3), those who are found to be persecutors of others under 8 U.S.C. § 1227(a)(4)(D) or those who were previously granted cancellation of removal. See 8 U.S.C. § 1229b(c), Sec. 240A(c).

charge, after admission, a person may only be subject to removal if she becomes a public charge within five years "from causes not affirmatively shown to have arisen since entry." This would require that the person received public benefits from a state or federal agency and that there was a demand for repayment that the person failed to pay.[18]

Waiver for economic grounds. There is no waiver for this ground of deportability except in the case of long-term permanent residents and certain victims of domestic violence.[19]

Health Grounds. The primary health grounds for deportability are for persons who at any time after admission have been narcotics or drug abusers or addicts.[20]

Waivers for health grounds. The statute does not provide a specific waiver for the health grounds except in the case of long-term permanent residents, long-term residents and certain victims of domestic violence.[21]

Political, Foreign Policy and Security Grounds. Separate from the provisions relating to the removal of terrorists in the inadmissibility grounds related to foreign policy and security discussed in the previous chapter are parallel grounds of deportability. Many of these provisions do not require more than a showing of "activity" as opposed to a conviction for specific actions, and 8 U.S.C. § 1227(a)(4)(A), Sec. 237(a)(4)(A) makes deportable any person who "has engaged, is engaged, or at any time after admission engages" in a myriad of activities, including the following: (1) espionage, sabotage or laws prohibiting the export of goods, technology or sensitive information from the United States; (2) any other criminal activity which endangers the public safety or national security including threats on the life of the President; or (3) any activity, a purpose of which is to control or overthrow by force or violence the U.S. government. Similarly, 8 U.S.C. § 1227(a)(4)(D), Sec. 237(a)(4)(D) make deportable anyone who has engaged either in genocide or Nazi persecution as defined in the inadmissibility provisions.[22] The Board of Immigration Appeals has interpreted the espionage provision as not requiring evidence that the person either engaged in an act of espionage or was convicted of violating a law relating to espionage.[23] The Board has also interpreted the public safety provisions as not contemplating only criminal activity but matters contrary to the national security.

8 U.S.C. § 1227(a)(4)(C), Sec. 237(a)(4)(C) makes deportable persons whose presence or activities in the United States the Secretary of State has reasonable grounds

---

18. 8 U.S.C. § 1227(a)(5), Sec. 237(a)(5). *See Matter of A*, 19 I. & N. Dec. 867 (Comm'r 1988).

19. See previous discussion of cancellation of removal.

20. 8 U.S.C. § 1227(a)(2)(B)(ii), Sec. 237(a)(2)(B)(ii).

21. See previous discussion of cancellation of removal.

22. The inadmissibility provision is cross-referenced to 8 U.S.C. § 1182(a)(3)(E)(i)–(ii), Sec. 212(a)(3)(E)(i)–(ii).

23. *See In re Luis-Rodriguez*, 22 I. & N. Dec. 747, 756–58 (BIA 1999).

to believe would have potentially serious adverse foreign policy consequences.[24] These provisions are rarely invoked, and the statute contemplates individualized determinations by the Secretary of State.

Waivers for security, foreign policy and political grounds. Persons who are deportable for espionage, past Nazi persecution, participation in genocide, sabotage or sedition are not eligible for waivers.

Criminal Grounds. These grounds of deportability include persons convicted of a crime involving moral turpitude within five years of entry (a person who became a permanent resident based on his admission under the "S" nonimmigrant visa has ten years) for which a sentence of one year or more could be imposed. The term "five years of entry" refers to the person's last admission to the United States.[25] A person will also be deportable if at any time after entry he is convicted of more than one crime (not arising out of single scheme of misconduct) irrespective of whether the person was imprisoned.[26] Unless a juvenile alien was tried as an adult, criminal convictions for persons under the age of 18 are not grounds for deportability.[27] Further, foreign statute convictions of aliens under 18 are evaluated under the Federal Juvenile Delinquency Act.[28] Other criminal grounds of deportability include conviction for the use of fraudulent documents such as visas, permits or other admission papers.[29] A person may also be criminally prosecuted and, if convicted, subject to removal for failure to register an address change either under 8 U.S.C. § 1306(c), Sec. 266(c) or § 36(c) of the Alien Registration Act.[30]

A person who at any time after entry commits a crime termed an "aggravated felony" will be deportable.[31] An aggravated felony includes a wide range of crimes, including the following: murder; rape; sexual abuse of a minor; illicit trafficking in a controlled substance, firearms or destructive devices; any crime of violence including statutory rape; theft[32] (including receipt of stolen property) for which the term of imprisonment was at least one year; RICO offenses; certain prostitution offenses; and obstruction of justice.[33] There are also a myriad of crimes which have separate deportability grounds,

---

24. A similar provision can be found under the inadmissibility grounds. *See* 8 U.S.C. § 1182(a)(3)(C)(i), Sec. 212(a)(3)(C)(i).

25. As was noted in our discussion of the *Fleuti* doctrine in the previous chapter, BIA considers *Fleuti* to no longer be viable and will treat new returns under 8 U.S.C. § 1101(a)(13)(C), Sec. 101(a)(13)(C). *See Matter of Collado-Muñoz*, 22 I. & N. Dec. 1061, 1065 (BIA 1998)

26. 8 U.S.C. § 1227(a)(2)(A)(ii), Sec. 237(a)(2)(A)(ii).

27. *See Matter of Devison-Charles*, I. & N. Dec. 1362 (BIA 2000); *Vierira Garcia v. INS*, 239 F.3d 409 (1st Cir. 2001).

28. *See Matter of Ramirez-Rivero*, 18 I. & N. 135 (BIA 1981).

29. 18 U.S.C. § 1546.

30. 8 U.S.C. § 1227(a)(3)(B), Sec. 237(a)(3)(B).

31. A foreign conviction is treated as an aggravated felony if the term of imprisonment was completed within the previous 15 years. *U.S. v. Maturin*, 499 F.3d 1243 (11th Cir. 2007).

32. *Gonzales v. Duenas-Alvarez*, 549 U.S. 183 (2007).

33. Aggravated felonies are described in detail at 8 U.S.C. § 1101(a)(43), Sec. 101(a)(43). As will be seen later, conviction for an aggravated felony will preclude the person from most forms of im-

which include persons convicted of violating, conspiring or attempting to violate the following: certain firearms offenses,[34] domestic violence,[35] travel restrictions during war or national emergency,[36] neutrality laws, threats to the President, selective service laws[37] and high speed flight from an immigration checkpoint.[38]

The initial question in these cases is whether the person has met the requirement for having been "convicted" of a crime. The statutory definition requires the imposition of some form of penalty or restraint on the person's liberty, along with a formal finding of guilt by a judge or jury which could include a plea of nolo contendre.[39] After determining whether there has been a conviction, the next question must be to determine how the crime should be viewed and applied to the immigration statute.[40] One approach is called "categorical," which looks only at the language of the criminal statute and not to any of the underlying circumstances of the offense.[41] The other approach, called the "modified categorical," permits a court to look at a limited set of sentencing documents such as the indictments, jury instructions, plea agreement, or the transcript of the plea colloquy to determine which alternative of a divisible statute of conviction formed the basis of the defendant's prior conviction.[42]

---

migration relief. While the statute makes the aggravated felony provisions applicable to a crime committed at any time, the analysis of whether it is retroactive to a particular crime is extremely complex and requires analysis on a case-by-case basis. Such analysis is beyond the breadth of this casebook. *See e.g. Choeum v. INS*, 129 F.3d 29 (1st Cir. 1997); *Valderrama-Fonseca v. INS*, 116 F.3d 853 (1997); *Mendez-Morales v. INS*, 119 F.3d 738 (8th Cir. 1997).

34. 8 U.S.C. § 1227(a)(2)(C), Sec. 237(a)(2)(C).

35. 8 U.S.C. § 1227(a)(2)(E), Sec. 237(a)(2)(E). *Leocal v. Ashcroft*, 543 U.S. 1 (2004) (holding that a Florida DUI statute did not meet the requirement of a "crime of violence" under the aggravated felony provision).

36. 8 U.S.C. § 1227(a)(2)(D), Sec. 237(a)(2)(D).

37. 8 U.S.C. § 1227(a)(2)(D)(iii), Sec. 237(a)(2)(D)(iii).

38. 8 U.S.C. § 1227(a)(2)(A)(iv), Sec. 237(a)(2)(A)(iv).

39. 8 U.S.C. § 1101(a)(48)(A), Sec. 101(a)(48)(A); *Matter of Cabrera*, 24 I. & N. Dec. 459 (BIA 2008). A deferral of adjudication which included a guilty plea and was accompanied by costs and charges was upheld as a conviction. *De Vega v. Gonzales*, 503 F.3d 45 (1st Cir. 2007); *Mejia-Rodriguez v. DHS*, 629 F.3d 1223, 1228 (11th Cir. 2011); *but see Retuta v. Holder*, 591 F.3d 1181, 1188 (9th Cir. 2010) (a suspended "non-incarceratory" sentence would not meet the "punishment" requirement of the statute). However, if the state law allows the entry of a judgment under a standard short of "beyond a reasonable doubt," it will not be deemed a conviction. *Matter of Eslamizar*, 23 I. & N. Dec. 684 (BIA 2004). A conviction is not final until appeals have been exhausted or waived. *Orabi v. Att'y Gen'l*, 738 F.3d 535, 739 (3d Cir. 2014).

40. In essence, the INA lists types of crimes that form the basis for the deportability grounds. Whether the crime involves a federal or state conviction, it must be analyzed to determine whether it meets the federal definition under 8 U.S.C. §§ 1101(a)(43) or 1227(a)(2).

41. *Moncrieffe v. Holder*, 569 U.S. 184 (2013); *Descamps v. U.S.*, 570 U.S. 254 (2013)

42. *Descamps v. U.S.*, 570 U.S. 254 (2013). The use of this approach is meant to assist in effectuating the categorical analysis. *Id.* at 261. A divisible statute is one which defines multiple offenses with alternative elements of which one falls in the removal ground and the other which doesn't. *Shepard v. U.S.*, 544 U.S. 13 (2005). *See also Nijhawan v. Holder*, 557 U.S. 29 (2009).

Waivers of Criminal Grounds. The criminal grounds of deportability involving crimes of moral turpitude, multiple convictions, aggravated felonies or high speed flight from an immigration checkpoint will not be applied where the person has received a full and unconditional pardon from the President of the United States or the Governor of any of the states.[43] Otherwise, waivers available for the criminal grounds of deportability are very limited.

Quasi-criminal. Included within this category are provisions for the removal of persons who have committed any one of a variety of frauds or misrepresentations in gaining admission or securing status in the United States. Included within this group are persons who entered into a fraudulent marriage with the purpose of gaining admission.[44] Persons who have assisted or encouraged others to illegally enter the country prior to or within five years after the person's entry into the United States are also deportable.[45] Other violations include a final administrative order finding that the person has used a fraudulent document for purposes of meeting the employment verification requirements of the statute[46] and a person's making a false claim to U.S. citizenship in order to obtain benefits under federal or state laws[47] or to unlawfully vote in any federal, state or local election.[48] Finally, anyone who has engaged in genocide or the persecution of others, acts of torture, extra-judicial killing, severe violations of religious freedom or the recruitment child soldiers is also deportable.[49]

Waivers of quasi-criminal. Document fraud under 8 U.S.C. § 1227(a)(3)(C)(i) may be waived if the person is a lawful permanent resident, there was no previous civil monetary penalty imposed and the violation was to assist or support the person's spouse or child.[50]

Immigration Law Violations. There is a category of actions unique to the grounds of deportability which can render a person deportable, and it can best be described as immigration law violations. These violations would include those who were in-

43. 8 U.S.C. § 1227(a)(2)(A)(vi), Sec. 237(a)(2)(A)(vi). Strictly interpreted, this is not a waiver, as a waiver is a benefit accorded by the agency to avoid the application of the grounds of deportability or inadmissibility. The effect of a pardon is to wipe out the conviction to prevent its application as a ground of deportability. The pardon is not effective to prevent the application for crimes involving a controlled substance, "miscellaneous crimes" under 8 U.S.C. 1227(a)(2)(D) and crimes of domestic violence.

44. 8 U.S.C. § 1227(a)(1)(G), Sec. 237(a)(1)(G).

45. 8 U.S.C. § 1227(a)(1)(E)(i), Sec. 237(a)(1)(E)(i). The statutory language is very broad and provides for removal where the person "encouraged, induced, assisted, abetted, or aided any other alien to enter or to try to enter the United States." Unlike other grounds of deportability, this one could have occurred prior to the violator's admission to the United States.

46. 8 U.S.C. § 1227(a)(3)(C)(i).

47. 8 U.S.C. § 1227(a)(3)(D), Sec. 237(a)(3)(D).

48. 8 U.S.C. § 1227(a)(6), Sec. 237(a)(6). This provision is retroactive and does not require that the person was convicted under a federal, state or local statute.

49. 8 U.S.C. §§ 1227(a)(4)(D), (E) and (F), Sections 237(a)(4)(D), (E) and (F).

50. 8 U.S.C. § 1227(a)(3)(C)(ii), Sec. 237(a)(3)(C)(ii).

admissible at entry,[51] whose visa had been revoked,[52] who violated the conditions of their admission[53] or who failed to register their address change within the time prescribed in the law.[54]

Waivers for immigration law violations. The only violations which may be waived are situations where the person's nonimmigrant status has been reinstated, where the failure to submit the address change was either not willful or excusable[55] or where the person is receiving status as a special immigrant juvenile.[56]

1. Comparison Chart of Grounds of Inadmissibility and Deportability

The chart which appears on the following pages are designed to provide a better understanding of the grounds of inadmissibility and deportability. These grounds are listed in the statute and appear at 8 U.S.C. § 1182 and 1227.[57] The chart is broken into the categories which make up the multiple and overlapping grounds of inadmissibility and deportability. These have been previously broken down into the following economic, political, health, crimes, quasi criminal, security, and miscellaneous.

At the top of the chart we begin with certain general propositions which relate to how the grounds of inadmissibility and deportability are applied. The inadmissibility provisions triggered when a person makes a visa application, is seeking admission, is applying for adjustment of status and in some cases even when a lawful permanent resident is returning to the U.S. [Some of these rules are the ones which were discussed in the context of the definition of admission found at 8 U.S.C. § 110(a)(13) (Section 101(a)(13).] When contrasted with the deportability provisions we seek some major differences as these only apply following a person's lawful admission and or when she is seeking citizenship. The chart further highlights the numerous grounds of inadmissibility that do not have comparable deportability provisions and vice versa.

The remaining categories of the chart bear the headings of the inadmissibility and deportability provisions which were discussed respectively in Chapters 3 and 4 of the text. The underlying purpose is to highlight the categories of inadmissibility and deportability and to focus on the differences between them.

---

51. 8 U.S.C. § 1227(a)(1)(A), Sec. 237(a)(1)(A).

52. 8 U.S.C. § 1227(a)(1)(B). The statute prescribes that such persons are "in the U.S. in violation of law."

53. 8 U.S.C. § 1227(a)(1)(C), Sec. 237(a)(1)(C). The conditions of admission for nonimmigrants are described more fully in Chapter 6 and include complying with the terms of the visa such as the time limitations set by the immigration inspector at the port of entry.

54. U.S.C. § 1227(a)(3)(A), Sec. 237(a)(3)(A). Such violations are also subject to criminal prosecution under 8 U.S.C. § 1306(b), Sec. 266(b).

55. *Id.* Such determinations are discretionary.

56. 8 U.S.C. § 1227(c), Sec. 237(c).

57. Sections 212 and 237.

	Grounds of Inadmissibility	Grounds of Deportability
General		
Application	Visa application, admission, adjustment of status, certain returns to the United States after permanent residency. Issues arise when seeking citizenship.	Following admission or entry or when seeking citizenship.
Unique Grounds	Admission of acts constituting a crime even without conviction, labor certification requirement, most health grounds, communists or totalitarian party, unqualified physicians or health care workers, prostitution, commercialized vice, persons asserting immunity from prosecution for "serious" crimes, polygamy, unlawful presence bars to returns, stowaways, student visa abusers, not in possession of proper documents, persons previously removed or unlawfully present, ineligible to citizenship, renunciation of citizenship to avoid taxation, accompanying certain inadmissible persons, international child abductors.	Inadmissibility at entry, present in violation of law, violation of condition of entry, termination of conditional residence status, failure to register change of address, high speed flight, certain firearm offenses, selective service act crimes, violators of protection orders, domestic violence, stalking or child abuse or neglect crimes, false citizenship claim.
Economic		
Public Charges	Likely to become public charge.	Becomes a public charge within five years.
Political		
Foreign Policy	Secretary has reasonable ground to believe admission would have potentially serious adverse consequences.	Same but person is in the United States
Health		
Drug Abusers	An abuser at the time seeking admission.	At any time after admission.
Crimes		
Moral Turpitude	A single crime involving moral turpitude.	Convicted within five years of a crime involving moral turpitude for which a sentence of one year or more could be imposed (Convicted within ten years if admitted under "witness protection" visa).
Controlled Substance	Any such crime.	Same.
Multiple Crimes	Two or more offenses w/aggregate sentence imposed of greater than or equal to five years.	Two or more crimes involving moral turpitude.

	Grounds of Inadmissibility	Grounds of Deportability
Crimes		
Petty Offenses	Petty offense and juvenile exception to crimes.	No equivalent.
Aggravated Felonies	Inadmissible.	Conviction any time after admission (summary removal for non residents).
Quasi-Criminal		
Marriage Fraud	Permanently ineligible to receive family immigration visa.	Marriage ends within two years unless a *bona fide* is established.
Fraud or Misrepresentation	Seeks or has sought to procure visa, documentation or admission into the United States.	(See false documents below).
	Person admitted as nonimmigrant who obtains benefits for which ineligible through fraud or material misrepresentation ineligible to return for five years.	
Smuggling	A person who at any time has engaged in "alien smuggling."	Five years from "any entry."
Security		
Espionage	Government "knows or has reasonable ground to believe, seeks to enter to engage in" espionage.	Has or is engaged in espionage at any time after admission.
Nazis	Participated in Nazi persecutions between 3/23/1933–5/8/1945.	Same.
Genocide	Engaged in genocide.	Same.
Terrorists	Has or likely will engage in terrorism according to the consular officer or Attorney General.	Has engaged or is engaging in terrorism.
Miscellaneous		
Illegal Entrants	Exempts battered spouses or children.	Persons illegally in U.S. subject to removal.
Failure to Appear	Inadmissible for five years.	May be ordered removed *in absentia*.
False Citizenship	False claim of U.S. citizenship for any purpose or benefit.	Same.
Document Fraud	Document fraud related to employer sanction compliance.	Same.

B. Removal of "Foreign" Terrorists

The Antiterrorism and Effective Death Penalty Act (AEDPA) created a special procedure to deport foreign "terrorists," or persons who commit or materially support the activities of terrorism or a terrorist organization.[58] Removal is accomplished through instituting proceedings in a special court of five judges appointed by the Chief Justice. The Attorney General files a petition to initiate the proceedings, which states the facts and circumstances relied on by the Justice Department in establishing probable cause that the alien is a terrorist physically present in the United States and the reasons that removal is necessary for national security.[59] An individual detained under this provision may face prolonged detention upon certification by the Attorney General or the Deputy Attorney General every six months.[60] The application is submitted *ex parte* and under seal to the court. The hearing is conducted in public, and the alien is entitled to "reasonable notice" of the "nature" of the charges against her. In the case of indigency, she may have counsel appointed by the court. Classified information may be used to support a deportation order, and the respondent is entitled to review an "unclassified summary" of the evidence prepared by the Attorney General.[61] However, the judge will examine the classified information *ex parte*, and the Federal Rules of Evidence will not apply in the proceedings.[62] The government must prove by a preponderance of the evidence that the alien is subject to removal because she is an alien terrorist.[63] Both the government and the alien may appeal the decision to the U.S. Court of Appeals for the D.C. Circuit by filing a notice of appeal within twenty days of the order.[64] A decision on the appeal is made by the appellate court within sixty days and is based upon the record of the court below and the briefs submitted. Questions of law are reviewed *de novo*, and findings of facts may only be set aside if they are "clearly erroneous."[65] The respondent may not be removed pending her appeal to the Court of Appeals. However, if the order is affirmed, the removal may be enforced unless the alien obtains an order from either the Court of Appeals or the Supreme Court.

C. Expedited Removal of Aggravated Felons

8 U.S.C. § 1228, Sec. 238 provides an expedited removal process for any noncitizen who has been convicted of an aggravated felony. (This is to be distinguished from

---

58. 8 U.S.C. § 1531–1537, Sec. 501–507.

59. See 8 U.S.C. §§ 1532 and 1533, Sections 502 and 503.

60. 8 U.S.C. § 1537(b)(2)(C), Sec. 507(b)(2)(C); *Nadarajah v. Gonzales*, 443 F.3d 1069, 1077–79 (9th Cir. 2006).

61. The respondent is not entitled to discovery of classified material where the disclosure would present a risk to the national security, nor can she suppress evidence which may have been illegally obtained. *See* 8 U.S.C. § 1534(e).

62. The respondent is not entitled to see the classified information.

63. 8 U.S.C. § 1534(g), Sec. 504(g).

64. 8 U.S.C. § 1535(c), Sec. 505(c).

65. 8 U.S.C. § 1535(a)(3), Sec. 505(a)(3).

the expedited removal discussed in Chapter 3.) According to this procedure, the respondent is served with a notice of the charges and of the opportunity to inspect the evidence and rebut the charges within ten days, and she is advised of the privilege of being represented by counsel of her own choice at no expense to the government. Although the regulations require that the notice be presented in a language the respondent understands, the proceedings do not have to be conducted in a language familiar to her.[66] In order to expedite the removal of aggravated felons, the proceedings are conducted by an officer of the Department of Homeland Security (DHS) rather than an Immigration Judge.[67] In general, an aggravated felon is ineligible for all forms of relief from deportation other than under the Convention Against Torture.[68] However, an alien convicted of an aggravated felony prior to the 1996 INA revision may still be eligible for cancellation of removal.[69]

D. Regular Removal Procedures

1. Detention or Release

Following a person's arrest, consideration is given to whether she will be detained or released. If the person is not released on her own recognizance, a bond will be set. There are three types of bonds or sureties commonly used in immigration cases: delivery, maintenance and public charge bonds. The delivery bonds are the most common and may be forfeited if the person fails to appear at a scheduled appearance. Maintenance bonds are forfeited when a person admitted to the United States fails to maintain her status. Public charge bonds are rarely imposed; the surety is forfeited upon the person admitted to the United States becoming a public charge.[70] Depending on the type of bond, the surety will be returned upon the person's death, departure or attainment of lawful permanent resident status.[71]

While there is no absolute right to bond, it is generally granted unless an individual poses a threat to national security. The principal factors in setting the amount of the bond are local family ties; prior arrests, convictions and immigration history; employment status; membership in community organizations; manner of entry and length of stay in the United States; and financial ability to post bond.[72]

One of the significant changes made by the enactment of AEDPA and IIRAIRA in 1996 were the institution of mandatory detention for persons who are subject to

66. 8 C.F.R. § 238.1.

67. 8 C.F.R. § 238.1(a). Any DHS officer can preside over the proceeding as long as she is not the same person who issued the notice to appear.

68. 8 C.F.R. §§ 208.31 and 1208.31.

69. *See INS v. St. Cyr*, 533 U.S. 289 (2001).

70. See 8 C.F.R. § 103.6(a)(2).

71. 8 C.F.R. § 103.6(c).

72. See *Matter of Daryoush*, 18 I. & N. Dec. 352 (BIA 1982); *Matter of Patel*, 15 I. & N. Dec. 666 (BIA 1976).

removal due to aggravated felonies or other criminal convictions or for those charged with being terrorists.[73] In non-mandatory detention cases, the minimum bond is statutorily set at $1,500, and work authorization is prohibited. Persons deemed to be inadmissible due to criminal convictions are also ineligible for release on bond. The statute further precludes judicial review of discretionary determinations on bond.[74] In October 1996, the Attorney General invoked Transition Provisional Custody Rules (TPCR) due to lack of detention space, which were enacted to afford the Attorney General sufficient time to implement the broad detention requirements imposed by IIRAIRA. As a result, only certain categories of persons with criminal convictions are subject to mandatory detention. Notwithstanding the transition rules, many persons, including lawful permanent residents, remain subject to mandatory detention. Challenges to the mandatory detention rules as applied to permanent residents have been successful on constitutional grounds because of their retroactive application.[75]

While the legality of pre-removal order detention remains an open question, post-removal order continued detention is not allowed beyond a period of six months, with the exception of those aliens the Attorney General certifies are terrorists or pose dangers to national security.[76] As was noted in the previous chapter, thus far the courts have only allowed for the indefinite detention of persons who have not been legally admitted into the United States, including those paroled into the country. In *Zadvydas v. Davis*,[77] the government had argued unsuccessfully for an extension of the plenary power doctrine to allow for the indefinite detention of persons for whom removal could not be completed after they had been admitted to the United. Drawing on the entry/admission distinction, the Court found that persons may avail themselves of constitutional protections once admitted or within the country. Justice Breyer writing for the Court, noted that,

> A statute permitting indefinite detention of an alien would raise a serious constitutional problem. The Fifth Amendment's Due Process Clause forbids the Government to "depriv[e]" any "person ... of ... liberty ... without due process of law." Freedom from imprisonment—from government custody, detention, or other forms of physical restraint—lies at the heart of the liberty that Clause protects ... And this Court has said that government detention violates that Clause unless the detention is ordered in a *criminal* proceeding with adequate procedural protections, *See United States v. Salerno,* 481 U.S. 739, 746 (1987), or, in certain special and "narrow" non-punitive "circumstances," *Foucha, supra*, at 80, where a special justification, such as harm-

73. 8 U.S.C. §§1226(a) and (c), Section 236(a) and (c).

74. 8 U.S.C. §1226(e), Sec. 236(e).

75. *See e.g. Ekekhor v. Aljets*, 979 F.Supp. 640 (N.D. Ill. 1997); *Pastor-Camarena v. Smith*, 977 F. Supp. 1416 (W.D. Wa. 1997); *St. John v. McElroy*, 917 F.Supp. 243 (S.D. N.Y. 1996); *Caballero v. Caplinger*, 914 F.Supp 1374 (E.D. La. 1996).

76. 8 U.S.C. §1226(a), Sec. 236(a).

77. 533 U.S. 678 (2001).

threatening mental illness, outweighs the "individual's constitutionally protected interest in avoiding physical restraint." *Kansas v. Hendricks,* 521 U.S. 346, 356 (1997).

The proceedings at issue here are civil, not criminal, and we assume that they are nonpunitive in purpose and effect. There is no sufficiently strong special justification here for indefinite civil detention—at least as administered under this statute....

2. The Removal Hearing

Removal proceedings begin with the service of the "Notice to Appear" (NTA) on the person who has been arrested.[78] This is normally carried out by an Immigration and Customs Enforcement (ICE) officer authorized to arrest and detain noncitizens.[79] If ICE determines that a bond will be required, they will also set the amount of the bond.[80] The respondent can seek a redetermination of the bond by written request (motion) to an immigration judge (IJ) at any time before a final order of removal has been entered.[81] Relevant factors in determining the amount of the bond are similar to most criminal proceedings, such as employment history, length of residence in the community, family ties, a record of nonappearance at court proceedings, and previous criminal or immigration law violations.[82] The bond decision itself is subject to administrative review by the Board of Immigration Appeals (BIA), and that decision may be reviewed in federal court through a habeas petition.[83]

---

78. 8 C.F.R. § 1003.13. Service is accomplished by personal delivery on the respondent; if by mail, it must be by certified mail or to her attorney. The NTA must contain the following: the nature of the proceedings; the time and place of the hearing; the legal authority under which the proceeding is being conducted; the acts alleged to have been violated; a notice of the right of representation; explanation of the respondent's obligation to inform the agency promptly of any change of address; and explanation of the consequences of a failure to appear at the removal hearing when scheduled. 8 U.S.C. § 1229(a), Sec. 239(a).

79. Under 8 C.F.R. § 239.1(a), Customs and Border Patrol Officers and ICE detention officers may also issue the NTA.

80. Release from custody pending and throughout the hearing process can be based on parole or without a bond. However, if bond is set, it must be for at least $1,500. 8 U.S.C. § 1226(a)(2), Sec. 236(a)(2).

81. If the respondent has posted bond, she may seek review of the bond by application to the immigration judge within 7 days. 8 C.F.R. §§ 236.1(d), 1236.1(d)(1). Afterwards, review must be sought before the ICE district director and then to the BIA. 8 C.F.R. §§ 236.1(d)(2) and (d)(3); *In re Valles-Perez,* 21 I. & N. Dec. 769 (BIA 1997); 8 C.F.R. § 236.1(d)(1). Once the IJ has made a determination on the amount of the bond, it can only be reset by an appeal to the Board of Immigration Appeals or upon a showing that there has been a material change in circumstances. 8 C.F.R. § 1003.19(e). Bond redetermination hearings are informal and are not part of the removal hearing itself, and the IJ can consider a wide body of information in making her decision. 8 C.F.R. § 1003.19(d).

82. *Matter of Patel,* 15 I. & N. Dec. 666 (BIA 1976); *Matter of Daryoush,* 18 I. & N. Dec. 352 (BIA 1982); Immigration Judge Benchbook 3.I.H. (2001).

83. *Al-Najjar v. Reno,* 97 F. Supp. 2d 1329 (S.D. Fla. 2000).

The first stage in the removal process is the Master Calendar hearing, which is essentially the initial pleading stage. At this initial hearing, the respondent is brought before an immigration judge to make an initial determination of the charges. The person may admit to the charges and agree to depart "voluntarily" from the U.S. with the permission of ICE.[84] If the respondent contests any of the charges against her or is seeking any form of immigration relief from removal which is contested by the government, the immigration judge will schedule the matter for a separate "merits" hearing at a later date. A person's failure to appear after having been properly served notice of the hearing can result in an *in absentia* order being entered.[85]

The merits hearing is conducted by an immigration judge. The judge has the authority to administer oaths, receive evidence, interrogate and cross-examine witnesses.[86] While the respondent has the right to be represented, the government does not provide counsel except in cases involving incompetency.[87] While strict rules of evidence do not apply in these proceedings, evidence may be admitted to the extent that it is probative and would not be fundamentally unfair to allow its consideration.[88] Hearings are conducted in English, and translation is provided for the primary purpose of creating a record upon which a decision can be made and assuring that the respondent understands the nature of the proceedings.

In the removal proceeding, the respondent may contest the charge of inadmissibility or deportability and/or apply for a waiver or discretionary relief. Where the respondent is found physically within or has been admitted, they may choose to contest the charge in the NTA, thereby forcing the government to meet its statutory burden of proof.[89] If inadmissibility or deportability is established, the respondent may either seek a waiver or relief of the ground. At the conclusion of the hearing, the IJ may either immediately decide the case or adjourn the proceeding and decide the case at

---

84. Voluntary departure is discussed in greater detail as a form of relief from removal in Chapter 10.

85. *In absentia* hearings cannot be conducted against minors. *Matter of Gomez-Gomez*, 23 I. & N. Dec. 522 (BIA 2002).

86. 8 U.S.C. § 1229a(b)(1), Sec. 240(b)(1); *Agyeman v. INS*, 296 F.3d 871, 884 (9th Cir. 2002); *In re J-F-F-*, 23 I. & N. Dec. 912, 922 (A.G. 2006). The statute authorizes hearings to be conducted by video or telephonic conferences by consent of the parties. 8 U.S.C. §§ 1229a(b)(2)(A)(ii)–(iv), Sec. 240(b)(2)(A)(ii)–(iv).

87. 8 U.S.C. § 1362, Sec. 292. In September of 2015, USCIS entered into a settlement of a class action case involving non-citizens with mental disabilities who had been detained for prolonged periods in immigration detention facilities after being determined to be mentally incompetent to represent themselves in their removal proceedings. In *Franco v. Holder*, 767 F. Supp. 2d 1034 (C.D. Ca. 2010), the court held that the Section 504 of the Rehabilitation Act required competency determinations, appointment of counsel and custody hearings in cases involving detained individuals in California, Arizona and Washington. *See* Sarah Sherman-Stokes, *Sufficiently Safeguarded: Competency Evaluations of Mentally Ill Respondents in Removal Proceedings*, 67 Hastings L.J. 1023 (2016).

88. 8 U.S.C. § 1229a(c)(3)(A), Sec. 240(c)(3)(A); *Ezeagwuna v. Ashcroft*, 325 F.3d 396, 405 (3d Cir. 2003); *Alexandrov v. Gonzales*, 442 F.3d 395, 404–07 (6th Cir. 2006); *but see Angov v. Holder*, 736 F.3d 1263, 1268 (9th Cir. 2013).

89. The burden of proof in these proceedings is discussed further in this Chapter.

a later date or issue a written opinion. An appeal of the decision must be filed within 30 days of the decision by the IJ.[90] The respondent's failure to file an appeal will render the decision final, and the respondent may be subject to removal.

3. Place for "Removal"

Another issue is the place to where a person may be removed once a removal order is obtained. In a case decided by the Supreme Court, the respondent argued in a *habeas petition* that the government should not be able to send him to his native Somalia, since there was no existing government there. In *Jama v. ICE*,[91] the Court held that the statute in question, 8 U.S.C. § 1231(b)(2), did not prohibit the removal of a person to a country without the explicit and advanced consent of that country's government. Keyse Jama, a citizen of Somalia, had been previously admitted to the United States as a refugee but had his status terminated due to a conviction for a crime involving moral turpitude. Following the decision, the government attempted to deport him unsuccessfully to Somalia, and upon his return to the country in May 2005, a Federal District Judge ordered his release.[92]

The rule as interpreted by the Supreme Court in *Jama*:

> (1) An alien shall be removed to the country of his choice, unless one of the conditions eliminating that command is satisfied; (2) otherwise he shall be removed to the country of which he is a citizen, unless one of the conditions eliminating that command is satisfied; (3) otherwise he shall be removed to one of the countries with which he has a lesser connection; or (4) if that is "impractical, inadvisable or impossible," he shall be removed to "another country whose government will accept the alien into that country."[93]

In the fourth stage, the government may designate a place such as the country from which the person came, a contiguous territory or other country willing to accept the person.[94]

Reinstatement of Removal. 8 U.S.C. § 1231(a)(5), Sec. 241(a)(5) provides for another procedure called "reinstatement of removal."[95] This is a situation where a person was found removable or ordered removed in a prior procedure and is once again discovered by immigration authorities. In this situation the prior order can be "reinstated" and the person can be removed. In order to reinstate the original order, the DHS

---

90. 8 C.F.R. § 1003.38(b). Administrative appeals are explored at greater length in Chapter 12.

91. 543 U.S. 335, 352 (2005).

92. *See Jama v. ICE*, No. Civ. 01-1172JRT/AJB, 2005 WL 1205160 (D. Minn. May 20, 2005). At some point, Jama failed to appear at the regular intervals as required under his release order. ICE, believing that he had moved to Canada, moved unsuccessfully to have the district court's writ dismissed. See *Jama v. ICE*, No. Civ 01-1172 JRT/AJB, 2006 WL 3610809 (D. Minn. Dec 11, 2006).

93. 543 U.S. at 341. The immigration judge may not designate a country which she knows is not the person's country of citizenship or nationality. *Hadera v. Gonzales*, 494 F.3d 1154, 1156 (9th Cir. 2007).

94. 8 U.S.C. § 1231(b)(2)(E), Sec. 241(b)(2)(E).

95. 8 C.F.R. §§ 241.8 and 1241.8.

must determine that the person was subject to a prior order, whether in fact it involved the same person and that the person unlawfully reentered. An unlawful reentry could include going through inspection and admission through deception or fraud. *Martinez v. Johnson*, 740 F.3d 1040, 1043 (5th Cir. 2014); *Tamayo-Tamayo v. Holder*, 725 F.3d 950 (9th Cir. 2013). The fact that reinstatement is invoked without an opportunity to appear before an immigration judge has withstood constitutional challenge. *Garcia-Villeda v. Mukasey*, 531 F.3d 141 (2d Cir. 2008); *Lorenzo v. Mukasey*, 508 F.3d 1278, 1283 (10th Cir. 2007). A person subject to reinstatement may still seek withholding of removal or relief under the Convention Against Torture which are discussed in Chapter 5. *Herrera-Molina v. Holder*, 597 F.3d 128, 138 (2d Cir. 2010).

Removal Proceedings (Timeline)
persons in the U.S.

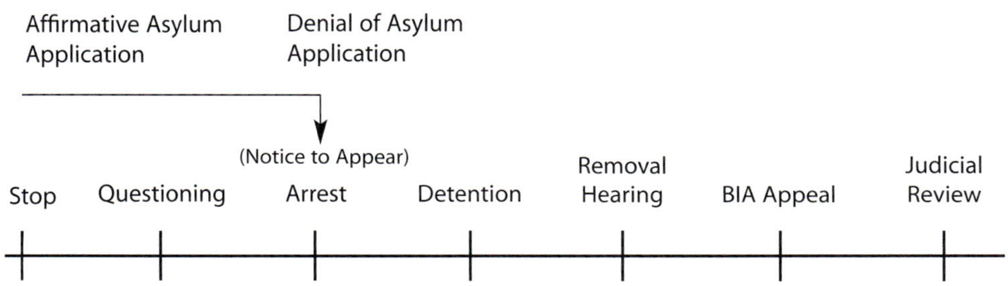

E. The Burden of Proof in Removal Proceedings

Elizabeth Rosalia Woodby and Joseph Sherman v. Immigration and Naturalization Service

385 U.S. 276 (1966)

Mr. Justice Stewart delivered the opinion of the Court.

The question presented by these cases is what burden of proof the Government must sustain in deportation proceedings. We have concluded that it is incumbent upon the Government in such proceedings to establish the facts supporting deportability by clear, unequivocal, and convincing evidence.

In Sherman (No. 80), the petitioner is a resident alien who entered this country from Poland in 1920 as a 14-year-old boy. In 1963 the Immigration and Naturalization Service instituted proceedings to deport him upon the ground that he had re-entered the United States in 1938, following a trip abroad, without inspection as an alien. After a hearing before a special inquiry officer, the petitioner was ordered to be deported, and the Board of Immigration Appeals dismissed his appeal. The Government's evidence showed that the petitioner had obtained a passport in 1937 under the name of Samuel Levine, representing himself as a United States citizen. Someone using this passport sailed to France in June 1937, proceeded to Spain, returned to the United States in December 1938, aboard the S.S. Ausonia, and was admitted without being examined as an alien. To establish that it was the petitioner who had traveled under this passport, the Government introduced the testimony of Edward Morrow, an American citizen who had fought in the Spanish Civil War. Morrow was at first unable to remember the name Samuel Levine or identify the petitioner, but eventually stated that he thought he had known the petitioner as "Sam Levine," had seen him while fighting for the Loyalists in Spain during 1937 and 1938, and had returned with him to the United States aboard the S.S. Ausonia in December 1938. Morrow conceded that his recollection of events occurring 27 years earlier was imperfect, and admitted that his identification of the petitioner might be mistaken.

It is not clear what standard of proof the special inquiry officer and the Board of Immigration Appeals on de novo review applied in determining that it was the petitioner who had traveled to Spain and re-entered the United States under the Samuel Levine passport. At the outset of his opinion, the special inquiry officer stated that the Government must establish deportability "by reasonable, substantial and probative evidence," without discussing what the burden of proof was. Later he concluded that the Government had established its contentions "with a solidarity far greater than required," but did not further elucidate what was "required." The Board of Immigration Appeals stated that it was "established beyond any reasonable doubt" that the petitioner had obtained the Samuel Levine passport, and added that this established a "presumption" that the petitioner had used it to travel abroad. The Board further stated that it was a "most unlikely hypothesis" that someone other than the petitioner had obtained and used the passport, and asserted that "the Service has borne its burden of establishing" that the petitioner was deportable, without indicating what it considered the weight of that burden to be.

Upon petition for review, the Court of Appeals for the Second Circuit originally set aside the deportation order, upon the ground that the Government has the burden of proving the facts supporting deportability beyond a reasonable doubt. The court reversed itself, however, upon a rehearing en banc, holding that the Government need only prove its case with "reasonable, substantial, and probative evidence." We granted certiorari, 384 U.S. 904.

In Woodby (No. 40), the petitioner is a resident alien who was born in Hungary and entered the United States from Germany in 1956 as the wife of an American soldier. Deportation proceedings were instituted against her on the ground that she had engaged in prostitution after entry. A special inquiry officer and the Board of Immigration Appeals found that she was deportable upon the ground charged.

At the administrative hearing the petitioner admitted that she had engaged in prostitution for a brief period in 1957, some months after her husband had deserted her, but claimed that her conduct was the product of circumstances amounting to duress. Without reaching the validity of the duress defense, the special inquiry officer and the Board of Immigration Appeals concluded that the petitioner had continued to engage in prostitution after the alleged duress had terminated. The hearing officer and the Board did not discuss what burden of proof the Government was required to bear in establishing deportability, nor did either of them indicate the degree of certainty with which their factual conclusions were reached. The special inquiry officer merely asserted that the evidence demonstrated that the petitioner was deportable. The Board stated that the evidence made it "apparent" that the petitioner had engaged in prostitution after the alleged duress had ended, and announced that "it is concluded that the evidence establishes deportability...."

In denying a petition for review, the Court of Appeals for the Sixth Circuit did not explicitly deal with the issue of what burden of persuasion was imposed upon the Government at the administrative level, finding only that "the Board's underlying order is 'supported by reasonable, substantial, and probative evidence on the record considered as a whole....'" We granted certiorari, 384 U.S. 904.

In the prevailing opinion in the Sherman case, the Court of Appeals for the Second Circuit stated that "[i]f the slate were clean," it might well agree that the standard of persuasion for deportation should be similar to that in denaturalization, where the Supreme Court has insisted that the evidence must be "clear, unequivocal, and convincing" and that the Government needs "more than a bare preponderance of the evidence" to prevail.... But here, the court thought, "Congress has spoken...." 350 F.2d at 900. This view was based upon two provisions of the Immigration and Nationality Act which use the language "reasonable, substantial, and probative evidence" in connection with deportation orders. The provisions in question are § 106(a)(4) of the Act which states that a deportation order, "if supported by reasonable, substantial, and probative evidence on the record considered as a whole, shall be conclusive," and § 242(b)(4) of the Act which provides inter alia that "no decision of deportability shall be valid unless it is based upon reasonable, substantial, and probative evidence."

It seems clear, however, that these two statutory provisions are addressed not to the degree of proof required at the administrative level in deportation proceedings, but to quite a different subject—the scope of judicial review. The elementary but crucial difference between burden of proof and scope of review is, of course, a commonplace in the law. The difference is most graphically illustrated in a criminal case. There the prosecution is generally required to prove the elements of the offense beyond a reasonable doubt. But if the correct burden of proof was imposed at the trial, judicial review is generally limited to ascertaining whether the evidence relied upon by the trier of fact was of sufficient quality and substantiality to support the rationality of the judgment. In other words, an appellate court in a criminal case ordinarily does not ask itself whether it believes that the evidence at the trial established guilt beyond a reasonable doubt, but whether the judgment is supported by substantial evidence.

That § 106(a)(4) relates exclusively to judicial review is made abundantly clear by its language, its context, and its legislative history. Section 106 was added to the Act in 1961 in order "to create a single, separate, statutory form of judicial review of administrative orders for the deportation and exclusion of aliens from the United States." The section is entitled "Judicial Review of Orders of Deportation and Exclusion," and by its terms provides "the sole and exclusive procedure for" the "judicial review of all final orders of deportation." Subsection 106(a)(4) is a specific directive to the courts in which petitions for review are filed.

It is hardly less clear that the other provision upon which the Court of Appeals for the Second Circuit relied, § 242(b)(4) of the Act, is also addressed to reviewing courts, and, insofar as it represents a yardstick for the administrative factfinder, goes, not to the burden of proof, but rather to the quality and nature of the evidence upon which a deportation order must be based. The provision declares that "reasonable, substantial, and probative evidence" shall be the measure of whether a deportability decision is "valid" — a word that implies scrutiny by a reviewing tribunal of a decision already reached by the trier of the facts. The location of this provision in a section containing provisions dealing with procedures before the special inquiry officer has little significance when it is remembered that the original 1952 Act did not itself contain a framework for judicial review — although such review was, of course, available by habeas corpus or otherwise. See *Marcello v. Bonds*, 349 U.S. 302. And whatever ambiguity might be thought to lie in the location of this section is resolved by its legislative history. The Senate Report explained § 242(b)(4) as follows: "The requirement that the decision of the special inquiry officer shall be based on reasonable, substantial and probative evidence means that, where the decision rests upon evidence of such a nature that it cannot be said that a reasonable person might not have reached the conclusion which was reached, the case may not be reversed because the judgment of the appellate body differs from that of the administrative body."

We conclude, therefore, that Congress has not addressed itself to the question of what degree of proof is required in deportation proceedings. It is the kind of question which has traditionally been left to the judiciary to resolve, and its resolution is necessary in the interest of the evenhanded administration of the Immigration and Nationality Act.

The petitioners urge that the appropriate burden of proof in deportation proceedings should be that which the law imposes in criminal cases — the duty of proving the essential facts beyond a reasonable doubt. The Government, on the other hand, points out that a deportation proceeding is not a criminal case, and that the appropriate burden of proof should consequently be the one generally imposed in civil cases and administrative proceedings — the duty of prevailing by a mere preponderance of the evidence.

To be sure, a deportation proceeding is not a criminal prosecution. *Harisiades v. Shaughnessy*, 342 U.S. 580. But it does not syllogistically follow that a person may be banished from this country upon no higher degree of proof than applies in a negligence case. This Court has not closed its eyes to the drastic deprivations that may follow when a resident of this country is compelled by our Government to forsake all the bonds formed here and go to a foreign land where he often has no contemporary identification. In words apposite to the question before us, we have spoken of "the solidity of proof that is required for a judgment entailing the consequences of deportation, particularly in the case of an old man who has lived in this country for forty years...." *Rowoldt v. Perfetto*, 355 U.S. 115, 120.

In denaturalization cases the Court has required the Government to establish its allegations by clear, unequivocal, and convincing evidence. The same burden has been imposed in expatriation cases. That standard of proof is no stranger to the civil law.

No less a burden of proof is appropriate in deportation proceedings. The immediate hardship of deportation is often greater than that inflicted by denaturalization, which does not, immediately at least, result in expulsion from our shores. And many resident aliens have lived in this country longer and established stronger family, social, and economic ties here than some who have become naturalized citizens.

We hold that no deportation order may be entered unless it is found by clear, unequivocal, and convincing evidence that the facts alleged as grounds for deportation are true....

Notes

1. The Immigration Act of 1990 removed 8 U.S.C. § 1252(b)(4), which provided that "no decision of deportability shall be valid unless it is based upon reasonable, substantial and probative evidence." If instead, Congress had used the word "substantial" in place of "reasonable, substantial and probative," what would be the result in light of *Woodby*? Is there any significance which can be attached to Congress' elimination of the "reasonable, substantial and probative" requirement? If Congress changed the burden of proof in deportation so as only to necessitate a preponderance of the evidence, would this be constitutional?

2. Although the burden of proof is on the government, deportability is usually easily and clearly established. As a result, in most cases deportability is generally conceded, and the respondent seeks some form of discretionary relief such as asylum (Chapter 5), cancellation of removal (Chapter 11), or adjustment of status (Chapter 7).

3. **Voluntary departure.** The Court noted that Woodby had been granted voluntary departure, which is a benefit described in 8 U.S.C. § 1229c, Sec. 240B that requires the applicant to establish that she is a person of good moral character and is ready, willing and able to leave the United States.[96] In effect, it allows the person protection from the adverse consequences of a deportation order. If a person is the subject of an order of deportation and does not have voluntary departure, she will not be allowed to return to the United States for five years unless she has first received permission from the Attorney General.[97] The usual period of voluntary departure is thirty days, although longer periods may be granted at the discretion of the immigration judge.[98]

---

96. *See also* 8 C.F.R. § 1240.26(c)(1).

97. *See also* discussion in Chapter 11 on relief from deportation.

98. *Matter of M-*, 4 I. & N. Dec. 626 (BIA 1969). For additional guidance on voluntary departure, see 8 C.F.R. §§ 1240.11(b) and 1240.26.

F. The Burden of Proof Applied

Matter of Vivas

16 I. & N. Dec. 68 (BIA 1977)

BY: Milhollan, Chairman; Wilson, Torrington, Maniatis, and Appleman, Board Members

The respondent appeals from an immigration judge's decision dated August 9, 1976. In this decision the respondent was found deportable under section 241(a)(1) of the Immigration and Nationality Act as excludable at entry under section 212(a)(14) and section 212(a)(20) of the Act and was granted the privilege of voluntary departure. The appeal will be dismissed.

The respondent is a 24-year-old native and citizen of Mexico. He entered the United States as an immigrant on August 31, 1974. At issue is whether the respondent's deportability has been established by clear, convincing and unequivocal evidence.

The record reveals that the respondent obtained his immigrant visa and his exemption from the labor certification on account of his marriage to a United States citizen. The Service must prove by the required degree of evidence that the respondent was not exempt at the time of entry from the labor certification and that the visa he presented to gain admission as a lawful permanent resident was invalid.

To prove its case, the Service presented as a witness a person claiming to be the individual referred to in the birth certificate used to establish the United States citizenship of the respondent's wife. The immigration judge concluded, on the basis of her testimony at the hearing and the other evidence in the record, that the birth certificate used to establish the citizenship of the respondent's wife belonged to the witness. The immigration judge's finding of fact carries great weight and will not ordinarily be set aside. *Matter of T-*, 7 I. & N. Dec. 417 (BIA 1957).

The witness testified that she has never gone through a marriage ceremony with the respondent, that she had never met him previously and that she is married to someone else presently. The respondent testified that he had not married the witness and that he had never seen her before. However, the respondent claimed that he married someone who was using the same name as the witness. The respondent presented no evidence to clarify his wife's identity or to prove that she is a United States citizen.

Since we have decided that the witness is the United States citizen referred to in the birth certificate, the question is, more concretely, whether the respondent's deportability as one who was excludable at entry under section 212(a)(14) of the Act is established by clear, convincing and unequivocal evidence when the Service establishes that the respondent is not married to the person whose birth certificate was used to establish the exemption from the labor certification and the respondent has not gone forward with evidence to establish the real identity of the person to whom he claims to have been married at the time he entered the United States. We hold in the affirmative for this proposition.

It is not a novel principle in immigration law that, notwithstanding the requirement of clear, convincing and unequivocal evidence to establish deportability, a respondent may properly be required to go forward with evidence to rebut prima facie showings by the Service. See *Matter of Tijerina-Villarreal*, 13 I. & N. Dec. 327 (BIA 1969); *Matter of Conliffe*, 13 I. & N. Dec. 95 (BIA 1968); *Matter of Vosganian*, 12 I. & N. Dec. 1 (BIA 1966). In the case at hand, the rule is justified.

In this situation, manifestly, the Service is under a serious practical handicap if it must prove the negative proposition: that the respondent did not marry a United States citizen when he married on June 9, 1973. The possibilities are of such magnitude as to defy inclusive rebuttal. On the other hand, the burden of affirmatively identifying the person whom he married is not an oppressive one for the respondent to undertake; the relevant facts to do that are peculiarly within his knowledge. He is only being called to identify properly the person; the Service still retains the obligation to prove by clear, convincing and unequivocal evidence that the respondent is deportable on the charges brought against him.

The rule that we are enunciating for this situation is not new to either criminal or civil proceedings. The burden of going forward with evidence can be placed on a party not bearing the burden of proof when the facts are within his particular knowledge or control. See *United States v. Fleischman*, 339 U.S. 349 (1950); *Commercial Molasses Corp. v. New York Tank Barge Corp.*, 314 U.S. 104 (1941); *Williams v. Administrator of Nat. Aero. & Space Admin.*, 463 F.2d 1391 (C.C.P.A.1972); *United States v. Hayes*, 369 F.2d 671 (9 Cir.1966). The burden of going forward with evidence also arises under certain circumstances when a prima facie case is made by the opponent. See *Government of Virgin Islands v. Lake*, 362 F.2d 770 (3 Cir.1966); *Rhay v. Browder*, 342 F.2d 345 (9 Cir.1965). And, more in line with the factual situation at hand, the burden of going forward with the evidence is placed on a party not having the burden of proof when he has better control or knowledge of the evidence and his adversary makes a prima facie showing of his case. See *Campbell v. United States*, 365 U.S. 85 (1961); *Rossi v. United States*, 289 U.S. 89 (1933).

The Service has shown that the respondent has not married the person whose birth certificate was used to establish his exemption from the labor certification as the spouse of a United States citizen. The respondent has not gone forward with evidence to establish the identity of the person he married.

Counsel for the respondent argues on appeal that the respondent is not deportable as excludable at entry under section 212(a)(14) because the record is silent as to the purpose of the respondent's entry. We reject counsel's contention.

The record shows that the respondent was employed in Chicago prior to his trek to Mexico to obtain his visa. The respondent when asked his occupation on the visa application said "labores." The respondent was employed at the time of the hearing. There is an affidavit in the record from the purported wife of the respondent, dated June 24, 1974, stating that he was permanently employed by the Crane Company in Chicago. That evidence is sufficient to establish that his purpose to enter the United

States was to perform skilled or unskilled labor. See *Matter of Lee*, Interim Decision 2424 (BIA 1975); *Matter of Becerra*, 13 I. & N. Dec. 19 (BIA 1968). The respondent's deportability as one who was excludable at entry under section 212(a)(14) has been established clearly, convincingly, and unequivocally.

It is established that the birth certificate accompanying the documentation presented to the consul to prove the eligibility of the respondent for his immigrant visa did not refer to the respondent's wife. If that fact had been known to the consul at the time he issued the visa, he would not have issued it since there was no evidence before him that would establish the respondent's eligibility to receive the visa.

Where the true facts would have required a consul to rule that an applicant for a visa had not borne the burden of establishing eligibility, we must hold that concealment of those facts resulted in the procurement of a visa which was not valid. *Matter of F-M-*, 7 I. & N. Dec. 420 (BIA 1957). The fact that the applicant might have obtained a visa at a later date, establishing his full eligibility with evidence other than the one submitted at the time, does not mean that the visa obtained on August 14, 1974 is a valid visa. See *Ablett v. Brownell*, 240 F.2d 625 (D.C.Cir.1957). Cf. *United States ex rel. Fink v. Reimer*, 96 F.2d 217 (2 Cir.1938). The respondent's inadmissibility under section 212(a)(20) of the Act at the time of entry has been established.

Counsel for the respondent seems to argue on appeal that the respondent cannot be found deportable as excludable at entry under section 212(a)(20) because there is no evidence of fraud on the part of the respondent concerning the obtainment of his visa. We agree with counsel for the respondent that there is no evidence of fraud on the part of the respondent. However, that does not affect deportability since fraud or willfulness is unnecessary for a charge under section 212(a)(20) of the Act. *Matter of F-M-, supra*. The appeal will be dismissed.

Notes

1. *Matter of Vivas* is presented to illustrate that the burden does not remain static. At some point, it is the responsibility of the respondent to rebut the contrary evidence. In cases involving a relevant criminal conviction, the government must "prove up" the conviction. If, however, the respondent establishes that the conviction was vacated, the burden then switches back to the government. *Barakat v. Holder*, 621 F.3d 398 (6th Cir. 2010).

2. In *Ward v. Holder*,[99] Ward, a lawful permanent resident, had returned in 2003 to the U.K, the country of his nationality, to tend to his mother who was suffering from dementia. He returned to the U.S. in 2006. The government called Ward as its only witness in attempting to meet its burden of showing that Ward had abandoned his permanent residency. The green card that Ward used to return had expired and

---

99. 733 F.3d 601 (6th Cir. 2013).

he was charged with not possessing "a valid unexpired immigrant visa, reentry permit, border crossing identification card, or other valid entry document" under 8 U.S.C. § 1182(a)(7)(A)(i)(I). Since the charge was that Ward had abandoned his LPR status, the burden fell on the government. The court stated that the burden was a steep one, and that the use of the "the term 'unequivocal,' taken by itself, means proof that admits of no doubt, a burden approximating, if not exceeding, that used in criminal cases."[100]

3. However once alienage has been established, respondent must show the time, place and manner of her entry to the U.S. 8 U.S.C. § 1361.[101] Therefore a person who has entered the U.S. by avoiding inspection and has admitted to alienage or the government has established alienage, will have the burden of going forward that she is clearly and beyond a doubt entitled to be admitted and not inadmissible. and of presenting convincing evidence that she is lawfully present. 8 U.S.C. 1229a(c)(2).[102]

4. In cases involving the invocation of deportability grounds, the Supreme Court has long held that the Rule of Lenity should be applied, meaning that it will apply a rule of strict construction in interpreting the statute in question.[103]

Removal Procedure and Burdens of Proof

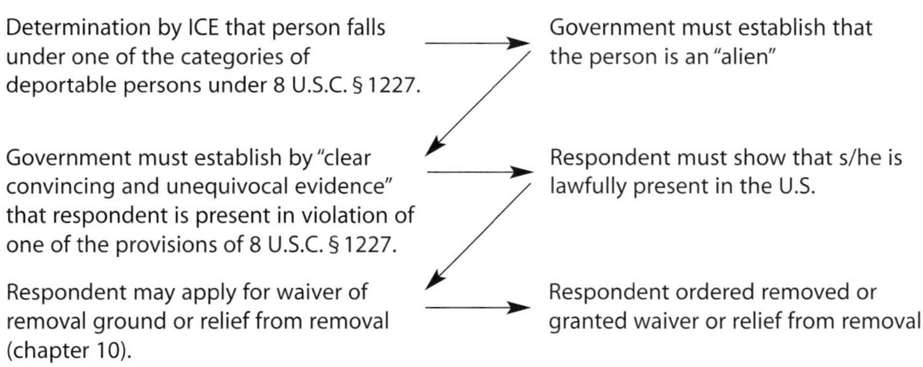

G. The Evolution of Search and Seizure Law

United States v. Felix Humberto Brignoni-Ponce

422 U.S. 873 (1975)

Mr. Justice Powell delivered the opinion of the Court.

This case raises questions as to the United States Border Patrol's authority to stop automobiles in areas near the Mexican border. It differs from our decision in *Almeida-*

---

100. 733 F.3d at 605.

101. Sec. 291.

102. Sec. 240(c)(2).

103. *See, e.g., Fong Haw Tan v. Phelan*, 333 U.S. 6 (1948); *INS v. Cardoza-Fonseca*, 480 U.S. 421 (1987); *Moncrieffe v. Holder*, 569 U.S. 184, 205 (2013).

Sanchez v. United States, 413 U.S. 266 (1973), in that the Border Patrol does not claim authority to search cars, but only to question the occupants about their citizenship and immigration status.

As a part of its regular traffic-checking operations in southern California, the Border Patrol operates a fixed checkpoint on Interstate Highway 5 south of San Clemente. On the evening of March 11, 1973, the checkpoint was closed because of inclement weather, but two officers were observing northbound traffic from a patrol car parked at the side of the highway. The road was dark, and they were using the patrol car's headlights to illuminate passing cars. They pursued respondent's car and stopped it, saying later that their only reason for doing so was that its three occupants appeared to be of Mexican descent. The officers questioned respondent and his two passengers about their citizenship and learned that the passengers were aliens who had entered the country illegally. All three were then arrested, and respondent was charged with two counts of knowingly transporting illegal immigrants, a violation of § 274(a)(2) of the Immigration and Nationality Act, 66 Stat. 228, 8 U.S.C. § 1324(a)(2). At trial respondent moved to suppress the testimony of and about the two passengers, claiming that this evidence was the fruit of an illegal seizure. The trial court denied the motion, the aliens testified at trial, and respondent was convicted on both counts.

Respondent's appeal was pending in the Court of Appeals for the Ninth Circuit when we announced our decision in *Almeida-Sanchez v. United States, supra*, holding that the Fourth Amendment prohibits the use of roving patrols to search vehicles, without a warrant or probable cause, at points removed from the border and its functional equivalents. The Court of Appeals, sitting en banc, held that the stop in this case more closely resembled a roving-patrol stop than a stop at a traffic checkpoint, and applied the principles of *Almeida-Sanchez*.[1] The court held that the Fourth Amendment, as interpreted in *Almeida-Sanchez*, forbids stopping a vehicle, even for the limited purpose of questioning its occupants, unless the officers have a "founded suspicion" that the occupants are aliens illegally in the country. The court refused to find that Mexican ancestry alone supported such a "founded suspicion" and held that respondent's motion to suppress should have been granted.[2] 499 F.2d 1109 (1974). We granted certiorari and set the case for oral argument with No. 73-2050, *United States v. Ortiz*, 422 U.S. 891, and No. 73-6848, *Bowen v. United States*, 422 U.S. 916 (1974).

---

1. For the Court of Appeals' purposes, the distinction between a roving patrol and a fixed checkpoint was controlling. The court previously had held that the principles of *Almeida-Sanchez v. United States* applied retrospectively to the activities of roving patrols but not to those of fixed checkpoints. *See United States v. Peltier*, 500 F.2d 985 (CA9 1974), *rev'd*, 422 U.S. 531; *United States v. Bowen*, 500 F.2d 960 (CA9 1974), *aff'd*, 422 U.S. 916.

2. There may be room to question whether voluntary testimony of a witness at trial, as opposed to a Government agent's testimony about objects seized or statements overheard, is subject to suppression as the fruit of an illegal search or seizure. *See United States v. Guana-Sanchez*, 484 F.2d 590 (CA7 1973), *cert. dismissed as improvidently granted*, 420 U.S. 513 (1975). But since the question was not raised in the petition for certiorari, we do not address it.

The Government does not challenge the Court of Appeals' factual conclusion that the stop of respondent's car was a roving-patrol stop rather than a checkpoint stop. Brief for United States 8. Nor does it challenge the retroactive application of Almeida-Sanchez, Brief for United States 9, or contend that the San Clemente checkpoint is the functional equivalent of the border. The only issue presented for decision is whether a roving patrol may stop a vehicle in an area near the border and question its occupants when the only ground for suspicion is that the occupants appear to be of Mexican ancestry. For the reasons that follow, we affirm the decision of the Court of Appeals.

The Government claims two sources of statutory authority for stopping cars without warrants in the border areas. Section 287(a)(1) of the Immigration and Nationality Act, 8 U.S.C. § 1357(a)(1), authorizes any officer or employee of the Immigration and Naturalization Service (INS) without a warrant, "to interrogate any alien or person believed to be an alien as to his right to be or to remain in the United States." There is no geographical limitation on this authority. The Government contends that, at least in the areas adjacent to the Mexican border, a person's apparent Mexican ancestry alone justifies belief that he or she is an alien and satisfies the requirement of this statute. Section 287(a)(3) of the Act, 8 U.S.C. § 1357(a)(3), authorizes agents, without a warrant, "within a reasonable distance from any external boundary of the United States, to board and search for aliens any vessel within the territorial waters of the United States and any railway car, aircraft, conveyance, or vehicle...."

Under current regulations, this authority may be exercised anywhere within 100 miles of the border. 8 CFR § 287.1(a) (1975). The Border Patrol interprets the statute as granting authority to stop moving vehicles and question the occupants about their citizenship, even when its officers have no reason to believe that the occupants are aliens or that other aliens may be concealed in the vehicle.[3] But "no Act of Congress can authorize a violation of the Constitution," *Almeida-Sanchez, supra*, 413 U.S. at 272, and we must decide whether the Fourth Amendment allows such random vehicle stops in the border areas.

III

The Fourth Amendment applies to all seizures of the person, including seizures that involve only a brief detention short of traditional arrest. *Davis v. Mississippi*, 394 U.S. 721 (1969); *Terry v. Ohio*, 392 U.S. 1, 16–19 (1968). "[W]henever a police officer accosts an individual and restrains his freedom to walk away, he has 'seized' that person," *id.*, at 16, and the Fourth Amendment requires that the seizure be "reasonable." As with other categories of police action subject to Fourth Amendment constraints, the reasonableness of such seizures depends on a balance between the public interest

3. We cannot accept respondent's contention that, even though § 287(a)(3) does not mention probable cause, its legislative history establishes that Congress meant to condition immigration officers' authority to board and search vehicles on probable cause to believe that they contained aliens. The legislative history simply does not support this contention.

and the individual's right to personal security free from arbitrary interference by law officers. *Id.*, at 20–21; *Camara v. Municipal Court*, 387 U.S. 523, 536–537 (1967).

The Government makes a convincing demonstration that the public interest demands effective measures to prevent the illegal entry of aliens at the Mexican border. Estimates of the number of illegal immigrants in the United States vary widely. A conservative estimate in 1972 produced a figure of about one million, but the INS now suggests there may be as many as 10 or 12 million aliens illegally in the country.[4] Whatever the number, these aliens create significant economic and social problems, competing with citizens and legal resident aliens for jobs, and generating extra demand for social services. The aliens themselves are vulnerable to exploitation because they cannot complain of substandard working conditions without risking deportation. See generally Hearings on Illegal Aliens before Subcommittee No. 1 of the House Committee on the Judiciary, 92d Cong., 1st and 2d Sess., ser. 13, pts. 1–5 (1971–1972).

The Government has estimated that 85% of the aliens illegally in the country are from Mexico. *United States v. Baca*, 368 F.Supp. 398, 402 (SD Cal.1973). The Mexican border is almost 2,000 miles long, and even a vastly reinforced Border Patrol would find it impossible to prevent illegal border crossings. Many aliens cross the Mexican border on foot, miles away from patrolled areas, and then purchase transportation from the border area to inland cities, where they find jobs and elude the immigration authorities. Others gain entry on valid temporary border-crossing permits, but then violate the conditions of their entry. Most of these aliens leave the border area in private vehicles, often assisted by professional "alien smugglers." The Border Patrol's traffic-checking operations are designed to prevent this inland movement. They succeed in apprehending some illegal entrants and smugglers, and they deter the movement of others by threatening apprehension and increasing the cost of illegal transportation.

Against this valid public interest we must weigh the interference with individual liberty that results when an officer stops an automobile and questions its occupants. The intrusion is modest. The Government tells us that a stop by a roving patrol "usually consumes no more than a minute." Brief for United States 25. There is no search of the vehicle or its occupants, and the visual inspection is limited to those parts of the vehicle that can be seen by anyone standing alongside. According to the Government, "[a]ll that is required of the vehicle's occupants is a response to a brief question or two and possibly the production of a document evidencing a right to be in the United States." *Ibid.*

Because of the limited nature of the intrusion, stops of this sort may be justified on facts that do not amount to the probable cause required for an arrest. In *Terry v. Ohio, supra*, the Court declined expressly to decide whether facts not amounting to

---

4. The estimate of one million was produced by the Commissioner of the INS for the Immigration and Nationality Subcommittee of the House Judiciary Committee. Hearings on Illegal Aliens before Subcommittee, No. 1 of the House Committee on the Judiciary, 92d Cong., 2d Sess., ser. 13, pt. 5, pp. 1323–1325 (1972). The higher estimate appears in the INS Ann.Rep. iii (1974).

probable cause could justify an "investigative seizure" short of an arrest, 392 U.S., at 19 n. 16, but it approved a limited search—a pat-down for weapons—for the protection of an officer investigating suspicious behavior of persons he reasonably believed to be armed and dangerous. The Court approved such a search on facts that did not constitute probable cause to believe the suspects guilty of a crime, requiring only that "the police officer ... be able to point to specific and articulable facts which, taken together with rational inferences from those facts, reasonably warrant" a belief that his safety or that of others is in danger. *Id.*, at 21; see id., at 27.

We elaborated on *Terry* in *Adams v. Williams*, 407 U.S. 143 (1972), holding that a policeman was justified in approaching the respondent to investigate a tip that he was carrying narcotics and a gun.

> "The Fourth Amendment does not require a policeman who lacks the precise level of information necessary for probable cause to arrest to simply shrug his shoulders and allow a crime to occur or a criminal to escape. On the contrary, *Terry* recognizes that it may be the essence of good police work to adopt an intermediate response.... A brief stop of a suspicious individual, in order to determine his identity or to maintain the status quo momentarily while obtaining more information, may be most reasonable in light of the facts known to the officer at the time." *Id.*, at 145–146.

These cases together establish that in appropriate circumstances the Fourth Amendment allows a properly limited "search" or "seizure" on facts that do not constitute probable cause to arrest or to search for contraband or evidence of crime. In both *Terry* and *Adams v. Williams* the investigating officers had reasonable grounds to believe that the suspects were armed and that they might be dangerous. The limited searches and seizures in those cases were a valid method of protecting the public and preventing crime. In this case as well, because of the importance of the governmental interest at stake, the minimal intrusion of a brief stop, and the absence of practical alternatives for policing the border, we hold that when an officer's observations lead him reasonably to suspect that a particular vehicle may contain aliens who are illegally in the country, he may stop the car briefly and investigate the circumstances that provoke suspicion. As in *Terry*, the stop and inquiry must be "reasonably related in scope to the justification for their initiation." 392 U.S., at 29. The officer may question the driver and passengers about their citizenship and immigration status, and he may ask them to explain suspicious circumstances, but any further detention or search must be based on consent or probable cause.

We are unwilling to let the Border Patrol dispense entirely with the requirement that officers must have a reasonable suspicion to justify roving-patrol stops. In the context of border area stops, the reasonableness requirement of the Fourth Amendment demands something more than the broad and unlimited discretion sought by the Government. Roads near the border carry not only aliens seeking to enter the country illegally, but a large volume of legitimate traffic as well. San Diego, with a metropolitan population of 1.4 million, is located on the border. Texas has two fairly large metropolitan areas directly on the border: El Paso, with a population of 360,000, and the Brownsville-McAllen area, with a combined population of 320,000. We are confident that substantially all of the traffic in these cities is lawful and that relatively few of their residents have any connection with the illegal entry and transportation of aliens. To approve roving-patrol stops of all vehicles in the border area, without any suspicion that a particular vehicle is carrying illegal immigrants, would subject the residents of these and other areas to potentially unlimited interference with their use of the highways, solely at the discretion of Border Patrol officers. The only formal limitation on that discretion appears to be the administrative regulation defining the term "reasonable distance" in § 287(a)(3) to mean within 100 air miles from the border. 8 CFR § 287.1(a) (1975). Thus, if we approved the Government's position in this case, Border Patrol officers could stop motorists at random for questioning, day or night, anywhere within 100 air miles of the 2,000-mile border, on a city street, a busy highway, or a desert road, without any reason to suspect that they have violated any law.

We are not convinced that the legitimate needs of law enforcement require this degree of interference with lawful traffic. As we discuss in Part IV, infra, the nature of illegal alien traffic and the characteristics of smuggling operations tend to generate articulable grounds for identifying violators. Consequently, a requirement of reasonable suspicion for stops allows the Government adequate means of guarding the public interest and also protects residents of the border areas from indiscriminate official interference. Under the circumstances, and even though the intrusion incident to a stop is modest, we conclude that it is not "reasonable" under the Fourth Amendment to make such stops on a random basis.[8]

The Government also contends that the public interest in enforcing conditions on legal alien entry justifies stopping persons who may be aliens for questioning about their citizenship and immigration status. Although we may assume for purposes of this case that the broad congressional power over immigration, see *Kleindienst v. Mandel*, 408 U.S. 753, 765–767 (1972), authorizes Congress to admit aliens on condition that they will submit to reasonable questioning about their right to be and remain in the country, this power cannot diminish the Fourth Amendment rights of citizens who may be mistaken for aliens. For the same reasons that the Fourth Amendment forbids stopping vehicles at random to inquire if they are carrying aliens who are illegally in the country, it also forbids stopping or detaining persons for questioning about their citizenship on less than a reasonable suspicion that they may be aliens.

8. Our decision in this case takes into account the special function of the Border Patrol, the importance of the governmental interests in policing the border area, the character of roving-patrol stops, and the availability of alternatives to random stops unsupported by reasonable suspicion. Border Patrol agents have no part in enforcing laws that regulate highway use, and their activities have nothing to do with an inquiry whether motorists and their vehicles are entitled, by virtue of compliance with laws governing highway usage, to be upon the public highways. Our decision thus does not imply that state and local enforcement agencies are without power to conduct such limited stops as are necessary to enforce laws regarding drivers' licenses, vehicle registration, truck weights, and similar matters.

IV

The effect of our decision is to limit exercise of the authority granted by both § 287(a)(1) and § 287(a)(3). Except at the border and its functional equivalents, officers on roving patrol may stop vehicles only if they are aware of specific articulable facts, together with rational inferences from those facts, that reasonably warrant suspicion that the vehicles contain aliens who may be illegally in the country.[9]

Any number of factors may be taken into account in deciding whether there is reasonable suspicion to stop a car in the border area. Officers may consider the characteristics of the area in which they encounter a vehicle. Its proximity to the border, the usual patterns of traffic on the particular road, and previous experience with alien traffic are all relevant. See *Carroll v. United States*, 267 U.S. 132, 159–161 (1925); *United States v. Jaime-Barrios*, 494 F.2d 455 (CA9), cert. denied, 417 U.S. 972 (1974).[10] They also may consider information about recent illegal border crossings in the area. The driver's behavior may be relevant, as erratic driving or obvious attempts to evade officers can support a reasonable suspicion. See *United States v. Larios-Montes*, 500 F.2d 941 (CA9 1974); *Duprez v. United States*, 435 F.2d 1276 (CA9 1970). Aspects of the vehicle itself may justify suspicion. For instance, officers say that certain station wagons, with large compartments for fold-down seats or spare tires, are frequently used for transporting concealed aliens. See *United States v. Bugarin-Casas*, 484 F.2d 853 (CA9 1973), cert. denied, 414 U.S. 1136 (1974); *United States v. Wright*, 476 F.2d 1027 (CA5 1973). The vehicle may appear to be heavily loaded, it may have an extraordinary number of passengers, or the officers may observe persons trying to hide. See *United States v. Larios-Montes, supra*. The Government also points out that trained officers can recognize the characteristic appearance of persons who live in Mexico, relying on such factors as the mode of dress and haircut. Reply Brief for United States 12–13, in *United States v. Ortiz*, 422 U.S. 891. In all situations the officer is entitled to assess the facts in light of his experience in detecting illegal entry and smuggling. *Terry v. Ohio*, 392 U.S., at 27.

In this case the officers relied on a single factor to justify stopping respondent's car: the apparent Mexican ancestry of the occupants. We cannot conclude that this furnished reasonable grounds to believe that the three occupants were aliens. At best the officers had only a fleeting glimpse of the persons in the moving car, illuminated by headlights. Even if they saw enough to think that the occupants were of Mexican descent, this factor alone would justify neither a reasonable belief that they were aliens, nor a reasonable belief that the car concealed other aliens who were illegally in the

9. As noted above, we reserve the question whether Border Patrol officers also may stop persons reasonably believed to be aliens when there is no reason to believe they are illegally in the country. *See Cheung Tin Wong v. INS*, 152 U.S.App.D.C. 66, 468 F.2d 1123 (1972); *Au Yi Lau v. INS*, 144 U.S.App.D.C. 147, 445 F.2d 217, *cert. denied*, 404 U.S. 864 (1971). The facts of this case do not require decision on the point.

10. The Courts of Appeals decisions cited throughout this part are merely illustrative. Our citation of them does not imply a view of the merits of particular decisions. Each case must turn on the totality of the particular circumstances.

country. Large numbers of native-born and naturalized citizens have the physical characteristics identified with Mexican ancestry, and even in the border area a relatively small proportion of them are aliens. The likelihood that any given person of Mexican ancestry is an alien is high enough to make Mexican appearance a relevant factor, but standing alone it does not justify stopping all Mexican-Americans to ask if they are aliens.[12]

The judgment of the Court of Appeals is affirmed.

Mr. Justice REHNQUIST, concurring.

I join in the opinion of the Court. I think it quite important to point out, however, that that opinion, which is joined by a somewhat different majority than that which comprised the *Almeida Sanchez* Court, is both by its terms and by its reasoning concerned only with the type of stop involved in this case. I think that just as travelers entering the country may be stopped and searched without probable cause and without founded suspicion, because of "national self protection reasonably requiring one entering the country to identify himself as entitled to come in, and his belongings as effects which may be lawfully brought in," *Carroll v. United States*, 267 U.S. 132, 154 (1925), a strong case may be made for those charged with the enforcement of laws conditioning the right of vehicular use of a highway to likewise stop motorists using highways in order to determine whether they have met the qualifications prescribed by applicable law for such use. See *Cady v. Dombrowski*, 413 U.S. 433, 440–441 (1973); *United States v. Biswell*, 406 U.S. 311 (1972). I regard these and similar situations, such as agricultural inspections and highway roadblocks to apprehend known fugitives, as not in any way constitutionally suspect by reason of today's decision.

Mr. Justice DOUGLAS, concurring in the judgment.

I join in the affirmance of the judgment. The stopping of respondent's automobile solely because its occupants appeared to be of Mexican ancestry was a patent violation of the Fourth Amendment. I cannot agree, however, with the standard the Court adopts to measure the lawfulness of the officers' action. The Court extends the "suspicion" test of *Terry v. Ohio*, 392 U.S. 1 (1968), to the stop of a moving automobile. I dissented from the adoption of the suspicion test in *Terry*, believing it an unjustified weakening of the Fourth Amendment's protection of citizens from arbitrary interference by the police. I remarked then:

---

12. The 1970 census and the INS figures for alien registration in 1970 provide the following information about the Mexican-American population in the border States. There were 1,619,064 persons of Mexican origin in Texas, and 200,004 (or 12.4%) of them registered as aliens from Mexico. In New Mexico there were 119,049 persons of Mexican origin, and 10,171 (or 8.5%) registered as aliens. In Arizona there were 239,811 persons of Mexican origin, and 34,075 (or 14.2%) registered as aliens. In California there were 1,857,267 persons of Mexican origin, and 379,951 (or 20.4%) registered as aliens. Bureau of the Census, Subject Report PC(2)-1C: Persons of Spanish Origin 2 (1970); INS Ann.Rep. 105 (1970). These figures, of course, do not present the entire picture. The number of registered aliens from Mexico has increased since 1970, INS Ann.Rep. 105 (1974), and we assume that very few illegal immigrants appear in the registration figures. On the other hand, many of the 950,000 other persons of Spanish origin living in these border States, see Bureau of the Census, supra, at 1, may have a physical appearance similar to persons of Mexican origin.

> "The infringement on personal liberty of any 'seizure' of a person can only be 'reasonable' under the Fourth Amendment if we require the police to possess 'probable cause' before they seize him. Only that line draws a meaningful distinction between an officer's mere inkling and the presence of facts within the officer's personal knowledge which would convince a reasonable man that the person seized has to commit a particular crime." *Id.*, at 38.

The fears I voiced in *Terry* about the weakening of the Fourth Amendment have regrettably been borne out by subsequent events. Hopes that the suspicion test might be employed only in the pursuit of violent crime—a limitation endorsed by some of its proponents—have now been dashed, as it has been applied in narcotics investigations, in apprehension of "illegal" aliens, and indeed has come to be viewed as a legal construct for the regulation of a general investigatory police power. The suspicion test has been warmly embraced by law enforcement forces and vigorously employed in the cause of crime detection. In criminal cases we see those for whom the initial intrusion led to the discovery of some wrongdoing. But the nature of the test permits the police to interfere as well with a multitude of law-abiding citizens, whose only transgression may be a nonconformist appearance or attitude. As one commentator has remarked:

> "Police power exercised without probable cause is arbitrary. To say that the police may accost citizens at their whim and may detain them upon reasonable suspicion is to say, in reality, that the police may both accost and detain citizens at their whim." Amsterdam, *Perspectives on the Fourth Amendment*, 58 Minn.L.Rev. 349, 395 (1974).

The uses to which the suspicion test has been put are illustrated in some of the cases cited in the Court's opinion. In *United States v. Wright*, 476 F.2d 1027 (CA5 1973), for example, immigration officers stopped a station wagon near the border because there was a spare tire in the back seat. The court held that the officers reasonably suspected that the spare wheel well had been freed in order to facilitate the concealment of aliens. In *United States v. Bugarin-Casas*, 484 F.2d 853 (CA9 1973), the Border Patrol officers encountered a man driving alone in a station wagon which was "riding low"; stopping the car was held reasonable because the officers suspected that aliens might have been hidden beneath the floorboards. The vacationer whose car is weighted down with luggage will find no comfort in these decisions; nor will the many law-abiding citizens who drive older vehicles that ride low because their suspension systems are old or in disrepair. The suspicion test has indeed brought a state of affairs where the police may stop citizens on the highway on the flimsiest of justifications.

The Court does, to be sure, disclaim approval of the particular decisions it cites applying the suspicion test. But by specifying factors to be considered without attempting to explain what combination is necessary to satisfy the test, the Court may actually induce the police to push its language beyond intended limits and to advance as a justification any of the enumerated factors even where its probative significance is negligible.

Ultimately the degree to which the suspicion test actually restrains the police will depend more upon what the Court does henceforth than upon what it says today. If my Brethren mean to give the suspicion test a new bite, I applaud the intention. But in view of the developments since the test was launched in *Terry*, I am not optimistic. This is the first decision to invalidate a stop on the basis of the suspicion standard. In fact, since *Terry* we have granted review of a case applying the test only once, in *Adams v. Williams*, 407 U.S. 143 (1972), where the Court found the standard satisfied by the tip from an informant whose credibility was not established and whose information was not shown to be based upon personal knowledge. If in the future the suspicion test is to provide any meaningful restraint of the police, its force must come from vigorous review of its applications, and not alone from the qualifying language of today's opinion. For now, I remain unconvinced that the suspicion test offers significant protection of the "comprehensive right of personal liberty in the face of governmental intrusion," *Lopez v. United States*, 373 U.S. 427, 455 (1963) (dissenting opinion), that is embodied in the Fourth Amendment.

Note

1. In *Brignoni-Ponce*, the government argued that along the border, a person's Mexican ancestry satisfied the requirements of 8 U.S.C. § 1357. This argument was specifically rejected by the Court where they stated that "[t]he likelihood that any given person of Mexican ancestry is an alien is high enough to make Mexican appearance a relevant factor, but standing alone it does not justify stopping all Mexican Americans to ask if they are aliens."[104] Similarly, the Ninth Circuit has held that race or alienage alone is insufficient to establish "specific articulable facts together with rational inferences" that suggest that an undocumented person is present.[105] However, the BIA, in *Matter of King and Yang*,[106] held that the reasonable suspicion requirement was met where the person was of "oriental appearance" and worked at an establishment with a history of violations, and the INS had received an anonymous tip. Would the fact that 8 U.S.C. § 1304(e) requires every adult person who is not a U.S. citizen to carry her "certificate of alien registration" or other identifying DHS-issued document justify an ICE officer's request for the document?

2. In *U.S. v. Arvizu*,[107] the Court elaborated on the principles laid out in *Brignoni-Ponce*:

> The Fourth Amendment prohibits "unreasonable searches and seizures" by the Government, and its protections extend to brief investigatory stops of persons or vehicles that fall short of traditional arrest.... Because the "balance between the public interest and the individual's right to personal

---

104. 422 U.S. at 887.
105. *U.S. v. Rodriguez*, 976 F.2d 592 (9th Cir. 1992).
106. 16 I. & N. Dec. 502 (BIA 1978).
107. 534 U.S. 266 (2002).

> security," *United States v. Brignoni-Ponce*, 422 U.S. 873, 878 (1975), tilts in favor of a standard less than probable cause in such cases, the Fourth Amendment is satisfied if the officer's action is supported by reasonable suspicion to believe that criminal activity " 'may be afoot,' " See also *Cortez*, 449 U.S., at 417 ("An investigatory stop must be justified by some objective manifestation that the person stopped is, or is about to be, engaged in criminal activity").
>
> When discussing how reviewing courts should make reasonable-suspicion determinations, we have said repeatedly that they must look at the "totality of the circumstances" of each case to see whether the detaining officer has a "particularized and objective basis" for suspecting legal wrongdoing. See, e.g., *id.*, at 417–418. This process allows officers to draw on their own experience and specialized training to make inferences from and deductions about the cumulative information available to them that "might well elude an untrained person." *Id.*, at 418. See also *Ornelas v. United States*, 517 U.S. 690, 699 (1996) (reviewing court must give "due weight" to factual inferences drawn by resident judges and local law enforcement officers). Although an officer's reliance on a mere " 'hunch' " is insufficient to justify a stop, *Terry*, *supra*, at 27, the likelihood of criminal activity need not rise to the level required for probable cause, and it falls considerably short of satisfying a preponderance of the evidence standard, *Sokolow*, *supra*, at 7.

534 U.S. at 274.

---

1. The Warrant Requirement

Blackie's House of Beef, Inc., v. Leonel J. Castillo, Commissioner of the I.N.S.

659 F.2d 1211 (D.C. Cir. 1981)

Before McGowan, Edwards and Ginsburg, Circuit Judges.

McGowan, Circuit Judge:

* * *

Blackie's House of Beef, Inc. ("Blackie's"), plaintiff-appellee, operates the Blackie's House of Beef Restaurant and Deja Vu Cocktail Lounge located in Washington, D.C. The Immigration and Naturalization Service ("INS"), defendant-appellant, is the federal agency charged with enforcement of federal immigration laws. Through its limited number of agents, the INS is empowered, inter alia, without warrant

> (1) to interrogate any alien or person believed to be an alien as to his right to be or to remain in the United States;
>
> (2) to arrest any alien ... in the United States, if he (the INS agent) has reason to believe that the alien so arrested is in the United States in violation of any

> such law or regulation and is likely to escape before a warrant can be obtained for his arrest ...

8 U.S.C. § 1357(a)(1) & (2) (Supp. III 1979).

In 1976, the INS began to receive information that illegal aliens were employed at Blackie's. One such indication was a sworn statement by an illegal alien who had been apprehended by the INS and was in the process of undergoing deportation hearings. This informant swore that he had worked at Blackie's and, furthermore, that he had personal knowledge that approximately 20 other illegal aliens were currently employed there. (App. 8). Another such affidavit was executed by an apprehended alien claiming to have worked at Blackie's. In addition to verifying the information provided in the first affidavit, the second informant indicated that "there were many Hispanics employed there and that the names of two illegal aliens who worked there were Rogelio and Pedro." (App. 9, P 2). Other information included three anonymous telephone calls in which informants notified the INS that Blackie's was employing illegal aliens. (App. 9, P 3, 5, 6). Finally, INS officers apprehended two illegal aliens who were carrying wage statements from Blackie's. (App. 9, 10). The latter of the two swore by affidavit that Blackie's was employing illegal aliens from El Salvador and Africa, and supplied the first names of three such employees (App. 10).

On the basis of this information, INS Agent Foster twice asked the owner and manager of Blackie's for permission to enter the restaurant and question suspected illegal aliens. Ulysses "Blackie" Auger twice refused such consent. (App. 10, P 8). After receiving the last of the above-described tips, Agent Foster again requested Auger's consent, which was again refused. (App. 10, P 10).

On March 17, 1978, Agent Foster presented the assembled evidence and accompanying affidavits to a federal magistrate, asking that "a search warrant be issued to any Agent of the Immigration and Naturalization Service authorizing him or them to enter with proper assistance ... (Blackie's) and there to search for and arrest the individuals subject to arrest pursuant to Title 8, United States Code, Section 1357." (App. 10). On March 27, 1978, the magistrate issued the requested warrant, which provided that INS agents might, within five days of the issuance of the warrant, search the "entire premises of Blackie's House of Beef" because "there is now being concealed certain persons namely Aliens who are believed to be in the United States in violation of ... Title 8, Section 1325 and Section 241(a)(2)." (App. 13). It was a standard form warrant, with the word "property" marked out and the word "persons" inserted in the above-quoted passage and in a subsequent passage providing that "there is probable cause to believe that the persons so described are being concealed on the person or premises above described." (App. 13).[3]

3. On the bottom portion of the warrant, the magistrate failed to change the word "property" to "persons" in several instances. Therefore, the bottom portion of the warrant orders the agents to seize the "property described above." Inasmuch as the top portion of the warrant orders agents to enter Blackie's for the purpose of questioning aliens, we think the allusions to "property" in the concluding provision of the warrant are most reasonably interpreted as the magistrate's oversights. The district judge thought otherwise, however, and found that the warrant could most reasonably be interpreted

On March 30, 1978, INS agents executed the warrant, entering Blackie's Restaurant during the dinner hour. (App. 14). As noted on the return document, 15 employees were seized, at least 10 of whom proved to be illegal aliens subject to deportation. (App. 15).

Blackie's subsequently filed suit in the District Court for a declaratory judgment, injunctive relief, and damages, alleging that the search warrant was not supported by probable cause and thus violated the fourth amendment. In a memorandum opinion issued October 5, 1978, the District Court agreed that the warrant was invalid. *Blackie's House of Beef, Inc. v. Castillo*, 467 F.Supp. 170 (D.D.C.1978) (hereinafter "*Blackie's I*"). Recognizing that the word "property" had been scratched out on the upper portion of the warrant, the court was nevertheless impressed by the bottom portion of the warrant, which directed INS agents to search the person or place named for the property specified, ... and if the property be found there to seize it, leaving a copy of this warrant and receipt for the property taken, and prepare a written inventory of the property seized and promptly return this warrant. (App. 13). From this, the court concluded that the warrant most nearly resembled a warrant for the seizure of property, and was invalid inasmuch as it had been used to authorize a search for persons. See note 3 *supra*....

The INS continued to receive information that illegal aliens were being employed at Blackie's. The information that upwards of 30 illegal aliens were currently employed at Blackie's was supplied in an affidavit, dated October 27, 1978, by a previously reliable source. (App. 45–46). The affiant was quite specific, revealing names of suspected illegal aliens, explanations as to how he knew the suspects to be illegal aliens, and details as to the places in which such persons might be hiding. *Id.*

To supplement this information, INS Agent Parry then surveyed Blackie's restaurant for several hours on October 23 and 24, 1978, and observed employees working both inside and outside the restaurant, eighteen of whom Parry believed to be aliens of Hispanic descent, principally because of their attire and seeming inability to speak any language but Spanish. (App. 43, P 4). In addition, Agent Riordan staked out Blackie's on October 27, and observed numerous persons of apparent Hispanic descent entering through the back doors of the restaurant. (App. 43, P 5).

Parry also stated that Blackie's was a known employer of illegal aliens. In support of this assertion, it was said that INS records showed that 48 illegal aliens employed by Blackie's have been apprehended by the Service since January 30, 1974. Further, attached to the affidavit was a recent Washington Post news story which reported the manager of Blackie's as having said that he hires foreign workers because of their reliability and that he does not demand to see their green cards (proof of legal immigrant status) except in Virginia. (App. 43, P 6).

Armed with this information, the INS sought another warrant to search Blackie's. This time the INS claimed to derive its power to search not from Rule 41 but from

---

as an order to search and seize property. Since we affirm *Blackie's I* on other grounds, we do not reach this issue....

its general powers to question aliens and to enforce the immigration laws. 8 U.S.C. §§1357, 1103(a) (Supp. III 1979).

On November 16, 1978, the magistrate issued a warrant, concluding that the INS had established probable cause to believe illegal aliens were present on Blackie's premises. (App. 40–41). Unlike the first warrant, this was not a form warrant, and Rule 41 was nowhere mentioned. Rather, the authority to search was premised upon sections 1357 and 1103 of the Immigration and Nationality Act, and the warrant was entitled "Order For Entry on Premises to Search for Aliens in the United States Without Legal Authority." (App. 40).

The warrant directed the INS to "enter the premises located on 22nd and M Street, North West, Washington, D.C., in order to search for persons believed to be aliens in the United States without legal authority."(App. 40). The magistrate limited the INS's search to "the daylight hours and within 10 days of this order," and required a return within 10 days after completion of the search. (App. 41). The area for permissible search included "any locked rooms on the premises in order to locate aliens in the United States without legal authority." (App. 40–41).

On November 17, 1978, INS agents conducted a search of the public area, kitchen, and second-floor offices of Blackie's beginning at 11:12 A.M. and continuing for 23 minutes. During the 23-minute search, the INS removed 14 suspected illegal aliens from Blackie's, who were detained for an additional 10 minutes in an alley behind the restaurant while transportation to the local INS office was being arranged. The required warrant return was made on November 20, 1978, reciting the names and country of origin of 14 illegal aliens found on the premises. Ten patrons were observed in the restaurant during the search, and four more came in during the course of it.

Blackie's again filed suit for injunctive and declaratory relief, and for damages in the amount of $500,000, alleging that this second warrant violated the fourth amendment and that the search as executed was disruptive and exceeded all reasonable limits. Again the District Court, on defendants' motion to dismiss and cross-motions for summary judgment, held the warrant invalid, ruling that this second warrant failed to satisfy the fourth amendment requirement that "no Warrant shall issue, but upon probable cause, ... particularly describing ... the persons or things to be seized", because it failed to describe with particularity each alien sought. The court also objected to the magistrate's failure to signify, on the face of the warrant, that the magistrate had balanced the enforcement interests of the INS against the privacy interests of Blackie's, its employees, and its patrons. The district judge enjoined the INS from entering plaintiff's premises (except in exigent circumstances) without a warrant complying with the standards set forth in his second memorandum opinion. *Blackie's House of Beef, Inc. v. Castillo*, 480 F.Supp. 1078 (D.D.C.1979) (hereinafter "*Blackie's II*"). The plaintiff's actions against the defendants in their individual capacities were dismissed with prejudice.

The United States appealed the District Court's rulings in *Blackie's I* and *II*, arguing that both search warrants were valid under the fourth amendment and Rule 41. We consolidated the cases for hearing and decision.

Our task on appeal is to determine whether either or both of the warrants were sufficient to protect the fourth amendment rights of Blackie's. Neither party challenges the proposition that a warrant was necessary to support the INS searches of Blackie's premises. We agree that, in light of *Almeida-Sanchez v. United States*, 413 U.S. 266 (1973), the applicability of the Warrant Clause of the fourth amendment to INS enforcement activities can no longer be doubted.

The District Court focused on completely different aspects of the problem in its two memorandum opinions, properly refusing to reach the issue of whether the INS may obtain a hybrid "administrative warrant" upon a lesser showing of probable cause until that issue was squarely presented in *Blackie's II*. Therefore, we are confronted with two distinct questions on appeal. The first, in *Blackie's I*, is primarily a question of statutory construction, i.e., whether the INS may rely upon Rule 41, Fed.R.Crim.P., to obtain a search warrant, given that INS investigations are conducted pursuant to a civil law enforcement power. In *Blackie's II*, the issue is, first, the authority of the INS to seek, and of the District Court to grant, authority by warrant for access to commercial premises to question persons believed to be aliens as to their status, and second, the level of probable cause required for such a warrant.

We address first the issue in *Blackie's II*. Our analysis leading to reversal of the District Court in that case, establishing that warrants to search premises for illegal aliens are civil (administrative) in nature, compels affirmance of *Blackie's I* because the INS's proceeding there under Rule 41 was inappropriate.

A. *Blackie's II*

The fourth amendment prohibits "unreasonable searches and seizures," requiring that "no Warrants shall issue, but upon probable cause, supported by Oath or affirmation, and particularly describing the place to be searched, and the persons or things to be seized." U.S.Const. Amend. IV. The warrant procedure contemplates that the necessity for every intrusion upon the privacy of an individual first be considered by a "neutral and detached magistrate instead of being judged by the officer engaged in the often competitive enterprise of ferreting out crime." *Johnson v. United States*, 333 U.S. 10, 14 (1948). This prior consideration must be more than pro forma: "(T)he magistrate must judge the reasonableness of every warrant in light of the circumstances of the particular case, carefully considering the description of the evidence sought, the situation of the premises, and the position and interests of the owner or occupant." *Zurcher v. Stanford Daily*, 436 U.S. at 570. (Powell, J., concurring). Our task in this case is to determine whether this warrant reflects careful and informed consideration by the magistrate, and reasonably "advise(s) the (subject) of the scope and objects of the search, beyond which limits the (officer) is not expected to proceed," *Marshall v. Barlow's, Inc.*, 436 U.S. 307, 323 (1978).

* * *

We think the District Court perceived correctly that the warrant at issue in this case was not comparable to the OSHA "routine inspection" warrant that the Supreme Court found to be constitutionally required in *Marshall v. Barlow's, Inc.*, 436 U.S.

307 (1978), because the nature of the two enforcement activities differs significantly. The INS sought to enter Blackie's to search for a particular violation, not to conduct a routine inspection of regulated industry premises, and therefore the "neutral standards" principle is inapposite.

The District Court erred, however, in failing to take this argument one step further and acknowledged that the situation also was not analogous to a criminal investigation. The Supreme Court has explicitly held that the detention and deportation of illegal aliens is not criminal law enforcement activity. *Harisiades v. Shaughnessy*, 342 U.S. 580, 594 (1952). There are no sanctions of any kind, criminal or otherwise, imposed by law upon a knowing employer of illegal aliens. This warrant in particular was issued to aid the agency in the enforcement of its statutory mandate, not to aid police in the enforcement of criminal laws.

We think that the District Court failed to recognize the unique aspects of an INS search, and thus erroneously concluded that Blackie's fourth amendment rights were violated by the second search warrant. Our decision rests on three determinations. First, we think that Congress, in passing the Immigration and Nationality Act, contemplated a vigorous enforcement program that might include INS entries onto private premises for the purpose of questioning "any alien or person believed to be an alien," and of detaining those aliens believed to be in this country illegally. Second, since an INS search is conducted pursuant to a civil administrative mandate, the warrant issued to permit such a search may therefore be evaluated under a standard of probable cause different from that applied to criminal warrants. *Marshall v. Barlow's, Inc.*, 436 U.S. 307 (1978). Last, we hold that the warrant in *Blackie's II* was properly tailored both to protect the fourth amendment rights of Blackie's and to aid the enforcement interests of the United States.

1. INS Authority to Search

In styling the warrant as an "Order for Entry on Premises To Search for Aliens in the United States Without Legal Authority," and in invoking the Immigration and Nationality Act ("the Act") as authority for the search, the magistrate made clear his understanding that the INS gains its authority to search from its general statutory authority to question aliens suspected of entering the United States illegally. The Act does not by its terms authorize INS entries of private premises for this purpose.[6] Nonetheless, we agree with the magistrate that there is ample authority to infer such a power from the general provisions of the Act.

---

6. The Act authorizes the INS to conduct warrantless searches of vessels "within the territorial waters of the United States and any railway car, aircraft, conveyance, or vehicle, and within a distance of twenty-five miles from any external boundary to have access to private lands, but not dwellings, for the purpose of patrolling the border to prevent the illegal entry of aliens into the United States." 8 U.S.C. § 1357(a)(3) (Supp. III 1979). It expressly disallows warrantless searches of dwellings. From this, one could infer either that dwellings may never be searched by the INS or that dwellings may never be subjected to warrantless searches or routine inspections. For the reasons set forth below, we adopt the latter interpretation. *See* text accompanying notes 7–13 *infra*.

In 1952, Congress passed the Act in an attempt to deal systematically with its decision to restrict illegal immigration into the United States. The Act outlines the requirements for legal immigration into the United States and those circumstances under which an immigrant is subject to deportation. 8 U.S.C. § 1251 et seq. (Supp. III 1979). Of primary importance to this case is section 103(a), 8 U.S.C. § 1103(a) (Supp. III 1979), which grants general enforcement powers to the Attorney General and empowers him to delegate his authority as follows:

> The Attorney General shall be charged with the administration and enforcement of this chapter and all other laws relating to the immigration and naturalization of aliens.... He shall have control, direction, and supervision of all employees and of all the files and records of the (Immigration and Naturalization) Service.... He is authorized, in accordance with the civil-service law, ... to appoint such employees of the Service as he deems necessary, and to delegate to them ... any of the duties and powers imposed upon him in this chapter ...

Section 287, 8 U.S.C. § 1357(a) (Supp. III 1979), then grants INS agents general powers to investigate possible violations:

> (a) Any officer or employee of the Service authorized under regulations prescribed by the Attorney General shall have power without warrant
>
> > (1) to interrogate any alien or person believed to be an alien as to his right to be or to remain in the United States;
> >
> > (2) to arrest any alien who in his presence or view is entering or attempting to enter the United States in violation of any law or regulation ... or to arrest any alien in the United States, if he has reason to believe that the alien so arrested is in the United States in violation of any such law or regulation.

Together, these statutes reveal Congress's strong interest in effectively enforcing the immigration laws, rather than merely creating a set of normative prohibitions devoid of any means of enforcement. Also significant is INS's vigorous exercise of its enforcement powers, and Congress's failure to cut back on these powers in light of the INS's activities. As the plethora of INS cases attests, the INS has been as zealous in its pursuit of illegal aliens as is possible, given its considerable manpower limitations and the enormous increase in illegal immigration over the past 20 years. Yet, Congress has never attempted to diminish the INS's powers or in any way to undercut the effectiveness of the enforcement program. On the contrary, Congress has considered supplementing the INS's enforcement powers with a law that would penalize employers who knowingly hire illegal aliens, which in itself attests to the seriousness of the public interest in enforcement of the immigration laws.

The Supreme Court has recognized that the public interest in enforcement of the immigration laws is significant. *United States v. Martinez-Fuerte*, 428 U.S. 543, 556–58 (1976); *United States v. Brignoni-Ponce*, 422 U.S. 873, 878–79 (1975); *Almeida-Sanchez v. United States*, 413 U.S. 266, 276 (1973) (Powell, J., concurring). This court, too, has adverted to the seriousness of the INS enforcement effort, in the context of addressing the constitutionality of section 287. In *Yam Sang Kwai v. INS*, 411 F.2d 683 (D.C. Cir.), cert. denied, 396 U.S. 877 (1969), this court held that the fourth amendment allows immigration officials to conduct warrantless interrogations of persons reasonably believed to be of alien origin. We reasoned that "the minimum invasion of privacy of the individual approached for questioning was justified by the special needs of immigration officials to make such interrogations." 411 F.2d at 687, explained in *Au Yi Lau v. INS*, 445 F.2d at 222. In *Yi Au Lau v. INS*, 445 F.2d 217 (D.C. Cir.), cert. denied, 404 U.S. 864 (1971), we were next confronted with the question of whether the INS might temporarily detain a suspected illegal alien for purposes of interrogation. We held that under the standards for temporary detention enunciated in *Terry v. Ohio*, 392 U.S. 1 (1968), the INS might "make forcible detentions of a temporary nature" pursuant to the general investigatory powers described in section 287. *Au Yi Lau v. INS*, 445 F.2d 223.

Underlying these decisions was the understanding that Congress, in passing the Act, clearly contemplated the creation of a mechanism for the vigorous enforcement of its prohibition against illegal immigration. In *Yam*, *Au*, and other cases as well, courts have balanced the government's interest in enforcing the immigration laws against the privacy interests of those whom the INS seeks to investigate. Although courts have, in several instances, ordered the INS to refrain from practices which proved too intrusive under the circumstances, in all such cases it was assumed that the public interest in effective enforcement was both urgent and substantial. Even the District Court did not challenge as a general proposition the INS's right to obtain a warrant in aid of its considerable investigatory powers.

Almeida-Sanchez v. United States, 413 U.S. 266 (1973), supports this conclusion. In *Almeida-Sanchez* the Supreme Court ruled upon the constitutionality of the Border Patrol's warrantless, random search of an automobile 25 air miles north of the Mexican border. The Court held that a search conducted pursuant to the INS's general power to question and detain suspected aliens requires a search warrant, except in exigent circumstances, and thus disapproved random, warrantless searches of automobiles not qualifying as border searches. The Court assumed that under some circumstances the INS might obtain a warrant to search in aid of its general powers to question and detain aliens, if the INS first made some showing of probable cause.

We, too, infer from the provisions of the Immigration and Nationality Act some predicate power to obtain search warrants in aid of the enforcement activities specifically delineated in the statute, although the statute does not explicitly authorize such warrants. The power to obtain warrants "in aid of jurisdiction" is an indispensable law enforcement tool in the field of criminal justice. Rule 41, Fed.R.Crim.P.; cf. 28 U.S.C. § 1615 (Supp. III 1979) (All Writs Act). The Supreme Court has held that, in the civil area, administrative agencies also may obtain warrants when such searches will aid in the performance of regulatory functions. See *Marshall v. Barlow's, Inc.*, 436 U.S. 307 (1978); See v. Seattle, 387 U.S. 541 (1967); *Camara v. Municipal Court*, 387 U.S. 523 (1967).

The same holds true for the INS. Its primary statutory enforcement function is to seek out, question, and detain suspected illegal aliens. See 8 U.S.C. § 1357(a), quoted at text following note 4 *supra*. Although the statute does not provide by its terms for INS entry into dwellings or commercial premises, it is logical to suppose, as did the *Almeida-Sanchez* Court, that INS agents are not always restricted to questioning only those whom they see on the street or in public places.

We conclude that the INS's right to enter commercial premises, with a proper warrant, for the purpose of searching out a suspected violation of the immigration laws derives from its general statutory power to seek out and question suspected illegal aliens.[13] We rest upon the Almeida-Sanchez Court's assumption that this is a valid exercise of the INS's statutory mandate, naturally to be implied from the serious nature of the INS enforcement effort and the statutory language.

2. Probable Cause to Search

The harder question is the showing of probable cause necessary to support an INS warrant to search for a suspected violation. The District Court held that the warrant in this case was invalid because it did not attain the level of "particularized description" necessary to justify a criminal search. It especially deplored the lack of detailed description of each individual alien, and the magistrate's failure to balance, on the face of the warrant, the public interest in law enforcement against Blackie's interest in privacy. The Government asserts in opposition that an INS search warrant need not and, moreover, cannot meet such a standard of probable cause, given the nature of the particular law enforcement activity. We agree that the District Court's stringent formulation of probable cause was inappropriate in the present situation, and that *Marshall v. Barlow's, Inc.*, 436 U.S. at 320, calls for a more flexible definition of probable cause to comport with the multiplicity of "hybrid" administrative law enforcement activities in a non-criminal context.

The reasoning of the *Marshall* Court is central to our decision. In *Marshall v. Barlow's, Inc.*, 436 U.S. 307 (1978), the Supreme Court held unconstitutional a statute which allowed OSHA officials to conduct a warrantless search of the work area of any facility within the agency's jurisdiction. 29 U.S.C. § 657 (Supp. III 1979). Although the statute required the OSHA inspector first to show his credentials, he was not required to obtain a warrant prior to entry, Congress having believed that the value of surprise in a routine inspection outweighed any privacy interests of the employer. *Marshall v. Barlow's, Inc.*, 436 U.S. at 316.

The Supreme Court concluded that, even though Congress had apparently given its express consent to a warrantless search in that instance, such a search would nev-

---

13. We express no opinion as to whether the INS could ever obtain an "area search warrant" allowing agents to enter buildings randomly to inspect for illegal aliens or otherwise justifying random searches. The Supreme Court declined to decide that question in *Almeida-Sanchez v. United States*, 413 U.S. at 270 n.3, noting that the Justices joining in the opinion were divided on the question. *See* Justice Powell's discussion of area warrants in his *Almeida-Sanchez* concurrence, 413 U.S. at 283–85 (Powell, J., concurring).

ertheless violate the fourth amendment. The Court established a principle which holds in this case, namely, that an intrusion upon commercial premises, even if motivated by a valid regulatory purpose, is unconstitutional absent a proper warrant or exigent circumstances. The Court rejected the contention that a party's privacy is of minimal importance when balanced against the state's need to enforce its regulatory laws. Rather, "the privacy interest suffers whether the government's motivation is to investigate violations of criminal laws or breaches of other statutory or regulatory standards."[14]

The second portion of *Marshall* is of primary importance to the resolution of this case. Having determined that the warrantless search provision of OSHA was unconstitutional, the Court then discussed the type of warrant sufficient to support a routine inspection conducted by OSHA in fulfillment of its regulatory responsibilities. To the argument that OSHA could only obtain a warrant on a showing that illegal working conditions existed on those very premises, the Court replied unequivocally:

> Probable cause in the criminal law sense is not required. For purposes of an administrative search such as this, probable cause justifying the issuance of a warrant may be based not only on specific evidence of an existing violation but also on a showing that "reasonable legislative or administrative standards for conducting an ... inspection are satisfied with respect to a particular (establishment).

Marshall v. Barlow's, Inc., 436 U.S. at 320, quoting *Camara v. Municipal Court*, 387 U.S. at 538.

In so holding, the Court clarified the standards set forth in an earlier "administrative warrant" case, *Camara v. Municipal Court*, 387 U.S. 523 (1967). Since *Camara*, the law has been that "[w]here considerations of health and safety are involved, the facts that would justify an inference of "probable cause" to make an inspection are clearly different from those that would justify such an inference where a criminal investigation has been undertaken." *Camara v. Municipal Court*, 387 U.S. at 538, quoting *Frank v. Maryland*, 359 U.S. at 383 (Douglas, J., dissenting). The Court in *Camara* noted that the ultimate question, for purposes of compliance with the fourth amendment, is the "reasonableness" vel non of a particular warrant. 387 U.S. at 536–37.

In the context of routine agency inspections, such as those involved in *Marshall* and *Camara*, the reasonableness of a search warrant obviously cannot depend on evidence of the condition of the particular building sought to be searched. In those cases, the Supreme Court held that the probable cause requirement would be satisfied if "reasonable legislative or administrative standards for conducting an area inspection are satisfied with respect to a particular dwelling." *Camara v. Municipal Court*, 387 U.S. at 538. Such standards could be based upon "the passage of time, the nature of the building, or the condition of the entire area," id., in the case of the *Camara* fire

14. *Id.* at 312–13. Heeding the lessons of *Marshall*, the INS agents in this case did not attempt to conduct a warrantless search of Blackie's but, rather, twice attempted to obtain a valid search warrant.

inspection warrant, or upon the nature of the business being conducted, in the case of the *Marshall* OSHA warrant. Both the *Camara* and *Marshall* Courts turned deaf ears to the plea that a flexible probable cause requirement impermissibly lessens the protections of the Fourth Amendment. *Marshall v. Barlow's, Inc.*, 436 U.S. at 328 (Stevens, J., dissenting). Instead, both Courts agreed that "[t]he warrant procedure is designed to guarantee that a decision to search private property is justified by a reasonable governmental interest. But reasonableness is still the ultimate standard." *Camara v. Municipal Court*, 387 U.S. at 539.

Since *Marshall*, the Court has reiterated its conviction that "the permissibility of a particular law enforcement practice is judged by balancing its intrusion on the individuals Fourth Amendment interests against its promotion of legitimate governmental interests." *Delaware v. Prouse*, 440 U.S. 648, 654 (1979). "In those situations in which the balance of interests precludes insistence upon 'some quantum of individualized suspicion,' other safeguards are generally relied upon to assure that the individual's reasonable expectation of privacy is not 'subject to the discretion of the official in the field.'" *Id.* at 655 (citation omitted), quoting *Camara v. Municipal Court*, 387 U.S. at 532.

In the present case, the District Court did not directly address the question of whether a flexible standard of probable cause would justify the type of warrant obtained in this case, but simply assumed that a formulation of probable cause differed from the traditional requirement of "particularized description" is appropriate only in the context of routine inspections. Blackie's has set forth the argument in more detail. It contends that *Marshall* and *Camara* stood only for the proposition that routine inspections cannot be evaluated under stringent standards of probable cause, and not for the broader proposition that administrative warrants generally may be evaluated differently from criminal warrants.

We do not read *Marshall* so narrowly, however. Several courts since then have joined us in recognizing that not only routine inspections but agency enforcement activities in general are Protean, taking many forms which are not susceptible to treatment as traditional law enforcement activities. Most notably, the Seventh Circuit recently held that criminal probable cause standards are inappropriately applied to OSHA search warrants issued in aid of searches for specific violations as well as for routine inspections. *Burkart Randall Division of Textron, Inc. v. Marshall*, 625 F.2d 1313 (7th Cir. 1980). The court formulated the standard of probable cause broadly, remarking that "when a warrant is sought for an inspection to be conducted pursuant to a legislative or administrative plan, probable cause is to be judged according to the relaxed or flexible standard of administrative probable cause established in *Camara*." *Id.* at 1316–17. The court rejected the employer's interpretation of *Marshall*, which was that the "application of this standard is inappropriate where the warrant is sought on the basis of 'specific evidence of an existing location,'" *id.* at 1317. Instead, the court quoted *Marshall* for the proposition that probable cause in the context of administrative investigations may be established either by specific evidence of an existing violation or by a showing of a reasonable legislative or administrative plan. *Marshall v. Barlow's, Inc.*, 436 U.S. at 320. Thus, the *Burkart* court concluded, "the more logical interpretation of the Court's language is that criminal probable cause is not required for either an employee complaint or administrative plan inspection." *Burkart Randall Division of Textron, Inc. v. Marshall,* 625 F.2d 1317 n.4.

We find Judge Sprecher's excellent opinion in *Burkart* highly persuasive and adopt this reasoning fully, for we think that the search undertaken in this case was as unsuited to the application of traditional probable cause standards as were the routine inspections at issue in *Marshall* or the searches for specific violations involved in *Burkart.* It is difficult to imagine any instance in which INS agents could satisfy the District Court's requirement and obtain the names of each illegal alien employed in the nonpublic areas of a restaurant, or even physical descriptions any more particularized than those proffered to the magistrate in this instance. Since an illegal alien is essentially a fugitive outside the law, it is unlikely that his vital statistics will be on file anywhere in the United States or even that he will customarily use his real name, either in his contacts with the Government or with anyone else. Obviously he would never subject himself to more than the minimum of public scrutiny.

Furthermore, and most important to our way of thinking, is the fact that the stringent requirements laid down by the District Court would, in practical terms, have little effect on the activities of the law enforcement officers operating pursuant to the "stringent" warrant. If the INS agents in this case had entered Blackie's with a more "particularized" warrant, perhaps one setting out the first names of certain aliens, the agents would still have been forced to pursue exactly the same course of conduct as was pursued here: the questioning of those employees appearing to be aliens and found in nonpublic areas of the restaurant. The INS could perhaps never have obtained in advance information specific enough to allow it to pick a dozen suspected illegal aliens out of a large crowd of employees without the need for further questioning. Thus, it is unlikely that the INS could meet the standard of probable cause applicable in criminal cases, at least as formulated by the District Court, except in the rare instance when an INS informer tips as to one specific violator and supplies the description and name of that person. The effect of the court's rule, then, is highly ironic; it leaves the INS free to combat isolated instances of illegal immigration and powerless to combat the much more serious problem of illegal alien employee congregations at one central place, such as a restaurant.

In short, we are not persuaded that *Marshall, Camara* or *Delaware* require the INS to meet a standard of probable cause so unrealistically restrictive as to cripple the statutory mandate to enforce the Act, and we think the District Court erred in holding to the contrary. This is one of "those situations in which the balance of interests precludes insistence upon 'some quantum of individualized suspicion,'" at least as to the persons sought. *Delaware v. Prouse*, 440 U.S. at 654. Rather, the court should have examined the warrant and supporting affidavits with an eye to whether the warrant satisfied the alternative requirement of *Delaware v. Prouse*: sufficient specificity and reliability to prevent the exercise of unbridled discretion by law enforcement officials. *Id.*

3. Sufficiency of the Warrant

With the correct probable cause standard firmly in mind, we are forced to conclude that the District Court erred in striking down the warrant in *Blackie's II*. This warrant was as descriptive as was reasonably possible with respect to the persons sought, the place to be searched, and the time within which the search might take place. In our view, the warrant contained sufficient safeguards to assure that nothing impermissible would be left to the discretion of the INS agents. *Delaware v. Prouse*, 440 U.S. at 654.

The warrant was duly restricted to the location in which there was cause to believe aliens could be found: "the premises located at 22nd and M Streets, North West, Washington, D.C." (App. at 40). It was also restricted as to the time within which the warrant could be executed, providing that execution must occur within 10 days of the order and during the daylight hours.

Furthermore, the INS was restricted as to how it could act once inside the premises. A search could only be conducted where aliens were likely to be hiding. Thus, the INS was proscribed from searching the files or books of Blackie's, and it is uncontroverted that they searched only those areas in which aliens were likely to be found. No private property of Blackie's within the premises was searched or seized.

Nor did the warrant leave impermissible discretion in the hands of the INS agents with respect to the persons sought to be questioned. The affidavits filed along with the application for search warrant suggested that numerous persons working in nonpublic areas of the restaurant were possibly illegal aliens, and gave credible reasons for the affiants' suspicions as well. See Affidavit of Immigration and Naturalization Service Officer Russell G. Parry, Jr., app. at 42 (describing evidence as to Ulysses Auger's suspected employment of illegal aliens, including a few first names of suspects and descriptions of suspected illegal aliens based on affiant's surveillance of restaurant); Affidavit of Anonymous Informant, app. at 45 (describing knowledge of employment of illegal aliens at Blackie's, describing such suspects' personal appearances and naming several suspects). These affidavits also contained very general, but not irrelevant descriptions of the suspects: persons dressed in foreign-style apparel, who appeared to speak no English.

Taken in conjunction with the warrant, which authorized the INS to enter the premises and make a search "including, but not limited to, the search of any locked rooms on the premises in order to locate aliens in the United States without legal authority," these papers establish that the INS agents were empowered to enter Blackie's only for the purpose of questioning those employees whom the agents might reasonably suspect of being illegal aliens, on the basis of the information in the warrant and the standards set down for the questioning of suspected aliens in *Yam Sang Kwai v. INS*, 411 F.2d 687. As we noted above, some amount of questioning is always necessary in such a situation, as this court recognized when it held in *Yam*

Sang Kwai that INS agents may question a person merely upon the "articulable" suspicion that the person is an alien. *Id.* This warrant and accompanying affidavits narrowed down the field of potentially vulnerable persons to those employees whom INS agents might reasonably believe to be aliens. We think this was precisely within the contemplation of the Act, and "reasonable" within the meaning of the fourth amendment.[17]

Our view as to the propriety of this warrant is also influenced by the significant amount of supporting evidence that accompanied the application for warrant. These included one affidavit summarizing two separate day-long surveillances of Blackie's, and a lengthy affidavit from an anonymous informant who claimed to have worked at Blackie's. The informant identified suspects by first names, described the layout of Blackie's Restaurant, and gave other indicia as to his credibility. The officers' surveillance of Blackie's corroborated the information set forth in the anonymous affiant's statement to the effect that Blackie's employed numerous persons of foreign appearance who were unable to speak English.

On the basis of these three independent sources of information, it could be reasonably supposed that persons likely to be illegal aliens were being employed in Blackie's. The magistrate was therefore correct in assuming that the public interest in conducting a search justified the intrusion into Blackie's Restaurant. In the event, that intrusion occurred at 11:12 A.M.; 23 minutes in all were spent by the agents inside the restaurant, and at a time when, as might be expected, the number of patrons was small.

* * *

III

In conclusion, we hold that the warrant in *Blackie's II* was within the statutory authority of the INS to seek, and was, on the showing of probable cause made to the magistrate, sufficient, under the standards set out by the Supreme Court in Marshall and Delaware, to protect the fourth amendment rights of Blackie's and the enforcement interests of the United States. We think that the warrant curbed the discretion of the INS agents sufficiently to guard against the exercise of unbridled discretion on the part of the INS. The District Court's fundamental error lay in requiring that the

17. Blackie's has argued that reversal of Blackie's II would amount to a ruling that INS agents may obtain a warrant merely upon showing that persons inside the building have "foreign appearances." This misconceives our holding. The supporting affidavits included evidence that Blackie's was employing persons of foreign appearance, but this was certainly not the only evidence that Blackie's was employing illegal aliens. In addition, there was a lengthy affidavit from a person claiming to have worked at Blackie's. He claimed to know several of the suspected illegal aliens personally, described their appearances, supplied a few first names of suspects, and gave numerous other indicia as to his reliability. Furthermore, even the two INS agents did not base their conclusions solely on the "foreign appearance" of suspects, but also marked the suspects' foreign style clothes, inability to speak English, and unwillingness to venture far from the restaurant. All this evidence taken together constituted probable cause to search.

INS meet the same level of probable cause as is appropriate in the case of criminal warrants. For these reasons, we affirm *Blackie's I* and reverse *Blackie's II.*

* * *

---

2. Search or Seizure?

Immigration and Naturalization Service, et al., v. Herman Delgado, et al.

466 U.S. 210 (1984)

Justice REHNQUIST delivered the opinion of the Court.

In the course of enforcing the immigration laws, petitioner Immigration and Naturalization Service (INS) enters employers' worksites to determine whether any illegal aliens may be present as employees. The Court of Appeals for the Ninth Circuit held that the "factory surveys" involved in this case amounted to a seizure of the entire work forces, and further held that the INS could not question individual employees during any of these surveys unless its agents had a reasonable suspicion that the employee to be questioned was an illegal alien. International Ladies' Garment Worker's Union, AFL-CIO v. Sureck, 681 F.2d 624 (9th Cir.1982). We conclude that these factory surveys did not result in the seizure of the entire work forces, and that the individual questioning of the respondents in this case by INS agents concerning their citizenship did not amount to a detention or seizure under the Fourth Amendment. Accordingly, we reverse the judgment of the Court of Appeals.

Acting pursuant to two warrants, in January and September, 1977 the INS conducted a survey of the work force at Southern California Davis Pleating Co. (Davis Pleating) in search of illegal aliens. The warrants were issued on a showing of probable cause by the INS that numerous illegal aliens were employed at Davis Pleating, although neither of the search warrants identified any particular illegal aliens by name. A third factory survey was conducted with the employer's consent in October, 1977, at Mr. Pleat, another garment factory.

At the beginning of the surveys several agents positioned themselves near the buildings' exits, while other agents dispersed throughout the factory to question most, but not all, employees at their work stations. The agents displayed badges, carried walkie-talkies, and were armed, although at no point during any of the surveys was a weapon ever drawn. Moving systematically through the factory, the agents approached employees and, after identifying themselves, asked them from one to three questions relating to their citizenship. If the employee gave a credible reply that he was a United States citizen, the questioning ended, and the agent moved on to another employee. If the employee gave an unsatisfactory response or admitted that he was an alien, the employee was asked to produce his immigration papers. During the survey, employees continued with their work and were free to walk around within the factory.

Respondents are four employees questioned in one of the three surveys.[1] In 1978 respondents and their union representative, the International Ladies Garment Workers' Union, filed two actions, later consolidated, in the United States District Court for the Central District of California challenging the constitutionality of INS factory surveys and seeking declaratory and injunctive relief. Respondents argued that the factory surveys violated their Fourth Amendment right to be free from unreasonable searches or seizures and the equal protection component of the Due Process Clause of the Fifth Amendment.

The District Court denied class certification and dismissed the union from the action for lack of standing, App. to Pet. for Cert. 58a–60a. In a series of cross-motions for partial summary judgment, the District Court ruled that respondents had no reasonable expectation of privacy in their workplaces which conferred standing on them to challenge entry by the INS pursuant to a warrant or owner's consent. Id., at 49a–52a, 53a–55a, 56a–57a. In its final ruling the District Court addressed respondents' request for injunctive relief directed at preventing the INS from questioning them personally during any future surveys. The District Court, with no material facts in dispute, found that each of the four respondents was asked a question or questions by an INS agent during one of the factory surveys. Id., at 46a. Reasoning from this Court's decision in Terry v. Ohio, 392 U.S. 1 (1968), that law enforcement officers may ask questions of anyone, the District Court ruled that none of the respondents had been detained under the Fourth Amendment during the factory surveys, either when they were questioned or otherwise. App. to Pet. for Cert. 47a. Accordingly, it granted summary judgment in favor of the INS.[2]

The Court of Appeals reversed. Applying the standard first enunciated by a Member of this Court in United States v. Mendenhall, 446 U.S. 544 (1980) (opinion of Stewart, J.), the Court of Appeals concluded that the entire work forces were seized for the duration of each survey, which lasted from one to two hours, because the stationing of agents at the doors to the buildings meant that "a reasonable worker 'would have believed that he was not free to leave.'" 681 F.2d, at 634 (quoting United States v. Anderson, 663 F.2d 934, 939 (CA9 1981)). Although the Court of Appeals conceded that the INS had statutory authority to question any alien or person believed to be an alien as to his right to be or remain in the United States, see 66 Stat. 233, 8 U.S.C. § 1357(a)(1), it further held that under the Fourth Amendment individual employees could be questioned only on the basis of a reasonable suspicion that a particular employee being questioned was an alien illegally in the country. 681 F.2d, at 639–645. A reasonable suspicion or probable cause to believe that a number of illegal aliens

1. Respondents Herman Delgado, Ramona Correa, and Francisca Labonte worked at Davis Pleating, while Marie Miramontes, the fourth respondent, was employed by Mr. Pleat. Both Delgado and Correa are United States citizens, while Labonte and Miramontes are permanent resident aliens.

2. The District Court never ruled directly on respondents' Fifth Amendment claim, apparently reasoning that since respondents' Fourth Amendment rights had not been violated, their Fifth Amendment right had also not been violated. The Court of Appeals also never ruled on respondents' Fifth Amendment claim, and we decline to do so.

were working at a particular factory site was insufficient to justify questioning any individual employee. Id., at 643. Consequently, it also held that the individual questioning of respondents violated the Fourth Amendment because there had been no such reasonable suspicion or probable cause as to any of them.

We granted certiorari to review the decision of the Court of Appeals, 461 U.S. 904 (1983), because it has serious implications for the enforcement of the immigration laws and presents a conflict with the decision reached by the Third Circuit in Babula v. INS, 665 F.2d 293 (1981).

The Fourth Amendment does not proscribe all contact between the police and citizens, but is designed "to prevent arbitrary and oppressive interference by enforcement officials with the privacy and personal security of individuals." United States v. Martinez-Fuerte, 428 U.S. 543, 554 (1976). Given the diversity of encounters between police officers and citizens, however, the Court has been cautious in defining the limits imposed by the Fourth Amendment on encounters between the police and citizens. As we have noted elsewhere: "Obviously, not all personal intercourse between policemen and citizens involves 'seizures' of persons. Only when the officer, by means of physical force or show of authority, has restrained the liberty of a citizen may we conclude that a 'seizure' has occurred." Terry v. Ohio, supra, 392 U.S., at 19, n. 16. While applying such a test is relatively straightforward in a situation resembling a traditional arrest, see Dunaway v. New York, 442 U.S. 200, 212–216 (1979), the protection against unreasonable seizures also extends to "seizures that involve only a brief detention short of traditional arrest." United States v. Brignoni-Ponce, 422 U.S. 873, 878 (1975). What has evolved from our cases is a determination that an initially consensual encounter between a police officer and a citizen can be transformed into a seizure or detention within the meaning of the Fourth Amendment, "if, in view of all the circumstances surrounding the incident, a reasonable person would have believed that he was not free to leave." Mendenhall, supra, 446 U.S. at 554 (footnote omitted); see Florida v. Royer, 460 U.S. 491, 502 (1983) (plurality opinion).

Although we have yet to rule directly on whether mere questioning of an individual by a police official, without more, can amount to a seizure under the Fourth Amendment, our recent decision in Royer, supra, plainly implies that interrogation relating to one's identity or a request for identification by the police does not, by itself, constitute a Fourth Amendment seizure. In Royer, when Drug Enforcement Administration agents found that the respondent matched a drug courier profile, the agents approached the defendant and asked him for his airplane ticket and driver's license, which the agents then examined. A majority of the Court believed that the request and examination of the documents were "permissible in themselves." Id., at 501 (plurality opinion), see id., at 523, n. 3 (opinion of Rehnquist, J.). In contrast, a much different situation prevailed in Brown v. Texas, 443 U.S. 47 (1979), when two policemen physically detained the defendant to determine his identity, after the defendant refused the officers' request to identify himself. The Court held that absent some reasonable suspicion of misconduct, the detention of the defendant to determine his identity violated the defendant's Fourth Amendment right to be free from an unreasonable seizure. Id., at 52.

What is apparent from Royer and Brown is that police questioning, by itself, is unlikely to result in a Fourth Amendment violation. While most citizens will respond to a police request, the fact that people do so, and do so without being told they are free not to respond, hardly eliminates the consensual nature of the response. Cf. Schneckloth v. Bustamonte, 412 U.S. 218, 231–234 (1973). Unless the circumstances of the encounter are so intimidating as to demonstrate that a reasonable person would have believed he was not free to leave if he had not responded, one cannot say that the questioning resulted in a detention under the Fourth Amendment. But if the person refuses to answer and the police take additional steps—such as those taken in Brown—to obtain an answer, then the Fourth Amendment imposes some minimal level of objective justification to validate the detention or seizure. United States v. Mendenhall, 446 U.S., at 554; see Terry v. Ohio, 392 U.S., at 21.

The Court of Appeals held that "the manner in which the factory surveys were conducted in this case constituted a seizure of the workforce" under the Fourth Amendment. 681 F.2d, at 634. While the element of surprise and the systematic questioning of individual workers by several INS agents contributed to the court's holding, the pivotal factor in its decision was the stationing of INS agents near the exits of the factory buildings. According to the Court of Appeals, the stationing of agents near the doors meant that "departures were not to be contemplated," and thus, workers were "not free to leave." Ibid. In support of the decision below, respondents argue that the INS created an intimidating psychological environment when it intruded unexpectedly into the workplace with such a show of officers. Besides the stationing of agents near the exits, respondents add that the length of the survey and the failure to inform workers they were free to leave resulted in a Fourth Amendment seizure of the entire work force.

We reject the claim that the entire work forces of the two factories were seized for the duration of the surveys when the INS placed agents near the exits of the factory sites. Ordinarily, when people are at work their freedom to move about has been meaningfully restricted, not by the actions of law enforcement officials, but by the workers' voluntary obligations to their employers. The record indicates that when these surveys were initiated, the employees were about their ordinary business, operating machinery and performing other job assignments. While the surveys did cause some disruption, including the efforts of some workers to hide, the record also indicates that workers were not prevented by the agents from moving about the factories.

Respondents argue, however, that the stationing of agents near the factory doors showed the INS's intent to prevent people from leaving. But there is nothing in the record indicating that this is what the agents at the doors actually did. The obvious purpose of the agents' presence at the factory doors was to insure that all persons in the factories were questioned. The record indicates that the INS agents' conduct in this case consisted simply of questioning employees and arresting those they had probable cause to believe were unlawfully present in the factory. This conduct should have given respondents no reason to believe that they would be detained if they gave truthful answers to the questions put to them or if they simply refused to answer. If mere questioning does not constitute a seizure when it occurs inside the factory, it is no more a seizure when it occurs at the exits.

A similar conclusion holds true for all other citizens or aliens lawfully present inside the factory buildings during the surveys. The presence of agents by the exits posed no reasonable threat of detention to these workers while they walked throughout the factories on job assignments. Likewise, the mere possibility that they would be questioned if they sought to leave the buildings should not have resulted in any reasonable apprehension by any of them that they would be seized or detained in any meaningful way. Since most workers could have had no reasonable fear that they would be detained upon leaving, we conclude that the work forces as a whole were not seized.

The Court of Appeals also held that "detentive questioning" of individuals could be conducted only if INS agents could articulate "objective facts providing investigators with a reasonable suspicion that each questioned person, so detained, is an alien illegally in this country." 681 F.2d, at 638. Under our analysis, however, since there was no seizure of the work forces by virtue of the method of conducting the factory surveys, the only way the issue of individual questioning could be presented would be if one of the named respondents had in fact been seized or detained. Reviewing the deposition testimony of respondents, we conclude that none were.

The questioning of each respondent by INS agents seems to have been nothing more than a brief encounter. None of the three Davis Pleating employees were questioned during the January survey. During the September survey at Davis Pleating, respondent Delgado was discussing the survey with another employee when two INS agents approached him and asked him where he was from and from what city. When Delgado informed them that he came from Mayaguez, Puerto Rico, the agent made an innocuous observation to his partner and left. App. 94. Respondent Correa's experience in the September survey was similar. Walking from one part of the factory to another, Correa was stopped by an INS agent and asked where she was born. When she replied "Huntington Park, [California]," the agent walked away and Correa continued about her business. Id., 115. Respondent Labonte, the third Davis Pleating employee, was tapped on the shoulder and asked in Spanish, "Where are your papers?" Id., 138. Labonte responded that she had her papers and without any further request from the INS agents, showed the papers to the agents, who then left. Finally, respondent Miramontes, the sole Mr. Pleat employee involved in this case, encountered an agent en route from an office to her worksite. Questioned concerning her citizenship, Miramontes replied that she was a resident alien, and on the agent's request, produced her work permit. The agent then left. Id., at 120–121.

Respondents argue that the manner in which the surveys were conducted and the attendant disruption caused by the surveys created a psychological environment which made them reasonably afraid they were not free to leave. Consequently, when respondents were approached by INS agents and questioned concerning their citizenship and right to work, they were effectively detained under the Fourth Amendment, since they reasonably feared that refusing to answer would have resulted in their arrest. But it was obvious from the beginning of the surveys that the INS agents were only questioning people. Persons such as respondents who simply went about their business in the workplace were not detained in any way; nothing more occurred than that a question was put to them. While persons who attempted to flee or evade the agents may eventually have been detained for questioning, see d., at 50, 81–84, 91–93, respondents did not do so and were not in fact detained. The manner in which respondents were questioned, given its obvious purpose, could hardly result in a reasonable fear that respondents were not free to continue working or to move about the factory. Respondents may only litigate what happened to them, and our review of their description of the encounters with the INS agents satisfies us that the encounters were classic consensual encounters rather than Fourth Amendment seizures. See Florida v. Royer, 460 U.S. 491 (1983); United States v. Mendenhall, 446 U.S. 544 (1980).

Accordingly, the judgment of the Court of Appeals is Reversed.

* * *

Justice Brennan, with whom Justice Marshall joins, concurring in part and dissenting in part.

As part of its ongoing efforts to enforce the immigration laws, the Immigration and Naturalization Service (INS) conducts "surveys" of those workplaces that it has reason to believe employ large numbers of undocumented aliens who may be subject to deportation. This case presents the question whether the INS's method of carrying out these "factory surveys" violates the rights of the affected factory workers to be secure against unreasonable seizures of one's person as guaranteed by the Fourth Amendment. Answering that question, the Court today holds, first, that the INS surveys involved here did not result in the seizure of the entire factory work force for the complete duration of the surveys, ante, at 1763–1764, and, second, that the individual questioning of respondents by INS agents concerning their citizenship did not constitute seizures within the meaning of the Fourth Amendment, ante, at 1764–1765. Although I generally agree with the Court's first conclusion, I am convinced that a fair application of our prior decisions to the facts of this case compels the conclusion that respondents were unreasonably seized by INS agents in the course of these factory surveys.

* * *

At first blush, the Court's opinion appears unremarkable. But what is striking about today's decision is its studied air of unreality. Indeed, it is only through a considerable feat of legerdemain that the Court is able to arrive at the conclusion that the respondents were not seized. The success of the Court's sleight of hand turns on the proposition that the interrogations of respondents by the INS were merely brief, "consensual encounters," ante, at 1765, that posed no threat to respondents' personal security and freedom. The record, however, tells a far different story.

Contrary to the Court's suggestion, see ante, at 1762, we have repeatedly considered whether and, if so, under what circumstances questioning of an individual by law enforcement officers may amount to a seizure within the meaning of the Fourth

Amendment. See, e.g., Terry v. Ohio, 392 U.S. 1 (1968); Davis v. Mississippi, 394 U.S. 721 (1969); Adams v. Williams, 407 U.S. 143 (1972); Brown v. Texas, 443 U.S. 47 (1979); United States v. Mendenhall, 446 U.S. 544 (1980); Florida v. Royer, 460 U.S. 491 (1983). Of course, as these decisions recognize, the question does not admit of any simple answer. The difficulty springs from the inherent tension between our commitment to safeguarding the precious, and all too fragile, right to go about one's business free from unwarranted government interference, and our recognition that the police must be allowed some latitude in gathering information from those individuals who are willing to cooperate. Given these difficulties, it is perhaps understandable that our efforts to strike an appropriate balance have not produced uniform results. Nevertheless, the outline of what appears to be the appropriate inquiry has been traced over the years with some clarity.

The Court launched its examination of this issue in Terry v. Ohio, supra, by explaining that "the Fourth Amendment governs 'seizures' of the person which do not eventuate in a trip to the station house and prosecution for crime—'arrests' in traditional terminology. It must be recognized that whenever a police officer accosts an individual and restrains his freedom to walk away, he has 'seized' that person." Id., at 16. Such a seizure, the Court noted, may be evidenced by either "physical force or show of authority" indicating that the individual's liberty has been restrained. Id., at 19, n. 16. The essential teaching of the Court's decision in Terry—that an individual's right to personal security and freedom must be respected even in encounters with the police that fall short of full arrest—has been consistently reaffirmed. In Davis v. Mississippi, 394 U.S., at 726–727, for example, the Court confirmed that investigatory detentions implicate the protections of the Fourth Amendment and further explained that "while the police have the right to request citizens to answer voluntarily questions concerning unsolved crimes they have no right to compel them to answer." Id., at 727, n. 6. Similarly, in Brown v. Texas, supra, we overturned a conviction for refusing to stop and identify oneself to police, because, in making the stop, the police lacked any "reasonable suspicion, based on objective facts, that the individual [was] involved in criminal activity." Id., at 51. The animating principle underlying this unanimous decision was that the Fourth Amendment protects an individual's personal security and privacy from unreasonable interference by the police, even when that interference amounts to no more than a brief stop and questioning concerning one's identity.

Although it was joined at the time by only one other Member of this Court, Part IIA of Justice Stewart's opinion in United States v. Mendenhall, supra, offered a helpful, preliminary distillation of the lessons of these cases. Noting first that "as long as the person to whom questions are put remains free to disregard the questions and walk away, there has been no intrusion upon that person's liberty or privacy," Justice Stewart explained that "a person has been 'seized' within the meaning of the Fourth Amendment only if, in view of all of the circumstances surrounding the incident, a reasonable person would have believed that he was not free to leave." Id., at 554. The opinion also suggested that such circumstances might include "the threatening presence of several officers, the display of a weapon by an officer, some physical touching of the person of the citizen, or the use of language or tone of voice indicating that compliance with the officer's request might be compelled." Ibid.

A majority of the Court has since adopted that formula as the appropriate standard for determining when inquiries made by the police cross the boundary separating merely consensual encounters from forcible stops to investigate a suspected crime. See Florida v. Royer, 460 U.S., at 502 (plurality opinion); id., at 511–512 (Brennan, J., concurring in result); id., at 514 (Blackmun, J., dissenting). This rule properly looks not to the subjective impressions of the person questioned but rather to the objective characteristics of the encounter which may suggest whether or not a reasonable person would believe that he remained free during the course of the questioning to disregard the questions and walk away. See 3 W. LaFave, Search and Seizure §9.2, p. 52 (1978). The governing principles that should guide us in this difficult area were summarized in the Royer plurality opinion:

> [L]aw enforcement officers do not violate the Fourth Amendment by merely approaching an individual on the street or in another public place, by asking him if he is willing to answer some questions, by putting questions to him if the person is willing to listen, or by offering in evidence in a criminal prosecution his voluntary answers to such questions. Nor would the fact that the officer identifies himself as a police officer, without more, convert the encounter into a seizure requiring some level of objective justification. The person approached, however, need not answer any question put to him; indeed, he may decline to listen to the questions at all and may go on his way. He may not be detained even momentarily without reasonable, objective grounds for doing so; and his refusal to listen or answer does not, without more, furnish those grounds. 460 U.S., at 497–498 (citations omitted).

Applying these principles to the facts of this case, I have no difficulty concluding that respondents were seized within the meaning of the Fourth Amendment when they were accosted by the INS agents and questioned concerning their right to remain in the United States. Although none of the respondents was physically restrained by the INS agents during the questioning, it is nonetheless plain beyond cavil that the manner in which the INS conducted these surveys demonstrated a "show of authority" of sufficient size and force to overbear the will of any reasonable person. Faced with such tactics, a reasonable person could not help but feel compelled to stop and provide answers to the INS agents' questions. The Court's efforts to avoid this conclusion are rooted more in fantasy than in the record of this case. The Court goes astray, in my view, chiefly because it insists upon considering each interrogation in isolation as if respondents had been questioned by the INS in a setting similar to an encounter between a single police officer and a lone passerby that might occur on a street corner. Obviously, once the Court begins with such an unrealistic view of the facts, it is only a short step to the equally fanciful conclusion that respondents acted voluntarily when they stopped and answered the agents' questions.

The surrounding circumstances in this case are far different from an isolated encounter between the police and a passerby on the street. Each of the respondents testified at length about the widespread disturbance among the workers that was sparked by the INS surveys and the intimidating atmosphere created by the INS's investigative tactics. First, as the respondents explained, the surveys were carried out by surprise by relatively large numbers of agents, generally from 15 to 25, who moved systematically through the rows of workers who were seated at their work stations. See App. 77–78, 81–85, 102–103, 122–123. Second, as the INS agents discovered persons whom they suspected of being illegal aliens, they would handcuff these persons and lead them away to waiting vans outside the factory. See id., at 88, 140–141. Third, all of the factory exits were conspicuously guarded by INS agents, stationed there to prevent anyone from leaving while the survey was being conducted. See id., at 48, 82, 125–126, 144–145, 158. Finally, as the INS agents moved through the rows of workers, they would show their badges and direct pointed questions at the workers. In light of these circumstances, it is simply fantastic to conclude that a reasonable person could ignore all that was occurring throughout the factory and, when the INS agents reached him, have the temerity to believe that he was at liberty to refuse to answer their questions and walk away.

Indeed, the experiences recounted by respondents clearly demonstrate that they did not feel free either to ignore the INS agents or to refuse to answer the questions posed to them. For example, respondent Delgado, a naturalized American citizen, explained that he was standing near his work station when two INS agents approached him, identified themselves as immigration officers, showed him their badges, and asked him to state where he was born. Id., at 95. Delgado, of course, had seen all that was going on around him up to that point and naturally he responded. As a final reminder of who controlled the situation, one INS agent remarked as they were leaving Delgado that they would be coming back to check him out again because he spoke English too well. Id., at 94. Respondent Miramontes described her encounter with the INS in similar terms: "He told me he was from Immigration, so when I showed him the [work permit] papers I saw his badge. If I hadn't [seen his badge], I wouldn't have shown them to him." Id., at 121. She further testified that she was frightened during this interview because "normally you get nervous when you see everybody is scared, everybody is nervous." Ibid. Respondent Labontes testified that while she was sitting at her machine an immigration officer came up to her from behind, tapped her on the left shoulder and asked "Where are your papers?" Explaining her response to this demand, she testified: "I turned, and at the same time I didn't wish to identify myself. When I saw [the INS agents], I said, 'Yes, yes, I have my papers.'" Id., at 138.

In sum, it is clear from this testimony that respondents felt constrained to answer the questions posed by the INS agents, even though they did not wish to do so. That such a feeling of constraint was reasonable should be beyond question in light of the surrounding circumstances. Indeed, the respondents' testimony paints a frightening picture of people subjected to wholesale interrogation under conditions designed not to respect personal security and privacy, but rather to elicit prompt answers from completely intimidated workers. Nothing could be clearer than that these tactics amounted to seizures of respondents under the Fourth Amendment.

The Court's eagerness to conclude that these interrogations did not represent seizures is to some extent understandable, of course, because such a conclusion permits the Court to avoid the imposing task of justifying these seizures on the basis of reasonable, objective criteria as required by the Fourth Amendment.

The reasonableness requirement of the Fourth Amendment applies to all seizures of the person, including those that involve only a brief detention short of traditional arrest. But because the intrusion upon an individual's personal security and privacy is limited in cases of this sort, we have explained that brief detentions may be justified on "facts that do not amount to the probable cause required for an arrest." United States v. Brignoni-Ponce, 422 U.S. 873, (1975). Nevertheless, our prior decisions also make clear that investigatory stops of the kind at issue here "must be justified by some objective manifestation that the person stopped is, or is about to be, engaged in criminal activity." United States v. Cortez, 449 U.S. 411, 417 (1981). As the Court stated in Terry, the "demand for specificity in the information upon which police action is predicated is the central teaching of this Court's Fourth Amendment jurisprudence." 392 U.S., at 21, n. 18. Repeatedly, we have insisted that police may not detain and interrogate an individual unless they have reasonable grounds for suspecting that the person is involved in some unlawful activity. In United States v. Brignoni-Ponce, supra, for instance, the Court held that "[Border Patrol] officers on roving patrol may stop vehicles only if they are aware of specific articulable facts, together with rational inferences from those facts, that reasonably warrant suspicion that the vehicles contain aliens who may be illegally in the country." Id., 422 U.S., at 884. This requirement of particularized suspicion provides the chief protection of lawful citizens against unwarranted governmental interference with their personal security and privacy.

* * *

In this case, the individual seizures of respondents by the INS agents clearly were neither "based on specific, objective facts indicating that society's legitimate interests require[d] the seizure," nor "carried out pursuant to a plan embodying explicit, neutral limitations on the conduct of individual officers." Brown v. Texas, supra, 443 U.S., at 51. It is undisputed that the vast majority of the undocumented aliens discovered in the surveyed factories had illegally immigrated from Mexico. Nevertheless, the INS agents involved in this case apparently were instructed, in the words of the INS Assistant District Director in charge of the operations, to interrogate "virtually all persons employed by a company." App. 49. See also id., at 77, 85–86, 151–152, 155. Consequently, all workers, irrespective of whether they were American citizens, permanent resident aliens, or deportable aliens, were subjected to questioning by INS agents concerning their right to remain in the country. By their own admission, the INS agents did not selectively question persons in these surveys on the basis of any reasonable suspicion that the persons were illegal aliens. See id., at 55, 155. That the INS policy is so indiscriminate should not be surprising, however, since many of the employees in the surveyed factories who are lawful residents of the United States may have been born in Mexico, have a Latin appearance, or speak Spanish while at work. See id., at 57, 73. What this means, of course, is that the many lawful workers who constitute the clear majority at the surveyed workplaces are subjected to surprise questioning under intimidating circumstances by INS agents who have no reasonable basis for suspecting that they have done anything wrong. To say that such an indiscriminate policy of mass interrogation is constitutional makes a mockery of the words of the Fourth Amendment.

* * *

No one doubts that the presence of large numbers of undocumented aliens in this country creates law enforcement problems of titanic proportions for the INS. Nor does anyone question that this agency must be afforded considerable latitude in meeting its delegated enforcement responsibilities. I am afraid, however, that the Court has become so mesmerized by the magnitude of the problem that it has too easily allowed Fourth Amendment freedoms to be sacrificed. Before we discard all efforts to respect the commands of the Fourth Amendment in this troubling area, however, it is worth remembering that the difficulties faced by the INS today are partly of our own making.

The INS methods under review in this case are, in my view, more the product of expedience than of prudent law enforcement policy. The Immigration and Nationality Act establishes a quota-based system for regulating the admission of immigrants to this country which is designed to operate primarily at our borders. See 8 U.S.C. §§ 1151–1153, 1221–1225. See generally Developments, 96 Harv. L. Rev., at 1334–1369. With respect to Mexican immigration, however, this system has almost completely broken down. This breakdown is due in part, of course, to the considerable practical problems of patrolling a 2,000-mile border; it is, however, also the result of our failure to commit sufficient resources to the border patrol effort. See Administration's Proposals on Immigration and Refugee Policy: Joint Hearing before the Subcommittee on Immigration, Refugees, and International Law of the House Committee on the Judiciary, and the Subcommittee on Immigration and Refugee Policy of the Senate Committee on the Judiciary, 97th Cong., 1st Sess., 6 (1981) (statement of Attorney General Smith); see also Developments, 96 Harv. L. Rev., at 1439. Furthermore, the Act expressly exempts American businesses that employ undocumented aliens from all criminal sanctions, 8 U.S.C. § 1324(a), thereby adding to the already powerful incentives for aliens to cross our borders illegally in search of employment.[8]

8. The enormous law enforcement problems resulting from this combination of practical difficulties in patrolling this border and the incentives for illegal aliens to secure employment have been noted by the Congress, *see* Hearings on Oversight of the Immigration and Naturalization Service before the Subcommittee on Immigration, Citizenship and International Law of the House Committee on the Judiciary, 95th Cong., 2d Sess. (1978); and also by a Select Commission on Immigration and Refugee Policy, *see* United States Immigration Policy and the National Interest, Final Report of the Select Commission on Immigration and Refugee Policy 46, 61–62, 72–73 (1981)

In the face of these facts, it seems anomalous to insist that the INS must now be permitted virtually unconstrained discretion to conduct wide-ranging searches for undocumented aliens at otherwise lawful places of employment in the interior of the United States. What this position amounts to, I submit, is an admission that since we have allowed border enforcement to collapse and since we are unwilling to require American employers to share any of the blame, we must, as a matter of expediency, visit all of the burdens of this jury-rigged enforcement scheme on the privacy interests of completely lawful citizens and resident aliens who are subjected to these factory raids solely because they happen to work alongside some undocumented aliens. The average American, as we have long recognized, see Carroll v. United States, 267 U.S. 132, 154 (1925), expects some interference with his or her liberty when seeking to cross the Nation's borders, but until today's decision no one would ever have expected the same treatment while lawfully at work in the country's interior. Because the conditions which spawned such expedient solutions are in no sense the fault of these lawful workers, the Court, as the guardian of their constitutional rights, should attend to this problem with greater sensitivity before simply pronouncing the Fourth Amendment a dead letter in the context of immigration enforcement. The answer to these problems, I suggest, does not lie in abandoning our commitment to protecting the cherished rights secured by the Fourth Amendment, but rather may be found by re-examining our immigration policy.

Notes

1. The following sections of the statute were enacted two years after *INS v. Delgado* by the Immigration Reform and Control Act of 1986.[108]

8 U.S.C. §§ 1357(a) and (e)

(a) Any officer or employee of the Service authorized under regulations prescribed by the Attorney General shall have power without warrant—

(1) to interrogate any alien or person believed to be an alien as to his right to be or to remain in the United States;

(2) to arrest any alien who in his presence or view is entering or attempting to enter the United States in violation of any law or regulation made in pursuance of law regulating the admission, exclusion, expulsion, or removal of aliens, or to arrest any alien in the United States, if he has reason to believe that the alien so arrested is in the United States in violation of any such law or regulation and is likely to escape before a warrant can be obtained for his arrest, but the alien arrested shall be taken without unnecessary delay for examination before an officer of the Service having authority to examine aliens as to their right to enter or remain in the United States;

---

108. Pub. L. No. 99-603, 100 Stat. 3359.

(3) within a reasonable distance from any external boundary of the United States, to board and search for aliens any vessel within the territorial waters of the United States and any railway car, aircraft, conveyance, or vehicle, and within a distance of twenty-five miles from any such external boundary to have access to private lands, but not dwellings for the purpose of patrolling the border to prevent the illegal entry of aliens into the United States ...

* * *

(e) Notwithstanding any other provision of this section other than paragraph (3) of subsection (a), *an officer or employee of the Service may not enter without the consent of the owner (or agent thereof) or a properly executed warrant onto the premises of a farm or other outdoor agricultural operation for the purpose of interrogating a person believed to be an alien as to the person's right to be or to remain in the United States* (emphasis supplied).

2. What possible justifications might there be for the enactment of 8 U.S.C. § 1357(e) which requires that ICE obtain a warrant or permission of the farmowner prior to conducting a search? Is the warrant requirement for farm searches constitutional in light of the previous case?

3. In March 2005, the Supreme Court held in *Muehler v. Mena*[109] that the defendant who was being kept in handcuffs for two to three hours and questioned by government officers regarding his immigration status was not protected under the Fourth Amendment. The Court reasoned that the search which had been conducted pursuant to a warrant, and therefore the detention which followed, necessary flowed as part of the search. The Court, citing *Florida v. Bostick*[110] and *Illinois v. Caballes*[111] concluded that the questioning of Mena regarding her immigration status by immigration officers called to the scene did not violate her Fourth Amendment rights, since mere questioning by authorities neither constitutes a seizure nor requires reasonable suspicion. *Caballes* involved a defendant who had been convicted of trafficking in cannabis. The defendant had appealed the denial of a motion to suppress evidence which had been obtained during a traffic stop. The Court held that the stop had not gone on for an unreasonable period of time and that the use of a drug sniffing dog around the exterior of the car did not rise to the level of an infringement on the defendant's Fourth Amendment rights.

4. **Stop, Questioning and Arrests.** Although the plenary power doctrine gives Congress and the president broad authority to determine who may be admitted and become citizens of the United States,[112] noncitizens within the country's borders are afforded basic constitutional rights.

---

109. 544 U.S. 93 (2005).
110. 501 U.S. 429, 434 (1991).
111. 543 U.S. 405 (2005).
112. *See Chae Chan Ping v. U.S.*, 130 U.S. 581 (1889).

8 U.S.C. § 1357(a)(1) allows the warrantless questioning of any person who an officer believes to be an alien as to her right to remain in the United States irrespective of whether the officer suspects the person to be in the country illegally. The questioning does not violate the person's Fourth Amendment rights against unreasonable searches and seizures as long as the person is given the impression that she can leave at any time[113] and the officer has reasonable suspicion that the person has no right to be in the United States based on more than mere ethnic appearance; thus, the alien is free to walk away without answering the officer's questions. However, an officer has the authority to detain or arrest any person who voluntarily admits to being an alien but to not having her immigration papers on her person, who makes an effort to escape[114] or who is identified by a reliable informant as being an illegal alien.[115] A person may also be detained if the officer can point to specific and articulable facts suggesting that the she has committed a crime.[116] Similarly, officers may stop any vehicle if they have specific and articulable facts suggesting that persons on board are in the United States illegally,[117] but they may not conduct a warrantless vehicular search incident to arrest after the occupants have been secured and there is no continuing threat to their safety or need to preserve evidence relevant to the crime of arrest from being accessed by the arrestee.[118]

Under 8 U.S.C. § 1357(a)(2), an officer can arrest any person without a warrant if there exists probable cause suggesting that the person is in the country illegally or has violated an immigration law[119] and is likely to escape prior to the issuance of a warrant.[120] After a proper investigatory stop, a person may be arrested for such acts as failing to provide documents relating to her status;[121] providing fabricated identification documents and being unable to give details affirming his legal right to be in the United States;[122] matching a reliable informant's description of an alleged alien;[123] or confessing to having made an illegal entry, being in possession of an expired visa and being unable to provide documents establishing legal presence in the country.[124]

---

113. *See INS v. Delgado*, 466 U.S. 210 (1984).

114. *See Babula v. INS*, 665 F.2d 293 (3d Cir. 1981); *Lee v. INS*, 590 F.2d 497 (3d Cir. 1979); *Au Yi Lau v. INS*, 445 F.2d 217 (D.C. Cir. 1971).

115. *See State v. Nebar*, 529 So. 2d 117 (La. Ct. App. 4th Cir. 1988).

116. *See Terry v. Ohio*, 392 U.S. 1 (1968).

117. *See United States v. Brignon-Ponce*, 422 U.S. 873 (1975).

118. *See Arizona v. Gant*, 556 U.S. ___, 129 S.Ct. 1710, 1719 (2009).

119. *See Murillo v. Musegades*, 809 F. Supp. 487 (W.D. Tex. 1992); *Pearl Meadows Mushroom Farm, Inc. v. Nelson*, 723 F. Supp. 432 (N.D. Cal. 1989).

120. *See Murillo v. Musegades*, 809 F. Supp. 487 (W.D. Tex. 1992).

121. *See U.S. v. Sanchez*, 635 F.2d 47 (2d Cir. 1980).

122. *See U.S. v. Alvarado-Bermudez*, 499 F. Supp. 1070 (E.D.N.Y. 1980); *U.S. v. Hernandez-Rojas*, 470 F. Supp. 1212 (E.D. N.Y. 1979), *aff'd*, 615 F. 2d 1351 (2d Cir. 1979).

123. *See Chairez v. Van Buren County*, 542 F. Supp. 706 (W.D. Mich. 1982), *judgment rev'd on other grounds*, 790 F. 2d 544 (6th Cir. 1986).

124. *See U.S. v. Galindo-Hernandez*, 674 F. Supp. 979 (E.D.N.Y. 1987).

Unlike persons stopped for questioning, once a person is arrested, she must be given Miranda warnings.[125] If the officer decides to initiate formal proceedings, the Sixth Amendment guarantees the right to counsel at all "critical" stages of the proceedings,[126] which includes interrogation.[127] The person can waive her right to counsel as long as the waiver is "voluntary, knowing and intelligent,"[128] but once the person invokes her right to counsel, the officers may not continue the interrogation unless she initiates the contact.[129] In *Montejo v. Louisiana*,[130] the Court held that there may be circumstances in which a defendant may knowingly give up her right to counsel without having counsel present at the time of the waiver. In *Montejo*, the Court reaffirmed that the waiver of the right to counsel could not be secured through coercion or badgering.[131]

H. The Exclusionary Rule

Immigration and Naturalization Service v. Adan Lopez-Mendoza, et al.

468 U.S. 1032 (1984)

Justice O'Connor announced the judgment of the Court and delivered the opinion of the Court with respect to Parts I, II, III, and IV, and an opinion with respect to Part V, in which Justice Blackmun, Justice Powell, and Justice Rehnquist joined. [The Chief Justice joined in all but the last part of this opinion.]

This litigation requires us to decide whether an admission of unlawful presence in this country made subsequent to an allegedly unlawful arrest must be excluded as evidence in a civil deportation hearing. We hold that the exclusionary rule need not be applied in such a proceeding.

Respondents Adan Lopez-Mendoza and Elias Sandoval-Sanchez, both citizens of Mexico, were summoned to separate deportation proceedings in California and Washington, and both were ordered deported. They challenged the regularity of those proceedings on grounds related to the lawfulness of their respective arrests by officials of the Immigration and Naturalization Service (INS). On administrative appeal the Board of Immigration Appeals (BIA), an agency of the Department of Justice, affirmed the deportation orders.

125. *See Babula v. INS*, 665 F.2d 293 (3d Cir. 1981).

126. *See United States v. Wade*, 388 U.S. 218 (1967); *Powell v. Alabama*, 287 U.S. 45 (1932).

127. *See Massiah v. U.S.*, 377 U.S. 201 (1964); *see also United States v. Henry*, 447 U.S. 264 (1980).

128. *See Patterson v. Illinois*, 487 U.S. 285 (1988); *Brewer v. Williams*, 430 U.S. 387 (1977); *Johnson v. Zerbst*, 304 U.S. 1938).

129. *See Edwards v. Arizona*, 451 U.S. 477 (1981).

130. 556 U.S. ___, 129 S.Ct. 2079 (2009).

131. Id. at 2086 (2009).

The Court of Appeals for the Ninth Circuit, sitting en banc, reversed Sandoval-Sanchez' deportation order and vacated and remanded Lopez-Mendoza's deportation order. 705 F.2d 1059 (1983). It ruled that Sandoval-Sanchez' admission of his illegal presence in this country was the fruit of an unlawful arrest, and that the exclusionary rule applied in a deportation proceeding. Lopez-Mendoza's deportation order was vacated and his case remanded to the BIA to determine whether the Fourth Amendment had been violated in the course of his arrest. We granted certiorari, 464 U.S. 1037 (1984).

Respondent Lopez-Mendoza was arrested in 1976 by INS agents at his place of employment, a transmission repair shop in San Mateo, Cal. Responding to a tip, INS investigators arrived at the shop shortly before 8 a.m. The agents had not sought a warrant to search the premises or to arrest any of its occupants. The proprietor of the shop firmly refused to allow the agents to interview his employees during working hours. Nevertheless, while one agent engaged the proprietor in conversation another entered the shop and approached Lopez-Mendoza. In response to the agent's questioning, Lopez-Mendoza gave his name and indicated that he was from Mexico with no close family ties in the United States. The agent then placed him under arrest. Lopez-Mendoza underwent further questioning at INS offices, where he admitted he was born in Mexico, was still a citizen of Mexico, and had entered this country without inspection by immigration authorities. Based on his answers, the agents prepared a "Record of Deportable Alien" (Form I-213), and an affidavit which Lopez-Mendoza executed, admitting his Mexican nationality and his illegal entry into this country.

A hearing was held before an Immigration Judge. Lopez-Mendoza's counsel moved to terminate the proceeding on the ground that Lopez-Mendoza had been arrested illegally. The judge ruled that the legality of the arrest was not relevant to the deportation proceeding and therefore declined to rule on the legality of Mendoza's arrest. *Matter of Lopez-Mendoza*, No. A22 452 208 (INS, Dec. 21, 1977), reprinted in App. to Pet. for Cert. 97a. The Form I-213 and the affidavit executed by Lopez-Mendoza were received into evidence without objection from Lopez-Mendoza. On the basis of this evidence the Immigration Judge found Mendoza deportable. Lopez-Mendoza was granted the option of voluntary departure.

The BIA dismissed Lopez-Mendoza's appeal. It noted that "[t]he mere fact of an illegal arrest has no bearing on a subsequent deportation proceeding," *In re Lopez-Mendoza*, No. A22 452 208 (BIA, Sept. 19, 1979), reprinted in App. to Pet. for Cert. 100a, 102a, and observed that Lopez-Mendoza had not objected to the admission into evidence of Form I-213 and the affidavit he had executed. *Id.*, at 103a. The BIA also noted that the exclusionary rule is not applied to redress the injury to the privacy of the search victim, and that the BIA had previously concluded that application of the rule in deportation proceedings to deter unlawful INS conduct was inappropriate. *Matter of Sandoval*, 17 I. & N. Dec. 70 (BIA 1979).

The Court of Appeals vacated the order of deportation and remanded for a determination whether Lopez-Mendoza's Fourth Amendment rights had been violated when he was arrested.

Respondent Sandoval-Sanchez (who is not the same individual who was involved in Matter of Sandoval, supra) was arrested in 1977 at his place of employment, a potato processing plant in Pasco, Wash. INS Agent Bower and other officers went to the plant, with the permission of its personnel manager, to check for illegal aliens. During a change in shift, officers stationed themselves at the exits while Bower and a uniformed Border Patrol agent entered the plant. They went to the lunchroom and identified themselves as immigration officers. Many people in the room rose and headed for the exits or milled around; others in the plant left their equipment and started running; still others who were entering the plant turned around and started walking back out. The two officers eventually stationed themselves at the main entrance to the plant and looked for passing employees who averted their heads, avoided eye contact, or tried to hide themselves in a group. Those individuals were addressed with innocuous questions in English. Any who could not respond in English and who otherwise aroused Agent Bower's suspicions were questioned in Spanish as to their right to be in the United States.

Respondent Sandoval-Sanchez was in a line of workers entering the plant. Sandoval-Sanchez testified that he did not realize that immigration officers were checking people entering the plant, but that he did see standing at the plant entrance a man in uniform who appeared to be a police officer. Agent Bower testified that it was probable that he, not his partner, had questioned Sandoval-Sanchez at the plant, but that he could not be absolutely positive. The employee he thought he remembered as Sandoval-Sanchez had been "very evasive," had averted his head, turned around, and walked away when he saw Agent Bower. App. 137, 138. Bower was certain that no one was questioned about his status unless his actions had given the agents reason to believe that he was an undocumented alien.

Thirty-seven employees, including Sandoval-Sanchez, were briefly detained at the plant and then taken to the county jail. About one-third immediately availed themselves of the option of voluntary departure and were put on a bus to Mexico. Sandoval-Sanchez exercised his right to a deportation hearing. Sandoval-Sanchez was then questioned further, and Agent Bower recorded Sandoval-Sanchez' admission of unlawful entry. Sandoval-Sanchez contends he was not aware that he had a right to remain silent.

At his deportation hearing Sandoval-Sanchez contended that the evidence offered by the INS should be suppressed as the fruit of an unlawful arrest. The Immigration Judge considered and rejected Sandoval-Sanchez' claim that he had been illegally arrested, but ruled in the alternative that the legality of the arrest was not relevant to the deportation hearing. *Matter of Sandoval-Sanchez*, No. A22 346 925 (INS, Oct. 7, 1977), reprinted in App. to Pet. for Cert. 104a. Based on the written record of Sandoval-Sanchez' admissions the Immigration Judge found him deportable and granted him voluntary departure. The BIA dismissed Sandoval-Sanchez' appeal. *In re Sandoval-Sanchez*, No. A22 346 925 (BIA, Feb. 21, 1980). It concluded that the circumstances of the arrest had not affected the voluntariness of his recorded admission, and again declined to invoke the exclusionary rule, relying on its earlier decision in *Matter of Sandoval, supra.*

On appeal the Court of Appeals concluded that Sandoval-Sanchez' detention by the immigration officers violated the Fourth Amendment, that the statements he made were a product of that detention, and that the exclusionary rule barred their use in a deportation hearing. The deportation order against Sandoval-Sanchez was accordingly reversed.

A deportation proceeding is a purely civil action to determine eligibility to remain in this country, not to punish an unlawful entry, though entering or remaining unlawfully in this country is itself a crime. 8 U.S.C. §§ 1302, 1306, 1325. The deportation hearing looks prospectively to the respondent's right to remain in this country in the future. Past conduct is relevant only insofar as it may shed light on the respondent's right to remain. See 8 U.S.C. §§ 1251, 1252(b); *Bugajewitz v. Adams*, 228 U.S. 585, 591 (1913); *Fong Yue Ting v. United States*, 149 U.S. 698, 730 (1893).

A deportation hearing is held before an immigration judge. The judge's sole power is to order deportation; the judge cannot adjudicate guilt or punish the respondent for any crime related to unlawful entry into or presence in this country. Consistent with the civil nature of the proceeding, various protections that apply in the context of a criminal trial do not apply in a deportation hearing. The respondent must be given "a reasonable opportunity to be present at [the] proceeding," but if the respondent fails to avail himself of that opportunity the hearing may proceed in his absence. 8 U.S.C. § 1252(b). In many deportation cases the INS must show only identity and alienage; the burden then shifts to the respondent to prove the time, place, and manner of his entry. See 8 U.S.C. § 1361; *Matter of Sandoval*, 17 I. & N.Dec. 70 (BIA 1979). A decision of deportability need be based only on "reasonable, substantial, and probative evidence," 8 U.S.C. § 1252(b)(4). The BIA for its part has required only "clear, unequivocal and convincing" evidence of the respondent's deportability, not proof beyond a reasonable doubt. 8 CFR § 242.14(a) (1984). The Court of Appeals have held, for example that the absence of Miranda warnings does not render an otherwise voluntary statement by the respondent inadmissible in a deportation case. *Navia-Duran v. INS*, 568 F.2d 803, 808 (CA1 1977); *Avila-Gallegos v. INS*, 525 F.2d 666, 667 (CA2 1975); *Chavez-Raya v. INS*, 519 F.2d 397, 399–401 (CA7 1975). See also *Abel v. United States*, 362 U.S. 217, 236–237 (1960) (search permitted incidental to an arrest pursuant to an administrative warrant issued by the INS); *Galvan v. Press*, 347 U.S. 522, 531 (1954) (Ex Post Facto Clause has no application to deportation); *Carlson v. Landon*, 342 U.S. 524, 544–546 (1952) (Eighth Amendment does not require bail to be granted in certain deportation cases); *United States ex rel. Bilokumsky v. Tod*, 263 U.S. 149, 157 (1923) (involuntary confessions admissible at deportation hearing). In short, a deportation hearing is intended to provide a streamlined determination of eligibility to remain in this country, nothing more. The purpose of deportation is not to punish past transgressions but rather to put an end to a continuing violation of the immigration laws.

The "body" or identity of a defendant or respondent in a criminal or civil proceeding is never itself suppressible as a fruit of an unlawful arrest, even if it is conceded that an unlawful arrest, search, or interrogation occurred. See *Gerstein v. Pugh*, 420 U.S. 103, 119 (1975); *Frisbie v. Collins*, 342 U.S. 519, 522 (1952); *United States ex rel. Bilokumsky v. Tod, supra*, 263 U.S., at 158. A similar rule applies in forfeiture proceedings directed against contraband or forfeitable property. See, e.g., *United States v. Eighty-Eight Thousand, Five Hundred Dollars*, 671 F.2d 293 (CA8 1982); *United States v. One (1) 1971 Harley-Davidson Motorcycle*, 508 F.2d 351 (CA9 1974); *United States v. One 1965 Buick*, 397 F.2d 782 (CA6 1968).

* * *

Respondent Sandoval-Sanchez has a more substantial claim. He objected not to his compelled presence at a deportation proceeding, but to evidence offered at that proceeding. The general rule in a criminal proceeding is that statements and other evidence obtained as a result of an unlawful, warrantless arrest are suppressible if the link between the evidence and the unlawful conduct is not too attenuated. *Wong Sun v. United States*, 371 U.S. 471 (1963). The reach of the exclusionary rule beyond the context of a criminal prosecution, however, is less clear. Although this Court has once stated in dictum that "[i]t may be assumed that evidence obtained by the [Labor] Department through an illegal search and seizure cannot be made the basis of a finding in deportation proceedings," *United States ex rel. Bilokumsky v. Tod, supra*, 263 U.S., at 155, the Court has never squarely addressed the question before. Lower court decisions dealing with this question are sparse.

In *United States v. Janis*, 428 U.S. 433 (1976), this Court set forth a framework for deciding in what types of proceeding application of the exclusionary rule is appropriate. Imprecise as the exercise may be, the Court recognized in Janis that there is no choice but to weigh the likely social benefits of excluding unlawfully seized evidence against the likely costs. On the benefit side of the balance "the 'prime purpose' of the [exclusionary] rule, if not the sole one, 'is to deter future unlawful police conduct.'" *Id.*, at 446, quoting *United States v. Calandra*, 414 U.S. 338, 347 (1974). On the cost side there is the loss of often probative evidence and all of the secondary costs that flow from the less accurate or more cumbersome adjudication that therefore occurs.

At stake in *Janis* was application of the exclusionary rule in a federal civil tax assessment proceeding following the unlawful seizure of evidence by state, not federal, officials. The Court noted at the outset that "[i]n the complex and turbulent history of the rule, the Court never has applied it to exclude evidence from a civil proceeding, federal or state." 428 U.S., at 447 (footnote omitted). Two factors in Janis suggested that the deterrence value of the exclusionary rule in the context of that case was slight. First, the state law enforcement officials were already "punished" by the exclusion of the evidence in the state criminal trial as a result of the same conduct. *Id.*, at 448. Second, the evidence was also excludable in any federal criminal trial that might be held. Both factors suggested that further application of the exclusionary rule in the federal civil proceeding would contribute little more to the deterrence of unlawful conduct by state officials. On the cost side of the balance, *Janis* focused simply on the loss of "concededly relevant and reliable evidence." *Id.*, at 447. The Court concluded that, on balance, this cost outweighed the likely social benefits achievable through application of the exclusionary rule in the federal civil proceeding.

While it seems likely that the deterrence value of applying the exclusionary rule in deportation proceedings would be higher than it was in Janis, it is also quite clear that the social costs would be very much greater as well. Applying the Janis balancing test to the benefits and costs of excluding concededly reliable evidence from a deportation proceeding, we therefore reach the same conclusion as in Janis.

The likely deterrence value of the exclusionary rule in deportation proceedings is difficult to assess. On the one hand, a civil deportation proceeding is a civil complement to a possible criminal prosecution, and to this extent it resembles the civil proceeding under review in Janis. The INS does not suggest that the exclusionary rule should not continue to apply in criminal proceedings against an alien who unlawfully enters or remains in this country, and the prospect of losing evidence that might otherwise be used in a criminal prosecution undoubtedly supplies some residual deterrent to unlawful conduct by INS officials. But it must be acknowledged that only a very small percentage of arrests of aliens are intended or expected to lead to criminal prosecutions. Thus the arresting officer's primary objective, in practice, will be to use evidence in the civil deportation proceeding. Moreover, here, in contrast to *Janis*, the agency officials who effect the unlawful arrest are the same officials who subsequently bring the deportation action. As recognized in *Janis*, the exclusionary rule is likely to be most effective when applied to such "intrasovereign" violations.

Nonetheless, several other factors significantly reduce the likely deterrent value of the exclusionary rule in a civil deportation proceeding. First, regardless of how the arrest is effected, deportation will still be possible when evidence not derived directly from the arrest is sufficient to support deportation. As the BIA has recognized, in many deportation proceedings "the sole matters necessary for the Government to establish are the respondent's identity and alienage—at which point the burden shifts to the respondent to prove the time, place and manner of entry." *Matter of Sandoval*, 17 I. & N. Dec., at 79. Since the person and identity of the respondent are not themselves suppressible, see *supra*, at 3485, the INS must prove only alienage, and that will sometimes be possible using evidence gathered independently of, or sufficiently attenuated from, the original arrest. See *Matter of Sandoval, supra*, at 79; see, e.g., *Avila-Gallegos v. INS*, 525 F.2d 666 (CA2 1975). The INS's task is simplified in this regard by the civil nature of the proceeding. As Justice Brandeis stated: "Silence is often evidence of the most persuasive character.... [T]here is no rule of law which prohibits officers charged with the administration of the immigration law from drawing an inference from the silence of one who is called upon to speak.... A person arrested on the preliminary warrant is not protected by a presumption of citizenship comparable to the presumption of innocence in a criminal case. There is no provision which forbids drawing an adverse inference from the fact of standing mute." *United States ex rel. Bilokumsky v. Tod*, 263 U.S., at 153–154.

The second factor is a practical one. In the course of a year the average INS agent arrests almost 500 illegal aliens. Brief for Petitioner 38. Over 97.5% apparently agree to voluntary deportation without a formal hearing. 705 F.2d, at 1071, n. 17. Among the remainder who do request a formal hearing (apparently a dozen or so in all, per officer, per year) very few challenge the circumstances of their arrests. As noted by the Court of Appeals, "the BIA was able to find only two reported immigration cases since 1899 in which the [exclusionary] rule was applied to bar unlawfully seized evidence, only one other case in which the rule's application was specifically addressed, and fewer than fifty BIA proceedings since 1952 in which a Fourth Amendment challenge to the introduction of evidence was even raised." *Id.*, at 1071. Every INS agent knows, therefore, that it is highly unlikely that any particular arrestee will end up challenging the lawfulness of his arrest in a formal deportation proceeding. When an occasional challenge is brought, the consequences from the point of view of the officer's overall arrest and deportation record will be trivial. In these circumstances, the arresting officer is most unlikely to shape his conduct in anticipation of the exclusion of evidence at a formal deportation hearing.

Third, and perhaps most important, the INS has its own comprehensive scheme for deterring Fourth Amendment violations by its officers. Most arrests of illegal aliens away from the border occur during farm, factory, or other workplace surveys. Large numbers of illegal aliens are often arrested at one time, and conditions are understandably chaotic. See Brief for Petitioner in *INS v. Delgado*, O.T.1983, No. 82-1271, pp. 3–5. To safeguard the rights of those who are lawfully present at inspected workplaces the INS has developed rules restricting stop, interrogation, and arrest practices. *Id.*, at 7, n. 7, 32–40, and n. 25. These regulations require that no one be detained without reasonable suspicion of illegal alienage, and that no one be arrested unless there is an admission of illegal alienage or other strong evidence thereof. New immigration officers receive instruction and examination in Fourth Amendment law, and others receive periodic refresher courses in law. Brief for Petitioner 39–40. Evidence seized through intentionally unlawful conduct is excluded by Department of Justice policy from the proceeding for which it was obtained. See Memorandum from Benjamin R. Civiletti to Heads of Offices, Boards, Bureaus and Divisions, Violations of Search and Seizure Law (Jan. 16, 1981). The INS also has in place a procedure for investigating and punishing immigration officers who commit Fourth Amendment violations. See Office of General Counsel, INS, U.S. Dept. of Justice, The Law of Arrest, Search, and Seizure for Immigration Officers 35 (Jan. 1983). The INS's attention to Fourth Amendment interests cannot guarantee that constitutional violations will not occur, but it does reduce the likely deterrent value of the exclusionary rule. Deterrence must be measured at the margin.

Finally, the deterrent value of the exclusionary rule in deportation proceedings is undermined by the availability of alternative remedies for institutional practices by the INS that might violate Fourth Amendment rights. The INS is a single agency, under central federal control, and engaged in operations of broad scope but highly repetitive character. The possibility of declaratory relief against the agency thus offers a means for challenging the validity of INS practices, when standing requirements for bringing such an action can be met. Cf. *INS v. Delgado*, 466 U.S. 210 (1984).

Respondents contend that retention of the exclusionary rule is necessary to safeguard the Fourth Amendment rights of ethnic Americans, particularly the Hispanic-Americans lawfully in this country. We recognize that respondents raise here legitimate and important concerns. But application of the exclusionary rule to civil deportation proceedings can be justified only if the rule is likely to add significant protection to these Fourth Amendment rights. The exclusionary rule provides no remedy for completed wrongs; those lawfully in this country can be interested in its application only insofar as it may serve as an effective deterrent to future INS misconduct. For the reasons we have discussed we conclude that application of the rule in INS civil deportation proceedings, as in the circumstances discussed in Janis, "is unlikely to provide significant, much less substantial, additional deterrence." 428 U.S., at 458, 96 S.Ct., at 3034. Important as it is to protect the Fourth Amendment rights of all persons, there is no convincing indication that application of the exclusionary rule in civil deportation proceedings will contribute materially to that end.

On the other side of the scale, the social costs of applying the exclusionary rule in deportation proceedings are both unusual and significant. The first cost is one that is unique to continuing violations of the law. Applying the exclusionary rule in proceedings that are intended not to punish past transgressions but to prevent their continuance or renewal would require the courts to close their eyes to ongoing violations of the law. This Court has never before accepted costs of this character in applying the exclusionary rule.

* * *

Other factors also weigh against applying the exclusionary rule in deportation proceedings. The INS currently operates a deliberately simple deportation hearing system, streamlined to permit the quick resolution of very large numbers of deportation actions, and it is against this backdrop that the costs of the exclusionary rule must be assessed. The costs of applying the exclusionary rule, like the benefits, must be measured at the margin.

The average immigration judge handles about six deportation hearings per day. Brief for Petitioner 27, n. 16. Neither the hearing officers nor the attorneys participating in those hearings are likely to be well versed in the intricacies of Fourth Amendment law. The prospect of even occasional invocation of the exclusionary rule might significantly change and complicate the character of these proceedings. The BIA has described the practical problems as follows:

> Absent the applicability of the exclusionary rule, questions relating to deportability routinely involve simple factual allegations and matters of proof. When Fourth Amendment issues are raised at deportation hearings, the result is a diversion of attention from the main issues which those proceedings were created to resolve, both in terms of the expertise of the administrative decision makers and of the structure of the forum to accommodate inquiries into search and seizure questions. The result frequently seems to be a long, confused record in which the issues are not clearly defined and in which there is voluminous testimony.... The ensuing delays and inordinate amount of

> time spent on such cases at all levels has an adverse impact on the effective administration of the immigration laws.... This is particularly true in a proceeding where delay may be the only "defense" available and where problems already exist with the use of dilatory tactics. *Matter of Sandoval*, 17 I. & N., at 80 (footnote omitted).

The BIA's concerns are reinforced by the staggering dimension of the problem that the INS confronts. Immigration officers apprehend over one million deportable aliens in this country every year. *Id.*, at 85. A single agent may arrest many illegal aliens every day. Although the investigatory burden does not justify the commission of constitutional violations, the officers cannot be expected to compile elaborate, contemporaneous, written reports detailing the circumstances of every arrest. At present an officer simply completes a "Record of Deportable Alien" that is introduced to prove the INS's case at the deportation hearing; the officer rarely must attend the hearing. Fourth Amendment suppression hearings would undoubtedly require considerably more, and the likely burden on the administration of the immigration laws would be correspondingly severe.

Finally, the INS advances the credible argument that applying the exclusionary rule to deportation proceedings might well result in the suppression of large amounts of information that had been obtained entirely lawfully. INS arrests occur in crowded and confused circumstances. Though the INS agents are instructed to follow procedures that adequately protect Fourth Amendment interests, agents will usually be able to testify only to the fact that they followed INS rules. The demand for a precise account of exactly what happened in each particular arrest would plainly preclude mass arrests, even when the INS is confronted, as it often is, with massed numbers of ascertainably illegal aliens, and even when the arrests can be and are conducted in full compliance with all Fourth Amendment requirements.

In these circumstances we are persuaded that the Janis balance between costs and benefits comes out against applying the exclusionary rule in civil deportation hearings held by the INS. By all appearances the INS has already taken sensible and reasonable steps to deter Fourth Amendment violations by its officers, and this makes the likely additional deterrent value of the exclusionary rule small. The costs of applying the exclusionary rule in the context of civil deportation hearings are high. In particular, application of the exclusionary rule in cases such as Sandoval-Sanchez', would compel the courts to release from custody persons who would then immediately resume their commission of a crime through their continuing, unlawful presence in this country. "There comes a point at which courts, consistent with their duty to administer the law, cannot continue to create barriers to law enforcement in the pursuit of a supervisory role that is properly the duty of the Executive and Legislative Branches." *United States v. Janis*, 428 U.S., at 459. That point has been reached here.

We do not condone any violations of the Fourth Amendment that may have occurred in the arrests of respondents Lopez-Mendoza or Sandoval-Sanchez. Moreover, no challenge is raised here to the INS's own internal regulations. Our conclusions concerning the exclusionary rule's value might change, if there developed good reason to believe that Fourth Amendment violations by INS officers were widespread. Cf. *United States v. Leon*, 468 U.S. 897, 928 (Blackmun, J., concurring). Finally, we do not deal here with egregious violations of Fourth Amendment or other liberties that might transgress notions of fundamental fairness and undermine the probative value of the evidence obtained. At issue here is the exclusion of credible evidence gathered in connection with peaceful arrests by INS officers. We hold that evidence derived from such arrests need not be suppressed in an INS civil deportation hearing.

Justice Brennan, dissenting.

I fully agree with Justice White that under the analysis developed by the Court in such cases as *United States v. Janis*, 428 U.S. 433 (1976), and *United States v. Calandra*, 414 U.S. 338 (1974), the exclusionary rule must apply in civil deportation proceedings. However, for the reasons set forth today in my dissenting opinion in *United States v. Leon, ante*, 468 U.S. 897, I believe the basis for the exclusionary rule does not derive from its effectiveness as a deterrent, but is instead found in the requirements of the Fourth Amendment itself. My view of the exclusionary rule would, of course, require affirmance of the Court of Appeals. In this case, federal law enforcement officers arrested respondents Sandoval-Sanchez and Lopez-Mendoza in violation of their Fourth Amendment rights. The subsequent admission of any evidence secured pursuant to these unlawful arrests in civil deportation proceedings would, in my view, also infringe those rights. The Government of the United States bears an obligation to obey the Fourth Amendment; that obligation is not lifted simply because the law enforcement officers were agents of the Immigration and Naturalization Service, nor because the evidence obtained by those officers was to be used in civil deportation proceedings.

Justice White, dissenting.

The Court today holds that the exclusionary rule does not apply in civil deportation proceedings. Because I believe that the conclusion of the majority is based upon an incorrect assessment of the costs and benefits of applying the rule in such proceedings, I respectfully dissent.[1]

The paradigmatic case in which the exclusionary rule is applied is when the prosecutor seeks to use evidence illegally obtained by law enforcement officials in his case-in-chief in a criminal trial. In other classes of cases, the rule is applicable only when the likelihood of deterring the unwanted conduct outweighs the societal costs imposed by exclusion of relevant evidence. *United States v. Janis*, 428 U.S. 433, 454 (1976). Thus, the Court has, in a number of situations, refused to extend the exclusionary rule to proceedings other than the criminal trial itself. For example, in *Stone v. Powell*, 428 U.S. 465 (1976), the Court held that the deterrent effect of the

---

1. I also question the Court's finding that Lopez-Mendoza failed to object to admission of the evidence. *Ante*, at 3485, and n.1. The Court of Appeals held that he had made a proper objection, 705 F.2d 1059, 1060, n.1 (CA9 1983), and the INS did not seek review of that conclusion. Brief for Petitioner 8, n.8. Moreover, the fact that changes in an opinion are made between the time of the slip opinion and the bound volume has never before been considered evidence that the holding of a case is "unsettled." *See ante*, at 3484, n.1.

rule would not be reduced by refusing to allow a state prisoner to litigate a Fourth Amendment claim in federal habeas corpus proceedings if he was afforded a full and fair opportunity to litigate it in state court. Similarly, in *United States v. Calandra*, 414 U.S. 338, 351 (1974), we concluded that "[a]ny incremental deterrent effect which might be achieved by extending the rule to grand jury proceedings is uncertain at best." And in *United States v. Janis, supra*, we declined to extend the exclusionary rule to bar the introduction in a federal civil proceeding of evidence unconstitutionally seized by a state law enforcement officer. In all of these cases it was unquestioned that the illegally seized evidence would not be admissible in the case-in-chief of the proceeding for which the evidence was gathered; only its collateral use was permitted.

Civil deportation proceedings are in no sense "collateral." The majority correctly acknowledges that the "primary objective" of the INS agent is "to use evidence in the civil deportation proceeding" and that "the agency officials who effect the unlawful arrest are the same officials who subsequently bring the deportation action." *Ante*, at 3485. The Immigration and Naturalization Service likewise concedes that INS agents are "in the business of conducting searches for and seizures of illegal aliens for the purpose of bringing about their deportation." Brief for Petitioner 37. Thus, unlike the situation in *Janis*, the conduct challenged here falls within "the offending officer's zone of primary interest." 428 U.S., at 458. The majority nonetheless concludes that application of the rule in such proceedings is unlikely to provide significant deterrence. Because INS agents are law enforcement officials whose mission is closely analogous to that of police officers and because civil deportation proceedings are to INS agents what criminal trials are to police officers, I cannot agree with that assessment.

The exclusionary rule rests on the Court's belief that exclusion has a sufficient deterrent effect to justify its imposition, and the Court has not abandoned the rule. As long as that is the case, there is no principled basis for distinguishing between the deterrent effect of the rule in criminal cases and in civil deportation proceedings. The majority attempts to justify the distinction by asserting that deportation will still be possible when evidence not derived from the illegal search or seizure is independently sufficient. *Ante*, at 3485–3486. However, that is no less true in criminal cases. The suppression of some evidence does not bar prosecution for the crime, and in many cases even though some evidence is suppressed a conviction will nonetheless be obtained.

The majority also suggests that the fact that most aliens elect voluntary departure dilutes the deterrent effect of the exclusionary rule, because the infrequency of challenges to admission of evidence will mean that "the consequences from the point of view of the officer's overall arrest and deportation record will be trivial." *Ante*, at 3486. It is true that a majority of apprehended aliens elect voluntary departure, while a lesser number go through civil deportation proceedings and a still smaller number are criminally prosecuted. However, that fact no more diminishes the importance of the exclusionary sanction than the fact that many criminal defendants plead guilty dilutes the rule's deterrent effect in criminal cases. The possibility of exclusion of evidence quite obviously plays a part in the decision whether to contest either civil deportation or criminal prosecution. Moreover, in concentrating on the incentives under which the individual agent operates to the exclusion of the incentives under which the agency as a whole operates neglects the "systemic" deterrent effect that may lead the agency to adopt policies and procedures that conform to Fourth Amendment standards. See, e.g., *Dunaway v. New York*, 442 U.S. 200, 221 (1979) (Stevens, J., concurring).

The majority believes "perhaps most important" the fact that the INS has a "comprehensive scheme" in place for deterring Fourth Amendment violations by punishing agents who commit such violations, but it points to not a single instance in which that scheme has been invoked.[2] *Ante*, at 3486. Also, immigration officers are instructed and examined in Fourth Amendment law, and it is suggested that this education is another reason why the exclusionary rule is unnecessary. *Ibid.* A contrary lesson could be discerned from the existence of these programs, however, when it is recalled that they were instituted during "a legal regime in which the cases and commentators uniformly sanctioned the invocation of the rule in deportation proceedings." 705 F.2d 1059, 1071 (CA9 1983). Thus, rather than supporting a conclusion that the exclusionary rule is unnecessary, the existence of these programs instead suggests that the exclusionary rule has created incentives for the agency to ensure that its officers follow the dictates of the Constitution. Since the deterrent function of the rule is furthered if it alters either "the behavior of individual law enforcement officers or the policies of their departments," *United States v. Leon*, 468 U.S., at 918, it seems likely that it was the rule's deterrent effect that led to the programs to which the Court now points for its assertion that the rule would have no deterrent effect.

The suggestion that alternative remedies, such as civil suits, provide adequate protection is unrealistic. Contrary to the situation in criminal cases, once the Government has improperly obtained evidence against an illegal alien, he is removed from the country and is therefore in no position to file civil actions in federal courts. Moreover, those who are legally in the country but are nonetheless subjected to illegal searches and seizures are likely to be poor and uneducated, and many will not speak English. It is doubtful that the threat of civil suits by these persons will strike fear into the hearts of those who enforce the Nation's immigration laws.

It is also my belief that the majority exaggerates the costs associated with applying the exclusionary rule in this context. Evidence obtained through violation of the Fourth Amendment is not automatically suppressed, and any inquiry into the burdens associated with application of the exclusionary rule must take that fact into account. In

---

2. The INS suggests that its disciplinary rules are "not mere paper procedures" and that over a period of four years 20 officers were suspended or terminated for misconduct toward aliens. Brief for Petitioner 45, n.28. The INS does not assert, however, that any of these officers were disciplined for Fourth Amendment violations, and it appears that the 11 officers who were terminated were terminated for rape or assault. See Brief for Respondents 60, n. 42.

United States v. Leon, 468 U.S. 897, we have held that the exclusionary rule is not applicable when officers are acting in objective good faith. Thus, if the agents neither knew nor should have known that they were acting contrary to the dictates of the Fourth Amendment, evidence will not be suppressed even if it is held that their conduct was illegal.

As is noted, *ante*, at 3489, n. 5, the BIA has already held that evidence will be suppressed if it results from egregious violations of constitutional standards. Thus, the mechanism for dealing with suppression motions exists and is utilized, significantly decreasing the force of the majority's predictions of dire consequences flowing from "even occasional invocation of the exclusionary rule." *Ante*, at 3488. Although the standard currently utilized by the BIA may not be precisely coextensive with the good-faith exception, any incremental increase in the amount of evidence that is suppressed through application of *Leon* is unlikely to be significant. Likewise, any difference that may exist between the two standards is unlikely to increase significantly the number of suppression motions filed.

Contrary to the view of the majority, it is not the case that Sandoval-Sanchez' "unregistered presence in this country, without more, constitutes a crime." *Ante*, at 3487. Section 275 of the Immigration and Nationality Act makes it a crime to enter the United States illegally. 8 U.S.C. § 1325. The first offense constitutes a misdemeanor, and subsequent offenses constitute felonies. *Ibid.* Those few cases that have construed this statute have held that a violation takes place at the time of entry and that the statute does not describe a continuing offense. *Gonzales v. City of Peoria*, 722 F.2d 468, 473–474 (CA9 1983); *United States v. Rincon-Jimenez*, 595 F.2d 1192, 1194 (CA9 1979). Although this Court has not construed the statute, it has suggested in dictum that this interpretation is correct, *United States v. Cores*, 356 U.S. 405, 408, n. 6 (1958), and it is relatively clear that such an interpretation is most consistent with the statutory language. Therefore, it is simply not the case that suppressing evidence in deportation proceedings will "allo[w] the criminal to continue in the commission of an ongoing crime." *Ante*, at 3488. It is true that some courts have construed § 276 of the Act, 8 U.S.C. § 1326, which applies to aliens previously deported who enter or are found in the United States, to describe a continuing offense. *United States v. Bruno*, 328 F.Supp. 815 (WD Mo.1971); *United States v. Alvarado-Soto*, 120 F.Supp. 848 (SD Cal.1954); *United States v. Rincon-Jimenez, supra* (dictum). But see *United States v. DiSantillo*, 615 F.2d 128 (CA3 1980). In such cases, however, the Government will have a record of the prior deportation and will have little need for any evidence that might be suppressed through application of the exclusionary rule. See *United States v. Pineda-Chinchilla*, 712 F.2d 942 (CA5 1983) (illegality of arrest does not bar introduction of INS records to demonstrate prior deportation) cert. denied, 464 U.S. 964 (1983); 8 U.S.C. § 1326.

Although the majority relies on the registration provisions of 8 U.S.C. §§ 1302 and 1306 for its "continuing crime" argument, those provisions provide little support for the general rule laid down that the exclusionary rule does not apply in civil deportation proceedings. First, § 1302 requires that aliens register within 30 days of entry into the country. Thus, for the first 30 days failure to register is not a crime.

Second, § 1306 provides that only willful failure to register is a misdemeanor. Therefore, "unregistered presence in this country, without more," *ante*, at 3487, does not constitute a crime; rather, unregistered presence plus willfulness must be shown. There is no finding that Sandoval-Sanchez willfully failed to register, which is a necessary predicate to the conclusion that he is engaged in a continuing crime. Third, only aliens 14 years of age or older are required to register; those under 14 years of age are to be registered by their parents or guardian. By the majority's reasoning, therefore, perhaps the exclusionary rule should apply in proceedings to deport children under 14, since their failure to register does not constitute a crime.

Application of the rule, we are told, will also seriously interfere with the "streamlined" nature of deportation hearings because "[n]either the hearing officers nor the attorneys participating in those hearings are likely to be well versed in the intricacies of Fourth Amendment law." *Ante*, at 3488. Yet the majority deprecates the deterrent benefit of the exclusionary rule in part on the ground that immigration officers receive a thorough education in Fourth Amendment law. *Ante*, at 3488. The implication that hearing officers should defer to law enforcement officers' superior understanding of constitutional principles is startling indeed.

Prior to the decision of the Board of Immigration Appeals in *Matter of Sandoval*, 17 I. & N.Dec. 70 (1979), neither the Board nor any court had held that the exclusionary rule did not apply in civil deportation proceedings. 705 F.2d at 1071. The Board in *Sandoval* noted that there were "fewer than fifty" BIA proceedings since 1952 in which motions had been made to suppress evidence on Fourth Amendment grounds. This is so despite the fact that "immigration law practitioners have been informed by the major treatise in their field that the exclusionary rule was available to clients facing deportation. See 1A C. Gordon and H. Rosenfield, Immigration Law and Procedure § 5.2c at 5–31 (rev. ed. 1980)." 705 F.2d, at 1071. The suggestion that "[t]he prospect of even occasional invocation of the exclusionary rule might significantly change and complicate the character of these proceedings," *ante*, at 3488, is thus difficult to credit. The simple fact is that prior to 1979 the exclusionary rule was available in civil deportation proceedings, and there is no indication that it significantly interfered with the ability of the INS to function.

Finally, the majority suggests that application of the exclusionary rule might well result in the suppression of large amounts of information legally obtained because of the "crowded and confused circumstances" surrounding mass arrests. *Ante*, at 3489. The result would be that INS agents would have to keep a "precise account of exactly what happened in each particular arrest," which would be impractical considering the "massed numbers of ascertainably illegal aliens." *Ante*, at 3489. Rather than constituting a rejection of the application of the exclusionary rule in civil deportation proceedings, however, this argument amounts to a rejection of the application of the Fourth Amendment to the activities of INS agents. If the pandemonium attending immigration arrests is so great that violations of the Fourth Amendment cannot be ascertained for the purpose of applying the exclusionary rule, there is no reason to think that such violations can be ascertained for purposes of civil suits or internal disciplinary proceedings, both of which are proceedings that the majority suggests provide adequate deterrence against Fourth Amendment violations. The Court may be willing to throw up its hands in dismay because it is administratively inconvenient to determine whether constitutional rights have been violated, but we neglect our duty when we subordinate constitutional rights to expediency in such a manner. Particularly is this so when, as here, there is but a weak showing that administrative efficiency will be seriously compromised.

In sum, I believe that the costs and benefits of applying the exclusionary rule in civil deportation proceedings do not differ in any significant way from the costs and benefits of applying the rule in ordinary criminal proceedings. Unless the exclusionary rule is to be wholly done away with and the Court's belief that it has deterrent effects abandoned, it should be applied in deportation proceedings when evidence has been obtained by deliberate violations of the Fourth Amendment or by conduct a reasonably competent officer would know is contrary to the Constitution.

Justice MARSHALL, dissenting.

I agree with Justice White that application to this case of the mode of analysis embodied in the decisions of the Court in *United States v. Janis*, 428 U.S. 433 (1976), and *United States v. Calandra*, 414 U.S. 338 (1974), compels the conclusion that the exclusionary rule should apply in civil deportation proceedings. *Ante*, at 3490–3491. However, I continue to believe that that mode of analysis fails to reflect the constitutionally mandated character of the exclusionary rule. See *United States v. Leon*, 468 U.S., at 931–938 (Brennan, J., joined by Marshall, J., dissenting); *United States v. Janis, supra*, at 460 (Brennan, J., joined by Marshall, J., dissenting). In my view, a sufficient reason for excluding from civil deportation proceedings evidence obtained in violation of the Fourth Amendment is that there is no other way to achieve "the twin goals of enabling the judiciary to avoid the taint of partnership in official lawlessness and of assuring the people—all potential victims of unlawful government conduct—that the government would not profit from its lawless behavior, thus minimizing the risk of seriously undermining popular trust in government." *United States v. Calandra, supra*, at 357 (Brennan, J., joined by Marshall, J., dissenting).

Justice STEVENS, dissenting.

Because the Court has not yet held that the rule of *United States v. Leon*, 468 U.S. 897 has any application to warrantless searches, I do not join the portion of Justice White's opinion that relies on that case. I do, however, agree with the remainder of his dissenting opinion.

Notes

1. Amendments made to the immigration laws by the 1986 Immigration Reform and Control Act imposed sanctions against certain employers for hiring undocumented aliens. In addition, the immigration statute in its present form imposes

criminal penalties on aliens for avoiding inspection at the border. What considerations, if any, would you give to these provisions if you were deciding *Lopez-Mendoza*? What considerations would you give these factors if you were the Board of Immigration Appeals?

2. A noncitizen who has had her rights violated by government officials has at least four types of remedies: (1) actions under the civil rights statutes, (2) actions under the Federal Tort Claims Act (FTCA), (3) *Bivens* actions and (4) private causes of action.

The civil rights statutes[132] protect all persons from civil rights violations by federal and state officials.[133] Noncitizens are protected from racial discrimination upon the basis of ancestry or ethnic characteristics[134] and discrimination upon the basis of alienage,[135] and federal and state officials are prohibited from depriving persons of their constitutional and federal rights.[136] Actual and punitive damages may be granted to a noncitizen who has had her civil rights violated,[137] and declaratory and injunctive relief may be available in certain circumstances. A noncitizen who has won her civil rights suit may still pursue a claim under the FTCA or *Bivens* if remedies under the latter actions are available.[138]

The FTCA waives sovereign immunity in cases where persons have been injured "by the negligent or wrongful act or omission of any employee of the Government while acting within the scope of his office or employment,"[139] allowing them to bring claims against the United States for certain torts committed by its federal employees.[140] Liability may be imposed for the intentional torts of assault and battery, false imprisonment, false arrest, abuse of process and malicious prosecution committed by U.S. investigative or law enforcements officers.[141] Courts have held that legacy INS officers, and therefore current DHS officers, carrying out their immigration control functions are considered law enforcement officers for purposes of FTCA.[142] Exceptions to FTCA liability include certain acts of discretion under 28 U.S.C. § 2680(a),[143] and FTCA li-

132. 42 U.S.C. §§ 1981, 1983, 1985 and 1986.

133. *Plyler v. Doe*, 457 U.S. 202 (1982).

134. *See St. Francis College v. Al-Khazraji*, 481 U.S. 604 (1987); *Shaare Tefila Congregation v. Cobb*, 481 U.S. 615 (1987).

135. *See Anderson v. Conboy*, 156 F.3d 167 (2d Cir. 1998); *but see Bhandari v. First Bank of Commerce*, 829 F.2d 1343 (5th Cir. 1987) (*en banc*).

136. *See Mena v. City of Simi Valley*, 332 F.2d 1255 (9th Cir. 2003).

137. *See City of Newport v. Facts Concerts, Inc.*, 453 U.S. 247 (1981).

138. *See Baker v. F & F Inv. Co.*, 489 F.2d 829 (7th Cir. 1973); *Peck v. United States*, 470 F. Supp. 1003 (S.D.N.Y. 1979).

139. 28 U.S.C. § 1346(b).

140. 28 U.S.C. §§ 2671–2680.

141. 28 U.S.C. § 2680.

142. *See Caban v. INS*, 671 F.2d 1230 (2d Cir. 1982); *Medina v. U.S.*, 92 F. Supp. 2d 545 (E.D. Va. 2000).

143. *See Medina v. U.S.*, 259 F.3d 220 (4th Cir. 2001) (INS agents' decision to detain and subsequently terminate removal proceedings is considered a discretionary function under FTCA); *Adras v. Nelson*, 917 F.2d 1552 (11th Cir. 1990) (detention of Haitian nationals seeking asylum and denial of their parole is a discretionary function); *Flammia v. U.S.*, 739 F.2d 202 (5th Cir. 1984) (decision to allow Cuban refugee known to be a felon convicted of a violent crime to enter the United States

ability generally does not apply to actions committed outside the United States.[144] A prevailing noncitizen may collect compensatory but not punitive damages.[145]

Unlike the FTCA, which allows noncitizens to bring claims against the United States alone for tortious actions committed by federal officers, a *Bivens* action allows the noncitizen to bring an action against the federal officer in his private capacity for violating her First, Fourth, Fifth, Sixth or Eighth Amendment rights.[146] In order to bring a *Bivens* action, no other alternate remedies must be available and no special factors exist that would counsel against the claim.[147] Noncitizens may recover punitive damages in a *Bivens* claim; however, if a noncitizen brings both a FTCA and *Bivens* claim, a money judgment may not be recovered against both the United States and the individual federal employee, so she may only choose one of the two remedies if she is successful in both actions.[148]

Private rights of action may be brought under various provisions of the INA and related statutes as long as the court determines that Congress intended noncitizens to have such a claim under that particular statute.[149] However, most private causes of actions considered by the courts have been rejected thus far.[150]

3. From a policy standpoint, what, if anything, should be done about an immigration officers' Fourth Amendment transgressions?[151] Is this an important factor to be weighed by a court faced with an application of the exclusionary rule?

---

as well as broad policy decisions to admit or release Cuban refugees in general are discretionary functions not subject to FTCA liability). *But see Garcia v. U.S.*, 826 F.2d 806 (9th Cir. 1987) (border patrol's use of force not discretionary); *Caban v. INS*, 728 F.2d 68 (2d Cir. 1984) (Decision to arrest and detain at a port of entry is not discretionary).

144. *See Romero v. Consulate of the U.S. in Barranquilla, Columbia*, 860 F.Supp. 319 (E.D. Va. 1994); *Maffei v. Nieves-Reta*, 412 F. Supp. 43 (S.D. Cal. 1976).

145. 28 U.S.C. § 2674.

146. *Bivens v. Six Unknown Named Agents of the Federal Bureau of Narcotics*, 403 U.S. 388 (1971) (Fourth Amendment); *Davis v. Passman*, 442 U.S. 228 (1979) (Fifth Amendment); *Carlson v. Green*, 446 U.S. 14 (1980) (Eighth Amendment); *Garcia v. U.S.*, 666 F.2d 960 (5th Cir. 1982) (First Amendment); *Wounded Knee Legal Defense/Offense Committee v. FBI*, 507 F.2d 1281 (8th Cir. 1974) (Sixth Amendment).

147. *See Schweiker v. Chilicky*, 487 U.S. 412 (1988); *Bush v. Lucas*, 462 U.S. 367 (1983).

148. *See Carlson v. Green*, 446 U.S. 14 (1980); *Arevalo v. Woods*, 811 F.2d 487 (9th Cir. 1987); *Serra v. Pichardo,* 786 (F.2d 237 (6th Cir. 1986); *Sanchez v. Rowe*, 651 F. Supp. 571 (N.D. Tex. 1986).

149. *See Standt v. City of New York*, 153 F.Supp.2d 417 (S.D.N.Y. 2001).

150. *See Urbina-Mauricio v. INS*, 989 F.2d 1085 (9th Cir. 1993); *Prieto v. Gluch*, 913 F.2d 1159 (6th Cir. 1990); *Gonzalez v. INS*, 867 F.2d 1108 (8th Cir. 1989); *Medina v. O'Neill*, 838 F.2d 800 (5th Cir. 1988); *Chairez v. Van Buren*, 790 F.2d 544 (6th Cir. 1986); *Ortega v. Rowe*, 796 F.2d 765 (5th Cir. 1986).

151. *See* The September 11 Detainees: A Review of the Treatment of Aliens Held on Immigration Charges in Connection with the Investigation of the September 11 Attacks, issued June 2, 2003, which is located on the OIG's website at https://oig.justice.gov/special/0306/, for an in-depth discussion of the actions and broad policies established in processing and detaining noncitizens in the aftermath of the terrorist attacks on September 11, 2001, the problems that arose in connection with these actions in the treatment of noncitizens and the recommendations made by the Inspector General in order to improve the handling of detainees in the future.

4. **Suppression of evidence.** While the Court refused to endorse an exclusionary rule in removal proceedings, the BIA noted in one case that where the violation "prejudiced [the] interests of the alien ... protected by the regulation" the evidence would be excluded.[152] The validity of this case is not clear given that the BIA was adopting a standard set by the Ninth Circuit prior to *Lopez-Mendoza.* However, suppression may still be possible where the Fifth Amendment is implicated.[153] Finally, when exclusion of evidence is not possible, injunction may be an alternative remedy.[154]

5. **Privilege against self-incrimination.** It has been well established that a person who has been detained or questioned enjoys the privilege of being free from self-incrimination.[155] The privilege can only be asserted to avoid prosecution for crimes. Similarly, several courts have held that *Miranda* warnings are not required in removal proceedings.[156] However, what happens if the person in removal proceedings remains silent? Can his silence be interpreted as an admission of deportability? While negative inferences can be drawn from a refusal to testify, it will not be sufficient standing alone to meet the government's burden of establishing deportability by clear, convincing and unequivocal evidence.[157]

By regulation, ICE officers are required to provide Miranda warnings to aliens subject to removal, with the exception of those subject to expedited removal. 8 C.F.R. § 287.3(c) (emphasis supplied) provides the following:

> (c) Notifications and information. Except in the case of an alien subject to the expedited removal provisions of section 235(b)(1)(A) of the Act, an alien arrested without warrant and placed in formal proceedings under section 238 or 240 of the Act *will be advised of the reasons for his or her arrest and the right to be represented at no expense to the Government.* The examining officer will provide the alien with a list of the available free legal services provided by organizations and attorneys qualified under 8 CFR part 3 and organizations recognized under § 292.2 of this chapter that are located in the district where the hearing will be held. The examining officer shall note on Form I-862 that such a list was provided to the alien. *The officer will also advise the alien that any statement made may be used against him or her in a subsequent proceeding.*

---

152. *See Matter of Garcia-Flores,* 17 I. & N. Dec. 325, 328 (BIA 1980).

153. *See Matter of Toro,* 17 I. & N. Dec. 340 (BIA 1980); *Wall v. INS,* 722 F.2d 1442 (9th Cir. 1984).

154. *See, e.g., Int'l Moulders' & Allied Workers' Local Union 164 v. Nelson,* 799 F.2d 547 (9th Cir. 1986); *Pearl Meadows Mushroom Farm, Inc. v. Nelson,* 723 F. Supp. 432 (N.D. Ca. 1989).

155. *See U.S. v. Soliz,* 129 F.3d 499 (9th Cir. 1997); *also see U.S. v. Balsys,* 119 F.3d 122 (2d Cir. 1997) (court interpreted the right to extend to possible foreign prosecution).

156. *U.S. v. Solano-Godines,* 120 F.3d 357 (9th Cir. 1997); *Bustos-Torres v. I.N.S.,* 898 F.2d 1053 (5th Cir. 1990).

157. *See Matter of Guevara,* 20 I. & N. Dec. 238 (BIA 1991).

1. Special Registration—Post 9/11 Enforcement

During the Fall of 2002, the government announced a program termed "Special Registration," or "NSEERS." NSEERS was the acronym for the National Security Entry-Exit Registration System and required non-U.S. citizen males 16 and over in the United States from Iran, Iraq, Libya, Sudan and Syria to submit themselves to questioning by legacy INS.[158] Those who were inspected and admitted were required to present themselves 30 days following their arrival and every 12 months thereafter. The program was highly controversial as it targeted persons from predominantly Muslim or Middle Eastern countries for special review, which resembled similar efforts initiated against Japanese Americans following the outbreak of hostilities during World War II.[159] The program, which was expanded to include other nationalities, relied on statutory authority from 8 U.S.C. § 1305(b), Sec. 265(b). Beginning in December 2002, it required persons from selected countries who had been admitted to the United States on or before September 10, 2002, and had remained in the country beyond the cutoff date to report for questioning. Over the next several months, additional groups were added to the list.[160] By December 2003, the Department of Homeland Security[161] had suspended the thirty-day and annual registration requirements;[162] however, persons subject to NSEERS were still required to register and could be removed if they failed to do so.[163] Although the Special Registration program has largely been replaced by US-VISIT, which requires the photographing and fingerprinting of all non-immigrants who enter the country, DHS or consular officers could still identify persons from selected countries on a case-by-case basis to comply with the program upon their entry into the United States. While federal court challenges to removal orders based on the NSEERS program were uniformly unsuccessful, there were some favorable individual suppression motions.[164]

Eventually the program was terminated, based in part on an Office of the Inspector General's report which found that it was highly inefficient and relied on an inaccurate

---

158. Registration and Monitoring of Certain Nonimmigrants, 67 Fed. Reg. 52,584 (Aug. 12, 2002).

159. While the registration program was arguably based on concerns revolving around national security, it initially omitted persons from Saudi Arabia and Yemen, notwithstanding the fact that most of the 9/11 hijackers had been identified as coming from those two countries. Registrants had also been confused by a constantly changing list of persons covered, deadlines and the other requirements of the program.

160. *See Registration of Certain Nonimmigrant Aliens From Designated Countries,* 67 Fed. Reg. 66,765–68 (2002); 67 Fed. Reg. 77,642 (2002); 68 Fed. Reg. 2363 (2003); 68 Fed. Reg. 8047 (2003).

161. Legacy INS by this time had been folded into a new federal agency called the Department of Homeland Security (DHS).

162. *See Suspending the 30-Day and Annual Interview Requirements From the Special Registration Process for Certain Nonimmigrants,* 68 Fed. Reg. 67578 (2003).

163. *See* Memorandum from Victor X. Cerda, Acting Principal Legal Advisor, ICE, (Jan. 8. 2004) (posted on AILA InfoNet at Doc. No. 06050512, May 5, 2004).

164. *See* Mario Russell, *A New York Immigration Court's Cure for Regulatory Due Process Violations in NSEERS Special Registration: Suppress Evidence and Terminate Proceedings,* 82 Interpreter Releases 1505 (2005).

database.[165] In its place the agency instituted US-VISIT along with modifications to the visa waiver program. In December of 2016 DHS officially removed the enabling regulations related to the program.[166]

I. Practice Questions

Exercise 1

B was not born in the U.S., she came to the U.S. with her parents when they immigrated here when B was only 2 years old (yr. -30). When B was 12 (yr. -20) she began drinking heavily and when she reached 18 (yr. -14) she had really gotten involved with the wrong crowd and began using drugs. In (yr. -9) when B was 23, she and a friend went into a supermarket, made a purchase and forged a check for $19.83, which was $10 over the purchase price so they could buy alcohol. She was caught and because the forgery constituted a violation of her probation from an earlier marijuana possession charge, she was sentenced to six years in prison. Ultimately, she served less than a year in jail.

Some time after serving her time in jail in (yr. -7), B got into a serious treatment program, stopped drinking, and got a job with a computer company, where she has worked for the last 5 years. She married 4 years ago, and she and her husband have bought a house, and are raising their two children together. The DHS has initiated removal proceedings against her, with the intent of sending her back to her native country. She does not speak the language of her native country, and has no family there.

What are the deportability provisions that she likely faces?

Exercise 2

Max is a native and citizen of Country A. He came to the United States on a tourist visa, which he purchased from an underground operation in Country A which sold fraudulent travel documents. He was admitted to the United States on August 1, (yr. -4) at JFK International Airport on the fraudulent B-2 visa. According to his admission documents, Max's period of authorized stay expired on November 1, (yr. -4).

After being admitted to the U.S. Max met Mary, who is a U.S. citizen. After a very short "courtship," they were married on August 1, (yr. -3) in a civil ceremony in New York City where Max and Mary were living. Mary filed an immediate relative petition and adjustment of status petition on behalf of Max on that same day. The petition was finally approved on December 1, (yr. -1). Max was able to adjust his status after convincing the USCIS officer that he had been admitted on another date by showing

---

165. Department of Homeland Security, Office of Inspector General, *Information Sharing on Foreign Nationals: Border Security*, OIG—12–39 (Feb. 2012).

166. Removal of Regulations Relating to Special Registration Process for Certain Nonimmigrants, 51 Cust. B. & Dec. 19 (Dec. 23, 2016), 2016 WL 7912863.

him a date stamp that appears in his passport showing that he was admitted on September 1, (yr. -4).

In the application for adjustment of status, Max, instead of providing information that he had been inspected and admitted with false documents, indicated that he had entered the United States without inspection on August 1 (yr. -1) at a location along the Canadian-U.S. border. He had been concerned about telling the truth, because the false document had the name of someone else.

Max remains married to Mary, and they lived together as husband and wife until recently when they separated. Apparently, Mary and Max continue to be friends but decided that they cannot stay together.

Max comes to you, because he is interested in applying for citizenship given the strong anti-immigrant sentiment that pervades the country. He is finding it increasingly oppressive to deal with immigration authorities every time he returns to the United States. Max is doing very well financially and would like to petition for his parents who are living in Country A.

Provide Max with advice and counsel on how he might deal with his immigration problems.

Exercise 3

"D" is a native and citizen of Iran and was born in Tehran, Iran, on January 1, yr. -35. D became a lawful permanent resident when her parents immigrated to the United States in yr. -20 when she was 15. In yr. -15 at the age of 20, D had mixed with the wrong crowd in college, got involved in criminal activity and was convicted of credit card fraud under 18 U.S.C. § 1029(a)(2). Even though D was involved in a conspiracy with a number of other people and had extensive involvement in their fraud schemes, because of her cooperation with the authorities and her vital testimony, she was able to negotiate an agreement that allowed her to plead guilty to one count of fraud and receive a sentence of 364 days imprisonment, a sentence which was suspended for five years.

Since that time, D has changed her life and has become a role model in her community. She continued her studies and started a new high tech company creating sophisticated exam software for educational use. In January, yr. -2 while traveling in Country A, in a chance encounter, D was seated across from Frank Fine, a person from her past criminal life. Apparently, unbeknownst to D, Fine was still involved in criminal activity. Without going into the details of Fine's criminal activities, D once again found herself on the other end of the law, and in an effort to get herself out of her predicament, pleaded guilty to receipt of stolen property. While the possible sentence under the Country A's laws was 1–7 years, the criminal court allowed D to leave and she did not serve any prison time upon assurances that she would not return to that country for 5 years. She gladly accepted the terms and returned to the U.S. on April 15 where, upon questioning by the immigration inspector, was detained. [Country A's relevant criminal code provision appears at the end of this question.]

You learn in the course of your interview with D that she is very concerned about a possible removal (she refers to it as "deportation") to Iran because she is Christian and has lived in the U.S. since she was very young. While she does speak Farsi, she has no known family in that country. Her parents remain living in the U.S. as lawful permanent residents. She would like to eventually become a U.S. citizen. Assume for purposes of this question that the official record of the proceedings indicate that D was carrying a camera which Mr. Fine had given to her to hold for a short while. An undercover officer witnessed this and arrested both D and Mr. Fine. According to D's appointed lawyer, D was frightened and decided to accept the offer from the authorities instead of risking more serious consequences. Assume for purposes of this exam that the government (DHS) is fully aware of the facts in this case. Provide D with advice as to what could likely occur and how you would defend her and help her to accomplish her objectives.

Statutory References for Exercise 3

18 U.S.C. § 1029. Fraud and related activity in connection with access devices

(a) Whoever—

(1) knowingly and with intent to defraud produces, uses, or traffics in one or more counterfeit access devices;

(2) knowingly and with intent to defraud traffics in or uses one or more unauthorized access devices during any one-year period, and by such conduct obtains anything of value aggregating $1,000 or more during that period;

(3) knowingly and with intent to defraud possesses fifteen or more devices which are counterfeit or unauthorized access devices;

(4) knowingly, and with intent to defraud, produces, traffics in, has control or custody of, or possesses device-making equipment;

(5) knowingly and with intent to defraud effects transactions, with 1 or more access devices issued to another person or persons, to receive payment or any other thing of value during any 1-year period the aggregate value of which is equal to or greater than $1,000;

(6) without the authorization of the issuer of the access device, knowingly and with intent to defraud solicits a person for the purpose of—

(A) offering an access device; or

(B) selling information regarding or an application to obtain an access device;

* * *

(c) Penalties.—

(1) Generally.—The punishment for an offense under subsection (a) of this section is—

(A) in the case of an offense that does not occur after a conviction for another offense under this section—

(i) if the offense is under paragraph (1), (2), (3), (6), (7), or (10) of subsection (a), a fine under this title or imprisonment for not more than 10 years, or both; and

(ii) if the offense is under paragraph (4), (5), (8), or (9) of subsection (a), a fine under this title or imprisonment for not more than 15 years, or both;

(B) in the case of an offense that occurs after a conviction for another offense under this section, a fine under this title or imprisonment for not more than 20 years, or both; and

(C) in either case, forfeiture to the United States of any personal property used or intended to be used to commit the offense.

(2) Forfeiture procedure.—The forfeiture of property under this section, including any seizure and disposition of the property and any related administrative and judicial proceeding, shall be governed by section 413 of the Controlled Substances Act, except for subsection (d) of that section.

* * *

(e) As used in this section—

(1) the term "access device" means any card, plate, code, account number, electronic serial number, mobile identification number, personal identification number, or other telecommunications service, equipment, or instrument identifier, or other means of account access that can be used, alone or in conjunction with another access device, to obtain money, goods, services, or any other thing of value, or that can be used to initiate a transfer of funds (other than a transfer originated solely by paper instrument);

(2) the term "counterfeit access device" means any access device that is counterfeit, fictitious, altered, or forged, or an identifiable component of an access device or a counterfeit access device;

(3) the term "unauthorized access device" means any access device that is lost, stolen, expired, revoked, canceled, or obtained with intent to defraud;

(4) the term "produce" includes design, alter, authenticate, duplicate, or assemble;

(5) the term "traffic" means transfer, or otherwise dispose of, to another, or obtain control of with intent to transfer or dispose of;

(6) the term "device-making equipment" means any equipment, mechanism, or impression designed or primarily used for making an access device or a counterfeit access device;

(7) The term "credit card system member" means a financial institution or other entity that is a member of a credit card system, including an entity, whether affiliated with or identical to the credit card issuer, that is the sole member of a credit card system;

* * *

(h) Any person who, outside the jurisdiction of the United States, engages in any act that, if committed within the jurisdiction of the United States, would constitute an offense under subsection (a) or (b) of this section, shall be subject to the fines, penalties, imprisonment, and forfeiture provided in this title if—

(1) the offense involves an access device issued, owned, managed, or controlled by a financial institution, account issuer, credit card system member, or other entity within the jurisdiction of the United States; and

(2) the person transports, delivers, conveys, transfers to or through, or otherwise stores, secrets, or holds within the jurisdiction of the United States, any article used to assist in the commission of the offense or the proceeds of such offense or property derived therefrom.

Country A's Criminal Code

Criminal Code § 22-3232. Receiving stolen property.

(a) A person commits the offense of receiving stolen property if that person buys, receives, possesses, or obtains control of stolen property, knowing or having reason to believe that the property was stolen, with intent to deprive another of the right to the property or a benefit of the property.

(b) It shall not be a defense to a prosecution for an attempt to commit the offense described in this section that the property was not in fact stolen, if the accused engages in conduct which would constitute the crime if the attendant circumstances were as the accused believed them to be.

(c)(1) Any person convicted of receiving stolen property shall be fined not more than $5,000 or imprisoned not more than 7 years, or both, if the value of the stolen property is $250 or more.

(2) Any person convicted of receiving stolen property shall be fined not more than $1,000 or imprisoned not more than 180 days, or both, if the value of the stolen property is less than $250.

J. Employer Sanctions

1. Employer Sanctions—Extending the Enforcement Powers of DHS

As we have seen, the power to control the persons who may enter or remain in the United States is extensive. However, once the person gains entry, albeit surreptitiously, this power does not flow unfettered, for once the non-citizen is "within" the borders, she receives a certain measure of constitutional protections. The notion of constitutional protection inuring once a person has gained entry provides an excellent backdrop for a discussion of the power of the enforcement arm of the immigration power (the U.S. Immigration and Customs Enforcement (ICE)) to search for and seize foreigners and to ultimately remove them from the country. Sanctions on employers for hiring unauthorized workers is an important enforcement tool not just because of the penalties that can be imposed on violating employers, but also because they provide a justification for entering the workplace.

Immigration authorities had long sought authority to add to its enforcement arsenal the authority to penalize employers for hiring undocumented persons. One rationale for employer sanctions has been the understanding that the economic disparities between the "sending" nations and the United States are a strong force for illegal immigration.[167] Another is that making finding work more difficult is an effective disincentive to the migrant. Notwithstanding these arguments since the enactment of the original employer sanction legislation in 1986, illegal migration has been more impacted by the overall strength of the U.S. economy rather than whether employers might face sanctions.[168]

Largely in response to its frustration with controlling the flow of illegal migrants and what was perceived as a threat to the integrity of the system of legal migration, in 1986 Congress enacted a system of sanctioning employers who hired unauthorized workers.[169] It was long thought that a system which penalized employers would deter the flow of unauthorized migration to the country.[170] In order for the sanctions to be effective, they would have to be uniformly applied to both citizens and noncitizens in a non-discriminatory fashion. As a result, employers are required to "verify" the legal status of all persons hired irrespective of their U.S. citizenship.[171]

The sanction provisions operate as an enforcement tool to assist ICE when they inspect employers' records or conduct searches for unauthorized workers. The immigration laws impose duties on the employer, which when not adhered to, expose them to civil and possible criminal penalties. The more important elements of the

---

167. *See* Gerald Lopez, *Undocumented Mexican Migration: In Search of a Just Immigration Law and Policy*, 28 U.C.L.A. L. Rev. 615 (1981); J. Card, *Push and Pull Factors at Origin and Destination as Determinants of Migration* (Aug. 1980) (study prepared for the Select Commission on Immigration and Refugee Policy).

168. *See* Peter H. Schuck, *Taking Immigration Federalism Seriously*, 2007 Univ. Chi. Legal F. 57, 78. Undocumented migration has hardly been abated as a result. Office of Policy & Planning, U.S. Immigration & Naturalization Serv., Estimates of the Unauthorized Immigrant Population Residing in the United States: 1990 to 2000, at 1, 2 n.1 (2003).

169. These sanctions are in the form of fines and/or criminal penalties. *See generally* Section Immigration Reform and Control Act of 1986, Pub. L. No. 99-603, 100 Stat. 3359, amending 8 U.S.C. § 1324.

170. For many years, individual states had laws which prohibited employers from hiring unauthorized persons. *See* California Labor Code section 2805 (repealed 1988); 1977 Fla. Laws 1192; 1979 La. Acts 1498; 1977 Vt. Acts & Resolves 320; 1977 Va. Acts 651.

171. 8 U.S.C. § 1324a. While the regulations do not require employers to review documentation of potential employees, it has been argued that because certain aliens are ineligible for employment and the antidiscrimination provisions require that *all* employees be verified, it behooves the employer to question all prospective employees. The verification procedures are described at 8 C.F.R. § 274a.2(b).

sanction provisions are described below. What follows is a mostly descriptive discourse on the employer sanctions regime found in federal immigration law.

2. Covered Employees

All employees except "casual hires" and "independent contractors" must be verified by the employer.[172] Casual hires are those hired sporadically, irregularly or intermittently as domestic employment.[173] An employer violates the law when she *knowingly* hires someone who is not authorized to work under the Act.[174] The statute defines an unauthorized alien as an "alien [who] is not at that time either (A) an alien lawfully admitted for permanent residence, or (B) authorized to be so employed by this chapter or by the Attorney General."[175] Whether an employer has knowingly hired or continues to employ an "unauthorized" individual will be governed by the facts and will often turn on what information the employer had available at the time or what information would lead a reasonable person to inquire further. The test to be applied is whether, under the totality of the circumstances, the employer had constructive knowledge that an employee was working without authorization.[176]

Good faith compliance with the verification system is a properly asserted affirmative defense to sanctions. This means that if the employer reviewed the proper documents and the documents appeared to be genuine or if the person was referred by a state agency which conducted the verification, the charge will not be sustained unless the government can establish actual knowledge.

3. Verification Requirements

Employers are required to inspect two types of documents for each person actually hired and must attest to the review of these documents under penalty of perjury by completing Form I-9 within three business days of hiring, and the form must be signed by the person hired.[177] The employee must present either an original document that establishes both employment authorization and identity or two separate original

---

172. 8 C.F.R. §§ 274a.1(f) and 1274a.1(f) define an employee as "an individual who provides services or labor for an employer for wages or other remuneration but does not mean independent contractors as defined in paragraph (j) of this section or those engaged in casual domestic employment as stated in paragraph (h)."

173. 8 C.F.R. § 274a.1(h). This provision was found as not protecting an employer where the work involved hiring casual laborers to do construction work where previously the employer had sought cost estimates from different companies. *Jenkins v. INS*, 108 F.3d 195, 199 (9th Cir. 1997). At the same time, it does not include volunteers.

174. 8 U.S.C. § 1324a(a)(1)(A), Sec. 274A(a)(1)(A).

175. 8 U.S.C. § 1324a(h)(3), Sec. 274A(h)(3).

176. *See* Memo, Paul Virtue, Gen. Counsel INS, posted on AILA Infonet at Doc. 01061431 (Apr. 12, 1999)

177. 8 C.F.R. §§ 274a.2(b), 1274a.2(b).

documents: one establishing employment authorization and the other for identity.[178] If the individual is unable to provide the required documentation showing eligibility to work, or if they have applied for a replacement of the document, the employer must allow the employee at least ninety days to provide the actual document.[179]

Even after an employer has completed the verification requirements, if the employment eligibility document of the person hired expires, the employer, recruiter or referrer, for a fee, must update the I-9 to reflect that the individual is still authorized to work in the United States; otherwise the individual may no longer be employed, recruited or referred. In order to update Form I-9, the employee or referred individual must present a document that either shows continuing employment eligibility or a new grant of work authorization. The employer, recruiter or referrer is required to review the document, and if it appears to be genuine and relate to the individual in question, Form I-9 should be updated.

The verification requirements do not contemplate that the employer establishing the legitimacy of the document has a duty to determine whether it is fraudulent. The standard imposed on the employer in the verification process is that of whether the employer has reviewed the original document and if it appears on reasonable inspection to be genuine.[180] The verification requirements provide the entirety of the documentation required of a worker.[181]

What Documents are Required for Verification?

Documentation establishing employment authorization and identity.[182] A U.S. passport or certificate of U.S. citizenship (N-560 or N-561); Naturalization Certificate (N-550 or N-570); a foreign passport containing a temporary I-551 stamp or temporary I-551 printed notation on a machine-readable immigrant visa; an Employment Authorization Document which contains a photograph (Form I-766); Alien Registration Receipt Card (I-151); Temporary Resident Card (I-688); where the person being hired is a nonimmigrant authorized to work for a specific employer incident to status, a foreign passport with a Form I-94 or Form I-94A bearing the same name as the passport and containing an endorsement of the alien's nonimmigrant status, as long as the period of endorsement has not yet expired and the proposed employment is not in conflict with any restrictions or limitations identified on the Form;[183] a military identification card for a person lawfully enlisted but it must be one accepted by the

---

178. 8 C.F.R. §§ 274a.2(b)(1)(v), 1274a.2(b)(1)(v). If the person is hired for less than three days, the verification must be completed at the time of hire. 8 C.F.R. §§ 274a.2(b)(1)(iii), 1274a.2(b)(1)(iii).

179. 8 C.F.R. §§ 274a.2(b)(1)(vi), 1274a.2(b)(1)(vi). The replacement documents that are covered under this rule are the temporary proof of permanent residency (Form I-551) or the arrival departure record (Form I-94 or I-94A), which also establishes the persons status.

180. *See* 43 Interpreter Releases 1562 (2003).

181. The employer's demand for excessive documentation coupled with a showing of discriminatory intent could provide the basis for an unfair immigration-related employment practice. *See* 8 U.S.C. § 1324b(a)(6); *Robison Fruit Ranch, Inc. v. U.S.*, 147 F.3d 798 (9th Cir. 1998).

182. 8 C.F.R. §§ 274a.2(b)(1)(v)(A), 1274a.2(b)(1)(v)(A).

183. 8 C.F.R. §§ 274a.2(b)(1)(A)(5), 1274a.2(b)(1)(A)(5).

Armed Forces as proof of current service; or a passport from the Federated States of Micronesia (FSM) or the Republic of the Marshall Islands (RMI) with Form I-94 or Form I-94A indicating nonimmigrant admission under the Compact of Free Association Between the United States and the FSM or RMI.

Documentation establishing identity only.[184] *For individuals 16 years of age or older*: A state-issued driver's license or state-issued identification (with a photograph and identifying information, such as name, date of birth, sex, height, color of eyes and address). If the driver's license or identification card does not contain a photograph, the following documentation will satisfy the identification requirement: school identification card with a photograph; voter's registration card; U.S. military card or draft record; identification card issued by federal, state or local government agencies or entities; military dependent's identification card; Native American tribal documents; United States Coast Guard Merchant Mariner Card; or driver's license issued by a Canadian government authority. For those under the age of 18 and unable to produce any of the documents listed above, the minor's parent or legal guardian completes Form I-9 and writes "minor under age 16."

Documentation establishing employment authorization only.[185] A social security card other than one which on its face indicates that it is not valid for employment purposes; a Certification of Birth issued by the Department of State, Form FS-545; a Certification of Birth Abroad issued by the Department of State, Form DS-1350; an original or certified copy of a birth certificate issued by a state, county or municipal authority bearing an official seal; an employment authorization document issued by USCIS; Native American tribal document; United States Citizen Identification Card, INS Form I-197; identification card for use of resident citizen in the United States, Form I-179.

4. What Penalties Can Be Imposed?

An employer who continues the employment of someone, knowing that the employee is or has become an unauthorized alien with respect to that employment, is in violation of the sanction provisions.[186] A respondent determined by DHS or by an administrative law judge (after a hearing)[187] to have failed to comply with the employment verification requirements shall be subject to a civil penalty in an amount of not less than $110 and not more than $1,100 for each individual with respect to whom such violation occurred.[188] In determining the amount of the penalty, con-

184. 8 C.F.R. §§ 274a.2(b)(1)(v)(B), 1274a.2(b)(1)(v)(B).

185. 8 C.F.R. §§ 274a.2(b)(1)(v)(C), 1274a.2(b)(1)(v)(C).

186. 8 U.S.C. § 1324a(a)(2), Sec. 274A(a)(2). The effective date is when the statute came into force, which is November 6, 1986. That date is not used here for ease of discussion and because very few situations will arise in which the person was not hired after November 6, 1986.

187. Decisions of the administrative law judge are reviewable in a court of appeals upon the filing of a petition for review within 45 days. The administrative law judges are granted subpoena powers to compel the appearance of witnesses and the production of witnesses.

188. The original fee schedule is set forth in the statute and was in effect until 1999, which was 10% less than what appears below. *See* 8 U.S.C. § 1324(e)(4), Sec. 274A(e)(4). The regulations also

sideration shall be given to: (i) the size of the business of the employer being charged; (ii) the good faith of the employer; (iii) the seriousness of the violation; (iv) the status of the individual as an unauthorized alien; and (v) the history of previous violations of the employer.

If ICE has reasonable cause to believe that a person or entity is engaged in a pattern or practice of employment, recruitment or referral violations, it may bring civil action in the appropriate U.S. district court to request relief, including a permanent or temporary injunction, restraining order or other order against the person or entity as the Attorney General deems necessary.[189] The Attorney General may also seek criminal penalties of not more than $3,000 for each unauthorized person or imprisonment for not more than six months for the entire pattern or practice, or both, notwithstanding the provisions of any other federal law relating to fine levels.[190]

5. Enforcement Procedures

Any person or entity having knowledge of a violation or potential violation may submit a signed, written complaint in person or by mail to the ICE office with jurisdiction over the business or residence of the potential violator. The signed, written complaint must contain sufficient information to identify both the complainant and the potential violator, including their names and addresses. The complaint should also contain detailed factual allegations relating to the potential violation, including the date, time and place that the alleged violation occurred and the specific act or conduct of the employer alleged to constitute a violation of the Act. Written complaints may be delivered either by mail to the appropriate ICE office or by personally appearing before any immigration officer at an ICE office.

ICE conducts investigations for possible violations on its own initiative and without having received a written complaint; however, it is governed by the same standards necessary for immigration searches and will need articulable facts concerning possible violations. When ICE receives a complaint from a third party, it likely will investigate only those complaints which have a reasonable probability of validity. If it is determined after investigation that the person or entity has violated the sanction provisions, the agency will issue and serve upon the alleged violator a citation in the form of "Notice of Intent to Fine." ICE officers are allowed reasonable access to examine any relevant evidence of any person or entity being investigated. ICE also has the authority to conduct random audits, known as compliance audits,

---

describe some of the civil sanctions according to the following schedule: first violation, not less than $250 and not more than $2,200 for each unauthorized person; second violation, not less than $2,200 and not more than $5,500 for each unauthorized person; and more than two violations, not less than $3,300 and not more than $11,000 for each unauthorized person. 8 C.F.R. § 274a.10(b)(1)(ii), 1274a.10(b)(1)(ii).

189. 8 U.S.C. § 1324a(f)(2), Sec. 274A(f)(2).

190. 8 U.S.C. § 1324a(f)(1), Sec. 274A(f)(1).

which it conducts using statistical methods designed to assure random selection of employers.[191] The audits may provide the basis for further investigation and alone may cause a complaint to be filed.

If after investigation ICE determines that a person or entity has committed a violation for the first time during the citation period (June 1, 1987 through May 31, 1988), the agency issues a citation. If after investigation the ICE determines that a person or entity has violated the law for the second time during the citation period or for the first time after May 31, 1988, it will commence the proceeding to assess administrative penalties. Notice is accomplished through service on the person or entity identified in the Notice of Intent to Fine, which is issued by an ICE officer after consultation with the attorney for the agency or her designee.

The Notice of Intent to Fine should contain a concise statement of factual allegations informing the respondent (employer) of the act or conduct alleged to be in violation of law, a designation of the charge(s) against the respondent, the statutory provisions alleged to have been violated and the penalty that will be imposed.

The Notice of Intent to Fine will provide the following notice to the respondent: (i) the person or entity has the right to representation by counsel of her own choice at no expense to the government; (ii) any statement given may be used against the person or entity; (iii) the person or entity has the right to request a hearing before an administrative law judge pursuant to 5 U.S.C. §§ 554–57 within thirty days from the service of the Notice of Intent to Fine; (iv) ICE will issue a final order in 45 days if a written request for a hearing is not timely received; and (v) there will be no appeal of the final order.

If a respondent contests the issuance of a Notice of Intent to Fine, she must, by mail, serve a written answer responding to each allegation listed in the notice and request a hearing within thirty days from the issuance of the notice. If the respondent does not file an answer within thirty days, ICE shall issue a final order to which there is no appeal.

Notes

1. Employer sanctions for hiring persons who are ineligible to work under the immigration laws require that employers be particularly careful when making their hiring decisions. In enacting the sanction provisions, Congress directed USCIS to study the implementation of a verifiable identification system. Given that an identification card would have to be used by all persons seeking work, how might the concerns of those who fear the abuse of such a identity system be allayed?

2. **E-Verify Program.** More formally known as the Electronic Verification Program is a program which commenced in 1996 designed to provide a mechanism for employers to be able to electronically verify a person's eligibility for employment. Once a person who has been hired has provided documentation to the employer as required

191. 47 Interpreter Releases v1696 (1998).

in the I-9 process, the employer has complied with her requirements and cannot be held in violation. However, if the employer receives information from the Social Security Administration (SSA) that a number of its employees have names that do not match with records held by the agency, a question arises as to whether the employee has constructive knowledge such that further inquiry should be undertaken. The use of SSA records as a method for verifying employment authorization status has been very controversial. In 2007 DHS issued a rule which set forth the procedure to be followed by employers following receipt of a SSA generated "no-match" letter.[192] While the enforcement of the regulation was based on a balancing of harms, the plaintiffs also argued that the use of no-match letters improperly shifted the burden to the employers.[193] In October, 2008 the agency reissued the regulations which had been previously enjoined.[194] In October 2009 the 2008 regulation was formally rescinded.[195] DHS some time earlier created a program known as "E-verify" which is an internet based document verification system which can be used by employers for verification. An employer's use of E-verify along with other steps such as in-house audits is now considered as a best practice to avoid liability and making a showing of good faith compliance with the verification requirements under the immigration laws.[196]

192. *See* 72 Fed. Reg. 45,611 (Aug. 15, 2007).

193. *American Federation of Labor v. Chertoff*, 552 F. Supp. 2d 999, 1013–14 (N.D. Cal. 2007).

194. *See* 73 Fed. Reg. 63,863 (Oct. 28, 2008).

195. *See* 74 Fed. Reg. 51,447 (Oct. 7, 2009).

196. Austin T. Fragomen, Jr., Alfred J. Del Rey, Jr., and Sam Bernsen, 3 IMMIGRATION LAW & BUSINESS § 11.7 (2009). For a critique of E-verify, see Naomi Barrowclough, *E-Verify: A Long Awaited "Magic Bullet" or Weak Attempt to Substitute Technology for Comprehensive Reform*, 62 RUTGERS L. REV. 791 (2010).

Chapter 5

Protections from Harm

Introduction

The period following World War II has seen a tremendous growth in the international community's concern for the rights of refugees and others whose life or well-being are at risk. Modern immigration law provides a variety of protections for those facing different forms of peril upon removal. The main forms of protection under U.S. immigration law come in the form of "refugee" status, "asylum," "safe-haven" or "temporary protective status." Most of our discussion will focus on the refugee definition and asylum. At the conclusion of this chapter, we will explore the mechanisms for providing safety for those facing a range of harms, which as interpreted, do not fit the refugee definition.

Originally, U.S. immigration law did not recognize a formalized right of asylum for persons seeking admission or within the country. Up until 1952, the only way that a person who feared persecution could obtain refuge in this country was either through special legislation or through admission as a parolee.[1] As will be seen in the following discussion, until 1980 the laws protecting refugees were enacted as a reaction to refugee crises rather than as part of a well thought-out plan to assure the orderly admission of persons who were fleeing persecution.[2]

There were tens of thousands of refugees and displaced persons in the post-World War II era, which resulted in numerous legislative efforts by Congress to allow the admission of refugees. The first major legislative enactment was the Displaced Persons Act of 1948.[3] This statute allowed for the admission of more than 400,000 refugees as immigrants under the immigration quota system.[4] One writer has described the Displaced Persons Act as "mortgaging" the regular immigration quotas into the future,

1. Though many refugees obtained sanctuary in the United States, they came as immigrants, not asylees, under the general authorization of the immigration laws. The terms "parole" and "parolee" were discussed in Chapter 3. Those facing removal or deportation might be able to obtain a deferral of prosecution.

2. One major distinction between refugees and other persons coming to a country is that the refugee is fleeing some type of harm considered to be persecution within the meaning of the relevant statute. On the other hand, many people do leave their country voluntarily: either for work (economic migrants) or to join family members (family unification).

3. Act of June 25, 1948, 62 Stat. 1009.

4. As will be discussed later, persons seeking permanent admission because of their family ties or the unavailability of U.S. workers are admitted in limited numbers under an immigrant quota system. *See* Chapter 7.

meaning that the admission of these 400,000 refugees was at the expense of quotas normally allocated to immigrants.[5]

The next important refugee provision, in effect from 1953 until 1956, was referred to as the Refugee Relief Act of 1953.[6] The Refugee Relief Act ameliorated some of the adverse impacts of refugee admissions on the admission of other immigrants. This statute permitted legacy INS to admit 214,000 refugees without any effect on the quota system. The Hungarian revolt of 1956 brought confusion to the plans of the Refugee Relief Act as it occurred toward the end of 1956, coinciding with the expiration of the Refugee Relief Act. Ultimately, more than 38,000 Hungarian refugees were admitted to the United States. Only 6,000 were admitted under the Refugee Act, and the remaining 32,000 were paroled into the country.

A. Protecting Refugees with Parole

The legislative approach used to respond to the refugee problems which followed World War II and continued until 1956 became the pattern for refugee relief until the major statutory enactment known as the Refugee Act in 1980. This pattern was one of reacting to crisis either by allowing the admission of the refugees through an act of grace by Congress or through the administrative grant of parole. The grant of parole would be followed within a short period by Congress' enactment of legislation adjusting the refugee's status to lawful permanent residence.[7] Prior to 1950, there was no special procedure for the protection of a person who feared persecution upon return to a particular country. The remedies available were either to admit the person under parole or defer her deportation.[8] In 1950, Section 243(h)[9] of the Act was amended to prevent the Attorney General from deporting a person to a country where she would be subjected to "physical" persecution."[10] Section 243(h) was modified in 1952 to emphasize the discretionary nature of the Attorney General's power to "withhold" deportation.[11]

---

5. *See* 1 Charles Gordon & Stanely Mailman, Immigration Law and Procedure 2–184 (rev. ed. 1990). This borrowing against future admissions was terminated in 1957. Act of Sept. 11, 1957, 71 Stat. 642.

6. Act of Aug. 7, 1953, 67 Stat. 400.

7. *See e.g.*, Cuban Adjustment Act of 1966, Pub. L. No. 89-732, 80 Stat. 1161; Indochina Refugee Adjustment Act of 1977, Pub. L. No. 95-145, 91 Stat. 1223.

8. *See* discussion of parole in Chapter 2. The administrative practice of deferred action, or "deferral of prosecution", is discussed at Chapter 11.

9. 8 U.S.C. § 1253(h). This section of the statute deals with the deportation of persons from the United States.

10. *See* Sec. 20(a), Act of Feb. 5, 1917, 39 Stat. 890, as amended by Sec. 23, Internal Security Act of 1950, 64 Stat. 987.

11. Sec. 243(h), Act of 1952, 66 Star. 214. This amendment provided that

> The Attorney General is *authorized* to withhold deportation of any alien within the United States to any country in which *in his opinion* the alien would be subject to physical persecution and for such period of time as he deems to be necessary for such reason (emphasis supplied).

A 1965 amendment eliminated the requirement that persecution be physical.[12] The 1965 amendments also included a special provision for admitting a limited number of refugees through a procedure known as conditional entry status. This device was similar to the parole status discussed earlier. It provided for the admission and grant of permanent residence to certain groups fleeing persecution from Communist-dominated or Middle Eastern countries and to persons fleeing a presidentially declared "natural calamity."[13]

The most significant legislation affecting refugees was the Refugee Act of 1980,[14] which was intended to bring U.S. law into compliance with the U.N. Protocol Relating to the Status of Refugees.[15] The definition of "refugee" in the Act directly tracks the language of the U.N. Protocol.[16] Passage of the Refugee Act was also intended to improve the cumbersome manner in which refugee admissions were previously handled and to eliminate the use of parole as a means for admitting refugee groups.[17] The 1980 Act instead established a separate annual allocation for the admission of refugees, fixed at 50,000 annually for 1980, 1981, and 1982. Admissions quotas for the years following 1982 were established by the President after consultation with Congress.

In order to understand asylum and refugee law, the following similarity and distinctions between the two should be noted.

1. An important distinction between asylum and refugee status is that of the physical location of the person when applying for protection from anticipated or experienced persecution. If the person is outside the United States, she must apply for refugee status. If the person is at a port of entry or inside the United States, she must apply

---

12. Sec. 11(f), Act of October 3, 1965, Pub. L. No. 89-236, 79 Stat. 918. This amendment added the words "persecution on account of race, religion, or political opinion" in place of "physical persecution."

13. *See* Sec. 20, Act of Oct. 3, 1965, Pub. L. No. 89-236, 79 Stat. 912. The Act defined the Middle East as the area

> [B]etween and including (1) Libya on the west, (2) Turkey on the north, (3) Pakistan on the east, and (4) Saudi Arabia and Ethiopia on the south....

The statute also provided a similar benefit for persons who were physically present in the United States. In 1976, the Act was again amended to make the provisions for conditional entrants applicable to aliens from the Western Hemisphere quota. The requirements of flight from a Communist-dominated country or national calamity were preserved in the statute.

14. Act of March 17, 1980, Pub. L. No. 96-212, 93 Stat. 102.

15. The United Nations Convention Relating to the Status of Refugees was adopted in 1951 and was incorporated into U.S. law by the United Nations Protocol Relating to the Status of Refugees. 19 U.S.T. 6223, T.I.A.S. No. 6577 (entered into force with respect to the U.S. on November 1, 1968).

16. In tracking international standards, the Refugee Act eliminated the requirement that a person be fleeing persecution from a Communist government or the government of a specific geographical area. In so doing, the Refugee Act made the definition of refugee fact-specific and not ideologically based. On its face, this would enable a person in the United States seeking asylum from a nation friendly with the United States to also receive protection.

17. It should be noted that almost immediately after the enactment of the Refugee Act, the United States paroled approximately 125,000 Cuban refugees from the Freedom Flotilla who had been allowed by Fidel Castro to leave the country.

for asylum. Refugee determinations are made overseas, and the admission categories are set by consultation between the executive and Congress, whereas asylum adjudications are without congressional involvement and are subject to judicial review.

2. Asylum and refugee applicants must both show that they have a "well-founded fear of persecution" and that the basis for the persecution is on account of "race, religion, nationality, membership in a particular social group or political opinion." Applicants for asylum and refugee status must meet the same statutory definition and the same burden of a well-founded fear of persecution. However, an important difference is that there is no limit on the number of asylum applications which may be granted annually yet an annual limit on the number of refugees admitted to this country.[18] These refugee quotas are set by the President in consultation with Congress. Therefore, even if the refugee meets the statutory definition, she may not necessarily be allowed to enter the country. The applicant for asylum does not have this problem, since there is no quota on the number of asylum applications granted. The control of the number of refugees admitted and their country of origin provides a mechanism for the injection of political and foreign policy considerations into the decision-making process.[19]

3. A person admitted as a refugee or granted asylum may apply for lawful permanent residency in the United States one year after her admission date or the date on which she received asylum.[20]

B. Asylum Procedure

An individual who is within the United States and who is not in removal proceedings—either because she is here legally or because she has not come to the notice of the DHS—may file an *affirmative* application for political asylum. Prior to April 1991, these applications were adjudicated by regular immigration examiners. As one commentator noted, the examiners had no specialized training in asylum law, and

18. Persons granted asylum because they are fleeing persecution in the form of a forced sterilization or family planning policy are limited to 1,000 persons per year. *See* 8 U.S.C. § 1157(a)(5), Sec. 207(a)(5).

19. There is some question as to the degree to which these quotas operate to reinstate the old geographical limitation on who could seek refuge. For example, in each of the fiscal years since enactment of the Refugee Act, the overwhelming majority of refugee admissions were from the former Soviet Union and Asia with the fewest from Latin America and Africa. *See,* e.g., Presidential Determination No. 83-2, 47 Fed. Reg. 46,483 (1982); Presidential Determination No. 87-1, 51 Fed. Reg. 39,637 (1986); Presidential Determination No. 88-1, 52 Fed. Reg. 42,073 (1987).

20. Emergency Supplemental Appropriations Act for Defense, the Global War on Terror, and Tsunami Relief, 2005 (REAL ID Act of 2005), Pub. L. No. 109-13, § 101(g), 119 Stat. 231, 305 (2005). Until the enactment of the REAL ID Act in 2005, only 10,000 asylees per year were allowed to receive permanent residence due to quota restrictions. *See* 8 U.S.C. § 1159(b) (2004). The quota on asylees who could adjust to permanent resident status created serious problems for those who had been granted asylum following enactment of the Refugee Act of 1980.

the adjudication process was "little more than a reflection of United States foreign policy."[21] The commentator went on to detail that:[22]

> From 1983 through 1991, approval rates for people fleeing communist, or other countries considered "hostile to United States foreign policy interests (such as China, U.S.S.R. And Iran), exceeded 50% while approval rates for those fleeing three countries the United States supported—El Salvador, Guatemala and Haiti—were less than 3% despite extensive documentation of widespread human rights abuses and political violence in all three countries.

Regulations in force during this time required that the Department of State issue an advisory opinion on every application for political asylum. Studies demonstrated that the immigration examiners followed the State Department recommendations in more than 95% of their decisions, leading to the consistency between approval rates and U.S. foreign policy considerations.[23] The ongoing criticism of arbitrary and discriminatory adjudication finally led to reforms in the affirmative adjudication system.

The reforms were implemented by regulations promulgated in October 1990.[24] The regulations created a corps of "professional" Asylum Officers who were to receive "special training in international relations and in international law."[25] The adjudicatory function for affirmative applications was transferred from immigration examiners to the Asylum Officer corps.[26] The 1990 regulations also required the creation of a human rights documentation center to "compile and disseminate to Asylum Officers information concerning the persecution of persons in other countries ... and other information relevant to asylum determinations...."[27] State Department advisory letters became optional rather than mandatory, and in an attempt to change previous practice where such opinions were considered dispositive, the regulations identified the letters as only one of a number of relevant sources of information:

> In deciding applications for asylum or restriction on removal[28] the Asylum Office may rely upon material provided by the Department of State, the Asylum Policy or Review Unit, the Office of Refugees, Asylum and Parole, the District Director ... or other credible sources, such as international organizations, private voluntary agencies, or academic institutions....[29]

---

21. Sarah Ignatius, National Asylum Study Project: An Assessment of the Asylum Process of the Immigration and Naturalization Service 17 (1993) [hereinafter referred to as "Ignatius Report"].

22. *Id.* at 18.

23. *Id.* at 17.

24. Asylum and Withholding of Deportation Procedures, 55 Fed. Reg. 30,674 (1990).

25. *Id.* at 30,680 [amending 8 C.F.R. § 208.1(b)].

26. The asylum officer corp is under the Office of International Affairs. 8 C.F.R. § 208.2(a).

27. *Id.*

28. IIRAIRA changed the term "withholding of deportation" and replaced it with "restriction on removal." References in the cases and discussion may use these terms interchangeably.

29. 8 C.F.R. § 208.12(a).

The procedures set forth in the changes established in 1990 have continued in place to the present through the reorganization of the INS into the DHS, with the asylum officers falling under USCIS. Every applicant for asylum is required to be interviewed by an Asylum Officer, and applications are filed with the USCIS Regional Center. The Regional Center forwards the applications to the appropriate regional Asylum Office, which is responsible for scheduling and carrying out the interview. The asylum interview is contemplated as being "non-adversarial" and less formal than a court adjudication. One result of the non-adversarial format is that the role of the asylum seeker's counsel is greatly curtailed. The regulations provide that: "Upon completion of the interview, the applicant or his representative shall have an opportunity to make a statement or comment on the evidence presented. The Asylum Officer in his discretion may limit the length of such comments or statements or may require their submission in writing."[30] In contrast to immigration court proceedings where interpretation is provided by the court, the Asylum Office does not provide interpreters for non-English speaking applicants, who are required to bring their own translators. Failure to bring a translator will result in the interview being rescheduled.

The Asylum Officer may issue a positive or negative decision on a request for asylum. A positive decision will be issued in the form of a grant of asylum, while a negative decision may issue as either a *denial* or a *referral*. Whether an Asylum Officer denies or refers a case depends upon whether the asylum applicant is lawfully present in the United States. If the applicant is not here legally, the Asylum Officer will refer the case to an immigration judge for the initiation of what was previously deportation but now would be removal proceedings. However, if the applicant is lawfully present in the country, the Asylum Officer may simply deny the case, which leaves the applicant in her previous lawful status.

Prior to January 1995, asylum applicants who filed non-frivolous claims were entitled to receive work authorization. A frivolous claim has been defined as one which is without merit or lacks "an arguable basis in either law or fact."[31] There were consistent allegations that individuals who did not have legitimate asylum claims were filing simply to receive work authorization. In response to these allegations, the 1995 USCIS regulations attempted to de-link the asylum application process with the granting of work authorization by precluding a grant of work authorization to an asylum applicant unless her application has been pending for more than 180 days. The regulations contemplated that applications would be processed before the 180-day period runs, thus precluding a grant of work authorization.

30. 8 C.F.R. § 208.9(d).

31. *Ramos v. Thornburgh*, 732 F. Supp. 696 (E.D. Tex. 1989).

1. Affirmative Asylum Application

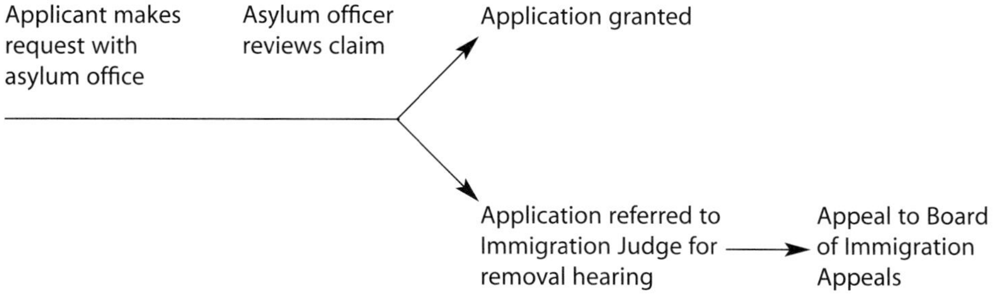

2. Asylum Applications as a Defense to Removal

As noted above, individuals who file affirmatively and are denied asylum are referred to the immigration court for removal proceedings, where they may renew their claims for protection. A person who files for asylum at the port of entry will have her case determined by an immigration judge in immigration court.[32] However, the denial of an affirmative application is not the only route by which an asylum seeker may end up in removal proceedings. Any individual not lawfully present in the United States may be placed in removal proceedings upon apprehension by the ICE.

In contrast to the non-adversarial affirmative interview process, removal proceedings are adversarial in nature. The applicant may be represented by counsel, and the government is represented by a trial attorney, who will have an opportunity to cross-examine the applicant and other witnesses who may appear on her behalf. It is not uncommon for the immigration judge to also question the applicant and her witnesses. 8 U.S.C. § 1230(b)(4)(B), Sec. 240(b)(4)(B) details the applicant's hearing rights, including the right to present evidence and cross-examine witnesses. All testimony is given under oath and tape-recorded for the purpose of producing a written transcript for administrative and possibly judicial review.

The immigration judge who presides over the hearing is not an employee of DHS but is part of the Executive Office for Immigration Review (EOIR), a separate adjudicatory body under the supervision of the Associate Attorney General within the Department of Justice. Prior to 1983, immigration judges were part of legacy "INS," which resulted in criticism regarding the impropriety of institutionally combining neutral adjudicatory functions with the enforcement and prosecutorial arms of the agency. Historically, a significant percentage of immigration judges were former INS trial attorneys. Therefore, notwithstanding the formal separation of judicial and pros-

32. 8 C.F.R. §§ 208.2(b) and 1208.2(b). The initial claim will likely be addressed by an asylum officer in the context of a credible fear interview and could be reviewed by an immigration judge. Ultimately, the asylum application will be considered by an immigration judge.

ecutorial functions, there were continued complaints that the neutral judicial role was tainted by a pro-enforcement bias. The creation of EOIR was viewed as a positive step towards securing a more impartial adjudicatory environment.

At the end of proceedings, the immigration judge may make an oral decision or take the case under submission and issue a subsequent written decision. If either the applicant or the ICE is not satisfied with the immigration judge's decision, either may appeal to the Board of Immigration Appeals (BIA). The Board, also part of the EOIR, is the administrative appellate tribunal which reviews immigration court decisions. The BIA conducts a *de novo* review of both facts and law based on the entire record of immigration court proceedings. Although it is physically located in Falls Church, Virginia, the BIA has nationwide jurisdiction.

Over the years, the Board has been subject to criticism for adjudicatory bias. One commentator compared the claims of applicants from different countries and detailed how claims with similar facts were decided differently depending on the nationality of the applicant.[33] Others have pointed out that, for example, in cases based upon conscientious objection to military service, relief was granted to Afghanis but not to Central Americans. Similarly, a number of circuit court decisions have harshly criticized the Board over the years for a lack of professionalism. In *Bastanipour v. INS*, 980 F.2d 1129 (7th Cir. 1992), Judge Posner declared that "[t]he Board's handling of the question of apostasy [religious conversion] makes us wonder whether the Board's knowledge of Iran is any greater than its knowledge of Biafra, about which we commented critically in *Osaghae v. INS*...."

Similar to immigration judges, a substantial number of BIA judges came from legacy INS and brought that perspective, prompting one scholar to note that it was like "staffing a criminal court predominantly with prosecutors."[34] Pursuant to regulations finalized in 1997, the Board was reorganized into a sixteen member body. The expanded size of the Board permitted its members to decide cases in three judge panels or to sit *en banc* for the consideration of selected appeals. It also has allowed the Board to increase its productivity in an attempt to reduce the substantial backlog of cases which have long been pending.

Decisions rendered by the BIA may be appealed to the federal circuit courts of appeal, and either side may petition the Supreme Court for *certiorari* following the appellate court decision.

a. Defensive Asylum Claim

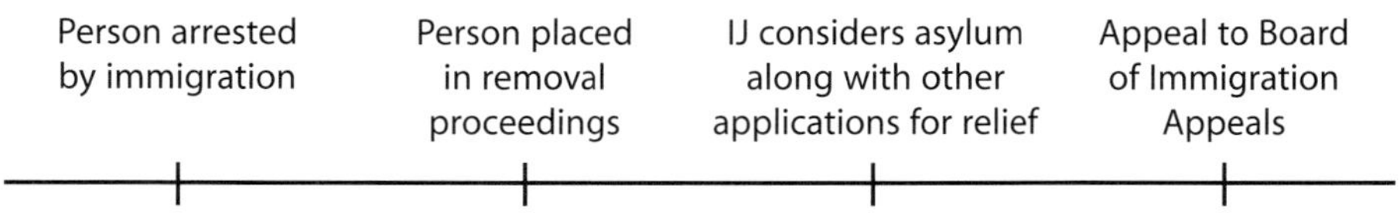

33. *See A Refugee by Any Other Name: An Examination of the Board of Immigration Appeals' Actions in Asylum Cases*, 75 VA. L. REV. 681 (1989).

34. Keith Donoghue, *Immigration Board Revitalized*, LEGAL TIMES, Sept. 18, 1995 at p. 6.

3. Refugee Procedure

Even if a person meets the definition of "refugee," the statute does not require her admission. Each year, the President and Congress establish not only the numbers but the regions or countries from which refugees will be admitted to the United States. USCIS is required to admit refugees in accordance with this presidential determination of special humanitarian concern.[35]

The refugee applicant must apply at a designated consular office overseas where she is interviewed by a USCIS officer and a determination is made as to her eligibility.[36] The decision by the officer, although reviewable informally within USCIS, cannot be appealed. Although the person is required to be given a copy of the denial letter, it is not uncommon for the refugee to lack a clear understanding of why her application was denied. If the application is approved, the refugee is allowed to travel to the United States and be admitted as a refugee.

4. Refugee Processing

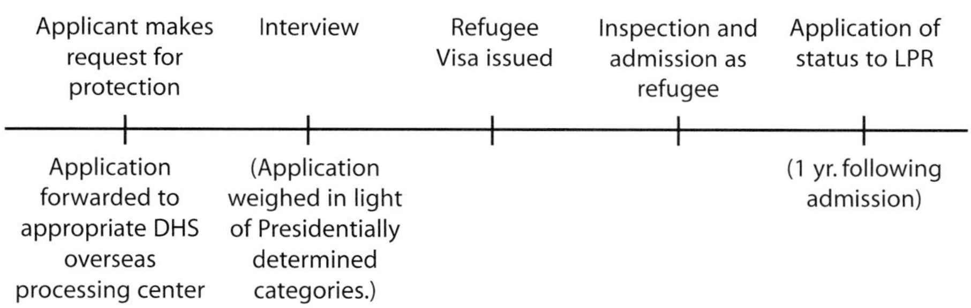

C. Credibility and the Presentation of Asylum Claims

At the heart of every asylum claim is the issue of credibility.[37] Applicants travel long distances and invariably must rely on presenting their own stories in a compelling way to a listener from a very different culture who may be unfamiliar with the circumstances in the applicant's country. The following article describes the present state of asylum law as it relates to credibility and the burden of proof on persons who claim persecution.

---

35. Although it is difficult to determine in advance and from year to year which refugees will be admitted, the following general guidelines have been used in the past: (1) past or present ties with the United States; (2) advancement of foreign policy objectives; (3) opportunities for resettlement in other countries; (4) ability of the United States to absorb the refugees; and (5) present or former political prisoners. *See* 8 C.F.R. § 207.1.

36. Under some circumstances the refugee applicant may be interviewed by a U.S. consul if there are no asylum officers nearby.

37. Throughout the discussion, the reference will be to asylum claims because refugee claims are handled overseas. While credibility is also an important factor in those claims, they are by nature less adversarial and not subject to review.

Karen Musalo, Credibility and Burden of Proof in Asylum Claims after the Board of Immigration Appeals' Four 1998 Decisions

31st Annual Immigration and Naturalization Institute
277 (Austin E. Fragomen ed. 1998)

I. Introduction

The applicant in an asylum or restriction on removal case bears the burden of proof in establishing eligibility for relief. Establishing credibility is a key element of meeting that burden. In 1998 the Board of Immigration Appeals (BIA) issued four significant precedent decisions which impact the substantive law on credibility and burden of proof. The decisions are: *Matter of O-D-*, Int. Dec. 3334 (BIA 1998), *Matter of A-S-*, Int. Dec. 3336 (BIA 1998), *Matter of Y-B-*, Int. Dec. 3337 (BIA 1998), and *Matter of M-D-*, Int. Dec. 3339 (BIA 1998). This article will discuss these decisions, looking at them in the context of existing jurisprudence, and considering their practical implications.

II. Burden of Proof and Applicant's Credibility

Commentators have often remarked that the burden of proof for asylum seekers may be a difficult one, given that the events at issue occurred thousands of miles away, making it unlikely that the applicant will be able to produce witnesses, forensic evidence, or other documentary evidence corroborative of the claim. In recognition of these inherent difficulties, in its decision in *Matter of Mogharrabi*, 19 I.&N. Dec. 439 (BIA 1987), the Board of Immigration Appeals (BIA) articulated the principle that an applicant's testimony alone could suffice to meet the required burden of proof. In relevant part, the BIA held:

> In determining whether the alien has met his burden of proof, we recognize, as have the courts, the difficulties faced by many aliens in obtaining documentary or other corroborative evidence to support their claims of persecution. Although every effort should be made to obtain such evidence, the lack of such evidence will not necessarily be fatal to the application. The alien's own testimony may in some cases be the only evidence available, and it can suffice where the testimony is believable, consistent, and sufficiently detailed to provide a plausible and coherent account of the basis for his fear.

Matter of Mogharrabi, at 15–16.

INS regulations affirmed the rule pronounced in *Mogharrabi*, providing at 8 C.F.R.§ 208.13(a) that: "The testimony of the applicant, if credible, may be sufficient to sustain the burden of proof without corroboration." In *Matter of S-M-J-*, Int. Dec. 3303 (BIA 1997) the Board elaborated on the issue of corroboration, noting that although it is not a requirement, it should be supplied where it is reasonably available.

The Board's four recent published decisions addressing burden of proof and credibility do not repudiate the letter of this well-established rule. However, the decisions run counter to the spirit of the rule, which recognized the unique obstacles facing the asylum seeker, and tended to afford such individuals the "benefit of the doubt."[1] The Board in these decisions—rather than giving the benefit of the doubt—appears to raise the bar for asylum seekers in several respects. First, the Board appears to impose more stringent requirements for a finding that testimony is credible—expecting an increased degree of detail and consistency. Second, the Board expresses an expectation that corroborating evidence would be available in a wide range of circumstances. Third, the Board appears willing to rule that an otherwise credible applicant has failed to meet his burden of proof if such applicant is unable to provide corroborating evidence.

III. The 1998 BIA Decisions

A. *Matter of O-D-*., Int. Dec. 3334 (BIA 1998)

Matter of O-D-, Int. Dec. 3334 (BIA 1988), 1998 WL 24904 (BIA) involved the claim of an individual who testified that he was a native and citizen of Mauritania. He testified that he and other young people from his village had been arrested by soldiers, detained for four years, and compelled to perform hard labor. Upon his release he went to a refugee camp in Senegal where he received an identity document, which he testified that he subsequently lost. As evidence in his behalf, he had submitted an identification card and a birth certificate. The Immigration and Naturalization Service (INS) Forensic Document Lab reported that the identification card was a "known counterfeit" and that the birth certificate was "probably counterfeit." The immigration judge (IJ) found the applicant not credible primarily on the basis of inconsistencies between his testimony and two I-589 asylum applications that he had submitted. The Board upheld the immigration judge's adverse credibility determination. It did so, relying principally on the INS Forensic Lab report, although it took the inconsistencies into account, referring to its own jurisprudence on deference to an immigration judge's adverse credibility finding. Because the majority found the applicant not credible, it ruled that he had failed to meet his burden of proof in establishing eligibility for relief.

Board Chair Paul Schmidt, and Board Members Lory Rosenberg and John Guendelsberger dissented,[2] finding that the applicant had established his credibility and met the requisite burden of proof notwithstanding his submission of an identification

1. The United Nations High Commissioner for Refugees (UNHCR) has recommended that asylum seekers be given the "benefit of the doubt." The UNHCR HANDBOOK ON PROCEDURES AND CRITERIA FOR DETERMINING REFUGEE STATUS recognizes that "the requirement of evidence should ... not be too strictly applied in view of the difficulty of proof inherent in the special situation in which an applicant for refugee status finds himself." HANDBOOK, ¶ 197. Because "it is hardly possible for a refugee to 'prove' every part of his case and, indeed, if this were a requirement the majority of refugees would not be recognized ... [it] is frequently necessary to give the applicant the benefit of the doubt." HANDBOOK ¶ 203.

2. In addition to the majority decision, and the dissent herein discussed, there was a concurrence by Board Member Gustavo Villageliu, and a concurrence and dissent by Board Members David Holmes and Mary Maguire Dunne.

card which the INS Lab reported to be counterfeit. In ruling that the applicant was credible, the dissenting members examined the applicant's testimony in light of country conditions. According to the dissent, the IJ's decision "indicated that Mauritania is controlled by 'white' moors of Arabic descent and that since 1989, thousands of the 'black' Hal Fular (Halpulaar) segment of the population, of which respondent is a member, have been arrested, tortured, killed and expelled from their country." *Id.* at 26. The applicant claimed that he and his family were members of the Fulani tribe, and were known as supporters of the African Liberation Forces of Mauritania (FLAM), an organization which protested the Mauritanian government abuses. He had testified in detail regarding his "Mauritanian identity and Fulani membership" as well as the circumstances of his arrest, conditions of detention, and manner of escape. *Id.* The details included descriptions regarding the content of the prison meals on which he subsisted and the manner in which he was interrogated and physically abused during his detention. The dissent found that his testimony was consistent with descriptions of the human rights situation reported by the U.S. Department of State, Amnesty International and the Africa Report. *Id.*

The dissent also analyzed the nature of the inconsistencies between the applicant's two I-589 applications and his testimony, which had formed the basis for the IJ's adverse credibility determination. The dissenting Board members concluded that the discrepancies relied upon were inadequate to support an adverse credibility because they were not true inconsistencies, but rather omissions of detail in the prior statements. Nor, in the dissent's opinion were these issues which went to the heart of the applicant's claim.

The dissent did not ignore the INS Forensics Lab report finding the applicant's identity card to be counterfeit. However, it invoked the spirit of the UNHCR HANDBOOK in rejecting: "the majority's implicit presumption that an adverse forensics report, or even an admittedly false document, undermines the case of an otherwise meritorious asylum applicant. Such a bright-line rule ignores the exigencies faced by asylum seekers in terms of trauma, fear and cultural and language barriers, and would defeat the principle of case-by-case consideration of an asylum claim based on the totality of circumstances as required by the Handbook[.]" *Id.* at 42. Applying the totality of the evidence standard, the dissent found that the applicant was credible and that he met his burden of proof.

B. *Matter of A-S-*, Int. Dec. 3336 (BIA 1998)

Matter of A-S-, Int. Dec. 3336 (BIA 1998), is the second in this quartet of decisions published by the Board in 1998. The applicant in *Matter of A-S-* was a twenty-nine year old native and citizen of Bangladesh whose claim was based on alleged beatings and threats as a result of his participation with the Jatiyo party of President Ershad in his home country. The applicant testified that he had been a member of the Jatiyo party since 1985, and that in 1987 he had been appointed to the high level position of Organizing Secretary. He claimed that beginning in 1991 when Ershad was defeated, members of opposing parties sought him out; on several occasions either he or his family members where physically attacked by the individuals affiliated with these parties. By the time he finally decided to leave Bangladesh in 1994, the police had issued a warrant for his arrest.

The immigration judge found the applicant in *Matter of A-S-* not credible, ruling that his testimony was inconsistent and lacked "specifics and details" which a high-level member of the Jatiyo party would be expected to know. Id. at 6. In support of his adverse credibility finding, the IJ had pointed to: (1) inconsistent dates between the respondent's I-589 asylum application and his testimony; (2) the applicant's failure to testify at his hearing about a demonstration at which he was attacked by the police, which was mentioned in his asylum application; and (3) "some confusion" regarding the details of the 1991 Bangladesh elections. The IJ also relied upon the applicant's demeanor to support the adverse credibility determination, finding that he testified in a "very halting" and "hesitant" manner. *Id.* at 7. Finally, the IJ ruled that the documentary evidence, which included two letters from the president and secretary of the local chapter of the Jatiyo party failed to support his claim.

In ruling on the respondent's appeal, the Board majority announced a seemingly new rule as to when it is appropriate to defer to an immigration judge on credibility, rather than conduct the de novo review which is within its authority. According to this rule, the Board will not disturb an IJ's credibility determination where:

> (1) the discrepancies and omissions described by the Immigration Judge are actually present; (2) these discrepancies and omissions provide specific and cogent reasons to conclude that the respondent provided incredible testimony; and (3) the respondent has not provided a convincing explanation for the discrepancies and omissions.

Id. at 9.

The Board held that these three elements were present in the case at bar, and found no reason to "disturb the Immigration Judge's adverse credibility determination." *Id.* at 9. The Board further relied upon the IJ's evaluation of demeanor, citing authority for the proposition that "credibility findings based on demeanor findings deserve more deference than those based on testimonial analysis" since the immigration judge has had the opportunity to observe the witness. *Id.* at 14.

Three Board members filed two separate dissents to this majority decision. The first dissent, by Board Chair Schmidt and Board Member Guendelsberger, took exception to what it characterized as the "enhanced standard of deference" accorded to immigration judges under the majority new rule. In their dissent, they observed that such deference is not appropriate in the special circumstances under which asylum cases are determined.

> In my view, the majority basically concludes that if the Immigration Judge's credibility finding is within a zone that could be reached by a reasonable adjudicator, cites problems that actually are reflected in the record, and is not convincingly challenged on appeal, it must be upheld upon appellate review....
>
> [T]he majority's standard is more appropriate to an appellate court of general jurisdiction than it is to a specialized, expert administrative appellate

> body such as our Board. This is of particular concern in the important area of asylum adjudication. Asylum applicants are entitled to a practical, deferential adjudication that recognizes both the frailties of the human mind and the chaotic, traumatic situations in which asylum cases arise. *See, e.g., Matter of Mogharrabi* [citation omitted].
>
> In many cases, the expertise, independence, and sound judgment of this Board is all that stands between an asylum applicant and return to a place where he or she will face persecution or death. It is quite possible that we review more asylum adjudications than any other tribunal in the world. Certainly, each Board Member adjudicates many more asylum cases, from a wider variety of nationalities, than an individual Immigration Judge....
>
> While we may lack the advantage of a face-to-face observation of the witness, we have the very substantial, and much underrated, advantage of being able to review a written transcript. We also have a talented professional staff to assist us in reviewing the record.... Moreover, we have the opportunity for collegial discussion and the application of shared expertise to difficult appellate issues.
>
> Therefore, it is not clear to me why our vantage point is necessarily less revealing than that of the Immigration Judge and why we want to give such great deference to the Immigration Judge, rather than relying on our own expertise and sound, independent judgement after review of the written record on appeal....

Id. at 18–22.

After expressing disagreement with the majority's rule which diminishes de novo review, Schmidt and Guendelsberger conducted a de novo review, and reached the conclusion that the applicant was credible. Their consideration of the evidence began with a discussion of the two letters submitted by the applicant corroborating his membership in the Jatiyo party. The IJ had ruled that the letters deserved little weight since the respondent "seemed to have very little knowledge as to how those letters were obtained." *Id.* at 26. Schmidt and Guendelsberger disagreed that the letters merited little weight, observing that the applicant did know how they had been obtained, testifying that he had asked his father, who still lived in Bangladesh, to obtain letters confirming his party membership. *Id.* at 27. The two dissenting Board Members also disagreed that the respondent's testimony was too vague to establish credibility, recounting the numerous details to which he had testified.

The dissent spent a significant amount of time addressing the issues of demeanor and inconsistencies. This discussion is especially useful because it is based in an explicit recognition of the manner in which cultural and psychological factors may impact credibility. The dissent issued a strong cautionary note against reliance upon demeanor, as follows:

> ... [A]lthough I obviously did not have the benefit of observing the manner in which the respondent testified, I decline to assume that his 'halting' man-

> ner of testifying indicated that he was untruthful, especially when considering the nervousness that is often precipitated by appearing at a tribunal in any country, let alone a foreign country. *See Matter of B-*, Interim Decision 3251 (BIA 1995) (finding that the respondent's tendency to look at the wall or table, instead of at the Immigration Judge, did not necessarily indicate deception). *See* generally *Paredes-Urrestarazu v. INS*, 36 F.3d 801, 818 (9th Cir. 1994) (stating that nervousness is a factor properly considered in assessing credibility). My own professional experience and observation is that halting delivery of a presentation in a formal setting often has causes other than untruthfulness.

Id. at 27–28.

The dissent issued an equally strong cautionary note against reliance upon inconsistency regarding dates to make an adverse credibility determination. The applicant, who had testified that he had difficulty recalling dates, had given different dates in his application than in his testimony for various attacks and threats by opposition party members. In rejecting these differences in dates as a sufficient basis for assuming untruthfulness, the dissent observed:

> Difficulties in remembering dates are certainly a common problem with respect to victims of persecution. *See* generally Tina Rosenberg, *To Hell and Back*, NEW YORK TIMES MAGAZINE, Dec. 28, 1997, at 32, 34. For example, according to that recent article on refugees who had been victims of torture: "Early studies suggest that the brain processes a traumatic event very differently from an everyday one and might keep the trauma from being integrated with other memories. That may explain why trauma sufferers have amnesia or can retrieve only fragments, like a smell or a sound, or cannot put the events behind them." *Id.* at 34.

Id. at 31–32.

After conducting its de novo review of the evidence in the record, Schmidt and Guendelsberger found the applicant credible and ruled that he had established eligibility for the relief of political asylum.[3]

C. *Matter of Y-B-*, Int. Dec. 3337 (BIA 1998)

Matter of Y-B-, Int. Dec. 3337 (BIA 1988), like *Matter of O-D-*, involved a black Mauritanian. The applicant in *Matter of Y-B-* worked as a farmer and herder. He claimed that he was outside his town with a cousin and friends when white Maur soldiers came with the intention of taking their cattle. He testified that the white Maurs killed his cousin, and then tied up the applicant. According to the applicant, he was beaten and threatened, and taken into town to his home. There his captors found his father, and tied him up also while they searched the house for other things

3. Board Member Lory Rosenberg filed a separate dissent in which she reached the same conclusion as members Schmidt and Guendelsberger, but wrote a more extensive critique of the majority's decision.

to take. His uncle was also taken into captivity. He and his uncle were taken to one prison detention site by their captors, while his father was taken to another site. Three weeks later he and his uncle were released "because a lot of prisoners were dying and the captors did not want them to die in Mauritania; they were told to go die in Senegal." *Id.* at 2. He testified that he searched in a number of refugee camps for his family, and found his mother and paternal grandmother, but did not locate his father. He lived in the refugee camp for more than two years, and in Dakar for a year, and then traveled through a number of African countries before coming to the United States.

To support his request for asylum, the applicant had submitted a copy of his and his mother's Mauritanian identity card, as well as documentation regarding conditions in Mauritania. He was not, however, able to obtain corroboration of his stay at the refugee camp in Senegal. In response to a request for confirmation, the UNHCR wrote that the applicant was "not known" to the UNHCR office in Senegal. *Id.* at 6.

The immigration judge denied the applicant's request for relief. In contrast to the previous two cases discussed, the denial did not rest on a finding that the applicant was not credible. Although the IJ found that the applicant's testimony was "lacking in specific detail" he "determined that [it] was, for the most part, internally consistent, and ... not ... incredible." *Id.* at 4. The denial was premised upon a finding that the respondent had failed to meet his burden of proof.

The BIA affirmed the IJ's denial, focusing on the failure of the applicant to provide corroboration of his stay in the refugee camp in Senegal. In order to justify this corroboration requirement, the Board characterized the applicant's testimony as weak, and announced that "the weaker an alien's testimony, the greater the need for corroborative evidence." *Id.* at 7. The weakness of the testimony consisted in the respondent's failure, in the opinion of the Board, to give adequate details regarding his cousin's killing, his arrest and the arrest of his father and uncle, the circumstances of his detention, the circumstances of his entry into Senegal and his stay at the refugee camp there. The BIA also considered the fact that his testimony gave greater detail than had been provided in his asylum application. *Id.* at 5.

As in the previous two cases, Board Chair Schmidt, and Board Members Rosenberg and Guendelsberger filed a lengthy dissent, finding the majority's decision contrary to established precedent that, "testimony alone, if unrefuted and credible, is perfectly adequate to satisfy an asylum applicant's burden of proof[.]" *Id.* at 36. The dissent's discussion of burden of proof, and the relationship between credibility and burden of proof is instructive:

> I regard the decisions of both the Immigration Judge and the majority as divergent from this established precedent. To conclude that the burden has not been satisfied, an adjudicator must either reject the testimony as lacking in credibility, or find that the testimony, even if credible, does not adequately give rise to an inference that the applicant is a "refugee" as defined in the Act. If the adjudicator requires more than the testimony provided, then, in essence the adjudicator is asserting that the witness cannot be believed on

> his or her testimony alone, or that the testimony does not support the necessary inference [citations omitted]....

Id. at 37–38.

The BIA majority did not rule that the respondent was not credible. Therefore, in the opinion of the dissent, the only question left was whether the testimony gave rise to the inference that the respondent was a refugee. The dissent concluded that it did, in that the respondent established that he was "harmed by government military forces because he is black, and he has related that such harm was inflicted, at least in part, to seize his property and exile him because of his race...." *Id.* at 38.

The dissent also discussed the Board's 1997 decision *Matter of S-M-J-*, *supra*, which addressed circumstances under which it is reasonable to expect corroboration to be submitted. *Matter of S-M-J-* held that "specific documentary corroboration of an applicant's particular experiences is not required unless the supporting documentation is of the type that would normally be created or available in the particular country and is accessible to the alien, such as through friends, relatives, or co-workers." *Id.* at 41. The dissent concluded that it was not reasonable to expect the respondent to be able to corroborate his stay in the refugee camp in Senegal.

A factor in concluding that corroboration of the applicant's 1989 stay in the refugee camp was not reasonable was the fact that the United States "Department of State ... reported that of the approximately 70,000 Afro-Mauritanians who were expelled or fled to Senegal in 1989–1991, an estimated 55,000 remain in camps in Senegal, and the UNHCR has only recently begun to assist in the issuance of identity documents to refugees...." *Id.* at 41. In the opinion of the dissent, the recent UNHCR assistance in issuing documents could indicate that in the earlier time period when the applicant fled, such documents were not readily available. In addition, the dissent observed that it might be appropriate to take administrative notice of the fact that "refugee camps in developing third world countries often lack the staff or advanced computer resources" to accurately document any individual's presence in a refugee camp. *Id.* at 42, n4.

Finally, as in *Matter of A-S-*, the dissent invoked the cultural and psychological reality of refugees in general, and the applicant in particular—in critiquing the majority's decision. The majority found that the respondent's testimony was lacking in details on a number of issues, including the murder of his cousin. The dissent disagreed, finding that the respondent provided "significant detail" but also noting that documentation in the record indicated that "herders of the Halpulaar tribe, like the respondent, are completely unschooled, generally illiterate, and possibly even unable to count." *Id.* at 24. These cultural norms would also be impacted by psychological factors:

> The majority, echoing the Immigration Judge, states that the respondent's failure to provide 'detail' about his arrest and his cousin's death compromises his claim. The respondent's testimony that his cousin was killed is detail related to his own arrest. A large group of white Maur soldiers approached, ordered the animals seized, grabbed and beat the respondent, tied him up and even killed one of the people with him—his cousin. It is difficult to un-

> derstand what further information would satisfy the majority: that his cousin bled to death, that he was struck unconscious, that he cried, flinched, or had a seizure, that the ground where he fell was muddy, sandy, or hard clay? Do they expect the respondent to describe his emotions at witnessing his cousin being killed and his animals seized?
>
> Clearly, a medical diagnosis or autopsy report is not likely to be forthcoming under such circumstances. Similarly, the recounting of a violent event by one without an education or unaccustomed to lengthy written or spoken discourse as a means of communication is hardly likely to find expression in an elaborated verbal narrative. Even those with a formal education or from a tradition in which such detail may be valued and nurtured may consciously or unconsciously suppress such expression as a consequence of the traumatic experience itself.

Id. at 25–27.

D. *Matter of M-D-*, Int. Dec. 3339 (BIA 1998)

The asylum applicant in *Matter of M-D-*, Int. Dec. 3339 (BIA 1998), was a half-black Mauritanian. He testified that in June 1990 five white and two black Maurs from the military came to his house and accused him and his family of being Senegalese. They ordered them to produce their identify documents, which they then destroyed. His parents, wife and siblings, with whom he lived, were arrested and forced to cross the river into Senegal. He was separated from them, was blindfolded and beaten and taken to the village of M'Bagne. In M'Bagne he was imprisoned, forced to perform hard labor, and was beaten and burned with cigarettes. He was held under these conditions for a year and half. In December 1991 his captors took him and other prisoners and forced them into the river, ordering them to swim to Senegal. A passing fisherman from Senegal helped them cross to the other shore. The respondent located his family at one of the refugee camps in Senegal. He remained in the camp for eleven months before traveling to Dakar, and then to the United States, where he sought asylum.

In support of his application, the applicant had submitted "numerous articles and reports regarding general country conditions in Mauritania and the oppression of black Mauritanians on account of their race." *Id.* at 7. However, he had not provided specific corroboration of elements of his claim, and it was on this basis that the immigration judge ruled that he had not met his burden of proof. The BIA affirmed the denial, noting that the applicant had failed to corroborate his Mauritanian nationality, his arrest and detention, his and his family's expulsion from Mauritania, and proof of his eleven month stay at a refugee camp in Senegal. The majority pointed to the fact that the respondent's family remained in a refugee camp in Senegal and could send documentary evidence to him. On this basis, and citing to *Matter of S-M-J-, supra,* the majority ruled that the corroboration they required was "of the type that would normally be created or available in the particular country and is accessible to the alien." *Id.* at 10.

Board Chair Schmidt and Board Member Rosenberg each filed separate dissents to this decision. Schmidt's dissent reiterated the rule that an applicant can meet his burden of proof through credible testimony alone. Schmidt engaged in an extensive review of the respondent's testimony, finding it to be specific, detailed and consistent, and supported by the "uncontroverted evidence" that:

> [T]hose who control the Mauritanian Government have systematically forced blacks into detention, even slavery, and exile from their own country because of their race.... [D]uring the period of 1989 to 1991, when the respondent claims to have been arrested, imprisoned, and exiled, there were massive human rights abuses committed against African Mauritanians, and that some 70,000 were expelled or fled, hundreds were killed, and hundreds more were tortured and maimed ... [citations omitted]
>
> Thus, we have in this case not just testimony which is believable, consistent and detailed, and which provides a plausible and coherent account of the basis for the respondent's fear. We also have documentary evidence to substantiate that fear.

Id. at 16–18.

Schmidt's dissent also addressed the majority's conclusory finding that documentary corroboration of the respondent's stay in the refugee camp in Senegal would be readily available. Schmidt noted that in June 1996—two years after the respondent's flight from Senegal—the UNHCR entered into an agreement with the Mauritanian government to assist in the issuance of identity and other document to returning Mauritanian refugees, indicating that many of the refugees in the camps were not in possession of such documents. *Id.* at 19.

The majority's decision in *Matter of M-D-* indicates the increasing importance of an adjudicator's finding that corroboration of a specific fact is "readily available." In her separate dissent, Board Member Rosenberg excerpted portions of various UNHCR documents, and appended a letter from Anne Willem Bijleveld, UNHCR Regional Representative in the U.S. which cautioned against an assumption that Mauritanian refugees would be able to corroborate camp residency. In relevant part, the UNHCR letter observed:

> It has come to our attention that the lack of specific documentation from our office in support of asylum claims for Mauritanians has been given undue weight in determining the credibility of such claims. We suggest that other methods for establishing identity and credibility be employed.... [I]t is frequently necessary to give the applicant the benefit of the doubt. It should be borne in mind that it is often difficult or impossible to obtain documentary support of an asylum seekers' claim, especially from countries that have suffered and continue to suffer from periods of turbulence, or from countries that have hosted refugees as a result of such turbulence.

Id. at Appendix A at 43–44.

IV. Implications of the Board's Four Published Decisions

The Board's four published decisions make it more difficult for an asylum seeker to meet his or her burden of proof. Increasingly, the Board appears inclined to require corroboration of specific elements of an applicant's claim. In addition the Board—without acknowledging that it is doing so—appears to be raising the bar as to what constitutes credible testimony. Testimony which is detailed and specific is found lacking because it does not demonstrate *enough* detail or *enough* specificity. In addition, an applicant is expected to comprehensively recount his or her story from the inception, i.e., on the asylum application, because an adverse credibility ruling may arise if testimony is subsequently given as to issues which were not addressed in the original I-589. This may be the case even where the applicant has provided an explanation for the earlier omission.

The strong dissents filed in each of the four decisions demonstrates a fundamental disagreement among the Board Members regarding proper interpretation of the law on the issues of burden of proof and credibility. Attorneys who are challenging adverse credibility findings may wish to make extensive use of the dissents at all levels of advocacy; and it is for this reason that this article went into such an in-depth discussion of the dissenting opinions.

In the meantime, attorneys representing asylum applicants would be well-advised to be even more diligent in the preparation and presentation of their cases. Where corroboration is available, it should be submitted. Where it is not available, information regarding its unavailability should be made of record. The asylum application should provide as comprehensive a recounting of the applicant's claim as possible. The direct examination of the applicant should be prepared with an eye towards eliciting an extensive amount of detail on all relevant aspects of the claim. If the hearing testimony will cover matters which did not appear in the asylum application, an explanation for the earlier omission should be offered. In many cases, the applicant—due to cultural or psychological factors—may simply be unable to recall and provide the level of detail indicated necessary by these Board decisions. If the inability is a consequence of cultural norms, an expert on the applicant's culture—an anthropologist or political scientist—might be called in to explain the cultural factors. If the applicant is impacted by psychological trauma, a psychologist or other mental health expert can be asked to provide a psychological report addressing the effects of the trauma on the applicant.

Note

1. A number of recent federal court decisions have reversed the Board in cases where the applicant has been determined to be not credible.[38]

2. Amendments enacted in 2005 added the following language to 8 U.S.C. § 1158(b)(1)(B), Sec:

> (i) In General—The burden of proof is on the applicant to establish that the applicant is a refugee, within the meaning of section 101(a)(42)(A). To establish that the applicant is a refugee within the meaning of such section,

38. *See, e.g., Campos-Sanchez v. INS*, 162 F.3d 448, 449 (9th Cir. 1999); *Garrovillas v. INS*, 156 F.3d 1010, 1013–14 (9th Cir. 1998).

the applicant must establish that *race, religion, nationality, membership in a particular social group, or political opinion was or will be at least one central reason for persecuting the applicant* (emphasis supplied).

(ii) Sustaining burden—The testimony of the applicant may be sufficient to sustain the applicant's burden without corroboration, but only if the applicant satisfies the trier of fact that the applicant's testimony is credible, is persuasive, and refers to specific facts sufficient to demonstrate that the applicant is a refugee. In determining whether the applicant has met the applicant's burden, the trier of fact may weigh the credible testimony along with other evidence of record. Where the trier of fact determines that the applicant should provide evidence that corroborates otherwise credible testimony, such evidence must be provided unless the applicant does not have the evidence and cannot reasonably obtain the evidence.

(iii) Credibility Determination—Considering the totality of the circumstances, and all relevant factors, a trier of fact may base a credibility determination on the demeanor, candor, or responsiveness of the applicant or witness, the inherent plausibility of the applicant's or witness's account, the consistency between the applicant's or witness's written and oral statements (whenever made and whether or not under oath, and considering the circumstances under which the statements were made), the internal consistency of each such statement, the consistency of such statements with other evidence of record (including the reports of the Department of State on country conditions), and any inaccuracies or falsehoods in such statements, without regard to whether an inconsistency, inaccuracy, or falsehood goes to the heart of the applicant's claim, or any other relevant factor. There is no presumption of credibility, however, if no adverse credibility determination is explicitly made, the applicant or witness shall have a rebuttable presumption of credibility on appeal.

D. Restriction on Removal—Burden of Proof[39]

8 U.S.C. § 1231(b)(3, Sec. 241(b)(3)

(3) Restriction on removal to a country where alien's life or freedom would be threatened.—

(A) In general.—Notwithstanding paragraphs (1) and (2), the Attorney General may not remove an alien to a country if the Attorney General decides

39. As was noted earlier, the benefit termed "restriction on removal" refers to what used to be called "withholding of deportation." The change in terminology was required by replacement replacing what used to be called "exclusion" and "deportation proceedings" with "removal proceedings." Since these changes were made in the 1996 Amendments, the reference to restriction does not appear in this case.

that the alien's life or freedom would be threatened in that country because of the alien's race, religion, nationality, membership in a particular social group, or political opinion.

(B) Exception.—Subparagraph (A) does not apply to an alien deportable under section 237(a)(4)(D) or if the Attorney General decides that—

(i) the alien ordered, incited, assisted, or otherwise participated in the persecution of an individual because of the individual's race, religion, nationality, membership in a particular social group, or political opinion;

(ii) the alien, having been convicted by a final judgment of a particularly serious crime, is a danger to the community of the United States;

(iii) there are serious reasons to believe that the alien committed a serious nonpolitical crime outside the United States before the alien arrived in the United States; or

(iv) there are reasonable grounds to believe that the alien is a danger to the security of the United States.

Immigration and Naturalization Service v. Predrag Stevic

467 U.S. 407 (1984)

Justice Stevens delivered the opinion of the Court.

For over 30 years the Attorney General has possessed statutory authority to withhold the deportation of an alien upon a finding that the alien would be subject to persecution in the country to which he would be deported. The question presented by this case is whether a deportable alien must demonstrate a clear probability of persecution in order to obtain such relief under § 243(h) of the Immigration and Nationality Act of 1952, 8 U.S.C. § 1253(h) (1976 ed.), as amended by § 203(e) of the Refugee Act of 1980, Pub. L. 96-212, 94 Stat. 107.

Respondent, a Yugoslavian citizen, entered the United States in 1976 to visit his sister, then a permanent resident alien residing in Chicago. Petitioner, the Immigration and Naturalization Service (INS), instituted deportation proceedings against respondent when he overstayed his 6-week period of admission. Respondent admitted that he was deportable and agreed to depart voluntarily by February 1977. In January 1977, however, respondent married a United States citizen who obtained approval of a visa petition on his behalf. Shortly thereafter, respondent's wife died in an automobile accident. The approval of respondent's visa petition was automatically revoked, and petitioner ordered respondent to surrender for deportation to Yugoslavia.

Respondent moved to reopen the deportation proceedings in August 1977, seeking relief under § 243(h) of the Immigration and Naturalization Act....

Respondent's supporting affidavit stated that he had become active in an anti-Communist organization after his marriage in early 1977, that his father-in-law had been imprisoned in Yugoslavia because of membership in that organization, and that he feared imprisonment upon his return to Yugoslavia.

In October 1979, the Immigration Judge denied respondent's motion to reopen without conducting an evidentiary hearing. The Board of Immigration Appeals (BIA) upheld that action, explaining:

> A Motion to reopen based on a section 243(h) claim of persecution must contain prima facie evidence that there is a clear probability of persecution to be directed at the individual respondent. See *Cheng Kai Fu v. INS*, 386 F.2d 750 (2 Cir.1967), cert. denied, 390 U.S. 1003 (1968). Although the applicant here claims to be eligible for withholding of deportation which was not available to him at the time of his deportation hearing, he has not presented any evidence which would indicate that he will be singled out for persecution.

Respondent did not seek judicial review of that decision.

After receiving notice to surrender for deportation in February 1981, respondent filed his second motion to reopen. He again sought relief pursuant to § 243(h) which then—because of its amendment in 1980—read as follows:

> The Attorney General shall not deport or return any alien ... to a country if the Attorney General determines that such alien's life or freedom would be threatened in such country on account of race, religion, nationality, membership in a particular social group, or political opinion.

8 U.S.C. § 1253(h)(1).

Although additional written material was submitted in support of the second motion, like the first, it was denied without a hearing. The Board of Immigration Appeals held that respondent had not shown that the additional evidence was unavailable at the time his first motion had been filed and, further, that he had still failed to submit prima facie evidence that "there is a clear probability of persecution" directed at respondent individually. Thus, the Board applied the same standard of proof it had applied regarding respondent's first motion to reopen, notwithstanding the intervening amendment of § 243(h) in 1980.

The United States Court of Appeals for the Second Circuit reversed and remanded for a plenary hearing under a different standard of proof. *Stevic v. Sava*, 678 F.2d 401 (1982). Specifically, it held that respondent no longer had the burden of showing "a clear probability of persecution,"....

Because of the importance of the question presented, and because of the conflict in the Circuits on the question, we granted certiorari, 460 U.S. 1010 (1983). We now reverse and hold that an alien must establish a clear probability of persecution to avoid deportation under § 243(h).

The basic contentions of the parties in this case may be summarized briefly. Petitioner contends that the words "clear probability of persecution" and "well-founded fear of persecution" are not self-explanatory and when read in the light of their usage by courts prior to adoption of the Refugee Act of 1980, it is obvious that there is no "significant" difference between them. If there is a "significant" difference between them, however, petitioner argues that Congress' clear intent in enacting the Refugee Act of 1980 was to maintain the status quo, which petitioner argues would mean continued application of the clear-probability-of-persecution standard to withholding of deportation claims. In this regard, petitioner maintains that our accession to the United Nations Protocol in 1968 was based on the express "understanding" that it would not alter the "substance" of our immigration laws.

Respondent argues that the standards are not coterminous and that the well-founded-fear-of-persecution standard turns almost entirely on the alien's state of mind. Respondent points out that the well-founded-fear language was adopted in the definition of a refugee contained in the United Nations Protocol adhered to by the United States since 1968. Respondent basically contends that ever since 1968, the well-founded-fear standard should have applied to withholding of deportation claims, but Congress simply failed to honor the Protocol by failing to enact implementing legislation until adoption of the Refugee Act of 1980, which contains the Protocol definition of refugee.

Each party is plainly correct in one regard: in 1980 Congress intended to adopt a standard for withholding of deportation claims by reference to pre-existing sources of law. We begin our analysis of this case by examining those sources of law.

United States Refugee Law prior to 1968

Legislation enacted by the Congress in 1950, 1952, and 1965 authorized the Attorney General to withhold deportation of an otherwise deportable alien if the alien would be subject to persecution upon deportation. At least before 1968, it was clear that an alien was required to demonstrate a "clear probability of persecution" or a "likelihood of persecution" in order to be eligible for withholding of deportation under § 243(h) of the Immigration and Nationality Act of 1952, 8 U.S.C. § 1253(h) (1964 ed.). E.g., *Cheng Kai Fu v. INS*, 386 F.2d 750, 753 (CA2 1967), cert. denied, 390 U.S. 1003 (1968). With certain exceptions, this relief was available to any alien who was already "within the United States," albeit unlawfully and subject to deportation.

The relief authorized by § 243(h) was not, however, available to aliens at the border seeking refuge in the United States due to persecution. See generally *Leng May Ma v. Barber*, 357 U.S. 185 (1958). Since 1947, relief to refugees at our borders has taken the form of an "immigration and naturalization policy which granted immigration preferences to 'displaced persons,' 'refugees,' or persons who fled certain areas of the world because of 'persecution or fear of persecution on account of race, religion, or political opinion.' Although the language through which Congress has implemented this policy since 1947 has changed slightly from time to time, the basic policy has remained constant—to provide a haven for homeless refugees and to fulfill American responsibilities in connection with the International Refugee Organization of the United Nations." *Rosenberg v. Yee Chien Woo*, 402 U.S. 49, 52, (1971).

Most significantly, the Attorney General was authorized under § 203(a)(7) of the Immigration and Nationality Act of 1952, 8 U.S.C. § 1153(a)(7)(A)(i) (1976 ed.), to permit "conditional entry" as immigrants for a number of refugees fleeing from a Communist-dominated area or the Middle East "because of persecution or fear of persecution on account of race, religion, or political opinion." See also § 212(d)(5) of the Act, 8 U.S.C. § 1182(d)(5) (granting Attorney General discretion to "parole" aliens into the United States temporarily for emergency reasons). An alien seeking admission under § 203(a)(7) was required to establish a good reason to fear persecution. Compare *In re Tan*, 12 I. & N. Dec. 564, 569–570 (BIA 1967), with *In re Ugricic*, 14 I. & N. Dec. 384, 385–386 (Dist. Dir.1972).[8]

The United Nations Protocol

In 1968 the United States acceded to the United Nations Protocol Relating to the Status of Refugees, Jan. 31, 1967, [1968] 19 U.S.T. 6223, T.I.A.S. No. 6577. The Protocol bound parties to comply with the substantive provisions of Articles 2 through 34 of the United Nations Convention Relating to the Status of Refugees, 189 U.N.T.S. 150 (July 28, 1951) with respect to "refugees" as defined in Article 1.2 of the Protocol.

Two of the substantive provisions of the Convention are germane to the issue before us. Article 33.1 of the Convention provides: "No Contracting State shall expel or return ('refouler') a refugee in any manner whatsoever to the frontiers of territories where his life or freedom would be threatened on account of his race, religion, nationality, membership of a particular social group or political opinion." 19 U.S.T., at 6276. Article 34 provides in pertinent part: "The Contracting States shall as far as possible facilitate the assimilation and naturalization of refugees...." *Ibid.*

The President and the Senate believed that the Protocol was largely consistent with existing law. There are many statements to that effect in the legislative history of the accession to the Protocol. E.g., S.Exec.Rep. No. 14, 90th Cong., 2d Sess., 4 (1968) ("refugees in the United States have long enjoyed the protection and the rights which the protocol calls for"); *id.*, at 6, 7 ("the United States already meets the standards of the Protocol"); see also, *id.*, at 2; S.Exec. K, 90th Cong., 2d Sess., III, VII (1968); 114 Cong.Rec. 29391 (1968) (remarks of Sen. Mansfield); id., at 27757 (remarks of Sen. Proxmire). And it was "absolutely clear" that the Protocol would not "requir[e] the United States to admit new categories or numbers of aliens." S.Exec.Rep. No. 14, *supra*, at 19. It was also believed that apparent differences between the Protocol and existing statutory law could be reconciled by the Attorney General in administration and did not require any modification of statutory language. See, e.g., S.Exec. K, supra, at VIII.

United States Refugee Law: 1968–1980

Five years after the United States' accession to the Protocol, the Board of Immigration Appeals was confronted with the same basic issue confronting us today in

---

8. Notably, during this period of time, neither immigration judges nor the Board of Immigration Appeals had jurisdiction over asylum claims under § 203(a)(7). While the Board had jurisdiction over § 243(h) requests for withholding of deportation, § 203(a)(7) claims for asylum rested in the jurisdiction of Immigration and Naturalization Service District Directors. *See generally In re Lam*, Interim Dec. No. 2857, p. 5, n. 4 (BIA, Mar. 24, 1981).

the case of *In re Dunar*, 14 I. & N. Dec. 310 (1973). The deportee argued that he was entitled to withholding of deportation upon a showing of a well-founded fear of persecution, and essentially maintained that a conjectural possibility of persecution would suffice to make the fear "well founded." The Board rejected that interpretation of "well founded," and stated that a likelihood of persecution was required for the fear to be "well founded." *Id.*, at 319. It observed that neither § 243(h) nor Article 33 used the term "well-founded fear,"....

The Board concluded that "Article 33 has effected no substantial changes in the application of section 243(h), either by way of burden of proof, coverage, or manner of arriving at decisions," *id.*, at 323, and stated that Dunar had failed to establish "the likelihood that he would be persecuted.... Even if we apply the nomenclature of Articles 1 and 33, we are satisfied that respondent has failed to show a well-founded fear that his life or freedom will be threatened," *id.*, at 324.

Although before *In re Dunar*, the Board and the courts had consistently used a clear-probability or likelihood standard under § 243(h), after that case the term "well-founded fear" was employed in some cases. The Court of Appeals for the Seventh Circuit, which had construed § 243(h) as applying only to "cases of clear probability of persecution" in a frequently cited case decided before 1968, *Lena v. INS*, 379 F.2d 536, 538 (1967), reached the same conclusion in a case decided after the United States' adherence to the Protocol. *Kashani v. INS*, 547 F.2d 376 (1977). In that opinion Judge Swygert reasoned that the"well founded fear of persecution" language could "only be satisfied by objective evidence," and that it would "in practice converge" with the "clear probability" standard that the Seventh Circuit had previously "engrafted onto [§] 243(h)." *Id.*, at 379. Other Courts of Appeals appeared to reach essentially the same conclusion. See e.g., *Fleurinor v. INS*, 585 F.2d 129, 132, 134 (CA5 1978); *Pereira-Diaz v. INS*, 551 F.2d 1149, 1154 (CA9 1977); *Zamora v. INS*, 534 F.2d 1055, 1058, 1063 (CA2 1976).

While the Protocol was the source of some controversy with respect to the standard for § 243(h) claims for withholding of deportation, the United States' accession did not appear to raise any questions concerning the standard to be applied for § 203(a)(7) requests for admission. The "good reason to fear persecution" language was employed in such cases. See, e.g., *In re Ugricic*, 14 I. & N. Dec., at 385–386.

Section 203(e) of the Refugee Act of 1980 amended the language of § 243(h), basically conforming it to the language of Article 33 of the United Nations Protocol. The amendment made three changes in the text of § 243(h), but none of these three changes expressly governs the standard of proof an applicant must satisfy or implicitly changes that standard. The amended § 243(h), like Article 33, makes no mention of a probability of persecution or a well-founded fear of persecution. In short, the text of the statute simply does not specify how great a possibility of persecution must exist to qualify the alien for withholding of deportation. To the extent such a standard can be inferred from the bare language of the provision, it appears that a likelihood of persecution is required. The section literally provides for withholding of deportation only if the alien's life or freedom "would" be threatened in the country to which he would be deported; it does not require withholding if the alien "might" or "could" be subject to persecution. Finally, § 243(h), both prior to and after amendment, makes no mention of the term "refugee"; rather, any alien within the United States is entitled to withholding if he meets the standard set forth.

Respondent understandably does not rely upon the specific textual changes in § 243(h) in support of his position that a well-founded fear of persecution entitles him to withholding of deportation. Instead, respondent points to the provision of the Refugee Act which eliminated the ideological and geographical restrictions on admission of refugees under § 203(a)(7) and adopted an expanded version of the United Nations Protocol definition of "refugee." This definition contains the well-founded-fear language and now appears under § 101(a)(42)(A) of the Immigration and Nationality Act, 8 U.S.C. § 1101(a)(42)(A). Other provisions of the Immigration and Nationality Act, as amended, now provide preferential immigration status, within numerical limits, to those qualifying as refugees under the modified Protocol definition and renders a more limited class of refugees, though still a class broader than the Protocol definition, eligible for a discretionary grant of asylum.

Respondent, however, is not seeking discretionary relief under these provisions, which explicitly employ the well-founded-fear standard now appearing in § 101(a)(42)(A). Rather, he claims he is entitled to withholding of deportation under § 243(h) upon establishing a well-founded fear of persecution. Section 243(h), however, does not refer to § 101(a)(42)(A). Hence, there is no textual basis in the statute for concluding that the well-founded-fear-of-persecution standard is relevant to a withholding of deportation claim under § 243(h).

* * *

The principal motivation for the enactment of the Refugee Act of 1980 was a desire to revise and regularize the procedures governing the admission of refugees into the United States. The primary substantive change Congress intended to make under the Refugee Act, and indeed in our view the only substantive change even relevant to this case, was to eliminate the piecemeal approach to admission of refugees previously existing under § 203(a)(7) and § 212(d)(5) of the Immigration and Nationality Act, and § 108 of the regulations, and to establish a systematic scheme for admission and resettlement of refugees. S.Rep. No. 96-256, p. 1 (1979) (S.Rep.); U.S.Code Cong. & Admin. News 1980, p. 141; H.R.Rep. No. 96-608, pp. 1–5 (1979) (H.R.Rep.). The Act adopted, and indeed, expanded upon, the Protocol definition of "refugee," S.Rep., at 19; H.R.Rep., at 9–10, and intended that the definition would be construed consistently with the Protocol, S.Rep., at 9, 20. It was plainly recognized, however, that "merely because an individual or group of refugees comes within the definition will not guarantee resettlement in the United States. The Committee is of the opinion that the new definition does not create a new and expanded means of entry, but instead regularizes and formalizes the policies and practices that have been followed in recent years." H.R.Rep., at 10. The Congress distinguished between discretionary grants of refugee admission or asylum and the entitlement to a withholding of deportation if the § 243(h) standard was met. See *id.*, at 17–18.

Elimination of the geographic and ideological restrictions under the former § 203(a)(7) was thought to bring the United States' scheme into conformity with its obligations under the Protocol, see S.Rep., at 4, 15–16, and in our view these references are to the United States' obligations under Article 34 to facilitate the naturalization of refugees within the definition of the Protocol. There is, as always, some ambiguity in the legislative history—the term "asylum," in particular, seems to be used in various ways, see, e.g., S.Rep., at 9, 16—but that is understandable given that the same problem with nomenclature has been evident in case law as well. See In re Lam, Interim Dec. No. 2857, p. 5 (BIA, Mar. 24, 1981). Going to the substance of the matter, however, it seems clear that Congress understood that refugee status alone did not require withholding of deportation, but rather, the alien had to satisfy the standard under § 243(h), S.Rep., at 16. The amendment of § 243(h) was explicitly recognized to be a mere conforming amendment, added "for the sake of clarity," and was plainly not intended to change the standard. H.R.Rep., at 17–18.

The Court of Appeals' decision rests on the mistaken premise that every alien who qualifies as a "refugee" under the statutory definition is also entitled to a withholding of deportation under § 243(h). We find no support for this conclusion in either the language of § 243(h), the structure of the amended Act, or the legislative history.

We have deliberately avoided any attempt to state the governing standard beyond noting that it requires that an application be supported by evidence establishing that it is more likely than not that the alien would be subject to persecution on one of the specified grounds. This standard is a familiar one to immigration authorities and reviewing courts, and Congress did not intend to alter it in 1980. We observe that shortly after adoption of the Refugee Act, the Board explained: "As we have only quite recently acquired jurisdiction over asylum claims, we are only just now beginning to resolve some of the problems caused by this addition to our jurisdiction, including the problem of determining exactly how withholding of deportation and asylum are to fit together." *In re Lam*, Interim Dec. No. 2857, p. 6, n. 4 (BIA, Mar. 24, 1981). Today we resolve one of those problems by deciding that the "clear probability of persecution" standard remains applicable to § 243(h) withholding of deportation claims. We do not decide the meaning of the phrase "well-founded fear of persecution" which is applicable by the terms of the Act and regulations to requests for discretionary asylum. That issue is not presented by this case.

The Court of Appeals granted respondent relief based on its understanding of a standard which, even if properly understood, does not entitle an alien to withholding of deportation under § 243(h). Our holding does, of course, require the Court of Appeals to reexamine this record to determine whether the evidence submitted by respondent entitles him to a plenary hearing under the proper standard.

The judgment of the Court of Appeals is reversed, and the cause is remanded for further proceedings consistent with this opinion.

1. Restriction on Removal Flow Chart

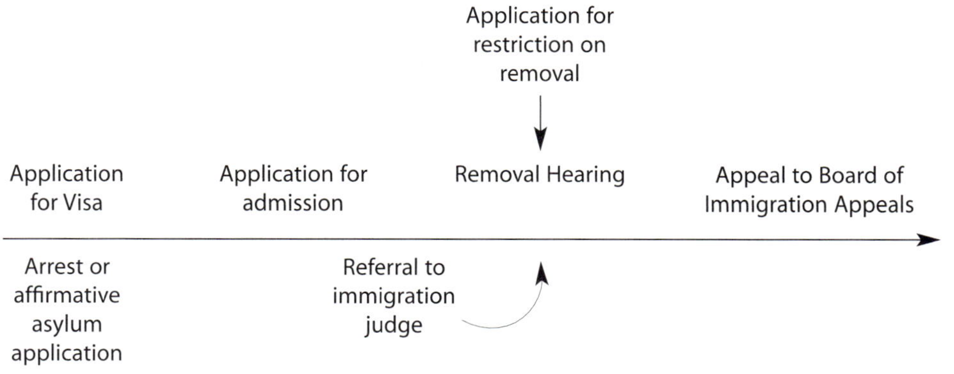

E. Asylum

Immigration and Naturalization Service v. Luz Marina Cardoza-Fonseca

480 U.S. 421 (1987)

Justice BLACKMUN filed a concurring opinion.

Justice SCALIA filed an opinion concurring in judgment.

Justice POWELL filed a dissenting opinion in which Chief Justice REHNQUIST and Justice WHITE joined.

Justice STEVENS delivered the opinion of the Court.

* * *

Respondent is a 38-year-old Nicaraguan citizen who entered the United States in 1979 as a visitor. After she remained in the United States longer than permitted, and failed to take advantage of the Immigration and Naturalization Service's (INS) offer of voluntary departure, the INS commenced deportation proceedings against her. Respondent conceded that she was in the country illegally, but requested withholding of deportation pursuant to § 243(h) and asylum as a refugee pursuant to § 208(a).

To support her request under § 243(h), respondent attempted to show that if she were returned to Nicaragua her "life or freedom would be threatened" on account of her political views; to support her request under § 208(a), she attempted to show that she had a "well-founded fear of persecution" upon her return. The evidence supporting both claims related primarily to the activities of respondent's brother who had been tortured and imprisoned because of his political activities in Nicaragua. Both respondent and her brother testified that they believed the Sandinistas knew that the two of them had fled Nicaragua together and that even though she had not been active politically herself, she would be interrogated about her brother's whereabouts and activities. Respondent also testified that because of her brother's status, her own political opposition to the Sandinistas would be brought to that government's attention. Based on these facts, respondent claimed that she would be tortured if forced to return.

The Immigration Judge applied the same standard in evaluating respondent's claim for withholding of deportation under § 243(h) as he did in evaluating her application for asylum under § 208(a). He found that she had not established "a clear probability of persecution" and therefore was not entitled to either form of relief. App. to Pet. for Cert. 27a. On appeal, the Board of Immigration Appeals (BIA) agreed that respondent had "failed to establish that she would suffer persecution within the meaning of section 208(a) or 243(h) of the Immigration and Nationality Act."

In the Court of Appeals for the Ninth Circuit, respondent did not challenge the BIA's decision that she was not entitled to withholding of deportation under § 243(h), but argued that she was eligible for consideration for asylum under § 208(a), and contended that the Immigration Judge and BIA erred in applying the "more likely than not" standard of proof from § 243(h) to her § 208(a) asylum claim. Instead, she asserted, they should have applied the "well-founded fear" standard, which she considered to be more generous. The court agreed. Relying on both the text and the structure of the Act, the court held that the "well-founded fear" standard which governs asylum proceedings is different, and in fact more generous, than the "clear probability" standard which governs withholding of deportation proceedings. 767 F.2d 1448, 1452–1453 (CA9 1985). Agreeing with the Court of Appeals for the Seventh Circuit, the court interpreted the standard to require asylum applicants to present " 'specific facts' through objective evidence to prove either past persecution or 'good reason' to fear future persecution." *Id.*, at 1453 (citing *Carvajal-Munoz v. INS*, 743 F.2d 562, 574 (CA7 1984)). The court remanded respondent's asylum claim to the BIA to evaluate under the proper legal standard. We granted certiorari to resolve a Circuit conflict on this important question.

Issue: whether the standard requires asylum applicants to . . .

* * *

Under this section, eligibility for asylum depends entirely on the Attorney General's determination that an alien is a "refugee," as that term is defined in § 101(a)(42), which was also added to the Act in 1980. That section provides:

> The term 'refugee' means (A) any person who is outside any country of such person's nationality or, in the case of a person having no nationality, is outside any country in which such person last habitually resided, and who is unable or unwilling to return to, and is unable or unwilling to avail himself or herself of the protection of, that country because of persecution or a well-founded fear of persecution on account of race, religion, nationality, membership in a particular social group, or political opinion.... 94 Stat. 102, 8 U.S.C. 1101(a)(42)....

Thus, the "persecution or well-founded fear of persecution" standard governs the Attorney General's determination whether an alien is eligible for asylum.[5]

---

5. It is important to note that the Attorney General is not required to grant asylum to everyone who meets the definition of refugee. Instead, a finding that an alien is a refugee does no more than

In addition to establishing a statutory asylum process, the 1980 Act amended the withholding of deportation provision, § 243(h). See *Stevic*, 467 U.S., at 421, n. 15. Prior to 1968, the Attorney General had discretion whether to grant withholding of deportation to aliens under § 243(h). In 1968, however, the United States agreed to comply with the substantive provisions of Articles 2 through 34 of the 1951 United Nations Convention Relating to the Status of Refugees. See 19 U.S.T. 6223, 6259–6276, T.I.A.S. No. 6577 (1968); see generally *Stevic, supra*, at 416–417. Article 33.1 of the Convention, 189 U.N.T.S. 150, 176 (1954), reprinted in 19 U.S.T. 6259, 6276, which is the counterpart of § 243(h) of our statute, imposed a mandatory duty on contracting States not to return an alien to a country where his "life or freedom would be threatened" on account of one of the enumerated reasons. See *infra*, at 1217–1218. Thus, although § 243(h) itself did not constrain the Attorney General's discretion after 1968, presumably he honored the dictates of the United Nations Convention. In any event, the 1980 Act removed the Attorney General's discretion in § 243(h) proceedings.

In *Stevic* we considered it significant that in enacting the 1980 Act Congress did not amend the standard of eligibility for relief under § 243(h). While the terms "refugee" and hence "well-founded fear" were made an integral part of the § 208(a) procedure, they continued to play no part in § 243(h). Thus we held that the prior consistent construction of § 243(h) that required an applicant for withholding of deportation to demonstrate a "clear probability of persecution" upon deportation remained in force. Of course, this reasoning, based in large part on the plain language of § 243(h), is of no avail here since § 208(a) expressly provides that the "well-founded fear" standard governs eligibility for asylum.

The Government argues, however, that even though the "well-founded fear" standard is applicable, there is no difference between it and the "would be threatened" test of § 243(h). It asks us to hold that the only way an applicant can demonstrate a "well-founded fear of persecution" is to prove a "clear probability of persecution." The statutory language does not lend itself to this reading.

To begin with, the language Congress used to describe the two standards conveys very different meanings. The "would be threatened" language of § 243(h) has no subjective component, but instead requires the alien to establish by objective evidence that it is more likely than not that he or she will be subject to persecution upon deportation. See Stevic, supra. In contrast, the reference to "fear" in the § 208(a) standard obviously makes the eligibility determination turn to some extent on the subjective mental state of the alien. "The linguistic difference between the words 'well-founded fear' and 'clear probability' may be as striking as that between a subjective and an objective frame of reference.... We simply cannot conclude that the standards are identical." *Guevara-Flores v. INS*, 786 F.2d 1242, 1250 (CA5 1986), cert. pending, No. 86- 388; see also *Carcamo-Flores v. INS*, 805 F.2d 60, 64 (CA2 1986); 767 F.2d, at 1452 (case below).

---

establish that "the alien may be granted asylum *in the discretion of the Attorney General.*" § 208(a) (emphasis added). See *Stevic*, 467 U.S., at 423, n. 18; see also *infra*, at 1218–1220.

That the fear must be "well-founded" does not alter the obvious focus on the individual's subjective beliefs, nor does it transform the standard into a "more likely than not" one. One can certainly have a well-founded fear of an event happening when there is less than a 50% chance of the occurrence taking place. As one leading authority has pointed out:

> "Let us ... presume that it is known that in the applicant's country of origin every tenth adult male person is either put to death or sent to some remote labor camp.... In such a case it would be only too apparent that anyone who has managed to escape from the country in question will have 'well-founded fear of being persecuted' upon his eventual return." 1 A. Grahl-Madsen, The Status of Refugees in International Law 180 (1966).

This ordinary and obvious meaning of the phrase is not to be lightly discounted. See *Russello v. United States*, 464 U.S. 16, 21 (1983); *Ernst & Ernst v. Hochfelder*, 425 U.S. 185, 198–199 (1976). With regard to this very statutory scheme, we have considered ourselves bound to "assume 'that the legislative purpose is expressed by the ordinary meaning of the words used'" *INS v. Phinpathya*, 464 U.S. 183, 189 (1984) (quoting *American Tobacco Co. v. Patterson*, 456 U.S. 63, 68, (1982), in turn quoting *Richards v. United States*, 369 U.S. 1, 9 (1962).

Congress' intent

The different emphasis of the two standards which is so clear on the face of the statute is significantly highlighted by the fact that the same Congress simultaneously drafted § 208(a) and amended § 243(h). In doing so, Congress chose to maintain the old standard in § 243(h), but to incorporate a different standard in § 208(a). "[W]here Congress includes particular language in one section of a statute but omits it in another section of the same Act, it is generally presumed that Congress acts intentionally and purposely in the disparate inclusion or exclusion." *Russello v. United States, supra*, 464 U.S., at 23 (quoting *United States v. Wong Kim Bo*, 472 F.2d 720, 722 (CA5 1972)). The contrast between the language used in the two standards, and the fact that Congress used a new standard to define the term "refugee," certainly indicate that Congress intended the two standards to differ.

The message conveyed by the plain language of the Act is confirmed by an examination of its history.[12] Three aspects of that history are particularly compelling: The pre-1980 experience under § 203(a)(7), the only prior statute dealing with asylum; the abundant evidence of an intent to conform the definition of "refugee" and our asylum law to the United Nation's Protocol to which the United States has been bound since 1968; and the fact that Congress declined to enact the Senate version of the bill

12. As we have explained, the plain language of this statute appears to settle the question before us. Therefore, we look to the legislative history to determine only whether there is "clearly expressed legislative intention" contrary to that language, which would require us to question the strong presumption that Congress expresses its intent through the language it chooses. See *United States v. James*, 478 U.S. 597, 606 (1986).

that would have made a refugee ineligible for asylum unless "his deportation or return would be prohibited by § 243(h)."

* * *

Section § 203(a)(7) of the pre-1980 statute authorized the Attorney General to permit "conditional entry" to a certain number of refugees fleeing from Communist-dominated areas or the Middle East "because of persecution or fear of persecution on account of race, religion, or political opinion." 79 Stat. 913, 8 U.S.C. § 1153(a)(7) (1976 ed.). The standard that was applied to aliens seeking admission pursuant to § 203(a)(7) was unquestionably more lenient than the "clear probability" standard applied in § 243(h) proceedings. *In Matter of Tan*, 12 I. & N. Dec. 564, 569–570 (1967), for example, the BIA "found no support" for the argument that "an alien deportee is required to do no more than meet the standards applied under section 203(a)(7) of the Act when seeking relief under section 243(h)." Similarly, in *Matter of Adamska*, 12 I. & N. Dec. 201, 202 (1967), the Board held that an alien's inability to satisfy § 243(h) was not determinative of her eligibility under the "substantially broader" standards of § 203(a)(7). One of the differences the Board highlighted between the statutes was that § 243(h) requires a showing that the applicant "would be" subject to persecution, while § 203(a)(7) only required a showing that the applicant was unwilling to return "because of *persecution or fear of persecution*." 12 I. & N., at 202 (emphasis in original). In sum, it was repeatedly recognized that the standards were significantly different.

At first glance one might conclude that this wide practice under the old § 203(a)(7), which spoke of "fear of persecution," is not probative of the meaning of the term "well-founded fear of persecution" which Congress adopted in 1980. Analysis of the legislative history, however, demonstrates that Congress added the "well-founded" language only because that was the language incorporated by the United Nations Protocol to which Congress sought to conform. See infra, at 1215–1216. Congress was told that the extant asylum procedure for refugees outside of the United States was acceptable under the Protocol, except for the fact that it made various unacceptable geographic and political distinctions. The legislative history indicates that Congress in no way wished to modify the standard that had been used under § 203(a)(7). Adoption of the INS's argument that the term "well-founded fear" requires a showing of clear probability of persecution would clearly do violence to Congress' intent that the standard for admission under § 207 be no different than the one previously applied under § 203(a)(7).

* * *

If one thing is clear from the legislative history of the new definition of "refugee," and indeed the entire 1980 Act, it is that one of Congress' primary purposes was to bring United States refugee law into conformance with the 1967 United Nations Protocol Relating to the Status of Refugees, 19 U.S.T. 6223, T.I.A.S. No. 6577, to which the United States acceded in 1968.... Not only did Congress adopt the Protocol's standard in the statute, but there were also many statements indicating Congress' intent that the new statutory definition of "refugee" be interpreted in conformance with the Protocol's definition. The Conference Committee Report, for example, stated that the definition was accepted "with the understanding that it is based directly upon the language of the Protocol and it is intended that the provision be construed consistent with the Protocol." S.Rep. No. 96-590, p. 20 (1980). It is thus appropriate to consider what the phrase "well-founded fear" means with relation to the Protocol.

The origin of the Protocol's definition of "refugee" is found in the 1946 Constitution of the International Refugee Organization (IRO). See 62 Stat. 3037. The IRO defined a "refugee" as a person who had a "valid objection" to returning to his country of nationality, and specified that "fear, based on reasonable grounds of persecution because of race, religion, nationality, or political opinions ..." constituted a valid objection. See IRO Constitution, Annex 1, Pt. 1, § C1(a)(i). The term was then incorporated in the United Nations Convention Relating to the Status of Refugees, 189 U.N.T.S. 150 (July 28, 1951). The Committee that drafted the provision explained that "[t]he expression 'well-founded fear of being the victim of persecution ...' means that a person has either been actually a victim of persecution or can show good reason why he fears persecution." U.N.Rep., at 39. The 1967 Protocol incorporated the "well-founded fear" test, without modification. The standard, as it has been consistently understood by those who drafted it, as well as those drafting the documents that adopted it, certainly does not require an alien to show that it is more likely than not that he will be persecuted in order to be classified as a "refugee."

In interpreting the Protocol's definition of "refugee" we are further guided by the analysis set forth in the Office of the United Nations High Commissioner for Refugees, Handbook on Procedures and Criteria for Determining Refugee Status (Geneva, 1979). The Handbook explains that "[i]n general, the applicant's fear should be considered well-founded if he can establish, to a reasonable degree, that his continued stay in his country of origin has become intolerable to him for the reasons stated in the definition, or would for the same reasons be intolerable if he returned there."[22] *Id.*, at Ch. II B(2)(a) § 42; see also *id.*, §§ 37–41.

* * *

Both the House bill, H.R. 2816, 96th Cong., 1st Sess. (1979), and the Senate bill, S. 643, 96th Cong., 1st Sess. (1979), provided that an alien must be a "refugee" within the meaning of the Act in order to be eligible for asylum. The two bills differed, how-

---

22. We do not suggest, of course, that the explanation in the U.N. Handbook has the force of law or in any way binds the INS with reference to the asylum provisions of § 208(a). Indeed, the Handbook itself disclaims such force, explaining that "the determination of refugee status under the 1951 Convention and the 1967 Protocol ... is incumbent upon the Contracting State in whose territory the refugee finds himself." Office of the United Nations High Commissioner for Refugees, Handbook on Procedures and Criteria for Determining Refugee Status 1(ii) (Geneva, 1979).

Nonetheless, the Handbook provides significant guidance in construing the Protocol, to which Congress sought to conform. It has been widely considered useful in giving content to the obligations that the Protocol establishes. *See McMullen v. INS*, 658 F.2d 1312, 1319 (CA9 1981); *Matter of Frentescu*, 18 I. & N. Dec. 244 (BIA 1982); *Matter of Rodriguez-Palma*, 17 I. & N. Dec. 465 (BIA 1980).

ever, in that the House bill authorized the Attorney General, in his discretion, to grant asylum to any refugee, whereas the Senate bill imposed the additional requirement that a refugee could not obtain asylum unless "his deportation or return would be prohibited under section 243(h)." S.Rep., at 26. Although this restriction, if adopted, would have curtailed the Attorney General's discretion to grant asylum to refugees pursuant to § 208(a), it would not have affected the standard used to determine whether an alien is a "refugee." Thus, the inclusion of this prohibition in the Senate bill indicates that the Senate recognized that there is a difference between the "well-founded fear" standard and the clear probability standard. The enactment of the House bill rather than the Senate bill in turn demonstrates that Congress eventually refused to restrict eligibility for asylum only to aliens meeting the stricter standard. "Few principles of statutory construction are more compelling than the proposition that Congress does not intend sub silentio to enact statutory language that it has earlier discarded in favor of other language." *Nachman Corp. v. Pension Benefit Guaranty Corporation*, 446 U.S. 359, 392–393 (1980) (Stewart, J., dissenting).

* * *

The INS makes two major arguments to support its contention that we should reverse the Court of Appeals and hold that an applicant can only show a "well-founded fear of persecution" by proving that it is more likely than not that he or she will be persecuted. We reject both of these arguments: the first ignores the structure of the Act; the second misconstrues the federal courts' role in reviewing an agency's statutory construction.

First, the INS repeatedly argues that the structure of the Act dictates a decision in its favor, since it is anomalous for § 208(a), which affords greater benefits than § 243(h), see n. 6, *supra*, to have a less stringent standard of eligibility. This argument sorely fails because it does not take into account the fact that an alien who satisfies the applicable standard under § 208(a) does not have a right to remain in the United States; he or she is simply eligible for asylum, if the Attorney General, in his discretion, chooses to grant it. An alien satisfying § 243(h)'s stricter standard, in contrast, is automatically entitled to withholding of deportation. In *Matter of Salim*, 18 I. & N. Dec. 311 (1982), for example, the Board held that the alien was eligible for both asylum and withholding of deportation, but granted him the more limited remedy only, exercising its discretion to deny him asylum. See also *Walai v. INS*, 552 F.Supp. 998 (SDNY 1982); *Matter of Shirdel*, Interim Decision No. 2958 (BIA Feb. 21, 1984). We do not consider it at all anomalous that out of the entire class of "refugees," those who can show a clear probability of persecution are entitled to mandatory suspension of deportation and eligible for discretionary asylum, while those who can only show a well-founded fear of persecution are not entitled to anything, but are eligible for the discretionary relief of asylum.

There is no basis for the INS's assertion that the discretionary/mandatory distinction has no practical significance. Decisions such as *Matter of Salim, supra*, and *Matter of Shirdel, supra*, clearly demonstrate the practical import of the distinction. Moreover, the 1980 Act amended § 243(h) for the very purpose of changing it from a discretionary to a mandatory provision. See *supra*, at 1211–1212. Congress surely considered the discretionary/mandatory distinction important then, as it did with respect to the very definition of "refugee" involved here....

This vesting of discretion in the Attorney General is quite typical in the immigration area, see, e.g., *INS v. Jong Ha Wang*, 450 U.S. 139 (1981). If anything is anomalous, it is that the Government now asks us to restrict its discretion to a narrow class of aliens. Congress has assigned to the Attorney General and his delegates the task of making these hard individualized decisions; although Congress could have crafted a narrower definition, it chose to authorize the General to determine which, if any, eligible refugees should be denied asylum.

The INS's second principal argument in support of the proposition that the "well founded fear" and "clear probability" standard are equivalent is that the BIA so construes the two standards. The INS argues that the BIA's construction of the Refugee Act of 1980 is entitled to substantial deference, even if we conclude that the Court of Appeals' reading of the statutes is more in keeping with Congress' intent. This argument is unpersuasive.

* * *

The question whether Congress intended the two standards to be identical is a pure question of statutory construction for the courts to decide. Employing traditional tools of statutory construction, we have concluded that Congress did not intend the two standards to be identical.[30] ...

The BIA has answered the question of the relationship between the objective § 243(h) standard and the fear-based standard of §§ 203(a)(7), 208, and the United Nations Protocol in at least three different ways. During the period between 1965, when § 203(a)(7) was enacted, and 1972, the BIA expressly recognized that § 203(a)(7) and § 243(h) prescribed different standards. See supra, at 1213–1214. Moreover, although the BIA decided in 1973 that the two standards were not irreconcilably different, see *Matter of Dunar*, 14 I. & N. Dec. 310 (1973), as of 1981 the INS was still instructing its officials to apply a "good reason" test to requests for asylum from aliens not within the United States. See Dept. of Justice, INS Operating Instructions Regulations TM 101, § 208.4, p. 766.9 (Nov. 11, 1981) (explaining that "well-founded fear" is satisfied if applicant "can show good reason why he/she fears persecution"). In 1984, when this case was decided by the BIA, it adhered to the view that the INS now espouses—complete identity of the standards. In 1985, however, the BIA decided to reevaluate its position and issued a comprehensive opinion to explain its latest understanding of the "well-founded fear" standard. *Matter of*

30. An additional reason for rejecting INS's request for heightened deference to its position is the inconsistency of the positions the BIA has taken through the years. An agency interpretation of a relevant provision which conflicts with the agency's earlier interpretation is "entitled to considerably less deference" than a consistently held agency view. *Watt v. Alaska*, 451 U.S. 259, 271 (1981).

Acosta, Interim Decision No. 2986 (Mar. 1, 1985). In *Acosta*, the BIA noted a number of similarities between the two standards and concluded that in practical application they are "comparable" or "essentially comparable," and that the differences between them are not "meaningful," but the agency never stated that they are identical, equivalent, or interchangeable. On the contrary, the *Acosta* opinion itself establishes that the two standards differ. In describing the objective component of the asylum standard, the BIA concluded that the alien is not required to establish the likelihood of persecution to any "particular degree of certainty." *Id.*, at 22. There must be a "real chance" that the alien will become a victim of persecution, *ibid.*, but it is not necessary to show "that persecution 'is more likely than not' to occur." *Id.*, at 25. The *Acosta* opinion was written after we had decided in *Stevic* that the § 243(h) standard "requires that an application be supported by evidence establishing that it is more likely than not that the alien would be subject to persecution," 467 U.S., at 429–430. The decision in *Acosta* and the long pattern of erratic treatment of this issue make it apparent that the BIA has not consistently agreed, and even today does not completely agree, with the INS's litigation position that the two standards are equivalent.

> "The judiciary is the final authority on issues of statutory construction and must reject administrative constructions which are contrary to clear congressional intent. [Citing cases.] If a court, employing traditional tools of statutory construction, ascertains that Congress had an intention on the precise question at issue, that intention is the law and must be given effect." *Id.*, at 843, n. 9, 104 S.Ct., at 2782, n. 9 (citations omitted).

* * *

Our analysis of the plain language of the Act, its symmetry with the United Nations Protocol, and its legislative history, lead inexorably to the conclusion that to show a "well-founded fear of persecution," an alien need not prove that it is more likely than not that he or she will be persecuted in his or her home country. We find these ordinary canons of statutory construction compelling, even without regard to the longstanding principle of construing any lingering ambiguities in deportation statutes in favor of the alien.

Deportation is always a harsh measure; it is all the more replete with danger when the alien makes a claim that he or she will be subject to death or persecution if forced to return to his or her home country. In enacting the Refugee Act of 1980 Congress sought to "give the United States sufficient flexibility to respond to situations involving political or religious dissidents and detainees throughout the world." H.R.Rep., at 9. Our holding today increases that flexibility by rejecting the Government's contention that the Attorney General may not even consider granting asylum to one who fails to satisfy the strict § 243(h) standard. Whether or not a "refugee" is eventually granted asylum is a matter which Congress has left for the Attorney General to decide. But it is clear that Congress did not intend to restrict eligibility for that relief to those who could prove that it is more likely than not that they will be persecuted if deported.

The judgment of the Court of Appeals is Affirmed.

Justice BLACKMUN, concurring.

I join the Court's opinion and judgment. Thus, I accept its "narrow" conclusion that "the Immigration Judge and the BIA were incorrect in holding that the [standards for withholding of deportation and granting asylum] are identical." *Ante*, at 1222. In accordance with this holding, the Court eschews any attempt to give substance to the term "well-founded fear" and leaves that task to the "process of case-by-case adjudication" by the INS, the agency in charge of administering the immigration laws. Ante, at 1221. I write separately and briefly to emphasize my understanding that, in its opinion, the Court has directed the INS to the appropriate sources from which the agency should derive the meaning of the "well-founded fear" standard, a meaning that will be refined in later adjudication. This emphasis, I believe, is particularly needed where, as here, an agency's previous interpretation of the statutory term is so strikingly contrary to plain language and legislative history.

Thus, as the Court observes, *ante*, at 1212–1213, the very language of the term "well-founded fear" demands a particular type of analysis—an examination of the subjective feelings of an applicant for asylum coupled with an inquiry into the objective nature of the articulated reasons for the fear. Moreover, in describing how, in the 1980 Act, Congress was attempting to bring this country's refugee laws into conformity with the United Nations Protocol, the Court notes that the Act's definition of refugee, wherein the "well-founded fear" term appears, *ante*, at 1211, tracks the language of the Protocol. See *ante*, at 1216. Such language has a rich history of interpretation in international law and scholarly commentaries. See *ante*, at 1216–1218, and nn. 20, 24. While the INS need not ignore other sources of guidance, the above directions by the Court should be significant in the agency's formulation of the "well-founded fear" standard.

Finally, in my view, the well-reasoned opinions of the Courts of Appeals, that almost uniformly have rejected the INS's misreading of statutory language and legislative history, provide an admirable example of the very "case-by-case adjudication" needed for the development of the standard. Although the Court refers to a conflict among these courts, see *ante*, at 1210, n. 2, with one exception, see ibid., all the Courts of Appeals that have addressed this question have concluded that the standards for withholding of deportation and granting asylum are not the same. Rather, differences in opinion have arisen as to the precise formulation of the "well-founded fear" standard. Such differences can arise only when courts or agencies seriously grapple with the problems of developing a standard, whose form is at first given by the statutory language and the intimations of the legislative history, but whose final contours are shaped by the application of the standard to the facts of specific cases. The efforts of these courts stand in stark contrast to—but, it is sad to say, alone cannot make up for—the years of seemingly purposeful blindness by the INS, which only now begins its task of developing the standard entrusted to its care.

Justice SCALIA, concurring in the judgment.

I agree with the Court that the plain meaning of "well-founded fear" and the structure of the Immigration and Nationality Act (Act) clearly demonstrate that the "well-founded fear" standard and the "clear probability" standard are not equivalent. I concur in the judgment rather than join the Court's opinion, however, for two reasons. First, despite having reached the above conclusion, the Court undertakes an exhaustive investigation of the legislative history of the Act. *Ante*, at 1213–1219. It attempts to justify this inquiry by relying upon the doctrine that if the legislative history of an enactment reveals a " 'clearly expressed legislative intention' contrary to [the enactment's] language," the Court is required to "question the strong presumption that Congress expresses its intent through the language it chooses." *Ante*, at 1213, n. 12. Although it is true that the Court in recent times has expressed approval of this doctrine, that is to my mind an ill-advised deviation from the venerable principle that if the language of a statute is clear, that language must be given effect—at least in the absence of a patent absurdity. Judges interpret laws rather than reconstruct legislators' intentions. Where the language of those laws is clear, we are not free to replace it with an unenacted legislative intent.

Even by its own lights, however, the Court's explication of the legislative history of the Act is excessive. The INS makes a number of specific arguments based upon the legislative history of the Act. It would have sufficed, it seems to me, for the Court to determine whether these specific arguments establish a "clearly expressed legislative intent" that the two standards be equivalent. I think it obvious that they do not, as apparently does the Court. That being so, there is simply no need for the lengthy effort to ascertain the import of the entire legislative history. And that effort is objectionable not only because it is gratuitous. I am concerned that it will be interpreted to suggest that similarly exhaustive analyses are generally appropriate (or, worse yet, required) in cases where the language of the enactment at issue is clear. I also fear that in this case the Court's conduct of that inquiry will be interpreted as a betrayal of its assurance that it does "not attempt to set forth a detailed description of how the well-founded fear test should be applied," *ante*, at 1222. See, e.g., *ante*, at 1217–1218 (appearing to endorse a particular interpretation of "well-founded fear").

Justice POWELL, with whom The CHIEF JUSTICE and Justice WHITE join, dissenting.

* * *

The Court's opinion seems to assume that the BIA has adopted a rigorous mathematical approach to asylum cases, requiring aliens to demonstrate an objectively quantifiable risk of persecution in their homeland that is more than 50%. The Court then argues that such a position is inconsistent with the language and history of the Act. But this has never been the BIA's position. Thus, it is useful to examine the BIA's approach in some detail before evaluating the Court's rejection of the BIA's approach. After all, the BIA is the tribunal with the primary responsibility for applying the Act and the greatest experience in doing so.

... Under the BIA's analysis, an immigration judge evaluating an asylum application should begin by determining the underlying historical facts. The burden of persuasion rests on the applicant, who must establish the truth of these facts by a preponderance of the evidence. See *id.*, at 7 (citing, inter alia, 1A C. Gordon & H. Rosenfield, Immigration Law and Procedure § 5.10b, p. 5–121 (rev. ed. 1986)).

* * *

[T]he requirement that the fear be "well-founded" rules out an apprehension which is purely subjective.... Some sort of showing must be made and this can ordinarily be done only by objective evidence. The claimant's own testimony as to the facts will sometimes be all that is available; *but the crucial question is whether the testimony, if accepted as true, makes out a realistic likelihood that he will be persecuted. Acosta, supra*, at 18–19 (quoting *Dunar, supra*, at 319) (emphasis added by Acosta Board). The Acosta Board went on to caution:

> "By use of such words [as 'realistic likelihood'] we do not mean that 'a well-founded fear of persecution' requires an alien to establish to a particular degree of certainty, such as a 'probability' as opposed to a 'possibility,' that he will become a victim of persecution. Rather as a practical matter, what we mean can best be described as follows: the evidence must demonstrate that (1) the alien possesses a belief or characteristic a persecutor seeks to overcome in others by means of punishment of some sort; (2) the persecutor is already aware, or could easily become aware, that the alien possesses this belief or characteristic; (3) the persecutor has the capability of punishing the alien; and (4) the persecutor has the inclination to punish the alien." *Acosta, supra*, at 22.

One might conclude that "a well-founded fear of persecution," which requires a showing that persecution is likely to occur, refers to a standard that is different from "a clear probability of persecution," which requires a showing that persecution is 'more likely than not' to occur. As a practical matter, however, the facts in asylum and withholding cases do not produce clear-cut instances in which such fine distinctions can be meaningfully made. Our inquiry in these cases, after all, is not quantitative, i.e., we do not examine a variety of statistics to discern to some theoretical degree the likelihood of persecution. Rather our inquiry is qualitative: we examine the alien's experiences and other external events to determine if they are of a kind that enable us to conclude the alien is likely to become the victim of persecution. In this context, we find no meaningful distinction between a standard requiring a showing that persecution is likely to occur and a standard requiring a showing that persecution is more likely than not to occur.... Accordingly, we conclude that the standards for asylum and withholding of deportation are not meaningfully different and, in practical application, converge. *Id.*, at 25.

In sum, contrary to the Court's apparent conclusion, the BIA does not contend that both the "well-founded fear" standard and the "clear probability" standard require proof of a 51% chance that the alien will suffer persecution if he is returned to his homeland. The BIA plainly eschews analysis resting on mathematical probabilities. Rather, the BIA has adopted a four-part test requiring proof of facts that demonstrate a realistic likelihood of persecution actually occurring. The heart of the *Acosta* decision is the BIA's empirical conclusion, based on its experience in adjudicating asylum applications, that if the facts establish such a basis for an alien's fear, it rarely will make a difference whether the judge asks if persecution is "likely" to occur or "more likely than not" to occur. If the alien can establish such a basis, he normally will be eligible for relief under either standard.

* * *

... The critical question presented by this case is whether the objective basis required for a fear of persecution to be "well-founded" differs in practice from the objective basis required for there to be a "clear probability" of persecution. Because both standards necessarily contemplate some objective basis, I cannot agree with the Court's implicit conclusion that the statute resolves this question on its face. In my view, the character of evidence sufficient to meet these two standards is a question best answered by an entity familiar with the types of evidence and issues that arise in such cases. Congress limited eligibility for asylum to those persons whom "the Attorney General determines" to be refugees. See § 208(a), 8 U.S.C. § 1158(a). The Attorney General has delegated the responsibility for making these determinations to the BIA. That Board has examined more of these cases than any court ever has or ever can. It has made a considered judgment that the difference between the "well-founded" and the "clear probability" standards is of no practical import: that is, the evidence presented in asylum and withholding of deportation cases rarely, if ever, will meet one of these standards without meeting both. This is just the type of expert judgment—formed by the entity to whom Congress has committed the question—to which we should defer.

* * *

Common sense and human experience support the BIA's conclusion. Governments rarely persecute people by the numbers. It is highly unlikely that the evidence presented at an asylum or withholding of deportation hearing will demonstrate the mathematically specific risk of persecution posited by the Court's hypothetical. Taking account of the types of evidence normally available in asylum cases, the BIA has chosen to make a qualitative evaluation of "realistic likelihoods." As I read the *Acosta* opinion, an individual who fled his country to avoid mass executions might be eligible for both withholding of deportation and asylum, whether or not he presented evidence of the numerical reach of the persecution. See Acosta, Interim Decision No. 2986, at 18–25. Nowhere does the Court consider whether the BIA's four-element interpretation of "well-founded" is unreasonable. Nor does the Court consider the BIA's view of the types of evidentiary presentations aliens generally make in asylum cases.

In sum, the words Congress has chosen—"well-founded" fear—are ambiguous. They contemplate some objective basis without specifying a particular evidentiary threshold. There is no reason to suppose this formulation is inconsistent with the analysis set forth in Acosta. The BIA has concluded that a fear is not "well-founded" unless the fear has an objective basis indicating that there is a "realistic likelihood" that persecution would occur. Based on the text of the Act alone, I cannot conclude that this conclusion is unreasonable.

The Court bolsters its interpretation of the language of the Act by reference to three parts of the legislative history. A closer examination of these materials demonstrates that each of them is ambiguous. Nothing the Court relies on provides a positive basis for arguing that there is a material difference between the two standards.

* * *

In my view, the legislative history indicates that Congress' choice of the words "well-founded" fear as the standard of eligibility for asylum was intended to carry forward the practice of the Attorney General in adjudicating asylum applications. The Attorney General had concluded that the standard for asylum was substantially identical to the standard for withholding of deportation. His decision to interpret the language of § 208 in the same way is entirely reasonable.

* * *

Even if I agreed with the Court's conclusion that there is a significant difference between the standards for asylum and withholding of deportation, I would reverse the decision of the Court of Appeals and uphold the decision of the BIA in this case. A careful reading of the decisions of the BIA and the Immigration Judge demonstrates that the BIA applied the lower asylum standard to this case.

Respondent's claim for asylum rested solely on testimony that her brother had experienced difficulties with the authorities in Nicaragua. The Immigration Judge rejected respondent's claim because he found "no evidence of any substance in the record other than her brother's claim to asylum."

* * *

I would reverse the decision of the Court of Appeals.

Notes

1. In deciding *Cardoza-Fonseca,* the Court noted that "[t]here is obviously some ambiguity in a term like 'well-founded fear' which can only be given concrete meaning through a process of case-by-case adjudication."[40] Following the Court's decision, the BIA elaborated on the well-founded fear standard, noting that the requirements were satisfied where "a reasonable person in his circumstances would fear persecution."[41] This position taken by the Board is in harmony with decisions in a number of circuits.[42] While *Mogharrabi* is good law today, the BIA acknowledged in its decision that it was merely a starting point in its "effort to formulate a workable and useful definition" of the standard.[43]

---

40. *Cardoza-Fonseca,* 480 U.S. 421, 448 (1987).

41. *See Matter of Mogharrabi,* 19 I. & N. Dec. 439, 445 (BIA 1987).

42. *See Guevara-Flores v. INS,* 786 F.2d 1242, 1249 (5th Cir. 1986), *cert. denied,* 480 U.S. 930 (1987); *Carcamo-Flores v. INS,* 805 F.2d 60 (2d Cir. 1986); *Ipina v. INS,* 868 F.2d 511, 514 (9th Cir. 1989).

43. *Matter of Mogharrabi,* 19 I. & N. Dec. 439, 442 (BIA 1987).

2. A basic principle of administrative law and a matter which should be considered is that courts will defer to an agency's interpretation where the statute is ambiguous, because the agency is seen as formulating policy or filling in the gaps left by Congress in the legislation.[44] In cases where the statute or congressional intent is clear, the agency interpretation will not be followed if it conflicts with the statute. However, if the statute is not clear, the courts will determine if the agency's interpretation is a "permissible construction of the statute."[45]

3. **Discretionary nature of asylum.** The asylum determination is discretionary, which means that a person who has established a well-founded fear can be denied relief if the negative equities of her case outweigh the positive ones. In *Matter of Pula,* Interim Dec. 3044 (BIA 1987), the Board modified a position it had taken in an earlier case, *Matter of Salim,* 18 I. & N. Dec. 311 (BIA 1982), where it had denied asylum to an individual who had entered the United States with fraudulent documents, thereby evading the normal refugee admission procedures. In *Pula,* the Board held that an applicant's manner of entry or attempted entry is a proper and relevant discretionary factor to consider but that it should not automatically result in a denial of relief. It noted that the exercise of discretion requires a balancing of all of the countervailing equities.[46]

4. **Credible fear and expedited removal.** Although unrelated to the issue of discretion, the expedited removal procedures impose requirements on asylum seekers who are not in possession of legitimate travel documents. They must establish a credible fear of persecution in order to be permitted to apply for asylum. What is a "credible fear," and how is it different from a well-founded fear of persecution? The answer to this question cannot be obtained from the usual sources, such as reviewing a body of cases interpreting the statute, for the statute does not provide for administrative or judicial review of these determinations in published cases. The only basis for determining the definition of credible fear is the statute and regulations promulgated under Title 8 of the Code of Federal Regulations. The statute defines credible fear as "*a significant possibility,* taking into account the credibility of the statements made by the alien in support of the alien's claim and such other facts as are known to the officer, that the alien *could establish eligibility for asylum* under section 208."[47] While the regulations repeat the language contained in the statute, it also notes that an additional factor to be considered is whether "the case presents novel or unique issues that merit consideration in a full hearing before an immigration judge."[48] By this

---

44. *Morton v. Ruiz,* 415 U.S. 199 (1974).

45. *See Chevron U.S.A. Inc. v. Natural Resources Defense Council, Inc.,* 467 U.S. 837 (1984). For excellent discussions of the issues raised by *Morton* and *Chevron,* see Anthony, *Which Agency Interpretations Should Bind Citizens and the Courts,* 7 Yale J. Reg. 1 (1990); Stephen Breyer, *Judicial Review of Questions of Law,* 38 Admin. L. Rev. 363 (1986).

46. For an interesting discussion of discretion in the adjudication of asylum claims, see Anker, *Discretionary Asylum: A Protection Remedy for Refugees Under the Refugee Act of 1980,* 28 Va. J. Int'l Law 1 (1987); Arthur Helton, *The Proper Role of Discretion in Political Asylum,* 22 San Diego L. Rev. 999 (1985).

47. *See* 8 U.S.C. § 1225(b)(1)(B)(v), Sec. 235(b)(1)(B)(v) (emphasis supplied).

48. 8 C.F.R. § 208.30(e)(2) and (4). Regulations guiding the immigration judge's determination refer back to the USCIS rules. 8 C.F.R. § 1208.30(e).

definition, credible fear requires an assessment by either the asylum officer or the immigration judge that the applicant has a significant possibility of success on the claim. It is also important to note that the credible fear interview may take place within 48 hours of the person's arrival in the United States when she may not have obtained a representative. Some commentators criticize the process, saying that it disadvantages asylum seekers who may be fearful or traumatized upon arrival.

F. The Scope of Protection: Where Does the Statute Apply?

Chris Sale, Acting Comm'r, INS, et al. v. Haitian Centers Council, Inc., et al.

509 U.S. 918 (1993)

Justice STEVENS, delivered the opinion of the Court, in which Chief Justice REHNQUIST, and Justices WHITE, O'CONNOR, SCALIA, KENNEDY, SOUTER, and THOMAS, joined. Justice BLACKMUN, filed a dissenting opinion.

The President has directed the Coast Guard to intercept vessels illegally transporting passengers from Haiti to the United States and to return those passengers to Haiti without first determining whether they may qualify as refugees. The question presented in this case is whether such forced repatriation, "authorized to be undertaken only beyond the territorial sea of the United States," violates § 243(h)(1) of the Immigration and Nationality Act of 1952 (INA or Act). We hold that neither § 243(h) nor Article 33 of the United Nations Protocol Relating to the Status of Refugees applies to action taken by the Coast Guard on the high seas.

* * *

On September 23, 1981, the United States and the Republic of Haiti entered into an agreement authorizing the United States Coast Guard to intercept vessels engaged in the illegal transportation of undocumented aliens to our shores. While the parties agreed to prosecute "illegal traffickers," the Haitian Government also guaranteed that its repatriated citizens would not be punished for their illegal departure.[1] The agreement also established that the United States Government would not return any passengers "whom the United States authorities determine[d] to qualify for refugee status." On September 29, 1981, President Reagan issued a proclamation in which he characterized "the continuing illegal migration by sea of large numbers of undoc-

---

1. As a part of that agreement, "the Secretary of State obtained an assurance from the Haitian government that interdicted Haitians would "not be subject to prosecution for illegal departure." *See* Agreement on Migrant(s)-Interdiction, Sept. 23, 1981, United States-Haiti, 33 U.S.T. 3559, 3560, T.I.A.S. No. 10241."

umented aliens into the southeastern United States" as "a serious national problem detrimental to the interests of the United States." Presidential Proclamation No. 4865, 3 C.F.R. 50–51 (1981–1983 Comp.). He therefore suspended the entry of undocumented aliens from the high seas and ordered the Coast Guard to intercept vessels carrying such aliens and to return them to their point of origin. His executive order expressly "provided, however, that no person who is a refugee will be returned without his consent." Executive Order 12324, 3 C.F.R. § 2(c)(3), (1981–1983 Comp.).[2]

In the ensuing decade, the Coast Guard interdicted approximately 25,000 Haitian migrants. After interviews conducted on board Coast Guard cutters, aliens who were identified as economic migrants were "screened out" and promptly repatriated. Those who made a credible showing of political refugee status were "screened in" and transported to the United States to file formal applications for asylum.

On September 30, 1991, a group of military leaders displaced the government of Jean Bertrand Aristide, the first democratically elected president in Haitian history. As the District Court stated in an uncontested finding of fact, since the military coup "hundreds of Haitians have been killed, tortured, detained without a warrant, or subjected to violence and the destruction of their property because of their political beliefs. Thousands have been forced into hiding." Following the coup the Coast Guard suspended repatriations for a period of several weeks, and the United States imposed economic sanctions on Haiti.

On November 18, 1991, the Coast Guard announced that it would resume the program of interdiction and forced repatriation. The following day, the Haitian Refugee Center, Inc., representing a class of interdicted Haitians, filed a complaint in the United States District Court for the Southern District of Florida alleging that the Government had failed to establish and implement adequate procedures to protect Haitians who qualified for asylum. The District Court granted temporary relief that precluded any repatriations until February 4, 1992, when a reversal on appeal in the Court of Appeals for the Eleventh Circuit and a denial of certiorari by this Court effectively terminated that litigation. See *Haitian Refugee Center, Inc. v. Baker*, 949 F. 2d 1109 (1991) (per curiam), cert. denied, 502 U.S. (1992).

In the meantime the Haitian exodus expanded dramatically. During the six months after October 1991, the Coast Guard interdicted over 34,000 Haitians. Because so many interdicted Haitians could not be safely processed on Coast Guard cutters, the Department of Defense established temporary facilities at the United States Naval Base in Guantanamo, Cuba, to accommodate them during the screening process. Those temporary facilities, however, had a capacity of only about 12,500 persons. In the first three weeks of May 1992, the Coast Guard intercepted 127 vessels (many of which were considered unseaworthy, overcrowded, and unsafe); those vessels

---

2. That proviso reflected an opinion of the Office of Legal Counsel that Article 33 of the United Nations Convention Relating to the Status of Refugees imposed some procedural obligations on the United States with respect to refugees outside United States territory. That opinion was later withdrawn after consideration was given to the contrary views expressed by the legal advisor to the State Department.

carried 10,497 undocumented aliens. On May 22, 1992, the United States Navy determined that no additional migrants could safely be accommodated at Guantanamo.

With both the facilities at Guantanamo and available Coast Guard cutters saturated, and with the number of Haitian emigrants in unseaworthy craft increasing (many had drowned as they attempted the trip to Florida), the Government could no longer both protect our borders and offer the Haitians even a modified screening process. It had to choose between allowing Haitians into the United States for the screening process or repatriating them without giving them any opportunity to establish their qualifications as refugees. In the judgment of the President's advisors, the first choice not only would have defeated the original purpose of the program (controlling illegal immigration), but also would have impeded diplomatic efforts to restore democratic government in Haiti and would have posed a life-threatening danger to thousands of persons embarking on long voyages in dangerous craft. The second choice would have advanced those policies but deprived the fleeing Haitians of any screening process at a time when a significant minority of them were being screened in.

On May 23, 1992, President Bush adopted the second choice. After assuming office, President Clinton decided not to modify that order; it remains in effect today. The wisdom of the policy choices made by Presidents Reagan, Bush, and Clinton is not a matter for our consideration. We must decide only whether Executive Order No. 12807, 57 Fed. Reg. 23133 (1992), which reflects and implements those choices, is consistent with § 243(h) of the INA.

* * *

Both parties argue that the plain language of § 243(h)(1) is dispositive. It reads as follows:

> "The Attorney General shall not deport or return any alien (other than an alien described in section 1251(a)(4)(D) of this title) to a country if the Attorney General determines that such alien's life or freedom would be threatened in such country on account of race, religion, nationality, membership in a particular social group, or political opinion." 8 U.S.C. § 1253(h)(1) (1988 ed., Supp. IV).

* * *

Although § 243(h)(1) refers only to the Attorney General, the Court of Appeals found it "difficult to believe that the proscription of § 243(h)(1)—returning an alien to his persecutors—was forbidden if done by the attorney general but permitted if done by some other arm of the executive branch." Congress "understood" that the Attorney General is the "President's agent for dealing with immigration matters," and would intend any reference to her to restrict similar actions of any government official. As evidence of this understanding, the court cited 8 U.S.C. 1103(a). That section, however, conveys to us a different message. It provides, in part:

> "The Attorney General shall be charged with the administration and enforcement of this chapter and all other laws relating to the immigration and nat-

uralization of aliens, *except insofar as this chapter or such laws relate to the powers, functions, and duties conferred upon the President, the Secretary of State, the officers of the Department of State, or diplomatic or consular officers....*" (emphasis added).

Other provisions of the Act expressly confer certain responsibilities on the Secretary of State,[3] the President,[4] and, indeed, on certain other officers as well.[5] The 1981 and 1992 Executive Orders expressly relied on statutory provisions that confer authority on the President to suspend the entry of "any class of aliens" or to "impose on the entry of aliens any restrictions he may deem to be appropriate."[6] We cannot say that the interdiction program created by the President, which the Coast Guard was ordered to enforce, usurped authority that Congress had delegated to, or implicated responsibilities that it had imposed on, the Attorney General alone.The reference to the Attorney General in the statutory text is significant not only because that term cannot reasonably be construed to describe either the President or the Coast Guard, but also because it suggests that it applies only to the Attorney General's normal responsibilities under the INA. The most relevant of those responsibilities for our purposes are her conduct of the deportation and exclusion hearings in which requests for asylum or for withholding of deportation under § 243(h) are ordinarily advanced. Since there is no provision in the statute for the conduct of such proceedings outside the United States, and since Part V and other provisions of the INA obviously contemplate that such proceedings would be held in the country, we cannot reasonably construe § 243(h) to limit the Attorney General's actions in geographic areas where she has not been authorized to conduct such proceedings. Part V of the INA contains no reference to a possible extraterritorial application.

Even if Part V of the Act were not limited to strictly domestic procedures, the presumption that Acts of Congress do not ordinarily apply outside our borders would support an interpretation of § 243(h) as applying only within United States territory. See, e.g., *EEOC v. Arabian American Oil Co.*, 499 U.S. (1991). The Court of Appeals held that the presumption against extraterritoriality had "no relevance in the present context" because there was no risk that § 243(h), which can be enforced only in United States courts against the United States Attorney General, would conflict with the laws of other nations. We have recently held, however, that the presumption has a foundation broader than the desire to avoid conflict with the laws of other nations.

---

3. *See* 8 U.S.C. §§ 1104, 1105, 1153, 1201, and 1202 (1988 ed. and Supp. IV).

4. *See* 8 U.S.C. §§ 1157(a), (b), and (d); § 1182(f); §§ 1185(a) and (b); and § 1324a(d) (1988 ed. and Supp. IV).

5. *See* §§ 1161(a), (b), and (c) (Secretaries of Agriculture and Labor); § 1188 (Secretary of Labor); § 1421 (federal courts).

6. 8 U.S.C. § 1182(f) provides:

> "Whenever the President finds that the entry of any aliens or of any class of aliens into the United States would be detrimental to the interests of the United States, he may by proclamation, and for such period as he shall deem necessary, suspend the entry of all aliens or any class of aliens as immigrant or nonimmigrants, or impose on the entry of aliens any restrictions he may deem to be appropriate."

Respondents' expansive interpretation of the word "return" raises another problem: it would make the word "deport" redundant. If "return" referred solely to the destination to which the alien is to be removed, it alone would have been sufficient to encompass aliens involved in both deportation and exclusion proceedings. And if Congress had meant to refer to all aliens who might be sent back to potential oppressors, regardless of their location, the word "deport" would have been unnecessary. By using both words, the statute implies an exclusively territorial application, in the context of both kinds of domestic immigration proceedings. The use of both words reflects the traditional division between the two kinds of aliens and the two kinds of hearings. We can reasonably conclude that Congress used the two words "deport or return" only to make § 243(h)'s protection available in both deportation and exclusion proceedings. Indeed, the history of the 1980 amendment confirms that conclusion.

As enacted in 1952, § 243(h) authorized the Attorney General to withhold deportation of aliens "within the United States." Six years later we considered the question whether it applied to an alien who had been paroled into the country while her admissibility was being determined. We held that even though she was physically present within our borders, she was not "within the United States" as those words were used in § 243(h). *Leng May Ma v. Barber*, 357 U.S. 185, 186 (1958).... Under the INA, both then and now, those seeking "admission" and trying to avoid "exclusion" were already within our territory (or at its border), but the law treated them as though they had never entered the United States at all; they were within United States territory but not "within the United States." Those who had been admitted (or found their way in) but sought to avoid "expulsion" had the added benefit of "deportation proceedings"; they were both within United States territory *and* "within the United States." *Ibid.* Although the phrase "within the United States" presumed the alien's actual presence in the United States, it had more to do with an alien's legal status than with his location.

The 1980 amendment erased the long-maintained distinction between deportable and excludable aliens for purposes of § 243(h). By adding the word "return" and removing the words "within the United States" from § 243(h), Congress extended the statute's protection to both types of aliens, but it did nothing to change the presumption that both types of aliens would continue to be found only within United States territory. The removal of the phrase "within the United States" cured the most obvious drawback of § 243(h): as interpreted in *Leng May Ma*, its protection was available only to aliens subject to deportation proceedings.

Of course, in addition to this most obvious purpose, it is possible that the 1980 amendment *also* removed any territorial limitation of the statute, and Congress might have intended a double-barreled result. That possibility, however, is not a substitute for the affirmative evidence of intended extraterritorial application that our cases require. Moreover, in our review of the history of the amendment, we have found no support whatsoever for that latter, alternative, purpose.

The addition of the phrase "or return" and the deletion of the phrase "within the United States" are the only relevant changes made by the 1980 amendment to

§ 243(h)(1), and they are fully explained by the intent to apply § 243(h) to exclusion as well as to deportation proceedings. That intent is plainly identified in the legislative history of the amendment. There is no change in the 1980 amendment, however, that could only be explained by an assumption that Congress also intended to provide for the statute's extraterritorial application. It would have been extraordinary for Congress to make such an important change in the law without any mention of that possible effect. Not a scintilla of evidence of such an intent can be found in the legislative history.

In sum, all available evidence about the meaning of § 243(h)—the government official at whom it is directed, its location in the Act, its failure to suggest any extraterritorial application, the 1980 amendment that gave it a dual reference to "deport or return," and the relevance of that dual structure to immigration law in general—leads unerringly to the conclusion that it applies in only one context: the domestic procedures by which the Attorney General determines whether deportable and excludable aliens may remain in the United States.

Although the protection afforded by § 243(h) did not apply in exclusion proceedings before 1980, other provisions of the Act did authorize relief for aliens at the border seeking protection as refugees in the United States. See *INS v. Stevic*, 467 U.S., at 415–416. When the United States acceded to the Protocol in 1968, therefore, the INA already offered *some* protection to both classes of refugees. It offered *no* such protection to any alien who was beyond the territorial waters of the United States, though, and we would not expect the Government to assume a burden as to those aliens without some acknowledgment of its dramatically broadened scope. Both Congress and the Executive Branch gave extensive consideration to the Protocol before ratifying it in 1968; in all of their published consideration of it there appears no mention of the possibility that the United States was assuming any extraterritorial obligations. Nevertheless, because the history of the 1980 Act does disclose a general intent to conform our law to Article 33 of the Convention, it might be argued that the extraterritorial obligations imposed by Article 33 were so clear that Congress, in acceding to the Protocol, and then in amending the statute to harmonize the two, meant to give the latter a correspondingly extraterritorial effect. Or, just as the statute might have imposed an extraterritorial obligation that the Convention does not (the argument we have just rejected), the Convention might have established an extraterritorial obligation which the statute does not; under the Supremacy Clause, that broader treaty obligation might then provide the controlling rule of law. With those possibilities in mind we shall consider both the text and negotiating history of the Convention itself.

Like the text and the history of § 243(h), the text and negotiating history of Article 33 of the United Nations Convention are both completely silent with respect to the Article's possible application to actions taken by a country outside its own borders. Respondents argue that the Protocol's broad remedial goals require that a nation be prevented from repatriating refugees to their potential oppressors whether or not the refugees are within that nation's borders. In spite of the moral weight of that argument, both the text and negotiating history of Article 33 affirmatively indicate that it was not intended to have extraterritorial effect.

Two aspects of Article 33's text are persuasive. The first is the explicit reference in Article 33.2 to the country in which the alien is located; the second is the parallel use of the terms "expel or return," the latter term explained by the French word "refouler."

The full text of Article 33 reads as follows:

> "*Article 33.—Prohibition of expulsion or return ('refoulement')*
>
> "1. No Contracting State shall expel or return ('refouler') a refugee in any manner whatsoever to the frontiers of territories where his life or freedom would be threatened on account of his race, religion, nationality, membership of a particular social group or political opinion.
>
> "2. The benefit of the present provision may not, however, be claimed by a refugee whom there are reasonable grounds for regarding as a danger to the security of *the country in which he is*, or who, having been convicted by a final judgment of a particularly serious crime, constitutes a danger to the community of that country." Convention Relating to the Status of Refugees, July 28, 1951, 19 U.S.T. 6259, 6276, T.I.A.S. No. 6577 (emphasis added).

Under the second paragraph of Article 33 an alien may not claim the benefit of the first paragraph if he poses a danger to the country in which he is located. If the first paragraph did apply on the high seas, no nation could invoke the second paragraph's exception with respect to an alien there: an alien intercepted on the high seas is in no country at all. If Article 33.1 applied extraterritorially, therefore, Article 33.2 would create an absurd anomaly: dangerous aliens on the high seas would be entitled to the benefits of 33.1 while those residing in the country that sought to expel them would not. It is more reasonable to assume that the coverage of 33.2 was limited to those already in the country because it was understood that 33.1 obligated the signatory state only with respect to aliens within its territory. Article 33.1 uses the words "expel or return ('refouler')" as an obvious parallel to the words "deport or return" in §243(h)(1). There is no dispute that "expel" has the same meaning as "deport"; it refers to the deportation or expulsion of an alien who is already present in the host country. The dual reference identified and explained in our opinion in *Leng May Ma v. Barber*, suggests that the term "return ('refouler')" refers to the exclusion of aliens who are merely "on the threshold of initial entry." 357 U.S., at 187 (quoting *Shaughnessy v. Mezei*, 345 U.S. 206, 212 (1953)).

This suggestion—that "return" has a legal meaning narrower than its common meaning—is reinforced by the parenthetical reference to "refouler", a French word that is *not* an exact synonym for the English word "return." Indeed, neither of two respected English-French Dictionaries mentions "refouler" as one of many possible French translations of "return." Conversely, the English translations of "refouler" do not include the word "return." They do, however, include words like "repulse," "repel," "drive back," and even "expel." To the extent that they are relevant, these translations imply that "return" means a defensive act of resistance or exclusion at a border rather than an act of transporting someone to a particular destination. In the context of the Convention, to "return" means to "repulse" rather than to "reinstate."

The text of Article 33 thus fits with Judge Edwards' understanding "that 'expulsion' would refer to a 'refugee already admitted into a country' and that 'return' would refer to a 'refugee already within the territory but not yet resident there.' Thus, the Protocol was not intended to govern parties' conduct outside of their national borders." *Haitian Refugee Center v. Gracey*, 809 F. 2d, at 840 (footnotes omitted). From the time of the Convention, commentators have consistently agreed with this view.

The drafters of the Convention and the parties to the Protocol—like the drafters of § 243(h)—may not have contemplated that any nation would gather fleeing refugees and return them to the one country they had desperately sought to escape; such actions may even violate the spirit of Article 33; but a treaty cannot impose uncontemplated extraterritorial obligations on those who ratify it through no more than its general humanitarian intent. Because the text of Article 33 cannot reasonably be read to say anything at all about a nation's actions toward aliens outside its own territory, it does not prohibit such actions.

* * *

[The Court goes on to explore the negotiating history of the Convention concluding that the words "expel" and "return" covered only refugees who had entered the host country and that term "refouler" was included in the English version of the text to avoid the expressed concern about an inappropriately broad reading of the English word "return."]

* * *

Therefore, even if we believed that Executive Order 12807 violated the intent of some signatory states to protect all aliens, wherever they might be found, from being transported to potential oppressors, we must acknowledge that other signatory states carefully—and successfully—sought to avoid just that implication. The negotiating history, which suggests that the Convention's limited reach resulted from a deliberate bargain, is not dispositive, but it solidly supports our reluctance to interpret Article 33 to impose obligations on the contracting parties that are broader than the text commands. We do not read that text to apply to aliens interdicted on the high seas.

Respondents contend that the dangers faced by Haitians who are unwillingly repatriated demonstrate that the judgment of the Court of Appeals fulfilled the central purpose of the Convention and the Refugee Act of 1980. While we must, of course, be guided by the high purpose of both the treaty and the statute, we are not persuaded that either one places any limit on the President's authority to repatriate aliens interdicted beyond the territorial seas of the United States.

It is perfectly clear that 8 U.S.C. § 1182(f) grants the President ample power to establish a naval blockade that would simply deny illegal Haitian migrants the ability to disembark on our shores. Whether the President's chosen method of preventing the "attempted mass migration" of thousands of Haitians—to use the Dutch delegate's phrase—poses a greater risk of harm to Haitians who might otherwise face a long and dangerous return voyage, is irrelevant to the scope of his authority to take action that neither the Convention nor the statute clearly prohibits. As we have already noted, Acts of Congress normally do not have extraterritorial application unless such an intent is clearly manifested. That presumption has special force when we are construing treaty and statutory provisions that may involve foreign and military affairs for which the President has unique responsibility. Cf. *United States v. Curtiss-Wright Export Corp.*, 299 U.S. 304 (1936). We therefore find ourselves in agreement with the conclusion expressed in Judge Edwards' concurring opinion in *Gracey*, 809 F.2d, at 841:

> "This case presents a painfully common situation in which desperate people, convinced that they can no longer remain in their homeland, take desperate measures to escape. Although the human crisis is compelling, there is no solution to be found in a judicial remedy."

The judgment of the Court of Appeals is reversed.

Justice BLACKMUN, dissenting.

When, in 1968, the United States acceded to the United Nations Protocol Relating to the Status of Refugees, Jan. 31, 1967, [1968] 19 U.S.T. 6223, T.I.A.S. 6577, it pledged not to "return ('refouler') a refugee in any manner whatsoever" to a place where he would face political persecution. In 1980, Congress amended our immigration law to reflect the Protocol's directives. Refugee Act of 1980, 94 Stat. 102. See *INS v. Cardoza-Fonseca*, 480 U.S. 421, 429, 436–437, 440 (1987); *INS v. Stevic*, 467 U.S. 407, 418, 421 (1984). Today's majority nevertheless decides that the forced repatriation of the Haitian refugees is perfectly legal, because the word "return" does not mean return, because the opposite of "within the United States" is not outside the United States, and because the official charged with controlling immigration has no role in enforcing an order to control immigration.

I believe that the duty of nonreturn expressed in both the Protocol and the statute is clear. The majority finds it "extraordinary," that Congress would have intended the ban on returning "any alien" to apply to aliens at sea. That Congress would have meant what it said is not remarkable. What is extraordinary in this case is that the Executive, in disregard of the law, would take to the seas to intercept fleeing refugees and force them back to their persecutors—and that the Court would strain to sanction that conduct.

* * *

The terms [of Article 33] are unambiguous. Vulnerable refugees shall not be returned. The language is clear, and the command is straightforward; that should be the end of the inquiry. Indeed, until litigation ensued, the Government consistently acknowledged that the Convention applied on the high seas.

The majority, however, has difficulty with the Treaty's use of the term "return ('refouler')." "Return," it claims, does not mean return, but instead has a distinctive legal meaning. For this proposition the Court relies almost entirely on the fact that *American* law makes a general distinction between *deportation* and *exclusion*. Without explanation, the majority asserts that in light of this distinction the word "return" as used in the Treaty somehow must refer only to "the exclusion of aliens who are ...'on the threshold of initial entry.'"

Setting aside for the moment the fact that respondents in this case seem very much "on the threshold of initial entry"—at least in the eyes of the Government that has ordered them seized for "attempting to come to the United States by sea without necessary documentation,"—I find this tortured reading unsupported and unnecessary. The text of the Convention does not ban the "exclusion" of aliens who have reached some indeterminate "threshold"; it bans their "return." It is well settled that a treaty must first be construed according to its "ordinary meaning." Article 31.1 of the Vienna Convention on the Law of Treaties, 1155 U.N.T.S. 331, T.S. No. 58 (1980), 8 I.L.M. 679 (1969). The ordinary meaning of "return" is "to bring, send, or put (a person or thing) back to or in a former position." Webster's Third New International Dictionary 1941 (1986). That describes precisely what petitioners are doing to the Haitians. By dispensing with ordinary meaning at the outset, and by taking instead as its starting point the assumption that "return," as used in the Treaty, "has a legal meaning narrower than its common meaning," the majority leads itself astray.

The straightforward interpretation of the duty of nonreturn is strongly reinforced by the Convention's use of the French term "refouler." The ordinary meaning of "refouler," as the majority concedes, is "[t]o repulse, ...; to drive back, to repel." Dictionnaire Larousse 631 (1981).[1] Thus construed, Article 33.1 of the Convention reads: "No contracting state shall expel or [repulse, drive back, or repel] a refugee in any manner whatsoever to the frontiers of territories where his life or freedom would be threatened...." That, of course, is exactly what the Government is doing. It thus is no surprise that when the French press has described the very policy challenged here, the term it has used is "refouler." See, e.g., *Le bourbier hatien*, Le Monde, May 31–June 1, 1992 ("[L]es Etats-Unis ont decide de refouler directement les refugies recueillis par la garde cotire." (The United States has decided [de refouler] directly the refugees picked up by the Coast Guard)). And yet the majority insists that what has occurred is not, in fact, "refoulement." It reaches this conclusion in a peculiar fashion. After acknowledging that the ordinary meaning of "refouler" is "repulse," "repel," and "drive back," the majority without elaboration declares: "To the extent that they are relevant, these translations imply that 'return' means a defensive act of resistance or exclusion at a border...." I am at a loss to find the narrow notion of "exclusion at a border" in broad terms like "repulse," "repel," and "drive back." Gage was repulsed (initially) at Bunker Hill. Lee was repelled at Gettysburg. Rommel was driven back across North Africa. The majority's puzzling progression ("refouler" means repel or drive back; therefore "return" means only exclude at a border; therefore the treaty does not apply) hardly justifies a departure from the path of ordinary meaning. The text of Article

1. The Court seems no more convinced than I am by the Government's argument that "refouler" is best translated as "expel." That interpretation, as the Second Circuit observed, would leave the treaty redundantly forbidding a nation to "expel" or "expel" a refugee. *Haitian Centers Council, Inc. v. McNary*, 969 F.2d 1350, 1363 (1992).

33.1 is clear, and whether the operative term is "return" or "refouler," it prohibits the Government's actions.

Article 33.1 is clear not only in what it says, but also in what it does not say: it does not include any geographical limitation. It limits only where a refugee may be sent "to", not where he may be sent from. This is not surprising, given that the aim of the provision is to protect refugees against persecution.

Article 33.2, by contrast, *does* contain a geographical reference, and the majority seizes upon this as evidence that the section as a whole applies only within a signatory's borders. That inference is flawed....

The signatories' understandable decision to allow nations to deport criminal aliens who have entered their territory hardly suggests an intent to permit the apprehension and return of noncriminal aliens who have not entered their territory, and who may have no desire ever to enter it. One wonders what the majority would make of an exception that removed from the Article's protection all refugees who "constitute a danger to their families." By the majority's logic, the inclusion of such an exception presumably would render Article 33.1 applicable only to refugees with families.

Far from constituting "an absurd anomaly," the fact that a state is permitted to "expel or return" a small class of refugees found within its territory but may not seize and return refugees who remain outside its frontiers expresses precisely the objectives and concerns of the Convention. Non-return is the rule; the sole exception (neither applicable nor invoked here) is that a nation endangered by a refugee's very presence may "expel or return" him to an unsafe country if it chooses. The tautological observation that only a refugee already in a country can pose a danger to the country "in which he is" proves nothing.

The majority further relies on a remark by Baron van Boetzelaer, the Netherlands' delegate at the Convention's negotiating conference, to support its contention that Article 33 does not apply extraterritorially. This reliance, for two reasons, is misplaced. First, the isolated statement of a delegate to the Convention cannot alter the plain meaning of the Treaty itself. Second, placed in its proper context, van Boetzelaer's comment does not support the majority's position.

It is axiomatic that a treaty's plain language must control absent "extraordinarily strong contrary evidence." *Sumitomo Shoji America, Inc. v. Avagliano*, 457 U.S. 176 (1982). Reliance on a treaty's negotiating history (travaux preparatoires) is a disfavored alternative of last resort, appropriate only where the terms of the document are obscure or lead to "manifestly absurd or unreasonable" results. See Vienna Convention on the Law of Treaties, Art. 32, 1155 U.N.T.S., at 340, 8 I.L.M., at 692 (1969). Moreover, even the general rule of treaty construction allowing limited resort to travaux preparatoires "has no application to oral statements made by those engaged in negotiating the treaty which were not embodied in any writing and were not communicated to the government of the negotiator or to its ratifying body." *Arizona v. California*, 292 U.S. 341, 360 (1934). There is no evidence that the comment on which the majority relies was ever communicated to the United States' Government or to the Senate in connection with the ratification of the Convention.

The pitfalls of relying on the negotiating record are underscored by the fact that Baron van Boetzelaer's remarks almost certainly represent, in the words of the United Nations High Commissioner for Refugees, a mere "parliamentary gesture by a delegate whose views did *not* prevail upon the negotiating conference as a whole" (emphasis in original). Brief for Office of the United Nations High Commissioner for Refugees as Amicus Curiae 24. The Baron, like the Swiss delegate whose sentiments he restated, expressed a desire to reserve the right to *close borders* to *large groups* of refugees....

* * *

There is strong evidence as well that the Conference rejected the right to close land borders where to do so would trap refugees in the persecutors' territory. Indeed, the majority agrees that the Convention does apply to refugees who have reached the border. The majority thus cannot maintain that van Boetzelaer's interpretation prevailed.

* * *

In any event, even if van Boetzelaer's statement had been "agreed to" as reflecting the dominant view, this is not a case about the right of a nation to close its borders. This is a case in which a Nation has gone forth to seize aliens who are not at its borders and return them to persecution. Nothing in the comments relied on by the majority even hints at an intention on the part of the drafters to countenance a course of conduct so at odds with the Convention's basic purpose.

* * *

Like the Treaty whose dictates it embodies, § 243(h) is unambiguous.... "With regard to this very statutory scheme, we have considered ourselves bound to assume that the legislative purpose is expressed by the ordinary meaning of the words used." Ordinary, but not literal. The statement that "the Attorney General shall not deport or return any alien" obviously does not mean simply that the person who is the Attorney General at the moment is forbidden personally to deport or return any alien, but rather that her agents may not do so. In the present case the Coast Guard without question is acting as the agent of the Attorney General. "The officers of the Coast Guard insofar as they are engaged ... in enforcing any law of the United States shall ... be deemed to be acting as agents of the particular executive department ... charged with the administration of the particular law ... and ... be subject to all the rules and regulations promulgated by such Department ... with respect to the enforcement of that law." 14 U.S.C. § 89(b). The Coast Guard is engaged in enforcing the immigration laws. The sole identified purpose of Executive Order 12,807 is to address "the serious problem of persons attempting to come to the United States by sea without necessary documentation and otherwise illegally." The Coast Guard's task under the order is "to enforce the suspension of the entry of undocumented aliens by sea and the interdiction of any defined vessel carrying such aliens." The Coast Guard is authorized to return a vessel and its passengers *only* "when there is reason to believe that an offense is being committed against the United States immigration laws, or appropriate laws of a foreign country with which we have an arrangement to assist."

The majority suggests indirectly that the law which the Coast Guard enforces when it carries out the order to return a vessel reasonably believed to be violating the immigration laws is somehow not a law that the Attorney General is charged with administering. That suggestion is baseless. Under 8 U.S.C. § 1103(a), the Attorney General, with some exceptions, "shall be charged with the administration and enforcement of this chapter and all other laws relating to the immigration and naturalization of aliens. . . ." The majority acknowledges this designation, but speculates that the particular enforcement of immigration laws here may be covered by the exception for laws relating to "the powers, functions, and duties conferred upon the President, the Secretary of State, the officers of the Department of State, or diplomatic or consular officers. . . ." The majority fails to point out the proviso that directly follows the exception: "*Provided, however*, That ... the Attorney General. . . . shall have the power and duty to control and guard the boundaries and borders of the United States against the illegal entry of aliens. . . ." There can be no doubt that the Coast Guard is acting as the Attorney General's agent when it seizes and returns undocumented aliens.

Even the challenged Executive Order places the Attorney General "on the boat" with the Coast Guard. The Order purports to give the Attorney General "unreviewable discretion" to decide that an alien will not be returned. Discretion not to return an alien is of course discretion to return him. Such discretion cannot be given; Congress removed it in 1980 when it amended the Immigration Act to make mandatory ("*shall not* deport or *return*") what had been a discretionary function ("The Attorney General is authorized to withhold deportation"). The Attorney General may not decline to follow the command of § 243(h). If she encounters a refugee, she must not return him to persecution.

The laws that the Coast Guard is engaged in enforcing when it takes to the seas under orders to prevent aliens from illegally crossing our borders are laws whose administration has been assigned to the Attorney General by Congress, which has plenary power over immigration matters. *Kleindienst v. Mandel*, 408 U.S. 753, 766 (1972). Accordingly, there is no merit to the argument that the concomitant legal restrictions placed on the Attorney General by Congress do not apply with full force in this case.

Comparison with the pre-1980 version of § 243(h) confirms that the statute means what it says. Before 1980, § 243(h) provided:

> The Attorney General is authorized to *withhold deportation* of any alien ... *within the United States* to any country in which in his opinion the alien would be subject to persecution on account of race, religion, or political opinion and for such period of time as he deems to be necessary for such reason" (emphasis added).

The Refugee Act of 1980 explicitly amended this provision in three critical respects. Congress (1) deleted the words "within the United States"; (2) barred the Government from "return[ing]," as well as "deport[ing]," alien refugees; and (3) made the prohibition against return mandatory, thereby eliminating the discretion of the Attorney General over such decisions.

The import of these changes is clear. Whether "within the United States" or not, a refugee may not be returned to his persecutors. To read into § 243(h)'s mandate a territorial restriction is to restore the very language that Congress removed. "Few principles of statutory construction are more compelling than the proposition that Congress does not intend sub silentio to enact statutory language that it has earlier discarded in favor of other language." Moreover, as all parties to this case acknowledge, the 1980 changes were made in order to conform our law to the United Nations Protocol. As has been shown above, that Treaty's absolute ban on refoulement is similarly devoid of territorial restrictions.

The majority, however, downplays the significance of the deletion of "within the United States" to improvise a unique meaning for "return." It does so not by analyzing Article 33, the provision that inspired the 1980 amendments, but by reference to a lone case from this Court that is not even mentioned in the legislative history and that had been on the books a full 22 years before the amendments' enactment.

In *Leng May Ma v. Barber*, 357 U.S. 185 (1958), this Court decided that aliens paroled into the United States from detention at the border were not "within the United States" for purposes of the former § 243(h) and thus were not entitled to its benefits. Pointing to this decision, the majority offers the negative inference that Congress' removal of the words "within the United States" was meant only to extend a right of nonreturn to those in exclusion proceedings. But nothing in *Leng May Ma* even remotely suggests that the only persons not "within the United States" are those involved in exclusion proceedings. Indeed, such a suggestion would have been ridiculous. Nor does the narrow concept of exclusion relate in any obvious way to the amendment's broad phrase "return any alien."

The problems with the majority's *Leng May Ma* theory run deeper, however. When Congress in 1980 removed the phrase "within the United States," it did not substitute any other geographical limitation. This failure is exceedingly strange in light of the majority's hypothesis that the deletion was intended solely to work the particular technical adjustment of extending protection to those physically present in, yet not legally admitted to, the United States. It is even stranger given what Congress did elsewhere in the Act. The Refugee Act revised the immigration code to establish a comprehensive, tripartite system for the protection of refugees fleeing persecution. Section 207 governs overseas refugee processing. Section 208, in turn, governs asylum claims by aliens "physically present in the United States, or at a land border or entry port." Unlike these sections, however, which explicitly apply to persons present in specific locations, the amended § 243(h) includes no such limiting language. The basic prohibition against forced return to persecution applies simply to "any alien." The design of all three sections is instructive, and it undermines the majority's assertion that § 243(h) was meant to apply only to aliens physically present in the United States or at one of its borders. When Congress wanted a provision to apply only to aliens "physically present in the United States, or at a land border or port of entry," it said so. An examination of the carefully designed provisions of the INA—not an elaborate theory about a 1958 case regarding the rights of aliens in exclusion proceedings—is the proper basis for an analysis of the statute.

That the clarity of the text and the implausibility of its theories do not give the majority more pause is due, I think, to the majority's heavy reliance on the presumption against extraterritoriality. The presumption runs throughout the majority's opinion, and it stacks the deck by requiring the Haitians to produce "affirmative evidence" that when Congress prohibited the return of "any" alien, it indeed meant to prohibit the interception and return of aliens at sea.

The judicially created canon of statutory construction against extraterritorial application of United States law has no role here, however. It applies only where congressional intent is "unexpressed." *EEOC v. Arabian American Oil Co.*, 499 U.S., (1991). Here there is no room for doubt: a territorial restriction has been deliberately deleted from the statute.

Even where congressional intent is unexpressed, however, a statute must be assessed according to its intended scope. The primary basis for the application of the presumption (besides the desire—not relevant here—to avoid conflict with the laws of other nations) is "the common-sense notion that Congress generally legislates with domestic concerns in mind." *Smith v. United States*, 507 U.S., n. 5 (1993) (slip op., at 7–8). Where that notion seems unjustified or unenlightening, however, generally-worded laws covering varying subject matters are routinely applied extraterritorially. See, e.g., *Hellenic Lines Ltd. v. Rhoditis*, 398 U.S. 306 (1970) (extraterritorial application of the Jones Act); *Steele v. Bulova Watch Co.*, 344 U.S. 280 (1952) (Lanham Act applies extraterritorially)....

In this case we deal with a statute that regulates a distinctively international subject matter: immigration, nationalities, and refugees. Whatever force the presumption may have with regard to a primarily domestic statute evaporates in this context. There is no danger that the Congress that enacted the Refugee Act was blind to the fact that the laws it was crafting had implications beyond this Nation's borders. The "common-sense notion" that Congress was looking inwards—perfectly valid in a case involving the Federal Tort Claims Act, such as *Smith*—cannot be reasonably applied to the Refugee Act of 1980.

In this regard, the majority's dictum that the presumption has "special force" when we construe "statutory provisions that may involve foreign and military affairs for which the President has unique responsibility," is completely wrong. The presumption that Congress did not intend to legislate extraterritorially has less force—perhaps, indeed, no force at all—when a statute on its face relates to foreign affairs. What the majority appears to be getting at, as its citation to *United States v. Curtiss-Wright Export Corp.*, 299 U.S. 304 (1936), suggests, is that in some areas, the President, and not Congress, has sole constitutional authority. Immigration is decidedly not one of those areas. "[O]ver no conceivable subject is the legislative power of Congress more complete...." *Fiallo v. Bell*, 430 U.S. 787, 792 (1977). And the suggestion that the President somehow is acting in his capacity as Commander-in-Chief is thwarted by the fact that nowhere among Executive Order No. 12,807's numerous references to the immigration laws is that authority even once invoked.

If any canon of construction should be applied in this case, it is the well-settled rule that "an act of congress ought never to be construed to violate the law of nations if any other possible construction remains." *Murray v. The Charming Betsy*, 2 Cranch 64, 117–118 (1804). The majority's improbable construction of § 243(h), which flies in the face of the international obligations imposed by Article 33 of the Convention, violates that established principle.

The Convention that the Refugee Act embodies was enacted largely in response to the experience of Jewish refugees in Europe during the period of World War II. The tragic consequences of the world's indifference at that time are well known. The resulting ban on refoulement, as broad as the humanitarian purpose that inspired it, is easily applicable here, the Court's protestations of impotence and regret notwithstanding.

The refugees attempting to escape from Haiti do not claim a right of admission to this country. They do not even argue that the Government has no right to intercept their boats. They demand only that the United States, land of refugees and guardian of freedom, cease forcibly driving them back to detention, abuse, and death. That is a modest plea, vindicated by the Treaty and the statute. We should not close our ears to it.

Notes

1. The Supreme Court in *Sale* ruled that neither the U.N. Refugee Convention nor the 1980 Refugee Act prohibit the United States from seeking asylum seekers on the high seas and returning them to the country they are attempting to flee. The decision in *Sale* has been roundly criticized as being inconsistent with the letter and spirit of the Refugee Convention and the 1980 Refugee Act. Other commentators have argued that it also violates the principle of non-refoulement, which is a norm of customary international law.[49]

2. The policy of forcible interdiction and repatriation applied against the Haitian asylum seekers is indicative of an international trend to deny asylum seekers access to the asylum adjudicatory process. The expedited removal process, described separately in Chapter 3, may be seen as part of that trend. It precludes asylum seekers from applying for asylum unless they can establish the strength of their claim immediately upon arriving in the United States.

3. After reviewing the procedures used in expedited removal, do you think it might be difficult for an asylum seeker to express and to establish a "credible fear of perse-

---

49. For a fuller discussion of the events leading up to the *Sale* decision and of the arguments on behalf of the Haitian asylum seekers, see Harold Hongju Koh, *Reflections on Refoulement*, 35 HARV. INT'L LAW. J. 1 (1994). For a critique of the decision from the international law perspective, see Harry A. Blackmun, *The Supreme Court and the Law of Nations*, 104 YALE L.J. 39 (1994), and Louis Henkin, *Notes from the President* (Am. Soc'y of Int'l L. News.), Sept.–Oct. 1993.

cution" immediately upon arriving in the United States? Some commentators point to the fact that people fleeing repressive regimes may be reluctant to speak openly to U.S. officials upon arrival, while persons who are traumatized or women who have suffered rape or other humiliating forms of persecution may be unable to express themselves well in an expedited procedure where access to legal representation is unavailable. Consider the following actual case of expedited removal, summarized in Karen Musalo, Report on the Second Year of Implementation of Expedited Removal 95 (May 1999):

> Mr. M, an Ogoni man from Nigeria, was a spokesperson for his village. Mr. M was arrested on January 4, 1996, for attending a peaceful political demonstration in honor of Ogoni Day. The protesters were asking the government for compensation for Ogoni land that had been polluted and for the release of detainees. The police and military tried to stop the demonstration by shooting into the crowd and dispersing tear gas. Mr. M began to run, but stopped when his friend was shot. At this time, he was arrested, in addition to sixty others. Other members of his group were killed.
>
> Those arrested, including Mr. M, were taken to Boni Camp, a camp located approximately forty-five minutes from his village. Upon arrival at Boni Camp, he was accused of being involved with riots against the government. He was frequently beaten with electric wires and rifle butts. In 1996, he was raped by three male officers. Although he reported the rape, the superior officers did not believe his story. Mr. M was told by his captors that they had tried to arrest him on two different occasions because he was the spokesman for his village. Mr. M's father had also told him that the police had twice tried to capture him, in 1995 and 1996, and that his father had told them that he was not at home. Mr. M was detained for one year and five months at Boni camp. On June 12, 1997, Mr. M escaped from the camp with the aid of a guard, who was a friend from school. The guard agreed to leave a door open so that Mr. M could escape. Mr. M went to his mother's village for one day, to Lagos, Nigeria, to Abidjan, Ivory Coast, to Sierra Leone, to Brazil, and then to the United States.
>
> Mr. M sought admission to the United States at John F. Kennedy International Airport in New York on July 4, 1997. At secondary inspection, he stated that he had fled Nigeria because of a political problem and wanted to seek political asylum. When asked about the political problem he had, he stated: "The killing and all the rest." The immigration officer asked Mr. M when he fled Nigeria. The officer recorded Mr. M's response as two years ago. When the officer asked if he returned to Nigeria after he left two years prior, Mr. M responded negatively. Mr. M was referred to a credible fear interview and detained at the Wackenhut Detention Facility.
>
> Mr. M's credible fear interview was conducted on July 9, 1997. Mr. M did not have an attorney or representative present, although he had contacted the Lawyers Committee for Human Rights in New York, and had been told

to call back. During the interview, Mr. M said that he was Ogoni and told the AO of his experiences, as set forth above. He offered to show the AO his scars. Mr. M told the AO that after he escaped, he went to his mother's village for one day, to Lagos, Nigeria, to Abidjan, Ivory Coast, to Sierra Leone, to Brazil, and then to the United States. When asked what would happen to him upon return, he stated that he would be "tortured or worse." He told the AO that the police would know that he was back in Nigeria because "[t]hey have syndicates who follow up on people who return." When asked why he stated that he had never been arrested or persecuted in Nigeria when asked by the immigration officer at the airport, he stated: "I was afraid to tell them that I had been arrested for fear that they would send me back home." When asked why he told the immigration officer at the airport that he left Nigeria two years ago, and spent those two years mostly in Abidjan, while later telling the AO that he was in Boni Camp from January 1996 until June 1997, Mr. M stated: "This was a mistake. It should be two days not two years."

The AO found that Mr. M's testimony was not credible, and thus that he had not demonstrated a significant possibility that he could establish eligibility for asylum. The AO found that Mr. M had given two conflicting stories. She noted that during secondary inspection, he "stated … that he left Nigeria two years ago" and answered other questions regarding his two-year stay in Abidjan. She further noted that during his credible fear interview, he stated that he was arrested, imprisoned, and beaten during this time and that when he left Nigeria, he spent only two days in Abidjan. The AO found that Mr. M's explanation that this inconsistency was a mistake was not sufficient. Additionally, although the AO noted she did not consider it in assessing credibility, she found that Mr. M's escape was not plausible. She noted that it did not seem likely that Mr. M "would choose to remain in the deplorable conditions of the camp for one year and five months if he had the opportunity to escape in such an easy manner as described and probably could have escaped at any time."

Review by an IJ of the credible fear determination was held on July 18, 1997. During the review, testimony was taken regarding Mr. M's background and fear of return to Nigeria. The IJ vacated the negative credible fear determination by the AO, finding that Mr. M had established a significant possibility that he would be persecuted on the basis of his race, religion, nationality, membership in a particular social group, or political opinion.

Expedited removal decisions are not subject to review by the BIA or the federal courts, so if the immigration judge in this case had not ruled in his favor, Mr. M would have been immediately returned to Nigeria. What do you think about the asylum officer's ruling that Mr. M was not credible? Would you have reversed the asylum officer if you were the immigration judge?

G. Grounds of Persecution—Establishing Nexus

As was noted in the introduction to this chapter, it is not enough to establish a well-founded fear of persecution, as the persecution must be "on account" of one of more of the five enumerated statutory grounds. As courts review USCIS determinations on individual claims of persecution, they must interpret the meaning of each claim of persecution on account of "race, religion, nationality, membership in a particular social group, or political opinion." Below are excerpts from the U.N. High Commissioner for Refugees, United Nations Handbook on Procedures and Criteria for Determining Refugee Status (1979) on the meaning of the five enumerated grounds as well as on claims based on a refusal to serve in the military. As you recall from *Cardoza-Fonseca,* although it is not binding, the UNHCR Handbook is a significant source of guidance in interpreting the Refugee Convention, upon which U.S. law is based.

United Nations High Commissioner for Refugees, Handbook on Procedures for Determining Refugee Status

(1979)

Race

¶ 68 Race, in the present connexion, has to be understood in its widest sense to include all kinds of ethnic groups that are referred to as "races" in common usage. Frequently it will also entail membership of a specific social group of common descent forming a minority within a larger population. Discrimination for reasons of race has found world-wide condemnation as one of the most striking violations of human rights. Racial discrimination, therefore, represents an important element in determining the existence of persecution.

¶ 69 Discrimination on racial grounds will frequently amount to persecution in the sense of the 1951 Convention. This will be the case if, as a results of racial discrimination, a person's human dignity is affected to such an extent as to be incompatible with the most elementary and inalienable human rights, or where the disregard of racial barriers is subject to serious consequences.

¶ 70 The mere fact of belonging to a certain racial group will normally not be enough to substantiate a claim to refugee status. There may, however, be situations where, due to particular circumstances affecting the group, such membership will in itself be sufficient ground to fear persecution.

Religion

¶ 71 The Universal Declaration of Human Rights and the Human Rights Covenant proclaim the right to freedom of thought, conscience and religion, which right includes the freedom of a person to change his religion and his freedom to manifest it in public or private, in teaching, practise, worship and observance.

¶ 72 Persecution for "reasons of religion" may assume various forms, e.g. prohibition of membership of a religious community, of worship in private or in public, of religious instruction, or serious measures of discrimination imposed on persons because they practise their religion or belong to a particular religious community.

¶ 73 Mere membership of a particular religious community will normally not be enough to substantiate a claim to refugee status. There may, however, be special circumstances where mere membership can be a sufficient ground.

Nationality

¶ 74 The term "nationality" in this context is not to be understood only as "citizenship". It refers also to membership of an ethnic or linguistic group and may occasionally overlap with the term "race". Persecution for reasons of nationality may consist of adverse attitudes and measures directed against a national (ethnic, linguistic) minority and in certain circumstances the fact of belonging to such a minority may in itself give rise to well-founded fear of persecution.

¶ 75 The co-existence within the boundaries of a State of two or more national (ethnic, linguistic) groups may create situations of conflict and also situations of persecution or danger of persecution. It may not always be easy to distinguish between persecution for reasons of nationality and persecution for reasons of political opinion when a conflict between national groups is combined with political movements, particularly where a political movement is identified with a specific "nationality".

¶ 76 Whereas in most cases persecution for reason of nationality is feared by persons belonging to a national minority, there have been many cases in various continents where a person belonging to a majority group may fear persecution by a dominant minority.

Membership of a Particular Social Group

¶ 77 A "particular social group" normally comprises persons of similar background, habits or social status. A claim to fear of persecution under this heading may frequently overlap with a claim to fear of persecution on other grounds, i.e. race, religion or nationality.

¶ 78 Membership of such a particular social group may be at the root of persecution because there is no confidence in the group's loyalty to the Government or because the political outlook, antecedents or economic activity of its members, or the very existence of the social group as such, is held to be an obstacle to the Government's policies.

¶ 79 Mere membership of a particular social group will not normally be enough to substantiate a claim to refugee status. There may, however, be special circumstances where mere membership can be a sufficient ground to fear persecution.

Political Opinion

¶ 80 Holding political opinions different from those of the Government is not in itself a ground for claiming refugee status, and an applicant must show that he has a fear of persecution for holding such opinions. This pre-supposes that the applicant holds opinions not tolerated by the authorities, which are critical of their policies or methods. It also pre-supposes that such opinions have come to the notice of the authorities or are attributed by them to the applicant. The political opinions of a teacher or writer may be more manifest than those of a person in a less exposed position. The relative importance or tenacity of the applicant's opinions in so far as this can be established from all the circumstances of the case will also be relevant.

¶ 81 While the definition speaks of persecution "for reasons of political opinion" it may not always be possible to establish a causal link between the opinion expressed and the related measures suffered or feared by the applicant. Such measures have only rarely been based expressly on "opinion". More frequently, such measures take the form of sanctions for alleged criminal acts against the ruling power. It will, therefore, be necessary to establish the applicant's political opinion, which is at the root of his behaviour, and the fact that it has led or may lead to the persecution that he claims to fear.

¶ 82 As indicated above, persecution "for reasons of political opinion" implies that an applicant holds an opinion that either has been expressed or has come to the attention of the authorities. There may, however, also be situations in which the applicant has not given any expression to his opinions. Due to the strength of his convictions, however, it may be reasonable to assume that his opinions will sooner or later find expression and that the applicant will, as a result, come into conflict with the authorities. Where this can reasonably be assumed, the applicant can be considered to have fear of persecution for reasons of political opinion.

¶ 83 An applicant claiming fear of persecution because of political opinion need not show that the authorities of his country of origin knew of his opinions before he left the country. He may have concealed his political opinion and never have suffered any discrimination or persecution. However, the mere fact of refusing to avail himself of the protection of his Government, or a refusal to return, may disclose the applicant's true state of mind and give rise to fear of persecution. In such circumstances the test of well-founded fear would be based on an assessment of the consequences that an applicant having certain political dispositions would have to face if he returned. This applies particularly to the so-called refugee "sur place."[50]

¶ 84 Where a person is subject to prosecution or punishment for a political offence, a distinction may have to be drawn according to whether the prosecution is for political *opinion* or for politically-motivated *acts*. If the prosecution pertains to a punishable act committed out of political motives, and if the anticipated punishment

---

50. A person who was not a refugee when he left his country, but who becomes a refugee at a later date, is called a refugee "sur place." *See* HANDBOOK at ¶ 94. A person becomes a refugee "*sur place*" due to circumstances arising in his country of origin during his absence. Diplomats and other officials serving abroad, prisoners of war, students, migrant workers and others have applied for refugee status during their residence abroad and have been recognized as refugees during their residence abroad and have been recognized as refugees. *See* HANDBOOK at ¶ 95.

is in conformity with the general law of the country concerned, fear of such prosecution will not in itself make the applicant a refugee.

¶ 85 Whether a political offender can also be considered a refugee will depend upon various other factors. Prosecution for an offence may, depending upon the circumstances, be a pretext for punishing the offender for his political opinions or the expression thereof. Again, there may be reason to believe that a political offender would be exposed to excessive or arbitrary punishment for the alleged offence. Such excessive or arbitrary punishment will amount to persecution.

¶ 86 In determining whether a political offender can be considered a refugee, regard should also be had to the following elements: personality of the applicant, his political opinion, the motive behind the act, the nature of the act committed, the nature of the prosecution and its motives; finally, also, the nature of the law on which the prosecution is based. These elements may go to show that the person concerned has a fear of persecution and not merely a fear of prosecution and punishment—within the law—for an act committed by him.

* * *

Deserters and Persons Avoiding Military Service

¶ 167 In countries where military service is compulsory, failure to perform this duty is frequently punishable by law. Moreover, whether military service is compulsory or not, desertion is invariably considered a criminal offence. The penalties may vary from country to country, and are not normally regarded as persecution. Fear of prosecution and punishment for desertion or draft-evasion does not in itself constitute well-founded fear of persecution under the definition. Desertion or draft-evasion does not, on the other hand, exclude a person from being a refugee, and a person may be a refugee in addition to being a deserter or draft-evader.

¶ 168 A person is clearly not a refugee if his only reason for desertion or draft-evasion is his dislike of military service or fear of combat. He may, however, be a refugee if his desertion or evasion of military service is concomitant with other relevant motives for leaving or remaining outside his country, or if he otherwise has reasons, within the meaning of the definition, to fear persecution.

¶ 169 A deserter or draft-evader may also be considered a refugee if it can be shown that he would suffer disproportionately severe punishment for the military offence on account of his race, religion, nationality, membership of a particular social group or political opinion. The same would apply if it can be shown that he has well-founded fear of persecution on these grounds above and beyond the punishment for desertion.

¶ 170 There are, however, also cases where the necessity to perform military service may be the sole ground for a claim to refugee status, i.e. when a person can show that the performance of military service would have required his participation in military action contrary to his genuine political, religious or moral convictions, or to valid reasons of conscience.

¶ 171 Not every conviction, genuine though it may be, will constitute a sufficient reason for claiming refugee status after desertion or draft-evasion. It is not enough for a person to be in disagreement with his government regarding the political justification for a particular military action. Where, however, the type of military action, with which an individual does not wish to be associated, is condemned by the international community as contrary to basic rules of human conduct, punishment for desertion or draft-evasion could, in the light of all other requirements of the definition, in itself be regarded as persecution.

¶ 172 Refusal to perform military service may also be based on religious convictions. If an applicant is able to show that his religious convictions are genuine, and that such convictions are not taken into account by the authorities of his country in requiring him to perform military service, he may be able to establish a claim to refugee status. Such a claim would, of course, be supported by any additional indications that the applicant or his family may have encountered difficulties due to their religious convictions.

¶ 173 The question as to whether objection to performing military service for reasons of conscience can give rise to a valid claim to refugee status should also be considered in the light of more recent developments in this field. An increasing number of States have introduced legislation or administrative regulations whereby persons who can invoke genuine reasons of conscience are exempted from military service, either entirely or subject to their performing alternative (i.e. civilian) service. The introduction of such legislation or administrative regulations has also been the subject of recommendations by international agencies. In the light of these developments, it would be open to Contracting States, to grant refugee status to persons who object to performing military service for genuine reasons of conscience.

¶ 174 The genuineness of a person's political, religious or moral convictions, or of his reasons of conscience for objecting to performing military service, will of course need to be established by a thorough investigation of his personality and background. The fact that he may have manifested his views prior to being called to arms, or that he may already have encountered difficulties with the authorities because of his convictions, are relevant considerations. Whether he has been drafted into compulsory service or joined the army as a volunteer may also be indicative of the genuineness of his convictions.

Immigration and Naturalization Service v. Jairo Jonathan Elias-Zacarias

502 U.S. 478 (1992)

Justice Scalia delivered the opinion of the Court, in which Chief Justice Rehnquist, and Justices White, Kennedy, Souter, and Thomas joined. Justice Stevens filed a dissenting opinion, in which Justices Blackmun and O'Connor joined.

The principal question presented by this case is whether a guerilla organization's attempt to coerce a person into performing military service *necessarily* constitutes "persecution on account of ... political opinion" under § 101(a)(42) of the Immigration and Nationality Act.

Respondent Elias-Zacarias, a native of Guatemala, was apprehended in July 1987 for entering the United States without inspection. In deportation proceedings brought by petitioner Immigration and Naturalization Service (INS), Elias-Zacarias conceded his deportability but requested asylum and withholding of deportation.

The Immigration Judge summarized Elias-Zacarias' testimony as follows:

> "[A]round the end of January in 1987 [when Elias-Zacarias was 18], two armed, uniformed guerrillas with handkerchiefs covering part of their faces came to his home. Only he and his parents were there.... [T]he guerrillas asked his parents and himself to join with them, but they all refused. The guerrillas asked them why and told them that they would be back, and that they should think it over about joining them.
>
> "[Elias-Zacarias] did not want to join the guerrillas because the guerrillas are against the government and he was afraid that the government would retaliate against him and his family if he did join the guerrillas. [H]e left Guatemala at the end of March [1987] ... because he was afraid that the guerrillas would return."

The Immigration Judge understood from this testimony that Elias-Zacarias' request for asylum and for withholding of deportation was "based on this one attempted recruitment by the guerrillas." She concluded that Elias-Zacarias had failed to demonstrate persecution or a well-founded fear of persecution on account of race, religion, nationality, membership in a particular social group, or political opinion, and was not eligible for asylum. She further concluded that he did not qualify for withholding of deportation.

The Board of Immigration Appeals (BIA) summarily dismissed Elias-Zacarias' appeal on procedural grounds. Elias-Zacarias then moved the BIA to reopen his deportation hearing so that he could submit new evidence that, following his departure from Guatemala, the guerrillas had twice returned to his family's home in continued efforts to recruit him. The BIA denied reopening on the ground that even with this new evidence Elias-Zacarias had failed to make a prima facie showing of eligibility for asylum and had failed to show that the results of his deportation hearing would be changed.

The Court of Appeals for the Ninth Circuit, treating the BIA's denial of the motion to reopen as an affirmance on the merits of the Immigration Judge's ruling, reversed. The court ruled that acts of conscription by a nongovernmental group constitute persecution on account of political opinion, and determined that Elias-Zacarias had a "well-founded fear" of such conscription. We granted certiorari.

Section 208(a) of the Immigration and Nationality Act, 8 U.S.C. §1158(a), authorizes the Attorney General, in his discretion, to grant asylum to an alien who is a "refugee" as defined in the Act, i.e., an alien who is unable or unwilling to return to his home country "because of persecution or a well-founded fear of persecution on account of race, religion, nationality, membership in a particular social group, or political opinion." §101(a)(42)(A), 8 U.S.C. §1101(a)(42)(A). See *INS v. Cardoza-Fonseca*, 480 U.S. 421, 423, 428, n. 5 (1987). The BIA's determination that Elias-Zacarias was not eligible for asylum must be upheld if "supported by reasonable, substantial, and probative evidence on the record considered as a whole." 8 U.S.C. § 1105a(a)(4). It can be reversed only if the evidence presented by Elias-Zacarias was such that a reasonable factfinder would have to conclude that the requisite fear of persecution existed. *NLRB v. Columbian Enameling & Stamping Co.*, 306 U.S. 292, 300 (1939).[1]

The Court of Appeals found reversal warranted. In its view, a guerrilla organization's attempt to conscript a person into its military forces necessarily constitutes "persecution on account of ... political opinion," because "the person resisting forced recruitment is expressing a political opinion hostile to the persecutor and because the persecutors' motive in carrying out the kidnapping is political." 921 F.2d, at 850. The first half of this seems to us untrue, and the second half irrelevant. Even a person who supports a guerrilla movement might resist recruitment for a variety of reasons—fear of combat, a desire to remain with one's family and friends, a desire to earn a better living in civilian life, to mention only a few. The record in the present case not only failed to show a political motive on Elias-Zacarias' part; it showed the opposite. He testified that he refused to join the guerrillas because he was afraid that the government would retaliate against him and his family if he did so. Nor is there any indication (assuming, arguendo, it would suffice) that the guerrillas erroneously *believed* that Elias-Zacarias' refusal was politically based.

As for the Court of Appeals' conclusion that the guerrillas' "motive in carrying out the kidnapping is political": It apparently meant by this that the guerrillas seek to fill their ranks in order to carry on their war against the government and pursue their political goals. See 921 F.2d, at 850 (citing *Arteaga v. INS*, 836 F.2d 1227, 1232, n. 8 (9th Cir. 1988). But that does not render the forced recruitment "persecution on account of ... political opinion." In construing statutes, "we must, of course, start with the assumption that the legislative purpose is expressed by the ordinary meaning of the words used." *Richards v. U.S.*, 369 U.S. 1, 9 (1962). The ordinary meaning of the phrase "persecution on account of ... political opinion" in § 101(a)(42) is persecution on account of the *victim's* political opinion, not the persecutor's. If a Nazi regime persecutes Jews, it is not, within the ordinary meaning of language, engaging in persecution on account of political opinion; and if a fundamentalist Moslem regime persecutes democrats, it is not engaging in persecution on account of religion. Thus, the mere existence of a generalized "political" motive underlying the guerrillas' forced recruitment is inadequate to establish (and, indeed, goes far to refute) the proposition that Elias-Zacarias fears persecution *on account of* political opinion, as § 101(a)(42) requires.

---

1. Quite beside the point, therefore, is the dissent's assertion that "the record in this case is more than adequate *to support the conclusion* that this respondent's refusal [to join the guerrillas] was a form of expressive conduct that constituted the statement of a 'political opinion'" (emphasis added). To reverse the BIA finding we must find that the evidence not only *supports* that conclusion, but compels it—and also compels the further conclusion that Elias-Zacarias had a well-founded fear that the guerrillas would persecute him *because of* that political opinion.

Elias-Zacarias appears to argue that not taking sides with any political faction is itself the affirmative expression of a political opinion. That seems to us not ordinarily so, since we do not agree with the dissent that only a "narrow, grudging construction of the concept of 'political opinion,'" would distinguish it from such quite different concepts as indifference, indecisiveness and risk-averseness. But we need not decide whether the evidence compels the conclusion that Elias-Zacarias held a political opinion. Even if it does, Elias-Zacarias still has to establish that the record also compels the conclusion that he has a "well-founded fear" that the guerrillas will persecute him because of that political opinion, rather than because of his refusal to fight with them. He has not done so with the degree of clarity necessary to permit reversal of a BIA finding to the contrary; indeed, he has not done so at all.

Elias-Zacarias objects that he cannot be expected to provide direct proof of his persecutors' motives. We do not require that. But since the statute makes motive critical, he must provide *some* evidence of it, direct or circumstantial. And if he seeks to obtain judicial reversal of the BIA's determination, he must show that the evidence he presented was so compelling that no reasonable factfinder could fail to find the requisite rear of persecution. That he has not done.

The BIA's determination should therefore have been upheld in all respects, and we reverse the Court of Appeals' judgment to the contrary.

Justice STEVENS, with whom Justice Blackmun, and Justice O'Connor join, dissenting.

* * *

A political opinion can be expressed negatively as well as affirmatively. A refusal to support a cause—by staying home on election day, by refusing to take an oath of allegiance, or by refusing to step forward at an induction center—can express a political opinion as effectively as an affirmative statement or affirmative conduct. Even if the refusal is motivated by nothing more than a simple desire to continue living an ordinary life with one's family, it is the kind of political expression that the asylum provisions of the statute were intended to protect.

* * *

The narrow, grudging construction of the concept of "political opinion" that the Court adopts today is inconsistent with the basic approach to this statute that the Court endorsed in *INS v. Cardoza-Fonseca, supra*. In that case, relying heavily on the fact that an alien's status as a "refugee" merely makes him eligible for a discretionary grant of asylum—as contrasted with the entitlement to a withholding of deportation authorized by § 243(h) of the Act—the Court held that the alien's burden of proving a well-founded fear of persecution did not require proof that persecution was more likely than not to occur. We explained:

> "Our analysis of the plain language of the Act, its symmetry with the United Nations Protocol, and its legislative history, lead inexorably to the conclusion that to show a 'well-founded fear of persecution,' an alien need not prove that it is more likely than not that he or she will be persecuted in his or her home country. We find these ordinary canons of statutory construction com-

pelling, even without regard to the longstanding principle of construing any lingering ambiguities in deportation statutes in favor of the alien.

> "Deportation is always a harsh measure; it is all the more replete with danger when the alien makes a claim that he or she will be subject to death or persecution if forced to return to his or her home country. In enacting the Refugee Act of 1980 Congress sought to 'give the United States sufficient flexibility to respond to situations involving political or religious dissidents and detainees throughout the world.' H. R. Rep., at 9. Our holding today increases that flexibility by rejecting the Government's contention that the Attorney General may not even consider granting asylum to one who fails to satisfy the strict § 243(h) standard. Whether or not a 'refugee' is eventually granted asylum is a matter which Congress has left for the Attorney General to decide. But it is clear that Congress did not intend to restrict eligibility for that relief to those who could prove that it is more likely than not that they will be persecuted if deported." 480 U.S., at 449–450.

Similar reasoning should resolve any doubts concerning the political character of an alien's refusal to take arms against a legitimate government in favor of the alien. In my opinion, the record in this case is more than adequate to support the conclusion that this respondent's refusal was a form of expressive conduct that constituted the statement of a "political opinion" within the meaning of § 208(a).

It follows as night follows day that the guerrillas' implied threat to "take" him or to "kill" him if he did not change his position constituted threatened persecution "on account of" that political opinion. As the Court of Appeals explained in *Bolanos-Hernandez, supra*:

> "It does not matter to the persecutors what the individual's motivation is. The guerrillas in El Salvador do not inquire into the reasoning process of those who insist on remaining neutral and refuse to join their cause. They are concerned only with an act that constitutes an overt manifestation of a political opinion. Persecution because of that overt manifestation is persecution because of a political opinion."

It is important to emphasize that the statute does not require that an applicant for asylum prove exactly why his persecutors would act against him; it only requires him to show that he has a "well-founded fear of persecution on account of ... political opinion." As we recognized in *INS v. Cardoza Fonseca*, the applicant meets this burden if he shows that there is a " 'reasonable possibility' " that he will be persecuted on account of his political opinion. 480 U.S., at 440 (quoting *INS v. Stevic*, 467 U.S. 407, 425 (1984)). Because respondent expressed a political opinion by refusing to join the guerrillas, and they responded by threatening to "take" or to "kill" him if he did not change his mind, his fear that the guerrillas will persecute him on account of his political opinion is well founded.

H. Gender-Based Claims

Karen Musalo, The Developing Jurisprudence of Gender-Based Claims

1998–99 Annual Immigration and Nationality Handbook

I. Introduction

In the refugee context, women often suffer harms which are unique to women, that is, they suffer harms which are generally not suffered by men. Women may be subject to female genital mutilation, forced abortion or involuntary marriage. In addition, although women may suffer harm for the same reasons as men, i.e., race, nationality, religion, etc., in some cases they suffer harm simply and solely because of their gender, because they are women. For example, they may be forced into polygamy, banned from certain educational or professional endeavors, or suffer other forms of institutionalized discrimination.

Historically, these two factors—the unique *form* which the harm may take, and the fact that it may be inflicted exclusively *because of* gender—have often led adjudicators to deny protection to women under the Refugee Act. In some cases, the rationale for denial has been that the harm did not constitute persecution, while in others it was that harms imposed solely for reasons of gender were not "on account of" one of the five enumerated grounds: race, religion, nationality, political opinion, membership in a particular social group.

In this article we will look at the development of jurisprudence in the area of gender-based persecution. We will focus particularly on claims of persecution based on female genital mutilation (FGM), the imposition of discriminatory and repressive social norms, and domestic violence.

II. Canadian Guidelines, INS Considerations

There have been a number of developments which have resulted in increasing recognition that neither the unique form which the harm may take, nor the fact that the harm is imposed for reasons of gender brings the claim of a woman asylum seeker outside of the refugee definition. Significant among these developments have been pronouncements by the United Nations High Commissioner for Refugees (UNHCR)[2], and the issuance of guidance on the adjudication of women refugee

2. *See, e.g.*, Ex. Comm. Conclusion No. 39 (XXXVI) on Refugee Women and International Protection (36th Session 1985); UNHCR Guidelines on the Protection of Refugee Women (Geneva: Office of the UNHCR, EC/SCP/67, 22 July 1991); Ex. Comm. Conclusion No. 73 (XLIV) on Refugee Protection and Sexual Violence (44th Session 1993). For a review of the UNHCR's actions in the area of gender claims, see Karen Musalo et al., Refugee Law and Policy, Chapter 10 (Carolina Academic Press 1997).

claims by the Immigration and Refugee Board of Canada in 1993,[3] and the U.S. Immigration and Naturalization Service in 1995.[4] The Canadian Guidelines were updated in November 1996.

The 1993 Canadian Guidelines directly address the two issues mentioned above which repeatedly have been conceptual impediments to the granting of relief; namely that women may suffer forms of harm unique to their gender, and solely because of their gender. On the first point, the Guidelines clearly state that the unique form which harms suffered by women may take does not preclude such harms from constituting persecution. In fleshing out the concept of persecution in the context of gender claims, the Canadian Guidelines take a protection-oriented approach which defines persecution in relation to international human rights standards, including those specifically addressing the human rights of women.[6] The fact that a feared harm may be part of the social, cultural or religious norms of a country will not immunize it from being categorized as persecution if it violates international standards for the protection of women. On the second point, i.e., that in some instances harm may be imposed solely because of gender, the Canadian Guidelines encourage the use of the social group category as a basis for establishing the required nexus.

The INS Considerations adopt a tone similar to that of the Canadian Guidelines, although they do not go as far as the latter in referencing human rights standards as a framework for determining whether gender-specific harms constitute persecution. The INS Considerations do recognize, however, the significance of the international human rights framework in evaluating gender claims. They also discuss the potential of defining a social group by gender combined with other characteristics.

III. The Developing Jurisprudence: Federal Court, BIA and IJ Decisions

A. The Applicability of Traditional Asylum Norms

The Canadian Guidelines and the INS Considerations acknowledge the factors which may be unique to women's claims, while affirming the applicability of traditional asylum jurisprudence, informed by relevant international norms. A fair interpretation of the Guidelines and Considerations is that it is not necessary to reach beyond an informed application of well-accepted principles of asylum law in order to adjudicate

---

3. Guidelines Issued by the Chairperson Pursuant to Section 65(3) of the Immigration Act: Women Refugee Claimant Fearing Gender-Related Persecution (Immigration and Refugee Board, Ottawa, Canada, March 9, 1993).

4. Considerations for Asylum Officers Adjudicating Asylum Claims From Women (Memorandum from Phyllis Coven, Office of International Affairs, U.S. INS, to All INS Asylum Officers HQASM Coordinators, May 26, 1996).

6. The Guidelines list the following as relevant international instruments: Universal Declaration of Human Rights, International Covenant on Civil and Political Rights, International Covenant on Economic, Social and Cultural Rights, Convention on the Elimination of All Forms of Discrimination Against Women, Convention on the Political Rights of Women, and the Convention on the Nationality of Married Women.

the claims of women asylum seekers. Existing precedent which fleshes out the notion of persecution, and the definition of social group provides the over-arching adjudicatory framework. The applicability of traditional jurisprudence is important as a rejoinder to the criticism that the claims of women asylum seekers do not come within the scope of protection provided by the United Nations Refugee Convention and Protocol, and the U.S. Refugee Act.

* * *

D. The Imposition of Discriminatory and Repressive Social Norms—*Fatin,*[18] *Safaie*[19] & the *Fisher*[20] cases

In 1985 the U.N. Executive Committee issued a conclusion which provided that:

> ... States, in the exercise of their sovereignty, are free to adopt the interpretation that women asylum seekers who face harsh or inhuman treatment due to their having transgressed the social mores of the society in which they live may be considered as a "particular social group" within the meaning of ... the 1951 United Nations Refugee Convention.[21]

Notwithstanding this recommendation, which is echoed in the Canadian Guidelines and the INS Considerations, claims based upon the imposition of repressive, gender discriminatory norms have thus far not fared well in U.S. courts. Although courts have been willing to accept that a social group may be comprised of women subject to repressive norms, they have been reluctant to characterize the harm at issue as persecution.

In *Fatin*, *Safaie* and the *Fisher* cases, the Third, Eighth and Ninth Circuits, respectively, addressed claims arising out of the imposition of fundamentalist Islamic norms in Iran. The petitioners in *Fatin* and *Safaie* alleged persecution on the basis of social group membership, while *Fisher* alleged that imposition of the discriminatory and repressive norms constituted persecution on account of religion and political opinion.

The applicant in *Fatin* had been a supporter of the Shah, and identified herself as an educated, westernized feminist who believed in equal rights for women. She feared that if she returned to Iran she would be forced to comply with Islamic religious beliefs, including wearing of the traditional veil or "chador." The record demonstrated that the penalty for non-compliance with such gender specific norms included whippings, imprisonment, and in some cases, brutal rape and death. At her hearing, Fatin

---

18. *Fatin v. INS*, 12 F.3d 1233 (3d Cir. 1993).

19. *Safaie v. INS*, 25 F.3d 636 (8th Cir. 1994).

20. *Fisher v. INS*, 37 F.3d 1371 (9th Cir. 1994), amended 61 F.3d 1366 (9thCir. 1995), *Fisher v. INS*, 79 F.3d 955 (9th Cir. 1996).

21. Ex. Comm. Conclusion No. 39 (XXXVI) on Refugee Women and International Protection (36th Session 1985), para. k.

testified that she would have to submit to wearing the veil in order to avoid the severe physical sanctions for non-compliance.

The Third Circuit denied relief to Fatin, finding that her opposition to the Islamic norms was not so strong that her forced submission to them would constitute persecution. The court reasoned that if Fatin really found the fundamentalist Islamic requirements to be so abhorrent, she would resist and be willing to suffer the consequences. Since Fatin had testified that she would comply, the court declined to find persecution.

The Eight Circuit Court of Appeals subscribed to this same rationale in deciding *Safaie*. The petitioner in *Safaie,* who was a university student in Iran, opposed Islamic norms. Safaie testified that she had been discharged from a job as secretary to an Iranian official because she refused to wear traditional clothing. She had been confronted on other occasions regarding her refusal to conform, and had been threatened with punishment, and finally she had been expelled from the University for not accepting Islamic rules.

Safaie was denied relief because she had conceded that in the two years preceding her flight from Iran, she had complied with the Islamic dress code. The court interpreted her compliance as a lack of "missionary fever" in opposition to the requirements. Because she had chosen not to flout the norms, the court reached the conclusion that compliance with them was not so abhorrent that it rose to the level of persecution. Is the approach of the courts in *Fatin* and *Safaie* consistent with traditional asylum jurisprudence? Some commentators think not. In her article discussing gender cases, Professor Goldberg has noted:

> Nowhere else in asylum law has an applicant been required to meet such a high standard. It is difficult to present a clear analogy from existing caselaw in the context of social group membership. In comparing this analysis with the political opinion category, however, courts have not held that an individual must show that he or she would continue to express his or her beliefs regardless of the consequences. It is enough that the individual establish the holding of such beliefs, and persecution or a well-founded fear of persecution on account of those beliefs.[22]

The denial in *Fisher* was also premised partially upon a finding that the harm at issue did not constitute persecution, although the court did not evoke the "missionary fever" standard. The petitioner in *Fisher*, who also opposed the fundamentalist Islamic norms, had run afoul of governmental authorities on two occasions. On the first she was arrested and interrogated for having attended a party where she saw her male host in bathing attire; on the second she was stopped on the street and ordered at

22. Pamela Goldberg, *U.S. Law and Women Asylum Seekers: Where are They and Where Are They Going?*, 73 Interpreter Releases 889, 894 (July 8, 1996).

gunpoint into a car for allowing strands of her hair to stray outside her chador. The BIA rejected Fisher's claim, ruling in part that the two detentions did not constitute persecution. A panel of the Ninth Circuit reversed the Board, but was itself reversed in an *en banc* Ninth Circuit decision. The *en banc* court's denial rested on its determination that the harm Fisher had suffered did not rise to the level of persecution, but "only" constituted discrimination. The court also ruled that Fisher had failed to establish a nexus to an enumerated ground, finding that the imposition of these norms was not intended to punish her for religious or political beliefs.

Notwithstanding the decisions in *Fatin, Safaie*, and *Fisher*, traditional jurisprudence supports the argument that discriminatory norms which violate women's fundamental human rights may constitute persecution, and that this is the case regardless of whether or not a woman alleges that she would disobey them. A recent decision by an immigration judge in San Francisco is in accord with this notion. In *Matter of W-D-*, A73 490 183 (IJ July 3, 1996) (San Francisco) (King IJ) the applicant was a university educated woman from Afghanistan. She testified that after the ouster of Najibullah, the Islamic laws denied all education for women, even forbidding them from learning to read. The laws prohibited women from leaving the house without male accompaniment, and it required the wearing of the head covering, veil and shawl worn by traditional Muslim women. The applicant alleged that was opposed to these restrictions, that she tried to persuade others to oppose them, and that she did not wear the chador.

The immigration judge granted asylum, finding a well-founded fear of persecution on the alternative grounds of political opinion and social group membership. In her discussion of the social group basis of the claim, the judge ruled in relevant part:

> The Applicant has established that ... the Taliban have a definite political and religious philosophy which places women in a position subordinate to men. Under this philosophy women are to be wholly dependent on the men in society as either daughters, sisters, or wives. To ensure complete dependence, women are to be excluded from all forms of institutionalized education and precluded from earning money. The complete deprivation of education and exclusion from the workforce creates an atmosphere of oppression which goes beyond mere discrimination and rises to the level of virtual slavery, constituting persecution. Such persecution is"on account of" their being women and the desire of those holding power, for whatever reason, to keep women dependent upon, and at the service of men....
>
> [The Applicant] has and will refuse to abide by the restrictions and such defiance could lead to retaliation.... Indeed, even if the Applicant did not openly defy the Islamic law, she would be subject to persecution in the form of an almost complete loss of freedom because of her gender. The fact that she considers such restrictions to be abhorrant [sic] to her own beliefs and lifestyle increases the harm to her as a member of the social group in question, as does the fact that she would openly defy them. *Nevertheless, neither opposition nor abhorrance is necessary to a finding of persecution* ... [emphasis

> added]. Although this would not necessarily always be true, in this case, the form of persecution at issue includes not only retaliation for defiance, but also restrictions which in and of themselves are especially unconscionable....
>
> [A]s a member of the particular social group of Afghan women, who are subject to unconscionably restrictive gender-specific laws, the Applicant qualifies for asylum *simply because* such laws will be applied to her.

Was the immigration judge in *Matter of W-D-* ignoring the precedent set by *Fatin, Safaie* and *Fisher* in ruling that "neither opposition nor abhorrance" was necessary to a finding of persecution? No—rather she was able to distinguish *Fatin, Safaie* and *Fisher* from the case at bar because of the nature of the restrictions alleged in *Matter of W-D-*. The immigration judge found that the restrictions imposed went beyond "mere discrimination." They reduced the status of women to "the level of virtual slavery" and therefore constituted persecution in and of themselves. The immigration judge's decision in *Matter of W-D-* demonstrates the importance of fully detailing the nature and extent of the restrictive norms. The more extensive and repressive the norms, the stronger the argument that they constitute the type of harm recognized under traditional asylum jurisprudence as persecution.

D. Domestic Violence

The Canadian Guidelines and INS Considerations both recognize that under certain circumstances a successful claim to protection made be made by a woman who has fled her home country to escape domestic violence. Although the persecutor in these cases is a private actor, the domestic violence claims fit comfortably within traditional asylum jurisprudence. U.S. law has long accepted the principle that under the Refugee Act, the persecution may be at the hands of the government, or a non-governmental entity which the government cannot or will not control. Where there is a failure of State protection to the victims of domestic violence, a finding may be made that the government cannot or will not control the persecutor.

There have been a number of decisions in Canada granting asylum in claims involving domestic abuse, but there have been virtually no precedent decisions in the U.S.[27] There have, however, been a number of decisions by immigration judges, granting relief to women who were the victims of ongoing abuse by their domestic partners.

In *Matter of A and Z*, A72 190 893, A72 793 219 (IJ Dec. 20, 1994) (Arlington) (Nejelski, IJ) the immigration judge granted asylum to a Jordanian woman who had been physically and verbally abused throughout a thirty year marriage by her husband who was a wealthy and successful businessperson. The respondent had testified that

---

27. The Ninth Circuit's decision in *Lazo-Majano, v. INS*, 813 F.2d 1432 (9th Cir. 1987) may be considered to be one of the few precedent decisions involving domestic violence. It predated by a number of years the sensitivity to the issue engendered by the Canadian and U.S. guidelines.

she believed in Western values and was not "content to be a slave"[28] to her husband. The immigration judge found the wife to be a member of the social group of women who"are challenging the traditions of Jordanian society and government."[29] The court also noted that there was a failure of state protection because the respondent "could not go to the police to seek protection, nor could she divorce her husband."[30]

Matter of M and K, A72 374 558 (IJ Aug. 9, 1995) (Arlington) (Nejelski, IJ) involved both domestic abuse and forcible FGM. The applicant was from Sierra Leone, a country where FGM is widely practiced. Those who resist FGM are considered to be outcasts, and women are expected to be subservient to men. Although the applicant refused to voluntarily submit to mutilation, she was abducted from her parents' house and mutilated against her will at the age of twenty-three. In addition to the persecution of FGM, her husband verbally and physically abused her because she was "mouthy" and "attempted to assert her individual autonomy."[31]

The immigration judge found that the government was unable or unwilling to protect women from FGM or from spousal abuse, finding that the "police provides [sic] no protection to women who complain of physical spousal abuse."[32] The immigration judge granted asylum finding the FGM and spousal abuse to be persecution and finding a nexus to both political opinion and social group membership. The social group as to the harm of FGM was defined to include all women forced to undergo the practice, while the social group for the applicant's claim of domestic violence was comprised of "women who have been punished with physical spousal abuse for attempting to assert their individual autonomy."[33]

In *Matter of Sharmin*, A73 556 833 (IJ Sept. 27 1996) (New York) (Bukszpan, IJ) the immigration judge granted asylum to a Bangladeshi woman who was active in the women's section of the Jayto Party, against her husband's wishes who had ordered her not to leave the house, or to talk to other people.[34] Ms. Sharmin testified that her husband beat her, and she had scars, as well as a letter from a clinic corroborating physical injuries and hospitalization. The immigration judge found that Ms. Sharmin's persecution was on account of both social group membership and political opinion: "As a young, Westernized, educated Muslim wife, voicing political opinion by both word and deed in her political party involvement and in her de facto feminism, she was the target of persecution because of membership in a particular social group and because of political opinion." The immigration judge found that the government, and the society at large, condoned a husband's oppression of his wife, and that the

28. *Matter of A and Z, supra*, at 14.
29. *Matter of A and Z, supra*, at 15.
30. *Matter of A and Z, supra*, at 6.
31. *Matter of M and K, supra*, at 9.
32. *Matter of M and K, supra*, at 13.
33. *Matter of M and K, supra*, at 15.
34. A detailed summary of the decision appears in *IJ Grants Asylum to Battered Bangladeshi Woman*, 74 Interpreter Releases 174 (January 27, 1997).

Muslim religious laws consigned women to an inferior status, from which they could not escape.

* * *

The fact that women may suffer in ways unique to their gender, or because of their gender, should not defeat their claims. The definition of persecution clearly covers practices such as FGM, institutionalized discrimination and many of the other unique harms inflicted on women. Furthermore, as the courts have affirmed, where the persecution a woman suffers is not inflicted on the basis of race, religion, nationality or political opinion, the required nexus may be established by use of the social group ground, which may be defined in part or whole by the attribute of gender.

Note

For a comparative perspective on how other countries have dealt with gender-based claims, see Audrey Macklin, *Cross-border Shopping for Ideas: A Critical Review of United States, Canadian, and Australian approaches to Gender-Related Asylum Cases*, 13 GEO. IMMIGR. L.J. 25–71 (1998).

Olimpia Lazo-Majano v. Immigration and Naturalization Service

813 F.2d 1432 (9th Cir. 1986)

Before PREGERSON, POOLE and NOONAN, Circuit Judges.

NOONAN, Circuit Judge:

Olimpia Lazo-Majano is a thirty-four year old woman. She is the mother of three children. In 1981, when she was twenty-nine, her husband left El Salvador for political reasons: he had been in the rightist paramilitary group known as ORDEN; when he quit he was wanted by the guerrillas and distrusted by the government. Olimpia had always lived in the same small town. For five years she had been working as a domestic for another woman, getting a day off every fifteen days. In the middle of April 1982, she received a telephone call from Sergeant Rene Zuniga who had known her since childhood. He asked her to wash his clothes. Olimpia agreed.

On her day off during the next six weeks Olimpia worked for Zuniga at Zuniga's place. Zuniga then pointed out that Olimpia's husband was no longer in El Salvador and raped her. In Olimpia's words: "With a gun in his hand he made me be his." In the following months Olimpia accepted Zuniga's domination. She continued to wash for him on her days off. She accepted taunts, threats, and beatings from him. He broke her identity card in pieces and forced her to eat the pieces. He dragged her by the hair about a public restaurant. He pummeled her face, causing a blood clot to form in one eye; she thought that she had lost the eye. Olimpia became nervous, preoccupied, and depressed, ate little, and became thin and frail. She wanted to escape her tormentor but saw no way of doing so.

Central to the situation was the fact that Zuniga was a sergeant in the Fuerza Armada, the Armed Force which is the Salvadoran military. Zuniga used his gun in forcing Olimpia to submit the first time. On another occasion Zuniga held two hand grenades against her forehead. On another occasion he threatened to bomb her. When he referred to her husband, Zuniga said that if he returned Zuniga himself would cut him apart, kill both Olimpia and her husband and say that they were both subversives. Zuniga told Olimpia that it was his job to kill subversives.

Zuniga said to Olimpia that if she ever told on him he would have her tongue cut off, her nails removed one by one, her eyes pulled out, and she would then be killed. As Olimpia recalls his statement, he said: "And I can just say that you are contrary to us; subversive." When he was angry with her in the restaurant, he told a friend from the police "in front of all the other people in the restaurant" that she was a subversive and that was why her husband had left: "because she was a subversive."

Olimpia believed the Armed Force would let Zuniga carry out his threat. She believed that in 1979 a nineteen-year old boy she knew by sight had been tied, tortured and killed by the Armed Force; that in 1981 the husband of a neighbor had been taken away in a truck at night with fifteen others and killed by the Armed Force; that the Armed Force had raped "young college girls," as had Zuniga himself. In her view there was nobody in El Salvador that could stop the Armed Force from doing such things. In her experience when Zuniga was dragging her by the hair in the restaurant no one helped because where the Armed Force is concerned, "no one will get involved."

In 1982 Olimpia escaped from Zuniga, left El Salvador and illegally entered the United States. In January 1983, Olimpia was ordered to show cause why she should not be deported for entry without inspection. See 8 U.S.C. § 1251(a)(2). She admitted deportability and applied for political asylum, claiming fear of persecution by Zuniga. Her request was denied by Immigration Judge William F. Nail on March 23, 1984. On May 9, 1985, The Board of Immigration Appeals upheld Judge Nail's decision and dismissed her appeal. It found that "the evidence attests to mistreatment of an individual, not persecution" and cited *In re Pierre*, 15 I & N Dec. 461 (BIA 1976) (a wife threatened with death by her husband, a high Haitian official, did not show persecution for a political opinion even though the government of Haiti would not restrain her husband). The Board declared as to the plight of Olimpia that it was "not unsympathetic with this deplorable situation" but "the fact remains that such strictly personal actions do not constitute persecution within the meaning of the Act."

* * *

Persecution is stamped on every page of this record. Olimpia has been singled out to be bullied, beaten, injured, raped, and enslaved. Olimpia's initial acquiescence does not alter the persecutory character of her treatment. That she continued to return to Zuniga's place after his initial attack upon her presents a pattern, all too familiar, of a victim identifying with the aggressor under conditions of terror. She lacked "sufficient ego-strength, self-confidence and willpower" to "escape or cry out for help." Cf. *United States v. Winters*, 729 F.2d 602, 605 (9th Cir.1984) (Pregerson, J.). The persecution has been conducted by a member of the Armed Force, a military power that exercises domination over much of El Salvador despite the staunchest efforts of the Duarte government to restrain it. Zuniga had his gun, his grenades, his bombs, his authority and his hold over Olimpia because he was a member of this powerful military group.

Uncontradicted evidence, then, pointed to both a clear probability of persecution and a well-founded fear of persecution. Olimpia relates that Zuniga said to her that if she ever left him, "[H]e would look for me, for my person, in all El Salvador." El Salvador is a small country. We take judicial notice of reports that persons being deported there from the United States have been tortured and have been killed. We are not in a position to verify these reports. We are in a position to say that they are sufficiently credible to show that Olimpia, the target of a police officer's persecution for her political opinion, would be in serious jeopardy if forced to return to her native land.

Was Olimpia, however, persecuted by an agent of the government because she had a political opinion, or was the relation of Olimpia and Zuniga purely personal? When "political opinion" in the sense used by the two statutes is analyzed, it must mean "the political opinion of the victim as seen by the persecutor." At times in the history of persecution the victims have been persons who did not share the prejudices and enthusiasms of their persecutors. Their opinions have been politically unacceptable only because of the opposition and hostility the persecutors have read into their silence or noncommitment to the persecutors' opinions. Cf. *Bolanos-Hernandez v. INS*, 749 F.2d 1316, 1324 (9th Cir.1985). So in this case, if the situation is seen in its social context, Zuniga is asserting the political opinion that a man has a right to dominate and he has persecuted Olimpia to force her to accept this opinion without rebellion. Zuniga told Olimpia that in his treatment of her he was seeking revenge. But Olimpia knew of no injury she had ever done Zuniga. His statement reflects a much more generalized animosity to the opposite sex, an assertion of a political aspiration and the desire to suppress opposition to it. Olimpia was not permitted by Zuniga to hold an opinion to the contrary. When by flight, she asserted one, she became exposed to persecution for her assertion. Persecution threatened her because of her political opinion.

Olimpia has suffered persecution because of one specific political opinion Zuniga attributed to her. She is, she has been told by Zuniga, a subversive. Her husband left the country, a policeman has been told, because she is a subversive. If she complained of Zuniga, she was informed, she would be killed as a subversive. One cannot have a more compelling example of a political opinion generating political persecution than the opinion that is held by a subversive in opposition to the government. Zuniga viewed Olimpia as having such an opinion.

The opinion, it may be said, is not Olimpia's. It is only imputed to her by Zuniga. And it is imputed by Zuniga cynically. Zuniga knows that Olimpia is only a poor domestic and washerwoman. She does not participate in politics.

Olimpia, however, does have a political opinion, camouflage it though she does. She believes that the Armed Force is responsible for lawlessness, rape, torture, and murder. Such views constitute a political opinion. And she has been persecuted for possessing it. Because she believes that no political control exists to restrain a brutal sergeant in the Armed Force she has been subjected to his brutality. Her subversive doubts about governmental law-abidingness have made her the prey of a hunter of subversives. Characterized as a subversive, she was forced to submit to Zuniga.Even if she had no political opinion and was innocent of a single reflection on the government of her country, the cynical imputation of political opinion to her is what counts under both statutes. In deciding whether anyone has a well-founded fear of persecution or is in danger of losing life or liberty because of a political opinion, one must continue to look at the person from the perspective of the persecutor. If the persecutor thinks the person guilty of a political opinion, then the person is at risk.

Seventeen years ago this basic issue was decided by this circuit. A Yugoslavian citizen, who had refused to work with the Yugoslav secret police, was denied the opportunity to follow his profession as a clerk in Yugoslavia. He eventually became a cook on a Yugoslavian merchant vessel, which he left to seek asylum in the United States. He had no established political views beyond his unwillingness to be a police informer. The persecution he feared was punishment for defecting from a police state. This court, overruling the Board, recognized that such fear of persecution was fear of punishment on account of a political opinion. *Kovac v. INS*, 407 F.2d 102, 104 (9th Cir.1969) (Browning, J). The opinion on account of which he would have been punished was the one the masters of Yugoslavia would have attributed to him. So here Olimpia fears persecution on account of the opinion Zuniga attributes to her.

* * *

Here, when Zuniga manipulatively chooses to regard Olimpia as a subversive, he attributes to her the political opinion of a subversive, and she is being persecuted on account of a political opinion. The fact that Zuniga gave Olimpia the choice of being subjected to physical injury and rape or being killed as a subversive does not alter the significance of political opinion for Olimpia. Because of the status attributed to her by Zuniga and the political opinion that accompanied that status, Olimpia had to suffer the series of indignities that everyone sees as persecution.

Reversed and Remanded.

Note

The Ninth Circuit decided *Lazo-Majano* prior to the U.S. Supreme Court decision in *Elias Zacarias.* Are there elements of the court's decision that are no longer valid after *Zacarias?* You may want to defer your answer to that question until you read the BIA's decision in *Matter of R-A-*, which appears at the end of this section and involves a woman who suffered brutal treatment at the hands of a man with whom she was intimately involved.

In re Fauziya Kasinga

21 I. & N. Dec. 357 (BIA 1996)

Board En Banc: Schmidt, Chairman; Dunne, Vice Chairman; Holmes, Hurwitz, Villageliu, Cole, Mathon, and Guendelsberger, Board Members. Concurring Opinions: Fillpu, Board Member, joined by Heilman, Board Member; Rosenberg, Board Member. Dissenting: Vacca, Board Member.

Schmidt, Chairman:

* * *

A fundamental issue before us is whether the practice of female genital mutilation ("FGM") can be the basis for a grant of asylum under section 208 of the Immigration and Nationality Act, 8 U.S.C. § 1158 (1994). On appeal, the parties agree that FGM can be the basis for a grant of asylum. We find that FGM can be a basis for asylum.

Nevertheless, the parties disagree about 1) the parameters of FGM as a ground for asylum in future cases, and 2) whether the applicant is entitled to asylum on the basis of the record before us. In deciding this case, we decline to speculate on, or establish rules for, cases that are not before us.

We make seven major findings in the applicant's case. Those findings are summarized below.

First, the record before us reflects that the applicant is a credible witness. Second, FGM, as practiced by the Tchamba-Kunsuntu Tribe of Togo and documented in the record, constitutes persecution. Third, the applicant is a member of a social group consisting of young women of the Tchamba-Kunsuntu Tribe who have not had FGM, as practiced by that tribe, and who oppose the practice. Fourth, the applicant has a well-founded fear of persecution. Fifth, the persecution applicant fears is "on account of" her social group. Sixth, the applicant's fear of persecution is country-wide. Seventh, and finally, the applicant is eligible for and should be granted asylum in the exercise of discretion. Each finding is explained below.

The applicant is a 19-year-old native and citizen of Togo. She attended 2 years of high school. She is a member of the Tchamba-Kunsuntu Tribe of northern Togo. She testified that young women of her tribe normally under FGM at age 15. However, she did not because she initially was protected from FGM by her influential, but now deceased, father.

The applicant stated that upon her father's death in 1993, under tribal custom her aunt, her father's sister, became the primary authority figure in the family. The applicant's mother was driven from the family home, left Togo, and went to live with her family in Benin. The applicant testified that she does not currently know her mother's exact whereabouts.

The applicant further testified that her aunt forced her into a polygamous marriage in October 1994, when she was 17. The husband selected by her aunt was 45 years old and had three other wives at the time of marriage. The applicant testified that, under tribal custom, her aunt and her husband planned to force her to submit to FGM before the marriage was consummated.

The applicant testified that she feared imminent mutilation. With the help of her older sister, she fled Togo for Ghana. However, she was afraid that her aunt and her husband would locate her there. Consequently, using money from her mother, the applicant embarked for Germany by airplane.

Upon arrival in Germany, the applicant testified that she was somewhat disoriented and spent several hours wandering around the airport looking for fellow Africans who might help her. Finally, she struck up a conversation, in English, with a German woman.

After hearing the applicant's story, the woman offered to give the applicant temporary shelter in her home until the applicant decided what to do next. For the next 2 months, the applicant slept in the woman's living room, while performing cooking and cleaning duties.

The applicant further stated that in December 1994, while on her way to a shopping center, she met a young Nigerian man. He was the first person from Africa she had spoken to since arriving in Germany. They struck up a conversation, during which the applicant told the man about her situation. He offered to sell the applicant his sister's British passport so that she could seek asylum in the United States, where she has an aunt, an uncle, and a cousin. The applicant followed the man's suggestion, purchasing the passport and the ticket with money given to her by her sister.

The applicant did not attempt a fraudulent entry into the United States. Rather, upon arrival at Newark International Airport on December 17, 1994, she immediately requested asylum. She remained in detention by the Immigration and Naturalization Service ("INS") until April 1996.

The applicant testified that the Togolese police and the Government of Togo were aware of FGM and would take no steps to protect her from the practice. She further testified that her aunt had reported her to the Togolese police. Upon return, she would be taken back to her husband by the police and forced to undergo FGM. She testified at several points that there would be nobody to protect her from FGM in Togo.

In her testimony, the applicant referred to letters in the record (Exh. 3) from her mother. Those letters confirmed that the Togolese police were looking for the applicant and that the applicant's father's family wanted her to undergo FGM.

The applicant testified that she could not find protection anywhere in Togo. She stated that Togo is a very small country and her husband and aunt, with the help of the police, could locate her anywhere she went. She also stated that her husband is well known in Togo and is a friend of the police. On cross-examination she stated that it would not be possible for her to live with another tribe in Togo.

The applicant also testified that the Togolese police could locate her in Ghana. She indicated that she did not seek asylum in Germany because she could not speak German and therefore could not continue her education there. She stated that she did not have relatives in Germany as she does in the United States.

The applicant's written asylum application was filed on April 18, 1995, while she was in INS detention (Exh. 3). That application is consistent with the above testimony in all material respects.

A number of documents are attached to the applicant's asylum application. First, there are copies of two letters, dated December 27, 1994, and December 30, 1994, respectively, signed by the applicant's mother. The letters are in English. One letter confirms that the applicant's father's family wishes to have the applicant marry an older man and be subjected to FGM. That letter further confirms that the applicant's mother gave the applicant money to assist her escape. The other letter confirms that the Togolese police were looking for the applicant following her escape in October 1994.

The applicant testified that 1) her mother cannot write English; 2) the letters were prepared by the applicant's sister, at her mother's request; and 3) the letters are signed by the applicant's mother (Tr. at 62–63).

A translated copy of the applicant's marriage certificate also is appended to the asylum application. That document, dated October 7, 1994, is signed by the applicant's husband, but not by the applicant.

Finally, an untranslated document in French, perhaps from the police in Togo, is attached to the asylum application. The applicant did not rely on the untranslated document at the hearing. The INS trial attorney neither objected to the admission of the untranslated document nor cross-examined the applicant with respect to it. The Immigration Judge did not mention the untranslated document.

* * *

The applicant also submitted pictures of herself in tribal ceremonial dress at the time of her marriage. Those pictures were admitted into evidence (Exh. 5), and the applicant testified to their authenticity (Tr. at 70–71).

The applicant's prior counsel also filed a lengthy pre-hearing brief accompanied by extensive documentation. That documentation included information on the practice of FGM, its harmful effects on women, its lack of legitimate justification, and its condemnation by the international community. The documentation also confirmed the generally poor human rights situation in Togo, particularly for women. These background materials are designated "Group Exhibit" 4 in the record.

According to the applicant's testimony, the FGM practiced by her tribe, the Tchamba-Kunsuntu, is of an extreme type involving cutting the genitalia with knives, extensive bleeding, and a 40-day recovery period (Tr. 30–31, 41). The background materials confirm that the FGM practiced in some African countries, such as Togo, is of an extreme nature causing permanent damage, and not just a minor form of genital ritual. See, e.g., Nahid Toubia, Female Genital Mutilation: A Call for Global Action 9, 24–25 (Gloria Jacobs ed., Women Ink. 1993).

The record material establishes that FGM in its extreme forms is a practice in which portions of the female genitalia are cut away. In some cases, the vagina is sutured partially closed. This practice clearly inflicts harm or suffering upon the girl or woman who undergoes it.

FGM is extremely painful and at least temporarily incapacitating. It permanently disfigures the female genitalia. FGM exposes the girl or woman to the risk of serious, potentially life-threatening complications. These include, among others, bleeding, infection, urine retention, stress, shock, psychological trauma, and damage to the urethra and anus. It can result in permanent loss of genital sensation and can adversely affect sexual and erotic functions. See generally, Toubia, *supra*; INS Resource Information Center, Alert Series—Women—Female Genital Mutilation," Ref. No. Al/NGA/94.001 (July 1994) [hereinafter FGM Alert].

The FGM Alert, compiled and distributed by the INS Resource Information Center, notes that "few African countries have officially condemned female genital mutilation and still fewer have enacted legislation against the practice." FGM Alert, *supra*, at 6. Further, according to the FGM Alert, even in those few African countries where legislative efforts have been made, they are usually ineffective to protect women against FGM. The FGM Alert notes that "it remains practically true that [African] women have little legal recourse and may face threats to their freedom, threats or acts of physical violence, or social ostracization for refusing to undergo this harmful traditional practice or attempting to protect their female children." *Id.* at 6–7. Togo is not listed in the FGM Alert as among the African countries that have made even minimal efforts to protect women from FGM.

The record also contains a May 26, 1995, memorandum from Phyllis Coven, Office of International Affairs, INS, which is addressed to all INS Asylum Officers and sets forth guidelines for adjudicating women's asylum claims. Coven, U.S. Dep't of Justice, Considerations For Asylum Officers Adjudicating Claims From Women (1995). Those guidelines state that "rape..., sexual abuse and domestic violence, infanticide and genital mutilation are forms of mistreatment primarily directed at girls and women and they may serve as evidence of past persecution on account of one or more of the five grounds." Coven, *supra*, at 4.

The record also contains two reports compiled by the United States Department of State. The first of these, dated January 31, 1994, 1) confirms that FGM is practiced by some ethnic groups in Togo; 2) notes that while some reports indicate that the practice may be diminishing, an expert indicates that as many as 50% of Togolese females may have been mutilated; and 3) notes that various acts of violence against women occur in Togo with little police intervention. Committees on Foreign Affairs and Foreign Relations, 103d Cong., 2d Sess., Country Report on Human Rights Practices for 1993 (Joint Comm. Print 1994) [hereinafter 1993 Country Reports].

The second Department of State Report on Togo, prepared by the Bureau of Democracy, Human Rights and Labor, is dated April 1995. Bureau of Democracy, Human Rights and Labor, U.S. Dep't of State, Togo—Profile of Asylum Claims & Country Conditions (April 1995) [hereinafter Profile]. While not specifically addressing FGM, that report states that the President of Togo has a poor human rights record and confirms that the government's military and security forces have been involved in serious human rights abuses.

* * *

During the hearing before the Immigration Judge, the INS had an opportunity to cross-examine the applicant and to offer documentary evidence of its own having a bearing on the case. The INS submitted no documentary evidence.

As discussed below, the INS general attorney's cross-examination of the applicant revealed no meaningful inconsistencies in her testimony. The INS does not claim that the applicant is incredible, nor does the INS argue that the Immigration Judge's adverse credibility determination was correct. Rather, the INS requests that the record be remanded for further examination of the applicant's credibility. The INS cites four specific matters in support of its request.

First, the INS asserts that the applicant testified in an inconsistent manner because she gave several different answers regarding who performs FGM in her tribe. At one point, the applicant stated that an older man of the tribe performed the procedure (Tr. at 24). At another point, she indicated that an old lady or an official circumcisor performed the operations (Tr at 31–32).

These are not inconsistencies that undermine credibility. It is understandable that a teenage girl, who has been protected from FGM by her father, and who has never been subjected to the process, might have an imperfect understanding of who actually performs the procedure in her tribe. We also note that the applicant had been attending high school outside Togo, in Ghana, during the time *immediately* preceding her father's death. The INS does not challenge the applicant's membership in the Tchamba-Kunsuntu Tribe, not does it contend that the tribe does not practice FGM. When viewed in the context of the entire record, the ambiguous answers as to who performs FGM in the tribe do not undermine the applicant's credibility. See *Matter of B-*, Interim Decision 3251 (BIA 1995).

We reject the INS's second suggestion that there is a material discrepancy in the applicant's testimony regarding her marital status. The record establishes that the applicant was married against her will to an older man of her tribe, and the marriage was never consummated. The marriage certificate was not signed by the applicant. She fled the country shortly after the marriage, before she had been delivered to her husband's house. Understandably, in the particular circumstances of this case, the teenage applicant may, in her own mind, be uncertain as to whether she is actually "married" to her husband in Togo. The statement in her asylum application that she "would be forced to marry an old man, and be [circumcised]" is basically consistent with her testimony and the corroborating evidence she presented.

We also reject the INS's third challenge to the applicant's credibility. During oral argument, the General Counsel referred to the need to explore the matter of the "untranslated document" attached to the asylum application (O.A. at 33). However, he acknowledged that the INS had an opportunity to explore this matter below and did not do so (O.A. at 34). The INS is not entitled to another opportunity to try this issue. See *Matter of Guevara*, 20 I&N Dec. 238, 249 (BIA 1991).

We acknowledge the INS's fourth point—that a number of the applicant's answers on both direct and cross-examination were "inaudible" in the transcript. Nevertheless, there is ample audible testimony from the applicant that supports her asylum application. It is very unlikely that any of the "inaudible" portions of the transcript contained highly relevant material impeaching the applicant's credibility. If that were the case, we certainly would expect the INS to have brought it to our attention through an affidavit or declaration from its general attorney who was present at the haring below.

Finally, the INS has not suggested that it has any newly discovered, previously unavailable documentary evidence relating to conditions in Togo or the likelihood of country-wide persecution.

For the foregoing reasons, a remand is not necessary. This is particularly true in light of the length of time the applicant's asylum application has been pending.

We have conducted an independent review of the applicant's credibility. We note that the Immigration Judge's adverse credibility determination was based on a perceived lack of "rationality," "persuasiveness," and "consistency." The Immigration Judge did not rely on the applicant's demeanor. We, like the Immigration Judge, can determine from the record whether the applicant's testimony is "rational, plausible, and consistent."

We find that the applicant's testimony in support of her asylum application is plausible, detailed, and internally consistent. See *Matter of B-, supra.* It is consistent with her asylum application and with the substantial background information in the record. The latter includes information from the Department of State and the INS Resource Information Center.

The applicant is a 19-year-old woman, who was a 17-year-old high school student at the time the events in question occurred. The applicant's father had died, she was separated from her mother, and she was under the control of an unsympathetic aunt. Her arrival in the United States followed flight from her homeland and a lonely journey of thousands of miles that took her through a strange country. Her testimony followed more than 8 months of continuous INS detention, in several facilities, one of which was closed by a riot.*

We specifically reject the Immigration Judge's findings that the applicant's failure to know the present whereabouts of her mother; her claim to have avoided FGM through her father's efforts; the incident involving the German woman; or the incident with the Nigerian man were irrational, unpersuasive, or inconsistent. Each of those matters was adequately and reasonably explained by the applicant during her testimony and each of them reasonably could have happened to a teenage girl in the applicant's situation. Her testimony on these points was not impeached by the INS through cross-examination.

---

* Although not before us, the applicant's detention obviously had an impact on the trial and presentation of this case. The INS General Counsel characterizes the applicant's case as a "venture into new and difficult territory" of great importance (INS Reply Brief at 12). In light of that characterization, the applicant's young age, and her lack of any known criminal record, it is not apparent how the resolution of such important issues was facilitated by the applicant's long-term detention. The Commissioner and the General Counsel might well wish to review this policy should future cases of this type arise.

For the foregoing reasons, on the basis of the record before us, we find the applicant to be a credible witness.

For the purposes of this case, we adopt the description of FGM drawn from the record and summarized in Part I.B.4 of this opinion. We agree with the parties that this level of harm can constitute "persecution" within the meaning of section 101(a)(42)(A) of the Act, 8 U.S.C. § 1101(a)(42)(A)(1994).

While a number of descriptions of persecution have been formulated in our past decisions, we have recognized that persecution can consist of the infliction of harm or suffering by a government, or persons a government is unwilling or unable to control, to overcome a characteristic of the victim. See *Matter of Acosta*, 19 I&N Dec. 211, 222–23 (BIA 1985), modified on other grounds, *Matter of Mogharrabi*, 19 I&N Dec. 439 (BIA 1987). The "seeking to overcome" formulation has its antecedents in concepts of persecution that predate the Refugee Act of 1980, Pub. L. No. 96-212, 94 Stat. 102. See, e.g., *Matter of Diaz*, 10 I&N Dec. 199, 204 (BIA 1963).

As observed by the INS, many of our past cases involved actors who had a subjective intent to punish their victims. However, this subjective "punitive" or "malignant" intent is not required for harm to constitute persecution. See *Matter of Kulle*, 19 I&N Dec. 318 (BIA 1985); *Matter of Acosta, supra*.

Our characterization of FGM as persecution is consistent with our past definitions of that term. We therefore reach the conclusion that FGM can be persecution without passing on the INS's proposed "shocks the conscience" test. We also agree with the parties that this case is not controlled by *Matter of Chang*, 20 I&N Dec. 38 (BIA 1989) (holding that China's population control policy is not persecution).

To be a basis for a grant of asylum, persecution must relate to one of five categories described in section 101(a)(42)(A) of the Act. The parties agree that the relevant category in this case is "particular social group." Each party has advanced several formulations of the "particular social group" at issue in this case. However, each party urges the Board to adopt only that definition of social group necessary to decide this individual case.

In the context of this case, we find that particular social group to be the following: Young women of the Tchamba-Kunsuntu Tribe who have not had FGM, as practiced by that tribe, and who oppose the practice. This is very similar to the formulations suggested by the parties.

The defined social group meets the test set forth in *Matter of Acosta, supra*, at 233. See also Matter of H-, Interim Decision 3276 (BIA 1996) (finding that identifiable shared ties of kinship warrant characterization as social group). It also is consistent with the law of the United States Court of Appeals for the Third Circuit, where this case arose. *Fatin v. INS*, 12 F.3d 1233, 1241 (3d Cir. 1993) (stating that Iranian women who refuse to conform to the Iranian Government's gender-specific laws and social norms may well satisfy the Acosta definition).

In accordance with Acosta, the particular social group is defined by common characteristics that members of the group either cannot change, or should not be required to change because such characteristics are fundamental to their individual identities. The characteristics of being a "young woman" and a "member of the Tchamba-Kunsuntu Tribe" cannot be changed. The characteristic of having intact genitalia is one that is so fundamental to the individual identity of a young woman that she should not be required to change it.

* * *

Both parties have advanced, and the background materials support, the proposition that there is no legitimate reason for FGM. Group Exhibit 4 contains materials showing that the practice has been condemned by such groups as the United Nations, the International Federation of Gynecology and Obstetrics, the Council on Scientific Affairs, the World Health Organization, the International Medical Association, and the American Medical Association. Record materials state that FGM "has been used to control woman's sexuality," FGM Alert, *supra*, at 4. It also is characterized as a form of "sexual oppression" that is "based on the manipulation of women's sexuality in order to assure male dominance and exploitation." Toubia, *supra*, at 42 (quoting Raqiya Haji Dualeh Abdalla, Somali Women's Democratic Organization). During oral argument before us, the INS General Counsel agreed with the latter characterization. (O.A. at 41). He also stated that the practice is a "severe bodily invasion" that should be regarded as meeting the asylum standard even if done with "subjectively benign intent" (O.A. at 42).

We agree with the parties that, as described and documented in this record, FGM is practiced, at least in some significant part, to overcome sexual characteristics of young women of the tribe who have not been, and do not wish to be, subjected to FGM. We therefore find that the persecution the applicant fears in Togo is "on account of" her status as a member of the defined social group.

The INS suggests, in its brief and at oral argument, that a remand is necessary because the applicant has not established that she would be unable to avoid FGM by moving to some other part of Togo. As we found in Part I of our opinion, the applicant presented credible testimony that her husband is a well-known individual who is a friend of the police in Togo. She testified that her aunt and her husband were looking for her and that there could be no refuge for her because Togo is a small country and the police would not protect her (Tr. at 59, 61, 65, 73, 74, 78, 86, 87).

The applicant's testimony is consistent with the background information in the record. That information confirms that 1) FGM is widely practiced in Togo; 2) acts of violence and abuse against women in Togo are tolerated by the police; 3) the Government of Togo has a poor human rights record; and 4) most African women can expect little governmental protection from FGM. See 1993 Country Reports, *supra*; Profile, *supra*; FGM Alert, *supra*, at 6–7. We also take notice that Togo is a small country of approximately 22,000 square miles, slightly smaller than West Virginia.

Neither in its briefs nor at oral argument did the INS raise any claim of "new evidence" that might show changed country conditions. We assume that if the INS had any new documentation showing that the applicant could find safety from FGM elsewhere in Togo, it would have offered that evidence in support of its motion to remand.

For the foregoing reasons, we find that this record adequately supports the applicant's claim that she has a country-wide fear of persecution in Togo.

We have determined that the applicant is eligible for asylum because she has a well-founded fear of persecution on account of her membership in a particular social group in Togo. A grant of asylum to an eligible applicant is discretionary. The final issue is whether the applicant merits a favorable exercise of discretion. The danger of persecution will outweigh all but the most egregious adverse factors. *Matter of Pula*, 19 I&N Dec. 467, 474 (BIA 1987). The type of persecution feared by the applicant is very severe.

To the extent that the Immigration Judge suggested that the applicant had a legal obligation to seek refuge in Ghana or Germany, the record does not support such a conclusion. The applicant offered credible reasons for not seeking refuge in either of those countries in her particular circumstances.

The applicant purchased someone else's passport and used it to come to the United States. However, upon arrival, she did not attempt to use the false passport to enter. She told the immigration inspector the truth. See *Matter of Y-G-*, 20 I&N Dec. 794 (BIA 1994).

We have weighed the favorable and adverse factors and are satisfied that discretion should be exercised in favor of the applicant. Therefore, we will grant asylum to the applicant.

* * *

Concurring Opinion: Lauri Steven Filppu, Board Member, in which Michael J. Heilman, Board Member, joined.

* * *

The questions necessarily presented to the Board by virtue of the positions advanced by the parties in this case are narrow. The majority resolves the case on those grounds, and properly declines to address issues raised by the Service that go well beyond those essential to the disposition of this appeal.

* * *

The parties naturally understand that this case may well have implications beyond its facts. But only the Service asks that we adopt a framework of analysis which is specifically intended to address issues, such as past persecution question, that are not presented by the facts of this case. It is unclear whether there is an immediate need for a more comprehensive analytical framework in which to assess FGM claims. To the extent it is needed to address the concerns raised by the Service, that comprehensive guidance could more appropriately be issued through the legislative or regulatory process, not the Board's case adjudication process.

* * *

Despite the absence of any major dispute between the parties in this case, the Service requests that we adopt its broad "framework of analysis" for claims of this type. Its suggestion candidly is aimed at addressing issues it sees arising in relation to claims that may be made by women from other "parts of the world where FGM is practiced" and by those "who have been subjected to it in the past." (Brief at 15).

The Board engages in case adjudication. It decides those issues that lead to the resolution of the cases before it. Our published rulings act as precedent under the regulations, 8 C.F.R. § 3.1(g) (1995), and can affect many related cases. But the Board is not well positioned, in the context of a single disposition of a novel issue, to establish comprehensive rules or guidelines for the adjudication of all cases presenting variations on the case at hand. Yet, it is the cases that are *not* before us that seem to draw much of the Service's attention in its brief.

The Service points out that it is "estimated that over eighty million females have been subjected to FGM." (Brief at 13). It further notes that there is "no indication" that "Congress considered application of [the asylum laws] to broad cultural practices of the type involved here." (Brief at 14) ... The Service further argues that "the Board's interpretation in this case must assure protection for those most at risk of the harms covered by the statute, but it cannot simply grant asylum to all who might be subjected to a practice deemed objectionable or a violation of a person's human rights." (Brief at 15)....

The Service then offers its "framework of analysis." That framework includes a new "shocks the conscience" test for persecution. The advantages seen by the Service of this test evidently include: 1) the ability to define FGM as "persecution" notwithstanding any lack of intent to "punish" FGM victims on the part of the victims' parents or tribe members who may well "believe that they are simply performing an important cultural rite that bonds the individual to the society"; 2) the ability to exclude other cultural practices, such as "body scarring," from the definition of persecution as these do not shock the conscience; and 3) the ability to exclude past victims of FGM from asylum eligibility if "they consented" to it or "at least acquiesced," as in the case of a woman who experienced FGM as "a small child," since FGM would not shock the conscience unless inflicted on "an unconsenting or resisting individual." (Brief at 16–18).

With respect to the past persecution question, the Service references 8 C.F.R. § 208.13(b)(1) (1995), and notes "that a woman once circumcised cannot ordinarily be subjected to FGM a second time." (Brief at 18 n.3). The regulation cited by the Service provides in part for a presumption of future persecution that arises from past persecution, and allows only one way of overcoming the presumption, namely, a change in country conditions. As conditions in countries where FGM is practiced may not have changed, it may be anomalous to have a binding presumption of future persecution where the act of persecution will never again take place for the individual past victim.[2]

* * *

2. It might also be anomalous if persons facing death in their homelands because of religious or political persecution were denied protection for having "assisted, or otherwise participated in the persecution" of their children simply by virtue of being parents of FGM victims and having followed tribal custom. *See* section 243(h)(2)(A) of the Act, 8 U.S.C. § 1253(h)(2)(A); 8 C.F.R. § 208.13(c).

The Service does not offer its new framework of analysis for our consideration as part of an effort to harmonize a line of past rulings, or otherwise to put some order into a series of decisions that have addressed FGM questions in a variety of contexts. Instead, the Service offers its new analysis in the context of a case of first impression for the Board.... It then tries to develop a unifying theory or approach that would support grants of asylum to persons who may prospectively fact FGM, but would not routinely make asylum available to persons who have simply previously suffered FGM.

It may be that the Board will end up with an analysis along the lines proposed by the Service as it confronts various issues involving asylum and FGM in the future. Then again the Board may settle upon a different view, which may be better or worse from the perspective of particular parties. But I am fully in agreement with the majority's decision not to attempt to set forth a comprehensive analytical framework in the context of this one case.

The Board certainly is not oblivious to immigration policy considerations in the disposition of cases falling within our jurisdiction. But we are not fundamentally a policy-making body. There may be some unsettling or unsatisfying aspects to the slower and less predictable development of legal guidelines that inures in the Board's case adjudication system. But there are alternatives if resort to the Board's issuance of precedent is not satisfactory in a particular context. The Service can seek to have the Attorney General issue regulations that comprehensively address competing concerns, or it can work within the Administration for appropriate legislative action by Congress.[3] The Service should not, however, expect the Board to endorse a significant new framework for assessing asylum claims in the context of a single novel case, especially when that framework seems intended primarily to address cases that are not in fact before the Board yet.

Concurring Opinion: Lory D. Rosenberg, Board Member

* * *

This case falls squarely within the formulation adopted by Congress in the Refugee Act of 1980, Pub. L. No. 96-212, 94 Stat. 102, which was enacted in large part to establish compliance with this country's domestic and international humanitarian obligations under the 1967 United Nations Protocol Relating to the Status of Refugee, Jan. 31, 1967 [1968] 19 U.S.T. 6223, T.I.A.S. No. 6577, 606 U.N.T.S. 268, to which the United States is a signatory country, and which incorporates by reference the 1951 United Nations Convention Relating to the Status of Refugees, July 28, 1951, 189 U.N.T.S. 150 ("Convention"). See sections 208, 243(h) of the Act, 8 U.S.C. §§ 1158, 1243(h) (1994). As I read the record, both the Service and the applicant call upon us, in their briefs and at oral argument, to recognize and articulate a framework to provide a context for our decision in this case. However, unlike the Service, which

---

3. Indeed, appropriate new legislation might prove to be the better answer if principles of asylum law in fact end up creating the types of anomalies identifies by the Service.

urges us to consider a new standard and a new framework which exceeds the bounds of this case (Service Brief at 12–15; O.A. at 26), the applicant contends that we should draw on traditional principles of asylum jurisprudence to adopt a framework that is consistent and appropriate with the Refugee Act and international law. (Applicant's Brief at 27–36, Applicant's Reply Brief at 13–15, O.A. at 4).

* * *

In this case, I conclude that the applicant's fear is of imminent female genital mutilation, related to being forced to enter an arranged marriage, documented in the record as constituting a mandatory tribal custom. The harm or abuse amounting to persecution is the genital mutilation opposed by the applicant. The reason the persecution would be inflicted, the "on account of" element, is because of the persecutor's intent to overcome her state of being non-mutilated and accordingly, free from male-dominated tribal control, including an arranged marriage.

I see no reason to depart from our existing jurisprudence in order to determine the claim set forth here. In my view, this issue is controlled by our precedent decisions, interpreting the statute and agency regulations, in which, only recently, we have recognized that government-tortured Sri Lankans; imprisoned and beaten Somalia tribesmen; persecuted Afghani Mujahedin fighters; and Haitian women, raped for political retribution, can set forth claims which deserve and warrant protection within our laws. *Matter of H-*, Interim Decision 3276 (BIA 1996); *Matter of D-V-*, Interim Decision 3252 (BIA 1993); *Matter of B-*, Interim Decision 3251 (BIA 1995).

In adjudicating any asylum claim, we use a "reasonableness" standard to determine whether an asylum applicant has established the presence of these essential elements. See *INS v. Cardoza-Fonseca*, 480 U.S. 421 (1987) (addressing the distinct burdens of proof for asylum, which requires that the applicant's fear be reasonable, and for withholding of deportation, which requires that there be a likelihood or clear probability of persecution). In my view, while Cardoza-Fonseca and its progeny, including our decision in *Matter of Mogharrabi*, 19 I&N Dec. 439 (BIA 1987), invoked that standard principally to assess the fear of persecution asserted by the applicant, it is equally appropriate to employ that standard in our determination regarding the "on account of" element.

In this case, the applicant has met her burden of establishing that her fear of female genital mutilation is not only reasonable, but that its infliction on her is probable. In addition, she has shown this practice to be persecution since she has met her burden of establishing that it is both reasonable to believe and probable that the mutilation she faces is on account of her status as a young woman of the tribe, that she opposes the practice of mutilation, and that it will be inflicted in satisfaction of tribal customs or norms because of her status.

* * *

There is nothing about a social group definition based upon gender that requires us to treat it as either an aberration, or as an unanticipated development requiring a new standard. While this is the first time that this Board has addressed the particular type of harm or abuse feared by the respondent—female genital mutilation—it is not the first time that the Board has addressed the "particular social group category," see, e.g., *Matter of Sanchez and Escobar*, 19 I&N Dec. 276 (BIA 1985); *Matter of Acosta*, 19 I&N Dec. 211 (BIA 1985), modified on other grounds, *Matter of Mogharrabi, supra*. Indeed, this Board has specifically addressed the category of particular social group persecution in a recent decision. *Matter of H-*, Interim Decision 3276 (BIA 1996) (holding that membership in an identifiable subclan of a Somalian tribe constitutes membership in a particular social group and that harm suffered on account of that membership constitutes persecution).

The social group category within the refugee definition incorporated into the Act has been recognized as having deliberately been included as a "catch-all" for individuals not falling into the first four specifically enumerated categories of political opinion, race, religion, or ethnicity. See Kristin E. Kandt, *United States Asylum Law: Recognizing Persecution Based on Gender Using Canada as a Comparison*, 9 Geo. Immigr. L.J. 137, 145 (1995) (citing T. Alexander Aleinikoff, *The Meaning of "Persecution" on United States Asylum Law*, 3 Int'l J. Refugee L 5, 11 (1991); see also Nancy Kelly, *Guidelines for Women's Asylum Claims*, 26 Cornell Int'l. L.J. 625 (1993), Pamela Goldberg, *Anyplace But Home: Asylum in the United States for Women Fleeing Intimate Violence*, 26 Cornell Int'l. L.J. 565, 591–92 (1993). As Professor Goldberg discusses, the scope of the social group category has been addressed by preeminent international law scholars. For example, Atle Grahl-Madsen considers it to be broader than the other categories and to have been added to the Convention precisely to protect against persecution that would arise from unforeseeable circumstances. In addition, Guy Goodwin Gill asserts that the category allows states to expand it to various classes susceptible to persecution. In her article, Professor Goldberg proposes one definition of a gender-identified social group which would include a group of women characterized by circumstances or similar treatment, not unlike the definition we propose here.

Unlike requests for asylum premised upon political opinion, social group claims, like those involving race, ethnicity, or religion, are status based and do not necessarily require a showing of the presence of an individual's opinions or activities which spurs the persecutor's wrath or otherwise motivates the harm or persecution. *Matter of H-, supra*. Rather, such requests involve a determination of whether the shared characteristics are those which motivate an agent of persecution to seek to overcome or otherwise harm the individual. Matter of Acosta, supra. Consequently, while not inaccurate, it is surplusage to define the social group in this case by including as an element the applicant's opposition to the practice of female genital mutilation.

It may be true that sometimes an individual woman's political opinion may overlap or co-exist with her membership in a group designated as a particular social group; however, that does not detract from the fact that social group membership is a status-based ground protected under the Act, just as is religion or ethnicity. While it is not impossible that a political or social opinion, either actual or imputed, may be shared by persons whom, as a result, we would characterize as constituting a particular social group within the meaning of the Act, that is not the case here. As I have stated, the applicant's political or social views—her attitude or intent—is not relevant to our definition of the social group to which she belongs, but rather to whether the harm or abuse she faces constitutes persecution.

In *Matter of H-, supra*, this Board found, without difficulty or the need to qualify, that a man who was a member of a tribe in Somalia whose members were being systematically attacked by other tribes in retribution for the corruption and brutality of former ruler and tribe member, Siad Barre, had established persecution based on his clan membership alone. That his father and brother were killed and that he himself was brutally treated during detention was found to be persecution on account of his membership in a subclan in Somalia, a particular social group. His attitude towards that persecution was neither examined nor relevant.

The only distinguishing characteristic about this case that I can perceive to set it apart from others we already have decided is that it involves a woman. Reliance upon such a distinction to support a separate category for treatment of women's asylum claims, to my mind, would be impermissible. See, e.g., *Kandt, supra*, at 143–151. Here, the applicant is a member of a group—girls and women of a given tribe, some perhaps of marriageable age, whose members are routinely subjected to the harm which the majority finds to constitute persecution. The applicant's opposition (which happens to be present in this case) or the lack of it, is neither determinative, nor necessary to define the social group in accordance with the statutory language.

* * *

Consideration of gender-based, or gender-related, asylum claims within the "membership in a particular social group" construct that exists within the Act is entirely appropriate and consistent with the developing trend of jurisprudence in the United States and Canada as well as with international norms. *Fatin v. INS, supra*; *Cheung v. Canada*, 102 D.L.R. 4th 214 (1993); cf. *Gomez v. INS*, 947 F.2d 660 (2d Cir. 1991). Further, the United Nations High Commissioner for Refugees explicitly encourages the use of "particular social group" analysis to extend protection to women asylum seekers who otherwise satisfy the refugee definition. See United Nations High Commissioner for Refugees, Memorandum: Female Genital Mutilation (Geneva, UNHCR, Division of International Protection, May 1994). Our recognition of a particular social group based upon tribal affiliation and gender is also in harmony with the guidelines for adjudicating women's asylum claims issued by the Service, see Coven, U.S. Dep't of Justice, Considerations for Asylum Officers Adjudicating Asylum Claims From Women (1995), and with the Canadian guidelines for women refugees facing gender-related persecution, see, Immigration and Refugee Board, Guidelines Issued by the Chairperson Pursuant to Section 65(B) of the Immigration Act: Women Refugee Claimants Fearing Gender-Related Persecution (1993) ("Canadian gender guidelines").

In an endorsement of the viability of the present statutory structure, the Service itself saw fit to develop gender guidelines to assist in the adjudication of asylum claims brought by women. Coven, *supra*. Curiously, the position of the Service in this case makes no reference to its published guidance in that regard. However, it is notable that the guidelines recognize the important of considering gender-based claims in light of international human rights instruments and the framework they provide. Indeed, the Service itself recognizes that gender-based asylum claims are "developments in refugee protection" and that its guidelines are a natural and multifaceted outgrowth of a set of gender guidelines issued by the UNHCR in 1991, the 1993 Canadian gender guidelines and other sources of expertise including the Women's Refugee Project of the Harvard Immigration and Refugee Program.

What we have done here, while we do not explicitly say so, is to posit, by example, the proper framework in which the individual facts of such claims made before the Service and before Immigration Judges should be considered and judged. In sum, we have, in the majority opinion, set forth a road map for analysis appropriate for this case, which may easily be extrapolated and applied in upcoming adjudications, not only of gender-based asylum claims, but in many other asylum applications....

Notes

1. ***Abebe v. Ashcroft.***[51] In 2004, the Ninth Circuit denied asylum to Abebe and Mengistu, the parents of Amen, despite Mengistu's alleged fear of persecution on the basis of his involvement in an opposition political party and of both parents' fear that their daughter would be subjected to female genital mutilation upon return to their native Ethiopia. At their asylum hearing, the Immigration Judge was unconvinced that Mengistu's fear was well-founded given the extent of his involvement in the Medhin organization, nor that Amen's mutilation was of sufficient likelihood given the opposition of both her parents to the practice. The 2004 panel's majority distinguished the Sixth Circuit's grant of asylum in *Abay*, in part because Abay had testified that she might be unable to prevent her future husband and his family from subjecting her daughter Amare to FGM.

Dissenting from the majority opinion, Judge Ferguson emphasized the lack of certainty that Mengistu and Abebe could protect Amen from mutilation and the Supreme Court's decision in *Cardoza-Fonseca* mandating eligibility for asylum even where the risk of persecution is one in ten. Ferguson relied on *Olowo v. Ashcroft*[52] to signify that parents faced with the "anguishing dilemma" of their child's persecution should be granted asylum when they seek to protect their son or daughter from "a form of physical torture causing grave and permanent harm."[53] Ferguson's dissent seemed to an-

51. 379 F.3d 755 (9th Cir. 2004).
52. 368 F.3d 692 (7th Cir. 2004).
53. *Abebe*, 379 F.3d at 762, 763.

ticipate the Ninth Circuit's approach in *Tchoukhrova v. Gonzales*,[54] decided a few months later in 2005, where the court linked the suffering of a disabled child with cerebral palsy to the well-founded fear of persecution of his parents. The court in *Tchoukhrova* refused to require the parents to choose between leaving their child with strangers in the United States or subjecting him to abuse in their country of origin. Ferguson also cites *Moore v. City of East Cleveland*[55] in support of the principal of family unity, as does the court in *Tchoukhrova*. Compare *Abebe* with *Tchoukhrova*. (The Ninth Circuit considered a petition for rehearing *en banc* in *Tchoukhrova*, and voted to deny the petition in December 2005.)

In March 2005, the Ninth Circuit granted a petition for rehearing in *Abebe*. On December 30, 2005, an en banc panel of the Ninth Circuit reversed and remanded *Abebe* and *Mengistu*'s case.[56] Much of the opinion centered on whether the Respondent's FGM-based social group claim was properly before the court in light of the fact that the issue was mentioned only briefly in the statement of facts in their brief to the BIA. Because the Board had adopted and affirmed the decision of the Immigration Judge, which itself did analyze the Respondents' social group as well as political opinion claims, the Ninth Circuit found jurisdiction to consider the FGM claim.

In the part of his opinion analyzing the merits of the FGM claim, Judge Clifton cited the "well-settled" precedent "that FGM constitutes persecution sufficient to warrant a grant of asylum." Considering documentary evidence that "90% of women in Ethiopia were subjected to FGM," the court concluded that "the probability that Amen would have to undergo this ritual greatly exceeded the threshold required to establish eligibility for asylum." The en banc panel then remanded on the issue of whether parents can claim asylum based on their citizen daughter's fear of persecution in the form of FGM.

In partial dissent, Judge Tallman disagreed with the majority that the FGM claim was properly before the court. Moreover, he dissented on the appropriateness of remanding on the issue of parents claiming asylum based on their child's fear in cases where the child, like Amen, is a U.S. citizen and cannot be removed. Nevertheless, even in disapproving remand on this issue, Judge Tallman conceded a more basic point concerning the inherent interconnectedness of parents' and children's claims: "when addressing the parents' application for asylum, it is proper to consider not only the potential persecution the child may face, but also any hardship to the alien child due to the deportation of her parents."

2. Recent analysis on the issue provides further insight into the interrelated claims of parents and their daughters in cases involving the fear of female genital mutilation.[57]

---

54. 404 F.3d 1181 (9th Cir. 2005).

55. 431 U.S. 494 (1977).

56. *Abebe v. Gonzales*, 432 F.3d 1037 (9th Cir. 2005).

57. *See* Marcelle Rice, *Protecting Parents: Why Mothers and Fathers Who Oppose Female Genital Cutting Qualify for Asylum*, Immigration Briefings, No. 04-11 (November 2004).

Matter of A-R-C-G*

26 I. & N. Dec. 388 (BIA 2014)

Before: Adkins-Blanch, Vice Chairman; Miller and Greer, Board Members.

Adkins-Blanch, Vice Chairman:

In a decision dated October 14, 2009, an Immigration Judge found the respondents removable and denied their applications for asylum and withholding of removal under sections 208(a) and 241(b)(3) of the Immigration and Nationality Act, 8 U.S.C. §§ 1158(a) and 1231(b)(3) (2006). The respondents have appealed from that decision, contesting only the denial of their applications for relief from removal. We find that the lead respondent, a victim of domestic violence in her native country, is a member of a particular social group composed of "married women in Guatemala who are unable to leave their relationship." The record will be remanded to the Immigration Judge for further proceedings.

The lead respondent is the mother of the three minor respondents. The respondents are natives and citizens of Guatemala who entered the United States without inspection on December 25, 2005. The respondent filed a timely application for asylum and withholding of removal under the Act. The Immigration Judge found the respondent to be a credible witness, which is not contested on appeal. It is undisputed that the respondent, who married at age 17, suffered repugnant abuse by her husband. This abuse included weekly beatings after the respondent had their first child. On one occasion, the respondent's husband broke her nose. Another time, he threw paint thinner on her, which burned her breast. He raped her.

The respondent contacted the police several times but was told that they would not interfere in a marital relationship. On one occasion, the police came to her home after her husband hit her on the head, but he was not arrested. Subsequently, he threatened the respondent with death if she called the police again. The respondent repeatedly tried to leave the relationship by staying with her father, but her husband found her and threatened to kill her if she did not return to him. Once she went to Guatemala City for about 3 months, but he followed her and convinced her to come home with promises that he would discontinue the abuse. The abuse continued when she returned. The respondent left Guatemala in December 2005, and she believes her husband will harm her if she returns.

The Immigration Judge found that the respondent did not demonstrate that she had suffered past persecution or has a well-founded fear of future persecution on account of a particular social group comprised of "married women in Guatemala who are unable to leave their relationship." The Immigration Judge determined that there was inadequate evidence that the respondent's spouse abused her "in order to overcome" the fact that she was a "married woman in Guatemala who was unable to leave

---

* Footnotes have been omitted.

the relationship." He found that the respondent's abuse was the result of "criminal acts, not persecution," which were perpetrated "arbitrarily" and "without reason." He accordingly found that the respondent did not meet her burden of demonstrating eligibility for asylum or withholding of removal under the Act.

On appeal, the respondent asserts that she has established eligibility for asylum as a victim of domestic violence. The Department of Homeland Security ("DHS") initially responded that the Immigration Judge's decision should be upheld. We subsequently requested supplemental briefing from both parties and amici curiae to address the issue whether domestic violence can, in some instances, form the basis for a claim of asylum or withholding of removal under sections 208(a) and 241(b)(3) of the Act. *See Matter of R-A-*, 22 I&N Dec. 906 (BIA 1999) (en banc), *vacated*, 22 I&N Dec. 906 (A.G. 2001), remanded, 23 I&N Dec. 694 (A.G. 2005), *remanded and stay lifted*, 24 I&N Dec. 629 (A.G. 2008).

In response to our request for supplemental briefing, the DHS now concedes the respondent established that she suffered past harm rising to the level of persecution and that the persecution was on account of a particular social group comprised of "married women in Guatemala who are unable to leave their relationship." However, the DHS seeks remand, arguing that "further factual development of the record and related findings by the Immigration Judge are necessary on several issues" before the asylum claim can be properly resolved. The respondent opposes remand and maintains that she has met her burden of proof regarding all aspects of her asylum claim. We accept the parties' position on the existence of harm rising to the level of past persecution, the existence of a valid particular social group, and the issue of nexus under the particular facts of this case. We will remand the record for further proceedings.

The question whether a group is a "particular social group" within the meaning of the Act is a question of law that we review de novo. 8 C.F.R. § 1003.1(d)(3)(ii) (2014); *see Malonga v. Mukasey*, 546 F.3d 546, 553 (8th Cir. 2008). The question whether a person is a member of a particular social group is a finding of fact that we review for clear error. 8 C.F.R. § 1003.1(d)(3)(i).

We initially considered whether victims of domestic violence can establish membership in a particular social group in *Matter of R-A-*, 22 I&N Dec. at 907. We reversed an Immigration Judge's finding that the respondent in that case was eligible for asylum on account of her membership in a particular social group consisting of "Guatemalan women who have been involved intimately with Guatemalan male companions, who believe that women are to live under male domination." *Id.* at 911. The majority opinion reasoned that the proffered social group was "defined principally, if not exclusively, for purposes of the asylum case and that it was unclear whether "anyone in Guatemala perceives this group to exist in any form whatsoever," including spousal abuse victims themselves or their male oppressors. *Id.* at 918. We further reasoned that even if the proffered social group was cognizable, the respondent did not establish that her husband harmed her on account of her membership in the group. *Id.* at 920–23.

The Acting Commissioner of the former Immigration and Naturalization Service ("INS") referred the decision to the Attorney General for review. In 2001, Attorney General Janet Reno vacated our decision in *Matter of R-A-*, 22 I&N Dec. 906. She remanded the case for the Board's reconsideration following final publication of proposed regulations that addressed the meaning of various terms in asylum law, including "persecution," "membership in a particular social group," and "on account of a protected characteristic. *See* Asylum and Withholding Definitions, 65 Fed. Reg. 76,588, 76,597–98 (proposed Dec. 7, 2000).

On February 21, 2003, Attorney General John Ashcroft certified *Matter of R-A-* for review and provided an opportunity for additional briefing. He remanded the case to the Board in 2005, directing us to reconsider our decision "in light of the final rule." *Matter of R-A-*, 23 I&N Dec. 694. The proposed regulations were not finalized. On September 25, 2008, Attorney General Michael Mukasey certified the case for his review and issued a decision ordering us to reconsider it, removing the requirement that we await the issuance of the final regulations. *Matter of R-A-*, 24 I&N Dec. 629. *Matter of R-A-* is no longer pending.

The DHS has conceded that the respondent established harm rising to the level of past persecution on account of a particular social group comprised of " 'married women in Guatemala who are unable to leave their relationship.' The DHS's position regarding the existence of such a particular social group in Guatemala under the facts presented in this case comports with our recent precedents clarifying the meaning of the term "particular social group." *Matter of M-E-V-G-*, 26 I&N Dec. 227 (BIA 2014); *Matter of W-G-R-*, 26 I&N Dec. 208 (BIA 2014). In this regard, we point out that any claim regarding the existence of a particular social group in a country must be evaluated in the context of the evidence presented regarding the particular circumstances in the country in question.

In *Matter of W-G-R-* and *Matter of M-E-V-G-*, we held that an applicant seeking asylum based on his or her membership in a "particular social group" must establish that the group is (1) composed of members who share a common immutable characteristic, (2) defined with particularity, and (3) socially distinct within the society in question. The "common immutable characteristic" requirement incorporates the standard set forth in *Matter of Acosta*, 19 I&N Dec. 211, 233–34 (BIA 1985). The "particularity" requirement addresses "the question of delineation." *Matter of W-G-R-*, 26 I&N Dec. at 214. That is, it clarifies the point that "not every 'immutable characteristic' is sufficiently precise to define a particular social group." *Matter of M-E-V-G-*, 26 I&N Dec. at 239. The "social distinction" requirement renames the former concept of "social visibility" and clarifies "the importance of "perception' or 'recognition' to the concept of the particular social group." *Matter of W-G-R-*, 26 I&N Dec. at 216.

In this case, the group is composed of members who share the common immutable characteristic of gender. See *Matter of Acosta*, 19 I&N Dec. at 233 (finding that sex is an immutable characteristic); see also *Matter of W-G-R-*, 26 I&N Dec. at 213 ("The critical requirement is that the defining characteristic of the group must be something that either cannot be changed or that the group members should not be required to change in order to avoid persecution."). Moreover, marital status can be an immutable characteristic where the individual is unable to leave the relationship. A determination of this issue will be dependent upon the particular facts and evidence in a case. A range of factors could be relevant, including whether dissolution of a marriage could be contrary to religious or other deeply held moral beliefs or if dissolution is possible when viewed in light of religious, cultural, or legal constraints. In evaluating such a claim, adjudicators must consider a respondent's own experiences, as well as more objective evidence, such as background country information.

The DHS concedes that the group in this case is defined with particularity. The terms used to describe the group—"married," "women," and """unable to leave the relationship"—have commonly accepted definitions within Guatemalan society based on the facts in this case, including the respondent's experience with the police. In some circumstances, the terms can combine to create a group with discrete and definable boundaries. We point out that a married woman's inability to leave the relationship may be informed by societal expectations about gender and subordination, as well as legal constraints regarding divorce and separation. *See Matter of W-G-R-*, 26 I&N Dec. at 214 (observing that in evaluating a group's particularity, it may be necessary to take into account the social and cultural context of the alien's country of citizenship or nationality.... In this case, it is significant that the respondent sought protection from her spouse's abuse and that the police refused to assist her because they would not interfere in a marital relationship.

The group is also socially distinct within the society in question. *Matter of M-E-V-G-*, 26 I&N Dec. at 240 ("To be socially distinct, a group need not be seen by society; rather it must be perceived as a group by society."). To have """social distinction," there must be "evidence showing that society in general perceives, considers, or recognizes persons sharing the particular characteristic to be a group." *Matter of W-G-R-*, 26 I&N Dec. at 217. The group's recognition is "determined by the perception of the society in question, rather than by the perception of the persecutor." *Matter of M-E-V-G-*, 26 I&N Dec. at 242 ... (noting that there is some degree of overlap between the particularity and social distinction requirements because both take societal context into account).

When evaluating the issue of social distinction, we look to the evidence to determine whether a society, such as Guatemalan society in this case, makes meaningful distinctions based on the common immutable characteristics of being a married woman in a domestic relationship that she cannot leave. Such evidence would include whether the society in question recognizes the need to offer protection to victims of domestic violence, including whether the country has criminal laws designed to protect domestic abuse victims, whether those laws are effectively enforced, and other sociopolitical factors. *Cf. Davila-Mejia v. Mukasey*, 531 F.3d 624, 629 (8th Cir. 2008) (finding that competing family business owners are not a particular social group because they are not perceived as a group by society).

Supporting the existence of social distinction, and in accord with the DHS's concession that a particular social group exists, the record in this case includes unrebutted evidence that Guatemala has a culture of "machismo and family violence." See Guatemala Failing Its Murdered Women: Report, Canadian Broad. Corp. (July 18, 2006), http://www.cbc.ca/news/world/guatemala-failing-its-murdered-women-report-1.627240. Sexual offenses, including spousal rape, remain a serious problem. See Country Reports, supra, at 2608. Further, although the record reflects that Guatemala has laws in place to prosecute domestic violence crimes, enforcement can be problematic because the National Civilian Police "often failed to respond to requests for assistance related to domestic violence." *Id.* at 2609.

We point out that cases arising in the context of domestic violence generally involve unique and discrete issues not present in other particular social group determinations, which extends to the matter of social distinction. However, even within the domestic violence context, the issue of social distinction will depend on the facts and evidence in each individual case, including documented country conditions; law enforcement statistics and expert witnesses, if proffered; the respondent's past experiences; and other reliable and credible sources of information.

The DHS stipulates that the respondent suffered mistreatment rising to the level of past persecution. The DHS also concedes in this case that the mistreatment was, for at least one central reason, on account of her membership in a cognizable particular social group. We note that in cases where concessions are not made and accepted as binding, these issues will be decided based on the particular facts and evidence on a case-by-case basis as addressed by the Immigration Judge in the first instance. *See generally Matter of N-M-*, 25 I&N Dec. 526 (BIA 2011); *Matter of J-B-N& S-M-*, 24 I&N Dec. 208 (BIA 2007). In particular, the issue of nexus will depend on the facts and circumstances of an individual claim.

We will remand the record for the Immigration Judge to address the respondent's statutory eligibility for asylum in light of this decision. Under controlling circuit law, in order for the respondent to prevail on an asylum claim based on past persecution, she must demonstrate that the Guatemalan Government was unwilling or unable to control the "private" actor. *See Gutierrez-Vidal v. Holder*, 709 F.3d 728, 732–33 (8th Cir. 2013).

If the respondent succeeds in establishing that the Government was unwilling or unable to control her husband, the burden shifts to the DHS to demonstrate that there has been a fundamental change in circumstances such that the respondent no longer has a well-founded fear of persecution. 8 C.F.R. § 1208.13(b)(1)(i)(A), (ii) (2014). Alternatively, the DHS would bear the burden of showing that internal relocation is possible and is not unreasonable. 8 C.F.R. § 1208.13(b)(1)(i)(B), (ii); *see also Matter of M-Z-M-R-*, 26 I&N Dec. 28 (BIA 2012). The Immigration Judge may also consider, if appropriate, whether the respondent is eligible for humanitarian asylum. *See* 8 C.F.R. § 1208.13(b)(1)(iii).

Notes

1. **Social group persecution.** In *Ananeh-Firempong v. INS*,[58] the court of appeals reversed the BIA's denial of a motion to reopen the petitioner's deportation case to apply for withholding of deportation. The petitioner, a citizen of Ghana, had submitted extensive documentation alleging that she was subject to persecution based on membership in a social group. She argued that she was a member of three groups of people subject to persecution in her native country: (1) those associated with the former government; (2) members of the Ashanti tribe; and (3) professional business people and other highly educated individuals. In analyzing the claim, the court of appeals cited the Handbook and also noted that

> "[S]ocial group" persecution must be based on a "characteristic" that either is beyond the power of an individual to change or is so fundamental to individual identity or conscience that it ought not be required to be changed. [766 F.2d 621, 626 (citing) 1 A. GRAHL-MADSEN, THE STATUS OF REFUGEES IN INTERNATIONAL LAW 217 (1966).]

2. In *Matter of Acosta*,[59] the Board described social group persecution as

> persecution that is directed toward an individual who is a member of a group of persons all of whom share a common, immutable characteristic. The shared characteristic might be an innate one such as sex, color, kinship ties, or in some circumstances it might be a shared experience such as former military leadership or landownership. The particular kind of group characteristic that will qualify under this construction remains to be determined on a case-by-case basis. [*Matter of Acosta*, 19 I. & N. Dec. 211 (BIA 1985).]

In this case the applicant was a member of a taxicab cooperative that was being persecuted by the guerillas for refusal to participate in work stoppages. The Board, in rejecting the claim, stated that the characteristic was not immutable and, that the applicant could quit being a cab driver or agree to participate in work stoppages and the problem would be resolved. Recalling *Clark v. Martinez*,[60] discussed in Chapter 3, could a person who came to the United States in early 1980 from Cuba as part of the Freedom Flotilla be considered a member of a social group? What would be needed to establish such a claim?[61]

3. In *Aguirre-Cervantes v. INS*,[62] a Ninth Circuit panel held that a family was a cognizable social group and that the petitioner, who was unable to avail herself of protection from the Mexican government, had a well-founded fear of persecution

58. 766 F.2d 621 (1st Cir. 1985).
59. 19 I. & N. Dec. 211 (BIA 1985).
60. 543 U.S. 371 (2005).
61. *See Sanchez-Trujillo v. INS*, 801 F.2d 1371 (9th Cir. 1986).
62. 232 F.3d 1169 (9th Cir. 2001).

on account of her membership in a particular social group. In another case, the court held that a gay man with "female sexual identity" from Mexico comprised a particular social group and that the petitioner, who had repeatedly been assaulted by police officers, feared persecution on account of membership in the social group.[63] For an interesting article discussing persons with disabilities constituting a particular social group for asylum purposes, see Arlene Kanter & Kristin Dadey, *The Right of Asylum for People With Disabilities*, 73 Temp. L. Rev. 1117 (2000).

4. **Social Group and "Social Visibility."** In a case decided in 2006, the BIA further limited social group claims by requiring that the "social group" also have "visibility" as a group in order to qualify.[64] The Board concluded that a person who passed along information concerning the Cali drug cartel to the Colombian Government could not be a considered a social group because his acts as an informant were not socially visible. In *Matter of S-E-G-*,[65] the Board noted that social group claims must be described with particularity:

> The essence of the "particularity" requirement, therefore, is whether the proposed group can accurately be described in a manner sufficiently distinct that the group would be recognized, in the society in question, as a discrete class of persons. While the size of the proposed group may be an important factor in determining whether the group can be so recognized, the key question is whether the proposed description is sufficiently "particular," or is "too amorphous ... to create a benchmark for determining group membership."

When the Board established the social visibility requirement, it cited to interpretations of the United Nations High Commissioner for Refugees, which recently submitted an amicus curiae brief in a case pending in the U.S. Court of Appeals for the Third Circuit. The UNHCR noted in its submission that the BIA had "misconstrued" the meaning of the UNHCR Social Group Guidelines[66] and that its use of a social visibility requirement was also inconsistent. It noted that the social perception analysis is only engaged if the group is found to not share a characteristic that can be defined as either innate or fundamental. It then went on to state that an exploration into whether the group is perceived as a cognizable group in the society only occurs when the group's characteristics are neither innate nor fundamental.

In the following case involving social group persecution a 7th Circuit panel critiques an evolving line of decisions addressing the BIA's requirement that an asylum applicant establish social visibility in order to sustain a persecution claim.

---

63. *See Hernandez-Montiel v. INS*, 225 F.3d 1084 (9th Cir. 2000).

64. *See Matter of C-A-*, 23 I. & N. Dec. 951, 960–61 (BIA 2006), *aff'd*, *Castillo-Arias v. U.S. Att'y Gen.*, 446 F.3d 1190 (11th Cir. 2006), *cert. denied sub nom. Castillo-Arias v. Gonzales*, 549 U.S. 1115 (2007).

65. 24 I. & N. Dec. 579, 584 (BIA 2008).

66. Brief Amicus Curiae in Support of the Petitioner at 6, *Mauricio Edgardo Valdivieso-Galdamez v. Eric Holder, Atty. Gen'l*, No. 08-4564 (3rd Cir. Apr. 14, 2009).

Oliverto Pirir-Boc v. Eric H. Holder, Jr., Att'y Gen'l

750 F.3d 1077 (9th Cir. 2014)

Before: Stephen Reinhardt and Sidney R. Thomas, Circuit Judges, and William K. Sessions, District Judge.

Reinhardt, Circuit Judge:

Oliverto Pirir-Boc ("Pirir-Boc") was granted asylum by the Immigration Judge ("IJ") based on his well-founded fear of persecution as a member of a particular social group characterized as individuals "taking concrete steps to oppose gang membership and gang authority." The Board of Immigration Appeals ("BIA") vacated the grant of asylum on the ground that Pirir-Boc's "purported social group lacks the requisite particularity and social visibility." Pirir-Boc filed a petition for review. After briefing was complete, this court issued the en banc decision, *Henriquez-Rivas v. Holder*, 707 F.3d 1081, 1083 (2013) (en banc), holding that "witnesses who testify against gang members" may be cognizable as a particular social group for the purposes of asylum. We then ordered supplemental briefing in this case. Three days before oral argument, the BIA issued two published decisions designed to clarify its interpretation of the phrase "particular social group": *Matter of W-G-R-*, 26 I. & N. Dec. 208 (2014), and *Matter of M-E-V-G-*, 26 I. & N. Dec. 227 (2014). We hold that these two decisions do not affect the validity of *Henriquez-Rivas*, and we remand Pirir-Boc's petition to the BIA for consideration in light of *W-G-R, M-E-V-G-*, and *Henriquez-Rivas.*

The IJ granted Pirir-Boc asylum after finding his testimony credible. Pirir-Boc is a native and citizen of Guatemala who identifies as Cakchiquel, an indigenous minority ethnic group, and did not learn Spanish until age 10. He was recruited by the Mara Salvatrucha, a violent Central American gang, but refused to join. His younger brother, however, joined the gang and pledged himself to it for life. Pirir-Boc viewed the Mara Salvatrucha as "criminals who rape women and rob people" and disapproved of his brother's decision to join. Within the hearing of members of the Mara Salvatrucha, Pirir-Boc told his brother that he must leave the gang. Pirir-Boc was eventually able to help his brother defect and move to their grandparents' village, three hours away.

After his brother left the gang, members of the Mara Salvatrucha came looking for Pirir-Boc at his home several times. He sent his wife and small child away and went into hiding in the cliffs. Gang members continued to look for him at all hours, but he evaded them by not returning home. When Mara Salvatrucha members had not come to his house for eight days, Pirir-Boc returned. Ten or eleven gang members caught him and beat him severely, telling him that "[he has] to die." He continues to suffer effects from that beating.

Out of the "fear of losing [his] life" and never being able to "sleep in [his] own house" again, Pirir-Boc fled Guatemala with his younger brother. His wife subsequently informed him that the Mara Salvatrucha was still looking for him in Guatemala.

The IJ found Pirir-Boc eligible for asylum based on his past persecution and his well-founded fear of future persecution "on account of his membership in a particular social group of persons taking concrete steps to oppose gang membership and gang authority." She found that Pirir-Boc "took specific action to dissuade his brother from continuing in his membership in a criminal gang" and, by taking this action, allied himself with a particular social group of persons directly in opposition to gang activities and gang membership. Although [Pirir-Boc] does not belong to an organization, per se, the Country Reports and background material ... indicate that there are concerted efforts in Guatemala to combat gang activity. The Court notes that voluntarily associating oneself with a group may be evidence of membership in a particular social group.

The IJ also found that Pirir-Boc "has been visible and outspoken in his actions against the gang." In addition, she found that the authorities in Guatemala were unwilling or unable to protect him. The IJ did not consider whether Pirir-Boc was eligible for relief under the Convention Against Torture ("CAT"), noting that he had not applied for such relief.

The government appealed the IJ's decision, and the BIA sustained the appeal and vacated the IJ's finding of eligibility. The BIA incorporated the IJ's fact-finding in its decision, noting that "[t]he facts of this case are not in dispute." It then applied intervening authority from the BIA and this court to those facts and held that the purported social group of "those who have taken direct action to oppose criminal gangs" was not meaningfully distinguishable from Salvadoran "youths who have resisted gang recruitment, or family members of such Salvadoran youth," the group the BIA had rejected in *Matter of S-E-G-*, 24 I. & N. Dec. 579, 582 (2008). The BIA decided that "[a]lthough the respondent was seen by gang members to tell his brother to leave the gang, his purported social group lacks the requisite particularity and social visibility" and reversed the IJ's finding of eligibility. The BIA denied Pirir-Boc's claim for withholding of deportation because he had failed to satisfy the less burdensome standard for asylum. The BIA also rejected Pirir-Boc's claim for relief under the Convention Against Torture, finding that he had "failed to establish a prima facie case for eligibility" for that type of relief.

We review questions of law *de novo*. *Cordoba v. Holder*, 726 F.3d 1106, 1113 (9th Cir. 2013). Whether a group constitutes a "particular social group" is a question of law. *Mendoza-Alvarez v. Holder*, 714 F.3d 1161, 1163 (9th Cir. 2013). The BIA's construction of ambiguous statutory terms in precedential decisions is entitled to deference under *Chevron U.S.A., Inc. v. Natural Res. Def. Council, Inc.*, 467 U.S. 837, 844 (1984). *Henriquez-Rivas*, 707 F.3d at 1087; *Lezama-Garcia v. Holder*, 666 F.3d 518, 524 (9th Cir. 2011). We must accept the BIA's construction if it is reasonable. *Henriquez-Rivas*, 707 F.3d at 1087 (citing *Nat'l Cable & Telecomms. Ass'n v. Brand X Internet Servs.*, 545 U.S. 967, 980 (2005)).

A petitioner is eligible for asylum if he is determined to be a refugee within the meaning of section 101(a)(42)(A) of the Immigration and Nationality Act ("INA"), 8 U.S.C. § 1101(a)(42)(A). An individual qualifies as a refugee when he is "unable or unwilling to return to [his last country of residence] ... because of persecution or a well-founded fear of persecution on account of race, religion, nationality, membership in a particular social group, or political opinion." INA § 101(a)(42)(A), 8 U.S.C. § 1101(a)(42)(A); *Cordoba*, 726 F.3d at 1108.

Pirir-Boc's petition involves the construction of the term "particular social group." Since the BIA considered Pirir-Boc's petition, the term has been interpreted in an en banc decision of this court, *Henriquez-Rivas v. Holder*, 707 F.3d 1081 (2013), and in two published decisions by the BIA, *W-G-R-*, 26 I. & N. Dec. 208 (2014), and *M-E-V-G-*, 26 I. & N. Dec. 227 (2014). We first consider whether the BIA's new decisions affect the interpretation we set forth in *Henriquez-Rivas*, and conclude that *Henriquez-Rivas* remains valid in both holding and reasoning, with one minor qualification.

Prior to *Henriquez-Rivas*, the BIA defined "particular social group" as a group (1) that consisted of people who share an "immutable characteristic 'so fundamental to one's identity that a person should not be required to abandon it,'" *Henriquez-Rivas*, 707 F.3d at 1084 (quoting *Hernandez-Montiel v. INS*, 225 F.3d 1084, 1093 (9th Cir. 2000)); and (2) that had what the BIA called "social visibility" and "particularity." *Henriquez-Rivas*, 707 F.3d at 1084–85. In *S-E-G-*, the BIA had found that a proposed social group of "Salvadoran youth who have been subjected to recruitment efforts by MS-13 and who have rejected or resisted membership in the gang based on their own personal, moral, and religious opposition to the gang's values and activities" did not have "particularity" because it was too "amorphous," and that it did not have "social visibility" because there was little evidence that such youths would be "perceived as a group by society." *Henriquez-Rivas*, 707 F.3d at 1085; *S-E-G-*, 24 I. & N. Dec. at 584–85, 587.

In *Henriquez-Rivas* we considered whether witnesses who testify against gang members constitute a particular social group under the BIA's precedent. 707 F.3d at 1081. As in Pirir-Boc's case, the IJ found Henriquez-Rivas eligible for asylum but the BIA reversed that determination, holding that the proposed social group "lacks the requisite social visibility." *Id.* at 1091. The BIA did not fully explain its position, but instead cited *S-E-G-* and other cases now subject to the revised standard of *W-G-R-* and *M-E-V-G-*. *Id.* We vacated the BIA's decision, holding that the BIA had "erroneously assumed" that the putative social group was not cognizable under its precedent, and that because of this erroneous assumption, the BIA had ignored "significant evidence" that Salvadoran society recognizes the group in question as a particular social group. *Id.* at 1092. We noted that the evidence before the BIA strongly suggested that the putative group had sufficient social visibility—which, we clarified, refers to "'perception' rather than 'on-sight visibility,'" *id.* at 1089, 1092–93—and sufficient particularity to be cognizable. We remanded to the BIA for further proceedings so that it could consider that evidence. *Id.* at 1094.

The BIA took up these issues in a pair of precedential decisions. In *W-G-R-*, the BIA considered the putative social group of "former members of the Mara 18 gang in El Salvador who have renounced their gang membership" and rejected it as a social group due to a lack of evidence to that effect introduced at the proceedings. 26 I. & N. Dec. at 221. The BIA rejected the group on the ground that the record contained no evidence demonstrating that Salvadoran society recognized former gang members who have renounced their gang membership as a distinct social group. *Id.* at 222. The record contained "documentary evidence describing gangs, gang violence, and the treatment of gang members but very little documentation discussing the treatment or status of former gang members." *Id.* The "scant evidence" provided by *W-G-R-* was insufficient to meet the social distinction requirement. *Id.* The BIA also found that the proposed group lacked particularity because "the boundaries of a group are not sufficiently definable unless the members of society generally agree on who is included in the group, and evidence that the social group proposed ... is recognized within the society is lacking in this case." *Id.* at 221. "The group would need further specificity to meet the particularity requirement." *Id.*

In *M-E-V-G-*, decided on the same day as *W-G-R-*, the BIA declined to make a ruling on whether Honduran youths who were actively recruited by gangs but who refused to join constituted a particular social group because further factfinding was required. 26 I. & N. Dec. at 251. The BIA stated that there is no "blanket rejection of all factual scenarios involving gangs" and that "[s]ocial group determinations are made on a case-by-case basis." *Id.* Because the BIA's "guidance on particular social group claims ha[d] been clarified" since the IJ had last considered the question, it remanded the case to "enable the Immigration Judge to engage in any fact-finding that may be necessary to resolve the issues in this case." *Id.* at 251–52.

The new BIA decisions *W-G-R-* and *M-E-V-G-* are consistent with *Henriquez-Rivas,* in which the thrust of our holding was that the BIA had ignored specific evidence of whether Salvadoran society considered witnesses who testified against gang members to be a social group. The critical issue in each of the new decisions is whether there is evidence to support social recognition of the proposed group. In *W-G-R-* the BIA refused to find a social group because "evidence that the social group ... is recognized within the society is lacking in this case," 26 I. & N. Dec. at 221, and in *M-E-V-G-*, the BIA determined that the case-by-case analysis required remand for further factual development, 26 I. & N. Dec. at 251. The rule that thus emerges is the following: To determine whether a group is a particular social group for the purposes of an asylum claim, the agency must make a case-by-case determination as to whether the group is recognized by the particular society in question. To be consistent with its own precedent, the BIA may not reject a group solely because it had previously found a similar group in a different society to lack social distinction or particularity, especially where, as here, it is presented with evidence showing that the proposed group may in fact be recognized by the relevant society.

Here, the BIA did not perform the required evidence-based inquiry as to whether the relevant society recognizes Pirir-Boc's proposed social group. It failed to consider how Guatemalan society views the proposed group, and it did not consider the society-specific evidence submitted by Pirir-Boc in the form of U.S. State Department Country Reports on Guatemala, a Congressional Research Service Report for Congress on Gangs in Central America with a section on Guatemala, and background documents including news articles and Amnesty International Reports on Guatemala. The IJ, in contrast, did consider that evidence and found that in openly opposing the Mara Salvatrucha in Guatemala, Pirir-Boc "allied himself with a particular social group of persons directly in opposition to gang activities." The IJ found that there were "concerted efforts in Guatemala to combat gang activity" and that through his opposition to the Mara

Salvatrucha in that country, Pirir-Boc was "voluntarily associating" himself with that group. These are the type of findings that are relevant to determining "whether the people of a given society would perceive a proposed group as sufficiently separate or distinct to meet the 'social distinction' test." *M-E-V-G-*, 26 I. & N. Dec. at 241. "Evidence such as country conditions reports, expert witness testimony, and press accounts of discriminatory laws and policies, historical animosities, and the like may establish that a group exists and is perceived as 'distinct' or 'other' in a particular society." *Id.*

Because it is not clear to us from the record whether the evidence presented by Pirir-Boc is sufficient to meet the revised standard in *W-G-R-* and *M-E-V-G-*, we remand the petition to the BIA to consider Pirir-Boc's asylum claim in light of those decisions. See *Cordoba*, 726 F.3d at 1117. Because Pirir-Boc's claim for withholding of deportation was denied solely on the basis of his failure to satisfy the burden required for asylum, that claim is also remanded. We also advise the BIA to consider Pirir-Boc's petition in light of *Henriquez-Rivas*, which addressed a group comparable to Pirir-Boc's proposed group and found it to be potentially cognizable. In *Henriquez-Rivas*, the proposed group was "witnesses who testify against gang members." 707 F.3d at 1083. Here, the proposed group is "persons taking concrete steps to oppose gang membership and gang authority." The concrete and open steps Pirir-Boc took in opposition to the gang may fall within the framework of *Henriquez-Rivas*.

In remanding this case to the BIA, we do not decide whether the BIA's requirements of "social distinction" and "particularity" constitute a reasonable interpretation of "particular social group." We owe deference to the agency's construction of an ambiguous term, but only if the interpretation is reasonable. See *Brand X Internet*, 545 U.S. at 981 ("If a statute is ambiguous, and if the implementing agency's construction is reasonable, *Chevron* requires a federal court to accept the agency's construction of the statute, even if the agency's reading differs from what the court believes is the best statutory interpretation.") (citation omitted). If we were to conclude that the BIA's interpretation is not reasonable, we need not accept it; two circuits have in fact heretofore invalidated the BIA's previous formulation of the criteria of "particularity" and "social visibility." In *Henriquez-Rivas*, we held that the term "particular social group" is ambiguous, but we declined to decide whether the agency's construction was reasonable. 707 F.3d at 1087, 1091.

Here, once again, we leave open the question of whether the BIA's construction of "particular social group" is reasonable. First, we have not been asked to do so. Second, and more important, as is clear from *W-G-R-* and *M-E-V-G-*, the term is in flux, and it is premature to determine precisely how the rule will be implemented. After the BIA has on remand had the opportunity to apply the revised rule to this case, we may be in a better position to determine whether its revised construction of the term is reasonable. To qualify for CAT relief, Pirir-Boc must show that "it is more likely than not that he ... would be tortured if removed" to Guatemala. *Cole v. Holder*, 659 F.3d 762, 770 (9th Cir. 2011) (quoting 8 C.F.R. § 208.16(c)(2)). He does not need to show that he would be tortured on account of a protected ground. *Kamalthas v. I.N.S.*, 251 F.3d 1279, 1283 (9th Cir. 2001). The BIA denied Pirir-Boc relief under CAT in a single sentence, stating that he "has failed to establish a prima facie case for eligibility for relief under the Convention Against Torture." The BIA gave no explanation for its decision; nor did it mention any evidence that it had considered. "In order for the court to exercise our limited authority, there must be a reasoned explanation by the BIA of the basis for its decision." *Franco-Rosendo v. Gonzales*, 454 F.3d 965, 966 (9th Cir. 2006) (citing *Movsisian v. Ashcroft*, 395 F.3d 1095, 1098 (9th Cir. 2005)). Under the regulations, "[i]n making a CAT decision, ...'all evidence relevant to the possibility of future torture shall be considered." *Cole*, 659 F.3d at 771 (quoting 8 C.F.R. 1208.16(c)(3)). While the BIA is not required to "discuss each piece of evidence submitted," where there is "any indication that the BIA did not consider all of the evidence before it, a catchall phrase does not suffice, and the decision cannot stand. Such indications include ... failing to mention highly probative or potentially dispositive evidence." *Id.* at 771–72.

We therefore remand Pirir-Boc's CAT claim to the BIA for reconsideration. See *Movsisian*, 395 F.3d at 1099; *Tapia Madrigal v. Holder*, 716 F.3d 499, 509 (9th Cir. 2013).

Notes

1. **Overlapping grounds for persecution.** Asylum claims do not fall into neat packages conforming to the Protocol, and the standards and interpretations in the Handbook have taken this into account. One example of persecution which may be based on overlapping grounds is that of the individual who for reasons of conscience refuses to serve in the military.

Matter of Cañas[67] presented the issue of whether religious conscientious objectors from El Salvador, a country with compulsory military service without the possibility of exemption, could qualify for asylum in the United States. The petitioners in *Cañas* argued that their refusal to serve in the military would result in prosecution and punishment and that this punishment constituted persecution on account of their religion (Jehovah's Witness). In addition, they argued that their refusal to serve would be interpreted as a sign of disloyalty to the government on account of their "imputed" political opinion, i.e., the political opinion attributed to them by the Salvadoran government, which would result in their torture or death. The Board denied the claim of persecution based on political opinion, ruling that the evidence failed to establish that the applicants would be tortured or killed for their refusal to serve. It also held that punishment of religious conscientious objectors did not amount to persecution "on account of religion" unless it could be shown that the government's motive was to punish conscientious objectors for their religious beliefs rather than for their refusal to serve in the military. The Ninth Circuit rejected the Board's interpretation.[68]

---

67. 19 I. & N. Dec. 697 (BIA 1988).

68. *Cañas-Segovia v. INS*, 902 F.2d 717 (9th Cir. 1990), *cert. granted, vacated*, 502 U.S. 1086 (1992) (*Cañas I*).

After the decision in *Cañas I*, the Supreme Court ruled in *INS v. Zacarias* (which appeared earlier in this chapter) that in order to establish that persecution is on account of one of the five grounds, an applicant must prove that the persecutor was motivated to harm him because of his race, religion, political opinion, etc. On the basis of this decision, the government petitioned for certiorari in *Cañas I*. The Supreme Court vacated the decision, and on remand, the Ninth Circuit ruled that forced recruitment of Jehovah's Witnesses was not religious persecution, as the government recruited them to raise an army, not to punish them for their religion. However, the Ninth Circuit still found that the applicants qualified for asylum on the basis of their imputed political claim.[69]

2. A recognized principle of international law is that nations have the right to raise armies through conscription. In the absence of exemptions from military service for conscientious objectors, should the prosecution and punishment imposed for refusal to serve be considered a form of persecution? Should it matter whether human rights abuses are attributable to the military and that this forms the basis for objection? Should it matter that the military of a country is used to enforce a system, such as apartheid, which has been condemned by the community of nations? The *Handbook* notes that these factors should matter and recommends refugee status where the military action "is condemned by the international community as contrary to the basic rules of human conduct."[70] In a Fourth Circuit *en banc* decision, the language of the *Handbook* regarding condemnation by the international community was interpreted to require an explicit U.N. resolution condemning the military action at issue.[71] The *en banc* panel had rejected a prior ruling that did not require a U.N. resolution but had held that proof of the violation of the Geneva Convention rules of war would be adequate to meet the *Handbook* requirement.[72] Which is the better rule? During World War II, should individuals who were asked to collaborate with the Nazis have waited for a U.N. resolution before refusing to participate?

3. **Neutrality as political opinion.** In *Maldonado-Cruz v. INS*,[73] the court of appeals extended a position taken earlier where it held that a person who refused to take sides in the civil war in El Salvador had established a well-founded fear of persecution on account of political opinion where the persecution was by non-governmental (guerrilla) forces. The earlier case had found that persecution by the government on account of neutrality could form the basis for asylum.[74]

4. **Past persecution.** In *Matter of Chen*,[75] the BIA held that past persecution or a well-founded fear of future persecution could be the basis for an asylum appli-

---

69. *Cañas-Segovia v. I.N.S.*, 970 F.2d 599, 601 (9th Cir. 1992) (*Cañas II*).

70. Handbook at ¶ 171.

71. *M.A. v. INS*, 899 F.2d 304 (4th Cir. 1990).

72. *M.A. v. INS*, 858 F.2d 219 (4th Cir. 1988).

73. 883 F.2d 788 (9th Cir. 1989).

74. *See Bolanos-Hernandez v. INS*, 767 F.2d 1277 (9th Cir. 1984); *Perlera-Escobar v.INS*, 894 F.2d 1292 (11th Cir. 1990).

75. 20 I. & N. Dec. 16 (BIA 1989).

cation claim, as the existence of past persecution raises the rebuttable presumption of future persecution. The BIA also held that asylum could be denied where, as a matter of discretion, "there was little likelihood of future persecution." Is the BIA's use of discretion as a basis for denying asylum a proper exercise of its authority? The principle in *Chen* is set forth in regulations, which describe how the presumption of future persecution can be rebutted by evidence of changed country conditions.

I. Statutory Bars to Relief

As demonstrated by the previous cases, in order to establish eligibility for political asylum, an individual must demonstrate a well-founded fear of persecution on account of race, religion, nationality, political opinion or membership in a particular social group. Eligibility for restriction on removal (formerly called "withholding of deportation") requires a showing of a threat to life or freedom on account of the five grounds. However, even if individuals make this required showing, they may be denied protection if:

- in the case of political asylum, there are reasons for denial in the exercise of discretion; or
- in the case of both political asylum and restriction on removal, they come within the statutory bars for these forms of relief. Pursuant to the relevant statutes, an individual is barred from both asylum and restriction on removal if it is determined that she: (1) is a persecutor of others; (2) has been convicted of a particularly serious crime; (3) has committed a serious non-political crime outside the United States; (4) is a danger to the security of the United States; or (5) is inadmissible or deportable on terrorism grounds.

In addition to the bars which apply to both asylum and restriction on removal, there are bars which apply only to asylum. An individual is precluded from asylum if the person: (1) was firmly resettled in a third country prior to coming to the United States; (2) could be removed to a "safe third country" with which the United States has a treaty and where she would not be at risk and could apply for some form of protection; (3) did not apply within a year of arriving in the United States; or (4) previously applied for and was denied political asylum.

The next two cases provide examples of the application of two of the asylum bars. *Diallo v. Ashcroft* focuses on the application of the bar to asylum for persons who are considered firmly-resettled. *Aguirre-Aguirre* addresses the serious non-political crime preclusion, which applies to both asylum and restriction on removal.

Mamadou Diallo v. Ashcroft

381 F.3d 687 (7th Cir. 2004)

Before Bauer, Manion, and Rovner, Circuit Judges.

Rovner, Circuit Judge.

Mamadou Diallo, a native citizen of Mauritania, requested that the Immigration and Naturalization Service (INS)[1] grant him asylum. The Agency refused, reasoning that Diallo had not been persecuted in Mauritania, did not have a well-founded fear of future persecution there, and had firmly resettled in Senegal prior to his arrival in the United States. Because the Agency (1) ignored its own regulations regarding the proper factors to consider in a firm resettlement analysis, (2) failed to make a credibility determination, and (3) failed to support its decision on fear of future prosecution with reasonable or substantial evidence, we must remand for further proceedings consistent with this opinion.

Diallo was born in Mauritania in 1958 and lived there for the first thirty-five years of his life. According to Diallo's testimony, in 1986 he joined the African Liberation Force of Mauritania (FLAM) an organization seeking to fight against slavery, torture, and discrimination in Mauritania. Diallo's brother, Saidou, was also a member of FLAM, and because of his leadership role in the organization, in approximately 1989 or 1990, he was arrested and imprisoned for six months. Through newspaper accounts, Diallo learned that Saidou had been tortured and eventually killed while in prison. Diallo himself was not a leader in the organization; he did not pass out political leaflets or brochures and did not speak at political rallies, but he did support the organization monetarily from the proceeds of his work as a merchant and did not hide his support for FLAM.

In approximately May 1993, uniformed police officers arrived at Diallo's house at night searching for a member of FLAM. They handcuffed him, searched his apartment, confiscated all of his documents, and took him to jail without the opportunity to appear before a judge or to be represented by a lawyer. For the six months that he remained in jail, he was forced to perform hard labor, cutting and hauling wood and digging holes. During one incident when he was working too slowly, a guard slashed his arm with a knife.

After six months, Diallo's captors released him and immediately placed him on a boat to Senegal with nothing but his Mauritanian national identification card. Diallo spent four years in Senegal "selling small things" and living with a former acquaintance from Mauritania in a rented apartment. He attended church, but had no familial ties in Senegal. Although he had neither a work permit nor official permission to remain

1. Congress transferred the functions of the former INS to the Department of Homeland Security (DHS) on March 1, 2003. The transfer does not affect any legal issue in the case, and the DHS did not exist during any of the underlying administrative proceedings. To avoid confusion, however, we will refer to the former INS as the "Agency."

there, he was not bothered by the Senegalese government. Diallo left Senegal and traveled as a stowaway on a boat to Baltimore, Maryland where he arrived in June 1997. Two months later, he submitted his application for asylum, withholding of removal, and for protection under the United Nations Convention Against Torture and Other Forms of Cruel, Inhuman or Degrading Treatment or Punishment (CAT). Diallo appeared for his scheduled asylum interview, but because his privately hired interpreter never arrived and Diallo could not participate in the interview, he was deemed to have failed to appear, he was charged with removal, and his asylum application was referred to an immigration judge pursuant to 8 C.F.R. § 1208.14(c)(1).

* * *

Diallo appealed the immigration judge's decision to the Board of Immigration Appeals (BIA), which summarily affirmed the decision of the immigration judge, making it the decision of the agency for purposes of our appellate review. 8 C.F.R. § 1003.1(e)(4); *Szczesny v. Ashcroft*, 358 F.3d 464, 465 (7th Cir. 2004). That decision held that the final blow to Diallo's asylum claim was that he had firmly resettled in Senegal prior to his arrival in the United States. "Firm resettlement," however, is an odd tool to use to strike the final blow to an asylum claim, since under the current statutory iteration of the doctrine of firm resettlement, an immigration court must deny asylum to any refugee if "the alien was firmly resettled in another country prior to arriving in the United States." 8 U.S.C. § 1158(b)(2)(A)(vi).[4] That being said, it seems the logical place to begin rather than end an assessment of whether a refugee is entitled to asylum in this country. If the doctrine of firm resettlement sounds the death knell on the asylum-seeker's claim, there is simply no need to continue on to determine whether an asylum-seeker was the victim of past persecution or has a well-founded fear of future persecution.

The question of how to determine whether a refugee has firmly resettled in another country prior to her arrival in the United States appears to be an issue of first impression for this circuit. The only published Seventh Circuit opinion discussing firm resettlement was decided in 1954, long before the enactment of the current statute and agency rules on the subject. See *United States v. Rumsa*, 212 F.2d 927 (7th Cir. 1954). Although the statute mandating the denial of asylum for refugees who have firmly resettled (8 U.S.C. § 1158(b)(2)(A)(vi)) does not itself define "firm resettlement" or offer instruction on how firm resettlement should be determined, the agency regulations set forth in straightforward language how an immigration judge should proceed in making that determination. 8 C.F.R. § 208.15. The regulations provide that:

> [a]n alien is considered to be firmly resettled if, prior to arrival in the United States, he or she entered into another country with, or while in that country

---

4. Prior to 1990, firm resettlement was but one factor that an immigration judge weighed in deciding whether to grant asylum. See *Abdille v. Ashcroft*, 242 F.3d 477, 483 n. 4 (3d Cir.2001) (reviewing the history of the firm resettlement bar to asylum claims). Consequently, the immigration judge's citation to *Matter of Soleimani*, 20 I. & N. Dec. 99, 1989 WL 331872 (BIA 1989) for the proposition that "firm resettlement in another country is a factor to be evaluated in determining whether asylum should be granted as a matter of discretion" is incorrect. Because firm resettlement is currently a mandatory bar to the grant of asylum, it is no longer merely "one factor" to be considered.

received, an offer of permanent resident status, or some other form of permanent resettlement unless he or she establishes:

(a) That his or her entry into that country was a necessary consequence of his or her flight from persecution, that he or she remained in that country only as long as was necessary to arrange onward travel, and that he or she did not establish significant ties in that country; or

(b) That the conditions of his or her residence in that country were so substantially and consciously restricted by the authority of the country of refuge that he or she was not in fact resettled. In making his or her determination, the asylum officer or immigration judge shall consider the conditions under which other residents of the country live; the type of housing, whether permanent or temporary, made available to the refugee; the types and extent of employment available to the refugee; and the extent to which the refugee received permission to hold property and to enjoy other rights and privileges, such as travel documentation that includes a right of entry or reentry, education, public relief, or naturalization, ordinarily available to others resident in the country.

8 C.F.R. § 208.15. After the government meets its initial burden of demonstrating firm resettlement, the asylum-seeker may rebut the presumption by presenting evidence to the contrary. *Mussie v. U.S. INS*, 172 F.3d 329, 332 (4th Cir.1999); *Cheo v. INS*, 162 F.3d 1227, 1229 (9th Cir.1998); *Salazar v. Ashcroft*, 359 F.3d 45, 50 (1st Cir.2004). For the refugee who has failed to rebut the presumption of firm resettlement, all hope is not lost. She may also demonstrate that she falls within one of the two exceptions to firm resettlement articulated in section (a) and (b) of the regulation. 8 C.F.R. § 208.15(a), (b).

The primary and initial consideration, therefore, is a simple one-whether or not the intermediary country has made some sort of offer of permanent resettlement. The regulations do allow the immigration judge to consider factors such as the length of time spent in the country, housing, and the type and extent of the refugee's employment, among others, but only after making a preliminary finding of a genuine offer *vel non* of permanent resettlement, and only then when the applicant seeks to demonstrate that she falls into one of the two exceptions. 8 C.F.R. § 208.15. See *Rife v. Ashcroft*, 374 F.3d 606, 610–11 (8th Cir.2004); *Abdille*, 242 F.3d at 486.

As we noted earlier, see footnote 4, supra, this was not always the case. Prior to 1990, "firm resettlement" was just one of the factors to be considered in the Agency's exercise of discretion in granting asylum. See *Rosenberg v. Yee Chien Woo*, 402 U.S. 49, 56, 91 S.Ct. 1312, 28 L.Ed.2d 592 (1971); *Abdille*, 242 F.3d at 483 n. 4. Under a discretionary scheme, where firm resettlement is but one factor to consider in granting or denying an asylum application, an adjudicator could consider factors such as the length of stay, ability to work, familial ties, economic conditions in the third country, and the like as other factors that militate for or against a grant of asylum. In 1990, however, the INS amended its regulations to make firm resettlement a mandatory bar to asylum. 8 C.F.R. § 208.14 (1990). Later, Congress codified the mandatory prohibition on grants of asylum to firmly resettled refugees when it passed the Illegal Immigration Reform and Illegal Immigrant Act of 1996. 8 U.S.C. § 1158(b)(2)(A)(vi). These new regulations "reoriented the central inquiry of firm resettlement to focus the adjudicator on the actual existence vel non of an offer of permanent resettlement." Robert D. Sloane, *An Offer of Firm Resettlement*, 36 Geo. Wash. Int'l L.Rev. 47, 57 (2004). Such a focus is consistent with the goals of asylum law. As the Third Circuit points out, "[a]bsent some government dispensation, an immigrant who surreptitiously enters a nation without its authorization cannot obtain official resident status no matter his length of stay, his intent, or the extent of the familial and economic conditions he develops. Citizenship or permanent residency cannot be gained by adverse possession." *Abdille*, 242 F.3d at 487.

Despite the metamorphosis in the focus of firm resettlement inquiries, some circuits continue to hang on to the "totality of the circumstances" test, looking at the applicant's length of stay and social and economic ties in the third country either instead of or on par with governmental offers of permanent resettlement. See, e.g., *Mussie*, 172 F.3d at 331–32, *Cheo*, 162 F.3d at 1229. The Third and Eighth Circuits' obedience to the language and purpose of the regulation seems the more rational path, and for this reason we agree that the primary and most important inquiry in any analysis of firm resettlement is whether or not the stopover country has made some type of offer of permanent resettlement. *Abdille*, 242 F.3d at 480; Rife, 374 F.3d at 610–11.

We recognize, as did the Third Circuit, that "circumstances may arise in which the INS may not be able to secure direct evidence of a formal government offer of some type of permanent resettlement, and thus may be [sic] not be able to make the prima facie showing of firm resettlement under § 208.15 in that manner." *Abdille*, 242 F.3d at 486–87. In that case, the Third Circuit noted in dicta, the immigration judge or BIA "may find it necessary to rely on non-offer-based factors, such as the length of an alien's stay in a third country, the alien's intent to remain in the country, and the extent of the social and economic ties developed by the alien, as circumstantial evidence of a government-issued offer." *Id.* at 487. The Third Circuit sees these non-offer-based elements as surrogates for direct evidence of a formal offer only "if they rise to a sufficient level of clarity and force, which we need not delineate here." *Id.*

The immigration judge in Diallo's case, however, did not consider whether there was an offer at all. The immigration judge's determination that Diallo had permanently resettled in Senegal was based entirely on his two-sentence finding that: "prior to his arrival in the United States, [Diallo] resided in neighboring Senegal for four years. Indeed, the respondent worked as a merchant and lived with a friend and a family member." In short, the immigration judge relied on three factors in determining that Diallo had firmly resettled: (1) his four-year stay, (2) his work as a merchant, and (3) the fact that he shared an apartment with a friend and family member. Nothing suggests that the immigration judge was using these factors as indirect evidence of a formal offer. Rather, it seems clear that the immigration judge simply ignored the Agency's own regulations requiring the immigration judge to consider the existence vel non of an offer of permanent resettlement, and completely ignored Diallo's testimony that he had no such formal offer or permission to live or work in Senegal. (R. at 131, 137, 139).

The government argues that residency documents are not required in order for the government to establish firm resettlement, and cites *Cheo* for the proposition that the passage of time alone is enough to establish "some other type of permanent resettlement." *Id.* 162 F.3d at 1229. But *Cheo* is not the case to turn to in order to alleviate our concern that the immigration judge failed to consider any evidence or lack thereof of an offer *vel non* of permanent resettlement. In fact, in *Cheo*, the Ninth Circuit considered the length of the stay only after concluding that there was no direct evidence one way or another as to whether the applicants had the right to return to the third country. *Id.* at 1229. In this way, its analysis was not much different from the Third Circuit's in *Abdille* when it announced that non-offer based elements may be used as surrogates for direct evidence only when there is no evidence of some formal offer of permanent resettlement. *Abdille*, 242 F.3d at 486–87. Neither the Ninth Circuit's approach in *Cheo* nor the Third Circuit's approach in *Abdille* allows an immigration judge to ignore completely the regulation's requirement to consider the existence of a formal offer or the lack thereof. The applicants in the *Cheo* case did not present any evidence of a lack of a formal offer. In this case, Diallo has presented evidence to the contrary. He presented undisputed testimony that he had no legal right to live or work in Senegal. The immigration judge erred by failing to consider this evidence at all.

A finding of firm resettlement is a factual determination that must be upheld if it is supported "by reasonable, substantial, and probative evidence on the record considered as a whole." *INS v. Elias-Zacarias*, 502 U.S. 478 (1992); *Krouchevski v. Ashcroft*, 344 F.3d 670, 673 (7th Cir.2003). We reverse only if the evidence is such that a reasonable fact-finder would be compelled to reach an opposite conclusion. *Krouchevski*, 344 F.3d at 673. This "substantial evidence" review is highly deferential and does not allow this court to overturn an agency determination simply because we would have decided the case differently. *Capric*, 355 F.3d at 1086. Nevertheless, the immigration judge below failed to consider the single factor that agency regulations require him to consider. Had he done so he would be, as we are, compelled to find that Diallo had not firmly resettled in Senegal.

Even if the immigration judge were applying the now outdated "totality of the circumstances" analysis, his finding of firm resettlement still would not be supported by substantial evidence and the reasonable fact-finder would be compelled to make a finding to the contrary. Most significantly, the immigration judge erred by ignoring Diallo's testimony that he had no documents permitting him to live or work in Senegal. An immigration judge may not simply ignore record evidence that favors the applicant's case. See *Vujisic* v. INS, 224 F.3d 578, 581 (7th Cir. 2000) (immigration judge and BIA erred by ignoring evidence of feared persecution and current conditions in applicant's native country). Diallo's testimony, if credible (and the immigration judge never found that it was not) was "sufficient to sustain the burden of proof without corroboration." 8 C.F.R. § 208.13(a). Furthermore, in assessing Diallo's social and familial ties, the immigration judge found it significant that Diallo lived with a friend and family member while in Senegal. In the first instance, the immigration judge's factual determination was simply incorrect. While in Senegal, Diallo lived with a man he had met in Mauritania. The record firmly establishes that the men were not related. (R. at 131–32). Moreover, we fail to see how living with a Mauritanian acquaintance in Senegal offers any evidence whatsoever of firm resettlement.

Consequently, we are left with a four-year stay and work as a "seller of small things"—the type of itinerant work that many refugees pick up in hopes of making ends meet until they reach their final destination. Four years does indeed constitute a lengthy stay, but not so lengthy that it, in and of itself, could support a finding of firm resettlement. The cases from our sister circuits—even those employing a "totality of the circumstances" test—have never held that a stay of this length in and of itself compels a finding of firm resettlement. The closest case comes from the Ninth Circuit's decision in *Cheo v. INS*, discussed earlier, which held that a peaceful, undisturbed stay of three years in a third country was enough to "establish[] that the ground of 'firm resettlement' in [the third country] might apply" thus shifting the burden to the applicants to prove that they were not firmly resettled. *Id.* at 1229. The applicants in that case did not present any evidence to the contrary. Significantly, the Ninth Circuit considered the length of the stay only after concluding that there was no direct evidence one way or another as to whether the applicants had the right to return to the third country. *Id.* In this case, Diallo has presented evidence to the contrary. He presented undisputed testimony that he had no legal right to live or work in Senegal.

The other circuit court cases cited by the government in its brief (the immigration judge cited no cases other than the no-longer-valid decision of the BIA in *Matter of Soleimani*, 20 I. & N. Dec. 99 (BIA 1989)) are no more helpful in supporting the immigration judge's conclusion that Diallo had firmly resettled in Senegal, as all contained compelling evidence of firm resettlement other than the mere passage of time. See *Mussie*, 172 F.3d at 332 (petitioner lived in Germany for four years; German government gave petitioner asylum, travel documents, government assistance for transportation, food, rent and education; petitioner held a job, paid taxes and rented her own apartment); *Vang v. INS*, 146 F.3d 1114, 1115 (9th Cir. 1998) (appellate court offered no details as to the factors the BIA applied in determining that petitioner was resettled, but in addition to living in France from the age of four to sixteen, applicant arrived in France as part of an official United Nations refugee program and also received French travel documents); *Yang v. INS*, 79 F.3d 932, 934 (9th Cir. 1996) (for purposes of the appeal, petitioners conceded that they were firmly resettled in France and argued only that the regulation on firm resettlement was beyond the authority of the INS; consequently the *Yang* Court had no opportunity to comment on the factors that constituted the Yang's firm resettlement in France.); *Farbakhsh v. INS*, 20 F.3d 877, 880 (8th Cir. 1994) (petitioner lived in Spain for four years, intended to stay there as evidenced by his application for asylum, and had strong familial ties there); *Abdalla v. INS*, 43 F.3d 1397, 1399 (10th Cir. 1994) (petitioner lived in and possessed a residence visa/permit for the United Arab Emirates); see also *Rife*, 374

F.3d at 609, 611 (finding firm resettlement where Israeli government offered petitioners permanent resettlement, issued certificates evidencing citizenship, and issued passports, none of which had ever been revoked); *Salazar v. Ashcroft*, 359 F.3d 45, 47–48 (1st Cir. 2004) (finding firm resettlement where petitioner lived in Venezuela for fourteen months, worked and rented an apartment, and received a Venezuelan passport with a resident stamp). In short, we cannot find a single published circuit court opinion that relied on as little as this immigration judge relied on to determine that an applicant for asylum had firmly resettled in a third country. We are compelled, therefore, to reverse the Agency's determination on firm resettlement.

Because we find that Diallo was not firmly resettled in Senegal, we can now turn to his claim that he is entitled to a grant of asylum....

* * *

In sum, we reverse the finding of the Agency that Diallo was firmly resettled in Senegal and we remand to the Department of Homeland Security for a credibility determination and for subsequent proceedings to determine whether Diallo suffered past persecution or had a well-founded fear of future persecution entitling him to asylum in this country. In view of our criticism of the immigration judge in this matter, we urge the Department of Homeland Security to refer this case to a different immigration judge on remand.

Notes

1. In firm resettlement cases, the initial burden is on the government to make out a prima facie case, such as evidence of the person having been granted asylum and issued travel documents.[76] But firm resettlement is not an issue where the person is able to show that they have a fear of persecution in the country of resettlement.[77]

2. Even though a person has not been firmly resettled, may she be removed to the country of last residence? In *Matter of Salim*,[78] the BIA held that withholding of deportation was country-specific. That is, it only protects the person from removal to a country where her life or freedom would be threatened. In *Salim*, the Board, in denying the asylum application of an Afghan national, ordered the person removed to Pakistan instead of Afghanistan. The Board agreed with the applicant that his claim of persecution in Afghanistan had been proven but that such a claim could not be made as to conditions in Pakistan, so Section 243(h) relief was granted only for Afghanistan. Assuming that the government could remove a person to another country, the person is entitled to assurances that the other country will not return her to the country where she would be persecuted.[79]

---

76. *Mussie v. INS*, 172 F.3d 329 (4th Cir. 1999).

77. *Siong v. INS*, 376 F.3d 1030 (9th Cir. 2004) (Laotian Hmong who resettled in France and was in fear of Laotians there for past CIA ties).

78. 18 I. & N. Dec. 311 (BIA 1982).

79. *See Amanullah v. Cobb*, 673 F. Supp. 28 (D. Mass. 1987), *aff'd* F.2d 362 (1st Cir. 1987), *vacated as moot*, 872 F.2d 11 (1st Cir. 1989).

3. Related to the issue of firm resettlement is that of "safe-haven." The issue of safe haven arises when an individual traveled through, or temporarily remained in, one or more countries en route to the United States. Legacy INS had argued that even though the individual did not have any of the rights and benefits associated with firm resettlement, she should be denied asylum because these countries provided refuge. This developing position or argument is commonly referred to as "safe-haven." The only case which even tangentially deals with the issue of safe-haven and firm resettlement as the basis for discretionary denial of asylum is *Diaz v. INS*.[80] In *Diaz*, the INS district director had denied work authorization because the asylum applicant had "failed" to apply for asylum in a third country prior to coming to the United States. The court, in discussing the "safe-haven" basis for denial, referred to the standards for firm resettlement.[81] In the 1996 amendments, Congress added a provision on "safe-third country" which allows for the denial of asylum and the removal of the person to a country where her life or freedom would not be threatened and where she would also have access to a full and fair procedure to determine her claim for asylum or temporary protection. In order for this provision to be invoked, there must first be a bilateral or multilateral agreement that provides these protections.[82]

4. **Failure to file for asylum within one year**. Included in the 1996 amendments was a provision which required the asylum applicant to apply for asylum within one year after the person's arrival in the United States. This one-year bar is inapplicable if the person is able to show changed country conditions "which materially affect the applicant's eligibility for asylum or extraordinary circumstances relating to the delay in filing the application" within the period.[83]

Immigration and Naturalization Service v. Juan Anibal Aguirre-Aquirre

526 U.S. 415 (1999)

Justice Kennedy delivered the opinion of the Court.

We granted certiorari to consider the analysis employed by the Court of Appeals in setting aside a determination of the Board of Immigration Appeals (BIA). The BIA ruled that respondent, a native and citizen of Guatemala, was not entitled to withholding of deportation based on his expressed fear of persecution for earlier political activities in Guatemala. The issue in the case is not whether the persecution is likely to occur, but whether, even assuming it is, respondent is ineligible for withholding because he "committed a serious nonpolitical crime" before his entry into the United States. 8 U.S.C. § 1253(h)(2)(C). The beginning point for the BIA's analysis was its determination that respondent, to protest certain governmental policies in Guatemala, had burned buses, assaulted passengers, and vandalized and destroyed

80. 648 F. Supp. 638 (E.D. Ca. 1986).

81. *Diaz* at 654. Cf. *Garcia-Ramos v. INS*, 775 F.2d 1370 (9th Cir. 1985).

82. *See* 8 U.S.C. § 1158(a)(2)(A), Sec. 208(a)(2)(A).

83. *See* 8 U.S.C. § 1158(a)(2)(D), Sec. 208(a)(2)(D).

property in private shops, after forcing customers out. These actions, the BIA concluded, were serious nonpolitical crimes. In reaching this conclusion, it relied on a statutory interpretation adopted in one of its earlier decisions, *Matter of McMullen*, 19 I. & N. Dec. 90 (BIA 1984), aff'd, 788 F.2d 591 (C.A.9 1986).

On appeal, the Court of Appeals for the Ninth Circuit concluded the BIA had applied an incorrect interpretation of the serious nonpolitical crime provision, and it remanded for further proceedings. In the Court of Appeals' view, as we understand it, the BIA erred by misconstruing the controlling statute and by employing an analytical framework insufficient to take account of the Court of Appeals' own precedent on this subject. According to the court, the BIA erred in failing to consider certain factors, including "the political necessity and success of Aguirre's methods;" whether his acts were grossly out of proportion to their objective or were atrocious; and the persecution respondent might suffer upon return to Guatemala.

... We disagree with the Court of Appeals and address each of the three specific areas in which it found the BIA's analysis deficient. We reverse the judgment of the court and remand for further proceedings.

The statutory provision for withholding of deportation that is applicable here provides that "[t]he Attorney General shall not deport or return any alien ... to a country if the Attorney General determines that such alien's life or freedom would be threatened in such country on account of race, religion, nationality, membership in a particular social group, or political opinion." 8 U.S.C. § 1253(h)(1). The provision was added to the Immigration and Nationality Act (INA), 66 Stat. 166, 8 U.S.C. § 1101 et seq., (1994 ed. and Supp. III), by the Refugee Act of 1980 (Refugee Act), Pub.L. 96-212, 94 Stat. 102. See *INS v. Stevic*, 467 U.S. 407, 414–416, 421–422 (1984). As a general rule, withholding is mandatory if an alien "establish[es] that it is more likely than not that [he] would be subject to persecution on one of the specified grounds," *id.*, at 429–430, 104 S.Ct. 2489, but the statute has some specific exceptions. As is relevant here, withholding does not apply, and deportation to the place of risk is authorized, "if the Attorney General determines that"

> "there are serious reasons for considering that the alien has committed a serious nonpolitical crime outside the United States prior to the arrival of the alien in the United States." 8 U.S.C. § 1253(h)(2)(C).

Under the immigration laws, withholding is distinct from asylum, although the two forms of relief serve similar purposes. Whereas withholding only bars deporting an alien to a particular country or countries, a grant of asylum permits an alien to remain in the United States and to apply for permanent residency after one year. See *INS v. Cardoza-Fonseca*, 480 U.S. 421, 428–429, n. 6(1987). In addition, whereas withholding is mandatory unless the Attorney General determines one of the exceptions applies, the decision whether asylum should be granted to an eligible alien is committed to the Attorney General's discretion. *Ibid.* As a consequence, under the law then in force, respondent was able to seek asylum irrespective of his eligibility for withholding.

* * *

We turn to the matter before us. In 1994, respondent was charged with deportability by the Immigration and Naturalization Service (INS) for illegal entry into the United States. Respondent conceded deportability but applied for asylum and withholding. At a hearing before an Immigration Judge respondent testified, through an interpreter, that he had been politically active in Guatemala from 1989 to 1992 with a student group called Estudeante Syndicado (ES) and with the National Central Union political party. App. 19–20, 36–37. He testified about threats due to his political activity. The threats, he believed, were from different quarters, including the Guatemalan Government, right-wing government support groups, and left-wing guerillas. App. to Pet. for Cert. 23a.

Respondent described activities he and other ES members engaged in to protest various government policies and actions, including the high cost of bus fares and the government's failure to investigate the disappearance or murder of students and others. App. 20–21; App. to Pet. for Cert. 22a–23a. For purposes of our review, we assume that the amount of bus fares is an important political and social issue in Guatemala. We are advised that bus fare represents a significant portion of many Guatemalans' annual living expense, and a rise in fares may impose substantial economic hardship. See Brief for Massachusetts Law Reform Institute et al. as Amicus Curiae 18–19. In addition, government involvement with fare increases, and other aspects of the transportation system, has been a focus of political discontent in that country. *Id.*, at 16–21.

According to the official hearing record, respondent testified that he and his fellow members would "strike" by "burning buses, breaking windows or just attacking the police, police cars." App. 20. Respondent estimated that he participated in setting about 10 buses on fire, after dousing them with gasoline. *Id.*, at 46. Before setting fire to the buses, he and his group would order passengers to leave the bus. Passengers who refused were stoned, hit with sticks, or bound with ropes. *Id.*, at 46–47. In addition, respondent testified that he and his group "would break the windows of ... stores," "t[ake] the people out of the stores that were there," and "throw everything on the floor." *Id.*, at 48.

The Immigration Judge granted respondent's applications for withholding of deportation and for asylum, finding a likelihood of persecution for his political opinions and activities if he was returned to Guatemala. App. to Pet. for Cert. 31a–32a. The INS appealed to the BIA. Respondent did not file a brief with the BIA, although his request for an extension of time to do so was granted. Brief for Petitioner 10, n. 6; Record 13–15. The BIA sustained the INS's appeal from this decision, vacated the Immigration Judge's order, and ordered respondent deported. App. to Pet. for Cert. 18a. With respect to withholding, the BIA did not decide whether respondent had established the requisite risk of persecution because it determined that, in any event, he had committed a serious nonpolitical crime within the meaning of § 1253(h)(2)(C).

In addressing the definition of a serious nonpolitical crime, the BIA applied the interpretation it first set forth in *Matter of McMullen*, 19 I. & N. Dec., at 97–98, 19 I. & N. Dec. 90: "In evaluating the political nature of a crime, we consider it important that the political aspect of the offense outweigh its common-law character. This would not be the case if the crime is grossly out of proportion to the political objective or if it involves acts of an atrocious nature." In the instant case, the BIA found, "the criminal nature of the respondent's acts outweigh their political nature." App. to Pet. for Cert. 18a. The BIA acknowledged respondent's dissatisfaction with the Guatemalan government's "seeming inaction in the investigation of student deaths and in its raising of student bus fares." *Ibid.* It said, however: "The ire of the ES manifested itself disproportionately in the destruction of property and assaults on civilians. Although the ES had a political agenda, those goals were outweighed by their criminal strategy of strikes...." *Ibid.* The BIA further concluded respondent should not be granted discretionary asylum relief in light of "the nature of his acts against innocent Guatemalans." *Id.*, at 17a.

A divided panel of the Court of Appeals granted respondent's petition for review and remanded to the BIA. 121 F.3d 521 (C.A.9 1997). According to the majority, the BIA's analysis of the serious nonpolitical crime exception was legally deficient in three respects. First, the BIA should have "consider[ed] the persecution that Aguirre might suffer if returned to Guatemala" and "balance[d] his admitted offenses against the danger to him of death." *Id.*, at 524. Second, it should have "considered whether the acts committed were grossly out of proportion to the[ir] alleged objective" and were "of an atrocious nature," especially with reference to Ninth Circuit precedent in this area. Ibid. (internal quotation marks and citation omitted). Third, the BIA "should have considered the political necessity and success of Aguirre's methods." *Id.*, at 523–524.

Judge Kleinfeld dissented. In his view, "[t]he BIA correctly identified the legal question, whether 'the criminal nature of the respondent's acts outweigh their political nature.'" *Id.*, at 524 (quoting *McMullen v. INS*, 788 F.2d 591, 592 (C.A.9 1986)). Given the violent nature of respondent's acts, and the fact the acts were in large part directed against innocent civilians, the BIA "reasonably conclude[d] that [his] crimes were disproportionate to his political objectives." 121 F.3d, at 525.

As an initial matter, the Court of Appeals expressed no disagreement with the Attorney General or the BIA that the phrase "serious nonpolitical crime" in § 1253(h)(2)(C) should be applied by weighing "the political nature" of an act against its "common-law" or "criminal" character. See *Matter of McMullen, supra*, at 97–98; App. to Pet. for Cert. 18a; Deportation Proceedings for Doherty, 13 Op. Off. Legal Counsel 1, 23 (1989) (an act "should be considered a serious nonpolitical crime if the act is disproportionate to the objective") (quoting *McMullen v. INS, supra*, at 595), rev'd on other grounds, *Doherty v. INS*, 908 F.2d 1108 (C.A.2 1990), rev'd, 502 U.S. 314 (1992). Nor does respondent take issue with this basic inquiry.

The Court of Appeals did conclude, however, that the BIA must supplement this weighing test by examining additional factors. In the course of its analysis, the Court of Appeals failed to accord the required level of deference to the interpretation of the serious nonpolitical crime exception adopted by the Attorney General and BIA. Because the Court of Appeals confronted questions implicating "an agency's construction of the statute which it administers," the court should have applied the principles of deference described in *Chevron U.S.A. Inc. v. Natural Resources Defense Council, Inc.*, 467 U.S. 837, 842 (1984). Thus, the court should have asked whether "the statute is silent or ambiguous with respect to the specific issue" before it; if so, "the question for the court [was] whether the agency's answer is based on a permissible construction of the statute." *Id.*, at 843. See also *INS v. Cardoza-Fonseca*, 480 U.S., at 448–449.

It is clear that principles of Chevron deference are applicable to this statutory scheme. The INA provides that "[t]he Attorney General shall be charged with the administration and enforcement" of the statute and that the "determination and ruling by the Attorney General with respect to all questions of law shall be controlling." 8 U.S.C. § 1103(a)(1) (1994 ed., Supp. III). Section 1253(h), moreover, in express terms confers decisionmaking authority on the Attorney General, making an alien's entitlement to withholding turn on the Attorney General's "determin[ation]" whether the statutory conditions for withholding have been met. 8 U.S.C. §§ 1253(h)(1), (2). In addition, we have recognized that judicial deference to the Executive Branch is especially appropriate in the immigration context where officials "exercise especially sensitive political functions that implicate questions of foreign relations." *INS v. Abudu*, 485 U.S. 94, 110 (1988). A decision by the Attorney General to deem certain violent offenses committed in another country as political in nature, and to allow the perpetrators to remain in the United States, may affect our relations with that country or its neighbors. The judiciary is not well positioned to shoulder primary responsibility for assessing the likelihood and importance of such diplomatic repercussions.

The Attorney General, while retaining ultimate authority, has vested the BIA with power to exercise the "discretion and authority conferred upon the Attorney General by law" in the course of "considering and determining cases before it." 8 C.F.R. § 3.1(d)(1) (1998). Based on this allocation of authority, we recognized in *Cardoza-Fonseca, supra*, that the BIA should be accorded *Chevron* deference as it gives ambiguous statutory terms "concrete meaning through a process of case-by-case adjudication" (though we ultimately concluded that the agency's interpretation in that case was not sustainable). 480 U.S., at 448–449. In the case before us, by failing to follow *Chevron* principles in its review of the BIA, the Court of Appeals erred.

The Court of Appeals' error is clearest with respect to its holding that the BIA was required to balance respondent's criminal acts against the risk of persecution he would face if returned to Guatemala. In *Matter of Rodriguez-Coto*, 19 I. & N. Dec. 208, 209–210 (1985), the BIA "reject[ed] any interpretation of the phras[e] ... 'serious nonpolitical crime' in [§ 1253(h)(2)(C)] which would vary with the nature of evidence of persecution." The text and structure of § 1253(h) are consistent with this conclusion. Indeed, its words suggest that the BIA's reading of the statute, not the interpretation adopted by the Court of Appeals, is the more appropriate one. As a matter of plain language, it is not obvious that an already-completed crime is somehow rendered less serious by considering the further circumstance that the alien may be subject to persecution if returned to his home country. See *ibid.* ("We find that the modifie[r] ... 'serious'... relate[s] only to the nature of the crime itself").

* * *

The U.N. Handbook may be a useful interpretative aid, but it is not binding on the Attorney General, the BIA, or United States courts. "Indeed, the Handbook itself disclaims such force, explaining that 'the determination of refugee status under the 1951 Convention and the 1967 Protocol ... is incumbent upon the Contracting State in whose territory the refugee finds himself.'" *INS v. Cardoza-Fonseca*, 480 U.S., at 439, n. 22 (quoting U.N. Handbook, at 1, & ¶ (ii)). See also 480 U.S., at 439, n. 22 ("We do not suggest, of course, that the explanation in the U.N. Handbook has the force of law or in any way binds the INS...."). For the reasons given, *supra*, at 1445–1446, we think the BIA's determination that § 1253(h)(2)(C) requires no additional balancing of the risk of persecution rests on a fair and permissible reading of the statute. See also *T. v. Secretary of State for the Home Dept.*, 2 All E.R. 865, 882 (H.L.1996) (Lord Mustill) ("The crime either is or is not political when committed, and its character cannot depend on the consequences which the offender may afterwards suffer if he is returned").

Also relying on the U.N. Handbook, the Court of Appeals held that the BIA "should have considered whether the acts committed were 'grossly out of proportion to the alleged objective.'... The political nature of the offenses would be 'more difficult to accept' if they involved 'acts of an atrocious nature.'" 121 F.3d, at 524 (quoting U.N. Handbook, & ¶ 152, at 36). The court further suggested that the BIA should have considered prior Circuit case law that "cast[s] light on what under the law are acts of [an] atrocious nature." 121 F.3d, at 524. Citing its own opinion affirming the BIA's decision in *Matter of McMullen*, see *McMullen v. INS*, 788 F.2d 591 (C.A.9 1986), the Court of Appeals stated that "[a] comparison of what the *McMullen* court found atrocious with the acts committed by Aguirre suggests a startling degree of difference." 121 F.3d, at 524. It reasoned that while *McMullen* had involved "indiscriminate bombing, murder, torture, [and] the maiming of innocent civilians," respondent's "only acts against innocent Guatemalans were the disruption of some stores and his use of methods that we would all find objectionable if practiced upon us on a bus in the United States but which fall far short of the kind of atrocities attributed to McMullen and his associates." 121 F.3d, at 524.

We do not understand the BIA to dispute that these considerations—gross disproportionality, atrociousness, and comparisons with previous decided cases—may be important in applying the serious nonpolitical crime exception. In fact, by the terms of the BIA's test (which is similar to the language quoted by the Court of Appeals from the U.N. Handbook) gross disproportion and atrociousness are relevant in the determination. According to the BIA, "[i]n evaluating the political nature of a crime, we consider it important that the political aspect of the offense outweigh its common-law character. This would not be the case if the crime is grossly out of proportion to the political objective or if it involves acts of an atrocious nature." *Matter of McMullen*, 19 I. & N. Dec., at 97–98. See also *Deportation Proceedings for Doherty*, 13 Op. Off. Legal Counsel, at 22–26, rev'd on other grounds, *Doherty v. INS*, 908 F.2d

1108 (C.A.2 1990), rev'd, 502 U.S., 314 (1992). The BIA's formulation does not purport to provide a comprehensive definition of the § 1253(h)(2)(C) exception, and the full elaboration of that standard should await further cases, consistent with the instruction our legal system always takes from considering discrete factual circumstances over time. See also 13 Op. Off. Legal Counsel, at 23 ("[T]he statute recognizes that cases involving alleged political crimes arise in myriad circumstances, and that what constitutes a 'serious nonpolitical crime' is not susceptible of rigid definition"). Our decision takes into account that the BIA's test identifies a general standard (whether the political aspect of an offense outweighs its common-law character) and then provides two more specific inquiries that may be used in applying the rule: whether there is a gross disproportion between means and ends, and whether atrocious acts are involved. Under this approach, atrocious acts provide a clear indication that an alien's offense is a serious nonpolitical crime. In the BIA's judgment, where an alien has sought to advance his agenda by atrocious means, the political aspect of his offense may not fairly be said to predominate over its criminal character. Commission of the acts, therefore, will result in a denial of withholding. The criminal element of an offense may outweigh its political aspect even if none of the acts are deemed atrocious, however. For this reason, the BIA need not give express consideration to the atrociousness of the alien's acts in every case before determining that an alien has committed a serious nonpolitical crime.

The BIA's approach is consistent with the statute, which does not equate every serious nonpolitical crime with atrocious acts. Cf. 8 U.S.C. § 1253(h)(2)(B) (establishing an exception to withholding for a dangerous alien who has been convicted of a "particularly serious crime," defined to include an "aggravated felony"). Nor is there any reason to find this equivalence under the statute. In common usage, the word "atrocious" suggests a deed more culpable and aggravated than a serious one. See Webster's Third New International Dictionary 139 (1971) (defining "atrocious" as, "marked by or given to extreme wickedness ... [or] extreme brutality or cruelty"; "outrageous: violating the bounds of common decency"; "marked by extreme violence: savagely fierce: murderous"; "utterly revolting: abominable"). As a practical matter, if atrocious acts were deemed a necessary element of all serious nonpolitical crimes, the Attorney General would have severe restrictions upon her power to deport aliens who had engaged in serious, though not atrocious, forms of criminal activity. These restrictions cannot be discerned in the text of § 1253(h), and the Attorney General and BIA are not bound to impose the restrictions on themselves.

In the instant case, the BIA determined that "the criminal nature of the respondent's acts outweigh their political nature" because his group's political dissatisfaction "manifested itself disproportionately in the destruction of property and assaults on civilians" and its political goals "were outweighed by [the group's] criminal strategy of strikes." App. to Pet. for Cert. 18a. The BIA concluded respondent had committed serious nonpolitical crimes by applying the general standard established in its prior decision, so it had no need to consider whether his acts might also have been atrocious. The Court of Appeals erred in holding otherwise.

We further reject the Court of Appeals' suggestion that reversal was required due to the BIA's failure to compare the facts of this case with those of *McMullen*. The court thought doing so was necessary because of the guidance provided by *McMullen* on the meaning of atrociousness. In light of our holding that the BIA was not required expressly to consider the atrociousness of respondent's acts, the BIA's silence on this point does not provide a ground for reversal.

The third reason given by the Court of Appeals for reversing the BIA was what the court deemed to be the BIA's failure to consider respondent's "offenses in relation to [his] declared political objectives" and to consider "the political necessity and success of [his] methods." 121 F.3d, at 523–524. As we have discussed, *supra*, at 1444, 1448–1449, the BIA did address the relationship between respondent's political goals and his criminal acts, concluding that the violence and destructiveness of the crimes, and their impact on civilians, were disproportionate to his acknowledged political objectives. To the extent the court believed the BIA was required to give more express consideration to the "necessity" and "success" of respondent's actions, it erred.

It is true the Attorney General has suggested that a crime will not be deemed political unless there is a "close and direct causal link between the crime committed and its alleged political purpose and object." *Deportation Proceedings for Doherty*, 13 Op. Off. Legal Counsel, at 23 (quoting *McMullen v. INS*, 788 F.2d 591 (C.A.9 1986)). The BIA's analysis, which was quite brief in all events, did not explore this causal link beyond noting the general disproportion between respondent's acts and his political objectives. Whatever independent relevance a causal link inquiry might have in another case, in this case the BIA determined respondent's acts were not political based on the lack of proportion with his objectives. It was not required to do more. Even in a case with a clear causal connection, a lack of proportion between means and ends may still render a crime nonpolitical. Moreover, it was respondent who bore the burden of proving entitlement to withholding, see 8 C.F.R. § 208.16(c)(3) (1995) ("If the evidence indicates that one or more of the grounds for denial of withholding of deportation ... apply, the applicant shall have the burden of proving by a preponderance of the evidence that such grounds do not apply"). He failed to submit a brief on the causal link or any other issue to the BIA, and the decision of the Immigration Judge does not address the point. In these circumstances, the rather cursory nature of the BIA's discussion does not warrant reversal.

Finally, respondent contends the record of his testimony before the Immigration Judge contains errors. He testified in Spanish and now contends there are errors in translation and transcription. Brief for Respondent 11–22. Respondent advanced this argument for the first time in his Brief in Opposition to Certiorari in this Court, see Brief in Opposition 1–5, having failed to raise it before either the BIA or the Court of Appeals. We decline to address the argument at this late stage.

Respondent has filed a motion in the BIA for a new hearing in light of the alleged errors. App. to Brief for Respondent 1a–6a. Should the BIA determine modification of the record is necessary, it can determine whether further consideration of the withholding

---

J. Temporary Protected Status and Extended Voluntary Departure

Temporary Protected Status or "TPS" is a relatively new statutory remedy designed to provide humanitarian protection to people of certain nationalities who face the possibility of being returned to countries facing armed conflict or natural disaster.[84] The legal status allows persons who might otherwise be subject to removal to remain in the United States for a relatively short period of time. Up until 1990, when asylum was not possible, some persons who faced the prospect of returning to their countries which were in the middle of a civil war could only hope for humanitarian reprieve of their removal in the form of what was known as extended voluntary departure (EVD). EVD, which was granted to nationals of certain countries, was an extra-statutory remedy granted by the Attorney General after consultation with the Secretary of State for limited periods of time. Extended voluntary departure was distinct from the statutory "voluntary departure" remedy in that the person was not contemplating departure within a relatively short period. If the person departed the United States while under EVD, she could not return. In short, the benefit was one of a humanitarian nature as a result of compelling circumstances in one's home country.

TPS has all of the indicia of EVD except that it is codified. The basic requirements of TPS are as follows: (1) while the status is available for nationals of a particular country in an area of conflict, the eligible person is not required to apply for the status but must only be provided notice of eligibility;[85] (2) the status may be terminated upon the review and determination made by the Attorney General; such determinations must be published in the Federal Register;[86] (3) the determination to terminate TPS is not subject to judicial review, though applicants for TPS are entitled to some type of administrative review, including assertion of relief in removal proceedings;[87] (4) those who receive TPS may not use the period while they are in TPS status to count towards other forms of discretionary relief such as cancellation of removal, unless the Attorney General determines that extreme hardship exists;[88] (5) applicants may be required to pay a registration fee not to exceed $50 to obtain the benefit;[89]

---

84. Temporary Protected Status was created in the 1990 Immigration Act and is codified at 8 U.S.C. § 1254a, Sec. 244A.

85. 8 U.S.C. § 1254a(a)(3), Sec. 244A(a)(3).

86. 8 U.S.C. § 1254a(b)(3)(A), Sec. 244A(b)(3)(A).

87. 8 U.S.C. § 1254a(b)(5), Sec. 244A(b)(5).

88. 8 U.S.C. § 1254a(e), Sec. 244A(e).

89. The TPS program for El Salvadoran nationals provided for a fee in an "amount sufficient to cover the costs of administration." *See* Sec. 303(b)(2), Immigration Act of 1990, Pub. L. No. 101-649, 104 Stat. 4978.

(6) persons who are inadmissible on grounds of crimes are ineligible for the benefit;[90] and (7) beneficiaries of TPS may not be granted adjustment of status under a special statutory provision except upon passage in by a super majority vote of three-fifths of both houses of Congress.[91]

A person granted TPS may not be removed or detained during the period of TPS designation and shall be granted employment authorization. In addition, the person may be authorized to travel outside of the United States and return under advance parole. The person, if she becomes eligible for adjustment of status independent of TPS status, may become a permanent resident through that procedure.[92] However, the TPS designation is treated as a period of authorized stay and does not create a lawful admission for purposes of any future immigration status.[93]

Temporary and Other Protected Status Designations (2009)

Authors Note: These are only examples of the TPS designations which were in effect at the time that these materials were published. A current listing of the TPS designations can be found at the USCIS website at http://www.uscis.gov.

Country	*First designated*	*Expiration*
El Salvador:	01/05/1999	09/09/2010
Honduras	01/05/1999	07/05/2010
Nicaragua	01/05/1999	07/05/2010
Liberia[94]	03/27/1991	03/31/2010
Somalia	09/16/1991	03/17/2011
Sudan	11/04/1997	05/02/2010

Hotel & Rest. Employees Union, Local 25, et al. v. William French Smith, Attorney General, et al.

594 F. Supp. 502 (D.D.C. 1984)*

Richey, District Judge.

Before the Court are defendants' two motions for partial summary judgment, along with memoranda in support thereof and in opposition thereto. This case involves two distinct issues relating to the status of the estimated hundreds of thousands of El Sal-

90. 8 U.S.C. § 1254a(c)(2), Sec. 244A(c)(2). Those persons with drug convictions involving simple possession of less than 30 grams of marijuana are excepted.

91. 8 U.S.C. § 244a(h), Sec. 244A(h).

92. 8 U.S.C. § 1254(f)(4), Sec. 244(f)(4). Adjustment of status is discussed in Chapter 9.

93. An interpretation by the INS Acting General Counsel in 1991 concludes that a person who originally entered the United States without having been inspected was ineligible for adjustment of status because he had no status, even though he had later been granted TPS. *See* 68 Interpreter Releases 483 (1991) (reprinting Legal Opinion, Acting General Counsel, Paul Virtue, Apr. 22, 1991). *But see* 69 Interpreter Releases 1400 (1992) of an unreported decision by an immigration judge in *Matter of Escobar-Turcios* reaching the opposite conclusion.

94. The designation for Liberia is for "Deferred Enforced Departure."

* The full case history is *Hotel & Rest. Employees Union, Local 25 v. Smith*, 563 F. Supp. 157 (D.D.C. 1983) (denial of motion to dismiss), 594 F. Supp. 502 (granting of summary judgment for defendants),

vadoran nationals currently residing illegally in the United States. Defendants' first summary judgment motion involves a decision by the Attorney General not to grant the El Salvadoran nationals "Extended Voluntary Departure," hereinafter "EVD," status, which, according to Count I of plaintiff's Complaint, would have had the effect of a blanket insulation from deportation procedures for all Salvadoran nationals now in the United States until such time as the turmoil in that country subsides. The second of defendants' motions for partial summary judgment relates to Count 11 of plaintiffs' Complaint and the procedures utilized by the Immigration and Naturalization Service (INS), after considering advisory opinions from the Department of State, in reviewing applications for asylum made by Salvadoran nationals now illegally in the United States.

Plaintiffs in this case are the Hotel and Restaurant Workers Union, whose membership is largely made up of Salvadoran nationals, and a plaintiff/intervenor, Mauro Hernandez, himself a Salvadoran national, currently residing in this country. They have brought this suit seeking both declaratory judgments and injunctive relief on both the EVD and asylum issues.

Plaintiffs claim that Salvadoran nationals are entitled to be granted blanket EVD status. They base this assertion on what they perceive as the controlling "humanitarian" standard for such action, which would require the Attorney General to extend EVD status to Salvadorans. Plaintiffs allege that the result of the Attorney General's denial of EVD is to deprive Salvadoran nationals of the protection of the Due Process Clause of the 5th Amendment to the U.S. Constitution. Defendant argues that this is a matter of the Attorney General's absolute discretion on issues of foreign and prosecutorial policy, and as such finds no basis for judicial review under the Administrative Procedure Act or the Constitution beyond whether the decision was rationally based. The Court agrees. Defendants further argue that EVD is extra-statutory, and as such is not a right or privilege to which due process considerations attach, an argument with which the Court also is in agreement.

[The court then discussed the second issue involving the procedures for processing and acting upon applications for asylum submitted by El Salvadoran nationals.]

* * *

... [T]he Court, while especially sympathetic to the plight of Salvadoran nationals and conscious of the tumultuous situation in that country, feels it is compelled by applicable law to grant the defendants' motions for summary judgment on both Counts I and II, and as hereinafter provided, the case will be dismissed.

... Initially, it must be noted that the issue presented in this case, that of judicial review of the Attorney General's determination regarding a grant of EVD, is one of first impression in the Courts. EVD is an extra-statutory form of discretionary relief from the deportation provisions of the Immigration and Nationality Act of 1952, as amended. It is granted to an entire class of persons, usually based upon nationality. It is a term not found anywhere in the Immigration and Nationality Act or in the ap-

---

804 F.2d 1256 (reversing in part and affirming in part), 808 F.2d 847 (rehearing granted judgment vacated), 846 F.2d 1499 (*en banc* panel evenly divided).

plicable regulations. Rather, the term Extended Voluntary Departure describes the Attorney General's discretion in determining the circumstances of both foreign and domestic policy which may give rise to a discretionary decision to grant a temporary suspension of deportation proceedings to members of a particular class of illegal aliens. As such, EVD is based on the prosecutorial discretion of the Attorney General after consultation or advice received from the State Department.

The Constitutional foundation for grants of EVD derives from the Executive's express and inherent authority in the areas of both foreign and prosecutorial policy. The Constitution places responsibility for the conduct of foreign affairs with the Executive branch. U.S. CONST. art. II, § 2. *United States v. Pink*, 315 U.S. 203 (1942). "Intricately interwoven" with this plenary authority over foreign relations are actions taken in the regulation of aliens. *Harisiades v. Shaughnessy*, 342 U.S. 580, 588–89 (1952). Regulation of immigration is an "inherent executive power." *United States ex rel. Knauff v. Shaughnessy*, 338 U.S. 537, 542 (1950).

The Attorney General's prosecutorial discretion finds its Constitutional basis under Article III, sections 1 and 3, which the Supreme Court has interpreted to mean that discretionary matters, such as in the immigration area, belong to the plenary, if not exclusive authority of the Executive. *United States v. Nixon*, 418 U.S. 683, 693 (1974). Specifically, it has been held that a determination "to commence a deportation proceeding or not to do so" is a matter of "prosecutorial discretion." *Johns v. Department of Justice*, 653 F.2d 884, 893 (5th Cir.1981); *Weisberg v. Department of Justice*, 489 F.2d 1195, 1201 (D.C.Cir.1973), cert. denied, 416 U.S. 993 (1974). This Constitutional authority to determine when or on what basis to prosecute a case is strongest when, as here, the matter involves enforcement of immigration laws. *Harisiades v. Shaughnessy, supra*, 342 U.S. at 596–97, *Ludecke v. Watkins*, 335 U.S. 160, 164 (1948). Further, grants of EVD do not relieve the aliens of individual adjudication and deportation procedures prescribed by the Act and regulations, but merely act to postpone those proceedings. Cf. *Attorney General v. Irish People, Inc.*, 684 F.2d 928, 984 (D.C.Cir.1982), cert. denied, 459 U.S. 1172 (1983). Thus, EVD is an exercise of the Executives "pure enforcement power." *Id.*

The statutory basis for the Attorney General's discretionary power to grant or deny EVD is found in the Immigration and Nationality Act of 1952, as amended by the Refugee Act of 1980. 8 U.S.C. § 1101 et seq. The Act provides the framework for the Attorney General's authority over aliens seeking residence or refuge in the United States. The statute charges the Attorney General "with the administration and enforcement of the Act," and empowers him to "establish such regulations ... and perform such other acts as he deems necessary for carrying out his authority...." 8 U.S.C. § 1103(a). See *Jean v. Nelson*, 727 F.2d 957, 964–65 (11th Cir.1984) (en banc). Thus, the Attorney General is vested with discretionary power to take actions and to "develop standards, principles and rules" so long as his actions are based upon "considerations rationally related to the statute he is administering." See *Fook Hong Mak v. INS*, 435 F.2d 728, 730 (2d Cir.1970). This Circuit has held that the Act "need not specifically authorize each and every action taken by the Attorney General, so long as his action is reasonably related to the duties imposed upon him." *Narenji v. Civiletti*, 617 F.2d 745, 747 (D.C.Cir.1979), cert. denied, 446 U.S. 957 (1980). Thus, the fact that EVD is extra-statutory in no way effects its validity as a discretionary action under the Act. "The Attorney General may govern the exercise of his discretion by written or unwritten rules." *Mak*, 435 F.2d at 731. Similarly, there can be no question that EVD is "rationally related to the statute [the Attorney General] is administering." *Id.* EVD is a tool utilized by the Attorney General, after consultation with the State Department, to respond to emergency situations which might require broad application of his authority under the Act, and which demand a speedy response.... There is no basis for the plaintiffs' blanket claims except for an abuse of discretion, which in this case cannot be said to exist.

* * *

The first step in the analysis is the Administrative Procedure Act, 8 U.S.C. §701 et seq. Under §704 of that title, an agency action may only be subject to review if it is "made reviewable by statute or if it is a final agency action for which there is no other adequate remedy in a court." 8 U.S.C. §704. The Attorney General's decision to deny EVD status to El Salvadorans is not made reviewable by any statute. Nor does the decision denying EVD status to Salvadorans in any way affect their remedies of appeal to the United States Courts of Appeal after exhausting the administrative process in deportation proceedings. The Salvadorans' "adequate remedy in a court" is found in the regulations under the Immigration and Nationality Act. Salvadorans subject to deportation, irrespective of the denial of EVD, retain the right to a hearing should such deportation proceedings be instituted. 8 C.F.R. Part 242 (1984). Nor does the Attorney General's decision not to grant EVD to Salvadoran nationals affect their right to appeal an adverse result in such a deportation hearing, both to the Board of Immigration Appeals and to the United States Court of Appeals. 8 C.F.R. Part 3 and 8 U.S.C. §1105(a). Therefore, judicial review of the Attorney General's decision, in this broad claim under the Administrative Procedure Act, is precluded.

In addition, judicial review of agency actions is precluded when such action is "committed to agency discretion by law." 5 8 U.S.C. §701(a)(2). The legislative history of the Administrative Procedure Act indicates that this that this is applicable where "statutes are drawn in such broad terms that in a given case there is no law to apply." S.Rep. No. 752, 79th Cong., 1st Sess., 26 (1945). *Citizens to Preserve Overton Park, Inc. v. Volpe*, 401 U.S. 402, 410 (1971). In the case of EVD, there is indeed "no law to apply" because of its extra-statutory nature, and these aliens at the case at bar have an adequate remedy in deportation proceedings....

The factors involved in determining the propriety of judicial review of an agency's exercise of discretion are the breadth of the discretionary power, the administrative expertise as balanced against judicial competence to evaluate the action at issue, whether there exists meaningful criteria by which a court may evaluate the action, and whether the decision is one based on policies to which a court must defer to the political branches. *Citizens to Preserve Overton Park v. Volpe*, 401 U.S. 402 (1971); *Panama Canal Co. v. Grace Line, Inc.*, 356 U.S. 309 (1958). Upon weighing these factors, the Court is faced with the inescapable conclusion that the Attorney General's decision is not subject to judicial review. It is clear from the discussion, supra, of the Constitutional basis for EVD that the decision here at issue is clearly a matter of the Attorney General's prosecutorial discretion, after his review of the evidence, to suspend, or, as here, not to suspend enforcement of the immigration laws in a specific case. It is well settled that the Executive has "exclusive authority and absolute discretion to decide whether to prosecute a case." *United States v. Nixon*, 418 U.S. 683, 693 (1974), citing, inter alia, *The Confiscation Cases*, 74 U.S. (7 Wall) 454, 457–58 (1868). The Attorney General was acting in this prosecutorial discretionary capacity when he made his decision in the case at bar, and, therefore, judicial review is inappropriate under this thread of the analysis.

There is no question that, under our system of separation of powers, matters involving an area such as foreign, military, or diplomatic policy, which has been entrusted exclusively to the Executive or Legislative branches, are subject, at most, to limited judicial review. *Baker v. Carr*, 369 U.S. 186, 217 (1962). It is also well settled that "any policy toward aliens is vitally and intricately interwoven" with the conduct of this country's foreign affairs. *Harisiades v. Shaughnessy, supra*, 342 U.S. at 589–90 (1952). The Supreme Court has recently affirmed that "matters relating 'to the conduct of foreign relations ... are so exclusively entrusted to the political branches of government as to be largely immune from judicial inquiry or interference.' *Regan v. Wald*, 468 U.S. ___, 104 S.Ct. 3026, 3039 (1984), citing *Harisiades v. Shaughnessy*, supra, 342 U.S. at 589. This Court cannot claim to have the expertise needed to decide such issues of foreign policy, and will defer to the Executive, to whom this area has been Constitutionally entrusted. Only in the case of a clear abuse of discretion may a Court impose its judgment over that of the Executive in a case such as the one at bar.

Before a Court can be assured that an abuse has occurred, there must first exist some kind of a standard by which to measure the Executive's action. In this case the plaintiffs would have us impose upon the Attorney General a "humanitarian" standard based upon what plaintiff perceives as a pattern or practice of past EVD grants in individual cases. While agreeing that such considerations may be a factor in EVD decisions, the Court does not agree that humanitarian concerns are, or can be, the sole or overriding factor in an EVD determination. The plaintiff points out, that humanitarian concerns have been a part of such decisions in the past. However, this does not mean that a standard based solely on such concerns has evolved. There is nothing in the Immigration and Nationality Act that would establish such a standard. Indeed, such a standard would be difficult to define and enforce. Humanitarianism is a vague concept, and by its terms overbroad. For a Court to order EVD in this case would set a far-reaching precedent, wholly within the prerogatives of Congress, and might then apply to all situations of widespread fighting, destruction and the breakdown of public services and order throughout the world. Also, such situations as famine, drought, or other natural disasters might at any time also raise "humanitarian" concerns, wherever they might occur. To require the Attorney General to grant blanket EVD status to all such nationals would be to open up irresponsibly the floodgates to illegal aliens, without regard to foreign policy and internal immigration concerns, or, of equal importance, to the concerns of American working men and women in the United States and our taxpayers generally.

The only remaining question concerning judicial review of the Attorney General's decision is whether the decision was rationally based. *Fiallo v. Bell*, 430 U.S. 787, 794–96, (1977). This requires that the Attorney General exhibit some facially legitimate reason for his decision. *Narenji v. Civiletti*, 617 F.2d 745, 747–48 (D.C.Cir.1979), cert. denied, 446 U.S. 957 (1980). The Court is satisfied that the Attorney General acted rationally in making his decision. Besides foreign policy considerations, the Attorney General advances several other factors. These include (i) the number of illegal Salvadoran aliens currently in the United States, (ii) the current crisis in generally controlling the "floodtide" of illegal immigration, (iii) the prospect of encouraging further illegal immigration, (iv) the effect of such illegal immigration upon this country's limited law enforcement capabilities, social services and economic resources, and (v) the availability under the Immigration and Nationality Act of alternate avenues of relief, such as asylum. The aggregate of these factors is that the Attorney General did fashion his decision in a considered and rational manner....

Plaintiffs also claim that this decision acts to deprive Salvadoran nationals of their Constitutional right to due process under the 5th Amendment of the U.S. Constitution. The Court holds that it does not. Again, EVD is extra-statutory in nature. In addition, it is clear that aliens have no Constitutional right to enter or remain in the United States. Therefore, no right or privilege is involved. There has been no denial of due process since the decision leaves unaffected the right to existing INS procedures, including hearing and appeal rights. There is no Equal Protection issue here, either. Historically, nationality-based distinctions have been seen as inevitable in the immigration field. Moreover, the Attorney General, acting for the Executive, has the authority to make such distinctions based upon nationality. *Narenji v. Civiletti*, 617 F.2d 745, 747 (D.C. Cir. 1979). Therefore, the Court concludes that there was no violation of due process involved in the EVD decision, particularly since the plaintiffs may invoke whatever rights they have in individual deportation proceedings including the right to appeal.

Notes

1. In lieu of answering the complaint in *Local 25*, the government moved to dismiss, and the district court, in denying the defendant's motion to dismiss, noted that:

> ... [T]he Court finds that the grant or denial of extended voluntary departure is not a nonjusticiable political question. As defendants admit, the control of immigration is not directly committed by the text of the Constitution to a coordinate federal branch. It is true that the political branches have been allowed broad leeway to regulate the flow of immigrants, but the Supreme Court has expressly left room for a "narrow standard of (judicial) review of decisions made by the Congress or the President in the area of im-

migration and naturalization." *Mathews v. Diaz*, 426 U.S. 67, 82 (1976).... Such review has long been exercised, as for instance in cases alleging a due process violation in immigration decisions. [*Hotel & Restaurant Workers Union, Local 25 v. Smith*, 563 F. Supp. 157, 159 (D.D.C. 1983).]

* * *

... [T]he Court does not lack a standard or the resources to decide the issues presented in this case. As plaintiff points out, defendants themselves have in the past articulated a cognizable standard for the grant of extended voluntary departure to a group of aliens—"wide-spread fighting, destruction and breakdown of public services and order" in the aliens' country of origin. 128 Cong. Rec. 5832 (daily ed. Feb. 11, 1982). At least one court has made findings as to the serious conditions that exist in El Salvador. *Orantes-Hernandez v. Smith*, 541 F.Supp. 351, 359 (C.D. Cal. 1982). [*Hotel & Restaurant Workers Union, Local 25 v. Smith*, 563 F. Supp. 157, 160 (D.D.C. 1983).]

In another case which raised some of the same issues brought in *Local 25*, a district court was willing to consider the claims raised by the litigants that the failure to accord EVD to El Salvadorans and Guatemalans could be subject to judicial review.[95] Subsequently, this case was settled, allowing Guatemalan asylum applicants who were in the United States prior to October 1, 1990, and El Salvadoran applicants who were in the United States prior to September 1, 1990, to have their cases re-adjudicated under new asylum regulations. El Salvadorans present in the United States were able to take advantage of the TPS which was granted by Congress in the 1990 Act.[96]

2. **Voluntary departure and EVD.** 8 U.S.C. § 1254(e) authorizes the Attorney General to grant voluntary departure to persons of good moral character who are ready, willing and able to depart the United States. Can an individual apply for a prolonged period of voluntary departure in lieu of requesting "extended voluntary departure"?[97] For additional discussion of voluntary departure, *see* Chapter 3.

3. Is asylum really an "alternative" to EVD, thereby providing a legitimate reason to justify the denial of the benefit? Are these persons who could not qualify for asylum but should nonetheless not be returned to their home countries?

4. Following the *Local 25* case, the BIA dealt with the question of individualized requests for relief. In *Matter of Medina*,[98] the Board rejected arguments that either the Geneva Convention Relative to the Protection of Civilian Persons in Time of War or customary international law created a remedy from removal akin to EVD. The Board held that exclusive remedies were provided for in the asylum and withholding statute and that neither EVD nor deferred action were statutory remedies.

---

95. *See American Baptist Churches v. Thornburgh*, 712 F. Supp. 756 (N.D. Cal. 1989).

96. *See American Baptist Churches v. Thornburgh*, 760 F. Supp. 796 (N.D. Cal. 1991); 67 INTERPRETER RELEASES 1480 (1990).

97. *See Matter of Quintero*, 18 I. & N. Dec. 348 (BIA 1982) (rejecting indefinite voluntary departure yet acknowledging authority of judge to grant voluntary departure, in this case for five months).

98. 19 I. & N. Dec. 734 (BIA 1988).

5. Below is a list of the many times when the Attorney General has conferred EVD status on certain persons based on their nationality and the conditions existing in their home countries.[99]

Cuba	granted effective November 29, 1960; terminated effective November 2, 1966 (*see* Public Law No. 89-732).
Dominican Republic	granted effective October 18, 1966 (for arrivals between April 24, 1965 and June 3, 1966); terminated effective April 26, 1978.
"Western Hemisphere"	granted July 1, 1968 (for certain individuals with visa preference dates from July 1, 1968 to December 31, 1976, inclusive, in response to the order entered in Silva v. Levi, Civil Action No. 76 C-4268 (N.D. Ill.)); terminated effective December 31, 1976; second grant effective August 1982; second grant terminated effective January 31, 1983.
Czechoslovakia	granted effective August 21, 1968; terminated effective December 30, 1977.
Chile	granted effective April 9, 1971; terminated effective December 30, 1977.
Cambodia	granted effective April 4, 1975; terminated effective October 28, 1977 (*see* Public Law No. 95-145).
Vietnam	granted effective April 4, 1975; terminated effective October 28, 1977 (*see* Public Law No. 95-145).
Laos	granted effective July 9, 1975; terminated effective October 28, 1977 (*see* Public Law No. 95-145).
Ethiopia	granted effective July 12, 1977 (for arrivals prior to June 30, 1980); expired March 1, 1989.
Uganda	granted effective June 8, 1978; terminated effective September 30, 1986.
Iran	granted effective April 16, 1975; renewed effective August 9, 1979; terminated effective December 13, 1979.
Nicaragua	granted effective July 3, 1979; renewed effective August 29, 1979, and January 4 and July 1, 1980; terminated effective September 28, 1980.
Mexico	granted effective December 31, 1979 (for certain second preference visa holders, in response to the order entered in Contreras v. Bell,

99. This list was extracted from the defendants' June 13, 1983, response to plaintiff's First Set of Interrogatories [No. 1(d)]. *See Hotel & Restaurant Employees Union, Local* 25 v. *Smith,* 563 F. Supp. 157 (D.D.C. 1983). This list was updated to conform with then-existing EVD policies. *See* Bill Ong Hing, Handling Immigration Cases § 6.36 (Supp. 1988), *citing EVD Update,* 65 Interpreter Releases 964 (1988). For INS policy regarding the handling of persons who are recipients of EVD, see O.I. 242.10e(3).

	Civil Action No. 80-1590 (N.D. Ill.)); terminated effective August 25, 1981.
Afghanistan	granted effective December 2, 1980 (for arrivals prior to June 30, 1980), expired March 1, 1989.
Poland	granted effective December 23, 1981 (for arrivals prior to December 24, 1981); renewed effective March 25, June 21, and December 20, 1982, and June 30, 1983; expired March 1, 1989.
China (PRC)	granted effective April 11, 1990 to January 1, 1994 (for arrivals between 1989 to April 11, 1990) (Exec. Order No. 12,711).

Additionally, from February 12, 1976, through 1990, it was the policy to view sympathetically requests by Lebanese nationals for extensions of the time permitted for voluntary departure where an individual's request was based on compelling humanitarian circumstances. Because such policy does not include the cessation of removal proceedings and provided only for the extension of grants of voluntary departure in individual cases, it differs significantly from the grants listed above.[100]

In 1987, Congress passed special legislation to provide for the legalization (adjustment of status) for nationals of Poland, Afghanistan, Ethiopia and Uganda who had been eligible for EVD status prior to July 21, 1984, and resided continuously in the United States since that time. This legalization program ended on December 22, 1989.[101]

K. Protection under the Convention against Torture

While asylum and other forms of relief from removal are generally unavailable to persons who have been convicted of aggravated felonies or who present a serious threat to the community, leaving them vulnerable to removal, the United Nations Convention Against Torture and Other Cruel, Inhuman or Degrading Treatment or Punishment (CAT) provides some form of protection.[102] Under CAT, a person who can establish that she is likely to be tortured or experience other forms of cruel or inhumane treatment may be able to avoid being sent back to the country where she will likely experience the mistreatment.

Article 1 of the CAT defines torture as:

> any act by which severe pain or suffering, whether physical or mental, is intentionally inflicted on a person for such purposes as obtaining from him

---

100. *Cf.* 8 U.S.C. §1254(e); 8 C.F.R. §244.2.

101. *See* Foreign Relations Authorization Act of 1987, Pub. L. No. 100-204, 101 Stat. 1331 (1987).

102. Convention Against Torture and Other Cruel, Inhuman or Degrading Treatment or Punishment, Dec. 10, 1984, 1465 U.N.T.S. 113 (entered into force June 26, 1987). While the Convention was ratified by the United States in 1994, it took an additional five years before proposed regulations were promulgated. U.S. Dep't of State, Treaties in Force 466 (1999) (effective Nov. 20, 1994).

> or a third person information or a confession, punishing him for an act he or a third person has committed or is suspected of having committed, or intimidation or coercing him or a third person, or for any reason based on discrimination of any kind when such pain and suffering is inflicted by or at the instigation of or with the consent or acquiesence of a public official or other person acting in an official capacity. It does not include pain or suffering arising only from, inherent in or incidental to lawful sanctions.

Based on this the key components of torture are: (1) intentional acts which cause severe physical or mental pain; (2) carried out for an impermissible purpose (i.e. for coercion or intimidation or based on discrimination—in contrast to acts which may constitute lawful sanctions); (3) with the involvement (instigation, consent or acquiescence) of public authority.

> The Convention's *non-refoulement* provision contained in Article 3 is becoming a basis for at least a limited form of protection. Under CAT, a person, while not receiving status that could lead to permanent residency, will still be able to avoid removal to the country of persecution.[103] This is in contrast to restriction on removal and asylum, which are not available to certain persons either because they are unable to show that their persecution is *on account* of one of the five grounds of persecution or because of their criminal convictions. In order to establish eligibility for relief under CAT, the applicant must show that the feared mistreatment is at the hands of a government. Where persons are otherwise eligible for CAT relief but have been convicted of crimes making them serious risks to the community, the regulations provide for continued detention. However, in cases where persons were admitted into the United States, prolonged detention may not be allowed under *Zadvydas v. INS.*[104]

Li Chen Zheng, aka Zheng Li Chen v. John Ashcroft, Attorney General

332 F.3d 1186 (9th Cir. 2003)*

Before: James R. Browning, Harry Pregerson, and Stephen Reinhardt, Circuit Judges.

Pregerson, Circuit Judge:

Li Chen Zheng ("Zheng"), a Chinese native and citizen, petitions this court for review of the Board of Immigration Appeals' ("BIA") final order. The BIA vacated the Immigration Judge's ("IJ") decision granting Zheng's application for relief under Article 3 of the United Nations Convention Against Torture and Other Forms of Cruel, Inhuman or Degrading Treatment or Punishment ("Convention Against Tor-

103. The CAT was implemented by legacy INS through regulations promulgated at 8 C.F.R. § 208.30.

104. 533 U.S. 678 (2001). *See* Discussion of indefinite detention and *Zadvydas*.

* Some footnotes have been omitted.

ture" or "Convention")[1] and ordered Zheng removed to China. Under the Convention Against Torture, the United States will not "expel, extradite, or otherwise effect the involuntary return of any person to a country in which there are substantial grounds for believing the person would be in danger of being subjected to torture." Foreign Affairs Reform and Restructuring Act of 1998 ("FARRA"), Pub. L. No. 105-277, Div. G, Title XXII, § 2242, 112 Stat. 2681–822 (1998) (codified as note to 8 U.S.C.A. § 1231 (1999)). To qualify for relief under the Convention, the torture must be "inflicted by or at the instigation of or with the consent or *acquiescence* of a public official or other person acting in an official capacity." 8 C.F.R. § 208.18(a)(1) (emphasis added). Zheng believes that if he is returned to China he will be killed by the smugglers who brought him to the United States because he reported the names of the smugglers to the American government; Zheng contends that the Chinese government will not protect him because public officials are connected to the smugglers. The IJ found that Zheng had "established a clear probability of torture and that there is [a] sufficient nexus between the [Chinese] public officials" and the smugglers; thus, the IJ granted Zheng relief under the Convention. But the BIA vacated the IJ's decision. Relying upon its previous decision in *Matter of S-V-*,[2] the BIA ruled that Zheng had to demonstrate that government officials "are willfully accepting of" the torturous activities of a third party. The BIA determined that—even assuming government officials were involved with smuggling—Zheng failed to show that Chinese officials would acquiesce to the torture inflicted by the smugglers.

We conclude that the BIA's interpretation of acquiescence to require that government officials "are willfully accepting" of torture to their citizens by a third party is contrary to clearly expressed congressional intent to require only "awareness," and not to require "actual knowledge" or "willful[ ] accept[ance]" in the definition of acquiescence. Therefore, we grant Zheng's petition, vacate the BIA's decision, and remand to the BIA for further proceedings consistent with this opinion.

I. Background

A. Factual and Procedural History

Zheng was born on February 19, 1983, in the Fujian Province in the People's Republic of China. In 1991 or 1992, his father left China to come to the United States; his father now lives in New York. In 1997, Zheng's mother left China to come to the United States; his mother now lives in Guam. On April 9, 1999, Zheng left China to come to the United States. He was 16 years old.

Zheng left China because he "was in a very low position." His parents had violated China's birth control policy. Under China's policy, if the "first born is a boy, you cannot have a second child"; Zheng's parents had two daughters after Zheng was born.

---

1. United Nations Convention Against Torture and Other Forms of Cruel, Inhuman or Degrading Treatment or Punishment, Dec. 10, 1984, 23 I.L.M. 1027, 1465 U.N.T.S. 85.

2. 22 I. & N. Dec. 1306 (BIA 2000) (en banc).

Human smugglers who transport Chinese immigrants from China to the United States and other countries—known as "snakeheads"[3] or "seaman"—brought Zheng, along with approximately one-hundred and fifty Chinese nationals, into the United States on a large boat. On or about April 23, 1999, Zheng was apprehended seeking to enter Guam. In the custody of the United States Marshal, Zheng lived on Tinian Island until June 1999.

Rojek testified that the snakeheads were, "an enormous organization," "very, very pervasive," and "very, very powerful." Those who failed to pay debts owed to the snakeheads would have to pay "the ultimate price," by facing "torture" involving "dismemberment of some sorts or other" and even death. Rojek testified that ... the PRC would not protect [Chen] from the snakeheads because the existence of the snakeheads as a criminal syndicate was not acknowledged by the PRC. "To intercede" for Jian Chen would be to admit their existence and so "to lose face," which "the Chinese government simply is not going to do...." *Id.*

While on Tinian Island, Zheng was a material witness in a criminal proceeding against the smugglers and "reported all the names of the seamen and said that they tortured me, tortured us." The same evening that Zheng reported the names of his smugglers, a snakehead nicknamed Lu Son approached Zheng as he waited for the restroom. Zheng testified that the snakehead told him "you be careful, you [will] be dead for sure." Zheng thought that the snakehead was going to "beat me." But a "police officer using [a] flashlight" came by and the snakehead left. Zheng told "an adult" about the snake-head's death threat. The adult told Zheng "this is not a big problem. Since we are here in the United States the American Government will protect us. We become their witnesses and they will be responsible for us." Zheng stated that "after" I heard this, I did not report" the snakehead's threat.

On June 17, 1999, Zheng was transferred to a juvenile detention center in Guam. Zheng stated that in Guam, he was "allowed to write a letter [to his parents], but I was not allowed to call. One letter only.... I cried and asked to call them, but ... it was refused." When Zheng asked why he was not allowed to contact his parents "[the officers] said, one of them said because we were witnesses, we were under protection."

In March 2000, Zheng was flown to Los Angeles, California. On April 5, 2000, Zheng first appeared before the Immigration Judge in Los Angeles for removal proceedings.

On May 10, 2000, Zheng again appeared before the IJ. When asked why he was afraid to return to China, Zheng testified, through an interpreter, that "the smugglers

3. We recently recounted the testimony of Dean G. Rojek, an associate professor of sociology at the University of Georgia: Professor Rojek testified on behalf of Jian Chen, a Chinese national also smuggled into the United States by "snakeheads." *Chen v. Ashcroft*, 289 F.3d 1113, 1114 (9th Cir. 2002), vacated on other grounds by *Chen v. Ashcroft*, 314 F.3d 995 (9th Cir. 2002). Professor Rojek has written extensively on the methods of social control practiced by the government of the People's Republic of China ("PRC"), and has lectured four times in China at the invitation of the government's Ministry of Justice. *Id.*

they will hurt me ... because I [have] been testifying." In addition, Zheng testified that because his family had violated the one child policy, the Chinese government "will not allow me to further my studies. Whatever school, I tried to apply to, they will expel me." The IJ completed an asylum application for Zheng.

On May 31, 2000, Zheng appeared before the IJ and testified concerning the "very low position" of his family because his parents had violated the birth control policy. If returned to China, Zheng stated that the government would not allow him to go to school because his family had violated the birth control policy of the government and "secondly" [he] was smuggled from China."

Zheng also testified that while still in China, before leaving by boat for the United States, "I was beaten ... [by] the snakehead. The one who watched over us ... unintentionally I stepped on his foot and he beat me up.... He struck my abdomen and kicked me and asked me to kneel down on the ground and I was not allowed to block with my arm." When asked why he was afraid of being sent back to China, Zheng stated that "[t]he snakehead will kill me ... [b]ecause I am a witness for the American Government against them.... I reported all the names of the seaman and said that they tortured me, tortured us.... I am afraid that the snakehead will kill me." Zheng told the IJ of the snakehead's threat "you be careful, you [will] be dead for sure." Zheng testified that there was "[n]o way" the Chinese government would protect him from the snakeheads "[b]ecause snakeheads are connected with the Chinese government officials." As an example of the collusion between the government officials and the snakeheads, Zheng testified that he saw the snakeheads give three cartons of cigarettes to the police at the harbor before they were allowed to board the boat.

The IJ admitted the following into the record: declarations of Wu Ming He and Qing He, Chinese immigrants also smuggled into the United States by snakeheads, the United States Department of State Country Report for China dated April 14, 1998, and the Trafficking Victims Protection Act of 2000 ("TVPA"), H.R. 3244, 106th Cong. (1999), which became the Trafficking Victims Protection Act, Pub. Law 106-386, 114 Stat. 1464 (2000) (codified at 22 U.S.C. §§7101–7110). The declaration of Wu Ming He stated that: "It is my personal knowledge that alien smugglers have connections with local government officials. I saw with my own eyes at least four times alien smugglers feasting and patronizing night clubs with local police officers in Fujian." The declaration of Qing He stated that: "I was smuggled into the United States from the Fujian Province of China on a boat. On my way to Guam, I saw with my own very eyes one of my fellow smugglees being tortured by the smugglers."

The State Department Country Report for China states that "China appears to be taking active measures to target people smugglers and stop illegal departures by economic migrants. Several scores of people smugglers and Fujian officials reportedly have been convicted, fired from jobs, or expelled from the Communist Party." Zheng argued before the IJ that this report indicated that there was official participation in alien smuggling in Fujian, the province Zheng is from.

In passing the TVPA, Congress found, in relevant part, that "[t]rafficking often is aided by official corruption in countries of origin[;] ... enforcement against traffickers is also hindered by official indifference, by corruption, and sometimes even by active official participation in trafficking." 22 U.S.C. §§7101(b)(8) & (16). In addition, Congress found that traffickers often resort to violence and torture, or threats of violence and torture, to keep their victims in line. 22 U.S.C. §§7101(b)(6) & (7). The INS unsuccessfully objected to the admission of the TVPA.

Before stating her decision, the IJ found that Zheng "testified credibly and consistently throughout his entire hearing.... Therefore, I find that the respondent is credible." The IJ, however, ruled that Zheng "failed to establish the standard for asylum ... [and] failed to establish the standard for withholding of deportation."

After ruling that Zheng was ineligible for asylum, the IJ stated that "[t]he Court is more concerned with the respondent's request for protection under the Convention Against Torture." The IJ found that:

> The observations of the respondent where police surrounded the home where he was being detained and then, withdrew after being spoken to by smugglers. Furthermore, the journey along the highway where he was not questioned in the truck where he was traveling in, though other trucks and vehicles were stopped. Then, his final observation of smugglers giving cigarettes to the police and then, the respondent and others being allowed to board the ship, is some evidence of collusion between the government. If not collusion as to the violence, at least some collusion that the government condones or at least is not willing to interfere and, in a way, acquiesces to the smuggler's conduct.

The IJ concluded:

> This Court is very concerned with smuggling. The Government of the United States is very concerned with smuggling. I believe that the respondent has established a clear probability of torture and that there is [a] sufficient nexus between the public officials and therefore, his application for protection under the Convention [] will be granted.

Zheng did not appeal the denial of asylum or withholding of removal. But the INS appealed the portion of the IJ's ruling that granted Zheng withholding of removal to China under the Convention Against Torture. The issue presented to the BIA was "[w]hether the Respondent failed to demonstrate acquiescence of a public official or other person acting in an official capacity as required by 8 C.F.R. 208.18," (emphasis omitted). According to the INS, "[t]he main flaw in the [Immigration] Judge's analysis was her failure to recognize the *qualitative* difference between localized government corruption in regard to day-to-day smuggling operations, and *prior* and *knowing* government acquiescence in regard to murder or other violent crimes," (emphases in original). The INS argued that the Chinese government turning a blind eye to its citizens being smuggled out of the country was not tantamount to acquiescing to torture:

> Even if some Chinese police take bribes to let refugees pass through checkpoints, this is a purely non-violent and relatively benign offense[.] It does

> not raise any inference whatsoever that such bribe-takers would be amenable to violence; i.e., that with *prior knowledge* they would allow the commission of acts of ... torture,

The BIA sustained the INS's appeal: "The Service contends that the Immigration Judge's decision misapplied the law. We agree." Citing an en banc BIA opinion, the BIA stated that "[w]hen the alien alleges a likelihood of torture from non-governmental sources, he or she must demonstrate that government officials 'are willfully accepting of' the non-governmental source's 'torturous activities.' See *Matter of S-V-*, Interim Decision 3430, at 8 (BIA 2000)." The BIA found that, even assuming Chinese government officials knew about the smuggling operations and failed to stop them, Zheng did not show that government officials would acquiesce in harm that rises to the level of torture. The BIA vacated the IJ's decision that granted Zheng's application for withholding of removal pursuant to the Convention and ordered Zheng removed to China.

Zheng now seeks review of the final order of the BIA vacating the IJ's grant of relief under the Convention Against Torture.

B. The Convention Against Torture

The United Nations drafted the Convention Against Torture in an effort to "make more effective the struggle against torture and other cruel, inhuman or degrading treatment or punishment throughout the world." Convention Against Torture, Preamble, 23 I.L.M. at 1027. On December 10, 1984, the United Nations General Assembly adopted the Convention by unanimous agreement. Committee on Foreign Relations, Convention Against Torture and Other Cruel, Inhuman or Degrading Treatment or Punishment, S. Exec. Rep. 101-30, at 2 (1990). President Reagan signed the Convention on April 18, 1988. Id. One month later, the President transmitted to the Senate the Convention for approval with nineteen proposed United States conditions, many of which concerned the human rights community, American Bar Association, and other groups. *Id*; 136 Cong. Rec. 36,193 (1990) (statement of Sen. Pell). One of those conditions was an understanding that the United States interpreted the term *acquiescence* to "re-quire[ ] that the public official, prior to the activity constituting torture, have *knowledge* of such activity." S. Exec. Rep. 101-30, at 15 (emphasis added). According to the Senate Foreign Relations Committee, "[t]hose conditions, in number and substance, created the impression that the United States was not serious in its commitment to end torture worldwide." *Id.* at 4. In January 1990, the Bush administration submitted a revised and reduced list of proposed United States conditions on the Convention: "the conditions proposed ... in large measure eliminate[d] th[e] problem" that the United States appeared insincere in its commitment to end torture world-wide. *Id.* at 2, 4. Under one of the new proposed understandings, the United States no longer required a public official to have "knowledge of [torture]" to acquiesce to torture; rather the public official need only an "awareness" of torture. *Id.* at 9, 30. The Committee stated that the purpose of requiring awareness, and not knowledge, "is to make it clear that both actual knowledge and 'willful blindness' fall within the definition of the term 'acquiescence.'" *Id.* at 9. In recommending ratification of the Convention with the new conditions, including the understanding that acquiescence required only awareness and not actual knowledge, the Committee found that "[r]atification is a natural follow-on to the active role that the United States played in the negotiating process for the Convention and is consistent with long-standing U.S. efforts to promote and protect basic human rights and fundamental freedoms throughout the world." *Id.* at 3.[4] The Senate adopted its resolution of advice and consent to ratification on October 27, 1990. 136 Cong. Rec. 36,198 (1990). On October 21, 1994, President Clinton deposited the instrument of ratification with the United Nations, and the Convention Against Torture was entered into force for the United States thirty days later. See Regulations Concerning the Convention Against Torture, 64 Fed. Reg. 8478 (1999).

In 1998, Congress passed the Foreign Affairs Reform and Restructuring Act of 1998, implementing Article 3 of the Convention Against Torture.[5] FARRA § 2242, 8 U.S.C.A. § 1231, note. This implementing legislation states that it is "the policy of the United States not to expel, extradite, or otherwise effect the involuntary return of any person to a country in which there are substantial grounds for believing the person would be in danger of being subjected to torture." *Id.*, § 2242(a). FARRA instructed "heads of the appropriate agencies [to] prescribe regulations to implement the obligations of the United States under Article 3 of the [Convention], subject to any reservations, understandings, declarations, and provisos contained in the United States Senate resolution of ratification of the Convention." *Id.*, § 2242(b). The INS's regulations to implement Article 3 are found in 8 C.F.R. §§ 208.16–208.18.

II. Standard of Review

Because the BIA conducted an independent review of the IJ's findings, we review the BIA's decision and not that of the IJ. *Sidhu v. INS*, 220 F.3d 1085, 1088 (9th Cir. 2000). We review for substantial evidence the factual findings underlying the BIA's determination that Zheng was not eligible for relief under the Convention Against Torture. See *Kamalthas v. INS*, 251 F.3d 1279, 1281 (9th Cir. 2001); see also Li v. Ashcroft, 312 F.3d 1094, 1103 (9th Cir. 2002).

We review de novo the BIA's interpretation of purely legal questions. See *Murillo-Espinoza v. INS*, 261 F.3d 771, 773 (9th Cir. 2001). The BIA's interpretations and applications of immigration law, however, are "subject to established principles of deference." *Id.* But deference is not required when the intent of Congress is clear. *Bel-*

---

4. Before the Senate voted to adopt its advice and consent to ratification of the Convention, Senator Moynihan stated:

> The United States has invested enormous resources in this convention. For 7 years our diplomats labored to make the convention more than just words on paper. They made its obligation concrete, meaningful, and, as never before, enforceable. I believe that this is an important step in the continuing battle to end man's inhumanity to man.

136 Cong. Rec. 36,196 (1990).

5. Article 3 of the Convention provides that "[n]o State Party shall expel, return ('refouler') or extradite a person to another State where there are substantial grounds for believing that the person would be in danger of being subjected to torture." Convention Against Torture, art. 3, 23 I.L.M. at 1028.

tran-Tirado v. INS, 213 F.3d 1179, 1185 (9th Cir. 2000); see also *Murillo-Espinoza*, 261 F.3d at 773 ("If the intent of Congress is clear, that is the end of the matter; for the court, as well as the agency, must give effect to the unambiguously expressed intent of Congress.) (quoting *Chevron, U.S.A., Inc. v. Natural Res. Def. Council, Inc.*, 467 U.S. 837, 842–43, 81 L. Ed. 2d 694, 104 S. Ct. 2778 (1984)).

III. Discussion

The outcome of this case hinges on the interpretation of the term acquiescence as used in 8 C.F.R. § 208.18. To qualify for relief under the Convention Against Torture, Zheng must establish that it is more likely than not that if removed to China, the snakeheads would torture him and that the torture would be inflicted with the acquiescence of Chinese government officials. The Convention does not require, as the INS purports, the government to "knowingly acquiesce" to such torture. And contrary to the BIA's ruling, the Convention does not require that Zheng prove that Chinese government officials would be "willfully accepting of" the torture inflicted on Zheng by the smugglers. As explained below, Congress made its intent clear that actual knowledge, or willful acceptance, is not required for a government to "acquiesce" to the torture of its citizens. Rather, subject to the understanding contained in the Senate's ratification of the Convention, "[a]cquiescence of a public official requires that the public official, prior to the activity constituting torture, have *awareness* of such activity and thereafter breach his or her legal responsibility to intervene to prevent such activity." 8 C.F.R. § 208.18(a)(7) (emphasis added). We conclude that the BIA's interpretation of the term acquiescence to require that Zheng must prove that the government is "willfully accepting of" torture, instead of proving that public officials are aware of the torture, impermissibly narrows Congress' clear intent in implementing relief under the Convention Against Torture.

Under INS regulations, Zheng has the burden of proof "to establish that it is more likely than not that he ... would be tortured if removed" to China. *Al-Saher v. INS*, 268 F.3d 1143, 1147 (9th Cir. 2001) (alteration in original) (quoting 8 C.F.R. § 208.16(c)(2)). The regulations define torture as:

> any act by which severe pain or suffering ... is intentionally inflicted on a person for such purposes as ... punishing him or her for an act he or she or a third person has committed ... when such pain or suffering is inflicted by or at the instigation of or with the consent or *acquiescence* of a public official or other person acting in an official capacity.

8 C.F.R. § 208.18(a)(1) (emphasis added). As stated above, "[a]cquiescence of a public official requires that the public official, prior to the activity constituting torture, have *awareness* of such activity and thereafter breach his or her legal responsibility to intervene to prevent such activity." 8 C.F.R. § 208.18(a)(7) (emphasis added).

Thus, to qualify for relief under the Convention, Zheng has to prove that the torture inflicted by the snakeheads would be carried out with the awareness of the Chinese government officials. That awareness includes "both actual knowledge and 'willful blindness.'" S. Exec. Rep. 101-30, at 9; see also *Ontunez-Tursios v. Ashcroft,* 303 F.3d 341, 354–55 (5th Cir. 2002) (stating that "'[w]illful blindness' suffices to prove 'acquiescence'" and finding that the evidence presented did not show that Honduran public officials "would turn a blind eye to torture"); *Ali v. Reno,* 237 F.3d 591, 597 (6th Cir. 2001) ("both actual knowledge and 'willful blindness' fall within the definition of the term 'acquiescence.'") (citation omitted). The Senate did not in its understandings to the Convention modify the terms awareness and acquiescence with the adjective "knowing" as the INS does in their briefs to the BIA and this court. Nor did the Senate require willful acceptance. Rather, the Senate ratified a version of the Convention that eliminated an understanding that acquiescence required a public official's knowledge and replaced it with an under-standing that acquiescence required only a public official's awareness. The Senate Committee on Foreign Relations expressly stated that the purpose of requiring awareness, and not knowledge, "is to make it clear that both actual knowledge and 'willful blindness' fall within the definition of the term 'acquiescence.'" S. Exec. Rep. 101-30, at 9.

The BIA in Zheng's case, however, required Zheng to prove more than awareness of torture by public officials. Instead, the BIA required that "[w]hen the alien alleges a likelihood of torture from non-governmental sources, he or she must demonstrate that government officials 'are *willfully accepting of* the non-governmental source's 'torturous activities.' See *Matter of S-V-*, Interim Decision 3430, at 8 (BIA 2000)," (emphasis added).

In *Matter of S-V-*, the BIA en banc denied relief under the Convention Against Torture to a respondent who asserted that if he were removed to Columbia he would be tortured by non-governmental guerrilla, narcotrafficking, and paramilitary groups. In discussing acquiescence, the BIA stated:

> In its resolution of advice and consent to the Convention Against Torture, the United States Senate included an understanding replacing the word "knowledge" in this definition of acquiescence with the word "awareness," indicating that actual knowledge of activity constituting torture is not required.... The Senate Committee on Foreign Relations clarified the point by stating that "(t)he purpose of this condition is to make it clear that both actual knowledge and 'willful blindness' fall within the definition of the term 'acquiescence.'"

22 I. & N. 1306 (citations omitted). After directly quoting the Senate's intent, the BIA then "interpret[ed] the regulation at 8 C.F.R. § 208.18(a) [defining acquiescence] to be limiting"—more limiting than the Senate's just quoted intent to require awareness and not actual knowledge. *Id.* Creating a standard more stringent than Congress clearly intended, the BIA held that to demonstrate acquiescence "the respondent must do more than show that the officials are aware of the activity constituting torture but are powerless to stop it. He must demonstrate that the Colombian officials are willfully accepting of the guerillas' torturous activities." *Id.* (emphases added). Quoting the Oxford Universal Dictionary, the BIA stated "[t]o interpret the term [acquiescence] otherwise would be to misconstrue the meaning of 'acquiescence,' the dictionary defi-

nition of which is 'silent or passive assent.'" *Id.* (quoting Oxford Universal Dictionary 17 (3d ed. 1955)).[6]

To interpret the term acquiescence as the BIA did, however, misconstrues and ignores the clear Congressional intent quoted by the BIA merely a paragraph above its restrictive holding. The BIA's interpretation and application of acquiescence impermissibly requires more than awareness and instead requires that a government be willfully accepting of a third party's tortuous activities. There is nothing in the understandings to the Convention approved by the Senate, or the INS's regulations implementing the Convention, to suggest that anything more than awareness is required. Yet, the BIA ignored the Senate's clear intent and constructed its own interpretation of acquiescence, an interpretation that requires more than awareness, includes "willfully accepting of," and seemingly excludes "willful blindness." Under this narrowed interpretation of acquiescence, the BIA stated that "[t]he relevant inquiry under the Convention Against Torture ... is whether governmental authorities would ... 'willfully accept' atrocities committed against persons in the respondent's position." *In re Y-L-, A-G-, R-S-R-*, 23 I. & N. 270, 283 (BIA 2002). The correct inquiry as intended by the Senate is whether a respondent can show that public officials demonstrate "willful blindness" to the torture of their citizens by third parties, or as stated by the Fifth Circuit, whether public officials "would turn a blind eye to torture." *Ontunez-Tursios*, 303 F.3d at 355.

Citing *INS v. Aguirre-Aguirre*, 526 U.S. 415, 143 (1999), the INS argues that "[t]he definition of torture has been properly left to INS." See *Aguirre-Aguirre*, 526 U.S. at 425 (citation omitted) ("[J]udicial deference to the Executive Branch is especially appropriate in the immigration context where officials 'exercise especially sensitive political functions that implicate questions of foreign relations.'"). The INS, however, is wrong. The definition of torture has been properly left, not to the INS, but to Congress, who instructed the INS to "prescribe regulations to implement the obligations of the United States under Article 3 of the [Convention], subject to any reservations, understandings, declarations, and provisos contained in the United States Senate resolution of ratification of the Convention." FARRA § 2242(b) (emphasis added). One of the "understandings" in the Senate resolution of ratification of the Convention Against Torture was that acquiescence of a public official requires "awareness" and not "knowledge" or "willful[] accept[ance]." Because the intent of Congress is clear, that is the end of the matter; for th[is] court, as well as the agency, must give effect to the unambiguously expressed intent of Congress." *Chevron*, 467 U.S. at 842–43.

To the extent that decisions such as *Matter of S-V-* and *In re Y-L, A-G, R-S-R-*, require actual knowledge and "willful[] accept[ance]"—contrary to clear congressional intent to require only awareness—we disapprove of those decisions. We note

6. But see The American Heritage Dictionary of the English Language (4th ed. 2000) ("Synonyms: assent, agree, accede, acquiesce, consent.... These verbs denote acceptance of and often belief in another's views, proposals, or actions. Assent implies agreement, especially as a result of deliberation: They readily assented to our suggestion.... Acquiesce suggests passive assent because of inability or unwillingness to oppose: I acquiesced in their decision despite my misgivings.") (http:// dictionary.reference.com/search?q=assent) (last visited May 30, 2003).

that "we have taken care not to exceed our authority, and not to second-guess the BIA. Our decision[] simply give[s] effect to the will of Congress"[7] that the BIA adhere to the definition of acquiescence intended by Congress when it ratified the Convention Against Torture and created legislation implementing Article 3 of the Convention Against Torture; the BIA may not construe its own, more limited definition of acquiescence.

In light of the Supreme Court's recent decision in *INS v. Ventura,* 537 U.S. 12 (2002) (per curiam), we do not now review the evidence under the correct standard of acquiescence to determine if substantial evidence supports the BIA's conclusion that Zheng does not qualify for relief under the Convention Against Torture. Rather, following Ventura, we remand to the BIA to give the BIA the first opportunity to apply the correct standard of "acquiescence" as intended by the Senate in ratifying the Convention—a standard that includes awareness and willful blindness and does not require actual knowledge or "willful[ ] accept[ance]." See *id.* at *355* ("Generally speaking, a court of appeals should remand a case to an agency for decision of a matter that statutes place primarily in agency hands.").

We note that the government maintains in its possession significant information about Chinese smuggling rings and their relationship to the Chinese government that may support the petitioner's "awareness" claim. For example, the U.S. Department of State International Information Programs website includes a useful collection of articles and reports under the heading Chinese Human Smuggling. Given that the regulations implementing the Convention Against Torture provide that "all evidence relevant to the possibility of future torture shall be considered," 8 C.F.R. § 208.16(c)(3), it would further the purposes of the Convention were the BIA, on remand, to supplement the record with such material information.

IV. Conclusion

In sum, we disapprove of the BIA's decision in *Matter of S-V-* that—contrary to clear congressional intent—requires a showing that a government is willfully accepting of the torture of its citizens by a third party. We grant Zheng's petition for review, vacate the BIA's decision, and remand this case to the BIA for further proceedings consistent with this opinion.

Note

For additional resources on CAT, see generally Joseph Voyame & Peter Burns, The Convention Against Torture and Other Cruel, Inhuman or Degrading Treatment or Punishment, in Manual on Human Rights Reporting 367 (1997). For a full account of the origins of CAT and how it applies, see generally Matthew Lippman, *The Development and Drafting of the United Nations Convention Against Torture and Other Cruel, Inhuman or Degrading Treatment or Punishment,* 17 B.C.

---

7. *Borja v. INS,* 175 F.3d 732, 739 (9th Cir. 1999) (en banc).

Int'l & Comp. L. Rev. 275 (1994); J. Herman Burgers & Hans Danelus, The United Nations Convention Against Torture and Other Cruel, Inhuman or Degrading Treatment or Punishment (1988); Peter Burns Q.C. & Obiora Okafor, *The United Nations Convention against Torture and Other Cruel, Inhuman or Degrading Treatment or Punishment or How It Is Still Better to Light a Candle than to Curse the Darkness*, 9 Otago L. Rev. 399 (1998).

L. Problem Exercise

The Case of Tomas Becerra

Tomas Becerra was born in Cali, Colombia, and is over 21 years old. He came to the United States seeking admission on a tourist visa (B-2) issued to him by the U.S. Consul in Bogota, Colombia. Upon his arrival at John F. Kennedy Airport in New York on March 1, 2009, he was routed to secondary inspection.

At secondary inspection, he was questioned by a CBP officer in Spanish with some help from an interpreter. When questioned about his purpose in coming to the United States, he stated that he was coming "to visit with relatives." The CBP officer was reluctant to admit Tomas and decided that instead of immediately returning him to Columbia, he would allow Tomas to proceed on parole status to "deferred inspection" to be completed by San Francisco District Office, the applicant's U.S. destination where his family was located.

Tomas comes to your office and tells you that he doesn't know the procedure that he is facing and is afraid of returning to Colombia, but he will go back there or to another country only "if it is necessary." He explains that in September 2005, his father was kidnapped by guerrillas for ransom money while going to his farm in a nearby city. He learned two months later from the police that his father was buried in a place near where he had been kidnapped. Because the ransom was not paid, the guerrillas began to call Tomas' home and stated that they wanted the money. (The money demand was for approximately $250,000, which the family had available.) Out of fear for his mother's safety, Tomas sent her to England to stay with family and paid the money to the people who contacted them. He remains afraid for his mother, because even though she later returned to a different location in Colombia, the guerillas seemed to know where she was all the time. When you question him about the guerrilla group involved, he tells you that he believes the ransom demands came either from a group called the Fuerzas Armadas Revolucionarios de Colombia (FARC) or a splinter group of the FARC.

In response to a question about his prior encounters with immigration authorities, he states that he, his mother and his sister had overstayed their tourist visas when they entered the United States in 1999. He had remained in the country without INS authorization for three years until sometime in 2002. His sister is married to a U.S. citizen, became a permanent resident some time ago and is now awaiting naturalization. He insists that he has never been removed and that he doubts that USCIS has a record of his departure in 2002.

Tomas tells you that he will tell the immigration authorities whatever you say is appropriate. He explains that his fear of returning to Colombia is because he doesn't believe that the police, military or authorities will do anything for him. Often, he says that "one learns later that the police are the very kidnappers, and are using the guerillas as a way to make extort money." Prior to the kidnapping, Tomas' father had told him that he was receiving phone calls from people he thought were the FARC who had demanded money. He is also very frightened because he and his siblings inherited his father's land, money and possessions. While his brothers who remain in Colombia are afraid, they have decided not to leave yet because they are "foolish, stubborn and too proud."

Questions

1. What additional questions would you have for Tomas?

2. Advise Tomas on the applicable law as it relates to all potential grounds of inadmissibility.

3. Advise Tomas on what possible things could happen when he returns to the immigration office to complete the inspection process, including a removal hearing if you believe one is likely.

4. Can Tomas apply for asylum? What can you tell him about his prospects of gaining asylum?

Chapter 6

Persons Coming to the U.S. Temporarily — Nonimmigrants

Introduction

There are four ways for persons who are not U.S. citizens to legally seek admission to the United States. They are (1) obtaining a visa from a U.S. consul abroad, (2) being granted parole by U.S. Customs and Border Protection (CBP), (3) seeking admission as an asylum seeker upon arrival, or (4) attempting to return to a residence in the United States after having been previously granted lawful permanent resident status. Since we have already discussed parole and asylum in Chapter 5 and will be discussing lawful permanent residency in the following chapter, our discussion here will be limited to nonimmigrant visas issued by U.S. consuls.[1]

It is easier to understand the role of the "visa" in the admission process by extending the analogy of the person "knocking at the door" discussed in the section on admission (Chapter 3). A person traveling to the United States in possession of a visa is merely applying for permission to seek admission, which is similar to a visitor who comes to your home and wishes to be allowed to stay for a period of time. The individual must obtain a visa as a condition precedent to seeking permission to enter, but the issuance of the visa is not a guarantee that the person will be admitted. The applicant must show that she qualifies for admission under the visa and must overcome all of the applicable inadmissibility grounds enumerated in 8 U.S.C. § 1182, Sec. 212.

Nonimmigrant visas are issued to persons outside the United States who wish to enter the country temporarily for a specific purpose. There are twenty-two separate categories of nonimmigrant visas described at 8 U.S.C. § 1101(a)(15), Sec. 101(a)(15).[2] In enacting the INA, Congress created a legal presumption that all visa applicants, including those who seek nonimmigrant visas, desire to come to the United States

1. There are two types of visas which can be issued: immigrant visas and nonimmigrant visas. Nonimmigrant visas may be issued only to persons who meet the specific requirements of the controlling statute and can show that they have a residence abroad to which they will return after completing their temporary stay in the United States. There are two broad categories of immigrant visas: family and employment based immigrants, which are discussed in Chapters 7 and 8. Immigrant visas for long-term residency can only be issued to persons who establish the requisite family ties or a specific need for their work skills in the United States.

2. *See also* 8 C.F.R. § 214.2 and 22 C.F.R. § 41.12.

to stay permanently. This presumption places a heavy burden on the applicant to clearly show her eligibility for one of the nonimmigrant visa categories. The person's inability to meet this burden effectively precludes her from legal admission.[3] Below is a brief summary of the different types of nonimmigrant visas. It should be noted that these visas are commonly referred to by letter designation, which reference the subparts of 8 U.S.C. § 1101(a)(15), Sec. 101(a)(15) to which the type of visa corresponds. For example, a tourist visa is called a "B" visa and is described at 8 U.S.C. § 1101(a)(15)(B), Sec. 101(a)(15)(B), while a visa for a crew member of a ship or airline is called a "D" visa and is described at 8 U.S.C. § 1101(a)(15)(D), Sec. 101(a)(15)(D).

In December 2000, Congress enacted amendments to the immigration laws which included a provision that covers all adjudications of the U.S. Citizenship and Immigration Services (USCIS), allowing them to collect a "premium" fee of $1,000 in addition to the regular filing fee.[4] Applications submitted with this premium fee will be adjudicated within fifteen calendar days. If the application is not adjudicated within the fifteen days, the fee must be returned and USCIS must still expeditiously adjudicate the application. The fee structure is designed for the convenience of businesses, which require speedy adjudications.

The applications covered under this rule are changes or extensions of status for the following nonimmigrant classifications: E-1 Treaty Traders; E-2 Treaty Investors; H-1B Temporary Workers in Specialty Occupations; H-2B Temporary Workers performing nonagricultural services; H-3 Trainees; L-1 Intracompany Transferees; O-1 and O-2 Aliens of Extraordinary Ability or Achievement; P-1, P-2 and P-3 Athletes and Entertainers; Q-1 International Cultural Exchange Aliens; R-1 Aliens in Religious Occupations; and TN NAFTA Professionals. The fee also covers dependent spouses and children. Interim rules governing the premium fees were promulgated in the Federal Register.[5]

A. Categories of Nonimmigrant Visas

Foreign Government Officials (Diplomatic Personnel)—A Visas[6]

The "A" or diplomatic visa is for heads of state, high members of government, justices of the highest courts and presiding members of the legislature, as well as am-

---

3. A person's ineligibility for a nonimmigrant visa does not necessarily act as a permanent bar to admission. While each visa application and denial is prejudicial to new requests, each application is a new opportunity to establish eligibility unless the person's ineligibility is one of the inadmissibility grounds which cannot be overcome. This should be contrasted with findings of inadmissibility or removal after entry, which may result in bars against the person's reentry. *See* discussion in Chapters 3 and 4. However, if the person's ineligibility is based on one of the grounds of inadmissibility which cannot be overcome, she will be ineligible for future admission.

4. *See* District of Columbia Appropriations Act, 2001, Public Law 106-553, 114 Stat. 2762 (2000).

5. 66 Fed. Reg. 29,682 (2001).

6. *See* 8 U.S.C. § 1101(a)(15)(A), Sec. 101(a) (15)(A); 8 C.F.R. § 214.2 (a); 22 C.F.R. §§ 41.21, 41.22, 41.26.

bassadors, career diplomats, consular officers and members of their immediate family who are coming to the United States on official business.[7] A person who has not been approved as a diplomat by the President or Secretary of State should not be issued an A visa. Diplomatic status, which can only be conferred by the President or Secretary of State, confers special immunity from prosecution and jurisdiction by the United States. Issues such as unauthorized employment and violation and maintenance of status are referred to the Department of State before any action can be taken by USCIS. Children of diplomats born in the United States are considered to be lawful permanent residents until such time that they abandon their residency by returning to their home country.[8] The removal of a diplomat is the declaration that she is a *persona non grata*.

The A-1 visa is issued to ambassadors, public ministers, career diplomatic or consular officers and members of their immediate families. The A-2 visa is issued to foreign government employees or officials and their families. The A-3 visa is issued to persons such as personal employees and servants of persons holding A-1 and A-2 visas. The A-1 and A-2 visas are valid for as long as they are recognized by the Secretary of State, while A-3 visas are valid for one year.

Visitors—B Visas[9]

The "B" visa is for visitors entering for business or pleasure. The B-1 visa is for a person visiting the United States for activities such as conducting business and attending conferences so long as the activities are on behalf of a foreign employer. The person can also be admitted for training and provided with room, board and expenses, but her salary must be paid by the foreign employer.

The B-2 visa is for tourists, and it is the largest of the nonimmigrant visa categories.[10] The B-2 visa may also be granted to such persons coming to obtain medical treatment or participate in amateur entertainment or athletic activities, in addition to dependents accompanying nonimmigrant crewman or U.S. Armed Forces officers temporarily stationed in the United States. The prospective visitor entering for pleasure must demonstrate to the satisfaction of the U.S. consul abroad that residence is not being abandoned in the home country, that the applicant has sufficient funds to support herself without engaging in work while in the country and that she will depart at the end of the visit. Some special provisions are made for persons entering for commercial reasons who are citizens of Canada or Mexico.[11]

---

7. *See* 22 C.F.R. §41.26.

8. *See Nikoi v. Attorney General*, 939 F.2d 1065 (D.C. Cir. 1991); *Matter of Huang*, 11 I. & N. Dec. 190 (Reg. Comm'r 1965).

9. *See* 8 U.S.C. §1101(a)(15)(B), Sec. 101(a)(15)(B); 8 C.F.R. §§214.1 and 214.2; 22 C.F.R. §41.31.

10. *See* DHS Report, "Temporary Admissions of Nonimmigrants to the United States" (May 2005), *published on* AILA InfoNet at Doc. No. 05051663 (*posted* May 5, 2005).

11. *See discussion infra;* The North American Free Trade Agreement, Pub. L. No. 103-322, 108 Stat 1796 (1994).

Persons in Transit or Traveling Without a Visa (TWOV)—C Visa

Persons traveling through the United States may either obtain a special "C" visa or be allowed in transit under a special program called the Transit Without Visa (TWOV) program.[12] The C visa is issued to persons who are in "immediate and continuous transit through the U.S."[13] The visa may also be issued to a non-member representative of the United Nations or a foreign representative passing through the country. In addition, it can be issued to members of a shipping crew who are joining another ship. In order to qualify, the person must have either a ticket or other proof that demonstrates that she is traveling on to her destination.[14] The TWOV program was suspended in 2003 for security reasons, which means that all persons, except foreign government officials, who could previously travel through the United States in transit are now required to obtain a visa.[15]

Crew Members—D Visas[16]

The D-1 visa is issued to crew members (including flight crew) remaining with their vessels. The D-2 visa is issued to a member discharged from her vessel with the intent of working on another vessel. Both D-1 and D-2 visas are valid for a maximum of 29 days. In order to be admitted as a crew member, the person must be employed by the carrier. No extension or change of status to any other classification is allowed.

Treaty Traders or Investors—E Visas[17]

"E" visas are issued to persons when the following requirements are met: (1) a "treaty of commerce and navigation" exists between the United States and the applicant's country, (2) the applicant is a national of that country and (3) the applicant is coming to the United States solely to "carry on substantial trade" (E-1), where "substantial" has been interpreted as constituting more than 50% of the international trade by the applicant's business,[18] or to "develop and direct an enterprise in which he has invested ... a substantial amount of capital" (E-2), where "substantial" has been interpreted as constituting an amount sufficient to successfully develop and operate a viable, not marginal, enterprise.[19] These visas are also available for the spouse and children of the holder of an E-1 or E-2 visa. Both visas are valid for two years, but unlimited extensions may be granted by USCIS in increments of up to two years as long as the business is maintained. The requirement of temporariness of stay in

12. *See* 8 U.S.C. § 1182(d)(4)(C), Sec. 212(d)(4)(C). Note that persons from selected countries may continue to come to the United States under the Visa Waiver Program.

13. 8 U.S.C. § 1101(a)(15)(C), Sec. 101(a)(15)(C).

14. *See* 8 C.F.R. § 214.2(c)(3) and 22 C.F.R. § 41.71.

15. 68 Fed. Reg. 46,926–28 (2003).

16. *See* 8 U.S.C. § 1101(a)(15)(D), Sec. 101(a)(15)(D); 8 C.F.R. § 214.2 (2)(d); and 22 C.F.R. § 41.41.

17. *See* 8 U.S.C. § 1101 (a) (15) (E), Sec. 101 (a) (15) (E); 8 C.F.R. § 214.2(e); 22 C.F.R. § 41.51.

18. *See* 8 C.F.R. § 214.2(e)(10)–(11); 22 C.F.R. 41.51(a)(9); 9 FAM 41.51 N.6–7.

19. Under 8 U.S.C. § 1101(a)(45), Sec 101(a)(45), the definition of "substantial" shall be established by the Department of State following consultation with appropriate government agencies. *See also* 8 C.F.R. § 214.2(e)(14)–(15); 9 FAM 41.51 N.10–11; 22 C.F.R. § 41.51(b)(9)–(10).

the United States and unrelinquished domicile abroad are not as strict under this visa classification as for the B visa. Special reciprocal provisions exist for the entry of investors and traders from Canada and Mexico.[20] Provisions for additional reciprocal visas under the E visa (treaty investor/trader) program for nationals of Australia in "specialty occupations"[21] in the amount of 10,500 per fiscal year were made in 2005.[22]

Students—F Visas[23]

The F-1 visa is issued to persons who are entering the United States temporarily and solely to pursue a full course of study at an established elementary school, academic high school, college, university, seminary, conservatory or language school approved by the Attorney General.[24] A "full course of study" is defined in 8 C.F.R. §214.2(f)(6). The prospective student visa applicant must satisfy the consular officer that she (1) fits under the statutory definition of student, (2) will attend an institution approved by the Attorney General for attendance by foreign students,[25] (3) has sufficient funds to meet expenses for the entire period of anticipated study without having to resort to employment in the United States, and (4) has sufficient scholastic preparation and knowledge of the English language (unless English is not an essential requirement or arrangements have been made for tutoring).[26] Following entry, the student visa holder is monitored by a "designated school official" (DSO), who can assist with such matters as transferring between schools and on- and off-campus employment for the duration of the student's course of study at the educational institution. The F-2 visa is issued to the spouse and children of the student visa holder.

Work Authorization for Students: The 1990 Act created an experimental program which has since become permanent that allows students to work off-campus in fields unrelated to the person's field of study. This work authorization is non-discretionary once the student meets the following three requirements: (1) she has completed at

---

20. *See* The United States-Canada Free-Trade Agreement Implementation Act of 1988, Pub. L. No. 100-449, 102 Stat. 1851 (1988); The North American Free Trade Agreement, Pub. L. No. 103-322, 108 Stat 1796 (1994).

21. Specialty occupations are defined under 8 U.S.C. §1184(i)(1).

22. *See* Sec. 501, REAL ID Act of 2005, Pub. L. No. 109-13, 119 Stat. 231 (2005).

23. *See* 8 U.S.C. §1101(a)(15)(F), Sec. 101(a)(15)(F); 8 C.F.R. §214.2(f); 22 C.F.R. §41.61.

24. The 1996 amendments prohibit student visa applicants from studying at public elementary, secondary or higher education institutions unless they plan to attend for less than twelve months and have reimbursed the school the full, unsubsidized per capita cost of their education. Applicants who fail to comply with this condition may be inadmissible under 8 U.S.C. §1184(m)(1), Sec. 214(m)(1).

25. Presentation of Form I-20, a form filled out by the student's accepting school, is prima facie evidence of admission to an accredited institution. The I-20 is surrendered to the CBP officer upon arrival at the U.S. border.

26. When a person enters the United States in one status (e.g., as a visitor for pleasure), then seeks to change to some other status (e.g., to that of student), unless a significant period of time has lapsed, it will be presumed by USCIS that the person was attempting to evade the normal procedures for obtaining a visa abroad. The burden shifts to the applicant to prove that she really changed her intention after she entered the country. The denial of a change of status application is appealable to the Administrative Appeals Office (AAO). (*See* Administrative Appeals which are discussed in Chapter 12.)

least one year in good academic standing as a nonimmigrant; (2) the employer provides an attestation that it has recruited for the position for at least sixty days and will pay the applicant either the rate of that occupation at that particular place of business or, if greater, the market wage level; and (3) the student will not work for more than twenty hours per week during the school year but may work full-time during vacation periods.[27]

Representatives to or Employees of International Organizations—G Visas[28]

G-1 visas are issued to principal representatives of governments recognized *de jure* by the United States or representatives of international organizations and their family members. G-2 visas are for other accredited representatives of foreign governments to international organizations and their family members. G-3 visas are for persons (and their families) who would otherwise qualify for a G-1 or G-2 visa, but the government they represent is not recognized *de jure* by the United States. G-4 visas are for officers and employees of international organizations and their family members. G-5 visas are issued to holders of C visas (persons who are entering to attend United Nations' meetings). All G visas are issued for one year and are renewable. Only family members of G-4 visa holders may accept employment in the United States, and such employment must be approved by USCIS.

Temporary Workers—H Visas[29]

Oversubscription under the immigrant visa quotas has caused an unavailability of visas and the subsequent increased use of the temporary work visas.[30] H visas generally take less time to adjudicate, and their requirements for documentation and evidence are less stringent than for immigrant visas. One of the most significant changes codified in the 1990 amendments was the formal recognition of the notion of dual intent for holders of or applicants for H-1 visas, which allow beneficiaries to pursue permanent residence in the United States while seeking nonimmigrant visas. The temporary intent requirement remains for all other H visas other than the H-1. While an employer in the past would have been required to show that the position was temporary, all that is required to be shown presently is that the foreign worker is willing to comply with the temporary terms of her nonimmigrant visa.

The H-1A visa allowed the admission of licensed registered nurses from foreign countries, but the program no longer exists. Exceptions exist for those applicants

---

27. *See* Sec. 221, Immigration Act of 1990, Pub. L. No. 101-649, 104 Stat. 4978.

28. *See* 8 U.S.C. § 1101(a)(15)(G); 8 C.F.R. § 214.2(g); 22 C.F.R. § 41.24, Sec. 101(a)(15)(G).

29. *See* 8 U.S.C. § 1101(a)(15)(H), Sec. 101(a)(15)(H); 8 C.F.R. § 214.2(h); 22 C.F.R. § 41.53.

30. This increased demand on the nonimmigrant visas is due to the fact that in most of the categories, there are no limits on the number of visas that can be issued. Even though the applicant may be successful in obtaining her H visa, she may eventually be confronted with the denial of a request for adjustment of status due to USCIS's determination that she had a "preconceived intent" to immigrate when she applied for the H visa. *See* Chapter 9 on permanent residency through adjustment of status.

who were pending for adjustment of status before September 30, 1997.[31] The H-1A program was originally created by the Immigration Nursing Relief Act of 1989 and was extended through the end of September 1997 by special legislation. Nurses who formerly could have qualified under the H-1A visa may still be able to qualify for a H-1B visa if they are able to establish that the position is for specialty occupation, pass the foreign nurse's exam (CGFNS) and obtain a state license. In addition, under NAFTA, Canadian and Mexicans may be able to enter as nurses under the TN visa.

The H-1B visa[32] is for persons coming to work in a "specialty occupation," or one which requires the theoretical and practical application of a body of highly specialized knowledge and the minimum entry requirement of a bachelor's or higher degree.[33] The H-1B is also for fashion models of distinguished merit and ability or persons providing services related to the Department of Defense's cooperative research and development project. However, applicants who are sponsored by higher education institutions or affiliated nonprofit entities or by nonprofit or governmental research organizations are not subject to the H-1B quotas.[34]

Before an applicant is granted an H-1B visa, the employer must have first obtained a certification of labor condition application (LCA). This requires that the employer attest to the Department of Labor (DOL) that (1) the H-1B will be offered the wage paid to similarly qualified employees or the prevailing wage in the area where the person will be employed, whichever is greater; (2) the employer is providing working conditions for the H-1B employee that will not adversely affect similarly employed

---

31. Pub. L. No. 101-238, 103 Stat. 2099 and amended by Sec. 162 of the Immigration Act of 1990, Pub. L. No. 101-649, 104 Stat. 4978 (1990).

32. Historically, there has never been a limit imposed on the number of nonimmigrants admitted in a given year. One of the more dramatic policy shifts of the 1990 Act was that it imposed a quota on the admission of nonimmigrants under the H-1B, H-2B, P-1 and P-3 categories. Under this amendment, the annual quota for H-1B workers was 65,000 and for H-2B workers was 66,000 (not counted within this annual quota are the derivative beneficiaries of the H workers and trainees). Legislation enacted in 1998 expanded the numbers for H-1B workers to 115,000 in fiscal years 1999 and 2000 and 107,500 for fiscal year 2001, and the quota then returns to 65,000 in the succeeding fiscal years. *See* Sec. 401, American Competitiveness and Workforce Improvement Act of 1998, Pub. L. No. 105-277, 112 Stat. 2681 (1998). Notwithstanding the additional visas, by June 1999, legacy INS announced that the 115,000 visa cap had already been reached for fiscal year 1999 and could only assure persons who had filed their applications before April 9, 1999 would be granted visas. *See Information Regarding the H-1B Numerical Limitation for Fiscal Year 1999*, 64 Fed Reg. 32151 (1999).

However, due to the recurring exhaustion of the 115,000 visas allocated for H-1B workers, Congress in the fall of 2000 increased the quota to 195,000 through fiscal year 2003. *See* Immigration Services and Infrastructure Improvements Act of 2000, Pub. L. No. 106-313, § 102, 114 Stat. 1251 (2000). The law also provided additional visas and therefore relief for persons who had previously filed applications or had been denied because of exhaustion of available H-1B visas over the prior two fiscal years.

33. *See*, 8 U.S.C. § 1184(i)(1), Sec. 214(i)(1) for the definition of "specialty occupation." The 1990 Act removed artists, entertainers and athletes from the H visa category and created the O and P visas discussed below.

34. 8 U.S.C. § 1184(g)(5), Sec. 214(g)(5).

U.S. workers; (3) there is no strike, lockout or work stoppage at the place of business; and (4) notice of the LCA has been provided to the bargaining representative or has been posted at the place of business.[35] (The notice must be posted in two or more places over a ten-day period prior to submission of the labor certification application, which must be submitted within thirty days of the posting.). The H-1B visa may be granted for a period of up to three years and may be extended for a total of six years with few exceptions. A visa holder qualifies for an exception to the six-year duration of the H-1B visa if she has submitted a labor certification or employment-based immigrant application one year prior to the six year visa expiration date, so she is entitled to renew her H-1B visa in one-year increments until a final decision is made on her application.[36] A visa holder is also eligible for an exception if she has an approved petition but is unable to complete the permanent residency process as a result of quota restrictions.

Due to the increased frustration of businesses in securing timely approval of temporary worker petitions because of quota restrictions as well as adjudications backlog, Congress included provisions allowing greater "portability" of H-1B status for nonimmigrants. One amendment allows employers to hire an H-1B visa holder upon the filing of a new petition rather than to wait until after its approval.[37] The provision is retroactive and applies to any application submitted before enactment of the statute as long as the beneficiary was lawfully admitted to the United States and has not worked in the country without employment authorization. Furthermore, if the H-1B visa holder has filed for permanent residency, she may also change employers as long as her permanent residency application has been pending for over 180 days and her new job would fall under a similar occupation.[38]

H-1C visas are available for professional nurses who come to the United States to work temporarily in health care professional shortage areas, but this program is subject to sunset.[39] This visa is only granted when the hospital attests that it has taken significant steps to recruit nurses in the United States and employs no more than thirty-three percent of H-1C nurses. Persons granted H-1C visas are ineligible for extensions beyond three years, and the quota for this category is set at 500 per year.

The H-2 visas are for temporary workers coming to "perform agricultural labor or services" of a "temporary or seasonal nature" (H-2A)[40] and for persons coming to

---

35. 20 C.F.R. §§ 655.705(c) and 655.730(d).

36. *See* American Competitiveness in the Twenty-First Century Act of 2000 (AC21), Pub. L. No. 106-313, § 106, 114 Stat. 1251, 1253–55 (2000).

37. Section 105 of the American Competitiveness in the Twenty First Century Act, Pub. L. No. 106 313, 105, 114 Stat. 1251 (2000).

38. 8 U.S.C. § 1184(j), Sec. 214(j).

39. *See* The Nursing Relief for Disadvantaged Areas Act of 1999, Pub. L. No. 106-95, 113 Stat. 1312 (original legislation statutorily implementing sunset four years following the implementation of final regulations); Nursing Relief for Disadvantaged Areas Reauthorization Act of 2005, Pub. L. No. 109-423, 120 Stat. 2900 (statutorily implementing sunset to December 2009).

40. Amendments to the statute in 1986 created special procedures for the adjudication of these applications and broadly defined agricultural labor or services by incorporating definitions set out

perform "other temporary services or labor" (H-2B). Unlike the H-1 visa, the person must be coming temporarily to the United States, and dual intent is not allowed. While no skill or experience of the type necessary for an H-1 visa is required, a condition precedent for approval is that the prospective employer attain a "temporary labor" certification which confirms that able, willing and qualified domestic workers[41] cannot be found at the time and place where they are needed and that hiring the aliens will not adversely affect the wages and working conditions of similarly employed U.S. workers.[42] The H-2A and H-2B visas may not be issued for more than one-year increments and for no more than a total of three years.

The H-3 visa is for persons coming to the United States to receive training not available in their home country; medical training is statutorily excluded. The program must be one that is not meant as a substitute for productive employment.[43] The training program is not one in which citizens or resident workers are usually employed but is one which intends to benefit the beneficiary in pursuing a career outside of the United States. The person will be admitted for the length of the training program but not for more than two years, and the H-3 visa holder will not be able to gain readmittance under an H or L visa until she has been outside of the United States for at least six months.[44]

The H-4 visa is for the spouse and children of H-1, H-2 and H-3 visa holders. The H-4 visa holder cannot accept employment unless specifically approved by USCIS.

An employer who dismisses an H-1B or H-2B worker before the expiration of her visa must pay the reasonable cost of her return trip abroad.

Media Representatives—I Visas

I visas are for representatives of foreign press, radio, film, television or other media, provided that U.S. citizens are granted reciprocal privileges.

Exchange Visitors—J Visas[45]

The J-1 visa is issued to persons accepted to participate in exchange visitor programs designated by the United States Information Agency (USIA). J visas are valid for up to one year and may be extended according to the length of the program. J visa holders cannot change their status to any other visa classification except "A" (foreign government official) or "G" (representative to international organization). A person

---

in the Internal Revenue Code of 1954 and the Fair Labor Standards Act of 1938. The annual quota for H-2B workers is 66,000.

41. Domestic workers are defined as U.S. citizens or lawful permanent residents.

42. Additional requirements imposed by the Department of Labor include the following: (1) the job must be in the employer's regular business, (2) the contemplated time period for the work must be reasonable, (3) the number of foreign workers being requested must be reasonable for the job, and (4) the employer is not hiring foreign workers in lieu of looking for domestic workers. 20 C.F.R. §§621 and 655.

43. 8 C.F.R. §214.2(h)(7).

44. 8 C.F.R. §214.2(h)(13)(v).

45. *See* 8 U.S.C. §1101 (a) (15) (J), Sec. 101(a)(15)(j); 8 U.S.C. §1182(e), Sec. 212(e); 8 C.F.R. §214.2(j); 22 C.F.R. §§41.65, 514.

entering on a J visa may be subject to a two-year foreign residency requirement, where she must first return to her home country for two years prior to being eligible to return to the United States except as an A, G, H or L nonimmigrant.[46] Whether or not a person is required to fulfill the residency requirement will depend on (1) whether the program sponsoring the applicant was funded in whole or in part by either the United States or the applicant's government, (2) whether the applicant's educational or skills training was designated as one needed by her home country (as certified by the USIA), or (3) whether the applicant came to the United States in order to receive graduate medical training or education.

The J-2 visa is for the spouse and children of J-1 visa holders. The J-2 visa holder may obtain permission to work from USCIS, provided it is work for her own support and not for the support of the principal exchange visitor.

Within the broader category of exchange visas is a program which permits nearly 23,000 youth from abroad to work for American families as childcare workers under the "au pair program." The program was initially limited to nationals of Europe when it began in 1986 but was broadened in 1996 to include nationals of any country with which the United States has diplomatic relations.[47] As with other J visa holders, au pairs come to the United States and are subsequently hired by individual families through approved programs.[48]

Fiancées or Fiancés of U.S. Citizens—K Visas[49]

The K-1 visa is designed to allow a person who intends to marry a U.S. citizen to enter the country. The K-1 visa entrant and the U.S. citizen must have met at least two years prior to filing the petition, and the visa holder is allowed to enter the country for 90 days and get married within that time. The K-2 visa is available for the minor children of the K-1 visa holder.

The enactment of the Legal Immigration Family Equity Act[50] included a provision creating a special K-3 nonimmigrant visa for persons who are overseas and married to U.S. citizens and the beneficiaries of a petition filed on their behalf by their citizen spouses. The visa was created due to the lengthy period for adjudicating immediate relative immigrant visas by USCIS and the Department of State. K-3 visa holders and their minor children, who are issued K-4 visas, are permitted to enter the country for two years while awaiting approval of their immigrant visas. Holders of K visas may not change their nonimmigrant classification.

---

46. *See* 8 U.S.C. § 1258(3), Sec. 248(3).

47. *See* 22 C.F.R. § 514.31.

48. For a critique of the program, *see* Joan Fitzpatrick, *The Gender Dimension of U.S. Immigration Policy*, 9 Yale J. L. & Feminism 23, 35–37 (1997); *see also A Response to "Nannygate": Untangling U.S. Immigration Law to Enable American Parents to Hire Foreign Childcare Providers*, 70 Ind. L. J. 305 (1993).

49. 8 U.S.C. § 1101 (a)(15)(K), 101(a)(15)(K); 8 C.F.R. § 214.2(k); 22 C.F.R. § 41.81.

50. Pub. L. No. 106-553, § 1101–04, 114 Stat. 2762A-141 (2000).

Intracompany Transferees—L Visas

The L-1 visa allows international corporations to transfer employees temporarily to the United States. The person must have been continuously employed by the petitioning firm outside the United States at least one year within the three preceding years. The law further requires that the prospective employment in the United States be in a managerial or executive capacity or require specialized knowledge.[51] The L visa holder is generally allowed to remain in the United States for five to seven years and may apply for lawful permanent residency while in the country. L visas are available to small, closely-held companies, large international corporations,[52] as well as religious and nonprofit organizations.[53] In certain instances, employers may apply for "blanket" permits to allow for more than one employee to enter the United States at a time under the L visa instead of applying for each employee individually.[54] The spouse and children of the L-1 recipient may be allowed to enter the country as L-2 visa holders but may not work.

Vocational Students—M Visas[55]

The M-1 visa is for students who wish to enter the country temporarily to pursue a course of study at a recognized vocational or non-academic institution.[56] The period of stay is granted for either one year or for the period of study plus 30 days, whichever is less, and is renewable. The M-2 visa is issued to family members who may stay as long as the M-1 visa holders. M visa holders ordinarily cannot accept employment, but M-1 holders may work if the employment is part of their course of study.

Extraordinary Ability in Arts and Science—O Visas

The O-1A visa is for persons of extraordinary ability in the sciences, arts, education, business or athletics which has been demonstrated by "sustained national or international acclaim." USCIS interprets the statute as encompassing a broad field of activities, which include the culinary arts, choreographers, directors, set designers, makeup artists and animal trainers.[57] The O-1B visa is for persons in the motion picture or television production business who have a "demonstrated record of extraordinary achievement." There is no foreign residence requirement for persons in the O-1A or O-1B categories, though they must demonstrate an intent to remain in the United States only temporarily. The O-2 visa is for persons entering for the purpose of assisting in a performance where the beneficiary is "an integral part" of the performance. The issuance of this visa requires "consultation" with the appropriate

---

51. For additional guidance on the requirement of "specialized knowledge," see Campbell and Taggert, *The International Business Client and Nonimmigrant Visas*, 11 Colo. Law. 2545, 2550 (1982).

52. *See Matter of Aphrodite Investments, Ltd.*, 17 I. & N. Dec. 530 (Reg. Com. 1980).

53. *See Matter of Church of Scientology Int'l*, 19 I & N Dec. 593 (Comm'r 1988); 9 FAM 41.54 N7.3.

54. *See* 8 U.S.C. § 1184(c)(2)(A), Sec. 214(c)(2)(A).

55. *See* 8 C.F.R. § 214.2(M); 22 C.F.R. § 41.61.

56. 8 U.S.C. § 1101(a)(15)(M), Sec. 101 (a)(15)(M).

57. 8 C.F.R. § 214.2(o)(3)(ii).

union. The O-3 visa is for the spouse and minor children of the O visa recipient. The beneficiary of the O visa may be admitted at the discretion of the Attorney General for a sufficient period to attend the event for which she is admitted,but not to exceed three years.[58]

Athletes and Performing Artists—P Visas[59, 60]

The P-1A visa is for a person who either performs as an athlete, individually or as part of a group or team, at an internationally recognized level of performance, while the P-1B visa is for a person who performs as part of an entertainment group that has been recognized internationally as being outstanding in the discipline for a sustained and substantial period of time.[61] The applicant must have had a substantial relationship with the group for at least one year, though waivers are available for the international recognition and one-year substantial relationship requirements.[62] This visa designation is also for persons who are entering as athletes or entertainers for a specific competition or performance. USCIS has not allowed persons to enter as P-1s when they come solely for promotional and non-performance guest appearances or sport camps. The P-2 visa is issued to a person coming to the United States as an artist or entertainer under a reciprocal exchange program. P-3 visas are for persons entering the country as artists or entertainers, individually or with a group, "under a program which is culturally unique." P-4 visas are for the spouse and children of P visa recipients.

The P visa applicant must have a residence abroad which she has no intention of abandoning, though she is permitted to demonstrate dual intent. In general, P visa recipients may remain in the United States for as long as the Attorney General specifies in order to perform in the event for which the nonimmigrant is admitted. In the case of an individual athlete, she may be admitted for an initial period of up to five years and may be granted an extension for five additional years. A P-2 and a P-3 entrant may not be readmitted in that status unless she has remained outside the United States for three months after the most recent admission (the Attorney General may waive this provision in cases of individual tours if undue hardship would result).[63]

International Cultural Exchange Program—Q Visas[64]

The Q visa is for persons who enter to participate in specially designated programs by the Attorney General, providing the participant the opportunity to obtain practical training and to share the history, culture and traditions of her country in a school, museum, business or similar establishment.[65] The Q visa recipient must receive the

58. 8 C.F.R. §214.2(o)(6).

59. *See* 8 U.S.C. §§1101(a)(15)(P) and 1184(a)(2)(B), Sections 101(a)(15)(P) and 214(a)(2)(B).

60. The 1990 Act placed a limit of 25,000 per year on the P-1 and P-3 visas. *See* 8 U.S.C. §1184(g)(1)(C), Sec. 214(g)(1)(C).

61. The P-1A visa is for an athlete, and the P-1B visa is for a person performing as part of an entertainment group. Individual entertainers must get an O-1 visa.

62. 8 U.S.C. §1184(c)(4)(B), Sec. 214(c)(4)(B).

63. *See* 8 U.S.C. §1184(a)(2), Sec. 214(a)(2).

64. *See* 8 U.S.C. §1101 (a)(15)(Q), Sec. 101(a)(15)(Q).

65. 8 C.F.R. §214.2(q)(3)(iii)(A).

same wage and be employed under the same working conditions as U.S. workers. The person entering with a Q visa is allowed to remain for a period not to exceed fifteen months. Persons who enter the United States cannot be readmitted until they have been physically outside of the country for a minimum of one year.[66]

Q-2 visas are for persons from Northern Ireland and certain countries of Ireland under the age of 35 who may enter the United States to gain practical training and experience in conflict resolution.[67] These visas have an annual quota of 4,000, and the Q-2 visa holder is allowed to remain in the country for a maximum of three years.

Religious Occupations—R Visas[68]

Religious workers who have been members, not employees,[69] of a religious organization for two years preceding their application for admission may qualify for R visas. The religious organization must have a bona-fide not-for-profit status in the United States, and religious workers include ministers and persons working in their professional capacities in a religious vocation, such as cantors, liturgical workers, translators and broadcasters.[70] These visa recipients may not stay in the country for more than five years. The R visa does not require prior USCIS approval but must be approved by a U.S. consul if the applicant is overseas.[71]

Informants Against Criminal or Terrorist Organizations—S Visas

As part of the Violent Crime Control and Law Enforcement Act of 1994[72] Congress established a new S visa for the admission of persons possessing "critically reliable" information concerning a criminal or terrorist organization or enterprise and whose life would be in danger for providing the information. Persons determined by the Attorney General to possess critical information concerning a criminal enterprise or organization are granted S-5 visas while persons determined by both the Attorney General and the Secretary of State to possess critical information concerning a terrorist organization or enterprise are granted S-7s. No more than 250 persons per year may be admitted on S visas, and they may not remain in that status for more than three years. In order to maintain her status, the S visa holder is required to report to USCIS every three months and to not be convicted of any crime punishable by a term of imprisonment exceeding one year. Special provisions are provided for the adjustment of status of S visa holders, where a person who has provided substantial information leading to a successful investigation may be granted lawful permanent residency. S-7 visas are granted to family members of S visa holders.

---

66. 8 C.F.R. § 214.2(q)(2)(ii).
67. 8 U.S.C. § 1101(a)(15)(Q)(ii), Sec 101(a)(15)(Q)(ii).
68. *See* Chapter 8; *also see* 8 U.S.C. § 1101 (a)(15)(R), Sec. 101(a)(15)(R).
69. *Ten Acre Foundation. v. INS*, 892 F. Supp. 289 (D. D.C. 1995), *aff'd* 78 F.3d 693 (D.C. Cir. 1996).
70. 8 C.F.R. § 214.2(r)(2).
71. The 1990 Act also revised the special immigrant provisions relating to religious workers. *See* Discussion *infra* at Chapter 8.
72. Pub. L. No. 103-322, 108 Stat 1796 (1994).

North American Free Trade Agreement—TN and Other Visas

The North American Free Trade Agreement (NAFTA), which became effective on January 1, 1994, included a section dealing with nonimmigrant immigration issues.[73] The purpose of the immigration chapter of the agreement was to remove some of the restrictions on cross-border business travel at a professional level by persons from the signatory countries (Canada,[74] Mexico and the United States). NAFTA creates separate procedures for business travelers and provides a list of specified professions (e.g. research and design, manufacture, production, marketing, sales, distribution, public relations, etc.) which, if met by the applicant, would permit her entry. Applicants within these professions are not required to obtain a visa if they are from Canada, while persons from Mexico are required to obtain either a B-1 visa or a border crossing card.

Another category of visas created by NAFTA is the TN visa, which is similar to the H-1B except that the person may stay indefinitely; however, applicants must demonstrate that they do not plan to stay permanently. The visa covers a broader range of occupations, and the definition of "activities at a professional level" is work which requires a minimum of a "baccalaureate degree or appropriate credentials demonstrating status as a professional." Some examples of the professions included in this definition are accountants, architects, computer systems analysts, engineers, librarians, social workers and urban planners. A person coming to the United States on a TN visa must have an employer in the country and be able to prove qualification for the position. In addition, she must possess the requisite educational level and, if required in the jurisdiction where she will work, a license to engage in the profession in the United States. Canadians entering on a TN visa need only present the documentation at a pre-inspection point in Canada or at the border. Mexicans must apply first through a U.S. consul and submit the appropriate labor condition application required of H-1B's. Additionally, TN visas for Mexico are limited to 5,500 per year and must be renewed annually. Canadians and Mexicans seeking admission under TN visas must overcome the presumption of immigrant intent.

Victims of Severe forms of Trafficking in Persons—T Visa

The T visa was created as part of a larger effort to combat human trafficking and has an annual quota of 5,000. It is for persons who have been the victims of severe forms of human trafficking, where the person has assisted in the investigation or prosecution of trafficking and would suffer extreme hardship should she be forced to leave the United States.[75] T visa holders are allowed to remain in the United States for three years, although they may seek lawful permanent residency. The T visa is also available to the spouse, children and immediate family of the trafficking victim.

---

73. North American Free-Trade Agreement Implementation Act of 1993, Pub. L. No. 103-182, 107 Stat. 2057 (1993). Implementing regulations can be found at 58 Fed. Reg. 68, 526–28 (1993) and 58 Fed. Reg. 69, 226–28 (1993); *also see* 8 C.F.R. §§ 214.2(b)(4) and 214.6.

74. In addition, there was a previously signed agreement with Canada. *See* United States-Canada Free-Trade Agreement Implementation Act of 1988, Pub. L. No. 100-449, 102 Stat. 1851 (1988).

75. *See* Victims of Trafficking and Violence Protection Act of 2000, Pub. L. No. 106-386, § 1513, 114 Stat. 1478, 1533 (2000).

Humanitarian/Material Witness—U Visa

The U visa, like the T visa, was created as part of the Victims of Trafficking and Violence Protection Act of 2000[76] for law enforcement to be able to provide protection for material witnesses in the prosecution of a whole host of local, federal or state crimes beyond trafficking, including

> rape; torture; trafficking; incest; domestic violence; sexual assault; abusive sexual contact; prostitution; sexual exploitation; female genital mutilation; being held hostage; peonage; involuntary servitude; slave trade; kidnapping; abduction; unlawful criminal restraint; false imprisonment; blackmail; extortion; manslaughter; murder; felonious assault; witness tampering; obstruction of justice; perjury; or attempt, conspiracy, or solicitation to commit any of the above mentioned crimes.

U visas are limited to 10,000 per year and are granted for three years, although visa holders are allowed to seek lawful permanent residency after the three-year limit.

Spouse and Children of Certain Permanent Residents—V Visas

Due to the immigration quotas, many persons who were married to lawful permanent residents would not be able to obtain an immigrant visa for a number of years. As intending immigrants, they were ineligible for most nonimmigrant visas because they were unable to overcome the immigrant-intent presumption. To deal with this hardship, Congress created the V visa,[77] which was for persons who were the spouse or child under the age of 21 of a permanent resident of the United States and are beneficiaries of a visa petition filed on their behalf on or before the enactment of the Act of Congress[78] creating the new V visa and who have been waiting for at least three years following the filing of the original application.[79] The V visa was not for the "sons or daughters" of permanent residents, meaning children of permanent residents who are over the age of 21. By its terms. while this visa category still exists, it is would only be available to a select small number of people.

B. Nonimmigrant Visa Procedure

What follows below are flow charts which represent a variety of common scenarios encountered by persons going through the visa issuance and admission process. The first scenario involves an applicant who obtains a visa through a U.S. Consul abroad and then seeks admission, the second involves an applicant who has been inspected and admitted and then seeks extension or change and the third involves an applicant seeking an extension which is denied by USCIS.

76. Pub. L. No. 106-386, § 1513, 114 Stat. 1478, 1533 (2000).

77. See Legal Immigration Family Equity Act, Pub. L. No. 106-553, § 1102, 114 Stat. 2762 (2000).

78. The LIFE Act was enacted on December 21, 2000.

79. The statute contemplates that either a preference petition had been pending for three years or that the preference petition has been approved and the person has been waiting for at least three years for the issuance of an immigrant visa.

1. Overseas Applicant

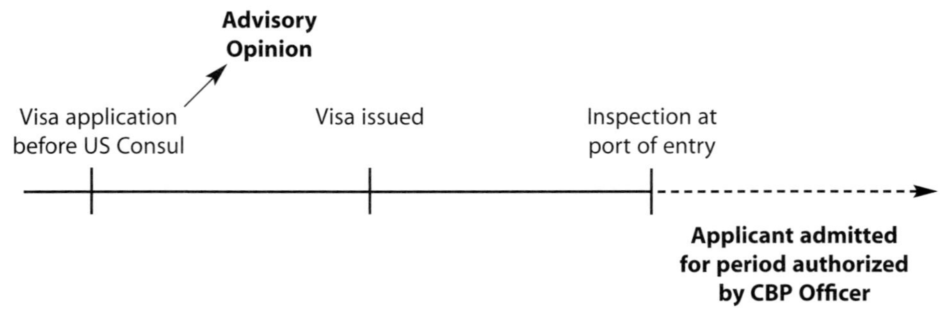

Visas may only be sought by making an application at a U.S. Consulate. Consular offices are only found outside of the United States. In issuing a visa, the consular officer may seek a legal opinion in the form of an "advisory opinion" from the Visa Office of the Department of State, though most applications do not involve advisory opinions and are made or rejected based upon the application. The approved visa, once issued, is placed on a page in the applicant's passport, and this allows the person to seek admission to the United States. On its face, the visa includes the date of issue, the type of visa and its period of validity. Upon arrival the traveler must present herself for "inspection" at the port of entry before a CBP officer. The CBP inspection officer determines how long the person may remain in the country based upon the visa which was issued. This determination is based upon information received from the applicant at the time of inspection. (The person may also face the removal process based upon the information received at inspection.)

2. Applicant Seeking Extension or Change of Status

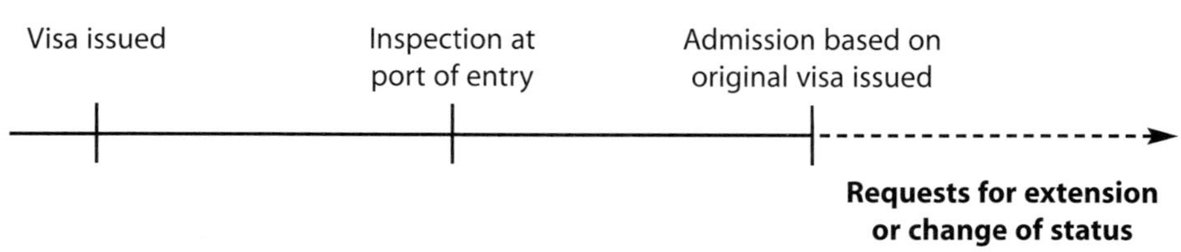

The third chart shows the process from visa issuance to admission. Following admission, the applicant's stay in the United States is controlled by USCIS. While the applicant's initial period of authorized stay is set by a CBP officer, future extensions or changes of nonimmigrant visa status are set by USCIS. At a later point in this chapter, there will be a more extensive discussion on extensions, maintenance and change of status. As will be seen, an applicant's ability to extend or change status will be contingent on her compliance with the conditions of her initial permission to enter.

3. Applicant's Request for Change or Extension of Status Is Denied

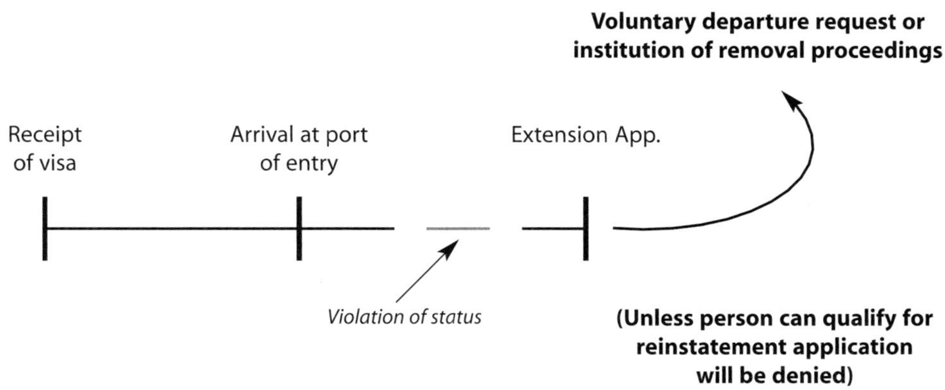

In the above chart, we follow the consequence of a violation of status on a request for change of status. In the event there is no justifiable reason for the violation, the application will be denied, and the person will be forced to either leave the country voluntarily or face removal proceedings.

* * *

The Chart below attempts to present the many nonimmigrant visas according to their broader categories, which are pleasure, study, work and miscellaneous. The chart further notes the limits, if any, which the statute places on extensions following admission to the United States, as well as other special characteristics of the visa.

In recent years, increased attention has been focused on immigration law, particularly insofar as it affects our domestic economy. The public's perception that increases in the admission of foreign workers diminishes opportunities for domestic workers has had a significant impact on the formulation of policy. This perception clashes with the traditional policy in immigration law of encouraging family reunification and protecting those fleeing persecution. Further strains are added to the formulation of a coherent immigration policy when the industry demands for skilled and unskilled workers are not met by the available pool of U.S. workers.[80] Congress has thus far

80. The provision for temporary agricultural workers which was discussed earlier is an example of one of these clashes. The "temporary" agricultural worker provisions were designed to accommodate the important domestic agricultural industry, but these provisions conflict with the restrictions on nonimmigrant visas for persons coming to the United States for a short period of time. A strong argument could be made that if the rules applicable to H-2A's were applied to nonimmigrant workers under the H-1B, L, O and P categories, many would be denied admission.

Nonimmigrant Visa Chart

	Length of Stay	Remarks
Pleasure (no work)		
B-1, B-2 Tourist	Increments of not less than six months but not more than one year.	Very limited stays in the United States.
Visa Waiver	No longer than 90 days.	Very limited rights.
Study (work must be authorized)		
F-1 Student	Duration of status in consideration of the full course of study.	Can be used to gain experience for later permanent residency qualification. Status monitored by Designated School Official (DSO). Must reimburse school district if attending a public elementary/ secondary school.
M-1 Vocational Student	Short periods.	Must show proof of need for education for use in home country.
H-3 Trainee	Length of training.	Cannot remain in the United States for more than two years.
J-1 Exchange Student	Duration of status.	Two-year foreign residency requirement for some.
Work (with specific employer)		
A Diplomats	Duration of assignment at Embassy or Consulate.	Only taken away by Secretary of State.
G International Organization	Duration of work with organization.	Indefinite stay.
NATO	Duration of work with NATO.	Indefinite stay.
H-1B Specialty Occupation	Increments of three years with a maximum of six years.	Subject to a quota. Allows for dual intent. Bridge to LPR. Status is portable.
H-2A Agricultural Worker	Maximum of three years. May return to the United States again after six months.	No quota. No bridge to LPR. Requires employer's "serious recruitment" of U.S. workers.
H-2B Other Workers	Increments of one year with a maximum of three years.	195,000 quota. Labor certification required. Must be for a temporary position.
L-1 Intracompany Transferee	Three years plus possible extension of a maximum of seven years for executives and five years for those with specialized knowledge.	Allows for dual intent. Statutory expedited treatment of application.
O Extraordinary Ability in Arts and Science	Maximum of three years.	No foreign residence requirement.
P Athletes	Five years plus possible five-year extension.	

	Length of Stay	Remarks
Work (with specific employer)		
E Treaty Trader and Investor	Possible indefinite stay in the United States as long as investment or trade is maintained. Extensions of up to two-year increments.	Nonimmigrant alternative to permanent residency.
R Religious Worker	Maximum of five years.	
TN NAFTA	Indefinite extensions.	Similar to H-1B visas. Canadians in certain professions may be admitted without having to seek visas at a U.S. Consulate. Mexican visas limited to 5,500 and must be renewed annually.
Miscellaneous		
D Crewmember	29-day validity.	Severely restricts ability to change status or obtain permanent benefits.
C Transit	Very short with no extension.	No change of status.
S Informants Against Criminals and Terrorists	Increments of three months for a maximum of two years.	Limited to 100 annually.
T Victims of Severe Trafficking	Unclear, but probably one-year extensions.	Limited to 5,000 annually. Eligible for permanent residency after three years.
U Humanitarian/ Material Witness	Not clear but probably one-year extensions.	Limited to 10,000 annually. Eligible for permanent residency after three years.
K Fiancé	90 days.	Must marry. No change of status.
K3 Spouse and Children of U.S. Citizen	None (admitted until adjustment of status).	Must be married to a U.S. citizen and seeking admission in lieu of an immigrant visa. Must be in the country where the marriage took place.

been unable to address most of these issues, and the inability on the part of the executive and legislative branches to adequately resolve these issues may cause the Department of Homeland Security to deal with the problems through regulations.[81]

An important point to remember when reading the following cases is that there is a much greater supply of foreign workers and willing employers in the United States

81. The reader should compare the period nonimmigrants are generally permitted to stay in the United States with that allowed for holders of H, L and E visas.

than can be accommodated under the immigrant quota system. Since there are fewer limits on the number of nonimmigrant visas which may be issued, employers and foreigners are constantly searching for new methods of using nonimmigrant visas to alleviate the labor supply shortage.

C. Pleasure Visa (B-2)

Matter of Healy and Goodchild

17 I. & N. Dec. 22 (BIA 1979)

BY: Milhollan, Chairman; Maniatis, Appleman, Maguire, and Farb, Board Members

* * *

Mr. Healy, a native and citizen of Ireland and a resident of Australia, applied for a nonimmigrant visa at the United States Consulate General in Melbourne, Australia, for the stated purpose of visiting this country for a 1-month period. On September 7, 1977, he was issued a B-2 nonimmigrant visitor for pleasure visa, valid for multiple applications for admission to the United States within 3 months from the date of issuance. On that same date, Mr. Goodchild, a native and citizen of Great Britain, was issued a B-2 nonimmigrant visitor visa at the United States Embassy in London, England, which was valid for multiple applications for admission to this country within 6 months from the date of issuance.

In the course of inspection upon their respective arrivals in New York, each applicant was found to be in possession of a letter of acceptance for admission to a 9-month course of study at the Claymont School for Continuing Education, an institution which has not been approved for attendance by nonimmigrant students. The applicants were thereupon charged with excludability under section 212(a)(26) as nonimmigrant students not in possession of valid nonimmigrant student visas and under section 212(a)(19) as aliens who procured their visas by willfully misrepresenting material facts.

In the consolidated exclusion proceedings that ensued, the immigration judge found Mr. Goodchild excludable as charged under section 212(a)(26) but held that the charge under section 212(a)(19) could not be sustained in his case. As noted above, Mr. Healy was found excludable under both section 212(a)(26) and section 212(a)(19). The immigration judge's findings as to each charge will be examined in turn.

* * *

Under section 101(a)(15) of the Act, every alien is considered to be an immigrant unless he is able to establish that he is entitled to nonimmigrant status under one of the specified classes of nonimmigrants designated by Congress in section 101(a)(15)(A) through section 101(a)(15)(L). Section 214(b) of the Act, 8 U.S.C. 1184(b); 22 C.F.R. 41.10. Moreover, the burden is upon the alien to establish that he is entitled to the nonimmigrant classification and type of nonimmigrant visa for which he is an applicant. 22 C.F.R. 41.10; cf. section 291 of the Act, 8 U.S.C. 1361.

The applicants conceded that they are not entitled to status as nonimmigrant students under section 101(a)(15)(F) inasmuch as the Claymont School has not been approved by the Attorney General or his delegate.[1] Each applicant further acknowledged that the principal purpose of his visit was to participate in the basic course to which he was admitted at the Claymont School, that he had paid a deposit of $100 toward the $2,750 tuition for the course prior to seeking admission to the United States, and that he had been in attendance at the school since his parole into this country.

Counsel does not seriously contest the fact that the Claymont School is a school and that the applicants are students within the ordinary usage of those terms and we are satisfied that they are properly classifiable as such. Counsel argues instead that section 101(a)(15)(F) is solely concerned with alien students destined for approved schools. Since the Claymont School has not been accredited by the Service, he insists that the applicants are not subject to the provisions of section 101(a)(15)(F) of the Act but are admissible as visitors for pleasure. We disagree.

It is clear that absent Service approval of the school to which an alien student is destined, he may not establish eligibility for a nonimmigrant student visa under section 101(a)(15)(F). It does not follow ipso facto, however, that an alien bound for the United States for the primary purpose of pursuing a course of study at an unapproved school is entitled to status as a nonimmigrant visitor for pleasure under section 101(a)(15)(B). That such alien is not entitled to status as a nonimmigrant visitor is evident from the express terms of section 101(a)(15)(B) which includes among those classifiable as nonimmigrants:

> an alien (other than one coming for the purpose of study or of performing skilled or unskilled labor or as a representative of foreign press, radio, film, or other foreign information media coming to engage in such vocation) having a residence in a foreign country which he has no intention of abandoning and who is visiting the United States temporarily for business or temporarily for pleasure; ...

1. The purpose and program of the basic course at the Claymont School are described as follows in excerpts from the institution's 1977–78 catalog:

> The Claymont School for Continuous Education is founded on the principle that true education must include techniques of self-perfecting in mind, body, and spirit and must realize the potential latent in normal men and women.... The daily schedule normally begins at 6 a.m. All students and staff share in psychological and spiritual exercises until breakfast. After breakfast, 4–5 hours are devoted to practical activities involving the acquisition of a wide variety of skills such as cooking, breadmaking, carpentry, housepainting, plumbing and electrical work, gardening, logging, animal and vegetable husbandry, repairs and special crafts and skills such as spinning, woodworking and pottery to meet particular needs....

While the statutory term "pleasure" is not defined in the Act, State Department regulation 22 C.F.R. 41.25 provides the following definition:

> (c) The term "pleasure", as used in section 101(a)(15)(B) of the Act, refers to legitimate activities of a recreational character, including tourism, amusement, visits with friends or relatives and rest; medical treatment, or activities of a fraternal, social or service nature.

It is thus apparent from the explicit language of section 101(a)(15)(B), as supplemented by the foregoing regulation, that the B-2, or visitor for pleasure, nonimmigrant category was not intended to be a "catch-all" classification available to all who wish to come to the United States temporarily for whatever purpose. Instead, as is the case with the other nonimmigrant classes enumerated by Congress in section 101(a)(15), section 101(a)(15)(B) was designed to encompass a specific, defined class of aliens; by the express terms of the statute, that class does not include aliens coming for the purpose of study. To accept counsel's theory would not only disregard the explicit language of section 101(a)(15)(B) but would undermine the requirements for entitlement to student status under section 101(a)(15)(F) and the detailed regulations which have been promulgated to implement that section. See 8 C.F.R. 214.2(f); 8 C.F.R. 214.3; 8 C.F.R. 214.4.

We accordingly hold that an alien bound for the United States for the primary purpose of study is not admissible as a nonimmigrant visitor for pleasure as defined by section 101(a)(15)(B) but must instead establish his entitlement to nonimmigrant student status under section 101(a)(15)(F) and the pertinent regulations. Cf. *Matter of Le Floch*, 13 I & N. Dec. 251 (BIA 1969). We recognize that our decision in effect declares unapproved educational institutions such as the Claymont School to be unavailable to alien students. Our holding, however, is in keeping with the clear statutory scheme drawn by Congress which deems all aliens to be immigrants unless they can demonstrate that they qualify for status under one of the distinct nonimmigrant classes enumerated in section 101(a)(15). The dispositive fact is that Congress made no provision thereunder for aliens destined for the United States for the primary purpose of pursuing a course of study at an unapproved school.

* * *

The remaining issue before us concerns the finding of excludability under 212(a)(19) with respect to Mr. Healy. At the hearing, Mr. Goodchild testified that he had requested a visa valid for 9 months, telling the consul at the Embassy in London that he was "coming to a community where we practice all sorts of living" (Tr. p. 27). He conceded that he did not disclose to the counsul that he intended to take an actual course of study here but accepted as accurate the immigration judge's summation that he had "more or less told them everything about the place except that it was a school" (Tr. p. 29). On the basis of this testimony, the immigration judge concluded, with the concurrence of the Service, that a charge under section 212(a)(19) had not been sustained with respect to Mr. Goodchild.

Mr. Healy testified that he had had but one brief conversation with a State Department employee at the United States Consulate in Melbourne prior to obtaining his visa. He stated that he was told by that employee when he visited the Consulate to inquire about procedures for coming to the United States, that he need only fill out a visitor visa application form if he planned to remain here for 1 month or less but that he would have to produce documentary evidence of his intention to return to Australia if he contemplated a longer stay. He testified that he told the employee that he would apply for a 1-month visit but would probably seek an extension of his stay from the Service after his arrival in this country.

Mr. Healy maintained that his visa was issued on the basis of that single conversation, which involved no discussion as to the purpose of his trip, and of the visitor visa application form which he contemporaneously completed and returned to the Consulate employee. On his application form, Mr. Healy responded to Items 18 and 19 as follows:

18. What is the purpose of your trip? "to visit America"

19. How long do you plan to stay in the USA? "one month"

In response to the inquiry set forth in Item 20, "At what address will you reside in the USA?", Mr. Healy provided the address of the Claymont School.

At several points in the course of the hearing, Mr. Healy indicated that notwithstanding his acceptance at the Claymont School for a 9-month course of study and his payment of a $100 deposit to the school, he had not firmly decided to remain in this country for the duration of the course at the time he applied for his visa. He stated that he instead intended to visit the school and, if he found that course to be suitable, to apply to the Service for an extension of his stay. Mr. Healy explained that he would have requested additional time for his visit when he initially applied for a visa but felt he would have encountered difficulties in producing documentation to establish the requisite ties in Australia since he had terminated his employment in that country.

* * *

The immigration judge held that Mr. Healy had willfully misrepresented a material fact within the ambit of section 212(a)(19) by indicating that he was destined for a 1-month visit to the United States when he in fact knew that he was coming to study for a 9-month period. While the record is not free of ambiguities, we are, on balance, unable to agree with the conclusion reached by the immigration judge.

In determining whether an alien has procured his visa by fraud or willful misrepresentation of a material fact within the meaning of section 212(a)(19), it is appropriate to examine the circumstances as they existed at the time the visa was issued. Under the rule of law announced herein, an alien's trip to the United States for the primary purpose of participating in a course of study at an educational institution that has not been approved by the Service may not be characterized as a "visit" of a nature which would qualify him for status as a visitor for pleasure under section 101(a)(15)(B). This precise issue, however, has not previously been addressed by the Board. Given the uncertain state of the law at the time Mr. Healy applied for his visa, it is not unlikely that he considered the declared purpose of his trip, "to visit America," to be an accurate statement of his intent.[6] Moreover, we find Mr. Healy's explanation with respect to his stated anticipated length of stay plausible, if not compelling.

In interpreting the term "willful" for purposes of section 212(a)(19), the Court of Appeals for the Third Circuit held in a recently decided case that knowledge of the falsity of a representation satisfies the fraud and willfulness requirements of that section. Suite v. INS, 594 F.2d 972 (3 Cir.1979). We are not persuaded that a finding of willfulness is warranted on the particular facts of this case, and we accordingly hold that Mr. Healy in not inadmissible under section 212(a)(19) of the Act for having procured his visa by fraud or by willfully misrepresenting a material fact.

In so holding, we recognize that the Act places the burden on the alien to demonstrate that he is not inadmissible under one of the exclusionary grounds enumerated in section 212(a). Section 291 of the Act, 8 U.S.C. 1361. We believe, however, that given the harsh consequences of a finding of excludability under the first clause of section 212(a)(19), the factual basis of such finding should be subject to close scrutiny. This is particularly true where the alleged fraud or misrepresentation involves a disputed issue with respect to an alien's subjective intent.

In accordance with the foregoing discussion, we shall order each applicant excluded and deported solely on the ground of inadmissibility set forth in section 212(a)(20) of the Act.

Notes

1. Had these applicants for admission come to the United States following enactment of IIRAIRA, how might their cases have been handled?

2. Each nonimmigrant classification has its own peculiar rules which the applicant must qualify for in order to be admitted. The role of the CBP officer at the port of entry, in addition to determining whether the person falls within one of the grounds of inadmissibility, is to make sure that the person is entering under the proper visa.

3. An applicant who arrives at a port of entry with a tourist visa and is seeking admission to the United States must overcome a presumption that she is an intending immigrant. 8 U.S.C. § 1184(b), Sec. 214(b) provides that "[e]very alien (other than a nonimmigrant described in subparagraph (H)(i) or (L) of section 101(a)(15)) shall be presumed to be an immigrant until he establishes to the satisfaction of the consular officer, at the time of application for a visa, and the immigration officers, at the time of application for admission, that he is entitled to a nonimmigrant status under section 101(a)(15)." How can this presumption be overcome by the applicant at the border? Why should it not be enough that the person has already been screened once by a consular officer when obtaining the visa in the first place?

---

6. We note that unlike Mr. Goodchild, Mr. Healy apparently was not afforded an opportunity to fully discuss the purpose of his trip with a consular officer prior to the issuance of his visa.

4. In addition to the requirement that a nonimmigrant have an unrelinquished domicile abroad, she must also satisfy the consular officer and CBP that the visit will be temporary, that she will depart the United States at the end of her stay, that she has permission to enter a foreign country at the end of the visit, that she has sufficient funds to carry out the purpose of the visit and that her passport is valid for at least six months following admission.[82] (The passport requirement does not apply to Canadians, Mexicans and citizens of certain countries with reciprocity agreements with the United States.) What might be the reason for the requirement that the person seeking admission has advance permission to enter a foreign country at the end of her visit to the United States?

5. **Expedited Removal and the Admission of Nonimmigrants.** Consider the following scenario which was reported by the Expedited Removal Study and detailed in its report:[83]

> Mr. G is a thirty-two year old Russian software engineer. He has an advanced degree, a successful job, and a wife and children in Russia. At the suggestion of a friend of his who worked in the same field in Silicon Valley, he decided to visit the United States to explore the possibilities of finding future employment in the computer industry and the various legal avenues open to him for obtaining this employment. His friend suggested that he bring his resume and his diploma so that he could talk with the representatives of some California-based companies. Mr. G arrived in the United States on September 25, 1998. He was traveling with a valid passport and visitor's visa. He intended to return to his family and job in Russia at the end of his authorized stay in the United States.
>
> Mr. G had filled out an I-94 (Arrival-Departure Record) on the plane, but did not provide his address. He was planning to stay with his friend in California, but did not have the address readily accessible. When he arrived at San Francisco International Airport, an immigration officer addressed him in English. When it was apparent that his English was limited, the immigration officer asked an employee of the airlines to interpret. The interview was conducted in Russian, but because the employee's ability to speak Russian was limited, Mr. G had a difficult time understanding what was happening.
>
> The immigration officer asked Mr. G to fill in the address where he would be staying. Mr. G pulled out a folder which contained the address and other personal papers. The officer then asked to search the folder and found copies of Mr. G's resume and diploma. At this point, the immigration officer concluded that Mr. G had come to the United States to seek or accept unauthorized employment. He would not listen to Mr. G's explanation that he had

82. *See* 8 C.F.R. § 212.1.

83. *See* Karen Musalo, Expedited Removal Study: Report on the First Two Years of Implementation 76–77 (1999).

> a job and a family in Russia. Mr. G was then given two choices: to either sign some papers and withdraw his application for admission, or be barred from entry into the United States for five years. Because all the papers were in English, Mr. G could not read what he was signing. He chose to withdraw his application for admission to the United States. He was handcuffed to a chair at the airport and held for two hours before being taken to Oakland County Jail.
>
> Mr. G was not allowed to contact anyone until he arrived at the jail. He called the friend with whom he planned to stay. His friend tried to contact an attorney, but was unsuccessful because it was a Friday night. His friend was finally able to retain an attorney on Sunday, and they went together to San Francisco International Airport to try to intercept Mr. G before he was returned to Russia. The INS did not allow Mr. G to speak with the attorney. The INS claimed that Mr. G had twice been offered the options of withdrawing his application for admission or being barred for five years from entry into the United States. The attorney asked the immigration officer whether Mr. G had understood the options. The immigration officer stated that he had understood his options because they were translated in Russian with the assistance of a telephonic interpreter. Nevertheless, Mr. G was never given copies of the papers he signed. Nor were the papers ever translated for him. Mr. G was sent back to Russia and told that he had to begin anew the process of applying for entrance into the United States. According to his friend in California, Mr. G was shocked at the way he was treated, especially since he was traveling with valid documents. At this point he is very discouraged with his exposure to what he ironically calls American "democracy" and is not sure whether he will ever return.

Is this what would have happened to Healy and Goodchild if they had arrived after expedited removal went into effect?

1. Visa Waiver Program for Selected Countries

Under the 1986 Act, Congress established a pilot program, which was made permanent and is now referred to as the "Visa Waiver Program (VWP)," to expedite the admission of visitors to the United States from certain countries for which the Department of State has substantially high approval rates for the issuance of tourist visas. Persons from these so-called low risk countries are allowed to board flights as long as they possess authorization to travel under the VWP through the Electronic System for Travel Authorization (ESTA),[84] a machine-readable passport with biometric

---

84. As of January 2009, ESTA approval is required for all travelers under the VWP for entry into the United States. This free, automated system allows DHS to screen eligible visitors for security purposes, and the application collects the same information as the paper I-94 arrival-departure form.

identifiers and a roundtrip airline ticket.[85] Persons who enter the United States under the waiver program are in essence traveling without a visa and are admitted to the United States for a period of not more than ninety days. The person is either admitted as a "waiver" visitor for business (WB) or tourism (WT). Those applying to enter under the waiver program remain subject to all of the grounds of inadmissibility[86] and are ineligible for an extension, change of status or adjustment of status to permanent residency unless they are immediate relatives or spouses of U.S. citizens.[87] If the person is found to be inadmissible at the port of entry or is determined to have been ineligible for entry under the waiver program, she is subject to removal without a hearing except where she claims a fear of persecution. However, the CBP inspector may, at his discretion, allow the applicant to withdraw her request for admission in order to avoid future inadmissibility consequences. The waiver program has thus far survived court challenges.[88]

In December 2015, the President signed into law an omnibus appropriations bill which included amendments to the Visa Waiver Program styled as the "Visa Waiver Improvement and Terrorist Travel Prevention Act of 2015" imposing additional requirements on certain persons otherwise eligible for the VWP. A person who is a national (including dual nationals of or who traveled to) Iran, Iraq, Libya, Somalia, Sudan, Syria and Yemen after March 1, 2011 are required to obtain visas to come to the U.S. The Secretary of DHS is authorized under certain circumstances to waive these requirements and may also expand the countries to which these requirements might be applied.

As of October 2017, the following countries were designated under the VWP: Andorra, Australia, Austria, Belgium, Brunei, Chile, Czech Republic, Denmark, Estonia, Finland, France, Germany, Greece, Hungary, Iceland, Ireland, Italy, Japan, Latvia, Liechtenstein, Lithuania, Luxembourg, Malta, Monaco, Netherlands, New Zealand, Norway, Portugal, San Marino, Singapore, Slovakia, Slovenia, South Korea, Spain, Sweden, Switzerland, Taiwan and the United Kingdom. For the most up to date list of countries, visit: https://www.dhs.gov/visa-waiver-program-requirements.

Notes

1. The VWP has been found to be constitutional notwithstanding equal protection and due process challenges. *See Gjerjaj v. Holder*, 691 F.3d 288, 292–93 (2d Cir. 2012) (signature on I-94W was sufficient to waive rights). However, one court has held that consideration should be made to whether the waiver was actually knowing and voluntary. *Bayo v. Napolitano*, 593 F.3d 495, 502–04 (7th Cir. 2010) (en banc).

---

85. According to the regulations, those arriving at a land border must also show proof of financial solvency. 8 C.F.R. § 217.2(c).

86. 8 C.F.R. § 217.4.

87. 8 C.F.R. § 217.3(a).

88. *See Prasil v. Meissner*, 941 F. Supp. 91 (N.D. Ill. 1996); *McGuire v. INS*, 804 F. Supp 1229 (N.D. Cal. 1992).

2. A person who enters the country as a VWP entrant remains eligible to apply for asylum or other forms of relief which provide protections from harm. 8 C.F.R. §§ 1208.2(c)(1)(iv) and (c)(3)(iii); *Matter of D-M-C-P-*, 26 I. & N. Dec. 644, 645–47 (BIA 2015).

D. Study Visas (F, J and M)

Matter of Yazdani

17 I. & N. Dec. 626 (BIA 1981)

BY: Milhollan, Chairman; Maniatis, Appleman, and Maguire, Board Members

In a decision dated May 2, 1980, an immigration judge found the respondent deportable under section 241(a)(9) of the Immigration and Nationality Act, 8 U.S.C. 1251(a)(9), for failure to comply with the conditions of her nonimmigrant student status, but granted her the privilege of voluntary departure in lieu of deportation. The respondent appealed from that decision. The appeal will be dismissed.

The respondent is a 19-year-old native and citizen of Iran who entered the United States as a nonimmigrant student bound for a course of study at the University of Utah. She was admitted for the duration of her student status. Prior to her embarkation for this country, the respondent had been accepted for admission by both the University of Utah and the University of San Francisco and had obtained the requisite Form I-20, Certificate of Eligibility for Nonimmigrant "F-1" Student Status, from each institution. The Form I-20 from the University of San Francisco apparently arrived too late for the respondent to secure a visa to attend that school, however, and her visa was issued for attendance at the University of Utah.

The record reflects that upon her arrival in the United States, the respondent proceeded to the University of Utah, met with the Director of International Student Services there, and obtained that official's permission to transfer to the University of San Francisco together with his signature on her transfer request, Form I-538. The Form I-538 was submitted with the respondent's Form I-94 and her Form I-20 from the University of San Francisco to the Salt Lake City office of the Immigration and Naturalization Service.[1] The respondent then enrolled at the University of San Francisco, beginning classes on September 24, 1979.

---

1. The I-538, I-94 and I-20 package was transmitted for processing to the Service office in Raymond, Montana, which returned the package to the respondent for completion of one of the forms. The respondent supplied the additional information and sent the forms back to Raymond. The respondent was subsequently informed in response to an inquiry regarding the status of her application that the package had been returned to the Salt Lake City office. The forms were apparently lost along the way and it appears that the respondent's application for permission to transfer was never adjudicated on the merits.

In December 1979, the respondent reported to the Service's San Francisco office pursuant to 8 C.F.R. 214.5. These deportation proceedings were thereafter instituted by the issuance of an Order to Show Cause charging the respondent with deportability for having violated the conditions of her status by transferring from the school which she was authorized to attend to another school without obtaining advance permission from the Service. At the deportation hearing that ensued on May 2, 1980, the immigration judge found the respondent deportable as charged. The District Director subsequently reviewed the respondent's file to determine whether she should be reinstated to student status and on October 17, 1980, decided against reinstatement.

Section 214(a) of the Act, 8 U.S.C. 1184(a), provides in pertinent part:

> The admission to the United States of any alien as a nonimmigrant shall be for such time and under such conditions as the Attorney General may by regulations prescribe....

Under the regulations promulgated by the Attorney General, a nonimmigrant student must establish as a condition for admission that she is destined to and intends to attend the school specified in her visa. 8 C.F.R. 214.2(f)(2). She may not transfer to another school unless she submits a valid Form I-20 completed by that school and the Service grants her permission to transfer. 8 C.F.R. 214.2(f)(4). The regulations further provide that a nonimmigrant applying for admission must agree to abide by all the terms and conditions of her admission. 8 C.F.R. 214.1(a).

On appeal, the respondent through counsel argues (1) that advance permission to transfer is not required by the regulations, and (2) that the respondent is in any event not deportable because she substantially complied with the terms of her status in making application for a transfer. The respondent's arguments must be rejected.

In support of her first contention, the respondent points to language in Service Operations Instruction 214.2(f)(2) which she quotes as follows:

> ... if a school transfer has been effected, and the transfer request is submitted to the office having jurisdiction over the school to which he has transferred, the receiving office may adjudicate the request unless there is good reason not to do so.

The respondent maintains that the foregoing Operations Instruction casts doubt upon whether it is necessary for a student, in order to remain in status, to make application for permission to transfer prior to transferring schools. We disagree.

As previously noted, a nonimmigrant student is admitted for the purpose of attending a specified school and the regulations expressly provide that a student shall not be eligible to transfer to another school unless the Service grants her permission to transfer. 8 C.F.R. 214.2(f). An alien who transfers to a school other than that which she was authorized to attend without first securing Service permission is in breach of the conditions of her status and is thereby deportable under section 241(a)(9).

There is no question but that the District Director in charge of a Service office may through a retroactive grant of a transfer request reinstate an alien's student status, and Operations Instruction 214.2(f)(2) recognizes that power.[2] The power, however, to reinstate student status or grant an extension of nonimmigrant stay lies within the exclusive jurisdiction of the District Director and neither the immigration judge nor the Board may review the propriety of the District Director's determinations. *Matter of Teberen*, 15 I & N. Dec. 689 (BIA 1976); *Matter of Hosseinpour*, 15 I & N. Dec. 191 (BIA 1975), aff'd, 520 F.2d 941 (5 Cir.1975 (tabled case); *Matter of Gallares*, 14 I & N. Dec. 250 (BIA 1972); *Matter of Sourbis*, 11 I & N. Dec. 335 (BIA 1965). In the instant case, the District Director considered and denied reinstatement.[3]

We find the cases relied upon by the respondent as authority for her alternative argument to be inapposite. At issue in *Mashi v. INS*, 585 F.2d 1309 (5 Cir.1978), was the proper interpretation to be given the statutory requirement that a nonimmigrant student "pursue a full course of study" (see 101(a)(15)(F)(i) of the Act, 8 U.S.C. 1101(a)(15)(F)(i)) under superceded regulations which, unlike the present regulations, set forth no specific objective criteria for compliance with that requirement. Noting that the "12 credit" minimum requirement of the present regulations (8 C.F.R. 214.2(f)(1a)(ii)) did not apply to Mr. Mashi, the court found that he was in fact pursuing a full course of study and could not be deported for failure to comply with the conditions of his status simply because his academic load briefly dropped below 12 credits in the course of one semester.

Although the court in *Mashi*, id., suggested in dictum that the same result might be reached on the facts before it under the present regulations, there is room for interpretation in determining whether the "12 credit" rule of 8 C.F.R. 214.2(f)(1a)(ii) has been satisfied that does not exist in determining whether an alien has received permission from the Service to transfer as required by 8 C.F.R. 214.2(f)(4). The question is whether there has been compliance, not whether there has been substantial compliance, with the regulation in question.

We likewise find the respondent's reliance on the Board's decisions in *Matter of Murat-Kahn*, 14 I & N. Dec. 465 (BIA 1973), and *Matter of C-*, 9 I & N. Dec. 100 (BIA 1960), to be misplaced. We held in those cases that a student's conviction which does not interfere with her studies so as to meaningfully disrupt her education does not constitute a failure to maintain status. The instant case is concerned not with an alleged disruption of studies but rather with a separate, distinct violation of status, transferring schools without Service permission, a breach specifically defined by the regulations.

Finally, we cannot agree with the respondent's characterization of her failure to secure advance permission to transfer as a "minor, highly technical" violation of her

---

2. The portion of the Operations Instruction quoted by the respondent is jurisdictional, concerned solely with designating the Service office which may assume jurisdiction over a given application for transfer.

3. Although the District Director gave no reasons for his denial of reinstatement in this case, it is possible that his decision was based upon a determination, which finds some support in the record (*see* Ex. 2, Form I-213), that the respondent never intended to attend the school specified on her visa. *See* Operations Instruction 214.2(f)(2). However, we need not speculate as to the District Director's rationale in view of our lack of jurisdiction over the question.

status. The regulation in question, 8 C.F.R. 214.2(f)(4), like other regulations governing the activities of nonimmigrant students, is an essential tool in the administration of our immigration laws. The widespread disregard of those regulations which would likely result from lax enforcement thereof would severely hamper the Service in fulfilling its responsibilities of keeping track of the thousands of alien students within our borders and of enforcing the immigration laws with respect to those students.

We note that the respondent appears to have acted in good faith in all of her dealings with the Government. However, so long as the enforcement officials of the Service choose to initiate proceedings against an alien and to prosecute those proceedings to a conclusion, the immigration judge and the Board must order deportation if the evidence supports a finding of deportability on the ground charged. See *Lopez-Telles v. INS*, 564 F.2d 1302 (9 Cir.1977); *Guan Chow Tok v. INS*, 538 F.2d 36 (2 Cir.1976); *Matter of Merced*, 14 I & N. Dec. 644 (BIA 1974).

The respondent admittedly transferred from the school designated on her visa to another school without first receiving permission from the Service, an action that constitutes a violation of the conditions of her nonimmigrant student status and a ground for deportation under section 241(a)(9) of the Act. We find that deportability has been established by clear, unequivocal and convincing evidence on the basis of the respondent's concessions.

E. Business Visas (B-1, E)

Jose Garavito, et al. v. Immigration and Naturalization Service

901 F.2d 173 (5th Cir. 1990)

Before Breyer, Torruella and Selya, Circuit Judges.

Breyer, Circuit Judge.

On June 20, 1987, the appellant, Jose Garavito, a lawyer from Colombia who owns a gasoline service station in San Juan, Puerto Rico, entered the United States with a B-1 visa, a visa that the law makes available to an "alien" who is "visiting the United States temporarily for business." 8 U.S.C. § 1101(a)(15)(B); see 22 C.F.R. § 41.12 (providing for classification symbols).

He subsequently asked the Immigration and Naturalization Service ("INS") to change his visa "classification" to category E-2, a classification available to an "alien," as well as to his "spouse and children," provided he comes from a country with an appropriate treaty and he comes here "solely to develop and direct the operations of an enterprise in which he has invested ... a substantial amount of capital." 8 U.S.C. § 1101(a)(15)(E)(ii). See also 8 U.S.C. § 1258 ("The Attorney General may ... authorize a change from any nonimmigrant classification to any other nonimmigrant classification...."); 8 C.F.R. § 248.1 (providing for changes between nonimmigrant classifications). The INS denied the request for the change in classification. The appellant claims that the denial is "arbitrary, capricious, an abuse of discretion or otherwise not in accordance with law," and therefore unlawful under the Administrative Procedure Act, 5 U.S.C. § 706(2)(A).

While we recognize that the INS has broad discretionary authority to decide when, or whether, a change in visa classification is proper, see, e.g., *Patel v. INS*, 738 F.2d 239, 242 (7th Cir.1984); *Wing Ding Chan v. INS*, 631 F.2d 978, 980–81 (D.C.Cir.1980), cert. denied, 450 U.S. 921, 101 S.Ct. 1371, 67 L.Ed.2d 349 (1981), we believe that, in this instance, its determination is indeed an "abuse of discretion." That is because one important reason the INS gave for denying the visa change rests upon an obviously false factual premise, namely that the appellant, in 1987, obtained a visa to visit the United States "for pleasure," rather than the "for business" visa that he actually obtained. In the circumstances of this case, that factual mistake is not simply harmless; rather, it could well determine the outcome.

The key background facts are the following:

1. The appellant, as we have said, is a citizen of Colombia, a nation that has a treaty with the United States entitling its citizens to enter the United States for commercial purposes. He is an attorney; he has a wife and two children; he owns an apartment and an office suite in Colombia.

2. In 1983 the appellant came to Puerto Rico to visit his brother, an American citizen. The appellant went to the INS offices, where the INS explained how he could stay in the United States, as a commercial investor, if he invested a "substantial amount of capital."

3. The appellant organized an investment corporation, acquired a gasoline service station, and invested $80,000 in the enterprise. In October 1983 the INS consequently changed his visa classification to "E" (but, by mistake, gave him a one year "E-1" foreign trade visa, instead of the proper "E-2" investor visa).

4. In June 1984 the appellant, who was in Curacao at the time, went to the American consulate to obtain an "E" visa, permitting him to reenter the United States. The consulate told him it could not give him the visa because he did not have with him the papers that showed he had invested $80,000 in an American commercial enterprise. Appellant then flew to San Juan and asked the immigration officers at the airport for an "E" visa. They admitted him provisionally, and in December the INS approved a "waiver," thereby permitting the appellant to remain in the United States with an "E-2" visa classification. The INS also permitted his wife and his children to come to San Juan with the same visa classification. The visa was valid until the end of 1986.

5. Between 1985 and 1987 the appellant's business in San Juan employed five to six persons. It took in revenues of $700,000 to $1 million annually.

6. In December 1986, the appellant left the United States, and returned in June 1987. He obtained a "B-1," "visiting ... for business" visa. In September he again ap-

plied to change the classification to "E-2" investor. This time, however, the INS denied his request; and it denied reconsideration of that denial.

In determining the significance of these background facts, we have examined the reasons the INS gave for denying the change of visa status. It gave four reasons for its initial denial. First, it said that the appellant had "been working without authorization from this Service." Second, it said that he had to show that he had not invested "in a marginal enterprise, solely for the purpose of earning a living," and he had not made this showing. Third, it said that he had not shown his investment was "substantial," and of an amount sufficient to permit him to function as an investor and not "simply as a skilled or unskilled worker." Fourth, it said that when he entered the United States in June, he had not done so as "a bona fide nonimmigrant visitor for pleasure," and he had therefore used his "tourist" visa as a "bridge" to enter without going to the American Embassy to get his visa. The INS seemed to find this last reason particularly important, for it quoted language from an administrative decision saying that the "B-2, visitor for pleasure, nonimmigrant category is not a 'catch all classification available to all who wish to come to the United States for whatever purposes....'" Immediately thereafter, the appellant submitted a request for reconsideration, accompanied by massive documentation of the scope and legitimacy of his business, and an explanation of why he did not go to the American Embassy in Colombia for the visa, namely that he had the relevant documentation in San Juan and thought it was easier to request a change of status there. The INS, while conceding that the documentation "might have overcome the issue of marginality and substantiality of investment," denied reconsideration.

We believe the INS must reconsider appellant's visa application because its denial of the application rests upon a mistake of fact. The INS opinion rests in significant part upon its belief that appellant entered the United States in 1987 using, not a "business" visa, but a "pleasure" visa. The INS in effect concedes the mistake. The only possible question is whether the mistake is significant—whether it is likely to have affected the outcome. In our view, the mistake is important enough to warrant a fuller reconsideration than the INS has given, for the following reasons:

First, the mistake is important in respect to the work-related reason that the INS provided for the denial. The only evidence in the record that the appellant improperly engaged in work consists of a four-sentence "special agent" report. According to the report, on January 8, 1988, two special agents went to appellant's service station and saw him "taking a client out to his car." The agents "oriented" the appellant about the 1986 immigration law, and "noticed during the orientation that [he] was answering the telephone and giving other employees instructions on what to do."

Given the fact that INS regulations say that "a temporary visitor for pleasure ... may not engage in any employment," 8 C.F.R. § 214.1(e), one can understand how the INS might have concluded that appellant violated the law on the false assumption that he was a pleasure visitor. The INS nowhere explains, however, what law would prevent a business visitor from making phone calls, giving employees instructions, or taking clients to their cars. Indeed, were the INS regulations to make such activity unlawful, it is difficult to see how foreign businessmen could conduct business within the United States, and it is equally difficult to see how any such regulation could fall within the lawful scope of the relevant statute. See 8 U.S.C. § 1101(a)(15)(B). Although appellant might not "qualify as a business visitor if his business activities almost exclusively involved the fulltime management of a United States enterprise," *In re Lawrence*, 15 I. & N. Dec. 418, 420 (1975); see *Pereira-Diaz v. INS*, 551 F.2d 1149, 1152–53 (9th Cir.1977), nothing in the record shows that this was the case.

Second, the investment-related reasons are not adequately supported. Nothing in the record suggests that the INS, on reconsideration, would find plaintiff's investments "marginal" or "insubstantial." The INS seemed to concede this fact in its reconsideration denial.

Third, to correct the description of appellant's October 1987 visa also helps overcome the implication (present in the INS's explanation of why it denied the change) that appellant somehow acted dishonestly or improperly or surreptitiously when he entered the United States in October 1987. The record evidence in this respect, even if we read it in the INS's favor, tends to favor the appellant. For one thing, the correct description of appellant's October 1987 visa—the "for business" description—is also a correct description of why appellant wanted the visa; he did intend to enter the United States at that time, not "for pleasure," but "for business." We know of nothing that suggests the "B-1" (business) and "E-2" (investor) visa qualifications are somehow mutually exclusive—that a foreign visitor could not be eligible for both. For another thing, appellant, in entering the United States on a B-1 visa and applying for an E-2 change, was following the same procedure he followed before, a procedure that (as far as the record indicates) no one ever told him was improper. Moreover, nothing in the record suggests he was trying to avoid some special requirement that he appear at the American Embassy in Colombia. Indeed, neither the record nor the briefs suggest that there is any such special requirement. The only rule the government cites to that effect is a rule that says "every alien applying for a regular ... visa" shall apply at the consulate in the district where he resides, see 22 C.F.R. § 41.101, a rule that, by its terms, applies to all visas—tourist, business, pleasure, investor, trader-alike, and a rule that appellant (apparently like millions of businessmen) violated no more in respect to his E-2 visa than in respect to the B-1 visa which he obtained and for which the record suggests he was qualified. Nor does the record support the United States Attorney's contention that appellant misrepresented a material fact in his change-of-status application when he stated that he had never applied for an immigrant visa. As far as we can tell, appellant never has applied for such a visa. Appellant's brother did file an immigrant visa petition on appellant's behalf, but appellant clearly reports this fact on the change-of-status application.

On the other hand, the record does contain one potentially misleading statement that appellant made on his application for change of status. Under the heading "I did not apply to the American Consul for a visa in the nonimmigrant classification to which I wish to be changed," appellant wrote:

> I was unaware that I might qualify for E-2 status. Furthermore, I do not have with me all the documents necessary to establish my eligibility for E-2 status.

The United States Attorney argues that the first sentence is literally false, and shows an intent to mislead. Even though the first sentence looks more innocent in context (particularly against the background of the Curacao consulate's previous denial of an E-2 visa for lack of documentation, the very reason appellant cites), we are not now prepared to hold that the INS could not read the first sentence as reflecting an effort to mislead.

Nonetheless, the record suggests that the United States Attorney seems to have first raised this point in court. The INS, in its administrative proceedings, seems to have been more concerned with appellant's having misled immigration officials by stating he wanted to enter the United States "for pleasure"—a concern that a proper reading of the record removes. Given this state of the record, it would seem important that the INS have an opportunity to reconsider the matter under, and to provide an explanation that reflects, correct factual assumptions.

Finally, we note that the United States Attorney, in court (but not the INS in the administrative proceedings), points out that the appellant's brother has petitioned for an immigrant visa for appellant, that the petition has been approved, and that appellant could return to Colombia, wait about a year for his priority date to be reached, and then obtain the immigrant visa and return to the United States. We do not see how this fact helps the government, however. The United States Attorney points to no legal rule that requires the appellant to follow this course of action. (The mere fact that appellant is the beneficiary of a petition for an immigrant visa, for example, does not render his nonimmigrant visa invalid. See, e.g., *Brownell v. Carija*, 254 F.2d 78, 80 (D.C.Cir.1957) (intent to remain permanently in the United States if one can do so lawfully is not inconsistent with the intent, necessary for obtaining a nonimmigrant visa, to remain only temporarily); *In re Chartier*, 16 I. & N. Dec. 284 (1977) (same).) Moreover, insofar as the INS, in deciding whether to exercise statutory discretion, looks to the "equities" or the "common sense" of a particular case, this fact would seem to argue in favor of permitting the appellant to stay. After all, it would seem sensible to permit a legitimate investor, with a family in San Juan, apparently meeting all the substantive requirements for an investor's visa, to remain in San Juan for a few months with that visa until he qualifies for the immigrant visa to which he is also entitled; and it would seem inhumane (unless there is more to the matter than currently appears) to force him to remove his children from school, and return with his family to Colombia for a few months, moving back to San Juan thereafter. What reason is there to think that the INS, given the choice, would follow other than the more humane, more sensible course of action?

For these reasons, we conclude that the INS's failure to reconsider the appellant's application under a correct set of factual assumptions amounts to an "abuse of discretion." We vacate the judgment of the district court and order it to remand this case to the INS for reconsideration.

Notes

1. Visitors for business may be admitted to conduct commercial transactions such as negotiating contracts, litigating and consulting with business clients. Similarly, a B-1 visitor may come for scientific or professional reasons, such as attending a conference.

2. Consider the possibility where a person wishes to come to the United States for short periods as a musician, not to perform at engagements but to sell compact disks of ethnic music while engaging in sidewalk performances. Is this a legitimate use of the B-1 visa? Would it matter how often the person comes to the United States? Or how long she stays? Courts will defer to the agency's interpretation of what constitutes business activity and when the line is crossed to prohibited employment. *Chevron U.S.A. v. Natural Resources Defense Council*, 467 U.S. 837, 843 (1984). The BIA has held that if the function performed "is a necessary incident to international trade or commerce," it is within the range of activity of a B-1 visa but not if it was for employment. *Matter of Duckett*, 19 I. & N. Dec. 493, 497 (BIA 1987). In describing what constituted employment, the BIA did not find that the rule had been violated where truck drivers were delivering goods from Canada and picking up goods for sale in Canada. *Matter of Camilleri*, 17 I. & N. Dec. 441, 444 (BIA 1980). Similarly, a railroad clerk employed by a Canadian railroad who entered the country each day for a portion of his shift in order to clear his employer's railroad cars for transport from the United States to Canada was considered as properly under the B-1 visa. *Matter of Duckett*, 19 I. & N. Dec. at 493 (BIA 1987). On the other hand, the BIA has found that a non-citizen's engineer activities were not incident to international trade when his repeated, short visits to the United States were for the purpose of "extending his professional engineering practice to the United States." *Matter of Neill*, 15 I. & N. Dec. 331, 334 (BIA 1975).

3. B-1 classification has been allowed for personal domestic servants of a nonimmigrant under the following classifications: B, E, F, H, I, J, L, O, P, Q and R. The applicant is required to show that she maintains a foreign residence and has either worked for the employer for one year or has prior experience as a domestic worker for one year.

Matter of Nago

16 I. & N. Dec. 446 (BIA 1978)

BY: Milhollan, Chairman; Maniatis, Appleman, and Maguire, Board Members

On February 14, 1977, the immigration judge issued an order finding that the applicant, Osami Nago, qualifies for admission to the United States as a nonimmigrant treaty investor under section 101(a)(15)(E)(ii) of the Immigration and Nationality Act, 8 U.S.C. 1101(a)(15)(E)(ii). He ordered that the applicant be admitted to the United States as an "E-2 nonimmigrant" for a period to expire on August 14, 1977. The Immigration and Naturalization Service appealed from that decision. Subsequent to its appeal, the Service waived oral argument before this Board. The Service appeal will be dismissed.

The applicant is a 23-year-old single male alien who is a native and citizen of Japan. He arrived in the United States at Honolulu, Hawaii, on November 11, 1976. The applicant, at that time, was in possession of a valid passport issued by the Government of Japan and a nonimmigrant (E-2) visa. He applied for admission as a nonimmigrant treaty investor under section 101(a)(15)(E)(ii) of the Act.

The applicant was served by an immigration officer with a notice (Form I-122) informing him that he appeared to be an immigrant not in possession of a valid unexpired immigrant visa; that it did not appear that he was exempt from presentation of such a document; and that he may come within the exclusion provisions of section 212(a)(20) of the Act, 8 U.S.C. 1182(a)(20). He was also notified of the time and date of his hearing in exclusion proceedings. The hearing was conducted on February 14, 1977.

The record reveals that the applicant is a Japanese specialty cook who is employed for a one-year period at "Yakiniku House Osaka", a Japanese restaurant located in Honolulu. The restaurant is owned by a Japanese nonimmigrant treaty investor who seeks the culinary services of the applicant who is apparently well versed in a specialized type of Japanese cooking known as "Nabemono." The applicant will cook in the "Nabemono" style and train other employees of the restaurant in this form of cooking. It appears that "Nabemono" chefs are scarce in the United States and that the applicant's employer has been searching for such a chef for several years. The applicant's employer testified that the applicant is a graduate of a leading Japanese cooking school and experienced in the art of "Nabemono" cooking. The applicant's employer also testified that the applicant will teach other employees to carry on the "Nabemono" style of cooking; that the "Nabemono" process can be learned in one year, and that the applicant intends to return to Japan after one year. The immigration judge found that the "Nabemono" type of cooking "... requires a highly trained or specially qualified technical person for the preparation of the food and for the purpose of teaching others to perform the process."

The applicant seeks admission as a nonimmigrant treaty investor. Section 101(a)(15)(E)(ii) of the Act defines a treaty investor as:

> ... an alien entitled to enter the United States under and in the pursuance of the provisions of a treaty of commerce and navigation between the United States and the foreign state of which he is a national, and the spouse and children of any such alien if accompanying or following to join him:
>
> (i) ...
>
> (ii) solely to develop and direct the operation of an enterprise in which he has invested, or of an enterprise in which he is actively in the process of investing, a substantial amount of capital....

In *Matter of Udagawa*, 14 I. & N. Dec. 578 (BIA 1974), we pointed out that a reasonable construction of section 101(a)(15)(E)(ii) is contained in 22 C.F.R. 41.41. The relevant portion of this Department of State regulation states:

> (a) An alien shall be classifiable as a nonimmigrant treaty investor if he establishes to the satisfaction of the consular officer that he qualifies under the provisions of section 101(a)(15)(E)(ii) of the Act and that: (1) He intends

> to depart from the United States upon the termination of his status; and (2) he is an alien who has invested or is investing capital in a bona fide enterprise and is not seeking to proceed to the United States in connection with the investment of a small amount of capital in a marginal enterprise solely for the purpose of earning a living; or that (3) he is employed by a treaty investor in a responsible capacity and the employer is a foreign person having the nationality of the treaty country who is maintaining the status of a nonimmigrant treaty investor, or an organization which is principally owned by a person or persons having the nationality of the treaty country, and if not residing abroad, maintaining nonimmigrant treaty investor status.

We construe the above regulation to mean that an alien such as the applicant will qualify as a "treaty investor" if he has the necessary intent to depart and if he meets the conditions imposed by subdivision (3) of the quoted portion of the regulation. Since the evidence adduced at the hearing indicates that the applicant's employer is a foreign person of the same nationality as the applicant and that the applicant possesses the requisite intent to return to Japan, the remaining issue in this case is whether he can be considered to be "employed ... in a responsible capacity...."[1] *Matter of Udagawa, supra*; *Matter of Tamura*, 10 I. & N. Dec. 717 (R.C.1964).

It is clear that the applicant is a highly trained chef who is engaged in a specialized form of Japanese cooking. The applicant has been brought to the United States to impart his knowledge and share his experiences with other employees of the treaty investor in order to enable them to become proficient in "Nabemono" cooking. We conclude that the applicant is employed by a treaty investor in a responsible capacity. Therefore, the applicant qualifies for admission as a nonimmigrant alien within the meaning of section 101(a)(15)(E)(ii) of the Act.

Notes

1. While the B-1 visa is designed to facilitate a commercial activity, the E visa is designed to meet reciprocal treaties of nationals with certain countries. Below is a list of the countries which have current and in-force treaties with the United States. Note: The specific treaties should be consulted, for there are provisions which may exclude certain territories or have peculiar restrictions.

1. Treaty Investor Countries

Albania, Argentina, Armenia, Australia, Austria, Azerbaijan, Bahrain, Bangladesh, Belgium, Bolivia, Bosnia and Herzegovina, Bulgaria, Cameroon,

---

1. An elaboration of the provisions of 22 C.F.R. §41.41 are contained in Note Number 4 of Volume 9 (Visas) of the Department of State Foreign Affairs Manual. That note provides, in pertinent part, that highly trained technical and managerial personnel employed by firms having the nationality of a country which has entered into a treaty with the United States providing for the investor classification are entitled to treaty investor status if they are engaged in the training or supervision of technicians employed in manufacturing, maintenance, and repair functions

Canada, Chile, China (Taiwan), Colombia, Congo (Brazzaville), Congo (Kinshasa), Costa Rica, Croatia, Czech Republic, Ecuador, Egypt, Estonia, Ethiopia, Finland, France, Georgia, Germany, Grenada, Honduras, Iran, Ireland, Italy, Jamaica, Japan, Jordan, Kazakhstan, Korea (South), Kyrgyzstan, Latvia, Liberia, Lithuania, Luxembourg, Macedonia (the Former Yugoslav Republic of (FRY)), Mexico, Moldova, Mongolia, Morocco, Netherlands, Norway, Oman, Pakistan, Panama, Paraguay, Philippines, Poland, Romania, Senegal, Singapore, Slovak Republic, Slovenia, Spain, Sri Lanka, Suriname, Sweden, Switzerland, Thailand, Togo, Trinidad & Tobago, Tunisia, Turkey, Ukraine, United Kingdom, Yugoslavia.

2. Treaty Trader Countries

Argentina, Australia, Austria, Belgium, Bolivia, Bosnia and Herzegovina, Brunei, Canada, Chile, China (Taiwan), Colombia, Costa Rica, Croatia, Denmark, Estonia, Ethiopia, Finland, France, Germany, Greece, Honduras, Iran, Ireland, Israel, Italy, Japan, Jordan, Korea (South), Latvia, Liberia, Luxembourg, Macedonia (the Former Yugoslav Republic of (FRY)), Mexico, Netherlands, Norway, Oman, Pakistan, Paraguay, Philippines, Poland, Singapore, Slovenia, Spain, Suriname, Sweden, Switzerland, Thailand, Togo, Turkey, United Kingdom, Yugoslavia.

2. Regulations attempted to clarify a number of issues, including the definition of "trade" investor and the substantiality requirement.[89]

22 C.F.R. §41.51(a)—Treaty Traders

(7) *Trade.* The term "trade" as used in this section means the existing international exchange of items of trade for consideration between the United States and the treaty country. Existing trade includes successfully negotiated contracts binding upon the parties that call for the immediate exchange of items of trade. This exchange must be traceable and identifiable. Title to the trade item must pass from one treaty party to the other.

(8) *Item of trade.* Items that qualify for trade within these provisions include but are not limited to goods, services, technology, monies, international banking, insurance, transportation, tourism, communications, and some news gathering activities.

(9) *Substantial trade.* Substantial trade for the purposes of this section entails the quantum of trade sufficient to ensure a continuous flow of trade items between the United States and the treaty country. This continuous flow contemplates numerous exchanges over time rather than a single transaction, regardless of the monetary value. Although the monetary value of the trade item being exchanged is a relevant consideration, greater weight is given to more numerous exchanges of larger value. In the case of smaller businesses, an income derived from the value of numerous transactions that

89. 62 Fed. Reg. 149 (1997).

is sufficient to support the treaty trader and his or her family constitutes a favorable factor in assessing the existence of substantial trade.

22 C.F.R. § 41.51(b) — Treaty Investors

(7) *Investment.* Investment means the treaty investor's placing of capital, including funds and other assets, at risk in the commercial sense with the objective of generating a profit. The treaty investor must be in possession of and have control over the capital invested or being invested. The capital must be subject to partial or total loss if investment fortunes reverse. Such investment capital must be the investor's unsecured personal business capital or capital secured by personal assets. Capital in the process of being invested or that has been invested must be irrevocably committed to the enterprise. The alien has the burden of establishing such irrevocable commitment given to the particular circumstances of each case. The alien may use any legal mechanism available, such as by placing invested funds in escrow pending visa issuance, that would not only irrevocably commit funds to the enterprise but that might also extend some personal liability protection to the treaty investor.

(8) *Bona fide enterprise.* The enterprise must be a real and active commercial or entrepreneurial undertaking, producing some service or commodity for profit and must meet applicable legal requirements for doing business in the particular jurisdiction in the United States.

(9) *Substantial amount of capital.* A substantial amount of capital constitutes that amount that is:

(i)(A) Substantial in the proportional sense, i.e., in relationship to the total cost of either purchasing an established enterprise or creating the type of enterprise under consideration;

(B) Sufficient to ensure the treaty investor's financial commitment to the successful operation of the enterprise; and

(C) Of a magnitude to support the likelihood that the treaty investor will successfully develop and direct the enterprise.

(ii) Whether an amount of capital is substantial in the proportionality sense is understood in terms of an inverted sliding scale; i.e., the lower the total cost of the enterprise, the higher, proportionately, the investment must be to meet these criteria.

3. The treaty investor or trader is envisioned as engaging in active investment or trade and does not contemplate a passive investment, such as in stocks or undeveloped land, or trade which is inactive.[90]

---

90. *See Matter of Heitland,* 14 I. & N. Dec. 563 (BIA 1974).

F. Work Visas (H, L)

1. Temporary Workers (H visas)

Hong Kong T.V. Video Program, Inc. v. David N. Ilchert, District Director, I.N.S.

685 F. Supp. 712 (N.D. Ca. 1988)

SCHWARZER, District Judge.

On September 19, 1985, plaintiff Hong Kong T.V. Video Program, Inc., submitted a visa petition to the Immigration and Naturalization Service ("INS") to classify See Soo Chuan ("beneficiary") as a temporary worker of "distinguished merit and ability" pursuant to section 101(a)(15)(H)(i) of the Immigration and Nationality Act ("Act"), 8 U.S.C. § 1101(a)(15)(H)(i). The visa would enable the beneficiary to work as the plaintiff's president and chief executive officer.

The INS denied the petition on the grounds that a president and chief executive officer is not a member of a profession, that the beneficiary was not a professional because he did not have a university degree, that the person holding the position of president and chief executive officer of plaintiff was not required to be preeminent, and that the beneficiary was not preeminent in his field. The Administrative Appeals Unit ("AAU") dismissed plaintiff's appeal on July 8, 1986.

On April 30, 1987, plaintiff filed this action in federal court, seeking a declaration that the INS's denial of the petition was an abuse of discretion. Plaintiff moved for summary judgment, and defendant filed a cross-motion for summary judgment. A hearing on the motions was held on October 2, 1987. At the hearing, the Court stated that on the record as it then stood, the INS's denial appeared to be arbitrary and capricious and not supported by substantial evidence. However, the Court deferred ruling on the motions and gave the INS an opportunity to show cause why the plaintiff's nonimmigrant visa petition on behalf of the beneficiary should not be granted. The purpose of the deferral was to allow the INS to reconsider its decision.

The INS reopened plaintiff's visa petition proceedings for consideration of the factors set forth by the Court on the record and on December 29, 1987, issued a revised decision which again dismissed plaintiff's appeal and denied plaintiff's visa petition. That decision is now before the Court on the parties' previously filed and deferred cross-motions for summary judgment.

Facts

Plaintiff, a California corporation, imports and distributes motion picture and drama series foreign language video cassettes in Cantonese, Mandarin, Vietnamese, Cambodian, Thai, Korean, and Spanish languages. It is the largest Asian language video cassette distributor in the United States. It employs over seventy United States workers and has gross annual sales revenues of over eight million dollars.

Plaintiff seeks to employ the beneficiary as its president and chief executive officer. The beneficiary has twenty years of experience in business including temporary chief executive officer and president of plaintiff from 1981 to the present; special business advisor at Lumistar International Ltd. in Hong Kong from 1979 to the present; commission agent and coordinator for Lumistar International (Canada) Ltd. in Ontario from 1977 to 1980; joint venture in Dek's Corporation, an import/export business in Singapore from 1971 to 1976; sales manager with Star Trade Electronics Ltd. from 1969 to 1971; sales representative at Bright Office Equipment from 1964 to 1966; sales representative at Hageneyer Trading Co. Pte. Ltd. in Singapore from 1966 to 1969; sales executive with NCR Singapore, 1967–68; and special accounts sales representative for Olivetti in Singapore from 1967 to 1968.

As plaintiff's president, the beneficiary oversees monthly operating expenses of $150,000; controls a standard inventory of $500,000; is responsible for corporate, financial planning, marketing, and promotional strategy; negotiates contracts with United States licensees and Hong Kong HKTVB; supervises legal actions against video "pirates"; works on videotape anti-pirate technology; and makes high level decisions involving technical, legal and fiscal matters, capital improvements, and copyright infringement.

In support of the visa petition, plaintiff submitted a report from Oren Harari, a professor at McLaren College of Business, University of San Francisco. Professor Harari evaluates the professional experiences of students to determine whether their work experience may be translated into university credit. He found that the beneficiary was operating at a senior executive level of management and that his position, as president and chief executive officer, normally required an MBA. He also concluded that the beneficiary's record was "far more superior and impressive than the records which are ordinarily granted graduate credit" and that the beneficiary's work experience was equivalent to the content of a typical MBA program.

Professor Harari stated that the beneficiary could teach university level courses in Business Law (domestic and international, customs, copyright, trade, litigation), International Business (banking and currency exchange, capital budgeting, portfolio analysis, international strategic management and marketing), and Marketing Management (strategy, promotion, advertising, pricing, distribution, subcontracting, brokering and sales). He also stated that the beneficiary's impressive and extensive experience, permitted him to be a guest lecturer in MBA courses dealing with marketing, sales, finance, operation, law, and personnel relations.

Discussion

A. Standard of Review

The Court reviews an administrative denial of a visa petition for abuse of discretion. *Occidental Eng'g Co. v. INS*, 753 F.2d 766, 768 (9th Cir.1985). If a decision is based on an improper understanding of the law, or if it is not supported by substantial evidence, the INS has abused its discretion. *Lee v. INS*, 573 F.2d 592, 594 (9th Cir.1978); *Song Jook Suh v. Rosenberg*, 437 F.2d 1098, 1102 (9th Cir.1971). Judicial relief may also be warranted if it affirmatively appears that the application was turned down for a reason outside the contemplation of Congress. *Kaloudis v.*

Shaughnessy, 180 F.2d 489 (2d Cir.1950); see also *Hintopoulos v. Shaughnessy*, 353 U.S. 72 (1957).

Section 101(a)(15)(H)(i) permits "an alien having a residence in a foreign country which he has no intention of abandoning ... who is of distinguished merit and ability and who is coming temporarily to the United States to perform services of an exceptional nature requiring such merit and ability" to obtain an H-1 nonimmigrant visa.

The distinguished merit and ability test under this statute involves a two-step assessment. First, a person must occupy a position classifiable as a profession within the meaning of section 101(a)(32) to be classifiable as an alien of distinguished merit and ability. Secondly, the person must herself be a professional. *Matter of Gen. Atomic Co.*, 17 I. & N. Dec. 537 (Comm.1980); *Matter of Essex Cryogenics Indus., Inc.*, 14 I. & N. Dec. 196 (Dep.Assoc.Comm.1972). Alternatively, aliens of prominence, renown, or preeminence in their field may be classified as aliens of distinguished merit and ability. *Matter of Shaw*, 11 I. & N.Dec. 277 (D.D.1965).

B. The Occupation of President as a Profession

In the December 29, 1987 dismissal of plaintiff's appeal, the INS concluded that the beneficiary's position, president and chief executive officer of a multi-million dollar company, was not a profession. The INS stated:

> Absent actual evidence a specific academic degree is necessary to perform the beneficiary's duties as a company president and chief executive officer and is, in fact, an industry standard for that position, it may not be concluded that the proposed employment is professional employment within the meaning of section 101(a)(32).

Decision of the AAU at 4 (Dec. 29, 1987). The INS concluded that since a president is a type of business manager and only forty percent of business managers have academic degrees, the occupation of president does not require a degree and therefore is not a profession.

The INS assumes that in order for an occupation to be a profession under section 101(a)(32), entrance into that occupation must, under the industry's standards, require at least a baccalaureate degree.

> Examination of the occupations named in section 101(a)(32) of the Act indicates the following characteristics common to all: (1) recognition as a member of those professions normally requires the successful completion of a specified course of education on the college or university level, culminating in the attainment of a specific type of degree or diploma; and (2) the attainment of such a degree or diploma is usually the minimum requirement for entry into those occupations.

Matter of Asuncion, 11 I. & N. Dec. 660 (R.C.1966). In this case the INS maintains, therefore, that only occupations which have a degree requirement may be professions under 8 U.S.C. § 1011(a)(32). See *Matter of Huckenbeck*, 13 I. & N.Dec. 118 (R.C.1969); *Matter of Ahmed*, 12 I. & N.Dec. 498 (R.C.1967).

Section 101(a)(32) of the Act states:

> The term "profession" *shall include but not be limited to* architects, engineers, lawyers, physicians, surgeons, and teachers in elementary or secondary schools, colleges, academies, or seminaries.

8 U.S.C. § 1011(a)(32) (emphasis added). Thus the statute specifically states that the term "profession" is not limited to the occupations enumerated. The fact that certain professions are listed which usually require academic specialization as an entry level qualification does not preclude other kinds of professions or endeavors from being treated as professions within the meaning of subsection 32.

Subsection 32 covers a wide spectrum of "professions." It includes architects, engineers, physicians, surgeons and elementary teachers. Each listed profession requires different levels and types of higher education. Certainly the academic qualifications for an elementary school teacher cannot be considered equivalent to those of a surgeon or physician. Therefore, Congress clearly intended to permit a broad spectrum of occupations or positions with varying educational requirements to be treated as professions.

Since the statute is open-ended and encompasses occupations requiring varying levels of academic training, its text does not support the INS's conclusion that, to qualify as a profession, an occupation must require at least a baccalaureate degree.

Moreover, the INS itself has not consistently required a degree as a prerequisite to classifying occupations as professions. See *Matter of Sun*, 12 I. & N. Dec. 535 (Reg. Comm.1967). In *Matter of Sun*, the INS held that the vocation of hotel manager is a profession based on the complexity of the duties involved, not the existence of a degree. *Id.* at 536. The INS concluded that the complex duties of personnel administration, establishing performance standards, allocating funds, planning budgets, authorizing expenditures, delegating authority, controlling and supervising performance of personnel, and insuring efficient and profitable operation of the hotel raised the occupation of hotel manager to a profession. *Id.* The INS noted that as applied to the particular petitioner his degree supported his status as a professional. However, the INS did not consider the manager's degree in holding the occupation of hotel manager to be a profession. *Id.*

The president of a multi-million dollar corporation, such as the plaintiff, performs all the duties performed by the hotel manager in *Matter of Sun* and numerous other duties including determining legal strategies and evaluating technical data. Therefore, like the hotel manager, the position of company president may be considered a profession based on the complexity of the duties alone.

The INS's determination in this case that the position of president and chief executive officer is not a profession simply because it does not require an academic degree is based on an erroneous interpretation of the statute and is in conflict with its own prior interpretation of the statute.

For support of its determination, the INS relies on the Dictionary of Occupational Titles, (4th ed. 1977). The Dictionary lists the occupation of president (DOT code

189.117-026) under the group of miscellaneous managers and officials not classified elsewhere. The classifications in the Dictionary include both professional and non-professional occupations and the locations do not purport to classify on the basis of whether an occupation is a profession. In any event president is listed in the Dictionary under the general heading of professional, technical and managerial occupations. Its worker function code, 117, which describes the responsibility level and functions of an occupation, is identical to that of a corporate lawyer (110.117-022), a patent lawyer (110.117-026), a hotel manager (187.117-038), and numerous other occupations which are classified as professions. Therefore, the location of the listing of president in the Dictionary of Occupational Titles contradicts rather than supports the INS's conclusion that president is not a profession.

Accordingly, the INS's determination that the position of president and chief executive officer is not a profession is arbitrary and capricious and unsupported by substantial evidence.

C. Classifying the beneficiary as a professional

On the second step of the distinguished merit and ability test under § 101(a)(15)(H)(i), the INS concluded that the beneficiary was not a professional since he did not have at least a baccalaureate degree or its equivalent. As previously stated, a degree requirement is not a prerequisite to classifying an occupation as a profession. Similarly, a person does not necessarily have to possess a degree to qualify as a professional under the statute. A university degree or its equivalent may demonstrate that the person is a member of a profession and a professional, but is not necessarily required. See *Matter of Retino*, 13 I. & N. Dec. 286 (R.C.1969); *Matter of Che*, 12 I. & N. 146 (D.D. 1967).

The INS concluded that the beneficiary had neither a university degree nor its equivalent. While the beneficiary does not have an academic degree, substantial evidence supports the conclusion that he has the equivalent of a degree.

Professor Harari's opinion is the only evidence concerning the beneficiary's educational status. Professor Harari concluded that the beneficiary had at least the equivalent of an MBA. The INS did not question Professor Harari's qualifications to present this expert opinion during the initial determination, the first appeal or the Court's October 2, 1987 hearing. Nor has the INS presented any evidence to contradict Professor Harari's testimony.

In its December 29, 1987 decision, the INS disregarded what it called Professor Harari's "allegedly advisory" opinion principally because he failed to specify "which aspects of the beneficiary's work experience may be equated to which courses and at which level." Decision at 5. However, after extensively discussing the beneficiary's past and present work experiences, Professor Harari specifically said that the beneficiary could "teach university courses in: Business Law (domestic and international, customs, copyright, trade, litigation), International Business (banking and currency exchange, capital budgeting, portfolio analysis ...) and Market Management courses (strategy, promotion, advertising ...)," and be a guest lecturer in MBA courses covering marketing, sales, finance, operations, law, and personnel relations. Supplemental Administrative Record at 64. Obviously, if the beneficiary's experiences permit him to teach a course, those same experiences may be equated with the specific enumerated course he is qualified to teach.

The INS determination that the beneficiary is not a professional because he lacks the equivalent of a university degree is, therefore, arbitrary and capricious and unsupported by substantial evidence.

In view of the foregoing deposition, it is unnecessary to consider whether the beneficiary may qualify on the basis of preeminence.

For the previously stated reasons, the INS's denial of the petition was an abuse of discretion. Plaintiff's motion for summary judgment is granted and defendant's cross-motion for summary judgment is denied. Defendant is ordered to issue the visa petition as requested.

Notes

1. The situation presented in *Hong Kong Video,* where the only evidence available had been presented on behalf of the beneficiary, is common to most USCIS adjudications. From the advocate's perspective, *Hong Kong Video* is a lesson in the importance of painstaking case preparation. As the representative of the USCIS's interest, how would you have presented the case differently?

2. *Hong Kong Video* demonstrates the nature of the disputes involving interpretations of the INA, which can be characterized as a conflict between agency policy and legislative mandates. As the court stated here, the proper standard for review is "abuse of discretion." Courts will defer to reasonable agency interpretations of their statutory mandate and will rely on the agency's expertise. *See Chevron v. NRDC*, 467 U.S. 837 (1984).

3. As noted earlier, H-1 visas are designated for persons of "distinguished merit and ability,"[91] which may be established in two separate ways. First, a person may be a "professional" within the meaning of 8 U.S.C. § 1101(a)(32).[92] Second, a person who is prominent or preeminent in her field may be classifiable as being of "distinguished merit and ability."[93]

4. The traditional position of USCIS has been that an occupation may be classifiable as "professional" where a baccalaureate degree is the minimal entrance requirement.[94]

---

91. *See* 8 U.S.C. § 1101(a)(15)(H)(i).

92. *See Matter of General Atomic Co.*, 17 I. & N. Dec. 532 (Comm. 1980); *Matter of Essex Cryogenics Industries, Inc.*, 14 I. & N. Dec. 196 (Dep. Assoc. Comm. 1972).

93. *See Matter of Shaw*, 11 I. & N. Dec. 277 (Dist. Dir. 1966).

94. *See Matter of Portugues Do Atlantico*, 19 I. & N. Dec. 194 (Comm. 1984).

While this restrictive definition of professional has been modified, it has been criticized by reviewing courts.[95]

5. It does not matter that the hiring of the foreign worker as an H-1 could displace a U.S. worker or that there might be an adverse effect on domestic wages and working conditions. In *Matter of Essex Cryogenics Industries, Inc.*,[96] where the INS district director had denied the employer's petition to classify an engineer as an H-1 employee in part because it would grant foreign workers benefits not available to domestic workers, the claim was specifically rejected. Should this type of nonimmigrant visa include a requirement that the hiring of the foreign worker not displace U.S. workers? If so, what type of procedure might be devised to accomplish this objective?

Matter of St. Pierre

18 I. & N. Dec. 308 (Reg. Comm. 1982)

This matter is before me on appeal from the District Director's decision of August 3, 1981, denying the petition to classify the beneficiary as a nonimmigrant trainee in accordance with section 101(a)(15)(H)(i) of the Immigration and Nationality Act, as amended, 8 U.S.C. 1101(a)(15)(H)(i). The appeal will be sustained.

The petitioner is an environmental consulting firm established in 1954 and located in Southfield, Michigan. Its business is to help industry and government identify and solve pollution problems. It has 65 employees and annual sales of $2.5 million. The beneficiary is a 44-year-old native and citizen of Canada. He is a professor of Chemical Engineering at the University of Windsor. He asked for and was granted an educational sabbatical with pay, of one year by his university in order to study industrial hygiene in the United States.

The beneficiary made application to the petitioner in 1980 for a one-year internship to learn survey and laboratory procedures in industrial hygiene such as:

> Evaluation of worker exposure to toxic chemicals such was lead, silica, benzene, and other potential cancer-causing chemicals.
>
> Evaluation and control of noise in the workplace.
>
> Evaluation and control of other physical stresses, such as radiation and heat and cold stress in industrial work environments.
>
> Development of new controls and procedures for minimizing/eliminating workplace hazards.

---

95. *See Matter of Caron*, 19 I. & N. Dec. 791 (Comm. 1988) (recognizing substantial course work combined with experience as satisfactory of the requirement); 55 Fed. Reg. 2606, 2623 (1990) [to be codified at 8 C.F.R. § 214.2(h)(3)(ii)(A)]. For cases critical of the INS position, see *Augat v. Tovar*, 719 F. Supp. 1158 (D. Mass. 1989); *Hird/Blaker, Corp.*, 712 F. Supp. 1095 (S.D.N.Y. 1989).

96. 14 I. & N. Dec. 196 (Dep. Assoc. Comm. 1972).

The petitioner accepted the beneficiary as an intern because of his superior credentials: Ph.D from Northwestern University in Chemical Engineering (1965), engineering consultant and university professor since 1965. The beneficiary wanted to take his training with the petitioner in Southfield, Michigan because it was the only laboratory with facilities to provide industrial hygiene training close to Windsor.

The petitioner had had five intern-trainees in the past and was training one at the time this petition was filed. The beneficiary will not receive any payment from the petitioner. Thus the suggestion of productive employment which would displace a resident worker which was noted in *Matter of Kraus Periodicals*, 11 I & N. Dec. 63 (R.C.1964), is absent. The beneficiary will continue to receive his professor's salary from the University of Windsor. He will return to his employment there at the end of one year's training. Thus the beneficiary is not being trained for eventual employment in the United States which was found impermissible in *Matter of Glencoe Press*, 11 I & N. Dec. 764 (R.C.1966).

Although the beneficiary's training is primarily on-the-job training, no productive labor will be involved because the beneficiary will be merely observing, not conducting field tests. The petitioner states that:

> Industrial hygiene, by its very nature, can only be learned in the work setting. It involves chemicals, noise, dust, gas and vapor measurement and testing done at the work site. Laboratory and office procedures involve research and evaluation of field tests and procedures. Thus it can only be learned by going into the field with trained professionally qualified regular company personnel.

However, the beneficiary will not be displacing a resident worker by his participation in this training program as required by *Matter of Treasure Craft of California*, 14 I & N. Dec. 190 (R.C.1972). The petitioner states that the beneficiary:

> ... will "tag along" on most field testing ... he will perform little or no actual testing as most of the test procedures are performed under strict governmental reporting and sign-off requirements.... Obviously, the company could not jeopardize the credibility of its report by having [the beneficiary, an intern] do such work. The field work he would do is thus, in fact, extra or make-work work for his use and benefit only. He would be the third man on a normal two man crew which would only need two men.

Thus the beneficiary will not, as required by *Matter of Miyaki Travel Agency, Inc.*, 10 I & N. Dec. 644 (R.C.1964), "be employed in a position which is in the normal operation of a business and in which citizens and resident aliens are regularly employed" (*id.* at 645).

I am satisfied that training in Industrial Hygiene is not available abroad as required by Matter of Treasure Craft of California, supra. The petitioner states that:

Industrial hygiene in the United States is the outgrowth of procedures and technology developed under the standards and specifications of Federal Occupational Safety and Health Act of 1970 and the various statutes and regulations enacted in implementation thereof. The United States procedures and technology are vastly different than any other country.... There is in fact no similar or even related training in Canada.

I find that all the requirements of 8 C.F.R. 214.2(h)(2)(i) (1981) and the precedent decisions relating to the H-3 classification have been met. The petitioner has specifically described a training program which will prepare the beneficiary to return to his position as Professor of Chemical Engineering with a sub-specialty in environmental engineering—a field just developing in Canada. The petitioner has demonstrated that this training is not available in Canada and must be taken here. The petitioner has established that the beneficiary will not be engaged in productive employment that might displace a resident worker [see 8 C.F.R. 214.2(h)(2)(ii) (1981)].

Therefore, I conclude that this training program is a suitable one by which a beneficiary may be classified as a nonimmigrant trainee under section 101(a)(15)(H)(i) of the Act.

ORDER: The appeal is sustained and the petition is approved.

Matter of Artee Corp.

18 I. & N. Dec. 366 (Comm. 1982)

* * *

The sole issue in this case is the temporary need of the petitioner for the services of the beneficiary. In a situation involving a "temporary help" service, the Service has found that such a service is qualified to be and remains the actual employer of the beneficiary. See *Matter of Smith*, 12 I & N. Dec. 772 (D.D.1968). The petitioner in this case is a temporary help service and I agree with the Regional Commissioner that it qualifies as a petitioner and is the actual employer of the beneficiaries. The Regional Commissioner found that, because of the current wide-spread shortage of machinists in the United States, the nature of the employment offered must be viewed as permanent and not temporary. The decision examined the use of the beneficiaries' services by the customer of the help service in reaching this conclusion. I do not believe that this is the proper view of the employment situation involved. The test of the true nature of the temporary need for the position lies in examination of the temporary need of the temporary help service, not its customers.

Section 101(a)(15)(H)(ii) defines an H-2 temporary worker as an alien "who is coming temporarily to the United States to perform temporary services or labor, if unemployed persons capable of performing such services or labor cannot be found in this country ..." As noted in *Matter of Contopoulos*, 10 I & N. Dec. 654, 657 (Acting R.C.1964), "... both the coming to the United States and the performance of service or labor must be temporary, the term 'temporary' being used twice." The nature of the duties to be performed were controlling, not the intent of the petitioner and the beneficiary concerning the time that the individual beneficiary would be employed in that position.

The Service now views this interpretation as incorrect. It is not the nature or the duties of the position which must be examined to determine the temporary need. It is the nature of the need for the duties to be performed which determines the temporariness of the position. Under this interpretation the key question in *Contopoulos* is: "Can the petitioner credibly establish that she has not employed a mother's helper in the past and that her need for a mother's helper will end in the near, definable future?" Likewise, in the instant case, the primary question becomes: "Can Artee establish that they have not employed machinists in the past and will not need the services of machinists in the near, definable future?" Here, as in *Contopoulos*, we are considering the second temporary requirement of the statute which concerns the position itself and not the first requirement which relates to the intent of the alien to enter for a temporary period. The function of a temporary help service is to provide for the fluctuating needs of other enterprises for specified services. In this case the petitioner provides technically-oriented personnel of a skilled nature to industries requiring such services. The customers of the petitioner do not have a steady need for a specific number of employees. Their business fluctuates and in so changing, their personnel needs change. To meet their needs, the customers of the petitioner turn to the petitioner to provide temporary help. While it is true that the temporary help may be needed for periods of 2 to 3 years, it is also true that shorter periods can be involved and that the need of the customer may not continue.

The situation of a temporary help service differs, however. The business of a temporary help service is to meet the temporary needs of its clients. To do this they must have a permanent cadre of employees available to refer to their customers for the jobs for which there is frequently or generally a demand. By the very nature of this arrangement, it is obvious that a temporary help service will maintain on its payroll, more or less continuously, the types of skilled employee most in demand. This does not mean that a temporary help service can never offer employment of a temporary nature. If there is no demand for a particular type of skill, the temporary help service does not have a continuing and permanent need. Thus a temporary help service may be able to demonstrate that in addition to its regularly employed workers and permanent staff needs it also hires workers for temporary positions. For a temporary help service company, temporary positions would include positions requiring skill for which the company has a non-recurring demand or infrequent demand.

There is currently a wide-spread shortage of skilled machinists in the United States. Because of this shortage, the petitioner, as a prudent business measure, has ensured that it can supply machinists to its customers. Its need to supply machinists to its customers is ongoing. Therefore, as long as this universal shortage of machinists exists, the nature of the need for the position with the petitioner is such that the duties are not temporary and will persist as long as the shortage.

In the absence of evidence that the petitioner has a non-recurring or infrequent demand for skilled machinists, the following order is entered:

Order: The petition is denied.

---

2. Intracompany Transferees (L Visas)

Matter of Chartier

16 I. & N. Dec. 284 (BIA 1977)

BY: Milhollan, Chairman; Wilson, Maniatis, Appleman, and Maguire, Board Members

In a decision dated November 18, 1976, the respondent was found deportable upon the charges contained in the Order to Show Cause, but granted the privilege of departing voluntarily in lieu of deportation. The immigration judge has certified his decision to us for review, in accordance with the provisions of 8 C.F.R. 3.1(c). We have decided to reverse the immigration judge's decision.

The respondent is a 52-year-old native and citizen of Canada. Immediately preceding the time of his application for admission to the United States, the respondent had been employed in Canada, as Canadian Manager of Technical Services, by Grow Chemical Company, a Michigan corporation.

Grow Chemical Company is a wholly owned subsidiary of Grow Chemical Corporation, headquartered in New York City. The parent corporation had sales of $92.8 million in 1975. The Michigan company forms part of the Automotive Group of the parent corporation. Other subsidiaries, which are part of this Automotive Group, are located in California and Belgium.

Grow Chemical Company manufactures and sells high efficiency thinners, solvents and specialty coatings for industrial applications. Its principal customers are manufacturers of automobiles, trucks and automotive parts in the United States, Canada and Western Europe.

Grow Chemical Company's sales to Canadian customers are approximately one million dollars a year. Despite this substantial Canadian business, the company has never established a Canadian subsidiary or even an office in Canada. Nor is the company officially licensed to do business in Canada. However, the company has stated that it intends to establish a Canadian sales and service subsidiary at some point, when market conditions and the supply of raw materials permit this.

When the respondent was employed by Grow in Canada, he worked out of his home. His job involved visiting automotive assembly plants on a regular basis to make sure that Grow's paint products were being applied properly.[1]

In 1974, Grow decided to transfer the respondent to the United States, in order to perform similar services here.

1. In his affidavit of December 12, 1975, Leslie Stott, Vice-President and General Sales Manager of Grow Chemical Company, stated: "The painting of an automobile is an extremely complex process, and our technical service representative is required to know the process in detail, to know the chemical and other properties of the material being coated, and the coating materials as well as the conditions under which paints and lacquers are prepared and applied in the automotive plants."

The company filed a visa petition to classify the respondent as an intra-company transferee under section 101(a)(15)(L) of the Immigration and Nationality Act. The petition was approved by the District Director in Detroit, Michigan. The respondent entered the United States on June 14, 1974, with an L-1 nonimmigrant visa. He received extensions of stay, in the same status, until May 18, 1976. On September 17, 1974, the respondent brought his wife and four children from Etibicoke, Ontario, to Walled Lake, Michigan, to join him.

In July, 1975, the respondent filed an application for a labor certification from the Department of Labor. This event precipitated an investigation into the respondent's immigration status by the Immigration and Naturalization Service office in Detroit.

The District Director now decided that he had made a mistake in approving an L-1 visa petition in behalf of the respondent. The respondent was informed that he was not qualified for L-1 nonimmigrant status, and that he would be required to leave the United States. The respondent contested the District Director's interpretation of the law, and refused to leave the country voluntarily.

An Order to Show Cause was issued on November 14, 1975. In it, the Service charged that the respondent was not entitled to his L-1 visa classification because he was "not the representative of a foreign subsidiary or entity conducting business in Canada."

By this inartful language, what the Service meant to say was that the respondent's company did not have a subsidiary or affiliate in Canada, and that therefore he did not qualify as an intra-company transferee. The wording of the Order to Show Cause did not, however, cause any confusion.

Because he did not qualify as an intra-company transferee, continued the Order to Show Cause, the respondent was deportable under section 241(a)(1) of the Immigration and Nationality Act, in that, at the time of his entry he was within one or more of the classes of aliens excludable by the law, to wit, aliens who are nonimmigrants not in possession of a valid nonimmigrant visa, as described in section 212(a)(26) of the Act.

The Order to Show Cause also charged that the respondent was excludable under section 212(a)(20) of the Act as an immigrant not in possession of a valid, unexpired immigrant visa. In charging that the respondent entered the United States as an immigrant, the Service was alleging, somewhat redundantly, that, at the time of his entry, the respondent did not come within any of the defined classes of nonimmigrants set out in section 101(a)(15) of the Act. That same section of the Act defines the term "immigrant" as every alien who does not come within one of the defined classes of nonimmigrants.

The respondent denied deportability, claiming that, under a correct interpretation of section 101(a)(15)(L), he did qualify as an intra-company transferee. The respondent also argued that, even if the Service's interpretation of the Act was correct, it should be equitably estopped from deporting him, since it had approved his L-1 visa petition, and he had relied on that approval to his substantial detriment.

On April 7, 1970, the 91st Congress amended the Immigration and Nationality Act, to facilitate the entry of certain aliens into the United States, by creating additional categories of nonimmigrants. See Public Law 91-225. This law added section 101(a)(15)(L) to the Act, 8 U.S.C. 1101(a)(15)(L). It reads as follows:

> (L) an alien who, immediately preceding the time of his application for admission into the United States, has been employed continuously for one year by a firm or corporation or other legal entity or an affiliate or subsidiary thereof and who seeks to enter the United States temporarily in order to continue to render his services to the same employer or a subsidiary or affiliate thereof in a capacity that is managerial, executive, or involves specialized knowledge, and the alien spouse and minor children of any such alien if accompanying him or following to join him.

The Service concedes that the express statutory language does not require the employer to have a subsidiary or other legal entity abroad. The Service argument is that such a requirement should be implied from the statutory requirement that the employment in the United States be temporary. The Service contends that if the corporation has no established foreign branch, there is no place for the alien to return to, and therefore his employment in the United States cannot be deemed temporary.

There are several reasons why this argument fails to convince us.

In the first place, we are reluctant to read implied restrictions into the statute, particularly in the context of a deportation proceeding. It is settled doctrine that deportation statutes must be construed in favor of the alien. "Since the stakes are considerable for the individual, we will not assume that Congress meant to trench on his freedom beyond that which is required by the narrowest of several possible meanings of the words used." *Lennon v. INS*, 527 F.2d 187, 193 (2 Cir.1975). See *Rosenberg v. Fleuti*, 374 U.S. 449, 459 (1963); Bonetti v. Rogers, 356 U.S. 691, 699 (1958); *Fong Haw Tan v. Phelan*, 333 U.S. 6, 10 (1948).

Furthermore, the Service has given us no reason to believe that its interpretation of the statute accords with Congress' intent. Section 101(a)(15)(L) was added to the Act in order to make it easier for corporations doing business in the United States to bring key foreign employees here to work.

The Service's interpretation of the statute would restrict the ability of companies such as Grow, which have not gone through the formalities of establishing subsidiaries or branch offices abroad, to bring their executives or technical specialists to the United States. We see no reason why a distinction should be made between United States companies with subsidiaries abroad and United States companies with employees abroad who work directly for the parent company.

The Service contends that this distinction is necessary to guarantee that the employee's stay in the United States be temporary. However, the Service ignores the possibility of sending the respondent back to his previous job in Canada. It also ignores the fact that Grow has an affiliate in Belgium to which the respondent could be sent after his sojourn in the United States.

Finally, the Service itself has consistently interpreted section 101(a)(15)(L) generously, so as to facilitate intra-company transfers.

The Service appears to be concerned by the fact that the respondent has applied for a labor certification, which may indicate that he intends to become a permanent resident if he can. However, there is nothing in the law which prevents the respondent from seeking to change his status to that of a lawful permanent resident. In fact, section 245 of the Act, which enables an alien to adjust his status to that of a lawful permanent resident without having to leave the United States to obtain an immigrant visa abroad, is designed to facilitate such changes of status.[5]

In view of our interpretation of section 101(a)(15)(L), we need not reach the estoppel issue raised by the respondent.

ORDER: The decision of the immigration judge is reversed. The deportation proceeding will be terminated.

Matter of Siemens Medical Systems, Inc.

19 I. & N. Dec. 362 (Comm. 1986)

This appeal is before the Commissioner from the February 27, 1985, decision of the district director denying the visa petition to classify the beneficiary under section 101(a)(15)(L) of the Immigration and Nationality Act, 8 U.S.C. § 1101(a)(15)(L) (1982). The district director found that the petitioner had failed to establish an affiliation with the beneficiary's foreign employer. The appeal will be sustained.

I. Facts

The petitioner, Siemens Medical Systems, Inc., seeks to classify the beneficiary as an intracompany transferee under section 101(a)(15)(L) of the Act to enable the beneficiary to provide services as a senior technical representative for medical x-ray equipment for its operation in the United States. Section 101(a)(15)(L) requires the beneficiary to be coming to the United States to continue employment in a managerial, executive, or specialized knowledge capacity with the same employer, its parent, branch, subsidiary, or affiliate with which the beneficiary was continuously employed abroad for the immediate prior year.

The petitioner is a United States wholly-owned subsidiary of Siemens AG, a multinational corporation headquartered in West Germany, and is involved in the development and sale of medical and dental equipment and systems. The beneficiary was employed as an x-ray engineer by wholly-owned subsidiaries of Siemens AG from

---

5. The Service has not raised the issue of the respondent's subjective intent when he applied for his L-1 nonimmigrant visa. If the Service had claimed that the respondent was really an intending immigrant when he entered the United States, and therefore not entitled to a nonimmigrant visa, it would have to prove more than the mere fact (assuming it is a fact) that he hoped from the beginning to be able to adjust his status to that of a lawful permanent resident. *See Bong Young Choy v. Barber*, 279 F.2d 642, 646 (9 Cir.1960); *Brownell v. Carija*, 254 F.2d 78 (D.C. Cir.1957); *Chryssikos v. Commissioner of Immigration*, 3 F.2d 372 (2 Cir.1924); *Matter of Hosseinpour*, Interim Decision 2349 (BIA 1975); *Matter of Wellhofer*, 12 I. & N. Dec. 522 (R.C.1967); *Matter of H-R-*, 7 I. & N. Dec. 651 (R.C.1958). *See also Matter of Bocris, supra.*

1975 until 1982. In July 1982, the beneficiary was transferred to Hospitalia International GmbH, a 50–50 joint venture between Siemens AG and Phillips International, to work on an x-ray maintenance project at King Hussein Medical Center, Amman, Jordan. After the project terminated in January 1985, he was reassigned to Siemens AG headquarters.

II. Case History, Decision, and Appeal

The petition was filed on February 14, 1985. On February 27, 1985, the district director denied the petition after determining, following Matter of Hughes, 18 I&N Dec. 289 (Comm. 1982), that the petitioner submitted no evidence that Siemens AG controls Hospitalia International and, therefore, failed to establish that affiliation exists between Siemens Medical Systems and Hospitalia International. On April 15, 1985, the petitioner filed a motion to reopen and reconsider in which it argued that the beneficiary's identity as an employee of Siemens AG was not terminated or otherwise affected by his assignment to Hospitalia. The district director denied the motion, noting that there is nothing in the record to indicate that the beneficiary should be considered an employee of Siemens during the time he was at Hospitalia; nor is there evidence that Siemens exercises control over the management or policies of Hospitalia, which is required for affiliation.

On appeal, the petitioner contends that a qualifying affiliation under the statute exists between itself and Hospitalia through Siemens AG and makes the following argument:

> Control does not nor should not mean total control. In the case at hand, it has previously been documented that Siemens AG supplies most of the technical personnel to Hospitalia International and owns 50% of the assets and 50% of the outstanding shares of stock in Hospitalia International. These three items, as indicated in the above section, should be sufficient to show control in order to establish affiliation as is defined under the immigration laws. However, it should be further noted that Siemens AG also participates in profits from Hospitalia International on a 50–50 basis; Hospitalia International's board of directors is comprised by 50% of people from Siemens AG; Hospitalia International does not manufacture equipment, but installs all necessities used in hospitals—to wit, beds, x-ray machinery, and other diagnostic equipment. The medical equipment used by Hospitalia International in the equipping of these hospitals is manufactured by Siemens AG.

The petitioner also notes that the beneficiary's identity as an employee of Siemens AG remained constant despite the beneficiary's assignment to Hospitalia. When the beneficiary went to Hospitalia International, he was assigned by Siemens AG and did not seek employment with Hospitalia International on his own volition and, at the end of his term with Hospitalia International, remained an employee of Siemens AG.

III. Analysis and Conclusion

Classification under section 101(a)(15)(L) of the Act requires consideration of several factors including, among others, whether or not there is a qualifying relationship between the petitioner and the entity from which the beneficiary will be transferred; whether or not the beneficiary has been employed abroad continuously for the immediate prior year in a managerial, executive, or specialized knowledge capacity by a parent, branch, subsidiary, or affiliate of the petitioner; and whether the proposed employment in the United States will be in a qualifying capacity.

A. Relationship Between the Entities

In this case, it must be established that there is a qualifying relationship between Siemens Medical Systems, Inc. (a wholly-owned subsidiary of Siemens AG) and Hospitalia International GmbH (a 50–50 joint venture established by Siemens AG and Phillips International).

The Service will accept the interpretation that a 50–50 joint venture creates a subsidiary relationship for purposes of section 101(a)(15)(L) of the Act. Where each of two corporations (parents) owns and controls 50 percent of a third corporation (joint venture), the joint venture is a subsidiary of each of the parents. There is no majority control, but where each parent through ownership and control of 50 percent of the voting shares of the joint venture has the power to prevent action by that company through exercise of its veto power, it "negatively" controls that company. That company is, therefore, properly regarded as a subsidiary of each parent.

The petitioner has the burden of establishing that the parent owns and controls 50 percent of the claimed subsidiary. To enable the Service to determine whether de facto control exists, the petition must identity all agreements between the parents relating to voting of the shares, management and direction of the subsidiary, and similar factors which affect actual control over 50 percent of the subsidiary. Unless such agreements restrict actual control of one parent, the 50-percent ownership will be deemed per se control.

The petitioner has provided sufficient evidence to establish that Hospitalia is a subsidiary of Siemens AG. The evidence shows that Siemens AG has de facto control over 50 percent of the voting shares. It jointly manages the joint venture, shares equally in its profits, and manufacturers the equipment sold and installed by Hospitalia. Since Siemens Medical Systems, Inc. is a subsidiary of Siemens AG, it is an affiliate of Hospitalia. The subsidiary and affiliate relationships in this case conform to the holdings of Matter of Hughes, supra, where it was held that: (1) The term "subsidiary" is a more specific form of affiliation in which the company so described is subordinate to the control of another, and (2) the term "affiliate" is sometimes more specifically used to describe the relationship between two companies which have no direct linkage, but are directed, controlled, and at least partially owned by the same parent corporation. We conclude that there is a qualifying relationship for purposes of section 101(a)(15)(L) of the Act between the petitioner and the beneficiary's employers abroad.

B. Beneficiary's Employment

It is evident from the facts of the case that the beneficiary had been employed abroad continuously by subsidiaries of the same parent corporation since 1975 until his reassignment to that parent in January 1985. His employment was in a specialized knowledge capacity and the proposed employment in the United States will be in a specialized knowledge capacity. It has been established that the beneficiary's employment qualifies him for classification under section 101(a)(15)(L) of the Act.

Order: The appeal is sustained. The decision of the district director is withdrawn and the petition is approved.

G. Limitations on Status

1. Extension of Status

Egil D. Lauvik v. Immigration and Naturalization Service

910 F.2d 658 (9th Cir. 1990)

Before Canby, Wiggins and Fernandez, Circuit Judges.

Canby, Circuit Judge:

The district court granted summary judgment to the Immigration and Naturalization Service (INS), affirming the denial of Egil Lauvik's request for an extension of treaty investor status. Lauvik appeals. We reverse and remand.

Background

Egil Lauvik, a citizen of Norway, invested $150,000 as a down payment on the purchase of a $375,000 motel/trailer park in Westport, Washington. INS granted him permission to stay one year as an E-2 nonimmigrant treaty investor. INS later extended his status for an additional year. On his application form, Lauvik wrote that he came to the United States "to immigrate to U.S.A. and go in bussiness [sic]." In the space for "date to which extension is requested," Lauvik wrote "4 more years till I get my citizenship," but then crossed that out and wrote "1 year."

On Lauvik's application for a second one-year extension, he listed $212 weekly income from the business and described his duties as "manage and do all work and repairs, rent rooms and trailer spaces, yard work, plombing [sic], etc." The INS District Director denied Lauvik's second extension request. INS found that Lauvik did not intend to depart the United States upon termination of his status and that Lauvik's duties gave him the status of a skilled or unskilled laborer rather than that of a treaty investor. Lauvik filed two unsuccessful motions to reconsider. He provided evidence of property and investments in Norway to show his intent to return there. His Norwegian assets included a $100,000 furnished home leased yearly, a $45,000 waterfront property co-owned with his brother, and over $6,000 in bonds and bank accounts. The INS District Director concluded that this additional financial information showed that Lauvik's investment in the United States, whether or not it was substantial, was his sole source of income and that precluded treaty investor status. Having exhausted all administrative remedies, Lauvik sought relief in district court. The district court granted the INS motion for summary judgment, and dismissed Lauvik's cross-motion for summary judgment. Lauvik appeals.

Analysis

1. Standard of Review

We review a grant of summary judgment de novo to determine whether, with the evidence viewed in the light most favorable to the nonmoving party, there are any genuine issues of material fact and whether the district court applied the relevant substantive law. *Tzung v. State Farm Fire and Casualty Co.*, 873 F.2d 1338, 1339–40 (9th Cir.1989). The district court, in turn, was under a duty to set aside the decision of the INS if it was "arbitrary, capricious, an abuse of discretion, or otherwise not in accordance with law." 5 U.S.C. § 706(2)(A).

The district court found no abuse of discretion because it concluded that there was some evidence to support the INS District Director's findings. The district court relied on *Song Jook Suh v. Rosenberg*, 437 F.2d 1098 (9th Cir.1971), which stated that "[a]buse of discretion may be found only if there is *no* evidence to support the decision or if the decision is based on an improper understanding of the law." *Id.* at 1102 (emphasis added). We have said, however, that this reference to "no evidence" cannot be read literally. *Tongatapu Woodcraft Hawaii, Ltd. v. Feldman*, 736 F.2d 1305, 1308 (9th Cir.1984). It cannot be read to mean any evidence, no matter how little. Id. There is some point at which evidence, though it exists, becomes so slight and so thoroughly outweighed by contrary evidence, that it would be an abuse of discretion to base a decision upon it.

Lauvik argues, with considerable force, that the findings of the INS must be supported by "substantial evidence." See *id.* at 1309. We need not decide whether that is the standard that the INS must meet, however, for in this case the evidence in support of the INS' decision fell below not only that standard, but below any lesser standard that we might reasonably employ.

2. Intention to Depart

A treaty investor is a nonimmigrant who enters the United States "solely to develop and direct the operations of an enterprise in which he has invested ... [a] substantial amount of capital." 8 U.S.C. § 1101(a)(15)(E)(ii). INS determined that Lauvik did not intend to depart the United States upon termination of his treaty investor status, as required by 22 C.F.R. § 41.51(b)(2).

Lauvik wrote on a form that he wanted an extension of his status for "4 more years till I get my citizenship." Lauvik disavowed those words by drawing a line through them. Such crossed out and disavowed words shed little light on Lauvik's true intentions.

Lauvik also wrote that he came to the United States, "to immigrate to U.S.A. and go in bussiness [sic]." INS points to those words as showing his intent to permanently settle here.

We note that Lauvik filled out the form in English, his second language, without benefit of counsel. There was no evidence that Lauvik could distinguish in English between an alien who "immigrates" permanently, and one who enters as a "nonimmigrant" for a temporary stay. To the contrary, Lauvik's affidavit stated that he had been "under the impression that merely investing in business meant 'immigrating' to the United States ... [and he] did not know the difference between an immigrant and nonimmigrant, and merely intended to show that [he] was 'proceeding' to the United States to set up a business."

At most, Lauvik may have wanted to remain permanently, but there was no evidence that he intended to remain if that was not legally possible. On the contrary, Lauvik provided evidence of his furnished home and other investments in Norway to show his intent to return there if he must.[2] The INS District Director ignored the long line of precedent holding that an alien's desire to remain in the United States does not negate his intent to depart upon termination of his temporary status. See *Bong Youn Choy v. Barber*, 279 F.2d 642, 645–646 (9th Cir.1960) (even though an alien wanted to finish his and his children's education in America, he only intended to stay temporarily as a visitor unless he could arrange a permanent legal stay); see also *Brownell v. Carija*, 254 F.2d 78, 80 (D.C.Cir.1957) (nonimmigrant who entered for travel through the United States "does not become an unlawful entrant because he entertains a desire, purpose or intent to remain here if the laws of the country permit him to do so. Such a purpose, so limited, could at best be only a hope."); see also *Chryssikos v. Commissioner of Immigration*, 3 F.2d 372, 375 (2nd Cir.1924) (When a new bride entered the United States on a visitor's visa with her permanent resident husband, the court decided that she intended to depart when her visa expired, and to return only after her husband became a citizen. "[P]roof of a desire to stay is not proof of an intent to stay."); see also Matter of H-R-, 7 I & N Dec. 651, 654 (1958) ("The fact that the applicant previously expressed a desire to enter the United States as an immigrant—and may still have such a desire—does not of itself preclude the issuance of a nonimmigrant visa....").

We conclude that the INS District Director abused his discretion by finding that Lauvik was not "a bona fide immigrant intent upon departing upon termination of his status."

---

2. We note that E-2 treaty investors need not maintain a foreign home, but that Lauvik has done so. Although some nonimmigrants, such as students and visitors, must have an intent not to abandon a foreign residence, the Supreme Court found it significant that other nonimmigrants have no such requirement. "Congress' silence ... mean[s] that Congress, while anticipating that permanent immigration would normally occur through immigrant channels, was willing to allow nonrestricted nonimmigrant aliens to adopt the United States as their domicile." *Elkins v. Moreno*, 435 U.S. 647, 666, 98 S.Ct. 1338, 1349, 55 L.Ed.2d 614 (1978) (holding that no federal law prevented a G-4 nonimmigrant from having a state "domicile"). A nonimmigrant who enters as an employee or officer of an international treaty organization can "develop a subjective intent to stay indefinitely in the United States ... without violating the 1952 Act, the Service's regulations, or the terms of his visa." *Id.*

3. Labor Inconsistent with Treaty Investor Status

INS found that Lauvik engaged in unskilled or skilled labor inconsistent with his treaty investor status. A treaty investor "competes with other entrepreneurs to sell goods and services, but he does not compete directly in the market as a skilled or unskilled laborer." See *Cheung v. District Director*, 641 F.2d 666, 670 (9th Cir.1980) (optometrist's income primarily from labor, so not a treaty investor); see also *Matter of Udagawa*, 14 I & N, Dec. 578 (BIA 1974) (a tempura chef, with no personal funds invested, not entitled to treaty investor status.); see also *Matter of Ruangswang*, 16 I & N, Dec. 76, 80 (BIA 1976) (an alien who invested $13,000 in a dry cleaning business was not a treaty investor because what she called $1,000 monthly net profit was actually payment for her full-time labor).

However, Lauvik may perform some menial tasks without negating his treaty investor status if he primarily acts to direct, manage, and protect his investment. See *Matter of Ahmad*, 15 I & N, Dec. 81, 83 (BIA 1974) ("In many instances a bona fide investor will properly be able to engage in activities of a skilled or unskilled nature."); see also *Matter of Ko*, 14 I & N, Dec. 349, 350–351 (BIA 1973) (A treaty investor could work as a cashier in his own shoe store without labor certification.)

Lauvik is most similar to the alien who purchased and ran a small motel in *Bhakta v. INS*, 667 F.2d 771 (9th Cir.1982) (holding that the alien did not engage in unauthorized employment). We compared the motel owner in Bhakta to a treaty investor who competed with other entrepreneurs, but did not compete in the job market for skilled or unskilled labor. Id. at 773 (quoting *Cheung v. District Director*, 641 F.2d at 670). Similarly, Lauvik contends that he competes with other entrepreneurs for the sale of motel rooms and trailer spaces, not with individuals seeking maintenance work.

Lauvik invested $150,000 initially as a down payment on the purchase of his business. The total purchase price was $375,000. At the time of his motion to reconsider, he had paid an additional $67,500 toward the remaining debt and over $50,000 on business expenses and improvements. Lauvik did not invest over $250,000 in order to take a skilled or unskilled job away from an American citizen. Lauvik claims that INS ignored evidence that the former owners and a resident caretaker help maintain the motel/trailer park. We conclude that Lauvik is far more like the motel owner in Bhakta who competes with other entrepreneurs for the sale of rooms, than he is like the chef in Udagawa who takes jobs away from American citizens or the dry cleaner in Ruangswang who is paid for her labor. INS erred by not considering all relevant factors and assuming that all skilled and unskilled labor is inconsistent with treaty investor status. See *In Chung v. U.S. I.N.S.*, 662 F.Supp. 474, 476 (W.D. Wash.1987).

4. Lauvik's Investment as His Sole Source of Income

INS found that Lauvik's investment, whether or not it was substantial, was his sole source of income. A treaty investor must make a substantial investment, as "distinct from a relatively small amount of capital in a marginal enterprise solely for the purpose of earning a living." 22 C.F.R. § 41.51(b). Notes to this regulation suggest that an investment is marginal if it only provides a livelihood for the treaty investor and his family, and does not expand local job opportunities. Dept. of State Foreign Affairs Manual, Vol. 9, Note 5.4 to 22 C.F.R. §41.51. Lauvik hires a resident caretaker.

Lauvik's investment is not marginal and solely for earning a living if he has other substantial assets. See *Matter of Kung*, 17 I & N, Dec. 260, 262 (BIA 1978) (a treaty investor's $53,000 investment was not marginal and solely for the purpose of earning a living, when he had $46,000 in additional assets); see also *Choi v. INS*, 798 F.2d 1189 (8th Cir.1986) (remanded because INS did not consider evidence of stock ownership when it concluded that alien's gift shop was his sole source of income); see also *Dong In Chung v. INS*, 662 F.Supp. 474, 476 (W.D.Wash.1987) (remanded because INS ignored a $420 monthly pension, $75,000 real estate, and over $100,000 liquid assets when it concluded that the alien's investment was solely for the purpose of making a living); compare *Kun Young Kim v. District Director*, 586 F.2d 713 (9th Cir.1978) (investment was marginal and solely to earn a living when an alien earned $1,000 monthly on his $11,500 restaurant investment and he had no other assets).

Lauvik listed his income from the business as only $212 weekly. The record is not clear whether that amount represents the net profit from the business, or whether it was the amount Lauvik chose to draw at that time. We note that business owners may choose to draw small amounts from a new business, in hopes of reaping greater benefits later. Regardless, Lauvik also received income from the lease of his $100,000 Norwegian home, co-owned a $45,000 waterfront property, and had bonds and bank accounts worth more than $6,000. We conclude that he had substantial assets other than his investment, and that INS abused its discretion by failing to follow its own precedent in Kung.

Conclusion

We conclude that the district court erred in granting summary judgment, because Lauvik presented evidence that INS abused its discretion in denying him an extension of treaty investor status. We reverse and remand for further proceedings consistent with this opinion.

Notes

1. **Extensions of status**. Many people with temporary work visas wish to remain in the United States. Moreover, employers are also in need of their services. While E visas are indefinite, H1-B and L visas may not be extended indefinitely, but the H-1B visa may be extended for up to a total of six years while the L visa may be extended for a total of five to seven years. This six-year period can be extended in one-year increments for extraordinary circumstances. H-2B visas may be extended in one-year increments for up to three years.

2. In order to qualify for a change or extension of status, the applicant must have an unrelinquished domicile abroad which she has no intention of abandoning. How

can this be reconciled with the provision allowing E visa holders to stay in the United States indefinitely?

2. Change of Status

Lun Kwai Tsui v. Attorney General of the United States

445 F. Supp. 832 (D.D.C. 1978)

Flannery, District Judge

* * *

... On February 13, 1976, plaintiffs were denied nonimmigrant visas by the United States Consul in La Paz, Bolivia. Plaintiffs reapplied for admission on May 28, 1976. In their application, they stated that they would be coming to the United States for a period of one month as tourists and would stay at the Surf Comber Hotel in Miami, Florida.

Plaintiffs were granted visas on July 2, 1976 in La Paz and entered this country on July 3. At that time, they requested and were granted a stay of six months in the United States and they represented to the inspector that they would be staying at an Annandale, Virginia address. On August 12, 1976, plaintiffs obtained certificates of eligibility for nonimmigrant student status from a private school in Falls Church, Virginia. On October 18, 1976, plaintiffs filed for a change of nonimmigrant status under 8 U.S.C. § 1258. In their applications, plaintiffs stated that their objective was to obtain an American education and that they did not apply for a student visa prior to entry because their parents decided that such an education was desirable after their arrival in the United States and consultation with school officials. They also submitted with their applications bank statements which indicated that each plaintiff had a bank account with a balance of $40,000.

The applications were rejected by the District Director of the Immigration and Naturalization Service (INS) on April 12, 1977. The basis for rejection was that at the time the applications for nonimmigrant visas were filed, plaintiffs had stated that they were entering for the purpose of tourism and that they would only stay one month before returning to China. In addition, the Director noted that they misrepresented the address at which they would be staying in their visa applications and promptly requested a six-month stay. He also pointed out that shortly after arriving they obtained the certificates of eligibility from the school and money was deposited in bank accounts for the plaintiffs. The Director concluded from these facts that the plaintiffs entered the United States with the intent of being students and therefore, denied the requested change.

Plaintiffs appealed to the Regional Commissioner of INS and submitted three affidavits in support of their appeal. The Commissioner affirmed the Director's decision on August 17, 1977 and dismissed the appeal. The Commissioner held that plaintiffs were not bona fide visitors when they entered, but rather entered with the intent of becoming students. The Commissioner noted that the usual means for obtaining student visas was circumvented and that plaintiffs were excludable under 8 U.S.C. § 1182(a)(26), because they did not have proper documentation as nonimmigrants at that time. Therefore, the Commissioner held that plaintiffs were ineligible for a change of status under 8 U.S.C. § 1258.

* * *

Under 8 U.S.C. § 1258, a nonimmigrant alien may adjust his status from one classification to another subject to rules prescribed by the Attorney General provided that the alien has maintained his current nonimmigrant status. The burden of proof as to plaintiffs' eligibility for classification as nonimmigrant students is on them. See 8 U.S.C. § 1361; *Campos v. INS*, 402 F.2d 758, 760 (9th Cir. 1968). Thus, in this case at the administrative level the plaintiffs had to carry the burden of proof that they had maintained their status as nonimmigrant visitors for pleasure. The District Director and Regional Commissioner held that the plaintiffs do not possess valid nonimmigrant visas and therefore, they had not maintained their status. The basis for this conclusion was his opinion that the plaintiffs' obtaining visas as tourists was a pretext and that their original intent was to become students. Furthermore, they found that the plaintiffs were not properly documented as students at the time of entry and thus were inadmissible under 8 U.S.C. § 1182(a)(26). Thus, the Director and the Commissioner considered their present nonimmigrant visas invalid and the plaintiffs ineligible for a change of status under § 1258. See 8 U.S.C. § 1101(a)(15)(B).

The administrative record fully supports this finding with substantial evidence. The plaintiffs were issued visas as visitors for pleasure and gave the name of a hotel in Miami as their destination. Upon their arrival they obtained a six-month stay as temporary visitors and gave their destination as Annandale, Virginia. Prior to their arrival, their father transferred over $75,000 to a bank account in this country for their use. Within six weeks of their arrival, the plaintiffs obtained certificates of eligibility for nonimmigrant status as students from a private school in Virginia. On October 22, 1976, the plaintiffs filed applications for a change of status seeking student visas, including with the applications a bank certificate indicating that each plaintiff had a bank account of $40,000 to cover school expenses. Thus, it appears that the Director's and the Commissioner's conclusions that the plaintiffs' representations that they desired to enter this country for a brief visit were a pretext and that they actually intended to become students were not arbitrary, capricious, nor an abuse of discretion. Furthermore, the Commissioner and the Director properly understood and applied the relevant law in finding that the plaintiffs did not qualify for a change of status under § 1258. It is also apparent that the Commissioner and the Director fully considered all of the relevant factors and the affidavits and the other evidence presented by the plaintiffs.

Plaintiffs' basic assertion is that INS has charged the plaintiffs with fraud and found their actions to have been fraudulent. Plaintiffs then present an extensive review of the law of fraud including the elements that must be established and the standards to be applied. It does not appear, however, that a determination of fraud is necessary in order to find that a nonimmigrant visa is invalid under 8 U.S.C. § 1182(a)(26). Although there has been no determination by the courts as to whether a finding of fraud is required by that section, it should be noted that there is another section specifically dealing with fraud and the government must prove that there were wilful, material misrepresentations under that section. 8 U.S.C. § 1182(a)(19); *Castaneda-Gonzalez v. INS*, 564 F.2d 417, 434 (D.C.Cir.1977). In the present case, however, the government is not trying to deport the plaintiffs for misrepresentations under § 1182(a)(19). Therefore, it does not appear that a finding of fraud is necessary to a determination that a visa is invalid.

In any event, even if a finding of fraud is required by § 1182(a)(26), or the government is required to show wilful misrepresentations under § 1182(a)(19) to invalidate the visas, the grant of a change of nonimmigrant status is discretionary under § 1258. Thus, assuming arguendo that the facts in this case are insufficient to establish fraud by the plaintiffs, the questionable circumstances surrounding their entry certainly would warrant an exercise of discretion adverse to the plaintiffs. It was reasonable for the Commissioner and the Director to find that the plaintiffs were less than candid with immigration officials and therefore, a change in status from visitor to student was not warranted. It was not arbitrary, capricious, nor an abuse of discretion for these officials to decline to exercise their discretion in favor of the plaintiffs.

Plaintiffs also assert that the issuance of visas to them and their admission into this country preclude a challenge to the validity of their visas. Again, the exercise of discretion adverse to their applications can be upheld regardless of the validity of their visas. To address plaintiffs' point, however, it is evident that neither prior decisions of the State Department nor decisions of immigration inspectors are binding on the Attorney General and his delegates in subsequent proceedings. See *Alacron-Baylon v. Brownell*, 250 F.2d 45, 47 (5th Cir. 1957); *Yee v. Barber*, 210 F.2d 613, 614 (9th Cir.), cert. denied, 347 U.S. 988 (1954); cf. *Cartier v. Secretary of State*, 165 U.S.App.D.C. 130, 135–137, 506 F.2d 191, 196–98 (1974), cert. denied, 421 U.S. 947 (1975). Thus, the denial of a change in nonimmigrant status from visitor to student was not arbitrary, capricious, nor an abuse of discretion and the applicable law was properly applied. Therefore, defendant's motion for summary judgment will be granted.

Notes

1. Generally, a nonimmigrant is not allowed to work while in the United States unless special permission is granted or employment is the basis for her visa. Unauthorized employment is a violation of the conditions of a person's status, thereby making her subject to removal.[97]

2. Once the person has obtained her nonimmigrant status, she must "maintain" this status. A person's failure or inability to maintain her nonimmigrant status makes her deportable.

---

97. Unauthorized employment, in addition to being a violation of the conditions of an alien's status, may cause the person to be ineligible for "adjustment of status," which will be discussed in greater detail in Chapter 7.

3. When an applicant obtains a nonimmigrant visa and enters the country on that visa, it is analogous to having entered into a contract. In this contract, she is implicitly stating that she agrees to abide by all of the conditions relating to her nonimmigrant visa category. Violation of any one of those conditions can be grounds for removal.

4. The most common grounds for violating nonimmigrant status are the following: (1) unauthorized employment, (2) failure to timely file for an extension of one's status and (3) conviction of a crime of violence for which a sentence of more than one year could be imposed.

5. Most nonimmigrants (except those specifically prohibited from doing so by their nonimmigrant classification) may freely change from one nonimmigrant status to another.[98] A condition precedent to changing one's status is having properly maintained the status originally conferred upon entry. In addition, the applicant must show that she qualifies for the new status. There is also the requirement described in *Lun Kwai Tsui v. Attorney* General[99] that the applicant not have had a "preconceived intent" of obtaining the new status in the first place.

6. **Dual intent and permanent residency**. In recent years, the unavailability of visas for immigrants has caused applicants to obtain nonimmigrant visas and subsequently seek adjustment of status to lawful permanent residency. This has raised conflict as to whether the applicant is in fact a bona-fide nonimmigrant. In the 1980s, legacy INS amended its regulations for H-1 and L visa holders to recognize the doctrine of "dual intent," which allows a person to simultaneously intend to be a nonimmigrant as well as a permanent resident applicant.[100] Congress, through its enactment of the Immigration Act of 1990, removed the presumption of immigrant intent for H-1 and L visa applicants, making it much easier for these persons to sustain a claim of dual intent.[101] Notwithstanding these changes, a determination to deny an application to change or adjust status is rarely overturned, as it is reviewed on an abuse-of-discretion standard.[102]

7. Consider the following case from an independent review of the expedited removal process.[103]

> Mr. G.P., a Venezuelan national, is a long-term employee of F Corporation, a multinational corporation doing business in the U.S. and several other countries. Mr. G.P. serves as F's District Manager of Sales at F's Miami,

---

98. 8 U.S.C. § 1158 governs the requirements for change of nonimmigrant status. *See also* 8 C.F.R. § 248.

99. 445 F. Supp. 832 (D.D.C. 1978).

100. *See* 8 C.F.R. §§ 214.2(h)(16) and 214.2(l)(16); *see also Seiboon v. Levy*, 408 F. Supp. 1208, 1211 (M.D. La. 1976).

101. *See* Sec. 205(b), Immigration Act of 1990, Pub. L. No. 101-649, 104 Stat. 4978 *amending* 8 U.S.C. § 1184(b) and (h), Sec. 214(b) and (h).

102. *See Patel v. Minnix*, 663 F.2d 1042 (5th Cir. 1981); *Mohammad v. Morris*, 477 F. Supp. 702 (E.D. Pa. 1979).

103. See Karen Musalo & Deborah Anker, Report on the First Year of Implementation of Expedited Removal (May 1998).

Florida offices. Mr. G.P. obtained an L-1A visa, which permits certain non-U.S. citizen employees of multinational corporations to enter and temporarily stay in the United States as intracompany transferees. Between March 1996, and July 1996, Mr. G.P. traveled between Venezuela and Miami on numerous occasions without incident. In July, 1996, Mr. G.P.'s inspection was deferred. The immigration officer conducting the deferred inspection concluded that Mr. G.P.'s documents were proper and that he should be admitted. Thereafter, Mr. G.P. made several entries into the United States without incident.

On June 15, 1997, Mr. G.P. arrived in Miami International airport and presented the same documents he had presented in the past—a valid Venezuelan passport with an unexpired L-1A visa. However, this time, Mr. G.P. was questioned by immigration officials, detained at the airport overnight, and then returned to Venezuela the next morning. He was issued an expedited removal order, as he was deemed to have an immigrant intent. Under the order, Mr. G.P. would be barred from entering the U.S. for five years.

This was unacceptable to F Corporation, which needed Mr. G.P. to run its Miami office. F Corporation was also deeply distressed about the treatment of Mr. G.P. F Corporation filed a complaint against the INS and the Attorney General to the Miami U.S. District Court, alleging that the expedited removal order issued by the defendants violated the immigration statute and relevant regulations, as well as Mr. G.P.'s 5th Amendment due process rights.

After spending over $50,000 in attorney fees, F Corporation reached a settlement with INS whereby INS re-issued Mr. G.P. a valid visa and canceled the order of expediting removal against him. In addition, INS agreed that any computer-generated advisories concerning Mr. G.P.'s previous visa cancellations would be removed from its databases.

What was the problem with the INS' refusal to allow Mr. G.P. to enter the United States?

Presumption of Immigrant Intent

8 U.S.C. § 1184(b), Sec. 214(b)

Every alien (other than a nonimmigrant described in subparagraph (H)(i) or (L) of section 101(a)(15)) shall be presumed to be an immigrant until he establishes to the satisfaction of the consular officer, at the time of application for a visa, and the immigration officers, at the time of application for admission, that he is entitled to a nonimmigrant status under section 101(a)(15).

3. Maintenance of Status

Khalid Mahmood v. Raymond J. Morris, District Director, INS

477 F.Supp. 702 (E.D. Pa. 1979)

Troutman, District Judge.

Plaintiff, a native and citizen of Pakistan, entered the United States as a nonimmigrant visitor for pleasure on July 16, 1977. Ten days later plaintiff applied for admission to Edinboro State College (Edinboro), which admitted him the same day pursuant to its "rolling" admissions practice and issued a Form I-20, "Certificate of Eligibility for Nonimmigrant Student Status". Two weeks later plaintiff filed an application with the Immigration and Naturalization Service (INS) to adjust his status from nonimmigrant visitor for pleasure to student. The District Director of INS, relying in part on the fact that Edinboro issued Form I-20 thirty-one days prior to plaintiff's arrival in the United States, denied plaintiff's application.[1] Plaintiff then appealed to the INS Regional Commissioner, who relied on the following facts in sustaining the decision of the District Director. Plaintiff enrolled at Edinboro no later than ten days after his arrival. Within a short time Edinboro also confirmed several additional factors which must be considered in deciding to accept a foreign student. The college determined that the plaintiff had sufficient funds available to support himself and that he spoke English proficiently. Finally, the Commissioner considered a letter of employment presented with an affidavit of support filed by plaintiff's brother and dated March 31, 1977, nearly three months prior to plaintiff's arrival.

From these facts the Commissioner drew the inference that plaintiff entered the United States not as a visitor for pleasure as he claimed, but rather as a prospective college student. Plaintiff, claiming abuse of discretion, then instituted this action to declare defendant's denial of plaintiff's application for change of nonimmigrant status "null and void" and to direct defendant to grant the application]. Both plaintiff and defendants now move for summary judgment.

The administrative decision of INS must be sustained unless it is "arbitrary, capricious, an abuse of discretion, or otherwise not in accordance with law", Administrative Procedure Act, 5 U.S.C. § 706(2)(A), *Lun Kwai Tsui v. Attorney General of the United States*, 445 F.Supp. 832, 835 (D.D.C.1978), or if the administrative record as a whole contains no "substantial evidence" to support the administrative finding. *Seihoon v. Levy*, 408 F.Supp. 1208, 1209 (M.D.La.1976). Although this Court might disagree with the District Director's conclusions, it may not reevaluate the evidence and substitute its opinion. *Id.* at 1211. In the case at bar substantial evidence supports the administrative decision. The rapid sequence of events fol-

1. Originally, the date on Form I-20 read June 15, 1977. By a letter from the Dean of Admissions at Edinboro plaintiff later showed on appeal to the Regional Commissioner that the correct date of the I-20 form should have been July 26, 1977.

lowing plaintiff's entry into the United States permitted the inference that plaintiff's sole intention in gaining entry to this country was to locate a college which would accept him for enrollment. Such a finding of implicit bad faith on plaintiff's part in securing the nonimmigrant visitor for pleasure visa allowed the District Director and Regional Commissioner to conclude that plaintiff was ineligible for a status change.

Plaintiff contends that the District Director relied largely on conjecture in reaching his decision. Yet plaintiff attempts to explain the letter confirming the employment of plaintiff's brother by the same means. Furthermore, the District Director assigned little credibility to Edinboro's incorrectly dated letter. That conclusion is not so unreasonable or manifestly abusive of his discretion to warrant redetermination.

The District Director also found that plaintiff was ineligible for a change in status under 8 U.S.C. § 1258, which

> authorize(s) a change from a nonimmigrant classification to any other nonimmigrant classification in the case of any alien lawfully admitted to the United States as a nonimmigrant who is continuing to maintain that status.

To determine whether an applicant "continued to maintain that status" the District Director may consider "any conduct by the applicant relating to his maintenance of the status from which the applicant is seeking a change". 8 C.F.R. § 248.1(b). The District Director determined that plaintiff's behavior was inconsistent with his stated purpose of visiting for pleasure and therefore was ineligible for adjustment of his nonimmigrant status. As noted above, this conclusion is not so unreasonable or manifestly abusive to warrant redetermination. Accordingly, plaintiff's motion for summary judgment will be denied and defendants' motion for summary judgment will be granted.

Note

As was described in Chapter 4, during the Fall of 2004, the Attorney General instituted a special registration program for persons in the United States from certain countries. Under the conditions of the program, a person who failed to report or otherwise comply with the conditions set out in the regulation was deemed to have violated her status and was therefore ineligible for change or extension of status.[104]

---

104. A person shall be presumed to be inadmissible under 8 U.S.C. § 1182(a)(3)(A)(ii), Sec. 212(a)(3)(A)(ii), if she fails to register without good cause upon departure.

H. Nonimmigrant Visa Flowchart

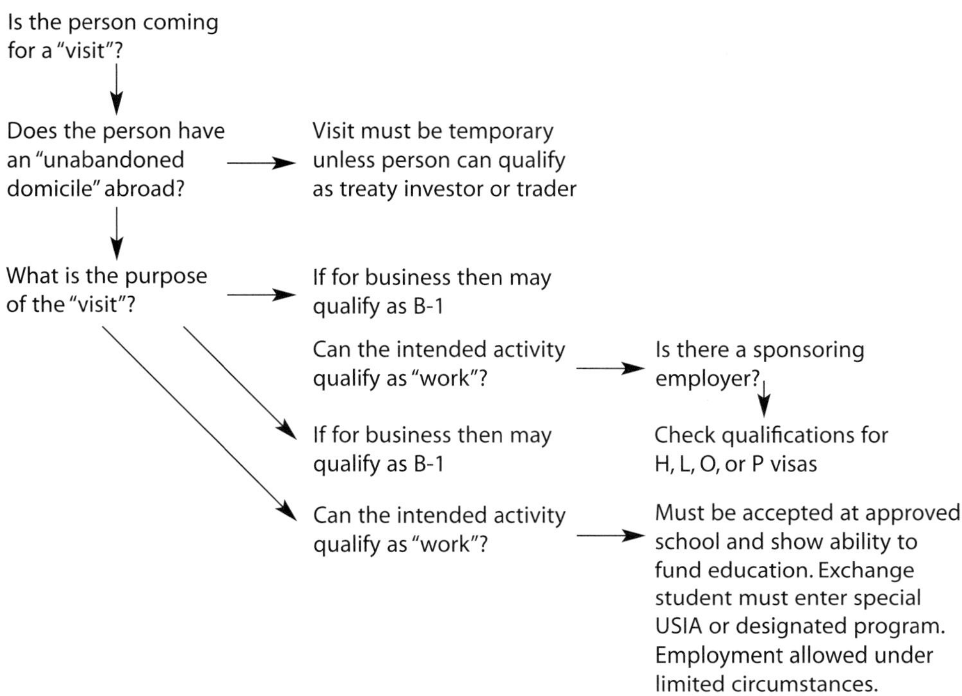

In conducting the analysis of the appropriate nonimmigrant visa and whether a person may qualify, there are some foundation questions which must be addressed: (1) Is the person an "intending immigrant"? The law presumes that she is, and the person must be prepared to show otherwise; (2) What is the applicant's nonimmigrant intentions? The law disfavors a person coming to the United States under one nonimmigrant classification and then changing her purpose to another unless that change in intent was normal or reasonable; and (3) A person may avoid the problem described in (2) if she clearly states her dual intention when she is applying for the nonimmigrant visa. In such a case, she may still qualify for the nonimmigrant visa as long as these two intents are not inconsistent. One example might be where the person is seeking admission as a tourist to search for the appropriate school to enroll in to learn English.

I. Revocation of Nonimmigrant Visas

As was noted earlier, the immigration laws provide a mechanism for the multilayered review of persons coming to the United States. The successful visa applicant who is issued a visa is subsequently subjected to inspection at the border. In order to assure that those who are ineligible but who have nevertheless managed to obtain a visa are not allowed to enter or remain, the INA provides a mechanism for visa revocation. The ultimate effect of a visa revocation is to render the person without a legal basis for remaining in the United States.[105]

The first case in this chapter deals with the issue of a nonimmigrant visa revocation by the Secretary of State after a person has entered the United States. Is a person who has entered the country entitled to notice of the grounds for issuance of an intent to revoke her visa? Should she have an opportunity to refute the charges spelled out in the notice of intent? What should be the standards for judicial review of a revocation? Consider these questions while reading the following case.

8 U.S.C. § 1201(i), Sec. 221(i)

After the issuance of a visa or other documentation to any alien, the consular officer or the Secretary of State may at any time, in his discretion, revoke such visa or other documentation. Notice of such revocation shall be communicated to the Attorney General, and such revocation shall invalidate the visa or other documentation from the date of issuance: Provided, That carriers or transportation companies, and masters, commanding officers, agents, owners, charterers, or consignees, shall not be penalized under section 1323(b) of this title for action taken in reliance on such visas or other documentation, unless they received due notice of such revocation prior to the alien's embarkation.

Nikolaas "Kallie" Knoetze v. Dep't of State

634 F.2d 207 (5th Cir. 1981)

* * *

Knoetze, a world-class boxer and former policeman from South Africa, came to the United States on a non-immigrant visa to take part in a prize fight. Knoetze then discovered through the news media that his visa had been revoked. The Secretary of State revoked his visa after concluding that Knoetze was convicted in South Africa of a crime corresponding to an American felony involving moral turpitude. The Immigration and Nationality Act renders such foreign convicts ineligible for a visa of entry into our country. 8 U.S.C. § 1182(a)(9).

Knoetze received a preliminary injunction against deportation and competed in the prize fight. He also applied for an H-class visa, which would have permitted him to work in this country. The Immigration and Nationalization Service (INS) denied this application because of the Secretary's act of revocation.

The trial court refused to grant a permanent injunction against the revocation of Knoetze's visa. The court agreed with Knoetze that the Secretary's act of revocation was subject to judicial review. The court also considered Knoetze's charge that civil rights leaders had exerted such intense political pressure upon the executive branch

105. Visa revocation may not necessarily preclude the person from receiving some other immigration benefit (such as asylum), allowing her to remain in the United States.

as to constitute impermissible levels of "political interference." Yet the court accepted the position of the Secretary that Knoetze's visa was lawfully revoked because of an admitted conviction in South Africa for a crime which the Secretary reasonably viewed as equivalent to an American felony involving moral turpitude.

This South African crime is entitled "Attempting to Obstruct or Impede the Process of Justice." The indictment to which Knoetze pled guilty alleged that he made several false statements while serving as a policeman in order to persuade citizens of his country to drop assault charges against a fellow police officer. The trial court accepted the conclusion of the Secretary that Knoetze's criminal conduct corresponded to the United States felony of "Influencing or Injuring an Officer, Juror or Witness," 18 U.S.C. § 1503, a felony involving moral turpitude. The trial court therefore upheld the Secretary's act of revocation.

* * *

We agree with the trial court that the judiciary may review a decision by the Secretary of State to revoke the visa of an alien within our country. On appeal, the government has dropped its argument of non-reviewability.

The proper standard of judicial review is expressed in the Administrative Procedure Act, 5 U.S.C. § 706(2). This is the limited standard of review applicable in the analogous context of deportation proceedings. *Wong Yang Sung v. McGrath*, 339 U.S. 33 (1950); *Jarecha v. Immigration and Nationalization Service*, 417 F.2d 220 (5th Cir. 1969).

* * *

Under this limited standard of review, we can enjoin the revocation of Knoetze's visa only if the Secretary has violated the law or committed a clear error of judgment. *Bowman Transportation, Inc. v. Arkansas-Best Freight Systems, Inc.*, 419 U.S. 281 (1974); *Refrigerated Transport Co. v. ICC*, 616 F.2d 748 (5th Cir. 1980). Our standard of review is the same as that of the trial court.

Congress has conferred upon the Secretary the power to revoke a visa in the following language: "After the issuance of a visa or other documentation to any alien, the consular officer, or the Secretary of State may at any time, in his discretion, revoke such visa or other documentation." 8 U.S.C. § 1201(i). No court has been called upon to decide whether this broad language confers authority upon the Secretary to revoke the visa of an alien after his entry into our country.

Knoetze argues that § 1201(i) merely confers revocation power prior to an alien's entry into the United States. He makes three supporting arguments. First, the overall statute to which this section belongs addresses the procedures for the issuance of visas to foreigners seeking initial entry. U.S.C. §§ 1151–1230. The language of § 1201(i) itself, after authorizing visa revocation, goes on to treat the liabilities of a transportation company that brings aliens into the country after the revocation of their visas.

Second, Congress entrusted major responsibility over aliens within the country to the Attorney General, rather than the Secretary of State, under a wholly different statutory scheme. 8 U.S.C. §§ 1251–60.

Third, Knoetze argues that the provision of due process safeguards in the Attorney General's deportation authorization, § 1252(b), coupled with the absence of any such safeguards in the Secretary's visa revocation authorization, § 1201(i), indicates a legislative intention of assigning responsibility for handling aliens within our country to the Attorney General, rather than the Secretary of State. Knoetze bolsters this argument by noting that aliens within the country are constitutionally entitled to procedural due process, while those outside the country receive no constitutional protection. *Shaughnessy v. United States*, 345 U.S. 206 (1953). He contends that in recognition of this distinction, Congress provided procedural safeguards in the Attorney General's deportation authorization because Congress intended the Attorney General to have responsibility over aliens after their arrival. We disagree.

We accept the argument of the government that § 1201(i) means exactly what it says: the Secretary may revoke an alien's visa "at any time." We reject Knoetze's invitation to limit this clear and broad language. We must assume that Congress used the unambiguous words "at any time" as they are commonly understood, even if a different interpretation would yield a result we would prefer. *United States v. Stewart*, 311 U.S. 60 (1940); *United States v. Porter*, 591 F.2d 1048 (5th Cir. 1979). Moreover, we accord considerable deference to the interpretation of § 1201(i) by the Department of State, the agency empowered by Congress to administer the issuance and revocation of visas. *E.I. duPont de Nemours & Co. v. Collins*, 432 U.S. 46 (1977). We hold that Congress has conferred upon the Secretary the authority to revoke the visa of an alien "at any time," even after he has entered our country.

We must now consider the substantive and procedural limitations upon the power conferred by § 1201(i). These limitations are implicit in the standard of review expressed in the Administrative Procedure Act, 5 U.S.C. § 706(2): (a) the Secretary must comply with any statutory procedures for the revocation of a visa; (b) the Secretary's act of revocation must not exceed his statutory authority; (c) the Secretary may not abuse his discretion by acting capriciously in revoking a visa; and (d) the Secretary must respect the constitutional rights enjoyed by visa holders within our borders.

The Secretary's method of revoking Knoetze's visa violated no statutory procedural requirements because the authorizing statute contains no procedural requisites. 8 U.S.C. § 1201(i). The Secretary acted within the bounds of his statutory authority because § 1201(i), as interpreted above, permitted the Secretary to revoke Knoetze's visa even after Knoetze had fully entered our country.

We further find that the Secretary lawfully acted within his discretion in revoking Knoetze's visa. The trial court determined that the Secretary revoked Knoetze's visa not because of impermissible "political interference," but because of Knoetze's conviction for a South African crime reasonably believed to correspond to an American felony involving moral turpitude.

Strong evidence of the politicalization of an otherwise routine, bureaucratic decision might raise a suspicion of discriminatory agency action. In this case, however, it is indisputed that Knoetze pled guilty to the South African crime of "Attempting to Obstruct or Impede the Process of Justice." ...

The American consul in South Africa issued Knoetze a visa because it believed that his offense fell within the misdemeanor petty offense exception of this Act. 8 U.S.C. § 1182(a)(9). The Secretary later concluded that Knoetze's conviction corresponded to a conviction for a felony involving moral turpitude. Because South African law differs greatly from American law, the Secretary compared the South African crime of "Attempting to Obstruct or Impede the Process of Justice" to the federal crime of "Influencing or Injuring an Officer, Juror or Witness," 18 U.S.C. § 1503. The acts prohibited by § 1503 constitute a felony. See 18 U.S.C. § 1(1). The misdemeanor petty offense exception is therefore inapplicable. The fraudulent acts prohibited by § 1503 also indicate moral turpitude: "fraud has consistently been regarded as such a contaminating component in any crime that American courts have, without exception, included such crimes within the scope of moral turpitude." *Jordan v. DeGeorge*, 341 U.S. 223, 229 (1951). The Secretary thus concluded that Knoetze was ineligible for a visa under 8 U.S.C. § 1182(a)(9).

... The conclusion reached by the Secretary in this case does not appear to be arbitrary or capricious or otherwise abusive of the discretion conferred upon him by § 1201(i). Even if experts differ as to whether Knoetze's foreign conviction corresponds to a felony involving moral turpitude, and even if hindsight shows that the Secretary has erred, his methods and conclusions appear entirely reasonable.

We must now determine whether the revocation of Knoetze's visa without notice complied with the due process rights guaranteed by the Constitution. The fifth amendment to the Constitution provides that "(n)o person shall be ... deprived of life, liberty, or property, without due process of law." Fifth amendment protection extends to all persons, including aliens, within the borders of the United States. *Kwong Hai Chew v. Colding*, 344 U.S. 590, (1953). Yet fifth amendment protection attaches only when the federal government seeks to deny a liberty or property interest. *Perry v. Sinderman*, 408 U.S. 593 (1972); *Downing v. Williams*, 624 F.2d 612 (5th Cir. 1980).

Knoetze argues that he has such a protected interest in the retention of his entry visa. He points out that he was denied a working visa by INS because of the revocation of his entry visa by the State Department. He contends that by denying him the opportunity to work in our country, the government effectively denied him the ability to remain here. Knoetze therefore urges us to recognize the constitutionally protected liberty and property interest in the retention of his visa. We decline.

We accept the position of the government that the revocation of an entry visa issued to an alien already within our country has no effect upon the alien's liberty or property interests. Revocation of an entry visa by the Secretary does not automatically lead to deportation of the alien. Congress has entrusted deportation to a different department of government, the Attorney General, and established different criteria for deportation than those for visa issuance and revocation. 8 U.S.C. § 1251 (Deportable Aliens-General Classes). Moreover, Congress has provided extensive procedural safeguards to those subject to deportation, including the right to reasonable notice, a fair hearing, opportunity for cross-examination and legal representation. 8 U.S.C. § 1252(b). Since deportation does not automatically follow visa revocation and any resulting deportation proceeding includes significant procedural safeguards, we hold that the revocation of an alien's visa jeopardizes no liberty or property interest entitled to constitutional protection.

We hold that the Secretary of State has the power under 8 U.S.C. § 1201(i) to revoke the visa of an alien even after an alien has entered the United States. We affirm the decision of the trial court that the revocation of a visa issued to an alien within the United States is subject to judicial review. We review such revocations under the Administrative Procedure Act, 5 U.S.C. § 706. We find no abuse of discretion in this case and no constitutional requirement of notice prior to revocation.

Notes

1. Do you agree with the court's conclusion that Knoetze had a liberty interest? What counter-arguments can be made to this point?

2. Was the court's statement that revocation of a visa is not necessarily followed by removal proceedings a fair characterization of the procedural posture in which Knoetze found himself? Does this make any difference to the underlying constitutional question?

3. If Knoetze had been denied a visa by the U.S. consul in South Africa, his case could not have been reviewed under the doctrine of non-reviewability of consular decisions.[106] However, litigants have been able to obtain review of visa revocations.[107] How would Knoetze have obtained review if his visa had been revoked prior to his arrival in the United States? A district court held that it had jurisdiction to review an overseas visa revocation where the litigant was in the United States. Apparently, the consul had granted the applicant a B-1 visa to allow him to tidy his affairs.[108] In another case involving the issuance of an immigrant visa, the Ninth Circuit held that while it could not review an immigrant visa determination, it could order the Consul to grant or deny a visa application that had been pending for eight years.[109]

4. The procedures governing visa revocation are found at 22 C.F.R. § 41.122. The notes to the Foreign Affairs Manual instruct consular officers not to revoke a visa if the person is "believed to be in the U.S. or has begun an uninterrupted journey to the U.S."[110] The procedure to be followed in such cases is for the consul to notify the

---

106. *See Kleindienst v. Mandel,* 408 U.S. 753, 766 (1972), and earlier discussion.

107. *See Wong v. Dep't of State,* 789 F.2d 1380 (9th Cir. 1986).

108. *Shimizu v. Dep't of State*, CV 89-2741 (C.D. Cal. 1990).

109. *Patel v. Reno*, 121 F.3d 1277 (9th Cir. 1997).

110. 9 FAM 41.122, note 2.

Department of State, which will then determine whether revocation and notification of USCIS is appropriate.[111]

5. **Visa revocation and expedited removal.** What might be the procedure used in the case of a person whom USCIS believes should not have been issued a visa in the first place? What kind of proof or information would they need in order to return a person without a hearing under expedited removal?

J. The Consular Non-Reviewability Doctrine

A recurring issue in immigration practice is the lack of effective administrative or judicial review in cases involving visa denials or revocations. As was described in our earlier discussion, these decisions are made by U.S. Consular officers located at embassies and consulates located overseas. An aggrieved party may seek an "advisory opinion" from the Visa Office of the Department of State. The advisory opinion does not force a specific result in the application process but is designed to provide guidance to the consular officer in applying the law to the facts. Judicial review of these decisions is narrowly proscribed under a doctrine commonly known as the "Doctrine of Consular Non-Reviewability." The restrictions are presented in greater detail in these materials at Chapter 12 (Administrative and Judicial Review).

The doctrine of consular non-reviewability is a natural extension of the plenary power doctrine and is reinforced by the generally limited jurisdiction of federal courts under U.S. law. The limits on judicial review were described in *Kleindienst v. Mandel*, where the Court held that it would only review a consular decision to determine if there was a "facially legitimate and bona fide reason" and that in conducting a review "the courts [would] neither look behind the exercise of that discretion, nor test it by balancing its justification" against constitutional rights.

K. Problem Exercises

Exercise 1

The potential client, a student from the Netherlands, is in her last year of a four-year undergraduate program in economics. She wishes to come to the United States to eventually complete a graduate program. Her English language skills are marginal, so she also wants to take a semester or so to study English. She is the beneficiary of a stipend from the Dutch government in the amount of approximately $2,000 per month, which is meant to cover all of her expenses. She has no other sources of income, as she has been disowned by her parents.

---

111. 9 FAM 41.122, procedural note 3.2.

What legal difficulties do you expect the client will have in gaining legal admission and status as a nonimmigrant in the United States?

Exercise 2

The client is a native and citizen of Algeria. She comes from a very wealthy family in Algeria and is now 20 years old. She studied art for one year at a French university and then returned to Algeria. She would like to come to the United States to study and has heard that there is a special government scholarship sponsored by the Algerian government which would help for her education. Her long-term goal is to stay in the United States, perhaps as a computer software engineer and maybe someday even starting her own company. The client's family is well-connected within the Algerian government and she believes that she can get the scholarship if she wants it. The client is currently in the United States on a tourist visa visiting with friends and requests legal advice as to the best way to proceed. The client is also a little worried about the political situation in Algeria and, if possible, would want to avoid going back there to apply for a visa.

1. What are the different visa options that might be used to accomplish her objectives?

2. Do any of these visas present potential problems for your client if she decides to remain after she has completed her studies? If so, what problems do you anticipate?

Exercise 3

The client works with George Soros (of the Soros Foundation) as Executive Director of the Open Society's office in Budapest, Hungary. She has worked with Open Society for 16 months. Mr. Soros wants the client to become the temporary director of the Soros Foundation's office in New York for a period of 18 months. There are a lot of problems at the NY office, and he will eventually appoint a permanent head of the organization. It is possible that the client could be considered for the position when it becomes open. The client has a graduate degree in Business Administration and extensive experience managing philanthropic organizations in Europe. The client has worked for several other European foundations and has eight years of cumulative experience running two major foundations in Paris and Rome in addition to her work for the Soros Foundation.

1. What nonimmigrant visa options would allow the client to come to the United States to manage the Soros Foundation office in New York?

2. What difficulties or problems do you see in bringing the client to the United States?

Chapter 7

Family-Based Immigrants

Introduction

In the next three chapters, we will explore the different avenues to lawful permanent resident status. Essentially there are two procedural routes—the immigrant visa and adjustment of status, and two bases—family and employment-based. In this chapter we will discuss the family-based immigration categories. In Chapter 8 we will cover the employment-based. Finally, in Chapter 9 we will discuss the special procedure of adjustment status which allows non-citizens to transition to permanent residency without having to get a visa.

During the early history of America, few restrictions were placed on immigration. Most of the action taken by the federal government in the area of immigration law was designed to encourage migration to this country. For instance, when Congress enacted the Act of March 2, 1819, its primary concern was the safety and health of the immigrants embarking on vessels bound for the United States.[1]

In the late 1800s, the official policy toward immigration began to become more restrictive. It initially took the form of health and welfare standards imposed on prospective citizens. Excluded were so-called "idiots, lunatics, convicts and persons likely to become a public charge,"[2] "persons suffering from a loathsome or dangerous contagious disease ... paupers and polygamists,"[3] and people convicted of certain criminal offenses. These restrictions sought to restrict legal immigration to those who were physically healthy and law-abiding.

Less rationally based and more controversial restrictions were later imposed. The first of these was a restriction on the grounds of national origin through the Chinese Exclusion Act of 1882.[4] The Chinese exclusion statutes were later expanded into the creation of what was called the Asiatic Barred Zone,[5] which rendered inadmissible natives of China, India, Burma, Siam, Polynesia, parts of Russia, Afghanistan and the countries of the Middle East.[6] The admission of Japanese and other Asian people not specifically barred by this 1917 Act was restricted by an in-

1. 3 Stat. 488.
2. Act of August 3, 1882, 22 Stat. 214.
3. Act of March 3, 1891, 26 Stat. 1084.
4. Act of May 6, 1882, 22 Stat. 58.
5. Act of Feb. 5, 1917, 39 Stat. 874 (1917).
6. Like a number of later immigration statutes, the 1917 Act was enacted over the President's veto.

formal undertaking to limit their emigration, which became known as "The Gentleman's Agreement."

In addition to the racial exclusion provisions, the 1917 Act imposed literacy requirements for aliens over the age of sixteen.[7] Interestingly, the literacy test did not require the ability to read English but rather excluded people "who could not read the English language or some other language or dialect." Each person could designate the particular language or dialect in which she desired the examination to be given.

These restrictions, and the value judgments inherent in them, were in part in response to the large influx of immigrants who came to this country in the period which preceded World War I. The two types of restrictions—a preference for people who were related to or culturally similar to citizens already here and for individuals who had achieved a certain level of education—have developed into recurring themes in our immigration laws.

The general preference for people with closer cultural ties with the dominant groups in the United States were reflected in the Quota Law of 1921.[8] The 1921 enactment attempted to freeze in place the then-existing national features of the country. The freeze was accomplished by limiting the number of persons of any nationality admitted annually to 3% of the foreign-born persons of that nationality who lived in this country in 1910. The McCarran-Walter Act continued the quota system, and it is the foundation of present immigration law.

These "national origin" quota provisions, though periodically modified, were eventually repealed by the Immigration and Nationality Act Amendments of 1965.[9] The 1965 amendments reflected two basic values. The first was a desire to promote the unification of families by issuing visas to close relatives of U.S. citizens and permanent residents. The second objective was a desire to promote the immigration of educated, skilled aliens who would enrich the community.[10]

In 1986, due in part to the existence of a large number of undocumented persons and in an effort to stem the flow of illegal migration, legislation was enacted to "legalize" or grant "amnesty" to these persons.[11] While the effect of the 1986 amendments

---

7. Section 3 of the Act of Feb. 5, 1917, 39 Stat. 874.

8. Act of May 19, 1921, 42 Stat. 5.

9. Pub. L. No. 89-236, 79 Stat. 911 (1965). For an excellent historical study of the legislation up to and including the 1952 Act, see 1952 U.S.C.C.A.N. 1680, 1692. The repeal of the national origin quota did not change the immigrant quota system or the racial biases reflected under the prior immigration statutes. Scholars have argued that because most immigration is based on close family ties, the closing out of racial minorities in the past was not remedied by the removal of the national origin quotas. Moreover, U.S. immigration laws continue to prohibit the immigration of more than 25,600 persons per year from each country. *See* 8 U.S.C. § 1152(a), Sec. 202(a). *See* Kevin R. Johnson, The "Huddled Masses" Myth: Immigration & Civil Rights 22–24 (2004).

10. Immigration and Nationality Act Amendments of 1965, Pub. L. No. 89-236, 1965 U.S.C.C.A.N. 3329.

11. The Immigration Reform and Control Act of 1986, Pub. L. No. 99-603, § 201, 100 Stat. 3359 (adding 8 U.S.C. § 1255a Sec. 245A).

on the immigrant quota system cannot be accurately measured, that legislation did not alter the allocation of immigrant visas. In 1990, at the culmination of the immigration reform process begun by the 1986 legislation, Congress modified the system of allocating immigrant visas.[12] This reform legislation expanded the number of immigrants permitted to enter the United States each year and, at the same time, shifted the allocation between the family-based and employment-based visas.

Under existing law, an immigrant is a person who seeks admission for the purpose of remaining permanently. As noted earlier, there is a statutory presumption that all persons coming to the United States are intending immigrants unless they can prove otherwise and establish their eligibility for an immigrant or nonimmigrant visa. These burdens on admission must be overcome both before the U.S. consul overseas and the U.S. Customs and Border Protection (CBP) officer at the border. If admitted as a lawful permanent resident, she may reside in this country indefinitely and is eligible to apply for citizenship within either three or five years.[13] All immigrants must meet certain personal qualitative standards[14] and complete the required administrative formalities prior to entry.[15] A person who is inadmissible to the United States and is unable to obtain a waiver of the grounds of inadmissibility will not receive an immigrant visa.

The statute requires that the arriving person be denied admission unless she fits into one of the specified immigrant visa categories (or otherwise establishes entitlement to a bona fide nonimmigrant visa). In addition to requiring that foreigners meet specific criteria of the immigrant visa categories, the immigration laws also limit their entry through an annual numerical quota. During the period from October 1991 through October 1994, the quota was set at 700,000, and in the following years at 675,000.[16] The statute precludes the admission of more than 25,600 immigrants in any year from any one country and further limits the immigration of persons from colonies to approximately 7,320.

As described earlier, the current system, which allows for those coming on a long-term basis, is divided into the broad categories of those with family ties with a U.S. citizen or lawful permanent resident, and those with desirable skills. Our discussion in this chapter will focus on the family-based immigrants and select categories of "special" immigrants.

---

12. *See* Sections 111, 121, 131 and 132 Immigration Act of 1990, Pub. L. No. 101-649, 104 Stat. 4978.

13. The time within which a person can apply for citizenship varies depending on how she obtained her permanent residency. Generally, if permanent residency was obtained through marriage to a U.S. citizen, the residency period is shorter. *See* Chapter 11.

14. These "personal qualitative standards" deal with the health, economic and criminal grounds of inadmissibility. *See generally* 8 U.S.C. § 1182(a), Sec. 212(a).

15. *See generally* 8 U.S.C. § 1181 (a), Sec. 211 (a).

16. *See* Sec. 101, Immigration Act of 1990, Pub. L. No. 101-649, 104 Stat. 4978.

A. Numerical Limits

1. Immigrants Admitted without Numerical Limits[17]

1. *Immediate Relatives.* There is no quota for this category, which includes spouses, certain widows/widowers (and their minor children),[18] parents and children of U.S. citizens. In the case of petitioning for parents, the petitioning "child" must be over the age of 21 in order to qualify the parents for admission.

2. *Special Immigrants.*[19] This category includes returning lawful permanent residents, certain persons who were former citizens and are returning to the country to regain their citizenship under 8 U.S.C. §§ 1435 or 1438,[20] certain children who are dependents of a juvenile court and are eligible for long-term foster care or are committed to the custody of a state agency[21] and certain religious workers.[22]

2. Immigrants Subject to Numerical Limits

The most significant changes made to the immigration laws by the 1990 Act related to the issuance of immigrant visas. The most important of these changes was in the immigrant selection system. Under prior law, "quota" visas were allocated to persons under six preference categories with a "catch-all" non-preference category. Changes made by the 1990 Act to the "quota" visas created the "family-based," "employment-based" and "diversity and transition" immigrant categories.[23] Our discussion of employment-based immigration will be covered in Chapter 8. The family-based immigrants are divided into four preferences:

1. *First Preference.* Unmarried sons and daughters of U.S. citizens.[24] This preference is limited to 23,400 visas plus any unused visas from the fourth preference visas.

2. *Second Preference.* Spouses and children of lawful permanent residents (2A) and unmarried sons and daughters of lawful permanent residents (2B).[25] This category is allocated 114,200 visas plus the unused portion designated for family immigration

---

17. While most of the immigrants described in this category are not restricted by an annual quota, approximately 254,000 of the first visas issued to immediate relatives are counted against the quota allocation for family-based immigrants. *See* 8 U.S.C. § 1151(c), Sec. 203(c). Juveniles described below under the "special immigrant" category are subject to the 4th Preference employment-based quota.

18. This change was enacted in 1990 and provides that the widow must have been married for at least two years and was not legally separated from the U.S. citizen spouse at the time of death. It also requires that she petition for status within two years of the spouse's death. Marriage by the surviving spouse eliminates the person's eligibility for immediate relative status. *See* 8 U.S.C. § 1151(b)(2)(A)(i), Sec. 201 (b)(2)(A)(i).

19. 8 U.S.C. § 1101(a)(27), Sec. 101(a)(27).

20. Sec. 324 and 327.

21. 8 U.S.C. § 1101(a)(27)(J), Sec. 101(a)(27)(J).

22. 8 U.S.C. § 1101(a)(27)(C)(ii), Sec. 101(a)(27)(C)(ii).

23. Diversity and transition visas are further described below. The complicated formula for determining diversity immigrants is described at 8 U.S.C. § 1153(c), Sec. 203(c).

24. 8 U.S.C. § 1153(a)(1), Sec. 203(a)(1).

25. 8 U.S.C. § 1153(a)(2)(A)–(B), Sec. 203(a)(2)(A)–(B).

not used by the first preference category; not less than 77% of the visas in this preference category are allocated for the spouse and minor children of lawful permanent residents.

3. *Third Preference.* Married sons and daughters of U.S. citizens.[26] This preference is allotted 23,400 plus whatever visas are not used by the first and second preferences.

4. *Fourth Preference.* Brothers and sisters of U.S.[27] This preference is allocated 65,000 plus whatever visas are not used by the first, second and third preferences.

A separate category of immigrant visas are termed *diversity immigrants.*[28] These visas are not based exclusively on the familial or employment relation normally required for immigration to the United States. Instead they are allocated on a formula intended to confer up to 55,000 visas to persons from low admission regions and countries of the world. These "diversity visas" are distributed in a lottery to persons from countries who have traditionally immigrated in fewer numbers (50,000). Northern Ireland is treated as a "diversity state for the purposes of this special program."[29] In establishing eligibility under the lottery, the applicant must establish that she has, as a minimum, the equivalent of a high school diploma and 2 years work experience in a field which requires at least 2 years of training or experience.[30]

Due to the extremely heavy demand for immigrant visas, most of the preference categories require that the applicant wait a lengthy period of time before actually obtaining a visa and becoming eligible for admission. A practitioner must fully understand each of the different preference categories and their relationships with the nonimmigrant categories in order to assure a client the speediest admission possible into the United States.

3. The Procedure

The prospective immigrant is either waiting overseas to come to the U.S. or is already in the country.[31] The most common procedure has the prospective immigrant overseas with a family member petitioner in the U.S. who files a petition to accord immediate relative or a family preference. This procedure is referred to variously as "overseas," "consular," or immigrant visa processing. Following the petition's approval, the beneficiary waits until there are available visas and appears at an interview with

---

26. 8 U.S.C. § 1153(a)(3), Sec. 203(a)(3).

27. 8 U.S.C. § 1153(a)(4), Sec. 203(a)(4).

28. The diversity visas are described at 8 U.S.C. § 1153(c), Sec. 203(c). The transition visas are not codified in the U.S. Code but are temporary provisions covered under the Act. *See* Sections 112, 132 and 133 of the Immigration Act of 1990, Pub. L. No. 101-649, 104 Stat. 4978 (1990).

29. 8 U.S.C. § 1153(c)(1)(F), Sec. 203(c)(1)(F).

30. 22 C.F.R. § 42.33 (2016). The applicant's spouse and immediate children are also eligible for admission, but visas issued will reduce the remaining eligible visas under the program. 8 U.S.C. § 1153(d), Sec. 203(d).

31. The prospective beneficiary with a family member who meets the immediate relative or one of the family-based preferences may qualify for the special procedure called "adjustment of status," which is described in greater detail in Chapter 9.

a U.S. Consular officer. At the interview, a determination is made as to whether the beneficiary remains qualified and is not subject to one of inadmissibility grounds.[32] Following the issuance of the visa, the beneficiary may travel to the U.S. for inspection at a port of entry. At the inspection point, the CBP officer reviews the documents in the beneficiary's file to determine whether there are any relevant inadmissibility grounds. If there are none, the person is admitted as a lawful permanent resident. If there are any applicable inadmissibility grounds, a determination will be made as to whether the person will be detained or paroled and proceedings instituted.[33]

B. Constitutional Issues

In our earlier discussion, we saw how immigration law is applied in removal whether it involved someone seeking admission or who had already been admitted. In the case below, we will see the breadth and power of Congress to decide who may be allowed admission as a lawful permanent resident. Even though this case is about a family based petition, the legal principles are applicable to all other types of immigrant visas.

Ramon Martin Fiallo, etc., et al., v. Griffin B. Bell, Attorney General of the United States

430 U.S. 787 (1976)

Mr. Justice White filed a dissenting statement.

Mr. Justice Marshall filed a dissenting opinion, in which Mr. Justice Brennan joined.

Mr. Justice Powell delivered the opinion of the Court.

This case brings before us a constitutional challenge to §§ 101(b)(1)(D) and 101(b)(2) of the Immigration and Nationality Act of 1952 (Act), 66 Stat. 182, as amended, 8 U.S.C. §§ 1101(b)(1)(D) and 1101(b)(2).

The Act grants special preference immigration status to aliens who qualify as the "children" or "parents" of United States citizens or lawful permanent residents. Under § 101(b)(1), a "child" is defined as an unmarried person under 21 years of age who is a legitimate or legitimated child, a stepchild, an adopted child, or an illegitimate child seeking preference by virtue of his relationship with his natural mother. The definition does not extend to an illegitimate child seeking preference by virtue of his relationship with his natural father. Moreover, under § 101(b)(2), a person qualifies as a "parent" for purposes of the Act solely on the basis of the person's relationship

32. If a ground of inadmissibility becomes apparent the waiver must be submitted. In most cases the waiver request must be decided by USCIS, which will delay the issuance of the immigrant visa.

33. Depending on the nature of the ground of inadmissibility, a waiver which can be adjudicated by USCIS might be available in lieu of a removal hearing before an immigration judge.

with a "child." As a result, the natural father of an illegitimate child who is either a United States citizen or permanent resident alien is not entitled to preferential treatment as a "parent."

The special preference immigration status provided for those who satisfy the statutory "parent-child" relationship depends on whether the immigrant's relative is a United States citizen or permanent resident alien. A United States citizen is allowed the entry of his "parent" or "child" without regard to either an applicable numerical quota or the labor certification requirement. 8 U.S.C. §§ 1151(a), (b), 1182(a)(14). On the other hand, a United States permanent resident alien is allowed the entry of the "parent" or "child" subject to numerical limitations but without regard to the labor certification requirement. 8 U.S.C. § 1182(a)(14).

Appellants are three sets of unwed natural fathers and their illegitimate offspring who sought, either as an alien father or an alien child, a special immigration preference by virtue of a relationship to a citizen or resident alien child or parent. In each instance the applicant was informed that he was ineligible for an immigrant visa unless he qualified for admission under the general numerical limitations and, in the case of the alien parents, received the requisite labor certification.[3]

Appellants filed this action in July 1974 in the United States District Court for the Eastern District of New York challenging the constitutionality of §§ 101(b)(1) and 101(b)(2) of the Act under the First, Fifth, and Ninth Amendments. Appellants alleged that the statutory provisions (i) denied them equal protection by discriminating against natural fathers and their illegitimate children "on the basis of the father's marital status, the illegitimacy of the child and the sex of the parent without either compelling or rational justification"; (ii) denied them due process of law to the extent that there was established "an unwarranted conclusive presumption of the absence of strong psychological and economic ties between natural fathers and their children born out of wedlock and not legitimated"; and (iii) "seriously burden(ed) and infringe(d) upon the rights of natural fathers and their children, born out of wedlock and not legitimated, to mutual association, to privacy, to establish a home, to raise

---

3. Appellant Ramon Martin Fiallo, a United States citizen by birth, currently resides in the Dominican Republic with his natural father, appellant Ramon Fiallo-Sone, a citizen of that country. The father initiated procedures to obtain an immigrant visa as the "parent" of his illegitimate son, but the United States Consul for the Dominican Republic informed appellant Fiallo-Sone that he could not qualify for the preferential status accorded to "parents" unless he legitimated Ramon Fiallo.

Appellant Cleophus Warner, a naturalized United States citizen, is the unwed father of appellant Serge Warner, who was born in 1960 in the French West Indies. In 1972 Cleophus Warner petitioned the Immigration and Naturalization Service to classify Serge as Warner's "child" for purposes of obtaining an immigrant visa, but the petition was denied on the ground that there was no evidence that Serge was Warner's legitimate or legitimated offspring.

Appellants Trevor Wilson and Earl Wilson, permanent resident aliens, are the illegitimate children of appellant Arthur Wilson, a citizen of Jamaica. Following the death of their mother in 1974, Trevor and Earl sought to obtain an immigrant visa for their father. We are informed by the appellees that although the application has not yet been rejected, denial is certain since the children are neither legitimate nor legitimated offspring of Arthur Wilson.

natural children and to be raised by the natural father." App. 11–12. Appellants sought to enjoin permanently enforcement of the challenged statutory provisions to the extent that the statute precluded them from qualifying for the special preference accorded other "parents" and "children."

* * *

At the outset, it is important to underscore the limited scope of judicial inquiry into immigration legislation. This Court has repeatedly emphasized that "over no conceivable subject is the legislative power of Congress more complete than it is over" the admission of aliens. *Oceanic Navigation Co. v. Stranahan*, 214 U.S. 320, 339 (1909); accord, *Kleindienst v. Mandel*, 408 U.S. 753, 766 (1972). Our cases "have long recognized the power to expel or exclude aliens as a fundamental sovereign attribute exercised by the Government's political departments largely immune from judicial control." *Shaughnessy v. Mezei*, 345 U.S. 206, 210 (1953); see, e.g., *Harisiades v. Shaughnessy*, 342 U.S. 580 (1952); *Lem Moon Sing v. United States*, 158 U.S. 538 (1895); *Fong Yue Ting v. United States*, 149 U.S. 698 (1893); *The Chinese Exclusion Case*, 130 U.S. 581 (1889). Our recent decisions have not departed from this long-established rule. Just last Term, for example, the Court had occasion to note that "the power over aliens is of a political character and therefore subject only to narrow judicial review." *Hampton v. Mow Sun Wong*, 426 U.S. 88, 101 n. 21 (1976), citing *Fong Yue Ting v. United States, supra*, at 713; accord, *Mathews v. Diaz*, 426 U.S. 67, 81–82 (1976). And we observed recently that in the exercise of its broad power over immigration and naturalization, "Congress regularly makes rules that would be unacceptable if applied to citizens." *Id.*, at 80.

Appellants apparently do not challenge the need for special judicial deference to congressional policy choices in the immigration context, but instead suggest that a "unique coalescing of factors" makes the instant case sufficiently unlike prior immigration cases to warrant more searching judicial scrutiny. Brief for Appellants 52–55. Appellants first observe that since the statutory provisions were designed to reunite families wherever possible, the purpose of the statute was to afford rights not to aliens but to United States citizens and legal permanent residents. Appellants then rely on our border-search decisions in *Almeida-Sanchez v. United States*, 413 U.S. 266 (1973), and *United States v. Brignoni-Ponce*, 422 U.S. 873 (1975), for the proposition that the courts must scrutinize congressional legislation in the immigration area to protect against violations of the rights of citizens. At issue in the border-search cases, however, was the nature of the protections mandated by the Fourth Amendment with respect to Government procedures designed to stem the illegal entry of aliens. Nothing in the opinions in those cases suggests that Congress has anything but exceptionally broad power to determine which classes of aliens may lawfully enter the country.

Appellants suggest a second distinguishing factor. They argue that none of the prior immigration cases of this Court involved "double-barreled" discrimination based on sex and illegitimacy, infringed upon the due process rights of citizens and legal permanent residents, or implicated "the fundamental constitutional interests of United States citizens and permanent residents in a familial relationship." Brief for

Appellants 53–54; see *id.*, at 16–18. But this Court has resolved similar challenges to immigration legislation based on other constitutional rights of citizens, and has rejected the suggestion that more searching judicial scrutiny is required. In *Kleindienst v. Mandel, supra*, for example, United States citizens challenged the power of the Attorney General to deny a visa to an alien who, as a proponent of "the economic, international, and governmental doctrines of World communism", was ineligible to receive a visa under 8 U.S.C. § 1182(a)(28)(D) absent a waiver by the Attorney General. The citizen-appellees in that case conceded that Congress could prohibit entry of all aliens falling into the class defined by § 1182(a)(28)(D). They contended, however, that the Attorney General's statutory discretion to approve a waiver was limited by the Constitution and that their First Amendment rights were abridged by the denial of Mandel's request for a visa. The Court held that "when the Executive exercises this (delegated) power negatively on the basis of a facially legitimate and bona fide reason, the courts will neither look behind the exercise of that discretion, nor test it by balancing its justification against the First Amendment interests of those who seek personal communication with the applicant." 408 U.S., at 770. We can see no reason to review the broad congressional policy choice at issue here under a more exacting standard than was applied in *Kleindienst v. Mandel*, a First Amendment case.[6]

We are dealing here with an exercise of the Nation's sovereign power to admit or exclude foreigners in accordance with perceived national interests. Although few, if any, countries have been as generous as the United States in extending the privilege to immigrate, or in providing sanctuary to the oppressed, limits and classifications as to who shall be admitted are traditional and necessary elements of legislation in this area. It is true that the legislative history of the provision at issue here establishes that congressional concern was directed at "the problem of keeping families of United States citizens and immigrants united." H.R.Rep. No. 1199, 85th Cong., 1st Sess., 7 (1957), U.S.Code Cong. & Admin.News, 1957, pp. 2016, 2020. See also H.R.Rep. No. 1365, 82d Cong., 2d Sess., 29 (1952), U.S.Code Cong. & Admin.News 1952, pp. 1653, 1680 (statute implements "the underlying intention of our immigration laws regarding the preservation of the family unit"). To accommodate this goal, Congress has accorded a special "preference status" to certain aliens who share relationships with citizens or permanent resident aliens. But there are widely varying relationships and degrees of kinship, and it is appropriate for Congress to consider not only the nature of these relationships but also problems of identification, administration, and the potential for fraud. In the inevitable process of "line drawing," Congress has determined that certain classes of aliens are more likely than others to satisfy national

6. The thoughtful dissenting opinion of our Brother Marshall would be persuasive if its basic premise were accepted. The dissent is grounded on the assumption that the relevant portions of the Act grant a "fundamental right" to American citizens, a right "given only to the citizen" and not to the putative immigrant. *Post*, at 1485, 1486, 1490. The assumption is facially plausible in that the families of putative immigrants certainly have an interest in their admission. But the fallacy of the assumption is rooted deeply in fundamental principles of sovereignty.

objectives without undue cost, and it has granted preferential status only to those classes.

Finally, appellants characterize our prior immigration cases as involving foreign policy matters and congressional choices to exclude or expel groups of aliens that were "specifically and clearly perceived to pose a grave threat to the national security," citing *Harisiades v. Shaughnessy*, 342 U.S. 580 (1952), "or to the general welfare of this country," citing *Boutilier v. INS*, 387 U.S. 118 (1967). Brief for Appellants 54. We find no indication in our prior cases that the scope of judicial review is a function of the nature of the policy choice at issue. To the contrary, "(s)ince decisions in these matters may implicate our relations with foreign powers, and since a wide variety of classifications must be defined in the light of changing political and economic circumstances, such decisions are frequently of a character more appropriate to either the Legislature or the Executive than to the Judiciary," and "(t)he reasons that preclude judicial review of political questions also dictate a narrow standard of review of decisions made by the Congress or the President in the area of immigration and naturalization." *Mathews v. Diaz*, 426 U.S., at 81–82. See *Harisiades v. Shaughnessy, supra*, at 588–589. As Mr. Justice Frankfurter observed in his concurrence in *Harisiades v. Shaughnessy*:

> The conditions of entry for every alien, the particular classes of aliens that shall be denied entry altogether, the basis for determining such classification, the right to terminate hospitality to aliens, the grounds on which such determination shall be based, have been recognized as matters solely for the responsibility of the Congress and wholly outside the power of this Court to control.

342 U.S., at 596–597.

As originally enacted in 1952, § 101(b)(1) of the Act defined a "child" as an unmarried legitimate or legitimated child or stepchild under 21 years of age. The Board of Immigration Appeals and the Attorney General subsequently concluded that the failure of this definition to refer to illegitimate children rendered ineligible for preferential nonquota status both the illegitimate alien child of a citizen mother, *Matter of A*, 5 I. & N.Dec. 272, 283–284 (A.G.1953), and the alien mother of a citizen born out of wedlock, *Matter of F*, 7 I. & N.Dec. 448 (B.I.A.1957). The Attorney General recommended that the matter be brought to the attention of Congress, *Matter of A, supra*, at 284, and the Act was amended in 1957 to include what is now 8 U.S.C. § 1101(b)(1)(D). See n. 1, *supra*. Congress was specifically concerned with the relationship between a child born out of wedlock and his or her natural mother, and the legislative history of the 1957 amendment reflects an intentional choice not to provide preferential immigration status by virtue of the relationship between an illegitimate child and his or her natural father.

* * *

This distinction is just one of many drawn by Congress pursuant to its determination to provide some but not all families with relief from various immigration restrictions that would otherwise hinder reunification of the family in this country. In addition to the distinction at issue here, Congress has decided that children, whether legitimate or not, cannot qualify for preferential status if they are married or are over 21 years of age. 8 U.S.C. § 1101(b)(1). Legitimated children are ineligible for preferential status unless their legitimation occurred prior to their 18th birthday and at a time when they were in the legal custody of the legitimating parent or parents. § 1101(b)(1)(C). Adopted children are not entitled to preferential status unless they were adopted before the age of 14 and have thereafter lived in the custody of their adopting or adopted parents for at least two years, § 1101(b)(1)(E). And stepchildren cannot qualify unless they were under 18 at the time of the marriage creating the stepchild relationship. § 1101(b)(1)(B).

* * *

Appellants suggest that the distinction drawn in § 101(b)(1)(D) is unconstitutional under any standard of review since it infringes upon the constitutional rights of citizens and legal permanent residents without furthering legitimate governmental interests. Appellants note in this regard that the statute makes it more difficult for illegitimate children and their natural fathers to be reunited in this country than for legitimate or legitimated children and their parents, or for illegitimate children and their natural mothers. And appellants also note that the statute fails to establish a procedure under which illegitimate children and their natural fathers could prove the existence and strength of their family relationship. Those are admittedly the consequences of the congressional decision not to accord preferential status to this particular class of aliens, but the decision nonetheless remains one "solely for the responsibility of the Congress and wholly outside the power of this Court to control." *Harisiades v. Shaughnessy*, 342 U.S., at 597. (Frankfurter, J., concurring). Congress obviously has determined that preferential status is not warranted for illegitimate children and their natural fathers, perhaps because of a perceived absence in most cases of close family ties as well as a concern with the serious problems of proof that usually lurk in paternity determinations. See *Trimble v. Gordon*, 430 U.S. 762, 771. In any event, it is not the judicial role in cases of this sort to probe and test the justifications for the legislative decision.

* * *

Mr. Justice MARSHALL, with whom Mr. Justice Brennan joins, dissenting.

Until today I thought it clear that when Congress grants benefits to some citizens, but not to others, it is our duty to insure that the decision comports with Fifth Amendment principles of due process and equal protection. Today, however, the Court appears to hold that discrimination among citizens, however invidious and irrational, must be tolerated if it occurs in the context of the immigration laws. Since I cannot agree that Congress has license to deny fundamental rights to citizens according to the most disfavored criteria simply because the Immigration and Nationality Act is involved, I dissent.

The Immigration and Nationality Act of 1952 (INA), 8 U.S.C. § 1101 et seq., establishes the terms and conditions for entry into the United States. Among its various conditions, the Act requires that an alien seeking to enter the United States as a legal permanent resident must come within a restrictive numerical quota and must satisfy certain labor certification requirements. INA §§ 201, 202, 212(a)(14), 8 U.S.C. §§ 1151, 1152, 1182(a)(14) (1976 ed.), as amended by the Immigration and Nationality Act Amendments of 1976, 90 Stat. 2703 (hereinafter 1976 Amendments). In recognition of the fact that such requirements frequently separate families, Congress has provided that American citizens may petition to have the requirements waived for their immediate families spouse, parents, children. INA §§ 201(a), (b), 212(a)(14), 8 U.S.C. §§ 1151(a), (b), 1182(a)(14).

The privilege is accorded only to those parents and children who satisfy the statute's definitions. Under INA § 101(b)(1), a "child" is defined as an unmarried person under 21 years of age who is a legitimate or legitimated child, a stepchild, an adopted child, or an illegitimate child by whom or on whose behalf a privilege is sought by virtue of the relationship of the child to its biological mother. 8 U.S.C. § 1101(b)(1). A "parent" is defined under INA § 101(b)(2) solely on the basis of the individual's relationship with a "child" as defined by § 101(b)(1). 8 U.S.C. § 1101(b)(2). The definitions cover virtually all parent-child relationships except that of biological father-illegitimate child. Thus while all American citizens are entitled to bring in their alien children without regard to either the numerical quota or the labor certification requirement, fathers are denied this privilege with respect to their illegitimate children. Similarly, all citizens are allowed to have their parents enter without regard to the labor certification requirement, and, if the citizen is over 21, also without regard to the quota. Illegitimate children, however, are denied such preferences for their fathers.

The unfortunate consequences of these omissions are graphically illustrated by the case of appellant Cleophus Warner. Mr. Warner is a naturalized citizen of the United States who, pursuant to 8 U.S.C. § 1154, petitioned the Attorney General for an immigrant visa for his illegitimate son Serge, a citizen of the French West Indies. Despite the fact that Mr. Warner acknowledged his paternity and registered as Serge's father shortly after his birth, has his name on Serge's birth certificate, and has supported and maintained Serge since birth, the special dispensation from the quota and labor certification requirements was denied because Serge was not a "child" under the statute. It matters not that, as the Government concedes, Tr. of Oral Arg. 25–26, Serge's mother has abandoned Serge to his father and has, by marrying another man, apparently rendered impossible, under French West Indies law, Mr. Warner's ever legitimating Serge. Mr. Warner is simply not Serge's "parent."

The Government contends that this legislation is not subject to judicial review. Pointing to the fact that aliens have no constitutional right to immigrate to the United States and to a long line of cases that recognize that policies pertaining to the entry of aliens and their right to remain here are peculiarly concerned with the political conduct of government, the Government concludes that "[t]he congressional decision whether or to whom to extend such a valuable privilege ... is not a subject of judicial concern." Brief for Appellees 22.

The Court rightly rejects this expansive claim and recognizes that "(o)ur cases reflect acceptance of a limited judicial responsibility ... even with respect to the power of Congress to regulate the admission and exclusion of aliens." *Ante*, at 1478 n. 5. It points out, however, that the scrutiny is circumscribed. Congress has "broad power to determine which classes of aliens may lawfully enter the country" and its political judgments warrant deference. *Ante*, at 1478–1479.

I wholeheartedly agree with the Court's rejection of the Government's claim of unreviewable discretion. Indeed, as I observed in *Kleindienst v. Mandel*, 408 U.S. 753, 781 (1972) (dissenting opinion), the old immigration cases that reflect an absolute "hands-off" approach by this Court "are not the strongest precedents in the United States Reports." I am pleased to see the Court reveal once again a "reluctance to rely on them completely." *Ibid.* I also have no quarrel with the principle that the essentially political judgments by Congress as to which foreigners may enter and which may not deserve deference from the judiciary.

My disagreement with the Court arises from its application of the principle in this case. The review the majority purports to require turns out to be completely "toothless." Cf. *Trimble v. Gordon*, 430 U.S., at 767. After observing the effects of the denial of preferential status to appellants, the majority concludes: "[B]ut the decision nonetheless remains one 'solely for the responsibility of the Congress and wholly outside the power of this Court to control.'" *Ante*, at 1481. Such "review" reflects more than due deference; it is abdication.[6] Assuming, arguendo, that such deference might be appropriate in some situations a supposition I find difficult to accept it is particularly inappropriate in this case.

This case, unlike most immigration cases that come before the Court, directly involves the rights of citizens, not aliens. "[C]oncerned with the problem of keeping families of United States citizens and immigrants united", H.R.Rep. No. 1199, 85th Cong., 1st Sess., 7 (1957), U.S. Code Cong. & Admin.News 1957, p. 2020, Congress extended to American citizens the right to choose to be reunited in the United States with their immediate families. The focus was on citizens and their need for relief from the hardships occasioned by the immigration laws. The right to seek such relief was given only to the citizen, not the alien. 8 U.S.C. § 1154. If the citizen does not petition the Attorney General for the special "immediate relative" status for his parent or child, the alien, despite his relationship, can receive no preference. 8 U.S.C. § 1153(d). It is irrelevant that aliens have no constitutional right to immigrate and that Americans have no constitutional right to compel the admission of their families. The essential fact here is that Congress did choose to extend such privileges to American citizens but then denied them to a small class of citizens. When Congress draws such lines among citizens, the Constitution requires that the decision comport with Fifth Amendment principles of equal protection and due process. The simple fact

6. The majority does not even engage in the modest degree of scrutiny required by *Kleindienst v. Mandel*, 408 U.S. 753 (1972). That failure, I submit, is due to the fact that the statute could not even pass that standard of review. See Part III, *infra*.

that the discrimination is set in immigration legislation cannot insulate from scrutiny the invidious abridgment of citizens' fundamental interests.

The majority responds that in *Kleindienst v. Mandel, supra*, the Court recognized that First Amendment rights of citizens were "implicated," but refused to engage in the close scrutiny usually required in First Amendment cases. Therefore, it argues, no more exacting standard is required here. In that case, Mandel, a Belgian "revolutionary Marxist," could visit this country only if the Attorney General waived the statutory prohibition of visas to "(a)liens who advocate the economic, international, and governmental doctrines of World communism." 8 U.S.C. § 1182(a)(28)(D). The Attorney General denied the waiver, and suit was brought by Mandel and several citizens who claimed that their First Amendment right to hear Mandel in person was abridged by the denial. Rejecting the Government's contention that it had "unfettered discretion, and any reason or no reason (for denying a waiver) may be given", the Court upheld the denial only after finding that it was based on a "legitimate and bona fide" reason Mandel's abuses of visa privileges on a prior visit. 408 U.S., at 769. At the same time, however, the Court chose not to scrutinize more closely and accepted the reason without weighing against it the claimed First Amendment interest. It feared becoming embroiled in the "dangerous and undesirable" task of considering, every time an alien was denied a waiver, such factors as the projected number of people wishing to speak with the alien and the probity of his ideas. *Id.*, at 769.

Whatever the merits of the Court's fears in *Mandel*, cf. *id.*, at 774 (Marshall, J., dissenting), the present case is clearly distinguishable in two essential respects. First, in Mandel, Congress had not focused on citizens and their need for relief. Rather, the governmental action was concerned with keeping out "undesirables." The impact on the citizens' right to hear was an incidental and unavoidable consequence of that political judgment. The present case presents a qualitatively different situation. Here, the purpose of the legislation is to accord rights, not to aliens, but to United States citizens. In so doing, Congress deliberately chose, for reasons unrelated to foreign policy concerns or threats to national security, to deny those rights to a class of citizens traditionally subject to discrimination. Second, in Mandel, unlike the present case, appellees conceded the ability of Congress to enact legislation broadly prohibiting the entry of all aliens with Mandel's beliefs. Their concern was directed instead to the exercise of the discretion granted the Attorney General to waive the prohibition. In the present case, by contrast, we are asked to engage in the traditional task of reviewing the validity of a general Act of Congress challenged as unconstitutional on its face. Totally absent therefore is the specter of involving the courts in second-guessing countless individual determinations by the Attorney General as to the merits of a particular alien's entrance.

The class of citizens denied the special privilege of reunification in this country is defined on the basis of two traditionally disfavored classifications gender and legitimacy. Fathers cannot obtain preferred status for their illegitimate children; mothers can. Conversely, every child except the illegitimate legitimate, legitimated, step-, adopted can obtain preferred status for his or her alien father. The Court has little tolerance for either form of discrimination. We require that gender-based classifications "serve important governmental objectives and ... be substantially related to achievement of those objectives." *Califano v. Webster*, 430 U.S. 313, 317; *Califano v. Goldfarb*, 430 U.S. 199, 210–211. We are similarly hostile to legislation excluding illegitimates from governmental beneficence, finding it "illogical and unjust" to deprive a child "simply because its natural father has not married its mother." *Gomez v. Perez*, 409 U.S. 535 538 (1973).

But it is not simply the invidious classifications that make the statute so vulnerable to constitutional attack. In addition the statute interferes with the fundamental "freedom of personal choice in matters of marriage and family life". *Cleveland Board of Education v. LaFleur*, 414 U.S. 632, 639–640 (1974); see also *Roe v. Wade*, 410 U.S. 133 (1973); *Wisconsin v. Yoder*, 406 U.S. 205, 231–233(1972); *Stanley v. Illinois*, 405 U.S. 645, 651 (1972). The right to live together as a family belongs to both the child who seeks the entrance of his or her father and the father who seeks to bring his child in.

In view of the legislation's denial of this right to these classes, it is clear that, whatever the verbal formula, the Government bears a substantial burden to justify the statute.

There is no dispute that the purpose of these special preference provisions is to reunify families separated by the immigration laws. As Congress itself declared "(t)he legislative history of the Immigration and Nationality Act clearly indicates that the Congress intended (in these provisions) to provide for a liberal treatment of children and was concerned with the problem of keeping families of United States citizens and immigrants united." H.R.Rep. No. 1199, 85th Cong., 1st Sess., 7 (1957), U.S.Code Cong. & Admin.News 1957, p. 2020. It is also clear that when Congress extended the privilege to cover the illegitimate-child-mother relationship in 1957, it did so to alleviate hardships it found in several cases denying preferential status to illegitimate children and their mothers. *Id.*, at 7–8. Accord, S.Rep. No. 1057, 85th Cong., 1st Sess., 4 (1957).

The legislative history, however, gives no indication of why these privileges were absolutely denied illegitimate children and their fathers. The Government suggests that Congress may have believed that "such persons are unlikely to have maintained a close personal relationship with their offspring." Brief for Appellees 17. If so, Congress' chosen shorthand for "closeness" is obviously overinclusive. No one can dispute that there are legitimate, legitimated, step-, and adoptive parent-child relationships and mother-illegitimate child relationships that are not close and yet are accorded the preferential status. Indeed, the most dramatic illustration of the overinclusiveness is the fact that while Mr. Warner can never be deemed a "parent" of Serge, nevertheless, if he should marry, his wife could qualify as a stepparent, entitled to obtain for Serge the preferential status that Mr. Warner cannot obtain. *Andrade v. Esperdy*, 270 F.Supp. 516 (S.D.N.Y. 1967); *Nation v. Esperdy*, 239 F.Supp. 531 (S.D.N.Y. 1965). Similarly, a man who, in an adulterous affair, fathers a child outside his marriage cannot be the "parent" of that child, but his wife may petition as stepparent. *Matter of Stultz*, 15 I. & N. Dec.—(1975).

* * *

This Court has been equally intolerant of the rationale when it is used to deny rights to the illegitimate child. While we are sensitive to "the lurking problems with respect to proof of paternity," *Trimble v. Gordon*, 430 U.S., at 771 quoting *Gomez v. Perez*, 409 U.S. 535, 538 (1973), we are careful not to allow them to be "made into an impenetrable barrier that works to shield otherwise invidious discrimination." *Trimble*, 430 U.S., at 771. We require, at a minimum, that the statute (be) "carefully tuned to alternative considerations," 430 U.S., at 772, quoting *Mathews v. Lucas*, 427 U.S., at 513, and not exclude all illegitimates simply because some situations involve difficulties of proof. *Ibid.*

... As I observed earlier, since Congress gave no indication that administrative costs were its concern we should scrutinize the hypothesis closely. The likelihood of such a rationale is diminished considerably by the comprehensive and elaborate administrative procedures already established and employed by the INS in passing on claims of the existence of a parent-child relationship. All petitions are handled on a case-by-case basis with the petitioner bearing the burden of proof. Moreover, the INS is no stranger to cases requiring proof of paternity. When, for example, a citizen stepmother petitions for the entrance of her husband's illegitimate child, she must necessarily prove that her husband is the child's father. Indeed, it is ironic that if Mr. Warner marries and his wife petitions for Serge, her proof will, in fact, be one step more complex than his would be not only must she prove his paternity, but she must also prove their marriage. Nevertheless, she would be entitled to an opportunity to prove those facts; he is not.

Nor is a fear of involvement with foreign laws and records a persuasive explanation of the omission. In administering the Act with respect to legitimated children, for example, the critical issue is whether the steps undertaken are adequate under local law to render the child legitimate, and the INS has become expert in such matters. I note, in this connection, that where a child was born in a country in which all children are legitimate, proof of paternity is the critical issue and the proof problems are identical to those involved with an illegitimate child.

Given the existence of these procedures and expertise, it is difficult indeed to give much weight to the hypothesized administrative-convenience rationale. Moreover, as noted previously, this Court will not allow concerns with proof to justify "an impenetrable barrier that works to shield otherwise invidious discrimination." *Gomez, supra*, at 538. As the facts of this case conclusively demonstrate, Congress has "failed to consider the possibility of a middle ground between the extremes of complete exclusion and case-by-case determination of paternity." *Trimble*, 430 U.S., at 770–771. Mr. Warner is a classic example of someone who can readily prove both paternity and closeness. Appellees concede this Tr. of Oral Arg. 21–22. The fact that he is denied the opportunity demonstrates beyond peradventure that Congress has failed to "carefully tun(e) (the statute) to alternative considerations." *Trimble*, 430 U.S., at 772, quoting *Mathews v. Lucas*, 427 U.S., at 513. That failure is fatal to the statute. *Trimble*, 430 U.S., at 772–773.

* * *

When Congress grants a fundamental right to all but an invidiously selected class of citizens, and it is abundantly clear that such discrimination would be intolerable in any context but immigration, it is our duty to strike the legislation down. Because the Court condones the invidious discrimination in this case simply because it is embedded in the immigration laws, I must dissent.

Mr. Justice WHITE also dissents, substantially for the reasons stated by Mr. Justice Marshall in his dissenting opinion.

Notes

1. Amendments enacted in 1986 removed some aspects of the discriminatory treatment challenged in *Fiallo*. The amendments, which are contained in 8 U.S.C. § 1101(b)(1)(D), allow a petition by the natural father "if the father has or had a bona fide parent-child relationship."

2. Statutes conferring citizenship by a child's overseas birth to a U.S. citizen apply a similar rule as used in determining the parent-child relation for purposes of permanent resident status. The Court held in *Miller v. Albright*[34] that imposing a different standard where the person claimed citizenship based on a child's out-of-wedlock birth to her U.S. citizen father was not unconstitutional.[35] More recently in *Sessions v. Morales-Santana*,[36] which involved a gender-differentiated standard in conferring U.S. citizenship on a child born abroad, the Court found that the statute was incompatible with the Fifth Amendment's equal protection requirements. It remains to be seen how courts will deal with future equal protection challenges.

3. The Supreme Court in *Nguyen v. INS*[37] held that differential requirements as between fathers and mothers of U.S. citizens withstood constitutional scrutiny. In *Nguyen*, the U.S. citizen father had custody of a child born out of wedlock but only completed the paternity proceedings after his son had reached the age of 22. The statute in question, 8 U.S.C. § 1409(a)(4), required that these steps be completed before the child reached the age of 18. Unlike *Fiallo*, *Nguyen* involved the application of a statute conferring U.S. citizenship on children born outside of the country to one or more U.S. citizen parents. In *Nguyen*, he would have been regarded as a citizen if the situation had been reversed, that is, his mother had been a U.S. citizen.

C. Allocation of Visas

As described previously, immigrant visas are allocated first to certain "immediate relatives" of U.S. citizens and then under a complex preference quota system to persons

---

34. 523 U.S. 420 (1998).
35. *Miller v. Albright* appears in Chapter 11 (Naturalization and Citizenship).
36. 137 S. Ct. 1678 (2017). This case is also explored at greater length in Chapter 11.
37. 533 U.S. 53 (2001).

based on their relationship with a U.S. citizen or permanent resident. The case below which discusses the distribution of visas within the employment-based preference system illustrates both the complexity of the system and the difficulty in resolving its problems.

Providing the reader with more than a general understanding of how the system is structured and works is not the objective of these materials. This complex visa allocation system is managed by the U.S. Department of State and has two basic principles that are embodied in the immigration statute.[38] The first that more immigrants than provided by law can be admitted to the U.S in any given year. The second is that immigrants be issued visas as closely as possible to the order in which they applied. One inevitable problem in such a system is that at the end of each fiscal year, a number of immigrant visas go unissued. The blogpost which is excerpted below does a good job in illustrating the system and this problem.

Brent Renison, How Does Uncle Sam Waste Immigrant Visas?

ENTRY LAW BLOG (Oct. 6, 2015)*

I'm going to explain exactly how the government wastes on average tens of thousands of immigrant visas every year, contrary to Congressional intent, systematically compromising the workforce and keeping families apart. Every number in this report represents a green card which could have been issued to a waiting immigrant, but was not handed out due to government mismanagement and ineptitude. This loss of numbers impacts the very lives of legal immigrants in significant and permanent ways. To understand how this happens, we have to look at numbers. Because the formulas and calculations get a little complicated, and because the system of numerical limits set up by Congress in 1990 doesn't make a lot of sense, I'm going to use an analogy. We'll talk about how the system is like a theater that distributes tickets. The show is the American Dream, and not everyone gets seated. In fact, in this theater, not every seat gets filled even though there are plenty of people wanting to see the show.

The theater analogy is based on real immigrant categories and numbers. First, the immediate relatives of U.S. citizens are spouses, parents and minor children of U.S. citizens. Immediate relatives can immigrate in an unlimited number, so we will call them the VIPs. Second, are the family immigrants, such as the spouses of permanent residents, adult children of citizens, and brothers and sisters of citizens. We'll just call them family immigrants. Third, are the employment immigrants, such as advance degree holders, individuals of extraordinary ability, outstanding

38. *De Avilia v. Civiletti*, 643 F.2d 471, 475 (7th Cir.1981).

* http://www.entrylaw.com/blog/thousands-more-wasted-visas. [https;//perma.cc/ELJ2-ZT4X].

researchers and professors, and other professionals. So the three categories are VIP, family and employment.

In 1990, Congress established a limit of 140,000 employment immigrants, and a limit of 480,000 family immigrants, except that the numbers of VIP immigrants who were given green cards from the previous year would subtract from the family limit. For example, in 1989, when Congress would have been considering what rules to enact, there were 217,000 VIPs. So the number of family immigrants would have been 480,000 minus 217,000, which is 263,000. As a protection against a situation where there were more VIPs in future years, Congress established a minimum of 226,000 immigrants for the family category. So even if the number of VIPs in the prior year was more than the 480,000, there would still be 226,000 family immigrants allowed for the year. Also, to protect against numbers going unused, Congress allowed unused family numbers to be used in the employment line the next year, and unused employment numbers to be used in the family line the following year. You can see Congress wanted all the numbers utilized.

Let's get to the theater. There is one particular theater employee who holds all the tickets to the show. Let's call him Uncle Sam, since he represents the government. Each night at the theater represents a year of immigration. For simplicity, let's not use thousands of tickets, but just hundreds. So Sam is holding 140 instead of 140,000 tickets for employment folks. He has 480 family tickets, but the theater boss—that's Congress, let's call her Big Boss—said he has to subtract the number of VIPs who came in the night before. Let's use the example of 1989 numbers, and say 217 VIPs came through the door last night. So, 480 minus 217 equals 263, which is the number of tickets that can be used for the family line. That night, Sam is so slow he only manages to distribute 130 tickets to the employment line before the show is over, leaving 10 seats unfilled. He also gives out only 210 of the 263 tickets for family, leaving 53 seats unfilled. That night 300 VIPs come to watch the show. Big Boss tells Sam to take the 10 employment tickets he failed to hand out in time and put them in the family pile for the next night, and the 53 undistributed family tickets into the employment pile. He does, and the next day he takes 140 new employment tickets and adds them to the 53 family tickets so he has 193 tickets. He takes 480 new family tickets, plus the 10 employment tickets, which is 490, but then Big Boss tells him to subtract last night's VIP numbers from the pile, leaving him with only 190. But since the family line always has a minimum of 226 tickets, he increases the tickets to that number.

Every night thereafter, Sam slowly hands out the tickets, failing to give them all out, and almost always leaving people waiting outside while empty seats remain inside for the American Dream show. He moves the undistributed employment tickets to the family pile for the next night, but because each night the VIPs are in the 400 to 500 range now, he always just has 226 family tickets the next night. The unused employment tickets essentially vanish. That is what is happening with our immigration system, and has been happening from 1990 until the present time.

The CIS Ombudsman's office, which is an independent office within the Department of Homeland Security which provides some independent oversight of the country's immigration agency the USCIS, issued a report in 2010 which showed that over the years, over half a million employment based green cards were wasted, and nearly a quarter million family green cards lost as well. In 2000, the AC21 law provided for recapture of 130,000 of the lost employment numbers, and in 2005 the REAL ID Act recaptured another 50,000 employment numbers, still leaving about 326,000 employment based green cards wasted, unused, and lost due to government mismanagement of the system.

You know, I gotta say, if Sam was my employee I would have put him on a performance improvement plan long ago, but Big Boss (i.e. Congress) has simply given him extra tickets to use, and in turn, waste and lose again. In fact, after the bail out of Sam's losses, he has continued to lose them. Even after the 2010 Ombudsman's report, the losses have continued. It is hard to tell, because in 2008, after the REAL ID Act bailout, Sam stopped providing the detailed calculations used to show the unused numbers. That's right, the reports abruptly stopped, leaving only the raw data. Well, I wanted to know just how many green cards were lost to Sam's slow moving hand in the five fiscal years from 2010 to 2014, so I got out my calculator, and started adding and subtracting. It was like helping my middle schooler all over again with math problems. But now, for the first time, everyone can see the waste that has occurred since the Ombudsman's 2010 report to Big Boss. More than 38,000 family numbers were lost, and over 8,500 employment green cards were wasted, just in the past 5 years alone. Those are more than just numbers. Those are lives hanging in the balance. Those numbers represent separated family members, dreams on hold, and children who age out and lose eligibility.

To be fair, Sam has a difficult job. Big Boss stuck him with a formula that was bound to fail from the get-go. While Congress may have intended all the unused visas to roll over from one category to the other and vice-versa, they failed to anticipate that the number of VIPs, the immediate relatives, would dwarf the 480,000 limit, leaving only the 226,000 minimum. If they had realized that back in 1989 or 90, perhaps they would have added the unused numbers in the employment column to the 226,000 minimum instead of the 480,000, and the numbers wouldn't be lost. But the VIP numbers have been over 400,000 for decades, and now every single unused visa in the employment category goes to waste.

The dual date Visa Bulletin, announced in September 2015 for October 2015, was an attempt to allow individuals to file earlier, and thus give the agency more time to process applications to final decision before the theater closed for the night. By providing two lists, one for those who could file, and one for those whose cases could finally be approved, the agency would have a better chance at finishing the work in time. The dual date Visa Bulletin was an attempt to work within the existing flawed system to simply give Sam more time to hand out tickets so they're fully distributed, and so the American Dream show would have all seats filled. But in its execution, the October 2015 Visa Bulletin failed because the two agencies which give out green cards, the Department of State and the USCIS, can't seem to communicate.

* * *

Notes

1. Below is the chart referenced in the preceding blogpost. USCIS Ombudsman, *Unused Family and Employment Preference Visas—FY 1992–2009*, ANNUAL REPORT 2010 at 39 (Jun. 30, 2010).

Fiscal Year	Unused Family Preference Numbers	Unused Employment Preference Numbers	Following FY's Family Preference Limit	Following FY's Employment Preference Limit
1992	5,435	21,207	232,483	161,207
1993	3,213	0	226,000	143,213
1994	6,503	29,430	253,721	146,503
1995	0	58,694	311,819	140,000
1996	0	21,173	226,000	140,000
1997	0	40,710	226,000	140,000
1998	20,906	53,571	226,000	160,906
1999	2,299	98,941	294,601	142,299
2000	52,074	31,098	226,000	192,074
2001	2,632	5,511	226,000	142,632
2002	31,532	0	226,000	171,532
2003	64,422	88,482	226,000	204,422
2004	8,449	47,305	226,000	148,449
2005	3,949	0	226,000	143,949
2006	7,148	10,288	226,000	147,148
2007	22,704	0	226,000	162,704
2008	0	0	226,000	140,000
2009	10,662	0	226,000	150,662
Total	241,928	506,410 (180,039 were recaptured by special legislation)		

2. As was highlighted in the blog article, when there are delays in issuing visas beyond the end of the fiscal year, those visas are lost and fewer people might be admitted than provided for under the statute.

3. In cases involving diversity visa applicants, these adjudication delays can lead to the applicant's ineligibility for the visa.[39] Challenges to these delays have been un-

39. 8 U.S.C. § 1154(a)(1); 22 C.F.R. § 42.33(a)(a).

successful.[40] However because eligibility for family and employment-based visas are based on proving a relationship, the person who does not receive a visa due to delay would continue to be eligible when the visa become available again in the following fiscal year.

4. *Zixiang v. Kerry*[41] rejected the plaintiff's claim that USCIS's misallocation of employment-based visas warranted the remedy of forcing the agency to make visas available to injured parties.

5. **Priority Dates.** A priority date establishes the applicant's place in the waiting line for a visa. Conceptually, it is the date on which the person manifested an intent to immigrate coupled with a prima facie showing of eligibility for the preference category. An applicant is accorded a priority date based on the date the preference petition was filed on her behalf (in the case of relative visa petitions) or the filing date of the labor certification application (for employment-based immigrants). The use of priority dates establishes a uniform method for determining the order of processing visa applications.

Family unification has long been a cornerstone of immigration law, and the INA allows dependent family members to immigrate under the same immigrant visa preference category and priority date as the primary immigrant they are "accompanying" or "following to join."[42] "Accompanying" family members are those who immigrate within six months of the primary immigrant's entry into the United States.[43] Family members "following to join" must have met the definition of spouse or child under the INA prior to the primary immigrant's admission into the United States under the immigrant visa, and they are chargeable to the country's quota which would ensure their quickest admittance.[44]

Review the statute and consider what changes USCIS could make to the existing rules on priority dates.[45] Could USCIS require that a priority date not be accorded where it is later determined that the beneficiary was in the United States when the application was filed? Could they ignore a person's priority date where it is later determined that the applicant had been working illegally in the United States and her whereabouts were not disclosed in the application?

6. **Chargeability.** The INA provides that immigrant visas must be "charged" against an annual quota. The immigrant visa statutory scheme allocates visa numbers to beneficiaries based on eligibility for preference classification, order of application and country of birth. Since the number of immigrants who may be admitted from each

40. *Mwasaru v. Napoitano*, 619 F.3d 545 (6th Cir. 2010); *Mohamed v. Gonzales*, 436 F.3d 79 (3d Cir. 2006) (court held that the case was moot since at the end of the fiscal year, the agency was without authority to issue a visa); *Iddir v. INS*, 301 F.3d 492, 499 (7th Cir. 2002) (court lacked jurisdiction to issue mandamus).

41. 710 F.3d 995, 1001–02 (9th Cir. 2013).

42. 8 U.S.C. § 1153(d), Sec. 203(d).

43. 22 C.F.R. § 40.1(a)(1).

44. 8 U.S.C. § 1152(b)(1)–(2), Sec. 202(b)(1)–(2).

45. *See* 8 U.S.C. § 1153(c), Sec. 203(c).

country is limited to 25,600 per year, the visas must, in effect, be charged to the country's allotment. As a general rule, immigrant visas are charged to the beneficiary's country of birth.[46] Exceptions have been provided to allow a child or spouse to be chargeable to the parent or accompanying spouse's country of birth in the interest of family unity,[47] and this is referred to as "cross chargeability." Furthermore, former U.S. citizens seeking to return to the country are charged to their present country of citizenship.

7. The table which appears below was issued by the Department of State Visa Office and is used by consular officers and USCIS as a guide in determining who might be eligible to receive a visa during a given month. It is used by lawyers to estimate how long it might take for an applicant to proceed from establishing eligibility for a visa to actually receiving the visa. The vertical column at the left margin represents the preference categories. The horizontal row across the top represents the beneficiary's country of nationality. The dates which appear in the columns represent the priority date which are being processed for family-based immigrant visas during the month of the bulletin. The most current bulletin can be found at

https://travel.state.gov/content/travel/en/legal/visa-law0/visa-bulletin.html

Family-Based Immigrants Visa Office Bulletin, November 2017

Family Sponsored	All Chargeability Areas Except Those Listed	China-Mainland Born	India	Mexico	Philippines
F1	22JAN11	22JAN11	22JAN11	01APR96	01JAN07
F2A	15NOV15	15NOV15	15NOV15	01NOV15	15NOV15
F2B	15NOV10	15NOV10	15NOV10	22JUL96	01JAN07
F3	15AUG05	15AUG05	15AUG05	08MAY95	01MAR95
F4	22MAY04	22MAY04	22OCT03	08OCT97	06JUN94

The "2A" category is for spouses and children of lawful permanent residents while the "2B" category is for unmarried sons and daughters of lawful permanent residents.

For example, assume that A, who was born in India, is the beneficiary of a third preference family application submitted on January 1, 2001. Even though A was eligible for third preference classification, she will not be issued an immigrant visa in August 2009, but she might be eligible later in the year.

8. In the event a visa application is denied by the United States consul, the applicant may have her case reviewed by the Bureau of Consular Affairs, Advisory Opinions

46. *See* 8 U.S.C. § 1152(b), Sec. 202(b); 22 C.F.R. § 42.12.
47. 8 U.S.C. § 1152(b)(1)–(2), Sec. 202(b)(1)–(2).

Office, which will issue its view on how the law should be interpreted.[48] Only the legal opinion issued by the Department are binding, and the consular officers are left to determine the facts based upon their interview.[49]

D. Definition of "Child"

We will now look more closely at the operation of family-based immigration provisions. We begin by examining the statutory definition of "child" and look at some of the fundamental constitutional issues raised in Congress' power to limit immigrant visas through this definition. The following case arises in the context of the rights of a U.S. citizen father to petition for his child as an immediate relative.

1. Statutory Definition

8 U.S.C. § 1101(b), Sec. 101(b)

(1) The term "child" means an unmarried person under twenty-one years of age who is—

(A) a child born in wedlock;

(B) a stepchild, whether or not born out of wedlock, provided the child had not reached the age of eighteen years at the time the marriage creating the status of stepchild occurred;

(C) a child legitimated under the law of the child's residence or domicile, or under the law of the father's residence or domicile, whether in or outside the United States, if such legitimation takes place before the child reaches the age of eighteen years and the child is in the legal custody of the legitimating parent or parents at the time of such legitimation;

(D) a child born out of wedlock, by, through whom, or on whose behalf a status, privilege, or benefit is sought by virtue of the relationship of the child to its natural mother or to its natural father if the father has or had a bona fide parent-child relationship with the person;

(E) a child adopted while under the age of sixteen years if the child has been in the legal custody of, and has resided with, the adopting parent or parents for at least two years: Provided, That no natural parent of any such

48. Initial internal review at the Consulate is conducted by the "principal consular officer." 22 C.F.R. § 42.81(c)–(d) (1989).

49. *See* Wolff, *The Non-Reviewability of Consular Visa Decisions: An Unjustified Aberration from American Justice,* 5 N.Y.L. Sch. J. Int'l Comp. L. 341, 347–50 (1984); Donald S. Dobkin, *Challenging the Doctrine of Consular Nonreviewability in Immigration Cases*, 24 Geo. Immig. L.J. 113 (2010).

adopted child shall thereafter, by virtue of such parentage, be accorded any right, privilege, or status under this Act; or

(F) a child, under the age of sixteen at the time a petition is filed in his behalf to accord a classification as an immediate relative under section 201(b), who is an orphan because of the death or disappearance of, abandonment or desertion by, or separation or loss from, both parents, or for whom the sole or surviving parent is incapable of providing the proper care and has in writing irrevocably released the child for emigration and adoption; who has been adopted abroad by a United States citizen and spouse jointly, or by an unmarried United States citizen at least twenty-five years of age, who personally saw and observed the child prior to or during the adoption proceedings; or who is coming to the United States for adoption by a United States citizen and spouse jointly, or by an unmarried United States citizen at least twenty-five years of age, who have or has complied with the preadoption requirements, if any, of the child's proposed residence: Provided, That the Attorney General is satisfied that proper care will be furnished the child if admitted to the United States: Provided further, That no natural parent or prior adoptive parent of any such child shall thereafter, by virtue of such parentage, be accorded any right, privilege, or status under this Act.

(G) (i) a child, younger than 16 years of age at the time a petition is filed on the child's behalf to accord a classification as an immediate relative under section 1151(b) of this title, who has been adopted in a foreign state that is a party to the Convention on Protection of Children and Co-operation in Respect of Intercountry Adoption, done at The Hague on May 29, 1993, or who is emigrating from such a foreign state to be adopted in the United States by a United States citizen and spouse jointly or by an unmarried United States citizen who is at least 25 years of age, Provided, That—

(I) the Secretary of Homeland Security is satisfied that proper care will be furnished the child if admitted to the United States;

(II) the child's natural parents (or parent, in the case of a child who has one sole or surviving parent because of the death or disappearance of, abandonment or desertion by, the other parent), or other persons or institutions that retain legal custody of the child, have freely given their written irrevocable consent to the termination of their legal relationship with the child, and to the child's emigration and adoption;

(III) in the case of a child having two living natural parents, the natural parents are incapable of providing proper care for the child;

(IV) the Secretary of Homeland Security is satisfied that the purpose of the adoption is to form a bona fide parent-child relationship, and the parent-child relationship of the child and the natural parents has been terminated (and in carrying out both obligations under this sub-clause the Secretary of Homeland Security may consider whether there is a petition pending to confer immigrant status on one or both of such natural parents); and

(V) in the case of a child who has not been adopted—

(aa) the competent authority of the foreign state has approved the child's emigration to the United States for the purpose of adoption by the prospective adoptive parent or parents; and

(bb) the prospective adoptive parent or parents has or have complied with any pre-adoption requirements of the child's proposed residence; and

(ii) except that no natural parent or prior adoptive parent of any such child shall thereafter, by virtue of such parentage, be accorded any right, privilege, or status under this chapter; or

(iii) subject to the same provisos as in clauses (i) and (ii), a child who—

(I) is a natural sibling of a child described in clause (i), subparagraph (E)(i), or subparagraph (F)(i);

(II) was adopted abroad, or is coming to the United States for adoption, by the adoptive parent (or prospective adoptive parent) or parents of the sibling described in clause (i), subparagraph (E)(i), or subparagraph (F)(i); and

(III) is otherwise described in clause (i), except that the child is younger than 18 years of age at the time a petition is filed on his or her behalf for classification as an immediate relative under section 1151(b) of this title.

2. Child Status Protection Act

In August 2002, the President signed the Child Status Protection Act of 2002 (CSPA).[50] The statute, effective August 6, 2002, was intended to protect children who would otherwise lose their ability to immigrate because they turned 21 before receiving an immigration benefit under a range of programs in the INA.[51] The benefit programs covered by the CSPA include family and employment-based immigrants, diversity applications, asylum and refugee applications and parole adjustment.[52] However, a person who fails to act within one year of becoming eligible (when the visa number becomes available or when the parent adjusts status) loses the benefits under CSPA.

---

50. Pub. L. No. 107-208, 116 Stat. 927 (2002).

51. *Arobelidze v. Holder*, 653 F.3d 513, 521 (7th Cir. 2011).

52. It does not apply to nonimmigrant visa applications. *Alvidrez v. Ridge*, 311 F. Supp. 2d 1163, 1165 (D. Kan. 2004).

The law is rather straight-forward for persons who were under the age of 21 before the effective date of the statute and were the derivative beneficiaries of an immigrant visa or other petition conferring status based on the definition of child.[53]

3. Adoption

Karen Yuen Fong Young v. Janet Reno, Att'y Gen'l

114 F.3d 879 (9th Cir. 1997)

Before: Wiggins, Trott, Circuit Judges, and Zapata, District Judge.

Trott, Circuit Judge.

* * *

Karen Yuen Fong Young was adopted as a child by a paternal aunt in Hong Kong and was permitted to immigrate to the United States because of this adoptive parent-child relationship. In 1984, she filed petitions seeking to confer preferential immigration status on her four biological siblings, pursuant to section 203(a)(4) of the INA, 8 U.S.C. § 1153(a)(4).[1] The INS approved the petitions and forwarded them to the U.S. State Department consulate in Hong Kong for processing as visas became available. Young's siblings applied for immigration visas in 1994, when visas first became available to fourth-preference individuals with 1984 priority dates. However, the consulate returned Young's petitions to the INS for visa-revocation proceedings, explaining that the petitions should not have been approved because Young's adoption had severed her legal relationship to her natural siblings. Young filed this action for a declaratory judgment in district court, before the INS revoked the petitions. The INS subsequently revoked three of the four petitions. Young challenged the revocation of these three petitions in the district court, and the district court granted summary judgment in favor of the INS.

* * *

At issue in this case is whether a child who was given up for adoption can seek to confer preferential immigration status on her natural siblings. The INA prevents a natural parent from receiving any immigration privilege through that adopted child. Adoption severs the legal relationship, for immigration purposes, between an adopted child and her natural parents. The INA, however, is silent as to the effect of adoption on the legal relationship between an adopted child and her natural siblings.

Section 203(a)(4) of the INA establishes a fourth-level preference for "[q]ualified immigrants who are the brothers and sisters of citizens of the United States." 8 U.S.C.

---

53. For a more detailed article on this subject see Tammy Fox-Isicoff & H. Ronald Klasko, *The Child Status Protection Act: Is Your Child Protected?*, 80 Interpreter Releases 973 (2003).

1. This section's original numbering was INA section 203(a)(5), 8 U.S.C. § 1153(a)(5).

§ 1153(a)(4). Although the Act does not define "brother" or "sister," it does define "child" and "parent." The term "child" includes:

> a child adopted while under the age of sixteen years if the child has been in the legal custody of, and has resided with, the adopting parent or parents for at least two years: Provided, That no natural parent of any such adopted child shall thereafter, by virtue of such parentage, be accorded any right, privilege, or status under this chapter.

INA § 101(b)(1)(E), 8 U.S.C. § 1101(b)(1)(E). The Act then defines "parent" by reference to the definition of "child":

> The terms "parent", "father", or "mother" mean a parent, father, or mother only where the relationship exists by reason of any of the circumstances set forth in subdivision (1) of this subsection....

Id. at § 1101(b)(2). In the absence of explicit provisions defining "brother" or "sister," the INS defines siblings by their relationship to a common parent. Young, on the other hand, argues that their ordinary, biological meaning must prevail.

A. The INS's Interpretation

The BIA's most recent decision in *Matter of Li* followed two prior cases which also addressed the impact of adoption on the sibling relationship.

In *Matter of Fujii*, 12 I. & N. Dec. 495 (Dist.Dir.1967), the INS District Director[3] held that a U.S. citizen could petition for visa preference on behalf of her natural brother, who had been given up for adoption as a child. Recognizing that the Act did not define the terms "brother" or "sister", the Director noted that the "normal definition is a person having the same parent or parents as another." *Id.* at 496. The petitioner established that the beneficiary was the legitimate child of her natural parents and was therefore her brother under this definition.[4] The Director reasoned:

> To conclude without judicial or precedent administrative determination to the contrary (and we find none) that the relationship of brother and sister created by the legitimate birth of the petitioner and beneficiary to the same parents was destroyed by the subsequent adoption of the latter would be to place upon the statute a harsher construction than that intended by Congress.

Id. The Director also observed that, although section 101(b)(1)(E) of the INA prevented the natural parent of an adopted child from obtaining an immigration right, privilege, or status via that child, there was no similar proscription regarding the natural siblings of an adopted child. *Id.* at 497.

---

3. A decision by a district director does not constitute a precedent for the BIA. *Matter of Li*, 20 I. & N. Dec. 700, at *6 n. 2 (citing 8 C.F.R. §§ 3.1(g), 103.3(c) (1993)).

4. The beneficiary's adoption was terminated prior to the his natural sister's visa petition, thereby restoring to his natural parents their original parental status under Japanese law. However, the District Director noted that the adoption and subsequent dissolution were irrelevant to his determination.

In *Matter of Kong*, 17 I. & N. Dec. 151 (BIA 1979), the petitioner had been adopted as a child by the natural parents of the beneficiary. However, that adoption was terminated after the petitioner's natural mother immigrated to the United States so that the natural mother could seek a familial visa preference on the petitioner's behalf. The petitioner subsequently immigrated to the United States and became a U.S. citizen. The petitioner then applied for preferential visa status pursuant to section 203(a)(4) on behalf of the natural son of her adoptive parents (and thus her adoptive brother).

The BIA held that a sibling relationship created by an adoption does not survive the termination of that adoption for immigration purposes. Clarifying a prior BIA statement suggesting that the status of "parent," once established, cannot be terminated, the BIA explained that to qualify as siblings under section 203(a)(5) of the INA, a petitioner must establish: (1) that both she and the beneficiary "once qualified as children of a common parent," and (2) that the parent is still a parent of each of them. *Id.* at 153. Although the petitioner and the beneficiary once qualified as children of a common parent, they no longer shared a common parent because the petitioner's adoption had been terminated. Her adoptive parents were no longer her parents for immigration purposes. *Id.*

Finally, in *Matter of Li*, the BIA considered "whether a petitioner, who qualifies as an adopted child within the provisions of section 101(b)(1)(E) of the Act, can successfully petition for a natural sibling on the basis of their relationship to a common natural parent?" 20 I. & N. Dec. 700. Relying on its decision in *Matter of Kong*, the Board stated that "to qualify as siblings under section 203(a)(5) of the Act, a petitioner must establish both that he and the beneficiary once qualified as children of a common parent and that the parental relationship has not been severed."

Focusing on the section 101(b)(1)(E) proviso which provides that, upon an adoption that meets the requirements of the section, no natural parent can thereafter be accorded any "right, privilege, or status" under the Act, the Board held that such an adoption (which meets the statutory requirements) severs the relationship between natural parent and adopted child. Because the natural parent no longer has the status of parent under the Act, the legal relationship between adopted child and natural sibling also ceases. They no longer have a common parent for immigration purposes.

The Board rejected the District Director's analysis in *Matter of Fujii*, which depended on the absence of a prohibition of benefits for natural siblings similar to that of the section 101(b)(1)(E) proviso. Recognizing that section 101(b) of the Act defined only the parent-child relationship, the Board concluded that "[a]ll other familial relationships are dependent on these [parent-child] definitions." *Id.* at *5. Because "[a] sibling relationship can only be recognized through the fact of having a common parent within the definition of the Act," no sibling relationship can be recognized through a natural parent who loses his or her "status" as a "parent" under the Act as a result of the proviso to section 101(b)(1)(E). *Id.* "To the extent that a relationship between the petitioner and his natural parents was terminated by virtue of his adoption, he cannot now establish that he and the beneficiary are children of a common parent as is required by the Act for the purpose of establishing a sibling relationship." *Id.* at *6. With this understanding of the statutory provisions and the INS's construction, we proceed with our Chevron analysis.

B. Congress has not spoken on this issue

In reviewing the INS's construction of these statutory provisions, *Chevron* dictates that we first consider whether Congress has directly spoken to the precise question at issue. Young urges that Congress has so spoken, through its use of the words "brothers and sisters." Young contends that the *Li* definition of "brothers and sisters" is contrary to the plain meaning of those terms. Additionally, Young faults the BIA's conclusion that the sibling relationship is terminated with the severance of the natural-parent/adopted-child relationship, because the statute does not explicitly preclude natural siblings from gaining an immigration benefit through the adopted child.

Young relies primarily on *Gee v. INS*, 875 F.Supp. 666 (N.D.Cal.1994), in which the district court faced the same question of the effect of adoption on natural-sibling relationships. The district court in *Gee* recognized that the first step of the *Chevron* inquiry was "to determine congressional intent, using "traditional tools of statutory construction." *Id.* at 670. The court determined that it need not proceed beyond this step, because it concluded that Congress intended to grant a natural sibling of an adopted child a "brother and sister" immigration preference, regardless of any intervening adoption. It based its conclusion on the plain meaning rule and the doctrine of "expressio unius est exclusio alterius."[5] *Id.*

First, because the statute does not define "brothers" and "sisters" as used in section 1153(a)(4), the Gee court looked to Webster's Dictionary for the settled meaning of the terms. The court concluded that the dictionary definition of "brother"—"a male human being considered in his relation to another person having the same parents or having one parent in common"—is not affected by adoption "because a natural sibling shares the same parents as an adopted sibling." *Id.* However, the court fails to recognize that under the statute's definitions of "parent" and "child," adoption terminates the legal relationship between a natural parent and an adopted child. See 8 U.S.C. § 1101(b)(1)(E) (proviso). An adopted child's only "parents" under the statute are her adoptive parents. The natural sibling therefore does not share the same legal parents.

The district court in this case also disagreed with *Gee*'s plain meaning analysis, observing that "[w]hat is clear is that Congress did not specifically define 'brothers' and 'sisters' as those terms are used in 8 U.S.C. § 1153(a)(5)." 931 F.Supp. at 1503. The district court concluded that the fact that the Act did define in detail "parent" and "child" (as well as the fact that those definitions are not identical to their ordinary

5. Meaning that "the expression of one thing is the exclusion of another." Black's Law Dictionary 521 (5th ed. 1979).

meanings) "suggests that it may be error to apply the 'ordinary' definitions of 'brother' and 'sister' in this analysis." *Id.* We agree with this conclusion and reject the Gee court's contrary reliance on the terms' dictionary definitions.

The *Gee* court next relied on the "expressio unius est exclusio alterius" statutory tool of construction, which provides that when a statute names the parties that come within its provisions, other unnamed parties are excluded. 875 F.Supp. at 671. Because Congress expressly precluded natural parents from gaining advantage through an adopted child but did not mention natural siblings, the *Gee* district court reasoned, it would be unreasonable to interpret the statute as impliedly excluding natural siblings from qualifying for family-based preferences. *Id.* Although the District Director relied on this construction in *Matter of Fujii*, 12 I. & N. Dec. at 497, the BIA explicitly rejected it in *Matter of Li*, 20 I. & N. Dec. 700, at *5, pointing out that the sibling relationship is dependent upon the parent-child relationship, which is the only familial relationship defined.

In rejecting the *Fujii* analysis, the BIA in *Li* also noted that "the restrictive proviso of section 101(b)(1)(E) could be rendered meaningless over time." *Id.* As the district court in this case cogently explained:

> Like the BIA in *Li*, this court recognizes that Plaintiff's interpretation of "brothers" and "sisters" may increase the potential for fraud and eviscerate the prohibition contained in section 1101(b)(1)(E), as ultimately, Plaintiff would be permitted to petition for preferential immigration status on behalf of her natural siblings, who in turn, would be able to petition on behalf of their (including the Plaintiff's) natural parents. In light of Congress's express language that "no natural parent of any [] adopted child shall, by virtue of such parentage," benefit from his or her status under the Act, and absent any indication to the contrary, the court cannot agree that Congress intended the result suggested by Plaintiff.

931 F.Supp. at 1503–04. The Gee court, however, thought this scenario "unrealistic" and concluded that Congress did not share this concern either, as evidenced by its failure to close this supposed loophole by including language regarding siblings in the statute. Since *Li*, however, Congress twice amended the INA but did not interfere with the Board's interpretation of section 203(a)(4).

We once again agree with the district court in the instant matter and reject the *Gee* court's analysis. Although Congress did not expressly address preferences for natural siblings, we must give full meaning to its clear intention to prevent natural parents from gaining benefits—regardless of whether the *Gee* court finds this possibility realistic. Thus, neither the plain language rule nor the failure by Congress to exclude preferences for natural siblings after adoption indicates that Congress clearly intended that the natural sibling relationship survive adoption for immigration purposes.

The legislative history of section 101(b)(1)(E) further indicates that, when Congress adopted these provisions, it was not concerned with, and did not contemplate, whether the legal relationship between natural siblings would survive adoption. Prior to the enactment of section 101(b)(1)(E) in 1957, United States citizens were unable to bring adopted children into the U.S. because the definition of "child" did not include adopted children. H.R.Rep. No. 1199, 85th Cong., 1st Sess. (1957), reprinted in 1957 U.S.C.C.A.N. 2016. Although Congress's general purpose in enacting this provision was to keep families intact, their concern was focused on the adoptive, not the natural, family. Indeed, many of the adopted children were orphans. However, Congress did contemplate the effect of adoption on the natural-parent/adopted-child relationship, specifically providing that adoption severs that relationship. While Young is correct that congressional intent in adopting this provision was to preserve the family unit, there is no indication that this intention extended to natural siblings of adopted children.

We therefore conclude that Congress has not spoken on this precise issue, and we disapprove of the *Gee* court's contrary conclusion.

C. The INS's construction is permissible

The second step of the *Chevron* analysis is to consider whether the INS's interpretation is a permissible construction of the statute. The district court considered the BIA's analysis in both *Matter of Kong* and *Matter of Li* and found permissible the INS's requirement that to qualify as legal siblings under the Act, a petitioner must show that she and the beneficiary once qualified as children of a common parent and that the parental relationship has not been severed. 931 F.Supp. at 1503.

We agree with the district court's analysis and conclusion. The INS's two-part test reasonably ties the sibling relationship to the primary familial relationship defined in the Act—the parent-child relationship. By so doing, the INS's construction: 1) stays within four corners of the INA and does not rely on external definitions; 2) gives full meaning to the express language of the section 101(b)(1)(E) proviso prohibiting natural parents from benefitting from adoption; 3) prevents a scenario specifically prohibited by Congress whereby adopted children obtain preferences for natural siblings who then obtain preferences for natural parents; and 4) is consistent with the overall structure of Act, which emphasizes the primacy of the parent-child relationship and confers more benefits on parents than other relatives.

We therefore hold that the INS's interpretation of the INA, as set forth in *Matter of Kong* and *Matter of Li*, is a reasonable and permissible construction of the statute.

II

We must next consider whether the INS abused its discretion by announcing a new rule in an adjudicative forum. Young insists that the BIA's decision in *Matter of Li* constituted a departure from the contrary, prevailing rule of *Matter of Fujii*. Because she had justifiably relied on the *Fujii* rule and because the change imposed a substantial hardship on her without notice, Young contends that the INS should have made this new rule pursuant to the rule-making procedures of the Administrative Procedures Act ("APA"), 5 U.S.C. § 553. See *Ruangswang v. INS*, 591 F.2d 39 (9th Cir.1978) (INS abused its discretion in establishing and applying new standard in adjudicatory process because alien relied on prior rule, did not have adequate notice, and suffered substantial adverse consequences). We reject this argument because we conclude that the BIA did not announce a new rule in *Li*.

Young argues that *Matter of Fujii* established the prevailing rule, which the INS applied until the *Matter of Li* decision. She insists that *Matter of Kong* is distinguishable from *Fujii* and *Li* because *Kong* dealt only with whether sibling relationships created by adoption survive dissolution of adoption, whereas *Fujii* and *Li* dealt with whether a child's adoption terminated her biological-sibling relationships. However, in determining whether an adoptive-sibling relationship survived termination of adoption, *Kong* set forth the requirements for all sibling relationships, regardless of their origin. In so doing, *Kong* effectively overruled *Fujii*, even though it did not cite the earlier case. The BIA in *Li* did not deviate from the *Kong* requirements. Notably, although Young contends that she did not have adequate notice that the standard announced in *Li* could be applied to her petitions, the INS cited not *Li* but *Kong* as the cause justifying revocation.

Additionally, we reject Young's allegation that the INS routinely applied *Fujii* and that it decided to apply the *Kong* requirements only after the *Li* decision. This contention is not supported by the record. Young's only evidence is the INS's initial approval of visa petitions in three cases—which occurred after *Kong* but before *Li*—and the subsequent revocation of those petitions after the *Li* decision. The approval and subsequent revocation of visa preference petitions in three cases does not establish that the INS routinely followed any particular policy. Further, *Fujii*, a decision by an INS district director, was not binding on the BIA. Therefore, the *Li* decision did not announce a new rule.

Finally, we must consider whether the Government erred by applying *Li* retroactively and revoking Young's approved visa petitions. Young contends that the relevant considerations set forth in *Retail, Wholesale & Dep't Store Union v. NLRB*, 466 F.2d 380, 390 (D.C.Cir.1972), militate against retroactively applying *Li* to her case. However, the INS did not apply *Li* retroactively to revoke Young's petitions. As discussed above, *Li* was not a new rule, but rather an extension of *Kong*. Further, the INS did not rely on *Li* in revoking Young's petitions; instead, it cited *Kong* as the cause for revocation. Finally, the revocation of a petition is not retroactive, but only prospectively affects the issuance of a visa in the future. Young had no vested right in the issuance of a visa for her siblings. See *De Avilia v. Civiletti*, 643 F.2d 471, 477 (7th Cir. 1981).

Conclusion

Congress did not address directly whether adoption severs the legal relationship between an adopted child and her natural siblings, and the INS's construction of the relevant INA provisions is permissible. Further, the BIA did not announce a new rule in *Matter of Li*. Therefore, we affirm the district court's grant of summary judgment in favor of the Government.

Matter of Garcia-Rodriguez

16 I. & N. Dec. 438 (BIA 1978)

BY: Milhollan, Chairman; Wilson, Maniatis, Appleman, and Maguire, Board Members

The United States citizen petitioner applied for immediate relative status for the beneficiary as her adopted daughter under section 201(b) of the Immigration and Nationality Act, 8 U.S.C. § 1151(b). In a decision dated October 5, 1976, the District Director denied the petition. The petitioner has appealed. The appeal will be dismissed.

The beneficiary, a 15-year-old native and citizen of Mexico, was "adopted" by the petitioner and her husband in H. Matamoros, State of Tamaulipas, Mexico, on August 6, 1974. The couple had natural children of their own living at the time of this "adoption." A visa petition was submitted on behalf of the beneficiary on August 16, 1976.

Certain adopted children of United States citizen parents can qualify for "immediate relative status" under section 201(b) of the Act. See section 101(b)(E), 8 U.S.C. 1101(b)(1)(E). The District Director, however, denied this petition based on his finding that the petitioner failed to establish that the beneficiary had been lawfully adopted. Noting that article 400 of the Civil Code of Tamaulipas authorizes only persons "who do not have natural descendants" to adopt minor children, he concluded that the beneficiary's adoption was not in compliance with controlling law as the petitioner and her spouse had other natural children living in August 1974.

On appeal, the petitioner submits that the District Director erred by looking only to article 400 of the Civil Code of Tamaulipas. She states that article 400 governs only adoptions by single persons and that article 401 authorizes a "married couple [to] adopt if both agree to consider the adopted one as their son." The petitioner maintains that the adoption of the beneficiary was in compliance with the requirements of the Civil Code of Tamaulipas and that her daughter should, therefore, be recognized as her "immediate relative."

The burden of establishing both controlling foreign law (*Matter of Annang*, 14 I. & N. Dec. 502 (BIA 1973)) and eligibility for the benefit sought (*Matter of Brantigan*, 11 I. & N. Dec. 493 (BIA 1966) rests with the petitioner. We conclude that the petitioner has failed to sustain either burden.

Article 400 of the Civil Code of Tamaulipas provides:

> Persons over 30 years of age, in the full exercise of their rights and who have no descendants, may adopt a minor or an incompetent, even if he is of legal age, provided the adopter is 17 years older than the person adopted, and that the adoption is beneficial to the latter.

Article 401 of the Code states:

> The man and wife can adopt when both are in accord in considering the adopted child as their own son or daughter.

It seems evident that the former article is a general provision governing all adoptions, while the latter article sets forth an additional requirement to be imposed upon married couples. Thus, it would appear that the petitioner and her spouse were subject to the restrictions in article 400 at the time they attempted to adopt the beneficiary.

The petitioner would have us conclude that article 400 applies only to single persons. On its face, however, no such limitation appears. Moreover, to accept such an interpretation would be to conclude that the age differential and "welfare of the child" provisions of article 400 do not apply to adoptions by married couples. We decline to so conclude, and find that the petitioner has failed to establish that her reading of articles 400 and 401 of the Civil Code of Tamaulipas is correct.

This conclusion is supported by the fact that an extract from the adoption order submitted by the petitioner cites article 400 among the "legal bases" for the adoption. No reference is made in the order to article 401 of the Code. It would, therefore, certainly appear that the provisions of article 400 did apply to the "adoption" of the beneficiary.

In light of the above, we find that the petitioner has failed to establish that the beneficiary qualifies as her "child" within the meaning of section 101(b)(1)(E) of the Act. Thus, the beneficiary has not been shown to be eligible for "immediate relative" status under section 201(b) of the Act. See *Matter of Allmon*, Interim Decision 2339 (BIA 1975).

Notes

1. The basic rule in adoption cases is that the applicant must show 1) that an adoption occurred under the laws of the country where it took place; 2) that a lawful permanent parent-child relationship between a child and someone who wasn't already the legal parent; and 3) the relationship between the natural or prior parent was legally terminated.[54]

2. Effectively, there are three separate ways to adopt a child: 1) non-orphan adoptions; 2) orphan adoptions in countries which have signed the Hague Convention on Adoptions; and 3) orphan adoptions where the country has not signed the Hague Convention.[55] Non-orphan adoptions require that the child be adopted before reaching the age of 16 with two yeas of legal custody and residence with the parent. Residency may occur before or after legal custody and can be fulfilled simultaneously. *See Matter of Cuello*, 20 I. & N. Dec. 94 (BIA 1989).[56] Adoptions under the Hague Convention only apply to married U.S. citizens or unmarried U.S. citizens who are 25 or older.[57]

---

54. Policy Memorandum, USCIS, *Guidance for Determining if an Adoption is Valid for INA Purposes*, PM-602-0070 (Nov. 6, 2012).

55. Convention on Protection of Children and Cooperation in Respect of Intercountry Adoption, opened for signature May 29, 1993, 1870 U.N.T.S. 167 (entered into force Apr. 1, 2008).

56. It is the policy of USCIS to waive the two year residency and custody requirement where the adopted child has been battered or the victim of extreme cruelty by the adopting parent or member of the household. Policy Memorandum, USCIS, *Exception to the Two Year Custody & Two Year Residency Requirement for Abused Adopted Children*, PM-602-0089 (Sep. 12, 2013).

57. In the case of married U.S. citizens, both spouses must adopt the child.

The Convention was intended to monitor and control adoption fraud and places the central authority within the Department of State and certain adjudicatory functions with USCIS.[58] The Convention applies to foreign adoptions where the adopting parent resides in the U.S. and the child resides abroad. The child must be overseas. The visa petition must be filed before the child reaches its 16th birthday, but the two year legal and residency requirements are inapplicable.

3. **Customary Adoptions.** Just as some countries have tribal or customary marriages, some also have what are termed "customary" adoptions. These adoptions are analyzed according to the same test which are applied to other adoptions—was it legally recognized in the country where it took place.[59]

4. Stepchildren

Matter of McMillan

17 I. & N. Dec. 605 (BIA 1981)

BY: Milhollan, Chairman; Maniatis, Appleman, and Maguire, Board Members

In a decision dated July 23, 1980, the Acting District Director denied the visa petitions filed by the United States citizen petitioner to accord the beneficiaries immediate relative status as her stepsons pursuant to section 201(b) of the Immigration and Nationality Act, 8 U.S.C. 1151(b). The petitioner has appealed from that decision. The appeal will be sustained and the visa petitions will be approved.

The record reflects that the beneficiaries, twin brothers, were born in London, England, on July 26, 1962, to the petitioner's husband and a woman who was not then and never became his wife. The beneficiaries' natural mother abandoned them when they were infants and they have since resided with their paternal grandmother in Grenada, West Indies. The petitioner and the beneficiaries' father married in March 1964. The Acting District Director determined that the beneficiaries do not qualify as stepchildren of the petitioner within the meaning of the Act (see section 101(b)(1), 8 U.S.C. 1101(b)(1)) inasmuch as the petitioner failed to establish the existence of a close family relationship between herself, her husband, and the beneficiaries.

Section 101(b)(1)(B) of the Act includes within the definition of the term "child": "... a stepchild, whether or not born in wedlock, provided the child had not reached the age of eighteen years at the time the marriage creating the status of stepchild occurred...." In construing section 101(b)(1)(B), we have long adhered to the view that given the underlying Congressional policy of reuniting families, the mere fact of a

---

58. Lori Scialabba & Don Neufeld, USCIS, *Domestic Operations Intercountry adoption under the Hague Adoption Convention and the USCIS Hague Adoption Convention rule at 8 CFR §204, 213a, and 322*, HQ DOMO 70/6.1.1-P (Oct. 31, 2008)

59. *Kaho v. Ilchert*, 765 F.2d 877, 881 (9th Cir. 1985) (Immigration Service erred in denying customary adoption claim when it concluded that Tongan law did not recognize such adoptions).

marriage which technically creates a steprelationship does not in itself establish a stepparent-stepchild relationship for purposes of the immigration laws. We had until recent date imposed the additional requirement, apparently applied by the Acting District Director in the instant case, that a close family unit be shown to exist between the stepparent, the stepchild, and the natural parent. See *Nation v. Esperdy*, 239 F.Supp. 531 (S.D.N.Y.1965); *Matter of The*, 11 I & N. Dec. 449 (BIA 1965).[1]

We recently reexamined that position in *Matter of Moreira*, Interim Decisions 2720 and 2792 (BIA 1979 and 1980), and established a new standard that modified to some extent the close family unit test. After careful review of relevant legislative history and pertinent Board and court decisions, we held that a steprelationship exists for immigration purposes where, prior to the stepchild's eighteenth birthday, the stepparent not only married the child's natural parent but evinced an active parental interest in the child's support, instruction and general welfare.

In *Palmer v. Reddy*, 622 F.2d 463 (9 Cir.1980), the United States Court of Appeals for the Ninth Circuit specifically rejected both the *Moreira* "active parental interest" test and its predecessor, the "close family unit" rule, concluding that persons who become stepchildren through the marriage of a natural parent prior to their eighteenth birthday are entitled to visa preference as a class under section 101(b)(1)(B) without further qualification. We found ourselves bound to follow *Palmer v. Reddy, id.*, in *Matter of Bonnette*, Interim Decision 2840 (BIA 1980), a subsequent case arising in the Ninth Circuit.

We have now determined, with some reluctance, to retreat from our position in *Matter of Moreira, supra*, and to apply the holding in *Palmer v. Reddy, supra*, nationwide. The difficulties inherent in the literal interpretation given section 101(b)(1)(B) by the Ninth Circuit are manifest. See generally concurring opinion of Board Member Appleman in *Matter of Bonnette, supra*. However, the Ninth Circuit is the only Circuit Court of Appeals to have construed the stepchild provision thus far. The Government appears to have acquiesced in the Ninth Circuit's interpretation of section 101(b)(1)(B). We shall accordingly adopt that interpretation as controlling outside as well as within the Ninth Circuit.

The record establishes that the petitioner married the beneficiaries' natural father when the beneficiaries were 20 months of age. Under the rule of *Palmer v. Reddy*, the beneficiaries thereupon qualified as stepchildren of the petitioner within the meaning of section 101(b)(1)(B) and are entitled to immediate relative status as the children of a United States citizen. The visa petitions will be approved.
ORDER: The appeal is sustained and the visa petitions are approved.

---

1. In *Andrade v. Esperdy*, 270 F.Supp. 516 (S.D.N.Y.1967), another judge of the same judicial district that decided the *Nation* case, the Southern District of New York, struck down the close family unit requirement in cases arising within that jurisdiction. We declined to apply *Andrade* outside the Southern District of New York. *Matter of Amado and Monteiro*, 13 I & N. Dec. 179 (BIA 1969).

Notes

1. In cases where it is determined that a marriage was entered into "fraudulently for the purpose of obtaining an immigration benefit," the stepchild relationship will not be recognized.[60]

2. When a visa petition was filed on behalf of a "second" wife by the child of the "first" wife and her husband, the relationship between the child and "second" wife was not recognized.[61] The reasoning for not recognizing the relationship was that the BIA was of the view that Congress did not intend to accord preference classification on the basis of polygamous relationships.[62]

3. The BIA has held that it will recognize the stepchild relationship between the first wife and the child of the "second" wife. In this case, the BIA also approved the petition by the child for his natural mother.[63] As long as there is no polygamy, the relationship will be recognized.

4. The Attorney General also recognized a stepchild relationship as existing between the child conceived as a result of an extramarital adulterous relationship and the "new" wife of the natural father.[64]

5. "Legitimacy"

Matter of Vizcaino

19 I. & N. Dec. 644 (BIA 1988)

BY: Milhollan, Chairman; Dunne, Morris, Vacca, and Heilman, Board Members

This is an appeal from a decision of the Immigration and Naturalization Service acting Regional Service Center (RSC) director, dated July 6, 1987, denying a visa petition filed by the petitioner on behalf of the beneficiary as his unmarried son under section 203(a)(1) of the Immigration and Nationality Act, 8 U.S.C. § 1153(a)(1) (1982). Oral argument was heard before the Board on November 5, 1987. The appeal will be sustained and the record will be remanded to the RSC director.

The petitioner is a 63-year-old native of the Dominican Republic and a citizen of the United States. He resides in New York. The beneficiary is a 33-year-old native and citizen of the Dominican Republic. He is purported to be the son of the petitioner by a woman the petitioner never married. The instant visa petition was filed on the beneficiary's behalf on February 3, 1987.

In denying the visa petition, the acting RSC director noted that to be classifiable as a son or daughter under section 203 of the Act, a person must at some point

---

60. *Matter of Teng,* 15 I. & N. Dec. 516 (BIA 1975).
61. *Matter of Man,* 16 I. & N. Dec. 543 (BIA 1978).
62. 16 I. & N. Dec. at 546.
63. *Matter of Fong,* 17 I. & N. Dec. 212 (BIA 1980).
64. *Matter of Stultz,* 15 I. & N. Dec. 362 (A.G. 1975).

have qualified as a child within the meaning of section 101(b)(1) of the Act, 8 U.S.C. § 1101(b)(1) (1982).[1] She then concluded that the beneficiary never qualified as the petitioner's legitimate or legitimated child, because the petitioner never married the beneficiary's mother, and both New York and the Dominican Republic require parents to marry in order to legitimate their child. See *Matter of Bullen*, 16 I&N Dec. 378 (BIA 1977) (New York); *Matter of Reyes*, 17 I&N Dec. 512 (BIA 1980) (Dominican Republic). Such further [sic]found that the beneficiary could not qualify as the petitioner's illegitimate child under the provisions of section 101(b)(1)(D) of the Act, because the beneficiary was over 21 at the time the law changed to allow, under certain prescribed circumstances, petitions between illegitimate children and their fathers.

Section 101(b)(1)(D) of the Act, as amended by the Immigration Reform and Control Act of 1986, Pub. L. No. 99-603, 100 Stat. 3359, provides as follows:

> (1) The term "child" means an unmarried person under twenty-one years of age who is—
>
> ....
>
> (D) an illegitimate child, by, through whom, or on whose behalf a status, privilege, or benefit is sought by virtue of the relationship of the child to its natural mother or to its natural father if the father has or had a bona fide parent-child relationship with the person....

Until November 6, 1986, when the Immigration Reform and Control Act became law, illegitimate children could only receive or bestow immigration benefits through their natural mothers, not their natural fathers.

As indicated above, the acting RSC director found that the beneficiary could not benefit from the change in the law because he was over 21 at the time the change went into effect. On appeal, however, the Immigration and Naturalization Service, after lengthy internal debate, now agrees with the petitioner that section 101(b)(1)(D), as amended, may be applied on behalf of persons who turned 21 before the law went into effect, so long as paternity can be established and there is a showing that a bona fide parent-child relationship existed at the time the son or daughter was under 21 and unmarried. We agree that this is the correct application of the law. The law as amended should apply to all petitions, such as the present one, filed after the effective date of the statute, even where the son or daughter was over 21 at the time the law went into effect. Moreover, we find that the amended version of section 101(b)(1)(D) should apply to all immediate relative petitions filed and pending at the time the law

---

1. The terms "son" and "daughter" as used in section 203 are not defined in the Act. However, since Congress, in amending section 101(b)(1)(D) of the Act, specifically required that a "parent-child relationship' with the father be shown" (see discussion *infra*), we find that in order to qualify under that section, it must be shown that the son or daughter once qualified as a child under section 101(b)(1). Such a requirement is also consistent with long-settled law regarding stepchildren under section 101(b)(1)(B) of the Act, legitimated children under section 101(b)(1)(C), and adopted children under section 101(b)(1)(E). *See, e.g., Kaho v. Ilchert*, 765 F.2d 877 (9th Cir. 1985).

went into effect.[2] In all cases, it must be shown that the parent-child relationship was established when the son or daughter was unmarried and under 21 years of age. Such a showing is necessary in order to satisfy the requirement that a son or daughter must once have met the definition of "child," as discussed above.

This approach is not inconsistent with the line of cases holding that where a country or a state eliminates all legal distinctions between legitimate and illegitimate children, persons born after the effective date of the legislation are deemed legitimate children under section 101(b)(1)(A) of the Act, and persons born, and under 18 years of age, prior to the effective date are deemed to have been legitimated by the change in law. Benefits for or through such persons may be had under section 101(b)(1)(C) of the Act regarding legitimated children. See, e.g., *Matter of Hernandez*, 19 I&N Dec. 14 (BIA 1983), and cases cited therein. In those cases, the state and foreign law changes had to be applied and examined under the unchanged provisions of the Immigration and Nationality Act. Because we have held that the change in the state or foreign law was the act legitimating these persons, we have found them to be legitimated, not legitimate, children. We have therefore held that the legitimating act (the change in law) must have occurred prior to the time the child reached the age of 18, as required by section 101(b)(1)(C). In the present situation, on the other hand, Congress itself has changed the underlying statutory definition of an illegitimate child. Moreover, unlike section 101(b)(1)(C) of the Act, section 101(b)(1)(D), regarding illegitimate children, does not include an age restriction. We therefore have no problem in applying the amended law to any person, regardless of his or her age when the law went into effect, who can establish that he or she once met the requirements for an illegitimate child.

Although the Service agrees that the new version of the law applies in this case, it is argued that the visa petition must still be denied because the petitioner has not met his burden of establishing either paternity or a "bona fide parent-child relationship" as required under the statute. The petitioner asserts that, since the acting RSC director did not mention these issues in her decision, it must be assumed that she considered these showings to have been made. Alternatively, the petitioner contends that the evidence clearly establishes both paternity and a bona fide parent-child relationship and that, accordingly, the Board should simply grant the petition.

We reject the petitioner's contention that the acting RSC director's silence on these issues shows that she considered the matters resolved, and in the petitioner's favor. Rather, it appears clear that, finding a legal basis for denying the petition, the acting RSC director simply did not reach the factual issues. Having reviewed the record, we find a remand is necessary so that the RSC director may fully consider all the evidence on this issue. On remand, the petitioner will have the burden of establishing both that he is in fact the beneficiary's biological father, and that he and the beneficiary

2. Pursuant to *Matter of Bardouille*, 18 I&N Dec. 114 (BIA 1981), the new law will not be applied to preference petitions which were filed before the effective date by or on behalf of illegitimate children through their fathers. *See also Matter of Atembe*, Interim Decision 3023 (BIA 1986); *Matter of Drigo*, 18 I&N Dec. 223 (BIA 1982).

had a bona fide parent-child relationship prior to the time the beneficiary reached the age of 21.

The term "bona fide parent-child relationship" is new in the Act, is not defined, and the legislative history is silent as to congressional intent regarding its meaning. The Service suggests that, as a starting point in defining the term, we use the "active parental interest test" set forth in *Matter of Moreira*, 17 I&N Dec. 41 (BIA 1979). In *Matter of Moreira*, we attempted to state what showing was necessary to establish a steprelationship under section 101(b)(1)(B) of the Act. We held that where a child has not lived with a stepparent, it must be shown that the stepparent had demonstrated "an active parental interest in the child's support, instruction, and general welfare." *Id.* at 47; see also *Matter of Moreira*, 17 I&N Dec. 370 (BIA 1980). Subsequently, we retreated from the *Moreira* decisions in steprelationship cases and adopted the holding of the court in *Palmer v. Reddy*, 622 F.2d 463 (9th Cir. 1980), that because of the "unqualified language" of the stepchild provision, no qualifications beyond a valid marriage creating the steprelationship should be imposed. See *Matter of McMillan*, 17 I&N Dec. 605 (BIA 1981); *Matter of Bonnette*, 17 I&N Dec. 587 (BIA 1980).

Unlike the stepchild provision, section 101(b)(1)(D) of the Act, as amended, does carry specific qualifying language. Since Congress qualified the language, we must give some meaningful effect to it. As noted, Congress has provided no guidance as to the intended meaning of the phrase "bona fide parent-child relationship," and we shall not attempt a specific definition here. We emphasize, however, that the expansion of section 101(b)(1)(D) to include the illegitimate children of their fathers clearly was intended as a generous provision, and it should therefore be generously interpreted. At the same time, Congress did not intend to place fathers on an equal basis with mothers, or it would not have required a "bona fide parent-child relationship" only with regard to fathers.

It is obvious that Congress intended that more than mere paternity be required under the amendment. In keeping with the immigration laws' historical and ongoing concern with true family reunification, the key is the existence of a parent-child relationship in fact, not merely a tie by blood. In assessing a relationship, some evidence of emotional and/or financial ties should be shown. The factfinders should look for proof that the parties at some point actually lived together, or that the father held out the child as his own, or that he provided for some or all of the child's needs, or that in general the father's behavior evidence a genuine concern for the child. The most persuasive evidence would be some sort of documentary evidence which was contemporaneous with the events in question, as opposed to, for example, affidavits or letters written just before or after the visa petition was filed. We recognize, however, that once parties are separated, barriers of distance, national boundaries, immigration restrictions, and, sometimes, difficulties with communications must be taken into account. Nevertheless, there should be evidence of some attempt to help support the child and/or some showing of communication with or about the child, which evinces a genuine interest in the child. To require less would be to ignore Congress' clear language. Beyond this very general guidance, we believe the meaning of the term "bona fide parent-child relationship" is best left to be developed on a case-by-case basis. We see no need to specifically adopt the "active parental interest" standard set forth in the *Moreira* decisions, *supra.*

For the reasons discussed above, the appeal will be sustained and the record will be remanded to the RSC director for further proceedings consistent with the foregoing decision.

* * *

Note

In *Matter of Pineda*,[65] the BIA elaborated on the meaning of "bona fide parent-child relationship":

> At minimum, however, some showing of emotional and/or financial ties must be made. There should be evidentiary proof that the parent and child live or lived together, or that the father held the child out as his own, or that he provided for some or all of the child's needs, financial or otherwise, or that in general the father's behavior evidenced a genuine concern for and interest in the child....
>
> The evidence relevant to establishing a parent-child relationship is varied and widespread in nature and is not confined to documents the beneficiary may have had in her possession during her residence in El Salvador. It may include money order receipts or cancelled checks showing the petitioner's financial support of the beneficiary at any point in her life, including the time subsequent to her entry into the United States; medical or insurance records; school records on the beneficiary, including those compiled during her schooling in the United States; correspondence between the parties, including correspondence that the petitioner may have received from the beneficiary while she was still in El Salvador; and notarized affidavits of friends, neighbors, school officials, or other knowledgeable associates attesting to the existence of the parent-child relationship.

6. Orphans

Matter of Greenwood

18 I. & N. Dec. 417 (BIA 1983)

BY: Milhollan, Chairman; Maniatis, Dunne, Morris, and Vacca, Board Members

This matter is before the Board on appeal from the District Director's decision of February 17, 1982, denying the petition to classify the beneficiary as the mother of a United States citizen under section 201(b) of the Immigration and Nationality Act, 8 U.S.C. 1151(b). The appeal will be dismissed.

---

65. 20 I. & N. Dec. 70, 73, 75 (BIA 1989).

The petitioner is a 23-year-old native of Jamaica and naturalized citizen of the United States. The beneficiary is a 41-year-old native and citizen of Jamaica. The unauthenticated, uncertified copy of the petitioner's purported "Birth Registration Form" contained in the record reflects that she was born, apparently out of wedlock, to a woman named Hyacinth Robinson, said to be the instant beneficiary. For purposes of this appeal, we will assume that the beneficiary is the petitioner's natural mother. We also note that the petitioner's alleged birth document does not identify her natural father, and there is no evidence that she has ever legitimated or otherwise acknowledged the petitioner.

The record reflects that the petitioner immigrated to the United States classified as an "eligible orphan," to be adopted by a United States citizen sometime after entry, pursuant to the provisions of section 101(b)(1)(F) of the Act, 8 U.S.C. 1101(b)(1)(F). Although the petitioner's adoption was never legally perfected, she subsequently did become a naturalized United States citizen based upon her admission into the United States for permanent residence as an eligible orphan.

In order for the beneficiary to be eligible for classification as the petitioner's mother, the petitioner must once have qualified as the beneficiary's "child" under section 101(b)(1) of the Act. See section 101(b)(2); *Matter of Hassan*, 16 I & N. Dec. 16 (BIA 1976); *Matter of Citino*, 12 I & N. Dec. 427 (BIA 1967).

* * *

Under the facts assumed here, it is clear that the petitioner once qualified as the beneficiary's "child" under section 101(b)(1)(D). The only remaining issue is whether the further proviso of section 101(b)(1)(F) bars the petitioner from conferring immigration benefits upon the beneficiary.

The petitioner argues that the further proviso should not preclude her from conferring immigration benefits upon her natural mother because she (the petitioner) was never legally adopted in the United States. The Service asserts that the statute does not require an adoption, but only an entry as an eligible orphan. We agree with the position advanced by the Service because it is both supported by the apparent purpose and rationale of the provision and, more importantly, is clearly mandated by the plain meaning of the words of the further proviso.

Who is intended to benefit by the provisions of section 101(b)(1)(F)? It is apparent that these provisions have a humanitarian purpose, being designed to facilitate the entry of alien minors whose parents are dead, whose parents have abandoned them, or whose parents cannot properly care for them and have chosen to release them for emigration and adoption. It should be noted that an absolute prerequisite to qualification as an eligible orphan is that the alien minor's previous parental relationships be permanently severed—whether by death, abandonment, or irrevocable release. This fact spawned inclusion of the further proviso of section 101(b)(1)(F), with its specific articulation of the attendant immigration consequences: a parent so permanently severed from his child will thereafter be unable to secure immigration benefits through such a child. In addition to this explicit acknowledgment of the practical effect of such a permanent termination of the parental relationship, the further proviso also serves to prevent the possible manipulation—whether innocent or contrived—of the eligible orphan provision whereby, e.g., an alien parent may be motivated to release his child for immigration to the United States in the hope that he might further his own prospects of obtaining entry into the United States at a future time. A parent who abandons his child or irrevocably releases a child for adoption by another in the United States can have no legitimate expectation of preserving a legal bond by which to lay claim to subsequent immigration benefits himself. The further proviso merely recognizes this situation by incorporating an explicit legal bar to that effect.

Wholly apart from this sensible and practical rationale of the further proviso's terms, as a matter of pure statutory construction we are convinced that the plain meaning of section 101(b)(1)(F) renders the mere entry of an alien minor as an "eligible orphan" sufficient to invoke application of the further proviso, even absent a subsequent legal adoption. The further proviso stipulates, in pertinent part, "That no natural parent ... of any *such child* shall thereafter, by virtue of such parentage, be accorded any ... status under this Act" (emphasis supplied). This "such child" language refers to the immediately preceding definition of "child" in the main provision of section 101(b)(1)(F), to wit, "a child ... who is an orphan" and who either (1) "has been adopted abroad" or (2) "is coming to the United States for adoption." In this latter case, the statute requires only that the orphan child be coming to the United States for adoption; the words nowhere require that the intended adoption for which the orphan child is coming be legally perfected. Classification as an "eligible orphan" does not mandate the subsequent completion of the intended United States adoption, but only that at the time of entry the child was in fact coming to be adopted. A change of intent after the child has already entered and "come" does not contravene any specific provision of section 101(b)(1)(F). Thus, by virtue of the statute's plain meaning, the mere "coming" of an alien minor to the United States under that provision is sufficient to invoke application of the further proviso.

In view of the foregoing, we hold that where an alien minor is admitted to the United States classified as an "eligible orphan" pursuant to section 101(b)(1)(F) of the Act—even absent a subsequent formal adoption—the further proviso therein operates to forever bar the eligible orphan from conferring immigration benefits upon his natural parents (or prior adoptive parents).

In this case, the petitioner entered the United States classified as an "eligible orphan." Therefore, the further proviso of section 101(b)(1)(F) of the Act bars her from conferring immigrant status upon the beneficiary as her immediate relative mother under section 201(b) of the Act. Under the natural reading of the statute, the fact that the petitioner's adoption in the United States was never legally perfected is of no moment. Accordingly, the beneficiary is ineligible for classification as the petitioner's immediate relative, and the District Director properly denied the petition.

7. Filial Relationships

Matter of Mahal

12 I. & N. Dec. 409 (BIA 1967)

The case come forward pursuant to certification by the District Director of his orders dated October 28, 1966 denying the visa petitions for the reason that the beneficiaries are the offspring of a second polygamous marriage, which while valid where performed in Pakistan, cannot be considered as valid for immigration purposes; and that the issue of such a marriage do not enjoy a brother-sister relationship with the issue of the original and recognized marriage and are not entitled to status as the brother and/or sister of a citizen of the United States.

The petitioner, a native of Pakistan, a citizen of the United States by naturalization on December 12, 1960, seeks preference status under section 203(a)(5) of the Immigration and Nationality Act on behalf of the beneficiaries as his half brother and half sister, respectively. The beneficiaries are both married. The male beneficiary was born December 3, 1929 in Pakistan and the female beneficiary was born October 17, 1936 in India.

The information submitted in support of the visa petitions established that the petitioner is the legitimate son of Udham Singh Mahal and Aupar Pirtam Kaur Mahal who were married June 1917 in India according to the Hindu Rites. The beneficiaries, the half brother and half sister of the petitioner, are the offspring of a second marriage of the same father to Aupar Kaur Mahal in October 1928 also under the Hindu Rites. According to information from the Consulate General of India at San Francisco dated September 7, 1966, before the enactment of the Hindu Code Bill in 1955/1956, a man could legally marry more than one wife in India. It is established then that the petitioner and the beneficiaries are the children of polygamous marriage. It has been ascertained from the Indian Embassy at Washington, D.C. that the children of these polygamous marriages, which, it must be remembered were legal in both India and Pakistan until 1955/1956, under the Hindu law are legitimate in every sense of the word.

The case therefore falls squarely within the decision in *Matter of K-W-S-*, 9 I. & N. Dec. 396 (A.G., 1961). In that case the parties were a sister and her half brother who were the offspring of a wife and a concubine, respectively, in China. Under Chinese law the child of a concubine who is acknowledged by the father, was equally as legitimate as the child of his lawful wife. In affirming the Board's order that these children, who were legitimated under the law of China, should be regarded as brother and sister, the Attorney General pointed out that neither the decision nor the 1952 Act implies any approval of the institution of concubinage or polygamy, which constitutes a class excluded from entry into the United States under section 212(a)(11) of the Immigration and Nationality Act. However, in the 1952 Act, Congress deemed it more in accordance with humanitarian principles to try to keep together those offspring of a common parent who have lived together as a family unit in accordance with the established laws and institutions of their place of residence, regardless of whether or not those laws are in conformity with the long social and family institutions.[1]

In the instant case the polygamous marriage of the father to two wives in India or Pakistan was legal under Hindu law prevailing at that time and the children of such polygamous marriages were under the law then prevailing considered legitimate. *Matter of K-W-S- (supra)*, is considered dispositive of the case to accord recognition of a brother and sister relationship such as will support a petition for preference status.

ORDER: It is ordered that the visa petitions be approved for fifth preference quota status on behalf of the beneficiaries.

E. Spousal Relationships

1. The Definition of "Marriage"

Matter of McKee

17 I. & N. Dec. 332 (BIA 1980)

BY: Milhollan, Chairman; Maniatis, Appleman, Maguire, and Farb, Board Members

The petitioner has appealed from the decision of a District Director, dated December 12, 1978, denying the visa petition filed on behalf of the beneficiary as his spouse under section 201(b) of the Immigration and Nationality Act, 8 U.S.C. 1151(b). The record will be remanded.

The petitioner, a 24-year-old United States citizen, married the beneficiary, a 25-year-old native and citizen of Australia, on August 12, 1977 in Pensacola, Florida. On October 12, 1977, the petitioner filed a visa petition on the beneficiary's behalf, seeking to accord her immediate relative status. In his decision, the District Director found that the parties had separated, and, on that basis, he denied the petition. On appeal, the petitioner has raised several arguments in support of his claim that the District Director erred in considering the unsworn statement of the beneficiary that she and the petitioner had separated, in not affording the petitioner an opportunity to rebut this adverse evidence, and in considering the separation of the parties as a valid basis upon which to deny the petition.

In connection with the petitioner's last argument, we requested the position of the Immigration and Naturalization Service on April 24, 1979. In a memorandum dated June 22, 1979, the Service indicated their agreement with the rationale of the recent decision of *Chan v. Bell*, 464 F.Supp. 125 (D.D.C.1978), thereby accepting the court's ruling that, where the parties to a marriage were living apart, but there was no contention that the marriage was a sham at its inception in that it had been entered

1. In the unreported case of *Matter of Aref Hasan Hamdan*, VPO 7-3592 (July 27, 1955), the children of a polygamous marriage which was legal under the Moslem faith were recognized as legitimate and eligible for preference quota status as brothers of the petitioner.

into for the purpose of evading the immigration laws, the Service could not deny the visa petition solely because the parties were no longer living together.

In the past, this Board has held that a visa petition would only be approved where the petitioner established that he and the beneficiary had entered into a bona fide marriage which is presently viable and ongoing. See *Matter of Mintah*, 15 I & N Dec. 540 (BIA 1975). We found support for our position in the Congressional objective of preservation of the family unit through the immigration laws. See generally *Matter of Lew*, 11 I & N Dec. 148 (D.D.1965). A marriage that is entered into for the primary purpose of circumventing the immigration laws, referred to as a fraudulent or sham marriage, has not been recognized as enabling an alien spouse to obtain immigration benefits. See *Lutwak v. United States*, 344 U.S. 604 (1953); *McLat v. Longo*, 412 F.Supp. 1021 (D.V.I.1976); *Matter of M-*, 8 I & N Dec. 118 (BIA 1958); see generally *Johl v. United States*, 370 F.2d 174 (9 Cir.1967). However, we have always recognized that a fraudulent or sham marriage is intrinsically different from a nonviable or nonsubsisting one, see, e.g., *Matter of Rahmati*, 16 I & N Dec. 538 (BIA 1978), although we have denied visa petition approval in both instances.

Chan v. Bell, supra, involved an appeal from the denial of a visa petition filed by a United States citizen petitioner on behalf of her husband. The parties in that case had known each other for several years prior to their marriage on January 10, 1975. The couple lived together for several months subsequent to their marriage during which time they jointly purchased property. In July 1975, they separated, but continued an amicable relationship and their joint property ownership. In May 1976, the petitioner informed the District Director by letter that she and her husband had separated. Based upon this separation, the District Director denied the visa petition on June 14, 1976. A subsequent appeal to the Board was denied on November 9, 1977.

In its decision, the *Chan* court characterized the Attorney General's role in the adjudication of immediate relative visa petitions under section 201(b) of the Act as "limited: he is required to approve any true petition of a spouse of an American citizen in order that such spouse may secure immediate relative status." *Id.* at 127. Compare *Menezes v. INS*, 601 F.2d 1028 (9th Cir.1979). See also *Dabaghian v. Civiletti*, 607 F.2d 868 (9th Cir.1979). The court noted that, at the time the visa petition was filed, the parties were lawfully married and that no divorce or legal separation had taken place, nor had any proceedings for divorce or legal separation been instituted. The court then went on to state its reasons for rejection of our decision affirming the District Director's denial of the visa petition based upon our characterization of the Chans' marriage as "nonviable."

The *Chan* court addressed the distinction between a sham and a nonviable marriage, recognizing that the Service is not precluded "from refusing to recognize fraudulent marriages." *Id.* at n. 8. However, the court found no support in the statute or regulations for our refusal to approve a visa petition based on a finding that the parties to a valid marriage did not have a subsisting relationship. We find the reasoning of the court's decision in this regard persuasive.

In the present case, the District Director denied the visa petition based upon his determination that—

> [I]t must be established that a viable marriage exists both at the time of filing of the petition and at this time. On October 16, 1978, the beneficiary of the petition related to an officer of this Service that you and she were no longer residing together as man and wife.

He, therefore, based his denial of the petition on the sole basis that the parties were not residing together. The record indicates that the parties entered into a marriage valid under the laws of Florida, the place of celebration; there is no evidence that they have since obtained a legal separation or dissolution of that marriage under the laws of any state. Accordingly, we find that it was error for the District Director to deny the instant visa petition based solely on the separation of the parties. To the extent the *Matter of Mintah, supra*, indicates otherwise, it is hereby modified.

However, it is important to recognize that, although a separation in and of itself is no longer a valid basis for denial of a visa petition based upon a determination that the marriage is not viable, it is a relevant factor in determining the parties' intent at the time of their marriage, i.e., whether the marriage is a sham. See *Bark v. INS*, 511 F.2d 1200 (9 Cir.1975). In *Bark*, the court held that a marriage was a "sham" if "the bride and groom did not intend to establish a life together at the time they were married." 511 F.2d at 1201. The court there found that the duration of a separation is relevant, but not dispositive, on the issue of intent, stating that—

> Conduct of the parties after marriage is relevant only to the extent that it bears upon their subjective state of mind at the time they were married. Evidence that the parties separated after their wedding is relevant in ascertaining whether they intended to establish a life together when they exchanged marriage vows. But evidence of separation, standing alone, cannot support a finding that a marriage was not bona fide when it was entered.... Of course, the time and extent of separation, combined with other facts and circumstances, can and have adequately supported the conclusion that a marriage was not bona fide.

511 F.2d at 1202 (citations omitted). See also *Matter of Phillis*, 15 I & N Dec. 385 (BIA 1975).

In the present case, no determination has been made regarding the parties' intent at the time of their marriage. Additionally, there is no evidence concerning the present status of the petitioner's marriage, i.e., whether the parties are legally separated or have dissolved their marriage, nor has there been compliance with the regulation requiring the Service to give the petitioner an opportunity to rebut any adverse evidence before rendering a decision. See 8 C.F.R. 103.2(b)(2); *Matter of Holmes*, 14 I & N Dec. 647 (BIA 1974). Accordingly, we will remand the record for further consideration and the entry of a new decision. See generally *Matter of To*, 14 I & N Dec. 679 (BIA 1974). The petitioner should be given an opportunity on remand to submit any additional evidence he may have in support of the petition.

2. Restrictions on Immigration Benefits Notwithstanding the Existence of a Marriage

Immigration and Marriage Fraud Amendments of 1986[66]

8 U.S.C. § 1154(g), Sec. 204(g)

Notwithstanding subsection (a), except as provided in section 245(e)(3), a petition may not be approved to grant an alien immediate relative status or preference status by reason of a marriage which was entered into during the period described in section 245(e)(2), until the alien has resided outside the United States for a 2-year period beginning after the date of the marriage.

8 U.S.C. § 1255(e), Sec. 245(e)

(1) Except as provided in paragraph (3), an alien who is seeking to receive an immigrant visa on the basis of a marriage which was entered into during the period described in paragraph (2) may not have the alien's status adjusted under subsection (a).

(2) The period described in this paragraph is the period during which administrative or judicial proceedings are pending regarding the alien's right to be admitted or remain in the United States.

(3) Paragraph (1) and section 204(g) shall not apply with respect to a marriage *if the alien establishes by clear and convincing evidence to the satisfaction of the Attorney General that the marriage was entered into in good faith and in accordance with the laws of the place where the marriage took place and the marriage was not entered into for the purpose of procuring the alien's admission as an immigrant and no fee or other consideration was given* (other than a fee or other consideration to an attorney for assistance in preparation of a lawful petition) for the filing of a petition under section 204(a) or 214(d) with respect to the alien spouse or alien son or daughter. In accordance with regulations, there shall be only one level of administrative appellate review for each alien under the previous sentence (emphasis supplied).

Paul and Mona Anetekhai v. Immigration and Naturalization Service

876 F.2d 1218 (5th Cir. 1989)

Before Aldisert, Reavley and Higginbotham, Circuit Judges.

Reavley, Circuit Judge.

Prior to the enactment of the IMFA in 1986, any United States citizen claiming that his or her alien spouse was entitled to immediate relative status could seek an

---

66. Pub. L. No. 99-639, 100 Stat. 3537 (1986), as amended by Immigration Technical Corrections Act of 1988, Pub. L. No. 100-525, 102 Stat. 2609 (1988).

adjustment in status for the alien spouse simply by "fil[ing] a petition with the Attorney General for such classification." 8 U.S.C. § 1154(a). If, after an investigation, the Attorney General determined that the facts stated in the petition were true—in other words, if the Attorney General concluded that the marriage was bona fide—then the status of the alien spouse was adjusted to that of permanent resident alien. 8 U.S.C. § 1154(b). If, on the other hand, the Attorney General determined that the marriage had been entered into fraudulently for the purpose of obtaining immigration benefits, no adjustment in status was made.

Perceived abuses of this process and the difficulty of ferreting out sham marriages prompted Congress to enact the IMFA. Under the IMFA, an alien who marries a United States citizen while no deportation proceedings are pending against him receives a two-year conditional adjustment of status so long as the investigation into the facts surrounding the marriage reveal that it is bona fide. See generally 8 U.S.C. § 1186a. In order for the conditional status to be removed at the end of the two-year period, the couple must submit a joint petition to the Attorney General in accordance with statutory requirements and must appear for a personal interview. 8 U.S.C. § 1186a(c)(1). If the Attorney General concludes that the facts and information provided by the couple are true, the condition is removed and the alien spouse obtains full permanent resident status. 8 U.S.C. § 1186a(c)(3)(B).

The procedure that a couple must follow in order for the alien spouse to obtain preferential status is different if, at the time of the marriage, the alien is involved in deportation proceedings. In that case the alien spouse is required to reside outside the United States for a two-year period before he or she may obtain an adjustment in status based on the marriage. 8 U.S.C. § 1154(h) and § 1255(e). It is this aspect of the IMFA which is at issue here.

In January 1982, Paul Anetekhai, a Nigerian citizen, entered the United States on a nonimmigrant student visa. In February 1986, the INS, having discovered that Paul was employed without authorization, commenced deportation proceedings against him. Also in early 1986, Paul met and began dating Mona Morris; they married in January 1987. Believing that his marriage to a United States citizen would entitle him to an immediate adjustment in status and thus make the deportation proceedings unnecessary, Paul moved to dismiss the proceedings. The immigration judge denied the motion and, finding Paul deportable, granted him until January 31, 1988, to depart voluntarily from the United States. The INS later extended the date for departure to February 28, 1988.

* * *

In addressing the constitutionality of an immigration provision, "it is important to underscore the limited scope of judicial inquiry into immigration legislation." *Fiallo* [*v. Bell*], 430 U.S. at 792. The broad power that Congress possesses to decide not only which classes of aliens may enter the United States but also the terms and conditions of their entry cannot be disputed. See *Oceanic Steam Navigation Co. v. Stranahan*, 214 U.S. 320, 339 (1909)....

... The Court also has recognized that, in exercising its broad discretion over immigration, "Congress regularly makes rules that would be unacceptable if applied to citizens." *Mathews v. Diaz*, 426 U.S. 67, 80 (1976).

The Anetekhais do not deny that, ordinarily, courts should be highly deferential in reviewing congressional enactments in the areas of immigration and naturalization. They argue, however, that we should apply strict scrutiny in analyzing the immigration provision at issue here since § 1154(h) "affects Mona's fundamental rights in the domestic area." The Supreme Court rejected this very argument in *Fiallo....*

Of prime importance in the Court's decision to review the INA provisions challenged in *Fiallo* with such deference was its conclusion that at issue there were the rights of the alien children, not the rights of United States citizens. Indeed, it was this very point which divided the majority from the dissent. *Fiallo*, 430 U.S. at 795 n. 6. Similarly, in this case we are concerned with whatever rights Mr. Anetekhai, the alien spouse, may possess—not the rights of Mrs. Anetekhai.[5] That Mrs. Anetekhai asserts her fundamental right to marry here does not alter our analysis.[6] In *Fiallo*, the Supreme Court, too, was dealing with the citizens' fundamental interests in familial relationships.

Applying the deferential standard of review articulated in *Fiallo* to the case before us, we have no difficulty in concluding that § 1154(h) passes constitutional muster.[7] The Anetekhais admit that Congress has a strong and legitimate interest in deterring marriages which are entered into for the purpose of obtaining immigration benefits. We, like the other courts that have considered this issue, believe that Congress logically could have concluded that aliens who are engaged in deportation proceedings are more likely than aliens not so situated to enter into fraudulent marriages as a means of avoiding expulsion from the United States. See, e.g., *Almario v. INS*, 872 F.2d 147 (6th Cir.1989); *Escobar v. INS*, 700 F.Supp. 609, 612 (D.D.C. 1988); *Smith v. INS*, 684 F.Supp. 1113, 1117 (D.Mass.1988). "Since marriage to a United States citizen will no longer allow an alien engaged in deportation proceedings to remain in this country, it is rational to conclude that the two-year non-residency requirement will have some effect in reducing the incidence of marriage fraud" within this class of aliens. *Smith*, 684 F.Supp. at 1117.

---

5. Obviously our decision will have a significant impact on Mrs. Anetekhai's interests. We note, however, that Mrs. Anetekhai has no constitutional right to have her alien spouse remain in the United States. *See Burrafato v. United States Department of State*, 523 F.2d 554, 555 (2d Cir.1975), *cert. denied*, 424 U.S. 910 (1976).

6. Nor does the fact that Mrs. Anetekhai asserts her "First Amendment rights to privacy and association" affect the outcome here. The Supreme Court made clear in *Fiallo* that, in ruling on the constitutionality of a provision, we are to apply the same standard regardless of whether Fifth Amendment or First Amendment rights are asserted....

7. The INS argues that the test for determining the constitutionality of an immigration provision is whether it is based upon a "facially legitimate and bona fide reason." *See Fiallo*, 430 U.S. at 794–95 (citing *Kleindienst*, 408 U.S. at 770). Because we conclude that § 1154(h) easily passes a rational basis test, we need not decide whether some lesser standard might be appropriate.

In its amicus brief, the American Civil Liberties Union ("ACLU") attempts to distinguish *Fiallo* from this case. It argues that the issue in *Fiallo* was the validity of a statute establishing classes of admissible aliens. The ACLU concedes that Congress has virtually unlimited power in making such policy decisions. It argues that in this case, however, no policy decision is at issue. Instead, according to the ACLU, "the statute recognizes that aliens who marry citizens are admissible and then establishes a procedure designed to deny immigrant visas to aliens who base their claims on a fraudulent marriage." The ACLU contends that, because the procedure does not afford couples the opportunity to demonstrate that their marriages are not fraudulent, the statute violates their rights to procedural due process. We disagree.

As an initial matter, we reject the ACLU's attempt to characterize § 1154(h) as a matter of procedure only. Inherent in Congress' broad policy making power in the area of immigration law is the power to prescribe reasonable procedures by which that policy may be implemented. Congress made a policy decision to distinguish aliens who marry while involved in deportation proceedings from aliens who marry at other times. This decision, in effect, created two classes of alien spouses. The first class, those aliens who marry United States citizens at a time when no deportation proceedings are pending against them, follows track one. Their citizen spouses may petition on their behalf for an adjustment in status at any time after they are married; if the petition is approved, the alien is granted preferred status on a conditional basis for a two-year period. The second class, those aliens who marry after deportation proceedings are initiated against them, follow track two. In order for these aliens to obtain immediate relative status, they must reside outside the United States for a two-year period before they may obtain an adjustment in status. We believe that Congress acted well within its power in establishing this policy and procedure.

In addition, we disagree with the ACLU's suggestion that § 1154(h) deprives alien spouses of any protected interests in "immigrant visas." Far from being a provision designed to deprive aliens of benefits to which that are entitled, § 1154(h) is part and parcel of the statutory scheme under which those benefits are conferred in the first instance. The section title itself states: "Procedure for *granting* immigrant status." 8 U.S.C. § 1154 (emphasis added). Procedural due process guarantees attach only when the government deprives a citizen or alien of life, liberty or property. *Plyler v. Doe*, 457 U.S. 202, 210 (1982).

In concluding that § 1154(h) does not deprive Mr. Anetekhai of a protected interest, we do not mean to suggest that he is entitled to absolutely no due process under that provision. We simply hold that the process which he is due is limited to fair procedures to determine whether § 1154(h) was invoked properly. In other words, if the Anetekhais had married before the INS initiated deportation proceedings against Mr. Anetekhai, he would be entitled to demonstrate that fact.

The Anetekhais argue, however, that § 1154(h) violates their due process rights by creating an irrebuttable presumption that their marriage, and every other marriage entered into during deportation proceedings, is fraudulent; they maintain that, before this conclusion can be reached, they must be afforded the opportunity to present contrary evidence. Certainly, if Congress had conditioned an alien's eligibility for a status adjustment on the existence of a bona fide marriage, procedural due process would require that the couple be given an opportunity to establish that fact before an adjustment could be denied. See *Smith*, 684 F.Supp. at 1118. That is not what Congress did here, however. Section 1154(h) does not require a two-year nonresidency because it presumes that the marriage is fraudulent. Instead, the statute requires an alien in Mr. Anetekhai's position to leave the United States for a two year period simply because the timing of his marriage places him in that class of aliens for whom a two-year nonresidency is required. Again, Congress rationally could conclude that this provision would deter those who are faced with imminent deportation from entering into fraudulent marriages for the purpose of gaining immigration benefits.

The Anetekhais also argue that, because there are several ways in which § 1154(h) can be avoided, it is not rationally related to the government's interest in deterring marriage fraud. We recognize that there are several ways in which a couple could avoid the seemingly harsh results of this provision, and that there may be better ways for Congress to accomplish its objective of deterring marriage fraud. However, we cannot conclude that because there might be a better way to write the statute, the statute as it exists is irrational.

Nor do we agree with the ACLU that § 1154(h) "suffers from precisely the same defect" that *Francis v. INS*, 532 F.2d 268 (2d Cir.1976), held to be irrational. In *Guan Chow Tok v. INS*, 538 F.2d 36, 38–39 (2d Cir.1976), the Second Circuit explained that "[i]n *Francis*, we held it irrational to distinguish between two categories of narcotic offenders on the basis of a brief visit out of the country. Here, the distinction is between narcotic offenders and other offenders, a distinction that has a rational basis." Similarly, in this case, the distinction is between aliens who marry while involved in deportation proceedings and aliens who marry at other times. This distinction, too, has a rational basis. Section 1154(h) withstands constitutional challenge under the Fifth and First Amendments.

The Anetekhais also challenge § 1154(h) under the Ninth and Tenth Amendments. They claim that, in enacting § 1154(h), "Congress overstepped its authority by purporting to regulate Louisiana marriages." This argument is without merit. The two-year nonresidency requirement of § 1154(h), by itself, does not in any way affect the legal status of the Anetekhais' marriage under state law. See La.Civ.Code Ann. art. 138 (West Supp.1989); La.Rev.Stat.Ann. § 9:301 (West Supp.1989).

* * *

Notes

1. While USCIS may not be able to challenge the viability of a marriage, other restrictions may apply to a person's ability to obtain an immigrant visa based on the marriage. As the *Anetekhai* case demonstrates, amendments enacted in 1986 provided that an immigrant visa cannot be accorded based upon a marriage entered into during

"the period ... [in] which administrative or judicial proceedings are pending regarding the person's right to enter or remain in the United States" until the beneficiary has resided outside of the United States for two years unless the person can establish by clear and convincing evidence that the marriage was entered into in good faith and not for immigration purposes. These amendments, termed the "Immigration Marriage Fraud Amendments" also modified provisions of the statute which allow persons to obtain lawful permanent resident status through "adjustment of status."[67] As will be discussed later, adjustment of status allows a person to obtain permanent residency without having to depart the United States and apply for an immigrant visa. The two year bar to receiving permanent residency based upon such a marriage has only been successfully challenged in one lower court case.[68]

2. In *Anetekhai*, the court noted with regard to the IMFA that "Congress rationally could conclude that this provision would deter those who are faced with imminent deportation from entering into fraudulent marriages for the purpose of gaining immigration benefits." Is this a legitimate exercise of the congressional power? Does this mean that Congress can do whatever it wishes as long as its goal is the control of immigration?

3. The IMFA precludes preference or immediate relative status to persons involved in removal proceedings. In *Matter of Enriquez*,[69] BIA, citing 8 C.F.R. § 3.14(a), noted that the case begins with the filing of the order to show cause with the office of the immigration judge. USCIS's position is that removal proceedings commence upon the service of the order to show cause.[70]

4. Can the two-year foreign residency requirement for persons described in 8 U.S.C. § 1154(h) be construed more broadly than applying to removal proceedings? Does the period following USCIS's denial of a request for change of status?

5. What would happen if the Anetekhais had divorced and then remarried after Paul had left the United States under voluntary departure?

6. **Good Faith Exception.** While the IMFA is harsh, there is an exception to the two year bar which provides that it can be set aside if the petitioner and beneficiary of the marriage petition are able to establish by "clear and convincing" evidence that the marriage was entered into in good faith.[71]

---

67. *See* 8 U.S.C. § 1255, Sec. 245.

68. *See Manwani v. U.S. DOJ*, 736 F. Supp. 1367 (W.D. N.C. 1990) (holding the provisions unconstitutional); *Almario v. Attorney General*, 872 F.2d 147 (6th Cir. 1989) (upholding the constitutionality of the provisions); *Smith v. INS*, 684 F. Supp. 1113, 1117 (D. Mass. 1988) (rejecting an equal protection and due process challenge); *compare Blancada v. Turnage*, 891 F.2d 688, 690 (9th Cir. 1989) (without deciding constitutional claims, the court reversed the denial of a stay of deportation request and motion to reopen to raise challenge to the IMFA).

69. 19 I. & N. Dec. 554 (BIA 1988).

70. See 8 C.F.R. § 242.1(2)(iii).

71. 8 U.S.C. § 1255(e)(3), Sec. 245(e)(3); *Matter of Fuentes*, 20 I. & N. Dec. 227 (BIA 1991).

Presumptions of Fraud

8 U.S.C. § 1154(a)(2), Sec. 204(a)(2)

(A) The Attorney General may not approve a spousal second preference petition for the classification of the spouse of an alien if the alien, by virtue of a prior marriage, has been accorded the status of an alien lawfully admitted for permanent residence as the spouse of a citizen of the United States or as the spouse of an alien lawfully admitted for permanent residence, unless—

(i) a period of 5 years has elapsed after the date the alien acquired the status of an alien lawfully admitted for permanent residence, or

(ii) the alien establishes to the satisfaction of the Attorney General by clear and convincing evidence that the prior marriage (on the basis of which the alien obtained the status of an alien lawfully admitted for permanent residence) was not entered into for the purpose of evading any provision of the immigration laws.

In this subparagraph, the term "spousal second preference petition" refers to a petition, seeking preference status under section 203(a)(2), for an alien as a spouse of an alien lawfully admitted for permanent residence.

(B) Subparagraph (A) shall not apply to a petition filed for the classification of the spouse of an alien if the prior marriage of the alien was terminated by the death of his or her spouse.

Matter of Patel

19 I. & N. Dec. 774 (BIA 1988)

BY: Milhollan, Chairman; Dunne, Morris, Vacca, and Heilman, Board Members

The petitioner appeals from the decision of the district director denying the visa petition filed on behalf of the beneficiary as his spouse under section 203(a)(2) of the Immigration and Nationality Act, 8 U.S.C. § 1153(a)(2) (1982). The appeal will be sustained.

The petitioner is a 30-year-old native of Kenya. He acquired lawful permanent resident status in the United States on February 3, 1985, as the spouse of a lawful permanent resident whom he had married on June 23, 1983. The petitioner and his first wife were divorced on November 25, 1985. The beneficiary is a 29-year-old native and citizen of India. The petitioner and the beneficiary were married on March 6, 1986. On June 12, 1986, the petitioner filed a visa petition on behalf of the beneficiary as his spouse.

On February 9, 1987, the district director denied the petition on the ground that the petitioner had failed to comply with section 204(a)(2)(A) of the Act, 8 U.S.C. § 1154(a)(2)(A) (Supp.IV 1986), which requires that the petitioner establish by clear and convincing evidence that his prior marriage was not entered into for the purpose of evading any provision of the immigration laws.

At the time he filed his appeal to the Board, the petitioner also filed a motion to reopen and/or reconsider with the district director. He argued that he had failed to comply with section 204(a)(2)(A) of the Act because that provision did not exist at the time he filed his visa petition. He pointed out that section 204(a)(2)(A) of the Act was not enacted into law until November 10, 1986, with the signing of the Immigration Marriage Fraud Amendments of 1986, Pub.L. No. 99-639, 100 Stat. 3537 ("Amendments"), 5 months after the filing of his visa petition. With his motion, the petitioner attached documentary evidence in an attempt to show that his marriage to his first wife was bona fide.

The first document submitted with the motion is the petitioner's own affidavit. In that affidavit, the petitioner describes how his marriage to his first wife was arranged by their parents, but he notes that they were free to accept or reject the arrangement. He states that he decided to marry his first wife because he fell in love with her and wanted to spend the rest of his life with her. The petitioner avers that they were married on June 23, 1983, in an Indian religious ceremony in Murfreesboro, Tennessee, attended by 700 to 1,000 guests. He states that his family spent about $5,000 for the ceremony but that he does not know how much money was spent by his first wife's parents. The petitioner further advises that he and his first wife were very happy and took trips together to visit relatives in South Carolina, Alabama, and Tennessee. He avers that his first wife eventually filed for divorce because she found it difficult to adjust to life in LaFayette, Georgia, where they were the only Indian nationals. He explains that because she had lived in India for many more years than he had, her ties to traditional Indian culture were stronger than his. He says that she missed the relatives, friends, and Indian cultural functions she had left behind in Murfreesboro.

The petitioner also submitted an affidavit from his first wife, who avers that she and the petitioner married because they were in love and were planning to spend their lives together. She states that they were married in an Indian religious ceremony in Murfreesboro attended by more than 700 relatives from as far away as Oregon and California, and that the wedding cost their parents over $10,000. She further asserts that she was very happy living with the petitioner at the beginning of their marriage and mentions their trips to visit relatives in nearby states. The petitioner's first wife also advises, however, that she began to miss her family and friends in Murfreesboro. She indicates that she and the petitioner lacked a social life in LaFayette, where they were the only Indian nationals. She says that although they entered into their marriage "in the best of faith," she became depressed about their marriage and filed for divorce on September 18, 1985.

In addition, the petitioner attached an affidavit from the former owner of a LaFayette appliance company who avers that he knows the petitioner and his first wife because he used to service the appliances, plumbing, and heating and air conditioning units at the petitioner's motel in LaFayette. He states that he ate meals with them in their home on six to eight occasions and thought that they had a good, solid marriage, although the petitioner once mentioned to him that his wife did not like life in a small town like LaFayette.

The petitioner further submitted affidavits from a cousin, who describes in detail an interstate trip he took with the petitioner and his first wife and the recreational stops they made while traveling; a life insurance salesman, who avers that he made several business calls on the petitioner and his first wife at their home, discussed life insurance for the petitioner's wife, and ate Indian food they served to him; and two older male relatives of the petitioner, each of whom states that he has known the petitioner since his birth, that he attended the large June 1983 wedding of the petitioner and his first wife, that he entertained the petitioner and his first wife in an overnight visit they made to his home during 1984 and they seemed to have a happy marriage, and that he went to LaFayette in an effort to resolve their marital problems when he heard that they were considering a divorce.

Among the other documents submitted by the petitioner with his motion were an ornate greeting card in a foreign language which refers in English to an event at the Elk's Lodge in Murfreesboro; 15 photographs which show many guests attending a ceremony at an Elk's Lodge featuring a young couple; copies of 3 Christmas cards with inscriptions to the petitioner and his first wife; copies of 1983 and 1984 federal and Georgia joint income tax returns for the petitioner and his first wife which are accompanied by form cover letters from their accountant containing instructions on how to sign and mail the returns; a June 4, 1984, letter to the petitioner and his first wife from the Internal Revenue Service regarding the refund of an overpayment of tax on their 1983 return; and copies of a $5,000 corporate bond and Daily Passport Cash Trust account statements in the names of both the petitioner and his first wife.

Finally, the petitioner submitted copies of the divorce decree terminating his first marriage and the property settlement agreement referenced in the decree. In the divorce decree, the petitioner's first wife is identified as the complainant. The property settlement agreement reflects that she executed a quitclaim deed to all of the petitioner's personal and real property, including the motel property which he and a third party had purchased in March 1982. The agreement further indicates that the petitioner and his first wife conveyed to each other all of their interest in the other's personal property.

In a decision dated March 25, 1987, the district director denied the petitioner's motion to reopen and/or reconsider. He nonetheless proceeded to consider each document submitted by the petitioner individually. He characterized the petitioner's affidavit as "self-serving" and offering no evidence which was not available to the petitioner previously and, citing *Seihoon v. Levy*, 408 F.Supp. 1208 (M.D.La.1976), asserted that the relatively short period of time between the petitioner's acquisition of lawful permanent resident status and his divorce from his first wife indicated a fraudulent intent. The district director discounted the other affidavits on the various grounds that they contained evidence which was known at the time of the original filing of the visa petition, that they provided no new meaningful evidence, and that the affiants could not attest to the intentions of the petitioner when he entered into his first marriage. In addition, he stated that he was not considering the untranslated document, the unidentified photographs, and the undated copies of Christmas cards. The district director did acknowledge that the copies of the tax returns, the corporate bond, and the financial statements lent credence to the marriage, but he noted that these documents, as well as the divorce decree and the property settlement agreement, were available to the petitioner at the time of the original filing of his visa petition. The district director further observed that the petitioner had not supplied evidence of any insurance policies, property leases, or bank accounts naming his first wife, and that she had gained nothing upon her divorce from the petitioner. He concluded by finding that the petitioner's evidence failed to sustain his burden of proof.

On appeal, the petitioner contends that he has shown by clear and convincing evidence that his first marriage was bona fide. He maintains that the district director erred in requiring his motion to reopen and/or reconsider to be accompanied only by evidence which was not known at the time he filed his visa petition. He also asserts that the district director's decision reflects a predisposition to deny the petition, overlooking the fact that the Amendments provide for a presumption of fraud which is rebuttable. He claims in this regard that while the district director considers his intent at the time of his marriage to be critical, it is impossible for him to prove that his intent was bona fide when the district director dismisses his affidavit as "self-serving" and refuses to give any weight to the affidavits of his first wife and of people who observed them during their marriage. Finally, the petitioner argues that the 5-year rule of section 204(a)(2)(A) of the Act is unconstitutional because it violates his right of privacy. With his brief on appeal, the petitioner submitted documents in an attempt to cure defects noted by the district director in his decision denying his motion. These documents include an affidavit from one of the petitioner's older male relatives, who states that he has reviewed the photographs submitted with the motion and recognizes them as having been taken at the wedding of the petitioner and his first wife, and a translation of the greeting card submitted with the motion which reveals that it is a wedding invitation for the wedding ceremony of the petitioner and his first wife.

The Service contends on appeal that the district director's disqualification under 8 C.F.R. § 103.5 (1988) of the new evidence submitted by the petitioner was proper, as all of the materials submitted by the petitioner could have been submitted with his original visa petition. It is further argued that the district director correctly concluded that even if the new evidence had been accepted, it would not have satisfied the petitioner's burden of proof. The Service claims that the petitioner's evidence failed to provide objective proof of marital commitment and asserts that the joint tax returns and acquisitions of bonds and stocks indicated a financial but not necessarily a marital bond. In addition, it is asserted that the district director's reliance on *Seihoon v. Levy*, *supra*, was proper, because the rapid course of events in the instant case, as in *Seihoon*, indicates presumptive fraud.

Section 204(a)(2)(A) of the Act[1] provides as follows:

---

1. This subparagraph was added to section 204 of the Act by section 2(c) of the Immigration Marriage Fraud Amendments of 1986, Pub.L. No. 99-639, 100 Stat. 3537, 3541.

> (2)(A) The Attorney General may not approve a spousal second preference petition filed by an alien who, by virtue of a prior marriage, has been accorded the status of an alien lawfully admitted for permanent residence as the spouse of a citizen of the United States or as the spouse of an alien lawfully admitted for permanent residence, unless—
>
> (i) a period of 5 years has elapsed after the date the alien acquired the status of an alien lawfully admitted for permanent residence, or
>
> (ii) the alien establishes to the satisfaction of the Attorney General by clear and convincing evidence that the prior marriage (on the basis of which the alien obtained the status of an alien lawfully admitted for permanent residence) was not entered into for the purpose of evading any provision of the immigration laws.

In this subparagraph, the term "spousal second preference petition" refers to a petition, seeking preference status under section 203(a)(2), for an alien as a spouse of an alien lawfully admitted for permanent residence.

The initial issue before us is the propriety of retroactive application of section 204(a)(2)(A) of the Act to a spousal second-preference petition which was pending adjudication when the Amendments became law. Generally, a new statute applies to cases pending on the date of its enactment unless manifest injustice would result or there is a statutory directive or legislative history to the contrary. *Bradley v. Richmond School Board*, 416 U.S. 696 (1974). In determining whether a retroactive application would cause manifest injustice, three factors must be assessed: "(a) the nature and identity of the parties, (b) the nature of their rights, and (c) the nature of the impact of the change in law upon those rights." *Id.* at 717.

The provision creating section 204(a)(2)(A) of the Act appears in section 2(c) of the Amendments. An examination of section 2 of the Amendments reveals the absence of any statutory directive prohibiting the retroactive application of section 2(c). Section 2 makes no mention whatsoever of an effective date. This omission of an effective date for section 2(c) is significant, as Congress showed its awareness of the retroactivity issue by providing effective dates in the other substantive sections of the Amendments. Sections 3, 4, 5, and 6 of the Amendments all specify that provisions they set forth shall apply prospectively, on or after the date of the enactment of the Amendments. Thus, rather than prohibit retroactive application of section 2(c), the text of the Amendments, by its omission of an effective date for section 2(c) when a prospective effective date has been prescribed in other sections of the Amendments, in fact gives rise to an inference that Congress intended for section 2(c) to be applied retroactively as well as prospectively. Cf. *Marshall v. Gibson's Products, Inc. of Plano*, 584 F.2d 668 (5th Cir.1978) (stating that because Congress had expressly conferred jurisdiction on district courts in other sections of a statute, the natural inference to be drawn from the omission of any grant of jurisdiction in one particular section of that statute was that no such grant was intended).

Further, the legislative history of the Amendments, which is scanty, does not address the issue of the retroactivity of section 2(c). See H.R.Rep. No. 99-906, 99th Cong., 2d Sess. 8, reprinted in 1986 U.S.Code Cong. & Ad. News 5978. Thus, no statutory directive or legislative history exists which indicates that section 204(a)(2)(A) of the Act should not be applied retroactively. Therefore, we must next determine whether retroactive application of section 204(a)(2)(A) of the Act would result in manifest injustice.

In deciding whether manifest injustice would occur, we look first at the nature and identity of the parties. *Bradley v. Richmond School Board, supra*, at 717. In this analysis, a distinction is made between routine lawsuits engaged in by private parties, and litigation involving "great national concerns" with litigants who are public entities. *Id.* at 718–19; *LTV Federal Credit Union v. UMIC Government Securities, Inc.*, 704 F.2d 199, 203–04 (5th Cir.1983); *City of Great Falls v. United States Department of Labor*, 673 F.2d 1065, 1068 (9th Cir.1982). That a change in the law involves an issue of great national concern is a factor militating in favor of the law's retroactive application. See *Bradley v. Richmond School Board, supra*, at 719. Immigration policy is a matter of great national concern. *DeGurules v. INS*, 833 F.2d 861, 863 (9th Cir.1987). Moreover, one of the parties before us is the Federal Government. Thus, an examination of the nature and identity of the parties points towards the retroactive application of section 204(a)(2)(A) of the Act.

The second of the three factors involved in an assessment of whether manifest injustice would occur is the nature of the rights affected by the change in the law. *Bradley v. Richmond School Board, supra*, at 720. In describing this factor, the Supreme Court stated that an intervening change in the law should not apply to a pending action where to do so would infringe upon or deprive a person of a right that had matured or become unconditional. *Id.* When the Amendments were enacted into law, the petitioner in the case before us had already petitioned for a second preference visa for the beneficiary but the petition had not yet been adjudicated. We have held that the approval of a visa petition vests no rights in the beneficiary of the petition, as approval of a visa petition is but a preliminary step in the visa application process; the beneficiary is not, by mere approval of the petition, entitled to an immigrant visa. *Matter of Ho*, Interim Decision 3051 (BIA 1988). In the case before us, where the petition had not even been adjudicated when the law changed, it is clear that the petitioner had no vested or unconditional right to a visa for the beneficiary. Therefore, the second factor also militates in favor of applying section 204(a)(2)(A) of the Act retroactively.

The third factor to examine in determining whether manifest injustice would occur is the nature of the impact of the change in law upon existing rights and the possibility that new and unanticipated obligations may be imposed upon a party without notice or an opportunity to be heard. *Bradley v. Richmond School Board, supra*, at 720. The change in the law in this case does impose a new obligation on the petitioner, i.e., that he meet the evidentiary burden of proving the bona fides of his prior marriage by clear and convincing evidence. Yet the imposition of this new obligation on any petitioner would not ordinarily occur without adequate notice and an opportunity to be heard. In any case where a petition was filed prior to the enactment of section 204(a)(2)(A) of the Act into law, the petition would not be denied on the basis of that section unless the petitioner had been informed of the new law and given the opportunity to comply with its evidentiary requirements. Were we to receive an appeal in a case where a petition had been denied under those circumstances, we would find it appropriate to remand the case to afford the petitioner an opportunity to have evidence regarding his prior marriage considered by the district director in a new decision.

Moreover, the new evidentiary burden is a procedural rather than a substantive change. In a case where a question arises regarding the lawful permanent resident status of a petitioner which affects his right to confer benefits under the immigration laws to other persons, that petitioner may be required to carry his burden of proving that he is entitled to confer benefits. See *Matter of Abdoulin*, 17 I & N Dec. 458 (BIA 1980); *Matter of Abdelhadi*, 15 I & N Dec. 383 (BIA 1975). Thus, even before the enactment of section 204(a)(2)(A) of the Act into law, a district director could have considered the bona fides of a prior marriage if the facts raised a question regarding whether a petitioner was entitled to confer benefits based on the lawful permanent resident status acquired through that prior marriage. Here, the district director found that the rapidity with which the petitioner divorced and remarried after receiving lawful permanent resident status based on his first marriage raised a question about whether his first marriage had been entered into in good faith. Had this petition been adjudicated before the enactment of the Amendments, the bona fides of the petitioner's first marriage might still have been an issue. The only difference would have been procedural: before the Amendments, the petitioner would have been required to satisfy his burden of proof by a preponderance of the evidence rather than by clear and convincing evidence as specified by section 204(a)(2)(A) of the Act.

Further, the petitioner's right to petition for a second-preference visa for the beneficiary has only been restricted by section 204(a)(2)(A) of the Act, not eliminated. After a lawful permanent resident has been in lawful permanent resident status for 5 years, he may apply for a second-preference visa for a new spouse without being subject to the requirement that he establish by clear and convincing evidence that his prior marriage was not entered into for the purpose of evading any provision of the immigration laws. The regulations provide that a denial of a second-preference visa petition for failure to meet the clear and convincing evidentiary requirement will be without prejudice to the filing of a new petition once the petitioner has acquired 5 years of lawful permanent residence. 8 C.F.R. § 204.1(a)(2)(ii) (1988). Thus, even if a petitioner cannot meet the new evidentiary requirement of section 204(a)(2)(A) of the Act, that section still makes provision for the granting of a second-preference visa petition for a new spouse, albeit after a delay of up to 5 years. Therefore, we do not find that the nature of the impact of the change in law upon existing rights is such that manifest injustice would result from its retroactive application.

Based on the foregoing three factors, we conclude that no manifest injustice would result from the retroactive application of section 204(a)(2)(A) of the Act. Accordingly, we will apply that section to the visa petition before us and determine whether the petitioner has met his burden of establishing by clear and convincing evidence that his prior marriage was not entered into for the purpose of evading any provision of the immigration laws.

In visa petition proceedings, the burden is on the petitioner to establish eligibility for the benefit sought. See *Matter of Brantigan*, 11 I & N Dec. 493 (BIA 1966). The burden on the petitioner in visa petition proceedings is usually that of a preponderance of the evidence. *Matter of Soo Hoo*, 11 I & N Dec. 151 (BIA 1965). Section 204(a)(2)(A) of the Act, however, sets forth a presumption of a fraudulent prior marriage in any visa petition in which fewer than 5 years will have elapsed between the time a petitioner acquired his lawful permanent resident status based on that prior marriage and the time his visa petition for a subsequent spouse is adjudicated. In order to rebut this presumption, the petitioner has the burden of establishing by the standard of clear and convincing evidence that the prior marriage was not entered into for the purpose of evading any provision of the immigration laws.

Clear and convincing evidence is a standard of proof which requires more than the preponderance of the evidence standard applied in most civil cases, but less than the beyond a reasonable doubt standard used in criminal proceedings. *Addington v. Texas*, 441 U.S. 418, 425 (1979). The clear and convincing standard imposes a lower burden than the clear, unequivocal, and convincing standard applied in deportation and denaturalization proceedings because it does not require that the evidence be unequivocal or of such a quality as to dispel all doubt. *Id.* at 432; *United States v. Mastrangelo*, 561 F.Supp. 1114, 1120 (E.D.N.Y.1983). We have defined clear and convincing evidence as "that degree of proof though not necessarily conclusive, which will produce in the mind of the court a firm belief or conviction, or as that degree of proof which is more than a preponderance but less than beyond a reasonable doubt." *Matter of Carrubba*, 11 I & N Dec. 914, 917 (BIA 1966).

In attempting to show by clear and convincing evidence that his prior marriage was not entered into for the purpose of evading any provision of the immigration laws, a petitioner should submit evidence which includes that considered in any visa petition where the validity of a marital relationship is in issue. The issue of whether a marriage is bona fide has typically arisen in visa petition proceedings in cases of suspected fraudulent or "sham" marriages. Such marriages, entered into for the primary purpose of circumventing the immigration laws, have not been recognized as enabling an alien spouse to obtain immigration benefits. *Matter of McKee*, 17 I & N Dec. 332 (BIA 1980); see also *Lutwak v. United States*, 344 U.S. 604 (1953); *McLat v. Longo*, 412 F.Supp. 1021 (D.V.I.1976); *Matter of M-*, 8 I & N Dec. 217 (BIA 1958). See generally *Johl v. United States*, 370 F.2d 174 (9th Cir.1966). The central question in such cases is whether the bride and groom intended to establish a life together at the time they were married. *Bark v. INS*, 511 F.2d 1200 (9th Cir.1975); *Matter of McKee, supra*. The conduct of the parties after marriage is relevant to their intent at the time of marriage. *Lutwak v. United States, supra*; *Bark v. INS, supra*. Evidence to establish intent could take many forms, including, but not limited to, proof that the beneficiary has been listed as the petitioner's spouse on insurance policies, property leases, income tax forms, or bank accounts, and testimony or other evidence regarding courtship, wedding ceremony, shared residence, and experiences together. *Matter of Phillis*, 15 I & N Dec. 385 (BIA 1975).

Two significant distinctions exist between the typical sham marriage visa petition case and a case in which section 204(a)(2)(A) of the Act applies, however. The first is that the typical sham marriage visa petition case involves an assessment of the validity of a petitioner's present marriage to his beneficiary, while the inquiry under section 204(a)(2)(A) of the Act is directed exclusively towards marriages which have already been terminated. Thus, in addition to the forms of evidence suggested in Matter of Phillis, supra, in a visa petition proceeding under section 204(a)(2)(A) of the Act, evidence regarding such matters as the length of time the petitioner and the prior spouse resided together and the reasons for the termination of their marriage is also relevant. See 8 C.F.R. §204.1(a)(2)(ii) (1988).

The second evidentiary distinction between the typical sham marriage visa petition case and a case in which section 204(a)(2)(A) of the Act applies is that the burdens of proof differ. The clear and convincing evidence standard in section 204(a)(2)(A) of the Act imposes a greater evidentiary burden on the petitioner than the preponderance of the evidence standard ordinarily applied in visa petition proceedings. As a result, while the petitioner in a case in which section 204(a)(2)(A) of the Act applies may be submitting evidence similar to that considered in a typical sham marriage visa petition case, his evidence must be stronger and more persuasive before his petition may be granted.

Further, it should be pointed out that Congress designed the presumption of fraud in a prior marriage in section 204(a)(2)(A) of the Act to be rebuttable by clear and convincing evidence. In order to have any possibility of rebutting the presumption by that high standard, a petitioner in a case under section 204(a)(2)(A) of the Act must be accorded the same fair and reasonable evaluation of his evidence and factual situation as that given to any petitioner in visa petition proceedings. Simply because there is a statutory presumption that a petitioner's prior marriage was fraudulent, it should not be presumed that the petitioner's evidence is false or contrived or that any possible adverse inference which may be drawn applies to the sequence of events surrounding the prior marriage. For example, because documents showing joint income tax returns and bank accounts are generally considered to be evidence supportive of a bona fide marital relationship, in the absence of an objective basis in the record for discrediting the evidence, dismissal of such evidence as indicative of a financial but not necessarily a marital commitment, as argued by the Service in the case before us, would be unwarranted.

We turn now to the evidence considered by the district director with regard to the petitioner's prior marriage. This evidence was submitted by the petitioner with his motion to reopen and/or reconsider. The district director denied the motion on the dual grounds that the evidence could have been submitted at the time of the filing of the visa petition and that it failed to show by clear and convincing evidence that the petitioner's prior marriage was not entered into for the purpose of evading any provision of the immigration laws. Although the petitioner appealed from the district director's original decision rather than from the decision on the motion, we note that we disagree with both grounds relied on by the district director in denying the petitioner's motion. First of all, at the time the petitioner filed his petition, section 204(a)(2)(A) of the Act had not yet become law; the petitioner was not then directed by the regulations or the statute to submit evidence with his petition to establish the bona fides of his prior marriage. It was therefore illogical and unreasonable to penalize the petitioner and reject his documents because he failed to submit with his visa petition evidence which was neither requested nor required to be submitted at that time.

Secondly, we have determined that the evidence submitted to the district director with the motion to reopen and/or reconsider is sufficient to establish by clear and convincing evidence that the petitioner's prior marriage was not entered into for the purpose of evading any provision of the immigration laws. The district director emphasized what he characterized as the "rapid sequence of events," in that the period of time between the petitioner's acquisition of lawful permanent resident status and his divorce from his first wife was "relatively short." It is true that a rapid sequence of events by an alien may suggest a lack of bona fide intent, as section 204(a)(2)(A) of the Act implicitly recognizes by requiring proof of a bona fide prior marriage from any petitioner who petitions for a visa for a spouse within 5 years after acquiring lawful permanent resident status based on the prior marriage. Yet what constitutes a "rapid" sequence of events depends on the circumstances of each case. Some cases do involve such hasty action by the alien that the inference of a lack of bona fide intent is virtually inescapable. See e.g., *Patel v. Minnix*, 663 F.2d 1042 (11th Cir.1981) (alien seeking treaty investor status consummated business deal 15 days after entry as nonimmigrant visitor); *Seihoon v. Levy, supra* (alien seeking student status applied to university program 9 days after entry as nonimmigrant visitor). In the case before us, however, the sequence of events was not so rapid as to indicate unequivocally a lack of bona fide intent. The divorce proceeding was initiated by the petitioner's first wife, not by the petitioner, and it did not occur until almost 2 and 1/2 years after their marriage and over 9 months after the petitioner's acquisition of lawful permanent resident status. Moreover, the petitioner has provided evidence which adequately explains the sequence of events in this case.

The evidence submitted by the petitioner to the district director includes affidavits from relatives and business acquaintances. We find the affidavits to be credible and worthy of considerable weight because they are detailed, internally consistent, and plausible; they include explanations of how the affiants acquired knowledge of the facts set forth; and they are corroborated by historical evidence. These sworn statements by people who attended the elaborate wedding ceremony of the petitioner and his first wife and observed them sharing a residence, visiting relatives together, and entertaining guests in their home, provide objective evidence of the conduct of the petitioner and his first wife which is supportive of their subjective bona fide intent at the time of their marriage. Conduct of the petitioner and his first wife supportive of a bona fide intent is further shown by evidence which documents joint financial dealings, such as their filing of joint state and federal income tax returns and their joint ownership of a Daily Passport Cash Trust account and a $5,000 corporate bond.

In addition, the petitioner submitted affidavits from himself and his first wife which indicate that they originally intended to have a lasting marriage, but that the petitioner's first wife eventually filed for divorce because she had become lonely living apart from her family and friends in a town where there were no other Indian nationals with whom they could socialize. Their account is corroborated by the actions of two of the affiants, relatives of the petitioner who traveled to LaFayette to try to help the couple reconcile. Obviously these relatives would not have made these efforts had they not regarded the marriage as a bona fide relationship worthy of salvaging. Further, unlike the district director, we do not find the failure of the petitioner's first wife to exact any financial advantage in the property settlement to be remarkable, as she was the one who wanted the divorce, there were no children from the marriage to provide for, and the only asset of considerable value, the motel operated by the petitioner, was purchased by the petitioner before the marriage and constituted the means by which he earned his livelihood.

Therefore, based on the evidence submitted to the district director with the motion to reopen and/or reconsider, we find that the petitioner has met his evidentiary burden under section 204(a)(2)(A) of the Act. Because we have reached our decision in this case without relying on the evidence submitted by the petitioner on appeal, remand to the district director for review of that additional evidence is not necessary. Moreover, we have not addressed the petitioner's allegation that section 204(a)(2)(A) of the Act violates his right to privacy as we do not entertain constitutional challenges to the statutes we administer. See *Matter of Awadh*, 15 I & N Dec. 775 (BIA 1976); *Matter of Bulos*, 15 I & N Dec. 645 (BIA 1976); *Matter of Chery and Hassan*, 15 I & N Dec. 380 (BIA 1975).

Accordingly, the appeal will be sustained and the visa petition will be approved.

Notes

1. How much should a visa applicant be required to show in order to overcome the presumption of fraud? When do the requirements violate due process rights? Will the rights be different depending on whether the applicant is applying from within or from outside the United States?

2. Would it be proper for Congress to create an irrebuttable presumption of fraud? Could Congress have provided, as it did in 8 U.S.C. § 1255(e)(2), that persons who were divorced within five years of their marriage were ineligible to receive immigrant visas for five years? Could Congress have made persons who divorced within five years of their marriage ineligible for any immigration benefits?

3. In *Matter of Patel*, BIA held that IMFA applied retroactively to a spousal second-preference petition which was pending adjudication when IMFA was enacted. In articulating the basis for reaching this conclusion, it stated that:

> Generally, a new statute applies to cases pending on the date of its enactment unless manifest injustice would result or there is a statutory directive or legislative history to the contrary. *Bradley v. Richmond School Board*, 416 U.S. 696 (1974). In determining whether a retroactive application would cause manifest injustice, three factors must be assessed: "(a) the nature and identity of the parties, (b) the nature of their rights, and (c) the nature of the impact of the change in law upon those rights." [19 I. & N. Dec. at 779.]

On balance, the BIA concluded that the legislative history was silent on the question of retroactivity. It reasoned that Congress was so concerned about the possibility of benefits being obtained through fraudulent marriage that BIA sought to apply the statute as quickly and strictly as possible. In light of this reasoning, should the two-year residency requirement be applicable to persons who had not received their permanent residency before the statute was passed?

4. **Others Barred from Petitioning.** In addition to this provision, the statute precludes others from petitioning for family members. For example, certain sex offenders against minors are barred from petitioning for their spouse and family members,[72] as well anyone who USCIS has determined has received a preference or immediate relative status as a result of a fraudulent marriage.[73]

F. Exemption from the Petition Requirement

One of the central principles of immigration law has been that a person who wants to immigrate must have a petitioner. While this is often the case with nonimmigrant visas, it has been essential in most immigrant cases. Due to the hardships experienced by beneficiaries and the rigid application of this requirement, Congress has over the years created exceptions to this requirement. In situations where the petitioner has died or where the beneficiary has been the subject of abuse, the petition requirement will not be enforced.

---

72. 8 U.S.C. § 1154(a)(1)(A)(viii), Sec. 204(a)(1)(A)(viii). The applicable offenses are spelled out in the Adam Walsh Child Protection and Safety Act, Pub. L. No. 109-248, 120 Stat. 587 (2006). A waiver may be obtained and is within the sole and unreviewable discretion of the Secretary upon the determination that the petitioner poses no risk to the beneficiary.

73. 8 U.S.C. § 1154(c), Sec. 204(c). The bar would also apply where the person attempted to obtain the status and there has been a determination that the marriage was entered into to evade the immigration laws. *Dorley v. Cardinale*, 119 F. Supp. 3d 345 (E.D. Pa. 2015). The bar only applies to the barred spouse. *Matter of Otiende*, 26 I. & N. Dec. 127 (BIA 2013).

Death of Petitioner. The death of the petitioner will not automatically result in revocation of the petition if USCIS concludes that the application should proceed for humanitarian reasons.[74] In enacting the Immigration Act of 1990, Congress expanded the definition of "immediate relatives" to include widows and widowers who seek permanent residency within two years of their spouse's death, provided that the person has not remarried.[75] This provision, in effect, allows the surviving spouse to "self-petition" for her own permanent residency. Note, however, that the deceased spouse must have been a U.S. citizen. In order to self-petition, the family petition must have been filed at some point preceding the U.S. citizen spouse's death, and the beneficiary must be able to show humanitarian reasons for not revoking the approval.

Widow/ers. Widows and widowers may self petition as long as they petition within two years and have not remarried or were separated at the time of their spouse's death.[76]

Family of Members of U.S. Armed Forces Killed in Combat. Where the member of the armed forces was a U.S. citizen who served honorably and died due to injury or disease which was incurred by combat and the beneficiary was the spouse, child or parent, they may self petition within two years of the death. In the case of a child, they may apply even if they were over the age of 21 and marry after the citizen parent's death.[77]

Battered Spouse or Children. The second exemption from the petition requirement allows persons who have suffered abuse to proceed on their own petition where the spouse or parent was a U.S. citizen or lawful permanent resident.[78] The battered spouse must show that she is living in the United States, previously resided with the U.S. citizen or permanent resident, was battered or subject to extreme cruelty, entered into the marriage in good faith and would suffer extreme hardship if ordered removed. Here, the legal termination or separation of the couple will not adversely affect the petition, and. the benefits are also applicable to the immediate relative children of the primary beneficiary. In order to be eligible for these benefits, the beneficiary must not be inadmissible under the criminal or terrorist grounds of inadmissibility or deportability nor be an aggravated felon. Applications for battered spouse and children are not adjudicated by local USCIS district directors; instead, they are reviewed at the USCIS Vermont Service Center.

---

74. 8 C.F.R. § 205.1(a)(3).

75. 8 U.S.C. § 1151(b)(2)(A)(i), Sec. 201(b)(2)(A)(i).

76. 8 C.F.R. § 204.2(b)(1). *But see Williams v. Sec'y of Homeland Security*, 741 F.3d 1228 (11th Cir. 2014).

77. 8 U.S.C. 1151(b), Sec. 201(b). *See* Memo from Acting Dir. Domestic Operations reprinted in 83 Interpreter Releases 869, 897–910 (May 8, 2006).

78. 8 U.S.C. § 1154(a)(1)(A)(iii)–(iv), (a)(1)(B)(ii)–(iii), Sec. 204(a)(1)(A)(iii)–(iv), (a)(1)(B)(ii)–(iii)(b)(2)(A)(I). The amendments which allowed battered spouses and children to "self-petition" were incorporated into the immigration laws with the enactment of the Violence Against Women Act (VAWA), a component of the Violent Crime Control and Law Enforcement Act of 1994, Pub. L. 103-322, 108 Stat. 1902–1955 (1994).

G. Procedural Flow Charts

1. Spousal Relation Flowchart

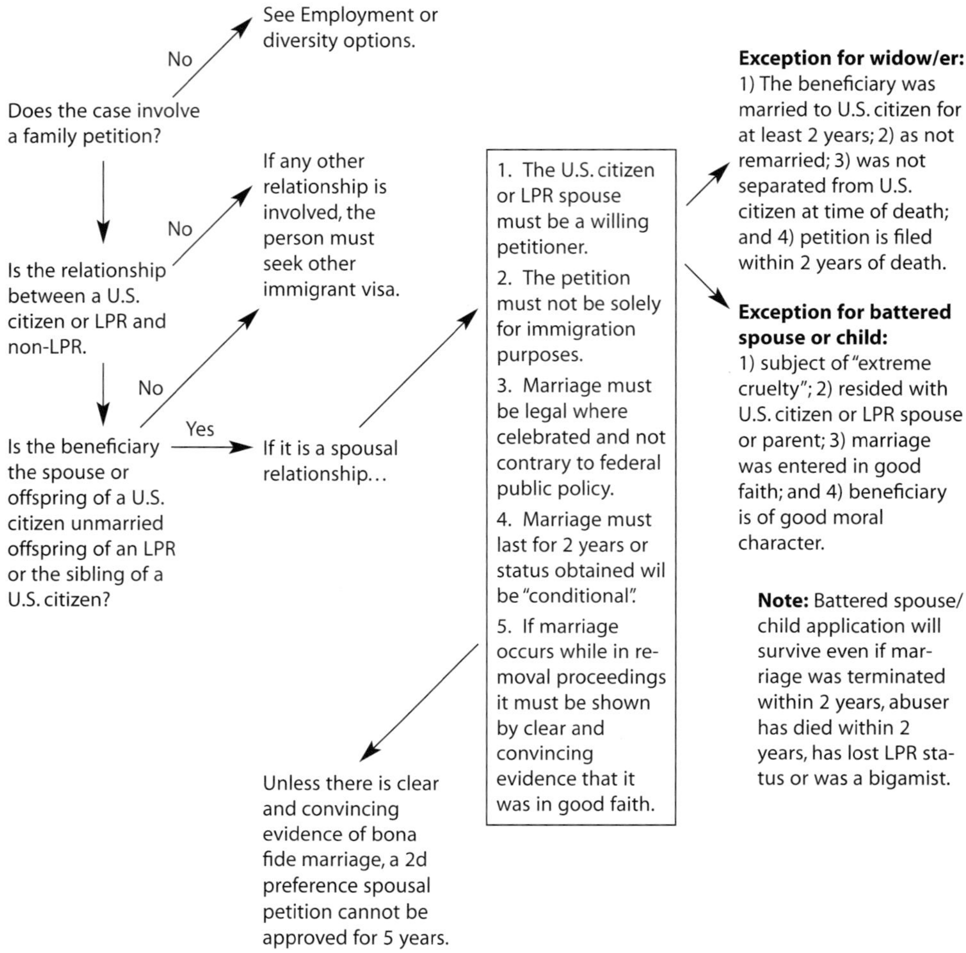

Note: Under "2" above, only where the adjustment of status application is denied will it be sent to the U.S. consul overseas where the beneficiary last resided.

2. Child-Parent Relation Flow Chart

The father-child relation will be recognized... →	1. Where parents were married at the time of the child's birth.		
	2. Where mother later marries father.		
	3. If mother doesn't marry father and a "bona fide" relation is created. →	Relationship is established before child marries or reaches 21.	
	4. If the father legally recognizes child through **legitimation**. *or if there is no legal distinction between legitimated and out of wedlock child* →	Child must be in custody and must occur before 18th birthday.	
The new parent-child relation will be recognized... →	Where mother marries different man the new relationship is "**stepchild**"-"stepparent." →	Child must be < 18 at time relation is created.	Continues to be recognized even after divorce as long as relation continues.
	Where **adoption** occurs before child reaches 16 and there is at least 2 years custody with adopting parent. →	If child remains with natural parent, the adopting parent must have primary parental control.	Adoption will not be recognized unless legal relation is cut off with natural parent and siblings.
	Where a U.S. citizen adopts an abandoned or "orphaned" child. →	Following adoption child becomes a U.S. citizen.	Parent must be at least 25 years of age.

H. Problem Exercises

Exercise 1

Juan would like to at some point in the future become a permanent resident of the U.S. along with all members of his immediate family. Juan is a native and citizen of Guatemala and you meet him on a flight bound for a U.S. port of entry. He presents his story below.

Juan and his wife, Sofia have three children, Adam, Beatriz and Carla, who are respectively 14, 16 and 18 years of age. None of the children are his natural children. Adam is the natural child of Sofia from a previous marriage, and Beatriz and Carla are the children of Sofia's sister and brother in law who were killed in a tragic accident. Beatriz and Carla have not been formally adopted by either Juan or Sofia.

As you talk more with Juan you learn the following: 1) His wife Sofia's sister is a U.S. citizen and lives in San Francisco; 2) Sofia's mother is a permanent resident of the U.S.; and 3) Juan operates a chain of fast food restaurants in Guatemala and El Salvador and as a result travels a great deal in the region as well as to the U.S. where he keeps most of his money. Juan is traveling under a indefinite multiple entry tourist visa (B-1/B-2).

Questions:

1) Juan is seeking advice about what he can reasonably expect to happen when he arrives at the U.S. port of entry?

2) What questions would you need to have answered before giving him advice?

3) Explain to him what the short and long term prospects are for him. Assume that his ultimate goal is to bring his entire family (wife and three children) in as permanent residents

Exercise 2 (short exercises)

Where relevant, for purposes of these exercises, assume that the relative petition was filed on June 1, (yr. -2), and the beneficiary is a native and citizen of the United Kingdom.

1. A, a U.S. Citizen through naturalization, marries B in a civil ceremony in the United Kingdom. What do A and B have to show in order to successfully establish that they are married and to be accorded benefits under the immigration laws?

2. M and F have a child, C. M is now a U.S. Citizen.

a. What does she have to show to successfully petition for C?

b. What preference status can C obtain, and how long will it take for C to be issued an immigrant visa?

c. Assume the same facts in (2) above but that F is a permanent resident. What result?

3. M and F1 are married and have a child, C1. They later divorce. Later, M is in a relationship with F2, and they have a child, C2. Assume further that C1 and C2 are in the United States and are both U.S. citizen, what needs to be established in order for

a. C1 to petition for F1?

b. C2 to petition for F2?

c. If C1 was a citizen and C2 was not, what would C1 need to show in order to petition for C2?

Chapter 8

Employment-Based Immigrants

Introduction

Our earlier discussion focused on the presumption that all foreigners coming to the United States are immigrants. This presumption is coupled with a requirement that the intending immigrant establish that she has the requisite relationship with a U.S. citizen or lawful permanent resident or that employment in the U.S. will not displace or adversely affect U.S. workers.[1] In the preceding chapter, we discussed the family relationships which provide a person with the means to immigrate to the United States. In this chapter, we will explore the employment relationships that enable a person to obtain permanent residence. Since the underlying policy issue of employment-related immigration is focused on protecting domestic workers, much of the discussion will be on the "labor certification" process, which is the primary tool used to determine if the employment of an immigrant will displace or adversely affect U.S. workers. Our discussion here will not focus on employment rights or the broad issue of international labor migration.[2]

A. An Overview

The concerns reflected in the labor certification requirements of U.S. immigration law are not unusual and can be found in the immigration laws of many countries. For example, Austria requires persons to obtain a labor permit or certificate of exemption prior to seeking employment.[3] Austria also utilizes a quota system, but, unlike the United States, provides for exceeding the quota in extraordinary

---

1. 8 U.S.C. § 1182(a)(5), Sec. 212(a)(5). This proscription does not apply to immigrants coming to the United States under the family-based immigration provisions of the statute, to refugees or to special immigrants. Persons entering as immediate relatives and "family preferences" need not obtain labor certification. In addition, persons entering as derivative beneficiaries under any of the preference categories including under the employment-based preferences are also exempted from the labor certifications requirement.

2. We discussed employment rights in the U.S. in Chapter 2. For an interesting exposition of these broader issues of trade and labor migration, see Valsamis Mitsilegas, *Immigration Control in an Era of Globalization: Deflecting Foreigners, Weakening Citizens, Strengthening the State,* 19 Ind. J. Global Legal Stud. 3 (2012); Jennifer Gordon, *People are Not Bananas: How Immigration Differs from Trade,* 104 Nw. U. L. Rev. 1109 (2010); Howard F. Chang, *The International Impact of International Labor Migration: Recent Estimates and Policy Implications,* 16 Temp. Pol. & Civ. Rts. L. Rev. 321 (2006).

3. W.R. Bohring, Studies in International Labour Migration 36 (1984).

circumstances.[4] In both the certificate of exemption and flexible quota systems, Austria seems to focus on macroeconomic and public interest concerns when issuing work permits.[5]

The United Arab Emirates applies a stricter limitation on the entry of foreign workers. Those brought in to work for the government as diplomats or domestics are the only persons exempt from obtaining an entry permit.[6] Under special circumstances, an employer may apply on behalf of individuals or groups of immigrants. In order to accomplish this, the employer must:

1. Submit written evidence that her business requires the particular worker(s),
2. Enter into an agreement with the Ministry of Labor and Social Affairs assuming responsibility for the workers, and
3. Enter into written work contracts with the immigrants and guarantee their return workers to the sending country.[7]

Such agreements place the initial burden on the employers, making it less likely that the employer will "import" foreign labor unless it is essential for the continued maintenance of the business. According to one scholar, similar policy is reflected in the 1986 reform legislation. Placing more of the burden on employers results from the belief that an employer has more to lose (in the way of reputation, financial losses, etc.), and hence can be more effectively sanctioned.[8]

While many countries enact laws which attempt to restrict the immigration of foreign workers, these laws may be selectively enforced or officially circumvented by regional agreements. For example, the European Union exempts member countries from immigration restrictions such that only citizens of non-member countries need obtain such labor certification requirements.[9] Similarly, Iraq and the Syrian Arab Republic treat all citizens of Arab states as nationals for purposes of immigration and employment.[10] Finally, the Scandinavian countries[11] have done the same since 1954.[12] Such agreements are clear evidence of the sense of identity these nations share. A valuable side effect is relief from the bureaucratic red tape involved in admitting foreign workers into a state.

---

4. *Id.* at 37. In contrast, the United States does not provide for flexibility for the immigration of workers even when the need is urgent.

5. *Id.*

6. *Id.* at 38.

7. *Id.*

8. Arnold Liebowitz, *The Immigration Challenge and the Congressional Response,* 1 La Raza L.J. 1 (1983).

9. *See* Treaty on European Union, Feb. 7, 1992, available at https://www.cvce.eu/content/publication/1997/10/13/5a6bfc79-757f-4d53-9379-ad23cc2cc911/publishable_en.pdf, Maastricht Treaty on February 7, 1992. In 1997 the Treaty of Amsterdam was signed, which incorporated the Schengen developments into the European Union's legal and institutional framework.

10. See Bohring, *supra* at 41.

11. Denmark, Finland, Norway and Sweden comprise this group. *Id.*

12. *Id.*

U.S. labor certification requirements have been criticized by virtually every political group. Those who believe in a more liberal (more open) immigration policy criticize the labor certification procedures for its inefficiency, as the procedures involve multiple levels of bureaucracy without effective protection for domestic workers.[13] Those who believe in greater restrictions have criticized existing policy for its emphasis on family reunification. As these critics point out, domestic workers are not protected under our present policy, because more than 85% of all immigrants are exempted from the labor certification requirements.[14] At the same time, agricultural interests desirous of bringing in workers point to the severe shortage of U.S. workers willing to harvest crops and note that U.S. farmers would not be able to compete in the world market if they paid significantly higher wages to domestic farm workers.

In 1990, as part of a reform package, legislation was enacted to deal with some of the problems of bringing in foreign workers.[15] The 1990 Act increased the number of employment-based immigrants who may enter the United States from 54,000 to 140,000.[16] It also retained the requirement that most employment-based immigrants must obtain certification from the Secretary of Labor that "there are not sufficient workers able, willing and qualified" to take the position to be filled by the foreigner. These employment-based visas are set out in following categories:

1. *First Preference (EB-1)—Priority Workers.*[17] 28.6% of the employment-based visas plus the unused investor and special immigrant visas are set aside for persons with extraordinary ability "in the sciences, arts, education, business, or athletics which has been demonstrated by sustained national or international acclaim and

---

13. The typical employment-based immigrant will have to deal with four government agencies: the local employment agency, the Department of Labor, USCIS and the Department of State.

14. *Id.* at 44. Some critics argue that this country should adopt a policy similar to Germany, which attempts to compromise between the competing interests of protecting native workers and reuniting families. Families of gainfully employed foreign workers are permitted to enter the country under the family reunification program but are restricted from the labor market for several years. While this may be perceived as a hardship to those immigrating, it is argued that this more restrictive approach protects the interests of German workers while recognizing some of the needs of immigrants residing in Germany.

While some of the criticism of immigration policy has been blunted by the Immigration Act of 1990, a careful analysis will show that only a relatively small number of people are actually required to meet the labor certification requirements. Following the 1990 Act, of the approximately 700,000 immigrant visas which might be issued in a given year in the period from 1991–1994, 140,000 were allocated to employment-based immigrants. Of those 140,000 visas, only 100,000 were in "certification preference categories," since many were issued to accompanying spouse and children, none of whom were required to obtain certification.

15. *See* Sections 121 and 122, Immigration Act of 1990, Pub. L. No. 101-649, 104 Stat. 4978 (1990).

16. The increase in the employment-based immigrant quota was based on the conclusion that there is an insufficient supply of trained domestic workers to meet the demands on the United States in an increasingly global economy. *See* Charles Gordon, Stanley Mailman, Stephen Yale-Loehr & Ronald Wada, Immigration Law & Procedure § 2.04[11][c] (rev. ed. 2017).

17. 8 U.S.C. § 1153(b)(1)(A), Sec. 203(b)(1)(A).

whose achievements have been recognized in the field through extensive documentation." Also within this group are "outstanding professors and researchers" and "certain multinational executives and managers."[18] These immigrants are not subject to the labor certification requirement.

Persons of "extraordinary ability" need not have an employer in the United States but must be coming to work in their field. The basic measure of their ability is that of a demonstrated "sustained or international acclaim."[19] Documentation can consist of evidence of attaining a major international award or three of the following: (1) lesser national or internationally recognized prizes or awards; (2) membership in an association which has outstanding achievement as judged by national or international experts (3) published material about the applicant in professional or other publications; (4) evidence of the person's participation as a judge of the works of others in the field; (5) evidence of significant original, scientific, scholastic, artistic, athletic or business-related contribution; (6) evidence of the applicant's authorship of scholarly publications; (7) prior participation in exhibitions; (8) performance in a leading or critical role for a distinguished organization; (9) high salary or remuneration in relation to others in the same field; or (10) commercial success in the performing arts.[20]

"Outstanding professors and researchers" must have at least three years experience and be recognized internationally in their field. Unlike persons of extraordinary ability, the outstanding professor or researcher must have an offer of ongoing employment from a sponsoring employer in the United States.[21] Evidence of the person's qualifications may consist of at least two of the following: (1) prizes or awards for outstanding achievement; (2) membership in a professional association which requires outstanding achievement; (3) published material about the applicant's work in professional publications; (4) publications by the person in her field; (5) evidence of the person's participation as a judge of the work of others; or (6) evidence of original research.[22]

Multinational executives and managers must have been employed for at least one year in the last three years by a firm, corporation or other legal entity. The person must be seeking permanent residency in order to continue to render services to the same employer or subsidiary in a managerial capacity.[23] Evidence of the person's qualification for the visa must include the following: (1) a statement from the U.S. em-

---

18. 8 U.S.C. § 1153(b)(1), Sec. 203(b)(1). While most employment-based immigrants are required to have a sponsoring employer, this is not required of those who meet the "extraordinary ability" requirement, even though these applicants must be coming to work in the United States. Exemption from the labor certification requirement is a significant procedural advantage, as the applicant does not have to proceed through the bureaucratic labyrinth of yet another government agency.

19. 8 C.F.R. § 204.5(h)(3).

20. 8 C.F.R. § 204.5(h)(3).

21. 8 C.F.R. § 204.5(i)(3)(iii).

22. 8 C.F.R. § 204.5(I)(3)(ii).

23. Unlike persons entering on an L-1 visa, the person cannot be a "skilled worker." This particular category of EB-1 visas is designed solely for multinational managers and executives.

ployer describing the person's employment relationship with the domestic entity; (2) evidence of the need to have the person in a managerial or executive capacity along with an offer of employment and description of the position; or (3) evidence that the company is operating abroad.[24]

2. *Second Preference (EB-2)—Professionals and Persons of "Exceptional Ability."*[25] 28.6% of the employment based visas are set aside for certain "members of the professions holding advanced degrees or their equivalent or who because of their exceptional ability in the sciences, arts, or business, will substantially benefit prospectively the national economy, cultural or educational interests, or welfare of the United States."[26] The number of EB-2 visas issued is augmented by any visas not used by the EB-1 category above. Exceptional ability is defined in terms of the benefit to the "national economy, cultural or educational interests" and may be shown by any three of the following: (1) a professional degree related to the area of claimed exceptional ability; (2) documentation showing at least ten years full-time experience in the field of expertise; (3) license to practice in the person's profession; (4) evidence of salary or remuneration which demonstrates the exceptional ability; (5) membership in a professional association; or (6) recognition of the person's achievement and contribution to the field by peers, governmental entities or professional or business organizations.[27]

In those cases where the Attorney General deems that the immigration of the person is in the "national interest", the job offer requirement may be waived.[28] The definition of "national interest" is not clear but should be viewed expansively, though it is within the discretion of the agency. In a 1992 non-precedent decision issued by legacy INS, *Matter of Mississippi Phosphate*,[29] the Administrative Appeals Unit listed seven criteria in determining what was in the national interest: (1) following a request by a federal agency; (2) improving the national economy; (3) improving the wages and working conditions of domestic workers; (4) improving education and training programs for children and under-qualified workers in the United States; (5) providing more affordable housing for young, older and poorer U.S. residents; (6) improving health care; or (7) improving the environment. These applicants are not required to have an employer and may bypass the formal labor certification process if they meet the criteria.

3. *Third Preference (EB-3)—Skilled Workers, Professionals and Other Workers.*[30] 28.6% of the employment-based visas plus any unused visas from the EB-1 and EB-2 categories are set aside for these applicants.[31] All but 5,000 of these visas are reserved for skilled workers, persons with baccalaureate degrees and members of the profes-

---

24. 8 C.F.R. § 204.5(j)(3).
25. 8 U.S.C. § 1153(b)(1)(C), Sec. 203(b)(1)(C).
26. 8 U.S.C. § 1153(b)(2)(A), Sec. 203(b)(2)(A).
27. 8 C.F.R. § 204.5(k)(3)(ii).
28. 8 U.S.C. § 1153(b)(2)(B), Sec. 203(b)(2)(B).
29. EAC 92 091 50126 (Jul. 21, 1992), reprinted in 69 Interpreter Releases 1364 (1992).
30. 8 U.S.C. § 1153(b)(3), Sec. 203(b)(3).
31. 8 U.S.C. § 1153(b)(3), Sec. 203(b)(3).

sions. When Congress enacted the Nicaraguan Adjustment and Central American Relief Act,[32] it provided for a "temporary reduction" of the "other workers" visa numbers from the 10,000 that had been created earlier. All workers under this category must satisfy the labor certification requirement.[33]

4. *Fourth Preference—Certain Special Immigrants.*[34] No more than 7.1%, or approximately 10,000 visas, may be issued to certain persons described as special immigrants under 8 U.S.C. §1101(a)(27).[35] This includes persons who have worked abroad for the U.S. government,[36] religious ministers and workers,[37] former U.S. government employees abroad, specified employees of the Panama Canal Treaty, employees of the U.S. Consulate General in Hong Kong[38] and certain retired employees of international organizations or family members of present or former employees of these international organizations.[39]

Provisions relating to special immigrant status for religious workers have been repeatedly extended by Congress.[40] There has been a great deal of concern with this category, as it has been perceived as vulnerable to abuse therefore favoring larger more established religious denominations.[41] The special immigrant religious worker may enter either as a minister or in a religious vocation or occupation for at least two years immediately before seeking admission to the U.S.[42]

---

32. Pub. L. No. 105-100, 11 Stat. 2160 (1997), Technical Corrections to the Nicaraguan Adjustment and Central American Relief Act, Pub. L. No. 105-139 111 Stat. 2644 (1997).

33. *See* 8 U.S.C. §§1182(a)(5)(A) and 1153(b)(3)(C), Sections 212(a)(5)(A) and 203(b)(3)(C).

34. 8 U.S.C. §§1153(b)(4) and 1101(a)(27), Sections 203(b)(4) and 101(a)(27).

35. As was noted in our discussion of special immigrants in the previous chapter, some persons, such as returning lawful permanent residents, are not subject to the quota.

36. 8 U.S.C. §1101(a)(27)(D), Sec. 101(a)(27)(D).

37. These visas originally were scheduled to phase out by October 1994 but have been extended by Congress through March 6, 2009. The provision applies to persons who have been members of a religious denomination for at least two years prior to their application for admission to the United States under the following conditions: (1) the sole purpose of their coming to the country is to carry on the vocation of minister in the religion; (2) the person seeks to enter before March 6, 2009, to work for an organization in the professional capacity of a "religious vocation or occupation"; or (3) the applicant seeks to enter the country before October 6, 2009, to work for an organization which is affiliated with the religious organization. *See* 8 U.S.C. §1101(a)(27)(C)(i)–(ii), Sec. 101(a)(27)(C)(i)–(ii).

38. *See* 8 U.S.C. §1101(a)(27)(D), Sec. 101(a)(27)(D), Sec. 152 of the Immigration Act of 1990, Pub. L. No. 101-649, 104 Stat. 4978.

39. The special immigrant provision relating to retired or present employees of international organizations was added by Section 312(1) of the Immigration Reform and Control Act, Pub. L. No. 99-603, 100 Stat. 3359 (1986).

40. An Act to Extend Certain Immigrant Programs, Pub. L. No. 111-9, 123 Stat. 989 (2009); Further Continuing and Security Assistance Appropriations Act of 2017, H.R. 2028, Pub. L. No. 114-254, 130 Stat. 1005 (2016); Resolution Making Continuing Appropriations, H.J. Res. 99, Pub. L. No. 115-30, 131 Stat. 134 (2017). The most recent of these provisions was scheduled to expire in May 2017.

41. Charles Gordon, Stanley Mailman, Stephen Yale-Loehr & Ronald Wada, Immigration Law & Procedure §26.04[2] (rev. ed. 2017).

42. 8 C.F.R. §204.5(m).

5. *Fifth Preference — Employment Creation (Investors).*[43] Persons who have invested or are actively in the process of investing at least $1 million in capital and employ ten or more full-time U.S. workers are allocated 10,000 visas. Of the 10,000 visas, 3,000 are set aside for investment in "targeted" employment areas, and investors investing in these areas may qualify with a lesser investment of $500,000. Investors are termed "entrepreneurs" and are admitted to permanent residence on a conditional basis for two years, whereupon their status is made permanent upon a timely petition. The status may be terminated for failure to file within the prescribed period, failure to invest or maintain the enterprise or fraud. The purpose of the conditional status is the deterrence of "immigration-related entrepreneurship fraud."[44]

The cases and the notes which follow them focus primarily on the labor certification requirement and its relation to the preference petitions.

B. Labor Certification Requirements

8 U.S.C. § 1182(a)(5)[45] provides that persons other than those immigrants seeking admission under a family preference category must first be certified by the Secretary of Labor as not displacing U.S. workers. The statute further requires that the Secretary certify that the employment of the foreign worker will not adversely affect the wages and working conditions of domestic workers. In the vast majority of cases, this certification can only be obtained after the employer has, in effect, surveyed the market to determine whether there are qualified, willing and able workers in the United States.[46]

The Program Electronic Review Management (PERM), a set of rules establishing a new labor certification process, went into effect on March 28, 2005.[47] The new system established a processing system with electronic filing and employer "attestations." PERM changes the recruitment process by requiring employers to conduct advance recruiting for a thirty-day period before filing for a certification using the electronic filing system. The program attempts to protect domestic workers with such requirements that if there has been a layoff within a six-month period, the employer must be able to attest to and document that the laid-off workers were notified and considered for the position,[48] or if a domestic worker could be trained to meet job requirements or could perform the duties satisfactorily given her background, the employer may not obtain a labor certification.[49]

---

43. 8 U.S.C. § 1153(b)(5)(A), Sec. 203(b)(5)(A).

44. 8 U.S.C. § 1186a(b), Sec. 216A(b).

45. Section 212(a)(5) of the INA, as amended.

46. For this reason, if the employer has provided training to the person on whose behalf she is seeking certification, she must be willing to provide training to domestic applicants.

47. Notice was made in the federal register in December 2004. See 69 Fed. Reg. 77,325 (2004).

48. 20 C.F.R. § 656.17(k).

49. 20 C.F.R. § 656.17(g)(2).

Basically, PERM is an attestation and audit system under which employers seeking permanent labor certification must proceed with advertising for the recruitment of domestic workers before they file for certification. The program does not remove but merely changes the procedure for obtaining the certification required under 8 U.S.C. § 1182.[50] In essence it is similar to the income tax system where a taxpayer must file a return but may be asked to produce other documentation when confronted with an audit. The requirements for obtaining a certification are not significantly different except where the employer must be ready to produce substantiating documents at the request for an audit by the Department of Labor or if questioned about whether the procedures were followed. Advertising must still conform to the existing prevailing wage (information which must be obtained from a local state employment agency), and employers must keep proof of the recruitment effort in the event that they are asked to show that they fulfilled the requirements.[51] After the employer has completed the recruitment effort, she may submit the labor certification application online with the Department of Labor or by mail to a national processing center. According to the Department of Labor, the adjudication process should take from 45–60 days, unless the case is selected for audit or the information provided raises the need to obtain additional information.[52] A remaining issue under the new regulations is the degree to which an employer seeking certification may need on-the-job work experience as a basis for requiring special skills for business necessity. The regulations do not alter the review process in the event that an application is denied.

If the certifying officer determines that the applicant has not met the requirements of 20 C.F.R. § 656.21 or that there is a U.S. worker who is "able, willing, qualified, and available" for the job, the officer issues a Notice of Findings setting forth the specific basis for the decision.[53] The employer may appeal the decision with the Board of Alien Labor Certification Appeals (BALCA).[54] However, if a labor certification is issued, the person must submit an immigrant visa petition within 180 days; otherwise, the certification expires.[55]

The labor certification procedures may appear simple, but the process is time consuming. Given that there is a widespread perception that foreigners take work from domestic citizens, USCIS and the Department of Labor have increased the problems faced by employers through narrow interpretations of 8 U.S.C. § 1182(a)(5). One should also remember that even if certification is obtained, the foreign worker may not be able to immigrate until there are visas available under the quota category.

---

50. Charles Gordon, Stanley Mailman, Stephen Yale-Loehr & Ronald Wada, Immigration Law & Procedure § 44.01[3] (rev. ed. 2017).

51. 69 Fed. Reg. 77.330 (2004).

52. 69 Fed. Reg. 77,328 (2004).

53. The employer may submit rebuttal evidence which must be reviewed by the certifying officer. If a final determination is made and the certification is denied, the employer may request administrative review by the Board of Alien Labor Certification Appeals (BALCA). *See* 20 C.F.R. § 656.25–656.27. The case can be taken to federal court through a declaratory judgment action.

54. 20 C.F.R. § 656.26.

55. 20 C.F.R. § 656.30(b)(1).

Employment-Based Immigrants Visa Office Bulletin, November 2017

Employment Based	All Chargeability Areas Except Those Listed	China-Mainland Born	India	Mexico	Philippines
1st	C	C	C	C	C
2nd	C	15JUN13	08OCT08	C	C
3rd	C	01FEB14	15OCT06	C	15JAN16
Other Workers	C	01APR06	15OCT06	C	15JAN16
4th	C	C	C	01APR16	C
Certain Religious Workers	C	01JUL14	C	01APR16	C
5th	C	01JUL14	C	C	C
Targeted Employment	C	01JUL14	C	C	C

Employment-Based Immigrants Visa Office Bulletin, November 2016

Employment Based	All Chargeability Areas Except Those Listed	China-Mainland Born	El Salvador Guatemala Honduras	India	Mexico	Philippines
1st	C	C	C	C	C	C
2nd	C	15JUL12	C	01NOV07	C	C
3rd	01JUL16	15APR13	01JUL16	08MAR05	01JUL16	01APR11
Other Workers	01JUL16	01SEP05	01JUL16	08MAR05	01JUL16	01APR11
4th	C	C	15JUL15	C	C	C
Certain Religious Workers	C	C	15JUL15	C	C	C
5th Non-Regional Center (C5 and T5)	C	08MAR14	C	C	C	C
5th Regional Center (I5 and R5)	C	08MAR14	C	C	C	C

Note: The priority date for an employment-based application is either the date on which the labor certification was filed or the date which the preference petition was submitted (discussed *infra*). C means that visas are available for all priority dates; U signifies that no visas are available for any priority date for that particular nationality and preference category.

C. Labor Certification and Its Relationship to the Employment-Based Preferences

Nooria Madany, et al. v. William French Smith, et al.

696 F.2d 1008 (D.C. Cir 1983)

Before Robinson, Chief Judge, and MacKinnon and Mikva, Circuit Judges.

Mikva, Circuit Judge:

* * *

Madany, a native citizen of Afghanistan, has successfully completed a three-year professional nursing course in India and is a member of the nursing profession for the purposes of the Immigration and Nationality Act, §§ 101–360, 8 U.S.C. §§ 1101–1503 (1976 & Supp. V 1981) (Act). See Appellee Brief 8. Madany entered the United States on July 3, 1979 as a business visitor, with authority to remain until February 20, 1980. In December 1979, Clinch Valley Community Hospital (Clinch Valley) submitted an application to DOL on Madany's behalf, seeking a labor certification as a nurse. The labor certification job description included the requirement that the prospective employee be able to obtain, or already have, a Virginia nursing license. Administrative Record (A.R.) 40. In her statement of qualifications, appellant claimed she had the "ability to obtain [a] nursing license in the State of Virginia" and that she "will obtain [a] Virginia R.N. license." A.R. 43. DOL granted the labor certification based on this claim.

Subsequently, on December 21, 1979, Clinch Valley filed with INS a petition, which included the DOL-issued labor certification, to obtain a third preference visa classification for appellant. Approximately nine months later, on September 10, 1980, the INS District Director denied the petition, finding that Clinch Valley had not met its burden of establishing that Madany met the "specific requirements of the individual labor certification"—in particular, that she was able to obtain a nursing license. A.R. 35. The only evidence presented on this issue was her eligibility to take a nursing license exam and her registration to take the July 1980 registered nurse's exam for the District of Columbia. INS concluded that this evidence was insufficient to sustain appellant's burden of proof, especially when coupled with the low 20% passing rate for foreign nurse candidates on licensing exams. A.R. 34. On appeal, the INS Regional Commissioner upheld the District Director's decision.

The Visa Preference Classification Design

Section 203(a)(3) of the Act establishes the criteria for the grant of a third preference visa classification. The alien must be a "qualified immigrant" who possesses membership in a profession or an exceptional ability in the arts or sciences, and whose services in the professions, arts, or sciences are sought by an employer. 8 U.S.C. § 1153(a)(3) (Supp. V 1981). Section 212(a)(14) of the Act additionally preconditions third preference classifications on the receipt of a labor certification from DOL. The purpose and content of the labor certification are explicit. The Secretary of Labor must certify that:

> (A) there are not sufficient workers who are able, willing, qualified (or equally qualified in the case of aliens who are members of the teaching profession or who have exceptional ability in the sciences or the arts), and available at the time of application for a visa and admission to the United States and at the place where the alien is to perform such skilled or unskilled labor, and (B) the employment of such aliens will not adversely affect the wages and working conditions of the workers in the United States similarly employed.

8 U.S.C. § 1182(a)(14) (Supp. V 1981). The purpose of the third preference classification petition, therefore, is to show that the alien is a member of a profession, has been offered employment in that profession, and has been issued a labor certification.

The Act also sets forth the procedure for granting the petition:

> After an investigation of the facts in each case, and after consultation with the Secretary of Labor with respect to petitions to accord a status under section 1153(a)(3) or 1153(a)(6) of this title, the Attorney General shall, if he determines that the facts stated in the petition are true and that the alien ... is eligible for a preference status under section 1153(a) of this title, approve the petition....

Act § 204(b), 8 U.S.C. § 1154(b) (1976); cf. 8 C.F.R. § 2.1 (1980) (delegating all powers of the Attorney General relating to the immigration and naturalization of aliens to INS). In addition to this broad mandate to investigate alien eligibility, the Act endows INS with the specific authority to reject a petition upon a finding that the alien procured any document offered in support of the petition through fraud or willful misrepresentation of a material fact, Act § 212(a)(19), 8 U.S.C. § 1182(a)(19) (1976), and to revoke a previously granted petition at any time for "good or sufficient cause," Act § 205, 8 U.S.C. § 1155 (1976). The failure to acquire a job qualification that was critical to the initial grant of the petition may constitute such sufficient cause. See *Navarro v. District Director*, 574 F.2d 379 (7th Cir.), cert. denied, 439 U.S. 861 (1978) (failure to acquire nursing license in two years is sufficient cause to permit revocation of a third preference classification); see also 8 C.F.R. § 204.4(b) (1980).

The Division of Authority

The essence of appellant's argument is that the content of the labor certification and the findings implicit therein are the product of DOL in performance of its statutory functions under section 212(a)(14). The grant of the labor certification, then, constitutes a final determination by DOL and, as such, is not the proper subject of review by INS. To the extent that the actions of DOL and INS interface, because a labor certification is a prerequisite to the preference classification, appellant urges that the scope of INS inquiry is limited to the fact of certification and nothing more.

It is true that determinations vested by statute with one agency are not normally subject to horizontal review by a sister entity, absent congressional authorization to that effect. But this case does not present an instance of INS trespass onto DOL territory. Appellant misreads the nature of DOL's findings and the arrangement that is implicitly, if not explicitly, set up by the Act. Although the Act allocates a limited role to DOL, it vests primary responsibility for implementation with INS.

* * *

The review here in question concerns the alien's skills or qualifications and is not one of the inquiries expressly allocated to DOL by section 212(a)(14). This does not mean that DOL cannot, or does not, undertake analysis of an alien's qualifications as it performs its statutory functions. Indeed, DOL may gauge an alien's skill level in evaluating the effect of the alien's employment on United States workers. The fact that DOL may find such an analysis useful, however, does not foreclose INS from considering alien qualifications in the preference classification decision.

* * *

We are aware that at least one district court addressed the identical issue in the context of a sixth preference classification petition. See *Singh v. Attorney General*, 510 F.Supp. 351 (D.D.C. 1980), aff'd on other grounds, 672 F.2d 894 (D.C. Cir.1981) (mem.). Sixth preference classifications are granted to "qualified immigrants who are capable of performing specified skilled or unskilled labor ... for which a shortage of employable and willing persons exists in the United States," Act § 203(a)(6), 8 U.S.C. § 1153(a)(6) (Supp. V 1981), and also are prefaced upon the receipt of a labor certification. The Singh court read the legislative history of the Act to signify that DOL is vested with primary authority to review alien qualifications, relying in part on the following statement by Senator Philip Hart:

> It is my understanding that when an immigrant seeks admission under these categories as special immigrants or preference immigrants and a determination by the Secretary of Labor is required, the Secretary will make a certification in the case of the individual immigrant. He must ascertain the prospective immigrant's skill and will match those skills with the employment and manpower reports he has available from the labor market area where the immigrant expects to reside. On the basis of such an analysis, the Secretary will be in a position to meet the requirement of the law, and provide the type of employment safeguards sought in this legislation.

111 Cong. Rec. 24,239 (1965) (quoted in *Singh*, 510 F.Supp. at 355). This statement must be placed in context, however, and considered in conjunction with the innumerable other statements of interpretation made during the floor debates. These statements describe DOL's labor certification functions almost exclusively in terms

of the two determinations specified in section 212(a)(14). See, e.g., 111 Cong. Rec. 21,579, 21,586, 21,767 (1965); H.R.Rep. No. 745, 89th Cong., 1st Sess. 21 (1965).

Given the language of the Act, the totality of the legislative history, and the agencies' own interpretations of their duties under the Act, we must conclude that Congress did not intend DOL to have primary authority to make any determinations other than the two stated in section 212(a)(14). If DOL is to analyze alien qualifications, it is for the purpose of "matching" them with those of corresponding United States workers so that it will then be "in a position to meet the requirement of the law," namely the section 212(a)(14) determinations. We therefore do not follow the ruling in *Singh* to the extent it suggests that INS does not have primary authority for preference classification decisions....

The License Requirement

Given that review of Madany's qualifications was within the discretionary authority of INS, its decision must be sustained if based on substantial evidence and not an abuse of discretion. *Wing Ding Chan v. INS*, 631 F.2d 978, 980–81 (D.C.Cir.1980), cert. denied, 450 U.S. 921 (1981). Appellant maintains that INS abused its discretion by imposing a job requirement on her beyond that contemplated by DOL.

The language at issue states that appellant "must be able to obtain Virginia nursing license or have Virginia nursing license." A.R. 40. Because appellant did not already possess a Virginia nursing license, the controversy focuses on the significance of the words "able to obtain." Appellant argues that this language means "eligible to sit" for the examination, and that she satisfies such a requirement through her foreign nursing education. In support of this interpretation, appellant cites to a letter solicited from DOL clarifying the requirement's purposes. This letter indicates that the requirement was designed to serve two purposes. First, it was intended to protect similarly situated United States workers who did not currently possess a Virginia license but who could sit for the exam. The second and primary purpose, however, was to ensure compliance with the state law requiring that professional nurses possess a license in order to be legally employed. Va.Code § 54-367.17 (1982); see 20 C.F.R. § 656.21(b)(16) (1979) (terms of job opportunity offered to alien must conform to the requirements of federal, state, and local law). This second purpose undermines the contention that mere eligibility to take the examination satisfies the requirement. INS' common sense interpretation that the prospective employee must have an actual ability to obtain the license within a reasonable time better comports with DOL's statement of purpose. Thus, it is not an abuse of discretion for INS to require that appellant show some likelihood of eventually passing the exam.

The next inquiry must be whether appellant sustained this burden. Appellant presented evidence of her nursing education, her registration to take the District of Columbia nursing exam, and possible reciprocity between the District of Columbia and Virginia. INS found this evidence to be insufficient, and the district court agreed.

We are wary of jumping too quickly to the conclusion that the evidence, because it did not show that appellant in fact would obtain the license, was thereby insufficient to sustain her burden. Insofar as it speaks to appellant's future potential, the "able to obtain" requirement is something that cannot, except in rare instances, be concretely proved or disproved now. In evaluating an individual alien's satisfaction of such a requirement, INS cannot require that the alien already have acquired the skill or met the qualification, thereby eliminating the grace period contained within the requirement when it states that future compliance is sufficient. Such a burden would effectively permit INS to impose an additional or different job requirement, something which it has no authority to do.

Between those two extremes, mere eligibility to sit for the examination and current possession of the license, lies the level of proof that balances the alien's ability to show a future qualification and INS' responsibility to ensure that, at some point, the alien will be able to perform the certified job. INS may require a preliminary showing that the alien intends to acquire and is reasonably likely to acquire the qualification in question within a reasonable period of time. This reasonable period of time should vary according to the nature of the qualification, the usual time period it takes to acquire the qualification, and the prospective employer's needs and expectations. But once this preliminary showing is made, the alien has satisfied her burden of demonstrating compliance with this type of job requirement. Thereafter, INS can deny the preference classification on that basis only if there is a finding, supported by substantial evidence, that the particular alien actually will not be able to acquire the specified qualification. For this reason, INS cannot rely on the low passing rate of foreign nurse candidates in general as the basis for rejecting appellant's petition once a preliminary showing is made.

* * *

We recognize that the statutory division of authority between DOL's labor certification determination and INS' preference classification decision can lead to some discontinuity insofar as DOL-imposed job requirements are subject to interpretation by INS in its review of the alien's qualifications. Accordingly, INS will need the sensitivity to coordinate DOL and INS interpretations and to follow the Act's directive to consult with DOL when correctable discrepancies between the alien's qualifications and the labor certification job requirements appear. INS must also recognize that DOL bears the authority for setting the content of the labor certification and that it cannot impose job qualifications beyond those contemplated therein. However delicate that task may be in future cases, we have no reason to upset the decision of INS in this case.

Notes

1. *Madany* highlights the limits of the certification. It is merely a certification by the Department of Labor and it must be coupled with two additional procedural filings—a preference petition and an application for adjustment of status, or a preference petition and an immigrant visa application. Armed with the certification, the beneficiary of the certification must proceed to establish both qualification for the

preference classification and ultimately the immigrant visa or adjustment of status. It is only at this final stage that the person acquires permanent residency.

2. Regulations promulgated after 2007 require that where a labor certification is required as a condition to the preference petition, the petition must be filed within 180 days. 8 C.F.R. § 204.5(a); 20 C.F.R. § 656.30(b). This regulation has withstood court challenges.[56]

3. **Relationship between Nonimmigrant and Immigrant Employment Visas.** As was discussed earlier, the immigration practitioner must be adept at protecting her client's interests through the nonimmigrant and immigrant visas. In order to remain in the United States, the applicant may need to pursue a strategy which includes maintaining a nonimmigrant status and later transitioning into immigrant status. Alternatively, the person may be required to leave the United States for a period of time before being able to obtain permanent residency. Understanding the interplay between these different forms of immigration status is made more important by the provisions in the immigration law which make a person inadmissible if she has been out of lawful status for a period of time exceeding 180 days.[57] Maneuvering between the different statutory provisions are made more difficult because of the immigrant quotas that may delay the person's adjustment of status to that of a lawful permanent resident or by limitations on maintaining nonimmigrant status while one is pursuing permanent resident status.[58]

4. A review of the many nonimmigrant classifications reveals connections to some of the employment-based immigrant preference categories. For example, the nonimmigrant religious worker (R-1) and special immigrant Employment-based 4 category, or the intracompany transfers (L-1) and temporary workers H-1B and the Employment-based 2 or Employment-based 3 categories. The availability of immigrant visas in these categories allows employers to bring in nonimmigrants and later transition some of them into permanent resident positions.

5. Consider the following scenario derived from the previous case. Ms. Madany comes to you as a graduate of a foreign nursing school. She has a tourist visa which allows her to remain for an additional three months. She explains that while her long-term goal is to find a position in the United States, she would like to receive additional training in this country and perhaps later take a licensing exam. What kind of visas might be available to her in the United States? What advice would you give her? For additional guidance, see 8 U.S.C. §§ 1182(a)(5)(C) and 1182(m), Sec. 212(a)(5)(C) and 212(m); also see 8 U.S.C. § 1101(a)(15)(H)(i), Sec. 101(a)(15)(H)(i).

---

56. *Elim Church of God v. Harris*, 722 F.3d 1137 (9th Cir. 2013); *Durable Mfg., Co. v. Dept. of Labor*, 578 F.3d 497, 501 (7th Cir. 2009).

57. *See* 8 U.S.C. § 1182(a)(9)(B), Sec. 212(a)(9)(B) and discussion in Chapter 3.

58. As was noted earlier, most persons are deemed to be immigrants until they can show otherwise, with the exception of certain H and L visa holders. *See* 8 U.S.C. § 1184(b), Sec. 214(b).

Production Tool Corp., et al. v. Employment and Training Administration, et al.

688 F.2d 1161 (7th Cir. 1982)

Before Bauer, Circuit Judge, Nichols, Associate Judge, and Wood, Circuit Judge.

Wood, Jr., Circuit Judge.

Production Tool Corp. and Kenall Manufacturing Co. appeal from separate orders affirming final decisions of the United States Department of Labor denying their applications for permanent alien labor certifications as provided for by the Immigration and Nationality Act, § 212(a)(14), 8 U.S.C. § 1182(a)(14) (as amended), and the regulations promulgated thereunder, 20 C.F.R. Pt. 656 (1980). Appellants challenge the validity and application of those regulations. For the following reasons, we affirm.

* * *

On May 3, 1977, Production Tool filed an application for labor certification on behalf of its employee Manuel Aguilar. The certifying officer denied that application in part for the stated reason that Production Tool "elected not to comply" with the advertising requirements of 20 C.F.R. § 656.21(b)(9). The hearing officer affirmed and the district court denied relief on the same ground. Production Tool admits that it did not comply with that regulation.

On June 13, 1977, Kenall filed an application on behalf of Blanca Fabian. Kenall had advertised the position in the Reader at a wage rate of $4.00. The Certifying Officer, after receiving Kenall's rebuttal evidence, denied certification on the ground, inter alia, that Kenall's newspaper advertisements did not satisfy 20 C.F.R. § 656.21(b)(9) because they did not offer the prevailing wage of $4.70 and were not placed in a newspaper of "general circulation." The Hearing Officer affirmed, noting that counsel for Kenall had conceded, and the record showed, that the advertising did not fully comply with the regulations: "This undisputed fact together with the unacceptable advertising in the Reader establishes a sufficient basis for affirming the denial." The district court entered summary judgment for appellees.

Production Tool and Kenall contend that the Secretary of Labor was without statutory authority to promulgate the regulations at issue and that, even if authorized, the regulations are invalid because they are inconsistent with the command and purpose of § 212(a)(14). Kenall separately argues that the denial of labor certification constituted an abuse of discretion because 1) it had offered to pay and advertise the prevailing wage and 2) the Reader, under Illinois law, is considered a newspaper of general circulation.

The validity of the advertising regulation, according to appellants, turns on the distinction between "legislative" and "interpretive" rules. Appellants assert that the regulation at issue is legislative because it "creates or changes existing rights and obligations" and, as such, "require(s) specific statutory authorization." In both decisions, the district courts found that promulgation of the advertising regulation was a valid exercise of the Secretary of Labor's inherent authority to adopt interpretive rules.

After examining the relevant case law, we believe that the distinction between legislative and interpretive rules is of little, if any, value in determining whether the Secretary must have a specific grant of rule making authority to promulgate the regulation at issue. That distinction nonetheless becomes important when reviewing the regulation to determine whether it constitutes a proper exercise of rule making authority.

* * *

... [T]he court in Silva sternly criticized the Secretary for failing to "promulgate suitable regulations": "in an area where the Secretary has considerable power under general statutory standards and must decide numerous cases in a routine fashion, the clarification of policy through rules or published pronouncements would protect against arbitrary action." 518 F.2d at 311. See also *White v. Roughton*, 530 F.2d 750, 752 (7th Cir. 1976); *Environmental Defense Fund, Inc. v. Ruckelshaus*, 439 F.2d 584, 598 (D.C. Cir. 1971). The absence of an express delegation of legislative power does not itself render the advertising regulation void.[1]

Appellants also contend that the advertising regulation shifts the burden of proving unavailability of domestic workers to the employer-applicant. This, they say, is contrary to the intent of Congress and to the greater weight of judicial decisions construing § 212(a)(14). Appellants' argument is not without merit, but we agree with the district court that the regulation constitutes a valid exercise of the Secretary's inherent authority to promulgate rules governing the administration of § 212(a)(14).

The interpretation of a statute by the agency charged with enforcement or administration is entitled to great deference provided it is consistent with the congressional purpose. *Morton*, 415 U.S. at 237; *Griggs v. Duke Power Co.*, 401 U.S. 424, 433–34 (1971). "[W]e need not find that [the agency's] construction is the only reasonable one, or even that it is the result we would have reached had the question arisen in the first instance in judicial proceedings." *Udall v. Tallman*, 380 U.S. 1, 16 (1965), quoting *Unemployment Commission v. Aragan*, 329 U.S. 143, 153 (1946). "[T]he rulings, interpretations and opinions (of the agency), while not controlling upon the courts by reason of their authority, do constitute a body of experience and informed judgment to which courts and litigants may properly resort for guidance." *Skidmore*, 323 U.S. at 140. Deference is especially appropriate where, as here, the rule was adopted only after all interested persons were given notice and an opportunity to comment pursuant to § 553 procedures. See *Pacific Gas & Electric Co. v. FPC*, 506 F.2d 33, 39 (D.C. Cir. 1974).

Congress enacted § 212(a)(14) to protect the domestic labor force from job competition and adverse working conditions as a result of foreign workers entering the labor market. H. Rep. No. 1365, 82nd Cong., 2d Sess. (1952), reprinted in 1952 U.S. Code Cong. & Ad. News 1653, 1705; S. Rep. No. 748, 89th Cong., 1st Sess. (1965), reprinted in 1965

1. We decide only that promulgation of the advertising requirement was a valid exercise of the Secretary's inherent rule making power. We therefore need not determine whether Congress intended to delegate "legislative" authority under § 212(a)(14), though other courts apparently have assumed such a grant. *See, e.g., Lewis-Mota v. Secretary of Labor*, 469 F.2d 478 (2d Cir. 1972); *Trimble House Corp. v. Marshall*, 497 F. Supp. 546 (N.D. Ga. 1980).

U.S. Code Cong. & Ad. News 3328, 3329, 3333–34. See *Alfred L. Snapp & Son, Inc. v. Puerto Rico ex rel. Barez*, ___ U.S. ___, ___, 102 S.Ct. 3260, 3264 (1982). The labor market findings the Secretary must make are designed to effectuate that purpose. The 1952 version of § 212(a)(14) provided that aliens will not be permitted to enter to perform work "*if* the Secretary of Labor has determined and certified ... that (A) sufficient workers in the United States who are able, willing, and qualified *are available* ... or (B) the employment of such aliens *will* adversely affect the wages and working conditions...." Act of June 27, 1952, ch. 477, § 212(a)(14), 66 Stat. 183 (emphasis added). In 1965 Congress sought to strengthen the protection of United States workers by amending § 212(a)(14) to require exclusion unless the Secretary affirmatively finds that there are not sufficient domestic workers available and that entry of the foreign worker will not adversely affect working conditions. Pub. L. No. 89-236, § 10(a), 79 Stat. 917. As the Senate Report stated, "Under the instant bill, (the present) procedure is substantially changed. The primary responsibility is placed upon the intending immigrant to obtain the Secretary of Labor's clearance prior to issuance of a visa establishing" the two statutory prerequisites. 1965 U.S. Code Cong. & Ad. News 3333–34. See H.R. Rep. No. 745, 89th Cong., 1st Sess. 14 (1965). Whereas the 1952 Act opened the door to immigrant workers unless the Secretary acted to exclude them, the 1965 amendment closed that door and placed direct responsibility on the alien to petition the Secretary to open it.

Appellees rely on *Pesikoff v. Secretary of Labor*, 501 F.2d 757 (D.C. Cir.), cert. denied, 419 U.S. 1038 (1974), wherein the D.C. Circuit found that, based on its assessment of the statutory language and legislative history, § 212(a)(14) sets up a presumption that aliens may not enter the United States for permanent employment. Id. at 761. Thus the court held:

> if the Secretary's consultation of the general labor market data readily available to him suggests that there is a pool of potential workers available to perform the job which the alien seeks, the burden should be placed on the alien or his putative employer to prove that it is not possible for the employer to find a qualified American worker.

Id. To support its conclusion the court cited the language change by the 1965 amendment and Senator Kennedy's remark on the Senate floor that the amendment "places the burden of proving no adverse effect on the applying alien." *Id.* at 762, citing 111 Cong. Rec. 24227 (1965).

Judge MacKinnon, in a strong dissent, commented that "(a)lthough this is consistent with the statutory structure, it does present some problems not considered in the majority opinion." *Id.* at 771. He noted that by bearing the "ultimate burden of persuasion," the employer is required to "prove the existence of the nonexistent, a sometimes difficult proposition." *Id.* Instead, he suggested that it would be reasonable and sufficient for the employer to bear the "burden of production" by documenting his efforts to find domestic workers "through newspaper advertisements, employment agencies and the assistance of friends." *Id.* If those efforts are shown to be unsuccessful, "(t)he Secretary then must introduce sufficient competent evidence to overcome that adduced by the employer, failing which certification must issue." *Id.*

As appellants point out, however, *Pesikoff* does not represent the law of this circuit. Several decisions of this court have held that it constitutes an abuse of discretion to deny labor certification on the basis of evidence which was challenged and not shown to be reliable. *Stenographic Machines, Inc. v. Regional Administrator for Employment & Training*, 577 F.2d 521 (7th Cir. 1978); *Shuk Yee Chan v. Regional Manpower Administrator*, 521 F.2d 592 (7th Cir. 1975); *First Girl, Inc. v. Regional Manpower Administrator*, 499 F.2d 122 (7th Cir. 1974) (per curiam); *Secretary of Labor v. Farino*, 490 F.2d 885, 889 (7th Cir. 1973); see also *Sherwin-Williams Co. v. Regional Manpower Administrator*, 439 F.Supp. 272 (N.D.Ill. 1976); *Bitang v. Regional Manpower Administrator*, 351 F.Supp. 1342 (N.D.Ill. 1972). The rationale for this circuit's position, first articulated in *Farino* and later crystalized in *First Girl*, is the basic principle of administrative law that a finding unsupported by reliable record evidence cannot be sustained. Thus, in *First Girl*, we affirmed a decision overturning a denial of certification on the district court's finding that the administrative record contained "no evidence to support defendant's determination that there was no shortage of applicants qualified, available, and willing to work in the type of employment offered by plaintiff." 499 F.2d at 124, quoting 361 F.Supp. 1339, 1340 (N.D. Ill. 1973) (Bauer, J.). The reviewing officer in that case had relied exclusively on raw ISES (Illinois State Employment Service) "availability data" which did not show "that the persons listed were in fact qualified, were still available for employment, or were willing to work for an employer such as plaintiff—as specified in the provisions of 8 U.S.C. § 1182(a)(14)." 361 F.Supp. at 1340. Implicit in this court's reasoning is the premise that labor certification must be granted under § 212(a)(14) unless the Secretary affirmatively determines that able, qualified, and willing United States workers are available or that employment of the alien will have an adverse effect. Appellants therefore contend that, under the law of this circuit, the burden of proof rests with the Secretary.

While this court has never addressed the statutory basis for that unstated assumption, we need not defend it here,[3] for we believe that the advertising rule, as written, is not inconsistent with Seventh Circuit precedent. In promulgating 20 C.F.R. § 656.21, the Secretary in effect adopted Judge MacKinnon's position in *Pesikoff*. An applicant-employer does not bear the ultimate burden of persuasion. The regulations require the certifying officer to look to various sources in determining whether a United States worker is available, able, and qualified and whether employment of the alien will have an adverse effect on wages and working conditions. 20 C.F.R. §§ 656.24(b)(2)(ii)–(iv), (b)(3). The documented results of the employer's recruitment efforts are considered

3. Senator Kennedy's reference to the alien's "burden of proof," to which the *Pesikoff* court attributed great weight, is somewhat ambiguous when viewed in light of his following remark that "there will be cases where the Secretary will be expected to ascertain in some detail the need for the immigrant in this country under the provisions of the law." 111 Cong. Rec. 24227 (1965).... "The remarks of a single legislator, even the sponsor, are not controlling in analyzing legislative history. (Any) statement must be considered with the Reports of both Houses and the statements of other Congressmen...." *Chrysler Corp.*, 441 U.S. at 311, The change in the wording of § 212(a)(14) may be explained, in view of remarks by other Congressmen and even the Senate Report, as a device which would ensure that certification decisions are made "on an individual case basis." *See* 111 Cong. Rec. 21579 (remarks of Rep. Madden); *id.* 21586....

only to determine whether a United States worker is willing to take the job opportunity. *Id.* § 656.24(b)(2)(1). Even on that inquiry, the certifying officer must also look to the Employment Service Office's recruitment efforts and, presumably, may consider any other sources that may be appropriate. Moreover, the regulations parallel this circuit's position that certification may be denied only upon an affirmative finding of availability and adverse effect.

We believe that Seventh Circuit precedent does not preclude the imposition of a "burden of production" that is well-defined, very specific, and not unduly burdensome. Rather, documentation of the employer's recruitment efforts will enable the Secretary to make an informed decision on the basis of reliable evidence. This was our primary concern in *Farino*, *First Girl*, and later cases. Indeed, the regulations may be viewed as a reaction to strong criticism by this and other circuits of the data upon which determinations had been made and the failure to determine the subsidiary questions of whether the available worker is able, qualified, and willing. In particular, the Secretary has found it a difficult task to establish that an available worker is "willing." See, e.g., *Ratnayake v. Mack*, 499 F.2d 1207, 1213 (8th Cir. 1974). These regulations seem reasonably designed to gather the most reliable information on that requirement. Finally, by specifying the information to be relied upon in determining whether a worker is willing, the regulations reduce the potential for arbitrariness, a major point of criticism under the prior regulations. See *Silva*, 518 F.2d at 311. Given the strong congressional intent to protect American workers and the statutory duty of the Secretary to determine worker availability and labor conditions, we find the Secretary's advertising regulation to be a reasonable exercise of rule making authority.

Having determined the advertising requirement to be a valid rule, it follows that the Secretary must be permitted to give effect to that rule by making substantial compliance[4] a prerequisite to approval of an application. See *Morrison & Morrison, Inc. v. Secretary of Labor*, 626 F.2d 771 (10th Cir. 1980). Production Tool admits that it did not comply. Kenall, however, argues in the alternative that the certifying officer abused his discretion by ruling that the Reader is not a newspaper of general circulation.

An agency's interpretation of its own regulation is controlling unless "plainly erroneous or inconsistent." *United States v. Larionoff*, 431 U.S. 864 (1977). We agree with the district court that the certifying officer's construction must stand.

Under the regulations, an employer must advertise the job opportunity "in such media as newspapers of general circulation, and ethnic and professional publications." 20 C.F.R. § 656.21(b)(9)(i). The obvious purpose of that requirement is, as the hearing officer noted, to test adequately the labor market in the area of intended employment. See *id.* §§ 656.24(b)(2)(i), (iv). The statute itself refers to workers who are available "at the place" of the job opportunity. 8 U.S.C. § 1182(a)(14). The hearing officer, however, found Kenall's advertisement deficient under the regulation since the Reader is a neighborhood weekly with a circulation of 92,000 in only a limited area of Chicago.

4. The current regulations specify that the certifying officer may grant certification if he determines that the employer has committed "harmless error." 20 C.F.R. § 656.24(b)(1) (1981).

The Tenth Circuit upheld a requirement that a Denver employer advertise in the eastern edition of the Wall Street Journal for a foreign investment representative. *Morrison & Morrison*, 626 F.2d at 773–74. In view of the sophisticated nature of the job sought, the court concluded that "(a) requirement that does not involve a significant expenditure of money which is likely to reach the pool of U.S. citizen prospects, is not inconsistent with the law or the regulations promulgated thereunder." *Id.* at 774.

Here, the job opportunity—quality control inspector—is centrally located in the city of Chicago. It is entirely reasonable for the Secretary to require advertisement for such a job to be run in one of the two major Chicago newspapers which circulate in the entire metropolitan area. The Illinois cases Kenall cites define "newspaper of general circulation" only for the purpose of publishing legal notices and have very little bearing on whether a job advertisement in the Reader adequately tests the relevant labor market. What constitutes the relevant labor market is a question that falls squarely within the Secretary's realm of expertise. Thus we are especially hesitant to second-guess that judgment.

Failure on the part of appellants substantially to comply with the Secretary of Labor's valid advertising regulation precluded the certifying officer from being able to determine whether any available United States worker was "willing" to take the job opportunities which appellants sought to fill with alien labor. The decisions of the district courts therefore are Affirmed.

D. The Significance of Labor Certification

Matter of Raol

16 I. & N. Dec. 466 (BIA 1978)

BY: Milhollan, Chairman; Maniatis, Appleman, Maguire, and Farb, Board Members

The respondent has appealed from a May 16, 1977, decision of an immigration judge denying a motion to reopen deportation proceedings for the purpose of applying for adjustment of status under section 245 of the Immigration and Nationality Act, 8 U.S.C. 1255, and also denying a request for reinstatement of voluntary departure. Oral argument was held on October 12, 1977. The appeal will be dismissed in part and sustained in part.

The record reflects the following facts. The respondent is a 27-year-old native and citizen of India who entered the United States as a nonimmigrant student on March 29, 1972. He graduated from Texas A & M University in December of 1974 with a B.S. degree in chemical engineering. The respondent was employed by the Louisiana Air Control Commission (hereinafter referred to as the LACC), with the permission of the Immigration and Naturalization Service, as an "on-the-job trainee" in connection with his student visa. This employment commenced in March of 1975 and the authorization of employment by the Immigration and Naturalization Service expired on March 13, 1976.

The record further indicates that a labor certification application was filed by the LACC on the respondent's behalf in early 1976. This application was denied on June 14, 1976, and on June 23, 1976, the District Director denied an application for adjustment of status filed by the respondent. The respondent was subsequently found deportable at a hearing held on October 14, 1976. He was granted voluntary departure until January 14, 1977, and this period was extended by the District Director through February 25, 1977. On January 24, 1977, a second application for a labor certification was filed by the LACC. This application was approved and a labor certification was issued on February 24, 1977. On March 1, 1977, the respondent filed a motion to reopen deportation proceedings for the purpose of applying for adjustment of status. Also filed on the same date was an application for adjustment of status and a petition to classify the respondent for sixth-preference status, accompanied by the labor certification.

The motion to reopen was denied by the immigration judge for the reason that the respondent was precluded from adjusting his status under section 245(c) of the Act, 8 U.S.C. 1255(c). This provision was added to the Immigration and Nationality Act by the 1976 Amendments, Public Law 94-571, 90 Stat. 2703, effective January 1, 1977. It provides, in pertinent part, that the benefits of section 245 are inapplicable to:

> (2) an alien (other than an immediate relative as defined in section 201(b)) who hereafter continues in or accepts unauthorized employment prior to filing an application for adjustment of status....

The respondent admits that he has continued his employment with the LACC as a chemical engineer beyond March 13, 1976, when the permission to work as an "on-the-job trainee" granted by the Service expired. He contends, however, that approval of a labor certification application by the Secretary of Labor for that position removes him from the unauthorized employment bar of section 245(c).

While sympathizing with the respondent's predicament, we disagree with his position that a labor certification issued pursuant to section 212(a)(14) of the Act, 8 U.S.C. 1182(a)(14), operates to authorize one's employment within the meaning of section 245(c). By issuing a labor certification, the Department of Labor, in conjunction with its regional divisions and local state employment offices, confirms that the employment of an alien in a particular job or profession will not displace a qualified American worker. An individual or blanket labor certification is a prerequisite for obtaining an approved third or sixth-preference visa petition. See 8 C.F.R. 204.2(c)(4); 20 C.F.R. 656.1 et seq. However, the Immigration and Naturalization Service is the entity that approves a third or sixth-preference visa petition and issues an immigrant visa to an alien already in this country. See 8 C.F.R. 204.2(c)(1); 8 C.F.R. 245.1(d).

The proposition that an alien's employment is unauthorized unless the Service has given specific approval has been affirmed in numerous administrative and Federal court decisions. See, e.g., *Ahmed v. United States*, 480 F.2d 531 (2 Cir.1973) (maintenance of status and departure bond); *Matter of Yarden*, Interim Decision 2513 (R.C.1976) (adjustment of status); *Matter of Boroumand*, 13 I. & N. Dec. 306 (BIA 1969) (deportation). Although Congress did not define the term "unauthorized employment" when it enacted section 245(c), we do not believe that a labor certification, standing alone, would shield an applicant for adjustment of status from the operation of that section.

Had the respondent obtained permission from the Service to continue his employment after January 1, 1977, his case would be on a different footing. Pursuant to the Service's Operations Instruction 245.9, an applicant for adjustment may be granted permission to work during the time his application for status as a permanent resident is pending. However, there is no evidence that the respondent's permission to work extended beyond March 13, 1976. Consequently, we must agree with the immigration judge that the respondent is statutorily precluded from adjusting his status due to his continuing in unauthorized employment after January 1, 1977, and at the time of applying for adjustment of status.

Counsel has notified the Board that the respondent's sixth-preference visa petition has been approved and that a visa is awaiting him in India. We have concluded that reinstatement of the privilege of voluntary departure is warranted at this time in order to facilitate the respondent's return to this country as an immigrant. Accordingly, the following order will be entered.

ORDER: The appeal is dismissed as to the denial of the motion to reopen for the purpose of applying for adjustment of status.

FURTHER ORDER: The outstanding order of deportation is withdrawn; the respondent is permitted to depart from the United States voluntarily within such time and under such conditions as the District Director shall direct; and in the event of failure so to depart, the respondent shall be deported as provided in the immigration judge's order.

Notes

1. *Matter of Raol* underscores that the labor certification standing alone does not give the person any legal status. It is merely a necessary step in pursuing an employment-based preference and then either adjustment of status or an immigrant visa. As will be discussed in Chapter 9, adjustment of status is a procedure through which a person may obtain permanent residency without having to leave the United States. In contrast, the immigrant visa is a procedure which requires the applicant seeking permanent residence to return to her home country to obtain the visa through a U.S. consul. While the person may pursue both of these procedures while physically present in the United States, only adjustment of status will confer permanent resident status without the necessity of leaving the country.

2. The labor certification process also does not include an inquiry of whether the person comes within one or more of the classes of inadmissible or deportable persons.[59] This is a separate inquiry that occurs at either adjustment of status or the immigrant visa interview.

---

59. *See* 8 U.S.C. §§ 1182(a) and 1227(a), Sections 212(a) and 237(a).

E. Recruitment as Part of the Certification Process

Recruitment is at the heart of the process, and the following case is included to highlight this requirement. Even though the case is dated and references the older citation for the governing statute, it remains good law.[60]

Industrial Holographics, Inc. et al. v. Raymond J. Donovan, Sect'y of Labor, et al.

722 F.2d 1362 (7th Cir. 1983)

Before Pell and Cudahy, Circuit Judges, and Wilkins, Senior District Judge.

Cudahy, Circuit Judge.

This case presents a challenge to a refusal by the Department of Labor to certify an alien for lawful employment in the United States. Specifically, the appellants challenge the Department's regulations equating an employer's offer of "prevailing wages and working conditions" with terms which "will not adversely affect the wages and working conditions" of American workers. The appellants also object to the prevailing wage determination in this case. The district court upheld the Secretary's action and we affirm.

Under section 212(a)(14) of the Immigration and Nationality Act, 8 U.S.C. §1182(a)(14), the State Department may not issue an alien a visa for admission to the United States for purposes of employment unless the Secretary of Labor certifies that American workers are not "able, willing, qualified..., and available" for the work, and that the employment of the alien "will not adversely affect the wages and working conditions" of similarly employed Americans. The Secretary of Labor has promulgated regulations which establish standards and procedures for the certification of alien workers under section 212(a)(14). See 20 C.F.R. §§656.20 et seq. (1983). If an employer wishes to hire an alien for work in the United States, these regulations require the employer first to recruit among American workers offering the "prevailing wage" and "prevailing working conditions" to determine whether any American workers are "able, willing, qualified, and available" for the job. See 20 C.F.R. §656.21(b)(1), (3) and (9) (1980). If an employer submits documentation showing it has been unable to recruit American workers on these terms, then the Secretary of Labor may certify the alien to enter the country and perform the work.

* * *

Plaintiff Industrial Holographics, Inc. (the "employer") manufactures and tests machinery used to make rubber tires. Plaintiff Roger K. Yu is an alien whom Industrial Holographics has sought to employ in Michigan as an export manager. The record indicates that Yu has never been in the United States. In June 1979, Industrial Holographics applied for labor certification on behalf of Yu. Industrial Holographics followed the various provisions in 20 C.F.R. §656.21 (1980), requiring it to post the job for internal re-

---

60. The predecessor statutory provision was 8 U.S.C. §1182(a)(14), Sec. 212(a)(14).

cruitment, to advertise the job in newspapers and to post the job with the state employment service. On August 24, 1979, the employer submitted to the certifying officer[61] documentation showing that it had complied with the requirements of section 656.21.

The employer, however, had advertised that the salary for the job of export manager was $1,000 per month. Section 656.21 requires the employer to advertise and post the job at the "prevailing wage" and "prevailing working conditions" in order to obtain certification. 20 C.F.R. § 656.21(b)(3) and (9) (1980). The Michigan Employment Security Commission (the "MESC") was responsible for determining the prevailing wage in this case, see 20 C.F.R. § 656.21(f) (1980), and it determined that the prevailing wage for export managers in the area was $1,666 per month. Therefore, the certifying officer issued to the employer a Notice of Findings proposing to deny labor certification for Yu because the employer had failed to advertise the job at the prevailing wage.

After receiving the Notice of Findings, the employer agreed to repeat the advertising and recruiting process at the higher salary of $1,666 per month. The employer advertised the job at the higher salary, but it failed to comply with all of the requirements of section 656.21. Specifically, the employer did not show it had posted the job for internal recruitment at the higher salary, § 656.21(b)(10), did not document the results of its recruitment efforts, § 656.21(b)(15), and did not recruit for thirty days through the state employment service, § 656.21(g)(1). Because the employer had failed to comply with the strict advertising requirements within the relevant time limits, the certifying officer denied the certification for Yu.[62] On review within the Department of Labor, the administrative law judge concluded that the employer had failed to comply with the regulations and that certification was properly denied.

* * *

Plaintiffs now appeal presenting three issues. First, they contend that the Secretary of Labor exceeded his statutory authority when he promulgated regulations requiring the employer to advertise the job at the "prevailing wage." Second, they argue that the prevailing wage determination in this case was incorrect. Finally, they argue that they substantially complied with the regulations and that they are therefore entitled to certification....

... The applicable statutory language says that the Secretary shall certify the alien only if his or her employment "will not adversely affect the wages and working conditions" of similarly employed workers in the United States. 8 U.S.C. § 1182(a)(14)(B).

---

61. The certifying officer is the regional official of the Employment and Training Administration who decides whether to grant or deny labor certification. The certifying officer's decision is then subject to review by an administrative law judge and later by the courts.

62. The employer had sought and received two written extensions of time to complete advertising at the higher wage. In the administrative hearings, the employer claimed that it had received a third oral extension and that it fulfilled the requirements within the time allowed by the third extension, but the administrative law judge rejected this claim. Appellants do not challenge the law judge's finding here, so we assume that appellants did not comply with the relevant time limits.

The district court relied upon our decision in *Production Tool Corp. v. Employment and Training Admin.*, 688 F.2d 1161 (7th Cir.1982), in holding that the Secretary had statutory authority to issue the prevailing wage standard. In Production Tool, the employers argued that the Immigration and Nationality Act did not authorize the Secretary to issue any interpretative regulations under section 212(a)(14), and that the regulations could not properly impose on the employer the burden of producing evidence showing that United States workers were not "able, willing, qualified, and available." This court held that the Secretary had inherent authority to issue the regulations requiring an employer to advertise positions among American workers and imposing on an employer the burden of producing evidence showing it had complied with the advertising procedures. 688 F.2d at 1170. On this appeal, appellants present us with a narrower challenge to the same regulations. They argue only that the regulations improperly equate the statute's standard of adverse effects with the payment of wages below "prevailing wages." This precise issue was not before the court in *Production Tool*, so we must go beyond that decision in considering the Secretary's authority to issue the prevailing wage requirement. However, the court's reasoning in *Production Tool* is highly relevant to this issue of statutory authority; hence, we believe that the *Production Tool* reasoning extends to the prevailing wage requirement.

In Production Tool this court clarified the authority under which the labor certification regulations were promulgated. The Immigration and Nationality Act does not expressly authorize the Secretary to issue regulations. However, the standards of section 212(a)(14) are quite broad. The Secretary must decide whether there are sufficient American workers who are "able, willing, qualified, and available," and whether the alien's employment would "adversely affect the wages and working conditions" of American workers. The statute leaves to the Department a broad area for the exercise of its discretion in issuing labor certificates. Where the agency must make a large number of individual discretionary decisions, it is entirely appropriate for it to issue regulations informing the public about the standards and procedures the agency intends to apply. *Production Tool, supra*, 688 F.2d at 1166. Those regulations simplify the administrative task and help guard against arbitrary agency action. See *Silva v. Secretary of Labor*, 518 F.2d 301, 310 (1st Cir.1975) (criticizing absence of regulations for certifying alien agricultural workers). As the court held in *Production Tool*, the labor certification regulations promote these ends, and the Secretary has inherent authority to issue them. 688 F.2d at 1167 & n. 1.

Because the Secretary did not act beyond his authority in issuing the advertising regulations, the only substantial reason appellants offer for finding the prevailing wage regulations invalid is that they are inconsistent with the language and underlying purpose of section 212(a)(14). In our view, the regulations as applied in this case are consistent with the statute and thus are not arbitrary, capricious or an abuse of discretion. The Secretary has exercised appropriately his inherent power to develop standards and procedures for achieving the statute's goals.

* * *

The language of section 212(a)(14) does little more than identify Congressional goals: aliens should not take jobs from "able, willing, qualified, and available" American workers, and an alien's employment should not "adversely affect" the wages and working conditions of American workers. The statute leaves to the Secretary the task of developing operational standards to effect the Congressional purpose. The breadth of the statutory language and the volume of decisions virtually require the Secretary to develop systematic standards and procedures for deciding upon labor certification applications. Each year the Department of Labor receives a large number of applications for permanent labor certification.[63] A complete and thorough analysis of all relevant factors affecting the impact of each individual alien's employment on the labor market is clearly out of the question. Sound administration and concern for consistency and fairness require simplified rules of general application for imposing the statutory standards.

The regulations here assume, as a general proposition, that the employment of an alien at wages below the prevailing wage will tend to affect adversely the wages and working conditions of American workers. Appellants have provided no evidence to persuade us that this general assumption is arbitrary or capricious.[64] While it may be possible to conceive of cases in which the prevailing wage standard would be inconsistent with the statute's purpose, that is not the case here.

* * *

In *Naporano Metal & Iron*, 529 F.2d 537 (3d Cir. 1976), the Secretary denied labor certification for an alien working in the United States as a welder and scrap metal cutter. The alien was paid a wage under a collective bargaining agreement, but the Secretary found that the union wage was below the "prevailing wage" required by the predecessor regulation of section 656.21. The Third Circuit held that payment of a union wage negotiated to cover both alien and United States workers could not, as a matter of law, adversely affect the wages and working conditions of similarly employed American workers. 529 F.2d at 541. The court also described the "adverse effect" standard of the statute as "substantially different" from the "prevailing wage" requirement of the regulation, but the court did not consider whether the regulation was consistent with the statute. 529 F.2d at 540 n. 9.[65] We agree that the statutory standard differs from the regulation's standard, but the standards are not necessarily inconsistent. The regulation simply gives operational meaning to the statute's expression of Congressional purpose. The Secretary clearly has authority to issue clarifying

---

63. In fiscal year 1981, the Department of Labor received approximately 33,000 applications for permanent labor certification, and it granted certification in 25,763 cases. Employment and Training Report of the President 51 (1982). In fiscal year 1980, the Department received 32,800 applications and granted certification in 29,000 cases. Employment and Training Report of the President 49 (1981).

64. The regulations were adopted after appropriate notice and comment procedures. *See* 42 Fed.Reg. 3440 (1977).

65. The Secretary amended the definition of "prevailing wage" in 1977 to reflect the *Naporano Metal & Iron* holding regarding union wages. *See* 20 C.F.R. §656.40(a)(2)(ii) (1983); 42 Fed.Reg. 3450 (1977). Because there is no union wage involved here, that provision does not apply to this case

regulations, and, as applied in this case, the regulations are not inconsistent with the statute.

Ozbirman v. Regional Manpower Adm'r, 335 F. Supp. 467 (S.D. N.Y. 1971) provides appellants more direct support. There an alien was denied labor certification as an auto mechanic. The wage he was offered matched the union negotiated wage in the area, but the Secretary found the wage to be below the "prevailing wage" as required by the predecessor regulation of section 656.21. The district court remanded the matter to the Secretary on two alternative grounds. First, the court held that the "prevailing wage" standard improperly construed the term "adverse effect" and did not implement the statutory purpose. Second, the court held that the denial was an abuse of discretion because the alien's wage would have been equal to that of his co-workers and was union negotiated. 335 F.Supp. at 472. The court discussed at length the complexity of a thorough determination of whether a particular package of wages and other benefits and working conditions would adversely affect American wages and working conditions. It concluded that the "prevailing wage" standard did not adequately take into account the other relevant variables. We agree with the *Ozbirman* court that a truly thorough analysis of adverse effects involves factors other than wages. However, we do not agree that the Secretary of Labor is without authority to issue regulations simplifying the inquiry so that decisions will be less arbitrary and more consistent.

We conclude that the Secretary acted reasonably in giving operational content to the language of section 212(a)(14) by applying the prevailing wage standard in this case. Therefore, the Secretary acted within his legal authority in relying on the prevailing wage standard of section 656.21(b) to deny labor certification in this case.

The second issue on appeal is whether the agency's determination of the prevailing wage was correct in this case. The employer contends that the agency did not properly calculate the prevailing wage for export managers in Michigan, and that the error was arbitrary, capricious or an abuse of discretion. See 5 U.S.C. §706(2)(A)....

The Department of Labor has promulgated regulations describing the calculation of the "prevailing wage" for labor certification. 20 C.F.R. §656.40 (1983). The section applicable to this case provides that the "prevailing wage" shall be:

> The average rate of wages, that is, the rate of wages to be determined, to the extent feasible, by adding the wage paid to workers similarly employed in the area of intended employment and dividing the total by the number of such workers. Since it is not always feasible to determine such an average rate of wages with exact precision, the wage set forth in the application shall be considered as meeting the prevailing wage standard if it is within 5 percent of the average rate of wages....

20 C.F.R. §656.40(a)(2)(i) (1983). In this case the MESC contacted five Michigan employers to determine the salary each paid its export manager.[66] From answers re-

66. The Secretary has delegated to local employment services the task of determining the prevailing wage according to federal standards. 20 C.F.R. §656.21(e) (1983); 20 C.F.R. §656.21(f) (1980).

ceived from these inquiries, the MESC calculated that the average wage of export managers in Michigan was $1,666 per month.

Appellants argue that this calculation was improper because the MESC surveyed employers in industries other than the rubber tire machinery business. They contend that the export managers for the other employers are not "similarly employed" as the regulations require. 20 C.F.R. §656.40(a)(2)(i) (1983). However, we do not believe that the agency acted arbitrarily and capriciously in surveying the other five employers. The agency concluded that jobs with similar functions in other industries were sufficiently comparable for purposes of determining a prevailing wage. Appellants have provided no evidence showing that the other jobs are not comparable.

Appellants rely on cases which are not apposite here. It is true that the prevailing wage calculation may be improper if the agency simply uses the wrong occupational category, see *Reddy, Inc. v. Department of Labor*, 492 F.2d 538, 544–45 (5th Cir.1974) (rate calculated for civil engineer where alien was mechanical engineer), but appellants have not shown that the job category used in this case was improper.[67] Therefore, we conclude that the agency's calculation of the prevailing wage in this case was not arbitrary, capricious or an abuse of discretion.

Finally, appellants contend that they are entitled to labor certification because they substantially complied with the advertising regulations when they recruited at the higher salary level. After the certifying officer issued the Notice of Findings informing the employer that it was not offering the prevailing wage, the employer tried to recruit American workers at the higher wage level. The employer sought and received two extensions of time to complete its second round of advertising. The employer submitted documents to show its compliance with the regulations. However, the certifying officer found that the employer failed to show it had posted the job at the higher salary level inside its own organization, 20 C.F.R. §656.21(b)(10) (1980), that it failed to document the results of its recruitment efforts among American workers, 20 C.F.R. §656.21(b)(15) (1980), and that it failed to show it had posted the job with the local employment service for thirty days, 20 C.F.R. §656.21(g)(1) (1980). The administrative law judge also concluded that the employer failed to comply with (b)(10), (b)(15), and (g)(1).

In *Production Tool, supra*, this court held that the Department of Labor may give the advertising regulations effect by requiring "substantial compliance" before granting labor certification. 688 F.2d at 1170. The employer here argues that its efforts amount to substantial compliance. Appellants have not shown that the agency erred

---

67. Appellants' reliance on two cases involving Montessori school teachers is misplaced. *See Ratnayake v. Mack*, 499 F.2d 1207, 1213–14 (8th Cir.1974); *Montessori Children's House and School, Inc. v. Secretary of Labor*, 443 F.Supp. 599, 608 (N.D. Tex. 1977). In both cases the employers had introduced evidence showing that the jobs of Montessori teachers differed substantially from those of public school teachers. By contrast, appellants in this case have made no attempt to show that the job offered to Yu differs from those surveyed by the MESC. The prevailing wage inquiry should be reasonably specific, but there is no reason to conclude a priori that it is improper to compare similar jobs in other industries.

in finding that appellants did not comply with (b)(10), (b)(15) and (g)(1).[68] Therefore, we need only consider whether appellants are entitled to certification despite these failures.

We find no abuse of discretion in the agency's denial of certification where the employer failed to comply with the internal posting requirement of section 656.21(b)(10), the documentation requirement of section 626.21(b)(15) and the employment service posting requirement of section 656.21(g)(1). The internal posting requirement insures that an employer's current employees—who are already familiar with the employer's products and organization—have an opportunity to apply for the job. The requirements that the employer advertise through the local employment service and document the results of its domestic recruitment efforts provide the agency with a means for monitoring the results of the employer's recruitment efforts. Therefore, we conclude that the Department of Labor did not abuse its discretion by denying labor certification because the employer failed to comply with the advertising regulations.

Notes

1. Under agency rules, the employer cannot delegate the recruiting process to others such as an attorney or another person. And the person for whom the certification is sought cannot participate in the process. 20 C.F.R. §656.10(b)(2). However, this does not mean that the prospective employee could not advise the employer. See *Fragomen Fires Back at Department of Labor*, 85 Interpreter Releases 2349 (2008).

2. In another case involving a challenge by the employer of the Department of Labor's (DOL) denial of a certification, the court affirmed the denial. In the recruitment process, the employer had expected the U.S. workers to personally appear at the interview. The court in *Warmtex Enterprises v. Martin*[69] stated first that the employer must demonstrate a good faith effort at recruitment

> In implementing these requirements, the Board [of Alien Labor Certification Appeals] has held the employer must make adequate inquiry by telephone or otherwise to determine whether United States workers who apply are qualified for the position, ... and that the employer may not reject as unqualified or unavailable United States workers who seem, after adequate inquiry, to be qualified but are unable or unwilling to appear for a personal interview at their own expense ... Failure to make a reasonable effort to determine whether United States applicants are qualified, or insisting upon a personal interview with an apparently qualified United States applicant at the applicant's

---

68. Appellants correctly argue that the agency has the discretionary power to waive some defects in compliance; however, this argument does not establish that the agency abused its discretion when it chose not to waive the defects here.

69. 953 F.2d 1133 (9th Cir. 1992).

expense, reflects a lack of good faith effort to recruit qualified United States workers.[70]

---

1. Business Necessity

As demonstrated in the previous case, the recruitment process involves a determination of whether there are U.S. workers who are qualified for the position for which the certification is being sought. The following case and the article which follows illustrate a related issue, which is the minimum level of experience and qualifications for the particular position and whether the employer could be expected to provide on the job training to bring the prospective employee up to that minimum. Here the employer argues (unconvincingly) that while at a previous stage it might have been able to provide such training, it was no longer able.

Pancho Villa Restaurant, Inc. v. U.S. Dep't of Labor

796 F.2d 596 (2d Cir. 1986)

Before Oakes, Meskill and Newman, Circuit Judges.

Oakes, Circuit Judge.

Conflicting determinations of the United States District Court for the Eastern District of New York relating to applications for alien labor certification filed by Pancho Villa Restaurant, Inc. ("Pancho Villa"), which, not surprisingly, serves Mexican food, are appealed here. Judge Charles P. Sifton, in Docket No. 85-6312 ("Pancho Villa I"), held that the decision of the Secretary of Labor to deny two applications for alien labor certification pursuant to section 212(a)(14) of the Immigration and Nationality Act, 8 U.S.C. §1182(a)(14) (1982), "appears arbitrary and without rational basis." In the second case, Docket No. 85-6348 ("Pancho Villa II"), then District Judge Frank X. Altimari upheld the denial of another such application. We agree with Judge Altimari that the Secretary did not act arbitrarily or capriciously or abuse his discretion in finding that a one-year minimum experience requirement for a Mexican specialty cook was unnecessary and that the restaurant had failed to show that it was unable to train a cook who lacked any experience. Indeed, the restaurant hired and trained the three aliens whose applications are at issue here when they had no experience as Mexican specialty cooks.

In 1983 Pancho Villa filed three applications seeking certification for three alien employees as specialty cooks for Mexican foods such as "Tacos, Enchiladas, Burritos, etc." The applications show that the aliens were paid $250 per week for a forty-hour week. Pancho Villa also informed the Department of Labor ("DOL") that it had employed two cooks and had sales of $337,560 in 1982, while in 1983 it had employed three cooks and had annual sales totalling $488,175.

---

70. 953 F.2d at 1135.

In February 1984 the DOL certifying officer issued a "Notice of Findings" in each case that Pancho Villa had not documented that its requirements for the job opportunity were the minimum necessary for the performance of the job and that it had not hired or it was not feasible for it to hire workers with less training or experience as mandated by 20 C.F.R. § 656.21(b)(6) (1986). In each case the certifying officer found that the alien had no prior experience before his employment and insisted that Pancho Villa document why it was not now feasible to train a United States worker. In response to these Notices of Findings, the restaurant argued that in 1977 when it opened for business in Huntington, Long Island, it had time to train inexperienced cooks, but business had increased to a point where it was no longer feasible to train someone without at least one year of experience. It also resubmitted its 1981/82 and 1982/83 annual sales data, arguing from these figures that it no longer had the time to train inexperienced cooks. In April, 1984, the certifying officer issued final determinations that Pancho Villa had not "adequately document[ed] why it is not feasible for [it] to train a U.S. worker at this time."

These decisions were affirmed by two administrative law judges. In a "Decision and Order" involving one of the aliens in Pancho Villa I, the ALJ found, "Employer has not shown why it can not train a new person with a staff of the three cooks when it was able to do so with a staff of two" and that "employer has not demonstrated that its business would suffer if an inexperienced cook were to join the staff." He made almost identical findings as to the other alien in Pancho Villa I. The ALJ in Pancho Villa II stated,

> If it is assumed that all of the cooks are responsible equally for the preparation and cooking of all the food which is sold by the Employer, then an analysis of the figures presented by the Employer shows that each cook who is currently working for the Employer is responsible for the preparation and cooking of approximately the same amount of food as was his counterpart in 1981.

Subsequently, the restaurant filed complaints in the United States District Court for the Eastern District of New York seeking review of the final decisions of the Secretary based upon the ALJs' conclusions....

By virtue of section 212(a)(14), Congress sought to exclude aliens competing for jobs that American workers could fill. *Ming Wang v. INS*, 602 F.2d 211, 213 (9th Cir.1979); S.Rep. No. 748, 89th Cong., 1st Sess. 15, reprinted in 1965 U.S.Code Cong. & Ad.News 3328, 3333–34. The DOL has adopted regulations requiring an employer to conduct a systematic recruitment of domestic workers. See 20 C.F.R. § 656.21 (1986). Failure to comply with these regulations may result in a denial of the labor certification. See 20 C.F.R. § 656.24(b)(1) (1986). We agree with the United States Court of Appeals for the District of Columbia that the scope of review of a denial of an alien labor certification is limited to a determination under section 706(2)(A) of the Administrative Procedure Act, 5 U.S.C. § 706(2)(A) (1982), as to whether the decision was "'arbitrary, capricious, an abuse of discretion, or otherwise not in accordance with law.'" *Pesikoff v. Secretary of Labor*, 501 F.2d 757, 761 n. 5 (D.C. Cir.) (quoting section 706(2)(A)), cert. denied, 419 U.S. 1038 (1974). In making this determination, we examine only the administrative record. *Doraiswamy v. Secretary of Labor*, 555 F.2d 832, 841–42 (D.C. Cir.1976).

We agree with the Secretary that Judge Sifton erred in finding the ALJ's decision "appear[ed]" to be arbitrary; Pancho Villa simply did not meet its burden of proving its entitlement to an exemption. See Mehta, 574 F.2d at 706. The restaurant's own figures indicate that each cook in 1983 had less work per sales volume than in the previous year. Thus, the employer presented insufficient evidence of a change in circumstances such that it could not train an inexperienced cook with three experienced cooks in 1983. Even if we interpret Judge Sifton's questionable use of the word "appears" to mean "is" arbitrary, we think the Secretary's finding that the employer has not shown that its business would suffer if an inexperienced cook joined the staff was rational and not an abuse of discretion. Judge Sifton also found the Secretary's determination that one year's experience was unnecessary to be "arbitrary and unconvincing." Because all three aliens were hired with no experience and because the employer failed to show that inexperienced cooks could not be trained, the Secretary acted rationally in concluding that one year's experience was not the employer's actual minimum requirement. Judge Sifton in effect impermissibly substituted his judgment for that of the Secretary by making his own factual determinations based upon a reevaluation of the record. Judge Altimari, on the other hand, correctly upheld the ALJ's determination. Appellant's contention that the DOL lacks authority to promulgate regulations pursuant to section 212(a)(14) is wholly without merit.

Actual Minimum Job Requirements in Labor Certifications: Application of Title 20, Section 656.21(b)(6)[71] of the Code of Federal Regulations to Experience or Training Gained with the Employer

Sandra Burgess, 23 San Diego L. Rev. 375 (1986)

Footnotes have been omitted.

Not infrequently a United States employer seeks labor certification for an alien who has worked for the employer previously. In such circumstances, it may be reasonable to require that the amount of experience the alien has gained be included in the application. Labor Department regulations preclude application requirements other than the actual minimum requirements of the employer. In addition, the employer must not have hired workers with less training or experience for a job similar to that in which the labor certification is sought. Departmental interpretation indicates that it is possible to require experience which the alien has gained working for the

---

71. Note: the regulations have been redesignated from 656.21 to 656.17(h) and (i).

employer in a different occupation. Inconsistent application of this interpretation by the Department of Labor adjudicators leaves an employer at peril of losing a labor certification whenever an alien has been previously employed in a position with the petitioning employer even though the position is different than the one for which certification is sought.

Introduction

The Immigration and Nationality Act provides for the exclusion of aliens seeking to enter the United States for the purpose of performing skilled or unskilled labor, unless the Secretary of Labor has granted them certification. In order to obtain a labor certification, the alien's prospective employer must demonstrate that it has attempted to recruit United States workers for the position which it desires the alien to fill. Furthermore, the employer must show that hiring the alien would not adversely affect the wages and working conditions of similarly employed United States workers. The procedure and requirements for this certification are set forth in title 20, section 656 of the Code of Federal Regulations.

* * *

Application of the Regulations

The general rule which accounts for the resolution of numerous cases is that a labor certification will be denied under section 656.21(b)(6) when the alien has been employed in the position for which certification is sought and has gained experience which is required by the job offer while working for the employer in that position. This rule is supported by the explanation in TAG [Technical Assistance Guide] and the language of the regulation itself. The rationale behind this basis for denial is that since the employer was willing to hire the alien without the experience, the experience must not be an actual minimum requirement for performance of the job.

This principle has been applied even though the alien gained the experience while working for the employer abroad. In *In re Speedent USA Corp.*, the employer contended that the alien gained the experience in China and that the Chinese employer was a different entity. The A.L.J. affirmed denial, however, because the names of the American and Chinese companies were similar, and insufficient documentation of their separateness had been provided.

* * *

In a situation in which the alien has on the job experience in the position for which certification is sought, and that experience is required in the application for labor certification, section 656.2(b)(6) requires proof that it is infeasible to hire workers with less training or experience than listed in the application for labor certification. In many cases, where the alien has acquired training and experience while working for the employer, the employer has attempted to show compliance with section 656.21(b)(6) by demonstrating that it is infeasible to hire workers with less training or experience.

Changed Business Conditions

A common approach to establishing infeasibility is through documentation that business conditions have changed since the alien was hired. Although at the time the alien was hired the business entity had been able to train an inexperienced worker on the job, it may no longer be feasible to train an employee because of changed business conditions. This exception was suggested in *In re Gartenhausfurs, Inc.*, where the A.L.J. found it 'highly unrealistic' to interpret the regulations in a way that failed to take change of business conditions over a six year period into consideration. 'Surely that is not the intent of the Regulation.'

In *In re McAliece Paper Co.*, a decrease in business scale justified a finding of infeasibility. The employer was able to show that since hiring the alien, his volume of business and labor force were so reduced as to preclude hiring an applicant in need of extensive training. The A.L.J. found this to be sufficient evidence of infeasibility since the 'employer no longer enjoys the sufficient manpower nor the economic resources to conduct such instruction.' A contrary result, however, was reached in *In re Lancer II, Restaurant Corp*. The A.L.J. held that documentation of a decrease in sales did not demonstrate infeasibility without a showing of the time needed to train, or evidence that the training would interfere with other workers. An increase in business has also justified infeasibility. In *In re Veselka Coffee Shop*, the employer adequately documented that expansion of business precluded hiring an inexperienced person as a cook. The A.L.J. observed that a good cook was indispensable to a successful restaurant and that the greater the pressure, the greater the gamble that an inexperienced cook would destroy the reputation of the restaurant.

In other cases, an increase in business was not sufficient evidence of infeasibility, because the employer either failed to document the business increase or failed to show why the business increase limited training capacity. In *In re Giulio Cesare Restorante Inc.*, increased volume was not sufficient to show infeasibility of training when the job was not that of chief cook. Moreover, in *In re Ace Grinding Co.*, the A.L.J. suggested expansion of business should make it easier to provide training. In *In re Pancho Villa Restaurant*, infeasibility to train due to a dramatic business increase was not substantiated. As a result of the increased sales, the A.L.J. concluded that the employer appeared more prosperous: "Employer has not shown why it cannot train a new person with a staff of three cooks when it was able to do so with a staff of two.... [He saw] no reason why the firing of an inexperienced cook would necessitate reducing the number of experienced cooks...," one of whom was the alien himself. Even when training has been shown to involve additional expenses and a slowing down in production, some ALJ's have found these grounds insufficient to show infeasibility.

These cases suggest that although it is a recognized principle that changed business conditions may constitute infeasibility to hire an inexperienced employee, many labor certifications are denied because the employer has not provided sufficient objective evidence of why the changed conditions limit the ability to train an inexperienced worker on the job.

Note

1. The case and article underscore another important part of the certification process, which is that the non-citizen for which certification is sought must also have the qualifications for the advertised position. However, if in *Pancho Villa*, the employer had been able to make the case for certification at the level of experience that the persons for whom certification had when they first started with the employer, the outcome could have been different.

2. Alternatively, if the workers at *Pancho Villa* had a different employer sponsoring their labor certification, would the arguments made by the DOL have had the same weight?

2. Qualifying "Experience" for Certification

Given what the certification is meant to establish, the following case brings out another point, which is what is "qualifying experience" for the non-citizen for whom certification is being sought? Keep in mind, however, that the case which follows was before employer sanctions which placed an employer at jeopardy for knowingly employing someone without proper work authorization.

Matter of Lam

16 I. & N. Dec. 432 (BIA 1978)

BY: Milhollan, Chairman; Wilson, Maniatis, Appleman, and Maguire, Board Members

This is an appeal from the immigration judge's denial of the relief of adjustment of status in a decision entered on February 3, 1977, in which the immigration judge granted to the respondent the privilege of voluntary departure. The appeal will be sustained.

The record relates to a married male alien, 40 years of age, who is a native and citizen of China. He was admitted to the United States on February 6, 1973, as a nonimmigrant visitor. He was originally found deportable in an earlier decision by the immigration judge on January 12, 1976. The finding of deportability rested on the respondent's admissions. The respondent did not appeal from that decision. He thereafter obtained reopening of the proceedings in order to apply for adjustment of status. This appeal is brought from the immigration judge's subsequent denial of that relief.

The respondent is a specialty cook of Chinese style food. He has been employed as a Chinese cook by the China Shoppe Restaurant in Maryland from May 1976 to the present time. He was previously employed by the Red Blazer Restaurant from January 1976 to April 1976 in New York, by the Horse River Restaurant in Maryland from May 1974 to December 1975, and by the Oriental Garden Restaurant in Virginia from April 1973 to April 1974. The China Shoppe Restaurant filed a labor certification application on behalf of the respondent, which was approved on April 15, 1976. A sixty-preference petition filed by the China Shoppe Restaurant on behalf of the respondent was approved on June 30, 1976.

On the labor certification application the China Shoppe Restaurant specified that two years experience was required for the position offered. All of the qualifying experience shown by the respondent in support of the labor certification was gained in the United States as listed above. At his deportation hearing the respondent testified that his sole experience as a cook prior to coming to the United States consisted of part-time work of about ten hours a week for several months during 1970 (Tr. p. 6). Inasmuch as that experience did not amount to the two years of experience required by the United States employer, the respondent's eligibility for a labor certification must necessarily depend upon the experience he gained while in the United States.

Because the respondent's qualifying employment experience was gained while he was here as a nonimmigrant visitor and later as an overstay, the immigration judge declined to exercise his discretion favorably to the respondent and denied him adjustment of status. The issue posed is whether the fact that qualifying experience for a labor certification was gained by employment which was not authorized under the immigration laws constitutes a factor adverse to the exercise of discretion, when considering an application for adjustment of status.

We have previously considered the general issue in the case of *Matter of Arai*, 13 I. & N. Dec. 494 (BIA 1970). *Arai*, like the present respondent, sought adjustment of status on the basis of an approved labor certification as a specialty cook. In that case, as in this, no finding was made by the immigration judge that the respondent was other than a bona fide visitor when he first arrived in the United States. The immigration judge, however, considered Arai's taking of employment as an adverse factor. We reversed the immigration judge and held that the case presented no adverse factors affecting the respondent's application. We characterized the employment as a potential benefit to the United States inasmuch as there was a shortage of United States workers in his field of employment. The Labor Department, by certifying the application, had so determined.

In the case before us the immigration judge, in declining to exercise discretion favorably, focused on the fact that the unauthorized employment was crucial to eligibility for the labor certification, rather than on the fact that the employment was unauthorized. While the focus is thus somewhat different from Arai's case, the immigration judge's consideration of the employment as an adverse factor is nonetheless inconsistent with the decision in *Matter of Arai*, supra. Inasmuch as the recitation of facts in *Arai* did not specify to the contrary, we must assume that Arai's work experience in the United States was crucial to his labor certification, as was the respondent's. The immigration judge's decision below that approval of a labor certification should be disregarded in the exercise of discretion when the experience was gained in the United States by means of unauthorized employment cannot, therefore, be reconciled with the decision in *Matter of Arai, supra*.

When a labor certification has been granted concerning employment, it has been determined that the employment is not detrimental to the United States labor market. An important concern of our immigration laws is the protection of our domestic economy. Taking unauthorized employment in violation of law may be an adverse discretionary factor. However, this is offset when unauthorized employment is not detrimental, and is in fact of potential benefit to our country, in view of the shortage of United States workers. In this case not only has a labor certification been granted for the employment, but a sixth-preference petition as well.

* * *

F. Issues Involving Labor Certifications

Business Necessity. In determining whether the job offer in the labor certification application has been tailor-made for the foreign worker-beneficiary, the U.S. employer may make the argument that the requirements are dictated by business necessity. According to 20 C.F.R. § 656.21(b)(2)(i), the requirements must "bear a reasonable relationship to the occupation in the context of the employer's business and are essential to perform" the job. Whether there is such a reasonable relationship to the requirements or whether they are "unduly restrictive" will be guided, in part, by the *Dictionary of Occupational Titles* (DOT) and the *Selected Characteristics of Occupations Defined in the Dictionary of Occupational Titles* (Selected Characteristics), which describe the skills, experience and educational requirements for occupations. In essence, compliance with DOT and Selected Characteristics makes a prima facie case.

Since the certification procedure is a way of testing whether there are available and qualified domestic workers, the reasonable job requirements, including those militated by business necessity, may form the basis for rejecting U.S. workers who apply for the advertised position.[72] The analysis of whether there in fact is a business necessity will require the consideration of a variety of factors which may include customer preference[73] or whether the purpose of the hire is to expand the business.[74]

How would one justify a foreign language requirement and how much evidence must the employer present in order to make out a case for business necessity?[75]

Ability to Pay the Prevailing Wage. The labor certification application requires the advertisement of the job at a particular wage, and both *Production Tool* and *Industrial Holographic* explore the meaning of the "prevailing wage." A corollary issue often arises after the certification has been approved and prior to the beneficiary's being accorded lawful permanent residence (which can take a number of years), which is

72. *See Ashbrook-Simon-Hartley v. McLaughlin*, 863 F.2d 410 (5th Cir. 1989); 20 C.F.R. § 656.24(a)(2)(ii).

73. *Matter of Alwya Computer Co.*, 88 INA-218 (BALCA 1989).

74. *Matter of Time Energy Systems, Inc.*, 92-INA-220 (BALCA 1994).

75. *See Matter of Akhtar Rahnama*, 93-INA-27 (BALCA 1994); *Matter of Advanced Digital Corp.*, 90-INA-137 (BALCA 1991).

whether the employer has the ability to pay the wage offered. Legacy INS took the position that the employer must show that she is able to pay the wages at the time the certification is filed.[76] While courts have upheld this power to investigate the ability of the employer to pay the wages offered, the imposition of unrealistic requirements of proof on the employer have been rejected.[77] The problem occurs, in part, because of the prospective nature of the application (when the foreign worker will begin working) and the retrospective interpretation by USCIS (when the certification was filed). The problem is further compounded by the two-step process for permanent residency. The employer must obtain a certification from the Department of Labor, and USCIS does not become involved until the preference petition is filed, which is often years later.[78]

Status of the Employer. A major issue arises when the petitioner and beneficiary of the labor certification are one and the same. While the Department of Labor recognizes corporate identity, if the foreign worker is a major shareholder in a closely-held corporation, she may not be the beneficiary of a labor certification. One appellate court has upheld the certifying officer's denial of a labor certification on grounds that there was no job opportunity clearly open to U.S. workers as there was no true employer-employee relationship.[79] The Department of Labor does not take an absolute position that these applications cannot be certified. Indeed, the issue is presented as a burden of proof problem.[80]

Some of the factors which will be evaluated in determining if the job offer is *bona fide* due to the close relationship between the foreign worker and the sponsoring employer are the following: (1) whether the beneficiary is in a position to control the hiring decision; (2) whether the beneficiary was involved in the founding of the company or is related to the officers; (3) whether the beneficiary has an ownership interest in the enterprise or on its board; (4) the size of the business; and (5) the unique qualifications of the beneficiary which make her so essential that the enterprise could not continue without her.[81]

Special Handling Applications. College and university teachers, aliens of exceptional ability in the arts and sheepherders are treated differently from other labor certification beneficiaries.[82] These applications are denoted as "special handling" primarily because the normal procedures are not required. The central difference with these applications is that the employer need only show that a U.S. worker "as qualified" as the foreign worker could not be found.[83] Notice that the measure for the job qualifications is that

76. *See Matter of Great Wall,* 16 I. & N. Dec. 142 (Reg. Comm. 1977); *Matter of Dial Auto Repair Shop, Inc.,* 19 I. & N. Dec. 481 (Comm. 1986).

77. *Masonry Masters v. Thornburgh,* 875 F.2d 898 (D.C. Cir. 1989).

78. 20 C.F.R. § 656.20(c)(2).

79. *See Hall v. McLaughlin,* 864 F.2d 868 (D.C. Cir. 1989).

80. *See* 20 C.F.R. §§ 656.20(c)(8) and 656.21(b).

81. *See Matter of Modular Container Systems, Inc.*, 89-INA-228 (BALCA 1991); *also see Matter of Paris Bakery Corp.*, 88-INA-337 (BALCA 1990).

82. *See* 20 C.F.R. § 656.21a.

83. *See* Hopper, *Special Handling Labor Certifications for College and Teachers,* 12 IMM. J. 77 (1989).

of the foreign worker, whereas in the normal labor certification, the position as defined in the *DOT* and *Selected Characteristics* determine the necessary qualifications.

With regards to college or university teachers, the application for certification need not be filed until eighteen months after the candidate has been selected, as long as it can be shown that there was a "competitive recruitment process" which should have included a national search. For persons in the performing arts with exceptional ability, the employer must document the person's renown in the field as well as the nature of the work which will be performed in the United States. In the case of sheepherders, special handling is allowed where she has worked as a nonimmigrant sheepherder for at least thirty-three of the preceding thirty-six months.

Schedule A Applications. While many occupations require that the foreigner seeking an immigrant visa first obtain a labor certification, some occupations have been designated by the Secretary as being *prima facie* certifiable. These "pre-certified" positions are referred to as "Schedule A occupations" and do not require a market survey.[84] These applications are filed directly with USCIS for the employment preference petition. The largest groups of persons who fall within Schedule A are nurses, therapists, persons of exceptional ability in the arts and sciences (with the exception of performing artists) and physical therapists. The 1990 Act directed the Secretary of Labor to designate up to ten occupational classifications for testing shortages and surpluses as pre-certified positions.[85] If a shortage is designated, the certification is deemed to have been issued, essentially having the same effect as Schedule A. If there is a surplus, the Secretary may only certify the position upon a showing that the position cannot be filled notwithstanding "extensive recruitment efforts."[86] The 1990 Act authorized this program for a three-year period beginning in October 1991.

Thus far, our discussion has focused on the labor certification application which is filed with the Department of Labor. This is only a small part of the process. There are two procedural routes that can be taken in employment immigration cases: (1) if the labor certification is approved, an application for a preference petition is filed with USCIS; or (2) if the foreign worker is eligible for Schedule A, the labor certification and preference application may be submitted directly to USCIS. In any event, upon approval, the beneficiary may apply for lawful permanent residence.[87]

Professionals. The INA defines the professions as "included but not limited to architects, engineers, lawyers, physicians, surgeons, and teachers in elementary or secondary schools, colleges, academies, or seminaries."[88] USCIS considers the attainment of a

84. This section of the statute was poorly drafted. Depending on how one reads the new law, it either requires or waives the labor certification requirement for persons in the teaching profession or who have exceptional ability in the sciences. *See* 8 U.S.C. § 1182(a)(5)(ii), Sec. 212(a)(5)(ii).

85. *See* Sec. 122, Immigration Act of 1990, Pub. L. No. 101-649, 104 Stat. 4978 (1990).

86. Sec. 122(a)(2)(B), Immigration Act of 1990, Pub. L. No. 101-649, 104 Stat. 4978 (1990).

87. *See Madany v. Smith,* at 642 for a discussion of the relationship between the preference petition and labor certification.

88. *See* 8 U.S.C. § 1101(a)(32), Sec. 101(a)(32).

baccalaureate degree to be the minimum requirement for entry into the occupation.[89] This rigid approach in determining professional workers has been rejected by the courts in favor of a standard which takes into account the nature of the work and the experience required for the position.[90]

For the first time, the INA, in the 1990 amendments attempted to define "managerial" and "executive."[91] *Managerial* is loosely defined as a person with the power (1) to manage an organization, function or component of an organization; (2) to supervise and control the work of other supervisory personnel or to supervise an essential function of the organization; (3) to hire and fire; and (4) to exercise discretion in the day-to-day operations. *Executive* is defined as a person with the power (1) to direct the management or a function or component of the organization; (2) to set goals and policies of the organization; and (3) to exercise a wide range of discretion in the decision-making process while receiving only general supervision.

G. Procedural Flow Chart

1. Labor Certification Chart

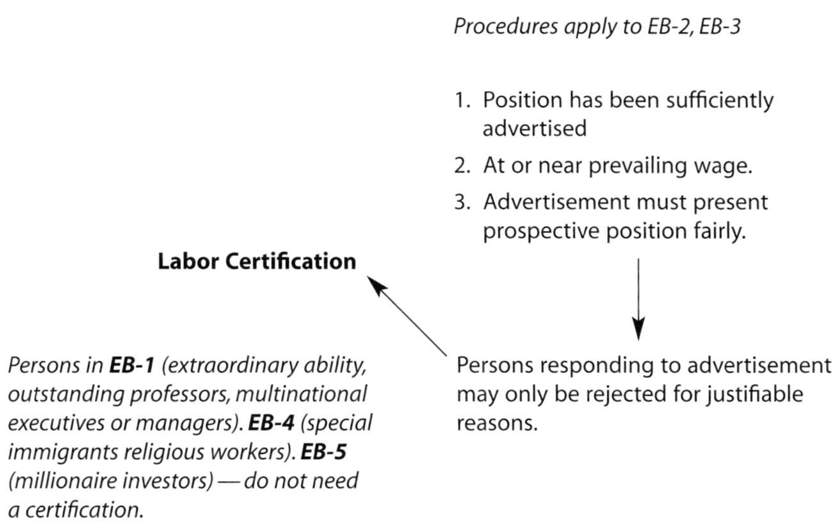

89. *Matter of Asuncion*, 11 I. & N. Dec. 660 (Reg. Comm. 1966); *Matter of Caron Industries, Inc.*, 19 I. & N. Dec. 791 (Comm. 1988).

90. *See, e.g., Shanti, Inc. v. Reno*, 36 F. Supp. 2d 1151 (D. Minn. 1999); *Hong Kong T.V. Video Program, Inc. Ilchert*, 685 F. Supp. 712, 716 (N.D. Cal. 1988); *Augat v. Tovar*, 719 F. Supp. 1158 (N.D. Mass. 1989).

91. *See* 8 U.S.C. § 1101(a)(44), Sec. 101(a)(44).

Chapter 9

Permanent Residency for Persons Already in the United States

Introduction

It has been said that obtaining lawful permanent resident status is one of the most important steps in a foreigner's efforts to remain permanently in this country. While lawful permanent residence may not be the goal of most persons arriving at our shores, it is nevertheless the objective of anyone who wishes to remain on a long term basis. As will be seen in the chapter on citizenship, permanent resident status is a condition precedent to U.S. citizenship.[1]

In Chapters 3 and 4, we discussed how persons who attempt to gain admission or who USCIS considers undeserving of the right to remain in the United States may be subject to removal. In Chapter 6, we explored the avenue of gaining temporary admission as a nonimmigrant. In Chapters 7 and 8, we explored the immigrant selection system and the process of immigrating to the United States. As was noted, a person must first qualify under the family or employment based preferences as a prerequisite to immigrating to the country. Once the person meets the requirements for a preference category, she may then apply for an immigrant visa. Armed with the visa, she may travel to the United States, and upon inspection and admission, she becomes a lawful permanent resident. In this chapter we will explore the special procedures for non-citizens who wish to obtain permanent resident status without ever having to leave the country, and proceeding abroad to apply for an immigrant visa.

As a general rule the immigration laws require that those who seek an immigration benefit must do so by first presenting their application at a United States Consulate overseas and then gain admission through the inspection process. The immigration laws limits those who can qualify for lawful permanent resident status outside of this overseas processing scheme.[2] The fact that a person might not qualify for this special procedure does not mean that they will not be eligible for an immigrant visa.

---

1. A person applying for permanent residence from *outside* the United States is an applicant for an immigrant visa, which upon obtaining the visa and passing inspection converts her to a lawful permanent resident (LPR) status. The immigrant preference system is discussed in Chapter 7 and 8.

2. Indeed, in recent years, with the perception that unauthorized immigration was on the rise, Congress has progressively limited access to permanent residency from within the country, as it has imposed bars to visa overstays and illegal entrants.

There are many people in the United States who find it preferable to become permanent residents without having to travel overseas and go through the immigrant visa procedures. In this chapter, we will explore the avenues to permanent residency available to those who are present in the United States. The major forms of immigration relief which result in the conferral of permanent residency without the necessity of having to travel abroad are adjustment of status, some forms of "cancellation of removal," amnesty and a series of special benefits enacted by Congress for narrowly defined groups of beneficiaries. We will explore all of them in this chapter with the exception of "cancellation of removal" which will be discussed in Chapter 10 when we cover relief from removal and waivers.

The different means by which an individual may obtain permanent residency from within the United States are unique in that they have their own peculiar origins and have changed over the years with the moods of Congress. Because of their unique requirements, it is important to remember that even if the person is unable to qualify for a particular form of relief, it does not mean that she will be forever barred from obtaining permanent residency through the immigrant visa process.[3] What these forms of relief share in common is that they confer lawful permanent residency on the beneficiary. In some cases, they may be sought by the individual or asserted as a defense in removal proceedings; in other cases, they may only be obtained by applying to USCIS. Obtaining permanent residency outside of the immigrant visa process has the advantage of providing a legal recourse from inside the United States. An applicant who proceeds through the immigrant visa process may become separated from loved ones and have limited access to counsel, whereas the person seeking permanent residency from within the United States may be able to renew her application in removal proceedings or seek other immigration remedies, all without leaving the country.[4]

A. Adjustment of Status

Perhaps the most widely used procedure for obtaining permanent residency from within the United States is "adjustment of status." Adjustment is a term of art, not to be confused with "change of status" which was explored in the context of nonimmigrant visas (see Chapter 6). Adjustment of status refers to the process by which a person otherwise eligible for an immigrant visa may obtain permanent residency without departing the country. Like most immigration benefits, adjustment of status

---

3. If, however, the reason for the person's disqualification is a ground of inadmissibility for which there is no available waiver, an immigrant visa may also be an unlikely prospect.

4. 8 C.F.R. § 1245.2(a)(1); *Matovski v. Gonzales*, 492 F.3d 722 (6th Cir. 2007). Despite the language in the regulation precluding adjustment for arriving "aliens," they may seek adjustment of status. *Clifton v. Holder*. 598 F.3d 486 (8th Cir. 2010).

is discretionary, requiring that the applicant establish why the benefit should be granted and discretion favorably exercised on her behalf. In all of these cases, the exercise of discretion amounts to a balancing of equities, requiring the fact-finder to weigh the social and humane considerations against the adverse factors presented in the application.

The statutory provisions which govern adjustment are found at 8 U.S.C. §§ 1255 and 1255a, Sections 245 and 245A. A condition precedent to qualifying for adjustment of status is proving the requisite familial relationship with a permanent resident or U.S. citizen,[5] a job offer in the country which would not displace a qualified, willing and able U.S. worker, or some other basis for obtaining an immigrant visa. Even after the person establishes the requisite familial relationship or job offer, she has only met the first step in a rather difficult process. She must also establish that:

1. She was "inspected and admitted or paroled into the United States."[6]
2. There is an immigrant visa number "immediately available" to her at the time the application for adjustment of status is filed.[7]
3. She was lawfully in status at the time that she filed the application, except in cases where the person seeking adjustment is an immediate relative of a U.S. citizen,[8] a battered spouses or child or certain special immigrants.
4. She is otherwise eligible for admission: the person must not be inadmissible, or if she is, she must be eligible for a waiver.[9]
5. The person, other than those applying as immediate relatives of U.S. citizens, has not engaged in unauthorized employment after January 1, 1977.

After meeting these requirements, the applicant must also establish that they merit the favorable exercise of this "discretionary relief." Factors considered include are the person's family ties in the United States, hardship in traveling abroad, length of residence in the country, prior violations of immigration law and preconceived intent.[10] In the following cases and notes we will explore each of the requirements noted above which constitute the elements of adjustment.

5. The familial relationship must meet the requirements that were discussed in the section on family-based immigrant visas. *See* Chapter 7.

6. 8 U.S.C. § 1255(a), Sec. 245(a).

7. 8 U.S.C. § 1255(a)(2), Sec. 245(a)(2).

8. Prior to enactment of the Immigration Reform and Control Act of 1986, Pub. L. No. 99-603, 100 Stat. 3359 (1986), an applicant could adjust her status even when her permission to stay in the United States had expired. The requirement of maintaining one's status does not apply if the person is out of status "through no fault of her own" or for technical reasons.

9. *Id.* Waivers of grounds of inadmissibility and deportability are discussed in Chapter 10.

10. Preconceived intent to immigrate when entering the United States as a nonimmigrant is a basis for denying an application for adjustment. *Jain v. INS*, 612 F.2d 683 (2d Cir. 1979), *cert. denied*, 446 U.S. 937 (1980). However, preconceived intent alone is not enough to deny an immediate relative petition. *Matter of Cavazos*, 17 I. & N. Dec. 215 (BIA 1980).

1. Procedural Flowcharts

What follows below is a flow chart presenting the procedures used to determine whether an applicant for adjustment of status should be granted.

a. Chart 1—Affirmative Adjustment Application before USCIS

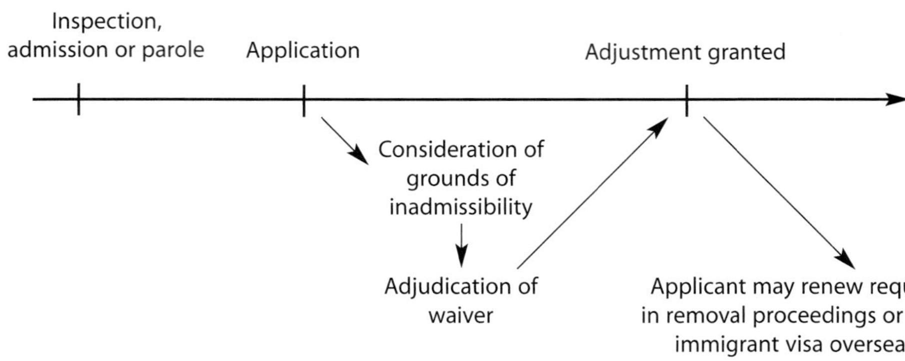

The first chart presents the affirmative application for adjustment of status which is made before the USCIS. To qualify the applicant must establish that they were admitted or paroled and that they can overcome the grounds of inadmissibility. Upon favorable adjudication the person is granted permanent resident status.

b. Chart 2—Adjustment Application as Defense from Removal

Once removal proceedings are instituted by Immigration and Customs Enforcement (ICE) by its service of a Notice to Appear, the applicant may submit an adjustment applicant as a defense to the removal. This application is submitted for consideration by the immigration judge. The immigration judge applies the same legal standards considered by USCIS, but her determination is *de novo*.

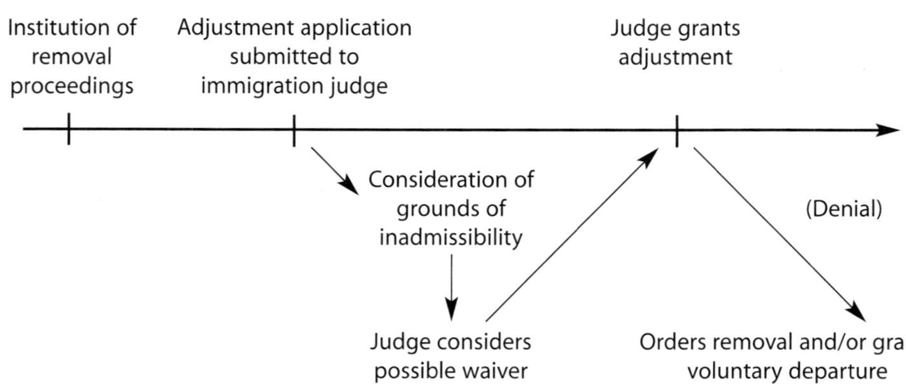

2. Qualifying for Adjustment

a. "[I]nspected and [A]dmitted ..."

8 U.S.C. § 1255, Sec. 245

(a) *The status of an alien who was inspected and admitted or paroled into the United States may be adjusted by the Attorney General, in his discretion* and under such regulations as he may prescribe, to that of an alien lawfully admitted for permanent residence if (1) the alien makes an application for such adjustment, (2) the alien is eligible to receive an immigrant visa and is admissible to the United States for permanent residence, and (3) an immigrant visa is immediately available to him at the time his application is filed.

(b) Upon the approval of an application for adjustment made under subsection (a), the Attorney General shall record the alien's lawful admission for permanent residence as of the date the order of the Attorney General approving the application for the adjustment of status is made, and the Secretary of State shall reduce by one the number of the preference visas authorized to be issued under sections 202 and 203 within the class to which the alien is chargeable for the fiscal year then current (emphasis supplied).

Matter of Areguillin

17 I. & N. Dec. 308 (BIA 1980)

BY: Milhollan, Chairman; Maniatis, Appleman, Maguire, and Farb, Board Members

In a decision dated January 25, 1978, an immigration judge found the respondent deportable as charged on the basis of her concessions at the hearing, denied her application for adjustment of status pursuant to section 245 of the Immigration and Nationality Act, 8 U.S.C. 1255, but granted her the privilege of voluntary departure in lieu of deportation. The respondent has appealed from the denial of relief under section 245. The appeal will be sustained and the record remanded for further proceedings before the immigration judge.

The respondent, a 45-year-old native and citizen of Mexico, claims eligibility for adjustment on the basis of her status as the beneficiary of an approved immediate relative visa petition which had been filed on her behalf by her United States citizen spouse. The immigration judge found that the respondent had not been inspected and admitted at the time of her last entry into the United States and therefore has not satisfied the statutory requirements for the relief sought under section 245 of the Act.

The respondent offered the following account with respect to the entry in issue. The respondent testified that she crossed the Mexican-United States border in a car with two couples and another woman. She had no travel or entry documents in her possession at the time. The respondent stated that the immigration officer at the port of entry looked inside the car, asked the driver a question,[2] then permitted the car

2. The respondent stated that she "think[s]" the driver was asked where he was from; at several points in the proceedings the respondent, who testified through a Spanish interpreter, indicated that

and its occupants to proceed into the United States. She testified that she personally was asked no questions by the immigration officer; she apparently volunteered no information.

The immigration judge concluded as a matter of law that the manner of entry described by the respondent does not establish an inspection and admission for purposes of section 245 inasmuch as the respondent was in fact inadmissible for lack of documentation at the time she presented herself for inspection. The immigration judge sought to distinguish the well-established line of cases which holds that an alien who physically presents himself for questioning is "inspected" even though he volunteers no information and is asked no questions by the immigration authorities. See *Matter of F__*, 1 I & N Dec. 90 (BIA 1941; A.G.1941); *Matter of F__*, 1 I & N Dec. 343 (BIA 1942); *Matter of G__*, 3 I & N Dec. 136 (BIA 1948).[3] He noted that the burden was on the Government in the foregoing cases to show, as part of its burden of establishing deportability, that inspection had not occurred while in the present case, the respondent bears the burden of proving she had been inspected as an element of establishing her eligibility for adjustment.

We agree with the respondent that the immigration judge's distinction is without a difference in determining what constitutes "inspection and admission." We find no basis for concluding that Congress, in first imposing the requirement that an alien be "inspected and admitted" or paroled into the United States as a condition for establishing eligibility for relief under section 245, intended to depart from the long-settled construction of that term in favor of the interpretation adopted by the immigration judge, i.e., that only an alien who has been "lawfully or legally" admitted to the United States may qualify for adjustment of status as one who has been inspected and admitted.[5] Regardless of which party bears the burden of establishing the presence or absence of an inspection and admission, that which must be proved remains unchanged. The rule that an alien has not entered without inspection when he presented himself for inspection and made no knowing false claim to citizenship applies in determining whether an alien has satisfied the inspection and admission requirement of section 245 of the Act.

---

she did not comprehend the verbal exchange between the immigration inspector and the driver since they spoke English.

3. That general rule notwithstanding, an alien who gains admission to the United States upon a knowing false claim to citizenship has not been "inspected and admitted." See *Reid v. United States*, 420 U.S. 619 (1975); *Matter of F__*, 9 I & N Dec. 54 (R.C.1960); *Matter of S__*, 9 I & N Dec. 599 (BIA 1962); *Matter of Woo*, 11 I & N Dec. 706 (BIA 1966); *Matter of Wong*, 12 I & N Dec. 733 (BIA 1968).

5. In 1952, Congress provided for adjustment of status, under prescribed conditions, to "an alien who was lawfully admitted to the United States as a bona fide nonimmigrant...." Section 245 was subsequently amended in 1958 and in 1960 to eliminate that restrictive terminology. The immigration judge's interpretation would in effect reenact the superseded law. Moreover, under the rationale set forth by the immigration judge, any alien found deportable under section 241(a)(1) of the Act, 8 U.S.C. 1251(a)(1), for having been excludable at the time of entry presumably would likewise be precluded from establishing statutory eligibility for section 245 relief for failure to satisfy the "inspection and admission" requirement.

We are satisfied that if the facts are found to be as claimed by the respondent, she was inspected and admitted within the contemplation of the law. The respondent, however, bears the burden of proving that she did, in fact, present herself for inspection. Inasmuch as the immigration judge found the respondent ineligible as a matter of law for adjustment under section 245, he made no finding with respect to the credibility or sufficiency of the evidence offered, which at present consists of the respondent's uncorroborated testimony. We shall accordingly remand the record to the immigration judge for further proceedings, during which the respondent should be accorded an opportunity to offer any additional evidence she may be able to produce in support of her assertions, and for the entry of a new decision. In the event the decision on remand is again adverse to the respondent, we direct that the case be certified back to the Board for review.

* * *

Order: The appeal is sustained and the record is remanded to the immigration judge for further proceedings consistent with the foregoing opinion and the entry of a new decision.

Notes

1. The BIA has expanded further on the meaning of "inspection and admitted" to include where a person is able to establish "procedural regularity" in the manner of their entry even where they might have otherwise been found to be inadmissible as long as the person did not make a false claim of citizenship.[11]

2. As was seen in *Areguillin*, adjustment of status may be sought in removal proceedings. A person who is not yet in removal proceedings may also seek adjustment. This application is sometimes referred to as an affirmative application for adjustment and is perhaps the most common. Indeed, most adjustment cases are presented to the USCIS where the person is seeking the benefit affirmatively as opposed to defensively as would be the case when the person is in removal proceedings. Where a person has sought the benefit affirmatively and the application has been denied by USCIS, they may renew the application if removal proceedings are instituted. Alternatively, they may seek an immigrant visa through the normal overseas visa process.

3. In addition to being in status the applicant must have continuously maintained a lawful status. Exempted from this requirement are person who are seeking adjustment as "immediate relatives."[12]

4. **Jurisdiction of the Immigration Judge.** As was noted in the previous two chapters, the immigration judge has limited jurisdiction. The judge does not have authority

---

11. *Matter of Quilantan*, 25 I. & N. Dec. 285, 292–94 (BIA 2010) (inquiry of citizenship was only made of the driver of the car and not of the applicant who was a passenger which was sufficient to establish inspection and admission).

12. 8 U.S.C. § 1255(c)(2), Sec. 245(c)(2).

to adjudicate preference petitions. This means that if a preference application has either not been granted or has been denied, the immigration judge is not able to grant the adjustment application. The judge however may within limits continue the case to allow the Service to adjudicate the pending preference petition.

3. Unauthorized Employment Restriction on Adjustment

8 U.S.C. § 1255, Sec. 245

> (c) Subsection (a) shall not be applicable to (1) an alien crewman; (2) an alien (other than an immediate relative as defined in section 201(b) or a special immigrant described in section 101(a)(27)(H), (I), (J), or (K)) *who hereafter continues in or accepts unauthorized employment prior to filing an application for adjustment of status or who is in unlawful immigration status on the date of filing the application for adjustment of status* or who has failed (other than through no fault of his own or for technical reasons) to maintain continuously a lawful status since entry into the United States; (3) any alien admitted in transit without visa under section 212(d)(4)(C); (4) an alien (other than an immediate relative as defined in section 201(b)) who was admitted as a nonimmigrant visitor without a visa under section 212(l) or section 217; (5) an alien who was admitted as a nonimmigrant described in section 101(a)(15)(S); (6) an alien who is deportable under section 237(a)(4)(B)(B); (7) any alien who seeks adjustment of status to that of an immigrant under section 203(b) and is not in a lawful nonimmigrant status; or (8) any alien who was employed while the alien was an unauthorized alien, as defined in section 274A(h)(3), or who has otherwise violated the terms of a nonimmigrant visa (emphasis supplied).

For many years unauthorized employment has been regarded as a magnet for undocumented immigrants. In 1976 Congress amended the Immigration and Nationality Act to prevent those who had engaged in unauthorized employment from being able to adjust their status to that of a lawful permanent resident. However, this bar to adjustment does not apply to those who are seeking adjustment as immediate relatives.[13] What is and is not employment is an important question, as there are many consequences of unauthorized employment, one of which is possible ineligibility for adjustment, another of which could be a violation of the conditions of ones nonimmigrant status making the person subject to removal.

---

13. As noted previously, immediate relatives are the spouses, unmarried minor children of U.S. citizens and parents of U.S. citizen where the petitioning son or daughter is over the age of 21. *See* discussion in Chapter 7.

Matter of Hall*

18 I. & N. Dec. 203 (BIA 1982)

BY: Milhollan, Chairman; Maniatis, Maguire, Morris, and Vacca, Board Members

At a deportation hearing conducted on December 19, 1978, an immigration judge found the respondent deportable as an overstayed nonimmigrant pursuant to section 241(a)(2) of the Immigration and Nationality Act, 8 U.S.C. 1251(a)(2), and statutorily ineligible for adjustment of status under section 245 of the Act, 8 U.S.C. 1255, by reason of the unauthorized employment bar of section 245(c)(2), 8 U.S.C. 1255(c)(2), but granted him the privilege of voluntary departure in lieu of deportation. The respondent concedes deportability but contests the denial of section 245 relief.

At the conclusion of the deportation hearing, as the immigration judge was stating his decision, the respondent through counsel made an oral motion to reopen the proceedings to permit further development of the record with respect to his eligibility for adjustment of status. The immigration judge declared the hearing closed and refused to entertain the respondent's motion to reopen.[1] Subsequent to the hearing, on December 26, 1978, the respondent submitted a formal, written motion to reopen which the immigration judge denied in a decision dated February 14, 1979. The respondent appealed from that decision and oral argument in the case was heard by the Board on May 1, 1980.

In seeking to reopen deportation proceedings, it is incumbent upon the alien to make a prima facie showing of eligibility for the relief sought. *Matter of Rodriguez*, 17 I & N. Dec. 105 (BIA 1979). The respondent has not sustained his burden. Upon careful consideration of the arguments advanced by the respondent since the hearing, we are satisfied that section 245(c)(2) operates to bar adjustment in his case. As no purpose would be served by reopening, the respondent's appeal from the denial of his motion to reopen will be dismissed.

The record reflects that the respondent, a 36-year-old single male, a native and citizen of Guyana, entered the United States at New York in May 1976 upon presentation of a nonimmigrant visitor visa. He came to the United States for the purpose of attending a rally sponsored by the Unification Church at Yankee Stadium. In July 1976, the respondent departed New York for Puerto Rico to "work ... as a missionary" for the Unification Church (Tr. p. 9), a pursuit in which he is apparently still engaged.

---

* Some footnotes have been omitted.

1. Prior to the deportation hearing, the District Director had denied the respondent's application for adjustment of status on a ground other than that cited by the immigration judge, i.e., section 212(a)(15) of the Act, 8 U.S.C. 1182(a)(15). The respondent contends that the Service did not raise the unauthorized employment bar of section 245(c)(2) as a possible basis for denial when he renewed his application at the hearing and that he was therefore denied an opportunity to show that the bar did not apply in his case. Despite this objection, the immigration judge ruled that the respondent had had adequate opportunity to demonstrate eligibility for the relief sought.

According to the respondent, his duties as a missionary consist of holding and attending seminars, witnessing, visiting houses and teaching people on the street the word of God, distributing literature, helping people financially under Church auspices, and visiting churches. Those duties also include selling toys, jewelry and trinkets as a means of raising funds for the Church. The respondent estimates that he spends from one-third to one-half of his time fund-raising.

The respondent testified that the proceeds of his fund-raising efforts are turned over to the Director of the Church in Puerto Rico with whom he shares a rented house. In return, the respondent receives full support from the Church which includes housing, food, clothing, medical expenses, transportation, entertainment, toiletries, and other personal expenses. In addition, the respondent is given approximately $25 in cash each month for "walking around" money, enough to ensure that he has $10 in pocket money at all times.

The unauthorized employment bar of section 245(c)(2), added by the 1976 Amendments to the Act, renders ineligible for adjustment of status aliens (other than immediate relatives) who, after the effective date of the bar, continued in or accepted authorized employment prior to filing an adjustment application. The respondent continued his activities on behalf of the Unification Church, which he does not contend were authorized by the Service, after the January 1, 1977, effective date of the bar. His adjustment application, based upon his status as the beneficiary of an approved second-preference visa petition submitted by his lawful permanent resident mother, was not filed until May 1977. The dispositive question, then, is whether those activities constitute "employment" within the contemplation of section 245(c)(2). The immigration judge answered that question in the affirmative, concluding that the respondent was employed as a fund-raiser for the Church.

The respondent contends that the activities in question may not properly be characterized as employment so as to bar him from the benefits of section 245. He describes his position with the Church as an unpaid volunteer, not an employee, arguing that he labors for no salary. He submits that his service as a missionary is not the type of pursuit Congress contemplated in enacting section 245(c)(2). Finally, the respondent argues that his fund-raising efforts and his teaching, proselytizing, and other religious duties are integral, indivisible parts of his missionary work and that it is not within the province of the Immigration and Naturalization Service or the immigration judge to determine what constitutes missionary work for any particular church.

The respondent's contention that he is an unpaid volunteer in the service of the Church is not persuasive. He clearly receives compensation in return for his efforts on behalf of the Church. By his own account, he is provided the wherewithal to cover both necessary and nonessential expenses, such as entertainment and recreation. He is, in addition, given discretionary funds as needed. The respondent's relationship with the Church in effect guarantees him a standard of living similar to that of many moderate-income wage earners. The fact that he receives no fixed salary or remuneration in an amount proportional to his success as a fund-raiser is, in our view, immaterial.

The respondent insists that his work on behalf of the Unification Church is not the sort of undertaking Congress intended to discourage with the imposition of the unauthorized employment bar inasmuch as his activities have no adverse impact on the United States labor force. As the respondent acknowledges, however, the legislative history of section 245(c)(2) provides little guidance as to the specific end or ends sought to be served by the bar. Congress' sole statement of purpose, contained in the House Judiciary Committee report to the 1976 Amendments,[3] reads as follows:

> ... [under the proposed legislation,] aliens who are not defined as immediate relatives and who accept unauthorized employment prior to filing their adjustment application would be ineligible for adjustment of status. *The Committee believes that this provision would deter many nonimmigrants from violating the conditions of their admission by obtaining unauthorized employment.* Similar provisions were included in legislation which passed by the House of Representatives during the 92d and 93rd Congresses (emphasis added).

Concern over the impact of a nonimmigrant's unauthorized employment upon the American labor force may well have been a motivating factor underlying the enactment of section 245(c)(2). However, Congress did not so indicate, either indirectly in the legislative history of the proposal ultimately enacted or directly in the express language of the statute.[4] Absent a clear expression of legislative intent, we are unwilling to conclude that detriment to American labor was Congress' sole or, for that matter, primary concern.

Manifest in the report language quoted above is Congress' substantial interest—apart from its arguable interest in protecting the domestic labor market—in the enforcement of our immigration laws with respect to nonimmigrant aliens within our borders. Cf. *Matter of Yazdani*, 17 I & N. Dec. 626 (BIA 1981).[5] Correlatively, by penalizing nonimmigrants who work in violation of the terms of their admission. Congress may well have sought to discourage aliens admitted to the United States for a temporary purpose from acquiring a source of funds to support a prolonged unlawful stay in this country.

In any event, we are not persuaded that the respondent's activities as a fund-raiser are without adverse impact on the United States labor market. Unlike the purely ministerial duties carried on by the respondent, we consider the raising of funds a secular

---

3. H.R.Rep. No. 94-1553, 94th Cong.2d Sess. (September 15, 1976), reprinted in 1976 U.S. Code Cong. & Ad. News 6073, 6084.

4. Congress could have, but did not exempt from the bar, nonimmigrants engaged in employment determined to be of benefit to the United States. *Cf. Matter of Raol*, 16 I & N. Dec. 466 (BIA 1978). Our reluctance to read a limitation into the statute not placed there by Congress is bolstered by the fact that an alien within the ambit of section 245(c)(2) is deprived of no ultimate right under the immigration laws since he remains free to apply to a United States consul abroad for an immigrant visa.

5. Pursuant to those immigration laws, a nonimmigrant is forbidden to work in this country unless he has been accorded a nonimmigrant classification which authorizes employment or has been granted specific work authorization from the Service; a nonimmigrant who is permitted to work may engage only in such employment as has been authorized.

function which could successfully be performed by persons or business enterprises outside the Church. We note, moreover, that the respondent does not merely solicit donations in the name of the Unification Church but engages in the sale of goods, an entrepreneurial undertaking which places the Church in competition with other sellers of such goods.

Under the circumstances here presented, were the institution or organization for which the respondent performs his fund-raising services not a church, we would have no difficulty in finding the section 245(c)(2) bar applicable. We find no basis in the language or history of the statute for carving out an exception to the bar in the case of a church, at least with respect to the secular activities of its adherents.

We reject the respondent's suggestion that the Government, by isolating his fund-raising activities, improperly seeks to dictate to the Unification Church the permissible scope of its missionaries' duties. Determining the status or the duties of an individual within a religious organization is one thing; determining whether that individual qualifies for status or benefits under our immigration laws is another. Authority over the latter determination lies not with the Unification Church or any other ecclesiastical body but with the secular authorities of the United States. See *Matter of Rhee*, 16 I & N. Dec. 607 (BIA 1978).

In sum, we conclude that the respondent, through his fundraising activities, engaged in employment without Service permission in contravention of section 245(c)(2) and consequently is not eligible to adjust his status in this country to that of a lawful permanent resident. His motion to reopen the proceedings to permit consideration of his application for adjustment of status under section 245 was, therefore, properly denied. The appeal will be dismissed.

Notes

1. Section 245(c) bars adjustment for persons who have engaged in unauthorized employment after January 1, 1977, and before the adjustment of application was filed. This means that a person who engages in unauthorized employment following the submission of the adjustment application would not be barred.

2. USCIS has taken the position that, except in limited categories of adjustment applicants, any unauthorized employment, even if it only began after the filing of the adjustment application, will bar the benefit.[14] However the bar to adjustment on account of unauthorized employment does not apply to persons seeking adjustment based on employment-based visas or as religious workers, where the total unauthorized work was for 180 days or less.[15] This special exemption for employment-based immigrants and religious workers also allows them to have been out of status "or oth-

---

14. *See* 8 C.F.R. § 245.1(b)(4). For a more extensive discussion of this bar to adjustment, see Charles Gordon, Stanley Mailman, Stephen Yale-Loehr & Ronald Wada, Immigration Law & Procedure § 51.04(b) (rev. ed. 2017).

15. *See* 8 U.S.C. § 1255(k), Sec. 245(k).

erwise violated the terms and conditions" of their status as long as it was not for more than 180 days.[16]

3. **Lawful Status.** This provision also requires that, except for immediate relatives and certain special immigrants, the applicant must be in lawful status *at the time* the application for adjustment was filed.[17] This provision was enacted at the time that the 1986 immigration amendments creating employer sanctions were instituted.

---

4. "Preconceived Intent" and Adjustment

Matter of Cavazos*

17 I. & N. Dec. 215 (BIA 1980)

BY: Milhollan, Chairman; Maniatis, Appleman, Maguire, and Farb, Board Members

This case is before us on appeal from the December 21, 1977, decision of an immigration judge, rendered in reopened deportation proceedings, which denied the respondent's application for adjustment of status pursuant to section 245 of the Immigration and Nationality Act, 8 U.S.C. 1255. The appeal will be sustained.

The respondent, a 26-year-old native and citizen of Mexico, entered the United States as a nonimmigrant visitor for pleasure on July 1, 1976, upon presentation of a border crossing card, Form I-186, issued to him in 1972. On that same date, he married his United States citizen spouse whom he had known for a considerable period of time prior to their marriage; a child was born in the United States in 1974 as a result of that relationship.

At the initial deportation hearing, the respondent conceded deportability as a nonimmigrant who remained longer than permitted and was granted the privilege of voluntary departure in lieu of deportation. Prior to the expiration of the authorized period of voluntary departure, the respondent filed the present motion to reopen for consideration of his application for section 245 relief predicated upon his status as the beneficiary of an approved immediate relative visa petition. The immigration judge granted the respondent's motion to reopen the deportation proceedings, found him statutorily eligible for adjustment at the reopened hearing that ensued, but denied him the relief sought in the exercise of discretion on the ground that he had entered the United States in July of 1976 with a preconceived intent to remain permanently.

We find that the record, while providing some support for the immigration judge's findings, is ambiguous at best with respect to the respondent's actual intentions at the time of his entry. We need not dwell on that question, however, in light of our conclusion that the adverse factor of preconceived intent, if it existed, has been overcome by the equities presented.

---

16. *See* 8 U.S.C. § 1255(k)(2)(C), Sec. 245(k)(2)(C).

17. 8 C.F.R. § 245.1(d)(1).

* Footnotes have been omitted.

We note with approval present Immigration and Naturalization Service policy, as reflected in Service Operations Instruction 245.3(b), regarding the discretionary grant or denial of an adjustment application. Operations Instruction 245.3(b) provides that notwithstanding evidence establishing an intent on the part of a nonimmigrant to circumvent the normal visa process, i.e., a preconceived intent to remain permanently at the time of entry as a nonimmigrant, an adjustment application should not be denied in the exercise of discretion where substantial equities are present in the case. Under that Instruction, substantial equities are considered to exist if the facts are such that the alien would be granted voluntary departure until he is invited to appear at a United States consulate to apply for an immigrant visa. The Code of Federal Regulations, 8 C.F.R. 242.5(a)(2)(vi)(A) and 245.5(a)(3), authorizes the District Director in his discretion, to grant voluntary departure to an immediate relative of a United States citizen, prior to the commencement of his deportation hearing, until such time as the United States consul abroad is ready to issue an immigrant visa.

The Service's internal Operations Instruction 245.3(b) binds neither the immigration judge nor the Board; moreover, under the express terms of the regulation which gives effect to the Instruction, whether an alien may benefit from the Instruction as one who would be granted extended voluntary departure is a discretionary determination to be made by the District Director prior to the commencement of the hearing. We believe, however, that the policy manifest in the Instruction, i.e., to favor immediate relatives seeking a grant of adjustment of status by essentially negating preconceived intent as an adverse factor in meritorious cases, may appropriately be adopted by the immigration judge and the Board in exercising discretion on applications for relief under section 245.

The finding of preconceived intent was the only negative factor cited by the immigration judge in denying the respondent's adjustment application and no additional adverse matters are apparent in the record. A significant equity is presented by the respondent's United States citizen wife and child. We conclude that a grant of adjustment of status is warranted in this case and will accordingly sustain the appeal and remand the record to the immigration judge for further processing of the application for adjustment of status filed by the respondent and for the entry of an order not inconsistent with this opinion. In light of our holding, we need not reach the alternative arguments advanced by the respondent on appeal.

Notes

1. Generally, being deportable does not in and of itself bar one from adjustment of status as long as all of the statutory requirements were met at the time the application was submitted. This means that if visa numbers were available and the situation has changed due to a "retrogression" in visa availability, the application is not barred.[18]

18. *See Matter of Rainford*, 20 I. & N. Dec. 598 (BIA 1992); *Malilia v. Holder*, 632 F.3d 598 (9th Cir. 2011).

2. Unlike the immigrant visa, an adjustment application is "discretionary" meaning that the applicant must merit the benefit.[19] However, in the absence of adverse factors, the application is generally granted.[20] One of those adverse factors could be an applicant's preconceived intent to immigrate by entering under a nonimmigrant visa. In the above case, the Board reasoned that the close family ties with his U.S. citizen spouse was a countervailing factor. In making a discretionary determination, factors which should be considered are family ties in the U.S., the hardship of traveling abroad, length of residence in the U.S., preconceived intent to immigrate, and previous immigration history.[21]

3. A person who seeks adjustment of status based upon marriage will not receive immediate lawful permanent residency. Instead, she will first receive conditional residency and have the opportunity to file for lawful permanent residency two years later if the marital relationship continues.

---

5. Marriage while in "Removal" Proceedings

As was noted in our discussion of family-based petitions (Chapter 7), the Immigration Marriage Fraud Amendments (IMFA) restricted immigration benefits, including adjustment of status, to persons who marry while they are in removal proceedings. The IMFA was amended in 1990 as follows: (1) where the applicant can establish by "clear and convincing evidence" satisfactory to USCIS that the marriage was entered into "in good faith," she will not be precluded from adjustment, because she was married after the commencement of removal proceedings; or (2) where the beneficiary (spouse or child) was the victim of cruelty caused by the U.S. citizen or lawful permanent resident spouse, the fact that the marriage no longer exists will not preclude the person from adjustment of status.[22] The statute has general language allowing for a discretionary hardship waiver for the beneficiary spouse who has entered into a bona fide marriage and can show that extreme hardship would result from the denial of the permanent residency petition. In addition, the statute provides that an applicant will receive conditional residence for two years and later permanent residence if the benefit being sought is on account of her marriage.[23] This conditional residence also applies to the children of the primary beneficiary. Congress' creation of a conditional residence status was without precedence in immigration law. In the past, persons would move from a nonimmigrant status to full permanent residency without

---

19. An immigrant visa cannot be denied in the exercise of discretion, it may only be denied based on ineligibility or an inadmissibility ground which cannot be cured by a waiver. *See* Charles Gordon, Stanley Mailman, Stephen Yale-Loehr & Ronald Wada, Immigration Law & Procedure §51.05[1] (rev. ed. 2017).

20. *Matter of Arai*, 13 I. & N. Dec. 494 (1970).

21. *Mamoka v. INS*, 43 F.3d 184 (5th Cir. 1995); *Jain v. INS*, 612 F.2d 683 (2d Cir. 1980).

22. *See* Section 702, of the Immigration Act of 1990, Pub. L. No. 101-649, 104 Stat. 4978 [amending 8 U.S.C. §1255(e), Sec. 245(e)]; 8 U.S.C. §1186(c)(4)(C), Sec. 216(c)(4)(C).

23. *See* 8 U.S.C. §1186a, Sec. 216.

passing through this intermediate step. As will be seen in our later discussion, this temporary or conditional status was also created for persons unlawfully present in the United States who receive "legalization."

Matter of Enriquez*

19 I. & N. Dec. 554 (BIA 1988)

BY: Milhollan, Chairman; Dunne, Morris, Vacca, and Heilman, Board Members

In a decision dated February 13, 1986, an immigration judge found the respondent deportable as charged and granted him the privilege of voluntary departure on or before August 1, 1986, in lieu of deportation to the Philippines. The respondent waived his right to appeal when the decision was rendered. On September 21, 1987, the respondent filed a motion to reopen deportation proceedings for the purpose of affording him an opportunity to apply for adjustment of status under section 245(a) of the Immigration and Nationality Act, 8 U.S.C. § 1255(a) (1982). In a decision dated October 8, 1987, the immigration judge denied the respondent's motion. The respondent has appealed. The appeal will be dismissed.

The respondent is a 44-year-old native and citizen of the Philippines who entered the United States on September 24, 1983, as a nonimmigrant visitor, with permission to remain in the United States until March 24, 1984. On September 10, 1985, an Order to Show Cause and Notice of Hearing (Form I-221) was issued, which alleges that the respondent remained in the United States beyond March 24, 1984, without permission and, therefore, that he is deportable under section 241(a)(2) of the Act, 8 U.S.C. § 1251(a)(2) (1982), on the ground that he has remained in the United States for a longer time than permitted. The respondent appeared before the immigration judge and conceded deportability on the basis of the charge in the Order to Show Cause. His deportability is not an issue in his appeal to this Board.

On July 21, 1986, the district director extended the time period for voluntary departure to September 1, 1986. The respondent remained in the United States instead of departing voluntarily. On March 15, 1987, he married a United States citizen in the State of California. On the basis of that marriage, he filed the motion that is presently before us on appeal. The immigration judge denied the motion on October 8, 1987, and the respondent was subsequently ordered to report for deportation on October 19, 1987. Three days before the date on which he was scheduled to be deported, he filed an appeal from the immigration judge's decision.

The immigration judge denied the respondent's motion on the ground that he is precluded from obtaining adjustment of status by the provisions of sections 245(e)(1) and (2) of the Act, 8 U.S.C. § 1255(e)(1) and (2) (Supp. IV 1986). These provisions were added to section 245 of the Act by section 5(a) of the Immigration Marriage

---

* Footnote has been omitted.

Fraud Amendments of 1986, Pub. L. No. 99-639, 100 Stat. 3537. The sections read as follows:

> (e) (1) An alien who is seeking to receive an immigrant visa on the basis of a marriage which was entered into during the period described in paragraph (2) may not have the alien's status adjusted under subsection (a).
>
> (2) The period described in this paragraph is the period during which administrative or judicial proceedings are pending regarding the alien's right to enter or remain in the United States.

We note further that section 5(a) of the Immigration Marriage Fraud Amendments of 1986 also added the provisions of section 204(h) of the Act, 8 U.S.C. § 1154(h) (Supp. IV 1986), which read as follows:

> Notwithstanding subsection (a), a petition may not be approved to grant an alien immediate relative status or preference status by reason of a marriage which was entered into during the period described in section 245(e)(2), until the alien has resided outside the United States for a 2-year period beginning after the date of the marriage.

If these provisions are applicable to the respondent, he is not eligible for adjustment of status under section 245(a) of the Act. *Matter of Egbunine*, Interim Decision 3034 (BIA 1987).

The respondent has contended on appeal that those provisions to not apply to his situation. We do not agree.

Although we applied the sections at issue in this case in *Matter of Egbunie, supra*, we did not decide in that case when administrative proceedings have been concluded.

The administrative proceedings in this case commenced with the issuance and service of the Order to Show Cause. *Matter of Ramirez-Sanchez*, 17 I&N Dec. 503 (BIA 1980). As of March 2, 1987, however, proceedings are commenced by filing the Order to Show Cause at the Office of the Immigration Judge. 8 C.F.R. § 3.14(a) (1987). The immigration judge's subsequent deportation 'order' became administratively final on February 13, 1986, when the respondent waived his right to appeal. *Matter of Lok*, 18 I&N Dec. 101 (BIA 1981). The deportation 'proceedings,' however, were still pending when the respondent married a United States citizen on March 15, 1987, because the proceedings had not been processed to a final conclusion at that point by the respondent's departure. *Matter of Chamizo*, 13 I&N Dec. 435 (BIA 1969). We note that this interpretation of 'the period during which administrative or judicial proceedings are pending' furthers the objective of the Immigration Marriage Fraud Amendments of 1986, which is to ensure that immigration benefits are not obtained through marriage fraud. The reason for this concern is that aliens who either cannot qualify for immigration to the United States or who, though qualified, are not willing to wait until an immigration visa becomes available, frequently find it expedient to engage in a fraudulent marriage to sidestep immigration law. H.R. Rep. No. 906, 99th Cong., 2d Sess. 6, reprinted in 1987 U.S. Code Cong. & Ad. News 5978. The contrary view of this issue would allow aliens to frustrate that objective by delaying their marriages. Moreover, if we did not interpret 'pending' to include aliens who have had deportation proceedings and then violated voluntary departure orders, such aliens would be rewarded for refusing to comply with voluntary departure orders. Also, they would be in a better position than aliens who have appealed the decisions in their cases to this Board. We conclude, therefore, that the respondent is not eligible for adjustment of status under section 245(a) of the Act.

Note

As was noted in our discussion on fraudulent marriages in Chapter 7 and above, USCIS has been concerned about "fraudulent" marriages entered into with the purpose of helping intending immigrants remain in the United States. When Congress enacted the reform legislation in 1986, it also enacted the Immigration Marriage Fraud Amendments of 1986 (IMFA).[24] One section of IMFA modified 8 U.S.C. § 1255(e), Sec. 245(e), by restricting adjustment of status of persons who marry *while* they are in removal proceedings, and the 1990 Act attempted to ameliorate the consequences of a marriage entered into during the pendency of removal proceedings.

Consider 8 U.S.C. § 1255(e), Sec. 245(e), as amended in 1990. Is this statute constitutional? How would you challenge the statute? What problems do you think will continue to plague persons in removal proceedings because of this bar to adjustment?[25]

6. Adjustment Problem Exercise

The following fact situation and questions should serve as a useful vehicle for discussing the interrelationship between a person's proper admission to the United States in a nonimmigrant status and her eventual attainment of lawful permanent residence.

In August (year -3), Smith went to the United States embassy in country A to apply for a student visa. Her sole means of *support* was her Uncle Ted, who owned an auto repair shop on the outskirts of city's capital. Smith was interviewed by the United States vice-consul and was asked whether she was married. Smith told the vice-consul that she was married but did not have proof of the marriage, because there had only been a tribal ceremony. This statement was not true, as she was not married to anyone.

Smith was issued a nonimmigrant student (F-1) visa by the consular office in Country A. She traveled to the United States and was inspected and admitted as a student pursuant to her visa. At the time of her admission, Smith was allowed to remain in the United States for the *"duration of her status."* Smith attended ABC University, where she studied

---

24. Pub. L. No. 99-639, 100 Stat. 3537

25. For an excellent exploration of the constitutional implications of IMFA, see Joe Tucker, *Assimilation to the United States: A Study of the Adjustment of Status and the Immigration Marriage Fraud Statutes,* 7 Yale L. & Pol'y Rev. 20, 82–100 (1989): *Manwani v. U.S. DOJ,* 736 F. Supp. 1367 (W.D.N.C. 1990) (holding the provisions unconstitutional); *Almario v. Attorney General,* 872 F.2d 147 (6th Cir. 1989) (upholding the constitutionality of the provisions).

accounting. During the time that Smith was in school, she was an excellent student. She dedicated all of her time to her studies, as she was receiving full financial support from her Uncle Ted in Country A. In August (year -1), Smith received news from her family that her uncle had died as a result of a massive heart attack. She also learned that she would not be receiving any money for some time to support her in school. Apparently, even though Smith was the sole heir of her Uncle Ted's estate, it would take a long time before she would be able to receive any money from the sizable estate.

After hearing the bad news, Smith applied to her school for permission to take on part-time employment while she continued her studies. She was informed by the foreign student advisor's office that they were not sure what to do and that they would be checking with USCIS on the application. After waiting for eight months for her work permit (March, year -0), a frustrated Smith went to the local USCIS office, where she was told that someone was looking into the problem and that she should "cool her jets." Smith ran out of money in April (year -0) and took on a part-time job off campus as a night guard. USCIS contacted Smith in June (year -0) by mail and requested that she provide them with a copy of her uncle's death certificate. Smith wrote home, received the certificate in August (year -0) and submitted the paper to both her foreign student advisor's office and USCIS. In September (year -0), in a routine check of Smith's employer's records, USCIS discovered that Smith and five other people were working without proper documentation. Smith and the five other people were arrested, served with OSCs (orders to show cause) for deportation and scheduled for hearings before an immigration judge. This all occurred notwithstanding Smith's protestations about her earlier attempts to properly obtain employment authorization.

Questions

1. If you were the arresting immigration officer in this case, how would you justify the issuance of the Notice to Appear (NTA)? What allegations would you set forth in the Notice?

2. If you were the USCIS trial attorney, what would be your arguments and what facts would you need to establish at the removal hearing?

3. If you were representing Smith, what would you advise her and what would you argue before the immigration judge?

4. If you were the immigration judge, what would be your ruling on the question of whether Smith had properly maintained her nonimmigrant status?

5. Did Smith follow the correct procedure for obtaining employment authorization?

6. Assume that when you interviewed Smith, she informed you that she has known a wonderful person for at least one year and that they have been planning to get married for some time and had planned on doing so next month. What would you advise Smith about what she should do at this time?

7. Did Smith's representations about her marital status to the U.S. vice-consul when she applied for her student visa jeopardize any future applications that might be filed with USCIS?

8. Why would the vice-consul ask Smith if she was married?

9. Would USCIS be justified in having Smith prove that she had not been married in her home country before adjudicating any application for lawful permanent residence?

10. Does Smith have a reasonable likelihood of obtaining lawful permanent residence in the future if she marries her friend? What additional information would you need to have before answering this question?

B. Additional Provisions Allowing for Adjustment of Status

1. Section 245(i) Adjustment

Until the enactment of amendments to the INA in 1994,[26] persons who violated the terms of their status or entered the country without status were precluded from adjustment, even if they were seeking permanent residence based upon an immediate relative petition. While the unauthorized employment bar did not apply to immediate relatives, the requirement of a legal admission or inspection was essential. The reasoning behind this bar was that adjustment should only be available for persons who had some kind of status "to adjust."

In an appropriations bill in 1994, Congress created a new provision that allowed those who had entered without inspection, worked without authorization or who otherwise violated the terms of their admission to avoid immigrant visa processing by paying what was in essence a $1,000 penalty per applicant, with the exception of minor children under the age of 17.[27] The Department of State found the program acceptable, because immigrant visa processing was a burden on consular officers and USCIS received significant additional money from the fees paid by adjustment applicants. From a bureaucratic standpoint, this program was efficient, and from the immigrant's perspective, it was generally less onerous and cheaper than a return trip to the U.S. Consul in her native country. The program, known as 245(i) adjustment, sunset on January 15, 1998, but remains available to persons who had filed preference petitions or labor certifications prior to that date. As part of an amendment to the Legal Immigration Family Equity Act,[28] Congress extended the availability of Section 245(i) relief to persons who could establish preference classifications by April 30, 2001. Thus, adjustment under 245(i) is available to a wide range of persons who would otherwise be ineligible for adjustment under section 245, including persons who entered without inspection, crewmen, stowaways, visa waiver entrants and persons who came to the country in transit without visas. Persons ineligible for this

26. Pub. L. No. 103-317, 108 Stat. 1765.

27. *See* Sec. 506(b), Departments of Commerce, Justice, and State, the Judiciary, and Related Appropriations Act, 1995, Pub. L. No. 103-317, 106 Stat. 1765 (1994).

28. Pub. L. No. 106-554, § 1102, 114 Stat. 2763, 2763A (2000).

special adjustment were J visa holders subject to the two-year foreign residency requirement but cannot qualify for a waiver,[29] persons who entered as fiancés but did not marry or persons seeking adjustment under the Chinese Student Protection Act of 1992.[30] An application for 245(i) adjustment may be submitted to USCIS or to an immigration judge in the course of a removal hearing, though such a petition may not necessarily stop the proceeding.

Though there have been continuing efforts to reinstate the program, its current unavailability presents problems for many who entered the country when relief was available under 245(i). By entering without inspection, these persons accrued "unlawful presence," which subjects them to the three- or ten-year bars of inadmissibility.[31]

2. Registry

In 1986, Congress enacted amendments to the immigration laws, which allowed millions of undocumented persons to legalize their status. The amnesty, or "legalization" program,[32] was accomplished through amendments to the adjustment of status provisions of the 1952 Act. Amnesty is very similar to the longstanding immigration benefit known as "registry," which from time to time has been used to legalize the immigration status of those with long-term residency in the country.[33] Registry allows undocumented persons who have resided continuously in the United States since January 1, 1972, to apply to have their status adjusted to that of lawful permanent residents.[34] The essential requirements for qualifying for registry are continuous residency, good moral character and not being inadmissible on grounds of criminal conviction(s), narcotics or subversive grounds or being otherwise ineligible for U.S. citizenship.[35]

3. Amnesty under the 1986 Act

One of the cornerstones of the Immigration Reform and Control Act of 1986 was the amnesty program. Amnesty and registry are interrelated and are policy tools which have been used in the past. The ostensible purpose of an amnesty program is to provide a legal mechanism to regularize the status of persons who in all likelihood will remain in the country. Proponents of amnesty believe that it will make the newly

---

29. *See* 8 U.S.C. § 1182(e), Sec. 212(e). For a discussion of the 212(e) waiver, see Chapter 10.

30. Pub. L. No. 102-404, 106 Stat. 1969 (1992); *Chan v. Reno*, 113 F.3d 1068 (9th Cir. 1997).

31. 8 U.S.C. § 1182(a)(9)(B), Sec. 212(a)(9)(B).

32. The Amnesty Program is described in greater detail later in this chapter.

33. The registry provisions are found at 8 U.S.C. § 1259, Sec. 249. Like all adjustment applications, a registry application is subject to a favorable exercise of discretion by the USCIS district director.

34. In addition to granting amnesty, the 1986 amendments changed the registry date from June 30, 1948, to January 1, 1972.

35. The original purpose of registry was to allow persons who had lived in the United States for a long time to obtain residency and citizenship. For this reason, if a person is ineligible for citizenship, she will be precluded from registry. As was seen earlier, certain grounds of ineligibility may be waived by the Attorney General.

legalized persons more productive members of society and prevent potential abuse often suffered by the undocumented who are forced to live underground.

The 1986 amnesty was instituted along with the creation of an employer sanctions program intended to be a disincentive to continued unauthorized immigration.[36] The 1986 amnesty program granted residency to large numbers of undocumented persons who had been in the United States for many years. The legalization program had two components: one for non-agricultural workers and the other for agricultural workers. Both of these programs provided for a two-tiered resident status for its beneficiaries and included cut-off dates for eligibility as well as requirements for residency. The primary difference between the plans was the cut-off date as to when the applicant had to have entered the United States in order to qualify. The cut-off date was more generous in the agricultural worker program, where agricultural workers must have worked for the equivalent of ninety days between May 1, 1985 and May 1, 1986.

Pursuant to the non-agricultural amnesty provisions, a qualified applicant received temporary or conditional status, which could be converted in two or more years to full lawful permanent residency. In order to obtain *temporary resident* status, the applicant must have resided unlawfully in the United States since January 1, 1982, and continuously to the present date. The application must be filed within a twelve-month period (beginning no later than six months after enactment of the amendments). The rules governing the applications for non-agricultural workers were as follows:

1. Persons upon whom a show cause order had been issued during the first eleven months of the amnesty must have applied for temporary resident status no later than thirty days after the implementation of rules regarding the application procedure or within thirty days from the issuance of the order to show cause.

2. In establishing physical residence since January 1, 1982, "brief, casual, and innocent absences" did not break the continuity of residence.[37]

3. Exchange visitors subject to the foreign residency requirement and ineligible for its waiver were not eligible for the amnesty.[38]

4. The applicant must also have established that she was otherwise admissible as an immigrant and had not been convicted of a felony or three or more misdemeanors committed in the United States. All grounds of inadmissibility were either disregarded or waived, except the following:

a. 8 U.S.C. § 1182(a)(14), (20), (21), (25), and (32) are inapplicable.[39]

---

36. Employer sanctions were discussed in Chapter 4.

37. *See* amendment to 8 U.S.C. § 1255a(a)(3)(B), Sec. 245A.

38. For further explanation of the foreign residency requirement, see 8 U.S.C. § 1101(a)(15)(J), Sec. 101(a)(15)(j); Chapter 6.

39. These provisions deal with the inadmissibility grounds barring most immigrants without labor certification, prohibiting the admission of illiterates and prohibiting the admission of foreign medical school graduates.

b. All grounds except 8 U.S.C. § 1182 (a)(9), (10), (15), (23), (27)–(29), and (33) are waivable.[40]

5. Temporary residents were not permitted to petition for their family members to join them in the United States, although they were allowed to travel abroad for "brief, casual trips as reflect an intention" to become a lawful permanent resident.[41]

In order to qualify for *permanent residence,* the applicant must first have been granted temporary residence and have remained lawfully in that status for at least one year. The requirements were as follows:

1. The alien *must* have applied during the one-year period beginning with the nineteenth month after she was granted temporary residence.

2. She must have demonstrated that she continuously resided in the country since obtaining temporary residence status. A break in the continuity of residence was to have been treated the same as it would if the person were applying for temporary residence.

3. The applicant must have continued to be admissible as an immigrant under the same provisions as when she applied for temporary residence.

4. The applicant must have demonstrated that she had certain "basic citizenship skills" described as a minimal understanding of ordinary English and knowledge of the history and government of the United States as required of applicants for naturalization. Alternatively, the applicant had to be "satisfactorily" pursuing a course of study to satisfy the language and history requirement. Meeting this requirement satisfies the language and civic knowledge requirement which would normally be required of applicants for United States citizenship.[42]

A person lost her temporary resident status if it appeared to the Attorney General that she was not entitled to it in the first place, she had committed an act rendering her inadmissible or she had not filed an application for permanent residence by the end of the forty-third month after the date upon which she obtained temporary residence as required under the bill.

The amnesty provisions for farmworkers varied from those for non-farmworkers. Farmworkers were permitted to make their applications before U.S. Consuls abroad. The only possible options for an otherwise qualified non-farmworker applicant who had left the country for a short period was to request parole (or enter the country surreptitiously) and then apply for amnesty.[43] The residency application was to have

40. These provisions deal with persons who are inadmissible because they are likely to become public charges, have been convicted of drug offenses (except for possession of small amounts of marihuana) are Communists, national security risks or Nazis.

41. It appears that the trips contemplated under the statute are those involving family obligations such as death or illness of a close relative or for another type of family need. *See* amendments to 8 U.S.C. § 1255a(b)(3)(A), Sec. 245A(b)(3)(A).

42. Persons 65 years or older may have the language and history requirements waived.

43. Absences caused by a person's having been on "advance parole" are specifically treated as not constituting a break in the period of continuous residence. Section 201, amending, 8 U.S.C.

been filed with the Attorney General or with a "designated entity"[44] if the applicant consented to the forwarding of the application to the Attorney General.

Residence and physical presence had to be "established" through documents and "independent corroboration," yet it was not clear from the legislation what specific documentation was required. The amendments clearly evidenced a preference for "employment-related documentation" whenever possible. Whatever the level of proof that was required of the applicant, it appeared from the language of the statute that Congress wished to leave the decision to the discretion of legacy INS adjudicators. This documentation provision had to be viewed in light of the section requiring the person to establish residency and employment by a "preponderance of the evidence" test. It appears only reasonable, given the tremendous benefit being granted to the farm worker for such a short period of residency, that a more rigorous test would be required.

a. Amnesty for Agricultural Workers

Agricultural workers who met the following requirements were eligible to become "alien[s] lawfully admitted for temporary residence."

1. The person must have applied within a period of eighteen months, beginning seven months after the enactment of the statute.

2. The person must have been able to show that she had worked for at least ninety days during the twelve-month period between May 1, 1985 and May 1, 1986.

3. She must have been otherwise admissible as an immigrant. (This provision was the same as that for other persons applying under the amnesty provisions.)

Following the granting of temporary residence, the Attorney General accorded "lawful permanent resident" status at the following times:

> Group 1, consisting of the first 350,000 applicants who had established eligibility, became lawful permanent residents one year after the date upon which they became "lawful temporary residents."
>
> Group 2, consisting of the remainder of persons qualified to become lawful permanent residents, became lawful permanent residents one year after the end of the application period for temporary status.

In addition, a person's status as a temporary resident was to be terminated upon a determination that she had become removable. The temporary resident was per-

---

§ 1254a(g)(2) (B)(ii), Sec. 245A(g)(2)(B) (ii). Advance parole is parole issued to a person prior to her departure from the United States, authorizing her return in the same status.

44. The statute provided for voluntary organizations to assist the government in processing applications under both the agricultural and non-agricultural workers' programs. The designated agency was not authorized to adjudicate the application but to act as a screener.

In order to make the amnesty program work, it was very important that the applicant believed that the adjudication system was fair. Given the great distrust of legacy INS, the voluntary agencies (organizations such as those involved in refugee resettlement) played a critical role in the legalization process.

mitted to travel abroad and was granted employment authorization in the form of a document issued by legacy INS.

The person applying for the farm labor benefit had the burden of establishing eligibility by a "preponderance of the evidence" test which was met by showing employment records. The applicant was also able to establish eligibility by producing sufficient evidence of the extent of the employment as a matter of just and reasonable inference. In these cases, the burden shifted to the Attorney General to negate the reasonableness of the inference.

There were no numerical limitations on the number of persons who could become permanent residents under the Act, excepting those described above. Moreover, most of the grounds for inadmissibility were inapplicable and others were waived.[45]

An anomaly was created by the amnesty provisions of the IRCA. The spouse and children of these legalized persons were not eligible for legalization unless they could show that they had entered the United States prior to January 1, 1982, or had worked for the requisite period on a farm before May 1, 1986. Since many family members could not meet these criteria, which would have resulted in family separation, Congress enacted family unity provisions in the 1990 Act, providing some family members with protection from removal and employment authorization.[46] In addition, the 1990 Act provided the spouse and minor children of legalized persons with the possibility of obtaining permanent residence outside of the traditional statutory scheme. In the fiscal years of 1992 through 1994, 55,000 immigrant visas were made available to the spouse and children of legalized persons under both amnesty programs.[47] The family unity provisions did not enable otherwise unqualified persons to adjust their status but instead allowed them to stay in the United States until they could have their immigrant visa petitions processed.[48]

While advocates for immigration reform have long encouraged additional amnesty programs, the election of President Trump in 2016 may diminish the prospects for such a program.

---

45. The applicability of the inadmissibility provisions were the same as those relating to the "general" amnesty. The primary difference was that 8 U.S.C. § 1182(a)(4), Sec. 212(a)(4) (public charge provision) was to be interpreted liberally by legacy INS, where the applicant's employment history evidenced self-support.

46. *See* Sec. 301, Immigration Act of 1990, Pub. L. No. 101-649, 104 Stat. 4978. The protected group includes those who are the spouses or unmarried children of legalized persons under the legalization program. Persons who have been convicted of a felony or three or more misdemeanors, who participated in the persecution of others, who presented a threat to the security of the United States or who had been convicted of a particularly serious crime constituting a danger to the community were not eligible for this benefit. Sec. 301(e), Immigration Act of 1990, Pub. L. No. 101-649, 104 Stat. 4978 (1990).

47. These visas were to be reduced by the number of visas exceeding 239,000 issued to immediate relatives and aliens born to lawfully admitted aliens, calculated as of the prior fiscal year. *See* Sec. 112(a)(1), Immigration Act of 1990, Pub. L. No. 101-649, 104 Stat. 4978.

48. Persons in this category are referred to as "transition immigrants" (Chapter 7).

4. The Chinese Student Protection Act

Following the massacre at Tiananmen Square in Beijing in October 1992, the President signed into law the Chinese Student Protection Act (CSPA).[49] The special legislation enabled Chinese nationals in the U.S. to more easily adjust their status to lawful permanent residency. It provided special procedures for Chinese nationals who had been described in an earlier Executive Order who had resided in the U.S. continuously since its signing on April 11, 1990.[50] These people were allowed to file for adjustment of status as employment-based third preference skilled workers irrespective of the availability of visa numbers or other normally disqualifying factors applied to most adjustment applicants.[51] The Act required the filing of the adjustment application for these people between July 1, 1993, and June 30, 1994.

5. Cuban Refugee Adjustment Act

As was discussed previously in the history of asylum protection preceding the enactment of the Refugee Act of 1980, persons fleeing persecution were traditionally admitted under parole in response to a humanitarian crisis and subsequently granted permanent residency through special adjustment statutes. Such was the pattern with nationals from countries such as Hungary and Indochina, who were paroled into the United States.[52] These adjustment statutes required that the applicant had entered the country within a specific time period and could show that she was a person of good moral character. The one notable exception to this pattern is in the case of Cuban refugees, who can apply for adjustment of status one year after they have been inspected, admitted or paroled into the country.[53] The benefits for Cuban nationals are so broad that they need only be admitted or paroled into the country and could have entered under any type of visa.[54] The Cuban Refugee Adjustment Act will be valid until such time as the President of the United States determines that a democratically elected government is in power in Cuba.[55]

---

49. Pub. L. No. 102-404, 106 Stat. 1969 (1992).

50. Policy Implementation With Respect to Nationals of the People's Republic of China, Exec. Order No. 12,711, 55 Fed. Reg. 13,897 (1990). The Act permitted brief, casual and innocent absences and were not in the Peoples Republic of China for more than 90 days between April 11, 1990 and October 9, 1992.

51. For example, ineligibility for lapse in status, unauthorized employment, and most grounds of inadmissibility were either inapplicable or could be waived. However, the Act was not interpreted as allowing for adjustment where the applicant had entered the country without being inspected. *See Chang v. Reno*, 113 F.3d 1068, 1074 (9th Cir. 1997) (rejecting plaintiff's argument that the amendments to 245(i) adjustment should be applied to them as CSPA applicants).

52. *See* Indochinese Refugee Adjustment Act, Pub. L. No. 95-145, 91 Stat. 1223 (1977); Hungarian Refugee Adjustment Act, Pub. L. No. 85-559, 72 Stat. 419 (1958).

53. Cuban Refugee Adjustment Act of 1966, Pub. L. No. 89-732, 80 Stat. 1161 (1966).

54. Presumably, the only exception would be if the person entered the United States and was never inspected by CBP.

55. *See* Section 606, The Illegal Immigration Reform and Immigrant Responsibility Act, Pub. L. No. 104-208, 110 Stat. 3009 (1996)

6. Nicaraguans, Cubans, Guatemalans, Salvadorans and Eastern Europeans (NACARA)

In 1997, Congress enacted the Nicaraguan Adjustment and Central American Relief Act (NACARA), which was designed to grant permanent resident status to large numbers of people from Nicaragua, Cuba, Guatemala, El Salvador and Eastern Europe. The primary beneficiaries of the legislation were Nicaraguans who came to the country during the war between the Sandinista government of Nicaragua and the Contras. The second beneficiaries were Eastern Europeans and certain Cubans who came to the United States but could not qualify under the Cuban Refugee Adjustment, because they had entered the country illegally without inspection. The final group benefitting under this legislation were Guatemalans and Salvadorans who were beneficiaries of the "ABC" class action litigation against legacy INS and Department of State over the handling of their asylum claims during the civil wars in their countries.[56] Whether or not a person could qualify for adjustment of status depended on of the following factors:

- Nicaraguans and Cubans physically present in the United States since December 1, 1995 may be adjusted if they apply before April 1, 2000. Applicants must show only that they were here, even if they had been ordered deported and never left. They must also show that they were not absent during this time for more than an aggregate period of 180 days since December 1, 1995.
- Salvadorans or Guatemalans who were members of the ABC class action or who filed asylum applications on or before April 1, 1990 may be considered for permanent residency under "cancellation of removal" upon the showing that: (1) they have been in the United States for at least seven years and (2) their removal from the country would cause them or their United States citizen or LPR spouse, parent or children extreme hardship. (Under proposed regulations issued by legacy INS, hardship was presumed for class members.[57]) The benefits of this protection extended to the person's spouse and children, even if they do not qualify independently. Also, the person must not have been convicted of an aggravated felony as defined in the statute.[58]
- Eastern Europeans or persons who were nationals of the former Soviet Union, Albania, Bulgaria, the former Czechoslovakia, former East Germany, Estonia,

56. *See American Baptist Churches v. Meese*, 712 F. Supp. 756 (N.D. Ca. 1989); *American Baptist Churches v. Thornburgh*, 760 F. Supp. 796 (N.D. Ca. 1991). The plaintiffs in ABC alleged that the asylum claims of Salvadorans and Guatemalans were being adjudicated in a biased manner. As the lawsuit was entering its discovery phase, the government agreed to settle. Pursuant to the settlement, legacy INS agreed to re-adjudicate asylum applications filed by the class members under new rules which professionalized the asylum officer corp. However, before the asylum claims were ever adjudicated, Congress enacted the IIRAIRA, which eliminated many forms of immigration relief to the class members and resulted in the need for further legislative action.

57. *See* Suspension of Deportation and Special Rule Cancellation of Removal for Certain Nationals of Guatemala, El Salvador, and Former Soviet Bloc Countries, 64 Fed. Reg. 27,856 (1999).

58. *See* 8 U.S.C. § 1101(a)(43), Sec. 101(a)(43).

Hungary, Latvia, Poland, Romania, Yugoslavia or any part of the former state of Yugoslavia may avail themselves of the same "cancellation of removal" described above for El Salvadorans and Guatemalans if they entered the United States on or before December 31, 1990 and filed for asylum before January 1, 1992.

7. Haitian Relief and Adjustment Act

Due in large part to the lack of benefits granted to Haitians as compared to that given to Nicaraguans, Cubans, Eastern Europeans, Guatemalans and Salvadorans,[59] in 1998, Congress enacted the Haitian Refugee Immigration Fairness Act of 1998.[60] This law allowed certain nationals of Haiti to adjust their status to that of lawful permanent residents. In order to be eligible for permanent residency, a Haitian must have been physically present in the United States for a continuous period beginning no later than December 31, 1995, and ending not earlier than the date the application for adjustment was filed (not counting any absence or absences totaling 180 days or less in the aggregate). The specific category of persons included any Haitian who: (1) filed for asylum before December 31, 1995; (2) was paroled into the United States prior to December 31, 1995, after being identified as having a credible fear of persecution or for emergent reasons or reasons deemed strictly in the public interest; (3) arrived in the United States without parents and remained without parents in the country since arrival; (4) were children who became orphaned subsequent to arrival in the United States; or (5) were children who were abandoned by their parents or guardians prior to April 1, 1998, and remained abandoned since that time. In order to qualify for the benefit, the person must have submitted her application before April 1, 2000. The statute further waived the application of grounds of inadmissibility paralleling the NACARA legislation.[61]

8. USA PATRIOT Act of 2001

Under the Uniting and Strengthening America by Providing Appropriate Tools Required to Intercept and Obstruct Terrorist (USA PATRIOT) Act of 2001,[62] nonimmigrants injured in the 9/11 attacks or who were unable to obtain status under the diversity immigration lottery in addition to spouses and children of United States

---

59. *See* discussion above on the Nicaraguan Adjustment and Central American Relief Act of 1997, Pub. L. No. 105-100, 111 Stat. 2160, 2193 (1997).

60. Pub. L. 105-277, 112 Stat. 2681 (1998).

61. Specifically waived were the inadmissibility grounds such as: (1) the requirement that the person had been inspected and admitted or paroled; (2) the bars to adjustment for persons who had accepted or continued in unauthorized employment; and (3) the bars to adjustment for persons who remained in the United States longer than authorized or were admitted as crewmen, in transit without visa or under the visa waiver pilot program.

62. Pub. L. No. 107-56, §§421–28, 115 Stat. 272, 356–63 (2001).

citizens or lawful permanent residents who were killed in the 9/11 attacks were able to apply for adjustment of status.

C. Loss of Permanent Residency

1. Abandonment of Permanent Residency

Once acquired, lawful permanent residency may be lost through removal proceedings any time before the person has become naturalized. In addition, one's actions can constitute an abandonment of the status, subjecting the person to removal. The removal can occur when the person returns from a trip overseas or after the person has reentered the United States. Proceedings can also be instituted when a person seeks to become a citizen through naturalization, but it is learned that the person had abandoned their permanent resident status. As can be seen in the following Board of Immigration Appeals decision, whether or not someone has "abandoned" her residency can be a very difficult factual and legal question.

Matter of Huang

19 I. & N. Dec. 749 (BIA 1988)

BY: Milhollan, Chairman; Dunne and Morris, Board Members. Concurring and Dissenting Opinion: Heilman and Vacca, Board Members.

In a decision dated May 13, 1986, an immigration judge found the applicants excludable under section 212(a)(20) of the Immigration and Nationality Act, 8 U.S.C. § 1182(a)(20) (1982), as aliens with no valid immigrant visas, and ordered them excluded and deported from the United States. The applicants have appealed from that decision. The appeal will be dismissed. The request for oral argument before the Board is denied.

The applicants are natives and citizens of Taiwan and include a female adult who is 38 years old, and her two minor children, ages 8 and 11. They were initially admitted to the United States as lawful permanent residents on June 5, 1982. The applicant's husband, the father of the children in question, was admitted as a lawful permanent resident a week earlier. The record reflects that the applicant's husband, after receiving his Alien Registration Receipt Card (Form I-551), returned to Japan to continue studying and working at a university's medical school as a medical doctor in the field of neurosurgery. Both the applicant and the Immigration and Naturalization Service stipulated at the exclusion hearing that the applicant's husband had entered into a contract with the medical school for this purpose in May 1981, and that the contract was for a period of 5 years. The applicant and the two children remained in Los Angeles, California, for approximately 3 to 4 weeks at the home of her husband's sister, a United States citizen. Thereafter, she and the children returned to Japan. The applicant and her two children last sought to reenter the United States on May 10, 1986, at which time they were placed in exclusion proceedings. In a sworn statement dated that same day, the applicant reported that she intended for her children to go to school in the United States and to live in this country forever, while she planned to return to Japan in 2 months.

The applicant testified at the exclusion hearing that her husband had been a medical doctor in Taiwan and had entered into the contract with the medical school in Japan, as they thought that it would take a great deal of time before they would be granted visas to enter the United States as immigrants on the basis of a visa petition filed by her husband's sister. She also related that she and her two children had returned to the United States every year since 1982 for 3 or 4 weeks in March or April in order to maintain her lawful permanent resident status. According to the applicant, she and the children would stay with her husband's sister. She reported that her children attended a Chinese school in Japan, but that they had also attended a preschool in the United States for a short period in 1982 and had also attended school in this country for a short period in 1984. According to the applicant, her husband had not returned to the United States since 1982 and had never worked in the United States. She also related that she had worked at the Taiwan consulate in Japan for 3 years, until February 1985, and that they had sold their property in Japan in October 1985.

At the exclusion hearing, the applicant reported that she and her husband had invested in a condominium in Long Beach, California, through a partnership or joint venture, beginning in 1980, and had paid investment taxes to the United States. She also related that she and her husband had purchased a house in Los Angeles, California, in 1985 and paid property taxes on the house. She additionally noted that she had a bank account in the United States.

Additional documents have been submitted by the applicants on appeal, including a June 18, 1986, letter from the chairman of the department of neurosurgery at Osaka University Medical School. In the letter, the chairman related that the applicant's husband had come to Japan on May 23, 1981, and since June 1, 1981, had been working as a research fellow in the department of neurosurgery. According to the chairman, he had been working as a staff neurosurgeon at another hospital since July 1, 1985, and had passed the Japanese National Board of Medical License in May 1982. An additional certificate from the dean of the medical school certifies that the applicant's husband had been a research student at the school's department of neurological surgery from July 1, 1983, to the present time.

A letter from the applicant's husband, dated June 12, 1987, has also been submitted. In the letter, her husband reported that he had been a neurological surgeon in Taiwan until 6 years earlier, when he decided to research and study more in that field and therefore entered a doctorate program at a medical school in Japan. According to the applicant's husband, he still needed to complete his dissertation and might have his doctorate degree in 1987. He indicated that he desired to stay in the United States after he passed an examination for neurological specialists the following year. Noting that he and his wife had a house in California as well as a bank account, he stated that they intended to stay and live in the United States even though they had been unable to do so for the past 5 years.

The immigration judge concluded that the applicant and her two children were excludable under section 212(a)(20) of the Act as aliens not in possession of valid immigrant visas, as they had never established their lawful permanent resident status. He concluded that even if they had, they had abandoned that status. He determined that they had never established a residence in the United States, and that their intent regarding their residence or domicile was irrelevant, noting that the Act defined "residence" as the actual dwelling place in fact, without regard to intent.

On appeal, the applicant contends that her and her family's intent is relevant to the question of whether their lawful permanent resident status has been abandoned. She asserts that she and her children never abandoned that status, as they had always intended to settle in the United States following the completion of her husband's doctoral program in Japan, which was now expected in 1988. She points out that when her husband began his training in 1981, they were unaware that his priority date for coming to the United States would be reached in early 1982. Noting that her family's Japanese residency documents submitted at the exclusion hearing show that her family was residing only in a temporary status which had to be renewed yearly, the applicant asserts that their purchase of investment property in 1980 and a house in 1985, as well as their bank account and payment of taxes in the United States, also show her intent.

The Service contends on appeal that the applicants have abandoned their lawful permanent resident status. In doing so, it points out that the applicant's husband has never returned to the United States, that the applicant herself has worked for years in Japan, that the applicant's children attend school in Japan, and that they own a home in Japan and have never had a residence in the United States. It further notes that the applicant's visits to the United States have been brief, and only for the purpose of giving the appearance of maintaining a residence in this country.

Section 212(a)(20) of the Act requires the exclusion of immigrants seeking admission to the United States if they do not possess a valid immigrant visa, re-entry permit, or other valid entry document. Section 211(b) of the Act, 8 U.S.C. §1181(b) (1982), however, permits the Attorney General to waive those documentary requirements and, hence, the section 212(a)(20) ground of excludability, for any alien who is a returning resident immigrant.

A returning resident is "an immigrant, lawfully admitted for permanent residence, who is returning from a temporary visit abroad." Section 101(a)(27)(A) of the Act, 8 U.S.C. §1101(a)(27)(A) (1982). The phrase "lawfully admitted for permanent residence" means "the status of having been lawfully accorded the privilege of residing permanently in the United States as an immigrant in accordance with the immigration laws, such status not having changed." Section 101(a)(20) of the Act. Under the applicable regulation, a returning resident may present an Alien Registration Receipt Card in lieu of an immigrant visa if returning to an unrelinquished lawful permanent residence in the United States after a temporary absence abroad not exceeding 1 year. 8 C.F.R. §211.1(b) (1988). Thus, in order to qualify as a returning resident alien, an alien must have acquired lawful permanent resident status in accordance with our laws, must have retained that status from the time that he acquired it, and must be returning to an "unrelinquished lawful permanent residence" after a "temporary visit abroad." *Santos v. INS*, 421 F.2d 1303, 1305 (9th Cir.1970); sections 101(a)(20) and (27)(A) of the Act; 8 C.F.R. §211.1(b) (1988).

The term "temporary" is not subject to inflexible definition and varies in application depending upon the facts and circumstances of each particular case. See *Gamero v. INS*, 367 F.2d 123 (9th Cir.1966). What is a temporary visit cannot be defined in terms of elapsed time alone. *United States ex rel. Polymeris v. Trudell*, 49 F.2d 730 (2d Cir.1931), aff'd, 284 U.S. 279 (1932). Rather, the intention of the alien, when it can be ascertained, will control. *Id.*; *Matter of Kane*, 15 I & N Dec 258 (BIA 1975); see also *United States ex rel. Alther v. McCandless*, 46 F.2d 288 (3d Cir.1931). We have in the past ascertained an alien's intention by examining the location of his family ties, property holdings, and job, and whether he intended to return to the United States as a place of employment or business or as an actual home. *Matter of Muller*, 16 I & N Dec. 637 (BIA 1978); *Matter of Quijencio*, 15 I & N Dec. 95 (BIA 1974). We have also considered the applicant's purpose in departing from the United States, whether the visit abroad can be expected to terminate within a relatively short period of time, and whether the termination date can be fixed by some early event. *Matter of Kane, supra.*

We emphasize that "unrelinquished lawful permanent residence," as used in 8 C.F.R. §211.1(b) (1988), can have reference to something less than a permanent dwelling place in the United States. See *Saxbe v. Bustos*, 419 U.S. 65 (1974); *Matter of Kane, supra*. Consequently, the applicant's lack of an actual dwelling place in this country is not, in and of itself, determinative in ascertaining whether he is returning from a temporary absence abroad. See *Matter of Kane, supra*; see also *Matter of Guiot*, 14 I & N Dec. 393 (D.D.1973).

It is important to note that the Service has the burden in this case of proving that the applicant is not eligible for admission as a returning permanent resident alien. While the burden of proving admissibility is generally on the applicant in exclusion proceedings, see section 291 of the Act, 8 U.S.C. §1361 (1982), where an applicant for admission has a colorable claim to returning resident status, the burden is on the Service to show that the applicant should be deprived of his or her status as a lawful permanent resident. *Matter of Salazar*, 17 I & N Dec. 167 (BIA 1979); *Matter of Kane, supra.*

This Board has not previously articulated what burden of proof the Service must meet in order to establish that an applicant's lawful permanent resident status has changed. We now conclude that the Service's burden is to show that the applicant's status has changed by clear, unequivocal, and convincing evidence. In *Woodby v. INS*, 385 U.S. 276 (1966), the Supreme Court observed that drastic deprivation may follow if a resident of the United States is compelled to forsake all bonds formed in this country and go to a foreign land where the resident often has no current ties. The Court therefore held in that case that in deportation hearings the Service must establish facts supporting deportability by clear, unequivocal, and convincing evidence. An applicant for admission to this country who has a colorable claim to returning resident status similarly may often have much at stake in retaining his or her lawful permanent resident status.

For purposes of the constitutional right to due process, a returning lawful permanent resident's status is assimilated to that of an alien continuously residing and physically present in the United States. *Kwong Hai Chew v. Colding*, 344 U.S. 590 (1953). Although these differently situated groups of aliens do not have a right to identical treatment, and a returning lawful permanent resident's admissibility may be properly determined in an exclusion hearing, *Landon v. Plasencia*, 459 U.S. 21 (1982), the returning lawful permanent resident should be given reasonable notice of the charges against her and afforded a fair hearing. *Kwong Hai Chew v. Colding, supra.* Given what the alien may have at stake, it has also been held, as noted above, that a returning lawful permanent resident may only be deprived of that status in proceedings in which the Service bears the burden of proof. The Board similarly concludes that the deprivation that may follow also requires that the Service establish that such status has changed by clear, unequivocal, and convincing evidence.

In the case at hand, the immigration judge concluded that the applicants had never established a lawful permanent resident status in the United States. This conclusion was incorrect. The applicants acquired lawful permanent resident status in the United States at the time of their June 5, 1982, admission to this country. See section 101(a)(20) of the Act. See generally 2 C. Gordon and H. Rosenfield, Immigration Law and Procedure, §6.17 (rev. perm. ed. 1986). At that point, the applicants attained "the status of having been lawfully accorded the privilege of residing permanently in the United States as an immigrant in accordance with the immigration laws," and were thus aliens "lawfully admitted for permanent residence" pursuant to section 101(a)(20) of the Act.

The immigration judge also found that the applicants, if they ever had attained lawful permanent resident status, had abandoned that status. The Board agrees. However, the Board would point out that the immigration judge was incorrect in concluding that the applicant's intent was irrelevant in determining whether she had abandoned that status. Although section 101(a)(33) of the Act defines "residence" as the principal, actual dwelling place in fact, without regard to intent, we are concerned with whether the applicant abandoned her lawful permanent resident status in this country, and not whether she abandoned a particular dwelling place. See Matter of Kane, supra. As noted above, an "unrelinquished lawful permanent residence" as used in 8 C.F.R. §211.1(b) (1988) can refer to something less than a permanent dwelling place in the United States. See *Saxbe v. Bustos, supra.* The definition of "residence" in section 101(a)(33) of the Act, which would preclude consideration of the alien's "intent" in proceeding or remaining abroad, is inapplicable in determining whether an alien has abandoned her lawful permanent resident status. *Matter of Guiot, supra.* Nevertheless, the Board concludes that the Service has met its burden of proving by clear, unequivocal, and convincing evidence that the applicants in this case abandoned their lawful permanent resident status.

While the applicant's professed intent was to return to the United States, her actions have not supported that intent. An alien's desire to retain her status, without more, is not sufficient. *Matter of Kane, supra.* The length of the applicant's absence from the United States is a significant factor in showing her intent to abandon her lawful permanent resident status. Except for brief 3- to 4-week visits each year, the applicant and her children had been absent from the United States for approximately 4 years at the time of their last attempted entry in May 1986. During these brief visits, the applicant and her children resided with the sister of the applicant's husband. Although the applicant and her husband have owned a house in Los Angeles, California, since 1985, they have never maintained a residence in the United States since being granted lawful permanent resident status in 1982. Since being granted that status, the applicant and her children have been living in Japan. The applicant's children have received their schooling in Japan and have reportedly only gone to school in this country for brief periods in 1982 and 1984 while visiting the sister of the applicant's husband. Additionally, the applicant and her husband owned a home in Japan until 1985.

Moreover, the applicant was employed in Japan for 3 years from 1982 to 1985. Her husband has studied and worked as a doctor in the field of neurosurgery at a university in Japan since June 1981 and, since returning to Japan in 1982, has never returned to the United States. The applicant asserts on appeal that her husband was required to remain in Japan, thus requiring that she and their children do the same, because her husband had entered into a 5-year contract in May 1981 to study and work at the university before they were notified that they could come to the United States as immigrants. As noted above, an extended period of absence from the United States, in appropriate circumstances, can be viewed as a temporary visit abroad if the end of the period of absence can be fixed by some early event. In the case at hand, the applicant argues that the period of absence was fixed by her husband's completion of his studies and work in the field of neurosurgery by attaining his doctorate degree at the university in question. However, the Board concludes that this does not provide a sufficiently definite point at which the applicant would return to the United States. In this regard, the Board would point out that the applicant initially testified that the time of her family's return was provided by the husband's 5-year contract with the university, which would have ended in June 1986. However, evidence submitted by the applicant, including a June 1987 letter from her husband, and statements made on appeal indicate that her husband did not plan on finishing his doctoral program and medical examinations until some time in 1988. In all, the record has not shown a clear demarcation as to when her husband's relationship with the university would end and she and her family could return to the United States.

The Board acknowledges that the applicant has some ties to the United States, including a sister-in-law living in California, investment property and a house in California, payment of investment and property taxes, and a bank account reportedly maintained somewhere in the United States. However, given that the applicants have never maintained a home or lived in the United States except for brief visits with the applicant's sister-in-law, these ties to the United States are minimal. Taking into account that the applicant has had extended absences from the United States, having lived and worked in Japan with her family for many years, the Board concludes that the status of the applicants as lawful permanent residents changed, that their absences were not temporary in nature, and that they are therefore not entitled to admission to the United States as returning permanent residents. The Service has met its burden of showing that they were excludable under section 212(a)(20) of the Act. Accordingly, the appeal will be dismissed.

Michael J. Heilman Board Member:

I respectfully concur in part and dissent in part.

In this decision, the majority rejects the immigration judge's finding that the applicants had failed to establish a permanent residence in the United States in 1982, when they were initially admitted as lawful permanent residents. Because the majority decision mischaracterizes the immigration judge's actual finding, the majority engages in a rather tangential analysis of section 101(a)(27) of the Immigration and Nationality Act, 8 U.S.C. § 1101(a)(27) (1982). I do not join in that portion of the majority decision, but do agree that the respondents should not be considered returning lawful permanent residents.

In my estimation, the immigration judge clearly found that the respondents had never established a permanent residence in the United States. The immigration judge stated that it was "obvious from this record" that the applicants "never actually resided in the United States, that they have never maintained a residence in this country." This finding is repeated twice more in the decision in similar terms: "I am satisfied that they did not establish a residence in this country...." "There is no evidence in this record to indicate or to suggest that any member of this family ever established residence in the United States...."

The majority focuses upon what is obviously an unintentional use of the word "status," in one sentence of the immigration judge's decision, where the word "residence" is certainly meant. The immigration judge stated: "To the contrary, I find that the applicants never established permanent status in the United States and that even if they did establish such *residence* that they have long since abandoned that status" (emphasis supplied). I am completely satisfied from the immigration judge's decision that he was quite aware of the distinction to be made between being admitted to the "status" of a lawful permanent resident, as the applicants were in 1982, and the actual acquisition of a permanent "residence" in the United States.

It is because of the mischaracterization of the immigration judge's decision that the majority rejects his finding that the respondents never established a permanent residence in the United States. This finding appears to me to be eminently justified and to provide the primary basis for denying the applicants admission under the terms of section 101(a)(27) of the Act, which provides for the admission of lawful permanent residents following a "temporary visit abroad."

It was recognized in *Matter of Kane*, 15 I & N Dec. 258, 261 (BIA 1975), that an alien who had been "lawfully admitted for permanent residence" could be denied admission subsequently under section 101(a)(27) of the Act if it was determined that the applicant had "no ties of residence or employment, either because he has abandoned them, or *because he never had them in the first place*" (emphasis supplied). If one does not take into account in this appeal the circumstances of the initial arrival of the applicants in this country when they first received permanent resident status, it seems to me that the analysis which follows is a bit awkward, and the Board and federal court decisions which are cited end up somewhat beside the point.

Here, the applicants were admitted, and returned to Japan 3 or 4 weeks after their admission, having stayed at a relative's home. Their visit was somewhat longer than that of their husband and father, the principal immigrant in the family, from whose immigrant status they derived their right to immigrate. He had come to the United States in 1982, been admitted as a permanent resident, and returned to Japan where he was studying and working. He apparently left before the applicants themselves arrived. He never returned to the United States after that. The applicants, as noted by the majority, made a number of short visits to the United States over a period of several years, during which time they established none of the ties ordinarily associated with permanent residence.

We are thus faced with a situation in which these applicants wish to be considered lawful permanent residents who are returning from "temporary" visits abroad under circumstances which clearly establish that no permanent residence was ever established. The applicants have never asserted that they intended to emigrate to the United States independently of their husband and father, or that they established a separate household. The record, to the contrary, shows without doubt that they continued to reside with him, that his employment and studies determined where they would live. It was his choice to live, study and work in Japan for an indefinite period, a choice to which he was obviously committed even prior to the time he journeyed to the United States to obtain his permanent resident status. It is not necessary to conjecture as to his intentions, or probe his mind; his conduct is ample evidence of what he desired to do and in fact did do. The applicants here followed his lead and merely returned to the United States when it was convenient, in order to maintain the pretense that they "intended" to reside in the United States, and so maintain their lawful permanent resident status.

Under these circumstances, the immigration judge was correct in finding that the applicants had never established a permanent residence in the United States. As this is so, they cannot be considered persons who are returning from "temporary" visits abroad. Their visits to the United States have been temporary, their permanent residence has been abroad.

For these reasons also I would dismiss the appeal.

Notes

1. USCIS's position is that if a person has been out of the United States for more than one year, residency has been abandoned.[63] However, from the preceding case, it should be clear that residency is a question of intent and may be treated as having

63. *See* 8 C.F.R. § 211.1(a)(2)(A).

been abandoned in less time or may be retained where absences are even longer. Factors considered include the purpose and dates of the temporary absence abroad as well as facts demonstrating an objective intention of the person to return to the United States, such as family ties, income tax returns, mortgages and employment.[64] The Sixth Circuit has held that notwithstanding the language in the statute, the burden is on the government to establish abandonment by "clear, unequivocal and convincing evidence." *Ward v. Holder*, 733 F.3d 601 (6th Cir. 2013).[65] At the same time, a person who lives and works in the U.S. may by his actions be deemed to have abandoned his residence. *Singh v. Reno*, 113 F.3d 1512 (9th Cir. 1997).

2. In *Matter of Kane*,[66] which was referred to in *Matter of Huang*, the Board provided what may be a useful analysis to determine whether residency has been abandoned:

> (1) Purpose for departing. The traveler should normally have a definite reason for proceeding abroad temporarily. See *U.S. ex rel Alther v. McCandless*, 46 F.2d 288 (C.A. 3, 1931); examples are education and professional training, *Serpico v. Trudell, supra*; employment for a definite, "albeit extended period," by accepting a two-year teaching position with a foreign university, *Matter of Guiot, supra*; indefinite employment abroad when assigned by one's United States employer, *Matter of Wu*, 14 I. & N. Dec. 290, (RC 1973), *Matter of Manion*, 11 I. & N. Dec. 261 (DD 1965); liquidation of assets, *Matter of Souqi*, 14 I. & N. Dec. 390, (RC 1973).
>
> (2) Termination date. The visit abroad should be expected to terminate "within a period relatively short, fixed by some early event," *U.S. ex rel. Lesto v. Day*, 21 F.2d 307, 309 (C.A. 2, 1927); *Matter of Castro*, 14 I. & N. Dec. 492 (BIA 1973). If unforeseen circumstances cause an unavoidable delay in returning, the trip would retain its temporary character, so long as the alien continued to intend to return as soon as his original purpose was completed. For example, war might inhibit travel or the alien might be drafted, *Serpico v. Trudell, supra*; there might be illness, *Transatlantica Italiana v. Elting*, 66 F.2d 542, 545 (C.A. 2, 1933); there might be a death requiring remaining abroad to settle an estate, *U.S. ex Polymeris v. Trudell, supra*.
>
> (3) Place of employment or actual home. The traveler must intend to return to the United States as a place of employment or business, *Saxbe v. Bustos, supra*; *Gooch v. Clark*, 433 F.2d 274 (C.A. 9, 1970), cert. den. 402 U.S. 995 (1971); *Matter of Bailey*, 11 I. & N. Dec. 466 (BIA 1965 and 1966); or as an actual home, *U.S. ex rel. Lesto v. Day, supra*; *Matter of D-C-*, 3 I. & N. Dec. 519 (BIA 1949). He must possess the requisite intention to return at the time of departure, *U.S. ex rel. Lesto v. Day*, supra; and must maintain it

64. *Matter of Huang*, 19 I. & N. Dec. 749 (BIA 1988); *Matter of Kane*, 15 I. & N. Dec. 258 (BIA 1975).

65. 8 U.S.C. §§ 1229a(c)(2)(A) and (3)(A), Sec. 240(c)(2)(A) and (3)(A) use the terms "clear and convincing" evidence.

66. 15 I. & N. Dec. 258 (BIA 1975).

> during the course of the visit, *Gamero v. INS, supra*; *Matter of B-*, 9 I. & N. Dec. 211, 213 ff (BIA 1961), reversed on other grounds, *Barrese v. Ryan*, 203 F.Supp. 880 (D.Conn.1962).
>
> * * *
>
> Since the number and nature of the ties will vary widely, the question is often one of determining whether the ties here are reasonably indicative of the alien's continuing desire and intent to return after a temporary absence. Nor will the bare claim of unawareness of possessing the status of a lawful permanent resident, establish a lack of intent to abandon, where the allegation falls short of establishing an affirmative intent to return to the United States after a temporary visit abroad. *Matter of Quijencio, supra.* On the other hand, a possible justifiable reliance on a misstatement of a United States official, contributing to extended absence and failure to return, has been held to be a factor that warrants full exploration. *Tejeda v. INS*, 346 F.2d 389 (C.A. 9, 1965). [15 I. & N. Dec. 258 at 262–64.]

3. A person does not lose her permanent residency until there has been a final administrative order of removal issued.[67]

---

2. Rescission of Adjustment

Under 8 U.S.C. § 1256,[68] a person who has obtained her lawful permanent resident status through the adjustment procedure can have that status "rescinded" if within the first 5 years, it appears that the person was ineligible for it in the first place. For example, it may be instituted where there was an error and the beneficiary was ineligible for adjustment or where there was a fraud such as a sham marriage.[69] The effect of a rescission order is that the adjustment applicant is returned to the status that they had before they were "adjusted" to permanent residence. In most cases, this would mean that the person becomes subject to removal. While the prevailing view is that the failure by the government to bring an action in rescission within five years does not bar removal on grounds of ineligibility for adjustment, that view is limited to the Third Circuit, in effect, creating a form of statute of limitations.[70]

---

67. 8 C.F.R. § 1.1(p); *Perez-Rodriguez v. I.N.S.*, 3 F.3d 1074 (7th Cir. 1993); *Matter of Gunaydin*, 18 I. & N. Dec. 326 (BIA 1982), aff'd, 742 F.2d 776 (3d Cir. 1984).

68. Sec. 246.

69. *Matter of Tayabji*, 19 I. & N. Dec. 264, 268 (BIA 1985) (even without misconduct on the part of the applicant because he was ineligible for the benefit, his status could be rescinded); *Matter of Athanasopoulos*, 13 I. & N. Dec. 827 (BIA 1971) (because of sham marriage, applicant was ineligible for adjustment).

70. *See Bamidele v. INS*, 99 F.3d 557, 562 (3d Cir. 1996); *Garcia v. Att'y Gen'l*, 553 F.3d 724 (3d Cir. 2009) (affirmed *Bamidele* following subsequent change in language in rescission statute). However, even in the Third Circuit, the LPR would not be eligible to naturalize. *Adegoke v. Fitzgerald*, 784 F. Supp. 2d 538 (E.D. Pa. 2011).

When seeking rescission, the government must bring its action within 5 years from adjustment.[71] However it may institute removal proceedings at any time where there is a basis to do so.[72] When the USCIS is seeking rescission, it sends the permanent resident a Notice of Intent to Rescind to which the LPR has 30 days to respond after which a hearing is held before an immigration judge.[73] The LPR's failure to file a proper response results in the loss of permanent residency. In *Ali v. Reno*,[74] the respondent's lawyer had filed a response to the Notice by requesting an additional 60 days to submit a reply and requesting copies of documentation supporting the government's allegations. The response was deemed improper and the LPR's residency was rescinded.[75]

a. Rescission or Removal Proceedings?

Matter of Awwal

19 I. & N. Dec. 617 (BIA 1988)

BY: Milhollan, Chairman; Dunne, Morris, Vacca, and Heilman, Board Members

* * *

The respondent is a 25-year-old native and citizen of Bangladesh. He apparently was paroled into the United States on September 9, 1972. On July 15, 1974, his status was adjusted to that of a lawful permanent resident of the United States. His adjustment was based on his status as the stepchild of his mother's United States citizen husband. See section 101(b)(1)(B) of the Immigration and Nationality Act, 8 U.S.C. s 1101(b)(1)(B) (1982). On August 18, 1975, a notice of intent to rescind was sent to the respondent. The notice alleged that the respondent's mother was separated from her husband at the time his adjustment was granted, and that the respondent therefore did not qualify as the stepchild of a United States citizen at that time. A similar notice was sent to the respondent's mother. Prior counsel of both the respondent and his mother apparently responded to the notices and requested a hearing. A rescission hearing relating only to the respondent's mother was held, and her adjustment was ordered rescinded on the ground that her marriage was a sham entered into in order to procure immigration benefits. This Board ultimately upheld the mother's rescission on August 15, 1979.

On March 5, 1981, the respondent's parole was terminated, and he was placed in exclusion proceedings, charged with excludability under section 212(a)(20) of the Act, 8 U.S.C. s 1182(a)(20) (1982), as an immigrant not in possession of a valid immigrant

---

71. Persons who obtained their permanent residency through the immigrant visa process may only be removed in removal proceedings under the normal procedures used there.

72. *Asika v. Ashcroft*, 362 F.3d 264, 266 (4th Cir. 2004), *cert. denied*, 543 U.S. 1049 (2005); *Stolaj v. Holder*, 577 F.3d 651 (655 (6thCir. 2009). In *Asika*, the Fourth Circuit acknowledged that the statute was ambiguous but accorded the agency *Chevron* deference.

73. 8 C.F.R. §§ 246.1 and 246.3, 1246.1 and 1246.3. These rules require personal service of the Notice.

74. 22 F.3d 442 (2d Cir. 1994).

75. 22 F.3d at 446. The regulations require that the response specifically contest, deny or request a hearing. 8 C.F.R. §§ 246.3 and 1246.3.

visa. Counsel for the respondent filed a trial brief in which it was argued, inter alia, that there was no jurisdiction to hold an exclusion hearing because the respondent's lawful permanent resident status had never been rescinded. The respondent noted that in rescission proceedings the Government bears the burden of proving ineligibility for adjustment by clear, unequivocal, and convincing evidence. See, e.g., *Waziri v. INS*, 392 F.2d 55 (9th Cir. 1968); *Matter of Suleiman*, 15 I&N Dec. 784 (BIA 1974). At a hearing held on May 18, 1982, counsel reiterated his contention that exclusion proceedings were improper because there had been no rescission proceedings. Because of the complex issues involved, the case was continued by the immigration judge.

A further hearing was held on October 4, 1983. On that date, the immigration judge stated that he was conducting a rescission hearing. Counsel made a motion to terminate the exclusion proceedings because the respondent had not had his lawful permanent resident status rescinded. The immigration judge again noted that he was conducting rescission, not exclusion, proceedings, so the motion was found to be premature. Counsel appeared to accede to this. However, counsel then moved for termination of the rescission proceedings because 8 years had passed since the notice of intent to rescind was served. It was argued that it would be 'inappropriate and unjust' to proceed with rescission after such a long delay. The immigration judge denied this motion, finding no affirmative misconduct on the part of the Government. See generally *INS v. Hibi*, 414 U.S. 5 (1973). The rescission hearing went forward.

Following the hearing, the immigration judge issued an oral decision rescinding the respondent's adjustment of status. He found the respondent to be a truthful witness and to be innocent of any wrongdoing. He further found that the respondent and his ex-stepfather had a familial relationship during and for some time after the marriage. However, he concluded that because the underlying marriage had been found to be a sham, there had never been a valid marriage under the immigration laws and thus the respondent could not obtain immigration benefits through that marriage. He relied for this holding on our decision in *Matter of Teng*, 15 I&N Dec. 516 (BIA 1975).

On appeal, the respondent first makes two arguments regarding the propriety of the proceedings. He argues that these are exclusion proceedings and the immigration judge was without authority to conduct a rescission hearing in exclusion proceedings. It is alternatively argued that, because the Immigration and Naturalization Service 'abandoned' the rescission proceedings for 8 years, it would be fundamentally unfair and excessively harsh to rescind the respondent's adjustment of status now. The primary focus of the respondent's appeal, however, is on the proper interpretation of *Matter of Teng, supra*. He contends that under that decision immigration benefits are available through a stepparent-stepchild relationship even where the underlying marriage was a sham, so long as there has been active parental interest shown by the stepparent in the stepchild.

On appeal, the Service argues first of all that the proceedings are proper. The Service notes that the respondent requested a rescission hearing, and that request was granted. It is further contended on this procedural issue that no prejudice to the respondent has been shown as a result of the delay in holding the hearing. As to the legal issue regarding steprelationships, the Service argues that there can be no steprelationship under section 101(b)(1)(B) of the Act without a valid underlying marriage.

Preliminarily, we find that these rescission proceedings are proper. As pointed out by Appellate Counsel for the Service, the respondent argued that he should be in rescission, not exclusion proceedings. The immigration judge agreed with the respondent and a rescission hearing was held. The respondent cannot now complain that a rescission hearing should not have been held. We note that counsel pled to the allegations set forth in the notice of intent to rescind and did not protest that he was not prepared for rescission proceedings. Nor has there been a showing that the respondent was prejudiced by the holding of these rescission proceedings, or by the delay in holding them. Moreover, even if we were to hold that, because of the delay, the proceedings were in some way unfair and should be terminated, that would not result in the end of all proceedings against the respondent. Exclusion proceedings could still be brought. See generally *Matter of Belenzo*, 17 I&N Dec. 374 (BIA 1980, 1981; A.G. 1981). While the delay in this case is unfortunate, we conclude that the rescission proceedings were properly held.[2]

We turn next to the issue which both parties have stated is the paramount one in this case. Simply stated, the question is, can there be a stepchild-stepparent relationship within the meaning of section 101(b)(1)(B) of the Act where the marriage creating the steprelationship was a sham from its inception. We agree with the immigration judge and the Service that the answer is no.

In *Matter of Teng, supra*, a stepfather had filed visa petitions on behalf of his wife's children. His marriage to their mother was subsequently determined to be a sham. We held that, 'where there is a sham marriage and no actual familial relationship between the stepchildren and the United States citizen stepparent has ever existed, the stepchildren are not entitled to be considered children of a United States citizen for purposes of the Immigration and Nationality Act.' *Id.* at 519. The immigration judge relied on this case in finding that, because there was no valid marriage between the respondent's mother and stepmother, the respondent was ineligible for immigration benefits through the stepfather. The Service agrees with this interpretation. The respondent, however, finds that *Matter of Teng, supra*, supports his position. He argues

2. The respondent cites *Matter of Quan*, 12 I&N Dec. 487 (D.A.C. 1967), for his contention that the Service should not have instituted rescission proceedings in this case because of the excessively harsh consequences that could result. *Matter of Quan* was a decision made by the Deputy Associate Commissioner for the Immigration and Naturalization Service, who noted in the decision that "the Service may exercise discretion in determining whether rescission proceedings should be instituted in any individual case." *Id.* at 488. In fact, what is complained of here is not the institution of rescission proceedings, but the delay in holding the rescission hearing. In any event, *Matter of Quan* can be of no help to the respondent since neither the immigration judge nor this Board has any authority to terminate proceedings as improvidently begun. The decision whether or not to institute proceedings is a matter of prosecutorial discretion, and once the Service, in the exercise of that discretion, institutes proceedings, we are required to go forward to determine whether the evidence warrants a decision to rescind. *See Matter of Saunders*, 16 I&N Dec. 326 (BIA 1977); *cf. Matter of Ramirez-Sanchez*, 17 I&N Dec. 503 (BIA 1980); *Matter of Lennon*, 15 I&N Dec. 9 (BIA 1974), and cases cited therein.

that because he did have an actual family relationship with his stepfather, he could obtain immigration benefits through him despite the sham nature of the marriage.

We can understand the respondent's view that *Matter of Teng, supra,* favors his position because it talks of a 'sham marriage *and* no actual familial relationship.' *Id.* at 519 (emphasis added). We are unwilling, however, to adopt that approach now that we are squarely faced with a situation involving not only a sham marriage but also an actual family relationship between the stepparent and child. A steprelationship under section 101(b)(1)(B) of the Act is, of course, based on a marriage, and it seems clear to us that the marriage forming the basis for the steprelationship must at some point have been a valid one. Where there is not and never has been a valid marriage, there cannot be a steprelationship under the immigration laws. Thus, a marriage which is a sham from the outset cannot form the basis for a steprelationship under section 101(b)(1)(B). We withdraw from the holding in *Matter of Teng, supra,* insofar as it may indicate that a sham marriage may form the basis for a steprelationship if there is an actual family relationship between the stepparent and stepchild.

The respondent cites *Matter of Pagnerre,* 13 I&N Dec. 688 (BIA 1971), as support for his position. See also *Matter of Mowrer,* 17 I&N Dec. 613 (BIA 1981). These cases are clearly distinguishable from the present one, however, since in *Pagnerre* and *Mowrer* there had been valid marriages at some point, whereas here there never was a valid marriage.

Counsel for the respondent recognizes the potential for fraud if steprelationships based on sham marriages are recognized under the immigration laws. However, he urges us to deal with the problem of fraud, not by adopting a 'per se' rule that sham marriages can never form the basis for steprelationships, but rather by placing the burden of proof on the party seeking to establish the steprelationship to show that there is no 'sham steprelationship.' The respondent's approach would not answer the real problem here: the fact that steprelationships, regardless of any family relationship, must be based on a marriage which has at one time been a valid marriage. A sham marriage is invalid from its inception. See, e.g., *Matter of Laureano,* Interim Decision 2951 (BIA 1983); *Matter of Romero,* 15 I&N Dec. 294 (BIA 1975); *Matter of M-,* 8 I&N Dec. 217 (BIA 1958). See generally *Lutwak v. United States,* 344 U.S. 604 (1952). It cannot under any circumstances be the basis of a steprelationship under section 101(b)(1)(B) of the Act.

The respondent's eligibility for immigration benefits depended entirely on his mother's marriage to a United States citizen. That marriage has been found to have been a sham, and the mother's own adjustment of status was rescinded because of the fraudulent marriage. Based on our discussion above, that marriage cannot form the basis for the respondent's adjustment of status. His adjustment was therefore properly ordered rescinded, and his appeal must be accordingly be dismissed.[3]

3. We note that the respondent may be eligible for legalization under section 201 of the Immigration Reform and Control Act of 1986, Pub. L. No. 99-603, 100 Stat. 3359. 19 I. & N. Dec. 617, Interim Decision (BIA) 3056.

Chapter 10

Relief from and Amelioration of Grounds for Removal

Introduction

As we have seen, there are numerous grounds under which a person may be found to be either inadmissible or removable. What relief is there from the prospect of removal? Which of the grounds of inadmissibility or deportability can be waived under the statute? What procedures are available to the person who has managed to gain entry but is faced with the possibility of removal? Can she avoid removal? In this section, we will explore the answers to these questions. The exploration of the forms of relief from removal and the ameliorative devices for the grounds for removal will also serve as a review of many of the issues which we have covered thus far.

Earlier, we discussed asylum, restriction on removal, temporary protected status, registry and adjustment of status, each of which are remedies which can be sought to prevent a person's removal. Three additional remedies falling under the category of relief from removal which we will explore at greater length are voluntary departure, deferred action and cancellation of removal for persons who are not permanent residents.

Like most immigration benefits, relief from removal are discretionary, requiring that the applicant establish eligibility and then demonstrate why she merits a favorable exercise of discretion. In all of these cases, the exercise of discretion will amount to a balancing of equities, requiring the fact finder to weigh the social and humane considerations presented in her application against the adverse factors evidencing her undesirability for the benefit being requested.[1] Each benefit will have its own rules and procedures, but all of them will serve to allow the person to remain in the United States for a short or extended period of time.

A. Relief from Removal

1. Voluntary Departure

The INA provides various provisions for a relief known as voluntary departure. Having been granted voluntary departure an individual agrees to depart from the

1. *See Matter of Edwards,* 20 I. & N. Dec. 191 (BIA 1990); *Matter of Marin,* 16 I. & N. Dec. 581 (BIA 1978).

United States and in exchange avoids a formal removal order.[2] Under most circumstances, the person seeking voluntary departure hopes at some point in the near future to return and secure a more permanent status. An individual might be seeking voluntary departure, because she has an approved family or employment-based preference petition which has not reached a point where an immigrant visa could be issued. Such a person might opt to leave the United States for a short period of time and then return later as an immigrant. Whether and under what circumstances voluntary departure might be sought is a question of strategy and case planning.

The statute contemplates two basic forms of voluntary departure—prehearing voluntary departure and voluntary departure while in proceedings. Prehearing voluntary departure pursuant to 8 U.S.C. § 1229c(a), Sec. 240B(a), provides that the Attorney General[3] may permit a person otherwise subject to removal to voluntarily depart the United States prior to the institution of removal proceedings. The period of voluntary departure which may be granted is a total of 120 days.[4] The benefit is only available to persons who agree to depart at their own expense and cannot be granted to aggravated felons or persons engaged in terrorist activities.[5] This form of voluntary departure is not available to someone who is arrested at the border.[6] Should a person granted voluntary departure fail to depart within the time allowed, she will be subject to the sanction of being ineligible for most forms of immigration relief for ten years plus civil penalties ranging from $1,000 to $5,000.[7]

The second form of voluntary departure, pursuant 8 U.S.C. § 1229c(b), Sec. 240B(b), may be sought after removal hearings have been instituted and may be available to certain persons who are otherwise subject to removal. This form of relief may be requested at two junctures: the first is prior to or at the pleading or "master calendar" stage of the removal proceeding or by stipulation of the parties, and the second is at the conclusion of the hearing at which time the immigration judge considers the person's eligibility for the relief.[8] A person who seeks voluntary departure before the pleading stage can obtain up to 120 days of voluntary departure as long as no other immigration relief is requested, and she waives appeal, concedes that she falls into one of the grounds of deportability, has not been convicted of an aggravated

---

2. The person might want to elect voluntary departure, because if a removal order is entered, she might not be able to reenter the United States for five years. *See* 8 U.S.C. § 1182(a)(9)(A), Sec. 212(a)(9)(A).

3. Like most forms of immigration relief, the Attorney General has delegated her powers to DHS, and the local ICE district directors review prehearing voluntary departure requests.

4. 8 U.S.C. § 1229c(a)(2), Sec. 240B(a)(2).

5. 8 U.S.C. § 1229c(a)(1), Sec. 240B(a)(1).

6. A person deemed inadmissible at the border may be permitted to withdraw her application for admission in lieu of having removal proceedings instituted. 8 U.S.C. § 1225(a)(4), Sec. 235(a)(4).

7. 8 U.S.C. § 1229c(d), Sec. 240B(d). The sanction for failure to depart may be avoided where it was not voluntary. *Matter of Zmijewska*, 24 I. & N. Dec. 87, 93–95 (BIA 2007) (where applicant unaware or physically unable to depart); *Singh v. Holder*, 658 F.3d 879, 386–88 (9th Cir. 2011) (where respondent was prejudiced by ineffective assistance of counsel and was not aware of order).

8. *Matter of Cordova*, 22 I. & N. Dec. 966, 968 (BIA 1999).

felony and is not removable for one of the security grounds of removal.[9] Eligibility for voluntary departure at the conclusion of the hearing requires that the person be of good moral character for at least five years preceding the application, have been physically present in the United States for at least one year prior to the issuance of the notice to appear and have not been granted voluntary departure after a finding of deportability for having entered the United States without permission[10] or for being an aggravated felon or terrorist. In addition, the person must be able to show that she has the ability to leave at her own expense and that she intends to do so. The period of voluntary departure granted by an immigration judge may not exceed 60 days.[11]

Voluntary departure assures that the person who leaves the country (notwithstanding the fact that she has been found to be removable by an immigration judge) may return to the United States, if admissible, without having to seek the special permission from the Attorney General that is required of persons returning within five years of their removal.[12] Voluntary departure only provides relief for persons who have accrued unlawful presence of less than one year.[13] Therefore a lawyer representing someone in proceedings will need to determine the period of unlawful presence which has accrued.[14] However there may be other considerations for seeking voluntary departure, such as to avoid detention or forcible return.[15]

A period of voluntary departure may be further extended.

Samson Taiwo Dada v. Michael B. Mukasey, Attorney General

554 U.S. 1 (2008)*

Justice Kennedy delivered the opinion of the Court.

We decide in this case whether an alien who has requested and been granted voluntary departure from the United States, a form of discretionary relief that avoids certain statutory penalties, must adhere to that election and depart within the time prescribed, even if doing so causes the alien to forgo a ruling on a pending, unresolved motion to reopen the removal proceedings. The case turns upon the interaction of relevant provisions of the Illegal Immigration Reform and Immigrant Responsibility Act of 1996, 110 Stat. 3009-546 (IIRIRA or Act). The Act provides that every alien ordered removed from the United States has a right to file one motion to reopen his or her removal proceedings. See 8 U.S.C. § 1229a(c)(7) (2000 ed., Supp. V). The

9. There is no requirement that the person be of "good moral character."
10. *See* 8 U.S.C. § 1182(a)(6)(A), Sec. 212(a)(6)(A).
11. 8 U.S.C. § 1229c(b)(2), Sec. 240B(b)(2).
12. 8 U.S.C. § 1254(e), Sec. 244(e).
13. 8 U.S.C. § 1182(a)(9)(B)(i)(I), Sec. 212(a)(9)(B)(i)(I).
14. This subject was explored at greater length in Chapter 3.
15. A person who leaves under voluntary departure may choose the destination of her departure, whereas the government will normally deport a person to their home country.

* Footnotes have been omitted.

statute also provides, however, that if the alien's request for voluntary departure is granted after he or she is found removable, the alien is required to depart within the period prescribed by immigration officials, which cannot exceed 60 days. See § 1229c(b)(2) (2000 ed.). Failure to depart within the prescribed period renders the alien ineligible for certain forms of relief, including adjustment of status, for a period of 10 years. § 1229c(d)(1) (2000 ed., Supp. V). Pursuant to regulation, however, departure has the effect of withdrawing the motion to reopen. See 8 CFR § 1003.2(d) (2007).

Without some means, consistent with the Act, to reconcile the two commands—one directing voluntary departure and the other directing termination of the motion to reopen if an alien departs the United States—an alien who seeks reopening has two poor choices: The alien can remain in the United States to ensure the motion to reopen remains pending, while incurring statutory penalties for overstaying the voluntary departure date; or the alien can avoid penalties by prompt departure but abandon the motion to reopen.

The issue is whether Congress intended the statutory right to reopen to be qualified by the voluntary departure process. The alien, who is petitioner here, urges that filing a motion to reopen tolls the voluntary departure period pending the motion's disposition. We reject this interpretation because it would reconfigure the voluntary departure scheme in a manner inconsistent with the statutory design. We do not have the authority to interpret the statute as petitioner suggests. Still, the conflict between the right to file a motion to reopen and the provision requiring voluntary departure no later than 60 days remains untenable if these are the only two choices available to the alien. Absent a valid regulation resolving the dilemma in a different way, we conclude the alien must be permitted an opportunity to withdraw the motion for voluntary departure, provided the request is made before the departure period expires....

Petitioner Samson Taiwo Dada, a native and citizen of Nigeria, came to the United States in April 1998 on a temporary nonimmigrant visa. He overstayed it. In 1999, petitioner alleges, he married an American citizen. Petitioner's wife filed an I-130 Petition for Alien Relative on his behalf. The necessary documentary evidence was not provided, however, and the petition was denied in February 2003.

In 2004, the Department of Homeland Security (DHS) charged petitioner with being removable under § 237(a)(1)(B) of the Immigration and Nationality Act (INA) ... 8 U.S.C. § 1227(a)(1)(B) (2000 ed., Supp. V), for overstaying his visa. Petitioner's wife then filed a second I-130 petition. The Immigration Judge (IJ) denied petitioner's request for a continuance pending adjudication of the newly filed I-130 petition and noted that those petitions take an average of about three years to process. The IJ found petitioner to be removable but granted the request for voluntary departure under § 1229c(b) (2000 ed.). The BIA affirmed on November 4, 2005, without a written opinion. It ordered petitioner to depart within 30 days or suffer statutory penalties, including a civil fine of not less than $1,000 and not more than $5,000 and ineligibility for relief under §§ 240A, 240B, 245, 248, and 249 of the INA for a period of 10 years.

Two days before expiration of the 30-day period, on December 2, 2005, petitioner sought to withdraw his request for voluntary departure. At the same time he filed with the BIA a motion to reopen removal proceedings under 8 U.S.C. § 1229a(c)(7) (2000 ed., Supp. V). He contended that his motion recited new and material evidence demonstrating a bona fide marriage and that his case should be continued until the second I-130 petition was resolved.

On February 8, 2006, more than two months after the voluntary departure period expired, the BIA denied the motion to reopen on the ground that petitioner had overstayed his voluntary departure period. Under § 240B(d) of the INA, 8 U.S.C. § 1229c(d) (2000 ed. and Supp. V), the BIA reasoned, an alien who has been granted voluntary departure but fails to depart in a timely fashion is statutorily barred from applying for and receiving certain forms of discretionary relief, including adjustment of status. See App. to Pet. for Cert. 3–4. The BIA did not address petitioner's motion to withdraw his request for voluntary departure.

* * *

Voluntary departure is a discretionary form of relief that allows certain favored aliens—either before the conclusion of removal proceedings or after being found deportable—to leave the country willingly. Between 1927 and 2005, over 42 million aliens were granted voluntary departure; almost 13 million of those departures occurred between 1996 and 2005 alone. See Dept. of Homeland Security, Aliens Expelled: Fiscal Years 1892 to 2005, Table 38 (2005)....

Voluntary departure was "originally developed by administrative officers, in the absence of a specific mandate in the statute." 6 C. Gordon, S. Mailman, & S. Yale-Loehr, Immigration Law and Procedure § 74.02[1], p. 74-15 (rev. ed.2007) (hereinafter Gordon). The practice was first codified in the Alien Registration Act of 1940, § 20, 54 Stat. 671. The Alien Registration Act amended § 19 of the Immigration Act of Feb. 5, 1917, 39 Stat. 889, to provide that an alien "deportable under any law of the United States and who has proved good moral character for the preceding five years" may be permitted by the Attorney General to "depart the United States to any country of his choice at his own expense, in lieu of deportation." § 20(c), 54 Stat. 672.

In 1996, perhaps in response to criticism of immigration officials who had expressed frustration that aliens granted voluntary departure were "permitted to continue their illegal presence in the United States for months, and even years," Letter from Benjamin G. Habberton, Acting Commissioner on Immigration and Naturalization, to the Executive Director of the President's Commission on Immigration and Naturalization, reprinted in Hearings before the House Committee on the Judiciary, 82d Cong., 2d Sess., 1954 (Comm. Print 1952), Congress curtailed the period of time during which an alien may remain in the United States pending voluntary departure....

* * *

When voluntary departure is requested at the conclusion of removal proceedings, as it was in this case, the statute provides a voluntary departure period of not more than 60 days. See § 1229c(b)(2). The alien can receive up to 120 days if he or she concedes removability and requests voluntary departure before or during removal proceedings. See § 1229c(a)(2)(A). Appropriate immigration authorities may extend the time to depart but only if the voluntary departure period is less than the statutory maximum in the first instance. The voluntary departure period in no event may exceed 60 or 120 days for §§ 1229c(b) and 1229c(a) departures, respectively. See 8 CFR § 1240.26(f) (2007) ("Authority to extend the time within which to depart voluntarily specified initially by an immigration judge or the Board is only within the jurisdiction of the district director, the Deputy Executive Associate Commissioner for Detention and Removal, or the Director of the Office of Juvenile Affairs.... In no event can the total period of time, including any extension, exceed 120 days or 60 days as set forth in section 240B of the Act").

The voluntary departure period typically does not begin to run until administrative appeals are concluded. See 8 U.S.C. § 1101(47)(B) ("The order ... shall become final upon the earlier of—(i) a determination by the [BIA] affirming such order; or (ii) the expiration of the period in which the alien is permitted to seek review of such order by the [BIA]"); § 1229c(b)(1)....

Voluntary departure, under the current structure, allows the Government and the alien to agree upon a *quid pro quo*. From the Government's standpoint, the alien's agreement to leave voluntarily expedites the departure process and avoids the expense of deportation—including procuring necessary documents and detaining the alien pending deportation. The Government also eliminates some of the costs and burdens associated with litigation over the departure. With the apparent purpose of ensuring that the Government attains the benefits it seeks, the Act imposes limits on the time for voluntary departure, see *supra*, at 2313, and prohibits judicial review of voluntary departure decisions, see 8 U.S.C. §§ 1229c(f) and 1252(a)(2)(B)(i).

Benefits to the alien from voluntary departure are evident as well. He or she avoids extended detention pending completion of travel arrangements; is allowed to choose when to depart (subject to certain constraints); and can select the country of destination. And, of great importance, by departing voluntarily the alien facilitates the possibility of readmission.... The current statute likewise allows an alien who voluntarily departs to sidestep some of the penalties attendant to deportation. Under the current Act, an alien involuntarily removed from the United States is ineligible for readmission for a period of 5, 10, or 20 years, depending upon the circumstances of removal.... An alien who makes a timely departure under a grant of voluntary departure, on the other hand, is not subject to these restrictions—although he or she otherwise may be ineligible for readmission based, for instance, on an earlier unlawful presence in the United States, see § 1182(a)(9)(B)(i).

A motion to reopen is a form of procedural relief that "asks the Board to change its decision in light of newly discovered evidence or a change in circumstances since the hearing." 1 Gordon § 3.05[8][c], at 3-76.32. Like voluntary departure, reopening is a judicial creation later codified by federal statute....

In 1958, when the BIA was established, the Attorney General promulgated a rule for the reopening and reconsideration of removal proceedings, 8 CFR § 3.2, upon which the current regulatory provision is based. See 23 Fed.Reg. 9115, 9118–9119 (1958), final rule codified at 8 CFR § 3.2 (1959) ("The Board may on its own motion reopen or reconsider any case in which it has rendered a decision" upon a "written motion"); see also BIA: Powers; and Reopening or Reconsideration of Cases, 27 Fed.Reg. 96–97 (1962). Until 1996, there was no time limit for requesting the reopening of a case due to the availability of new evidence.

Then, in 1990, "fear[ful] that deportable or excludable aliens [were] try[ing] to prolong their stays in the U.S. by filing one type of discretionary relief... after another in immigration proceedings," Justice Dept. Finds Aliens Not Abusing Requests for Relief, 68 Interpreter Releases 907, 908 (July 22, 1991) (No. 27), Congress ordered the Attorney General to "issue regulations with respect to ... the period of time in which motions to reopen ... may be offered in deportation proceedings," including "a limitation on the number of such motions that may be filed and a maximum time period for the filing of such motions," Immigration Act of 1990, § 545(d)(1), 104 Stat. 5066. The Attorney General found little evidence of abuse, concluding that requirements for reopening are a disincentive to bad faith filings. See 68 Interpreter Releases, supra. Because "Congress ... neither rescinded [n]or amended its mandate to limit the number and time frames of motions," however, the Department of Justice (DOJ) issued a regulation imposing new time limits and restrictions on filings. The new regulation allowed the alien to file one motion to reopen within 90 days. Executive Office for Immigration Review; Motions and Appeals in Immigration Proceedings, 61 Fed. Reg. 18900, 18901, 18905 (1996); see 8 CFR § 3.2 (1996).

* * *

We hold that, to safeguard the right to pursue a motion to reopen for voluntary departure recipients, the alien must be permitted to withdraw, unilaterally, a voluntary departure request before expiration of the departure period, without regard to the underlying merits of the motion to reopen. As a result, the alien has the option either to abide by the terms, and receive the agreed-upon benefits, of voluntary departure; or, alternatively, to forgo those benefits and remain in the United States to pursue an administrative motion.

If the alien selects the latter option, he or she gives up the possibility of readmission and becomes subject to the IJ's alternative order of removal. See 8 CFR § 1240.26(d). The alien may be removed by the DHS within 90 days, even if the motion to reopen has yet to be adjudicated. See 8 U.S.C. § 1231(a)(1)(A). But the alien may request a stay of the order of removal, see BIA Practice Manual § 6.3(a), http://www.usdoj.gov/eoir/vll/qapracmanual/apptmtn4.htm; cf. 8 U.S.C. § 1229a(b)(5)(C) (providing that a removal order entered in absentia is stayed automatically pending a motion to reopen); and, though the BIA has discretion to deny the motion for a stay, it may constitute an abuse of discretion for the BIA to do so where the motion states nonfrivolous grounds for reopening.

Notes

1. One of the changes instituted by IIRAIRA was the elimination of judicial review of voluntary departure determinations.[16] Although there is administrative review of voluntary departure, that review is limited to the issue of eligibility; the period of time granted cannot be appealed.[17] Regulations enacted in 2009 provide for the termination of voluntary departure 30 days after the filing of a petition for review in the federal appeals court. 8 C.F.R. § 1240.26(i). While prior to the promulgation of the 2009 rules, federal courts were in agreement that they could reinstate voluntary departure where the appellant was within the period at the time the petition was filed, no court has held that they have power to reinstate voluntary departure.[18]

2. In addition to determining whether the person is of good moral character to qualify for voluntary departure, the immigration judge may look at the applicant's prior immigration history, the nature of his entry, length of residence and family ties.[19] The statute further requires that the person post a bond of no less than $500 but at "an amount necessary to ensure that the [person] will depart."[20]

3. After the immigration judge has granted a period of voluntary departure, if the person leaves on his own after the period of voluntary departure has passed, the departure is treated as a self-removal.[21] In addition, once the period granted by the immigration judge has lapsed, only the local ICE district director can grant further extensions.[22] At the same time, an immigration judge or the BIA may reinstate voluntary departure in a proceeding that has been reopened. Similarly, the BIA will normally reinstate voluntary departure if it expired while a person's appeal was pending, unless the appeal was frivolous.[23]

2. Deferred Action

Recall that in Chapter 5, we discussed Temporary Protected Status (TPS) and Extended Voluntary Departure (EVD), the former being a statutory and the latter an

---

16. *See* 8 U.S.C. § 1229b(e)–(f), Sec. 240B(e)–(f); *see also Moosa v. INS*, 171 F.3d 994 (5th Cir. 1999) (acknowledging court's lack of jurisdiction to review voluntary departure denial).

17. 8 C.F.R. § 1240.26(g).

18. *Garfias-Rodriguez v. Holder*, 702 F.3d 504, 524–25 (9th Cir. 2012) (court is without authority to issue a stay of the voluntary departure period.

19. *Matter of Seda*, 17 I. & N. Dec. 550 (BIA 1980).

20. 8 U.S.C. § 1229c(b)(3), Sec. 240B(b)(3).

21. 8 C.F.R. § 241.7.

22. 8 C.F.R. § 1240.26(f). While the statute limits the period of voluntary departure to 120 days, it appears that District Directors continue the practice of extending that period. 6 Charles Gordon et al., Immigration Law & Procedure § 74.02[f], n. 92 and accompanying text (2017). The decisions by District Directors are not subject to court review.

23. *See Matter of Chouliaris*, 16 I. & N. Dec. 168 (BIA 1977).

extra-statutory remedy. Deferred action is different from TPS or EVD in that it is applied on a case-by-case basis, while TPS and EVD are generally granted to a class of individuals. It has been said that both EVD and deferred action are grounded in traditional notions of the exercise of prosecutorial discretion. In both cases, the ultimate benefit to the person is that she is allowed to stay in the United States for a period of time and is given permission to work. If, however, the person should ever depart the country, she may not be allowed to return.[24] The following description is from the prior INS Operating Instructions, which sheds some light on deferred action.[25] The citation of this regulation was subsequently changed to OI 242.1(a)(22) and then removed altogether without explanation. However, the policy of granting deferred action on an individual basis remains an important form of discretionary relief.[26]

O.I. 103.1a(l)(ii)

(ii) Deferred action. The district director may, in his discretion, recommend consideration of deferred action, an act of administrative choice to give some cases lower priority and in no way an entitlement, in appropriate cases.

The deferred action category recognizes that the Service has limited enforcement resources and that every attempt should be made administratively to utilize these resources in a manner which will achieve the greatest impact under the immigration laws. In making deferred action determinations, the following factors, among others, should be considered:

(A) the likelihood of ultimately removing the alien, including:

(1) likelihood that the alien will depart without formal proceedings (e.g., minor child who will accompany deportable parents);

(2) age or physical condition affecting ability to travel;

(3) likelihood that another country will accept the alien;

(4) the likelihood that the alien will be able to qualify for some form of relief which would prevent or indefinitely delay deportation;

(B) the presence of sympathetic factors which, while not legally precluding deportation, could lead to unduly protracted deportation proceedings, and which, because of a desire on the part of the administrative authorities or

---

24. It should also be noted that EVD has been effective in cases involving persons seeking admission. For example, many Afghans in the United States who were denied asylum and found removable were not removed due to the policy of EVD for Afghans.

25. For additional information on the deferred action, *see* Leon Wildes, *The Nonpriority Program of the Immigration and Naturalization Service Goes Public: The Litigative Use of the Freedom of Information Act,* 14 San Diego L. Rev. 42 (1976). For a broader discussion of discretionary relief from removal, see Shoba Sivasprasad Wadhia, Beyond Deportation: The Role of Prosecutorial Discretion in Immigration Cases (2015)

26. *See* Charles Gordon et al. 1 Immigration Law and Procedure § 1.03, n. 50 (2002).

the courts to reach a favorable result, could result in a distortion of the law with unfavorable implications for future cases;

(C) the likelihood that because of the sympathetic factors in the case, a large amount of adverse publicity will be generated which will result in a disproportionate amount of Service time being spent in responding to such publicity or justifying actions;

(D) whether or not the individual is a member of a class of deportable aliens whose removal has been given a high enforcement priority (e.g., dangerous criminals, large-scale alien smugglers, narcotic drug traffickers, terrorists, war criminals, habitual immigration violators).

Matter of Quintero

18 I. & N. Dec. 348 (BIA 1982)

BY: Milhollan, Chairman; Maniatis, Dunne, Morris, and Vacca, Board Members

In a decision dated October 22, 1981, the immigration judge found the respondent deportable on his own admissions and granted him voluntary departure on or before April 1, 1982. The respondent has appealed from that decision. The appeal will be dismissed.

The respondent is a native and citizen of Mexico who last entered the United States on April 5, 1977. The record reflects that his wife is a lawful permanent resident whose visa petition has been approved to accord the respondent second-preference classification. They have two children, one of whom is a United States citizen.

At his deportation hearing the respondent made a motion to adjourn the proceedings in order to allow the District Director to act on his request for termination of the proceedings or for deferred action status pursuant to Operations Instruction 103.1(a)(1)(ii). He argued that the District Director should have granted him permission to remain until a visa number was available because of the hardship his deportation would cause his family. He further contended that the immigration judge should grant him deferred action status or indefinite voluntary departure if the District Director declined to accord him relief. The immigration judge denied the respondent's motion to adjourn and found that he was without jurisdiction to grant deferred action status.

The respondent has reiterated his arguments on appeal and further contends that the immigration judge erred in refusing to adjourn the hearing so that the District Director could address his request for deferred action status. We find his contentions to be without merit.

As the Operations Instruction indicates, deferred action status is an informal administrative stay of deportation which is granted only where the District Director, with the Regional Commissioner's approval, finds it to be warranted. See *Wan Chung Wen v. Ferro*, 543 F.Supp. 1016 (W.D.N.Y.1982). Such permission to remain in this country indefinitely is bestowed as a matter of prosecutorial grace and accords no rights to permanent residence. See *Soon Bok Yoon v. INS*, 538 F.2d 1211 (5 Cir.1976); *Zacharakis v. Howerton*, 517 F.Supp. 1026 (S.D.Fla.1981); *Matter of Lennon*, 15 I & N. Dec. 9 (BIA 1974), rev'd on other grounds, *Lennon v. INS*, 527 F.2d 187 (2 Cir.1975).

Authority for a grant of deferred action status appears only in the Operations Instructions. It is mentioned nowhere in the statute or the regulations and is simply the result of an administrative policy to give low priority to the enforcement of the immigration laws in certain cases. See *Zacharakis v. Howerton, supra*. Consequently, the prosecutorial discretion exercised in granting deferred action status is committed exclusively to the Service enforcement officials. See *Soon Bok Yoon v. INS, supra*; *Vergel v. INS*, 536 F.2d 755 (8 Cir.1976); *Zacharakis v. Howerton, supra*; *Spata v. INS*, 442 F.2d 1013 (2 Cir.), cert. denied, 404 U.S. 857 (1971); *Discaya v. INS, supra*. Inasmuch as deferred action status is a function of the District Director's prosecutorial authority, neither the immigration judge nor the Board may grant such status or review a decision of the District Director to deny it. See *Lopez-Telles v. INS*, 564 F.2d 1302 (9 Cir.1977).

Furthermore, since the respondent can request deferred action status at any stage in the proceedings, the immigration judge did not err in refusing to adjourn the hearing to allow him to pursue that relief. See 1A C. Gordon and H. Rosenfield, Immigration Law and Procedure section 5.3e(7) (1982); *Manantan v. INS, supra*. Likewise, the immigration judge's refusal to continue the hearing until a visa number was available was proper because he may neither terminate nor indefinitely adjourn the proceedings in order to delay an alien's deportation. See *Bowes v. INS*, 443 F.2d 30 (9 Cir.1971). Once deportation proceedings have been initiated by the District Director, the immigration judge may not review the wisdom of the District Director's action, but must execute his duty to determine whether the deportation charge is sustained by the requisite evidence in an expeditious manner. See *Lopez-Telles v. INS, supra*; *Matter of Geronimo, supra*. In any case, the fact that the respondent has an approved visa petition does not entitle him to delay the completion of deportation proceedings pending availability of a visa number. See *Armstrong v. INS*, 445 F.2d 1395 (9 Cir.1971); *Manantan v. INS, supra*; *Matter of Merced, supra*; *Matter of Agarwal*, 13 I & N Dec. 171 (BIA 1969). We conclude therefore that the immigration judge did not abuse his discretion in denying the respondent's motion to adjourn.

The respondent has argued that the immigration judge's authority to grant voluntary departure confers on him the power to accord extended voluntary departure, which he contends is equivalent to deferred action status. Unlike extended voluntary departure which allows an alien to remain in this country indefinitely, voluntary departure is only granted to aliens who have established that they are willing and have the immediate means to depart promptly from the United States. See 8 C.F.R. 244.1. As the respondent notes, the immigration judge is not limited as to the period of time he may grant for voluntary departure. See *Hernandez-Rivera v. INS*, 630 F.2d 1352 (9 Cir.1980); *Matter of Chouliaris*, 16 I & N. Dec. 168 (BIA 1977). However, it is well established that the immigration judge may not grant voluntary departure for an indefinite period of time. See *Matter of Anaya*, 14 I & N. Dec. 488 (BIA 1973), aff'd sub nom. *Anaya-Perchez v. INS*, 500 F.2d 574 (5 Cir.1974); *Matter of Chamizo*, 13 I & N. Dec. 435 (BIA 1969). Furthermore, jurisdiction to grant extended voluntary departure, as well as deferred action status, lies solely with the District Director. See 8 C.F.R. 244.2; *Manantan v. INS, supra*; *Matter of Anaya, supra*. The respondent's argument is therefore without merit.

Finally, we conclude that the immigration judge did not abuse his discretion in declining to grant the respondent 2 years for voluntary departure as requested. The usual period of time allowed for voluntary departure is 30 days. See *Matter of M__*, 4 I & N Dec. 626 (BIA 1952). Taking into consideration the facts that the respondent has a lawful permanent resident wife and a United States citizen child and is the beneficiary of an approved visa petition, we find that the period of over 5 months granted by the immigration judge was more than adequate. Accordingly, the appeal will be dismissed.

ORDER: The appeal is dismissed.

FURTHER ORDER: Pursuant to the immigration judge's order and in accordance with our decision in *Matter of Chouliaris, supra*, the respondent is permitted to depart from the United States voluntarily within 30 days from the date of this order or any extension beyond that time as may be granted by the District Director; and in the event of his failure so to depart, the respondent shall be deported as provided in the immigration judge's order.

---

a. Deferred Action Programs—2012 and 2014

In June of 2012, the Secretary of the Department of Homeland Security announced a program called "Deferred Action for Childhood Arrivals" (DACA) that provided deferred action to certain people who had come to the U.S. as children.[27] In order to qualify, the applicant must have been under the age of 31, arrived in the U.S. before their 16th birthday, have been present in the U.S. on June 15, 2012, and satisfied numerous additional requirements.[28] Applicants were required to individually apply, providing supporting documentation and paying the requisite filing fees.[29] While it had been estimated that there were 1.2 million eligible persons, approximately 800,000 eventually received deferred action status.[30] Under a great deal of political pressure, the agency in November, 2014 announced a broader deferred action program called "Deferred Action for Parents of Americans and Lawful Permanent Residents" (DAPA)

27. Memo, Sect'y Janet Napolitano, Secretary DHS, *Exercising Prosecutorial Discretion with Respect to Individuals Who Came to the United States as Children* (June 15, 2012).

28. The additional criteria included among other things that they were either in school, graduated, obtained a degree or had been honorably discharged from the military and did not have any disqualifying criminal convictions.

29. The application consisted of a DACA application and an Application for Employment Authorization which had a combined cost of $495. *USCIS, Consideration for Deferred Action for Childhood Arrival Process* (Aug. 31, 2012).

30. Jeanne Batalova, Sarah Hooker & Randy Capps, *DACA at the Two-Year Mark: A National and State Profile of Youth Eligible and Applying for Deferred Action* (Migration Policy Institute 2014).

along with an expansion of the existing DACA program.[31] DAPA provided work authorization and withholding of immigration enforcement for certain undocumented parents of U.S. citizens or lawful permanent residents who had been residing in the U.S. before January 1, 2010. In response, the state of Texas along with 25 other states filed for and were granted injunctive relief in federal court to prevent the program's implementation.[32] Following appeals by the government from the District Court decision, the injunction was upheld with some modifications by the Fifth Circuit—that decision was later affirmed by a deadlocked Supreme Court.[33]

With the election of a new President in November 2016, the DACA program was eventually terminated under a complicated schedule that allowed those whose deferred action status would lapse before the termination date of March 2018 could apply for a two year renewal while the remainder would lose their status upon expiration of their DACA grant.[34] At this writing the termination has been temporarily stayed. *Regents of Univ. of Calif. v. US DHS*, 279 F. Supp. 3d 1011 (N.D. Ca. 2018).

The underlying justification for the DACA and DAPA programs was that DHS had inherent prosecutorial discretion authority to prioritize its enforcement of the immigration laws. At the time that the programs were announced, it was widely believed that there were more than 11 million undocumented persons in the U.S. and the government only had resources to remove approximately 400,000 in any given year. In addition, it was assumed that many of those who would be placed in proceedings would have many options for relief in immigration court and the number of people who would actually be deported would be further reduced. All of this begged the question of whether it made sense from a policy perspective to so aggressively pursue removal proceedings against these populations of undocumented persons.

Note

The Operating Instructions make it clear that negative publicity arising from a case may form a basis for granting deferred action. You might recall *Matter of R-A-*,[35] an asylum case where the Board denied relief to a Guatemalan woman who had been the victim of brutal domestic violence which resulted in widespread sympathetic

---

31. Memo, Jeh Johnson, Sect'y. DHS, *Exercising Prosecutorial Discretion with Respect to Individuals Who Came to the United Sates as Children and with Respect to Certain Individuals Whose Parents are U.S. Citizens or Permanent Residents* (Nov. 20, 2014).

32. *Texas v. U.S.*, 86 F. Supp. 3d 591, 609–10 (S.D. Tex. 2015). The district court entered a preliminary injunction against the institution of DAPA and the expansion of DACA. 86 F. Supp. 3d at 677.

33. The full citation for this case is *Texas v. U.S.*, 86 F. Supp. 3d 591, 609–10 (S.D. Tex. 2015) (preliminary injunction); 787 F.3d 733 (5th Cir. 2015) (denial of stay request), 809 F.3d 134 (5th Cir. 2015) (revised decision affirming order), *U.S. v. Texas*, 136 S. Ct. 2271 (2016) (affirmed by an equally divided Court).

34. One possible reason for this complicated termination schedule was that those who had been granted status received the status in 2 year increments and many had already had their applications renewed.

35. 22 I. & N. Dec. 906 (BIA 1999).

media coverage. In its opinion, the Board made the following observation about the case endorsing the possible application of deferred action:

> It is not possible to review this record without having great sympathy for the respondent and extreme contempt for the actions of her husband. The questions before us, however, are not whether some equitable or prosecutorial authority ought to be invoked to prevent the respondent's deportation to Guatemala. Indeed, the Service has adequate authority in the form of "deferred action" to accomplish that result if it deems it appropriate. Rather, the questions before us concern the respondent's eligibility for relief under our refugee and asylum laws. And, as explained below, we do not agree with the Immigration Judge that the respondent was harmed on account of either actual or imputed political opinion or membership in a particular social group.

22 I. & N. Dec. at 914.

3. Cancellation of Removal for Long-Term "Non-Permanent Residents"

There are two forms of cancellation of removal—one for long-term non-permanent residents and another for long-term permanent residents. Through cancellation, a person will have their removal proceedings "cancelled" and their status will be adjusted to that of a lawful permanent resident. The cancellation of removal which is available to long term permanent residents will be discussed separately under waivers of grounds of inadmissibility since it is more like a waiver than relief from removal. The underlying rationale behind cancellation is that the law recognizes that removal can be a severe sanction for a person who has resided in the United States for a long period of time and has possibly developed extensive ties with their family and community here.

Cancellation relief is found in the statute at 8 U.S.C. § 1229b(b)[36] and provides for relief for persons who are not lawful permanent residents but are either inadmissible or removable and meet the following criteria:

- A prerequisite for relief is that the person has been "physically present" in the United States for a continuous period of at least ten years immediately preceding the date of the application. The ten year period is counted up to the service of the Notice to Appear (NTA) or the commission of certain crimes.[37]
- Persons who have served honorably in active duty status in the U.S. military for at least 24 months (provided that they were in the United States at the time of

36. Sec. 240A(b).

37. 8 U.S.C. § 1229b(d)(1(A), Sec. 240A(d)(1)(A). This is referred to as the "stop-time" rule. *Cheung v. Holder*, 678 F.3d 66, 69 (1st Cir. 2012). The stop-time rule has been upheld as constitutional. *Padilla-Padilla v. Gonzales*, 463 F.3d 972, 978 (9th Cir. 2006). Although requiring a conviction, the crimes referenced are to those found in 8 U.S.C. §§ 1182(a)(2) or 1227(a)(2). *Santos-Reyes v. Att'y Gen'l*, 660 F.3d 196 (3d Cir. 2011).

their enlistment or induction) do not have to meet the ten-year physical presence requirement.[38]

- The applicant must be a person of good moral character for ten years and has not been convicted of a crime or act forming a ground of inadmissibility under 8 U.S.C. §§1182(a)(2) and 1227(a)(2)–(3), Sections 212(a)(2), and 237(a)(2)–(3).
- The applicant must also establish that her removal would cause "exceptional and extremely unusual hardship" to her spouse, parent or child who is either a U.S. citizen or permanent resident. The hardship that the applicant might experience as a result of removal is not relevant to the claim.

Whether an individual can qualify for cancellation relief will depend on the ground of inadmissibility or deportability which forms the basis for the removal proceedings. The predecessor relief was found at 8 U.S.C. §1254[39] and provided for a "suspension of deportation" upon a showing of continuous residency of seven years, good moral character during the statutory period and a showing that the applicant's removal would cause extreme hardship to the applicant or her U.S. citizen or LPR spouse, parent or child.[40] However, a person who was deportable on criminal or political grounds could only qualify for a second form of suspension which required ten years of residency, good moral character and a showing that removal would result in "exceptional and extremely unusual hardship" to the applicant or her U.S. citizen or LPR spouse, parent or child.

a. What Is "Hardship"?

The most difficult question in all cases where hardship must be established is in determining whether the statutory requisite has been met. Although the case which follows involved an interpretation of the predecessor statute, it remains instructive towards understanding the definition of hardship more generally.

In re O-J-O-

21 I. & N. Dec. 381 (BIA 1996)

Before: Board En Banc: Schmidt, Chairman; Hurwitz, Villageliu, Mathon, and Guendelsberger, Board Members. Concurring Opinions: Dunne, Vice Chairman; Holmes, Board Member; Rosenberg, Board Member. Dissenting Opinion: Filppu, Board Member, joined by Vacca, Heilman, and Cole, Board Members.

Guendelsberger, Board Member:

The respondent, a native of Nicaragua, conceded deportability. In a decision rendered on April 19, 1995, the Immigration Judge denied the respondent's requests for asylum, withholding of deportation, and suspension of deportation, but granted

38. 8 U.S.C. §1229b(d)(3), Sec. 240A(d)(3).

39. 8 U.S.C. §1254(a)(1)–(2), Sec. 244(a)(1)–(2).

40. Prior to 1986, former Nazis (persons deportable under what is now 8 U.S.C. §1227(a)(4)(D), Sec. 237(a)(4)(D)) were eligible for suspension of deportation under this broad category.

voluntary departure. The respondent has appealed the denials of discretionary relief. We sustain the appeal as to the denial of the application for suspension of deportation.

The respondent is a 24-year-old native of Nicaragua who lived with his family in Esteli, Nicaragua, until his early teens. The respondent's father was a captain there in the fire department. After a prolonged conflict with local Sandinista officials, including imprisonment and forced resignation from his position, the respondent's father left Nicaragua for the United States, arriving in May 1985. The respondent joined his father in the United States in November 1985. His mother and younger brother arrived soon thereafter.

The respondent attended school in the United States, where he successfully completed elementary school, junior high, and high school. He earned good grades, participated in school sporting events, and became fluent in speaking, reading, and writing English. He has held a number of jobs and has been active in his church and in community events. In particular, he is an avid fan of softball and baseball and participates as a player in local softball and baseball leagues. He is a deacon in his church, where he not only attends regularly but also participates in the youth ministry program. He has plans to continue his studies at the college level and hopes eventually to become a police officer.

The respondent's father applied for asylum in the United States in 1987, and included the respondent in the application, but the claim was never adjudicated. In 1994, the respondent's father and mother returned to Nicaragua for an interview for an employment-based immigrant visa at the United States consulate. The respondent's father, seriously ill at the time, died before visa processing could be completed. His mother remained in Nicaragua after her husband's death and now resides there. The respondent's brother has left the United States and is living in Guatemala.

The respondent's father had built up a business in the United States as an independent hauler. After his father's death in 1994, the respondent assumed responsibility for the family trucking business.

* * *

Matter of Anderson, [16 I. & N. Dec. 596 (BIA 1978)] *supra*, has been the starting point for many years in applying the extreme hardship requirement. *Anderson* involved a 55-year-old native of the Dominican Republic who had overstayed his nonimmigrant visa and resided in the United States for 8 years by the time of his deportation hearing. He claimed that the impoverished economy in his country of origin should be dispositive as to extreme hardship. The Board rejected such a broad approach to extreme hardship, holding that "it is only when other factors such as advanced age, severe illness, family ties, etc. combine with economic detriment to make deportation extremely hard on the alien or the citizen or permanent resident members of his family that Congress has authorized suspension of the deportation order." *Id.* at 598.

In assessing hardship in *Anderson*, the Board found guidance concerning "other adverse factors" in a House Judiciary Committee report on the issue of "extreme hardship" in the context of a bill providing discretionary adjustment of status for certain aliens. *Matter of Anderson, supra*, at 597. This report included the following factors:

1. family ties in the United States and abroad;
2. length of residence in the United States;
3. condition of health;
4. conditions in the country to which the alien is returnable-economic and political;
5. financial status-business and occupation;
6. the possibility of other means of adjustment of status;
7. special assistance to the United States or community;
8. immigration history;
9. position in the community.

This list was not meant to preclude consideration of aspects of hardship which do not fit squarely within one of these nine factors.

Although these factors provide a framework for analysis, the "elements required to establish extreme hardship are dependent upon the facts and circumstances peculiar to each case." *Matter of Ige*, 20 I & N Dec. 880, 882 (BIA 1994). "Relevant factors, though not extreme in themselves, must be considered in the aggregate in determining whether extreme hardship exists." *Id.* In each case, the trier of fact must consider the entire range of factors concerning hardship in their totality and determine whether the combination of hardships takes the case beyond those hardships ordinarily associated with deportation, e.g., economic detriment due to loss of a job or efforts ordinarily required in relocating or adjusting to life in the native country. Such ordinary hardships, while not alone sufficient to constitute extreme hardship, are considered in the assessment of aggregate hardship.

The respondent entered the United States in November 1985 when he was 13 years old. He has lived here for over 10 years, including the critical formative years of adolescence.

During his stay in the United States, the respondent has assimilated into American life and culture. He successfully completed elementary school, junior high, and high school in the United States. He won an award for his excellent scholarship in junior high school. He has become fluent in written and spoken English. During his hearing before the Immigration Judge he testified in English rather than Spanish.

Since he graduated from high school, he has held a number of jobs. From 1992 to 1994 he worked as a security guard. In 1994 he took over his father's trucking business and now works as an independent hauler. He hopes to continue his studies and then pursue a career as a police officer.

He is deeply involved in church activities, attending services regularly and serving as a voluntary deacon in his congregation. As a deacon he assists in various church activities, including cleaning the church, taking up collection, and working with young children. The president of the respondent's congregation provided a letter indicating that the respondent has taken preliminary theological classes and that his involvement in youth ministry includes counseling, campaign coordination, and evangelization. The respondent is currently participating in continuing education courses towards full theological requirements for ordination to the ministry.

The respondent is a baseball enthusiast who attends many games each year. He also participates as a player on city league baseball and softball teams. The manager of his baseball team provided a letter praising the respondent as an athlete who has been of great value to the team and the community.

The respondent has close friends in the Los Angeles area, including his cousin, his brother's fiancee, and his own fiancee. The respondent testified that he is very close to his cousin whom he sees on nearly a daily basis. He has also established a close relationship with his brother's fiancee who testified that she has known the respondent for 6 years and that he treats her like a sister. Respondent testified to a close relationship of nearly 3 years with his fiancee who is in the United States awaiting adjudication of her asylum claim.

The Immigration Judge noted that the respondent could participate in church activities and become involved in community activities, such as baseball, in Nicaragua. The hardship related to community involvement, however, derives from the loss of the personal and social bonds established during the course of such activities. We consider not only the length of residence, but also the degree of integration into American society and the strength of attachments to friends and community.

Ordinarily, "the readjustment of an alien to life in his native country after having spent a number of years in the United States is not the type of hardship that is characterized as extreme, since similar hardship is suffered by most aliens who have spent time abroad." *Matter of Ige, supra*, at 883. When an alien has strongly embraced and deeply immersed himself in the social and cultural life of the United States, however, the emotional and psychological impact of readjustment must be considered in assessing hardship. *Santana-Figueroa v. INS*, 644 F.2d 1354, 1357 (9th Cir. 1981) (finding that extreme hardship could result from "the combined effect of depriving the petitioner of his livelihood and uprooting him from a community to which he had belonged and contributed for more than a decade.").

The Supreme Court has noted that "deportation may result in the loss 'of all that makes life worth living.'" *Bridges v. Wixon*, 326 U.S. 135, 147 (1945) (quoting *Ng Fung Ho v. White*, 259 U.S. 276, 284 (1922)). In this case, the respondent has developed such strong ties that deportation to Nicaragua would result in significant hardship on a social and psychological level. We find that deportation in this case would cause significant hardship over and above the normal disruption of social and community ties involved in deportation.

Additional hardship factors in this case relate to the depressed economic conditions and volatile political situation throughout Nicaragua. Although somewhat speculative, these factors do provide some additional weight in the assessment of aggregate hardship. See *Tukhowinich v. INS*, 64 F.3d 460, 463 (9th Cir.1995) (holding that political unrest in the country of origin should be considered in assessing hardship).

While economic detriment alone is not enough to constitute extreme hardship, it "is still a factor to consider in determining eligibility for suspension of deportation." *Mejia-Carrillo v. United States INS*, 656 F.2d 520, 522 (9th Cir.1981). In this case, the respondent helped his father to develop and operate an independent trucking business which he continued to manage after his father's death. The respondent's recent tax returns indicate that he has had an income of about $13,000 per year from this trucking business. He testified that were he to return to Nicaragua he could not establish the same kind of business in his home country because of difficult economic and political conditions. His loss of income as well as the business good will he and his father built up over the years are hardships which should be considered.

The Department of State's January 1995 Country Profile for Nicaragua, made part of the record of proceedings below, indicates that "[u]nemployment and underemployment total about 50 percent." Bureau of Democracy, Human Rights, and Labor, U.S. Dep't of State, Nicaragua-Profile of Asylum Claims & Country Conditions 4 (Jan. 1995) [hereinafter Profile]. The economy continues to stagnate with annual per capita income "less than one-third of what it was in the mid-1970s." *Id.* "Nicaragua's political problems continue to hamper economic growth and investors remain wary." *Id.*

In regard to political conditions, the respondent provided testimony and newspaper reports concerning recent Sandinista-related security problems in Nicaragua. The Profile reports that "Sandinistas maintain important positions in the military, police, bureaucracy, judiciary and unions. They have followers throughout the population and are in a position to punish and harm their perceived enemies if they have sufficient motive to do so. Furthermore, the Sandinistas can carry out such acts with virtually assured impunity because of their positions within the public safety/security organizations, their influence upon the government and the government's repeated grants of amnesty for past misdeeds." Profile, *supra*, at 5. In light of the respondent's family's history of conflict with the Sandinistas, the current political situation in Nicaragua should be factored into the hardship assessment.

Family unity considerations do not add measurably to the hardship aspects of this case. As indicated above, the respondent is unmarried and has no children. His mother resides in Nicaragua. His brother in Guatemala hopes to return to the United States to marry a permanent resident with a pending naturalization application. The respondent also testified that he has a close relationship with his cousin living nearby and that he has a number of cousins in New York with whom he keeps in touch. The respondent's fiancee is an undocumented alien with a pending asylum claim. The expectation that a brother may obtain permanent resident status and the hope that his undocumented fiancee will be granted asylum, while relevant, add little to the overall assessment of hardship in this case.

That the respondent has relatively weak family ties in the United States does not preclude him from demonstrating extreme hardship under other factors in *Matter of Anderson, supra.* In *Tukhowinich v. INS, supra*, for example, the respondent had never been married and had no children. She had worked in the garment industry in the United States for over 10 years to support her retired parents and five sisters residing in Thailand and three sisters in undocumented status in the United States. The respondent had devoted her life to providing for her family. Although similar work was available in Thailand, she could not have supported her family with the wages she would earn there. The United States Court of Appeals for the Ninth Circuit concluded that "[b]ecause the loss of financially comparable employment would create not only an economic hardship for Ms. Tukhowinich but would severely frustrate what she regards as the overriding mission in her life—to provide for her parents and siblings—we think the BIA should have considered the implications of her economic loss." *Id.* at 464.

Hardship is diminished to the extent that alternate means of obtaining lawful permanent residence may be available. In this case, asylum and withholding of deportation having been denied, the respondent has no present means of obtaining lawful permanent residence.

There is nothing in the respondent's immigration history which would detract from any of the aspects of his hardship claim. He entered the United States when he was 13 years old and has not left since that time. He has worked with authorization of the Immigration and Naturalization Service and has paid taxes during all of his years of work.

This is a close case on the issue of "extreme hardship" but one which, in the final analysis, meets the requirement of significant hardships over and above the normal economic and social disruptions involved in deportation. The respondent has lived in the United States during his critical formative years. He has significant church and community ties in the United States. He is fully assimilated into American culture and society. This assimilation makes the prospect of readjustment to life in Nicaragua much harder than would ordinarily be the case. He would also face difficult economic and political circumstances in his native country, including the possible loss of an ongoing business concern. This combination of hardships amounts to extreme hardship.

With regard to the exercise of discretion, there are no significant adverse factors. The record reflects that the respondent pays his taxes and is law abiding. He holds a position as a deacon in his church, and is well regarded by friends and acquaintances in the community. The record indicates that he has become thoroughly assimilated to life in the United States. Due to his productive and constructive time in the United States, the respondent merits relief in the exercise of discretion.

Concurring Opinion: David B. Holmes, Board Member

The dissent notes, not unfairly, that *Matter of Anderson, supra*, "does little in the way of providing content to the ambiguous phrase 'extreme hardship.'" In my view, the best manner in which to provide "content" to this "ambiguous phrase" is to provide examples and discussion in published Board decisions of factual circumstances in which the Board has concluded that the "extreme hardship" requirement for suspension of deportation eligibility either has or has not been met. Although in recent years the Board has provided little published guidance in this regard, the fact remains there are over 20 published Board decisions that address the "extreme hardship" requirement in cases in which respondents have applied for suspension of deportation under section 244(a)(1) of the Act. These published decisions of the Board have not been overruled, amended, or otherwise modified by the Board. Under the regulations which govern Board and Immigration Judge practice, these decisions "shall serve as precedents in all proceedings involving the same issue or issues." See 8 C.F.R. s 3.1(g) (1995). While there is discussion of some of this Board precedent in the majority and separate opinions, much of it goes unreferenced.

This case is the first published Board decision in many years that involves the adjudication of an application for suspension of deportation under section 244(a)(1) of the Act. Therefore, in the interest of the discussion being as complete as possible, I think it useful to identify and briefly summarize existing Board precedent involving "merits" adjudications of suspension applications that include "extreme hardship" determinations. These decisions are categorized below chronologically by outcome (i.e., grouped into those cases in which the Board found the "extreme hardship" requirement not to have been met and those cases in which the Board concluded that the "extreme hardship" element had been established). Although brief summaries of the pertinent "extreme hardship" considerations in each of these cases are noted, I do not claim to set forth every relevant consideration in these cases or to reference every nuance of these decisions. The decisions themselves are there to be read.

This—hopefully complete—survey of published Board decisions only includes cases involving "merits" adjudications of applications for relief under section 244(a)(1), rather than motions to reopen to apply for such relief, which often present different issues.

The most recent published Board decision involving a "merits" adjudication of an application for suspension under section 244(a)(1) of the Act was decided by the Board some 17 years ago.

Extreme Hardship Requirement Not Been Established

1. *Matter of Saekow*, 17 I & N Dec. 138 (BIA 1979). Unmarried native and citizen of Thailand; 29 years old; entered as a nonimmigrant student; 9 years' residence in the United States; no evidence of family ties to this country; employment as a specialty cook. "Extreme hardship" not established.

2. *Matter of Chumpitazi*, 16 I & N Dec. 629 (BIA 1978). Unmarried native and citizen of Peru; 31 years old; 11 years' residence in the United States; claim of loss of job and inability to financially support mother in Peru; argued difficult readjustment to life in Peru. "Extreme hardship" not established.

3. *Matter of Anderson*, 16 I & N Dec. 596 (BIA 1978). Married native and citizen of the Dominican Republic; 55 years old; wife with "emotional difficulties" unlawfully

present in the United States; 10 children and siblings residing in the Dominican Republic; 8 years' residence in the United States; employed as carpenter; principal claim related to economic detriment; cousins are only relatives in the United States. "Extreme hardship" not established.

4. *Matter of Gibson*, 16 I & N Dec. 58 (BIA 1976). Unmarried respondent from Great Britain; 32 years old; 9 years of residence in the United States; entered as nonimmigrant student; 5 semesters of college in this country; primarily employed as a custodian; should have "no difficulty" finding suitable employment abroad; "accustomed to the American way of life"; no relatives in the United States. "Extreme hardship" not established.

5. *Matter of Marques*, 15 I & N Dec. 200 (BIA 1975). Single native and citizen of Spain; 41 years old; entered as nonimmigrant worker; length of residence not stated, but apparently entered as an adult; no family ties; principal hardship claim tied to future access to financial benefits (insurance and industrial commission award) that allegedly would not be available if deported; facts indicate respondent is "a man of substantial means." "Extreme hardship" not established.

6. *Matter of Kim*, 15 I & N Dec. 88 (BIA 1974). Korean husband and wife; both entered as nonimmigrant students after obtaining college educations in Korea; claimed personal hardship arising from unsuitable employment opportunities and hardship to 6 1/2- and 3-year-old United States citizen children based on diminished educational and economic advantages in Korea. "Extreme hardship" not established.

7. *Matter of Kajoory*, 12 I & N Dec. 215 (BIA 1967). Unmarried native and citizen of Iran; 32 years old; 11 years' residence in the United States; no family ties in this country; entered as nonimmigrant student; hardship claim principally related to fear of persecution if returned to Iran, severely limited economic opportunities in that country, lack of opportunities in his own particular field, and difficulty adjusting to lower standard of living in Iran. "Extreme hardship" not established.

8. *Matter of Sangster*, 11 I & N Dec. 309 (BIA 1965). Native and citizen of Jamaica; 36 years old; entered as nonimmigrant student when over 26 years old; no dependents in this country; married to lawful permanent resident, but marriage never consummated and possibly under annulment proceedings; principal hardship would simply be economic detriment; not a "scintilla of evidence" in the record that suitable employment was unavailable in Jamaica or England. "Extreme hardship" not established.

9. *Matter of Uy*, 11 I & N Dec. 159 (BIA 1965). Unmarried native of the Philippines and citizen of China; 28 years old; entered as nonimmigrant student when about "19 1/2 years old"; student and part-time worker; parents and siblings in Philippines, and all of his brothers employed; claim of hardship principally tied to difficulty in adjusting to new environment outside the United States and claim of limited opportunities in his field of academic training. "Extreme hardship" not established.

10. *Matter of Liao*, 11 I & N Dec. 113 (BIA 1965). Unmarried native of China; advanced training as a pilot, skill as contact lens technician, and college education; 39 years old; admitted as nonimmigrant worker when approximately 28 years old;

hardship claim tied to fear of persecution and to claim of diminished employment opportunities; employed as stockman; sought permanent residence to complete undergraduate degree and to do postgraduate work; claim that anticipated training would be of more benefit in this country than in Formosa; Board noted in part that the respondent would "be in a better position to obtain employment ... than when he entered the United States." "Extreme hardship" not established.

Extreme Hardship Requirement to Have Been Established

Following are the Board's published cases involving "merits" adjudications of applications for suspension of deportation under section 244(a)(1) of the Act in which the Board found the requirement of "extreme hardship" established and ultimately granted suspension of deportation or affirmed Immigration Judge grants of such relief.

1. *Matter of Loo*, 15 I & N Dec. 601 (BIA 1976). 53-year-old native and citizen of China; 25 years' residence in the United States; lawful permanent resident daughter; small investment in United States business in which he was employed. "Extreme hardship" requirement met.

2. *Matter of Piggott*, 15 I & N Dec. 129 (BIA 1974). Husband and wife respondents; natives of Antigua and citizens of the United Kingdom and Colonies; minor United States children; Immigration Judge finding that respondents would not be able to provide for their own necessities in Antigua and that respondents' children would suffer because of parents' inability to provide them with proper food, living facilities, and education in that country; youngest United States citizen daughter afflicted with rheumatic fever, under physician's care, and "equal medical care ... not available in Antigua." "Extreme hardship" requirement met.

3. *Matter of Ching*, 12 I & N Dec. 710 (BIA 1968). Native and citizen of China; 55 years old; lawful permanent resident spouse; 16 years' residence in the United States following deportation in 1952; employed as cook; no relatives of either the respondent or his wife residing in the United States. "Extreme hardship" requirement met. Board also concluded that, even if respondent's application were considered under the more stringent provisions of section 244(a)(2) of the Act, suspension of deportation would be granted.

4. *Matter of Wong*, 12 I & N Dec. 271 (BIA 1967), overruled on other grounds, *Matter of Dilla*, 19 I & N Dec. 54 (BIA 1984). Native and citizen of China; 36 years old; 15 years' residence in the United States; married to a native and citizen of China who resided in Canada with their three children, ages 16, 6, and 5; two youngest children born in Canada; partner in grocery store; speaks "acceptable English"; would suffer "considerable financial hardship" if deported. "Extreme hardship" requirement met.

5. *Matter of Gee*, 11 I & N Dec. 639 (BIA 1966). Native and citizen of China; 32 years old; entered the United States when 18 years of age; 14 years' residence, interrupted by 4 months' trip to Formosa in 1960 during which the respondent was married; respondent subsequently divorced from wife and did not know her whereabouts; employed in laundry; supports mother who resides in Hong Kong; father is deceased;

2 years' honorable service in the United States Army; respondent submitted that it would be "very difficult" to obtain a job outside this country and that he had "become accustomed to the way of life here." "Extreme hardship" requirement met.

6. *Matter of Lum*, 11 I & N Dec. 295 (BIA 1965). Native and citizen of China; 29 years old; lived in United States for 14 years after entry at age of 15 years; regularly employed; owned 1/2 interest in restaurant from which he derived monthly income; "doubtful" he would be able to earn a comparable income elsewhere; "probably would suffer a substantial loss on his investment in the restaurant"; last entered the United States in 1962 under false claim to citizenship; married to a native and citizen of China who was attending school in Hong Kong and supported by the respondent; no children; service in United States Army. "Extreme hardship" requirement met.

7. *Matter of Chien*, 10 I & N Dec. 387 (BIA 1963). Native and citizen of China; 32 years old; 9 years' residence; originally entered as nonimmigrant student; became exchange visitor and granted waiver of 2-year foreign residence requirement; respondent's wife apparently a native and citizen of China, who was beneficiary of a waiver of the 2-year foreign residence requirement; wife was a pediatrician, but not employed; two United States citizen children, ages 4 and 2; employed as assistant professor of psychology engaged in problems of "wound shock" under contract with the Office of the Army Surgeon General; although beneficiary of a visa petition, respondent could not "readily" obtain an immigrant visa to adjust his nonimmigrant status because the relevant quota was oversubscribed. "Extreme hardship" requirement met.

8. *Matter of Woo*, 10 I & N Dec. 347 (BIA 1963). Native and citizen of China; 28 years old; entered the United States at age 12 and resided here for 15 years; served in the United States Armed Forces; married a native and citizen of China in Hong Kong in 1959; wife and 2-year-old foreign-born son reside in Hong Kong; excellent employment record and reputation. "Extreme hardship" requirement met.

9. *Matter of Leong*, 10 I & N Dec. 274 (BIA 1963). Married, native of China; 31 years old; originally entered the United States at age 18; last entered 3 years before deportation proceedings; United States military service and service-incurred 30% degree of disability; wife was a native and citizen of China who resided in that country; graduated from high school in the United States; employed in various capacities in restaurants in this country; the respondent's "adult years" had been spent in the United States; his earning ability had been impaired by his service-incurred disability. "Extreme hardship" requirement met.

10. *Matter of McCarthy*, 10 I & N Dec. 227 (BIA 1963). Native and citizen of Canada; 45 years old; twice deported, but first entry at age 6; had presence in United States spanning some 40 years; lawful permanent resident spouse and three United States citizen children, ages 8, 16, and 19; otherwise ineligible for visa. "Extreme hardship" requirement met.

11. *Matter of Louie*, 10 I & N Dec. 223 (BIA 1963). Native and citizen of China; 42 years old; 11 years' residence in the United States; respondent's Chinese wife and child still resided in Hong Kong; respondent contributed to their support; employment

as waiter; permanently disabled, elderly United States citizen father, who resided in "International Guest Home" in Los Angeles; respondent contributed to cost of father's maintenance and took his father to the doctor weekly; respondent and his father had no other close relatives in the United States. In view of "the father's advanced age and physical condition, ... it would be extremely harsh, both to the respondent and his father, to deport [the respondent] from the United States. "Extreme hardship" requirement met, both as to the respondent and to his United States citizen father.

Notes

1. The previous suspension statute provided relief for persons removable for crimes where the applicant was able to show exceptional and extremely unusual hardship. One court said that this standard could only be met if the person's removal would be unconscionable.[41]

2. Recall that in our discussion of adjustment of status, the concept of "balancing of equities" was introduced. In cancellation cases, the analysis is focused more on the degree of hardship than in weighing positive and negative factors of the applicant's conduct. Therefore, the challenge for the immigration judge is in considering all of the factors cumulatively.[42]

3. The result of a successful application for cancellation of removal is that the applicant receives lawful permanent residency. Cancellation of removal for non-permanent residents was intended to be a very difficult benefit for persons to obtain.[43] Indeed, the original suspension remedy was also very difficult benefit to obtain.[44]

4. In fashioning an argument for extreme hardship, a lawyer must use creative approaches. In *Matter of Anderson*, the BIA outlined the criteria to be used in assessing the extreme hardship claim. What argument might be presented where the individual simultaneously applies for asylum *and* suspension of removal? What should be the burden of proof in such a claim?

5. In *In re Monreal-Aguinaga*,[45] the BIA rejected the notion that the standard of "extremely, exceptional and unusual" would have to amount to one where the person's removal would be "unconscionable." The case involved a 34-year-old man from Mexico who had lived in the United States since the age of 14. He had two children, both U.S. citizens aged eight and twelve, his parents resided in the United States as permanent residents since 1995 and he had worked regularly in his uncle's business since 1991. His wife had previously returned to Mexico believing that she was ineligible for cancellation relief. In rejecting the applicant's claim, the immigration judge noted

---

41. *Asikese v. Brownell*, 230 F.2d 34 (D.C. Cir. 1956).

42. *See Santana-Figueroa v. INS*, 644 F.2d 635 (7th Cir. 1981); *Barrera-Leyva v. INS*, 637 F.2d 640 (9th Cir. 1980); *Ramos v. INS*, 695 F.2d 181 (5th Cir. 1983).

43. *See* H.R. Conf. Rep. 828 104th Cong., 2d Sess. 213–14 (1996).

44. *See, e.g., Suspension of Deportation: Illusory Relief*, 14 San Diego L. Rev. 229 (1976); *but see Suspension of Deportation: A Revitalized Relief for the Alien*, 18 San Diego L. Rev. 65 (1980).

45. 23 I. & N. Dec. 56 (BIA 2001).

that "this was a 'sad' case, particularly in view of its effect on the United States citizen children", and the INS trial attorney stated that the applicant and his family were "really good people." The Board, in affirming the immigration judge's decision, attempted to elaborate on the meaning of the hardship standard, stating that

> ... The new standard requires a showing of hardship beyond that which has historically been required in suspension of deportation cases involving the "extreme hardship" standard. As the legislative history indicates, the hardship to an alien's relatives, if the alien is obliged to leave the United States, must be "substantially" beyond the ordinary hardship that would be expected when a close family member leaves this country. Cancellation of removal under section 240A(b) of the Act is to be limited to "truly exceptional" situations.
>
> At the same time, we recognize that some cases in which this Board or the Immigration Judges have found "extreme hardship" under the suspension statute may also have presented facts and circumstances that rose to the level of "exceptional and extremely unusual hardship." Moreover, although guidance as to this term's meaning can be provided, each case must be assessed and decided on its own facts.

6. USCIS district directors do not adjudicate requests for cancellation of removal; these cases are decided by Immigration judges in the course of removal proceedings. In the event of an adverse decision, it may, like other cases in removal, be appealed to the BIA.

7. Cancellation cases are brought in the following manner: (a) if the applicant is in custody or an order or notice to appear (NTA) has been issued, the application is presented before the judge at the commencement of the hearing; and (b) a person who intends to seek cancellation must appear before USCIS and request the issuance of the NTA so that the application can be presented to the judge. Counsel representing the applicant must be cautious before deciding to "turn the client in" to proceed with a cancellation of removal application. Finally, in many cases, cancellation may be seen as part of a strategy of preventing immediate removal, allowing the attorney an opportunity to seek alternative remedies.

8. Proving the claim of hardship requires a careful presentation of the facts initiated by the submission of application form EOIR-42B. A well-prepared case will include affidavits, letters, other documents and witnesses. Assume, for example, that you were attempting to show that an infirmity coupled with advanced age and sick children constituted sufficient hardship. You would first present the application, affidavits attesting to good moral character, police reports reflecting no derogatory information, income tax returns and pay receipts, birth certificates of the children, medical reports for the children and family and live testimony from experts such as treating physicians, psychiatrists and persons knowledgeable of the family's situation. Can you think of any additional information which you would present at the hearing? Would it make any difference if you were submitting the evidence as part of a motion to reopen? A motion to reopen is a request based upon newly discovered evidence in which the

applicant claims that she now qualifies for a benefit. (Motions to reopen are discussed at greater length in Chapter 12.)

B. Waivers of Grounds for Removal and Inadmissibility

As we discussed in Chapters 3 and 4, the grounds of inadmissibility and deportability are extensive and represent the exercise of congressional plenary power to exclude and remove those foreigners whom Congress deem undesirable. Most of the grounds of inadmissibility and deportability include waiver provisions which may be obtained depending upon (1) the applicant's length of residency; (2) the applicant's familial relationship to U.S. citizens or lawful permanent residents; (3) the degree of hardship that would be suffered by the applicant or her family members; (4) the applicant's employment history; (5) the applicant's property or business ties in the country; (6) the applicant's value, service and ties to the community; (7) the applicant's criminal history; and (8) any evidence of the applicant's moral character, whether good or bad. Waivers represent a recognition that persons considered to be undesirable might not—in the particular circumstances—be undesirable as a matter of fact. An apt analogy might be that of an angry person who makes a blanket statement as to persons she does not want to permit into her house. Later, she might realize that the blanket exclusion prevents her from inviting certain people she would like to welcome, so she might provide criteria and exceptions to the broad exclusion.

With the passage of the Anti-Drug Abuse Act in 1988[46] and the Immigration Act of 1990,[47] the available ameliorative devices for non-citizens with criminal convictions have decreased. For example, until November 28, 1990, sentencing judges could grant a person a judicial recommendation against removal, thereby precluding the use of the conviction in a later removal proceeding. In subsequent years, Congress enacted restrictive statutes designed to curb the numbers of people who would be able to remain in the United States following their convictions.[48] It remains to be seen what effect the limiting of discretionary ameliorative devices have had on criminal and immigration proceedings. The discussion and cases which follow attempt to present most of the mechanisms which may be used to protect persons from the many grounds of inadmissibility and deportability.

The waiver application is generally sought at the point where it will be necessary for gaining admission, preventing removal or obtaining an immigration benefit such as conditional or lawful permanent residence. The waiver application may be sub-

---

46. Pub. L. No. 100-690, 102 Stat. 4181 (1988).

47. Pub. L. No. 101-649, 104 Stat. 4978 (1990).

48. *See* Anti-Terrorism and Effective Death Penalty Act of 1996, Pub. L. No. 104-132, 110 Stat. 279 (1996).

mitted to the Consul in the case of a nonimmigrant, to USCIS in the case where a person is seeking adjustment of status or to the immigration judge if the person is in proceedings to determine admissibility or removability. Waivers have peculiar procedural requirements due in part to the separate roles of the Department of State, USCIS and immigration judge in determining whether a person may be admitted.

Non-waivable grounds. Before launching into a discussion of the waivers, it bears mentioning that there are certain categories of persons for whom there are no waivers. If such a person is in the United States, her only alternative may be to seek relief under one of the benefits described previously. The categories of persons for whom waivers are unavailable are the following:

- Certain aggravated felons—While aggravated felons are ineligible for most forms of immigration relief such as asylum and restriction of removal, they may be eligible for limited protection under the Convention Against Torture (see Chapter 5). Aggravated felons who committed crimes of torture or murder or who after being admitted as lawful permanent residents committed an aggravated felony are ineligible for waivers. Other persons may be eligible for relief under 8 U.S.C. § 1182(h), Sec. 212(h), which is discussed later.
- Participants in Nazi persecutions or in genocide—8 U.S.C. § 1182(a)(3)(E)(i), Sec. 212(a)(3)(E)(i), prohibits the admission of persons who participated in the persecution of others under a broad range of areas controlled or supported by the Nazi regime between March 23, 1933 and May 8, 1945. A subsection of the statute also prohibits persons who have engaged in conduct defined as Genocide under the International Convention on the Prevention and Punishment of Genocide.
- Narcotics traffickers—8 U.S.C. § 1182(a)(2)(C), Sec. 212(a)(2)(C), prohibits the admission of persons who a consular or immigration officer has "reason to believe" is or has engaged in the illicit trafficking of a "controlled substance." This provision is broad and encompasses those who have in any way participated in trafficking. Potentially included within this broad group are drug abusers or addicts who are otherwise eligible for cancellation of removal.[49]
- Persons who pose a risk to national security or terrorists.
- Certain graduates of foreign medical schools who have not passed the VQE.
- Certain persons likely to become a public charge.
- Persons coming to practice polygamy.

The discussion which follows begins by exploring the waivers for crimes and then for the broader categories of inadmissibility and deportability.

---

49. Under 8 U.S.C. § 1182(a)(1)(A)(iv), Sec. 212(a)(1)(A)(iv), drug abusers or addicts are ineligible for admission. While the statute does not provide for a waiver, the cancellation of removal provisions provide for granting of cancellation and eventual permanent residence for those who qualify.

1. Cancellation of Removal— Long-Term Permanent Residents

Previously, we discussed cancellation of removal for non-permanent residents.[50] That form of cancellation is more like relief from removal rather than the waivers which we discuss here. Here we will explore the cancellation of removal for permanent residents which allows a permanent resident who has become deportable or inadmissible to avail themselves of a one time waiver of most grounds of removal, essentially allowing the proceedings to be cancelled. When Congress amended the INA in 1996 it unified the former exclusion/deportation hearings into "removal proceedings" and created cancellation relief to replace a waiver provision which had been available for long-term permanent known as the "section 212(c)" waiver. Cancellation of removal accomplishes the same objective of the predecessor statute as it is available to persons who have been present in the United States for an extended period of time but have committed acts which render them inadmissible or deportable.

In order to qualify for this form of cancellation, the applicant must show that they have been a lawful permanent resident for 5 years; have resided in the U.S. continuously for 7 years; and warrant the positive exercise of discretion. Aggravated felons, terrorists, persecutors of others as well as those who entered as crewmen and certain persons who entered as J visa holders are ineligible. The stop-time rule which was discussed previously applies to the residence requirement of the benefit.[51]

Following the enactment of the cancellation of removal provision under IIRAIRA, persons who would have been eligible for §212(c) relief at the time of their conviction under the predecessor statute but would not be eligible for relief under the new cancellation of removal challenged the retroactive application of the statute. In the case which follows, *INS v. St. Cyr*,[52] the Court elaborates on the principle that statutes are presumptively non-retroactive unless there is an otherwise clear statement to the contrary.[53]

Immigration and Naturalization Service v. Enrico St. Cyr

533 U.S. 289 (2001)

Stevens, J., delivered the opinion of the Court, in which Kennedy, Souter, Ginsburg, and Breyer, JJ., joined. O'Connor, J., filed a dissenting opinion. Scalia, J., filed a dissenting opinion, in which Rehnquist, C.J., and Thomas, J., joined, and in which O'Connor, J., joined, as to Parts I and III.

---

50. 8 U.S.C. §1229b(a)–(b), Sec. 240A(a)–(b).

51. *Sinotes-Cruz v. Gonzales*, 468 F.3d 1190, 1197 (9th Cir. 2006).

52. 533 U.S. 289 (2001).

53. Note: Other portions of this case are excerpted and discussed in the chapter on judicial review. For a complete copy of *St. Cyr*, see the Casebook webpage under "Relief and Amelioration of Grounds for Removal."

Justice Stevens delivered the opinion of the Court.

* * *

The absence of a clearly expressed statement of congressional intent also pervades our review of the merits of St. Cyr's claim. Two important legal consequences ensued from respondent's entry of a guilty plea in March 1996:(1) He became subject to deportation, and (2) he became eligible for a discretionary waiver of that deportation under the prevailing interpretation of § 212(c). When IIRIRA went into effect in April 1997, the first consequence was unchanged except for the fact that the term "removal" was substituted for "deportation." The issue that remains to be resolved is whether IIRIRA § 304(b) changed the second consequence by eliminating respondent's eligibility for a waiver.

The INS submits that the statute resolves the issue because it unambiguously communicates Congress' intent to apply the provisions of IIRIRA's Title III-A to all removals initiated after the effective date of the statute, and, in any event, its provisions only operate prospectively and not retrospectively. The Court of Appeals, relying primarily on the analysis in our opinion in *Landgraf v. USI Film Products*, 511 U.S. 244 (1994), held, contrary to the INS' arguments, that Congress' intentions concerning the application of the "Cancellation of Removal" procedure are ambiguous and that the statute imposes an impermissible retroactive effect on aliens who, in reliance on the possibility of § 212(c) relief, pled guilty to aggravated felonies. See 229 F.3d, at 416, 420. We agree.

Retroactive statutes raise special concerns. See *Landgraf*, 511 U.S., at 266. "The Legislature's unmatched powers allow it to sweep away settled expectations suddenly and without individualized consideration. Its responsivity to political pressures poses a risk that it may be tempted to use retroactive legislation as a means of retribution against unpopular groups or individuals." *Ibid.* Accordingly, "congressional enactments ... will not be construed to have retroactive effect unless their language requires this result." *Bowen v. Georgetown Univ. Hospital*, 488 U.S. 204, 208 (1988).

> "[This] presumption against retroactive legislation is deeply rooted in our jurisprudence, and embodies a legal doctrine centuries older than our Republic. Elementary considerations of fairness dictate that individuals should have an opportunity to know what the law is and to conform their conduct accordingly; settled expectations should not be lightly disrupted. For that reason, the 'principle that the legal effect of conduct should ordinarily be assessed under the law that existed when the conduct took place has timeless and universal human appeal.' *Kaiser*, 494 U.S., at 855 (Scalia, J., concurring). In a free, dynamic society, creativity in both commercial and artistic endeavors is fostered by a rule of law that gives people confidence about the legal consequences of their actions." *Landgraf*, 511 U.S., at 265–266 (footnote omitted).

Despite the dangers inherent in retroactive legislation, it is beyond dispute that, within constitutional limits, Congress has the power to enact laws with retrospective effect. See *id.*, at 268. A statute may not be applied retroactively, however, absent a clear indication from Congress that it intended such a result. "Requiring clear intent assures that Congress itself has affirmatively considered the potential unfairness of retroactive application and determined that it is an acceptable price to pay for the countervailing benefits." *Id.*, at 272–273. Accordingly, the first step in determining whether a statute has an impermissible retroactive effect is to ascertain whether Congress has directed with the requisite clarity that the law be applied retrospectively. *Martin v. Hadix*, 527 U.S. 343, 352 (1999).

The standard for finding such unambiguous direction is a demanding one. "[C]ases where this Court has found truly 'retroactive' effect adequately authorized by statute have involved statutory language that was so clear that it could sustain only one interpretation." *Lindh v. Murphy*, 521 U.S. 320, 328, n. 4 (1997). The INS makes several arguments in favor of its position that IIRIRA achieves this high level of clarity.

First, the INS points to the comprehensive nature of IIRIRA's revision of federal immigration law. "Congress's comprehensive establishment of a new immigration framework," the INS argues, "shows its intent that, after a transition period, the provisions of the old law should no longer be applied at all." Brief for Petitioner 33–34. We rejected a similar argument, however, in *Landgraf*, a case that, like this one, involved Congress' comprehensive revision of an important federal statute. 511 U.S., at 260–261. By itself, the comprehensiveness of a congressional enactment says nothing about Congress' intentions with respect to the retroactivity of the enactment's individual provisions.

The INS also points to the effective date for Title III-A as providing a clear statement of congressional intent to apply IIRIRA's repeal of § 212(c) retroactively. See IIRIRA § 309(a). But the mere promulgation of an effective date for a statute does not provide sufficient assurance that Congress specifically considered the potential unfairness that retroactive application would produce. For that reason, a "statement that a statute will become effective on a certain date does not even arguably suggest that it has any application to conduct that occurred at an earlier date." *Landgraf*, 511 U.S., at 257.

The INS further argues that any ambiguity in Congress' intent is wiped away by the "saving provision" in IIRIRA § 309(c)(1). Brief for Petitioner 34–36. That provision states that, for aliens whose exclusion or deportation proceedings began prior to the Title III-A effective date, "the amendments made by [Title III-A] shall not apply, and ... the proceedings (including judicial review thereof) shall continue to be conducted without regard to such amendments." This rule, however, does not communicate with unmistakable clarity Congress' intention to apply its repeal of § 212(c) retroactively. Nothing in either § 309(c)(1) or the statute's legislative history even discusses the effect of the statute on proceedings based on pre-IIRIRA convictions that are commenced after its effective date. Section 309(c)(1) is best read as merely setting out the procedural rules to be applied to removal proceedings pending on the effective date of the statute. Because "[c]hanges in procedural rules may often be applied in suits arising before their enactment without raising concerns about retroactivity,"

Landgraf, 511 U.S., at 275, it was necessary for Congress to identify which set of procedures would apply in those circumstances. As the Conference Report expressly explained, "[Section 309(c)] provides for the transition to new *procedures* in the case of an alien already in exclusion or deportation proceedings on the effective date." H.R. Conf. Rep. No. 104-828, p. 222 (1996) (emphasis added).

Another reason for declining to accept the INS' invitation to read § 309(c)(1) as dictating the temporal reach of IIRIRA § 304(b) is provided by Congress' willingness, in other sections of IIRIRA, to indicate unambiguously its intention to apply specific provisions retroactively. IIRIRA's amendment of the definition of "aggravated felony," for example, clearly states that it applies with respect to "conviction[s] ... entered before, on, or after" the statute's enactment date. § 321(b). As the Court of Appeals noted, the fact that Congress made some provisions of IIRIRA expressly applicable to prior convictions, but did not do so in regard to § 304(b), is an indication "that Congress did not definitively decide the issue of § 304(b)'s retroactive application to pre-enactment convictions." See 229 F.3d, at 415. The "saving provision" is therefore no more significant than the specification of an effective date.

The presumption against retroactive application of ambiguous statutory provisions, buttressed by "the longstanding principle of construing any lingering ambiguities in deportation statutes in favor of the alien," *INS v. Cardoza-Fonseca*, 480 U.S. 421, 449 (1987), forecloses the conclusion that, in enacting § 304(b), "Congress itself has affirmatively considered the potential unfairness of retroactive application and determined that it is an acceptable price to pay for the countervailing benefits."[44] *Landgraf*, 511 U.S., at 272–273. We therefore proceed to the second step of *Landgraf's* retroactivity analysis in order to determine whether depriving removable aliens of consideration for § 212(c) relief produces an impermissible retroactive effect for aliens who, like respondent, were convicted pursuant to a plea agreement at a time when their plea would not have rendered them ineligible for § 212(c) relief.

* * *

IIRIRA's elimination of any possibility of § 212(c) relief for people who entered into plea agreements with the expectation that they would be eligible for such relief clearly " 'attaches a new disability, in respect to transactions or considerations already past.' " *Landgraf*, 511 U.S., at 269. Plea agreements involve a *quid pro quo* between a criminal defendant and the government. See *Newton v. Rumery*, 480 U.S. 386, 393,

44. The legislative history is significant because, despite its comprehensive character, it contains no evidence that Congress specifically considered the question of the applicability of IIRIRA § 304(b) to pre-IIRIRA convictions. Cf. *Harrison v. PPG Industries, Inc.*, 446 U.S. 578, 602 (1980) (Rehnquist, J., dissenting) ("In a case where the construction of legislative language such as this makes so sweeping and so relatively unorthodox a change as that made here, I think judges as well as detectives may take into consideration the fact that a watchdog did not bark in the night"), cited in *Chisom v. Roemer*, 501 U.S. 380, 396, n. 23 (1991) (citing A. Doyle, *Silver Blaze*, in The Complete Sherlock Holmes 335 (1927)).

n. 3 (1987). In exchange for some perceived benefit, defendants waive several of their constitutional rights (including the right to a trial) and grant the government numerous "tangible benefits, such as promptly imposed punishment without the expenditure of prosecutorial resources."[47] *Ibid.* There can be little doubt that, as a general matter, alien defendants considering whether to enter into a plea agreement are acutely aware of the immigration consequences of their convictions. See *Magana-Pizano v. INS*, 200 F.3d 603, 612 (C.A.9 1999) ("That an alien charged with a crime ... would factor the immigration consequences of conviction in deciding whether to plead or proceed to trial is well-documented."); see also 3 Bender, Criminal Defense Techniques §§ 60A.01, 60A.02[2] (1999) ("Preserving the client's right to remain in the United States may be more important to the client than any potential jail sentence"). Given the frequency with which § 212(c) relief was granted in the years leading up to AEDPA and IIRIRA, preserving the possibility of such relief would have been one of the principal benefits sought by defendants deciding whether to accept a plea offer or instead to proceed to trial.

The case of Charles Jideonwo, a petitioner in a parallel litigation in the Seventh Circuit, is instructive. Charged in 1994 with violating federal narcotics law, Jideonwo entered into extensive plea negotiations with the government, the sole purpose of which was to ensure that " 'he got less than five years to avoid what would have been a statutory bar on 212(c) relief.' " *Jideonwo v. INS*, 224 F.3d 692, 699 (C.A.7 2000) (quoting the Immigration Judge's findings of fact). The potential for unfairness in the retroactive application of IIRIRA § 304(b) to people like Jideonwo and St. Cyr is significant and manifest. Relying upon settled practice, the advice of counsel, and perhaps even assurances in open court that the entry of the plea would not foreclose § 212(c) relief, a great number of defendants in Jideonwo's and St. Cyr's position agreed to plead guilty.[51] Now that prosecutors have received the benefit of these plea agreements, agreements that were likely facilitated by the aliens' belief in their continued eligibility for § 212(c) relief, it would surely be contrary to "familiar considerations of fair notice, reasonable reliance, and settled expectations," *Landgraf*, 511 U.S., at 270, to hold that IIRIRA's subsequent restrictions deprive them of any possibility of such relief.[52]

The INS argues that deportation proceedings (and the Attorney General's discretionary power to grant relief from deportation) are "inherently prospective" and that,

47. "If every criminal charge were subjected to a full-scale trial, the States and the Federal Government would need to multiply by many times the number of judges and court facilities." *Santobello v. New York*, 404 U.S. 257, 260 (1971).

51. Ninety percent of criminal convictions today are obtained by guilty plea. See U.S. Dept. of Justice, Office of Justice Programs, Bureau of Justice Statistics, Section 5: Judicial Processing of Defendants, Tables 5.30, 5.51, in United States Sentencing Commission, 1999 Sourcebook of Criminal Justice Statistics (2000).

52. The significance of that reliance is obvious to those who have participated in the exercise of the discretion that was previously available to delegates of the Attorney General under § 212(c). See *In re Soriano*, 16 Immig. Rptr. B1-227, B1-238 to B1-239 (BIA 1996) (Lory D. Rosenberg, Board Member, concurring and dissenting) ("I find compelling policy and practical reasons to go beyond

as a result, application of the law of deportation can never have a retroactive effect. Such categorical arguments are not particularly helpful in undertaking *Landgraf's* commonsense, functional retroactivity analysis. See *Martin*, 527 U.S., at 359. Moreover, although we have characterized deportation as "look[ing] prospectively to the respondent's right to remain in this country in the future," *INS v. Lopez-Mendoza*, 468 U.S. 1032, 1038(1984), we have done so in order to reject the argument that deportation is punishment for past behavior and that deportation proceedings are therefore subject to the "various protections that apply in the context of a criminal trial." *Ibid.* As our cases make clear, the presumption against retroactivity applies far beyond the confines of the criminal law. See *Landgraf*, 511 U.S., at 272. And our mere statement that deportation is not punishment for past crimes does not mean that we cannot consider an alien's reasonable reliance on the continued availability of discretionary relief from deportation when deciding whether the elimination of such relief has a retroactive effect.

Finally, the fact that § 212(c) relief is discretionary does not affect the propriety of our conclusion. There is a clear difference, for the purposes of retroactivity analysis, between facing possible deportation and facing certain deportation. Cf. *Hughes Aircraft Co. v. United States ex rel. Schumer*, 520 U.S. 939, 949 (1997) (an increased likelihood of facing a *qui tam* action constitutes an impermissible retroactive effect for the defendant); *Lindsey v. Washington*, 301 U.S. 397, 401 (1937) ("Removal of the *possibility* of a sentence of less than fifteen years ... operates to [defendants'] detriment" (emphasis added)). Prior to AEDPA and IIRIRA, aliens like St. Cyr had a significant likelihood of receiving § 212(c) relief. Because respondent, and other aliens like him, almost certainly relied upon that likelihood in deciding whether to forgo their right to a trial, the elimination of any possibility of § 212(c) relief by IIRIRA has an obvious and severe retroactive effect.

We find nothing in IIRIRA unmistakably indicating that Congress considered the question whether to apply its repeal of § 212(c) retroactively to such aliens. We therefore hold that § 212(c) relief remains available for aliens, like respondent, whose convictions were obtained through plea agreements and who, notwithstanding those convictions, would have been eligible for § 212(c) relief at the time of their plea under the law then in effect.

The judgment is affirmed.

Notes

1. Courts are extremely reluctant to overturn denials of cancellation claims by the BIA, as they are discretionary exercises. However, some courts have been willing to

---

such a limited interpretation as the one the majority proposes in this case. All of these people, and no doubt many others, had settled expectations to which they conformed their conduct").

look more closely at the factors considered by the Board in assessing extreme hardship, thereby allowing for remand of the case to the Board for further consideration.[54] IIRAIRA eliminated judicial review of those determinations, which are committed to the discretion of the Attorney General. That does not mean that there is no judicial review, since aspects of decisions in cancellation cases involve issues of law and fact, which are subject to review.

2. On review, the individual applicant is entitled first to have her case decided on its own facts, and the weighing of these facts must be evident from the decision. In one case, a Ninth Circuit *en banc* panel criticized the BIA for its summary approach to a review of the evidence and for having invoked a floodgates argument in denying the applicant's claim.[55] For an excellent critique of this relief from removal, see Margaret H. Taylor, *What Happened to Non-LPR Cancellation? Rationalizing Immigration Enforcement by Restoring Durable Relief from Removal*, 30 J. of L. & Pol. 527 (2015).

3. The continuous physical presence requirement allows for breaks in physical presence of up to 180 days during the ten-year period.

4. Even if a person is successful in establishing eligibility for cancellation, there is a limit of 4,000 persons who may be adjusted to permanent residency each year.[56] The regulations provide that the person be placed on a waiting list and have a conditional grant of cancellation in the interim, which will be converted to permanent residency when it becomes available.[57] This limit only applies to cancellation for non-permanent residents.

5. Do you think that the Board's approach to interpreting the meaning of the cancellation statute is similar to the manner in which the Supreme Court has interpreted other immigration statutes?[58]

6. 8 U.S.C. § 1229a(c), Sec. 240(c), provides that the following persons are ineligible for both forms of cancellation: (1) those who entered as crewmen after June 30, 1964; (2) those who are admitted under a J visa for graduate medical training or subject to the two-year foreign residency requirement; (3) those inadmissible or removable under the terrorist grounds;[59] (4) those who have persecuted others;[60] or (5) those who were previously granted suspension of deportation, a § 212(c) waiver or cancellation of removal.

---

54. *See e.g. Ravancho v. INS*, 658 F.2d 169 (3d Cir. 1981); *Santana-Figueroa v. INS*, 644 F.2d 1354 (9th Cir. 1981); *Antoine-Dorcelli v. INS*, 703 F.2d 19 (1st Cir. 1983); *Carrete-Michel v. INS*, 749 F.2d 490 (8th Cir. 1984).

55. *See Prapavat v. INS*, 638 F.2d 87 (9th Cir. 1980), *aff'd en banc*, 662 F.2d 561 (1981).

56. 8 U.S.C. §§ 1229b(b)(3) and (e), Sections 240A(b)(3) and (e).

57. *See* 8 C.F.R. § 1240.21(a).

58. *See INS v. Phinpathya*, 464 U.S. 183 (1984); *INS v. Stevic*, 467 U.S. 407 (1984); *INS v. Cardoza-Fonseca*, 480 U.S. 421 (1987).

59. 8 U.S.C. §§ 1182(a)(3) and 1227(a)(3), Sections 212(a)(3) and 237(a)(3).

60. 8 U.S.C. § 1231(b)(3)(B)(i), Sec. 241(b)(3)(B)(i).

7. Much of the controversy following the enactment of IIRAIRA revolved around the issue of whether a person may be able to proceed under the old § 212(c) applications or be required to submit a cancellation of removal request. The statute's language provides that the effective date of the statute is April 1, 1997, meaning that cancellation would be available for cases brought after April 1, 1997 and that legacy INS had the option of terminating and then beginning the proceedings anew under IIRAIRA.[61]

8. A federal district court in New York rejected the BIA's interpretation in *Perez*.[62] Another court has refused to follow the analysis in *Henry*, noting that because *St. Cyr* involved the consideration of a plea rather than the commission of an act and cut off the period of continuous residence, "[i]t would border on the absurd to argue that these aliens might have decided not to commit ... crimes, or might have resisted conviction more vigorously, had they known that if they were not only imprisoned but also, when their prison term ended, [and] ordered deported, they could not ask for a discretionary waiver of deportation."[63]

---

2. Crimes

a. What Is a "Conviction"?

In re Salazar-Regino

23 I. & N. Dec. 223 (BIA 2002)

BEFORE: Board En Banc: Scialabba, Acting Chairman; Dunne, Vice Chairman; Hurwitz, Filppu, Cole, Grant, Ohlson, Hess and Pauley, Board Members. Concurring Opinions: Holmes, Board Member, joined by Guendeslberger, Miller and Osuna, Board Members; Brennan, Board Member. Concurring and Dissenting Opinion: Schmidt, Board Member. Dissenting Opinions: Rosenberg, Board Member, joined by Villageliu and Espenoza, Board Members; Moscato, Board Member, joined by Villageliu, Board Member, Grant, Board Member:

In a decision dated February 22, 1999, an Immigration Judge terminated the removal proceedings against the respondent. The Immigration and Naturalization Service has appealed from that decision.... The appeal will be sustained.

The respondent is a native and citizen of Mexico who entered the United States on May 14. 1977, as a nonimmigrant visitor. Her status was adjusted to that of a

---

61. See *Matter of Soriano*, Interim Dec. 3289 (Att'y Gen. 1997); *but see Mojica v. Reno*, 970 F. Supp. 828 (E.D.N.Y. 1997); *Yesil v. Reno*, 973 F. Supp. 372 (S.D.N.Y. 1997).

62. See *Henry v. Ashcroft*, 175 F. Supp. 2d 688, 691 (S.D.N.Y. 2001).

63. See *Worrell v. Ashcroft*, 207 F. Supp. 61, 67 (W.D.N.Y 2002) (quoting *La Guerre v. Reno*, 164 F.3d 1035, 1040 (7th Cir. 1998)).

lawful permanent resident on May 7, 1981. On October 11, 1996, an indictment was filed against the respondent in Texas, charging that she committed a third degree felony by "intentionally and knowingly possess[ing] a usable quantity of marijuana in an amount of 50 pounds or less but more than 5 pounds." The respondent pled guilty to the charge on January 7, 1997, and the District Court for Chambers County deferred adjudication of guilt pursuant to article 42.12, section 5(a) of the Texas Code of Criminal Procedure, placing her on probation for 10 years.

The Service commenced proceedings in this case when it filed a Notice to Appear (Form 1-862) with the Immigration Court on August 10, 1998. The Notice to Appear charged that the respondent is removable under section 237(a)(2)(A)(in) of the Immigration and Nationality Act, 8 U.S.C. § 1227(a)(2)(A)(iii) (Supp. IV 1998), as an alien convicted of an aggravated felony (a drug trafficking crime as defined in section 101(a)(43)(B) of the Act, 8 U.S.C. § 1101(a)(43)(B) (Supp. IV 1998)), and under section 237(a)(2)(B)(i) of the Act as an alien convicted of a controlled substance violation. In removal proceedings on January 20, 1999, the respondent denied the allegation that she had been "convicted" of the Texas felony offense, and she denied both charges of removability.

The Immigration Judge first determined that the conviction records established that the respondent had been convicted in Texas of a felony drug possession offense. He therefore concluded that the respondent was subject to removal under section 237(a)(2)(B)(i) of the Act as an alien convicted of a controlled substance violation. However, he found that the charge under section 237(a)(2)(A)(iii) was not proved because the respondent's offense was not a felony under federal law and was therefore not an aggravated felony under *Matter of L-G-, 20 I&N Dec. 905 (BIA 1994). Finally, the Immigration Judge determined that because the respondent was a first-time drug offender with a state deferred adjudication, she would have been eligible for federal first offender treatment pursuant to 18 U.S.C. § 3607 (1994) if she were prosecuted in federal court, and that she therefore met the requirements set* forth in *Matter of Manrique*, 21 I&N Dec. 58 (BIA 1995). Consequently, he concluded that she should not be deported and terminated the proceedings against her.

Two issues are presented for resolution in this case. The first is whether the respondent's deferred adjudication for felony possession of marijuana constitutes a "conviction" under the Act. Subsequent to the Immigration Judge's decision, we held in *Matter of Roldan,* Interim Decision 3377 (BIA 1999), that *Matter of Manrique, supra,* had been superseded in 1996 by the enactment of section 101(a)(48)(A) of the Act, 8 U.S.C. § 1101(a)(48)(A) (Supp. II 1996), However, in *Lujan-Armendariz v. INS,* 222 F.3d 728 (9th Cir, 2000), the United States Court of Appeals for the Ninth Circuit overruled *Matter of Roldan* in part and required application of the Board's former rule in *Matter of Manrique* in that circuit. We must therefore determine whether to apply the Ninth Circuit's decision on a nationwide basis.

Assuming that the respondent's deferred adjudication is a conviction for immigration purposes, the second issue before us is whether her offense is an aggravated felony under section 101(a)(43)(B) of the Act.

On the First issue, the Service asserts that *Matter of Roldan, supra,* is controlling. It relies as well on *Matter of Punu,* Interim Decision 3364 (BIA 1998), where we held that a deferred adjudication was a conviction under Texas law. According to the Service, therefore, the respondent was convicted of a drug offense for purposes of the immigration laws and is removable under section 237(a)(2)(B)(i) of the Act.

Regarding *Lujan-Armendariz v. INS, supra,* the Service argues that the Ninth Circuit's decision is contrary to the plain language of section 101(a)(48)(A) of the Act, which takes precedence over the federal first offender statute in immigration matters. The Service also cites the Ninth Circuit's later decision in *Murillo-Espinoza v. INS,* 261 F.3d 771 (9th Cir. 2001), a theft case in which the court deferred to the Board's interpretation of section 101(a)(48)(A) as precluding recognition of state rehabilitative expungements. In addition, it relies on several other circuit court decisions, which, according to the Service, consider section 101(a)(48)(A) to be controlling on questions regarding the effect of state rehabilitative actions. *Griffiths v. INS,* 243 F.3d 45 (1st Cir. 2001); *Herrera-Inirio v. INS,* 208 F.3d 299 (1st Cir. 2000); *Moosa v. INS,* 171 F.3d 994 (5th Cir. 1999); *United States* v, *Campbell,* 167 F.3d 94 (2d Cir. 1999). Finally, the Service claims that the Ninth Circuit improperly imparted constitutional status to the Board's earlier policy expressed in *Matter of Manrique, supra,* by finding our withdrawal from that policy to be a violation of equal protection. For these reasons, the Service urges us not to apply *Lujan-Armendariz* to cases outside the Jurisdiction of the Ninth Circuit. On the second issue, the Service argues that we should apply, in the immigration context, the Fifth Circuit's ruling in *United States v. Hinojosa-Lopez,* 130 F.3d 691 (5th Cir. 1997), which held that, for sentencing guidelines purposes, a state drug offense that is classified as a felony under state law is an aggravated felony, even if it is punishable only as a misdemeanor under federal law. Acknowledging the Board's ruling to the contrary in *Matter of K-V-D-,* Interim Decision 3422 (BIA 1999), the Service cites to the Fifth Circuit's recent decision in *United States v. Hernandez-Avalos,* 251 F.3d 505 (5th Cir.), *cert. denied,* 122 S. Ct. 305 (2001), where the court reaffirmed its holding in *United States v. Hinojosa-Lopez* and rejected our statements in *Matter of K-V-D-* that *Hinojosa-Lopez* was not binding in immigration cases. Based on this ruling, the Service asserts that the respondent has been convicted of an aggravated felony and is also removable under section 237(a)(2)(A)(iii) of the Act.

The respondent argues that *Lujan-Armendariz v. INS, supra,* was correctly decided and should be applied on a nationwide basis. She concurs with the court's conclusions (1) that when Congress enacted section 101(a)(48)(A) of the Act, it expressed no intent to amend or repeal by implication the federal first offender statute, and (2) that the principles of equal protection require that an alien who would have received the benefits of the Federal statute should get the same benefits if the alien's conviction was expunged under a state rehabilitative statute. She asserts that nationwide application of the Ninth Circuit's decision would foster the uniform administration of the immigration laws if *Matter of Manrique, supra,* is reinstated. Finally, she claims that because the Government did not seek further review of *Lujan-Armendariz,* it has essentially acquiesced in the court's ruling.

In regard to the Fifth Circuit's holding in *United States v. Hernandez-Avalos, supra,* the respondent notes that the court did not apply *Chevron, U.S.A., Inc. v. Natural Resources Defense Council, Inc.,* 467 U.S. 837 (1984), to our decision in *Matter of K-V-D-, supra,* but merely mentioned its disapproval of our holding in dicta. She therefore asserts that, in the absence of a direct ruling on the merits of our decision in *Matter of K-V-D-,* we are not required to apply a contrary rule.

The respondent pled guilty to felony possession of drugs and was granted deterred adjudication pursuant to Texas law. Under the law of the Fifth Circuit, the respondent would clearly be considered convicted of this offense. *Moosa v. INS, supra,* at 1005–06; *see also Matter of Punu, supra.* The question before us, therefore, is whether, because of the nature of the crime, we should carve out an exception to accord special treatment to first-time drug offenders who have received rehabilitative treatment under a state law. We find that, under the plain language of section 101(a)(48)(A) of the Act, we have no authority to make such an exception. Even if we did have such authority, we are unpersuaded by the Ninth Circuit's decision in *Lujan-Armendariz v. INS, supra,* that our interpretation of the statute in *Matter of Roldan* was incorrect. Accordingly, we decline to give the holding in *Lujan-Armendariz v. INS* nationwide application and will continue to apply the rule set forth in *Matter of Roland* to cases arising outside the jurisdiction of the Ninth Circuit.

The concept of conviction and the treatment of state rehabilitative provisions in immigration proceedings is long and complex. The complete history is adequately set forth in *Matter of Roldan, supra,* and it need not be repeated in full here. What follows is a brief discussion of the most significant developments of the law to date.

Prior to the enactment of section 101(a)(48)(A) of the Act, we held that an expunged conviction does not support a finding of deportability. *See Matter of Luviano,* 21 I&N Dec. 235, 237 (BIA 1996); *Matter of Ibarra-Obando,* 12 I&N Dec. 576, 578 (BIA 1966; A.G.1967); *Matter of G-,* 9 I&N Dec. 159, 161 (BIA 1960; A.G. 1961). The Attorney General, making an exception to that rule, found that a drug conviction expunged under a state rehabilitative statute was not eliminated for immigration purposes. *See Matter of A-F-,* 8 I&N Dec. 429, 432 (BIA; A.G. 1959). However, after considering the effect of the federal first offender statute, we later announced an exception to the Attorney General's ruling for those convictions expunged under a state law that was a counterpart to the federal first offender statute. *See, e.g., Matter of Werk,* 16 I&N Dec. 234 (BIA 1977). In *Matter of Deris,* 20 I&N Dec. 5 (BIA 1989), we further refined this exception, holding that an alien whose state drug offense was expunged could avoid deportation only if the state expungement statute was an exact counterpart to the federal statute.

The Ninth Circuit subsequently criticized *Matter of Deris* as unduly urn-row. *See Garberding* v. *INS,* 30 F.3d 1187 (9th Cir. 1994). In response to *Garberding,* we issued *Matter of Manrique, supra.* There we held that, in the interest of uniform application of the immigration laws, a first-time simple drug possession offender, whose conviction was set aside pursuant to a state statute, would not be deported if he or she would have been eligible for treatment under the federal first offender statute had the prosecution been in federal court.

Following the enactment of a definition of a "conviction" in section 101(a)(48)(A) of the Act, however, we determined in *Matter of Roldan, supra*, that we could no longer "apply a policy exception providing federal first offender treatment to certain drug offenders who have received state rehabilitative treatment, in the face of the definition provided by Congress." *Id.* at 19. We therefore concluded that *Matter of Manrique* had been superseded by the statute.

In *Lujan-Armendariz v. INS, supra*, the Ninth Circuit partially reversed our holding in *Matter of Roldan, supra.* The court held that enactment of the definition of a conviction at section 101(a)(48)(A) of the Act did not repeal the federal first offender statute, either on its face or by implication. *Id.* at 743–46. It concluded further, on constitutional equal protection grounds, that an alien whose first-time simple drug possession offense was expunged by a state rehabilitative statute cannot be deported if first offender treatment would have been accorded under 18 U.S.C. § 3607 had the alien been prosecuted in federal court. *Id.* at 748–49. While the Ninth Circuit's holding in *Lujan-Armendariz* is limited to cases in which aliens would have been eligible for rehabilitative treatment under the federal first offender statute, the court also indicated that no expunged conviction could constitute a conviction under section 101(a)(48)(A) of the Act. *Id.* at 745–46.

Subsequent to that decision, however, a different panel of Ninth Circuit held that a state court action setting aside a theft conviction under a rehabilitative scheme did not eliminate the immigration consequences of that offense. *Murillo-Espinoza v. INS, supra.* Affirming our decision in *Matter of Roldan, supra*, insofar as it applies to expunged convictions in general, the court stated that while our interpretation of section 101(a)(48)(A) of the Act is not the only plausible one, it is a permissible construction of the statute entitled to deference under the principles enunciated in *Chevron, U.S.A., Inc. v. Natural Resources Defense Council, Inc., supra.*

The starting point in cases involving statutory construction must be the language employed by Congress. It is assumed that the legislative purpose is expressed by the ordinary meaning of the words used. *INS v. Cardoza-Fonseca*, 480 U.S. 421, 431 (1987); *INS v. Phinpathya*, 464 U.S. 183, 189 (1984). The plain language of both section 101(a)(48)(A) of the Act and the federal first offender statute supports our holding in *Matter of Roldan, supra*, that the definition of a conviction for immigration purposes does not give effect to state rehabilitative treatment accorded to first-time simple drug possession offenders.

Section 101(a)(48)(A) of the Act clearly states the requirements for a conviction under the immigration laws. The statute contains no exception for offenders who have been accorded rehabilitative treatment under state law. Similarly, there is no provision in the federal first offender statute relating to convictions that have been vacated, set aside, or otherwise expunged under *state* law. Nothing in either statute indicates that Congress intended to excuse a first-time simple drug possession offender accorded rehabilitative treatment under state law from the definition of a conviction that it set forth in section 101(a)(48)(A).

The body of case law that sought to balance various policy interests and provide a uniform rule for when an alien is considered convicted for immigration purposes has now been superseded by Congress' enactment of section 101(a)(48)(A) of the Act. *See Matter of Roldan, supra.* Although this federal definition of a conviction raises the possibility that uniform results may not be accorded to similarly-situated aliens, Congress clearly chose not to provide otherwise. The mandate of Congress has been expressed by the straightforward language of the statute, and, as we concluded in *Roldan*, we are not at liberty to create exceptions where Congress has declined to provide them.

Our interpretation of section 101(a)(48)(A) of the Act in *Matter of Roldan, supra*, is consistent with its legislative history. Although legislative statements have less force than the plain language of the statute, such statements are helpful to corroborate and underscore a reasonable construction of the statute. *See Weinberger v. Rossi,* 456 U.S. 25, 32 (1982); *Matter of Punu, supra.* Here, the Conference Report states that Congress enacted the definition of a conviction for the express purpose of clarifying when a conviction exists for immigration purposes, in light of the disparities caused by varying state rehabilitative procedures. H.R. Conf. Rep. No. 104-828 (1996), at 224, *available in* 1996 WL 563320, at 496. According to the report, Congress was not satisfied with how the Board dealt with cases in which a judgment of guilt or imposition of sentence was suspended, conditioned upon an alien's future good behavior. The report explicitly states that Congress intended the definition of a conviction to include cases involving state deferred adjudication laws, noting that a conviction occurs upon a finding or confession of guilt, before the term of probation begins, regardless of whether the state requires further proceedings to determine the alien's guilt or innocence if probation is violated.

The legislative history of section 101(a)(48)(A) of the Act further indicates that Congress intended convictions that are expunged pursuant to state rehabilitative laws to remain convictions for immigration purposes, notwithstanding the nature of the offense. The Conference Report noted that "aliens who have clearly been guilty of criminal behavior and whom Congress intended to be considered 'convicted' have escaped the immigration consequences normally attendant upon a conviction" as a result of "a myriad of provisions [in state laws] for ameliorating the effects of a conviction." H.R. Conf. Rep. No. 104-828, at 224. Congress clearly desired to remedy this situation by passing a law to ensure that aliens whose guilt had been established could not avoid deportation as a result of some subsequent state action to eliminate the consequences of the conviction. Nothing in the legislative history suggests that Congress contemplated any exceptions, express or implicit, to the federal definition of a conviction that it mandated for immigration purposes. It would be inappropriate for us to create such exceptions where none were authorized by Congress.

We are unpersuaded by the Ninth Circuit's reasoning in *Lujan-Armendariz v. INS, supra,* that our withdrawal from the policy set forth in *Matter of Manrique, supra,* violates equal protection. The court found "no rational basis" for treating aliens whose convictions were expunged under state rehabilitative provisions differently from those who were prosecuted in federal court for the same offenses. *See also Garberding v. INS, supra.* This presupposes, of course, that aliens accorded first offender treatment in federal court would not be subject to removal, as the court concluded. We declined to address this issue in *Matter of Roldan, supra,* and continue to do so here. However, even if we were to find that aliens treated as first offenders in federal court are exempt, we would not be bound to hold that aliens convicted in state court are likewise exempt from removal.

We have long declared that we lack authority to rule on the constitutionality of the statutes we administer. *See, e.g., Matter of Rodriguez-Carrillo,* Interim Decision 3413 (BIA 1999); *Matter of C-,* 20 I&N Dec. 529 (BIA 1992); *Matter of Cenatice,* 16 I&N Dec.162 (BIA 1977). Here, however, any extension of *Lujan-Armendariz* outside the Ninth Circuit depends on whether that court's equal protection rationale is shared by the United States Supreme Court or the Fifth Circuit. We therefore consider it appropriate to examine the equal protection rationale that underpins *Lujan-Armendariz.*

The Ninth Circuit's equal protection analysis is based on speculation that a first-lime offender prosecuted under state law would have been granted first offender treatment in the federal courts. However, such treatment is not a right or entitlement and, indeed, is quite generous compared to many state sentencing and rehabilitative schemes. Under the federal first offender statute, no conviction is entered pending the successful completion of probation, and the length of such probation is limited by statute to 1 year. It simply cannot be known whether any particular defendant in state proceedings would have been found to warrant such treatment had they been prosecuted in federal court. We note that the respondent in this case was convicted of possession of between 5 and 50 pounds of marijuana and received a sentence of 10 years' probation, whereas the aliens at issue in *Lujan-Armendariz* received sentences that included jail time and 5 years' probation. While such sentences do not dictate what the outcome would have been in federal court, they illustrate the fruitlessness of trying to impose uniform consequences under the Act for aliens who were prosecuted for similar criminal conduct in the more than 50 jurisdictions comprising our federal system.

We find further reason for declining to follow the *Lujan-Armendariz* rule in the decision of the Eleventh Circuit in *Fernandez-Bernal v. Attorney General of the United States,* 257 F.3d 1304 (11th Cir. 2001). In that case, the court found that an alien whose first-time simple drug possession offense had been expunged under a state rehabilitative statute could not claim that he would have been eligible for federal first offender treatment because his sentence—2 years' probation and time in jail—exceeded the maximum penalty of 1-year probation set forth in 18 U.S.C. § 3607. Without reaching the question whether to adopt the rule in *Lujan-Armendariz,* the Eleventh Circuit concluded that aliens, such as the respondent in this case, who were sentenced in state court to more than 1 year of probation could not have received first offender treatment under the federal law. In light of our holding, it is unnecessary for us to consider whether to adopt the Eleventh Circuit's ruling outside that circuit. Nevertheless, we note that its decision clearly demonstrates the futility of seeking "uniform" results between federal and state prosecutions by engaging in speculation as to whether a particular first-time drug offender would have been adjudicated under. 18 U.S.C. § 3607.

In other contexts, the Supreme Court and, indeed, the Ninth Circuit itself, have rejected the argument that equal protection requires such an attempt at uniformity. *See McCleskey v. Kemp,* 481 U.S. 279, 312 (1987) (noting that apparent disparities in sentencing are an inevitable part of our criminal justice system): *United States v. Antelope,* 430 U.S. 641, 648–49 (1977) (asserting that because Congress has constitutional power to prescribe the criminal code applicable in Indian country, it is of no consequence that the federal scheme differs from the state criminal code that is otherwise applicable within the state); *Williams v. Illinois,* 399 U.S. 235, 243 (1970) (stating that the Constitution permits qualitative differences in meting out punishment and there is no requirement that two persons convicted of the same offense receive identical sentences); *see also United States v. Laughing,* 855 F.2d 1427, 1428 (9th Cir 1985); *United States v. Hall,* 778 F.2d 1427, 1428 (9th Cir. 1985); *United States v. Flores,* 540 F.2d 432, 438 (9th Cir.1976); *Schiller v. California,* 427 F.2d 1178, 1179 (9th Cir. 1970) (holding that nothing in the Constitution requires that persons convicted of the same crime receive identical penalties), *cert. denied,* 401 U.S. 929 (1971).

Furthermore, we find no indication that the Fifth Circuit, in whose jurisdiction the instant case arises, shares the Ninth Circuit's theory of equal protection as expressed in *Lujan-Armendariz.* In this regard, we note the Fifth Circuit's recent rulings that a first-time drug possession offense prosecuted as a felony under Texas state law constitutes a "drug trafficking crime" under 18 U.S.C. § 924(c), even though such an offense is only a misdemeanor under federal law and thus would not be prosecuted as a drug trafficking crime in federal court. *United States v. Hernandez-Avalos, supra* (reaffirming *United States v. Hinojosa-Lopez, supra).* Consequently, under the law of the Fifth Circuit, immigration consequences may vary dramatically depending on whether an alien's crime is prosecuted in state or federal court: the alien convicted in state court is an aggravated felon; the federal defendant is not.

In sum, neither the Supreme Court nor the Fifth Circuit follows the sweeping equal protection analysis set forth in *Lujan-Armendariz v. INS, supra.* There is no mechanism to extend the principles of the federal first offender statute to offenses expunged under state rehabilitative laws. Section 101(a)(48)(A) of the Act provides a clear and evenhanded standard for determining when a criminal proceeding in any jurisdiction has given rise to a "conviction" for purposes of the immigration laws. This provision does not exempt first-time simple drug possession offenders who have been accorded rehabilitative treatment under state law. Accordingly, we find that we are not compelled to apply *Lujan-Armendariz* to cases arising outside the jurisdiction of the Ninth Circuit.

5. Application of Section 101(a)(48)(A) to Expungements

As we noted previously, the court in *Lujan-Armendariz v. INS, supra,* also analyzed whether, in general, a criminal conviction expunged under a state rehabilitative provision constitutes a conviction under section 101(a)(48)(A) of the Act. While acknowledging congressional intent to treat all deferred adjudications as convictions for immigration purposes prior to their expungement, the court nevertheless stated its belief that Congress did not intend to eliminate the longstanding rule that, when a conviction or finding of guilt has been expunged, it may not thereafter be used as the basis for removal. *Id.* at 745–46. The court's discussion of this issue is contrary to our holding in *Matter of Punu, supra,* and, if taken to its logical conclusion, would vitiate our holding in that case. However, the subsequent decision of another panel of the Ninth Circuit in *Murillo-Espinoza v. INS, supra,* calls into question the continued validity of much of the analysis set forth in *Lujan-Armendariz* by giving deference to our holding in *Matter of Roldan, supra.* Consequently, it provides further reason for this Board to not apply the holding of that case nationwide.

Moreover, the decisions of several other circuit courts support our interpretation in *Matter of Roldan, supra,* of section 101(a)(48)(A) of the Act, by finding that state rehabilitative expungements have no effect in immigration proceedings. Most significantly, the Fifth Circuit found that a Texas deferred adjudication satisfies both prongs of the statutory definition and, consequently, is a conviction for immigration purposes. *Moosa v. INS, supra.* In this regard the court stated that the text of the statute "could not be more clear." *Id.* at 1005.

The First Circuit has also emphasized that the language of section 101(a)(48)(A) "leaves nothing to the imagination" *Herrera-Inirio v. INS, supra,* at 304. The court noted that the definition of a conviction clearly includes situations where adjudication of guilt has been withheld, and it concluded that a subsequent dismissal of charges based solely on rehabilitative goals does not vitiate the original admission of guilt. *See also Griffiths v. INS, supra* (holding that our interpretation of the treatment of withheld adjudications is wholly consistent with the plain language of the statute). Finally, the Second Circuit refused to recognize a Texas expungement of a drug offense, finding that no provision of the immigration laws gives controlling effect to state law or excepts from section 101(a)(48)(A) a conviction that has been vacated pursuant to a state rehabilitative statute. *United States v. Campbell, supra.*

We find clear support in these circuit court decisions for our conclusion in *Matter of Roldan* that Congress did not intend to provide any exceptions from its statutory definition of a conviction for expungements pursuant to state rehabilitative proceedings. For this reason and those stated above, we find that it would be inappropriate to give the Ninth Circuit's ruling in *Lujan-Armendariz v. INS, supra,* nationwide application.

B. Aggravated Felony

It is undisputed that the respondent pled guilty to possession of marijuana, which is a third degree felony under Texas law. Although the Fifth Circuit held that this offense is an aggravated felony for federal sentencing purposes in *United States v. Hi-*

nojosa-Lopez, supra, we declined to apply that decision in the immigration context in *Matter of K-V-D-, supra.* However, the Fifth Circuit recently concluded that our interpretation was "plainly incorrect" in *United States v. Hernandez-Avalos, supra,* at 509. The court stated that it found no validity to giving different interpretations to the definition of a drug trafficking crime in 18 U.S.C. §924(c) based on a distinction between sentencing and immigration cases. It therefore applied the holding in *United States v. Hinojosa-Lopez* to the alien in that case and found him to be an aggravated felon. We are bound to apply the law of the circuit in cases arising in that circuit. *See Matter of K-S-,* 20 I&N Dec. 715 (BIA 1993); *Matter of Anselmo,* 20 I&N Dec. 25 (BIA 1989). Because this case is in the Fifth Circuit, we find that the offense to which the respondent pled guilty is an aggravated felony. *United States v. Hernandez-Avalos, supra; United States v. Hinojosa-Lopez, supra; see also Matter of Olivares,* 23 I&N Dec. 148 (BIA 2001). *But see Matter of K-V-D-, supra; Matter of L-G-,* 21 I&N Dec. 89 (BIA 1995); *Matter of L-G-,* 20 I&N Dec. 905 (BIA 1994).

After considering the analysis set forth in *Lujan-Armendariz v. INS, supra,* we decline to apply the ruling in that decision to cases arising outside of the jurisdiction of the Ninth Circuit. We therefore conclude that, except in the Ninth Circuit, a first-time simple drug possession offense expunged under a state rehabilitative statute is a conviction under section 101(a)(48)(A) of the Act. Accordingly, pursuant to *Matter of Roldan, supra,* we find that the respondent has been convicted for immigration purposes. Inasmuch as the respondent's offense is an aggravated felony according to the rulings of the Fifth Circuit, we conclude that she is removable on both of the grounds charged. Accordingly, the Service's appeal will be sustained and the respondent will be ordered removed from the United States.

ORDER: The appeal of the Immigration and Naturalization Service is sustained.

FURTHER ORDER: The decision of the Immigration Judge is vacated, and the respondent is ordered removed from the United States.

b. Aggravated Felonies

As we saw in Chapter 4, there is an extensive list of crimes which fall under the category of "aggravated felonies."[64] The following case is illustrative of the approach that the Court has taken to how crimes should be analyzed to determine whether or not they should be treated as aggravated felonies.

Josue Leocal v. John D. Ashcroft

543 U.S. 1 (2004)

Chief Justice Rehnquist delivered the opinion of the Court.

Petitioner Josue Leocal, a Haitian citizen who is a lawful permanent resident of the United States, was convicted in 2000 of driving under the influence of alcohol (DUI) and causing serious bodily injury, in violation of Florida law. See Fla. Stat.

---

64. *See* 8 U.S.C. §1101(a)(43), Sec. 101(a)(43).

§ 316.193(3)(c)(2) (2003). Classifying this conviction as a "crime of violence" under 18 U.S.C. § 16, and therefore an "aggravated felony" under the Immigration and Nationality Act (INA), an Immigration Judge and the Board of Immigration Appeals (BIA) ordered that petitioner be deported pursuant to § 237(a) of the INA. The Court of Appeals for the Eleventh Circuit agreed, dismissing petitioner's petition for review. We disagree and hold that petitioner's DUI conviction is not a crime of violence under 18 U.S.C. § 16.

Petitioner immigrated to the United States in 1980 and became a lawful permanent resident in 1987. In January 2000, he was charged with two counts of DUI causing serious bodily injury under Fla. Stat. § 316.193(3)(c)(2), after he caused an accident resulting in injury to two people. He pleaded guilty to both counts and was sentenced to two and a half years in prison.

In November 2000, while he was serving his sentence, the Immigration and Naturalization Service (INS) initiated removal proceedings against him pursuant to § 237(a) of the INA. Under that provision, "[a]ny alien who is convicted of an aggravated felony ... is deportable" and may be removed upon an order of the Attorney General. 66 Stat. 201, 8 U.S.C. § 1227(a)(2)(A)(iii). Section 101(a)(43) of the INA defines "aggravated felony" to include, inter alia, "a crime of violence (as defined in section 16 of title 18, but not including a purely political offense) for which the term of imprisonment [is] at least one year."[1] 8 U.S.C. § 1101(a)(43)(F) (footnote omitted). Title 18 U.S.C. § 16, in turn, defines the term "crime of violence" to mean:

> (a) an offense that has as an element the use, attempted use, or threatened use of physical force against the person or property of another, or
>
> (b) any other offense that is a felony and that, by its nature, involves a substantial risk that physical force against the person or property of another may be used in the course of committing the offense.

Here, the INS claimed that petitioner's DUI conviction was a "crime of violence" under § 16, and therefore an "aggravated felony" under the INA.

In October 2001, an Immigration Judge found petitioner removable, relying upon the Eleventh Circuit's decision in Le v. United States Attorney General, 196 F.3d 1352 (1999) (per curiam), which held that a conviction under the Florida DUI statute qualified as a crime of violence. The BIA affirmed.[2] Petitioner completed his sentence

---

1. Congress first made commission of an aggravated felony grounds for an alien's removal in 1988, and it defined the term to include offenses such as murder, drug trafficking crimes, and firearm trafficking offenses. See Anti-Drug Abuse Act of 1988, §§ 7342, 7344, 102 Stat. 4469, 4470. Since then, Congress has frequently amended the definition of aggravated felony, broadening the scope of offenses which render an alien deportable. See, e.g., Antiterrorism and Effective Death Penalty Act of 1996, § 440(e), 110 Stat. 1277 (adding a number of offenses to § 101(a)(43) of the INA); Illegal Immigration Reform and Immigrant Responsibility Act of 1996 (IIRIRA), § 321, 110 Stat. 3009-627 (same). The inclusion of any "crime of violence" as an aggravated felony came in 1990. See Immigration Act of 1990, § 501, 104 Stat. 4978, 5048.

2. When petitioner first appealed, the BIA's position was that a violation of DUI statutes similar to Florida's counted as a crime of violence under 18 U.S.C. § 16. See, e.g., *Matter of Puente-Salazar*,

and was removed to Haiti in November 2002. In June 2003, the Court of Appeals for the Eleventh Circuit dismissed petitioner's petition for review, relying on its previous ruling in Le, supra. App. to Pet. for Cert. 5a–7a. We granted certiorari, 540 U.S. 1176 (2004), to resolve a conflict among the Courts of Appeals on the question whether state DUI offenses similar to the one in Florida, which either do not have a mens rea component or require only a showing of negligence in the operation of a vehicle, qualify as a crime of violence.... We now reverse the Eleventh Circuit.

Title 18 U.S.C. § 16 was enacted as part of the Comprehensive Crime Control Act of 1984, which broadly reformed the federal criminal code in such areas as sentencing, bail, and drug enforcement, and which added a variety of new violent and nonviolent offenses. § 1001(a), 98 Stat. 2136. Congress employed the term "crime of violence" in numerous places in the Act, such as for defining the elements of particular offenses, see, e.g., 18 U.S.C. § 1959 (prohibiting threats to commit crimes of violence in aid of racketeering activity), or for directing when a hearing is required before a charged individual can be released on bail, see § 3142(f) (requiring a pretrial detention hearing for those alleged to have committed a crime of violence). Congress therefore provided in § 16 a general definition of the term "crime of violence" to be used throughout the Act. See § 1001(a), 98 Stat. 2136. Section 16 has since been incorporated into a variety of statutory provisions, both criminal and noncriminal.

* * *

Our analysis begins with the language of the statute. See Bailey v. United States, 516 U.S. 137, 144 (1995). The plain text of § 16(a) states that an offense, to qualify as a crime of violence, must have "as an element the use, attempted use, or threatened use of physical force against the person or property of another." We do not deal here with an attempted or threatened use of force. Petitioner contends that his conviction did not require the "use" of force against another person because the most common employment of the word "use" connotes the intentional availment of force, which is not required under the Florida DUI statute. The Government counters that the "use" of force does not incorporate any mens rea component, and that petitioner's DUI conviction necessarily includes the use of force. To support its position, the Government dissects the meaning of the word "use," employing dictionaries, legislation, and our own case law in contending that a use of force may be negligent or even inadvertent.

Whether or not the word "use" alone supplies a mens rea element, the parties' primary focus on that word is too narrow. Particularly when interpreting a statute that

---

22 I. & N. Dec. 1006, 1012–1013, 1999 WL 770709 (BIA 1999) (en banc). Before petitioner received a decision from his appeal (due to a clerical error not relevant here), the BIA in another case reversed its position from Puente-Salazar and held that DUI offenses that do not have a mens rea of at least recklessness are not crimes of violence within the meaning of § 16. See *Matter of Ramos*, 23 I. & N. Dec. 336, 346, 2002 WL 1001049 (BIA 2002) (en banc). However, because the BIA held in Ramos that it would "follow the law of the circuit in those circuits that have addressed the question whether driving under the influence is a crime of violence," *id.*, at 346–347, and because it found the Eleventh Circuit's ruling in *Le* controlling, it affirmed the Immigration Judge's removal order. See App. to Pet. for Cert. 1a–4a.

features as elastic a word as "use," we construe language in its context and in light of the terms surrounding it. See *Smith v. United States*, 508 U.S. 223, 229 (1993); *Bailey, supra*, at 143. The critical aspect of § 16(a) is that a crime of violence is one involving the "use ... of physical force *against the person or property of another*" (emphasis added). As we said in a similar context in *Bailey*, "use" requires active employment. 516 U.S., at 145. While one may, in theory, actively employ something in an accidental manner, it is much less natural to say that a person actively employs physical force against another person by accident. Thus, a person would "use ... physical force against" another when pushing him; however, we would not ordinarily say a person "use[s] ... physical force against" another by stumbling and falling into him. When interpreting a statute, we must give words their "ordinary or natural" meaning. *Smith, supra*, at 228, 113 S.Ct. 2050. The key phrase in § 16(a)—the "use ... of physical force against the person or property of another"—most naturally suggests a higher degree of intent than negligent or merely accidental conduct. See *United States v. Trinidad-Aquino*, 259 F.3d, at 1145.... Petitioner's DUI offense therefore is not a crime of violence under § 16(a).

Neither is petitioner's DUI conviction a crime of violence under § 16(b). Section 16(b) sweeps more broadly than § 16(a), defining a crime of violence as including "any other offense that is a felony and that, by its nature, involves a substantial risk that physical force against the person or property of another may be used in the course of committing the offense." But § 16(b) does not thereby encompass all negligent misconduct, such as the negligent operation of a vehicle. It simply covers offenses that naturally involve a person acting in disregard of the risk that physical force might be used against another in committing an offense. The reckless disregard in § 16 relates not to the general conduct or to the possibility that harm will result from a person's conduct, but to the risk that the use of physical force against another might be required in committing a crime. The classic example is burglary. A burglary would be covered under § 16(b) not because the offense can be committed in a generally reckless way or because someone may be injured, but because burglary, by its nature, involves a substantial risk that the burglar will use force against a victim in completing the crime.

Thus, while § 16(b) is broader than § 16(a) in the sense that physical force need not actually be applied, it contains the same formulation we found to be determinative in § 16(a): the use of physical force against the person or property of another. Accordingly, we must give the language in § 16(b) an identical construction, requiring a higher mens rea than the merely accidental or negligent conduct involved in a DUI offense. This is particularly true in light of § 16(b)'s requirement that the "substantial risk" be a risk of using physical force against another person "in the course of committing the offense." In no "ordinary or natural" sense can it be said that a person risks having to "use" physical force against another person in the course of operating a vehicle while intoxicated and causing injury.

In construing both parts of § 16, we cannot forget that we ultimately are determining the meaning of the term "crime of violence." The ordinary meaning of this term, combined with § 16's emphasis on the use of physical force against another person (or the risk of having to use such force in committing a crime), suggests a category of violent, active crimes that cannot be said naturally to include DUI offenses. Cf. *United States v. Doe*, 960 F.2d 221, 225 (C.A.1 1992) (Breyer, C.J.) (observing that the term "violent felony" in 18 U.S.C. § 924(e) (2000 ed. and Supp. II) "calls to mind a tradition of crimes that involve the possibility of more closely related, active violence"). Interpreting § 16 to encompass accidental or negligent conduct would blur the distinction between the "violent" crimes Congress sought to distinguish for heightened punishment and other crimes. See *United States v. Lucio-Lucio*, 347 F.3d 1202, 1205–1206 (C.A.10 2003).

* * *

This case does not present us with the question whether a state or federal offense that requires proof of the reckless use of force against a person or property of another qualifies as a crime of violence under 18 U.S.C. § 16. DUI statutes such as Florida's do not require any mental state with respect to the use of force against another person, thus reaching individuals who were negligent or less. Drunk driving is a nationwide problem, as evidenced by the efforts of legislatures to prohibit such conduct and impose appropriate penalties. But this fact does not warrant our shoehorning it into statutory sections where it does not fit. The judgment of the United States Court of Appeals for the Eleventh Circuit is therefore reversed, and the case is remanded for further proceedings consistent with this opinion.

Notes

1. One of the lessons of statutory interpretation evidenced in the *Leocal* case is the close reading that a court is expected to take when parsing the statute. This is consistent with the "Rule of Lenity" discussed previously requiring a strict construction approach to aggravated felony statutes.[65] In *Lopez v. Gonzales*, the Court held that "illicit trafficking in a controlled substance" requires some sort of commercial activity.[66] Lopez had been convicted under a South Dakota statute for aiding and abetting cocaine possession. The Court concluded that this conviction was not an aggravated felony under 8 U.S.C. § 1101(a)(43)(B).

2. In another case involving the interpretation of whether a person who was convicted of "aiding and abetting" auto theft under a California statute, using the categorical approach, the Court concluded that the aggravated felony definition was met. *See Gonzales v. Duenas-Alvarez*, 549 U.S. 183, 189 (2007).[67]

---

65. *See* discussion infra at Chapter 4, following *Matter of Vivas*.

66. 549 U.S. 47, 54 (2006).

67. Similarly, a person who aids and assists in a tax violation met the aggravated felony definition. *See Kawashima v. Holder*, 565 U.S. 478 (2012).

3. **Foreign Convictions.** Aggravated felonies include crimes which meet the statutory definition and were committed in a foreign country if the term of imprisonment was completed within the previous fifteen years.[68]

4. **Anti-Drug Abuse Act of 1988.**[69] In 1988, Congress enacted the Anti-Drug Abuse Act, which was intended to expedite the removal of persons convicted of crimes involving drugs as well as other "aggravated felonies." The statute, which amended 8 U.S.C. § 1251(a)(2), Sec. 241(a)(2), creates a presumption of deportability for these convicted persons and requires them to appeal their removal orders within thirty days.

In 1990 and again in 1996, Congress redefined the aggravated felony provisions. Aggravated felonies now include illicit trafficking in controlled substances, money laundering, crimes of violence for which the sentence imposed is at least one year. and many other crimes.

There has been some controversy as to certain crimes and their characterization as aggravated felonies. For example, the BIA has held that a person convicted of "aggravated" driving while under the influence and sentenced to two-and-a-half years in prison is considered a person who has been convicted of a crime of violence, thereby qualifying the crime as an aggravated felony.[70] This view has been rejected by some courts.[71] At the same time, the Board has held that a person convicted under an Arizona statute for aggravated driving while under the influence had not been convicted of a crime involving moral turpitude. Further, while the crime might be an aggravated felony, it would not render the person ineligible for adjustment of status, since an aggravated felony is a ground for removal and not admissibility.[72]

c. Petty Offenses, Juvenile Exceptions and Pardons

8 U.S.C. § 1182(a), which provides for removal based on criminal acts, specifically exempts persons who would be removable because of a conviction for a petty crime.[73]

> An alien who would be excludable because of the conviction of an offense for which the sentence actually imposed did not exceed a term of imprison-

---

68. 8 U.S.C. § 1101(a)(43), Sec. 101(a)(43).

69. Pub. L. No. 100-690, 102 Stat. 4181 (1988).

70. *See Matter of Magallanes*, 22 I. & N. Dec. 1 (BIA 1998).

71. *See U.S. v. Chapa-Garza*, 243 F.3d 921 (5th Cir. 2001) (rejecting that DUI is a per se crime of violence or aggravated felony); *Dalton v. Ashcroft*, 2001 WL 8222454 (2d Cir. 2001); *but see Tapia-Garza v. INS*, 237 F.3d 1216 (10th Cir. 2001).

72. *See In re Fernando Torres-Varela*, 23 I. & N. Dec. 78 (BIA 2001) (distinguishing *Matter of Lopez-Meza*, 22 I. & N. Dec. 1188 (BIA 1999)).

73. 8 U.S.C. § 1182(a)(2) was amended retroactively effective November 1, 1986, by the Omnibus Crime Control Act of October 12, 1984, 98 Stat. 1837. The earlier statute required that the crime be a misdemeanor or petty offense under 18 U.S.C. § 1(3) and the punishment *imposed* be within the statutory definition of six months.

> ment in excess of six months, or who would be excludable as one who admits the commission of an offense for which a sentence not to exceed one year's imprisonment might have been imposed may be granted a visa and admitted to the United States if otherwise admissible: Provided. That the alien has committed only one such offense, or admits the commission of acts which constitute the essential elements of only one such offense.

The petty offense exception has been modified by Congress over the years. Amendments enacted in 1984 focused on the sentence actually imposed, rather than the sentence which could have been imposed. This changed with the 1990 Act, which looked to both the actual sentence and the possible sentence. A person whose sentence has been suspended might still be removable if the suspended sentence is greater than that associated with petty offenses.[74] A "petty crime"[75] is one in which the maximum possible penalty does not exceed imprisonment for one year and where the person's prison sentence did not exceed six months.[76]

In the case of foreign convictions, one must look to the sentence imposed by the foreign court. In the absence of a crime with a classification comparable to U.S. law (i.e., misdemeanor versus felony), one may look to the U.S. Code to find a similar crime. If no authority is found, the D.C. Code should be consulted.

Juvenile delinquency convictions are not considered "crimes" that fall under the inadmissibility and deportability grounds.[77] In the event that the minor is treated as an adult offender and the trial court expressly forgoes the juvenile proceeding, she will be subject to removal under 8 U.S.C. § 1182(a)(2).[78] If the person was convicted under a foreign statute, the conviction will be viewed according to the standards of the Federal Juvenile Delinquency Act.[79]

Pardons. A person might be able to avoid the immigration consequences of a criminal conviction through a pardon. In order for a pardon to be effective, it must be made by the President of the United States or by the supreme authority of the state which is empowered to extend pardons.[80] Foreign pardons are ineffective.[81] The pardon

---

74. *See Matter of Patel*, 15 I. & N. Dec. 212 (BIA 1975).

75. The term "petty crime" does not appear in the statute.

76. *See* 8 U.S.C. § 1182(a)(2)(A)(ii)(II), Sec. 212(a)(2)(A)(ii)(II). The statute allows the commission of only one petty crime.

77. *Matter of Denison-Charles*, 22 I. & N. Dec. 1362 (BIA 2001).

78. Juveniles convicted of violent crimes and tried as adults will be subject to inadmissibility under 8 U.S.C. § 1182(a)(9). *See* 18 U.S.C. § 1(1) and (16).

79. *See Matter of Ramirez-Rivero*, 18 I. & N. 135 (BIA 1981).

80. *See* 8 U.S.C. § 1251(a)(2)(A)(iv), Sec. 241(a)(2)(A)(iv). This is so, even though the statute specifically limits its coverage to pardons issued by the President or a governor. *See Matter of Tajer*, 15 I. & N. Dec. 125 (BIA 1974) (pardon issued by the parole board and recognized for immigration purposes where the parole board was the final authority in the state to issue pardons); 22 C.F.R. § 42.91 (a)(9)(vii).

81. *See Mullen-Cofee v. INS*, 976 F.2d 1375 (11th Cir. 1992).

cannot be used to waive the immigration consequences of crimes involving moral turpitude, multiple criminal convictions, aggravated felonies or high-speed flight from an immigration checkpoint.[82] In order to be effective, the pardon must be unconditional.[83] The pardon may also protect the person from DHS's use of the criminal conviction to negate an assertion of good moral character which is required to obtain voluntary departure, registry and U.S. citizenship.[84]

3. Waivers for Crimes

8 U.S.C. § 1182(h), Section 212(h)

The Attorney General may, in his discretion, waive the application of subparagraphs (A)(i)(I), (B), (D), and (E) of subsection (a)(2) and subparagraph (A)(i)(II) of such subsection insofar as it relates to a single offense of simple possession of 30 grams or less of marijuana if—

(1) (A) in the case of any immigrant it is established to the satisfaction of the Attorney General that—

(i) the alien is inadmissible only under subparagraph (D)(i) or (D)(ii) of such subsection or the activities for which the alien is inadmissible occurred more than 15 years before the date of the alien's application for a visa, admission, or adjustment of status,

(ii) the admission to the United States of such alien would not be contrary to the national welfare, safety, or security of the United States, and

(iii) the alien has been rehabilitated; or

(B) in the case of an immigrant who is the spouse, parent, son, or daughter of a citizen of the United States or an alien lawfully admitted for permanent residence if it is established to the satisfaction of the Attorney General that the alien's denial of admission would result in extreme hardship to the United States citizen or lawfully resident spouse, parent, son, or daughter of such alien; and

(2) the Attorney General, in his discretion, and pursuant to such terms, conditions and procedures as he may by regulations prescribe, has consented to the alien's applying or reapplying for a visa, for admission to the United States, or adjustment of status.

---

82. For example, pardons are ineffective against a charge that the person is removable for a controlled substance conviction. *See* 8 U.S.C. § 1227(a)(2)(B), Sec. 237(a)(2)(B).

83. *See Matter of Tajer*, 15 I. & N. Dec. 125 (BIA 1974).

84. *See Giambanco v. INS*, 531 F.2d 141 (3d Cir. 1976).

> No waiver shall be provided under this subsection in the case of an alien who has been convicted of (or who has admitted committing acts that constitute) murder or criminal acts involving torture, or an attempt or conspiracy to commit murder or a criminal act involving torture. No waiver shall be granted under this subsection in the case of an alien who has previously been admitted to the United States as an alien lawfully admitted for permanent residence if either since the date of such admission the alien has been convicted of an aggravated felony or the alien has not lawfully resided continuously in the United States for a period of not less than 7 years immediately preceding the date of initiation of proceedings to remove the alien from the United States. No court shall have jurisdiction to review a decision of the Attorney General to grant or deny a waiver under this subsection.

In re Jose Mendez-Moralez

21 I. & N. Dec. 296 (BIA 1996)

Before: Board En Banc: Dunne, Vice Chairman; Vacca, Heilman, Holmes, Hurwitz, Villageliu, Filppu, Cole, and Mathon, Board Members. Concurring and Dissenting Opinion: Schmidt, Chairman, joined by, Guendelsberger, Board Member. Dissenting Opinion: Rosenberg, Board Member.

VACCA, Board Member:

In a decision dated November 22, 1994, an Immigration Judge found the respondent deportable as charged under section 241(a)(2)(A)(i) of the Immigration and Nationality Act, 8 U.S.C. § 1251(a)(2)(A)(i) (1994), as an alien convicted of a crime involving moral turpitude committed within 5 years of entry into the United States. He also denied his application for adjustment of status under section 245(a) of the Act, 8 U.S.C. § 1255(a) (1994), as well as his corresponding application for a waiver of inadmissibility under section 212(h) of the Act, 8 U.S.C. § 1182(h) (1994), and ordered him deported from the United States to Mexico. The respondent has appealed from that decision. The appeal will be dismissed.

The respondent, a 42-year-old native and citizen of Mexico, was first admitted to the United States as a lawful permanent resident on May 2, 1988. He was convicted in a Nebraska court by a jury verdict on November 19, 1992, of first degree sexual assault, in violation of section 28-319(1)(c) of the Nebraska Revised Statutes. For this crime, committed in April or May 1992, the respondent was sentenced on January 5, 1993, to an indeterminate sentence of 2 to 3 years. Reportedly, he was released from prison on parole in January 1995, after having served 1 year of his sentence. The respondent conceded his deportability during the proceedings and has not contested his deportability on appeal. The only issue before us is whether the Immigration Judge properly denied the respondent's application for adjustment of status under section 245 of the Act and, in the exercise of discretion, the corresponding waiver of inadmissibility under section 212(h) of the Act. We find that he did.

Section 245 of the Act provides that the Attorney General may in her discretion adjust the status of an alien inspected and admitted or paroled into the United States to that of an alien lawfully admitted for permanent residence if the alien applies for adjustment, the alien is eligible to receive an immigrant visa and is admissible to the United States for permanent residence, and an immigrant visa is immediately available. An alien subject to deportation proceedings may also apply for adjustment of status before the Immigration Judge and, if inadmissible under section 212(a) of the Act, may also apply for a waiver of the ground of inadmissibility. See 8 C.F.R. § 242.17(a) (1995).

In the case before us the respondent's application for adjustment of status is based on his February 20, 1987, marriage to a United States citizen and the immediate relative visa petition she filed on his behalf, which was approved by the Immigration and Naturalization Service on November 21, 1994. As such, it appears that the respondent is eligible for an immigrant visa that is immediately available to him. The fact that he is a lawful permanent resident does not preclude him from applying for adjustment of status under section 245. *Tibke v. INS*, 335 F.2d 42 (2d Cir.1964); *Matter of Parodi*, 17 I & N Dec. 608 (BIA 1980); *Matter of Loo Bing Sun*, 15 I & N Dec. 307 (BIA 1975); *Matter of Krastman*, 11 I & N Dec. 720 (BIA 1966); see also *Matter of Gabryelsky*, 20 I & N Dec. 750 (BIA 1993).

However, the respondent is not admissible to the United States as required for eligibility under section 245. By virtue of his conviction for a crime involving moral turpitude, he is inadmissible under section 212(a)(2)(A)(i)(I) of the Act. An alien who is inadmissible under this section as an alien convicted of a crime involving moral turpitude may seek a waiver of inadmissibility under section 212(h) of the Act. Section 212(h) may be used to waive inadmissibility which would otherwise preclude adjustment of status. See *Osuchukwu v. INS*, 744 F.2d 1136, 1139 (5th Cir.1984); *Matter of Goldeshtein*, 20 I & N Dec. 382 (BIA 1991), rev'd on other grounds, 8 F.3d 645 (9th Cir.1993); *Matter of Parodi, supra*; *Matter of Sanchez*, 17 I & N Dec. 218 (BIA 1980); *Matter of Shaughnessy*, 12 I & N Dec. 810 (BIA 1968).

* * *

The amended version of section 212(h) essentially creates two categories of immigrants eligible for section 212(h) relief. The first category includes any immigrant who meets eligibility criteria that largely concern the type of exclusion ground involved or when the excludable activity occurred, as well as issues of the alien's rehabilitation and the national welfare, safety, or security of the United States. The second category includes immigrants who demonstrate the requisite relationship to a United States citizen or lawful permanent resident, and establish that their exclusion would result in extreme hardship to that relative. See *Matter of Alarcon*, 20 I & N Dec. 557 (BIA 1992). In the case at hand, the respondent, who is assimilated to the position of an immigrant for purposes of seeking adjustment of status, is married to a United States citizen and has three United States citizen children. As such, he may demonstrate eligibility under section 212(h)(1)(B) of the Act by establishing extreme hardship to his United States citizen wife or children if he were excluded.

In his decision the Immigration Judge in fact found that extreme hardship to the wife and children had been established, and that the respondent consequently was eligible for section 212(h) relief. However, he denied the section 212(h) waiver in the exercise of discretion, and accordingly found him ineligible for adjustment of status because of his inadmissibility resulting from his criminal conviction.

On appeal, the respondent has contested the discretionary denial of relief, arguing that he merited a favorable exercise of discretion in light of his equities and the hardship to his family if he were deported. In the respondent's view, the Immigration Judge erred in ruling that he had not demonstrated rehabilitation and in placing too much emphasis on his claim of innocence of the crime of which he was convicted. According to the respondent, the Immigration Judge also erred in requiring that rehabilitation be shown.

As is true for other discretionary forms of relief, the burden is on the applicant to establish that a grant of a waiver of inadmissibility under section 212(h)(1)(B) of the Act is warranted in the exercise of discretion. See *Matter of Fernandez*, 14 I & N Dec. 24 (BIA 1972). This has been held to be the case for other waivers of inadmissibility. See *Matter of Marin*, 16 I & N Dec. 581 (BIA 1978) (section 212(c) waiver). As is also true for other waivers of inadmissibility that would allow an alien to be admitted to the United States as a lawful permanent resident, the Immigration Judge must balance the adverse factors evidencing an alien's undesirability as a permanent resident with the social and humane considerations presented on his behalf to determine whether the grant of relief in the exercise of discretion appears to be in the best interests of this country. See *id.*

We find this use of *Matter of Marin, supra*, as a general guide to be appropriate. For the most part, it is prudent to avoid cross application, as between different types of relief, of particular principles or standards for the exercise of discretion. *Id.* However, our reference to *Matter of Marin, supra*, is only for the purpose of the approach taken in that case regarding the balancing of favorable and unfavorable factors within the context of the relief being sought under section 212(h)(1)(B) of the Act. See, e.g., *Palmer v. INS*, 4 F.3d 482 (7th Cir.1993) (balancing of discretionary factors under section 212(h)). We find this guidance to be helpful and applicable, given that both forms of relief address the question of whether aliens with criminal records should be admitted to the United States and allowed to reside in this country permanently.

* * *

... Section 212(h)(1)(B) relief is its own distinct form of waiver, with the balancing of factors to be undertaken in view of the particular purposes either stated or inherent in the statute. To exemplify, we would emphasize two considerations that do not often arise in an application for section 212(c) relief. First, a section 212(h) applicant seeking to adjust his status need not be, and in most cases is not already, a lawful permanent resident, and those lawful permanent residents that do apply may not necessarily have the length of residency attained by those eligible for section 212(c) relief. Secondly, those found eligible for relief under section 212(h)(1)(B) will by definition have already established extreme hardship to qualified family members, which would be a factor favorable to the alien in exercising discretion.

We emphasize that establishing extreme hardship and eligibility for section 212(h)(1)(B) relief does not create any entitlement to that relief. Extreme hardship is a requirement for eligibility, but once established it is but one favorable discretionary factor to be considered. We would note, however, that an application for discretionary relief, including a waiver under section 212(h), may be denied in the exercise of discretion without express rulings on the question of statutory eligibility. *Matter of Goldeshtein, supra*; see also *Silva v. Carter*, 326 F.2d 315, 320 (9th Cir.1963), cert. denied, 377 U.S. 917 (1964); cf. *INS v. Rios-Pineda*, 471 U.S. 444, 449 (1985); *INS v. Bagamasbad*, 429 U.S. 24, 25 (1976). We also emphasize that the discretionary analysis discussed is specifically applicable only to those aliens applying for relief under subsection (B) of 212(h)(1), subsection (A) having particular eligibility criteria that, if met, will affect the exercise of discretion.

In evaluating whether section 212(h)(1)(B) relief is warranted in the exercise of discretion, the factors adverse to the applicant include the nature and underlying circumstances of the exclusion ground at issue, the presence of additional significant violations of this country's immigration laws, the existence of a criminal record and, if so, its nature, recency and seriousness, and the presence of other evidence indicative of an alien's bad character or undesirability as a permanent resident of this country. See e.g., *Matter of Marin, supra*, and cases cited therein. The favorable considerations include family ties in the United States, residence of long duration in this country (particularly where the alien began his residency at a young age), evidence of hardship to the alien and his family if he is excluded and deported, service in this country's Armed Forces, a history of stable employment, the existence of property or business ties, evidence of value and service to the community, evidence of genuine rehabilitation if a criminal record exists, and other evidence attesting to the alien's good character (e.g., affidavits from family, friends, and responsible community representatives). See, e.g., *id.*, and cases cited therein.

Upon review of the record as a whole, the Immigration Judge is required to balance the equities and adverse matters to determine whether discretion should be favorably exercised. The basis for the Immigration Judge's decision must be enunciated in his opinion. See, e.g., *id.* The equities that the applicant for section 212(h)(1)(B) relief must bring forward to establish that he merits a favorable exercise of administrative discretion will depend in each case on the nature and circumstances of the ground of exclusion sought to be waived and on the presence of any additional adverse matters, and as the negative factors grow more serious, it becomes incumbent upon the applicant to introduce additional offsetting favorable evidence. See, e.g., *id.*

The underlying significance of the adverse and favorable factors is also to be taken into account. For example, if the alien has relatives in the United States, the quality of their relationship must be considered in determining the weight to be awarded this equity. Further, the equity of a marriage and the weight given to any hardship to the spouse is diminished if the parties married after the commencement of deportation proceedings, with knowledge that the alien might be deported. *Ghassan v. INS*, 972 F.2d 631 (5th Cir.1992), cert. denied, 507 U.S. 971 (1993). Similarly, if the alien has a history of employment, it is important to consider the type of employment and its length and stability. Further, when looking at the length of the alien's presence in the United States, the nature of his presence during this period must be evaluated. For example, a period of residency marked by a term of imprisonment diminishes the significance of the period of residency....

Having reviewed the record and the Immigration Judge's decision, and the contentions made on appeal, we agree with the Immigration Judge that a favorable exercise of discretion is not warranted. The respondent has demonstrated equities that may be characterized as substantial. Although he has only been in this country lawfully for a little more than 7 years, he does have significant family ties, including his United States citizen wife of 8 years. His United States citizen children include a 9-year-old stepson, a 7-year-old daughter, and a 4-year-old son. According to the wife's testimony, the respondent has been a loving father and the children are close to him emotionally. The respondent also has a consistent history of employment as an agricultural worker and mechanic at various ranches, and he has testified that his most recent employer has assured him of a position as a mechanic at $6 an hour upon his release from prison. The record also reflects that the respondent has continuously supported his family financially before his incarceration, except for a period in 1991 when he injured his back. The family began receiving food stamps that year, and since his incarceration they have also received welfare payments and housing assistance as well. The respondent's wife last worked as a cashier for a department store from 1989 to 1991, when she was terminated from her employment because she was pregnant.

The respondent also has other family ties in the United States, including two lawful permanent resident brothers living in Colorado and Kansas, a sister living in Colorado, and his lawful permanent resident parents, who also live in Colorado and who are self-supporting. The respondent testified that his sister was not a lawful permanent resident, but he did not elaborate as to her specific status in this country. The respondent also testified that he has two children in Mexico, but he has no contact with them and does not know their whereabouts.

As noted above, the Immigration Judge found that the respondent's departure would cause extreme hardship to his wife and children, as they are dependent upon him financially and are emotionally close to him. The wife testified that if her husband were deported she would remain in the United States with the children and likely move to Kansas with her adoptive father. She also testified that she was receiving psychiatric treatment for depression, noting that she had attempted to commit suicide in 1992 after the criminal charges were filed against her husband, and observing that she was attempting to obtain disability payments. She also observed that she had a medical condition involving her spine and hips that precluded her from lifting things.

In sum, the respondent has demonstrated substantial equities in his favor, including hardship to his wife and children if he were deported. Some hardship to the respondent is also apparent in view of his ties to this country and the poor economic conditions in Mexico, as documented by news articles submitted by the respondent, although he has not demonstrated that he would be virtually precluded from finding employment in Mexico. However, his equities must be balanced against the adverse factors in his case, particularly the serious crime of which he was convicted. The seriousness of his crime can be seen from a reading of the statute under which he was convicted and the surrounding circumstances.

* * *

The respondent was convicted under section 28-319(1)(c) of sexually penetrating a victim under the age of 16. In fact the record before the Immigration Judge made clear that the respondent's victim was 13 years old at the time of the sexual assault, at a time when he was 40 years of age. The young girl, who lived in the same apartment building, frequented the respondent's home. Apparently she practically lived there, reportedly because her own mother was mentally disabled to some degree and did not exert much parental control, and the respondent and his wife were not willing to force her to leave. The respondent has acknowledged that their unwillingness to force her to leave led to situations where the young girl was present when he and his wife were watching sexually explicit movies or engaging in sexual intercourse themselves. He has also admitted soliciting the victim's mentally disabled mother for sex, as repayment for money the mother had borrowed from him. According to the respondent, he did this in order to discourage her from asking to borrow more money. The circumstances of his crime clearly show its egregiousness.

We point out that as a matter of law, a 13-year-old child is incapable of consent where the act is being perpetrated by a grown man 27 years older. Where a statute makes sexual acts with a child under a specified age a crime, without regard to consent, such statutes are construed as fixing the age of consent. The purpose of these statutes is to protect children from illicit acts by rendering them incapable of consenting. See *Matter of Dingena*, 11 I & N Dec. 723 (BIA 1966).

Given the nature of the respondent's crime, we do not find that his equities are sufficient to counterbalance its seriousness. We find this to be particularly so given that his equities do not include any persuasive evidence of rehabilitation. We do not find his release from prison after 1 year due to his good conduct in following prison rules in a controlled setting to be persuasive evidence of rehabilitation from his criminal act of sexually assaulting a young child. At his hearing, the respondent denied that the sexual assault ever occurred, stated that he had been "falsely accused," and did not express remorse for his crime. In addition, when asked whether he had attempted to get any "sexual offender treatment," he responded, "I believe that I do not have a sexual problem."

The respondent argues on appeal that his assertion of innocence should not be used against him because he is, in fact, innocent and the criminal justice system makes mistakes, and he therefore should not be forced to be dishonest with himself. However, in ascertaining the effect of a criminal conviction, neither the Board nor the Immigration Judge may go beyond the judicial record to determine the guilt or innocence of an alien. See *Matter of Edwards*, 20 I & N Dec. 191 (BIA 1990); *Matter of Khalik*, 17 I & N Dec. 518 (BIA 1980). He must be considered guilty of the crime. Taking responsibility and showing remorse for one's criminal behavior does constitute some evidence of rehabilitation. See *Gonzalez v. INS*, 996 F.2d 804 (6th Cir.1993); *Villareal-San Miguel v. INS*, 975 F.2d 248 (5th Cir.1992); *Akrap v. INS*, 966 F.2d 267 (7th Cir.1992). This is not to say that an alien who claims innocence and does not express remorse could never present persuasive evidence of rehabilitation by other means. But the fact remains that in the case before us, there is no evidence of remorse or of acknowledgement of guilt. Moreover, the claim of innocence is inconsistent with the jury verdict and the respondent's own pre-trial admission that he had engaged in sexual intercourse with the victim.

The Board acknowledges the humanitarian concerns in this case, particularly the hardship to the respondent's wife and children, but the Board also has the obligation to consider the welfare and safety of the other citizens and residents of this country in making its discretionary determination. In the case before us, we have an individual who sexually assaulted a 13-year-old girl. After serving a short period of imprisonment, he has not offered any significant evidence that he is rehabilitated from his criminal behavior.

As pointed out by the respondent on appeal, a showing of rehabilitation is not an absolute prerequisite in all cases involving an alien with a criminal record. However, rehabilitation or the lack thereof is a factor to be considered in the exercise of discretion, and it may be ultimately determinative in some cases. See *Matter of Edwards, supra.* There will be cases where such a showing is necessary before a favorable exercise of discretion is warranted in view of the other aspects of the case. Thus, while the lack of persuasive evidence of rehabilitation may not in itself be an adverse factor, the absence of this equity in the alien's favor may ultimately be determinative in a given case, particularly where an alien has engaged in serious misconduct and there are questions whether the alien will revert to criminal behavior. Conversely, evidence of rehabilitation in some cases may constitute the factor that raises the significance of the alien's equities in total so as to be sufficient to counterbalance the adverse factors in the case and warrant a favorable exercise of discretion.

However, having weighed the respondent's equities in this case, which do not include persuasive evidence of rehabilitation, against the extremely serious nature of his criminal behavior involving a sexual offense against a child, the Board agrees that the respondent has not met his burden of establishing that a grant of section 212(h) relief is warranted in the exercise of discretion. Accordingly, the appeal will be dismissed.

Notes

1. How much of a factor did the applicant's continued assertion of innocence play in the denial of the waiver?

2. The 212(h) waiver is unavailable for persons who have been convicted of murder, acts of torture or conspiracy to commit such crimes.

3. The 212(h) waiver may be available to a person who has been convicted of an aggravated felony and is applying for adjustment of status but was never previously a lawful permanent resident.[85] In addition, for cases instituted after September 30, 1996, the waiver may not be granted to a lawful permanent resident who has not resided continuously in the United States for seven years before the notice to appear was issued.

4. Persons who have been admitted to the United States and are convicted of crimes making them subject to removal can only avail themselves of the other forms of relief from removal that were discussed earlier. In order to be eligible for the 212(h) waiver, they would in effect have to be seeking adjustment of status or an immigrant visa. Does this difference in treatment between persons who are seeking admission and those who have already been admitted raise any constitutional issues?[86]

5. A person cannot be found removable under 8 U.S.C. § 1227(a)(2)(A), for foreign convictions.

6. Do you see a disadvantage for obtaining a waiver where a short period of time has passed since a person's conviction? Congress, in its effort to expedite the removal of persons convicted of crimes, has appropriated funding to assure the speedy institution of proceedings as soon as possible after a person has been convicted. In the past, removal proceedings were often initiated after the person had served her sentence.

---

4. Other Waivers

A request for a waiver of a ground of inadmissibility or deportability is both an admission of the ground as well as an affirmative request for an exercise of discretion.[87] To understand the waiver provisions, one must first revisit the inadmissibility grounds discussed earlier.[88] Nonimmigrants have traditionally been accorded greater latitude with respect to the various grounds of inadmissibility. For example, nonimmigrants entering the United States for employment, with the exception of certain H visa applicants, need not obtain labor certifications as required under 8 U.S.C. § 1182(a)(5). In addition, applicants to the United States who are graduates of foreign medical

85. *See Matter of Michel*, Interim Dec. 3335 (BIA 1998).

86. *See Yeung v. INS*, 76 F.3d 337 (11th Cir. 1995).

87. Waivers, as distinguished from pardons, recommendations against deportation and petty and juvenile offense exceptions are discretionary.

88. *See* discussion *supra* Chapter 3.

schools are allowed admission in certain nonimmigrant classifications notwithstanding the foreign residency requirement of 8 U.S.C. § 1182(e). The difference in the treatment of nonimmigrants can be attributed to the fact that the nonimmigrant is seeking admission for a limited period of time.[89]

Insofar as waivers are concerned, certain categories of persons are viewed with disfavor irrespective of the length or purpose of their stay or visit to the United States. These include persons whose activities would have potentially serious adverse foreign policy consequences,[90] those likely to engage in espionage or overthrow of the government of the United States[91] and those associated with the Nazi regime in Germany during World War II or who have engaged in the persecution of others at any time.[92]

In the cases and notes which follow, we will explore some additional issues involved in ameliorating or waiving the grounds for inadmissibility and deportability.

5. Waivers for Nonimmigrants

Matter of Hranka

16 I. & N. Dec. 491 (BIA 1976)

BY: Milhollan, Chairman; Maniatis, Appleman, Maguire, and Farb, Board Members

This is an appeal from a decision of the District Director of the Immigration and Naturalization Service in Detroit, Michigan, dated August 9, 1977, denying the applicant's request for advance permission to enter the United States as a nonimmigrant visitor pursuant to section 212(d)(3)(B) of the Immigration and Nationality Act, 8 U.S.C. 1182(d)(3)(B). The appeal will be sustained.

The applicant is a 25-year-old native and citizen of Canada who is inadmissible to the United States because she was previously deported for having engaged in prostitution. See section 212(a)(12) of the Act, 8 U.S.C. 1182(a)(12).

Regardless of the fact that she is otherwise inadmissible, a nonimmigrant may be admitted into the United States temporarily in the discretion of the Attorney General. Congress provided for this procedure because it recognized that there are cases where the temporary admission of otherwise inadmissible aliens is desirable for humane reasons or for reasons of public interest.

The District Director denied the application for a waiver of inadmissibility for two reasons. He concluded that insufficient time had elapsed since the applicant's depor-

89. An example of an inadmissibility ground inapplicable to nonimmigrants is the provisions dealing with polygamists. *See* 8 U.S.C. § 1182(a)(9), Sec. 212(a)(9). Diplomats are also protected from the ideological inadmissibility provisions. *Id.* The general nonimmigrant waiver provision is described at 8 U.S.C. § 1182(d)(3), Sec. 212.

90. *See* 8 U.S.C. § 1182(a)(3)(C), Sec. 212(a)(3)(C).

91. 8 U.S.C. § 1182(a)(3)(A), Sec. 212(a)(3)(A).

92. 8 U.S.C. § 1182(a)(3)(E), Sec. 212(a)(3)(E). Another category of persons coming into this group are those involved in the trafficking of narcotics and terrorists. *See* Anti-Drug Abuse Act of 1988 Pub. L. No. 100-690, 102 Stat. 4181; 8 U.S.C. § 1182(a)(3)(B), Sec. 212(a)(3)(B).

tation to permit a determination that she had been rehabilitated. He also found that there were no "compelling humanitarian ... circumstances involved" in the applicant's desire to enter the United States.

The evidence in the record convinces us that the applicant has been rehabilitated. She was deported in April 1975. Her United States citizen mother informs us that the applicant has been holding down two jobs since September 1976, working between 60 and 70 hours a week. The applicant's mother also stated that her daughter had always been well-behaved until the time she began living with a certain man in Detroit. This man had a very negative influence upon her. She began using heroin and engaged in occasional acts of prostitution. She has had no contact at all with this man since June 1976, and has resumed living with her parents in Windsor, Ontario.

The statements of the applicant's mother impress us as being sincere and truthful. They are supported by a letter from the principal of the high school which the applicant attended. This man is a psychologist and a close friend of the applicant's family.

The applicant's reasons for desiring to enter the United States occasionally are stated by her mother as follows:

Being a border town it is a little more difficult to go about the every day life if she is unable to cross into Detroit. She is trying to put the past behind her as she is very embarrassed and ashamed and every time she is invited out on a date and the date suggests going to Detroit to a show or dinner or ball game it is all brought back to her and is very embarrassing.

As well as three uncles living in Detroit she has numerous cousins who are all marriageable age. She has already missed one of her cousins' weddings.

It is true that these reasons for wanting to enter the United States cannot be fairly characterized as "compelling." However, there is no requirement that the applicant's reasons for wishing to enter the United States be "compelling."

In deciding whether or not to grant an application under section 212(d)(3)(B), there are essentially three factors which we weigh together. The first is the risk of harm to society if the applicant is admitted. The second is the seriousness of the applicant's prior immigration law, or criminal law, violations, if any. The third factor is the nature of the applicant's reasons for wishing to enter the United States. In this case, the risk of harm to American society if the applicant is allowed to enter is very small. The applicant has no other criminal or immigration law violations. The fact that she has many close relatives living in Detroit is substantial reason for desiring a waiver. Balancing the three factors, we conclude that the requested waiver should be granted.

ORDER: The appeal is sustained.

FURTHER ORDER: The applicant for advance permission to enter as a nonimmigrant will be granted under such conditions as the District Director deems appropriate.

Notes

1. Even though the BIA sustained the appeal, it provided that the admission of the applicant would be allowed "under such conditions as the District Director deems appropriate." What kind of conditions would you expect to see imposed?

2. Should the fact that the nonimmigrant applicant lives across the U.S. border be a positive or negative factor in determining whether the grounds of inadmissibility should be waived?

3. Most of the major grounds of inadmissibility may be waived for nonimmigrants under this provision with the exception of some of the security grounds of inadmissibility and the Nazi exclusion provisions. To say that this includes the entirety of the provisions of the immigration laws applicable to nonimmigrants is somewhat misleading. For example, there may be other statutes not part of Section 212 which might provide for inadmissibility, such as the Cuban Liberty and Democratic Solidarity (Libertad) Act of 1996,[93] which provides that a person who is a corporate officer or controlling shareholder in an entity which has been involved in the confiscation of property in Cuba owned by a U.S. national may not be allowed into the United States. The only exemption allowed under this provision is for persons entering for medical reasons or for litigation. There are other provisions like this which have been enacted by Congress and signed by the President.

4. The procedure for securing a nonimmigrant waiver is that the applicant first applies for a visa before a U.S. consul. Upon a determination that the person is inadmissible, the consul determines if the person is eligible for a waiver. The consul then recommends to USCIS that a waiver be granted, whereupon it makes the final determination.

6. Waivers for Fraud or Material Misrepresentation — Sections 212(i) and 237(a)(1)(H) Waivers

In re Luis Felipe Cervantes-Gonzalez

22 I. & N. Dec. 560 (BIA 1999)

Before: Board En Banc: Dunne, Vice Chairman; Vacca, Heilman, Holmes, Hurwitz, Filppu, Cole, Mathon, Guendelsberger, Jones, Grant, and Scialabba, Board Members. Concurring Opinion: Villageliu, Board Member, joined by Schmidt, Chairman. Concurring and Dissenting Opinion: Rosenberg, Board Member.

GRANT, Board Member:

In an oral decision dated January 21, 1997, an Immigration Judge denied the respondent's requests for a waiver of inadmissibility and adjustment of status pursuant to sections 212(i) and 245 of the Immigration and Nationality Act, 8 U.S.C. §§ 1182(i) and 1255 (Supp. II 1996). The respondent's appeal from that decision will be dismissed.

---

93. Pub. L. No. 104-114, 110 Stat 785 (1996).

In a preliminary hearing held on October 26, 1995, the respondent admitted the allegations contained in the Order to Show Cause and Notice of Hearing (Form I-221) and was found deportable by the Immigration Judge. He then filed a request for adjustment of status on September 19, 1996, based on an approved visa petition filed by his United States citizen spouse. Because the respondent had been convicted of possession of false identification documents, the respondent also filed a request for a waiver of inadmissibility. See section 245 of the Act.

The Immigration Judge originally believed that the respondent required a waiver of inadmissibility under section 212(h) of the Act, but then determined that the respondent fell within an exception to section 212(a)(2)(A)(i)(I) of the Act (crime involving moral turpitude). Specifically, the Immigration Judge found that the respondent had not been incarcerated for more than 6 months, making a waiver under 212(h) unnecessary. See section 212(a)(2)(A)(ii)(II) of the Act. However, the Immigration Judge determined that the respondent's crime did fall within section 212(a)(6)(C) of the Act, which renders inadmissible any alien who procures or seeks to procure, by fraud, documentation or other immigration benefits under the Act. Therefore, the respondent still needed a waiver of inadmissibility under section 212(i) of the Act (waiver for fraud or misrepresentation).

In determining whether to grant the application for a section 212(i) waiver, the Immigration Judge found that the respondent had failed to establish extreme hardship to his spouse in the event he is deported. Additionally, the Immigration Judge denied the respondent's application for adjustment of status as a matter of discretion.

On appeal, the respondent argues that the Immigration Judge erred in finding no extreme hardship and that he also gave improper weight to the negative factors in this case. In addressing the respondent's arguments, we will engage in an independent review of the merits of the case. Prior to discussing the merits of the respondent's arguments, however, we will address several issues of statutory interpretation raised in his appeal.

The respondent first argues that he does not require a waiver of inadmissibility under section 212(i) of the Act because he is not inadmissible under section 212(a)(6)(C)(i) of the Act. Specifically, he states that his sole conviction for possession of a false identification document (namely, a counterfeit Texas birth certificate) with the intent to defraud the United States (by obtaining a United States passport) does not fall within the definition of fraud in the Act. As he was convicted only of possession, he asserts that it is error to find him guilty of seeking to procure a fraudulent document. We disagree. Section 212(a)(6)(C)(i) of the Act states:

> [A]ny alien who, by fraud or willfully misrepresenting a material fact, seeks to procure (or has sought to procure or has procured) a visa, other documentation, or admission into the United States or other benefit provided under this Act is inadmissible.

Obviously, the respondent admits to procuring one document in the form of a fraudulent birth certificate. The respondent testified that he purchased the birth certificate in Los Angeles, California, for approximately $400 or $500 so that he could obtain employment. He then used the birth certificate to procure by fraud a social security number, and he used both documents to seek to procure a passport. The latter document was necessary in order for the respondent to be able to travel into and out of the United States and to aid him in obtaining employment.

We note also that in finding the respondent's conviction fell within section 212(a)(6)(C) of the Act, the Immigration Judge and the Immigration and Naturalization Service did not improperly "go behind" the conviction record as contended by the respondent. Rather, they were merely establishing the facts regarding the respondent's fraud, which would have constituted grounds for inadmissibility whether or not the respondent had been convicted. See section 212(a)(6)(C) of the Act (no conviction is required in order to establish inadmissibility).

* * *

As we have stated in other cases involving discretionary relief, extreme hardship is not a definable term of fixed and inflexible meaning, and the elements to establish extreme hardship are dependent upon the facts and circumstances of each case. See *Matter of Chumpitazi*, 16 I&N Dec. 629 (BIA 1978). The Board has, however, enunciated factors relevant to the issue of the extreme hardship determination in previous decisions, albeit ones involving relief other than a section 212(i) waiver.

Although it is, for the most part, prudent to avoid cross application between different types of relief of particular principles or standards, we find the factors articulated in cases involving suspension of deportation and other waivers of inadmissibility to be helpful, given that both forms of relief require extreme hardship and the exercise of discretion. See *Matter of Mendez*, Interim Decision 3272 (BIA 1996) (applying discretionary factors articulated in a section 212(c) case to a waiver of inadmissibility under section 212(h)(1)(B) of the Act); see also *Hassan v. INS*, 927 F.2d 465, 467 (9th Cir. 1991) (noting that suspension cases interpreting extreme hardship are useful for interpreting extreme hardship in section 212(h) cases). These factors relate to the level of extreme hardship which an alien's "qualifying relative," in this case his spouse, would experience upon deportation of the respondent. *INS v. Hector*, 479 U.S. 85 (1986) (stating that the Board does not need to consider hardship to third parties other than the qualifying relatives delineated in the Act for purposes of deciding whether an alien is entitled to relief).

The factors deemed relevant in determining extreme hardship to a qualifying relative include, but are not limited to, the following: the presence of lawful permanent resident or United States citizen family ties to this country; the qualifying relative's family ties outside the United States; the conditions in the country or countries to which the qualifying relative would relocate and the extent of the qualifying relative's ties to such countries; the financial impact of departure from this country; and, finally, significant conditions of health, particularly when tied to an unavailability of suitable medical care in the country to which the qualifying relative would relocate. See *Jong Ha Wang v. INS*, 450 U.S. 139 (1981); *Gutierrez-Centeno v. INS*, 99 F.3d 1529

(9th Cir. 1996); *Shooshtary v. INS*, 39 F.3d 1049 (9th Cir. 1994); *Palmer v. INS*, 4 F.3d 482 (7th Cir. 1993); *Cerrillo-Perez v. INS*, 809 F.2d 1419 (9th Cir. 1987); *Ramirez-Durazo v. INS*, 794 F.2d 491 (9th Cir. 1986); *Sanchez v. INS*, 755 F.2d 1158 (5th Cir. 1985); *Contreras-Buenfil v. INS*, 712 F.2d 401 (9th Cir. 1983); *Ramirez-Gonzalez v. INS*, 695 F.2d 1208 (9th Cir. 1983); see also *Matter of Pilch*, Interim Decision 3298 (BIA 1996); *Matter of L-O-G-*, Interim Decision 3281 (BIA 1996); *Matter of O-J-O-*, Interim Decision 3280 (BIA 1996); *Matter of Ige*, 20 I&N Dec. 880 (BIA 1994); *Matter of Anderson*, 16 I&N Dec. 596 (BIA 1978).

* * *

The respondent is a 24-year-old native and citizen of Mexico. He has resided in the United States since 1989 and was recently married in 1995. At the time of the marriage, the respondent's wife was a lawful permanent resident; she became a naturalized United States citizen in 1996. Both the respondent and his wife reside with her family and provide them some financial support in return for room and board. Most of the respondent's family, however, resides in Mexico.

The respondent testified that he and his wife have very little money. Therefore, if forced to accompany the respondent to Mexico, the respondent's wife would be unable to travel back and forth to visit her family in the United States. In addition, the respondent's wife testified that she would have difficulty in obtaining employment in Mexico.

Having fully weighed the factors mentioned above, we find that the respondent has failed to establish extreme hardship to his spouse. As noted in the Immigration Judge's decision, the respondent's wife knew that the respondent was in deportation proceedings at the time they were married. In contrast to the respondent's assertions on appeal, this factor is not irrelevant. Rather, it goes to the respondent's wife's expectations at the time they were wed. Indeed, she was aware that she may have to face the decision of parting from her husband or following him to Mexico in the event he was ordered deported. In the latter scenario, the respondent's wife was also aware that a move to Mexico would separate her from her family in California. We find this to undermine the respondent's argument that his wife will suffer extreme hardship if he is deported. See Perez v. INS, 96 F.3d 390, 392 (9th Cir. 1996) (stating that "'(e)xtreme hardship' is hardship that is 'unusual or beyond that which would normally be expected' upon deportation. The common results of deportation are insufficient to prove extreme hardship." (quoting *Hassan v. INS, supra*, at 468)); *Shooshtary v. INS, supra*, at 1051 (holding that the uprooting of family and separation from friends does not necessarily amount to extreme hardship but rather represents the type of inconvenience and hardship experienced by the families of most aliens being deported); *Silverman v. Rogers*, 437 F.2d 102, 107 (1st Cir. 1970) (stating that "(e)ven assuming that the federal government had no right either to prevent a marriage or destroy it, we believe that here it has done nothing more than to say that the residence of one of the marriage partners may not be in the United States"), cert. denied, 402 U.S. 983 (1971).

Additionally, at no time during the hearing did the respondent's wife suggest that she would suffer any particular hardship, let alone extreme hardship, by moving to Mexico. See *Shooshtary v. INS, supra*, at 1051 (reviewing the Board's denial of a waiver of inadmissibility under section 212(h)(1)(B) of the Act, and stating that a "waiver should be granted only in those cases where 'great actual or prospective injury' to the qualifying party will occur. There must be an 'extreme impact' on the citizen or lawful permanent resident family member...." (quoting the Board's decision in the case, which in turn quoted *Matter of Ngai*, 19 I&N Dec. 245 (BIA 1984))). Furthermore, although the respondent's spouse would lose the physical proximity to her family, she speaks Spanish and the majority of her family is originally from Mexico. Therefore, she should have less difficulty adjusting to life in a foreign country. See *Ramirez-Durazo v. INS, supra*, at 498 (noting that the family spoke Spanish, which would ease the children's transition to Mexican society and schools, and that any hardship would be alleviated by numerous relatives living in the country to which the qualifying aliens would be relocating); *Ramirez-Gonzalez v. INS, supra*, at 1211 (holding that the hardship resulting from separation from extended family would be alleviated by immediate family relatives living in the alien's homeland); see also *Matter of Pilch, supra*, at 9 (noting that numerous family members in Poland may be able to provide an emotional base of support upon the aliens' return to that country).

In addition, neither the respondent nor his wife have any real financial ties to the United States. The respondent's wife is currently unemployed. Although the respondent is a musician in a band, he provided no evidence to prove that it had experienced success such that deportation would cause him to relinquish a lucrative career and, therefore, plunge his wife into unaccustomed poverty. Even if this were the case, we have generally not found financial hardship alone to amount to extreme hardship. See, e.g., *INS v. Jong Ha Wang, supra*, at 144 (holding that the mere showing of economic detriment to qualifying family members is insufficient to warrant findings of extreme hardship); *Ramirez-Durazo v. INS, supra*, at 499 (finding no extreme hardship where the child faced a lower standard of living in Mexico); *Hernandez-Patino v. INS*, 831 F.2d 750, 755 (7th Cir. 1987); *Holley v. INS*, 727 F.2d 189 (1st Cir. 1984); *Jong Shik Choe v. INS*, 597 F.2d 168 (9th Cir. 1979); see also *Shooshtary v. INS*, supra, at 1051 (stating that the "extreme hardship requirement of section 212(h)(2) was not enacted to insure that the family members of excludable aliens fulfill their dreams or continue in the lives which they currently enjoy").

In sum, the respondent has failed to show that his spouse would suffer extreme hardship over and above the normal economic and social disruptions involved in the deportation of a family member. See *Matter of Pilch, supra*; see also *Hassan v. INS, supra*, at 468 (finding that an alien attempting to establish extreme hardship must show a more severe impact than that of the common results of deportation); *Ramirez-Durazo v. INS, supra*, at 498. Therefore, we agree with the Immigration Judge's decision denying the respondent a waiver of inadmissibility under section 212(i) of the Act.

On appeal, the respondent cites several cases to support his assertion that the Immigration Judge erroneously focused on the underlying fraud as an adverse factor.

See *Matter of Alonzo*, 17 I&N Dec. 292 (Comm'r 1979); *Matter of Da Silva*, 17 I&N Dec. 288 (Comm'r 1979). As correctly noted by the respondent, these cases stand for the proposition that obtaining certain documentation by fraud, in order to achieve an immigration benefit, "shows disrespect for the law, but ... is the action for which (the applicants) seek to be forgiven and should not be held as an adverse factor." *Matter of Alonzo, supra*, at 294. However, this Board is not bound by decisions of the Commissioner of the Immigration and Naturalization Service. See *Matter of Fueyo*, 20 I&N Dec. 84, 87 n.3 (BIA 1989). In addition, since the writing of these decisions, several changes in law have required us to reevaluate the issue of use of underlying fraud as an adverse factor.

Specifically, the United States Supreme Court ruled in *INS v. Yueh-Shaio Yang*, 519 U.S. 26 (1996), that the Attorney General has the authority to consider any and all negative factors, including the respondent's initial fraud, in deciding whether or not to grant a waiver under section 241(a)(1)(H) of the Act. Therefore, as more thoroughly articulated in *Matter of Tijam*, Interim Decision 3372 (BIA 1998), the Supreme Court has undercut the rationale of *Matter of Da Silva, supra*, and *Matter of Alonzo, supra*. For this reason, as well as those stated in *Matter of Tijam, supra*, we find that the Immigration Judge properly considered the respondent's underlying fraud as an adverse factor in denying him relief under section 212(i) of the Act as a matter of discretion.

Board Member Anthony C. Moscato did not participate in the decision in this case.

Gustavo D. Villageliu, Board Member, in which Paul W. Schmidt, Chairman, joined

I respectfully concur.

* * *

First, in assessing the extreme hardship requirement, the majority cites *INS v. Hector*, 479 U.S. 85 (1986), for the proposition that hardship to relatives not listed under former section 244(a) of the Immigration and Naturalization Act, 8 U.S.C. § 1254(a) (1994), need not be considered. However, the Supreme Court in *INS v. Hector, supra*, at 86 n.1, specifically recognized the relevance of such relatives' suffering to the determination of the hardship the respondent will suffer if deported, citing *Contreras-Buenfil v. INS*, 712 F.2d 401, 403 (9th Cir. 1983) (separation from woman and her son respondent lived with), and *Antoine-Dorcelli v. INS*, 703 F.2d 19, 21–22 (1st Cir. 1983) (separation from family for whom respondent was caretaker). Moreover, the United States Court of Appeals for the Ninth Circuit, where this case arises, has ruled that in considering the totality of factors relevant to the extreme hardship determination in suspension applications, the Board abused its discretion in failing to consider the consequences of an alien's deportation on other relatives not specifically listed under section 244(a)(1). See *Tukhowinich v. INS*, 64 F.3d 460 (9th Cir. 1995). The majority's statement that nonqualifying relatives need not be considered should be read only as applicable to applications for relief under section 212(i) of the Act, 8 U.S.C. § 1182(i) (Supp. II 1996), where hardship to the applicant is not a listed factor.

Second, the majority's opinion may be read to imply that the time the respondent and his spouse wed is determinative as to whether to discount the spouse's hardship because of diminished expectations when marrying an alien in deportation proceedings. I disagree with that implication. Such diminished expectations clearly must relate to the actual circumstances, both of the marriage, and of the pending deportation proceedings, and the totality of the circumstances is paramount. Moreover, we only "discount" equities acquired after a final order of deportation. See *Matter of Correa*, 19 I&N Dec. 130 (BIA 1984). In this case no final order was entered since an appeal was pending. See *Matter of Lok*, 18 I&N Dec. 101 (BIA 1981) (stating that an order is final when the Board renders its decision on appeal).

Third, the majority's opinion correctly notes that in purchasing the fraudulent birth certificate, using it to procure a fraudulent social security card, and subsequently using these documents to seek to procure a United States passport in order to travel into and out of the United States and seek employment, the respondent sought to procure both "documentation" and "other benefits" under the Act. The majority's finding is consistent with the close scrutiny of such a finding required by *Matter of Healy and Goodchild*, 17 I&N Dec. 22 (BIA 1979), because of its harsh consequences. However, a small clarification is needed. The other benefits under the Act the respondent sought to procure are the right to travel with a United States passport pursuant to section 215(b) of the Act, 8 U.S.C. § 1185(b) (1994). The majority's language may be misinterpreted as suggesting that using the fraudulent passport to obtain employment is obtaining a benefit under the Act.

Although the use or possession of such document is punishable under section 274C of the Act, 8 U.S.C. § 1324c (1994 & Supp. II 1996), working in the United States is not "a benefit provided under this Act," and we have specifically held that a violation of section 274C and fraud or misrepresentation under section 212(a)(6)(C)(i) of the Act are not equivalent. See *Matter of Lazarte*, Interim Decision 3264 (BIA 1996); accord *Matter of Jimenez-Santillano*, Interim Decision 3291 (BIA 1996); cf. *Matter of Serna*, 20 I&N Dec. 579 (BIA 1992) (relating to possession or use of an altered immigration document). It is long settled that inadmissibility for immigration fraud does not ensue from the mere purchase of fraudulent documents, absent an attempt to fraudulently use the document for immigration purposes. *Matter of Kai Hing Hui*, 15 I&N Dec. 288 (BIA 1975); *Matter of Sarkissian*, 10 I&N Dec. 109 (BIA 1962); Matter of Box, 10 I&N Dec. 87 (BIA 1962); accord *Matter of D-L- & A-M-*, 20 I&N Dec. 409 (BIA 1991); cf. *Matter of Serna, supra* (stating that mere possession is not a crime involving moral turpitude).

Finally, the majority points out that the Supreme Court has indicated that we may permissibly construe the element of extreme hardship narrowly. However, such permissibility does not require a narrow construction of extreme hardship, and we have recently declined to do so, choosing instead to rely on our precedents for guidance in our case-by-case determinations. See *Matter of O-J-O-*, Interim Decision 3280 (BIA 1996). Consequently, this decision should not be misinterpreted as a change in our precedents regarding the level of hardship we will require for relief from deportation. See *Matter of O-J-O-, supra*, at 11, 13 (Dunne and Holmes, concurring), and cases cited therein.

Lory Diana Rosenberg, Board Member

I respectfully concur in part and dissent in part.

In my view the majority opinion is erroneous as a matter of law in every respect. I disagree with the majority opinion for four principal reasons.

First, I disagree that the respondent is inadmissible, as I do not believe that any of the documents he supposedly "procured" fall within the statutory ground of inadmissibility under section 212(a)(6)(C)(i) of the Immigration and Nationality Act, 8 U.S.C. § 1182(a)(6)(C)(i) (Supp. II 1996), which requires that "a visa (or) other documentation" was used to obtain "admission into the United States or other benefit provided under (the) Act." *Id.* Second, I disagree that section 212(i), as amended by the Illegal Immigration Reform and Immigrant Responsibility Act of 1996, Division C of Pub. L. No. 104-208, 110 Stat. 3009-546, 3009-639 ("IIRIRA"), applies to the respondent, as it contains no express legislative mandate making its application retroactive.

Third, even assuming that the respondent was required to satisfy the more restrictive standard imposed by the IIRIRA, requiring a showing of extreme hardship, and limiting the extreme hardship considered to hardship that would be experienced by his spouse, I find that the extreme hardship adjudication fails to consider all the relevant factors involved, contrary to the law of the United States Court of Appeals for the Ninth Circuit, in which this appeal arises. Fourth, I disagree that the Immigration Judge's denial of voluntary departure is not a proper matter for review, merely because the respondent has not addressed it in his appeal.

It is with regard to my second point of disagreement that I feel I must concur. Arguably, the reasoning in the Attorney General's decision in *Matter of Soriano*, Interim Decision 3289 (BIA, A.G. 1996) (interpreting the new restrictions on eligibility for discretionary section 212(c) waivers to present no retroactivity concerns, by comparing such waivers to prospective injunctive relief, a procedural mechanism that, under *Landgraf v. USI Film Products*, 511 U.S. 244 (1994), would be applicable immediately), may control the issue as to which version of section 212(i) of the Act applies to the respondent's case. Nevertheless, as discussed below, I believe the recent opinions of the Supreme Court, as well as the decisions of three federal circuit courts of appeals and several federal district courts rejecting the Attorney General's interpretation, warrant our reconsideration of *Matter of Soriano*, as well as a fresh interpretation of the statutory section at issue, unencumbered by the reasoning in that decision.

In sum, based on my findings that (1) the majority decision erroneously determines the respondent inadmissible when he is not inadmissible, and (2) even if inadmissible, the majority either erroneously judges the respondent's waiver application according to the wrong version of the statute, or erroneously applies the prevailing standard applicable to a discretionary determination of the presence of extreme hardship, I conclude that the respondent has been denied a fair hearing, and a reasoned decision. I do not believe that the respondent received a fair hearing as a matter of law, and I do not believe that the favorable and adverse factors present in this case were fairly weighed and balanced as our own standards, applicable circuit standards, and the principle of fundamental fairness require. Consequently, I dissent.

* * *

According to the record, the respondent pled guilty to and was convicted of a violation of 18 U.S.C. § 1028(a)(4) (1994), possession of a false identification document. That federal criminal provision under which the respondent was convicted states as follows:

> Whoever, in a circumstance described in subsection (c) of this section—
>
> (4) knowingly possesses an identification document (other than one issued lawfully for the use of the possessor) or a false identification document, *with the intent such document be used to defraud the United States* ... or attempts to do so, shall be punished as provided in subsection (b) of this section.

18 U.S.C. § 1028(a)(4) (emphasis added).

According to an "Information" in the record, the conviction refers to the respondent's possession of a false birth certificate, which he used in applying for a United States passport at a passport agency in San Francisco. This conduct occurred on September 27, 1994.

Putting aside, for a moment, the procedural defects in the decisions of the Immigration Judge and the majority related to their failure to consider the actual offense for which the respondent was convicted, the majority inexplicably focuses on the verb "procuring" in assessing inadmissibility. In fact, the operative word in section 212(a)(6)(C)(i) of the Act as it relates to the respondent's case is not whether he procured a document or was seeking to procure another document, but whether the procuring in which he engaged was for the purpose of obtaining "a visa, other documentation, or admission into the United States, *or other benefit provided under this Act*" (emphasis added).

Initially, I note that the conduct of the respondent on which the Immigration Judge and the majority rely in finding the respondent to be inadmissible under section 212(a)(6)(C)(i) of the Act is based on his conviction for offering a United States birth certificate obtained from a friend to obtain a United States passport. The statute under which the respondent was convicted covers conduct that is engaged in with an intent to defraud the United States. It does not require, in every instance, that the conduct engaged in be engaged in with the intent, or with the result, of obtaining a "benefit ... under this Act." The term "this Act" in section 212(A)(6)(C)(i) refers to the Immigration and Nationality Act.

Thus, an individual could be convicted under 18 U.S.C. § 1028(a)(4) without there being any specific evidence that the individual had any intent to act, or actually did act to obtain a "benefit under this Act." Cf. section 212(a)(6)(C)(i) of the Act. There is nothing in the record of conviction before us, nor in the testimony or other documentation in the record before us, that indicates that the respondent engaged in the conduct resulting in his conviction for possession of a false identification document to obtain a "benefit under (the) Act."

Moreover, neither employment, nor the ability to travel necessarily constitutes a "benefit under this Act." No matter how powerful the majority may wish to make the reach of the Immigration and Nationality Act, it does not extend to the constitutional rights to work and to travel. As should be self-evident, an individual may be prosecuted under federal criminal law for a violation of using false documents "to defraud the United States," but not be convicted of an offense that involves fraud or a material misrepresentation to obtain a "benefit under (the) Act." As the respondent argues, he was convicted only of possession of identification documents, not of using them to procure admission or any other benefit under the Act. His conviction is for possessing the document with the intent to defraud the United States. No more; no less.

Notes

1. The 212(i) waiver does not waive inadmissibility for persons who have made a false claim to U.S. citizenship, as the statute specifically applies to the first paragraph of section 212(a)(6)(C).

2. The central purpose of this waiver is to provide for family unification, and the failure to consider all relevant factors of extreme hardship have brought reversals from the courts.[94]

3. The 212(i) waiver requires a showing that "a refusal of admission to the United States of such immigrant alien would result in extreme hardship to the citizen or lawfully resident spouse or parent of such an alien." The equivalent waiver of the grounds of deportability is designed for persons who were inadmissible at the time of the admission on account of 212(a)(6)(C)(i).[95] The 237(a)(1)(H) waiver does not require a showing of hardship but merely requires that the person is the spouse, parent, or child of a U.S. citizen or lawful permanent resident and is in possession of an immigrant visa or equivalent document. The underlying purpose of the provision was to preserve families. Can you think of why the two provisions at 212(i) and 237(a)(1)(H) are different?

4. Persons who are found inadmissible due to the possession of an invalid visa, passport or other admission document may be eligible for a discretionary waiver if they are able to prove that they either did not know or could not reasonably have known of the invalidity of their documentation.[96]

7. Waiver for Prior Removal

Matter of Lee

17 I. & N. Dec. 275 (Comm'r 1978)

This matter is before the Commissioner on certification as provided by 8 C.F.R. 103.4, for review of the Regional Commissioner's decision to dismiss the appeal from

94. *See Delmundo v. INS*, 43 F.3d 436 (9th Cir. 1994).
95. *See* 8 U.S.C. § 1227(a)(1)(H), Sec. 237(a)(1)(H).
96. 8 U.S.C. § 1182(k), Sec. 212(k).

the District Director's order denying an application for permission to reapply for admission into the United States after deportation.

The applicant is a 39-year-old native and citizen of China residing in Hong Kong. He first came to Service attention as a crewman on board the M/V Eastern Star applying for permission to land temporarily in pursuit of his calling on June 1, 1965. His application was refused and he was ordered detained on board as a mala fide crewman. On a subsequent arrival on the same vessel on November 9, 1965, at Port Angeles, Washington, he was granted permission to land temporarily as a crewman. On November 18, 1965, the applicant, accompanied by two other crewmembers, left the vessel at Port Angeles, Washington, and traveled by bus to Seattle, Washington, despite a standing order issued by the Captain of the M/V Eastern Star that shore leave for all crewmembers was restricted to the immediate area of Port Angeles. The applicant and his two companions were taken into custody at the bus station in Seattle by immigration officers. They were charged with attempting to desert the vessel on which they arrived, permission to land was revoked, and they were ordered deported pursuant to section 252(b) of the Immigration and Nationality Act of 1952, as amended, 8 U.S.C. 1282(b). The applicant was returned to his vessel at Port Angeles on November 20, 1965, and ordered detained on board in custody of the Master. His deportation from the United States was effected on November 24, 1965, upon the vessel's departure from the United States. The applicant was refused landing privileges as a crewman on five subsequent occasions of arrival on foreign-registered vessels in the United States. On the fifth occasion of arrival (July 3, 1969), he deserted his vessel, the M/V Deganya, at Newark, New Jersey. Efforts by the Service to locate the applicant were unsuccessful. On July 21, 1975, a sixth-preference petition was submitted by the China Garden Restaurant, Incorporated, Raynham, Massachusetts, on the applicant's behalf. This petition was approved on May 21, 1976. At the request of this Service, the applicant surrendered himself to this Service at Boston, Massachusetts, and was granted the privilege of departing voluntarily from the United States. The record contains verification of departure on August 21, 1976, from Anchorage, Alaska, to Tokyo, Japan.

The applicant made application for an immigrant visa at the United States Consulate in Hong Kong and was informed on October 22, 1976, that he needed permission to reapply for admission into the United States after deportation. The instant application was then filed on October 29, 1976, at Boston and subsequently transferred to the Seattle office, which had jurisdiction in the matter pursuant to 8 C.F.R. 212.2(c).

The District Director denied the application as a matter of discretion and cited *Matter of Tin*, 14 I & N Dec. 371 (R.C.1973), and *Matter of Chim*, 14 I & N Dec. 357 (R.C.1973), as justification for his action. The Regional Commissioner affirmed the District Director's decision and dismissed the appeal.

Section 212(a)(17) of the Immigration and Nationality Act of 1952, as amended, 8 U.S.C. 1182(a)(17), has its roots in section 3 of the Act of 1917. Section 3 made prostitutes and other immoral classes who had been previously debarred or deported from the United States excludable unless they had received permission from the Secretary of Labor to reapply for admission. The Act of March 2, 1929, extended this provision, making it a felony to reenter the United States after having been deported unless the Secretary had granted permission to reapply for admission after deportation.

The Immigration and Nationality Act of 1952, as amended, incorporated the same language but made a distinction between those previously excluded (section 212(a)(16) of the Act) and those who had been deported (section 212(a)(17) of the Act). Those previously excluded require permission of the Attorney General to reapply for admission if that application was to be made within 1 year of the date of exclusion and deportation. Those previously deported require the permission of the Attorney General to reapply for admission at any time after deportation.

The intent of Congress in enacting section 212(a)(16) and (17) can best be found in the conclusions and recommendations of the Senate Committee on the Judiciary in their report (S.Rep. No. 1515, 81st Cong., 2nd Sess. (1950)) concerning the effectiveness and necessity of retaining the various laws affecting immigration. A study was conducted pursuant to S.Res. 137, 80th Cong., 1st Sess., for the purpose of bringing all laws pertaining to immigration and nationality under one composite heading. (The Immigration and Nationality Act of 1952 was the fruit of these labors.) The Committee report issuing from this study addressed the subject of previously deported or excluded aliens and made the following conclusions and recommendations.

Speaking of section 3 of the 1917 Act, the Committee stated:

> The subcommittee finds that the law as it is now written is adequate to prevent the abuse of the exclusion and deportation laws by aliens who attempt to reapply for admission to the United States soon after their exclusion or deportation, <u>as well as to allow reconsideration when the alien is able to overcome the handicaps which brought about the original exclusion and deportation</u>. Page 365. (Underscoring supplied.)

The second clause of these conclusions and recommendations directly concerns the instant application. The import of these words is to give a previously deported alien a second chance and connotes a remedial relief rather than a punitive provision of statute. In this regard, I find the several decisions affecting permission to reapply after deportation lacking this attitude. *Matter of H__R__*, 5 I & N Dec. 769 (C.O.1954), and *Matter of Chim, supra*, convey a punitive attitude and attach conditions beyond anything I believe Congress intended in granting the Attorney General authority to allow previously deported or excluded aliens to reapply for entry into the United States. The discussion of the issues raised in the instant case will be made with the foregoing in mind.

1. Moral character of the applicant:

In a recent case before me on certification, the Regional Commissioner also held that a record of immigration violations denoted poor moral character and cited this finding as one of the adverse factors considered. In that case, I ruled that contention was without merit, and reaffirmed *Matter of T__*, 1 I & N Dec. 158 (BIA 1941), in that a record of immigration violations standing alone will not conclusively support a finding of a lack of good moral character. In the instant case, I will likewise dismiss the contention that the applicant is a person lacking good moral character.

2. Recency of the deportation:

The recency of the deportation is mentioned as a factor to be considered in Matter of Tin, supra. However, there is but a passing reference to this factor. ("As a further example, an alien who was deported many years ago solely for a minor immigration violation and who has a bona fide reason for wanting to immigrate to the United States, may be granted permission to reapply....")

I believe that the recency of the deportation can only be considered when there is a finding of poor moral character based on moral turpitude in the conduct and attitude of a person which evinces a callous conscience. In such circumstances, there must be a measurable reformation of character over a period of time in order to properly assess an applicant's ability to integrate into our society. In all other instances when the cause of deportation has been removed and the person now appears eligible for issuance of a visa, the time factor should not be considered.

3. Need for the applicant's services in the United States:

The Regional Commissioner considered the need for the services of the applicant in the United States and dismissed this as a favorable factor. However, I find there is merit in counsel's contention that where the applicant will provide services to the public in a job category where sufficient workers in the United States are not available, this is a favorable factor in behalf of the applicant.

4. Applicant's contention that he did not know he was deported:

This contention will be dismissed without discussion. The record clearly shows he was deported pursuant to section 252(b) of the Act and does need permission of the Attorney General to apply for admission to the United States.

5. Length of time applicant had been in the United States:

I can only relate a positive factor of residence in the United States where that residence is pursuant to a legal admission or adjustment of status as a permanent resident.

If we were to reward a person for remaining in the United States in violation of law, the structure of all laws pertaining to immigration would be seriously threatened. Therefore, I will dismiss counsel's contention that this should be considered a favorable factor.

In item #1, the Regional Commissioner discussed the record of immigration violations in the context of equating these violations with a finding of a lack of good moral character. While I dismissed the finding of poor moral character, I will not lightly dismiss a serious record of immigration violations. An evinced callous attitude toward violating the immigration laws without a hint of reformation of character should be considered as a heavily weighted adverse factor. In the instant case, I do find that hint of reformation of character in the attitude of the applicant in surrendering himself to the Service and departing the United States voluntarily as requested.

While it may be argued that his motivation in doing so was predicated on self-interest, it is only natural that positive character reformation is more apt to take place when a benefit seems likely to accrue to a person.

In applying the principles set forth in this discussion and weighing all factors present, I find that the applicant should be granted permission to reapply for admission into the United States after deportation and will set aside the order of the District Director denying the application and the Regional Commissioner's dismissal of the appeal. *Matter of Chin, supra*, and *Matter of Tin, supra*, are modified insofar as the weight given to adverse factors is inconsistent with the weight accorded the adverse factors in this decision.

ORDER: The District Director's decision denying the application for permission to reapply for admission after deportation and the Regional Commissioner's dismissal of appeal to that decision is hereby set aside, and the application is granted.

Notes

1. The equivalent provision of the current statute referred to in the previous case is 8 U.S.C. § 1182(a)(9)(A)(iii), Sec. 212(a)(9)(A)(iii), which provides:

> Clauses (i) and (ii) shall not apply to an alien seeking admission within a period if, prior to the date of the alien's reembarkation at a place outside the United States or attempt to be admitted from foreign contiguous territory, the Attorney General has consented to the alien's reapplying for admission.

2. **Unlawful Presence.** As was noted in our discussion in Chapter 3, in 1996, Congress added a new ground of inadmissibility for persons who remained in the United States unlawfully for a period of more than 180 days and later seeks readmission.[97] The statute also provides for waivers of these grounds of inadmissibility in the interest of preserving family unity and for humanitarian reasons

> in the case of an immigrant who is the *spouse or son of daughter of a United States citizen or of an alien lawfully admitted for permanent residence*, if it is established to the satisfaction of the Attorney General that the refusal of admission to such immigrant alien would result in *extreme hardship* to the citizen or lawfully resident spouse or parent of such alien (emphasis supplied).

Similarly, a person who has earlier been in the United States unlawfully for more than one year or who has been ordered removed under expedited removal and then reenters or attempts to reenter without permission is inadmissible and may only apply to the Attorney General for permission for readmission ten years after the date of the last departure; however, this provision may be waived for battered spouses and children under the U, S or T visas. The determination of "extreme hardship" is not defined in the statute and has yet to be clarified by regulations.

---

97. *See* 8 U.S.C. § 1182(a)(9)(B), Sec. 212(a)(9)(B).

3. **Other Immigration Law Violations.** The deportability provision for failure to submit the appropriate change of address documentation may be waived if it was not willful but excusable. Also, persons who have had their visas revoked or who violated the conditions of their admission may obtain a waiver if their nonimmigrant status had been reinstated or if they are receiving special immigrant juvenile status.[98]

8. Miscellaneous Waivers

Economic Grounds. Persons found inadmissible based upon the public charge provisions may obtain a waiver by posting a bond in an amount determined by the Secretary of DHS.[99]

Health Grounds. Waivers for the health grounds are set forth in 8 U.S.C. § 1182(g), Sec. 212(g). Persons who are inadmissible on account of a communicable disease of public health significance or for a physical or mental disorder may have the provision waived if they are the parent, spouse, or unmarried child of a U.S. citizen or lawful permanent resident or are issued an immigrant visa. The person's admission may be permitted under terms and conditions that include a bond, proof of health insurance or other conditions set by the discretion of the Attorney General after consultation with the Secretary of Health and Human Services. A person who is inadmissible due to lack of vaccination against certain diseases may have the provision waived where the vaccination requirement would be contrary to the person's religious beliefs or moral conviction or where the vaccination would not be medically appropriate.

Quasi-Criminal and Moral Grounds. Persons who have engaged in or sought to engage in prostitution are eligible for a waiver upon a showing of extreme hardship to the U.S. citizen or LPR spouse, parent or child or if no acts of prostitution were committed within ten years preceding the application.[100] The inadmissibility grounds for document fraud may be waived for LPRs for humanitarian reasons if no prior fine was imposed and the fraudulent documents were used to assist support the person's spouse or child.[101]

Exchange Visitor Two-Year Foreign Residency Requirement. As was explained in our discussion of the exchange visitor visa (J visa) in Chapter 6, some if its beneficiaries are subject to the two-year foreign residence requirement. 8 U.S.C. § 1182(e), Sec. 212(e), provides a waiver for persons who are able to establish that (1) their U.S. citizen or lawful permanent resident spouse or child will experience "exceptional hardship"; (2) the beneficiary will be persecuted; (3) their country of nationality has no objection to the grant of a waiver;[102] (4) a U.S. government agency establishes

98. 8 U.S.C. § 1227(c), Sec. 237(c).

99. 8 U.S.C. § 1183, Sec. 213.

100. 8 U.S.C. § 1182(a)(2)(D)(i)–(ii), Sec. 212(a)(2)(D)(i)–(ii).

101. 8 U.S.C. §§ 1182(d)(12) and 1227(a)(3)(C)(ii), Sections 212(d)(12) and 237(a)(3)(C)(ii).

102. The "no objection" from their government is ineffective in the case of persons who were admitted as physicians practicing medicine.

that the admission of the person is in the public interest; or (5) a state department of health requests the beneficiary's services.[103]

J waivers are rarely successful, since the courts interpret the statute as granting a great deal of discretion to the Attorney General. Moreover, Congress, in enacting the statute, contemplated that exchange visitors would return to their countries except under rare circumstances. Therefore, the challenge for the advocate is to clearly lay out and document each element of the hardship, which in the aggregate may engender sympathy from USCIS or the reviewing court. The factors which can be considered in meeting the requirement of exceptional hardship are similar to other waivers; however, the applicant must present a compelling case.

The J-1 waiver for certain foreign medical graduates practicing in areas where there are medical shortages in the United States was initially set to expire in 2002 but has been extended further. The President signed the Modification of Visa Requirements with Respect to International Medical Graduates,[104] which extends the program through May 31, 2006. Beneficiaries of this program are not covered under the normal quota for H-1B workers,[105] and the legislation includes a provision which allows the physician to practice either primary care or specialty medicine. With respect to specialty medicine, the program is limited to areas where shortages in that particular specialty already exist. The bill also authorizes five of each state's recipients, if requested by an interested state agency, to practice in a facility that is not in a "designated geographic area."

One unique aspect of the J waiver is that while the ultimate decision is made by USCIS, the applicant must first receive a favorable recommendation from the U.S. Information Agency (USIA) of the Department of State.[106]

9. Waiver Chart

This chart is intended to assist in gaining a better understanding of the myriad of waivers spread throughout the immigration statute. The chart organizes the waivers according to the factors which apply to the inadmissibility or deportability grounds to which they apply. Each waiver includes one or more of the factors in the far left column—the column on the far right describes the grounds which can be waived upon satisfying the requirements. As we know from our previous discussion, most waivers have elements of discretion and may also require a level of hardship, familial relationship to a U.S. citizen or lawful permanent resident, or a period of residency or physical presence.

---

103. This program was created under the Immigration and Nationality Technical Corrections Act of 1994, Pub. L. No. 103-416, 108 Stat. 4305 (1994), and extended by IIRAIRA until June 1, 2002. Under this program, a special procedure is established where each state is allowed only twenty such waivers each year.

104. Pub. L. No. 108-441, 118 Stat. 2630 (2004).

105. See Chapter 6.

106. *See Matter of Tayabji*, 19 I. & N. Dec. 264 (BIA 1985).

Factors	Grounds Waived
No Discretion	Prohibits the removal of a person where there is a "clear probability" that the person's life or freedom would be threatened on account of her race, religion, nationality, membership in a particular social group or political opinion.
Discretion	
Pure Discretion	1. Physical or mental disorder [8 U.S.C. § 1182(a)(1)(A)(ii)]. 2. Previously removed persons under all forms of removal (expedited, removal following arrival or admission or self-removal), where the person seeks readmission within the applicable period [8 U.S.C. § 1182(a)(9)(A)].
Recommendations of Consular Officer	*For nonimmigrants.* Waives all grounds of inadmissibility except for persons coming to engage in terrorism or persons whose admission would cause adverse foreign policy consequences [8 U.S.C. § 1182(d)(3)].
Emergency, Reciprocity or for Persons in Transit	Waives the requirement of having a passport valid for six months following admission or a valid nonimmigrant visa [8 U.S.C. § 1182(a)(7)(B)].
Considerations of the Individual's Religious Beliefs or Moral Convictions & Bond or Other Assurances	Immigrants who fail to present proof of having received certain vaccinations for preventable diseases [8 U.S.C. § 1182(a)(1)].
Humanitarian Purposes, Family Unity or Public Interest	1. Waives inadmissibility for a LPR who is returning (not following a removal order) but remains subject to the document fraud violation under § 274C and is otherwise admissible [8 U.S.C. § 1182(d)(12)]. 2. Applicant for immigrant visa or adjustment who has had one document fraud violation under § 274C where fraud was to *support spouse or child* [8 U.S.C. § 1182(d)(12)]. 3. Person who has encouraged, induced, assisted, abetted or aided an individual who at the time of such action was the alien's spouse, parent or child to enter the United States in violation of law [8 U.S.C. § 1182(d)(11)].
"No Objection" Waiver by Diplomatic Note from Home Country & Favorable Recommendation from the Department of State	Waives two-year foreign residency requirement ("no objection" diplomatic note is not effective for J-visa graduate medical trainees) [8 U.S.C. § 1182(e)].
"Would be Subject to Persecution" in Home Country	Waives the two-year foreign residency requirement for persons who entered under a J-visa (exchange visitor visa) [8 U.S.C. § 1182(e)].
Well-founded Fear of Persecution	Waives all grounds except aggravated felons, persecutors of others and torturers (asylum).

Factors	Grounds Waived
Period of Time	
15 Years & Rehabilitation and Admission	Waives most crimes under 8 U.S.C. § 1182(a)(2), including simple possession of 30g or less of marihuana but not crimes involving murder or torture of persons previously removed. Waiver is inapplicable to lawful permanent residents convicted of aggravated felonies or those who have resided in the United States for less than seven years immediately preceding the initiation of removal proceedings
Lawful Permanent Resident for Five Years Who Has Resided Continuously in the United States for Seven Years	Waives all grounds of inadmissibility and deportability except under the aggravated felony and terrorist provisions. Persons admitted as exchange students, foreigners obtaining graduate medical education or persons previously granted relief are ineligible [8 U.S.C. § 1229b(a)].
Ten Years Continuous Physical Presence, GMC & Exceptional and Extremely Unusual Hardship to Person's U.S. Citizen or LPR spouse, parent or child	Waives all grounds except the criminal and security grounds. Statute restricts benefits to only 4,000 per year [8 U.S.C. § 1229b(b)].
Relationship	
Spouse, Minor, Unmarried Child or Parent of U.S. Citizen or LPR & Discretion	1. Waives communicable diseases of public health significance [8 U.S.C. 1182(a)(1)(A)(i)] but may require the posting of a bond [8 U.S.C. § 1182(g)]. 2. Waives fraud or willful misrepresentations of material facts [8 U.S.C. 1182(i)].
Spouse, Parent or Child of U.S. Citizen or LPR, Discretion, Note Contrary to the National Welfare, Safety or Security & Extreme Hardship & Rehabilitation	Waives crimes of moral turpitude [8 U.S.C. 1182(a)(2)(A)(i)(II)], two or more crimes irrespective of moral turpitude [8 U.S.C. § 1182(a)(2)(B)], prostitution and commercialized vices [8 U.S.C. 1182(a)(2)(D)], persons having asserted immunity from prosecution (diplomats) [8 U.S.C. § 1182(a)(2)(E)] and controlled substance violations for simple possession of less than 30g of marihuana [8 U.S.C. 1182(a)(2)(A)(I)(II)]. [Also see 8 U.S.C. § 1182(h)]. *This provision is unavailable to LPRs convicted of aggravated felonies or who have not lived in the United States for seven years preceding the initiation of proceedings.*
Spouse, Parent or Child of U.S. Citizen or LPR & Extreme Hardship to Spouse, Parent or Child	Waives unlawful presence for more than 180 days (normally three-year bar) or greater than one year (normally a ten-year bar) [8 U.S.C. § 1182(a)(9)(B)].
Spouse, Parent or Child of U.S. Citizen or LPR, Exceptional Hardship & Favorable Recommendation from the Department of State	1. Waives J-visa exchange visitors foreign residency requirements. 2. Waives unlawful presence for more than 180 days but less than one year.

Chapter 11

Citizenship — Acquisition and Loss

Introduction

Just as immigration law can be viewed as seeking to control the movement of persons between countries, the law of citizenship can be viewed as the rules governing membership and participation in the national community. While the laws governing who is or may become a citizen vary from country to country, the attainment of citizenship is always accompanied by rights and privileges greater than those enjoyed by foreigners. Generally, citizenship will allow a person the rights of entry and participation.[1] Naturalization is the term which refers to the acquisition of citizenship other than through birth.[2]

Naturalization and citizenship is one of the more complex areas of immigration and nationality law. In this chapter, we will explore the principles governing citizenship and naturalization as well as expatriation and denaturalization, which refer to the loss of citizenship.

Even though there are numerous references in the Constitution to citizenship, the original document never defined the term. Instead, the Constitution empowered Congress to enact a "uniform rule of naturalization."[3] The Fourteenth Amendment, which was adopted after the Civil War, was the first provision in the Constitution, which set the criteria for U.S. citizenship. The Fourteenth Amendment provides that:

> *All persons born or naturalized in the United States, and subject to the jurisdiction thereof, are citizens of the United States and of the state wherein they reside.*

The following case, which preceded the adoption of the fourteenth amendment, was the first major decision to deal with the issue of who is a citizen and whether citizenship enured to all persons born in the United States.

---

1. In the United States the rights of citizens include the full right of movement, participation (voting and holding of public office), and equality of treatment under the law.

2. Whether citizenship is acquired at birth depends upon whether birth was in the U.S. or if outside the U.S., whether one or both of the parents were U.S. citizens.

3. U.S. Const. art. 1, §8, cl. 4.

A. Citizenship, a Historical Perspective—Birth in the U.S.

Dred Scott v. John F.A. Sandford

60 U.S. (19 How.) 393 (1856)

[Note: Prior to the institution of the present suit, an action was brought by Scott for his freedom in the Circuit Court of St. Louis county (State court), where there was a verdict and judgment in his favor. On a writ of error to the Supreme Court of the State, the judgment below was reversed and the case remanded to the Circuit Court, where it was continued to await the decision of the case now in question. The declaration of Scott contained three counts: that Sandford had assaulted the plaintiff; that he had assaulted Harriet Scott, his wife; and that he had assaulted Eliza Scott and Lizzie Scott, his children.]

Chief Justice Taney delivered the opinion of the Court:

* * *

The question is simply this: Can a [N]egro, whose ancestors were imported into this country, and sold as slaves, become a member of the political community formed and brought into existence by the Constitution of the United States, and as such become entitled to all the rights, and privileges, and immunities guarantied by that instrument to the citizen, One of which rights is the privilege of suing in a court of the United States in the cases specified in the Constitution.

It will be observed, that the plea applies to that class of persons only whose ancestors were [N]egroes of the African race, and imported into this country, and sold and held as slaves. The only matter in issue before the court, therefore, is whether the descendants of such slaves, when they shall be emancipated, or who are born of parents who had become free before their birth, are citizens of a State, in the sense in which the word citizen is used in the Constitution of the United States....

The situation of this population was altogether unlike that of the Indian race. The latter, it is true, formed no part of the colonial communities, and never amalgamated with them in social connections or in government. But although they were uncivilized, they were yet a free and independent people, associated together in nations or tribes, and governed by their own laws. Many of these political communities were situated in territories to which the white race claimed the ultimate right of dominion. But that claim was acknowledged to be subject to the right of the Indians to occupy it as long as they thought proper, and neither the English nor colonial Governments claimed or exercised any dominion over the tribe or nation by whom it was occupied, nor claimed the right to the possession of the territory, until the tribe or nation consented to cede it. These Indian Governments were regarded and treated as foreign Governments, as much so as if an ocean had separated the red man from the white; and their freedom has constantly been acknowledged, from the time of the first emigration to the English colonies to the present day, by the different Governments which succeeded each other. Treaties have been negotiated with them, and their alliance sought for in war; and the people who compose these Indian political communities have always been treated as foreigners not living under our Government....

* * *

The words "people of the United States" and "citizens" are synonymous terms, and mean the same thing. They both describe the political body who, according to our republican institutions, form the sovereignty, and who hold the power and conduct the Government through their representatives. They are what we familiarly call the "sovereign people," and every citizen is one of this people, and a constituent member of this sovereignty. The question before us is whether the class of persons described in the plea in abatement compose a portion of this people, and are constituent members of this sovereignty. We think they are not, and that they are not included, and were not intended to be included, under the word "citizens" in the Constitution, and can therefore claim none of the rights and privileges which that instrument provides for and secures to citizens of the United States. On the contrary, they were at that time considered as a subordinate and inferior class of beings, who had been subjugated by the dominant race, and, whether emancipated or not, yet remained subject to their authority, and had no rights or privileges but such as those who held the power and the Government might choose to grant them.

In discussing this question, we must not confound the rights of citizenship which a State may confer within its own limits, and the rights of citizenship as a member of the Union. It does not by any means follow, because he has all the rights and privileges of a citizen of a State, that he must be a citizen of the United States. He may have all of the rights and privileges of the citizen of a State, and yet not be entitled to the rights and privileges of a citizen in any other State. For, previous to the adoption of the Constitution of the United States, every State had the undoubted right to confer on whomsoever it pleased the character of citizen, and to endow him with all its rights. But this character of course was confined to the boundaries of the State, and gave him no rights or privileges in other States beyond those secured to him by the laws of nations and the comity of States. Nor have the several States surrendered the power of conferring these rights and privileges by adopting the Constitution of the United States. Each State may still confer them upon an alien, or any one it thinks proper, or upon any class or description of persons; yet he would not be a citizen in the sense in which that word is used in the Constitution of the United States, nor entitled to sue as such in one of its courts, nor to the privileges and immunities of a citizen in the other States. The rights which he would acquire would be restricted to the State which gave them. The Constitution has conferred on Congress the right to establish an uniform rule of naturalization, and this right is evidently exclusive, and has always been held by this court to be so. Consequently, no State, since the adoption of the Constitution, can by naturalizing an alien invest him with the rights and privileges secured to a citizen of a State under the Federal Government, although, so far as the State alone was concerned, he would undoubtedly be entitled to the rights of a citizen, and clothed with all the rights and immunities which the Constitution and laws of the State attached to that character.

It is very clear, therefore, that no State can, by any act or law of its own, passed since the adoption of the Constitution, introduce a new member into the political community created by the Constitution of the United States. It cannot make him a member of this community by making him a member of its own. And for the same reason it cannot introduce any person, or description of persons, who were not intended to be embraced in this new political family, which the Constitution brought into existence, but were intended to be excluded from it.

* * *

It is true, every person, and every class and description of persons, who were at the time of the adoption of the Constitution recognised as citizens in the several States, became also citizens of this new political body; but none other; it was formed by them, and for them and their posterity, but for no one else. And the personal rights and privileges guarantied to citizens of this new sovereignty were intended to embrace those only who were then members of the several State communities, or who should afterwards by birthright or otherwise become members, according to the provisions of the Constitution and the principles on which it was founded. It was the union of those who were at that time members of distinct and separate political communities into one political family, whose power, for certain specified purposes, was to extend over the whole territory of the United States. And it gave to each citizen rights and privileges outside of his State which he did not before possess, and placed him in every other State upon a perfect equality with its own citizens as to rights of person and rights of property; it made him a citizen of the United States.

* * *

In the opinion of the court, the legislation and histories of the times, and the language used in the Declaration of Independence, show, that neither the class of persons who had been imported as slaves, nor their descendants, whether they had become free or not, were then acknowledged as a part of the people, nor intended to be included in the general words used in that memorable instrument.

* * *

The language of the Declaration of Independence is equally conclusive: It begins by declaring that, "when in the course of human events it becomes necessary for one people to dissolve the political bands which have connected them with another, and to assume, among the powers of the earth, the separate and equal station to which the laws of nature and nature's God entitle them, a decent respect for the opinions of mankind requires that they should declare the causes which impel them to the separation."

It then proceeds to say: "We hold these truths to be self-evident: that all men are created equal; that they are endowed by their Creator with certain unalienable rights; that among them is life, liberty, and the pursuit of happiness; that to secure these rights, Governments are instituted, deriving their just powers from the consent of the governed."

* * *

... The brief preamble sets forth by whom it was formed, for what purposes, and for whose benefit and protection. It declares that it is formed by the people of the United States; that is to say, by those who were members of the different political communities in the several States; and its great object is declared to be to secure the blessings of liberty to themselves and their posterity. It speaks in general terms of the people of the United States, and of citizens of the several States, when it is providing for the exercise of the powers granted or the privileges secured to the citizen. It does not define what description of persons are intended to be included under these terms, or who shall be regarded as a citizen and one of the people. It uses them as terms so well understood, that no further description or definition was necessary. But there are two clauses in the Constitution which point directly and specifically to the [N]egro race as a separate class of persons, and show clearly that they were not regarded as a portion of the people or citizens of the Government then formed.

* * *

... [I]t is said that a person may be a citizen, and entitled to that character, although he does not possess all the rights which may belong to other citizens; as, for example, the right to vote, or to hold particular offices; and that yet, when he goes into another State, he is entitled to be recognised there as a citizen, although the State may measure his rights by the rights which it allows to persons of like character or class resident in the State, and refuse to him the full rights of citizenship.

Undoubtedly, a person may be a citizen, that is, a member of the community who form the sovereignty, although he exercises no share of the political power, and is incapacitated from holding particular offices. Women and minors, who form a part of the political family, cannot vote; and when a property qualification is required to vote or hold a particular office, those who have not the necessary qualification cannot vote or hold the office, yet they are citizens.

So, too, a person may be entitled to vote by the law of the State, who is not a citizen even of the State itself. And in some of the States of the Union foreigners not naturalized are allowed to vote. And the State may give the right to free [N]egroes and mulattoes, but that does not make them citizens of the State, and still less of the United States. And the provision in the Constitution giving privileges and immunities in other States, does not apply to them.

Neither does it apply to a person who, being the citizen of a State, migrates to another State. For then he becomes subject to the laws of the State in which he lives, and he is no longer a citizen of the State from which he removed. And the State in which he resides may then, unquestionably, determine his status or condition, and place him among the class of persons who are not recognised as citizens, but belong to an inferior and subject race; and may deny him the privileges and immunities enjoyed by its citizens.

But so far as mere rights of person are concerned, the provision in question is confined to citizens of a State who are temporarily in another State without taking up their residence there. It gives them no political rights in the State, as to voting or holding office, or in any other respect. For a citizen of one State has no right to participate in the government of another. But if he ranks as a citizen in the State to which he belongs, within the meaning of the Constitution of the United States, then, whenever he goes into another State, the Constitution clothes him, as to the rights of person, with all the privileges and immunities which belong to citizens of the State. And if persons of the African race are citizens of a State, and of the United States, they would be entitled to all of these privileges and immunities in every State, and the State could not restrict them; for they would hold these privileges and immunities under the paramount authority of the Federal Government, and its courts would be bound to maintain and enforce them, the Constitution and laws of the State to the contrary notwithstanding....

Concurring opinion of Justice Daniel.

... For who, it may be asked, is a citizen? What do the character and status of citizen import? Without fear of contradiction, it does not import the condition of being private property, the subject of individual power and ownership. Upon a principle of etymology alone, the term citizen, as derived from civitas, conveys the ideas of connection or identification with the State or Government, and a participation of its functions. But beyond this, there is not, it is believed, to be found, in the theories of writers on Government, or in any actual experiment heretofore tried, an exposition of the term citizen, which has not been understood as conferring the actual possession and enjoyment, or the perfect right of acquisition and enjoyment, of an entire equality of privileges, civil and political.

Thus Vattel, in the preliminary chapter to his Treatise on the Law of Nations, says: "Nations or States are bodies politic; societies of men united together for the purpose of promoting their mutual safety and advantage, by the joint efforts of their mutual strength. Such a society has her affairs and her interests; she deliberates and takes resolutions in common; thus becoming a moral person, who possesses an understanding and a will peculiar to herself." Again, in the first chapter of the first book of the Treatise just quoted, the same writer, after repeating his definition of a State, proceeds to remark, that, "from the very design that induces a number of men to form a society, which has its common interests and which is to act in concert, it is necessary that there should be established a public authority, to order and direct what is to be done by each, in relation to the end of the association. This political authority is the sovereignty." Again this writer remarks: "The authority of all over each member essentially belongs to the body politic or the State."

By this same writer it is also said: "The citizens are the members of the civil society; bound to this society by certain duties, and subject to its authority; they equally participate in its advantages. The natives, or natural-born citizens, are those born in the country, of parents who are citizens. As society cannot perpetuate itself otherwise than by the children of the citizens, those children naturally follow the condition of their parents, and succeed to all their rights." Again: "I say, to be of the country, it is necessary to be born of a person who is a citizen; for if he be born there of a foreigner, it will be only the place of his birth, and not his country. The inhabitants, as distinguished from citizens, are foreigners who are permitted to settle and stay in the country." (Vattel, Book 1, cap. 19, p. 101.)

* * *

It is difficult to conceive by what magic the mere surcease or renunciation of an interest in a subject of property, by an individual possessing that interest, can alter the essential character of that property with respect to persons or communities unconnected with such renunciation. Can it be pretended that an individual in any State, by his single act, though voluntarily or designedly performed, yet without the cooperation or warrant of the Government, perhaps in opposition to its policy or its guaranties, can create a citizen of that State? Much more emphatically may it be asked, how such a result could be accomplished by means wholly extraneous, and entirely foreign to the Government of the State? The argument thus urged must lead to these extraordinary conclusions. It is regarded at once as wholly untenable, and as unsustained by the direct authority or by the analogies of history.

* * *

The proud title of Roman citizen, with the immunities and rights incident thereto, and as contradistinguished alike from the condition of conquered subjects or of the lower grades of native domestic residents, was maintained throughout the duration of the republic, and until a late period of the eastern empire, and at last was in effect destroyed less by an elevation of the inferior classes than by the degradation of the free, and the previous possessors of rights and immunities civil and political, to the indiscriminate abasement incident to absolute and simple despotism.

... [C]itizenship was not conferred by the simple fact of emancipation, but that such a result was deduced therefrom in violation of the fundamental principles of free political association; by the exertion of despotic will to establish, under a false and misapplied denomination, one equal and universal slavery; and to effect this result required the exertions of absolute power—of a power both in theory and practice, being in its most plenary acceptation the sovereignty, the state itself—it could not be produced by a less or inferior authority, much less by the will or the act of one who, with reference to civil and political rights, was himself a slave. The master might abdicate or abandon his interest or ownership in his property, but his act would be a mere abandonment. It seems to involve an absurdity to impute to it the investiture of rights which the sovereignty alone had power to impart. There is not perhaps a community in which slavery is recognised, in which the power of emancipation and the modes of its exercise are not regulated by law—that is, by the sovereign authority; and none can fail to comprehend the necessity for such regulation, for the preservation of order, and even of political and social existence.

* * *

Justice McLean dissenting.

* * *

Being born under our Constitution and laws, no naturalization is required, as one of foreign birth, to make him a citizen. The most general and appropriate definition of the term citizen is 'a freeman.' Being a freeman, and having his domicil in a State different from that of the defendant, he is a citizen within the act of Congress, and the courts of the Union are open to him.

It has often been held, that the jurisdiction, as regards parties, can only be exercised between citizens of different States, and that a mere residence is not sufficient; but this has been said to distinguish a temporary from a permanent residence.

In *Chirae v. Chirae*, (2 Wheat., 261; 4 Curtis, 99,) this court says: 'That the power of naturalization is exclusively in Congress does not seem to be, and certainly ought not to be, controverted.' No person can legally be made a citizen of a State, and consequently a citizen of the United States, of foreign birth, unless he be naturalized under the acts of Congress. Congress has power 'to establish a uniform rule of naturalization.'

It is a power which belongs exclusively to Congress, as intimately connected with our Federal relations. A State may authorize foreigners to hold real estate within its jurisdiction, but it has no power to naturalize foreigners, and give them the rights of citizens. Such a right is opposed to the acts of Congress on the subject of naturalization, and subversive of the Federal powers. I regret that any countenance should be given from this bench to a practice like this in some of the States, which has no warrant in the Constitution.

In the argument, it was said that a colored citizen would not be an agreeable member of society. This is more a matter of taste than of law. Several of the States have admitted persons of color to the right of suffrage, and in this view have recognised them as citizens; and this has been done in the slave as well as the free States. On the question of citizenship, it must be admitted that we have not been very fastidious. Under the late treaty with Mexico, we have made citizens of all grades, combinations, and colors. The same was done in the admission of Louisiana and Florida. No one ever doubted, and no court ever held, that the people of these Territories did not become citizens under the treaty. They have exercised all the rights of citizens, without being naturalized under the acts of Congress.

As to the locality of slavery. The civil law throughout the Continent of Europe, it is believed, without an exception, is, that slavery can exist only within the territory where it is established; and that, if a slave escapes, or is carried beyond such territory, his master cannot reclaim him, unless by virtue of some express stipulation. (Grotius, lib. 2, chap. 15, 5, 1; lib. 10, chap. 10, 2, 1; Wicqueposts Ambassador, lib. 1, p. 418; 4 Martin, 385; *Case of the Creole* in the House of Lords, 1842; 1 Phillimore on International Law, 316, 335.)

There is no nation in Europe which considers itself bound to return to his master a fugitive slave, under the civil law or the law of nations. On the contrary, the slave is held to be free where there is no treaty obligation, or compact in some other form, to return him to his master. The Roman law did not allow freedom to be sold. An ambassador or any other public functionary could not take a slave to France, Spain, or any other country of Europe, without emancipating him. A number of slaves escaped from a Florida plantation, and were received on board of ship by Admiral Cochrane; by the King's Bench they were held to be free.

I prefer the lights of Madison, Hamilton, and Jay, as a means of construing the Constitution in all its bearings, rather than to look behind that period, into a traffic which is now declared to be piracy, and punished with death by Christian nations. I do not like to draw the sources of our domestic relations from so dark a ground. Our independence was a great epoch in the history of freedom; and while I admit the Government was not made especially for the colored race, yet many of them were citizens of the New England States, and exercised the rights of suffrage when the Constitution was adopted, and it was not doubted by any intelligent person that its tendencies would greatly ameliorate their condition.

* * *

Justice Curtis dissenting.

Of this there can be no doubt. At the time of the ratification of the Articles of Confederation, all free native-born inhabitants of the States of New Hampshire, Massachusetts, New York, New Jersey, and North Carolina, though descended from African slaves, were not only citizens of those States, but such of them as had the other necessary qualifications possessed the franchise of electors, on equal terms with other citizens. The Supreme Court of North Carolina, in the case of the *State v. Manuel*, (4 Dev. and Bat., 20,) has declared the law of that State on this subject, in terms which I believe to be as sound law in the other States I have enumerated, as it was in North Carolina.

"According to the laws of this State," says judge Gaston, in delivering the opinion of the court, 'all human beings within it, who are not slaves, fall within one of two classes. Whatever distinctions may have existed in the Roman laws between citizens and free inhabitants, they are unknown to our institutions. Before our Revolution, all free persons born within the dominions of the King of Great Britain, whatever their color or complexion, were native-born British subjects—those born out of his allegiance were aliens. Slavery did not exist in England, but it did in the British colonies. Slaves were not in legal parlance persons, but property. The moment the incapacity, the disqualification of slavery, was removed, they became persons, and were then either British subjects, or not British subjects, according as they were or were not born within the allegiance of the British King. Upon the Revolution, no other change took place in the laws of North Carolina than was consequent on the transition from a colony dependent on a European King, to a free and sovereign State. Slaves remained slaves. British subjects in North Carolina became North Carolina freemen. Foreigners, until made members of the State, remained aliens. Slaves, manumitted here, became freemen, and therefore, if born within North Carolina, are citizens of North Carolina, and all free persons born within the State are born citizens of the State. The Constitution extended the elective franchise to every freeman who had arrived at the age of twenty-one, and paid a public tax; and it is a matter of universal notoriety, that, under it, free persons, without regard to color, claimed and exercised the franchise, until it was taken from free men of color a few years since by our amended Constitution."

* * *

The Constitution of New York gave the right to vote to "every male inhabitant, who shall have resided," &c.; making no discrimination between free colored persons and others. (See Con. of N.Y, Art. 2, Rev. Stats. of N.Y, vol. 1, p. 126.) That of New Jersey, to "all inhabitants of this colony, of full age, who are worth 50 proclamation money, clear estate."

* * *

The fact that free persons of color were citizens of some of the several States, and the consequence, that this fourth article of the Confederation would have the effect to confer on such persons the privileges and immunities of general citizenship, were not only known to those who framed and adopted those articles, but the evidence is decisive, that the fourth article was intended to have that effect, and that more restricted language, which would have excluded such persons, was deliberately and purposely rejected.

* * *

Among the powers expressly granted to Congress is "the power to establish a uniform rule of naturalization." It is not doubted that this is a power to prescribe a rule for the removal of the disabilities consequent on foreign birth. To hold that it extends further than this, would do violence to the meaning of the term naturalization, fixed in the common law, (Co. Lit., 8 a, 129 a; 2 Ves., sen., 286; 2 Bl. Com., 293,) and in the minds of those who concurred in framing and adopting the Constitution. It was in this sense of conferring on an alien and his issue the rights and powers of a native-born citizen, that it was employed in the Declaration of Independence. It was in this sense it was expounded in the Federalist, (No. 42,) has been understood by Congress, by the judiciary, (2 Wheat., 259, 269; 3 Wash. R., 313, 322; 12 Wheat., 277,) and by commentators on the Constitution. (3 Story's Com. on Con., 1–3; 1 Rawle on Con., 84–88; 1 Tucker's Bl. Com. App., 255–259.)

It appears, then, that the only power expressly granted to Congress to legislate concerning citizenship, is confined to the removal of the disabilities of foreign birth.

* * *

Undoubtedly, as has already been said, it is a principle of public law, recognised by the Constitution itself, that birth on the soil of a country both creates the duties and confers the rights of citizenship. But it must be remembered, that though the Constitution was to form a Government, and under it the United States of America were to be one united sovereign nation, to which loyalty and obedience on the one side, and from which protection and privileges on the other, would be due, yet the several sovereign States, whose people were then citizens, were not only to continue in existence, but with powers unimpaired, except so far as they were granted by the people to the National Government.

Among the powers unquestionably possessed by the several States, was that of determining what persons should and what persons should not be citizens. It was practicable to confer on the Government of the Union this entire power. It embraced what may, well enough for the purpose now in view, be divided into three parts. First: The power to remove the disabilities of alienage, either by special acts in reference to each individual case, or by establishing a rule of naturalization to be administered and applied by the courts. Second: Determining what persons should enjoy the privileges of citizenship, in respect to the internal affairs of the several States. Third: What native-born persons should be citizens of the United States.

The first-named power, that of establishing a uniform rule of naturalization, was granted; and here the grant, according to its terms, stopped. Construing a Constitution containing only limited and defined powers of government, the argument derived from this definite and restricted power to establish a rule of naturalization, must be admitted to be exceedingly strong. I do not say it is necessarily decisive. It might be controlled by other parts of the Constitution. But when this particular subject of citizenship was under consideration, and, in the clause specially intended to define the extent of power concerning it, we find a particular part of this entire power separated.

Notes

1. *Dred Scott is* included here for its discussion of citizenship, illustrating the principle that the status of citizenship is implicated with issues of membership in the national community. In *Dred Scott*, the U.S. Supreme Court considered that an African-American, even though born in the U.S., was not entitled to citizenship, because they were not worthy of being members of the national community. However, with the adoption of the Fourteenth Amendment in 1868, the ruling was effectively overturned.[4]

2. **Citizenship v. Lawful Permanent Residency.** While lawful permanent residency provides persons with most of the benefits of citizenship, there are still a few notable exceptions.

Lawful permanent residents are granted the right to live and work in the United States. However, even if they are allowed to leave and re-enter the country without a visa, those who are deemed to be seeking a new admission following a trip abroad are subject to the grounds of inadmissibility and deportability upon their return to the United States. These grounds have no statutes of limitation, and the lawful permanent resident's status can be revoked at any time. Furthermore, the government

---

4. Dred Scott was a significant decision for many other reasons including that of deciding the question of who was entitled to sue in United States courts, and the national government's power to legislate. *See* John Nowak, et al., Constitutional Law § 4.4 (3d ed. 1986).

may revoke lawful permanent residence status if the person seems to have abandoned her domestic residence by not maintaining sufficient ties to the United States. On the other hand, citizenship cannot be abandoned, even if a U.S. citizen chooses to reside in another country for long periods of time and does not maintain strong ties to the country.

One of the present-day rights of citizenship is the right to vote. In earlier times, the right to vote was determined by the states, and the qualification for voting did not necessarily include citizenship. As seen in the previous case, historically, the right to vote was limited on the basis of gender, race and property ownership.[5] In addition, citizenship has increasingly carried with it the advantage of being eligible for certain jobs for which non-citizens may be ineligible.[6]

B. U.S. Citizenship and Its Acquisition

As a general matter, United States citizenship is acquired when a person is: (1) born in the United States, subject to its jurisdiction; (2) naturalized in the United States; or (3) born outside of the United States to one or more parents who are citizens. The first two are constitutional guarantees provided for in the Constitution which cannot be changed by statute,[7] and the third is provided for by Congress, which has plenary power. Similarly, Congress' power to regulate other matters relating to the acquisition of citizenship outside of the fourteenth amendment is plenary.[8] For example, persons in the United States with diplomatic immunity are not subject to the jurisdiction of the United States, and therefore, their children born in the country are not United States citizens.

United States laws relating to the acquisition of citizenship derive from both the English common law and Roman law principles of *jus soli* and *jus sanguinis*.[9] The principle of *jus soli* derived from the common law rule that the place of a person's birth determined citizenship. *Jus sanguinis* derives from the Roman law rule that citizenship is conferred by relationship or descent.

---

5. For interesting discussion on this topic, see Virginia Harper-Ho, *Noncitizen Voting Rights: The History, the Law and Current Prospects for Change*, 18 LAW & INEQUALITY 271 (2000); *Gerald* Rosberg, *Aliens and Equal Protection: Why Not the Right to Vote*, 75 MICH. L. REV. 1092 (1977).

6. *See, e.g., Ambach v. Norwick*, 441 U.S. 68 (1979) (recognizing the political function exception to deny teaching licenses to non-citizens); *Foley v. Connelie*, 435 U.S. 291 (1978) (upholding New York statute denying employment as state troopers to noncitizens); *also see Cabell v. Chavez-Salido*, 454 U.S. 432 (1982); Gerald Rosberg, *The Protection of Aliens from Discriminatory Treatment by the National Government*, 1977 SUP. CT. REV. 275. For additional discussion on this subject, see Chapter 2.

7. *See Afroyim v. Rusk*, 387 U.S. 253, 263 (1967).

8. *See United States v. Wong Kim Ark*, 169 U.S. 649 (1898).

9. The statutory provisions governing citizenship can be found in the Act at section 301. 8 U.S.C. § 1401. In researching questions of citizenship and naturalization, USCIS's Adjudicator's Field Manual beginning at Chapter 72 should be consulted.

There are a number of principles helpful to understanding the acquisition of U.S. citizenship. First, the reference in the fourteenth amendment to birth "in the United States" includes birth in the U.S. Territories of the Virgin Islands, Panama Canal Zone, Puerto Rico and Guam. Second, legal questions regarding acquisition and retention of U.S. citizenship at birth are governed by the laws in effect at the time of the person's birth.[10] Third, in terms of the statutory provisions for the "passing of citizenship," the citizenship of a parent is not sufficient to confer the same status on the child. The rules concerning acquisition of citizenship in the case of a child born outside of the country where one or both parents are U.S. citizens are outlined below:

1. If both parents are U.S. citizens and at least one of the parents has lived in the United States, then the child is a U.S. citizen.[11] (Applies to births before May 24,1934)

2. Where one of the parents is a U.S. citizen and the other a "national" of the United States, then the child born outside of the country and its possessions is a citizen if the U.S. citizen parent has been physically present in the United States for a continuous period of at least one year prior to the child's birth.[12] (Applies to births between May 24, 1934 and January 13, 1941)

3. Where the child is born in an "outlying possession" of the United States, then the child will be a U.S. citizen if at least one of the parents is a U.S. citizen and has been physically present in the United States or its possessions for a continuous period of not less than one year.[13] (Applies to births between January 13, 1941 and December 24, 1952)

4. Where the child is born outside the United States and its outlying possessions, the child will be a citizen even if only one of the parents is a U.S. citizen if that parent has been physically present in the United States or its possessions for a period totaling

---

10. *See Montana v. Kennedy*, 366 U.S. 308 (1961). The retention requirements were removed from the statute in 1994. *See* Immigration and Nationality Technical Corrections Act of 1994, Pub. L. No. 103-416, 108 Stat. 4307–08 (1994).

11. *See* 8 U.S.C. § 1401(c).

12. *See* 8 U.S.C. § 1401(d). The Constitution makes numerous references to citizens of the United States but makes no reference to the term "nationals." Nationals describe persons (including both citizens and non-citizens) who owe permanent allegiance to the United States. *See* 8 U.S.C. § 1101(a)(22); *see also* 8 U.S.C. § 1408. A distinction was made between citizen and non-citizen nationals when the United States had more extensive insular possessions whose inhabitants were considered "nationals" of the United States but were not afforded full citizenship rights. For example, a person born in American Samoa or the Swain Islands is a "non-citizen national" with the unrestricted right to enter the United States and may obtain U.S. citizenship through relaxed naturalization procedures. *See* O.I. 325.1(a)(2).

13. 8 U.S.C. § 1401(e). The "outlying possession[s]" are defined as the Swain Islands and American Samoa. 8 U.S.C. § 1101(a)(29). Special provision is made granting citizenship to persons born in Puerto Rico after January 13, 1941 and some of those born in Puerto Rico between April 11, 1899 and January 13, 1941. *See* 8 U.S.C. § 1402. Similar provisions exist for persons born in the Panama Canal Zone, Alaska, Hawaii, the Virgin Islands and Guam.

ten years. Five of those ten years must have been after the citizen parent reached the age of 14.[14] (Applies to births after December 24, 1952)

5. A child born outside of the United States may also acquire U.S. citizenship derivatively through her parent's naturalization.[15]

6. **Child Citizenship Act of 2000.**[16] The Child Citizenship Act of 2000 (CCA), facilitates the acquisition of U.S. citizenship in cases involving adoptions. Under previous law, a child born to a U.S. citizen abroad would acquire U.S. citizenship, however a child adopted by a U.S. citizen would be eligible for admission as an immediate relative, unless she was adopted as an orphan, in which case she would acquire citizenship upon adoption.[17] The CCA provides for automatic citizenship when four conditions are satisfied: 1) at least one of the parents is a U.S. citizen; 2) the child is under 18; 3) the child is a lawful permanent resident; and 4) the child is residing in the U.S. "in the legal and physical custody of the citizen parent pursuant to a lawful admission for permanent residence."[18] The statute applies to children admitted after February 27, 2001.[19] Legal custody is presumed for the citizen parent unless there is evidence to the contrary. The provision applies to adopted children and those legitimated, but not step-children.[20]

As can be seen in the following case, citizenship transmitted at birth to a person born outside of the United States is vastly different from citizenship obtained at birth in the United States.

William P. Rogers, Sect'y of State v. Aldo Mario Bellei

401 U.S. 815 (1971)

Justice Blackmun delivered the opinion of the Court.

Under constitutional challenge here, primarily on Fifth Amendment due process grounds, but also on Fourteenth Amendment grounds, is § 301(b) of the Immigration and Nationality Act of June 27, 1952, 66 Star. 236, 8 U.S.C. § 1401(b).

Section 301(a) of the Act, 8 U.S.C. § 1401(a), defines those persons who "shall be nationals and citizens of the United States at birth." Paragraph (7) of § 301(a) includes in that definition a person born abroad "of parents one of whom is an alien, and the

14. Certain periods of service in the U.S. government, international organizations or the armed forces will qualify the person for residence purposes. *See* 8 U.S.C. § 1401(g).

15. *See* 8 U.S.C. §§ 1431, 1432.

16. Pub. L. No. 106-395, 114 Stat. 1631 (2000).

17. See discussion in Chapter 7.

18. 8 U.S.C. § 1431(a)(3).

19. The provisions of the statute are not retroactive. *See Jordan v. Att'y Gen'l*, 424 F.3d 320 (3d Cir. 2005); *Ali v. Ashcroft*, 395 F.3d 722, 725 (7th Cir. 2005).

20. According to the USCIS, step-children are not accorded automatic citizenship because they are not "children" under Title III of the Act. *compare* 8 U.S.C. §§ 1101(b)(1) and (c)(1).

other a citizen of the United States" who has met specified conditions of residence in this country. Section 301 (b), however, provides that one who is a citizen at birth under § 301(a)(7) shall lose his citizenship unless, after age 14 and before age 28, he shall come to the United States and be physically present here continuously for at least five years.

The plan thus adopted by Congress with respect to a person of this classification was to bestow citizenship at birth but to take it away upon the person's failure to comply with a post-age-14 and pre-age-28 residential requirement. It is this deprival of citizenship, once bestowed, that is under attack here.

The facts are stipulated:

1. The appellee, Aldo Mario Bellei (hereinafter the plaintiff), was born in Italy on December 22, 1939. He is now 31 years of age.

2. The plaintiff's father has always been a citizen of Italy and never has acquired United States citizenship. The plaintiff's mother, however, was born in Philadelphia in 1915 and thus was a native-born United States citizen. She has retained that citizenship. Moreover, she has fulfilled the requirement of § 301(a)(7) for physical presence in the United States for 10 years, more than five of which were after she attained the age of 14 years. The mother and father were married in Philadelphia on the mother's 24th birthday, March 14, 1939. Nine days later, on March 23, the newlyweds departed for Italy. They have resided there ever since.

3. By Italian law the plaintiff acquired Italian citizenship upon his birth in Italy. He retains that citizenship. He also acquired United States citizenship at his birth under Rev. Stat. § 1993, as amended by the Act of May 24, 1934, § 1, 48 Star. 797, then in effect. That version of the statute, as does the present one, contained a residence condition applicable to a child born abroad with one alien parent.

4. The plaintiff resided in Italy from the time of his birth until recently. He currently resides in England, where he has employment as an electronics engineer with an organization engaged in the NATO defense program.

5. The plaintiff has come to the United States five different times. He was physically present here during the following periods:

April 27 to July 31, 1948

July 10 to October 5, 1951

June to October 1955

December 18, 1962 to February 13, 1963

May 26 to June 13, 1965.

On the first two occasions, when the plaintiff was a boy of eight and 11, he entered the country with his mother on her United States passport. On the next two occasions, when he was 15 and just under 23, he entered on his own United States passport and was admitted as a citizen of this country. His passport was first issued on June 27, 1952. His last application approval, in August 1961, contains the notation "Warned abt. 301(b)." The plaintiff's United States passport was periodically approved to and including December 22, 1962, his 23d birthday.

6. On his fifth visit to the United States, in 1965, the plaintiff entered with an Italian passport and as an alien visitor. He had just been married and he came with his bride to visit his maternal grandparents.

7. The plaintiff was warned in writing by United States authorities of the impact of § 301(b) when he was in this country in January 1963 and again in November of that year when he was in Italy. Sometime after February 11, 1964, he was orally advised by the American Embassy at Rome that he had lost his United States citizenship pursuant to § 301(b). In November 1966 he was so notified in writing by the American Consul in Rome when the plaintiff requested another American passport.

8. On March 28, 1960, plaintiff registered under the United States Selective Service laws with the American Consul in Rome. At that time he already was 20 years of age. He took in Italy, and passed, a United States Army physical examination. On December 11, 1963, he was asked to report for induction in the District of Columbia. This induction, however, was then deferred because of his NATO defense program employment. At the time of deferment he was warned of the danger of losing his United States citizenship if he did not comply with the residence requirement. After February 14, 1964, Selective Service advised him by letter that, due to the loss of his citizenship, he had no further obligation for United States military service.

Plaintiff thus concededly failed to comply with the conditions imposed by § 301(b) of the Act.

* * *

The two cases primarily relied upon by the three-judge District Court are, of course, of particular significance here. *Schneider v. Rusk*, 377 U.S. 163 (1964). Mrs. Schneider, a German national by birth, acquired United States citizenship derivatively through her mother's naturalization in the United States. She came to this country as a small child with her parents and remained here until she finished college. She then went abroad for graduate work, was engaged to a German national, married in Germany, and stayed in residence there. She declared that she had no intention of returning to the United States. In 1959, a passport was denied by the State Department on the ground that she had lost her United States citizenship under the specific provisions of § 352(a)(1) of the Immigration and Nationality Act, 8 U.S.C. § 1484(a)(1), by continuous residence for three years in a foreign state of which she was formerly a national. The Court, by a five-to-three vote, held the statute violative of Fifth Amendment due process because there was no like restriction against foreign residence by native-born citizens.

The dissent (Mr. Justice Clark, joined by Justices Harlan and White) based its position on what it regarded as the long acceptance of expatriating naturalized citizens who voluntarily return to residence in their native lands; possible international complications; past decisions approving the power of Congress to enact statutes of that type; and the Constitution's distinctions between native-born and naturalized citizens.

Afroyim v. Rusk, 387 U.S. 253 (1967). Mr. Afroyim, a Polish national by birth, immigrated to the United States at age 19 and after 14 years here acquired United States citizenship by naturalization. Twenty-four years later he went to Israel and voted in a political election there. In 1960 a passport was denied him by the State Department on the ground that he had lost his United States citizenship under the specific provisions of §349(a)(5) of the Act, 8 U.S.C. §1481(a)(5), by his foreign voting. The Court, by a five-to-four vote, held that the Fourteenth Amendment's definition of citizenship was significant; that Congress has no "general power, express or implied, to take away an American citizen's citizenship without his assent," 387 U.S., at 257; that Congress' power is to provide a uniform rule of naturalization and, when once exercised with respect to the individual, is exhausted, citing Mr. Chief Justice Marshall's well-known but not uncontroversial dictum in *Osborn v. Bank of the United States*, 9 Wheat. 738 (1824); and that the "undeniable purpose" of the Fourteenth Amendment was to make the recently conferred "citizenship of Negroes permanent and secure" and "to put citizenship beyond the power of any governmental unit to destroy," 387 U.S., at 263. *Perez v. Brownell*, 356 U.S. 44 (1958), a five-to-four holding within the decade and precisely to the opposite effect, was overruled.

The dissent (Mr. Justice Harlan, Joined by Justices Clark, Stewart, and White) took issue with the Court's claim of support in the legislative history, would elucidate the Marshall dictum, and observed that the adoption of the Fourteenth Amendment did not deprive Congress of the power to expatriate on permissible grounds consistent with "other relevant commands" of the Constitution.

It is to be observed that both Mrs. Schneider and Mr. Afroyim had resided in this country for years. Each had acquired United States citizenship here by the naturalization process (in one case derivative and in the other direct) prescribed by the National Legislature. Each, in short, was covered explicitly by the Fourteenth Amendment's very first sentence: "All persons born or naturalized in the United States and subject to the jurisdiction thereof, are citizens of the United States and of the State wherein they reside." This, of course, accounts for the Court's emphasis in *Afroyim* upon "Fourteenth Amendment citizenship." 387 U.S., at 262.

The very first Congress, at its Second Session, proceeded to implement its power, under the Constitution's Art. 1, §8, cl. 4, to "establish an uniform Rule of Naturalization" by producing the Act of March 26, 1790, 1 Star. 103. That statute, among other things, stated,

> And the children of citizens of the United States, that may be born beyond sea, or out of the limits of the United States, shall be considered as natural born citizens: Provided, That the right of citizenship shall not descend to persons whose fathers have never been resident in the United States....

A like provision, with only minor changes in phrasing and with the same emphasis on paternal residence, was continuously in effect through three succeeding naturalization Acts. Act of January 29, 1795, § 3, 1 Stat. 415; Act of April 14, 1802, § 4, 2 Stat. 155; Act of February 10, 1855, c. 71, § 1, 10 Stat. 604. The only significant difference is that the 1790, 1795, and 1802 Acts read retrospectively, while the 1855 Act reads prospectively as well.

The Act of March 2, 1907, § 6, 34 Stat. 1229, provided that all children born abroad who were citizens under Rev. Stat. § 1993 and who continued to reside elsewhere, in order to receive governmental protection, were to record at age 18 their intention to become residents and remain citizens of the United States and were to take the oath of allegiance upon attaining their majority.

The change in § 1993 effected by the Act of May 24, 1934, ... eliminated the theretofore imposed restriction to the paternal parent and prospectively granted citizenship, subject to a five-year continuous residence requirement and an oath, to the foreign-born child of either a citizen father or a citizen mother. This was the form of the statute at the time of plaintiff's birth on December 22, 1939.

The Nationality Act of 1940, § 201, 54 Star. 1138, contained a similar condition directed to a total of five years' residence in the United States between the ages of 13 and 21.

The Immigration and Nationality Act, by its § 407, 66 Star. 281, became law in December 1952. Its § 301(b) contains a five years' continuous residence condition (alleviated, with the 1957 amendment, see n. 1, by an allowance for absences less than 12 months in the aggregate) directed to the period between 14 and 28 years of age.

The statutory pattern, therefore, developed and expanded from (a) one established in 1790 and enduring through the Revised Statutes and until 1934, where citizenship was specifically denied to the child born abroad of a father who never resided in the United States; to (b), in 1907, a governmental protection condition for the child born of an American citizen father and residing abroad, dependent upon a declaration of intent and the oath of allegiance at majority; to (c), in 1934, a condition for the child born abroad of one United States citizen parent and one alien parent, of five years' continuous residence in the United States before age 18 and the oath of allegiance within six months after majority; to (d), in 1940, a condition for that child, of five years' residence here, not necessarily continuous, between ages 13 and 21; to (e), in 1952, a condition for that child, of five years' continuous residence here, with allowance, between ages 14 and 28. The application of these respective statutes to a person in plaintiff Bellei's position produces the following results:

1. Not until 1934 would that person have had any conceivable claim to United States citizenship. For more than a century and a half no statute was of assistance. Maternal citizenship afforded no benefit. One may observe, too, that if Mr. Bellei had been born in 1933, instead of in 1939, he would have no claim even today.

2. Despite the recognition of the maternal root by the 1934 amendment, in effect at the time of plaintiff's birth, and despite the continuing liberalization of the succeeding statutes, the plaintiff still would not be entitled to full citizenship because, although

his mother met the condition for her residence in the United States, the plaintiff never did fulfill the residential condition imposed for him by any of the statutes.

3. This is so even though the liberalizing 1940 and 1952 statutes, enacted after the plaintiff's birth, were applicable by their terms to one born abroad subsequent to May 24, 1934, the date of the 1934 Act, and were available to the plaintiff.

Thus, in summary, it may be said fairly that, for the most part, each successive statute, as applied to a foreign-born child of one United States citizen parent, moved in a direction of leniency for the child. For plaintiff Bellei the statute changed from complete disqualification to citizenship upon a condition subsequent, with that condition being expanded and made less onerous, and, after his birth, with the succeeding liberalizing provisions made applicable to him in replacement of the stricter statute in effect when he was born. The plaintiff nevertheless failed to satisfy any form of the condition.

Over 70 years ago the Court, in an opinion by Mr. Justice Gray, reviewed and discussed early English statutes relating to rights of inheritance and of citizenship of persons born abroad of parents who were British subjects, *United States v. Wong Kim Ark*, 169 U.S. 649, 668–671 (1898). The Court concluded that "naturalization by descent" was not a common-law concept but was dependent, instead, upon statutory enactment. The statutes examined were 25 Edw. 3, Stat. 2 (1350); 29 Car. 2, c. 6 (1677); 7 Anne, c. 5, § 3 (1708); 4 Geo. 2, c. 21 (1731); and 13 Geo. 3, c. 21 (1773). Later Mr. Chief Justice Taft, speaking for a unanimous Court, referred to this "very learned and useful opinion of Mr. Justice Gray" and observed "that birth within the limits of the jurisdiction of the Crown, and of the United States, as the successor of the Crown, fixed nationality, and that there could be no change in this rule of law except by statute…." He referred to the cited English statutes and stated, "These statutes applied to the colonies before the War of Independence."

We thus have an acknowledgment that our law in this area follows English concepts with an acceptance of the jus soli, that is, that the place of birth governs citizenship status except as modified by statute.

The Constitution as originally adopted contained no definition of United States citizenship. However, it referred to citizenship in general terms and in varying contexts: Art. 1, § 2, House; Art. 1, § 3, cl. 3, qualifications for Senators; Art. 11, § 1, cl. 5, Art. III, § 2, cl. 1, citizenship of the States. And, as has been noted, Art. Article III, § 2, cl. 1, citizenship as affecting judicial power of the United States. And, as has been noted, Article 1, § 8, cl. 4, vested Congress with the power to "establish an uniform Rule of Naturalization." The historical reviews in the *Afroyim* opinions provide an intimation that the Constitution's lack of definitional specificity may well have been attributable in part to the desire to avoid entanglement in the then existing controversy between concepts of state and national citizenship and with the difficult question of the status of Negro slaves.

In any event, although one might have expected a definition of citizenship in constitutional terms, none was embraced in the original document or, indeed, in any of the amendments adopted prior to the War Between the States.

Apart from the passing reference to the "natural born Citizen" in the Constitution's Art. 11, § 1, cl. 5, we have, in the Civil Rights Act of April 9, 1866, 14 Stat. 27, the first statutory recognition and concomitant formal definition of the citizenship status of the native born: "[A]ll persons born in the United States and not subject to any foreign power, excluding Indians not taxed, are hereby declared to be citizens of the United States." This, of course, found immediate expression in the Fourteenth Amendment, adopted in 1868, with expansion to "[a]ll persons born or naturalized in the United States...." As has been noted above, the amendment's "undeniable purpose" was "to make citizenship of Negroes permanent and secure" and not subject to change by mere statute. *Afroyim v. Rusk*, 387 U.S., at 263. See H. Flack, Adoption of the Fourteenth Amendment 88–94 (1908). Mr. Justice Gray has observed that the first sentence of the Fourteenth Amendment was "declaratory of existing rights, and affirmative of existing law," so far as the qualifications of being born in the United States, being naturalized in the United States, and being subject to its Jurisdiction are concerned. *United States v. Wong Kim Ark*, 169 U.S., at 688. Then follows a most significant sentence:

> But it (the first sentence of the Fourteenth Amendment) has not touched the acquisition of citizenship by being born abroad of American parents; and has left that subject to be regulated, as it had always been, by Congress, in the exercise of the power conferred by the constitution to establish an uniform rule of naturalization.

Thus, at long last, there emerged an express constitutional definition of citizenship. But it was one restricted to the combination of three factors, each and all significant: birth in the United States, naturalization in the United States, and subjection to the jurisdiction of the United States. The definition obviously did not apply to any acquisition of citizenship by being born abroad of an American parent. That type, and any other not covered by the Fourteenth Amendment, was necessarily left to proper congressional action.

The Court has recognized that existence of this power. It has observed, "No alien has the slightest right to naturalization unless all statutory requirements are compiled with...." *United States v. Ginsberg*, 243 U.S. 472, 475 (1917). And the Court has specifically recognized the power of Congress not to grant a United States citizen the right to transmit citizenship by descent. As hereinabove noted, persons born abroad, even of United States citizen fathers who, however, acquired American citizenship after the effective date of the 1802 Act, were aliens. Congress responded to that situation only by enacting the 1855 statute. *Montana v. Kennedy*, 366 U.S., at 311. But more than 50 years had expired during which, because of the withholding of that benefit by Congress, citizenship by such descent was not bestowed. *United States v. Wong Kim Ark*, 169 U.S., at 673–674. Then, too, the Court has recognized that until the 1934 Act the transmission of citizenship to one born abroad was restricted to the child of a qualifying American father, and withheld completely from the child of a United States citizen mother and an alien father. *Montana v. Kennedy, supra.*

Further, it is conceded here both that Congress may withhold citizenship from persons like plaintiff Bellei and may prescribe a period of residence in the United States as a condition precedent without constitutional question.

Thus we have the presence of congressional power in this area, its exercise, and the Court's specific recognition of that power and of its having been properly withheld or properly used in particular situations.

This takes us, then, to the issue of the constitutionality of the exercise of that congressional power when it is used to impose the condition subsequent that confronted plaintiff Bellei. We conclude that its imposition is not unreasonable, arbitrary, or unlawful, and that it withstands the present constitutional challenge.

The Congress has an appropriate concern with problems attendant on dual nationality. *Savorgnan v. United States*, 338 U.S. 491, 500 (1950).... These problems are particularly acute when it is the father who is the child's alien parent and the father chooses to have his family reside in the country of his own nationality. The child is reared, at best, in an atmosphere of divided loyalty. We cannot say that a concern that the child's own primary allegiance is to the country of his birth and of his father's allegiance is either misplaced or arbitrary.

The duality also creates problems for the governments involved. Mr. Justice Brennan recognized this when, concurring in *Kennedy v. Mendoza-Martinez*, 372 U.S. 144, 187 (1963), a case concerning native-born citizens, he observed: "We have recognized the entanglements which may stem from dual allegiance...." In a famous case Mr. Justice Douglas wrote of the problem of dual citizenship. *Tomoya Kawakita v. United States*, 343 U.S. 717, 723–36 (1952). He noted that "[o]ne who has a dual nationality will be subject to claims from both nations, claims which at times may be competing or conflicting," *id.*, at 733; that one with dual nationality cannot turn that status "into a fair-weather citizenship," *id.*, at 736; and that "[c]ircumstances may compel one who has a dual nationality to do acts which otherwise would not be compatible with the obligations of American citizenship," *ibid.* The District Court in this very case conceded: "It is a legitimate concern of Congress that those who bear American citizenship and receive its benefits have some nexus to the United States." 296 F.Supp., at 1252.

There are at least intimations in the decided cases that a dual national constitutionally may be required to make an election. In *Perkins v. Elg*, 307 U.S. 325, 329 (1939), the Court observed that a native-born citizen who had acquired dual nationality during minority through his parents' foreign naturalization abroad did not lose his United States citizenship "provided that on attaining majority he elects to retain that citizenship and to return to the United States to assume its duties." In *Tomoya Kawakita v. United States*, 343 U.S., at 734, the Court noted that a dual national "under certain circumstances" can be deprived of his American citizenship through an Act of Congress. In *Mandoli v. Acheson*, 344 U.S. 133, 138 (1952), the Court took pains to observe that there was no statute in existence imposing an election upon that dual nationality litigant.

These cases do not flatly say that a duty to elect may be constitutionally imposed. They surely indicate, however, that this is possible, and in *Mandoli* the holding was based on the very absence of a statute and not on any theory of unconstitutionality. And all three of these cases concerned persons who were born here, that is, persons who possessed Fourteenth Amendment citizenship; they did not concern a person, such as plaintiff Bellei, whose claim to citizenship is wholly, and only statutory.

The statutory development outlined in Part IV above, by itself and without reference to the underlying legislative history, committee reports, and other studies, reveals a careful consideration by the Congress of the problems attendant upon dual nationality of a person born abroad. This was purposeful and not accidental. It was legislation structured with care and in the light of then apparent problems.

The solution to the dual nationality dilemma provided by the Congress by way of required residence surely is not unreasonable. It may not be the best that could be devised, but here, too, we cannot say that it is irrational or arbitrary or unfair. Congress first has imposed a condition precedent in that the citizen parent must have been in the United States or its possessions not less than 10 years, at least five of which are after attaining age 14. It then has imposed, as to the foreign-born child himself, the condition subsequent as to residence here.

* * *

We feel that it does not make good constitutional sense, or comport with logic, to say, on the one hand, that Congress may impose a condition precedent, with no constitutional complication, and yet be powerless to impose precisely the same condition subsequent. Any such distinction, of course, must rest, if it has any basis at all, on the asserted "premise that the rights of citizenship of the native born and of the naturalized person are of the same dignity and are coextensive," *Schneider v. Rusk*, 377 U.S., at 165 and on the announcement that Congress has no "power, express or implied, to take away an American citizen's citizenship without his assent," *Afroyim v. Rusk*, 387 U.S., at 257. But, as pointed out above, these were utterances bottomed upon Fourteenth Amendment citizenship and that Amendment's direct reference to "persons born or naturalized in the United States." We do not accept the notion that those utterances are now to be judicially extended to citizenship not based upon the Fourteenth Amendment and to make citizenship an absolute. That it is not an absolute is demonstrated by the fact that even Fourteenth Amendment citizenship by naturalization, when unlawfully procured, may be set aside. *Afroyim v. Rusk*, 387 U.S., at 267 n. 23.

A contrary holding would convert what is congressional generosity into something unanticipated and obviously undesired by the Congress. Our National Legislature indulged the foreign-born child with presumptive citizenship subject to subsequent satisfaction of a reasonable residence requirement, rather than to deny him citizenship outright, as concededly it had the power to do, and relegate the child, if he desired American citizenship, to the more arduous requirements of the usual naturalization process. The plaintiff here would force the Congress to choose between unconditional conferment of United States citizenship at birth and deferment of citizenship until a condition precedent is fulfilled. We are not convinced that the Constitution requires so rigid a choice. If it does, the congressional response seems obvious.

Neither are we persuaded that a condition subsequent in this area impresses one with "second-class citizenship." That cliche is too handy and too easy, and, like most cliche's, can be misleading. That the condition subsequent may be beneficial is apparent in the light of the conceded fact that citizenship to this plaintiff was fully deniable. The proper emphasis is on what the statute permits him to gain from the possible starting point of noncitizenship, not on what he claims to lose from the possible starting point of full citizenship to which he has no constitutional right in the first place. His citizenship, while it although conditional, is not "second-class."

The plaintiff is not stateless. His Italian citizenship remains. He has lived practically all his life in Italy. He has never lived in this country; although he has visited here five times, the stipulated facts contain no indication that he ever will live here. He asserts no claim of ignorance or of mistake or even of hardship. He was warned several times of the provision of the statute and of his need to take up residence in the United States prior to his 23d birthday.

We hold that § 301(b) has no constitutional infirmity in its application to plaintiff Bellei. The judgment of the District Court is reversed.

Notes

1. The statute, which required residency in the United States and was being challenged in the *Bellei* case, was repealed by the Immigration and Nationality Amendments of 1978, Pub. L. No. 95-432, 92 Stat. 1046.

2. While the repeal of the residency requirement is not retroactive, several courts have interpreted the requirement as being met where the person is not aware of her claim to citizenship or did not learn of the *claim* before reaching the age of 28.[21]

3. Citizenship can also be derived through the naturalization of one's parent. This can occur where one parent is a citizen and the other is a non-citizen, the non-citizen naturalizes before the child's 18th birthday and the child is in the legal custody of the parent and permanently residing in the United States. Derivative naturalization can also occur where both parents are naturalized or the parent having legal custody naturalizes before the child's 18th birthday.

4. **Passport and Citizenship Claims.** A U.S. passport is prima facie evidence of U.S. citizenship.[22] A person may apply for a passport at a United States consulate or at any number of designated facilities such as the United States Post Office. Even though application may be made at one of these facilities, the application is adjudicated at the Department of State, Passport Office. Issues involving citizenship may arise

---

21. *See Rucker v. Saxbe*, 552 F.2d 998 (3d Cir. 1977); *Ramos-Hernandez* v. INS, 566 F.2d 638 (9th Cir. 1977); 0.I. 349.1(c) and 301.1(b)(6)(ix).

22. *Matter of Villanueva*, 19 I. & N. 101 (BIA 1984).

in three different settings. First, an individual may be seeking admission at a port of entry. Second, a person may have his citizenship questioned when making a passport application abroad before a United States Consul. Third, a person could be applying in the United States for a passport or certificate of citizenship and have his status challenged.[23] In cases where a person's passport is denied, she may seek administrative review through the Board of Appellate Review (BAR), whose procedures are governed by 22 C.F.R. § 7.5. Judicial review is obtained through the district court under 8 U.S.C. § 1401.[24]

5. *Bellei* highlights the extent of the congressional power as well as the analysis required to resolve citizenship questions. In cases of persons born outside of the United States to citizen parents, one must review the law in effect at the time of the child's birth.

In the following case, one sees some of the same issues that arose in the context of the family-based petition which we discussed earlier in *Kleindienst v. Mandel* (Chapter 7). While in the context of determining who may immigrate to the United States, *Kleindienst* could be understood as standing for the vitality of the plenary power doctrine. Consider how the following case should be analyzed. While the solution in the case may seem unsatisfactory, the Court's majority position developed over a period of more than two decades.

Jefferson B. Sessions, Att'y Gen'l v. Luis Ramón Morales-Santana*

137 S. Ct. 1678 (2017)

GINSBURG, J., delivered the opinion of the Court, in which Roberts, C.J., and Kennedy, Breyer, Sotomayor, and Kagan, JJ., joined. Thomas, J., filed an opinion concurring in the judgment in part, in which Alito, J., joined. Gorsuch, J., took no part in the consideration or decision of the case.

Justice GINSBURG delivered the opinion of the Court.

This case concerns a gender-based differential in the law governing acquisition of U.S. citizenship by a child born abroad, when one parent is a U.S. citizen, the other, a citizen of another nation. The main rule appears in 8 U.S.C. § 1401(a)(7) (1958 ed.), now § 1401(g). Applicable to married couples § 1401(a)(7) requires a period of physical presence in the United States for the U.S.-citizen parent. The requirement, as initially prescribed, was ten years' physical presence prior to the child's birth, § 601(g) (1940 ed.); currently, the requirement is five years prebirth, § 1401(g) (2012

---

23. Certificates of citizenship are issued by USCIS and passports are issued by the Department of State.

24. *See* James, *The Board of Appellate Review of the Department of State: The Right to Appellate Review of Administrative Determinations of Loss of Nationality*, 23 SAN DIEGO L. REV. 261 (1986).

* Footnotes have been omitted.

ed.). That main rule is rendered applicable to unwed U.S.-citizen fathers by § 1409(a). Congress ordered an exception, however, for unwed U.S.-citizen mothers. Contained in 1409(c), the exception allows an unwed mother to transmit her citizenship to a child born abroad if she has lived in the United States for just one year prior to the child's birth.

The respondent in this case, Luis Ramón Morales-Santana, was born in the Dominican Republic when his father was just 20 days short of meeting § 1401(a)(7)'s physical-presence requirement. Opposing removal to the Dominican Republic, Morales-Santana asserts that the equal protection principle implicit in the Fifth Amendment1 entitles him to citizenship stature. We hold that the gender line Congress drew is incompatible with the requirement that the Government accord to all persons "the equal protection of the laws." Nevertheless, we cannot convert § 1409(c)'s exception for unwed mothers into the main rule displacing § 1401(a)(7) (covering married couples) and § 1409(a) (covering unwed fathers). We must therefore leave it to Congress to select, going forward, a physical-presence requirement (ten years, one year, or some other period) uniformly applicable to all children born abroad with one U.S.-citizen and one alien parent, wed or unwed. In the interim, the Government must ensure that the laws in question are administered in a manner free from gender-based discrimination.

... The primacy of § 1401 in the statutory scheme is evident. Comprehensive in coverage, § 1401 provides the general framework for the acquisition of citizenship at birth. In particular, at the time relevant here, § 1401(a)(7) provided for the U.S. citizenship of

> a person born outside the geographical limits of the United States and its outlying possessions of parents one of whom is an alien, and the other a citizen of the United States who, prior to the birth of such person, was physically present in the United States or its outlying possessions for a period or periods totaling not less than ten years, at least five of which were after attaining the age of fourteen years: *Provided,* That any periods of honorable service in the Armed Forces of the United States by such citizen parent may be included in computing the physical presence requirements of this paragraph.

Congress has since reduced the duration requirement to five years, two after age 14. § 1401(g) (2012 ed.).

Section 1409 pertains specifically to children with unmarried parents. Its first subsection, § 1409(a), incorporates by reference the physical-presence requirements of § 1401, thereby allowing an acknowledged unwed citizen parent to transmit U.S. citizenship to a foreign-born child under the same terms as a married citizen parent. Section 1409(c)—a provision applicable only to unwed U.S.-citizen mothers—states an exception to the physical-presence requirements of §§ 1401 and 1409(a). Under § 1409(c)'s exception, only one year of continuous physical presence is required before unwed mothers may pass citizenship to their children born abroad.

Respondent Luis Ramón Morales-Santana moved to the United States at age 13, and has resided in this country most of his life. Now facing deportation, he asserts

U.S. citizenship at birth based on the citizenship of his biological father, José Morales, who accepted parental responsibility and included Morales-Santana in his household.

José Morales was born in Guánica, Puerto Rico, on March 19, 1900. Record 55–56. Puerto Rico was then, as it is now, part of the United States, see *Puerto Rico v. Sanchez Valle*, 579 U.S. ___, ___, 136 S.Ct. 1863 (2016); 8 U.S.C. § 1101(a)(38) (1958 ed.) ("The term United States ... means the continental United States, Alaska, Hawaii, Puerto Rico, Guam, and the [U.S.] Virgin Islands." (internal quotation marks omitted)); § 1101(a)(38) (2012 ed.) (similar), and José became a U.S. citizen under the Organic Act of Puerto Rico, ch. 145, § 5, 39 Stat. 953 (a predecessor to 8 U.S.C. § 1402). After living in Puerto Rico for nearly two decades, José left his childhood home on February 27, 1919, 20 days short of his 19th birthday, therefore failing to satisfy § 1401(a)(7)'s requirement of five years' physical presence after age 14. Record 57, 66. He did so to take up employment as a builder-mechanic for a U.S. company in the then-U.S.-occupied Dominican Republic. *Ibid.*

By 1959, José attested in a June 21, 1971 affidavit presented to the U.S. Embassy in the Dominican Republic, he was living with Yrma Santana Montilla, a Dominican woman he would eventually marry. *Id.*, at 57. In 1962, Yrma gave birth to their child, respondent Luis Morales-Santana. *Id.*, at 166–167. While the record before us reveals little about Morales-Santana's childhood, the Dominican archives disclose that Yrma and José married in 1970, and that José was then added to Morales-Santana's birth certificate as his father. *Id.*, at 163–164, 167. José also related in the same affidavit that he was then saving money "for the susten[ance] of [his] family" in anticipation of undergoing surgery in Puerto Rico, where members of his family still resided. *Id.*, at 57. In 1975, when Morales-Santana was 13, he moved to Puerto Rico, *id.*, at 368, and by 1976, the year his father died, he was attending public school in the Bronx, a New York City borough, *id.*, at 140, 369.

In 2000, the Government placed Morales-Santana in removal proceedings based on several convictions for offenses under New York State Penal Law, all of them rendered on May 17, 1995. *Id.*, at 426. Morales-Santana ranked as an alien despite the many years he lived in the United States, because, at the time of his birth, his father did not satisfy the requirement of five years' physical presence after age 14. See *supra*, at 1686–1687, and n. 3. An immigration judge rejected Morales-Santana's claim to citizenship derived from the U.S. citizenship of his father, and ordered Morales-Santana's removal to the Dominican Republic. Record 253, 366; App. to Pet. for Cert. 45a–49a. In 2010, Morales-Santana moved to reopen the proceedings, asserting that the Government's refusal to recognize that he derived citizenship from his U.S.-citizen father violated the Constitution's equal protection guarantee. See Record 27, 45. The Board of Immigration Appeals (BIA) denied the motion. App. to Pet. for Cert. 8a, 42a–44a.

The United States Court of Appeals for the Second Circuit reversed the BIA's decision. 804 F.3d 520, 524 (2015). Relying on this Court's post-1970 construction of the equal protection principle as it bears on gender-based classifications, the court held unconstitutional the differential treatment of unwed mothers and fathers. *Id.*, at 527–535. To cure the constitutional flaw, the court further held that Morales-Santana derived citizenship through his father, just as he would were his mother the U.S. citizen. *Id.*, at 535–538. In so ruling, the Second Circuit declined to follow the conflicting decision of the Ninth Circuit in *United States v. Flores-Villar,* 536 F.3d 990 (2008), see 804 F.3d, at 530, 535, n. 17. We granted certiorari in *Flores-Villar,* but ultimately affirmed by an equally divided Court.). Taking up Morales-Santana's request for review, 579 U.S. ___ (2016), we consider the matter anew.

Because § 1409 treats sons and daughters alike, Morales-Santana does not suffer discrimination on the basis of *his* gender. He complains, instead, of gender-based discrimination against his father, who was unwed at the time of Morales-Santana's birth and was not accorded the right an unwed U.S.-citizen mother would have to transmit citizenship to her child. Although the Government does not contend otherwise, we briefly explain why Morales-Santana may seek to vindicate his father's right to the equal protection of the laws.

* * *

Sections 1401 and 1409, we note, date from an era when the lawbooks of our Nation were rife with overbroad generalizations about the way men and women are. See, *e.g., Hoyt v. Florida,* 368 U.S. 57, 62, (1961) (women are the "center of home and family life," therefore they can be "relieved from the civic duty of jury service"); *Goesaert v. Cleary,* 335 U.S. 464, 466 (1948) (States may draw "a sharp line between the sexes"). Today, laws of this kind are subject to review under the heightened scrutiny that now attends "all gender-based classifications." *J.E.B. v. Alabama ex rel. T. B.,* 511 U.S. 127, 136 (1994.

* * *

Prescribing one rule for mothers, another for fathers, § 1409 is of the same genre as the classifications we declared unconstitutional in *Reed, Frontiero, Wiesenfeld, Goldfarb,* and *Westcott.* As in those cases, heightened scrutiny is in order. Successful defense of legislation that differentiates on the basis of gender, we have reiterated, requires an "exceedingly persuasive justification." *Virginia,* 518 U.S., at 531 (internal quotation marks omitted)....

The defender of legislation that differentiates on the basis of gender must show "at least that the [challenged] classification serves important governmental objectives and that the discriminatory means employed are substantially related to the achievement of those objectives." *Virginia,* 518 U.S., at 533; alteration in original); see *Tuan Anh Nguyen v. INS,* 533 U.S. 53, 60, 70 (2001). Moreover, the classification must substantially serve an important governmental interest *today,* for "in interpreting the [e]qual [p]rotection [guarantee], [we have] recognized that new insights and societal understandings can reveal unjustified inequality ... that once passed unnoticed and unchallenged." *Obergefell v. Hodges,* 576 U.S. ___, ___, 135 S.Ct. 2584, 2603 (2015). Here, the Government has supplied no "exceedingly persuasive justification," *Virginia,* 518 U.S., at 531 (internal quotation marks omitted), for § 1409(a) and (c)'s "gender-based" and "gender-biased" disparity.

History reveals what lurks behind § 1409. Enacted in the Nationality Act of 1940 (1940 Act), see 54 Stat. 1139–1140, § 1409 ended a century and a half of congressional silence on the citizenship of children born abroad to unwed parents. During this era, two once habitual, but now untenable, assumptions pervaded our Nation's citizenship laws and underpinned judicial and administrative rulings: In marriage, husband is dominant, wife subordinate; unwed mother is the natural and sole guardian of a nonmarital child.

Under the once entrenched principle of male dominance in marriage, the husband controlled both wife and child. "[D]ominance [of] the husband," this Court observed in 1915, "is an ancient principle of our jurisprudence." *Mackenzie v. Hare,* 239 U.S. 299, 311 (1915). See generally Brief for Professors of History et al. as *Amici Curiae* 4–15. Through the early 20th century, a male citizen automatically conferred U.S. citizenship on his alien wife. Act of Feb. 10, 1855, ch. 71, § 2, 10 Stat. 604; see *Kelly v. Owen,* 7 Wall. 496, 498 (1869) (the 1855 Act "confers the privileges of citizenship upon women married to citizens of the United States"); C. Bredbenner, A Nationality of Her Own: Women, Marriage, and the Law of Citizenship 15–16, 20–21 (1998). A female citizen, however, was incapable of conferring citizenship on her husband; indeed, she was subject to expatriation if she married an alien. The family of a citizen or a lawfully admitted permanent resident enjoyed statutory exemptions from entry requirements, but only if the citizen or resident was male. See, *e.g.,* Act of Mar. 3, 1903, ch. 1012, § 37, 32 Stat. 1221 (wives and children entering the country to join permanent-resident aliens and found to have contracted contagious diseases during transit shall not be deported if the diseases were easily curable or did not present a danger to others); S.Rep. No. 1515, 81st Cong., 2d Sess., 415–417 (1950) (wives exempt from literacy and quota requirements). And from 1790 until 1934, the foreign-born child of a married couple gained U.S. citizenship only through the father.

For unwed parents, the father-controls tradition never held sway. Instead, the mother was regarded as the child's natural and sole guardian. At common law, the mother, and only the mother, was "bound to maintain [a nonmarital child] as its natural guardian." 2 J. Kent, Commentaries on American Law *215–*216 (8th ed. 1854); see *Nguyen,* 533 U.S., at 91–92, 121 S.Ct. 2053 (O'Connor, J., dissenting). In line with that understanding, in the early 20th century, the State Department sometimes permitted unwed mothers to pass citizenship to their children, despite the absence of any statutory authority for the practice. See Hearings on H.R. 6127 before the House Committee on Immigration and Naturalization, 76th Cong., 1st Sess., 43, 431 (1940) (hereinafter 1940 Hearings); 39 Op. Atty. Gen. 397, 397–398 (1939); 39 Op. Atty. Gen. 290, 291 (1939). See also Collins, *Illegitimate Borders:* Jus Sanguinis *Citizenship and the Legal Construction of Family, Race, and Nation,* 123 Yale L.J. 2134, 2199–2205 (2014) (hereinafter Collins).

In the 1940 Act, Congress discarded the father-controls assumption concerning married parents, but codified the mother-as-sole-guardian perception regarding unmarried parents. The Roosevelt administration, which proposed § 1409, explained: "[T]he mother [of a nonmarital child] stands in the place of the father ... [,] has a right to the custody and control of such a child as against the putative father, and is bound to maintain it as its natural guardian." 1940 Hearings 431 (internal quotation marks omitted).

This unwed-mother-as-natural-guardian notion renders § 1409's gender-based residency rules understandable. Fearing that a foreign-born child could turn out "more alien than American in character," the administration believed that a citizen parent with lengthy ties to the United States would counteract the influence of the alien parent. *Id.*, at 426–427. Concern about the attachment of foreign-born children to the United States explains the treatment of unwed citizen fathers, who, according to the familiar stereotype, would care little about, and have scant contact with, their nonmarital children. For unwed citizen mothers, however, there was no need for a prolonged residency prophylactic: The alien father, who might transmit foreign ways, was presumptively out of the picture. See *id.*, at 431; Collins 2203 (in "nearly uniform view" of U.S. officials, "almost invariably," the mother alone "concern[ed] herself with [a nonmarital] child" (internal quotation marks omitted)).

* * *

In accord with this eventual understanding, the Court has held that no "important [governmental] interest" is served by laws grounded, as § 1409(a) and (c) are, in the obsolescing view that "unwed fathers [are] invariably less qualified and entitled than mothers" to take responsibility for nonmarital children. *Caban v. Mohammed*, 441 U.S. 380, 382, 394 (1979). Overbroad generalizations of that order, the Court has come to comprehend, have a constraining impact, descriptive though they may be of the way many people still order their lives. Laws according or denying benefits in reliance on "[s]tereotypes about women's domestic roles," the Court has observed, may "creat[e] a self-fulfilling cycle of discrimination that force[s] women to continue to assume the role of primary family caregiver." *Nevada Dept. of Human Resources v. Hibbs*, 538 U.S. 721, 736 (2003). Correspondingly, such laws may disserve men who exercise responsibility for raising their children. See *ibid.* In light of the equal protection jurisprudence this Court has developed since 1971, see *Virginia*, 518 U.S., at 531–534, § 1409(a) and (c)'s discrete duration-of-residence requirements for unwed mothers and fathers who have accepted parental responsibility is stunningly anachronistic.

In urging this Court nevertheless to reject Morales-Santana's equal protection plea, the Government cites three decisions of this Court: *Fiallo v. Bell*, 430 U.S. 787 (1977); *Miller v. Albright*, 523 U.S. 420; and *Nguyen v. INS*, 533 U.S. 53. None controls this case.

The 1952 Act provision at issue in *Fiallo* gave special immigration preferences to alien children of citizen (or lawful-permanent-resident) mothers, and to alien unwed mothers of citizen (or lawful-permanent-resident) children. 430 U.S., at 788–789, and n. 1. Unwed fathers and their children, asserting their right to equal protection, sought the same preferences. *Id.*, at 791, 97 S.Ct. 1473. Applying minimal scrutiny (rational-basis review), the Court upheld the provision, relying on Congress' "exceptionally broad power" to admit or exclude aliens. *Id.*, at 792, 794. This case, however, involves no entry preference for aliens. Morales-Santana claims he is, and since birth has been, a U.S. citizen. Examining a claim of that order, the Court has not disclaimed, as it did in *Fiallo,* the application of an exacting standard of review.

The provision challenged in *Miller* and *Nguyen* as violative of equal protection requires unwed U.S.-citizen fathers, but not mothers, to formally acknowledge parenthood of their foreign-born children in order to transmit their U.S. citizenship to those children. See § 1409(a)(4) (2012 ed.). After *Miller* produced no opinion for the Court, see 523 U.S., at 423 we took up the issue anew in *Nguyen.* There, the Court held that imposing a paternal-acknowledgment requirement on fathers was a justifiable, easily met means of ensuring the existence of a biological parent-child relationship, which the mother establishes by giving birth. See 533 U.S., at 62–63. Morales-Santana's challenge does not renew the contest over § 1409's paternal-acknowledgment requirement (whether the current version or that in effect in 1970), and the Government does not dispute that Morales-Santana's father, by marrying Morales-Santana's mother, satisfied that requirement.

Unlike the paternal-acknowledgment requirement at issue in *Nguyen* and *Miller,* the physical-presence requirements now before us relate solely to the duration of the parent's prebirth residency in the United States, not to the parent's filial tie to the child. As the Court of Appeals observed in this case, a man needs no more time in the United States than a woman "in order to have assimilated citizenship-related values to transmit to [his] child." 804 F.3d, at 531. And unlike *Nguyen*'s parental-acknowledgment requirement, § 1409(a)'s age-calibrated physical-presence requirements cannot fairly be described as "minimal." 533 U.S., at 70.

Notwithstanding § 1409(a) and (c)'s provenance in traditional notions of the way women and men are, the Government maintains that the statute serves two important objectives: (1) ensuring a connection between the child to become a citizen and the United States and (2) preventing "statelessness," *i.e.,* a child's possession of no citizenship at all. Even indulging the assumption that Congress intended § 1409 to serve these interests, but see *supra,* at 1683–1693, neither rationale survives heightened scrutiny.

We take up first the Government's assertion that § 1409(a) and (c)'s gender-based differential ensures that a child born abroad has a connection to the United States of sufficient strength to warrant conferral of citizenship at birth. The Government does not contend, nor could it, that unmarried men take more time to absorb U.S. values than unmarried women do. See *supra,* at 1694. Instead, it presents a novel argument, one it did not advance in *Flores-Villar.*

An unwed mother, the Government urges, is the child's only "legally recognized" parent at the time of childbirth. Brief for Petitioner 9–10, 28–32. An unwed citizen father enters the scene later, as a second parent. A longer physical connection to the United States is warranted for the unwed father, the Government maintains, because of the "competing national influence" of the alien mother. *Id.,* at 9–10. Congress, the Government suggests, designed the statute to bracket an unwed U.S.-citizen mother with a married couple in which both parents are U.S. citizens, and to align an unwed U.S.-citizen father with a married couple, one spouse a citizen, the other, an alien.

Underlying this apparent design is the assumption that the alien father of a nonmarital child born abroad to a U.S.-citizen mother will not accept parental responsibility. For an actual affiliation between alien father and nonmarital child would create the "competing national influence" that, according to the Government, justifies imposing on unwed U.S.-citizen fathers, but not unwed U.S.-citizen mothers, lengthy physical-presence requirements. Hardly gender neutral, see *id.,* at 9, that assumption conforms to the long-held view that unwed fathers care little about, indeed are strangers to, their children. See *supra,* at 1690–1693. Lump characterization of that kind, however, no longer passes equal protection inspection. See *supra,* at 1692–1693, and n. 13.

* * *

The Government maintains that Congress established the gender-based residency differential in § 1409(a) and (c) to reduce the risk that a foreign-born child of a U.S. citizen would be born stateless. Brief for Petitioner 33. This risk, according to the Government, was substantially greater for the foreign-born child of an unwed U.S.-citizen mother than it was for the foreign-born child of an unwed U.S.-citizen father. *Ibid.* But there is little reason to believe that a statelessness concern prompted the diverse physical-presence requirements. Nor has the Government shown that the risk of statelessness disproportionately endangered the children of unwed mothers.

As the Court of Appeals pointed out, with one exception, nothing in the congressional hearings and reports on the 1940 and 1952 Acts "refer[s] to the problem of statelessness for children born abroad." 804 F.3d, at 532–533. See Collins 2205, n. 283 (author examined "many hundreds of pre-1940 administrative memos … defend[ing] or explain[ing] recognition of the nonmarital foreign-born children of American mothers as citizens"; of the hundreds, "exactly one memo by a U.S. official … mentions the risk of statelessness for the foreign-born nonmarital children of American mothers as a concern"). Reducing the incidence of statelessness was the express goal of *other* sections of the 1940 Act. See 1940 Hearings 430 ("stateless[ness]" is "object" of section on foundlings). The justification for § 1409's gender-based dichotomy, however, was not the child's plight, it was the mother's role as the "natural guardian" of a nonmarital child. See *supra,* at 1690–1693; Collins 2205 ("[T]he pronounced gender asymmetry of the Nationality Act's treatment of nonmarital foreign-born children of American mothers and fathers was shaped by contemporary maternalist norms regarding the mother's relationship with her nonmarital child—and the father's lack of such a relationship."). It will not do to "hypothesiz[e] or inven[t]" governmental purposes for gender classifications "*post hoc* in response to litigation." *Virginia,* 518 U.S., at 533, 535–536.

Infecting the Government's risk-of-statelessness argument is an assumption without foundation. "[F]oreign laws that would put the child of the U.S.-citizen mother at risk of statelessness (by not providing for the child to acquire the father's citizenship at birth)," the Government asserts, "would *protect* the child of the U.S.-citizen father against statelessness by providing that the child would take his mother's citizenship." Brief for Petitioner 35. The Government, however, neglected to expose this supposed "protection" to a reality check. Had it done so, it would have recognized the formidable impediments placed by foreign laws on an unwed mother's transmission of citizenship to her child. See Brief for Scholars on Statelessness as *Amici Curiae* 13–22, A1–A15.

* * *

In sum, the Government has advanced no "exceedingly persuasive" justification for § 1409(a) and (c)'s gender-specific residency and age criteria. Those disparate criteria, we hold, cannot withstand inspection under a Constitution that requires the Government to respect the equal dignity and stature of its male and female citizens.

While the equal protection infirmity in retaining a longer physical-presence requirement for unwed fathers than for unwed mothers is clear, this Court is not equipped to grant the relief Morales-Santana seeks, *i.e.,* extending to his father (and, derivatively, to him) the benefit of the one-year physical-presence term § 1409(c) reserves for unwed mothers.

There are "two remedial alternatives," our decisions instruct, *Westcott,* 443 U.S., at 89 (quoting *Welsh v. United States,* 398 U.S. 333, 361 (1970) (Harlan, J., concurring in result)), when a statute benefits one class (in this case, unwed mothers and their children), as § 1409(c) does, and excludes another from the benefit (here, unwed fathers and their children). "[A] court may either declare [the statute] a nullity and order that its benefits not extend to the class that the legislature intended to benefit, or it may extend the coverage of the statute to include those who are aggrieved by exclusion." *Westcott,* 443 U.S., at 89 (quoting *Welsh,* 398 U.S., at 361 (opinion of Harlan, J.)). "[W]hen the 'right invoked is that to equal treatment,' the appropriate remedy is a mandate of equal treatment, a result that can be accomplished by withdrawal of benefits from the favored class as well as by extension of benefits to the excluded class." *Heckler v. Mathews,* 465 U.S. 728, 740 (1984).... "How equality is accomplished ... is a matter on which the Constitution is silent." *Levin v. Commerce Energy, Inc.,* 560 U.S. 413, 426–427 (2010).

The choice between these outcomes is governed by the legislature's intent, as revealed by the statute at hand. See *id.,* at 427 ("On finding unlawful discrimination, ... courts may attempt, within the bounds of their institutional competence, to implement what the legislature would have willed had it been apprised of the constitutional infirmity."). See also *Ayotte v. Planned Parenthood of Northern New Eng.,* 546 U.S. 320, 330 (2006) ("the touchstone for any decision about remedy is legislative intent").

Ordinarily, we have reiterated, "extension, rather than nullification, is the proper course." *Westcott,* 443 U.S., at 89, 99 S.Ct. 2655. Illustratively, in a series of cases involving federal financial assistance benefits, the Court struck discriminatory exceptions denying benefits to discrete groups, which meant benefits previously denied were extended. See, *e.g., Goldfarb,* 430 U.S., at 202–204, 213–217 (plurality opinion) (survivors' benefits), aff'g 396 F.Supp. 308, 309 (E.D.N.Y.1975) (*per curiam*); *Jimenez v. Weinberger,* 417 U.S. 628, 630–631, and n. 2, 637–638 (1974) (disability benefits); *Department of Agriculture v. Moreno,* 413 U.S. 528, 529–530, 538 (1973) (food stamps); *Frontiero,* 411 U.S., at 678–679, and n. 2, 691, and n. 25 (plurality opinion) (military spousal benefits). Here, however, the discriminatory exception consists of *favorable* treatment for a discrete group (a shorter physical-presence requirement for unwed U.S.-citizen mothers giving birth abroad). Following the same approach as in those benefits cases—striking the discriminatory exception—leads here to extending the general rule of longer physical-presence requirements to cover the previously favored group.

The Court has looked to Justice Harlan's concurring opinion in *Welsh v. United States,* 398 U.S., at 361–367 in considering whether the legislature would have struck an exception and applied the general rule equally to all, or instead, would have broadened the exception to cure the equal protection violation. In making this assessment, a court should " 'measure the intensity of commitment to the residual policy' "—the main rule, not the exception—" 'and consider the degree of potential disruption of the statutory scheme that would occur by extension as opposed to abrogation.' " *Heckler,* 465 U.S., at 739, n. 5.

The residual policy here, the longer physical-presence requirement stated in §§ 1401(a)(7) and 1409, evidences Congress' recognition of "the importance of residence in this country as the talisman of dedicated attachment." *Rogers v. Bellei,* 401 U.S. 815, 834 (1971) ... (Congress "attached more importance to actual residence in the United States as indicating a basis for citizenship than it did to descent.... [T]he heritable blood of citizenship was thus associated unmistakeably with residence within the country which was thus recognized as essential to full citizenship." (internal quotation marks omitted)). And the potential for "disruption of the statutory scheme" is large. For if § 1409(c)'s one-year dispensation were extended to unwed citizen fathers, would it not be irrational to retain the longer term when the U.S.-citizen parent is married? Disadvantageous treatment of marital children in comparison to nonmarital children is scarcely a purpose one can sensibly attribute to Congress.

Although extension of benefits is customary in federal benefit cases, all indicators in this case point in the opposite direction. Put to the choice, Congress, we believe, would have abrogated § 1409(c)'s exception, preferring preservation of the general rule.

The gender-based distinction infecting §§ 1401(a)(7) and 1409(a) and (c), we hold, violates the equal protection principle, as the Court of Appeals correctly ruled. For the reasons stated, however, we must adopt the remedial course Congress likely would have chosen "had it been apprised of the constitutional infirmity." *Levin,* 560 U.S., at 427, 130 S.Ct. 2323. Although the preferred rule in the typical case is to extend favorable treatment, see *Westcott,* 443 U.S., at 89–90, 99 S.Ct. 2655 this is hardly the typical case. Extension here would render the special treatment Congress prescribed in § 1409(c), the one-year physical-presence requirement for U.S.-citizen mothers, the general rule, no longer an exception. Section 1401(a)(7)'s longer physical-presence requirement, applicable to a substantial majority of children born abroad to one U.S.-citizen parent and one foreign-citizen parent, therefore, must hold sway. Going forward, Congress may address the issue and settle on a uniform prescription that neither favors nor disadvantages any person on the basis of gender. In the interim, as the Government suggests, § 1401(a)(7)'s now-five-year requirement should apply, prospectively, to children born to unwed U.S.-citizen mothers. See Brief for Petitioner 12, 51; Reply Brief 19, n. 3.

The judgment of the Court of Appeals for the Second Circuit is affirmed in part and reversed in part, and the case is remanded for further proceedings consistent with this opinion.

It is so ordered.

Justice Gorsuch took no part in the consideration or decision of this case. Justice Thomas, with whom Justice Alito joins, concurring in the judgment in part....

Notes

1. The Court in *Miller v. Albright*,[25] delivered an opinion by Justice Stevens where the petitioner made a similar challenge to the constitutionality of the statutory provisions governing the acquisition of citizenship at birth by children born out of wedlock and outside of the United States. The Court in rejecting the challenge noted that:

> We find no merit in the challenge because the statute does not impose any limitation on the time within which the members of either class of children may prove that they qualify for citizenship. It does establish different qualifications for citizenship for the two classes of children, but we are persuaded that the qualifications for the members of each of those classes, so far as they are implicated by the facts of this case, are well supported by valid governmental interests. We therefore conclude that the statutory distinction is neither arbitrary nor invidious.

Id. at 425. Though argued in *Miller*, there was no majority resolution of the issue. Four Justices, in two different opinions, rejected the challenge to the gender-based distinction. Justice Stevens and Chief Justice Rehnquist found the statute consistent with the Fifth Amendment. Justices Scalia and Thomas found that the Court could not confer citizenship as a remedy even if the statute violated equal protection. While Justices Ginsburg, Souter and Breyer would have found the distinction unconstitutional, Justices O'Connor and Kennedy would not reach the constitutional question, since Miller lacked standing. In Justice Ginsburg's dissent, joined by Souter and Breyer, she argued that the statute should be found unconstitutional.

2. In a subsequent challenge to the statute, in *Nguyen v. INS*,[26] the issue was raised again and rejected by the Supreme Court. Tuan Anh Nguyen and his father, Joseph Boulais, challenged a determination rejecting his citizenship claim. Tuan Ahn Nguyen was born in Saigon, Vietnam, on September 11, 1969, to Joseph Boulais and a Viet-

---

25. 523 U.S. 420 (1998).
26. 533 U.S. 53 (2001).

namese citizen, who were not married. Boulais always has been a citizen of the United States, and he was in Vietnam under the employ of a corporation. After he and Nguyen's mother ended their relationship, Nguyen lived for a time with the family of Boulais' new Vietnamese girlfriend. In June 1975, Nguyen, then almost six years of age, came to the United States. He became a lawful permanent resident and was raised in Texas by Boulais. It was only following encounters with the criminal justice system after Nguyen had reached the age of 22 and when facing removal that efforts made to formally establish paternity were undertaken in state court. The Court, in an opinion by Justice Kennedy, rejected the equal protection claim on grounds that there was a legitimate governmental interest in the rules as established, requiring that the person either be legitimized or acknowledged in writing under oath or in a formal paternity action prior to the child's 18th birthday.

In addition to the actual blood relation with the U.S. citizen, the majority articulated another interest:

> The second important governmental interest furthered in a substantial manner by § 1409(a)(4) is the determination to ensure that the child and the citizen parent have some demonstrated opportunity or potential to develop not just a relationship that is recognized, as a formal matter, by the law, but one that consists of the real, everyday ties that provide a connection between child and citizen parent and, in turn, the United States.... In the case of a citizen mother and a child born overseas, the opportunity for a meaningful relationship between citizen parent and child inheres in the very event of birth, an event so often critical to our constitutional and statutory understandings of citizenship. The mother knows that the child is in being and is hers and has an initial point of contact with him. There is at least an opportunity for mother and child to develop a real, meaningful relationship.

Id. at 64–67. The dissent in *Nguyen*, written by Justice O'Connor and joined by Ginsburg, Souter and Breyer, argued that heightened scrutiny was called for in cases involving these classifications. *Id.* at 74.

3. What would be the result where the parents are married and a child is born, but it is not clear whether the father has a blood relationship with the child? In *Scales v. INS*,[27] a Ninth Circuit panel dismissed a deportation order against a person ordered removed as an aggravated felon. The court reasoned that the case was distinguishable from the situation where a child was born "out of wedlock," for the statute only requires that the child be born of parents, one of whom is a U.S. citizen. It was sufficient therefore that the parents were married, and there was no requirement that a blood relationship be established.

4. **Other Issues.** Cases involving assisted reproductive technology were clearly not contemplated when the statute was written. The Department of State has interpreted the statute as conferring citizenship when the citizen father is the genetic

27. 232 F.3d 1159 (9th Cir. 2000).

parent, and the citizen mother must either be the genetic or gestational and legal parent at the time and place of birth. 22 C.F.R. § 51.28. For an interesting discussion of the broader topic, see Victoria Degtyareva, *Defining Family in Immigration Law: Accounting for Nontraditional Families in Citizenship by Descent*, 120 Yale L.J. 862 (2011).

C. Citizenship through Naturalization

Naturalization is the procedure through which a person not otherwise a citizen may become a citizen of the United States. The statutory provisions dealing with naturalization are found at 8 U.S.C. §§ 1421–1459 and the applicable federal regulations, at 8 C.F.R. § 306 et seq.[28] To qualify for naturalization, the person must be a lawful permanent resident of the United States over the age of 18 who has resided continuously in the United States for five years following receipt of lawful permanent resident status (with certain exceptions);[29] if the naturalization applicant obtained permanent residence through marriage to a U.S. citizen and continues to be married to the U.S. citizen spouse, the applicant must establish three years of residence. Further, the person must have been physically present in the United States for at least half of the three or five years.[30]

The naturalization applicant must have been a resident in the place where the petition is filed for at least three months[31] prior to its filing. This three month residency is a jurisdictional requirement enabling the Attorney General to naturalize the applicant.[32] The applicant must also continue her residence in the United States from the date of filing the petition to the time the Attorney General approves citizenship. If the person is absent from the country for more than one year during the continuous residency period, the government will deem the application abandoned, and an absence of over six months raises a rebuttable presumption of abandonment, with few exceptions.[33] In addition, in order to make a successful naturalization application, the applicant must be a person of good moral character; adhere to the principles of the Constitution; be willing to take an oath of allegiance to the United States, including

---

28. For a helpful discussion of the rules governing many citizenship questions, USCIS's Adjudicator's Field Manual should be consulted.

29. For the exceptions, see 8 U.S.C. § 1427(b).

30. *See* 8 U.S.C. § 1427(c) for some exceptions to this rule.

31. *See* 8 U.S.C. § 1427(a)(1), Sec. 316(a)(1). This change was made by the 1990 Act. The earlier provision contained a six month residency period.

32. The power to confer naturalization was transferred from the courts to the Attorney General in the 1990 Act. *See* 8 U.S.C. § 1421 (a), Sec. 310; *but see In Re Duncan*, 713 F.2d 538 (9th Cir. 1983) (where the court construed the requirement of residency within the geographic jurisdiction as a venue and not a subject matter jurisdictional provision.)

33. 8 U.S.C. § 1427(b), Sec. 316(b); 8 C.F.R. § 316.5(c)(1)(i)–(ii).

the renunciation of citizenship in her native country; understand the English language; and have knowledge of the workings of the U.S. government and its history.[34]

The requirements listed above are generally in conformity with international law. International law requires that the acquisition of nationality will be recognized only if the state makes the legal bond of nationality accord with the individual's genuine connection with the state.[35]

The Act contains numerous exceptions to the conditions required by the naturalization provisions noted above. The statutory provisions dealing with these special exceptions are found at 8 U.S.C. §§ 1430(b)–(d), 1433, 1435, 1436, and 1438–1440.

From a procedural standpoint, naturalization is a power delegated to the Attorney General by Congress. In delegating the naturalization power to USCIS, Congress created a different form of review than is found in other areas of immigration law. An unfavorable decision may be appealed for administrative review within 30 days of receipt of the decision. If the administrative appeal fails, the applicant can seek relief in a *de novo* hearing before the U.S. district court, where the court makes its own findings of fact and conclusions of law.[36] Persons who have not had their naturalization applications adjudicated within 120 days may also seek relief in the district courts. Prior to the 1990 Act, the naturalization power was in the courts, with legacy INS having an administrative and investigative role.

D. Loss of Citizenship—Expatriation

Expatriation is the renunciation of citizenship. The immigration statute sets forth a series of actions, which in and of themselves constitute acts of renunciation.[37] Notwithstanding these statutes, case law instructs that expatriation must be voluntary to be effective. Early questions on the validity of the expatriation statutes turned on the issue of whether the power was part of the necessary and proper grant of the foreign affairs authority to the federal government or whether citizenship was itself an inalienable right.[38]

In *Afroyim v. Rusk*,[39] the Supreme Court struck down the statutory provision requiring expatriation for voting in a foreign election. Justice Black based his reasoning

---

34. Although the applicant must be at least 18 years old, a minor child will become a citizen upon the naturalization of her parents. The child must be residing in the United States as a lawful permanent resident, and the parent having legal custody must agree to the naturalization. 8 U.S.C. §§ 1431 and 1432.

35. *See Nottebohm Case (Liechtenstein v. Guatemala)*, I.C.J. Rep. 4 (1955).

36. *See* 8 U.S.C. § 1421(c), Sec. 310(c). This provision became effective for naturalization applications filed after October 30, 1991.

37. 8 U.S.C. 1481, Sec. 349.

38. *Perez v. Brownell*, 356 U.S. 44 (1958)

39. 387 U.S. 253 (1967).

on grounds that in the absence of a specific grant of power in the Constitution, Congress lacked the power to deprive a citizen of her citizenship without her assent, and the Fourteenth Amendment protects a citizen against the involuntary destruction of her citizenship. Four years later in *Rogers v. Bellei*,[40] the Court distinguished the expatriation of a citizen who obtained his citizenship derivatively through his American mother but failed to return to the United States within the time required by statute from persons who obtained their citizenship on other grounds.[41] The Court noted that Bellei's citizenship was not obtained under the Fourteenth Amendment formula but depended entirely on a statutory grant.[42] Justice Black's dissent argued that the Fourteenth Amendment protects all citizens, and that the requirement for proof of voluntary intent to relinquish should be uniform.

The statutory grounds for expatriation are found at 8 U.S.C. § 1481 and describe a long list of acts which cause the loss of citizenship. While the Supreme Court, in *Savorgan v. U.S.*,[43] upheld the expatriation of a person for naturalization in a foreign state, such a blanket provision seems questionable in light of the *Afroyim* requirement of specific voluntary intent to relinquish American citizenship. Similarly, while the statute provides that the foreign naturalization of a parent of a U.S. citizen child may result in the child's loss of citizenship if the child fails to establish residence before her twenty-fifth birthday, such a result is questionable following *Afroyim*.[44]

The statute also treats the taking of an oath of allegiance to a foreign state as a relinquishment of citizenship. However, a mere oath of allegiance for admission to the bar does not entail the transfer of allegiance.[45] Similarly, the essential act of relinquishment must be voluntary and meaningful.[46] In addition, courts have been unwilling to recognize renunciation when a person volunteered for military service in a foreign country[47] or worked for a foreign government.[48]

---

40. 401 U.S. 815 (1971).

41. The statutory provisions referred to in *Rogers v. Bellei*, 401 U.S. 815 (1971), are no longer in effect.

42. 401 U.S. at 827.

43. 338 U.S. 491 (1950).

44. 8 U.S.C. § 1481(a)(1). Note that this scenario is distinguishable from the *Rogers v. Bellei* situation, as it may result in the involuntary loss of citizenship of one "born in the United States." However, given the requirements of voluntariness in the relinquishment of citizenship and the Court's decision in *Afroyim*, it is not clear how a case such as this would be decided at this time. Even before *Afroyim*, there were some circumstances under which a child would not be considered as having lost her citizenship. *See Perri v. Dulles*, 230 F.2d 259 (3d Cir. 1956) (failure to return was out of person's control due to war); *see also Petition of Acchione*, 213 F.2d 845 (3d Cir. 1954); *Rueff v. Brownell*, 116 F. Supp. 298 (D.N.J. 1953) (misadvice by consular officials).

45. *Baker v. Rusk*, 296 F. Supp. 1246 (9th Cir. 1969).

46. A careful review of the cases reveals that only in extremely rare situations is an act viewed as voluntary and meaningful.

47. *See also Nishikawa v. Dulles*, 356 U.S. 129 (1958).

48. Expatriation of United States Citizens: Attorney General's Statement of Interpretation, 34 Fed. Reg. 1,079 (1969) (reprinted in this chapter). Committing an act of treason or attempting to overthrow the U.S. government might satisfy the *Afroyim* standard of an act that reasonably manifests

Perhaps the strongest case for an effective renunciation would be where a person makes a *formal* renunciation of nationality before a diplomatic or consular officer of the United States. Such an act would seem to meet the "voluntary" requirement if it was evidenced by a specific and knowing intent.

All of the expatriating provisions in the INA, with the exception of treason, also require that the expatriated American take up residence thereafter outside of the United States and its outlying possessions.[49]

Cyrus Vance, Sect'y of State v. Laurence J. Terrazas

444 U.S. 252 (1980)

Justice White delivered the opinion of the Court.

Justice Stewart dissents for the reasons stated in Part II of Mr. Justice Brennan's dissenting opinion, which he joins.

Mr. Justice Marshall, concurring in part and dissenting in part.

Section 349(a)(2) of the Immigration and Nationality Act (Act), 66 Stat. 267, 8 U.S.C. § 1481(a)(2), provides that "a person who is a national of the United States whether by birth or naturalization, shall lose his nationality by ... taking an oath or making an affirmation or other formal declaration of allegiance to a foreign state or a political subdivision thereof." The Act also provides that the party claiming that such loss of citizenship occurred must "establish such claim by a preponderance of the evidence" and that the voluntariness of the expatriating conduct is rebuttably presumed. § 349(c), as added, 75 Stat. 656, 8 U.S.C. § 1481(c).[1] The issues in this case are whether, in establishing loss of citizenship under § 1481(a)(2), a party must prove

---

an individual's intent to transfer or abandon allegiance to the United States. However, the constitutionality of this provision has not been tested.

49. 8 U.S.C. § 1483(a), Sec. 351(a).

1. The relevant statutory provisions are §§ 349(a)(2), (c) of the Act, 66 Stat. 267, as amended, 75 Stat. 656, as set forth in 8 U.S.C. § 1481:

> (a) From and after the effective date of this chapter a person who is a national of the United States whether by birth or naturalization, shall lose his nationality by—
>
> * * *
>
> (2) taking an oath or making an affirmation or other formal declaration of allegiance to a foreign state or a political subdivision thereof;
>
> * * *
>
> (c) Whenever the loss of United States nationality is put in issue in any action or proceeding commenced on or after September 26, 1961 under, or by virtue of, the provisions of this chapter or any other Act, the burden shall be upon the person or party claiming that such loss occurred, to establish such claim by a preponderance of the evidence. Except as otherwise provided in subsection (b) of this section, any person who commits or performs, or who has committed or performed, any act of expatriation under the provisions of this chapter or any other Act shall be presumed to have done so voluntarily, but such presumption may be rebutted upon a showing, by a preponderance of the evidence, that the act or acts committed or performed were not done voluntarily.

an intent to surrender United States citizenship and whether the United States Constitution permits Congress to legislate with respect to expatriation proceedings by providing the standard of proof and the statutory presumption contained in § 1481(c).

Appellee, Laurence J. Terrazas, was born in this country, the son of a Mexican citizen. He thus acquired at birth both United States and Mexican citizenship. In the fall of 1970, while a student in Monterrey, Mexico, and at the age of 22, appellee executed an application for a certificate of Mexican nationality, swearing "adherence, obedience, and submission to the laws and authorities of the Mexican Republic" and "expressly renounc[ing] United States citizenship, as well as any submission, obedience, and loyalty to any foreign government, especially to that of the United States of America, ..." App. to Brief for Appellant 5a.[2] The certificate, which issued upon this application on April 3, 1971, recited that Terrazas had sworn adherence to the United Mexican States and that he "has expressly renounced all rights inherent to any other nationality, as well as all submission, obedience, and loyalty to any foreign government, especially to those which have recognized him as that national." *Id.*, at 8a. Terrazas read and understood the certificate upon receipt. App. to Juris. Statement 21a.

A few months later, following a discussion with an officer of the United States Consulate in Monterrey, proceedings were instituted to determine whether appellee had lost his United States citizenship by obtaining the certificate of Mexican nationality. Appellee denied that he had, but in December 1971 the Department of State issued a certificate of loss of nationality. App. to Brief for Appellant 31a. The Board of Appellate Review of the Department of State, after a full hearing, affirmed that appellee had voluntarily renounced his United States citizenship. Juris. Statement 31a. As permitted by § 360(a) of the Act, 66 Stat. 273, 8 U.S.C. § 1503(a), appellee then brought this suit against the Secretary of State for a declaration of his United States nationality. Trial was de novo.

The District Court recognized that the first sentence of the Fourteenth Amendment, as construed in *Afroyim v. Rusk*, 387 U.S. 253, 268 (1967), "protect[s] every citizen of this Nation against a congressional forcible destruction of his citizenship" and that every citizen has "a constitutional right to remain a citizen ... unless he voluntarily relinquishes that citizenship." App. to Juris. Statement 25a. A person of dual nationality, the District Court said, "will be held to have expatriated himself from the United States when it is shown that he voluntarily committed an act whereby he unequivocally renounced his allegiance to the United States." *Ibid.* Specifically, the District Court found that appellee had taken an oath of allegiance to Mexico,

2. The application contained the following statement:

"I therefore hereby expressly renounce ____ citizenship, as well as any submission, obedience, and loyalty to any foreign government, especially to that of ____, of which I might have been subject, all protection foreign to the laws and authorities of Mexico, all rights which treaties or international law grant to foreigners; and furthermore I swear adherence, obedience, and submission to the laws and authorities of the Mexican Republic."

The blank spaces in the statement were filled in with the words "Estados Unidos" (United States) and "Norteamerica" (North America), respectively. Brief for Appellant 4.

that he had "knowingly and understandingly renounced allegiance to the United States in connection with his Application for a Certificate of Mexican Nationality," *id.*, at 28a, and that "[t]he taking of an oath of allegiance to Mexico and renunciation of a foreign country [sic] citizenship is a condition precedent under Mexican law to the issuance of a Certificate of Mexican Nationality." *Ibid.* The District Court concluded that the United States had "proved by a preponderance of the evidence that Laurence J. Terrazas knowingly, understandingly and voluntarily took an oath of allegiance to Mexico, and concurrently renounced allegiance to the United States," *id.*, at 29a, and that he had therefore "voluntarily relinquished United States citizenship pursuant to § 349(a)(2) of the ... Act."

* * *

The Secretary first urges that the Court of Appeals erred in holding that a "specific intent to renounce U. S. citizenship" must be proved "before the mere taking of an oath of allegiance could result in an individual's expatriation." 577 F.2d, at 11. His position is that he need prove only the voluntary commission of an act, such as swearing allegiance to a foreign nation, that "is so inherently inconsistent with the continued retention of American citizenship that Congress may accord to it its natural consequences, i.e., loss of nationality." Brief for Appellant 24. We disagree.

* * *

In *Afroyim v. Rusk*, 387 U.S. 253 (1967), the Court held that § 401(e) of the Nationality Act of 1940, 54 Stat. 1168–1169, which provided that an American citizen "shall lose his nationality by ... [v]oting in a political election in a foreign state," contravened the Citizenship Clause of the Fourteenth Amendment. Afroyim was a naturalized American citizen who lived in Israel for 10 years. While in that nation, Afroyim voted in a political election. He in consequence was stripped of his United States citizenship. Consistently with *Perez v. Brownell*, 356 U.S. 44 (1958), which had sustained § 401(e), the District Court affirmed the power of Congress to expatriate for such conduct regardless of the citizen's intent to renounce his citizenship. This Court, however, in overruling *Perez*, "reject[ed] the idea ... that, aside from the Fourteenth Amendment, Congress has any general power, express or implied, to take away an American citizen's citizenship without his assent." *Afroyim v. Rusk, supra*, 387 U.S., at 257. The *Afroyim* opinion continued: § 1 of the Fourteenth Amendment is "most reasonably ... read as defining a citizenship which a citizen keeps unless he voluntarily relinquishes it." 387 U.S., at 262.

The Secretary argues that *Afroyim* does not stand for the proposition that a specific intent to renounce must be shown before citizenship is relinquished. It is enough, he urges, to establish one of the expatriating acts specified in § 1481(a) because Congress has declared each of those acts to be inherently inconsistent with the retention of citizenship. But *Afroyim* emphasized that loss of citizenship requires the individual's "assent," 387 U.S., at 257, in addition to his voluntary commission of the expatriating act. It is difficult to understand that "assent" to loss of citizenship would mean anything less than an intent to relinquish citizenship, whether the intent is expressed in words or is found as a fair inference from proved conduct. *Perez* had sustained congressional

assent = intent to relinquish

power to expatriate without regard to the intent of the citizen to surrender his citizenship. *Afroyim* overturned this proposition. It may be, as the Secretary maintains, that a requirement of intent to relinquish citizenship poses substantial difficulties for the Government in performance of its essential task of determining who is a citizen. Nevertheless, the intent of the Fourteenth Amendment, among other things, was to define citizenship; and as interpreted in *Afroyim*, that definition cannot coexist with a congressional power to specify acts that work a renunciation of citizenship even absent an intent to renounce. In the last analysis, expatriation depends on the will of the citizen rather than on the will of Congress and its assessment of his conduct.

* * *

In any event, we are confident that it would be inconsistent with *Afroyim* to treat the expatriating acts specified in § 1481(a) as the equivalent of or as conclusive evidence of the indispensable voluntary assent of the citizen. "Of course," any of the specified acts "may be highly persuasive evidence in the particular case of a purpose to abandon citizenship." *Nishikawa v. Dulles*, 356 U.S. 129 (1958) (Black, J., concurring). But the trier of fact must in the end conclude that the citizen not only voluntarily committed the expatriating act prescribed in the statute, but also intended to relinquish his citizenship.

This understanding of *Afroyim* is little different from that expressed by the Attorney General in his 1969 opinion explaining the impact of that case. 42 Op.Atty.Gen. 397. An "act which does not reasonably manifest an individual's transfer or abandonment of allegiance to the United States," the Attorney General said, "cannot be made a basis for expatriation." *Id.*, at 400. Voluntarily relinquishment is "not confined to a written renunciation," but "can also be manifested by other actions declared expatriative under the [A]ct, if such actions are in derogation of allegiance to this country." *Ibid.* Even in these cases, however, the issue of intent was deemed by the Attorney General to be open; and, once raised, the burden of proof on the issue was on the party asserting that expatriation had occurred. Ibid. "In each case," the Attorney General stated, "the administrative authorities must make a judgment, based on all the evidence, whether the individual comes within the terms of an expatriation provision and has in fact voluntarily relinquished his citizenship." *Id.*, at 401. It was under this advice, as the Secretary concedes, that the relevant departments of the Government have applied the statute and the Constitution to require an ultimate finding of an intent to expatriate. Brief for Appellant 56–57, n. 28.

Accordingly, in the case now before us, the Board of Appellate Review of the State Department found that appellee not only swore allegiance to Mexico, but also intended to abandon his United States citizenship: "In consideration of the complete record, we view appellant's declaration of allegiance to Mexico and his concurrent repudiation of any and all submission, obedience, and loyalty to the United States as compelling evidence of a specific intent to relinquish his United States citizenship." Juris. Statement 50a. This same view—that expatriation depends on the will of a citizen as ascertained from his words and conduct—was also reflected in the United States' response to the petition for certiorari in *United States v. Matheson*, 532 F.2d 809, cert. denied,

429 U.S. 823 (1976). Insofar as we are advised, this view remained the official position of the United States until the appeal in this case.

As we have said, *Afroyim* requires that the record support a finding that the expatriating act was accompanied by an intent to terminate United States citizenship. The submission of the United States is inconsistent with this holding, and we are unprepared to reconsider it.

With respect to the principal issues before it, the Court of Appeals held that Congress was without constitutional authority to prescribe the standard of proof in expatriation proceedings and that the proof in such cases must be by clear and convincing evidence rather than by the preponderance standard prescribed in § 1481(c). We are in fundamental disagreement with these conclusions.

In *Nishikawa v. Dulles*, 356 U.S. 129 (1958), an American-born citizen, temporarily in Japan, was drafted into the Japanese Army. The Government later claimed that, under § 401(c) of the Nationality Act of 1940, 54 Stat. 1169, he had expatriated himself by serving in the armed forces of a foreign nation. The Government agreed that expatriation had not occurred if Nishikawa's army service had been involuntary. Nishikawa contended that the Government had to prove that his service was voluntary, while the Government urged that duress was an affirmative defense that Nishikawa had the burden to prove by overcoming the usual presumption of voluntariness. This Court held the presumption unavailable to the Government and required proof of a voluntary expatriating act by clear and convincing evidence.

Section 1481(c) soon followed; its evident aim was to supplant the evidentiary standards prescribed by *Nishikawa*. The provision "sets up rules of evidence under which the burden of proof to establish loss of citizenship by preponderance of the evidence would rest upon the Government. The presumption of voluntariness under the proposed rules of evidence, would be rebuttable—similarly—by preponderance of the evidence...." H.R.Rep. No. 1086, 87th Cong., 1st Sess., 41, U.S.Code Cong. & Admin. News, p. 2985 (1961).

We see no basis for invalidating the evidentiary prescriptions contained in § 1481(c). *Nishikawa* was not rooted in the Constitution. The Court noted, moreover, that it was acting in the absence of legislative guidance. *Nishikawa v. Dulles*, 356 U.S., at 135. Nor do we agree with the Court of Appeals that, because under *Afroyim* Congress is constitutionally devoid of power to impose expatriation on a citizen, it is also without power to prescribe the evidentiary standards to govern expatriation proceedings. 577 F.2d, at 10. Although § 1481(c) had been law since 1961, *Afroyim* did not address or advert to that section; surely the Court would have said so had it intended to construe the Constitution to exclude expatriation proceedings from the traditional powers of Congress to prescribe rules of evidence and standards of proof in the federal courts. This power, rooted in the authority of Congress conferred by Art. 1, § 8, cl. 9, of the Constitution to create inferior federal courts, is undoubted and has been frequently noted and sustained. See, e.g., *Usery v. Turner Elkhorn Mining Co.*, 428 U.S. 1, 31 (1976).

We note also that the Court's opinion in *Afroyim* was written by Mr. Justice Black who, in concurring in *Nishikawa*, said that the question whether citizenship has been voluntarily relinquished is to be determined on the facts of each case and that Congress could provide rules of evidence for such proceedings. *Nishikawa v. Dulles, supra*, 356 U.S., at 139. In this respect, we agree with Mr. Justice Black; and since Congress has the express power to enforce the Fourteenth Amendment, it is untenable to hold that it has no power whatsoever to address itself to the manner or means by which Fourteenth Amendment citizenship may be relinquished.

* * *

In sum, we hold that in proving expatriation, an expatriating act and an intent to relinquish citizenship must be proved by a preponderance of the evidence. We also hold that when one of the statutory expatriating acts is proved, it is constitutional to presume it to have been a voluntary act until and unless proved otherwise by the actor. If he succeeds, there can be no expatriation. If he fails, the question remains whether on all the evidence the Government has satisfied its burden of proof that the expatriating act was performed with the necessary intent to relinquish citizenship.

The judgment of the Court of Appeals is reversed, and the case is remanded for further proceedings consistent with this opinion.

Expatriation of United States Citizens: Attorney General's Statement of Interpretation

34 Fed. Reg. 1,079 (1969)

In *Afroyim v. Rusk*, 387 U.S. 253 (1967), the Supreme Court held unconstitutional section 401(e) of the Nationality Act of 1940, which provided that a citizen of the United States shall lose his citizenship by voting in a foreign political election.

The sweeping language of the *Afroyim* opinion raises questions as to its effect on the validity of expatriation provisions, other than those relating to voting, in the Immigration Service and Nationality Act ("the Act") or in former law preserved in section 405(c) of the Act, 8 U.S.C. 1101. These questions are of importance to the Department of State in the administration of the passport laws and to the Immigration and Naturalization in the administration of the immigration laws.

Of course, the ultimate determination of the effect of *Afroyim is* a matter for the courts. The Act empowers the Attorney General, however, to determine *Afroyim*'s effect on the Act for administrative purposes. This Statement of Interpretation will serve to guide both the Department of State and the Immigration and Naturalization Service in the performance of their functions insofar as they involve questions of loss of citizenship.

1. Section 401(e) of the 1940 Act had been ruled constitutional in the Court's earlier decision in *Perez v. Brownell*, 356 U.S. 44 (1958). The majority opinion in *Perez* rejected the argument that "the power of Congress to terminate citizenship depends upon the

citizen's assent." 356 U.S. at 61. *Afroyim* expressly overruled *Perez* and held, in agreement with the Chief Justice's dissent in *Perez,* that the Government is without power to deprive a citizen of his citizenship for voting in a foreign election, 387 U.S. at 267. The rule laid down in *Afroyim* is that a U.S. citizen has a constitutional right to remain a citizen "unless he voluntarily relinquishes that citizenship." 387 U.S. at 268.

Afroyim did not expressly address itself to the question of defining what declarations or other conduct can properly be regarded as a "voluntary relinquishment" of citizenship. As a consequence, it did not provide guidelines of sufficient detail to permit me to pass definitively upon the validity of other expatriating provisions of the Act. It did, however, stress the constitutional mandate that no citizen born or naturalized in the United States can be deprived of his citizenship unless he has voluntarily relinquished" it.

On the question of what constitutes "voluntary relinquishment," we must look to earlier cases in the Supreme Court. Some guidance may be found in earlier opinions of the Justices who joined in the Court's opinion in *Afroyim.* Particularly relevant are the Chief Justice's dissent in *Perez,* which was cited in *Afroyim* with approval, and the concurring opinion of Justice Black (who wrote the opinion of the court in *Afroyim*) in *Nisbikawa v. Dulles,* 356 U.S. 129, 138 (1958), decided the same day as *Perez.*

In *Perez,* the Chief Justice stated (356 U.S. at 68–69)

> It has long been recognized that citizenship may not only be voluntarily renounced through exercise of the right of expatriation but also by other actions in derogation of undivided allegiance to this country. While the essential qualities of the citizen-state relationship under our Constitution precludes the exercise of governmental power to divest U.S. citizenship, the establishment of that relationship did not impair the principle that conduct of a citizen showing a voluntary transfer of allegiance is an abandonment of citizenship. Nearly all sovereignties recognize that acquisition of foreign nationality ordinarily shows a renunciation of citizenship. Nor is this the only act by which the citizen may show a voluntary abandonment of his citizenship. Any action by which he manifests allegiance to a foreign state may be so inconsistent with the retention of citizenship as to result in loss of that status. In recognizing the consequences of such action, the Government is not taking away U.S. citizenship to implement its general regulatory powers, for, as previously indicated, in my judgment citizenship is immune from divestment under these powers. Rather, the Government is simply giving formal recognition to the inevitable consequences of the citizen's own voluntary surrender of his citizenship.

In *Nishikawa,* Mr. Justice Black stated (356 U.S. at 139):

> Of course a citizen has the right to abandon or renounce his citizenship and Congress can enact measures to regulate and affirm such abjuration. But whether citizenship has been voluntarily relinquished is a question to be determined on the facts of each case after a judicial trial in full conformity with the Bill of Rights. Although Congress may provide rules of evidence

> for such trials, it cannot declare that such equivocal acts as service in a foreign army, participation in a foreign election or desertion from our armed forces establish a conclusive presumption of intention to throw off American nationality....

The foregoing quotations do not come from majority opinions, and *Afroyim* does not adopt them. Indeed, *Afroyim* does not reach the question of whether it may be possible under some circumstances for allegiance to be transferred or abandoned without constituting a voluntary relinquishment of the status of citizenship. That question must await further court decision. Under any reading of *Afroyim*, however, it is clear that an act which does not reasonably manifest an individual's transfer or abandonment of allegiance to the United States cannot be made a basis for expatriation.

2. For administrative purposes, and until the courts have clarified the scope of *Afroyim*, I have concluded that it is the duty of Executive officials to apply the Act on the following basis. "Voluntary relinquishment" of citizenship is not confined to a written renunciation, as under section 345(a)(6) and (7) of the Act, 8 U.S.C. 1431(a)(6) and (7). It can also be manifested by other actions declared expatriative under the Act, if such actions are in derogation of allegiance to this country. Yet even in those cases, *Afroyim* leaves it open to the individual to raise the issue of intent.

Once the issue of intent is raised, the Act makes it clear that the burden of proof is on the party asserting that expatriation has occurred. *Afroyim* suggests that this burden is not easily satisfied by the Government. In the words of Justice Black quoted above from his concurring opinion in *Nishikawa,* the voluntary performance of some acts can "be highly persuasive evidence in the particular case of a purpose to abandon citizenship." Yet some kinds of conduct, though within the proscription of the statute, simply will not be sufficiently probative to support a finding of voluntary expatriation.

For instance, it is obviously not enough to establish a voluntary relinquishment of citizenship that an individual accepts employment as a public school teacher in a foreign country. This I have already decided in the case of a dual national.... A different case would be presented by an individual's acceptance of an important political post in a foreign government.

A similar approach can be taken with respect to service in a foreign army, depending on the particular circumstances involved. Thus, an individual who enlists in the armed forces of an allied country does not necessarily evidence that by so doing he intends to abandon his U.S. citizenship. But it is highly persuasive evidence, to say the least, of an intent to abandon U.S. citizenship if one enlists voluntarily in the armed forces of a foreign government engaged in hostilities against the United States.

The examples mentioned above are, of course, merely illustrative. In each case the administrative authorities must make a judgment, based on all the evidence, whether the individual comes within the terms of an expatriation provision and has in fact voluntarily relinquished his citizenship. In order to avoid conflicts in interpretation between the Department of State and the Immigration and Naturalization

Service, these agencies should undertake the consult with each other; if any substantial difference should arise as to any particular type of situation, it should be referred to the Attorney General for resolution.

3. Finally, note should be made as to the scope of this Statement of Interpretation. I believe the *Afroyim* principles reach, and therefore this Statement covers, all of section 349(a) of the Act, section 350, insofar as it relates to dual nationals born or naturalized in the United States, and section 405(c) insofar as it purports to continue the effectiveness of individual losses of nationality under the similar provisions of sections 401 and 404 of the Nationality Act of 1940.

There are additional considerations relating to dual nationals born abroad which may affect their acquisition and retention of U.S. citizenship. This matter is currently in litigation. Hence this statement does not necessarily apply to loss of U.S. citizenship acquired as a result of birth abroad to a citizen parent or parents.

This statement has no application to a revocation of naturalization unlawfully procured. See *Afroyim v. Rusk,* 387 U.S. at 267, n.23.

Attorney General, Ramsey Clark.

E. Dual Citizenship

The Court in *Rogers v. Bellei,* in holding that restrictions could be placed on the conferral of citizenship, expressed the often-held opinion that there are problems and concerns with dual nationality. It is important to note that dual nationality is more common than ever before. A person could become a dual national by birth in the United States to parents of a country which recognizes the principle of *jus sanguinis.* A person could also become a dual citizen when she becomes a U.S. citizen through naturalization, and her country recognizes the principle of *jus soli.* Similarly, it could happen when a U.S. citizen moves to another country and acquires citizenship there through a naturalization procedure. Finally, a person who is a dual national is not forced to choose between nationalities at a particular age.[50] All that is required of the dual national who is returning to the United States is that she enter with her U.S. passport, for she is not a foreign national as far as the United States is concerned.[51]

F. Loss of Citizenship — Denaturalization

Denaturalization is a legal proceeding to revoke the original judicial decree of naturalization, which is a direct attack on the original decree conferring citizenship. It

50. *See Mandali v. Acheson,* 344 U.S. 133 (1952).
51. *See* 8 U.S.C. § 1185(b), Sec. 215(b).

can therefore be brought only against a person who received her citizenship as a result of a judicial decree of naturalization rather than through birth in the United States or through U.S. citizen parents.

Since deprivation of citizenship is a severe loss, the constitutionality of denaturalization and expatriation has often been challenged. The authority to denaturalize has been upheld as an exercise of Congress' constitutional power to establish a uniform rule of naturalization.[52] Under the "necessary and proper" clause, the authority to revoke citizenship that was fraudulently obtained is viewed as a requisite safeguard to maintaining the integrity of the judicial naturalization proceeding.[53] Both the present statute and the 1906 Act provide for the retroactive revocation of naturalization previously granted under 8 U.S.C. § 1451(a). This revocation aspect of the 1906 Act was upheld against a challenge that it was an ex post facto law, because it was not punishment to deprive the alien of something to which he was entitled.[54]

1. Grounds for Denaturalization

Naturalization may be revoked following a hearing before a federal judge if it is found that citizenship was illegally procured or procured by concealment of a material fact or willful misrepresentation.[55] Illegal procurement, when separately charged, most often relates to some failure to meet the statutory requirements for naturalization. Examples include failure to comply with the residence requirements[56] or to take the required oath of allegiance.[57]

Although denaturalization is a civil, not a criminal, proceeding, the government is required to prove the illegality of the original naturalization by "clear, convincing, and unequivocal" evidence. In at least one case where the government was unable to establish to this high degree of certainty that an active Communist failed to meet the requirements of attachment to the United States, the naturalization decree was held to have been improperly revoked.[58]

The consequences of making a misstatement or concealment of fact are so severe that it is generally conceded that the misstatement or concealment must be material and willful.[59] Examples include concealment of a criminal record[60] or prior Nazi party membership.[61]

---

52. *Knauer v. U.S.*, 328 U.S. 654 (1945).
53. *Id.*
54. *Johannessen v. U.S.*, 225 U.S. 227, 242 (1912).
55. 8 U.S.C. § 1451(a).
56. *U.S. v. Parisi*, 24 F. Supp. 414 (D. Md. 1938).
57. *U.S. v. Sremzuch*, 312 F. Supp. 928 (E.D. Wis. 1970).
58. *Schneiderman v. U.S.*, 320 U.S. 118 (1943).
59. *Chaunt v. U.S.*, 364 U.S. 350 (1960). *U.S. v. Arango*, 670 F.3d 988, 994 (3d Cir 2012) (government bears heavy burden to establish that misrepresentation was willful).
60. *U.S. v. Oddo*, 314 F.2d 115 (2d Cir. 1963).
61. *Klapprott v. U.S.*, 335 U.S. 601 (1949).

Facts concealed by an applicant in a naturalization proceeding are considered material if disclosure could have justified a denial of citizenship.[62] The government must establish a nexus between the illegal conduct and the naturalization.[63] This is not the sole test, however; concealed facts are also material if their disclosure would have revealed to the government an avenue for investigating other facts relating to the applicant's eligibility for naturalization.[64]

The case which follows illustrates the nature of cases involving illegal procurement, concealment or willful misrepresentation. The case explores how there is effectively no limit on the impact, even though many years have passed since the original naturalization. Cases such as *Fedorenko* came about as a result of investigations into the admission of Nazi-era war criminals who managed to gain admission to the U.S. These investigations were led by a special unit within the Department of Justice called the Office of Special Investigations (OSI). *Fedorenko* was one of the first cases brought by the OSI.[65]

Feodor Fedorenko v. United States

449 U.S. 490 (1981)

Justice MARSHALL delivered the opinion of the Court.

Section 340(a) of the Immigration and Nationality Act of 1952, 66 Stat. 260, as amended, 8 U.S.C. § 1451(a), requires revocation of United States citizenship that was "illegally procured or ... procured by concealment of a material fact or by willful misrepresentation."[1] The Government brought this denaturalization action, alleging that petitioner procured his citizenship illegally or by willfully misrepresenting a material fact. The District Court entered judgment for petitioner, but the Court of Appeals reversed and ordered entry of a judgment of denaturalization. We granted certiorari, 444 U.S. 1070, to resolve two questions: whether petitioner's failure to disclose, in his application for a visa to come to this country, that he had served during the Second World War as an armed guard at the Nazi concentration camp at Treblinka, Poland, rendered his citizenship revocable as "illegally procured" or procured by willful misrepresentation of a material fact, and if so, whether the District

---

62. *Costello v. U. S.*, 365 U.S. 265 (1961).

63. *Maslenjak v. U.S.*, 137 S. Ct. 1918 (2017).

64. *U.S. v. Galato*, 171 F. Supp. 169 (D. Pa. 1959); *U.S. v. Chandler*, 152 F. Supp. 169 (D. Md. 1957).

65. In 2009, the functions of the OSI were merged into the Human Rights and Special Prosecutions of the Criminal Division of the Department of Justice.

1. Title 8 U.S.C. § 1451(a) provides in pertinent part:

It shall be the duty of the United States attorneys ... to institute proceedings ... in the judicial district in which the naturalized citizen may reside at the time of bringing suit, for the purpose of revoking and setting aside the order admitting such person to citizenship and canceling the certificate of naturalization on the ground that such order and certificate of naturalization were illegally procured or were procured by concealment of a material fact or by willful misrepresentation....

Court nonetheless possessed equitable discretion to refrain from entering judgment in favor of the Government under these circumstances.

Petitioner was born in the Ukraine in 1907. He was drafted into the Russian Army in June 1941, but was captured by the Germans shortly thereafter. After being held in a series of prisoner-of-war camps, petitioner was selected to go to the German camp at Travnicki in Poland, where he received training as a concentration camp guard. In September 1942, he was assigned to the Nazi concentration camp at Treblinka in Poland, where he was issued a uniform and rifle and where he served as a guard during 1942 and 1943. The infamous Treblinka concentration camp was described by the District Court as a "human abattoir" at which several hundred thousand Jewish civilians were murdered.[2] After an armed uprising by the inmates at Treblinka led to the closure of the camp in August 1943, petitioner was transferred to a German labor camp at Danzig and then to the German prisoner-of-war camp at Poelitz, where he continued to serve as an armed guard. Petitioner was eventually transferred to Hamburg where he served as a warehouse guard. Shortly before the British forces entered that city in 1945, petitioner discarded his uniform and was able to pass as a civilian. For the next four years, he worked in Germany as a laborer.

In 1948, Congress enacted the Displaced Persons Act (DPA or Act), 62 Stat. 1009, to enable European refugees driven from their homelands by the war to emigrate to the United States without regard to traditional immigration quotas. The Act's definition of "displaced persons" eligible for immigration to this country specifically excluded individuals who had "assisted the enemy in persecuting civil[ians]" or had "voluntarily assisted the enemy forces ... in their operations...." Section 10 of the DPA, 62 Stat. 1013, placed the burden of proving eligibility under the Act on the person seeking admission and provided that "[a]ny person who shall willfully make a misrepresentation for the purpose of gaining admission into the United States as an eligible displaced person shall thereafter not be admissible into the United States." The Act established an elaborate system for determining eligibility for displaced person status. Each applicant was first interviewed by representatives of the International Refugee Organization of the United Nations (IRO) who ascertained that the person was a refugee or displaced person. The applicant was then interviewed by an official of the Displaced Persons Commission, who made a preliminary determination about his eligibility under the DPA. The final decision was made by one of several State Department vice consuls, who were specially trained for the task and sent to Europe to administer the Act. Thereafter, the application was re-

2. Historians estimate that some 800,000 people were murdered at Treblinka. *See* L. Dawidowicz, The War Against the Jews, 1933–1945, p. 149 (1975); R. Hilberg, The Destruction of the European Jews 572 (1978). The District Court described Treblinka in this manner:

> It contained only living facilities for the SS and the persons working there. The thousands who arrived daily on the trains had no need for barracks or mess halls: they would be dead before nightfall. It was operated with a barbarous methodology—brutally efficient—and such camps surely fill one of the darkest chapters in the annals of human existence, certainly the darkest in that which we call Western civilization.

455 F.Supp. 893, 901, n.12 (SD Fla.1978).

viewed by officials of the Immigration and Naturalization Service (INS) to make sure that the applicant was admissible into the United States under the standard immigration laws.

In October 1949, petitioner applied for admission to the United States as a displaced person. Petitioner falsified his visa application by lying about his wartime activities. He told the investigators from the Displaced Persons Commission that he had been a farmer in Sarny, Poland, from 1937 until March 1942, and that he had then been deported to Germany and forced to work in a factory in Poelitz until the end of the war, when he fled to Hamburg. Petitioner told the same story to the vice consul who reviewed his case and he signed a sworn statement containing these false representations as part of his application for a DPA visa. Petitioner's false statements were not discovered at the time and he was issued a DPA visa, and sailed to the United States where he was admitted for permanent residence. He took up residence in Connecticut and for three decades led an uneventful and law-abiding life as a factory worker.

In 1969, petitioner applied for naturalization at the INS office in Hartford, Conn. Petitioner did not disclose his wartime service as a concentration camp armed guard in his application, and he did not mention it in his sworn testimony to INS naturalization examiners. The INS examiners took petitioner's visa papers at face value and recommended that his citizenship application be granted. On this recommendation, the Superior Court of New Haven County granted his petition for naturalization and he became an American citizen on April 23, 1970.

Seven years later, after petitioner had moved to Miami Beach and become a resident of Florida, the Government filed this action in the United States District Court for the Southern District of Florida to revoke petitioner's citizenship. The complaint alleged that petitioner should have been deemed ineligible for a DPA visa because he had served as an armed guard at Treblinka and had committed crimes or atrocities against inmates of the camp because they were Jewish. The Government charged that petitioner had willfully concealed this information both in applying for a DPA visa and in applying for citizenship, and that therefore petitioner had procured his naturalization illegally or by willfully misrepresenting material facts.

* * *

Our examination of the questions presented by this case must proceed within the framework established by two lines of prior decisions of this Court that may, at first blush, appear to point in different directions.

On the one hand, our decisions have recognized that the right to acquire American citizenship is a precious one and that once citizenship has been acquired, its loss can have severe and unsettling consequences. See *Costello v. United States*, 365 U.S. 265, 269 (1961); *Chaunt v. United States*, 364 U.S., at 353. For these reasons, we have held that the Government "carries a heavy burden of proof in a proceeding to divest a naturalized citizen of his citizenship." *Costello v. United States, supra*, 365 U.S. at 269. The evidence justifying revocation of citizenship must be "'clear, unequivocal, and convincing' and not leave 'the issue in doubt.'" *Schneiderman v. United States, supra*, 320 U.S. at 125 (quoting *Maxwell Land-Grant Case*, 121 U.S. 325, 381 (1887)). Any less exacting standard would be inconsistent with the importance of the right that is at stake in a denaturalization proceeding. And in reviewing denaturalization cases, we have carefully examined the record ourselves. See, e.g., *Costello v. United States, supra*.

At the same time, our cases have also recognized that there must be strict compliance with all the congressionally imposed prerequisites to the acquisition of citizenship. Failure to comply with any of these conditions renders the certificate of citizenship "illegally procured," and naturalization that is unlawfully procured can be set aside. 8 U.S.C. § 1451(a); *Afroyim v. Rusk*, 387 U.S. 253, 267 (1967). As we explained in one of these prior decisions:

> "An alien who seeks political rights as a member of this Nation can rightfully obtain them only upon terms and conditions specified by Congress....
>
> * * *
>
> "No alien has the slightest right to naturalization unless all statutory requirements are complied with; and every certificate of citizenship must be treated as granted upon condition that the government may challenge it ... and demand its cancellation unless issued in accordance with such requirements." *United States v. Ginsberg, supra*, at 474–475.

This judicial insistence on strict compliance with the statutory conditions precedent to naturalization is simply an acknowledgment of the fact that Congress alone has the constitutional authority to prescribe rules for naturalization, and the courts' task is to assure compliance with the particular prerequisites to the acquisition of United States citizenship by naturalization legislated to safeguard the integrity of this "priceless treasure." *Johnson v. Eisentrager*, 339 U.S. 763, 791 (1950) (Black, J., dissenting).

* * *

Petitioner does not and, indeed, cannot challenge the Government's contention that he willfully misrepresented facts about his wartime activities when he applied for a DPA visa in 1949. Petitioner admitted at trial that he "willingly" gave false information in connection with his application for a DPA visa so as to avoid the possibility of repatriation to the Soviet Union. The District Court specifically noted that there was no dispute that petitioner "lied" in his application. 455 F.Supp., at 914. Thus, petitioner falls within the plain language of the DPA's admonition that "[a]ny person who shall willfully make a misrepresentation for the purposes of gaining admission into the United States as an eligible displaced person shall thereafter not be admissible into the United States." 62 Stat. 1013. This does not, however, end our inquiry, because we agree with the Government that this provision only applies to willful misrepresentations about "material" facts. The first issue we must examine then, is whether petitioner's false statements about his activities during the war, particularly the concealment of his Treblinka service, were "material."

At the outset, we must determine the proper standard to be applied in judging whether petitioner's false statements were material. Both petitioner and the Government have assumed, as did the District Court and the Court of Appeals, that materiality under the above-quoted provision of the DPA is governed by the standard announced in *Chaunt v. United States*, 364 U.S. 350 (1960). But we do not find it so obvious that the *Chaunt* test is applicable here. In that case, the Government charged that *Chaunt* had procured his citizenship by concealing and misrepresenting his record of arrests in the United States in his application for citizenship, and that the arrest record was a "material" fact within the meaning of the denaturalization statute. Thus, the materiality standard announced in that case pertained to false statements in applications for citizenship, and the arrests that *Chaunt* failed to disclose all took place after he came to this country. The case presented no question concerning the lawfulness of his initial entry into the United States.

In the instant case, however, the events on which the Government relies in seeking to revoke petitioner's citizenship took place before he came to this country and the Government is seeking to revoke petitioner's citizenship because of the alleged unlawfulness of his initial entry into the United States. Although the complaint charged that petitioner misrepresented facts about his wartime activities in both his application for a visa and his application for naturalization, both the District Court and the Court of Appeals focused on the false statements in petitioner's application for a visa. Thus, under the analysis of both the District Court and the Court of Appeals, the misrepresentation that raises the materiality issue in this case was contained in petitioner's application for a visa. These distinctions plainly raise the important question whether the *Chaunt* test for materiality of misrepresentations in applications for citizenship also applies to false statements in visa applications.

It is, of course, clear that the materiality of a false statement in a visa application must be measured in terms of its effect on the applicant's admissibility into this country. See *United States v. Rossi*, 299 F.2d 650, 652 (CA9 1962). At the very least, a misrepresentation must be considered material if disclosure of the true facts would have made the applicant ineligible for a visa. Because we conclude that disclosure of the true facts about petitioner's service as an armed guard at Treblinka would, as a matter of law, have made him ineligible for a visa under the DPA, we find it unnecessary to resolve the question whether *Chaunt*'s materiality test also governs false statements in visa applications.

Section 2(b) of the DPA, 62 Stat. 1009, by incorporating the definition of "[p]ersons who will not be [considered displaced persons]" contained in the Constitution of the IRO, ... specifically provided that individuals who "assisted the enemy in persecuting civil[ians]" were ineligible for visas under the Act. Jenkins testified that petitioner's service as an armed guard at a concentration camp—whether voluntary or not—made him ineligible for a visa under this provision. Jenkins' testimony was based on his firsthand experience as a vice consul in Germany after the war reviewing DPA visa applications. Jenkins also testified that the practice of the vice consuls was to circulate among the other vice consuls the case files of any visa applicant who was shown to have been a concentration camp armed guard. Record 826. Thus, Jenkins and the other vice consuls were particularly well informed about the practice concerning the eligibility of former camp guards for DPA visas. The District Court evidently agreed that a literal interpretation of the statute would confirm the accuracy of Jenkins' testimony. 455 F.Supp., at 913. But by construing § 2(a) as only excluding individuals who voluntarily assisted in the persecution of civilians, the District Court was able to ignore Jenkins' uncontroverted testimony about how the Act was interpreted by the officials who administered it.

* * *

The Court of Appeals evidently accepted the District Court's construction of the Act since it agreed that the Government had failed to show that petitioner was ineligible for a DPA visa. 597 F.2d, at 953. Because we are unable to find any basis for an "involuntary assistance" exception in the language of § 2(a), we conclude that the District Court's construction of the Act was incorrect. The plain language of the Act mandates precisely the literal interpretation that the District Court rejected: an individual's service as a concentration camp armed guard—whether voluntary or involuntary—made him ineligible for a visa. That Congress was perfectly capable of adopting a "voluntariness" limitation where it felt that one was necessary is plain from comparing § 2(a) with § 2(b), which excludes only those individuals who "voluntarily assisted the enemy forces ... in their operations...." Under traditional principles of statutory construction, the deliberate omission of the word "voluntary" from § 2(a) compels the conclusion that the statute made all those who assisted in the persecution of civilians ineligible for visas. See *National Railroad Passenger v. National Assn. of Railroad Passengers*, 414 U.S. 453, 458 (1974).... Thus, the plain language of the statute and Jenkins' uncontradicted and unequivocal testimony leave no room for doubt that if petitioner had disclosed the fact that he had been an armed guard at Treblinka, he would have been found ineligible for a visa under the DPA. This being so, we must conclude that petitioner's false statements about his wartime activities were "willfu[l] [and material] misrepresentation[s] [made] for the purpose of gaining admission into the United States as an eligible displaced person." 62 Stat. 1013. Under the express terms of the statute, petitioner was "thereafter not ... admissible into the United States." *Ibid.*

Our conclusion that petitioner was, as a matter of law, ineligible for a visa under the DPA makes the resolution of this case fairly straightforward. As noted, *supra*, at 747–748, our cases have established that a naturalized citizen's failure to comply with the statutory prerequisites for naturalization renders his certificate of citizenship revocable as "illegally procured" under 8 U.S.C. § 1451(a). In 1970, when petitioner filed his application for and was admitted to citizenship, §§ 316(a) and 318 of the Immigration and Nationality Act of 1952, 8 U.S.C. §§ 1427(a) and 1429, required an applicant for citizenship to be lawfully admitted to the United States for permanent residence. Lawful admission for permanent residence in turn required that the individual possess a valid unexpired immigrant visa. At the time of petitioner's initial entry into this country, § 13(a) of the Immigration and Nationality Act of 1924, ch. 190, 43 Stat. 153, 161 (repealed in 1952), provided that "[n]o immigrant shall be admitted to the United States unless he (1) has an unexpired immigration visa...."] The courts at that time consistently held that § 13(a) required a valid visa and that a visa obtained through a material misrepresentation was not valid. See, e.g., *Ablett v. Brownell*, 240 F.2d 625, 629 (1957); *United States ex rel. Jankowski v. Shaughnessy*, 186 F.2d 580, 582 (CA2 1951). Section 10 of the DPA, 62 Stat. 1013, provided that "all immigration laws, ... shall be applicable to ... eligible displaced ... persons who apply to be or who are admitted into the United States pursuant to this Act." And as previously noted, petitioner was inadmissible into this country under the express terms of the DPA. Accordingly, inasmuch as petitioner failed to satisfy a statutory requirement which Congress has imposed as a prerequisite to the acquisition of citizenship by naturalization, we must agree with the Government that petitioner's citizenship must be revoked because it was "illegally procured." See *Polites v. United States*, 364 U.S. 426, 436–437 (1960). In the lexicon of our cases, one of the "jurisdictional facts upon which the grant [of citizenship] is predicated," *Johannessen v. United States, supra*, 225 U.S., at 240, was missing at the time petitioner became a citizen.

* * *

We agree with the Court of Appeals that district courts lack equitable discretion to refrain from entering a judgment of denaturalization against a naturalized citizen whose citizenship was procured illegally or by willful misrepresentation of material facts. Petitioner is correct in noting that courts necessarily and properly exercise discretion in characterizing certain facts while determining whether an applicant for citizenship meets some of the requirements for naturalization. But that limited discretion does not include the authority to excuse illegal or fraudulent procurement of citizenship. As the Court of Appeals stated: "Once it has been determined that a person does not qualify for citizenship, ... the district court has no discretion to ignore the defect and grant citizenship." 597 F.2d, at 954. By the same token, once a district court determines that the Government has met its burden of proving that a naturalized citizen obtained his citizenship illegally or by willful misrepresentation, it has no discretion to excuse the conduct.... We repeat here what we said in one of these earlier cases:

> "An alien who seeks political rights as a member of this Nation can rightfully obtain them only upon the terms and conditions specified by Congress. Courts are without authority to sanction changes or modifications; their duty is rigidly to enforce the legislative will in respect of a matter so vital to the public welfare." *United States v. Ginsberg*, 243 U.S., at 474–75.

Notes

1. In *Kungys v. U.S.*[66] the Court elaborated on the meaning of material misrepresentation. *Kungys* involved the denaturalization of Juoazas Kungys, who had been accused of participating in the extermination of 2,000 Lithuanian civilians, mostly

66. 485 U.S. 759 (1988).

Jewish, in 1941. Kungys had applied for and received an immigrant visa as a displaced person, which he used for his admission to the United States in 1948. He was naturalized in 1954. The Office of Special Investigations instituted denaturalization proceedings in 1982, charging Kungys with participation in the above described atrocities and with having misrepresented his date and place of birth, wartime occupation and residences in his immigrant visa and naturalization applications.

Justice Kennedy did not participate in the decision and five separate opinions, including a dissent by Justice White, were filed. Five Justices joined in that portion of the decision adopting a *natural tendency* test, or whether the

> misrepresentation or concealment ... had a natural tendency to affect the official decision. The official decision in question, of course, is whether the applicant meets the requirements for citizenship. This test must be met, of course, by evidence that is clear, unequivocal, and convincing.

485 U.S. at 771. The Court held that the test had not been met in *Kungys*.

2. The *Kungys* Court also held that 8 U.S.C. § 1101(f)(6), Sec. 101(f)(6), precludes good moral character for "one who has given false testimony for the purpose of obtaining any benefits under" the Act, irrespective of the materiality of the statement. As the Court stated, "it denominates a person to be of bad moral character on account of having given false testimony if he has told even the most immaterial of lies with the subjective intent of obtaining immigration or naturalization benefits."[67] Ultimately, on remand, the *Kungys* case was settled. Kungys was denaturalized with the condition that he be allowed to remain in the United States as a permanent resident for the remainder of his life.[68]

2. Other Grounds for Denaturalization

Denaturalization proceedings may also be invoked where the person has refused to testify before a congressional committee regarding prenaturalization subversive activities which were not revealed in their citizenship application if it occurs within 10 years of naturalization. Additionally, someone who was naturalized under special procedures for those in the military under 8 U.S.C. §§ 1439 and 1440 may have their citizenship revoked if they do not have at least 5 years of honorable service.[69]

---

67. 485 U.S. at 780.

68. *See* Richard Prinz, *Kungys and Materiality*, Immigration and Nationality Law 1989 Annual Symposium: Advanced Topics 154 (1989).

69. The statute is unclear about the procedure for revoking military service naturalization. In *Gorbach v. Reno*, 219 F.3d 1087, 1093–94 (9th Cir. 2000), the Ninth Circuit held that an administrative revocation of naturalization was without statutory authority notwithstanding the agency's promulgation of regulations to that effect.

G. Flow Charts

1. Naturalization

Naturalization applications are first submitted to USCIS. The applicant must have been a lawful permanent resident for at least 3 years if he obtained his status as an immediate relative. Otherwise the applicant is not eligible until they have been residents for 5 years. Those who have served. Children are exempted from the residency requirements when their parents naturalize as they obtain citizenship derivatively.

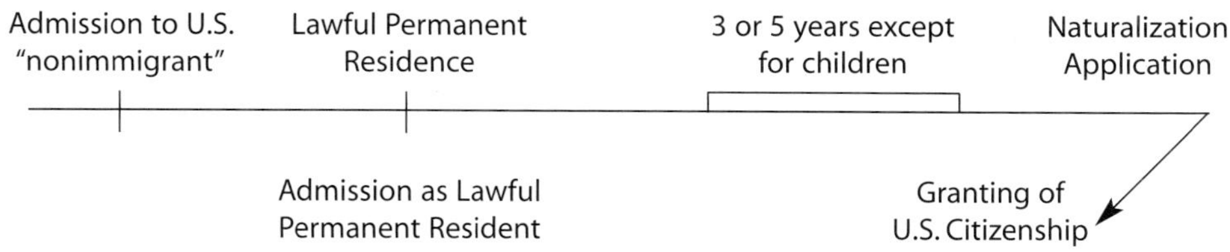

2. Denial of Naturalization and Denaturalization

Naturalization applications are initially submitted before USCIS and if denied, the applicant may seek *de novo* review in U.S. District Court [8 U.S.C. § 1421(c), Sec. 310(c)]. In many cases USCIS has failed to act promptly on naturalization applications, in which cases an action may lie in federal court under 8 U.S.C. § 1447(b), Sec. 336(b).

Denaturalization. Denaturalization begins by an action brought by the U.S. Attorney in the district where the person resides. The action is brought in the U.S. District Court. 8 U.S.C. § 1451(a), Sec. 340(a).

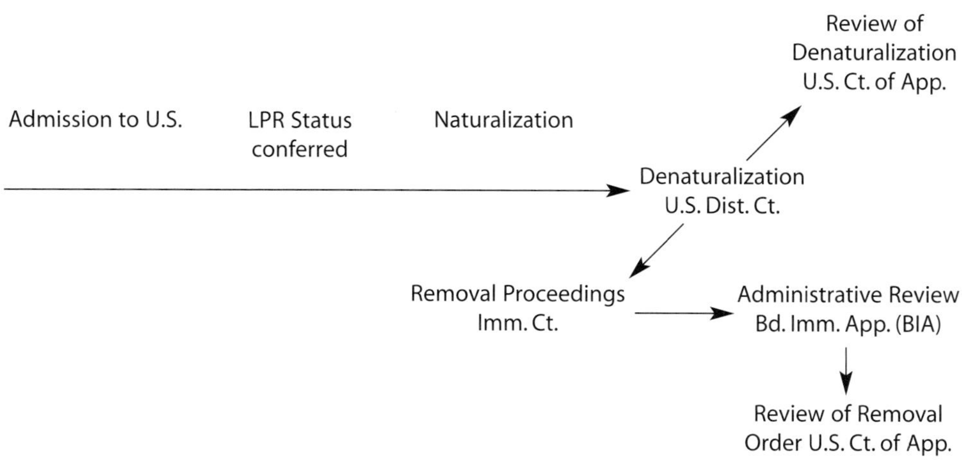

3. Loss of Nationality

Where a person has been denied a passport, or it has been revoked the matter can be reviewed administratively before the Board of Appellate Review at the Department of State (22 C.F.R. § 51.70). A person who is overseas or outside of the U.S. may seek admission where they are entitled to a hearing to establish their citizenship. If a passport request has been denied, or if a passport is cancelled the aggrieved party may seek declaratory judgment under 8 U.S.C. § 1503(a), Sec. 306(a). In addition to passport applications, a person may seek a certificate of citizenship, with review in federal district court under 8 U.S.C. § 1503, Sec. 360.

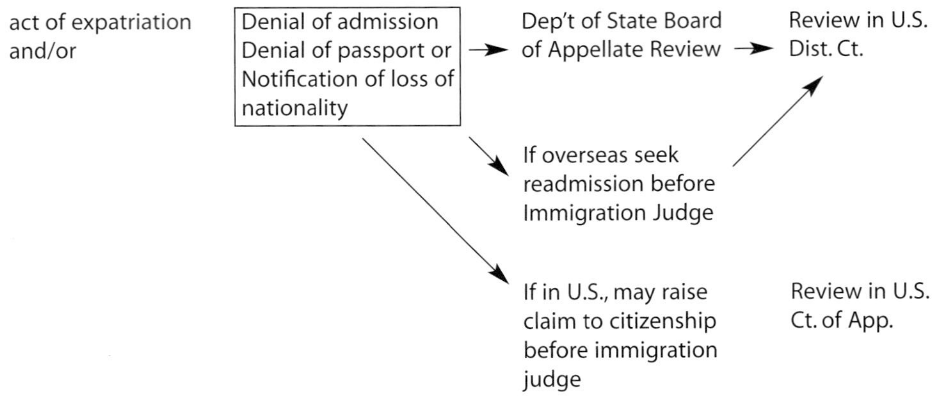

H. Problem Exercises

Exercise 1

A is a native of Country B. She is now a U.S. citizen having been naturalized 5 years ago. She originally obtained her permanent resident status approximately 10 years ago based on her marriage to C, who is a U.S. citizen. Presently she works for the World Bank in Washington, D.C. as an economist.

A learns that because non-U.S. citizen employees of the World Bank are exempt from state, local and federal taxes that her take home pay would be increased by more than 40% if she renounces her citizenship. In addition, non-U.S. citizen World Bank employees receive annual paid trips to their home country and free membership privileges at the World Bank Country Club in the suburbs of Washington, D.C. (Non-U.S. citizen employees of the World Bank enjoy "G" nonimmigrant visa status which is valid for as long as the person is an employee of the bank.) A comes to you because she would like to take advantage of the generous benefits offered by the bank and says that she would like to give up her U.S. citizenship. During the course of the interview, you learn that her husband is an undercover DEA agent working on the U.S.-Mexico border. A and C have two children, D and E—the children are respectfully 4 and 5 years of age.

What advice would you give her?

If she decides that she will go through with a renunciation, how would this be accomplished?

Exercise 2

A was born in Brownsville, Texas, on January 1, 1952, to B and C. His parents, B and C, are natives and citizens of Mexico. B and C become permanent residents but never naturalize, because at the time, Mexico did not recognize dual nationality and B and C were concerned about losing their family property.

When A reached his 18th birthday, B and C were concerned that he could be drafted into the U.S. army (the war in Vietnam was in full force, and college students were being drafted and called to serve) and encouraged A to renounce his U.S. citizenship and remain in Mexico to study at the public university. A completed the renunciation process before the U.S. Consul according to federal regulations in effect at the time. He studied at the UNAM (Universidad Nacional Autonoma de Mexico—The National Autonomous University) in Mexico City for four years.

Within a short while, A decided that he really didn't want to continue living in Mexico and returned to the U.S. at the age of 21. A was able to return and reenter the U.S.; he says that he was waved through by Border Patrol agents. He thinks the agents waved him through because he "looked" and sounded like he was an American and traveled back and forth and got to know a lot of the agents—A speaks with a Southwest Texas accent. In later years, A was able to travel to Mexico and reenter the US merely by showing his Texas issued driver license. He would carry a copy of his Texas birth certificate but doesn't recall ever having to show it.

A has settled into a "normal" life in Austin, Texas. He has developed a very successful business building homes. The company is one of the largest home builders in the region, and he now has over 100 employees in the Austin, Texas area. A comes to you for legal advice. A is married and his wife is a U.S. citizen. They have no children. Sadly, his wife is suffering from a terminal disease.

While in the past, A did not face any difficulties traveling back and forth to Mexico to visit family, he had to stop making these trips once the U.S. imposed mandatory passport rules requiring that all citizens returning from overseas trips have in their possession a valid U.S. passport. He comes to you for legal advice because he has heard that you are an expert in immigration law.

What if any questions would you want to ask of A?

What legal advice would you give to A regarding his citizenship status in the US?

Chapter 12

Administrative Appeals and Judicial Review

Introduction

Understanding the regulatory and statutory scheme for administrative appeals and judicial review of immigration decisions presents a challenge to both the inexperienced and seasoned practitioner. A careful inspection of the cases and statutes will reveal a number of important patterns which will help the student understand this difficult subject. The materials in this chapter are presented in a way that will give the reader a clear understanding of the jurisdiction of each of the decision-making bodies responsible for administering the immigration laws. The next step is to understand the jurisdiction of the federal courts and rules governing judicial review. As will be seen, because of the many agencies involved in matters relating to immigration law, the jurisdictional lines are sometimes difficult to follow. Consequently, our first task will be to explore some overarching principles governing the subject matter. Second we will examine the multi-layered agency review of the different types of cases that arise in immigration law, also identifying the types of decisions which are not subject to review. In the second section we will explore federal court jurisdiction and the scope of review in immigration cases.

The central theme running through the rules governing administrative and federal court review is the locus of the original determination which gives rise to the challenge. As will be seen, whether a matter is amenable to judicial review will depend on the nature of the decision. Similarly, the type of administrative review which may be sought will depend on the specific nature of the immigration relief and which agency had the power to grant it.[1] Therefore our discussion will begin with a review of the jurisdiction of the four federal agencies involved in immigration matters. Since the most complicated areas of administrative and judicial review involve appeals from decisions within different parts of DHS responsible for immigration matters, much of our discussion will concentrate on that agency.[2]

1. For example, whether the application was made before the Department of Labor, a consular officer or the USIA will determine both the administrative as well as judicial review which might be available.

2. Administrative review is governed by regulations promulgated by the head of the respective agency, which provide for appeals in clearly defined situations.

A. Administrative Review

As was noted earlier, there are many decisions which are made by government officials in matters relating to a person's efforts to obtain admission or remain in the U.S. In virtually all of these cases, the initial application is made before some U.S. government official. In some instances the decision by the government officer may be subject to review by another government official or an internal review body. This type of review is called "administrative review" and the rules governing these appeals will be set forth in regulations promulgated by the agency. Understanding the jurisdiction of these administrative review bodies is particularly important because there is a basic rule of administrative law that in order to be able to obtain judicial review a party must first exhaust all available administrative remedies.

1. The Department of State—Bureau of Consular Affairs, Exchange Visitor Waiver Review Board

As noted in previous chapters, there are three general areas in which agents of, or the Secretary herself may make decisions under the immigration and nationality laws. The first and broadest of these is where a consular officer determines whether a person is eligible for a visa.

The second type of case is those involving persons who come to the U.S. as exchange visitors with a J visa subject to the foreign residency requirement later seek to have the requirement waived. The third is where a decision is made as to whether the person who claims U.S. citizenship may be issued a passport.

Insofar as a person's admissibility to the U.S. as a visa applicant is concerned, neither the statute or the regulations contemplate any formal administrative review.[3] Further, decisions by consular officers are less likely to be challenged in the federal courts since they tend to occur outside of the U.S. far from the border. The only available review is an informal redress through the consular officer's supervisor or through a process known as an "advisory opinion."[4] The advisory opinion which is prepared in Washington at the Bureau of Consular Affairs is limited to legal issues and is not legally enforceable against a consular officer in court.[5] Persons who entered the U.S. as exchange visitors and are seeking a waiver of the 2 year foreign residency requirement may seek review of the denial of their request before the Exchange Visitor Waiver Review Board which is made up of officials within the United States Information Agency (USIA).[6] A decision involving the denial of U.S. passport or certificate

3. As will be seen later, for reasons of foreign policy and extraterritoriality, judicial review is very difficult to obtain for persons who are not in the United States or at the border. Moreover, courts have historically accorded the executive branch great deference in matters of foreign policy.

4. The Advisory Opinion section is within the Bureau of Consular Affairs of the Department of State.

5. *See generally* 22 C.F.R. §§ 41.121 and 42.81.

6. Review before the Board is allowed only in the following: (1) cases involving interested government agencies; (2) cases where the applicant has received a no objection letter from his own gov-

of citizenship must be based on the Bureau of Consular Affairs' assertion that the person is either not a U.S. citizen or under some type of travel restriction.[7] A person who has had any of these documents denied, revoked, invalidated or restricted may seek administrative review through the Board of Appellate Review of the Department of State.[8]

2. The Department of Labor — Board of Alien Labor Certification Appeals (BALCA)

As was seen earlier in our discussion of the employment-based immigrant visas and certain nonimmigrant visas, some individuals must obtain certification from the Secretary of Labor that the job that they are seeking in the U.S. will not displace U.S. workers. The administrative review of adverse decisions by the Department of Labor certifying officer is before the Board of Alien Labor Certification Appeals (BALCA). Appeals to the BALCA must be made by the sponsoring employer and the record will consist of the labor certification application and supporting documentation.[9] The appeal or a motion to reconsider must be filed within 35 days of the final determination.[10] Appeals are heard by a panel of 3 administrative law judges or the entire BALCA which consists of 13 judges.[11]

a. Procedural Flow Chart — Labor Certification Appeals

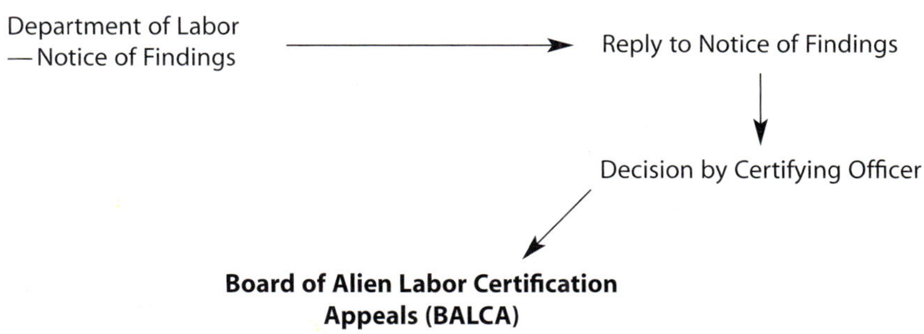

---

ernment; (3) cases involving a U.S. funded program which did not exceed $2,000; (4) where the applicant claimed persecution and the BHRHA gave an unfavorable recommendation; and (5) any case in which the waiver review board requests review. *See* 22 C.F.R. § 51.44(f).

7. Possession of a U.S. passport is prima facie evidence of U.S. citizenship and the refusal to issue such a document to a person who is trying to return to the U.S. is functionally equivalent to stripping the person of his citizenship.

8. *See* 22 C.F.R. §§ 51.70 and 51.71

9. 20 C.F.R. § 656.26(b)(4).

10. 20 C.F.R. § 656.26.

11. Because schedule "A" cases are not reviewed by the Department of Labor's certifying officer, denials are made by the USCIS and are therefore reviewed by the Administrative Appeals Office (AAO) discussed later.

3. Secretary of Health and Human Services—Public Health Service

In Chapter 3, we discussed the health grounds of inadmissibility. As was noted in that discussion, decisions involving the health grounds of inadmissibility are made by officers of the Public Health Service and are binding on ICE and USCIS.[12] These determinations which relate to inadmissibility of persons for psychological or health reasons are not routinely encountered and therefore will not be explored in detail here.[13]

4. The Department of Justice—Review by the Attorney General

Although the Secretary of Homeland Security is the primary official responsible for the enforcement of the immigration laws, large portions of the enforcement and some adjudicatory functions are overseen by immigration judges and also by the Board of Immigration Appeals. Board members as well as immigration judges are appointed by the Attorney General, and ultimate authority on legal interpretations rest with the Attorney General. It is also worth noting that the Department of Justice's Civil Division and U.S. Attorneys are responsible for defending the agencies' actions before the judiciary. This extensive authority of the Attorney General does not contemplate a formal and direct review to the Attorney General in all matters. At the same time, the Attorney General may occasionally assume jurisdiction over a case on her own or at the urging of an affected party.[14] Another method for obtaining review by the Attorney General is through "certification." A case may be certified to the Attorney General by the chairperson of the BIA, a majority of the BIA, or the Secretary of DHS and is provided for by regulation.[15] Whether and what type of judicial review may be obtained from a case which has been certified, will depend on the nature of the case, and whether or not the decision is construed as a "final order" of removal.[16]

---

12. *See* 8 U.S.C. § 1182(a)(1), Sec. 212(a)(1).

13. The review of these determinations is conducted before a panel of three doctors of the Public Health Service. The person who has been determined as falling within this category has the right to counsel and to present medical evidence by an independent doctor of her choice (at her own expense). *See* 42 C.F.R. §§ 34.4 and 34.14. Judicial review of these decisions may be obtained through the normal procedure available in removal proceedings. *See* discussion *infra.*

14. Since the Attorney General is vested with the power of administering the immigration laws, nothing precludes a party from seeking direct review in an appropriate case. However, since review by the Attorney General is not common, the case would have to be compelling and raise important policy issues. *Matter of Leon-Orosco & Rodriguez-Colas*, 19 I. & N. Dec. 136 (A.G. 1984).

15. 8 C.F.R. § 1003.1(h). The Attorney General's certification authority is limited to those matters within her jurisdiction, however, the regulations contemplate very broad authority. 8 C.F.R. § 1003.1(h)(iii).

16. "Final orders of removal" are defined at 8 U.S.C. § 1252(a), Sec. 242(a), and are discussed later in this chapter.

5. U.S. Citizenship and Immigration and Services (USCIS)—Administrative Appeals Office (AAO)

As was explained previously, the INA extends broad powers to government officials to make or review decisions under the immigration laws. Most cases are made initially by the INS district directors and are subject to administrative review at the USCIS central office at the Administrative Appeals Office (AAO). The AAO was originally created in 1983 and reorganized again in 1994 in an effort to expedite appeals and assure greater uniformity and consistency in decisionmaking.[17] The AAO has jurisdiction to review denials or revocations in the following cases:[18]

1. Breaching of bonds and forfeiture of collateral under 8 C.F.R. § 103.6.[19]

2. Employment-based preference petitions under 8 C.F.R. § 204.1(c), Hong Kong special immigrants, special immigrant juveniles or for entrepreneurs under 8 U.S.C. § 1153(b)(5), Sec. 203(b)(5), except when the denial of the petition is based upon lack of a certification by the Secretary of Labor under section 212(a)(5) of the Act.[20]

3. Indochinese refugee applications for adjustment of status under Section 103 of the Act of October 28, 1977.

4. Revocation of certain immigrant preference petitions or self-petitions under procedures set forth at 8 C.F.R. § 205.2. Revocation of nonimmigrant petition approvals.

5. Applications for permission to reapply for admission to the United States after a previous removal.[21]

---

17. 48 Fed. Reg. 43,160 (1983). The AAO was originally known as the Administrative Appeals Unit (AAU) and was created by transferring much of the jurisdiction originally held by INS Regional Commissioners within an office of the Associate Commissioner for Examinations. The only appeals which remain with Regional Commissioners is the power to review deferred action cases. These recommendations are initially made by the local ICE district director. 8 C.F.R. § 103.1(l). For a more extensive discussion of deferred action, see Charles Gordon, Stanley Mailman, Stephen Yale-Loehr & Ronald Wada, Immigration Law and Procedure § 72.03(h) (rev. 2017).

18. This is not a complete list of the cases which are reviewable by the AAO. For a more complete listing of the matters which are under the AAO's jurisdiction, see 8 C.F.R. §§ 103.3(a)(1) and 100.2(c)(3); former 8 C.F.R. § 103.1(f)(3).

19. A bond is breached when the person who has posted a bond either in lieu of being placed in custody or on condition of compliance with her status fails to comply with the obligation set forth in the bond agreement. The "breaching" of the bond is the first step in the INS' attempt to claim that the money posted has been forfeited.

20. As was discussed earlier, immigrants must establish entitlement to a "preference classification" in order to determine their position within the numerical quotas for persons seeking permanent residency in the U.S. A condition precedent to obtaining an employment based preference classification is an approved certification from the Secretary of Labor.

21. As was noted in our discussion in Chapter 3, a removal order prohibits the person from returning for a period of five years (if removal was initiated when the person arrived at the border) to ten years (in the case of proceedings instituted after the person's admission or physical entry). A summary removal order also carries a five year bar. Persons ordered "excluded" under prior law were inadmissible for only one year and those ordered "deported" were inadmissible for only five years. Under current law, a person ordered removed under "expedited" or summary removal is inadmissible for 5 years. 8 U.S.C. § 1182(a)(9)(A)(i), Sec. 212(a)(9)(A)(i). Persons ordered removed under normal re-

6. Applications for waiver of certain grounds of inadmissibility under 8 U.S.C. § 1182(h)(i), Sec. 212(h)(i).

7. Applications for waiver of the two-year foreign residence requirement for certain persons admitted to the U.S. as exchange students.[22]

8. Petitions to approve schools for attendance by foreign students as well as decisions by District Directors to withdraw school approvals under 8 C.F.R. § 214.1.

9. Petitions for temporary workers or trainees and fiancees or fiances of U.S. citizens seeking admission to the United States as nonimmigrants.[23]

10. Applications by permanent residents for reentry permits.[24]

11. Applications for issuance of refugee travel documents.

12. Adjustment of status of certain resident aliens to a nonimmigrant status under 8 C.F.R. § 247.12(b).

13. Applications to preserve residence for naturalization purposes under 8 C.F.R. § 316a.21(c).

14. Applications for Temporary Protected Status.

15. Petitions to classify certain Amerasians as the children of United States citizens.

16. Adjustment of status applications under the bona fide marriage exception to the 2 year foreign residency requirement where the marriage was entered into during the course of removal proceedings. *See* 8 U.S.C. § 1255(e), Sec. 245(e).

While AAO review is *de novo*, it does not have authority to rule on constitutional issues or to apply the doctrine of equitable estoppel in an individual case.[25] Generally, the party with standing to appeal is the petitioner not the beneficiary, and the appeal to the AAO must be filed within 30 days of the decision to the Regional Service Center.[26] Unlike other areas of administrative practice, since AAO review is not mandatory in all cases, the failure to appeal to the AAO is not subject to arguments under the exhaustion doctrine.[27]

---

moval proceedings after having been previously admitted are inadmissible for 10 years. 8 U.S.C. § 1182(a)(9)(A)(i), Sec. 212(a)(9)(A)(i). Persons removed for a second time are inadmissible for 20 years and those who are inadmissible on account of an aggravated felony are permanently barred. During these periods a person wishing to return to the U.S. must first obtain permission from the Attorney General. This permission to reapply for admission was discussed at Chapter 10.

22. One of the grounds prohibiting a person's change or "adjustment" of status is when the person was admitted into the U.S. with restrictions as an exchange alien (certain J-1 visas). Eligibility for "adjustment" or change of status requires prior approval from the Secretary of DHS following a recommendation by the Secretary of State. The review process for the J-1 visa holder is discussed at Chapter 10.

23. *See* Chapter 6.

24. Reentry permits are sought by lawful permanent residents who expect to remain outside of the U.S. for more than one year as a way of preserving their permanent resident status. The document allows the permanent resident to return during the period of the permit.

25. *Matter of Hernandez-Puente*, 20 I. & N. Dec. 335 (BIA 1991).

26. 8 C.F.R. §§ 103.3(a)(2)(i), 1103.3(a)(2)(i), 103.3(a)(1)(iii)(B), 1103.3(a)(1)(iii)(B).

27. 8 C.F.R. § 103.3(a)(1)(ii); *Olamide Olorunniyo v. Clinton*, 675 F. Supp. 2d 217, 222 (D. Mass. 2009).

The following flow chart presents the procedures followed in the above list of cases subject to appeal to the AAO. Note: cases involving a denial of an extension of stay as a nonimmigrant or change of nonimmigrant status is not subject to review by the AAO. In addition only the petitioner, not the beneficiary may appeal a decision.

a. Procedural Flow Chart—Administrative Review of USCIS Decisions

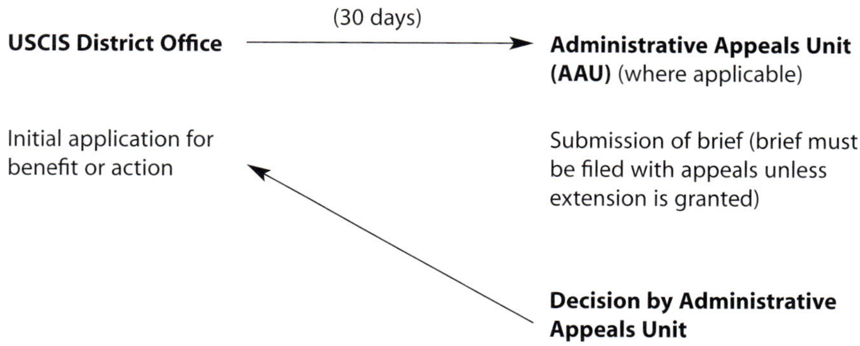

6. Office of the Chief Administrative Hearing Officer (OCAHO)

Earlier, we discussed the amendments to the Immigration and Nationality Act which established fines and other sanctions against employers who knowingly hired foreign workers without employment authorization or who failed to otherwise comply with the sanction provisions.[28] We also explored the legal remedies made available to persons who claimed that they were victims of "unfair immigration related employment practices." Employer sanctions and discrimination claims under the immigration laws are heard before a separate body of administrative law judges in the Office of the Chief Administrative Law Judge (OCAHO). These cases are heard initially by an administrative law judge and may be reviewed by the Chief Administrative Hearing Officer.[29] Judicial review is obtained by the aggrieved party's filing a petition for review within 45 days of the final order in the federal appellate court having jurisdiction over the place where the decision was made.[30]

7. Executive Office for Immigration Review—Board of Immigration Appeals and Immigration Judges

The Board of Immigration Appeals (BIA) is the body responsible for appeals from certain DHS and immigration judge decisions. The BIA is a regulatory and not a statu-

28. *See* Chapter 2.

29. There is no automatic appeal, but a party may seek review before the Chief Judge who may affirm, modify or vacate the previously issued order within 10 days. 28 C.F.R. § 68.54(a)(1). Interlocutory orders may be appealed within 30 days. 28 C.F.R. § 68.53(a).

30. The forty-five day period begins to run thirty days after the ALJ signs the order. 28 C.F.R. § 68.2(k).

tory creation and prior to 1983 the BIA was part of the INS. Amendments to the Code of Federal Regulations promulgated by the Attorney General in 1983, moved the BIA and immigration judges into a separate part of the Department of Justice called the Executive Office for Immigration Review (EOIR).[31] Immigration Judges have very limited jurisdiction to determine a person's admissibility or deportability in removal proceedings. The jurisdiction of the BIA is broader then immigration judges as the BIA reviews all IJ decisions as well as some other decisions of DHS district directors. The full range of cases which are reviewable by the BIA are set out at 8 C.F.R. § 1003.1(b). Below is a listing of the major areas of cases which fall within the Board's jurisdiction:

1. Decisions of immigration judges in removal proceedings, but not on the issue of the period of voluntary departure granted, or where an *in absentia* removal order was entered.[32]

2. Decisions on applications for cancellation of removal in the course of removal proceeding under 8 U.S.C. §§ 1229b(a) and (b), Sec. 240A(a) and (b).[33]

3. Decisions by district directors involving all family preferences and their revocation, but not the employment-based preferences or orphan petitions.[34]

4. Decisions by district directors on applications for the exercise of discretionary authority permitting the temporary admission of certain otherwise inadmissible nonimmigrants.

5. Decisions involving the imposition of administrative fines and penalties.

6. Decisions of immigration judges relating to bond or detention in cases of persons in removal proceedings except where they are seeking admission; and

7. Decisions of immigration judges regarding adjustment of status and rescission of adjustment of status.

The BIA's jurisdiction covers much of what is not encompassed within the AAO's jurisdiction. The BIA acts more like an administrative appeals court than does the AAO. Members of the Board are all lawyers, yet the AAO has many personnel who are not.

A case may reach the BIA on the Board's own certification,[35] or the commissioner or any other authorized DHS officers may certify the case if the Board could have had jurisdiction under 8 C.F.R. § 1003.1(b). A review of the above list demonstrates the difficulty in discerning a pattern for determining BIA reviewability. The cases in these materials begin with a case delineating the jurisdiction of the immigration

---

31. *See* 60 Interpreter Releases 155 (1983).

32. Included within its jurisdiction are cases under the predecessor statute involving exclusion and deportation cases.

33. This form of relief was formerly termed "212(c)" relief. Cancellation is available to long term permanent residents as well as persons who have resided illegally in the U.S. and are able to show a requisite level of hardship, and is discussed in Chapter 10.

34. The review of revocation cases only encompasses discretionary revocations, not for example automatic revocation, in the event of withdrawal or death of the petitioner.

35. *See* 8 C.F.R. § 3.1(c).

judge. As will be seen delineating the judge's jurisdiction is a significant aid in defining the limits of the Board's jurisdiction.[36]

The Board is not limited, as are appellate courts, to a determination of whether there exists substantial evidence in the record to support the immigration judge's findings. Generally when the BIA reviews cases it may make a *de novo* review of the record. On questions of law and fact and in exercising discretion, the Board may make an independent evaluation and arrive at its own decision.[37] However, like most administrative and judicial review bodies, the Board will defer to the immigration judge on questions of fact.

"Streamlining" of Administrative Appeals. In 2002, the Attorney General in effort designed to reduce the backlog of cases pending before the Board of Immigration Appeals instituted a program of accelerated adjudication of appeals. He later reduced the size of the Board. The streamlining measure provide for a single Board member to adjudicate cases without opinion.[38] The changes in both the composition of the Board of Immigration Appeals as well as the broader implications of limited administrative review have generated widespread criticism.[39]

a. Jurisdiction of the Immigration Judge

Matter of Roussis

18 I. & N. Dec. 256 (BIA 1982)

BY: Milhollan, Chairman; Maniatis, Dunne, Morris and Vacca, Board Members

In a decision dated February 1, 1982, an immigration judge granted the respondent's motion to reopen his deportation proceedings and to remand his case to the District Director for consideration of his application for adjustment of status under section 245 of the Immigration and Nationality Act, 8 U.S.C. § 1255. She then certified her decision to the Board for review pursuant to 8 C.F.R. § 3.1(c) and 8 C.F.R. § 242.8(a). The immigration judge's decision will be reversed.

---

36. Conversely, decisions made by district directors and not reviewable before an immigration judge can only be challenged in the U.S. district court.

37. While a creature of regulation and not a statutory body, the BIA's jurisdiction is quite extensive. For example, 8 C.F.R. § 3.1(d) provides that the Board shall exercise the discretion and authority conferred upon the Attorney General "as is appropriate and necessary for the disposition of the case." The Board reviews cases *de novo* and may even make new credibility findings or receive new evidence. *See, e.g., In re Villanova-Gonzalez,* 13 I. & N. Dec. 399, 403 (BIA 1969); *Cañas-Segovia v. INS,* 902 F.2d 717, 727 (9th Cir. 1990); *Platero-Cortez v. INS,* 804 F.2d 1127 (9th Cir. 1986). While making new credibility findings and receiving new evidence are not the Board's preferred method of fact adjudication, they are within its authority. *See In re Wong,* 12 I. & N. Dec. 417, 419 (BIA 1968).

38. Board of Immigration Appeals: Streamlining, 64 Fed. Reg. 56,135, 56,141 (Oct. 18, 1999).

39. Shruti Rana, *"Streamlining" the Rule of Law: How the Department of Justice is Undermining Judicial Review of Agency Action,* U. ILL. L. REV. 829 (2009); Jaya Ramji-Nogales, Andrew I. Schoenholtz & Philip G. Schrag, *Refugee Roulette: Disparities in Asylum Adjudication,* 60 STAN. L. REV. 295 (2007). *See also Benslimane v. Gonzales,* 430 F.3d 828, 830 (7th Cir. 2005); *Berishaj v. Ashcroft,* 378 F.3d 314, 331 (3d Cir. 2004); Pamela MacLean, *Immigration Bench Plagued by Flaws,* NAT'L L.J., Feb. 6, 2006, at 1.

The respondent, a 30-year-old native and citizen of Greece, was admitted to the United States on October 27, 1972, as a nonimmigrant student, authorized to remain until October 26, 1976. In deportation proceedings conducted on July 6, 1977, the respondent was found deportable as an overstay under section 241(a)(2) of the Act, 8 U.S.C. § 1251(a)(2), but was granted the privilege of voluntary departure in lieu of deportation.

On February 1, 1982, the immigration judge ordered the deportation proceedings reopened on the basis of an immediate relative visa petition which had been filed on the respondent's behalf by his United States citizen spouse.[40] Over the objection of the Immigration and Naturalization Service, she further ordered that the case be remanded to the District Director for adjudication of the respondent's adjustment application. She then certified her decision to us for review.

The precise issue presented is whether an immigration judge is authorized to remand a case involving a section 245 application to the District Director for adjudication notwithstanding the fact that an Order to Show Cause has been issued, deportation proceedings have begun, and the District Director objects to the remand order.

The immigration judge concluded that an order of remand to permit consideration by the District Director of an adjustment application, coupled with an order of conditional termination of the deportation proceedings, is a permissible exercise of her authority. Such procedure, she submits, promotes efficiency and the savings of resources for the District, the Immigration Court, the aliens and their representatives and, at the same time, does not contravene the applicable regulations. Moreover, she contends that "to deny to an alien the ability to move for a remand [a procedure available to the Service in certain circumstances pursuant to 8 C.F.R. 242.7] would unfairly favor the Service...."

* * *

For resolution of this question, reference must be made to provisions within the Code of Federal Regulations. The pattern set out in the code to govern the adjudication of applications for adjustment of status is quite clear. Pursuant to 8 C.F.R. 245.2(a)(1), "after an alien has been served with an Order to Show Cause or warrant of arrest, his application for adjustment of status under section 245 of the Act shall be made and considered only in proceedings under Part 242 of this Chapter."[41] It is evident then that the immigration judge is charged by regulation, which has the force of law, with the responsibility of accepting and adjudicating an application for section 245 relief if that application is submitted by an alien in deportation proceedings.

---

40. The respondent had already filed an earlier motion to reopen on August 27, 1977, in which he requested consideration of an adjustment application based upon a sixth preference petition. This motion was still pending when the immediate relative petition was substituted.

41. Section 242 governs the institution, conduct, and resolution of deportation proceedings. 18 I. & N. Dec. 256, Interim Decision (BIA) 2908.

The immigration judge acknowledges that 8 C.F.R. 245.2(a)(1) vests the immigration judge with exclusive jurisdiction to entertain adjustment applications, once an Order to Show Cause has been issued. It is her position, however, that nothing prevents the immigration judge from "ceding" that jurisdiction when practical and equitable considerations dictate. Thus, under the immigration judge's theory, the District Director could be forced to assume jurisdiction over a pending adjustment application simply because an immigration judge chooses to relinquish it. We do not believe that an issue as fundamental as jurisdiction is subject to ad hoc resolution, especially given the explicit mandate of the regulation in question.

Further, we agree with the Immigration and Naturalization Service that a sua sponte remand by an immigration judge impinges upon the District Director's exclusive authority to control the prosecution of deportable aliens. It has long been held that when enforcement officials of the Immigration and Naturalization Service choose to initiate proceedings against an alien and to prosecute those proceedings to a conclusion, the immigration judge is obligated to order deportation if the evidence supports a finding of deportability on the ground charged. Integral to a determination of whether an alien, although indisputably deportable, is to be ordered deported is whether or not he is eligible for any form of relief from deportation. See 8 C.F.R. 242.17. See *Lopez-Telles v. INS*, 564 F.2d 1302 (9 Cir.1977); *Guan Chow Tok v. INS*, 538 F.2d 36 (2 Cir.1976); *Matter of Merced*, 14 I & N. Dec. 644 (BIA 1974); *Matter of Geronimo*, 13 I & N. Dec. 680 (BIA 1971). See also *Matter of Chamizo*, 13 I & N. Dec. 435 (BIA 1969).

Aside from 8 C.F.R. 242.7, which authorized the District Director, in certain specified instances, to cancel an Order to Show Cause and thereby terminate proceedings prior to their commencement or to request dismissal or remand of a case after proceedings have begun, there is no provision in the regulations which authorizes the termination, whether conditional or final, of deportation proceedings. On the contrary, the regulations emphatically require the prompt completion of the deportation hearing if no action to terminate or remand is taken by the District Director. See 8 C.F.R. 242.7.

In conclusion, we find that the immigration judge's decision to grant the respondent's motion to remand and thereby conditionally divest herself of jurisdiction over his adjustment application is in clear derogation of the carefully defined jurisdictional scheme set out in the regulations pertaining to section 245. Further, the immigration judge's concern that an alien must be allowed to move for a remand of his adjustment application if the Service and the alien are to stand before her as equals is misplaced. While an alien is given the right to submit an application for relief under section 245, no authority of which we are aware suggests that he also has the right to dictate the procedures whereby his application is adjudicated.

Finally, we have noted the immigration judge's commendable interest in improving the efficiency of existing adjudicatory procedures. However, the fact remains that the suggested improvements are at variance with the applicable regulations. Thus, in the absence of regulatory amendment, we cannot sanction the procedures followed below.

Notes

1. *Matter of Roussis* highlights the peculiar jurisdiction of the immigration judge, who does not have authority to fully resolve cases presented to her. In addition to not having the authority over preference petitions, temporary protected status, deferred action and other immigration benefits for persons in removal proceedings, the immigration judge cannot grant parole or bond to a person seeking admission. As we will see later, these limitations will inform the available forms of judicial review.

2. While the immigration judge has the authority to set a person's release on bond in removal cases (where a person has been placed in proceedings after admission or entry), the power does not extend to the release of persons convicted of certain crimes or who are alleged to be terrorists.[42] Pursuant to a settlement agreement in a class action case, unaccompanied minors or juveniles may be released under certain conditions to approved agencies and to designated family members.[43] *See Reno v. Flores*, 507 U.S. 292 (1993) (upholding Constitutionality of unaccompanied minor policies); 8 C.F.R. § 236.3. Bond which is initially set by the district director may be appealed to the immigration judge within 10 days of release or at any time while the person is in custody. The respondent may seek an interlocutory review of the immigration judge's bond determination before the BIA.

b. Venue for the Removal Hearing

Matter of Rahman

20 I. & N. Dec. 480 (BIA 1992)

BY: Milhollan, Chairman; Dunne, Morris, Vacca, and Heilman, Board Members

On November 7, 1991, an immigration judge ordered that venue in this case be changed from Phoenix, Arizona, to Los Angeles, California. The Immigration and Naturalization Service has appealed. The appeal will be sustained, and the record will be remanded to the immigration judge.

This appeal is interlocutory. In order to avoid a piecemeal approach to the many issues that may arise in the course of an exclusion or deportation proceeding, this Board does not ordinarily entertain interlocutory appeals. See *Matter of Ruiz-Campuzano*, 17 I & N Dec. 108 (BIA 1979). However, we have on occasion ruled on the merits of an interlocutory appeal where we deemed it necessary to address important jurisdictional questions regarding the administration of the immigration laws, or to correct recurring problems in the handling of cases by immigration judges. See, e.g.,

---

42. Release of these persons is governed by rules issued by the Attorney General known as the Transitional Rules which were discussed in Chapter 4.

43. Stipulated settlement agreement, *Flores v. Reno*, No. 85-4544-RJK, ¶ 9 (C.D. Cal. Jan 19, 1997), available at https://www.aclu.org/files/pdfs/immigrants/flores_v_meese_agreement.pdf (last visited Dec. 31, 2017).

Matter of Guevara, Interim Decision 3143 (BIA 1990, 1991), and cases cited therein. In the instant case, the Service has shown the existence of many similar cases involving a recurring problem in the handling of certain motions to change venue in exclusion cases. We find consideration of this appeal appropriate.

The applicant in this case arrived at a port of entry to the United States in Los Angeles, California, on September 7, 1991, with an altered passport. He was issued a charging document, the Notice to Applicant for Admission Detained for Hearing Before Immigration Judge (Form 1-122), alleging that he had no valid entry documents, that he had committed fraud in an attempt to procure entry, and that he intended to enter the United States to perform labor without proper authorization.

In the judgment of the district director, there was insufficient detention space available to detain the applicant in the Los Angeles area. Therefore, the Service transferred the applicant and a number of others to a detention facility in Florence, Arizona, and filed the charging document with the Office of the Immigration Judge in Phoenix, Arizona.

Later, the applicant, through counsel, filed a motion to change venue to Los Angeles. The motion stated that the applicant's counsel of choice, his witnesses, and an interpreter would be available in Los Angeles, but not in Arizona. However, no witnesses were specified, nor was the nature of their possible testimony specifically indicated, nor was there any allegation that the applicant was unable to obtain counsel to represent him in Phoenix, Arizona. The motion did include an address in Los Angeles where the applicant could be reached, as the regulations required. 8 C.F.R. §3.19(c) (1991).[2] The address given, however, was simply that of the applicant's attorney. There was no evidence that the applicant himself had ever resided anywhere in the United States and there was apparently no specific indication of where he might reside if released. In any event, at the time of the motion, he was still detained in the custody of the Service.

The Service opposed the applicant's motion. Counsel for the Government argued that there was no good cause for the change of venue, and that granting the motion would require the Service either to transport the applicant, under guard, for hundreds of miles to his hearing and back again at considerable expense or, in the alternative, to release him on parole under 8 C.F.R. §212.5 (1991), with little or no assurance that he would later appear for his hearing. The Service presented specific evidence of prior cases in which similar changes of venue had been substantially prejudicial to the Government due to transportation and detention costs and the risk of flight from custody involved in such an operation.

However, the immigration judge granted the applicant's motion and, in a brief form order, ordered a change of venue to Los Angeles, "in order to permit respondent

2. This requirement is retained under newly revised regulations governing changes of venue. *See* 57 FED.REG. 11,568, 11,572 (1992) (to be codified at 8 C.F.R. §3.20) (interim Apr. 6, 1992).

[sic] to defend himself/herself in the area in which he/she resides." The Service represents that the immigration judge also stated his reasons orally as follows: "The Applicant landed at Los Angeles, has no connections at Florence, Arizona [the place of detention], and wants to go to Los Angeles."

On appeal, the Service argues that the immigration judge erred by changing venue in this case without a proper finding of good cause, where the Government had demonstrated that it would be prejudiced by such a change. We agree.

An immigration judge's discretion to change venue in both exclusion and deportation cases is subject to the existence of good cause for such a change. 57 Fed.Reg. 11,568, 11,572 (1992) (to be codified at 8 C.F.R. § 3.20) (interim Apr. 6, 1992) (an immigration judge may change venue for good cause only upon motion by one of the parties and only after the other party has been given notice and an opportunity to respond). Good cause is determined by balancing the factors we have found relevant to the venue issue. See *Matter of Rivera*, 19 I & N Dec. 688 (BIA 1988); *Matter of Velasquez*, 19 I & N Dec. 377 (BIA 1986) (relevant factors include administrative convenience, expeditious treatment of the case, location of witnesses, and cost of transporting witnesses or evidence to a new location); see also *Maldonado-Perez v. INS*, 865 F.2d 328 (D.C.Cir.1989); *La Franca v. INS*, 413 F.2d 686 (2d Cir.1969).

In the instant case, the immigration judge's order was perfunctory and showed no evaluation or balancing of the factors we have found relevant to a finding of good cause for a change of venue. We note that a brief statement of the reasons for an immigration judge's decision to grant or deny a change of venue over the objection of one of the parties would assist this Board in reviewing the decision and determining whether good cause exists. We have required such a statement in other contexts. See, e.g., *Matter of Correa*, 19 I & N Dec. 130 (BIA 1984) (immigration judge should state reasons for denial of motion to reopen to allow meaningful review by the Board); *Matter of Daryoush*, 18 I & N Dec. 352 (BIA 1982) (district director should provide reasons for bond determination to facilitate meaningful review). Here, no statement showing a balancing of the relevant factors was given, despite the Service's oral and written opposition to the motion and its showing of prejudice, as noted above. Upon review, we must conclude that no good cause for a change of venue existed.

Moreover, the reasons the immigration judge expressed for his order were not altogether appropriate under the circumstances. First, the place where an applicant happens to attempt to enter the United States, in and of itself, may have little, if any, significance to the question of where venue should lie in an exclusion proceeding. The alien cannot select a venue by deciding where to attempt to enter the United States. The venue question is rather entrusted in the first instance to the discretion of the district director, who files the charging document in the venue selected. *Matter of Victorino*, 18 I & N Dec. 259 (BIA 1982); 8 C.F.R. § 103.1(n)(1) (1992). Thereafter, the presiding immigration judge should not order a change of venue without a proper finding of good cause, as we have observed above.

Second, the immigration judge's order in this case focused upon the applicant's lack of connections to the place where he was detained. However, the question of where the applicant should be detained was not at issue. The issue upon a motion to change venue is rather where future hearings in the case shall take place. Accordingly, an order changing venue in a given case does not require the Service to change the place where the applicant is detained. The place of detention is a subject over which the immigration judge has no authority in an exclusion proceeding.[4]

Third, there was no evidence in this case that the applicant actually resided in Los Angeles, contrary to what the immigration judge's form order suggests. Moreover, while the factors commonly associated with the applicant's place of residence may be relevant to the question of proper venue, the mere fact that an applicant allegedly resides or wishes to reside in another city, without a showing of other significant factors associated with such residence, is insufficient cause to outweigh the Service's opposition to a motion for change of venue, particularly where the Service has demonstrated that it would be prejudiced by such a change. See *Matter of Rivera, supra*; cf. *Chlomos v. INS*, 516 F.2d 310 (3d Cir.1975) (deportation proceedings; residence already established prior to arrest).

Finally, there is no specific evidence in this case that the applicant himself would be prejudiced by proceeding with his hearing in Phoenix, Arizona. He argued, through counsel, that his counsel of choice and an interpreter would not be available in Phoenix. However, there is no evidence of any longstanding attorney-client relationship here, nor is there any persuasive evidence that the applicant could not have retained counsel and made arrangements for an interpreter to assist him in Phoenix. As the Service points out, Phoenix is a metropolitan area of about 2 million residents, with an experienced immigration bar. The Government is not required to accommodate the applicant's choice of a distant attorney and his acquisition of an interpreter by changing venue at considerable expense, especially where there is no showing that local counsel is unavailable or that an interpreter cannot otherwise be obtained. See section 292 of the Act, 8 U.S.C. § 1362 (1988) (alien may select attorney of choice, but at no expense to the Government); see also *El Rescate Legal Services v. EOIR*, ___ F.2d ___, No. 90-55292 (9th Cir. Mar. 10, 1992) (interpreters). We note that for purposes of the hearing itself, interpreters are provided by the Government. See *Matter of Exilus*, 18 I & N Dec. 276 (BIA 1982).

In view of the foregoing, the interlocutory appeal will be sustained.

---

4. The immigration judge can change the venue of the hearing in cases where the alien is detained. *Matter of Dobere*, Interim Decision 3133 (BIA 1990). However, the place of detention is a separate question entrusted to the sound discretion of the Service, the agency explicitly charged with the statutory duty to control and guard the boundaries of the United States. *See* section 103(a) of the Act, 8 U.S.C. § 1103(a) (1988); *see also* 8 C.F.R. §§ 212.5, 235.3(b) (1992); *Sasso v. Milhollan*, 735 F. Supp. 1045 (S.D. Fla. 1990).

Notes

1. While ICE sets venue by initiating proceedings at a particular location, it cannot change venue *sua sponte* by simply moving a person who has been detained. However, the respondent who challenges a case where venue has been changed without proper notice must be able to show prejudice in order to obtain a reversal of the removal order. *Jian v. INS*, 28 F.3d 256, 258–59 (2d Cir. 1994).

2. Additional factors to be considered in seeking a change of venue have included the nature of the evidence available in the place where venue was to be changed and its importance to the claim as well as prior continuances granted in the case. *Campos v. Nail*, 43 F.3d 1285 (9th Cir. 1994) (immigration judge had a personal policy of denying venue change to Salvadoran and Guatemalan asylum seekers).

3. The filing of a change of venue motion, until granted does not remove the requirement of appearance at the original place for the hearing. A person's failure to appear could cause an *in absentia* order to be entered. *Hernandez-Vivas v. INS*, 23 F.3d 1557 (9th Cir. 1994). If an *in absentia* order is entered there is no direct appeal to the BIA, the only remedy is to file a motion to reopen and then to appeal the denial of the motion to the BIA. 8 U.S.C. 1229a(b)(5)(C), Sec. 240(b)(5)(C).

4. **Interlocutory Review by the BIA**. As was pointed out by the BIA, interlocutory review is rarely granted and is only possible where a significant issue is raised that impacts on the administration of the immigration laws. *Matter of M-D-*, 24 I. & N. Dec. 138 (BIA 2007).

c. Motions to Reopen and Motions to Reconsider

In re H-A-

22 I. & N. Dec. 728 (BIA 1999)

Before: Board En Banc: Dunne, Vice Chairman; Vacca, Heilman, Filppu, Cole, Mathon, Jones, Grant, and Scialabba, Board Members. Dissenting Opinion: Villageliu, Board Member, joined by Schmidt, Chairman; Holmes, Hurwitz, Rosenberg, Guendelsburger, and Moscato, Board Members.

Scialabba, Board Member:

This case was last before us on April 17, 1997, when we denied the respondent's motion to reopen filed on September 25, 1996, for the purpose of applying for adjustment of status under section 245(i) of the Immigration and Nationality Act, 8 U.S.C. § 1255(i) (1994 & Supp. II 1996). The motion to reopen was denied because the visa petition filed on the respondent's behalf had not yet been approved. The respondent has submitted a motion to reconsider our April 17, 1997, denial of his motion and has also submitted a "Supplement to Motion to Reconsider" based on the fact that the immediate relative visa petition filed on his behalf was subsequently approved. We construe the respondent's May 20, 1998, "supplement" to be a motion to reopen because he has presented evidence that was previously unavailable. Such motion is both time and number barred under 8 C.F.R. § 3.2(c)(2) (1999). The respondent's motion to reconsider our April 17, 1997, decision will be denied.

The respondent is a 37-year-old male native and citizen of Sudan who entered the United States on January 26, 1990, as a nonimmigrant authorized to stay for 6 months. He overstayed his visa. The Immigration and Naturalization Service issued him an Order to Show Cause and Notice of Hearing (Form I-221) on June 24, 1993. The respondent filed an asylum application with the Immigration Court, which was denied on January 31, 1994. The Immigration Judge did, however, grant the respondent voluntary departure until March 7, 1994. The respondent appealed the Immigration Judge's decision to deny asylum. While the appeal was pending with this Board, the respondent married a United States citizen on July 27, 1994.

We dismissed the respondent's appeal on September 7, 1995, but gave him 30 days from the date of our order to voluntarily depart the United States. On September 18, 1996, nearly a year after the respondent's voluntary departure period ended and over 2 years after the couple were married, the respondent's spouse filed a Petition for Alien Relative (Form I-130) on his behalf with the Service. The respondent also filed an application to adjust his status with the Service on the same day. One week later, on September 25, 1996, the respondent filed with this Board a motion to reopen his deportation proceedings so that he could apply for adjustment of status. The Service did not file an opposition to the motion. Because the visa petition had been filed only a week earlier, the Service had not yet adjudicated it when the respondent filed his motion to reopen. We denied the respondent's motion on April 17, 1997, in accordance with *Matter of Arthur*, 20 I&N Dec. 475 (BIA 1992), which requires an approved immediate relative visa petition before a case may be reopened for adjustment of status. In Matter of Arthur, supra, we determined that we will not grant motions to reopen for the consideration of adjustment applications based upon unadjudicated visa petitions which fall within the ambit of sections 204(g) and 245(e) of the Act, 8 U.S.C. §§ 1154(g) and 1255(e) (Supp. II 1990), as discussed more fully infra.

On May 16, 1997, the respondent filed a timely motion to reconsider our April 17, 1997, decision denying his motion to reopen. See 8 C.F.R. § 3.2(b)(2) (1997). In the motion to reconsider, the respondent, through counsel, argues that the Board should revisit its decision in Matter of Arthur, supra, because it is inconsistent with the new motions regulations, which permit only one motion to reopen to be filed no later than 90 days after the final administrative decision. See 8 C.F.R. § 3.2(c)(2) (effective July 1, 1996). The respondent's motion to reconsider is based on the dissenting opinion that was part of our April 17, 1997, decision. The respondent contends that we should provide an exception to the Arthur rule because it is now inconsistent with due process, in light of the motions regulations. He argues that if we continue to apply Matter of Arthur without exception, we will be effectively foreclosing adjustment of status to eligible aliens because the motions regulations do not provide sufficient time for the visa petition adjudication process to be completed before the deadline for filing a motion to reopen expires.

* * *

In *Matter of Arthur, supra*, we modified our decision in *Matter of Garcia*, 16 I&N Dec. 653 (BIA 1978), based on Congress' 1986 enactment of the IMFA. Congress saw immigration-related marriage fraud as a serious problem and passed legislation designed to deter fraud by aliens seeking to acquire lawful permanent residence in the United States through marriage to a United States citizen or a lawful permanent resident alien. Section 5 of the IMFA provides, regarding an alien's right to enter or remain the United States, that if the alien marries while an administrative or judicial proceeding is pending, he or she may not use that marriage as a basis for adjustment of status or to gain immediate relative or preference status. See H.R. Rep. No. 99-906, at 11 (1986), reprinted in 1986 U.S.C.C.A.N. 5978, 5983; see also sections 204(g), 245(e)(1) of the Act.

In 1990, Congress amended the IMFA by creating a bona fide marriage exception. In section 702 of the IMMACT 90, 104 Stat. at 5086, Congress enacted a provision that allows an alien to overcome the marriage fraud presumption, but only if he or she is able to demonstrate by clear and convincing evidence the bona fides of the marriage. This provision also limits an alien to one administrative review in order to promote finality. See H.R. Rep. No. 101-723(I), at 51–52 (1990), reprinted in 1990 U.S.C.C.A.N. 6710, 6731–32.

It was within this framework that we issued our decision in *Matter of Arthur, supra*. In *Matter of Arthur*, we stated that the presumption established in *Matter of Garcia, supra*, was inconsistent and incompatible with the congressionally mandated presumption that marriages entered into after the institution of proceedings are fraudulent. *Matter of Arthur, supra*, at 479. We held that motions to reopen for adjustment of status based upon unadjudicated visa petitions which fall within the ambit of sections 204(g) and 245(e) of the Act will not be granted.

In section 545(d) of the IMMACT 90, 104 Stat. at 5066, Congress also addressed the problem of successive and frivolous administrative motions. See *Stone v. INS*, 514 U.S. 386, 400 (1995) ("(A) principal purpose of the 1990 amendments to the INA was to ... redress the related problem of successive and frivolous administrative appeals and motions."). Congress directed the Attorney General to issue regulations limiting the number of motions to reopen and the maximum time period during which a motion to reopen may be submitted. See H.R. Conf. Rep. No. 101-955, at 133 (1990), reprinted in 1990 U.S.C.C.A.N. 6784, 6798. In fact, the restrictions Congress had in mind were much more restrictive than those eventually issued by the Attorney General. "Unless the Attorney General finds reasonable evidence to the contrary, the regulations should state that such motions be made within 20 days of the date of the final determination...." *Id.*

Pursuant to the congressional mandate, the Attorney General revised the reopening regulations, effective July 1, 1996. Subject to certain exceptions, a party may file only one motion to reopen and it must be filed within 90 days of the final administrative decision, or on or before September 30, 1996, whichever is later. See 8 C.F.R. §§ 3.2(c)(2), 3.23(b)(4)(i) (1997); *Matter of J-J-*, Interim Decision 3323 (BIA 1997) (holding that reopening sua sponte is limited to exceptional circumstances and is not meant to cure filing defects or circumvent the regulations to prevent hardship).

While the Attorney General was in the process of revising the motion to reopen regulations, Congress codified the motions restrictions in section 304(a)(3) of the Illegal Immigration Reform and Immigrant Responsibility Act of 1996, Division C of Pub. L. No. 104-208, 110 Stat. 3009-546, 3009-593 ("IIRIRA"). This sent a clear message that Congress wanted an end to successive and frivolous motions to achieve finality in removal cases. See sections 240(c)(5), (6) of the Act, 8 U.S.C. §§ 1229a(c)(5), (6) (Supp. II 1996); see also Removal of Criminal and Illegal Aliens: Hearing before the Subcomm. on Immigration and Claims of the House Comm. on the Judiciary, 104th Cong., 1st Sess. 2 (Mar. 23, 1995) (statement of Hon. Lamar Smith, Subcomm. Chairman) (aliens "often file ... dilatory procedural motions ... in an effort to extend their stay and become eligible for relief. The time clock should stop when people are put in proceedings, and we must stop the abuse of this system to delay deportation.").

Contrary to the respondent's contention, we do not find an inconsistency between our holding in *Matter of Arthur, supra*, which is based on the IMFA, and the motions restrictions. The purpose of the IMFA is to deter immigration-related marriage fraud. The purpose of the motions regulations is to bring finality to administrative proceedings. These goals are distinct and separate [and] are in no way inconsistent. After examining Congress' activity and inactivity with these two matters, we see no need either to modify the Arthur rule or to create an exception to the motions regulations for aliens with unadjudicated immediate relative visa petitions, for two reasons. First, within the IMMACT 90, Congress both created the bona fide marriage exception and mandated that the Attorney General issue motions restrictions that include an exception for asylum claims arising from changed country conditions. In contemporaneously considering these two issues of marriage fraud and motions restrictions in 1990, Congress chose not to mandate an additional motions exception for marriage fraud cases.

Second, after we issued our 1992 holding in *Matter of Arthur*, Congress codified the motions restrictions in the IIRIRA in 1996. While Congress specifically included a time limit exception for asylum applicants based on changed country conditions, it did not create an exception for aliens who fall within the ambit of the *Arthur* rule and the 90-day motion deadline. Thus, Congress had two opportunities to amend the marriage fraud presumption or to create an additional exception to the restrictions for marriage fraud cases, but it declined to do either in both 1990 and 1996. The Supreme Court assumes that Congress is aware of existing law when it passes legislation. *South Dakota v. Yankton Sioux Tribe*, ___ U.S. ___, 118 S. Ct. 789, 801 (1998). We can therefore assume that Congress was aware of our holding in *Matter of Arthur* when it chose not to modify the marriage fraud presumption or to create an *Arthur* exception to the motions restrictions in the IIRIRA. Based on Congress' inactivity, we decline to modify the *Arthur* rule or to create an additional motions exception.

Furthermore, while there is now statutory authority for motions in removal cases, the authority for motions to reopen deportation proceedings is derived solely from regulations promulgated by the Attorney General. *INS v. Doherty*, 502 U.S. 314, 315 (1992); *INS v. Rios-Pineda*, 471 U.S. 444, 446 (1985). Any decision to grant a motion to reopen deportation proceedings is a matter within the discretion of this Board. See *INS v. Rios-Pineda, supra*, at 449; *INS v. Phinpathya*, 464 U.S. 183, 188 n.6 (1984). It is within this Board's discretion to determine that, in light of the marriage fraud presumption, visa petitions based on marriages entered into during proceedings must be approved before we will consider a motion to reopen for adjustment on that basis.

* * *

With respect to this particular case, we find that the respondent is not a victim of the motions regulations as he claims. The respondent was married for over a year before this Board issued a final order, which granted him 30 days to voluntarily depart the United States. If the respondent's wife had filed a visa petition in a timely manner, there is a very good possibility that the petition would have been adjudicated before this Board issued its final order. Furthermore, the respondent could have voluntarily departed the United States and pursued his immigrant visa abroad. However, the respondent chose not to depart the United States, and his spouse did not file a visa petition on his behalf until September 18, 1996, 2 years after the couple were married and 1 year after the respondent's voluntary departure period ended. One week later, on September 25, 1996, which was shortly before the September 30, 1996, motion deadline, the respondent filed his motion to reopen. It is not surprising that, when the respondent filed his motion 7 days after he filed the visa petition, the petition remained unadjudicated. This is the type of delay and dilatory tactics that Congress sought to halt in 1990 and again in 1996, in codifying the motions restrictions in section 304(a)(3) of the IIRIRA.

* * *

Dissenting Opinion: Gustavo D. Villageliu, Board Member, in which Paul W. Schmidt, Chairman; David B. Holmes, Gerald S. Hurwitz, Lory D. Rosenberg, John Guendelsberger, and Anthony C. Moscato, Board Members, join

I respectfully dissent from the denial of the respondent's motion to reconsider our denial of his motion to reopen seeking adjustment of status. The respondent is the husband and father of United States citizens and the beneficiary of an approved immediate relative visa petition. We should not as a matter of policy deprive him of his statutory right to apply for adjustment of status.

The majority inappropriately links legislation designed to end marriage fraud with general congressional intent to bring immigration cases to a close in order to preclude aliens eligible to adjust their status from the opportunity to do so. In so doing, the majority recognizes that certain aliens "will obviously run the risk of having to complete the immigration process from outside the country." *Matter of H-A-*, Interim Decision 3394, at 11 (BIA 1999). The majority reaffirms its 1992 policy of denying reopening to adjustment of status applicants with pending immediate relative visa petitions despite the fact that the 90-day period now prescribed for seeking reopening is often too short for the Immigration and Naturalization Service to adjudicate the visa petition. It compounds this mistaken policy by refusing to reconsider it or reopen when the Service finally approved the respondent's visa petition after we denied the original motion.

This harsh policy does not accomplish the congressional goal of bringing immigration cases properly to a close and does nothing to end marriage fraud. Instead, as a matter of course, the immigration of qualified spouses of United States citizens will be unduly delayed; the consular offices outside of the United States will be encumbered with applications more easily adjudicated in the United States; and this delay will cause needless hardship to the United States citizens whose bona fide marriages and families may disintegrate because their spouses will be deported and, as the majority dictates, be required to "complete the immigration process from outside the country." *Id.* The majority's policy is neither legally correct nor justified, as discussed below.

The respondent is a native and citizen of Sudan who came to the United States seeking asylum from his country, which has been designated for Temporary Protected Status due to its dangerous civil war and brutal regime. See 62 Fed. Reg. 59,737 (1997); cf. 63 Fed. Reg. 59,337 (1998) (extension of Temporary Protected Status); 1 Committees on Foreign Relations and International Relations, 106th Cong., 1st Sess., Country Reports on Human Rights Practices for 1998 392 (Joint Comm. Print 1999). His appeal from a denial of asylum was dismissed on September 7, 1995. On July 27, 1994, the respondent married a United States citizen who filed a visa petition on his behalf on September 18, 1996. Simultaneously with the visa petition, the respondent filed an Application to Register Permanent Residence or Adjust Status (Form I-485) in accordance with C.F.R. § 245.2(a)(2)(i) (1996).

On September 25, 1996, the respondent submitted a motion to reopen seeking adjustment of status. The motion was accompanied by the July 27, 1994, certificate of marriage; the couple's birth certificates; a copy of an immediate relative visa petition on Form I-130 (Petition for Alien Relative), filed on the respondent's behalf by his United States citizen spouse; their United States citizen child's birth certificate; and documents similarly evidencing the bona fides of the marriage, such as joint income tax returns, bank statements, a residential lease, a telephone bill, and a cable television bill. Finally, the motion included the application for adjustment of status, Biographic Information Sheets (Form G-325A), a fingerprint chart, and the fee receipt, as required by 8 C.F.R. § 3.2(c)(1) (1997). The Service did not oppose the motion. See 8 C.F.R. § 3.2(g)(3).

However, the Service had not adjudicated the underlying immediate relative visa petition prior to the September 30, 1996, deadline for filing such a motion. Accordingly, on April 17, 1997, we denied the motion under the policy set forth in *Matter of Arthur*, 20 I&N Dec. 475 (BIA 1992), modifying *Matter of Garcia*, 16 I&N Dec. 653 (BIA 1978), which requires prior Service approval of marital visa petitions before reopening for adjustment of status cases subject to the marriage fraud provisions of sections 204(g) and 245(e) of the Immigration and Nationality Act, 8 U.S.C. §§ 1154(g) and 1255(e) (1994 & Supp. II 1996).

On May 16, 1997, the respondent filed a timely motion to reconsider our April 17, 1997, decision, also unopposed by the Service, arguing that we should reconsider *Matter of Arthur*, supra, because it is inconsistent with the new motions regulations, effective July 1, 1996, which permit only one motion to reopen to be filed and imposes a 90-day time limit to do so. See 8 C.F.R. § 3.2(c)(2) (1999). On January 13, 1998, the Service approved the respondent's visa petition as an immediate relative of a United States citizen.

* * *

I believe that by refusing to reconsider or grant the motion, the majority, in effect, turns the rebuttable presumption that the marriage of an alien in proceedings is fraudulent into an irrebuttable presumption inconsistent with the 1990 congressional directive to provide the spouse of a United States citizen with an administrative process by which he can seek adjustment of status if he proves that this marriage is bona fide when the Service does not adjudicate the visa petition within 90 days.

* * *

The majority's analysis confuses the district director's ultimate determination in adjudicating visa petitions that a marriage is bona fide for purposes of adjustment of status with the preliminary determination by the Board and the Immigration Judge that the marriage is prima facie bona fide and that a hearing should be allowed to consider the merits of the application. There is no conflict between our concluding that a marriage appears bona fide for purposes of granting a hearing and the district director's ultimate determination of the visa petition.

The majority's assertion, that since Congress is presumed to be aware of the *Arthur* rule its inaction means its approval, is a fallacy. In fact, Congress had already acted by prescribing in 1990 that the presumption was rebuttable, and the marriage fraud regulations, as explained below, specifically prescribe an administrative determination in the adjustment of status process. What Congress could not anticipate is that the majority would interpret its regulations to preclude the adjustment of status forum for eligible applicants. In any event, the recent congressional extension of the availability of section 245(i) relief to beneficiaries of visa petitions filed before January 14, 1998, suggests that Congress prefers that we adjudicate the respondent's prima facie approvable application.

It is the Board and the Immigration Judges that bear the responsibility to determine whether an alien in deportation proceedings may pursue an application for adjustment of status based on a bona fide marriage. See section 245(e)(3) of the Act; 8 C.F.R. §§ 204.2(a)(1)(iii)(D), 245.1(c)(9)(vii) (1999). We must determine the applicant's prima facie eligibility for adjustment of status under a clear and convincing evidence standard in accordance with 8 C.F.R. § 245.1(c)(9)(iii)(F), as we consider the only motion to reopen allowed by regulation. See 8 C.F.R. § 3.2(c)(2).

We need only decide that there is a reasonable likelihood that the statutory requirements for the relief sought will be satisfied. *INS v. Abudu*, 485 U.S. 94 (1988); *INS v. Jong Ha Wong*, 450 U.S. 139 (1981) (per curiam); *Matter of Coelho*, 20 I&N Dec. 464 (BIA 1992). Regulations issued subsequent to the Board's decision in *Matter of Arthur* provide an adequate framework to consider the respondent's assertion that his marriage is a bona fide marriage. See 8 C.F.R. § 204.2(a)(1)(iii)(B) (listing evidence to be relied upon to meet the bona fide marriage exemption to the marriage fraud provisions in sections 204(g) and 245(e) of the Act; see also 8 C.F.R. § 245.2(a)(2)(i) (instructing that adjustment applications are to be retained when filed simultaneously with immediate relative visa petitions).

A review of the legal background relating to the *Arthur* rule shows that it is no longer justified. A motion to reopen for adjustment of status requires a prima facie showing of eligibility for such relief, including immediate visa availability. As a result of a 1976 amendment to section 245 of the Act, the regulations permit filing an adjustment application simultaneously with a visa petition, where the approval of the petition would make an immigrant visa immediately available. See 8 C.F.R. § 245.2(a)(2) (1978); *Matter of Garcia, supra*, at 654–55.

Prior to the 1976 amendment to section 245, visa availability was only required when the application for adjustment of status was approved. However, effective January 1, 1977, visa availability was required when the adjustment application was filed. Consequently, 8 C.F.R. § 245.2(a)(2) was amended to require immediate visa availability upon filing. See 41 Fed. Reg. 49,994 (November 12, 1976). As a result, the Board issued two precedent decisions addressing these changes. *Matter of Garcia, supra*; and *Matter of Kotte*, 16 I&N Dec. 449 (BIA 1978).

Matter of Garcia, supra, addressed adjustment applications simultaneously filed with the marital visa petition because there was immediate visa availability. *Matter of Kotte, supra*, in contrast, addressed applications for adjustment of status that could not be simultaneously filed because to file for third-preference status required prior approval by the United States Department of Labor of a labor certification. We ruled that 8 C.F.R. § 245.2(a)(2) did not require holding in abeyance pending deportation proceedings until the employment preference visa petition was adjudicated. *Id.* at 452; accord *Matter of Ficalora*, 11 I&N Dec. 592 (BIA 1966) (sixth preference); *Matter of M-*, 5 I&N Dec. 622 (BIA 1954) (ineligible nonimmigrant seaman overstay). Whether an alien qualified for third-preference status was solely within the exclusive jurisdiction of the district director, and an appeal from a denial was solely before the Service's Regional Commissioner under 8 C.F.R. §§ 103.1(m)(2) and (n) (1978), and specifically outside our appellate jurisdiction pursuant to 8 C.F.R. § 3.1(b)(5) (1978). *Matter of Kotte, supra*, at 452; cf. 8 C.F.R. § 3.1(b)(5) (Board appellate jurisdiction over most familial visa petitions). The remedy was to move to reopen once the third-preference visa petition was approved. *Matter of Kotte, supra*, at 452, and cases cited therein. The recently promulgated one-time and 90-day limits upon motions to reopen prescribed by 8 C.F.R. § 3.2(c)(2) no longer allow this remedy.

Matter of Garcia, supra, addressed, instead, applications simultaneously filed with immediate relative visa petitions. See *Matter of Guiragossian*, 17 I&N Dec. 161, 164 n.5 (BIA 1979); *Matter of Yodying*, 17 I&N Dec. 155 (BIA 1979). If the visa petition is subsequently approved, the adjustment application is deemed to have been properly filed with the accompanying petition. *Matter of Garcia, supra*, at 654–55. Since the date an adjustment application is filed determines whether a visa is immediately available, and the regulation allows a qualified applicant to preserve immediate visa availability, we decided that absent clear ineligibility, a motion to reopen should generally be granted for adjustment applications supported by simultaneously filed visa petitions with immediate visa availability. *Id.* at 657. A pending prima facie approvable visa petition would be treated as though it were already approved for purposes of reopening.

The Immigration Marriage Fraud Amendments of 1986, Pub. L. No. 99-639, 100 Stat. 3537, prohibited approval of visa petitions and adjustment applications based on marriages entered into while an alien was in proceedings. Thus, the rules prescribed in our decision in *Matter of Garcia, supra*, for purposes of reopening by beneficiaries of pending marital visa petitions, had no consequence after the 1986 Marriage Fraud Amendments were enacted. However, when Congress again amended the statute in 1990 to allow approval of such visa petitions and adjustment applications if the alien established by clear and convincing evidence that the marriage was bona fide, we had to devise a new policy regarding motions to reopen with visa petitions based on bona fide marriages entered into while in expulsion proceedings. We did not have to then consider the effect of the one-time and 90-day limitations which became effective 6 years later.

Under the amended statute, a marriage entered into while an alien was in proceedings was deemed presumptively fraudulent, the presumption was rebuttable by a showing of clear and convincing evidence that the marriage was entered into in good faith, and Congress expressed a legislative intent that aliens marrying after proceedings are initiated should be given an opportunity to present for administrative review such clear and convincing evidence that their marriage was bona fide. See H.R. Conf. Rep. No. 101-955, 101 at 128 (1990), reprinted in 1990 U.S.C.C.A.N. 6784, 6793. Because we perceived potential jurisdictional problems with the district director's primary role of adjudicating visa petitions, we held as a matter of policy that we would "hereafter decline to grant motions to reopen" where the alien married a United States citizen or lawful permanent resident while the alien's proceedings were pending until the Service approved the marital visa petition filed on the alien's behalf. *Matter of Arthur, supra*, at 479.

The subsequently enacted regulations prescribing procedures for bona fide marriage adjudications avoid such jurisdictional problems, and require that we provide a forum for adjustment applicants with bona fide marriages. The regulations at 8 C.F.R. §§245.1(c)(9)(iii)(F) and (iv) confer jurisdiction on the Immigration Court to at least consider prima facie evidence of a bona fide marriage for purposes of reopening. The regulation at 8 C.F.R. §245.1(c)(9)(iii)(F) specifically states that the prohibition against adjustment of status on the basis of a marriage while in deportation proceedings does not apply if the alien establishes that the marriage is bona fide by providing clear and convincing evidence that the marriage was entered into in good faith. The regulation at 8 C.F.R. §245.2(a)(2) permits simultaneous filing of the visa petition and adjustment application, and under 8 C.F.R. §245.2(a)(1) the Immigration Court has sole jurisdiction over adjustment applications after an alien is placed in deportation proceedings.

Since the Immigration Court has sole authority to entertain a bona fide marriage exemption request for adjustment relief under 8 C.F.R. §245.1(c)(9)(iii)(F), it follows that the Immigration Court can also make a preliminary assessment of evidence presented in connection with the exemption request for purposes of reopening. The regulation at 8 C.F.R. § 245.1(c)(9)(iv) specifies that the request for the bona fide exemption must be "submitted with the Form I-485, Application for Permanent Residence." Consequently, it is logical that the official who has sole authority to consider the application can also consider the accompanying bona fide marriage exemption request for purposes of reopening as part of the application.

After making this preliminary assessment, we may reopen, pending adjudication of the visa petition by the district director. Once the Service approves the visa petition, the Immigration Judge may rule on the application, consistent with the district director's authority to adjudicate visa petitions. Otherwise the Service could preclude adjustment of status simply by holding the visa petition without adjudicating it for more than 90 days since 8 C.F.R. § 3.2(c)(2) allows only one motion. Assuming arguendo that the Service could as a matter of discretion delay its adjudication such an intent should not be presumed when in fact the visa petition was approved and the Service did not oppose either motion in this case.

* * *

To deny reopening because the Service has not completed its adjudication of the visa petition, as the majority insists must be done, and then deny reconsideration of the denial after the Service approves the visa petition defeats the purpose of the regulations that allow for a United States citizen to file a simultaneous visa petition on behalf of a spouse. The record reflects that the Service did not oppose the motion to reopen and has not opposed the respondent's motion to reconsider. Why conclusively presume otherwise? The majority also disregards the authority of this Board and of the Immigration Judges to adjudicate whether a respondent is a party to a bona fide marriage under the regulations. No legitimate governmental interest is furthered by effectively precluding a forum to spouses of United States citizens who submit a visa petition within the strict limits prescribed by the regulations. It is only that result that is accomplished by the majority's disposition of this matter.

Finally, although the majority has declined to reconsider its denial of the motion, I note that in *Matter of J-J-*, Interim Decision 3323 (BIA 1997), we held that we would reopen or reconsider cases sua sponte in exceptional circumstances. On December 23, 1997, the Service issued instructions containing guidance as to when the Service may consent to reopening because of exceptional and compelling circumstances a case that is otherwise barred from such reopening by the 8 C.F.R. §§ 3.2(c)(2) and 3.23(b)(1) one-time and 90-day limitations. See 8 C.F.R. § 3.2(c)(3)(iii). These guidelines describe the following factors, all of which are present in the respondent's case:

> (1) whether the alien has presented new evidence that is material and was not available and could not reasonably have been discovered or presented at the former hearing; (2) whether the alien is statutorily eligible for the relief sought; (3) whether the alien merits a favorable exercise of discretion; (4) the hardship to the alien and/or his USC or LPR family members if the alien were required to procure a visa through consular processing (including the potential applicability of section 212(a)(9) should the alien depart the United

> States; (5) the alien's criminal history, if any; (6) the number and severity of the alien's immigration violations; (7) whether the alien has cooperated with, or his continued presence in the United States is desired for, a criminal or civil investigation or prosecution conducted by a federal, state or local law enforcement agency; and whether the alien's removal is consistent with INS objectives.

Memorandum from Office of the General Counsel to Regional and District Counsels, Motions to Reopen Policy (Dec. 23, 1997), reprinted in 75 Interpreter Releases, No. 7, February 23, 1998, app. III, at 275–76.

In this case, the visa petition was timely submitted but approved long after we denied the respondent's motion to reopen. The respondent appears prima facie eligible for relief and worthy of discretion. His United States citizen wife and child will undoubtedly suffer if he is forced to be deported, as section 212(a)(9) of the Act, 8 U.S.C. § 1182(a)(9) (Supp. II 1996), would render him inadmissible, and there appear to be no criminal or other violations present in the record before us. Moreover, as noted above, his country has been designated for Temporary Protected Status. Consequently, reopening these proceedings in order to adjudicate the respondent's application appears to be consistent with the Service's objectives.

On July 23, 1997, while promulgating regulations to implement section 245 of the Act, the Service recognized that the adjustment of status process is the preferred method of obtaining immigrant status for eligible aliens presently in the United States, and found that "Congress, having thus invited such applications, (could not have) intended to create the futile situation in which most entrants without inspection would be admissible solely for the purpose of filing an adjustment application, but would be precluded from ever being able to adjust status based on the same application." 62 Fed. Reg. 39,417, 39,422 (1997). Similarly, properly filed motions to reopen for adjustment of status in which a prima facie showing of a bona fide marital relationship is established should be granted. The goals of promoting family unity and efficiently resolving cases through the adjustment of status mechanism is better served by providing a forum to consider an adjustment application submitted by a qualifying spouse who has demonstrated a prima facie showing of a bona fide marriage. See *Matter of Cavazos*, 17 I&N Dec. 215 (BIA 1980); cf. *Matter of Ibrahim*, 18 I&N Dec. 55 (BIA 1981). See generally *INS v. Errico*, 385 U.S. 214 (1966) (congressional purpose to forestall deportation where it breaks up family of United States citizen); *Matter of Da Lomba*, 16 I&N Dec. 616 (BIA 1978).

Absent individual adverse factors we can not invoke discretion to deprive a class of eligible applicants of the sole forum prescribed by the regulations and section 245(e)(3) of the Act for consideration of their bona fide marriages. See 8 C.F.R. §§ 245.1(c)(9)(iii)(F), (iv); 245.2(a)(1), (2). It is well settled that the Attorney General from whom we derive our authority can not disregard the procedure prescribed by the regulations as they have the force of law. *United States ex rel. Accardi v. Shaughnessy*, 347 U.S. 260 (1954); *Matter of Ponce de Leon*, Interim Decision 3261 (BIA 1996). In determining whether to exercise our delegated power under 8 C.F.R. § 3.2(a)(2), we should apply the test prescribed in *Mathews v. Eldridge*, 424 U.S. 319, 335 (1976), which takes into account three factors: the interest at stake for the individual; the risk of erroneous deprivation of that interest; and the Government's administrative burden. See *Padilla-Agustin v. INS*, 21 F.3d 970 (9th Cir. 1994); *Hernandez v. Cremer*, 913 F.2d 230 (5th Cir. 1990); *Haitian Refugee Center, Inc. v. Nelson*, 872 F.2d 1555 (11th Cir. 1989), aff'd sub nom. *McNary v. Haitian Refugee Center, Inc.*, 498 U.S. 479 (1991). Here the fundamental nature of the marital relationship being threatened by our failure to provide a forum, and the reduced administrative burden entailed in proceedings likely to result in the prompt and fair resolution of the respondent's status favor reopening.

The fundamental role of marriage in our society requires access to our courts without creating an effectively irrebuttable presumption for purposes of adjustment of status, that the marriage is mala fide. Granting this timely filed motion to reopen would be consistent with the due process right to be heard at a meaningful time and in a meaningful manner in view of the 90-day and one-time limitations imposed by 8 C.F.R. §3.2(c)(2) (1997). See *Mathews v. Eldridge, supra*; *Bell v. Burson*, 402 U.S. 535 (1971); *Armstrong v. Manzo*, 380 U.S. 545 (1965). Under these circumstances the Service should consider joining in the respondent's motions pursuant to its December 23, 1997, guidelines.

Notes

1. What might be the tactical reasons for submitting a motion to reconsider instead of a motion to reopen? What advantages or disadvantages do you see in each of these motions? What type of motion should one file if the law changes (either by statute or court decision) after either the Board or Immigration Judge have made a decision in an individual case?

2. In *INS v. Abudu*, 485 U.S. 94 (1988), the court upheld the BIA's denial of a motion to reopen where the applicant had not applied for asylum at her deportation hearing and did not do so until three years later. The court noted that there were four bases for denying a motion to reopen: (1) the applicant failed to establish a *prima facie* case for the underlying substantive relief sought; (2) the applicant did not show that the evidence which was not introduced earlier was previously unavailable; (3) the applicant failed to explain her failure to apply initially (where the reason for reopening is a benefit not previously requested); and (4) the applicant was not deserving of a favorable exercise of discretion (where the benefit sought is discretionary). The appellate court, in determining whether a *prima facie* case had been presented, would have required the BIA to first treat the facts presented in the new application as true and then decide whether the case should be reopened. *See Abudu v. INS*, 802 F.2d 1096, 1102 (9th Cir. 1986).

3. While the four bases presented in *Abudu* may not seem expansive, in actuality they cover almost every request to reopen because most immigration benefits are discretionary. Although judicial deference to an agency's exercise of discretion is a well

settled principle of administrative law, can an argument be made in favor of less deference for the asylum applicant?

4. *Abudu* is seen by many as the death knell to a successful challenge to the denial of a motion to reopen. While abuse of discretion may be difficult to establish, it is essential that the application be presented with particularity on both the issue of eligibility, favorable exercise of discretion and an explanation for the failure to submit the application at the first hearing. For a review of other reopening cases with similar results, see *INS v. Wang*, 450 U.S. 139 (1981) (suspension of deportation); *INS v. Rios-Pineda*, 471 U.S. 444 (1985); *INS v. Bagamasbad*, 429 U.S. 24 (1976) (adjustment of status).

5. Motions and appeals to be decided by the Board must be filed directly with it along with the appropriate filing fee within the 90 day period designated by the regulations. Motions to reconsider must be filed within 30 days. 8 C.F.R. §§ 1003.2(b)(2), 1003.23(b)(3). Motions or appeals to the BIA from a decision by the IJ must be filed with the immigration court, which then is forwarded on to the BIA. 8 C.F.R. § 1003.2(g)(2)(iii). Appeals to the BIA must be filed within 30 days of service on the respondent and are not considered timely unless the appeal notice is received by the BIA with all of the necessary fees paid within that time. 8 C.F.R. §§ 1003.3(a)(1), 1003.38(c). "Service" on the respondent means the date that the decision was mailed by the immigration court to the respondent, or if presented orally, the date that it was rendered.

6. Insofar as appeals are concerned the BIA strictly follows its procedures in favor of finality such that it will not consider whether a person knowingly waived appeal when a later appeal was filed within the requisite period. *See Matter of Shih*, 20 I. & N. Dec. 697 (BIA 1993); *but see U.S. v. Zarate-Martinez*, 133 F.3d 1194, 1197 (9th Cir. 1998), *cert. denied* 525 U.S. 849 (1998) (court criticized refusal by the BIA to accept the appeal but found no prejudice and affirmed the decision). The major exceptions to the strict rules governing motions to reopen are if the BIA sua sponte reopens the proceedings, where both parties agree to reopening, where there are changed circumstances warranting an asylum claim or in limited cases involving in absentia orders. *See, e.g., Bolshakov v. INS*, 133 F.3d 1279, 1281 (9th Cir. 1998); 8 C.F.R. § 1003.2(c)(3).

7. The filing of a motion to reopen does not stay the order, but depending on the circumstances there may be due process concerns if a stay of the removal order is not granted. *See, e.g., Gutierrez-Roque v. I.N.S.*, 954 F.2d 769 (D.C. Cir. 1992); 8 U.S.C. § 1229a(b)(5)(C), Sec. 240(b)(5)(C) (filing of motion to reopen where the order for removal was entered *in absentia* stays the order pending adjudication). Generally, the appellant must seek a stay from the District Director, Immigration Judge or BIA. 8 C.F.R. §§ 241.6, 1003.6, 1003.23(b), 1241.6.

8. Departure of the appellant from the U.S. while a motion or appeal is pending is generally construed as an abandonment. *Matter of Yih-Hsiung Wang*, 17 I. & N. Dec. 565 (BIA 1980). Similarly, if a person departs between the time of the decision but before an appeal it will be treated as a withdrawal, 8 C.F.R. § 3.3(e), as are all other motions or requests. *See* 8 C.F.R. § 1003.2(d). However, under former exclusion

proceedings a departure pending an appeal was not treated as a withdrawal. *See Matter of Keyte*, 20 I. & N. Dec. 158 (BIA 1990); *Matter of Morales*, 21 I. & N. Dec. 130 (BIA 1996).

d. Procedural Flowchart—Board of Immigration Appeals

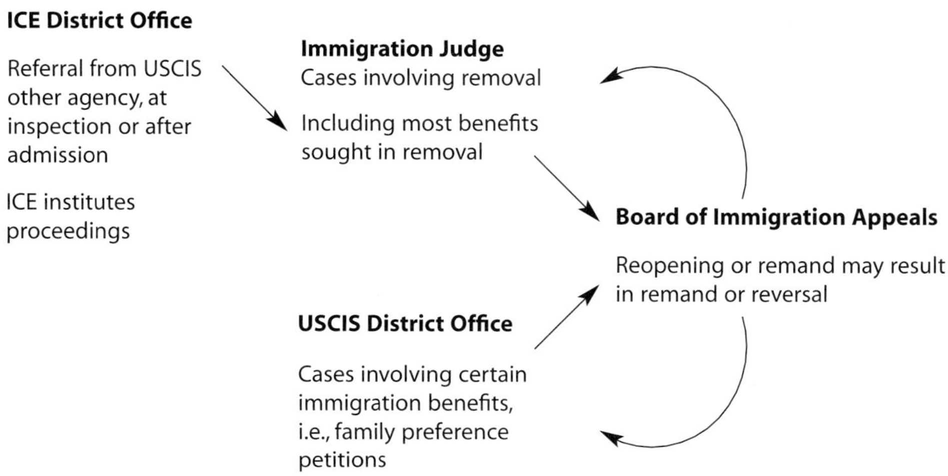

B. Judicial Review

Judicial review of immigration decisions has received much attention by Congress since the enactment of the McCarran-Walter Act in 1952. Congress, vexed by the delays in implementing deportation orders attempted to create legal mechanisms to limit judicial review. In an earlier period there were no provisions for judicial review and the only available remedy for those facing removal was a writ of habeas corpus filed in a U.S. district court. Later Congress established a truncated form of judicial review which bypassed the federal district courts by placing exclusive jurisdiction in the federal courts of appeals to review final orders of deportation.[44] This resulted in some cases being filed in U.S. district court and others in the appeals court. In 1996 Congress again amended the INA by joining exclusion and deportation cases into one removal proceeding and requiring that final removal orders be reviewable only in the court of appeals as well as stripping the courts of jurisdiction in a host of other immigration cases.[45] The result is that some actions are reviewable in the court of appeals, some limited cases may still be brought in the district court under the federal question statute and others through habeas petitions. The many changes enacted in 1996 make judicial review an even more complicated subject than it was before the amendments.

---

44. This remedy, known as "final order review" was originally codified at 8 U.S.C. § 1105a, Sec. 106(a) and was enacted in 1965.

45. *See* Anti-terrorism and Effective Death Penalty Act of 1966, Pub. L. No. 104-132, 110 Stat. 1214 (1996) ("AEDPA") and the Illegal Immigration Reform Amendments and Immigrant Responsibility Act of 1996 ("IIRAIRA"). The core judicial review provisions are now codified at 8 U.S.C. § 1252, Sec. 242.

Additional amendments enacted in 2005 sought to impose further constraints on federal court review. The Real ID Act of 2005[46] at Section 101(e) provides that

> [n]o court may reverse a determination made by a trier of fact with respect to the availability of corroborating evidence, as described in section 208(b)(1)(B), 240(c)(4)(B), or 241(b)(3)(C), unless the court finds, pursuant to section 242(b)(4)(B), that a reasonable trier of fact is compelled to conclude that such corroborating evidence is unavailable.

Section, 101(f) amended 8 U.S.C. § 1252(a)(2)(B)[47] and bars courts from reviewing discretionary judgments, decisions or actions made in the course of removal proceedings. Another prohibits habeas corpus review of removal orders and makes the federal appellate courts the only court with jurisdiction over the review of removal orders.[48] These provisions have been construed narrowly. For example, the habeas bar has been interpreted as not precluding review of matters which are not direct challenges of a removal order.[49] Similarly, the discretionary decision bar does not preclude review of questions of law.[50] Moreover the provision does not preclude review of constitutional claims and questions of law presented in petitions for review of final removal orders decisions not previously reviewable under the 1996 Amendments.[51] The relief can also be sought to outside of the U.S.[52]

1. Review of Final Orders of Removal

8 U.S.C. § 1252, Sec. 242 provides the exclusive procedure for judicial review of "final orders of removal." The term "final order" has its origins in the INA prior to the 1996 Amendments when the word "removal" replaced the terms "deportation" and "exclusion." Final orders were interpreted as including all determinations and or-

---

46. Pub. L. No. 109-13 (2005).

47. Sec. 242(a)(2)(B).

48. Indeed, the provision in the Real ID Act are consistent with the limits set on the review of final orders as discussed in the section which follows.

49. *Flores-Torres v. Mukasey*, 548 F.3d 708 (9th Cir. 2008) (does not preclude review of detention based on citizenship claim); *Nadarajah v. Gonzales*, 443 F.3d 1069 (9th Cir. 2006) (does not preclude challenge to detention before the entry of a final order of removal). Notwithstanding the broad language precluding review in the Real ID Act, the statute preserves review in the federal appellate courts. *See Zambrano-Reyes v. Holder*, 725 F.3d 744 (7th Cir. 2013); *Waldron v. Holder*, 688 F.3d 354 (8th Cir. 2012).

50. *IQ Sys., Inc. v. Mayorkas*, 667 F. Supp. 2d 105, 109 (D. D.C 2009) (while upholding the revocation of an employment based preference petition, court held that it had jurisdiction notwithstanding Real ID Act). *Yesil v. Reno*, 157 F.3d 106, 120–22 (2d Cir. 2009), *cert den. Reno v. Navas*, 526 U.S. 1004 (1999).

51. *Fernandez-Ruiz v. Gonzales*, 410 F.3d 585, 586 (9th Cir. 2005), rev. granted on other grounds 468 F.3d 1159 (9th Cir. 2006); *Hamid v. Gonzales*, 417 F.3d 642 645–46 (7th Cir. 2005); *Moallin v. Cangemi*, 427 F. Supp. 2d 908, 925–28 (D. Minn. 2006) (did not preclude custody challenge on constitutional grounds).

52. In *Boumediene v. Bush*, 553 U.S. 723 (2008) the Court held that the Suspension Clause could be applied extraterritorially in Guantanamo striking down a provision of the Military Commissions Act. *See also Al Maqaleh v. Gates*, 604 F.Supp2d 205 (D. D.C. 2009).

ders incident to a "deportation hearing" made by an immigration judge and reviewable by the Board of Immigration Appeals. Presumably a final order of removal includes determinations *incident* to a removal hearing and reviewable by the Board, unless specifically not subject to review under the statute.[53] The importance of understanding the preceding cases therefore become essential for matters which are not within the power of the immigration judge may not be amenable to review under Section 242. Section 242 review does not apply to expedited removal proceedings[54] and the case must be brought in the federal appeals court with jurisdiction over the immigration judge who entered the removal order of removal.[55] A condition for obtaining review before a U.S. Court of Appeals is that the person must have exhausted all administrative remedies and review of the case will be limited to the administrative record. In addition, the appellate court's scope of review is limited as the statute provides that the "administrative findings of facts are conclusive unless any reasonable adjudicator would be compelled to conclude to the contrary."[56] The reviewing court conducts *de novo* review of purely legal questions.[57] The filing of the petition for review does not automatically stay the removal order, which means that the person facing a removal order must seek and obtain an interim order of stay from the court with jurisdiction.[58] The petitioner's brief must be filed within 40 days after the administrative record is submitted to the court and will have 14 days in which to file a reply brief to the Attorney General's brief.[59]

As was noted earlier, one of the major objectives of the 1996 legislation was to eliminate most forms of judicial review in immigration cases. While some of the court stripping provisions are contained in 8 U.S.C. § 1252 many can be found in various sections of the INA. Some examples of the types of cases which may not be reviewed are the following:

a. A Rule of Thumb to Understanding "Final Orders"

Even though the 1996 Amendments significantly altered the law regarding Section 242 review, the restriction on the review of "final orders" is a carryover from the predecessor statute. Therefore it is useful to explore how final orders were defined before enactment of the 1996 Amendments. The seminal case on this issue was *Cheng Fan Kwok*

53. As will be seen in a later discussion, there are many forms of relief which may be sought in removal proceedings which the statute exempts from judicial review under this provision. *See infra*.

54. The statute specifically omits expedited removal orders from this form of judicial review. *See* 8 U.S.C. § 1252(a)(1), Sec. 242(a)(1).

55. 8 U.S.C. § 1252(b)(2), Sec. 242(b)(2). The petition for review must be filed within 30 days of when the order becomes final, which is within 30 days of when the BIA has issued its decision affirming or entering a removal order. 8 U.S.C. § 1252(b)(1), Sec. 242(b)(1). The predecessor statute allowed for the case to be brought where the petitioner resided.

56. 8 U.S.C. § 1252(b)(4), Sec. 242(b)(4).

57. *See, e.g., Arrieta v. INS*, 117 F.3d 429, 430 (9th Cir. 1997); *Tedeeva v. INS*, 88 F.3d 826, 827 (9th Cir. 1996).

58. 8 U.S.C. § 1252(b)(3)(B), Sec. 242(b)(3)(B).

59. 8 U.S.C. § 1252(b)(3)(C), Sec. 242(b)(3)(C).

v. INS,[60] where the petitioner had been admitted to the U.S. as a seaman and was required to depart within 29 days. Instead of departing, he absconded and was later found and placed in proceedings at which time he was granted voluntary departure. He later sought additional relief from the legacy INS District Director in the form of a stay of deportation and was preparing an application for conditional entrant status, as a native and citizen of China who was fleeing a communist country. The INS and the petitioner had argued that jurisdiction should rest exclusively with the court of appeals under Section 242. The Court held that it did not have jurisdiction under Section 242 as the section only provided review of matters that were part of the "deportation" proceeding, neither of which were matters which the immigration judge had authority to grant. As a result the petitioner in *Cheng Fan Kwok* would have to proceed in U.S. district court to review the denial of both the stay and the request for conditional entry status.

The lesson of *Cheng Fan Kwok* and understanding the meaning of what is a "final order" requires an analysis of whether the benefit which was denied was one which an immigration judge *could* have granted in the course of a removal hearing.[61] If the answer is in the affirmative then review must be sought by way of a "petition for review" only after the BIA has made a final determination. If the challenge is to an irregularity in the conduct of the hearing, something clearly within the power of the immigration judge, injunctive relief may be sought only under rare circumstances.[62] Generally, decisions which are within the *exclusive* province of the district directors, Administrative Appeals Office (AAO) or other agencies involved in deciding immigration cases may be reviewed by resorting to other forms of relief if they are available.[63] In using this "rule of thumb" consider the following fact situation:

A nonimmigrant exchange visitor is seeking lawful permanent resident status in the U.S. In order to be eligible to apply for permanent residence, exchange visitors are generally required to return and live in their native country for two years. The two-year foreign residency requirement may be waived by the Attorney General in cases where the applicant can establish that exceptional hardship would be experienced by the exchange visitor's U.S. citizen spouse or children and also receives a favorable recommendation from the Director of the U.S. Information Agency (USIA). If the person is placed in removal proceedings and is in the process of seeking a waiver,

---

60. 392 U.S. 206 (1963).

61. The use of this "rule of thumb" is helpful in most cases, however there are situations where there may be an overlap in jurisdiction. For example, in asylum and adjustment cases the applicant may pursue the benefit initially before the district director and later with the immigration judge in removal proceedings. The circuits are not in agreement on this issue. *See Galvez v. Howerton*, 503 F. Supp. 35 (D. Cal. 1980) (court found jurisdiction to review a denial of adjustment of status under 8 U.S.C. § 1254); *Chen Chaun-Fa v. Kiley*, 459 F. Supp. 762 (S.D.N.Y. 1978) (court found no jurisdiction to review a denial of asylum). However, it should be noted that when courts have dealt with this issue they have been more inclined to dismiss such cases on grounds that relief might be had in removal proceedings. *See Kashani v. Nelson*, 793 F.2d 818 (7th Cir. 1986).

62. Counsel will be required to show that all possibility of obtaining a fair hearing would be lost if the case is allowed to proceed as required by the immigration judge.

63. Given the limitations on judicial review as described earlier, the available legal remedies will be severely limited and depend on the relief sought and the person's claimed status in the U.S.

and the USCIS has recommended that the waiver be granted and the immigration judge denies adjustment because the Department of State will not grant the waiver, are any of these decisions subject to review under Section 242?

The answer to the question requires careful analysis. First, there is the question of whether the waiver request is really part of the removal hearing and within the jurisdiction of the immigration judge. One issue is whether the denial of the waiver request is subject to any administrative review. Another question is whether a denial of a stay of the removal proceedings pending administrative review is properly the subject of judicial review under Section 242. Finally, assuming that the waiver request is granted by the Secretary of State, would the denial of the adjustment of status be precluded under 8 U.S.C. § 1252(a)(2)(B)(i), Sec. 242(a)(2)(B)(i)?[64]

b. Procedural Flowchart—Judicial Review of Final Orders of Removal

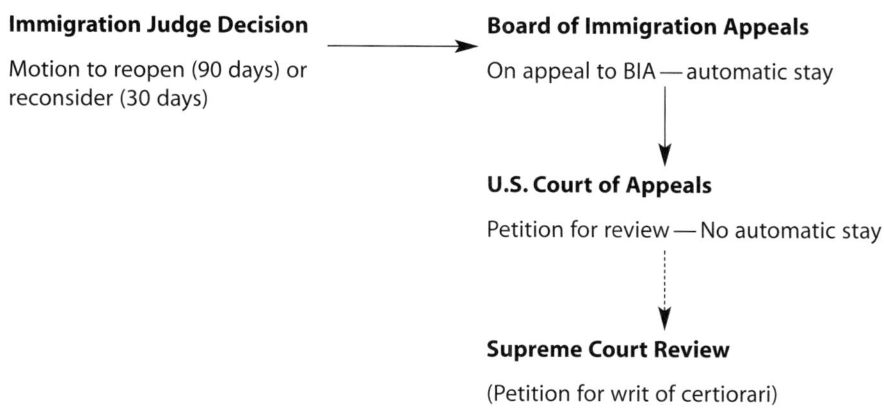

2. Review under the Administrative Procedure Act and Federal Question[65]

While it is clear that one can sue the government in immigration cases, the prevailing view is that the Administrative Procedure Act (APA) is not the proper basis

64. While an action for declaratory relief may be brought in federal district court under the Administrative Procedure Act, 5 U.S.C. § 706(2)(A), the courts have refused to review decisions of the United States Information Agency (USIA) in exchange visitor waiver cases under the theory that these decisions are made pursuant to 5 U.S.C. § 701(a) and are committed to agency discretion by law and therefore there is no meaningful standard of review to apply. *See Singh v. Moyer,* 867 F.2d 1035 (7th Cir. 1989); *Slyper v. Attorney General,* 827 F.2d 821 (D.C. Cir. 1987), *cert. denied sub nom. Slyper v. Meese*, 485 U.S. 941 (1988); *but see Chong v. Director, USIA,* 821 F.2d 171, 175 (3d Cir. 1987). The refusal by the USIA to favorably recommend a waiver presents an anomaly precluding review. Some of the problems presented in *Slyper* may have been remedied by the creation of an administrative review mechanism, which if not adhered to could create some legal remedy.

65. The Administrative Procedure Act, 5 U.S.C. § 551 *et seq.* (hereinafter referred to as the "APA"). The federal question statute, 28 U.S.C. § 1331, although the subject of extensive discussion, is a short statute and provides that

> The district courts shall have original jurisdiction of all civil actions arising under the Constitution, laws, or treaties of the United States.

for asserting jurisdiction in U.S. district court. Prior to 1976 the courts were divided on the question of whether the APA provided an independent basis for federal court jurisdiction.[66] Congress' amendment of the APA in 1976[67] and the later the Supreme Court's decision in *Califano v. Sanders*[68] made it clear that jurisdiction had not been conferred. Due to Congress' amendment of the federal question statute in 1980, the issue of whether the government could be sued is no longer at issue.[69] No doubt, due to the confusion caused by the split in circuits (prior to 1977) counsel in immigration cases continue to cite every conceivable jurisdictional statute. While one could argue that the APA does provide jurisdiction the question is now academic. Perhaps an easier way of conceptualizing the relationship between the APA and federal question statute is to view the federal question statute as providing jurisdiction, and the APA as granting a waiver of sovereign immunity and controlling the scope of judicial review and how the court will review the agency action.

While as was noted earlier, the APA does not apply to removal proceedings it does control the agency in actions such as in the notice and rulemaking procedures mandated by the statute.[70] For example the APA has been held as not providing a basis for mandating a removal hearing.[71] At the same time courts have held that DHS and Department of Labor are bound by the APA's notice, comment and rulemaking procedures.[72]

The problem for litigants challenging a decision in immigration matters is that the APA is limited to agency action where a person has suffered a legal wrong or has been adversely affected or aggrieved.[73] Not encompassed within the ambit of an actionable legal wrong is where the right asserted emanates from an internal policy directive.[74] The difficulty is that sometimes the policy which is published in the Operation Instructions is a statement of substantive right and at other times a policy.

---

66. *See Scanwell Labs, Inc. v. Thomas,* 521 F.2d 941 (D.C. Cir. 1975, *cert. denied,* 425 U.S. 910 (1975) (recognizing jurisdiction through the APA); *but see Chaudoin v. Atkinson,* 494 F.2d 1323 (3d Cir. 1983) (rejecting the claim that the APA granted jurisdiction).

67. Pub. L. No. 94-574 (1976), amending 5 U.S.C. §§702 and 703.

68. 430 U.S. 99 (1977).

69. The 1980 amendments removed the minimum amount in controversy requirement of $10,000 in all cases. *See* 28 U.S.C. §1331; *see also* 1980 U.S. Code Cong. & Admin. News 5063–69. While the government can clearly be sued, it *is not* clear that the APA is the proper basis for jurisdiction. For example, in *Grumman Ohio Corp. v. Dole,* 776 F.2d 338 (D.C. Cir. 1985), the court sidestepped the jurisdictional issue since the plaintiff had asserted jurisdiction under the federal question statute. Other courts have specifically stated that the APA provides no independent basis for jurisdiction. *See, e.g., Choctaw Mfg. Co. v. U.S.,* 761 F.2d 609 (11th Cir. 1985).

70. The notion that the APA does not apply to removal proceedings was settled in *Marcello v. Bonds,* 349 U.S. 302 (1955).

71. *Silveyra v. Moschorak,* 989 F.2d 1012 (9th Cir. 1993)

72. *See, e.g., DeBraun v. Meissner,* 958 F. Supp. 227 (E.D. Pa. 1997); *Kooritzky v. Reich,* 17 F.3d 1509 (D.C. Cir. 1994); *Dia Navigation Corp., Ltd. v. Pomeroy,* 34 F.3d 1255 (3d Cir. 1994).

73. 5 U.S.C. §702.

74. *See Haitian Refugee Center, Inc. v. Baker,* 953 F.2d 1498, 1511 (11th Cir. 1992), *cert denied,* 502 U.S. 1122 (1992).

Federal courts have enforced some Operation Instructions and DHS policy statements on grounds that they confer procedural rights.[75]

Even if there is no judicial review because the matter is not a "final order of removal," or the relief requested is not subject to review on account of one of the preclusion provisions listed previously, it may be subject to review as a federal question if it raises a serious constitutional question.[76] If this were the case, an action seeking judicial review would have to be brought in a U.S. District Court. This area of the law is still unsettled and will no doubt be the subject of cases which will be brought in the years ahead.

3. Limitations on Review

As previously noted, for some time, Congress has been determined to accelerate the removal process. Part of the effort to accelerate removal has been to limit the jurisdiction of federal courts. 8 U.S.C. § 1252 includes provisions which preclude injunctive relief from removal proceedings,[77] the review of decisions for discretionary relief such as for waivers under 8 U.S.C. §§ 1182(h) and (i), cancellation of removal under 8 U.S.C. § 1229b, adjustment of status under 8 U.S.C. § 1255, Sec. 245, and other forms of discretionary relief,[78] expedited removal orders,[79] final orders of certain persons with criminal convictions,[80] and for either the institution of removal proceedings or collateral attacks on removal orders.[81] Additional limitations on judicial review can be found scattered throughout the INA.[82]

---

75. *See, e.g., Pasquini v. Morris*, 700 F.2d 658 (11th Cir. 1983); *Zhang v. Slattery*, 840 F. Supp. 292 (S.D. N.Y 1994).

76. *See, e.g., McNary v. Haitian Refugee Center, Inc.*, 498 U.S. 479 (1991); *Wang v. Reno*, 81 F.3d 808 (9th Cir. 1996).

77. 8 U.S.C. § 1252(f), Sec. 242(f). Exempted are direct petitions to the Supreme Court or in individual cases where the person can show by clear and convincing evidence that the entry of the order of removal is prohibited as a matter of law.

78. 8 U.S.C. §§ 1252(a)(2)(B)(i) and (ii), Sections 242(a)(2)(B)(i) and (ii). This provision exempts asylum applications.

79. 8 U.S.C. § 1252(a)(2)(A), Sec. 242(a)(2)(A)

80. 8 U.S.C. § 1252(a)(2)(C), Sec. 242(a)(2)(C). This covers those removable as aggravated felons and others who are either inadmissible or deportable for crimes [8 U.S.C. §§ 1182(a)(2) and (a)(2)(A)(iii), 8 U.S.C. § 1227(a)(2)(B)], for firearm offenses or miscellaneous crimes [8 U.S.C. § 1227(a)(2)(D), Sec. 237(a)(2)(D)], or for persons convicted of 2 or more crimes of moral turpitude for which a sentence of more than 1 year could be imposed [8 U.S.C. § 1227(a)(2)(A)(ii)].

81. 8 U.S.C. §§ 1252(b)(1)(D) and (g), Sections 242(b)(1)(D) and (g).

82. These include decisions by the Attorney General regarding voluntary departure [8 U.S.C. §§ 1229b(e) and (f), Sections 240B(e) and (f)]; decisions involving detention or release including the grant, denial or revocation of bond or parole [8 U.S.C. § 1226(e), Sec. 236(e)]. Also precluded are decisions involving the right to apply for asylum on account of the availability of a safe third country, a previous denial of asylum, the failure to file for asylum within one year after arrival or on account of the person being a terrorist [8 U.S.C. §§ 1158(a)(3) and (b)(2)(D), Sections 208(a)(3) and (b)(2)(D)]; and decisions on waivers of grounds of inadmissibility or deportability because of a prior final order of removal under Sec. 274C [8 U.S.C. §§ 1182(d)(12) and 1227(a)(3)(C)(ii), Sections 212(d)(12) and 237(a)(3)(C)(ii)].

In the case excerpted below, the Court analyzes one of the jurisdictional limiting provisions written into the INA. Consider how the Court interprets what is and what is not a discretionary decision within the meaning of the specific statute in question.

Agron Kucana v. Eric H. Holder, Jr., Att'y Gen.

558 U.S. 233 (2010)

Justice Alito filed an opinion concurring in the judgment.

Justice Ginsburg, delivered the opinion of the Court.

Petitioner Agron Kucana moved to reopen his removal proceedings, asserting new evidence in support of his plea for asylum. An Immigration Judge (IJ) denied the motion, the Board of Immigration Appeals (BIA or Board) sustained the IJ's ruling, and the U.S. Court of Appeals for the Seventh Circuit concluded that it lacked jurisdiction to review the administrative determination. For that conclusion, the court relied on a provision added to the Immigration and Nationality Act (INA or Act), 66 Stat. 166, 8 U.S.C. § 1101 et seq., by the Illegal Immigration Reform and Immigrant Responsibility Act of 1996 (IIRIRA), 110 Stat. 3009-546. The provision found dispositive by the Seventh Circuit, 8 U.S.C. § 1252(a)(2) (B), states that no court shall have jurisdiction to review any action of the Attorney General "the authority for which is specified under this subchapter to be in the discretion of the Attorney General," § 1252(a)(2)(B)(ii) (emphasis added).

We granted certiorari to decide whether the proscription of judicial review stated in § 1252(a)(2)(B) applies not only to Attorney General determinations made discretionary by statute, but also to determinations declared discretionary by the Attorney General himself through regulation. We hold that the key words "specified under this subchapter" refer to statutory, but not to regulatory, specifications. We so rule based on the longstanding exercise of judicial review of administrative rulings on reopening motions, the text and context of § 1252(a)(2)(B), and the history of the relevant statutory provisions. We take account, as well, of the "presumption favoring interpretations of statutes [to] allow judicial review of administrative action." *Reno v. Catholic Social Services, Inc.*, 509 U.S. 43, 63–64 (1993) (quoting *McNary v. Haitian Refugee Center, Inc.*, 498 U.S. 479, 496 (1991)). Separation-of-powers concerns, moreover, caution us against reading legislation, absent clear statement, to place in executive hands authority to remove cases from the Judiciary's domain.

In IIRIRA, Congress for the first time codified certain rules, earlier prescribed by the Attorney General, governing the reopening process. The amended Act instructs that reopening motions "shall state the new facts that will be proven at a hearing to be held if the motion is granted, and shall be supported by affidavits or other evidentiary material." § 1229a(c)(7)(B). Congress also prescribed that "the motion to reopen shall be filed within 90 days of the date of entry of a final administrative order of removal." § 1229a(c)(7)(C)(i). Among matters excepted from the 90-day limitation are motions to reopen asylum applications because of changed conditions in the country of nationality or removal. § 1229a(c)(7)(C)(ii).

Section 1252(a)(2), captioned "Matters not subject to judicial review," contains the provision on which this case turns. Subparagraph (B) of that paragraph, headed "Denials of discretionary relief," states:

> "Notwithstanding any other provision of law (statutory or nonstatutory), ... except as provided in subparagraph (D), and regardless of whether the judgment, decision, or action is made in removal proceedings, no court shall have jurisdiction to review—
>
> "(i) any judgment regarding the granting of relief under section 1182(h), 1182(i), 1229b, 1229c, or 1255 of this title, or
>
> "(ii) any other decision or action of the Attorney General ... the authority for which is specified under this subchapter to be in the discretion of the Attorney General..., other than the granting of relief under section 1158(a) of this title."

A regulation, amended in 1996, just months before Congress enacted IIRIRA, 61 Fed. Reg. 18904, Pt. 3, § 3.2(a), states that "[t]he decision to grant or deny a motion to reopen ... is within the discretion of the Board." 8 CFR § 1003.2(a) (2009). As adjudicator in immigration cases, the Board exercises authority delegated by the Attorney General. See 8 U.S.C. § 1103(g)(2); 8 CFR § 1003.1. See also 8 CFR § 1003.23(b)(3) (governing motions to reopen filed with an IJ).

Kucana, a citizen of Albania, entered the United States on a business visa in 1995 and remained after the visa expired. Alleging that he would be persecuted based on his political beliefs if returned to Albania, Kucana applied for asylum and withholding of removal in 1996. An IJ determined that Kucana was removable and scheduled a hearing to evaluate his eligibility for asylum. When Kucana failed to appear for the hearing, the IJ immediately ordered his removal in absentia. Kucana filed a motion to reopen, explaining that he had missed his hearing because he had overslept. The IJ denied the motion, and the BIA affirmed in 2002. Kucana did not seek judicial review, nor did he leave the United States.

Kucana filed a second motion to reopen his removal proceedings in 2006, contending that conditions in Albania had worsened. The BIA denied relief; it concluded that conditions in Albania had actually improved since 1997. Arguing that the BIA had abused its discretion in denying his motion, Kucana filed a petition for review in the Seventh Circuit.

In a fractured decision, the Seventh Circuit dismissed the petition for lack of jurisdiction. *Kucana v. Mukasey*, 533 F.3d 534, 539 (2008). The court held that 8 U.S.C. § 1252(a)(2)(B)(ii) bars judicial review not only of administrative decisions made discretionary by statute, but also "when the agency's discretion is specified by a regulation rather than a statute." 533 F.3d, at 536. In so ruling, the Seventh Circuit created a split between itself and other Courts of Appeals, all of them holding that denials of reopening motions are reviewable in court.

* * *

The motion to reopen is an "important safeguard" intended "to ensure a proper and lawful disposition" of immigration proceedings. *Dada v. Mukasey*, 554 U.S. 1, ___, 128 S.Ct. 2307, 2317–19 (2008); cf. *Stone v. INS*, 514 U.S. 386, 401 (1995) (analogizing motions to reconsider immigration decisions to motions for relief from a judgment under Federal Rule of Civil Procedure 60(b)). Federal-court review of administrative decisions denying motions to reopen removal proceedings dates back to at least 1916. See *Dada*, 554 U.S., at ___, 128 S.Ct., at 2314–15 (citing cases). This Court has ultimately reviewed reopening decisions on numerous occasions. See, e.g., *INS v. Doherty*, 502 U.S. 314, 322–324 (1992); *INS v. Abudu*, 485 U.S. 94, 104–111 (1988).... Mindful of the Board's "broad discretion" in such matters, however, courts have employed a deferential, abuse-of-discretion standard of review. See *Doherty*, 502 U.S., at 323 (internal quotation marks omitted).

* * *

The Board's discretionary authority to act on a motion to reopen, we have thus far explained, is "specified" not in a statute, but only in the Attorney General's regulation, which instructs: "The decision to grant or deny a motion to reopen ... is within the discretion of the Board, subject to the restrictions of this section. The Board has discretion to deny a motion to reopen even if the party moving has made out a prima facie case for relief." 8 CFR § 1003.2(a). Nevertheless, in defense of the Seventh Circuit's judgment, amicus urges that regulations suffice to trigger 8 U.S.C. § 1252(a)(2)(B)(ii)'s proscription of judicial review.

* * *

Section 1252(a)(2)(B)(ii), the provision at issue here, is far from the only jurisdictional limitation in IIRIRA. See *Dada*, 554 U.S., at ___, 128 S.Ct., at 2317 ("In reading a statute we must not look merely to a particular clause, but consider in connection with it the whole statute." (internal quotation marks omitted)); *Davis v. Michigan Dept. of Treasury*, 489 U.S. 803, 809 (1989) ("[T]he words of a statute must be read in their context and with a view to their place in the overall statutory scheme."). Section 1252(a)(2), titled "Matters not subject to judicial review," lists a variety of agency determinations the federal courts lack jurisdiction to review. Those determinations divide into three categories. The first, § 1252(a)(2)(A), concerns immigration officers' determinations whether aliens applying for admission are admissible. Next in statutory order is the provision before us, § 1252(a)(2)(B), which involves denials of discretionary relief. The last category, § 1252(a)(2) (C), concerns final orders of removal entered against criminal aliens.

Both § 1252(a)(2)(A) and § 1252(a)(2)(C) depend on statutory provisions, not on any regulation, to define their scope. The latter provision, the criminal alien bar, precludes judicial review of "any final order of removal against an alien who is removable by reason of having committed a criminal offense covered in" § 1182(a)(2), § 1227(a)(2)(A)(iii), (B), (C), or (D), or certain offenses covered in § 1227(a)(2)(A)(ii). All the defining references are statutory; none invokes a regulation. The same holds for the admissibility bar in § 1252(a)(2)(A). Given § 1252(a)(2)(B)'s statutory placement, sandwiched between subsections (a)(2)(A) and (a)(2)(C), one would expect that it, too, would cover statutory provisions alone.

Focusing on § 1252(a)(2)(B), we note the lead line serving to introduce both of the subparagraph's two clauses: "[N]o court shall have jurisdiction to review...." Clause (i) then places within the no-judicial-review category "any judgment regarding the granting of relief under section 1182(h), 1182(i), 1229b, 1229c, or 1255." Each of the statutory provisions referenced in clause (i) addresses a different form of discretionary relief from removal, see supra, at 832, n. 2, and each contains language indicating that the decision is entrusted to the Attorney General's discretion. See, e.g., § 1182(h) ("The Attorney General may, in his discretion, waive [inadmissibility based on certain criminal offenses]."). Clause (i) does not refer to any regulatory provision.

To the clause (i) enumeration of administrative judgments that are insulated from judicial review, Congress added in clause (ii) a catchall provision covering "any other decision ... the authority for which is specified under this subchapter." The proximity of clauses (i) and (ii), and the words linking them—"any other decision"—suggests that Congress had in mind decisions of the same genre, i.e., those made discretionary by legislation. The clause (I) enumeration, we find, is instructive in determining the meaning of the clause (ii) catchall. Read harmoniously, both clauses convey that Congress barred court review of discretionary decisions only when Congress itself set out the Attorney General's discretionary authority in the statute. See *Hall Street Associates, L.L.C. v. Mattel, Inc.*, 552 U.S. 576, ___, 128 S.Ct. 1396, 1404 (2008) ("[W]hen a statute sets out a series of specific items ending with a general term, that general term is confined to covering subjects comparable to the specifics it follows.").

We also find significant the character of the decisions Congress enumerated in § 1252(a)(2)(B)(i), thereby insulating them from judicial review. As the Government explained at oral argument, the determinations there listed are "substantive decisions ... made by the Executive in the immigration context as a matter of grace, things that involve whether aliens can stay in the country or not." Tr. of Oral Arg. 14. They include waivers of inadmissibility based on certain criminal offenses, § 1182(h), or based on fraud or misrepresentation, § 1182(i); cancellation of removal, § 1229b; permission for voluntary departure, § 1229c; and adjustment of status, § 1255.

Other decisions specified by statute "to be in the discretion of the Attorney General," and therefore shielded from court oversight by § 1252(a)(2)(B)(ii), are of a like kind. See, e.g., § 1157(c)(1) (discretion to admit refugees "determined to be of special humanitarian concern to the United States"); § 1181(b) (discretion to waive requirement of documentation for readmission); § 1182(a)(3)(D)(iii) (discretion to waive, in certain cases, inadmissibility of aliens who have affiliated with a totalitarian party). Decisions on reopening motions made discretionary by regulation, in contrast, are adjunct rulings: The motion to reopen is a procedural device serving to ensure "that aliens [a]re getting a fair chance to have their claims heard." Tr. of Oral Arg. 17. A court decision reversing the denial of a motion to reopen does not direct the Executive to afford the alien substantive relief; ordinarily, it touches and concerns only the question whether the alien's claims have been accorded a reasonable hearing.

If Congress wanted the jurisdictional bar to encompass decisions specified as discretionary by regulation along with those made discretionary by statute, moreover, Congress could easily have said so. In other provisions enacted simultaneously with § 1252(a)(2)(B)(ii), Congress expressed precisely that meaning. See IIRIRA, § 213, 110 Stat. 3009-572 ("immigration benefits pursuant to this Act; or the regulations promulgated thereunder"), codified at 8 U.S.C. § 1324c(e)(2); IIRIRA, § 372, 110 Stat. 3009-646 ("any of the powers, privileges, or duties conferred or imposed by this Act or regulations issued thereunder"), codified at 8 U.S.C. § 1103(a) (10). "[W]here Congress includes particular language in one section of a statute but omits it in another section of the same Act, it is generally presumed that Congress acts intentionally and purposely in the disparate inclusion or exclusion." *Nken v. Holder*, 556 U.S. 418, ___ (2009) (internal quotation marks omitted).

* * *

Any lingering doubt about the proper interpretation of 8 U.S.C. § 1252(a)(2)(B)(ii) would be dispelled by a familiar principle of statutory construction: the presumption favoring judicial review of administrative action. When a statute is "reasonably susceptible to divergent interpretation, we adopt the reading that accords with traditional understandings and basic principles: that executive determinations generally are subject to judicial review." *Gutierrez de Martinez v. Lamagno*, 515 U.S. 417, 434 (1995). We have consistently applied that interpretive guide to legislation regarding immigration, and particularly to questions concerning the preservation of federal-court jurisdiction. See, e.g., *INS v. St. Cyr*, 533 U.S. 289, 298 (2001); *Catholic Social Services, Inc.*, 509 U.S., at 63–64; *McNary*, 498 U.S., at 496. Because the "presumption favoring interpretations of statutes [to] allow judicial review of administrative action" is "well-settled," *Catholic Social Services, Inc.*, 509 U.S., at 63–64 (quoting *McNary*, 498 U.S., at 496, 111 S.Ct. 888), the Court assumes that "Congress legislates with knowledge of" the presumption, id., at 496. It therefore takes "clear and convincing evidence" to dislodge the presumption. *Catholic Social Services, Inc.*, 509 U.S., at 64 (internal quotation marks omitted). There is no such evidence here.

* * *

A statute affecting federal jurisdiction "must be construed both with precision and with fidelity to the terms by which Congress has expressed its wishes." *Cheng Fan Kwok v. INS*, 392 U.S. 206, 212 (1968). As we have noted, see *supra*, at 838, and as amicus emphasizes, "many provisions of IIRIRA [we]re aimed at protecting [from court review exercises of] the Executive's discretion." *American-Arab Anti-Discrimination Comm.*, 525 U.S., at 486, 119 S.Ct. 936 (emphasis deleted). But "no law pursues its purpose at all costs, and ... the textual limitations upon a law's scope are no less a part of its 'purpose' than its substantive authorizations." *Rapanos v. United States*, 547 U.S. 715, 752 (2006) (plurality opinion). While Congress pared back judicial review in IIRIRA, it did not delegate to the Executive authority to do so. Action on motions to reopen, made discretionary by the Attorney General only, therefore remain subject to judicial review.

For the reasons stated, the judgment of the United States Court of Appeals for the Seventh Circuit is reversed, and the case is remanded for further proceedings consistent with this opinion.

Notes

1. For an excellent review of the Congressional efforts to limit federal court review, see Stephen H. Legomsky, *Deportation and the War on Independence*, 91 Cornell L. Rev. 369 (2006). Consistent with the analysis in *Kucana*, the federal courts have carefully scrutinized and limited the provisions which preclude court review. *See Dalton v. Ashcroft*, 257 F.3d 200, 203 (2d Cir. 2001) (reasoning that a court both has jurisdiction to determine its own jurisdiction and also to decide whether the person had in fact committed an aggravated felony); *Leocal v. Ashcroft*, 543 U.S. 1 (2004), *sub silentio* (holding that DUI conviction was not a "crime of violence" and therefore not an aggravated felony).

2. **Reinstatement of Removal Orders.** A reinstated removal order may be subject to constitutional or legal challenge under 8 U.S.C. 1252(a)(2)(D). *Debeato v. Att'y Gen'l*, 505 F.3d 231 (3d Cir. 2007); *Ramirez-Molina v. Ziglar*, 436 F.3d 508, 513 (5th Cir. 2006). Since the reinstated removal is not reviewed by an immigration judge or the BIA the time period within which the petition for review must be filed is 30 days from the signing of the DHS officer of the Decision, Order and Officer's Certification (I-871). *Ponta-Garca v. Ashcroft*, 386 F.3d 341 (1st Cir. 2004). The court on review may only determine whether the reinstatement order was valid or whether ICE followed the appropriate procedures in reinstating the original. *Anderson v. Napolitano*, 611 F.3d 275, 277 (5th Cir. 2010); *Morales-Izquierdo v. Gonzales*, 486 F.3d 484, 497–98 (9th Cir. 2007); *Arevalo v. Ashcroft*, 344 F.3d 1, 9 (1st Cir. 2003). Finally, habeas corpus review is also not appropriate because of the exclusive remedy found in the petition for review process of final orders. *Morales-Izquierdo* v. DHS, 600 F.3d 1076, 1081 (9th Cir. 2010).[83]

3. One very broad provision which precludes judicial review for persons removable under the criminal grounds has been interpreted as only limiting such review by the federal appeals courts under the petition for review leaving open review under habeas corpus under 28 U.S.C. § 2241.[84]

4. 8 U.S.C. § 1252(a)(2)(B) precludes review in a far reaching range of discretionary benefits decided by immigration judges and the BIA in removal cases such as cancellation and adjustment of status including waivers under 8 U.S.C. §§ 1182(h) and (i). However, courts in analyzing challenges have reasoned that they may review the predicate legal question of whether the immigration judge properly applied the law to the facts. *Rodriguez-Labato v. Sessions*, 868 F.3d 690 (8th Cir. 2017); *Gomez-Lopez*

---

83. One court has allowed a habeas corpus challenge to the original removal order where it was a predicate to a criminal conviction for illegal reentry. *Nolasco v. U.S.*, 358 F. Supp. 2d 224, 237 (S.D.N.Y. 2004).

84. *INS v. St. Cyr*, 533 U.S. 289 (2001); *Calcano-Martinez v. INS*, 533 U.S. 348 (2001). *See* 8 U.S.C. § 1252(a)(2)(C) for the limiting provision.

v. Ashcroft, 393 F.3d 882 (9th Cir. 2005) (however review does not encompass voluntary departure determinations).

5. The Section 242(g) preclusion provision has been found to prevent habeas review where the petitioner sought review of a district director's denial of his application for adjustment of status. *Morgan v. McElroy*, 981 F. Supp. 873 (S.D. N.Y 1997). A similar result occurred where the petitioner sought habeas review of a district director's denial of a request for a stay of deportation. *Bart-Addison v. Fisher*, 975 F. Supp. 1476 (N.D. Ga. 1997). However, a family preference petition is subject to administrative review by the BIA under 8 C.F.R. § 1003.1(b) and in federal district court under the APA and the INA. *See Bangura v. Hansen*, 434 F.3d 487 (6th Cir. 2006); *Hanif v. DHS*, 472 F. Supp. 2d 914, 920 (E.D. Mich. 2007).

6. In looking at the role of the judiciary in these matters, it is limited to interpreting the applicable law, and the court does not grant the underlying benefit being sought by the applicant. This was set out by the Supreme Court in *INS v. Ventura*, 537 U.S. 12 (2002), where the Court stated that:

> ... Within broad limits the law entrusts the agency to make the basic asylum eligibility decision here in question. E.g., 8 U.S.C. § 1158(a); 8 U.S.C. § 1253(h)(1) (1994 ed.); *Elias-Zacarias*, 502 U.S. at 481; *INS v. Aguirre-Aguirre*, 526 U.S. 415 (1999). See also 8 CFR § 3.1 (2002). In such circumstances a "judicial judgment cannot be made to do service for an administrative judgment." *SEC v. Chenery Corp.*, 318 U.S. 80, 88 (1943). Nor can an "appellate court ... intrude upon the domain which Congress has exclusively entrusted to an administrative agency." *Ibid.* A court of appeals "is not generally empowered to conduct a de novo inquiry into the matter being reviewed and to reach its own conclusions based on such an inquiry." *Florida Power & Light Co. v. Lorion*, 470 U.S. 729, 744 (1985). Rather, "the proper course, except in rare circumstances, is to remand to the agency for additional investigation or explanation." *Ibid.* Cf. *SEC v. Chenery Corp.*, 332 U.S. 194, 196 (1947) (describing the reasons for remand).

---

4. Habeas Corpus Review

David Cole, Jurisdiction and Liberty: Habeas Corpus and Due Process as Limits on Congress' Control of Federal Jurisdiction

86 Geo. L.J. 2481 (1998)

* * *

In 1996, Congress substantially rewrote the immigration laws in two steps. In April, it enacted the Antiterrorism and Effective Death Penalty Act. The jurisdictional aspects of AEDPA were, in retrospect, relatively minimal. Most significantly, it repealed a provision of the INA that authorized aliens in custody to seek habeas corpus review of their deportation orders, and substituted the following language: "Any final order of deportation against an alien who is deportable by reason of [certain enumerated criminal grounds] shall not be subject to review by any court." Thus, while most aliens could still seek review of their deportation orders in courts of appeals after the passage of AEDPA, those found deportable for having committed certain criminal offenses could not.

Several months later, Congress enacted a much more comprehensive revision of the immigration laws, the Illegal Immigration Reform and Immigrant Responsibility Act, which went far beyond AEDPA in restricting judicial review of immigration decisions. Under IIRIRA, the statutory distinctions between exclusion and deportation proceedings are largely eliminated, replaced by a single removal proceeding. IIRIRA continued AEDPA's ban on judicial review of removal orders against so-called "criminal aliens," but added many further restrictions. Criminal aliens, for example, are denied not only judicial review of their order of removal, but also of the INS's decision to detain them pending removal.

In provisions that affect not just "criminal aliens" but all aliens, IIRIRA bars judicial review of decisions by an immigration judge regarding most forms of relief from removal. Relief from removal allows eligible persons to remain in the country notwithstanding a finding that they are removable; relief usually turns on such considerations as family ties, personal hardship, likelihood of persecution abroad, and connections to the community. Questions concerning relief are litigated much more frequently and extensively than issues of whether the alien is deportable or removable under the INA.

In addition, IIRIRA creates an expedited removal procedure for aliens who arrive at the border without proper documentation, and severely restricts their access to judicial review. Aliens in this situation can be ordered removed after a truncated administrative procedure and may obtain judicial review only of certain very limited questions: whether the person is an alien; whether the person was ordered removed under the expedited removal process; and whether the person can prove that she or he is a lawful permanent resident or has been admitted as a refugee or granted asylum. The only remedy available is a court order that the person be given an ordinary rather than an expedited removal proceeding. The IIRIRA also severely restricts systemic judicial challenges to the validity of the expedited removal process, requiring that any such suits be filed within sixty days of the date on which the challenged provision or regulation was first implemented.

Finally, in a provision that the government has relied upon widely to seek dismissal of myriad challenges to immigration actions, IIRIRA's judicial review section contains a provision entitled "Exclusive Jurisdiction"....

* * *

The first constitutional constraint on Congress's power to restrict judicial review of immigration actions is that Congress may not deny all avenues for judicial redress of a constitutional claim. As the Supreme Court itself has acknowledged: "[All] agree that Congress cannot bar all remedies for enforcing federal constitutional rights." At least three constitutional problems would arise if all judicial review of an immigrant's constitutional challenge to removal were barred. First, such a bar would violate Article III of the Constitution because it would intrude on the courts' "essential function." As Justice Murphy stated, "Under our system there is no warrant for the view that the judicial power of a competent court can be circumscribed by any legislative arrangement designed to give effect to administrative action going beyond the limits of constitutional authority." Second, because removal entails a substantial deprivation of liberty, denial of a federal forum to review a constitutional challenge to removal would violate due process. Third, as I will argue below, denying a noncitizen any opportunity to challenge the constitutionality of his custody would violate the Suspension Clause, which requires the availability of habeas corpus relief for those detained by executive action contrary to law.

Even where physical liberty has not been at issue, and even where statutes on their face appear to bar all judicial review of administrative action, courts have consistently interpreted the statutes to preserve review of constitutional claims. In order to avoid the constitutional issues that would be raised were jurisdiction over constitutional claims wholly denied, courts have applied a kind of "clear statement" rule. Under this rule, courts construe statutes to preserve jurisdiction over constitutional claims unless Congress has expressly and unequivocally specified that it intended to bar such jurisdiction. Judge Posner recently summarized the law: "The circuits are in agreement: door-closing statutes do not, unless Congress expressly provides, close the door to constitutional claims." The presumption against such a result is so strong that the Supreme Court has never found that a jurisdictional statute barred judicial review of a constitutional claim.

* * *

The second restraint on Congress's power to limit the jurisdiction of the federal courts over immigration matters is contained in Article I, Section 9, which forbids suspension of the privilege of the writ of habeas corpus "unless when in cases of Rebellion or Invasion the public Safety may require it." As with the first restraint, the government does not dispute that this constitutional principle limits Congress's power to circumscribe the writ, but seeks to define those limits narrowly.

The government has argued, with some success in the courts thus far, that habeas review of an alien's removal must be preserved only when removal violates not just an immigration statute, but the Constitution itself. This argument collapses two distinct principles regarding, respectively, habeas corpus relief and judicial review of constitutional violations. I agree that the two principles are related, but in a very different way. The better view is that whenever the government detains an individual and bars all judicial review of the legality of her detention, it gives rise to a constitutional violation of both the Due Process Clause and the Suspension Clause. To hold someone in detention without affording her a judicial forum to test whether the detention is lawful (in any respect) is the very essence of a deprivation of liberty without due process. And a writ of habeas corpus provides a remedy for all executive detentions in violation of law, whether the immediate law violated is a statute, federal common law, or the Constitution. Thus, the Suspension Clause and the Due Process Clause, read together, impose a fundamental limit on Congress's control of federal jurisdiction: Congress may not authorize the executive to hold someone in detention without guaranteeing access to a court to test the legality of that detention.

This reliance on the writ of habeas corpus as a restraint on congressional control over jurisdiction resurrects an argument Henry Hart made in his classic Exercise in Dialectic. Hart's "sixty-four dollar question" was "what happens if the Government is hurting people and not simply refusing to help them ... [and] either limits the jurisdiction of the federal courts to inquire into what the officials do or denies it altogether." His answer was that the federal court's general habeas jurisdiction would nonetheless authorize it to determine whether the underlying conduct was invalid, and if so, "its duty is simply to declare the jurisdictional limit invalid also, and then proceed under the general grant of [habeas] jurisdiction." To the question of what would happen if "Congress says flatly that no court shall have jurisdiction in such ... a situation, even in habeas corpus," Hart answered, "The habeas corpus part of it would be in direct violation of the Constitution. Article I, Section 9, Clause 2."

This part of the Hart Dialogue has long been forgotten, as courts and scholars have focused almost entirely on the extent to which federal habeas corpus is required for review of state criminal convictions. But, even those who take a dim view of the Suspension Clause's relevance to federal habeas review of state court criminal convictions concede that it guarantees judicial review of federal executive detention. Thus, Chief Justice Burger, concurring in Swain v. Pressley, stated that "transfer of the historic habeas jurisdiction to an [Article] I court could raise separation-of-powers questions, since the traditional Great Writ was largely a remedy against executive detention." Similarly, Justice Jackson, concurring in *Brown v. Allen*, wrote, "the historic purpose of the writ has been to relieve detention by executive authorities without judicial trial."

Habeas corpus is implicated by every removal decision because in order to effect a noncitizen's removal from the country, the federal government must take the individual into custody. Moreover, forcibly removing someone from the country is as great a deprivation of liberty as any the government imposes short of incarceration itself; indeed, for many, deportation is worse than incarceration. As one court noted, "in severity [deportation] surpasses all but the most Draconian criminal penalties." An alien who is deported may "lose the right to [live with] her immediate family, a right that ranks high among the interests of the individual." Indeed, the Supreme Court has acknowledged that the deported alien may well lose "all that makes life worth living."

* * *

... The INS has generally conceded, and most courts have held, that even after the IIRIRA reforms, habeas corpus remains available to review orders of removal, even for "criminal aliens." The courts have generally held that absent an explicit statement by Congress showing it intended to repeal the pre-existing general habeas corpus jurisdiction under 28 U.S.C. § 2241, that statutory avenue for review remains available. This analysis follows the Supreme Court's reasoning in *Felker v. Turpin*[86] and *Ex parte Yerger*.[87] In both cases, the Supreme Court held that provisions explicitly cutting off judicial review would not be interpreted to deny general habeas corpus jurisdiction absent a clear statement to that effect. Felker concerned a provision of AEDPA that prohibited state inmates from filing successive habeas petitions absent permission from the court of appeals, and specified that a decision denying such permission "shall not be appealable and shall not be the subject of a petition for rehearing or for a writ of certiorari." In the face of this statutory prohibition, the Supreme Court held that its own habeas corpus jurisdiction, authorized by 28 U.S.C. § 2241, remained available to a prisoner who sought review of a court of appeals' denial of permission to file a successive petition. For the most part, courts interpreting IIRIRA and AEDPA have adopted similar reasoning: absent a clear statement that Congress intended to repeal habeas corpus jurisdiction for criminal aliens under 28 U.S.C. § 2241, that avenue for review remains.

* * *

The real debate thus concerns not whether habeas review is available at all, but what sorts of claims an alien is entitled to raise on habeas corpus. The government argues, and many lower courts have held, that habeas review need be maintained only for claims that the INS committed constitutional error or that deportation would constitute a "fundamental miscarriage of justice." That view is a mistake, as the history of habeas corpus review of immigration actions demonstrates. Professor Gerald Neuman has demonstrated through an exhaustive historical study of habeas corpus decisions reviewing deportation orders that courts exercising habeas jurisdiction routinely reviewed claims that INS officials violated statutes and regulations, abused their discretion, and entered orders unsupported by any evidence. Without repeating such a review, one need examine only four Supreme Court cases to see that the government's claim that only constitutional claims are reviewable is mistaken.

* * *

The 1996 immigration statutes may be Congress's most explicit attempt to cut off judicial review since *Ex parte McCardle*. Just as Congress did in *McCardle*, the 1996 statutes specifically restrict judicial review of federal executive detention, raising multiple constitutional questions. Yet those questions are not likely to be answered. In *McCardle* and virtually every other decision reviewing statutory restrictions on judicial review, the courts have been reluctant to address the constitutional issues raised. Instead, the courts have always interpreted statutory jurisdictional provisions to preserve judicial review where its preclusion would raise serious constitutional questions. If this trend continues, the courts are likely to read the 1996 statutes as preserving col-

86. 116 S. Ct. 2333, 2339 (1996) (refusing to interpret AEDPA's restriction on successive habeas petitions for state prisoners to repeal 28 U.S.C. § 2241 by implication).

87. 75 U.S. 85, 105 (1869) (refusing to interpret congressional repeal of one avenue of habeas jurisdiction as a repeal of another, more general habeas statute by implication).

lateral district court jurisdiction and habeas review for legal challenges to removal that would otherwise be unreviewable.

* * *

At least five doctrines of statutory construction point in that direction. First, as noted above, the courts interpret jurisdictional statutes to preserve constitutional claims unless Congress clearly and explicitly expresses its intention to deny review of such claims. Second, and relatedly, the general authority of the federal courts to hear habeas corpus claims under 28 U.S.C. § 2241 cannot be repealed by implication. Third, any ambiguity in an immigration statute must be construed in favor of the alien. Fourth, to bar judicial review of legal challenges to removal would mark a substantial change in the status quo, and statutes cannot be read to effect such change unless Congress makes its intent explicit in the language of the statute or legislative history. Finally, statutes should not be read to reach absurd results. To read IIRIRA to authorize executive detention without habeas review or to bar review of constitutional claims would achieve the absurd result of immunizing from review potentially lawless and unconstitutional detentions. As one court expressed the rule against absurdity, "the general rule honored even by interpretive literalists is that if a literal reading would produce an absurd result the interpreter is free (we would say compelled) to depart in the direction of sense." The Seventh Circuit relied on this maxim in *Czerkies* to preserve judicial review of constitutional claims in the face of a statute that broadly barred all judicial review, noting that it would be absurd to insulate even racially discriminatory decisions from judicial review.

The Supreme Court and lower federal courts have historically gone to great lengths to avoid squarely deciding the two types of constitutional issues presented by court-stripping in the immigration context: (1) the extent of Congress's power to restrict federal jurisdiction; and (2) the extent of Congress's power over immigration. On both issues, the courts have said that Congress has "plenary power." Only twice has the Court held an immigration statute unconstitutional, and only twice has it invalidated jurisdictional statutes for intruding on the judicial power.

The paucity of successful constitutional challenges in these areas, however, does not mean that challenges to immigration statutes or jurisdictional restrictions always lose. On the contrary, courts frequently rule for immigrants, and have always granted judicial review of constitutional claims in the face of statutes that would appear to require the opposite result. In both contexts, however, the courts do so by statutory construction rather than by constitutional invalidation.

There are clear advantages to this approach. Both immigration and jurisdiction are areas in which the Court has acknowledged that Congress has substantial power. The immigration authority not only touches on foreign affairs and is inherent in national sovereignty, but it almost inevitably involves somewhat arbitrary line-drawing between immigrants and citizens; for these reasons the Court has adopted a very deferential approach to constitutional review of immigration statutes. Congress's power to control the jurisdiction of federal courts finds solid support in the text of the Constitution, and plays an important structural role in legitimating the courts' antidemocratic decisions: the very fact that Congress could limit the federal courts' jurisdiction, but has not, affords the courts' decisions a degree of political legitimacy. Thus, the courts are loathe to confront Congress directly on either subject.

At the same time, by construing statutes in these areas to avoid particularly harsh and possibly unconstitutional results, the Court can and has imposed some limits on these otherwise plenary powers, without directly challenging Congress. In the jurisdictional area in particular, a direct challenge to Congress, drawing a line in the sand beyond which Congress may not go, would undermine the legitimating function that the unused potential for congressional restriction of jurisdiction creates. Once it becomes clear that Congress cannot exercise its jurisdictional power in certain ways, the Court loses the implicit legitimation given by Congress's silence.

In addition, judicial decisions which turn on statutory construction create an opportunity for dialogue between the Court and Congress. A statutory construction adopted to avoid a constitutional problem does not say to Congress, "you may not constitutionally do this," but only "we don't believe you intended to do this, because if you did it would raise grave constitutional questions." The latter statement leaves Congress the option to take the next step and bring the issue to a head, but also encourages Congress to consider carefully the results of its actions. If Congress really means to deprive the courts of habeas corpus jurisdiction over removal decisions, or of all review over certain constitutional matters, for example, it can state that intention in more clear terms, thereby mandating a constitutional decision. But in the light of a judicial construction preserving such review, Congress may well leave the statute as the Court construes it. In fact, I am not aware of a single instance in which Congress has responded to a statutory construction that preserved jurisdiction over constitutional claims by explicitly barring such jurisdiction.

Requiring Congress to be absolutely explicit about what it is doing when it seeks to deny judicial review may also improve the political process. Professor Hart argued that "the Court should use every possible resource of construction to avoid the conclusion that [Congress intended to effectuate an unconstitutional withdrawal of jurisdiction]" for the following reason: In the end we have to depend on Congress for the effective functioning of our judicial system, and perhaps for any functioning. The primary check on Congress is the political check—the votes of the people. If Congress wants to frustrate the judicial check, our constitutional tradition requires that it be made to say so unmistakably, so that the people will understand and the political check can operate.

Immigration and Naturalization Service v. Enrico St. Cyr

533 U.S. 289 (2001)

Stevens, J., delivered the opinion of the Court, in which Kennedy, Souter, Ginsburg, and Breyer, JJ., joined. O'Connor, J., filed a dissenting opinion. Scalia, J., filed a dissenting opinion, in which Rehnquist, C. J., and Thomas, J., joined, and in which O'Connor, J., joined, as to Parts I and III.

Justice STEVENS delivered the opinion of the Court.

Both the Antiterrorism and Effective Death Penalty Act of 1996 (AEDPA), enacted on April 24, 1996, 110 Stat. 1214, and the Illegal Immigration Reform and Immigrant Responsibility Act of 1996 (IIRIRA), enacted on September 30, 1996, 110 Stat. 3009-546, contain comprehensive amendments to the Immigration and Nationality Act (INA), 66 Stat. 163, as amended, 8 U.S.C. § 1101 et seq. This case raises two important questions about the impact of those amendments. The first question is a procedural one, concerning the effect of those amendments on the availability of habeas corpus jurisdiction under 28 U.S.C. § 2241. The second question is a substantive one, concerning the impact of the amendments on conduct that occurred before their enactment and on the availability of discretionary relief from deportation.

Respondent, Enrico St. Cyr, is a citizen of Haiti who was admitted to the United States as a lawful permanent resident in 1986. Ten years later, on March 8, 1996, he pled guilty in a state court to a charge of selling a controlled substance in violation of Connecticut law. That conviction made him deportable. Under pre-AEDPA law applicable at the time of his conviction, St. Cyr would have been eligible for a waiver of deportation at the discretion of the Attorney General. However, removal proceedings against him were not commenced until April 10, 1997, after both AEDPA and IIRIRA became effective, and, as the Attorney General interprets those statutes, he no longer has discretion to grant such a waiver.

In his habeas corpus petition, respondent has alleged that the restrictions on discretionary relief from deportation contained in the 1996 statutes do not apply to removal proceedings brought against an alien who pled guilty to a deportable crime before their enactment. The District Court accepted jurisdiction of his application and agreed with his submission. In accord with the decisions of four other Circuits, the Court of Appeals for the Second Circuit affirmed. 229 F.3d 406 (2000). The importance of both questions warranted our grant of certiorari.

I

The character of the pre-AEDPA and pre-IIRIRA law that gave the Attorney General discretion to waive deportation in certain cases is relevant to our appraisal of both the substantive and the procedural questions raised by the petition of the Immigration and Naturalization Service (INS). We shall therefore preface our discussion of those questions with an overview of the sources, history, and scope of that law.

Subject to certain exceptions, § 3 of the Immigration Act of 1917 excluded from admission to the United States several classes of aliens, including, for example, those who had committed crimes "involving moral turpitude." 39 Stat. 875. The seventh exception provided "[t]hat aliens returning after a temporary absence to an unrelinquished United States domicile of seven consecutive years may be admitted in the discretion of the Secretary of Labor, and under such conditions as he may prescribe." *Id.*, at 878. Although that provision applied literally only to exclusion proceedings, and although the deportation provisions of the statute did not contain a similar provision, the Immigration and Naturalization Service (INS) relied on § 3 to grant relief in deportation proceedings involving aliens who had departed and returned to this country after the ground for deportation arose. See, e.g., *Matter of L*, 1 I. & N. Dec. 1, 2 (1940).

Section 212 of the Immigration and Nationality Act of 1952, which replaced and roughly paralleled § 3 of the 1917 Act, excluded from the United States several classes of aliens, including those convicted of offenses involving moral turpitude or the illicit traffic in narcotics. See 66 Stat. 182–187. As with the prior law, this section was subject to a proviso granting the Attorney General broad discretion to admit excludable aliens. See *id.*, at 187. That proviso, codified at 8 U.S.C. § 1182(c), stated:

> Aliens lawfully admitted for permanent residence who temporarily proceeded abroad voluntarily and not under an order of deportation, and who are returning to a lawful unrelinquished domicile of seven consecutive years, may be admitted in the discretion of the Attorney General....

Like § 3 of the 1917 Act, § 212(c) was literally applicable only to exclusion proceedings, but it too has been interpreted by the Board of Immigration Appeals (BIA) to authorize any permanent resident alien with "a lawful unrelinquished domicile of seven consecutive years" to apply for a discretionary waiver from deportation. See *Matter of Silva*, 16 I. & N. Dec. 26, 30 (1976) (adopting position of *Francis v. INS*, 532 F.2d 268 (C.A.2 1976)). If relief is granted, the deportation proceeding is terminated and the alien remains a permanent resident.

The extension of § 212(c) relief to the deportation context has had great practical importance, because deportable offenses have historically been defined broadly. For example, under the Immigration and Nationality Act, aliens are deportable upon conviction for two crimes of "moral turpitude" (or for one such crime if it occurred within five years of entry into the country and resulted in a jail term of at least one year). See 8 U.S.C. §§ 1227(a)(2)(A)(i)–(ii) (1994 ed., Supp. V). In 1988, Congress further specified that an alien is deportable upon conviction for any "aggravated felony," Anti-Drug Abuse Act of 1988, 102 Stat. 4469–4470, § 1227(a)(2)(A)(iii), which was defined to include numerous offenses without regard to how long ago they were committed. Thus, the class of aliens whose continued residence in this country has depended on their eligibility for § 212(c) relief is extremely large, and not surprisingly, a substantial percentage of their applications for § 212(c) relief have been granted. Consequently, in the period between 1989 and 1995 alone, § 212(c) relief was granted to over 10,000 aliens.

Three statutes enacted in recent years have reduced the size of the class of aliens eligible for such discretionary relief. In 1990, Congress amended § 212(c) to preclude from discretionary relief anyone convicted of an aggravated felony who had served a term of imprisonment of at least five years. § 511, 104 Stat. 5052 (amending 8 U.S.C. § 1182(c)). In 1996, in § 440(d) of AEDPA, Congress identified a broad set of offenses for which convictions would preclude such relief. See 110 Stat. 1277 (amending 8 U.S.C. § 1182(c)). And finally, that same year, Congress passed IIRIRA. That statute, inter alia, repealed § 212(c), see § 304(b), 110 Stat. 3009-597, and replaced it with a new section that gives the Attorney General the authority to cancel removal for a narrow class of inadmissible or deportable aliens, see id., at 3009-594 (creating 8 U.S.C. § 1229b). So narrowed, that class does not include anyone previously "convicted of any aggravated felony." § 1229b(a)(3) (1994 ed., Supp. V).

In the Attorney General's opinion, these amendments have entirely withdrawn his § 212(c) authority to waive deportation for aliens previously convicted of aggravated felonies. Moreover, as a result of other amendments adopted in AEDPA and IIRIRA, the Attorney General also maintains that there is no judicial forum available to decide whether these statutes did, in fact, deprive him of the power to grant such relief. As we shall explain below, we disagree on both points. In our view, a federal court does have jurisdiction to decide the merits of the legal question, and the District Court and the Court of Appeals decided that question correctly in this case.

II

The first question we must consider is whether the District Court retains jurisdiction under the general habeas corpus statute, 28 U.S.C. § 2241, to entertain St. Cyr's challenge. His application for a writ raises a pure question of law. He does not dispute any of the facts that establish his deportability or the conclusion that he is deportable. Nor does he contend that he would have any right to have an unfavorable exercise of the Attorney General's discretion reviewed in a judicial forum. Rather, he contests the Attorney General's conclusion that, as a matter of statutory interpretation, he is not eligible for discretionary relief.

The District Court held, and the Court of Appeals agreed, that it had jurisdiction to answer that question in a habeas corpus proceeding. The INS argues, however, that four sections of the 1996 statutes—specifically, § 401(e) of AEDPA and three sections of IIRIRA (8 U.S.C. §§ 1252(a)(1), 1252(a)(2)(C), and 1252(b)(9) (1994 ed., Supp. V))—stripped the courts of jurisdiction to decide the question of law presented by respondent's habeas corpus application.

For the INS to prevail it must overcome both the strong presumption in favor of judicial review of administrative action and the longstanding rule requiring a clear statement of congressional intent to repeal habeas jurisdiction. See *Ex parte Yerger*, 8 Wall. 85, 102 (1869) ("We are not at liberty to except from [habeas corpus jurisdiction] any cases not plainly excepted by law"); *Felker v. Turpin*, 518 U.S. 651, 660–661 (1996) (noting that "[n]o provision of Title I mentions our authority to entertain original habeas petitions," and the statute "makes no mention of our authority to hear habeas petitions filed as original matters in this Court"). Implications from statutory text or legislative history are not sufficient to repeal habeas jurisdiction; instead, Congress must articulate specific and unambiguous statutory directives to effect a repeal. *Ex parte Yerger*, 8 Wall., at 105 ("Repeals by implication are not favored. They are seldom admitted except on the ground of repugnancy; and never, we think, when the former act can stand together with the new act").

In this case, the plain statement rule draws additional reinforcement from other canons of statutory construction. First, as a general matter, when a particular interpretation of a statute invokes the outer limits of Congress' power, we expect a clear indication that Congress intended that result. See *Edward J. DeBartolo Corp. v. Florida Gulf Coast Building & Constr. Trades Council*, 485 U.S. 568, 575 (1988). Second, if an otherwise acceptable construction of a statute would raise serious constitutional problems, and where an alternative interpretation of the statute is "fairly possible," see *Crowell v. Benson*, 285 U.S. 22, 62, (1932), we are obligated to construe the statute to avoid such problems. See *Ashwander v. TVA*, 297 U.S. 288, 341, 345–348 (1936) (Brandeis, J., concurring); *United States ex rel. Attorney General v. Delaware & Hudson Co.*, 213 U.S. 366, 408 (1909).

A construction of the amendments at issue that would entirely preclude review of a pure question of law by any court would give rise to substantial constitutional questions. Article I, § 9, cl. 2, of the Constitution provides: "The Privilege of the Writ of Habeas Corpus shall not be suspended, unless when in Cases of Rebellion or Invasion the public Safety may require it." Because of that Clause, some "judicial intervention in deportation cases" is unquestionably "required by the Constitution." *Heikkila v. Barber*, 345 U.S. 229, 235 (1953).

Unlike the provisions of AEDPA that we construed in *Felker v. Turpin*, 518 U.S. (1996), this case involves an alien subject to a federal removal order rather than a person confined pursuant to a state-court conviction. Accordingly, regardless of whether the protection of the Suspension Clause encompasses all cases covered by the 1867 Amendment extending the protection of the writ to state prisoners, cf. *id.*, at 663–664, or by subsequent legal developments, see *LaGuerre v. Reno*, 164 F.3d 1035 (C.A.7 1998), at the absolute minimum, the Suspension Clause protects the writ "as it existed in 1789." *Felker*, 518 U.S., at 663–664.

At its historical core, the writ of habeas corpus has served as a means of reviewing the legality of executive detention, and it is in that context that its protections have been strongest. See, e.g., *Swain v. Pressley*, 430 U.S. 372, 380, n. 13 (1977); *id.*, at 385–386 (Burger, C. J., concurring) (noting that "the traditional Great Writ was largely a remedy against executive detention"); *Brown v. Allen*, 344 U.S. 443, 533 (1953) (Jackson, J., concurring in result) ("The historic purpose of the writ has been to relieve detention by executive authorities without judicial trial"). In England prior to 1789, in the Colonies, and in this Nation during the formative years of our Government, the writ of habeas corpus was available to nonenemy aliens as well as to citizens. It enabled them to challenge executive and private detention in civil cases as well as criminal. Moreover, the issuance of the writ was not limited to challenges to the jurisdiction of the custodian, but encompassed detentions based on errors of law, including the erroneous application or interpretation of statutes. It was used to command the discharge of seamen who had a statutory exemption from impressment into the British Navy, to emancipate slaves, and to obtain the freedom of apprentices and asylum inmates. Most important, for our purposes, those early cases contain no suggestion that habeas relief in cases involving executive detention was only available for constitutional error.

Notwithstanding the historical use of habeas corpus to remedy unlawful executive action, the INS argues that this case falls outside the traditional scope of the writ at common law. It acknowledges that the writ protected an individual who was held without legal authority, but argues that the writ would not issue where "an official had statutory authorization to detain the individual but ... the official was not properly exercising his discretionary power to determine whether the individual should be released." Brief for Respondent, O.T.2000, No. 00-1011, p. 33. In this case, the INS points out, there is no dispute that the INS had authority in law to hold St. Cyr, as he is eligible for removal. St. Cyr counters that there is historical evidence of the writ issuing to redress the improper exercise of official discretion. See ... Hafetz, *The Untold Story of Noncriminal Habeas Corpus and the 1996 Immigration Acts*, 107 Yale L.J. 2509 (1998).

St. Cyr's constitutional position also finds some support in our prior immigration cases. In *Heikkila v. Barber*, the Court observed that the then-existing statutory immigration scheme "had the effect of precluding judicial intervention in deportation cases *except insofar as it was required by the Constitution*," 345 U.S., at 234–235 (emphasis added)—and that scheme, as discussed below, did allow for review on habeas of questions of law concerning an alien's eligibility for discretionary relief. Therefore, while the INS' historical arguments are not insubstantial, the ambiguities in the scope of the exercise of the writ at common law identified by St. Cyr, and the suggestions in this Court's prior decisions as to the extent to which habeas review could be limited consistent with the Constitution, convince us that the Suspension Clause questions that would be presented by the INS' reading of the immigration statutes before us are difficult and significant.

In sum, even assuming that the Suspension Clause protects only the writ as it existed in 1789, there is substantial evidence to support the proposition that pure questions of law like the one raised by the respondent in this case could have been answered in 1789 by a common law judge with power to issue the writ of habeas corpus. It necessarily follows that a serious Suspension Clause issue would be presented if we were to accept the INS's submission that the 1996 statutes have withdrawn that power from federal judges and provided no adequate substitute for its exercise. See Hart, *The Power of Congress to Limit the Jurisdiction of Federal Courts: An Exercise in Dialectic*, 66 Harv. L.Rev. 1362, 1395–1397 (1953). The necessity of resolving such a serious and difficult constitutional issue—and the desirability of avoiding that necessity—simply reinforce the reasons for requiring a clear and unambiguous statement of constitutional intent.

Moreover, to conclude that the writ is no longer available in this context would represent a departure from historical practice in immigration law. The writ of habeas corpus has always been available to review the legality of executive detention. See *Felker*, 518 U.S., at 663; *Swain v. Pressley*, 430 U.S., at 380, n. 13. Federal courts have been authorized to issue writs of habeas corpus since the enactment of the Judiciary

Act of 1789, and § 2241 of the Judicial Code provides that federal judges may grant the writ of habeas corpus on the application of a prisoner held "in custody in violation of the Constitution or laws or treaties of the United States." 28 U.S.C. § 2241. Before and after the enactment in 1875 of the first statute regulating immigration, 18 Stat. 477, that jurisdiction was regularly invoked on behalf of noncitizens, particularly in the immigration context. See, e.g., *In re Kaine*, 14 How. 103 (1853); *United States v. Jung Ah Lung*, 124 U.S. 621, 626–632 (1888).

Until the enactment of the 1952 Immigration and Nationality Act, the sole means by which an alien could test the legality of his or her deportation order was by bringing a habeas corpus action in district court. See, e.g., *United States v. Jung Ah Lung*, 124 U.S. 621 (1888); *Heikkila*, 345 U.S., at 235; *Chin Yow v. United States*, 208 U.S. 8 (1908); *Ng Fung Ho v. White*, 259 U.S. 276, 284 (1922). In such cases, other than the question whether there was some evidence to support the order, the courts generally did not review factual determinations made by the Executive. See *Ekiu v. United States*, 142 U.S. 651, 659 (1892). However, they did review the Executive's legal determinations. See *Gegiow v. Uhl*, 239 U.S. 3, 9 (1915) ("The statute by enumerating the conditions upon which the allowance to land may be denied, prohibits the denial in other cases. And when the record shows that a commissioner of immigration is exceeding his power, the alien may demand his release upon habeas corpus"); see also Neuman, *Jurisdiction and the Rule of Law after the 1996 Immigration Act*, 113 Harv. L.Rev.1963, 1965–1969 (2000). In case after case, courts answered questions of law in habeas corpus proceedings brought by aliens challenging Executive interpretations of the immigration laws.

Habeas courts also regularly answered questions of law that arose in the context of discretionary relief. See, e.g., *United States ex rel. Accardi v. Shaughnessy*, 347 U.S. 260 (1954); *United States ex rel. Hintopoulos v. Shaughnessy*, 353 U.S. 72, 77 (1957). Traditionally, courts recognized a distinction between eligibility for discretionary relief, on the one hand, and the favorable exercise of discretion, on the other hand. See Neuman, 113 Harv. L.Rev., at 1991 (noting the "strong tradition in habeas corpus law ... that subjects the legally erroneous failure to exercise discretion, unlike a substantively unwise exercise of discretion, to inquiry on the writ"). Eligibility that was "governed by specific statutory standards" provided "a right to a ruling on an applicant's eligibility," even though the actual granting of relief was "not a matter of right under any circumstances, but rather is in all cases a matter of grace." *Jay v. Boyd*, 351 U.S. 345, 353–354 (1956). Thus, even though the actual suspension of deportation authorized by § 19(c) of the Immigration Act of 1917 was a matter of grace, in *United States ex rel. Accardi v. Shaughnessy*, 347 U.S. 260 (1954), we held that a deportable alien had a right to challenge the Executive's failure to exercise the discretion authorized by the law. The exercise of the District Court's habeas corpus jurisdiction to answer a pure question of law in this case is entirely consistent with the exercise of such jurisdiction in *Accardi*. See also *United States ex rel. Hintopoulos v. Shaughnessy*, 353 U.S., at 77.

Thus, under the pre-1996 statutory scheme—and consistent with its common-law antecedents—it is clear that St. Cyr could have brought his challenge to the Board of Immigration Appeals' legal determination in a habeas corpus petition under 28 U.S.C. § 2241. The INS argues, however, that AEDPA and IIRIRA contain four provisions that express a clear and unambiguous statement of Congress' intent to bar petitions brought under § 2241, despite the fact that none of them mention that section. The first of those provisions is AEDPA's § 401(e).

While the title of § 401(e)—"Elimination of Custody Review by Habeas Corpus"—would seem to support the INS' submission, the actual text of that provision does not. As we have previously noted, a title alone is not controlling. *Pennsylvania Dept. of Corrections v. Yeskey*, 524 U.S. 206, 212 (1998) ("'[T]he title of a statute ... cannot limit the plain meaning of the text. For interpretive purposes [it is] of use only when [it] shed[s] light on some ambiguous word or phrase'" (quoting *Trainmen v. Baltimore & Ohio R. Co.*, 331 U.S. 519, 528–529 (1947)). The actual text of § 401(e), unlike its title, merely repeals a subsection of the 1961 statute amending the judicial review provisions of the 1952 Immigration and Nationality Act.... Neither the title nor the text makes any mention of 28 U.S.C. § 2241.

Under the 1952 Act, district courts had broad authority to grant declaratory and injunctive relief in immigration cases, including orders adjudicating deportability and those denying suspensions of deportability. See *Foti v. INS*, 375 U.S. 217, 225–226 (1963). The 1961 Act withdrew that jurisdiction from the district courts and provided that the procedures set forth in the Hobbs Act would be the "sole and exclusive procedure" for judicial review of final orders of deportation, subject to a series of exceptions. See 75 Stat. 651. The last of those exceptions stated that "any alien held in custody pursuant to an order of deportation may obtain review thereof by habeas corpus proceedings." See *id.*, at 652, codified at 8 U.S.C. § 1105a(10) (repealed Sept. 30, 1996).

The INS argues that the inclusion of that exception in the 1961 Act indicates that Congress must have believed that it would otherwise have withdrawn the pre-existing habeas corpus jurisdiction in deportation cases, and that, as a result, the repeal of that exception in AEDPA in 1996 implicitly achieved that result. It seems to us, however, that the 1961 exception is best explained as merely confirming the limited scope of the new review procedures. In fact, the 1961 House Report provides that this section "in no way disturbs the Habeas Corpus Act." H.R.Rep. No. 1086, 87th Cong., 1st Sess., 29 (1961). Moreover, a number of the courts that considered the interplay between the general habeas provision and INA § 106(a)(10) after the 1961 Act and before the enactment of AEDPA did not read the 1961 Act's specific habeas provision as supplanting jurisdiction under § 2241. *Orozco v. INS*, 911 F.2d 539, 541 (C.A.11 1990); *United States ex rel. Marcello v. INS*, 634 F.2d 964, 967 (C.A.5 1981); *Sotelo Mondragon v. Ilchert*, 653 F.2d 1254, 1255 (C.A.9 1980).

In any case, whether § 106(a)(10) served as an independent grant of habeas jurisdiction or simply as an acknowledgment of continued jurisdiction pursuant to § 2241, its repeal cannot be sufficient to eliminate what it did not originally grant—namely, habeas jurisdiction pursuant to 28 U.S.C. § 2241. See *Ex parte Yerger*, 8 Wall., at 105–106 (concluding that the repeal of "an additional grant of jurisdiction" does not "operate as a repeal of jurisdiction theretofore allowed"); *Ex parte McCardle*, 7 Wall. 506, 515 (1869) (concluding that the repeal of portions of the 1867 statute conferring appellate jurisdiction on the Supreme Court in habeas proceedings did "not affect the jurisdiction which was previously exercised").

The INS also relies on three provisions of IIRIRA, now codified at 8 U.S.C. §§ 1252(a)(1), 1252(a)(2)(C), and 1252(b)(9). As amended by § 306 of IIRIRA, 8 U.S.C. § 1252(a)(1) (1994 ed., Supp. V) now provides that, with certain exceptions, including those set out in subsection (b) of the same statutory provision, "[j]udicial review of a final order of removal ... is governed only by" the Hobbs Act's procedures for review of agency orders in the courts of appeals. Similarly, § 1252(b)(9), which addresses the "[c]onsolidation of questions for judicial review," provides that "[j]udicial review of all questions of law and fact, including interpretation and application of constitutional and statutory provisions, arising from any action taken or proceeding brought to remove an alien from the United States under this subchapter shall be available only in judicial review of a final order under this section." Finally, § 1252(a)(2)(C), which concerns "[m]atters not subject to judicial review," states: "Notwithstanding any other provision of law, no court shall have jurisdiction to review any final order of removal against an alien who is removable by reason of having committed" certain enumerated criminal offenses.

The term "judicial review" or "jurisdiction to review" is the focus of each of these three provisions. In the immigration context, "judicial review" and "habeas corpus" have historically distinct meanings. See *Heikkila v. Barber*, 345 U.S. 229 (1953). In *Heikkila*, the Court concluded that the finality provisions at issue "preclud[ed] judicial review" to the maximum extent possible under the Constitution, and thus concluded that the APA was inapplicable. *Id.*, at 235. Nevertheless, the Court reaffirmed the right to habeas corpus. *Ibid.* Noting that the limited role played by the courts in habeas corpus proceedings was far narrower than the judicial review authorized by the APA, the Court concluded that "it is the scope of inquiry on habeas corpus that differentiates" habeas review from "judicial review." *Id.*, at 236; see also, e.g., *Terlinden v. Ames*, 184 U.S. 270, 278 (1902) (noting that under the extradition statute then in effect there was "no right of review to be exercised by any court or judicial officer," but that limited review on habeas was nevertheless available); *Ekiu*, 142 U.S., at 663 (observing that while a decision to exclude an alien was subject to inquiry on habeas, it could not be "impeached or reviewed"). Both §§ 1252(a)(1) and (a)(2)(C) speak of "judicial review"—that is, full, nonhabeas review. Neither explicitly mentions habeas, or 28 U.S.C. § 2241. Accordingly, neither provision speaks with sufficient clarity to bar jurisdiction pursuant to the general habeas statute.

The INS also makes a separate argument based on 8 U.S.C. § 1252(b)(9) (1994 ed., Supp. V). We have previously described § 1252(b)(9) as a "zipper clause." *Reno v. American-Arab Anti-Discrimination Committee*, 525 U.S. 471, 483 (1999). Its purpose is to consolidate "judicial review" of immigration proceedings into one action in the court of appeals, but it applies only "[w]ith respect to review of an order of removal under subsection (a)(1)." 8 U.S.C. § 1252(b) (1994 ed., Supp. V). Accordingly, this provision, by its own terms, does not bar habeas jurisdiction over removal orders not subject to judicial review under § 1252(a)(1)—including orders against aliens who are removable by reason of having committed one or more criminal offenses. Subsection (b)(9) simply provides for the consolidation of issues to be brought in petitions for "[j]udicial review," which, as we note above, is a term historically distinct from habeas. See *Mahadeo v. Reno*, 226 F.3d 3, 12 (C.A.1 2000); *Flores-Miramontes v. INS*, 212 F.3d 1133, 1140 (C.A.9 2000). It follows that § 1252(b)(9) does not clearly apply to actions brought pursuant to the general habeas statute, and thus cannot repeal that statute either in part or in whole.

If it were clear that the question of law could be answered in another judicial forum, it might be permissible to accept the INS' reading of § 1252. But the absence of such a forum, coupled with the lack of a clear, unambiguous, and express statement of congressional intent to preclude judicial consideration on habeas of such an important question of law, strongly counsels against adopting a construction that would raise serious constitutional questions. Cf. *Felker*, 518 U.S., at 660–661. Accordingly, we conclude that habeas jurisdiction under § 2241 was not repealed by AEDPA and IIRIRA.

* * *

[The Court went on to discuss the statute, invoking the rule of statutory construction, that only if specifically and clearly stated otherwise a statute would not be given retroactive effect.]

The judgment is affirmed.

Notes

1. In *Richardson v. Reno*,[85] a case which was remanded by the Supreme Court in light of its decision in *Reno v. American-Arab Anti-Discrimination Comm.*, the 11th Circuit held on remand that it did not have jurisdiction under the habeas statute to review the petitioner's denial of bond pending his removal hearing because of 8 U.S.C. § 1252(g), Sec. 242(g).[86] The conclusion reached by the *Richardson* court has been rejected in other circuits.[87]

2. An issue which was not relevant under the predecessor statute because it was interpreted as allowing for review within a broadly defined group of persons who were "in custody," may become the subject of future litigation. Courts have taken dif-

85. 180 F.3d 1311 (11th Cir. 1999).

86. For additional history, see *Richardson v. Reno*, 994 F. Supp. 1466 (S.D. Fla. 1998), 162 F.3d 1338 (11th Cir.1998), 175 F.3d 898 (11th Cir.1999), 193 F.3d 525 (11th Cir. 1999) *pet. for reh'g denied, cert. granted, judg. vacated. Richardson v. Reno*, 526 U.S. 1142 (1999).

87. *See Liang v. INS*, 206 F.3d 208 (3d Cir. 2000); *Magaña-Pizano v. INS*, 200 F.3d 603, 608 (9th Cir.1999); *Pak v. Reno*, 196 F.3d 666, 671 (6th Cir.1999); *Requena-Rodriguez v. Pasquarell*, 190 F.3d 299, 305 (5th Cir. 1999); *Shah v. Reno*, 184 F.3d 719, 724 (8th Cir. 1999).

ferent views in habeas cases such that actual physical custody was not required, merely an order of deportation or other restraint on the person's liberty could be sufficient. This interpretation has been applied in the 7th and 9th Circuits.[88] On the other hand, actual physical custody was required in the 5th, 8th and 10th Circuits.[89]

3. One court held that it did not lose jurisdiction by virtue of the fact that the petitioner was no longer in the United States because his deportation had been carried out unlawfully.[90]

---

5. Declaratory and Injunctive Relief

Congress' enactment of 8 U.S.C. § 1252(f)[91] in the IIRAIRA sought to limit the application of injunctive relief to non-citizens and has narrowed its availability except in individual cases. Historically, federal district courts have had broad powers to fashion equitable relief to enjoin constitutional violations by administrative agencies, states or other parties in carrying out its responsibilities. Injunctions are a form of equitable relief and can be obtained by bringing a declaratory judgment action in the appropriate federal court under the Declaratory Judgment Act.[92] The Declaratory Judgment Act does not enlarge the court's jurisdiction but provides it with the authority to apply a remedy and is not appropriate in removal cases. In addition, the Administrative Procedure Act (APA) provides for relief in appropriate cases such as mandamus to compel action or to compel compliance with the notice and comment requirements in the promulgation of administrative rules. In cases where there are many individuals involved, the action could be brought in a "class action" challenging a pattern or practice of alleged violations.[93]

---

88. *See e.g. Nakaranurack v. U.S.*, 68 F.3d 290 (9th Cir. 1995); *Vargas v. Swan*, 854 F.2d 1028 (7th Cir. 1988).

89. *See, e.g., Campillo v. Sullivan*, 853 F.2d 593 (8th Cir. 1988); *Santana v. Chandler*, 961 F.2d 514 (5th Cir. 1992); *Galaviz-Medina v. Wooten*, 27 F.3d 487 (10th Cir. 1994) (court found jurisdiction only because the person was in the warden's custody and there was a final order of deportation).

90. *See Singh v. Walters*, 87 F.3d 346, 349 (9th Cir. 1996); *see also LaGuerre v. Reno*, 164 F.3d 1035, 1038 (7th Cir. Ill. 1998); *U.S. v. Fermin-Rodriguez*, 5 F. Supp. 2d 157, 163 (S.D.N.Y. 1998).

91. 8 U.S.C. § 1252(f)(1) provides

Regardless of the nature of the action or claim or of the identity of the party or parties bringing the action, no court (other than the Supreme Court) shall have jurisdiction or authority to enjoin or restrain the operation of the provisions of part IV of this subchapter, as amended by the Illegal Immigration Reform and Immigrant Responsibility Act of 1996, other than with respect to the application of such provisions to an individual alien against whom proceedings under such part have been initiated.

92. 28 U.S.C. §§ 2201 and 2202.

93. 8 U.S.C. § 1252 generally precludes review unless the action is seeking a collateral remedy apart from a removal order. *See, e.g. Nat'l Ctr. for Immigrants' Rights v. INS*, 743 F.2d 1365 (9th Cir. 1984); *Walters v. Reno*, 145 F.3d 1032, 1051–53 (9th Cir. 1998); *Orantes-Hernandez v. Gonzales*, 504 F. Supp. 2d 825 (C.D. Cal. 2007).

The jurisdiction stripping provisions of 8 U.S.C. §§ 1252(f)(1) and (2) have not been applied uniformly. For example, in one 10th Circuit case brought by immigration detainees challenging their transfer, the court determined that it did not have jurisdiction.[94] However, in another case brought in the First Circuit which challenged the transfer of immigration detainees, the court recognized that such a claim could survive a motion to dismiss on grounds that the transfers violated family integrity.[95] Similarly, several cases brought in the Ninth Circuit were not barred by the statute.[96]

The two cases below are meant to illustrate how these issues play out in the context of complaints.

Teodor G. Paunescu and Lelia A. Paunescu v. Immigration and Naturalization Service

76 F. Supp. 2d 896 (N.D. Ill. 1999)

Gettleman, District Judge.

On September 23, 1998, plaintiffs Teodor and Lelia Paunescu filed a complaint for mandamus and declaratory judgment against the Immigration & Naturalization Service, District Director Brian Perryman and the United States of America seeking to compel defendants to immediately issue all appropriate documents and take all appropriate action to execute and process plaintiffs' applications under the 1998 Diversity Immigrant Visa Program, and to grant plaintiffs legal permanent residence through an adjustment of status. The parties have filed cross-motions for summary judgment.

Teodor entered the United States in August 1995 on an F-1 Student Visa as a student at the University of Illinois. On August 19, 1997, he was appointed to the position of Graduate Teaching Assistant for the 1997–98 term. Lelia entered the United States on July 10, 1997, as a derivative spouse of Teodor. On July 29, 1997, Teodor was selected as a winner under the Fiscal Year 1998 Diversity Visa Lottery Program. Pursuant to instructions with the notification, plaintiffs applied for visas. Enclosed with those applications were the required fingerprint cards. The Department of Justice received plaintiffs' applications on November 5, 1997. The INS then scheduled plaintiffs' visa interviews on February 23, 1998. At that interview Teodor was told that his fingerprint card had been rejected by the FBI and that he was to go to an INS application support center to resubmit his fingerprints. He alleges that he was also told that absent the fingerprint problem his application would have been approved. That very same day Teodor delivered a new set of fingerprints via express mail to the interviewing officer. Five months later, on July 24, 1998, Teodor received a form letter informing him that his fingerprints had not yet cleared, without specifying any reason. The form letter

94. *Van Dinh v. Reno*, 197 F.3d 427, 433 (10th Cir. 1999).

95. *Aguilar v. USICE*, 510 F.3d 1, 17–20 (1st Cir. 2007).

96. *Rodriguez v. Hayes*, 591 F.3d 1105, 1118–21 (9th Cir. 2010) (statute did not bar class action claim to prolonged detention); *Duran-Gonzales v. DHS*, 508 F.3d 1227 (9th Cir. 2007).

contained the box to check if new fingerprints were required to be submitted. That box was not checked.

On September 18, 1998, just twelve days before the fiscal year ended, the INS directed plaintiffs to go to its office in Chicago. Teodor did so on September 21, 1998, and was informed that he had to submit a third set of prints. He immediately traveled to the INS support site in Hammond, Indiana and submitted his third set of fingerprints.

By September 23, 1998, plaintiffs, still without visa numbers, filed the instant action and moved for preliminary injunctive relief. On September 25, 1998, after a hearing, the court ordered defendants to "immediately complete adjudication of the applications for adjustment status" for both plaintiffs, without delay and by no later than September 30, 1998. The court order acknowledged, however, that the INS's ability to comply was contingent upon a favorable return of Teodor's fingerprints from the FBI and the final processing and issuance of visa numbers to plaintiffs by the Department of State on or before September 30, 1998.

The FBI failed to return Teodor's prints by the end of fiscal year September 30, 1998, leaving plaintiffs without visa numbers despite having fully complied with all requirements. In November 1998, plaintiffs moved for a rule to show cause, seeking to compel defendants to demonstrate why they failed to execute and process plaintiffs' adjustment of status. Defendants moved to vacate the court's September 25, 1998 order, contending that the court did not have jurisdiction to consider plaintiffs' request. The court concluded that it had jurisdiction and denied defendants' motion to vacate. The court also denied plaintiffs' petition for a rule to show cause, stating that the relief plaintiff requested could not be granted on the limited record before the court.

* * *

Plaintiffs assert in their complaint that this action arises under 8 U.S.C. § 1329, 28 U.S.C. § 1331, and 28 U.S.C. § 1361. In their cross-motion for summary judgment, defendants argue that the court does not have jurisdiction over the instant case. Defendants reiterate the argument they made in their motion to vacate that various sections of the INA, specifically 8 U.S.C. § 1252(g) and § 1252(a)(2)(B), deprive the court of jurisdiction. Defendants also argue that plaintiffs have not made a showing sufficient to allow the court to assume jurisdiction under the mandamus statute, 28 U.S.C. § 1361.

A. Section 1252(g)

The court once again rejects defendants' argument that § 1252(g) applies in the instant case. As the court explained in its order denying defendants' motion to vacate, the Supreme Court in *Reno v. American-Arab Anti-Discrimination Committee*, 525 U.S. 471 (1999) ("AADC"), held that § 1252(g) applies narrowly to the Attorney General's decision to "commence proceedings, adjudicate cases, or execute removal orders." If "[i]t is implausible that the mention of three discrete events along the road to deportation was a shorthand way of referring to all claims arising from deportation proceedings," *id.* 525 U.S. 471, it is even less plausible that the mention of these discrete events was a shorthand way of referring to all claims brought in immigration matters. Because this case does not involve any of the "specific steps in the deportation process," *id.* 525 U.S. 471 n. 9, or any aspect of the deportation process at all, § 1252(g) does not apply. See *Russell v. INS*, 1999 WL 675255, at *2 (N.D.Ill. Aug. 24, 1999) ("This case challenges denial of a visa petition, and the INS is not trying to deport Plaintiff; thus, this case does not fall under the ambit of the IIRIRA.").

B. Section 1252(a)(2)(B)

The remainder of defendants' jurisdictional arguments rest primarily on an issue the court has already decided in plaintiff's favor. In its March 15, 1999, order, the court held that plaintiffs request a ministerial, rather than a discretionary, decision. Defendants continue to contend, however, that the relief requested in the instant case implicates the Attorney General's discretion. Defendants argue that plaintiffs are complaining about the Attorney General's "decision" not to adjudicate an application for adjustment of status. Defendants suggest that this "decision" was made pursuant to 8 U.S.C. § 1255, which governs adjustments of status, and argue that therefore, 8 U.S.C.§ 1252(a)(2)(B)(i) deprives this court of jurisdiction.

Section 1252(a)(2)(B) is entitled "Denials of discretionary relief." Subsection (i) of this section reads, "no court shall have jurisdiction to review ... any judgment regarding the granting of relief under ... § 1255." 8 U.S.C. § 1252(a)(2)(B)(i). Defendants contend that the broad language "any judgment" means that this court does not have jurisdiction to "review" the Attorney General's refusal to entertain plaintiffs' applications. This argument is flawed in several respects. Subsection (i) clearly falls under a section of the statute that discusses denials of relief. Were plaintiffs contending that they had been denied relief, this court likely would not have jurisdiction over their claims. See, e.g., *Diallo v. Reno*, 61 F.Supp.2d 1361, 1367 (N.D.Ga.1999) ("8 U.S.C. § 1252(a)(2)(B)(i) precludes judicial review of a § 1255 denial of adjustment of status"); *Cruz v. INS*, 871 F.Supp. 1049, 1052 (N.D.Ill.1995) (holding that the plaintiff was not entitled to judicial review of a denial of adjustment of status) (citing *Massignani v. INS*, 438 F.2d 1276 (7th Cir.1971)). Because plaintiffs have neither been denied nor granted relief, § 1252(a)(2)(B)(i) does not bar jurisdiction.

Moreover, even reading the language of § 1252(a)(2)(B)(i) broadly, plaintiffs are not asking this court to review any discretionary judgment regarding the granting of relief. Defendants attempt to analogize this situation to the "deferred-action" decisions the INS formerly made in deportation cases (discretionary decisions to withhold or terminate deportation). The evidence demonstrates that the INS did not decide to defer action on plaintiffs' applications. Nor do plaintiffs contend that defendants refused to entertain their applications. See, e.g., *Alvidres-Reyes v. Reno*, 180 F.3d 199 (5th Cir.1999) (holding that, in the deportation context, § 1252(g) deprived the court of jurisdiction to compel the Attorney General to entertain the plaintiffs' applications for suspension of deportation) (cited by defendants). Defendants admit that they began entertaining plaintiff's applications. Moreover, Teodor attests in his affidavit that defendants' agent went so far as to tell plaintiffs that their applications would have been approved on that date if Teodor's fingerprints had cleared, a statement defendants neither admit nor deny. From this point forward, however, defendants simply failed to do anything at all. This was not a "decision," let alone a discretionary call. Plaintiffs do not ask this court to "review" a governmental action, but to examine and rectify a gross inaction.

C. Mandamus Jurisdiction

Because none of the cited provisions of the INA bar jurisdiction, the court must determine whether it has jurisdiction under the mandamus statute, 28 U.S.C. § 1361. This act grants district courts "jurisdiction of any action in the nature of mandamus to compel an officer or employee of the United States or any agency thereof to perform a duty owed to the plaintiff." Mandamus jurisdiction can be invoked when: (1) the plaintiff has a clear right to the relief sought; (2) the defendant has a clear duty to perform; and (3) no other adequate remedy is available. *Blaney v. United States*, 34 F.3d 509, 513 (7th Cir.1994). The court will address each of these factors.

Under 8 U.S.C. § 1255, the Attorney General may adjust an alien's status to that of a lawful permanent resident if the alien applies for such an adjustment and is eligible for a visa, and if a visa is available to him at the time his application is filed. Defendants contend that plaintiffs do not have a clear right to have their applications adjudicated because all decisions related to the processing of an application for adjustment of status are discretionary. The court agrees with Judge Grady that § 1255 "provide[s] a right to an adjudication ... within a reasonable time." *Agbemaple v. INS*, 1998 WL 292441, at *2 (May 18, 1998).

Defendants also contend that the INS does not have a clear duty to issue a decision on an adjustment of status at all, let alone to issue such a decision before the end of the fiscal year. See *Diallo*, at 1367–68. As discussed above, the court rejects defendants' argument that all decisions related to the processing of an application for adjustment of status are discretionary. The court does not mean to suggest that defendants have a duty to adjudicate applications on a "first-come, first-served basis." See, e.g., *Rahman v. McElroy*, 884 F.Supp. 782, 786–87 (S.D.N.Y.1995). Defendants nevertheless had a non-discretionary duty to issue a decision on plaintiffs' applications within a reasonable time. See *Yu v. Brown*, 36 F.Supp.2d 922, 931 (D.N.M.1999) ("All other courts addressing this question have held that INS has a *non-discretionary* duty to process applications for LPR status as well as all other immigration applications.") (emphasis added) (citing cases); *id.* at 932 (holding that the INS "owe[s] Plaintiffs a non-discretionary duty to complete processing of Plaintiffs' [LPR] applications in a reasonable time."); see also 2 Am.Jur. Administrative Law § 379 ("Even though agency action may be subject to no explicit time limit, a court may compel an agency to act within a reasonable time."). But see *Diallo*, at 1368–69 ("The decision of how to handle and investigate [a plaintiff's] application for adjustment of status and the District Director's denial of that application are clearly discretionary acts.").

Finally, defendants contend that plaintiffs have an adequate remedy: They can wait until the government institutes removal proceedings against them and raise their claims before the Immigration Judge. The court agrees that this may be the only remedy for an alien who is denied an adjustment of status. See, e.g., *Cruz*, 871 F.Supp. at 1052. But, as discussed above, the failure to adjudicate an application is different from the denial of an application. Defendant attempts to analogize the instant case to *Russell v. INS*, 1999 WL 675255 (N.D.Ill. Aug. 24, 1999), in which the plaintiff asked Judge Pallmeyer to issue an order of mandamus against an AAU who had allowed nineteen months to elapse without issuing a decision on Russell's case. Judge Pallmeyer held that the plaintiff had an adequate remedy: to wait until the judge issued his opinion. Following *Russell*, defendant argues that plaintiffs should simply wait until their applications are adjudicated. This suggestion is misguided. The character of the adjudication on Russell's application would not change no matter how long the AAU sat on the case. But the character of the adjudication on plaintiffs' applications changed forever on September 30, 1998 (in violation of this court's order), and this court alone can remedy plaintiffs' injury.

Judge Vasquez in the District of New Mexico found that the plaintiffs in *Yu v. Brown*, 36 F.Supp.2d 922 (D.N.M.1999), had established mandamus jurisdiction under nearly identical circumstances to those arise in the instant case. One of the plaintiffs in *Yu* had submitted her application for legal permanent residence two and a half years earlier. She later learned that her fingerprints had not cleared and refiled her fingerprint card. Judge Vasquez concluded that the defendants, including the INS, had a non-discretionary duty to process the plaintiffs' applications and held that the defendants had breached this duty by failing to act on plaintiff Yu's application within a year of the time she refiled her fingerprint card. See *id.* at 933.

The court concludes that it has mandamus jurisdiction over the instant case. Plaintiffs have a right to have their applications for adjustment of status adjudicated, defendants have a duty to perform this adjudication within a reasonable time, and no other remedy is available to plaintiffs. The court therefore proceeds to a consideration of the merits.

The Department of Justice received plaintiffs' applications on November 5, 1997, over ten months before the end of the fiscal year. Teodor attests that at plaintiffs' February 23, 1998, visa interview, they were informed that their applications were complete but for their fingerprint card. Defendants do not present any evidence to counter plaintiffs' claim that by February 23, 1998, they would have been eligible for an adjustment of status as soon as Teodor's fingerprints cleared. Over the next seven months plaintiffs made repeated efforts to force defendants to perform the one ministerial act that would complete their applications. For seven months defendants were on notice that plaintiffs' fingerprints had not cleared and were in wilful derogation of their duty to process plaintiff's applications.

Defendants contend that they attempted to comply with the court's September 25, 1998, order before the end of the fiscal year. According to a memo written by defendants' counsel on September 24, 1998, defendants planned to send the September 25, 1998, order to the FBI and to ask the FBI to expedite Teodor's fingerprints. Jeffrey

Gorski, a lawyer employed by the Department of State's Visa Office, attests that on September 30, 1998, the Assistant United States Attorney asked the Visa Office to issue a visa to the INS to allow plaintiffs' adjustment of incomplete, presumably because the FBI had not yet cleared Teodor's prints. The FBI's report shows that it did not receive Teodor's fingerprints until October 7, 1998. On October 8, 1998, Teodor's fingerprints cleared.

Plaintiffs were the victims of a bureaucratic nightmare. Although defendants have demonstrated that they made some efforts to comply with this court's September 25, 1998, order, the evidence demonstrates that none of the responsible parties coordinated their efforts to ensure that this court's order could be implemented. Plaintiffs should not be penalized for the government's misfeasance.

Plaintiffs' applications have been pending for over two years since they were first filed, for 19 months since Teodor refiled his fingerprint card, and for over a year since his fingerprints cleared. The court holds that defendants' failure to perform a non-discretionary duty within a reasonable time deprived plaintiffs of visas. Until September 30, 1998, plaintiffs had a right to have their applications adjudicated. Now that Teodor's fingerprints have cleared, plaintiffs are entitled to the visas they would have received but for defendants' failure to timely process their applications.

The court emphasizes that the instant case differs from cases in which immigrants who fail to timely apply for naturalization or citizenship and are later denied citizenship ask courts to use their equitable powers to reverse the denial. See, e.g., *INS v. Pangilinan*, 486 U.S. 875 (1988). The aliens requesting naturalization in Pangilinan did not take affirmative steps to be naturalized before the expiration of the statute under which they were eligible for naturalization. See *id.* at 880. The Ninth Circuit nevertheless reversed the district court decision and granted the aliens citizenship. It was in this context that the Supreme Court, reversing the Ninth Circuit, held: "[T]he power to make someone a citizen of the United States has not been conferred upon the federal courts, like mandamus or injunction as one of their generally applicable equitable powers." *Id.* at 883–84. The court reasoned that once the statute expired, the aliens in Pangilinan no longer qualified for citizenship, and the Ninth Circuit was bound to adhere to this Congressional mandate. See *id.* at 883–84. Plaintiffs in the instant case, in contrast, both timely applied for an adjustment of status and demonstrated to the INS investigating officer's satisfaction that, with the exception of the ministerial fingerprint clearance, they qualified for the adjustment they requested. Defendants did not deny plaintiffs' applications; they simply declined to finish processing them. The writ of mandamus confers upon this court the power to compel defendants to perform the duty they owe to plaintiffs.

Defendants argue that they do not have a legal duty to issue plaintiffs visas because the State Department has no legal authority to issue a visa under the FY 1998 Diversity Immigrant Visa Program. Other courts have ordered the INS and the State Department to procure visa numbers after the end of a fiscal year. In *Marcetic v. INS*, 1998 WL 173129 (N.D.Ill. April 6, 1998), Judge Moran ordered the INS "to complete all remaining process of [a] plaintiff's adjustment of status." *Id.* at *2. Defendants attempt to distinguish *Marcetic*, arguing that because an Immigration Judge had already granted the plaintiff in that case legal permanent residence, Judge Moran's order did not implicate the Attorney General's discretion to adjudicate residence, Judge Moran's order did not implicate the Attorney General's discretion to adjudicate an adjustment of status application. This court has already found, however, that defendants owe plaintiffs a non-discretionary duty to complete the processing of their applications. Plaintiffs are in the same position as the plaintiff in *Marcetic*: Their applications would have been complete and they would have received visas but for defendants' error.

The court therefore follows *Marcetic* and orders defendants to process plaintiffs' applications and to grant plaintiffs all relief to which they would have been entitled had defendants processed their applications in a timely fashion. Accordingly, the court denies defendants' motion for summary judgment and grants plaintiffs' motion for summary judgment.

Notes

1. If the plaintiff had waited for a removal hearing and requested an adjudication of the adjustment application, what would have been the likely result? Would the immigration judge be able to grant the applicant adjustment of status?

2. As the court here pointed out, a number of other courts have held that adjustment of status applications are not subject to review as a result of Congress' enactment of 8 U.S.C. § 1252(a)(2)(B)(i), Sec. 242(a)(2)(B)(i). *See e.g. Van Dinh v. Reno*, 197 F.3d 427, 432 (10th Cir. 1999); *Amoakowaa v. Reno*, 94 F. Supp. 2d 903 (N.D. Ill. 2000). However other courts have held that 242(a)(2)(B) was limited to discretionary applications which were part of the removal proceedings but that visa petitions were collateral to the removal process and as such not precluded from review. *See Shanti v. Reno*, 36 F. Supp. 2d 1151, 1158 (D. Minn. 1999); *Sabhari v. Reno*, 197 F.3d 938, 942 (8th Cir. 1999). Are these two different views reconcilable, or can it be said that whether a decision may be reviewed turns on the particular decision and whether review can be found under the APA and Federal Question statutes?

3. Does this decision mean that whenever the government unreasonably delays the adjudication of an application and it results in a substantial prejudice to the applicant, mandamus is the only available remedy?

As we have seen, the law on federal court review has been winding its way through the courts and there remains a great deal of uncertainty over its meaning. The increasing importance of immigration law, the compelling nature of the claims and political considerations have brought additional attention to the cases. The case which follows captured the attention of Presidential politics in the early part of 2000. While the case is *sui generis*, it provides an excellent backdrop for completing our discussion of this subject.

Elian Gonzalez, a Minor, by and through Lazaro Gonzalez, as Next Friend, or Alternately, as Temporary Legal Custodian v. Janet Reno, Attorney General of the United States, et al.

86 F. Supp. 2d 1167 (S.D. Fla. 2000)

K. Michael Moore, District Judge.

* * *

I. Background

The facts of this case are presented here in summary fashion. On November 25, 1999, the United States Coast Guard intercepted two fishermen who had rescued five-year-old Elian Gonzalez ("Plaintiff") from the Atlantic Ocean off the southeastern coast of Florida. The Coast Guard transported the boy, whose mother perished during the voyage from Cuba to the United States, to a local hospital. Later that day, the United States Immigration and Naturalization Service ("INS") granted Plaintiff a temporary deferral of his inspection and placed him in the care of his paternal great uncle, Lazaro Gonzalez, who resides in Miami, Florida.

On November 27, 1999, Plaintiff's father, Juan Gonzalez, sent a letter to the Cuban government requesting that his son be returned to him in Cuba. The letter stated that Plaintiff, who was born and had been raised in Cuba, "was taken out of [Cuba] in an illegal manner and without [Juan Gonzalez's] consent." Letter from Juan Gonzalez to Felipe Perez Roque, Minister of Foreign Relations of 11/27/99, Defendants' Notice of Filing Record and Exhibits, at 110 (English translation). The request was forwarded to the United States interests section in Havana that same day, and then to the INS. In a letter to Juan Gonzalez dated December 8, 1999, Robert Wallis, INS District Director, outlined the documentation required by the INS in order to release Plaintiff to his father's custody.

Two days later, an application for asylum for Plaintiff was submitted to the INS, signed by Lazaro Gonzalez. The alleged grounds for asylum were membership in a particular social group and/or political opinion. Shortly thereafter, another application—identical to the first—was submitted with Plaintiff's own printed name. On January 10, 2000, a Florida state court granted Lazaro Gonzalez "limited legal authority ... to assert and protect such rights as the child may have under United States immigration law." Lazaro Gonzalez then filed another asylum application on Plaintiff's behalf.

In the interim, an INS official conducted two interviews with Juan Gonzalez in Havana and obtained documentation of his request that Plaintiff be returned home to Cuba. During the first of those interviews, on December 13, 1999, Juan Gonzalez read from a handwritten statement and asked that any application for admission to the United States on his son's behalf be withdrawn. Silma L. Dimmel, Officer-in-Charge for the INS in Havana, conducted the interview in Spanish at Juan Gonzalez's home. Report of Interview with Juan Gonzalez, Defendants' Notice of Filing Record and Exhibits, at 48. When asked for his preference regarding Plaintiff, Juan Gonzalez stated the following:

> Elian, at the age of six, cannot make a decision on his own.... I'm very grateful that he received immediate medical assistance, but he should be returned to me and my family. As for him to get asylum, I am not allowing him to stay or claim any type of petition; he should be returned immediately to me.

Id. at 50.

During the interview, Juan Gonzalez also stated that Plaintiff "practically lived with me since he attended school closer to my residence [than to the residence of Plaintiff's mother]," and Plaintiff's paternal grandmother had cared for the boy while the parents worked. Juan Gonzalez asserted that he had been unaware that Plaintiff's mother was taking Plaintiff to the United States. He also stated that he wanted no claim or petition raised on Plaintiff's behalf, that Plaintiff's paternal relatives living in Miami have "no rights over Elian," and that he did "not want any law firm to represent Elian." Juan Gonzalez also expressed concern that Lazaro Gonzalez is "under pressure" and "unable to back off because of the circumstances of what could happen." *Id.* at 49–54.

In order to address concerns that the oral discussion might be monitored by external sources, the INS official provided Juan Gonzalez with a short written list of questions and possible answers for him to complete. His answers indicated that he felt he could "speak freely" and that it was his desire that Plaintiff "should return to Cuba." *Id.* at 57.

On December 20, 1999, officials from an INS District Office met with Lazaro Gonzalez, his daughter who resides in his home, and several attorneys. One of the INS officials present, Jorge L. Roig, Port Director for the INS at the Port of Miami, spoke directly with Lazaro Gonzalez and prepared a report of the interview (which was not recorded). According to Lazaro Gonzalez, Juan Gonzalez said that "if the boy made it to this country safe and sound that we should protect him by whatever means available." Declaration of Jorge L. Roig, Defendants' Notice of Filing Record and Exhibits, at 221. He also asserted that Juan Gonzalez is "under pressure" from the Cuban government, and that "whoever knows about the Castro system, knows this is how it works there." *Id.* When asked about any specific or objective reason to believe that Plaintiff would be harmed if he returned to Cuba, Lazaro Gonzalez stated that "everything he has, if he goes back, it's all changed," and that Plaintiff's "activities here are different from those that he would have over there." *Id.* at 222.

Subsequent to the meeting, attorney Roger Bernstein sent a letter to the General Counsel of the INS, claiming that in light of the "endemic and gross violations of human rights which exist in Cuba," Juan Gonzalez is not able to express his true wishes regarding Plaintiff "without dire repercussions to his person and family." Letter from Roger Bernstein to Owen Cooper, General Counsel, INS of 12/27/99, Defendants' Notice of Filing Record and Exhibits, at 225–26. Mr. Bernstein offered to provide written affidavits to support his assertions that Juan Gonzalez's movements are restricted, that his "tone drastically changed" in conversations with Lazaro Gonzalez, and that the Cuban government had "harassed" Plaintiff's mother. *Id.*

On December 31, 1999, the INS official in Havana again met with Juan Gonzalez—this time to "clarify some of the answers provided" during the first interview.

Declaration of Silma L. Dimmel, Defendants' Notice of Filing Record and Exhibits, at 229. During this meeting, which took place at the private residence of a United Nations official, Juan Gonzalez completed another written questionnaire, indicating that his actions were not restricted and that he did not want Plaintiff to stay in the United States. *Id.* at 231 (English translation). He expressed offense that the INS was "questioning my paternity over others that have no rights ... [and] giving more rights to others ... although they have no authority over Elian." *Id.* at 241.

The General Counsel for the INS prepared a Memorandum, dated January 3, 2000, which cited pertinent cases from the United States, as well as provisions of Cuban law, and expressly considered the following question: "May Plaintiff apply for asylum in direct opposition to the expressed wishes of his father?" Memorandum from Bo Cooper, General Counsel for Doris Meissner, Commissioner of 1/3/00, Defendants' Notice of Filing Record and Exhibits, at 7–17. The Memorandum addressed Florida law on the competency of a minor to enter into a contract and noted that the INS "generally assumes that someone under the age of 14 will not make representation or other immigration decisions without the assistance of a parent or legal guardian." *Id.*

In light of the attorneys' concerns regarding the voluntariness of Juan Gonzalez's statements, and a "general understanding of the practices of the Castro regime," the General Counsel found it "essential that the INS closely examine the voluntariness of the father's statements." *Id.* The General Counsel concluded that "the father is able to represent adequately the child's immigration interests," and that if Juan Gonzalez were to come to the United States, the INS "would be required to recognize Elian's father's interests ... [and] would necessarily change the custody arrangement we sought with his uncle in his absence." *Id.* The Memorandum also noted that while there are no age-based restrictions on applying for asylum, the INS need not process applications "if they reflect that the purported applicants are so young that they necessarily lack the capacity to understand what they are applying for or, failing that, that the applications do not present an objective basis for ignoring the parents' wishes." *Id.* The General Counsel concluded that Plaintiff "lacks the capacity to raise an asylum claim." *Id.*

The INS sent a letter to Roger Bernstein and Spencer Eig, two attorneys purporting to represent Plaintiff, reporting the decision of the Commissioner;

> After carefully considering all relevant factors, we have determined that there is no conflict of interest between Mr. Gonzalez-Quintana and his son, or any other reason, that would warrant our declining to recognize the authority of this father to speak on behalf of his son in immigration matters.
>
> * * *
>
> [W]e have determined that Elian does not have the capacity to apply for asylum without the assistance of his parent. Further, neither the applications you have submitted nor any other information available indicates that Elian would be at risk of harm in Cuba such that his interests might so diverge from those of his father that his father could not adequately represent him

> in this matter. Therefore, given Mr. Gonzalez-Quintana's decision not to assert Elian's right to apply for asylum, we cannot accept the asylum applications you have submitted on Elian's behalf.
>
> Mr. Gonzalez-Quintana has also repeatedly requested that Elian be returned immediately to his custody in Cuba. We consider this to be a request to withdraw Elian's application for admission to the United States, made by Elian's custodial parent with authority to speak for Elian in immigration matters. Therefore, we have granted Mr. Gonzalez-Quintana's request to withdraw Elian's application for admission to the United States.

Letter from Michael A. Pearson, Executive Associate Commissioner for Field Operations, to Roger Bernstein and Spencer Eig of 1/5/00, Defendants' Notice of Filing Record and Exhibits, at 5–6.

On January 6, 2000, James J. Burzynski, Director of the INS's Texas Service Center, sent a letter to Roger Bernstein, which indicated that the asylum applications that had been filed on Plaintiff's behalf were being returned, pursuant to the reasons articulated in the January 5, 2000 letter from Michael Pearson. Attached to the letter were the actual applications that had been filed, as well as a copy of the letter from Michael Pearson. Letter from James J. Burzynski, Director, TSC, to Roger Bernstein of 1/6/00, Complaint Ex. A.

The attorneys who claimed to represent Plaintiff in his asylum applications sought reconsideration of the Commissioner's decision to reject the applications, which had been articulated in the letters from Michael Pearson and James Burzynski. On January 12, 2000, Attorney General Janet Reno issued her decision upholding the INS's determination. Her letter is reproduced here, in pertinent part:

> While I am always open to considering new information that might arise, I am not currently aware of any basis for reversing Commissioner Meissner's decision that Juan Gonzalez—Elian's father—has the sole authority to speak for his son on immigration matters.
>
> * * *
>
> As a general matter, when dealing with a child this young, the immigration law, like other areas of law, looks to the wishes of the surviving parent.... Commissioner Meissner has determined that, under applicable law, Elian is too young to make legal decisions for himself, and that his father has the legal authority to speak for him in immigration matters. Commissioner Meissner reached her decision through a careful and thorough process. All of the available information was considered, including the reports from two lengthy and private interviews with Elian's father, Juan Gonzalez, and the report from the December 20 meeting with Elian's great uncle and cousin and each of you. Commissioner Meissner also carefully considered the allegation that Juan Gonzalez was under some form of coercion, and is confident, based on her representative's direct contact with Juan Gonzalez, the father's very close relationship with Elian, and the other evidence provided,

> that the father has expressed his true wishes in asking that his son be returned to him.
>
> The INS does not rule out the possibility of a case in which an asylum application would be accepted from a young child against the wishes of a parent.... The INS reviewed the asylum application you sought to file on Elian's behalf, considered all other relevant available information, and found no objective basis for overriding the father's wishes for his son. In particular, the INS found no credible information indicating that the child would be at risk of torture or persecution if returned to his father, and thus concluded that it had no reason to question the father's decision not to assert an asylum claim.
>
> * * *
>
> Nothing in the field guidance [referring to citations from the INS Inspector's Field Manual] suggests that a father's wishes regarding his six-year-old child should be overridden. On the contrary, in a related provision you do not cite, the Field Manual makes it clear that the first responsibility of the INS when confronted with an unaccompanied minor is to attempt to remedy the situation by finding the child's parent or legal guardian, even if that person is outside the United States....
>
> If Elian is not competent to "indicate[] a fear of persecution or intention to apply for asylum," then someone would have to decide in his behalf whether to do so. That someone, under universally accepted legal norms, is his father. And his father has stated, in no uncertain terms, that he does not wish for Elian to make an asylum claim. As noted above, the INS considered relevant information, including the statements of Elian's Miami relatives and information in the asylum application, and determined that there is no objective basis for a valid asylum claim. Consequently, it found no conflict between Elian and his father. Under these circumstances, the appropriate course of action was to honor the desires of the father regarding Elian's applications for admission and asylum. It is not appropriate to commence removal proceedings against this six-year-old boy.

Letter from Attorney General Janet Reno to Spencer Eig, Roger Bernstein, and Linda Osberg-Braun of 1/12/00, Defendants' Notice of Filing Record and Exhibits, at 25–28.

In a subsequent letter, the INS reaffirmed the agency's position with respect to the applications for asylum filed on behalf of Plaintiff, including the application filed on January 12, 2000:

> The new application, filed yesterday, is accompanied by a letter from you acknowledging that the information contained in this latest submission is the same as what you submitted last month. Thus, the only new factors in this case are Lazaro Gonzalez's signature on the new application and the Florida circuit judge's temporary protective order. The Commissioner has concluded that nothing in that order alters her determination that Juan Gonzalez has sole legal authority to speak for Elian on immigration matters, and

> that determination is ultimately one of federal immigration law. Thus, INS has determined that neither you nor Lazaro Gonzalez represents Elian before the INS. Accordingly, INS cannot accept the enclosed asylum application and I am returning it to you.

Letter from James Burzynski, Director, Texas Service, to Roger Bernstein of 1/13/00, Defendants' Notice of Filing Record and Exhibits, at 317–18.

Finally, on January 19, 2000, Plaintiff filed this lawsuit, alleging that the INS lacked the authority to reject the asylum applications and was required by federal statutes and regulations to accept and adjudicate those applications. Defendants urge this Court to dismiss the action or, alternatively, to grant summary judgment. Defendants attack the Complaint on various grounds, each of which is addressed below. Having carefully studied this matter, and mindful of the limits on this Court's authority, the Court concludes that Defendants' Motion To Dismiss or Alternative Motion for Summary Judgment must be granted.

* * *

For immigration purposes, Plaintiff is an unaccompanied minor alien who "arrived" in the United States because he was "brought to the United States after having been interdicted in international or United States waters." 8 U.S.C. § 1225(a)(1). An alien who arrives in the United States is deemed to be an applicant for admission. See id. Plaintiff has not been placed in removal proceedings, but rather has been temporarily "paroled" into the United States, and the INS has deferred his inspection. That deferral of processing for removal, originally issued on November 25, 1999, was extended until January 21, 2000, and reportedly has been extended indefinitely.

Although three applications were filed seeking asylum for Plaintiff—all of which were filed outside of the context of removal proceedings, each was returned by the INS without adjudication. Therefore, Plaintiff, now six years old, is an unaccompanied, unadmitted alien, subject to removal from the United States at the end of his period of temporary parole.

A. Subject Matter Jurisdiction

Federal courts are courts of limited jurisdiction, deriving their authority from both constitutional and legislative sources. See U.S. Const. art. III, § II; 28 U.S.C. § 1331: *Keene Corp. v. United States*, 508 U.S. 200 (1993). It is exclusively the power of Congress to restrict the jurisdiction of federal courts to adjudicate certain kinds of cases. See *Keene* Corp., 508 U.S., at 207; see also *United Gas Pipe Line Co. v. Whitman*, 595 F.2d 323, 330 (5th Cir.1979) (noting that only Congress may retract or expand the limits of federal judicial power).

In addition, federal courts will not infer congressional intent to restrict their jurisdiction. See *Block v. Community Nutrition Inst.*, 467 U.S. 340 (1984). The presumption in favor of judicial review may be rebutted only by a showing of "clear and convincing evidence" that Congress intended to preclude review. See *Board of Governors of the Fed. Reserve Sys. v. McCorp. Fin. Inc.*, 502 U.S. 32, 44 (1991). This is not a strict evidentiary burden, but rather one that may be met where a "congressional intent to preclude judicial review is 'fairly discernible in the statutory scheme.'" *Block*, 467 U.S. at 351 (quoting *Data Processing Serv. v. Camp*, 397 U.S. 150, 156 (1970)). In the event that there is "substantial doubt" as to congressional intent, the presumption in favor of judicial review controls. See *id.*

In applying these jurisdictional tenets to the case at bar, the Court looks first to the statutes that form the basis of Plaintiff's Complaint. See 8 U.S.C. §§ 1103, 1158. These statutes grant the Attorney General broad authority both to implement this nation's immigration laws and to exercise her discretionary authority over the grant of asylum. What is not included within either of the statutory provisions is a clear statement of congressional intent regarding judicial review of the processing of asylum applications by the INS. However, regarding section 1158(a), it is clear that the Attorney General's decision to permit an alien to apply for asylum relief itself is subject to review. See 8 U.S.C. § 1252(b)(4)(D) (providing that the decision whether to "grant relief under section 1158(a)" is "conclusive unless manifestly contrary to law and an abuse of discretion").

Plaintiff asserts that 28 U.S.C. § 1331, 28 U.S.C. § 1346, 28 U.S.C. § 1361, and 28 U.S.C. § 2201 provide this Court with subject matter jurisdiction over his claim that the INS must accept and adjudicate his applications for asylum pursuant to applicable constitutional, statutory, and regulatory provisions. Defendants assert that this Court lacks jurisdiction over the challenged agency action because such action is firmly committed to administrative discretion—similar to the agency's decision to commence removal proceedings. See 8 U.S.C. § 1252(g). Because the Attorney General's decision not to commence removal proceedings is unreviewable under section 1252(g), Defendants suggest that this Court lacks subject matter jurisdiction over this case.

In support of their position that there is no basis for judicial review over the action at issue, Defendants direct the Court's attention to *Heckler v. Chaney*, 470 U.S. 821 (1985), in which the Supreme Court found that agency decisions not to institute enforcement proceedings generally are not subject to judicial review under the Administrative Procedure Act ("APA"), 5 U.S.C. §§ 101 et seq. In so holding, the Court declared that "an agency's decision not to prosecute or enforce, whether through civil or criminal process, is a decision generally committed to an agency's absolute discretion." See *id.* at 831.

In contrast to *Chaney*, the INS decision in the instant case—affirmed by the Attorney General—involved not a matter of enforcement, but rather the refusal to accept an asylum application. Accordingly, the Court rejects Defendants' contention that *Chaney* is controlling in the instant context.

Defendants also rely on 8 U.S.C. § 1252(g), which bars judicial review of "any cause or claim by or on behalf of any alien arising from the decision or action by the Attorney General to commence proceedings, adjudicate cases, or execute removal orders against any alien," 8 U.S.C. § 1252(g). Plaintiff correctly argues that § 1252(g) is simply inapplicable, as he is not seeking the initiation of removal proceedings, but rather seeks simply for the INS to accept and consider his affirmative application for asylum.

Indeed, the Supreme Court in *Reno v. American-Arab Anti-Discrimination Committee*, 525 U.S. 471 (1999), declined to read the restriction on judicial review found in section 1252(g) as broadly as has been urged by the INS. In *American-Arab*, which involved allegations that the INS had unfairly targeted individuals for deportation proceedings, the Supreme Court concluded that judicial review was unavailable because the challenged action constituted one of the three discrete actions that was specified in 1252(g) (exempting from review decisions of the Attorney General to "'commence proceedings, adjudicate cases, or execute removal orders'"). The Supreme Court resisted a reading of section 1252(g) that would extend the application of the section, noting as follows:

> It is also implausible that the mention of three discrete events along the road to deportation was a shorthand way of referring to all claims arising from deportation proceedings. Not because Congress is too unpoetic to use synecdoche, but because that literary device is incompatible with the need for precision in legislative drafting. We are aware of no other instance in the United States Code in which language such as this has been used to impose a general jurisdictional limitation ...

Id. at 943. Based on the decision in *American-Arab*, this Court declines to read section 1252(g) as broadly as Defendants desire.

Defendants further argue that this case involves not only an application for asylum but also an application for admission to the United States, and that the INS decision to permit withdrawal of an application for admission is not subject to review by this Court. Although, as an arriving alien, Plaintiff is deemed to be an applicant for admission, see 8 U.S.C. § 1225(a)(1), Plaintiff asserts that this issue is not dispositive because the application for asylum is filed under a separate statutory provision, see 8 U.S.C. § 1158, with procedures independent of those related to applications for admission.

As to the application for admission, which was deemed to have been filed by Plaintiff through his mere presence as an arriving alien in this country, Defendants argue that 8 U.S.C. § 1252(a)(2)(B) bars review of any claim that the request to withdraw Plaintiff's application for admission was improperly granted:

> Notwithstanding any other provision of law, no court shall have jurisdiction to review (ii) any other decision or action of the Attorney General the authority for which is specified under this subchapter to be in the discretion of the Attorney General, other than the granting of [asylum] relief under section 1158(a) of this title.

8 U.S.C. § 1252(a)(2)(B)(ii). Specifically, Defendants point to 8 U.S.C. § 1225(a)(4), which provides that with respect to the withdrawal of applications for admission, "[a]n alien applying for admission may, in the discretion of the Attorney General and at any time, be permitted to withdraw the application for admission and depart immediately from the United States." 8 U.S.C. § 1225(a)(4). Thus, Defendants argue, the discretionary decision to prevent withdrawal of an application for admission may not be reviewed.

Plaintiff most strenuously urges that the INS decision not to accept the application for asylum filed under 8 U.S.C. § 1158 is the basis for his Complaint—not any purported withdrawal of the application for admission. And, as 8 U.S.C. § 1252(a)(2)(B)(ii) specifically exempts certain decisions under 8 U.S.C. § 1158(a) from the general elimination of judicial review, Plaintiff argues that this Court clearly has subject matter jurisdiction—or, at a minimum, the Court's subject matter jurisdiction is not eliminated by 8 U.S.C. § 1252(a)(2)(B)(ii). While the Defendants raise a compelling point regarding this Court's subject matter jurisdiction over an INS decision permitting withdrawal of an application for admission, it is clear that INS decisions regarding an application for asylum are governed by a different standard.

It also would appear that the provision relating to 8 U.S.C. § 1158(a) within 8 U.S.C. § 1252(a)(2)(B)(ii) can be read to exclude only 8 U.S.C. § 1158(a)(1) ("Any alien ... may apply for asylum") from the preclusion of judicial review, as decisions under 8 U.S.C. § 1158(a)(2) (excepting certain categories of aliens from the provisions of (a)(1)—for example, those who have previously unsuccessfully applied for asylum) expressly have been excluded from judicial review by 8 U.S.C. § 1158(a)(3). See 8 U.S.C. § 1158(a)(3) ("No court shall have jurisdiction to review any determination by the Attorney General under paragraph (2)."). Thus, clearly the only remaining portion of section 1158(a) that could be subject to judicial review by this Court is subsection (a)(1). The Court further observes that "where Congress includes particular language in one section of a statute but omits it in another section of the same Act, it is generally presumed that Congress acts intentionally and purposely in the disparate inclusion." *Russello v. United States*, 464 U.S. 16, 23 (1983) (quoting *United States v. Wong Kim Bo*, 472 F.2d 720, 722 (5th Cir.1972) (per curiam)).

Because of the parties' dispute regarding legislative intent and the absence of compelling evidence before the Court as to judicial review of the action challenged in this case, the Court conducted an inquiry into the relevant legislative history. This review, which included a study of the significant changes in immigration law enacted in 1996, does not compel a finding that the Court is without jurisdiction over this matter.

Upon review of the pertinent statutes, the applicable legislative history, and controlling case law, the Court finds that there is "substantial doubt" that Congress intended to establish a jurisdictional barrier to judicial review of the administrative decision at issue in the instant case, and the Court declines to strain in order to find any such intent. Accordingly, the Court concludes that Defendants' Motion must be denied as to subject matter jurisdiction.

* * *

The long-standing American common law rule that "'the parent stands in court [on his child's behalf] as the real party in interest upon his natural right of parent,'" *Lehman v. Lycoming County Children's Servs. Agency*, 458 U.S. 502, 524 (1982) (Blackmun, J., dissenting) (quoting Learned Hand, *Habeas Corpus Proceedings for the Release of Infants*, 56 Cent. L.J. 385, 389 (1903)), is not without exception. Indeed, concerns for a child's well-being in light of his parents' "'own wrongdoing or unfitness'" militate against the rule. See *id.* Furthermore, American jurisprudence has long held that minor children may be real parties in interest when they possess rights reserved to them. See *Martin v. Barbour*, 140 U.S. 634, 647 (1891). A real party in interest need not even have the ability to "realize that [his] fate is involved in these proceedings." *Gardner v. Alabama*, 385 F.2d 804, 806 (5th Cir.1967), cert. denied. 389 U.S. 1046 (1968) (conferring real party in interest status upon, among others, "innocent babies and children who are too immature" to realize that suit was brought on their behalf).

At the outset, the Court observes that the instant case was brought in Plaintiff's name. Moreover, the Court finds that Plaintiff, despite his tender age, possesses a "significant interest" in requiring the INS to follow its own procedures once asylum applications have been presented to the INS. This conclusion is based on the fact that a decision on one's asylum claim likely has enduring consequences. Thus, the Court finds that Plaintiff is a real party in interest for the narrow purpose of proceeding with this lawsuit to determine whether or not Defendants violated Plaintiff's rights to procedural due process.

* * *

In conclusion, the Court finds that Plaintiff has standing to bring the instant case, and that Plaintiff is the real party in interest in this litigation. However, due to his young age, Plaintiff does not have capacity to sue. Thus, he needs someone to represent his interests, and the Court is satisfied that Lazaro Gonzalez represents Plaintiff's interests sufficiently under the next friend test. The Court next turns to Defendants' attack on the specific allegations of the Complaint.

* * *

Under Count I of the Complaint, Plaintiff seeks relief for violations of constitutionally protected due process rights. Specifically, he charges that Defendants denied him due process by depriving him of the right to petition for asylum, declining to adjudicate his petitions for asylum and withholding of removal, and refusing to recognize his right to counsel. In their Motion, Defendants assert that Plaintiff's claim must be denied as a matter of law, and the Court agrees.

The procedural component of the Fifth Amendment's Due Process Clause protects against the deprivation of life, liberty, or property without "due process of law." U.S. Const. amd. V. The necessary first step in evaluating any procedural due process claim is determining whether a constitutionally protected interest has been implicated. See *Economic Dev. Corp. v. Stierheim*, 782 F.2d 952, 954–55 (11th Cir.1986) ("In assessing a claim based on an alleged denial of procedural due process a court must first decide whether the complaining party has been deprived of a constitutionally protected liberty or property interest. Absent such a deprivation, there can be no denial of due process."). However, "expectation does not equate with liberty or property, and a constitutionally protected interest cannot arise from relief that the executive exercises unfettered discretion to award." *Tefel v. Reno*, 180 F.3d 1286, 1300 (11th Cir.1999) (citing *Connecticut Bd. of Pardons v. Dumschat*, 452 U.S. 458, 465 (1981)).

In *Tefel* the Eleventh Circuit confirmed its prior holding in *Garcia-Mir v. Meese*, 788 F.2d 1446 (11th Cir.1986), "that the failure to receive discretionary relief in the immigration context does not deprive an alien of a constitutionally protected liberty interest." *Tefel*, 180 F.3d at 1300 (citing *Garcia-Mir*, 788 F.2d 1446).

Plaintiff is an unadmitted alien, and as such, is treated as being "on the threshold of initial entry" into the United States. *Shaughnessy v. United States ex rel. Mezei*, 345 U.S. 206, 212, 215 (1953). Plaintiff claims that because he has been paroled, he is entitled to the same constitutional protections as all persons in the territorial jurisdiction of the United States. However, this argument was expressly rejected in *Jean v. Nelson*, 727 F.2d 957, 969 (11th Cir.1984) (quoting *Leng May Ma v. Barber*, 357 U.S. 185, 188 (1958) ("The parole of aliens seeking admission is simply a device through which needless confinement is avoided while administrative proceedings are conducted. It was never intended to affect an alien's status.")).

Moreover, in *Jean v. Nelson*, the Eleventh Circuit specifically held that excludable (or unadmitted) aliens seeking parole pending determination of their claims for admission "are not within the protection of the Fifth Amendment." *Jean*, 727 F.2d at 968; see also *Landon v. Plasencia*, 459 U.S. 21, 32 (1982) ("[A]n alien seeking initial admission to the United States requests a privilege and has no constitutional rights regarding his application...."). Additionally, the asylum provisions established by Congress do not create any constitutionally protected interests. See *Jean*, 727 F.2d at 984 ("Excludable aliens cannot challenge the decisions of executive officials with regard to their applications for admission, asylum, or parole on the basis of the rights guaranteed by the United States Constitution.").

Accordingly, in light of Plaintiff's status as an unadmitted alien, no set of facts will support Plaintiff's claim for a denial of constitutional due process under Count I, and this Count must be dismissed.

Count II of Plaintiff's Complaint alleges a violation of 8 U.S.C. § 1103(a) and 8 U.S.C. § 1158(a). As to Count II, Defendants' Motion hinges on the following narrow question: Did the Attorney General have the authority to determine that, in light of the express contrary wishes of Plaintiff's father, an application filed by someone else on six-year-old Plaintiff's behalf did not require adjudication on its merits? After careful consideration, the Court finds that the Attorney General's determination is controlling, conclusive, not manifestly contrary to law, and not an abuse other congressionally delegated discretion.

As a starting point for its analysis, the Court looks to 8 U.S.C. § 1103(a), which provides the following general statement about decisions of the Attorney General on questions of law:

> (1) The Attorney General shall be charged with the administration and enforcement of this chapter and all other laws relating to the immigration and naturalization of aliens, except insofar as this chapter or such laws relate to the powers, functions, and duties conferred upon the President, the Secretary of State, the officers of the Department of State, or diplomatic or consular

> officers: Provided, however, *[t]hat determination and ruling by the Attorney General with respect to all questions of law shall be controlling.*

8 U.S.C. § 1103(a)(1) (emphasis added).

Under 8 U.S.C. § 1158(a), Congress provides some guidance on the issue of who may apply for asylum:

> Any alien who is physically present in the United States or who arrives in the United States (whether or not at a designated port of arrival and including an alien who is brought to the United States after having been interdicted in international or United States waters), irrespective of such alien's status, may apply for asylum in accordance with this section or, where applicable, section 1225(b) of this title.

8 U.S.C. § 1158(a)(1).

While section 1158(a) provides for authority to apply for asylum, it fails to set forth a standard of review. For direction, the Court looks to 8 U.S.C. § 1252(b)(4)(D), which provides as follows:

> Except as provided in paragraph (5)(B)—
>
> * * *
>
> (D) the Attorney General's discretionary judgment whether to grant relief under section 1158(a) of this title shall be conclusive unless manifestly contrary to the law and an abuse of discretion.

8 U.S.C. § 1252(b)(4)(D). This "manifestly contrary to the law and an abuse of discretion" standard provides strong support for the proposition that Congress did not intend to provide for much second-guessing of administrative decisions under section 1158(a).

Before evaluating the actions taken by the Attorney General with regard to Plaintiff's applications for asylum, the Court must properly characterize the Attorney General's decision at issue. On January 5, 2000, attorneys purporting to represent Plaintiff wrote to the Attorney General, asking that she determine whether the INS had properly followed its procedures in dealing with Plaintiff's applications.

Faced with an unprecedented set of circumstances—including a six-year-old child who had recently lost his mother, a father who had indicated (prior to his son's application for asylum) that he opposed any potential application for admission or asylum, the fact that the INS had conducted two in-person interviews with the father and had found no evidence of abuse, and principles of international standards that support the presumption that a parent speaks for his or her child—the Attorney General found that the INS Commissioner had correctly concluded that the wishes of Juan Gonzalez properly had been granted.

In her decision, the Attorney General concluded that Plaintiff is not competent to demonstrate an "intention to apply for asylum," and that "under universally accepted legal norms," Plaintiff's father should speak for Plaintiff. Letter from Attorney General

Janet Reno to Spencer Eig, Roger Bernstein, and Linda Osberg-Braun of 1/12/00, Defendants' Notice of Filing Record and Exhibits, at 25–28.

The Attorney General's finding of incompetency on the part of Plaintiff, much like a federal court's determination of a prospective witness's capacity or competency to testify, is a threshold matter in need of resolution prior to the processing of Plaintiff's application. And like such determinations in federal court, the Attorney General's finding as to Plaintiff's competency is best characterized as a question of law.

Under the facts alleged, and based on the nature of the issue of capacity to apply for asylum considered by the Attorney General—specifically its character as a question of law—the Attorney General's decision is controlling, see 8 U.S.C. § 1103(a), and thus dispositive of Count II.

* * *

The Administrative Procedure Act ("APA"), 5 U.S.C. §§ 101 et seq., defines the role of administrative agencies in the relationship among the three branches of government and the American citizenry. In doing so, the APA provides administrative agencies with broad discretion to establish policies and regulations, while imposing few limitations on that authority.

This broad discretion is extended by the manner in which federal courts assess the propriety of administrative decisionmaking. Under the applicable standards of review, courts give great deference to agency decisions. For example, pursuant to the APA, in the absence of congressional intent indicating otherwise, courts hold agency findings and decisions unlawful only if they are "'arbitrary, capricious, an abuse of discretion, or otherwise not in accordance with law.'" *Legal Environmental Assistance Foundation, Inc. v. EPA*, 118 F.3d 1467, 1473 (11th Cir.1997) (quoting 5 U.S.C. § 706(2)(A)).

In the event that courts reviewing an agency interpretation are presented with a statute that is "silent or ambiguous" with regard to intent, or there is otherwise a "gap left, implicitly or explicitly, by Congress," courts must ask whether the agency action at issue is based upon a permissible interpretation of the statute. *Chevron, U.S.A., Inc. v. Natural Resources Defense Council, Inc.*, 467 U.S. 837, 842–43 (1984) (citing *Morton v. Ruiz*, 415 U.S. 199, 231 (1974)).

* * *

The Supreme Court consistently has recognized, however, that the unique aspects of immigration law require a special approach. It is firmly established that immigration matters are within the plenary control of Congress. See U.S. Const. art. I, § 8, cl. 4 ("The Congress shall have Power … To establish an uniform Rule of Naturalization…."); see also *Fiallo v. Bell*, 430 U.S. 787, 792 (1977) ("'[O]ver no conceivable subject is the legislative power of Congress more complete than it is over' the admission of aliens.'" (quoting *Oceanic Steam Navigation Co. v. Stranahan*, 214 U.S. 320, 339 (1909))).

In the exercise of its plenary control, as evidenced in 8 U.S.C. § 1103 and other statutory provisions, Congress has made "sweeping … delegations of authority" to the Attorney General in the context of immigration matters. *Jean v. Nelson*, 727 F.2d 957, 965 (11th Cir.1984); see, e.g. *United States v. Shaughnessy*, 353 U.S. 72, 78 (1957) (holding that where Congress fails to specify standards to guide the Attorney General's discretion in immigration, the Attorney General may rely on any reasonable factors).

The Supreme Court has acknowledged this broad exercise of congressional authority, "recogniz[ing] that judicial deference to the Executive Branch is especially appropriate in the immigration context where officials exercise especially sensitive political functions that implicate questions of foreign relations." *INS v. Aguirre-Aguirre*, 526 U.S. 415 (1999). The Court has further observed that "[t]he judiciary is not well positioned to shoulder primary responsibility for assessing the likelihood and importance of [certain] diplomatic repercussions." *Id.*; see also *Hampton v. Mow Sun Wong*, 426 U.S. 88, 101–02 n. 21 (1976) ("[T]he power over aliens is of a political character and therefore subject only to narrow judicial review.").

Under *Chevron*, where a statute is "silent or ambiguous," actions by the Attorney General are to be reviewed for a determination of whether the agency's judgment call was based upon a "permissible construction of the statute." 467 U.S. at 842–43. As the Eleventh Circuit has noted in *Herman v. NationsBank Trust Co.*, 126 F.3d 1354 (11th Cir.1997).... Plaintiff asserts that the language of section 1158(a) is clear and unambiguous, thus precluding an analysis under *Chevron*. However, upon a closer examination of section 1158(a), in the context of other pertinent statutory provisions, the Court is unconvinced that Plaintiff's narrow reading is an appropriate construction of the statutory language. Rather, for the reasons discussed below, the Court agrees with Defendants' argument that 8 U.S.C. § 1158(a) falls into the category of statutes that are "silent or ambiguous," or otherwise contain a "gap left, implicitly or explicitly, by Congress." *Chevron*, 467 U.S. 837, 842–43 (1984) (citing *Morton v. Ruiz*, 415 U.S. 199, 231 (1974)).

To begin, 8 U.S.C. § 1158(a) fails to mention one particular class of aliens—children. This could be construed as silence, in light of the fact that in immigration law, Congress and the INS often make special provisions for children and others who may have difficulty acting in their own best interests. See, e.g., 8 U.S.C. § 1182(a)(9)(B)(iii)(I) ("No period of time in which an alien is *under 18 years of age* shall be taken into account in determining the period of unlawful presence in the United States under clause (i).") (emphasis added); *Perez-Funez v. District Director, INS*, 619 F.Supp. 656, 661 (C.D.Cal.1985) ("The Court notes that, as discussed above, INS policy treats *fourteen years of age and older* differently from younger class members.") (emphasis added); 8 C.F.R. § 236.2(a) ("If the respondent is confined, or if he or she is an incompetent, *or a minor under the age of 14*, the notice to appear, and the warrant of arrest, if issued, shall be served in the manner prescribed in § 239.1 of this chapter....") (emphasis added); 8 C.F.R. § 240.38 ("Every alien *14 years of age or older* who is excluded from admission to the United States by an immigration judge shall be fingerprinted....") (emphasis added). In light of these examples of age-specific provisions, it is apparent that Congress and the INS recognize that children deserve special treatment under immigration law.

Plaintiff would have the Court focus purely on 8 U.S.C. § 1158(a)(1) to the exclusion of the remainder of section 1158 and other portions of the INA. However, for the Court to do so would be to reject firmly established principles of statutory interpretation that guide this Court's analysis, as well as to accept the logical extension of Plaintiff's argument, which is that Congress requires the Attorney General to adjudicate asylum applications from all children—no matter how young in age, no matter who claims to speak for them, and no matter what their mental condition. This conclusion seems especially unreasonable in light of the potential harm that may result to a child on whose behalf an asylum application is filed.

Consider, as an example, the case in which a child is kidnapped abroad, brought to the United States, and an application for asylum is filed on his or her behalf by the kidnapper. In that case, Plaintiff would have the Court believe that even if the Attorney General were aware that the child had been kidnapped, the Attorney General would be obligated to accept the application. While it is true that the Attorney General would have an ability to deny the application following an adjudication, this would not alter the fact that the child's status under 8 U.S.C. § 1158(a) would have changed.

Moreover, if Congress truly intended section 1158(a) to permit any alien to apply for asylum, why enact 8 U.S.C. § 1252(b)(4)(D) at all? The fact that section 1252(b)(4)(D) provides a standard of review for "discretionary judgment" exercised by the Attorney General under section 1158(a) is the dagger to the heart of Plaintiff's request.

This conclusion is bolstered by the fact that within 8 U.S.C. § 1158(a)(2), Congress has provided for exceptions to the term "[a]ny alien." These include aliens who: 1) may be removed to a safe third country, 2) have failed to file for asylum within one year of arriving in the United States, or 3) have previously applied for and been denied asylum. See 8 U.S.C. § 1158(a)(2). Thus, "[a]ny alien" was evidently not intended by Congress literally to include all aliens.

Due to the failure of 8 U.S.C. § 1158(a) to address minors, as well as the fact that the word "[a]ny" in "[a]ny alien" is internally contradicted by 8 U.S.C. § 1158(a)(2), the Court concludes that the words "[a]ny alien" cannot be read as literally as Plaintiff suggests to the Court, and that 8 U.S.C. § 1158(a), regardless of the reason, is sufficiently "silent or ambiguous" to warrant an analysis under *Chevron*.

Having found that the statute is "silent or ambiguous," the pertinent question is whether the Attorney General's construction of 8 U.S.C. § 1158(a) was a "permissible interpretation." The Court finds that, in light of the discretion afforded to the Attorney General and the pertinent statutory provisions treating children differently from adults, the interpretation of the Attorney General was permissible, and relief cannot be awarded under Count II.

Following its determination that the decision of the Attorney General is controlling both on the issue of Plaintiff's capacity to file an application for asylum and on the question of who may speak for Plaintiff in the face of Plaintiff's incompetence, the

Court addresses briefly Plaintiff's claims under Counts III and IV that Defendants violated specific regulations.

Under Counts III and IV of the Complaint, Plaintiff sets forth claims under 8 C.F.R. § 208.9 and 8 C.F.R. § 208.14(b), which are regulatory provisions promulgated pursuant to the authority of the Attorney General to administer and enforce all laws relating to the immigration and naturalization of aliens. See 8 U.S.C. § 1103(a); 8 U.S.C. § 1158(d)(l) (expressly directing the Attorney General to "establish a procedure for the consideration of asylum applications").

As noted above, the Attorney General's determination as to Plaintiff's capacity to apply for asylum is controlling, and in light of that conclusion, no asylum applications are pending. Therefore, Counts III and IV must fail.

D. Count V: Petition for Writ of Mandamus

In Count V, Plaintiff seeks relief in the form of a writ of mandamus compelling Defendants to comply with their procedures for adjudicating asylum applications. Under 28 U.S.C. § 1361, this Court shall issue a writ "to compel an officer or employee of the United States or any agency thereof to perform a duty owed to the plaintiff" 28 U.S.C. § 1361.

A writ of mandamus is inappropriate, however, as to the exercise of a discretionary duty. See *Einhom v. DeWitt*, 618 F.2d 347, 349 (5th Cir.1980). In light of the Court's findings above, to the extent that any duty existed with respect to the consideration of Plaintiff's applications for asylum, that duty was discretionary. Accordingly, the issuance of a writ would be inappropriate in this case, and Count V must fail as a matter of law.

In the final analysis, a well-intended lawsuit filed on behalf of and for the benefit of Elian Gonzalez ran headlong into an equally well-intended Attorney General, sworn to uphold the letter and spirit of the immigration law, and determined to see that a father's wishes to be reunited with his six-year-old son be given primacy in law and fact.

At age six, Elian's recorded past is a profile of survival and courage in the face of adversity and the loss of his mother at sea. His future will undoubtedly unfold in due time, and it will surely remain a matter of interest to those who oppose his father's wishes.

Even this well-intended litigation has the capacity to bring about unintended harm. In light of the Attorney General's clearly articulated views on the matter of whether Elian Gonzalez should return home, as well as the reality that each passing day is another day lost between Juan Gonzalez and his son, the Court can only hope that those on each side of this litigation place the interests of Elian Gonzalez above all others.

From the outset, Plaintiff's counsel have urged that this lawsuit does not seek asylum, but rather seeks to vindicate a procedural right to apply for asylum. The determination to grant asylum is a matter within the discretion of the Attorney General. She has decided the issue of who may speak for Plaintiff, and her decision, by statute and in the exercise of congressionally delegated discretion, is controlling as a matter of law. A judicial review of the exercise of that discretion by the undersigned has found no abuse that would warrant a contrary conclusion.

Notes

1. After the district court entered its decision, Juan Gonzalez, the father of Elian traveled to the U.S. and intervened in the case which was on appeal. *See Gonzalez v. Reno*, 212 F.3d 1338 (11th Cir. 2000). After his arrival, Attorney General Reno changed the child's custody from the relatives in Miami to the father. The appellate court affirmed, and the Supreme Court later denied certiorari. The court of appeals decided the case on the grounds that while the INA provides that persons arriving at the border may apply for asylum, in this case, the father's wishes must be honored. The court noted that the asylum statute did not provide for the situation in which an application was submitted by or on behalf of a six year-old child and that it was proper for the INS to fill in those gaps and refuse the asylum application submitted by the minor. In deferring to the INS, the court stated that

> ... As a matter of law, it is not for the courts, but for the executive agency charged with enforcing the statute (here, the INS), to choose how to fill such gaps. See *Chevron*, 104 S. Ct. at 2793. Moreover, the authority of the executive branch to fill gaps is especially great in the context of immigration policy. See *Aguirre-Aguirre*, 119 S. Ct. at 1445. Our proper review of the exercise by the executive branch of its discretion to fill gaps, therefore, must be very limited. See *Pauley v. Bethenergy Mines, Inc.*, 111 S. Ct. 2524, 2534 (1991).
>
> That the courts owe some deference to executive policy does not mean that the executive branch has unbridled discretion in creating and in implementing policy. Executive agencies must comply with the procedural requirements imposed by statute. *Morton v. Ruiz*, 94 S. Ct. 1055, 1073 (1974). Agencies must respect their own procedural rules and regulations. And the policy selected by the agency must be a reasonable one in the light of the statutory scheme. To this end, the courts retain the authority to check agency policymaking for procedural compliance and for arbitrariness. But the courts cannot properly reexamine the wisdom of an agency-promulgated policy.

212 F.3d at 1349. The full history for this case is 86 F. Supp. 2d 1167 (S.D. Fla. 2000), *aff'd*, 212 F.3d 1338 (11th Cir. 2000), *reh'g and reh'g en banc denied*, 215 F.3d 1243 (11th Cir. 2000), *cert. denied*, 530 U.S. 1270 (2000).

2. Did the child's nationality as a citizen of Cuba have any legal bearing on the claims which were being presented and the available avenues for judicial review? To what extent does Elian Gonzalez's procedural posture bear on the outcome of the case?

3. Do you agree that the court properly had jurisdiction in this case to decide the issues? Are the issues wholly discretionary and therefore precluded from review? How can one articulate a constitutional claim, or is it enough to assert a statutory right?

Table of Cases

Cases which are referenced below in bold appear in the text at the page designate by asterisk (*).

Table of Authorities Cited

Citations with an asterisk (*) appear in the text of the materials at the page noted.

Miscellaneous Statutes and Treaties

REGULATIONS

POLICY MANUALS

Executive Orders and Federal Register

Articles and Books Cited

Citations with an asterisk (*) appear in the text at the referenced page number.

Kif Augustine-Adams, *The Plenary Power Doctrine After September 11*, 38 U.C. DAVIS L. REV. 701 (2005), 128

Raquel Aldana, *On Rights Federal Citizenship and the Alien*, 46 WASH. L.J. 263 (2007), 102

Anthony, *Which Agency Interpretations Should Bind Citizens and the Courts*, 7 YALE J. REG. 1 (1990), 329

Naomi Barrowclough, *E-Verify: A Long Awaited "Magic Bullet" or Weak Attempt to Substitute Technology for Comprehensive Reform*, 62 RUTGERS L. REV. 791 (2010), 285

Jeanne Batalova, Sarah Hooker & Randy Capps, *DACA at the Two-Year Mark: A National and State Profile of Youth Eligible and Applying for Deferred Action* (Migration Policy Institute 2014), 678

BLACK'S LAW DICTIONARY 112 (5th Ed. 1968), 184

BLACK'S LAW DICTIONARY 521 (5th ed. 1979), 542

BLACK'S LAW DICTIONARY 634 (10th Ed. 2014), 122

Harry A. Blackmun, *The Supreme Court and the Law of Nations*, 104 YALE L.J. 39 (1994), 345

Richard E. Blum, *Labor Standards Enforcement and the Results of Labor Migration*, 63 N.Y.U. L. REV. 1342 (1988), 78

W.R. BOHRING, STUDIES IN INTERNATIONAL LABOUR MIGRATION 36 (1984), 583

Richard A. Boswell, *Rethinking Exclusion: The Rights of Cuban Refugees Facing Indefinite Detention in the United States*, 17 VAND. J. TRANSNT'L L. 925 (1984), 128

Stephen Breyer, *Judicial Review of Questions of Law*, 38 ADMIN. L. REV. 363 (1986), 329

J. HERMAN BURGERS & HANS DANELUS, THE UNITED NATIONS CONVENTION AGAINST TORTURE AND OTHER CRUEL, INHUMAN OR DEGRADING TREATMENT OR PUNISHMENT (1988), 435

Peter Burns Q.C. & Obiora Okafor, *The United Nations Convention against Torture and Other Cruel, Inhuman or Degrading Treatment or Punishment or How It Is Still Better to Light a Candle than to Curse the Darkness*, 9 OTAGO L. REV. 399 (1998), 435

Sandra Burgess, *Actual Minimum Job Requirements in Labor Certifications: Application of Title 20, Section 656.21(B)(6) of the Code of Federal Regulations to Experience or Training Gained with the Employer*, 23 SAN DIEGO L. REV. 375 (1986), 615–617*

Janet Calvo, *Alien Status Restrictions on Eligibility for Federal Funded Assistance Programs*, 16 N.Y.U. REV. L. & SOC. CHANGE 395 (1988), 89

J. Card, Push and Pull Factors at Origin and Destination as Determinants of Migration (Aug. 1980), 279

Campbell and Taggert, *The International Business Client and Nonimmigrant Visas*, 11 Colo. Law. 2545, 2550 (1982), 447

Gilbert Paul Carrasco, *The Golden Moment of Legalization*, X In Defense of the Alien 32, 35 (1988), 64

Howard F. Chang, *The International Impact of International Labor Migration: Recent Estimates and Policy Implications*, 16 Temp. Pol. & Civ. Rts. L. Rev. 321 (2006), 583

Charnesky, *Protection for Undocumented Workers Under the FLSA: An Evaluation in Light of IRCA*, 25 San Diego L. Rev. 379 (1988), 78

Ming H. Chen, *Trust in Immigration Enforcement: State Noncooperation and Sanctuary Cities After Secure Communities*, 91 Chi. Kent L. Rev. 13 (2016), 125

Gabriel J. Chin, *Segregation's Last Stronghold: Racial Discrimination and the Constitutional Law of Immigration*, 46 UCLA L. Rev. 1 (1998), 128

Gabriel J. Chin, *Is There a Plenary Power Doctrine? A Tentative Apology and Prediction for Our Strange but Unexceptional Constitutional Immigration Law*, 14 Geo. Immigr. L.J. 257 (2000), 128

David Cole, *Jurisdiction and Liberty: Habeas Corpus and Due Process as Limits on Congress' Control of Federal Jurisdiction*, 86 Geo. L.J. 2481 (1998), 848–854*

Collins, *Illegitimate Borders: Jus Sanguinis Citizenship and the Legal Construction of Family, Race, and Nation*, 123 Yale L.J. 2134 (2014), 774–775, 777

L. Dawidowicz, *The War Against the Jews, 1933–1945* (1975), 796

Victoria Degtyareva, *Defining Family in Immigration Law: Accounting for Nontraditional Families in Citizenship by Descent*, 120 Yale L.J. 862 (2011), 782

Dictionary of Occupational Titles (Selected Characteristics), 480–481, 620

Donald S. Dobkin, *Challenging the Doctrine of Consular Nonreviewability in Immigration Cases*, 24 Geo. Immig. L.J. 113 (2010), 536

Keith Donoghue, *Immigration Board Revitalized*, Legal Times, Sept. 18, 1995, 294

EVD Update, 65 Interpreter Releases 964 (1988), 422

Joan Fitzpatrick, *The Gender Dimension of U.S. Immigration Policy*, 9 Yale J. L. & Feminism 23 (1997), 446

Robert Foss, *The Demise of Homosexual Exclusion: New Possibilities for Gay and Lesbian Immigration*, 29 Harv. C.R.-C.L. L. Rev. 439 (1994), 132

Tammy Fox-Isicoff & H. Ronald Klasko, *The Child Status Protection Act: Is Your Child Protected?*, 80 Interpreter Releases 973 (2003), 539

Fragomen Fires Back at Department of Labor, 85 Interpreter Releases 2349 (2008), 612

Austin T. Fragomen, Jr., Alfred J. Del Rey, Jr., and Sam Bernsen, 3 Immigration Law & Business § 11.7 (2009), 285

Barney Frank, *The Anti-Discrimination Amendment*, X In Defense of the Alien 67 (1988), 65

Lawrence Fuchs, *Immigration Policy and the Rule of Law*, 44 U. Pitt. L. Rev. 433 (1983), 127

Ebba Gebisa, *Constitutional Concerns with the Enforcement and Expansion of Expedited Removal*, 2007 U. Chi. Legal F. 565 (2007), 173

Pamela Goldberg, *U.S. Law and Women Asylum Seekers: Where are They and Where Are They Going?*, 73 Interpreter Releases 889 (1996), 360, 380

Charles Gordon, *The Need to Modernize Our Immigration Laws*, 13 San Diego L. Rev. 1 (1975), 10

Charles Gordon, Stanley Mailman, Stephen Yale-Loehr & Ronald Wada, Immigration Law and Procedure § 1.03 (rev. ed. 2017), 139, 675

Charles Gordon, Stanley Mailman, Stephen Yale-Loehr & Ronald Wada, Immigration Law & Procedure § 2.04 (rev. ed. 2017), 585

Charles Gordon, Stanley Mailman & Stephen Yale-Loehr, Immigration Law and Procedure § 26.04 (rev. ed. 2017), 588

Charles Gordon, Stanley Mailman, Stephen Yale-Loehr & Ronald Wada, Immigration Law & Procedure § 44.01[3] (rev. ed. 2017), 590

Charles Gordon, Stanley Mailman, Stephen Yale-Loehr & Ronald Wada, Immigration Law & Procedure § 51.04(b) (rev. ed. 2017), 636

Charles Gordon, Stanley Mailman, Stephen Yale-Loehr & Ronald Wada, Immigration Law & Procedure § 51.05[1] (rev. ed. 2017), 639

Charles Gordon, Stanley Mailman, Stephen Yale-Loehr & Ronald Wada, Immigration Law and Procedure § 72.03(h) (rev. 2017), 811

1 C. Gordon & S. Mailman, Immigration Law & Procedure 1–10 (rev. ed. 1990), 185

1 Charles Gordon & Stanley Mailman, Immigration Law and Procedure 2–184 (rev. ed. 1990), 288

6 C. Gordon, S. Mailman, & S. Yale-Loehr, Immigration Law and Procedure § 74.02 (rev. ed. 2007), 671

6 C. Gordon, S. Mailman,& S. Yale-Loehr, Immigration Law and Procedure § 72.03 [2][h] (1998), 811

Jennifer Gordon, *People are Not Bananas: How Immigration Differs from Trade*, 104 Nw. U. L. Rev. 1109 (2010), 583

A. Grahl-Madsen, The Status of Refugees in international Law 217 (1966), 318, 389

Hafetz, *The Untold Story of Noncriminal Habeas Corpus and the 1996 Immigration Acts*, 107 Yale L.J. 2509 (1998), 859

Virginia Harper-Ho, *Noncitizen Voting Rights: The History, the Law and Current Prospects for Change*, 18 Law & Inequality 271 (2000), 758

L. Tracy Harris, *Conflict or Double Deterrence? FLSA Protection of Illegal Aliens and the Immigration Reform and Control Act*, 72 Minn. L. Rev. 900 (1988), 78

H.L. Hart, *The Power of Congress to Limit the Jurisdiction of Federal Courts: An Exercise in Dialectic*, 66 Harv. L. Rev. 1362 (1953), 128

Roger C. Hartley, *Congressional Devolution of Immigration Policymaking: a Separation of Powers Critique*, 2 Duke J. Const'l L. & Pub. Pol'y 93 (2007), 100

Arthur Helton, *The Proper Role of Discretion in Political Asylum*, 22 San Diego L. Rev. 999 (1985), 329

Louis Henkin, *Notes From the President, American Society of International Law Newsletter* (Sept.-Oct. 1993), 345

Joshua Herndon, *Broken Border: De Canas v. Bica and the Standards that Govern the Validity of State Measures Designed to Deter Undocumented Immigration*, 12 TEX. HISPANIC J. L. & POL'Y 31 (2006, 103

R. Hilberg, *The Destruction of the European Jews* 572 (1978), 796

BILL ONG HING, HANDLING IMMIGRATION CASES, § 6.36 (Supp. 1988), 422

Bill Ong Hing, *Racial Disparity: The Unaddressed Issue of the Simpson-Mazzoli Bill*, 1 La Raza L. J. 21 (1983), 10

Bill Ong Hing, *Immigration Sanctuary Policies: Constitutional and Representative of Good Policing and Good Public Policy*, 2 U.C. IRVINE L. REV. 247 (2012), 125

Hopper, *Special Handling Labor Certifications for College and Teachers* 12 IMM. J. 77 (1989), 621

Lindsay Perez Huber, *"Make America Great Again!": Donald Trump, Racist Nativism and the Virulent Adherence to White Supremacy Amid U.S. Demographic Change*, 10 CHARLESTON L. REV. 215 (2016), 127

Elizabeth Hull, *The Unkindest Cuts: the 1996 Welfare Reform Acts Impact on Resident Aliens*, 33 GONZ. L. REV. 471 (1998), 102

SARAH IGNATIUS, NATIONAL ASYLUM STUDY PROJECT: AN ASSESSMENT OF THE ASYLUM PROCESS OF THE IMMIGRATION AND NATURALIZATION SERVICE 17 (1993), 291

IJ Grants Asylum to Battered Bangladeshi Woman, 74 INTERPRETER RELEASES 174 (1997), 363

INS Memorandum: Unaccompanied Minors Subject To Expedited Removal (Aug. 21, 1997) INTERPRETER RELEASES 155 (1983), 169

60 INTERPRETER RELEASES 155 (1983), 8, 814

65 INTERPRETER RELEASES 964 (1988), 422

67 INTERPRETER RELEASES 1480 (1990), 421

68 INTERPRETER RELEASES 483 (1991), 415

69 INTERPRETER RELEASES 1364 (1992), 587

69 INTERPRETER RELEASES 1400 (1992), 415

74 INTERPRETER RELEASES 1528 (1997), 169

James, *The Board of Appellate Review of the Department of State: The Right to Appellate Review of Administrative Determinations of Loss of Nationality*, 23 SAN DIEGO L. REV. 261 (1986), 770

Kevin R. Johnson, *The Antiterrorism Act, the Immigration Reform Act, and Ideological Regulation in the Immigration Laws: Important Lessons for Citizens and Noncitizens*, 28 ST. MARY'S L. J. 822 (1997), 130

KEVIN R. JOHNSON, THE "HUDDLED MASSES" MYTH: IMMIGRATION & CIVIL RIGHTS 22–24 (2004), 514

Arlene Kanter & Kristin Dadey, *The Right of Asylum for People With Disabilities*, 73 TEMP. L. REV. 1117 (2000), 390

Rebecca Kidder, *Administrative Discretion Gone Awry: The Reintroduction of the Public Charge Exclusion for HIV-Positive Refugees and Asylees*, 106 YALE L. J. 389 (1996), 133

Harold Hongju Koh, *Reflections on Refoulement*, 35 HARV. INT'L LAW. J. 1 (1994), 345

Jennifer Lee Koh, *Removal in the Shadows of Immigration Court*, 90 S. CAL. L. REV. 181 (2017), 173

Arnold Liebowitz, *The Immigration Challenge and the Congressional Response*, 1 LA RAZA L.J. 1 (1983), 584

EMMA LAZARUS, THE NEW COLOSSUS (1883), 127

Stephen H. Legomsky, *Deportation and the War on Independence*, 91 CORNELL L. REV. 369 (2006), 847

Matthew Lippman, *The Development and Drafting of the United Nations Convention Against Torture and Other Cruel, Inhuman or Degrading Treatment or Punishment*, 17 B.C. INT'L & COMP. L. REV. 275 (1994), 434

Gerald Lopez, *Undocumented Mexican Migration: In Search of a Just Immigration Law and Policy*, 28 U.C.L.A. L. REV. 615 (1981), 279

Pamela MacLean, *Immigration Bench Plagued by Flaws*, NAT'L L.J., Feb. 6, 2006, 815

Audrey Macklin, *Cross-Border Shopping for Ideas: A Critical Review of United States, Canadian, and Australian Approaches to Gender-Related Asylum Cases*, 13 GEO. IMMIGR. L.J. 25 (1998), 364

David A. Martin, *Immigration Policy and the Homeland Security Act Reorganization: An Early Agenda for Practical Improvements*, 80 INTERPRETER RELEASES 601 (2003), 6

Shadi Masri, *ICE's Initiation of Secure Communities Programs Draws More Criticism than Praise*, 25 GEO. IMM. L.J. 533 (2011), 115

Valsamis Mitsilegas, *Immigration Control in an Era of Globalization: Deflecting Foreigners, Weakening Citizens, Strengthening the State*, 19 IND. J. GLOBAL LEGAL STUD. 3 (2012), 583

Karen Musalo, *Credibility and Burden of Proof in Asylum Claims After the Board of Immigration Appeals Four 1998 Decisions*, 31ST ANNUAL IMMIGRATION AND NATURALIZATION INSTITUTE 277 (Austin E. Fragomen Ed. 1998), 296–306*

Karen Musalo, *The Developing Jurisprudence of Gender-Based Claims* 1998–99 ANNUAL IMMIGRATION AND NATIONALITY HANDBOOK, 357–364*

KAREN MUSALO ET AL., REFUGEE LAW AND POLICY (1997), 357

KAREN MUSALO, REPORT ON THE SECOND YEAR OF IMPLEMENTATION OF EXPEDITED REMOVAL 95 (May 1999), 346

KAREN MUSALO & DEBORAH ANKER, REPORT ON THE FIRST YEAR OF IMPLEMENTATION OF EXPEDITED REMOVAL (May, 1998), 501

James Nafziger, *The General Admission of Aliens Under international Law*, 77 Am. J. Int'l L. 804 (1983), 128

Gerald Neuman, *Jurisdiction and the Rule of Law after the 1996 Immigration Act*, 113 HARV. L. REV. 1963 (2000), 852

JOHN NOWAK, ET AL., CONSTITUTIONAL LAW §4.4 (3d Ed. 1986), 757

Office of Field Operations, *INS Memorandum: Policy Concerning Pre-1997 Parolees* (June 30, 1997), Reprinted in 74 Interpreter Releases 1528 (1997), 169

Office of the Deputy Commissioner, INS Memorandum: Implementation of Expedited Removal (Mar. 31, 1997), 173

Richard Prinz, *Kungys and Materiality*, Immigration and Nationality Law 1989 Annual Symposium: Advanced Topics 154 (1989), 802

A Response to "Nannygate": Untangling U.S. Immigration Law to Enable American Parents to Hire Foreign Childcare Providers, 70 Ind. L. J. 305 (1993), 446

Jaya Ramji-Nogales, Andrew I. Schoenholtz & Philip G. Schrag, *Refugee Roulette: Disparities in Asylum Adjudication*, 60 Stan. L. Rev. 295 (2007), 815

Shruti Rana, *"Streamlining" the Rule of Law: How the Department of Justice is Undermining Judicial Review of Agency Action*, U. Ill. L. Rev. 829 (2009), 815

Brent Renison, *How Does Uncle Sam Waste Immigrant Visas?* Entry Law Blog (Oct. 6, 2015), 530–532*

Marcelle Rice, *Protecting Parents: Why Mothers and Fathers Who Oppose Female Genital Cutting Qualify for Asylum*, Immigration Briefings, No. 04-11 (November 2004), 383

Gerald Rosberg, *The Protection of Aliens from Discriminatory Treatment by the National Government*, 1977 Sup. Ct. Rev. 275, 758

Gerald Rosberg, *Aliens and Equal Protection: Why Not the Right to Vote*, 75 Mich. L. Rev. 1092 (1977), 758

Mario Russell, *A New York Immigration Court's Cure for Regulatory Due Process Violations in NSEERS Special Registration: Suppress Evidence and Terminate Proceedings*, 82 Interpreter Releases 1505 (2005), 273

David S. Rubenstein & Pratheepan Gulasekaram, *Immigration Exceptionalism*, 111 Nw. U.L. Rev. 583 (2017), 158

Sharon Stanton Russell, *International Migration: Global Trends and National Responses*, 20 Fletcher F. World Aff. 1 (1996), 23–34*

2a C. Sands, Sutherland's Statutes and Statutory Construction § 48.05 (N. Singer 4th Ed. 1984), 65

Michael Scaperlanda, *Polishing the Tarnished Golden Door*, 1993 Wis. L. Rev. 165 (1993), 128

Samuel M. Silvers, *The Exclusion and Expulsion of Homosexual Aliens*, 15 Colum Hum. Rts. L. Rev. 295 (1984), 132

Brian Slocum, *The Immigration Rule of Lenity and Chevron Deference*, 17 Geo. Imm. L. J. 519 (2003), 195

Derek Smith, *A Refugee By Any Other Name: An Examination of the Board of Immigration Appeals Actions' in Asylum Cases*, 75 Va. L. Rev. 681 (1989), 294

Peter J. Spiro, *Explaining the End of Plenary Power*, 16 Geo. Immigr. L.J. 339 (2002), 128

Alan A. Stevens, *Give Me Your Tired, Your Poor, Your Destitute Laborers, Ready to be Exploited: The Failure of International Human Rights Law to Protect the Rights of Illegal Aliens in American Jurisprudence*, 14 Emory Int'l L. Rev. 205 (2000), 78

Sarah Sherman-Stokes, *Sufficiently Safeguarded: Competency Evaluations of Mentally Ill Respondents in Removal Proceedings*, 67 Hastings L.J. 1023 (2016), 207

Suspension of Deportation: Illusory Relief, 14 San Diego L. Rev. 229 (1976), 691

Suspension of Deportation: A Revitalized Relief For the Alien, 18 SAN DIEGO L. REV. 65 (1980), 691

THE TARNISHED GOLDEN DOOR: CIVIL RIGHTS ISSUES IN IMMIGRATION U.S. COMMISSION ON CIVIL RIGHTS, 7-12 (1980), 11–18*, 127

Margaret H. Taylor, *What Happened to Non-LPR Cancellation? Rationalizing Immigration Enforcement by Restoring Durable Relief from Removal*, 30 J. OF L. & POL. 527 (2015)., 701

LAWRENCE TRIBE, AMERICAN CONSTITUTIONAL LAW 344-45 (2d Ed. 1988), 100

Joe Tucker, *Assimilation to the United States: A Study of the Adjustment of Status and the Immigration Marriage Fraud Statutes*, 7 YALE L. & POL'Y REV. 20 (1989), 642

UNITED NATIONS HIGH COMMISSIONER FOR REFUGEES, HANDBOOK ON PROCEDURES FOR DETERMINING REFUGEE STATUS (1979), 297–298, 320, 348–352*

Vermeule, *Saving Constructions*, 85 GEO. L.J. 1945, 1960–1961 (1997), 165

Rose Cuison Villazor, *"Sanctuary Cities" and Local Citizenship*, 37 FORDHAM URB. L.J. 573 (2010), 125

Joseph Voyame & Peter Burns, *The Convention Against Torture and Other Cruel, Inhuman or Degrading Treatment or Punishment*, in MANUAL ON HUMAN RIGHTS REPORTING 367 (1997), 434

SHOBA SIVASPRASAD WADHIA, BEYOND DEPORTATION: THE ROLE OF PROSECUTORIAL DISCRETION IN IMMIGRATION CASES (2015), 675

Jack Wasserman, *Immigration Law and Procedure* 211 (1979), 185

Jack Wasserman, *The Undemocratic, Illogical and Arbitrary Laws of the United States*, 3 INT'L LAW. 254 (1969), 194

Charles D. Weisselberg, *The Exclusion and Detention from the Lives of Ellen Knauff and Ignatz Mezei*, 143 U. PA. L. REV. 933 (1995), 128

Leon Wildes, *The Nonpriority Program of the Immigration and Naturalization Service Goes Public: The Litigative Use of the Freedom of information Act*, 14 SAN DIEGO L. REV. 42 (1976), 675

Wolff, *The Non-Reviewability of Consular Visa Decisions: An Unjustified Aberration from American Justice*, 5 N.Y.L. SCH. J. INT'L COMP. L. 341, 347-50 (1984), 536

R. George Wright, *Federal Immigration Law and the Case for Open Entry*, 27 LOY. L.A. L. REV. 1265 (1994), 34–49*

Index